St Petersburg

TALLINN

ESTONIA

Pärnu • Tartu

Jūrmala • RĪGA LATVIA
Liepāja
NORTH
EASTERN EUROPE

Klaipėda LITHUANIA
Kaunas

VILNIUS

USSIAN
ERATION

BELARUS

WARSAW

EUROPE

MOSCOW

RUSSIAN
FEDERATION

**MOSCOW AND
ST PETERSBURG**
Pages 118–163

LITHUANIA
Pages 42–69

LATVIA
Pages 70–93

ESTONIA
Pages 94–117

UKRAINE

Košice

er

Debrecen

Cluj-Napoca
ROMANIA
Sighişoara

Timişoara
Braşov

LGRADE

BUCHAREST

ERBIA

SOUTH-EASTERN EUROPE Varna BLACK
SEA
SOFIA Veliko
Tûrnovo
Koprivshtitsa • Plovdiv Burgas

OVO

ACEDONIA BULGARIA TURKEY

GREECE

MOLDOVA

HUNGARY
Pages 332–397

ROMANIA
Pages 566–599

SERBIA
Pages 544–565

BULGARIA
Pages 600–641

EYEWITNESS TRAVEL

EASTERN AND CENTRAL EUROPE

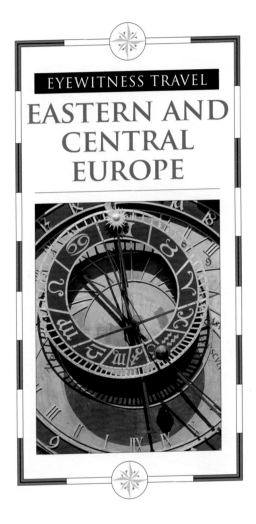

EYEWITNESS TRAVEL

EASTERN AND CENTRAL EUROPE

DK

LONDON, NEW YORK,
MELBOURNE, MUNICH AND DELHI
www.dk.com

MANAGING EDITOR Aruna Ghose
SENIOR EDITORIAL MANAGER Savitha Kumar
SENIOR DESIGN MANAGER Priyanka Thakur
PROJECT EDITOR Arundhti Bhanot
PROJECT DESIGNER Mathew Kurien
EDITORS Jyoti Kumari, Parvati M. Krishnan, Jayashree Menon,
Beverly Smart
DESIGNERS Kaberi Hazarika, Rajnish Kashyap, Neha Sethi
SENIOR CARTOGRAPHIC MANAGER Uma Bhattacharya
SENIOR CARTOGRAPHER AND ASSISTANT MANAGER Suresh Kumar
CARTOGRAPHER Mohammad Hassan
DTP DESIGNERS Rakesh Pal, Azeem Siddiqui
SENIOR PICTURE RESEARCH COORDINATOR Taiyaba Khatoon

MAIN CONTRIBUTORS
Jonathan Bousfield, Matthew Willis

MAIN PHOTOGRAPHER
Jonathan Smith

ILLUSTRATORS
Chinglemba Chingtham, Surat Kumar Mantoo,
Arun Pottirayil, T. Gautam Trivedi

Reproduced in Singapore by Colourscan
Printed and bound by L. Rex Printing Company Limited, China

First American Edition, 2010
10 11 12 13 10 9 8 7 6 5 4 3 2 1

Published in the United States by Dorling Kindersley Publishing, Inc.,
375 Hudson Street, New York 10014

Copyright © 2010 Dorling Kindersley Limited, London
A Penguin Company

Published in Great Britain by Dorling Kindersley Limited.

A CATALOGING IN PUBLICATION RECORD
IS AVAILABLE FROM THE LIBRARY OF CONGRESS.

ISSN: 1542-1554
ISBN: 978-0-7566-6194-6

FLOORS ARE REFERRED TO THROUGHOUT IN ACCORDANCE WITH
EUROPEAN USAGE; IE THE "FIRST FLOOR" IS AT GROUND LEVEL.

*Front cover main image: Štorch House with a painting of
St Wenceslas on horseback, Old Town Square, Prague*

MIX
Paper from
responsible sources
FSC™ C018179

◁ **Magnificent view of the clay-tiled rooftops of Dubrovnik, Croatia**

Forested hills, Western Tatras, Slovakia

CONTENTS

**Viru Street lined with cafés and
shops, Tallinn, Estonia**

Gilt-framed icons in the Russian Church, Sofia, Bulgaria

View of Drava riverfront, Maribor, Slovenia

Russian coat of arms, Peter and Paul Fortress, St Petersburg

Peleș Castle, Romania *(see pp582–3)*

HOW TO USE THIS GUIDE

This travel guide helps you to get the most from your visit to Eastern and Central Europe, providing detailed practical information and expert recommendations. *Eastern and Central Europe at a Glance* gives an overview of some of the main attractions and a brief history. The book is divided into three sections,

each covering five, six or seven countries. Each country chapter starts with a historical portrait and a map of the region. The main sightseeing section then follows, with maps of the capital cities. For each country there is a section on practical and travel information, followed by listings of recommended hotels and restaurants.

EASTERN AND CENTRAL EUROPE MAP

The coloured map on the inside front cover indicates the 14 country and 3 city chapters in this guide.

A locator map shows where the region lies in relation to the countries around it.

1 At a Glance

The map here highlights the most interesting cities, towns and sights in the countries covered by each of the guide's three sections, such as South Eastern Europe.

Each country chapter has colour-coded thumb tabs.

2 Country Introduction

This section gives the reader an insight into the country's history, geography and culture. A chart lists the key dates and events in the country's history.

Sights at a Glance lists the numbered sights in the chapter in alphabetical order.

3 Country Map

For easy reference, sights in each country are numbered and plotted on a map. The black bullet numbers indicate the order in which the sights are covered in the chapter.

4 Street-by-Street Map
This gives a bird's-eye view of interesting and important parts of each sightseeing area.

A suggested route takes in some of the area's most fascinating and attractive streets.

Numbers correspond to each sight's position on the country map and its place in the chapter.

5 Detailed Information
Cities, towns and other sights are described individually. Entries appear in the same order as the numbering on the country map.

A Visitors' Checklist gives all the practical information needed to plan one's visit.

6 Major Sights
Historic buildings are dissected to reveal their interiors, while museums have colour-coded floor plans to help one find the most important exhibits.

Stars indicate the features that no visitor should miss.

7 Practical Information
This section covers topics such as visas, security, travel, shopping and entertainment. The larger countries are covered in greater detail.

Directory boxes give contact information for the services and venues mentioned in the text.

Climate charts are provided for each country.

VISITING EASTERN AND CENTRAL EUROPE

Putting Eastern and Central Europe on the Map

The continent of Europe covers a total surface area of 10.4 million square km (4 million square miles) and stretches east as far as the Ural Mountains in the Russian Federation. This guide covers 14 countries, 10 of which belong to the European Union (EU), as well as the cities of Vienna, Moscow and St Petersburg. The featured countries are shown on this map in bright green. The principal international airports and major road links are also shown here, while the European rail network is shown on the inside back cover.

Satellite image showing the terrain of Europe
This image shows the range of landscapes in Eastern and Central Europe, from the broad plain that stretches from Poland to the Baltic States and Russia, to the rugged highlands of the Carpathian and Balkan mountain ranges.

BALTIC SEA

Koszalin
Gdynia
Gdańsk
Elbląg
Szczecin
Bydgoszcz
Toruń
GERMANY
Włocławek
Poznań
POLAND
Zielona Góra
Kalisz
Łódź
Legnica
Wrocław
Karlovy Vary
PRAGUE
Opole
Plzeň
Cracow
CZECH REPUBLIC
Ostrava
Olomouc
České Budějovice
Brno
Český Krumlov
SLOVAKIA
Danube
Trnava
VIENNA
BRATISLAVA
Esztergom
AUSTRIA
Győr
BUDAPEST
Veszprém
Kecskemét
Keszthely
Bled
Maribor
HUNGARY
LJUBLJANA
Varaždin
Pécs
SLOVENIA
ZAGREB
Rijeka
Osijek
Pula
Rab
Banja Luka
Novi Sad
CROATIA
BOSNIA AND HERZEGOVINA
Zadar
SARAJEVO
Trogir
Split
Vis
Brač
Hvar
Mostar
Korčula
MONTENEGRO
Dubrovnik
ADRIATIC SEA
PODGORICA
ITALY
ALBANIA

EUROPE

ATLANTIC OCEAN
NORWAY
FINLAND
SWEDEN
UNITED KINGDOM
NORTH SEA
BALTIC SEA
RUSSIAN FEDERATION
BELARUS
GERMANY
EASTERN AND CENTRAL EUROPE
UKRAINE
FRANCE
ITALY
BLACK SEA
SPAIN
MEDITERRANEAN SEA
TURKEY

◁ Outdoor café lining Cathedral Square in Rīga, Latvia

St Petersburg

TALLINN

Hiiumaa Island

ESTONIA

Lake Peipsi

Pärnu

Tartu

Saaremaa Island

RUSSIAN FEDERATION

Ventspils

Gulf of Riga

MOSCOW

RĪGA

LATVIA

iepāja

Jūrmala

Šiauliai

Daugavpils

laipėda

LITHUANIA

RUSSIAN *EDERATION*

Kaunas

VILNIUS

Olsztyn

Białystok

BELARUS

WARSAW

Radom

Lublin

Kielce

Rzeszów

UKRAINE

Košice

Aerial view of the medieval city of Dubrovnik, Croatia

Miskolc

Eger

Satu Mare

MOLDOVA

Debrecen

Oradea

Cluj-Napoca

Bacău

Targu Mureş

Arad

Sighişoara

ROMANIA

Timişoara

Sibiu

Braşov

Galaţi

Buzău

Brăila

Ploieşti

BELGRADE

Piteşti

Constanţa

BUCHAREST

SERBIA

Craiova

Danube

Ruse

Dobrich

Niš

Pleven

Varna

BULGARIA

Veliko Tûrnovo

SOFIA

Burgas

OSO...O

Koprivshtitsa

Stara Zagora

BLACK SEA

Plovdiv

ACEDONIA

TURKEY

GREECE

| 0 kilometres | 250 |
| 0 miles | 250 |

KEY

✈ Airport

—— Motorway

—— Major road

–·– International border

PRACTICAL INFORMATION

The countries in Eastern and Central Europe have undergone great transformation since the collapse of Communism in 1990. Some states have adapted quickly to the change and are now active members of the European Union (EU), while others continue to wrestle with serious economic and political problems. As a result, the quality of tourist facilities varies greatly

The European Union flag

throughout the region. Accommodation and public transport are well organized and reliable in North Eastern Europe. In the southeast, on the other hand, travel may be slower and standards less predictable. However, with an impressive diversity of history, culture and folklore to discover, Eastern and Central Europe makes for a rich and enjoyable travel experience.

WHEN TO GO

The best time to visit Eastern and Central Europe depends on the visitor's itinerary. However, most people prefer spring and summer, from April to September. Stretching from the Baltic Sea in the north to the Mediterranean Sea in the south, the region has a wide variety of climates. Summers in North Eastern Europe can be cool and rainy, while in South Eastern Europe they can be unbearably hot, especially in big cities. The Adriatic coast, with its hot, dry summers and relatively mild winters, has the balmiest climate, but crowds can be a drawback in the peak season of July and August, making May, June and September better times to visit.

Elsewhere in South Eastern Europe, long, hot summers and long, cold winters are the usual trends. The mountains of Slovenia, Slovakia, Romania and Bulgaria provide ideal conditions for skiing, with a season that runs from mid December to late March.

Winters in the north of the region, near the Baltic coast, can be long, cold and dark. During the depths of winter the sun sets at 3–4pm, and daytime temperatures rarely rise above 0° C (32° F). Summertime, on the other hand, offers the prospect of long daylight hours in St Petersburg and the northern Baltic States.

Visitors should bear in mind that August is a busy month in all parts of Eastern and Central Europe, when most Europeans take their vacations.

TIME ZONES

The countries covered in this guide sit across three time zones. Poland, the Czech Republic, Slovakia, Hungary, Austria, Slovenia, Croatia, Bosnia and Herzegovina, Montenegro and Serbia are all on Central European Time (CET), which is one hour ahead of Greenwich Mean Time (GMT) and 6 hours ahead of New York. Lithuania, Latvia, Estonia, Romania and Bulgaria are on East European Time (EET), which is 2 hours ahead of GMT and 7 hours ahead of New York. The Russian cities of Moscow and St Petersburg are on Moscow Standard Time (MST), which is 3 hours ahead of GMT and 8 hours ahead of New York.

In Europe, the clocks go forward by one hour in late March and go back by one hour in late October.

DOCUMENTATION

Of the 14 countries included in this guide, 11 (Lithuania, Latvia, Estonia, Poland, the Czech Republic, Slovakia, Hungary, Austria, Slovenia, Romania and Bulgaria) are members of the European Union (EU). EU citizens can visit all of these countries with a valid identity card. Citizens of the United States, Canada, Japan, New Zealand, Norway and Switzerland can also enter these countries with a valid passport.

All of the EU members listed above, except Romania and Bulgaria, are signatories of the Schengen Agreement. Borders between Schengen zone countries are open, and once inside the Schengen zone, identity documents do not usually need to be shown when crossing a common frontier. However, visitors should always keep their identity documents handy just in case random checks are made.

In the rest of Eastern Europe, entry requirements differ from country to country. Visitors from the EU, US, Canada, Australia and New Zealand can enter Croatia, Bosnia and Herzegovina, Serbia and Montenegro on the production of a valid passport. Citizens of other countries, however, should check current regulations before they travel.

Russia requires almost all foreign visitors to purchase a visa before travel, which usually involves applying in person or through a travel agent to the local Russian embassy or consulate several weeks before the trip. For visitors who want to include Moscow and St Petersburg in their itinerary, it is advisable to plan this part of the trip well in advance.

STUDENT CARDS

Various bus and rail tickets offer discounts on European travel (*see pp18–19*), but, in addition to these, students with a recognized student card may be eligible for a wider range of discounts. The best card is the International Student Identity Card (ISIC), which gives discounts on all kinds of goods and transport as well as cheaper admission to many museums, galleries and other sights. Most students can obtain this card from their educational establishment at home, but it can also be obtained abroad from an ISIC issuing office or from branches of STA travel *(see p17)*. For US students, this card also includes some medical cover.

CUSTOMS AND DUTY-FREE

Duty-free allowances are not available to visitors travelling from one EU country to another. However, duty-free goods can be purchased on entry or exit from the EU as a whole. The allowances are as follows: tobacco (200 cigarettes, 50 cigars or 250 g/ 9 oz of loose tobacco); alcohol (1 litre/2 pints of strong spirits, 2 litres/4 pints of alcohol under 22 per cent proof, and 2 litres/4 pints of wine); coffee (500 g/18 oz) and perfume (60 ml/0.1 pint).

When returning to their home country, visitors may be asked to declare any items purchased abroad and pay duty on any amount that exceeds their home country's allowance; the scope of these allowances will vary from one country to another.

VALUE ADDED TAX

In both EU member-states and most other countries in Eastern and Central Europe, all goods and services (except certain items such as food and children's clothing) are subject to Value Added Tax (VAT), which is included in most prices. Visitors may claim a refund on this tax if they are neither citizens of the EU nor of the particular country they are visiting, but it can be a lengthy process.

The easiest way to do this is to shop at places displaying the "Euro Free Tax" sign, although the stores that offer this service may be expensive or sell only luxury goods. Visitors need to show their passport to the shop assistant and complete a form, after which VAT will be deducted from the bill. In certain

countries, visitors need to keep their receipts and VAT forms and present them at a tax refund desk with their unopened purchases when they leave the country. These forms will be processed and a refund is eventually sent to their home address.

PERSONAL SECURITY

Although Eastern and Central Europe is a relatively safe region to travel, visitors should always take certain precautions. Pickpocketing and petty theft are by far the biggest threats to visitors, although these are more common in some countries than in others – specific information is given in the practical and travel information section of each country chapter.

The safest way of carrying money is in the form of traveller's cheques. Visitors should have their belongings adequately insured before leaving home and not leave them unattended. In the event of a robbery, it should be reported immediately to the local police and a copy of the report acquired. Visitors are advised to keep their valuables well concealed, especially in crowded areas or on public transport. If driving, it is safer to leave the car in a car park rather than on the street.

INSURANCE AND MEDICAL TREATMENT

Travel insurance is essential to cover any loss or damage to possessions and for unexpected medical and dental treatment. Many major credit cards offer some insurance if travellers purchase their flight tickets or holiday package through them, so it is advisable to check before buying a separate policy. If possible, it is better to buy a policy that pays for medical treatment on the spot, rather than one that reimburses later. Most general insurance policies do not cover potentially hazardous outdoor activities such as climbing, skiing and scuba diving, although these can be included at extra cost.

FACILITIES FOR THE DISABLED

Conditions for disabled travellers are improving rapidly throughout Eastern and Central Europe, however facilities can vary drastically from one country to the next.

In some cities, pavements, tourist attractions such as museums and public transport have been adapted for wheelchair users, while elsewhere much of this work still remains to be done. In general terms, the cities of South Eastern Europe lag behind those of Central and North Eastern Europe in serving disabled travellers.

Not all destinations provide adapted accommodation for those with special needs; wheelchair users should plan their itinerary carefully and much in advance. Hotels with ratings of four stars and above usually have rooms adapted for wheelchairs, but these are generally expensive and tend to be concentrated in and around the big cities and major tourist towns.

Spa tourism is well developed throughout the region, and many of the highly reputed health resorts offer excellent facilities for the disabled.

CONVERSION CHART

The metric system is used throughout Eastern and Central Europe.

Imperial to Metric
1 inch = 2.54 centimetres
1 foot = 30 centimetres
1 mile = 1.6 kilometres
1 ounce = 28 grams
1 pound = 454 grams
1 US pint = 0.47 litre
1 UK pint = 0.55 litre
1 US gallon = 3.8 litres
1 UK gallon = 4.6 litres

Metric to Imperial
1 millimetre = 0.04 inch
1 centimetre = 0.4 inch
1 metre = 3 feet 3 inches
1 kilometre = 0.6 mile
1 gram = 0.035 ounce
1 kilogram = 2.2 pounds
1 litre = 2.1 US pints
1 litre = 1.76 UK pints

Communications and Money

Communications in Eastern and Central Europe have improved vastly over the last two decades, and all countries in the region now have reliable postal services and extensive mobile phone networks. There is also a growing number of hotels and cafés which offer Internet services. Of the currencies in use in Eastern and Central Europe, some, such as the euro, can be purchased from banks in any country, while others are difficult to obtain until arrival. Credit cards are widely accepted throughout the region and ATM cash machines are not hard to find.

TELEPHONES

Mobile (cell) phone coverage extends across the region. Not all mobile phones, however, work everywhere. Visitors should check with their service provider before travelling to ensure that their mobile phone works abroad. Also, most US mobile phones do not work in Europe and vice versa, but visitors can buy phones that work in both continents.

Public telephone booths are becoming less common in Eastern and Central Europe, although they can still be found in the centre of towns and cities. Some public telephones are coin-operated, although most now accept phone cards, which can be bought from newspaper kiosks and post offices.

MAIL SERVICES

Mail services are generally efficient, with letters and cards typically taking 5 days to reach Western Europe and 7 days to reach North America or Australasia. Services do vary across the region, however,

and in some areas such as Serbia, Bulgaria and Russia, they may be slower. If the visitor's itinerary involves moving through countries rather than staying long-term at a particular address, they can still receive mail by using the Poste Restante system. This can be set up at main post offices in large towns. Travellers should ask for any mail to be sent "care of" poste restante to the main post office in the town in question. They will need to show their identity cards or passports to collect their mail. Mail from overseas is usually kept for one month.

INTERNET CAFÉS

Most towns and cities in Eastern and Central Europe will have a handful of Internet cafés offering computer access, scanning, printing and, frequently, cheap international telephone calls as well. A small but increasing number of city-centre cafés offer free wireless Internet to their customers. In addition, many hotels and hostels now offer wireless or cable Internet access to their guests. Many have a computer in the lobby which guests can use.

CHANGING MONEY

The majority of countries in Eastern and Central Europe have their own currency and, in most cases, visitors will need to change money every time they cross a border.

Money can usually be changed at banks, post offices, exchange bureaus (*bureaux de change*) and hotel reception desks. Banks and post offices are often open only from Monday to Friday (sometimes with the addition of a few hours on Saturday morning). Exchange bureaus are more likely to stay open at evenings and weekends. Those located at airports, railway stations and border crossings generally offer poor rates, so it is usually best to change only a small amount here and then proceed elsewhere to change the bulk of the spending money at a better rate. Many bureaus only offer advantageous rates on larger sums of money and apply a different rate of exchange to smaller transactions. Reception desks at hotels usually offer the worst rates of exchange and should only be used if other options are unavailable.

ATM cash machines are distributed widely throughout Eastern and Central Europe. Those visitors with a card belonging to a global network (Plus, Visa, Maestro, Cirrus or MasterCard) can withdraw cash anywhere, but a small fee will be charged for each ATM transaction carried out abroad. It is always a good idea to carry more than one card when travelling, in case one of them is refused or retained by an ATM due to a banking error. Although traveller's cheques remain the safest way to carry money, they are increasingly uncommon; trying to cash them in a bank can be a tedious and time-consuming process since cashiers are often unfamiliar with them.

INTERNATIONAL DIALLING CODES

The list below gives the international dialling codes for the countries covered in this guide. When calling from the US and Canada, prefix all numbers by "011"; from Australia by "0011"; from New Zealand by "00". When calling from within Europe, use the "00" prefix. If unsure, call international directory enquiries.

• Austria	43	• Lithuania	70
• Bosnia and Herzegovina	387	• Montenegro	82
• Bulgaria	359	• Poland	48
• Croatia	381	• Romania	40
• Czech Republic	420	• Russia	7
• Estonia	372	• Serbia	81
• Hungary	36	• Slovakia	21
• Latvia	371	• Slovenia	86

THE EURO

The euro (the common European Union currency) has so far been adopted by four of the countries in this guide: Austria, Slovenia, Slovakia and, despite not yet being an EU member, Montenegro. Several other countries in the region are planning to adopt the euro in the future, although this may take several years.

In countries outside the euro zone, the euro is sometimes accepted by hotels, restaurants and shops in big resorts, but it is always better to carry local currency in case it is not. The price of accommodation and transport is frequently quoted in euros in order to make it easier for visitors to calculate their expenditure, but actual payment is usually made in the local currency.

Bank Notes

Euro banknotes have seven denominations. The 5-euro note (grey in colour) is the smallest, followed by the 10-euro note (pink), 20-euro note (blue), 50-euro note (orange), 100-euro note (green), 200-euro note (yellow) and 500-euro note (purple). All notes feature the stars of the European Union.

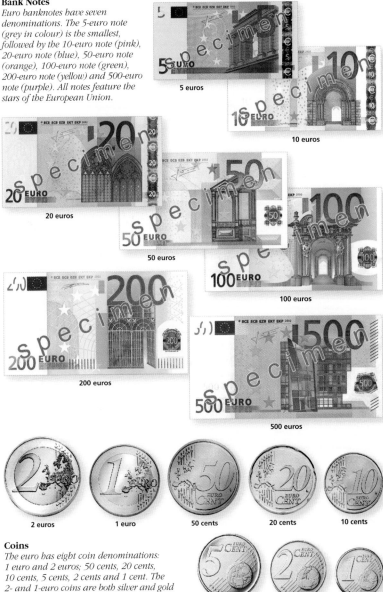

5 euros

10 euros

20 euros

50 euros

100 euros

200 euros

500 euros

2 euros

1 euro

50 cents

20 cents

10 cents

Coins

The euro has eight coin denominations: 1 euro and 2 euros; 50 cents, 20 cents, 10 cents, 5 cents, 2 cents and 1 cent. The 2- and 1-euro coins are both silver and gold in colour. The 50-, 20- and 10-cent coins are gold. The 5-, 2- and 1-cent coins are bronze.

5 cents

2 cents

1 cent

Eastern and Central Europe by Air

With a good network of international flights, the whole of Eastern and Central Europe is easily accessible by air. Most European nations have well-respected national carriers operating flights to Western Europe as well as North America. With the recent addition of budget airlines offering "no frills" flights in the area, several new destinations have opened up, resulting in an increase in the number of flights within countries in the region. Competition between various airlines ensures that air fares are relatively low, especially for travellers who book ahead over the Internet. Package tours and travel agencies help keep costs down as well and ensure great trips.

FLYING TO EASTERN AND CENTRAL EUROPE

Visitors travelling from a major international airport will find that a significant number of cities in Eastern and Central Europe are served by direct flights. National carriers offering direct flights from North America include **Austrian Airlines** to Vienna, **CSA Czech Airlines** to Prague, **LOT Polish Airlines** to Warsaw and Cracow and **Aeroflot** to Moscow. **Malév Hungarian Airlines** also flies from major cities in Europe and the US.

Most of the major North American airlines such as **Delta**, **Air Canada**, **American** and **Continental** offer one-stop flights to the region in conjunction with their European partner airlines, usually involving a change of flight in a city in Western Europe. From Australasia, **Qantas** and Air New Zealand offer one- or two-stop flights to the region in partnership with other airlines.

The biggest choice of flights is offered by airports in the UK and Ireland, and travellers from North America and Australasia may find it convenient to break their journey there before proceeding to Eastern and Central Europe. National carriers connect London directly with most of the capital cities in the region. In addition, budget airlines such as **easyJet**, **Ryanair** and **Wizzair** fly direct from London and many other regional UK and Irish airports

to several destinations in the region. Capitals such as Warsaw, Prague, Budapest and Rīga are well covered, along with a host of regional cities in Poland, the Adriatic resorts of Croatia, and a handful of destinations in Slovakia, Romania and Bulgaria. Travellers should bear in mind that flights with budget airlines do not provide passengers with much legroom and do not offer any complimentary food and drink.

FLIGHT TIMES

As a rough guide, flights from New York to Eastern and Central Europe take between 8 and 9 hours. Flights from Sydney will involve at least one change and are likely to take 23 to 25 hours. From London, flights to Austria, the Czech Republic, Slovenia and Croatia take around 2 hours and 30 minutes; flights to Poland and the Baltic States take around 3 hours and 30 minutes; and flights to Romania and Bulgaria take around 4 hours.

BUDGET TRAVEL AGENCIES

As a rule, European air fares are at their cheapest between November and March, with the exception of Christmas and Easter weeks. The high season is from June to mid-September. A "shoulder season" of moderate prices exists between these periods. It is always advisable to travel

mid-week, when tickets are cheaper and airports less busy. Many of the cheapest fares from North America or Australasia involve flights with more than one stop en route and long stopovers. While this may be an economical way to travel, it can also be tiring; it is best to check timings carefully before booking.

Whichever season visitors travel, there are several ways of saving money on air fares. A good way of finding out about cheap fares is to contact a travel agency that specializes in budget travel, such as **STA Travel** or **Trailfinders** in the US and the UK respectively. Youngsters (under 25), students and senior citizens will usually find that they are eligible for reduced fares. Generally speaking, the cheapest are return (round-trip) tickets, which have fixed dates rather than an "open" return. Depending on the distance, round-the-world (RTW) tickets can sometimes work out cheaper than a standard long-haul return. These enable travellers to fly around the world on specified routes, providing they do not backtrack. The number of Eastern and Central European cities that feature in RTW packages is relatively small, but it is always worth enquiring with established travel agents to see what is available.

Standby tickets are also economical, but visitors need to be flexible about the date and time of departure. Travelling this way may involve a wait of several days until a cancellation comes up.

PACKAGE DEALS

One of the easiest ways to arrange a visit to Eastern and Central Europe is to opt for a package vacation. They normally include flights, transfers, accommodation and sometimes, side trips and meals. Package trips often work out cheaper than if travellers were to book these deals separately. The downside is that such trips usually involve travelling in a group with a fixed itinerary, thereby cutting down on the independence of the visitor.

Several North American travel companies, including **Adventures Abroad**, **Gate 1** and **Tradesco**, offer week-long or 21-day holidays to the region, either focusing on one country or combining several in a busy itinerary.

Similar packages are offered by **Abercrombie & Kent**, which specializes in up market accommodation and is therefore slightly more expensive than the other operators. Those who specialize in Eastern and Central European destinations and provide the services of local guides include **Regent Holidays** in the UK, and **Gateway Travel** and **Contal Travel** in Australia.

Travellers who want to experience the great outdoors should consider adventure-holiday companies such as **Exodus** and **Explore**, which offer hiking and activity holidays with itineraries to suit all levels of fitness.

FLY-DRIVE

Many airlines and travel companies offer fly-drive packages, which combine flights and car rental. These deals are often worth considering, as they offer flexibility and save the effort of arranging for the two separately.

INTERNET BOOKING

The Internet has become a popular way of booking tickets. Many scheduled and budget airlines now offer their cheapest rates on the Internet, and these fares frequently undercut anything offered by the high-street travel agencies.

As well as checking individual airline websites, travellers should also browse the websites of Internet-based travel agents such as **Opodo**, **Expedia** and **Travelocity**. They are particularly useful for finding out the best deals on one-stop or two-stop flights to Eastern and Central Europe, which may involve more than one airline. These agents also offer bookings in select hotels, allowing visitors to sort out their flights and accommodation in one go. The US company **Europebyair** offers a FlightPass for non-European citizens, operating one-way flights between selected European cities for a reasonable price. Only a handful of East European airports are included in the FlightPass scheme, but it is still a useful way of getting around the vast European continent.

FLIGHTS WITHIN EASTERN AND CENTRAL EUROPE

Travelling from one end of the region to the other can be time consuming for those who attempt to do it by road or rail. Fortunately, there is an extensive network of flights between the major capitals.

National carriers such as CSA Czech Airlines, LOT Polish Airlines and Malév Hungarian Airlines offer the biggest choice of regional flights, with Prague, Budapest and Warsaw serving as the main hubs for their respective networks. Several budget airlines also operate regional flights, especially in the summer, when travellers from North Eastern Europe head for the Mediterranean and Black Sea beaches. The Latvian company AirBaltic has services linking the capitals of North Eastern Europe. In addition, the budget airline Wizzair offers summer flights from Poland and Hungary to the Bulgarian coast.

DIRECTORY

FLYING TO EASTERN AND CENTRAL EUROPE

Aeroflot
www.aeroflot.ru

Air Canada
www.aircanada.com

American
www.aa.com

Austrian Airlines
www.aua.com

Continental
www.continental.com

CSA Czech Airlines
www.czechairlines.com

Delta
www.delta.com

easyJet
www.easyjet.com

LOT Polish Airlines
www.lot.com

Malév Hungarian Airlines
www.malev.com

Qantas
www.qantas.com.au

Ryanair
www.ryanair.com

Wizzair
www.wizzair.com

BUDGET TRAVEL AGENCIES

STA Travel
www.statravel.com

Trailfinders
www.trailfinders.com

PACKAGE DEALS

Abercrombie & Kent
Tel 800 554 7016 (US).
www.abercrombiekent.com

Adventures Abroad
Tel 800 665 3998 (US),
0114 247 3400 (UK).
www.adventures-abroad.com

Contal Travel
Tel 02 9212 5077 (Aus).
www.contaltours.com.au

Exodus
Tel 020 8675 5550 (UK).
www.exodus.co.uk

Explore
Tel 0845 013 1537 (UK).
www.exploreworldwide.com

Gate 1
Tel 800 682 3333 (US).
www.gate1travel.com

Gateway Travel
Tel 02 9745 3333 (Aus).
www.russian-gateway.com.au

Regent Holidays
Tel 0845 277 3317 (UK).
www.regent-holidays.co.uk

Tradesco
Tel 800 448 4321 (US).
www.tradescotours.com

INTERNET BOOKING

Europebyair
www.europebyair.com

Expedia
www.expedia.com

Opodo
www.opodo.com

Travelocity
www.travelocity.com

Eastern and Central Europe by Train, Road and Ferry

Eastern and Central Europe is covered by an extensive and comprehensive rail network, but services vary in speed and comfort from one part of the region to another. Buses are a popular means of transport throughout, covering towns and villages that are not served by trains. Good-quality modern motorways connect the major cities but, away from the main routes, road surfaces can be poor. Boat trips are a great way to view the region's beautiful scenery, but can be expensive.

TRAINS AND TICKETS

The rail network in Eastern and Central Europe features every kind of train, at every speed. Among the fastest and most comfortable are the InterCity (IC) services, which link major centres and make few stops. Faster still are the Euro City (EC) international trains which connect big cities and may run through several countries en route. Most IC and EC routes are equipped with modern, air-conditioned carriages offering both first- and second-class seating.

Slightly slower are the regional express trains, which operate under different names in various countries. Slower still, regional passenger trains serve the local community and stop at all stations en route. These passenger trains only offer second-class seating and the carriages are frequently old and basic.

Tickets should be bought at the ticket counter in the station before boarding the train. Some stations have separate counters for domestic and international trains; it is best to confirm before queuing up. Many IC and EC trains offer seat reservations for a small extra cost. It is also advisable to check whether regional and international express services have buffet cars; many do not.

TRAIN ROUTES

The best IC and EC services are in Central Europe, where all major capitals and regional cities are served by fast, punctual trains. Using the rail network to tour Austria, the Czech Republic, Slovakia, Poland, Hungary, Slovenia and northern Croatia is very convenient and problem-free.

However, in South Eastern Europe, services between the main cities in Bosnia and Herzegovina, Serbia, Romania and Bulgaria are relatively slow, and visitors might consider travelling by bus instead. In North Eastern Europe, the capital cities of Lithuania, Latvia and Estonia are only connected by bus.

Several railway journeys are worth making for the fantastic scenery along the route. The express train from Belgrade, in Serbia, to Bar, in Montenegro, passes through dramatic mountain terrain. Much slower, but equally delightful, is the Bulgarian narrow-gauge line from Bansko to Septemvri, which goes through a bewitching highland landscape. The rail routes connecting central Romanian towns such as Brașov, Sibiu and Sighișoara pass through some of Europe's loveliest rural countryside, while travelling from Vienna in Austria to the Slovenian capital Ljubljana or the Croatian capital Zagreb features some gorgeous subalpine terrain.

INFORMATION AND TIMETABLES

Most of the national rail companies in the region have websites with relevant timetable details. However, information is not always available in English, and international rail routes across the whole continent are not consistently covered. The best source of information on international services is German Railways (Deutsche Bahn), whose website provides a timetable for most destinations in Eastern and Central Europe. Excellent advice on trans-European travel can also be found on The Man in Seat 61, a website run by dedicated rail enthusiasts. In addition, Thomas Cook publishes a European Railway Timetable which covers all the main routes in Europe. This can be bought from branches of Thomas Cook in the UK, or purchased online.

RAIL PASSES FOR NON-EUROPEANS

For non-Europeans, the cheapest way to explore the region by rail is to buy one of the many passes available from Eurail. For those travelling from North America or Australasia, it is cheaper to buy one before travelling. The official representative for Eurail in North America is Railpass. Eurail passes cover Austria, Bulgaria, the Czech Republic, Croatia, Hungary, Romania and Slovenia, but do not extend to Bosnia and Herzegovina, Estonia, Latvia, Lithuania, Montenegro, Serbia, Poland, Slovakia or Russia.

Several kinds of Eurail passes are available. Eurail Select covers unlimited first-class travel in a cluster of three to five countries of the visitor's choice, with passes valid for periods ranging from five days to two months. The Eurail Global pass covers first-class travel in the seven countries in Eastern and Central Europe mentioned above as well as in 14 countries in Western Europe, for periods ranging from 15 days to three months. The Eurail Youthpass is a cheaper, second-class version of the Global pass, available to those aged under 26.

RAIL PASSES FOR EUROPEANS

For Europeans, the best option is the Inter-Rail pass, which can be purchased from Rail Europe or from the main train operators in individual countries. This pass covers 30 countries across Europe, including most of the countries covered in this guide; Estonia, Latvia, Lithuania and Russia are the exceptions.

The pass comes in two versions – one for adults, and a less expensive one for travellers under the age 26. It covers periods ranging from five days to one month. It is not valid for the country in which it is purchased, where full-price individual rail tickets must be bought.

DRIVING PERMITS

Visitors planning to drive in Eastern and Central Europe are advised to acquire an International Driving Permit (IDP) before they travel.

The IDP is not compulsory everywhere in the region, but regulations differ from one country to the next, and many of the region's car-hire companies require an IDP in addition to a national driving permit issued in the visitor's home country. The IDP is valid for one year and can be obtained from the national motoring organization in a traveller's home country.

DRIVING IN EASTERN AND CENTRAL EUROPE

In Eastern and Central Europe, people drive on the right-hand side of the road and overtaking is from the left. Visitors should note that they are not allowed to overtake more than one car at a time. Distances are measured in kilometres. Speed limits are usually 120–130 kmph (75–80 mph) on motorways, 80–100 kmph (50–60 mph) on secondary roads, and 50 kmph (30 mph) in built-up areas, although there are differences from one country to the next.

Some countries charge toll fees on particular motorways, while others such as Austria and Slovenia charge a one-time fee which must be paid on entering the country. Elsewhere, the vast majority of roads are free. Filling stations are common on motorways and main roads but are less frequent in rural

areas. Unleaded fuel is available everywhere in most destinations. Driving at night can be dangerous in rural areas, where roads might be narrow and winding.

CAR RENTAL

Car rental is a competitive business in the region, so prices are generally affordable. The biggest car rental companies are **Avis**, **Budget**, **Europcar**, **Hertz** and **Sixt**, all of which offer excellent services.

TRAVELLING BY BUS

Domestic bus services offer an alternative to trains throughout Eastern and Central Europe, and provide the only means of getting to those places that are not served by the rail network. Buses running between major cities are often fast and comfortable, and may also have air conditioning. However, rural services frequently make use of slow, ageing vehicles.

Most towns and cities have a central bus station where visitors can check information and purchase tickets. Advance reservations are advisable when travelling on major intercity routes at weekends or during the summer holiday period.

There is a wide network of international buses, especially in the Baltic States and in South Eastern Europe, where international trains are slow or infrequent. International bus services are run by several local companies, but the international operator **Eurolines** runs an extensive network of routes across the continent.

TRAVELLING BY FERRY

Ferries constitute a lifeline in countries such as Estonia and Croatia, where they provide the only access to many of the offshore islands. A ride on the ferry which runs along the Croatian coast from Rijeka to Dubrovnik is one of South Eastern Europe's classic journeys. For visitors travelling from Western Europe,

one of the quickest ways to get there is to catch a ferry from Italy to Croatia. **Jadrolinija** and **SNAV** are the two biggest operators. Most ferries depart from the Italian port of Ancona, although there are services from Bari as well.

DIRECTORY

INFORMATION AND TIMETABLES

German Railways (Deutsche Bahn)
www.bahn.de

The Man in Seat 61
www.seat61.com

Thomas Cook
www.thomascooktimetables.com

RAIL PASSES FOR NON-EUROPEANS

Eurail
www.eurail.com

Railpass
Tel 1 877 724 5727 (US).
www.railpass.com

RAIL PASSES FOR EUROPEANS

Rail Europe
Tel 08448 484 064 (UK).
www.raileurope.co.uk

CAR RENTAL

Avis
www.avis.com

Budget
www.budget.com

Europcar
www.europcar.com

Hertz
www.hertz.com

Sixt
www.sixt.com

TRAVELLING BY BUS

Eurolines
Tel 0871 781 8181 (UK).
www.eurolines.co.uk

TRAVELLING BY FERRY

Jadrolinija
Tel 385 51 666 111 (Cro).
www.jadrolinija.hr

SNAV
Tel 39 71 207 6116 (Ita).
www.snav.it

EASTERN AND CENTRAL EUROPE AT A GLANCE

Landscapes

A range of climatic and geological conditions has forged an impressive variety of landscapes in Eastern and Central Europe. Despite the impact of human activity, there are many areas of wilderness that remain intact. From the bogs of North Eastern Europe and the wetlands of the Danube delta to striking mountain ranges such as the Carpathians, stretching from the Czech Republic to Romania, the region's diverse landscapes offer endless opportunities for exploration.

Slovakia
Running along Slovakia's border with Poland, the Tatra Mountains (see pp316–17) feature towering peaks and deep blue lakes. At 2,655 m (8,711 ft), Gerlachovský štít is the range's highest point.

Slovenia
Much of western Slovenia is made up of karst – dry limestone plateau dotted with caves. Show caverns at Postojna (see pp426–7) and Škocjan (see p428) contain a spectacular array of stalagmites and stalactites.

Croatia
Croatia's heavily indented Adriatic coast boasts stunning maritime scenery, with stark mountains overlooking turquoise seas. Charming stone-built villages and Mediterranean flora characterize the string of islands along its length.

Montenegro
The granite massif of Mount Durmitor offers some of the wildest landscapes in the western Balkans. The most dramatic feature is the Tara Gorge, hemmed in by jagged cliffs.

BALTIC SEA

POLAND

CZECH REPUBLIC

SLOVAKIA

Vienna ●

AUSTRIA

HUNGARY

SLOVENIA

CROATIA

BOSNIA AND HERZEGOVINA

SERBIA

ADRIATIC SEA

MONTENEGRO

◁ Stained–glass window at the St Vitus Cathedral, Prague, Czech Republic

Latvia

Eastern Latvia's Gauja National Park (see pp86–7) is dotted with green hills, sandstone cliffs and riverside castles. Highlights include the wildlife reserve at Līgatne and the Iron-Age Latvian village at Lake Āraiši.

St Petersburg

ESTONIA

RUSSIAN
FEDERATION

Moscow

LATVIA

LITHUANIA

Lithuania

Running parallel to the Baltic coast, the Curonian Spit (see pp62–3) is a thin sliver of land formed by wind-blown sand. Quaint fishing villages, such as Nida, are bordered by striking golden dunes.

| 0 km | 250 |
| 0 miles | 250 |

Romania

With its heavy concentration of marshes, lakes and floodplains, the reedy Danube delta is a paradise for flocks of migrating birds, while attracting a small population of fishermen and farmers.

ROMANIA

BLACK
SEA

BULGARIA

Bulgaria

Some of Eastern Europe's most exhilarating hiking terrain is found in the Rila Mountains, where bare grey summits loom over shimmering glacial lakes. At 2,925 m (9,596 ft), Mt Musala is Eastern Europe's highest peak.

Great Capitals

Until the 20th century, Eastern and Central Europe
were characterized by powerful empires rather than
independent nation states. These royal dynasties built
magnificent cathedrals, palaces and castles to symbolize
their greatness and assert their supremacy, giving rise
to some of Europe's most impressive capital cities.
Several imperial cities, including Vienna and Budapest,
were repositories of a fascinating mix of cultures, reflecting the rich ethnic diversity of the local population.

0 km   250

0 miles   250

Prague
*This remarkable city on the
Vltava river has long been
considered one of Europe's
most magical capitals, boasting cobbled medieval alleys,
soaring Gothic spires and
lively squares.*

BALTIC
SEA

POLAN

CZECH
REPUBLIC

Vienna
*In terms of
imperial grandeur,
few cities can
match Vienna,
once capital of the
Habsburg Empire
and still the epit-
ome of Central
European style.*

Vienna   SLOVAKI

AUSTRIA

SLOVENIA   HUNGAR

CROATIA

ADRIATIC SEA

BOSNIA AND
HERZEGOVIN

MONTENEGRO

Budapest
*Straddling the Danube
river, the Hungarian
capital enjoyed something
of an architectural golden
age in the 19th century,
endowing the city with an
array of fine buildings.*

Vilnius

The capital of the Grand Duchy of Lithuania, which stretched from the Baltic to the Black Sea in its 15th-century heyday, Vilnius is packed with grand architecture befitting its wide-ranging historical heritage.

ESTONIA

St Petersburg

RUSSIAN
FEDERATION

LATVIA

Moscow

LITHUANIA

Moscow

*Capital of Russia
since 1480, Moscow
rose to become the
nerve centre of
the Tsarist Empire.
Though displaced by
St Petersburg from
1712–1918, this
fascinating city
remained the heart-
land of Russian
Orthodox culture as
is evident from the
fine churches lining
its central squares.*

ROMANIA

BLACK
SEA

BIA)

BULGARIA

Warsaw

*Elegant Neo-Classical Warsaw was
almost completely destroyed by the
Germans in 1944. Painstakingly
reconstructed after World War II,
today it is an enduring symbol of
Polish national survival.*

Historic Cities

Since time immemorial, Eastern Europe has been crossed by major trade routes to Russia, Central Asia and the Near East. Market towns grew rich from this commerce, and their streets and squares were lined with fine architecture. Some trading towns, such as Cracow in Poland, became, for a time, the seat of royal dynasties and the centre of political power before being sidelined by history. Others, notably the prominent Baltic ports of Riga and Tallinn, spent centuries on the fringes of large empires before finally emerging as the capitals of independent states.

Cracow
The capital of Poland's medieval kings and the site of the biggest market square in Europe, Cracow is packed with buildings from the medieval and Renaissance periods.

Ljubljana
The Slovenian capital is rich in Baroque churches and red-tiled mansions. The tree-lined banks of the Ljubljanica river provide the perfect setting for a stroll.

Sarajevo
An important trading centre in the Ottoman Empire, Sarajevo has, over the centuries, been home to Muslim, Orthodox, Catholic and Jewish communities, all of whom have left their striking architectural imprint on the city.

Dubrovnik
The Adriatic port of Dubrovnik, in Croatia, was an independent city-state that thrived on trade with the Ottoman Empire. The Baroque Old Town, surrounded by stout defensive walls, has been well preserved.

BALTIC SEA

POLAND

CZECH REPUBLIC

SLOVAKI

Vienna ●

AUSTRIA

HUNGARY

SLOVENIA

CROATIA

BOSNIA AND HERZEGOVINA

SERB

MONTENEGRO

ADRIATIC SEA

Tallinn
The Estonian capital is one of the best-preserved medieval cities in Europe. Its cobbled streets are lined with churches and guild halls built by Baltic merchants of the past.

St Petersburg

ESTONIA

RUSSIAN
FEDERATION

Moscow

ATVIA

THUANIA

Rīga
Rīga has been a major Baltic port since the 12th century. It still enjoys the reputation of a city driven by commerce and business, while wonderfully restored Gothic buildings add character to the city centre.

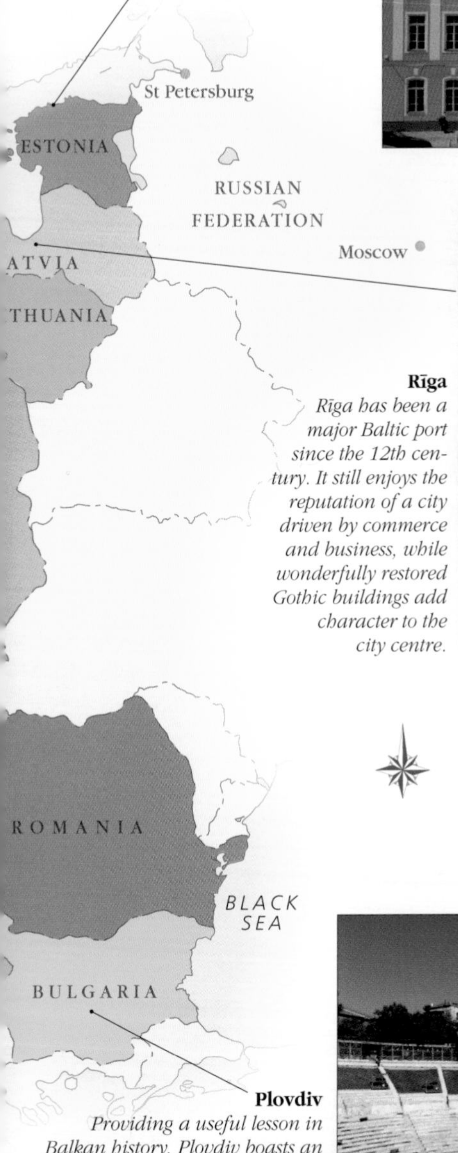

ROMANIA

| 0 km | 250 |
| 0 miles | 250 |

BLACK
SEA

BULGARIA

Plovdiv
Providing a useful lesson in Balkan history, Plovdiv boasts an impressive Roman amphitheatre and Ottoman mosques, as well as 19th-century mansions built by Bulgarian merchants.

Castles and Fortresses

The history of Eastern and Central Europe is one of shifting borders and military conquests. It is no surprise, therefore, that castles and fortresses are a ubiquitous feature of the landscape. Many of the castles became aristocratic residences once their military role was over and were often furnished lavishly by their owners. In modern times, a large number of the fortresses have been restored by governments eager to showcase their country's rich past. They now house some of the region's most prestigious museums, offering a good opportunity to understand the local history and culture.

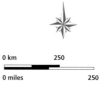

Malbork
A religious and political centre, Malbork Castle (see p207) was built to serve as the capital of the Teutonic knights, the Germanic crusaders who carved out an empire in North Eastern Europe. The castle contains an imposing medieval church.

Karlštejn
Residence of the Holy Roman Emperor Charles IV, Karlštejn Castle (see pp260–61) symbolizes the power and influence enjoyed by medieval Czech rulers. Paintings in the castle's chapel represent one of the high points of Gothic art.

Tvrđa
Built by the Austrians to serve as their military command centre in South Eastern Europe, the fort of Tvrđa (see p496) in Osijek is a virtual city-within-a-city. Complete with squares, mansions and churches, it is one of the best-preserved Baroque ensembles in the continent.

BALTIC
SEA

POLAND

CZECH
REPUBLIC

Vienna SLOVAK

AUSTRIA   HUNGAR

SLOVENIA
          CROATIA
ADRIATIC
              BOSNIA AND
              HERZEGOVIN

SEA   MONTENEG

0 km   250

0 miles   250

Trakai

Romantically situated on an island in the middle of a lake, Trakai Island Castle (see pp56–7) was the one-time residence of Grand Duke Vytautas the Great, who extended Lithuanian power as far as the Black Sea.

St Petersburg

RUSSIAN
FEDERATION

Moscow

ESTONIA

LATVIA

LITHUANIA

Bran

The captivating hilltop stronghold of Bran (see pp580–81) was built in the 14th century to defend Europe from the Turks. It was subsequently used as a holiday home by the Romanian royal family.

ROMANIA

RBIA

BULGARIA   BLACK
SEA

Tsarevets

A fortress that also served as Bulgaria's capital city, Tsarevets (see pp626–7) was home to the Bulgarian tsars from 1185 to 1393. It now plays host to a spectacular son-et-lumiere show on summer evenings.

Kalemegdan

Affording access to the Danube river, this medieval fortress (see pp550–51) was used by Serbian, Ottoman and Austrian rulers. It now serves as Belgrade's most popular park, offering sweeping views from its battlements.

Jewish Culture

Menorah candlestick

One of the key heartlands of Jewish culture, Eastern and Central Europe was home to two main groups of Jewish communities. The first to arrive were the Ashkenazi, who emigrated from the Rhine valley from the 12th century onwards. They were followed by the Sephardic Jews, who, after being expelled from Spain in 1492, resettled in South Eastern Europe. Although over 90 per cent of the region's Jewish population perished during World War II, traces of their heritage can still be seen in the carefully preserved historic quarters of many European cities.

A 19th-century line engraving
depicting the expulsion of Jews from Spain on the orders of King Ferdinand and Queen Isabella.

The old historic quarter of Třebíč (see p278), *in the Czech Republic, is a beautifully preserved example of one of the small towns once dominated by Jewish trading families.*

JEWISH HERITAGE
Eastern and Central Europe's rich Jewish heritage is evident in the large number of synagogues found across the region. Dating from the 1850s, Budapest's Great Synagogue *(see p353)* is a testament to the size and prestige of Hungary's Jewish community. Built in the Moorish Revival style, the interior features both Byzantine and Gothic elements.

Sofia Synagogue (see p606), *built in 1909 to serve the city's growing Jewish community, is an impressive combination of Oriental and Art Nouveau styles.*

Vilnius's Choral Synagogue *was the only one in the Lithuanian capital to survive World War II unscathed. It was completed in 1903 for a congregation that introduced choral singing into their religious services.*

Tallinn's Beit Bella Synagogue, *inaugurated in 2007, is the first synagogue to open in Estonia since the destruction of the earlier one during World War I. It hosts many concerts and events.*

LANGUAGE AND CULTURE

The everyday language of North Eastern European Jewry was Yiddish. By the early 19th century, Vilnius had emerged as a centre of Jewish learning. The religious customs of the Litvaks, as Lithuanian Jews are known in Yiddish, were marked by a rigid analysis of the Talmud, the Jewish laws and traditions. However, any proliferation of Yiddish literature was cut short by the devastation of Jewish communities in World War II.

The Sarajevo Haggadah, *illustrating the Jewish Passover, is a beautifully illuminated manuscript written by Sephardic Jews in 1350.*

The Jewish Museum *in Prague is spread between four historic synagogues. The museum's collections provide a fascinating insight into all aspects of Jewish culture.*

Vilnius *was regarded as the European Jewry's most vibrant cultural centre. It was famous as a centre of study as well as of art and literature.*

The Jewish Culture Festival in Cracow, *held in June each year, features films, theatre, choral performances and traditional* klezmer *music, and is one of the biggest festivals of Jewish culture in the world.*

EMINENT JEWS

Banned from taking up most professions until the late 19th century, Jews lived largely as traders. However, over time many gained recognition in the fields of art and literature.

Mark Rothko (1903–70), *a pioneer of brooding, meditative abstract art, was born in the Latvian city of Daugavpils. He later moved to New York.*

Sigmund Freud (1856–1939), *the father of modern psychoanalysis, spent much of his life in Vienna until Hitler's invasion of Austria drove him to London.*

Franz Kafka (1883–1924), *renowned for his surreal stories written in German, was part of a German-Jewish literary circle in Prague, where he spent most of his life.*

The History of Eastern and Central Europe

In this timeline of the history of Eastern and Central Europe, important political and social events appear on the upper half of the page, while the lower half charts contemporary developments in art and architecture. This lower section focuses on buildings and works of art that illustrate major historical trends and can still be seen today. They are described in more detail in the main sightseeing sections of the book.

AD 101 Roman Emperor Trajan completes the conquest of Dacia (modern-day Romania)

FROM PREHISTORY TO THE EARLY MIDDLE AGES

Civilization in Europe started in the southeast, with metalworking and clay-firing techniques developing in the Balkans before spreading to the rest of the continent. Much of Central and South Eastern Europe came under Roman rule, while the northeast remained isolated. The collapse of Rome and the period of great migrations changed the ethnic map of Europe and hastened the emergence of nation states such as Bulgaria, Serbia, Croatia, Hungary and Poland.

AD 45 Rome takes over Thrace (modern-day Bulgaria)

168 BC Romans conquer Illyria (modern-day Croatia, Bosnia, Serbia and Montenegro)

AD 276 Goth overrun Roma territories i the Balkan

4500 BC Start of the Copper Age in South Eastern Europe

700 BC Greeks establish colonies in the Adriatic Sea and the Black Sea

PREHISTORY			ROMAN EMPIRE	
4500 BC	**3000 BC**	**1500 BC**	**AD 1**	**AD 2**
NEOLITHIC			HELLENISTIC AND ROMAN	

4200 BC Gold and copper jewellery is made near Varna, Bulgaria *(see p628)*

2500 BC Sophisticated earthenware is produced in the Danube valley, most notably the Vučedol Dove *(see p493)* in present-day Croatia

300 BC Thracian goldsmiths produce jewellery, ceremonial goblets and funeral masks *(see p606)*

ART AND ARCHITECTURE

South Eastern Europe enjoyed long contact with Greek, Roman and Byzantine civilizations, which greatly enriched its art and culture over the centuries. The Romans were great admirers of the Greeks and the growth of the Roman Empire spread Greek aesthetics throughout Eastern Europe. North Eastern Europe, however, largely missed out on these cultural links until the region's gradual conversion to Christianity, when Western art and architecture left an impact.

AD 81 Construction of the Roman Amphitheatre at Pula, Croatia completed *(see p483)*

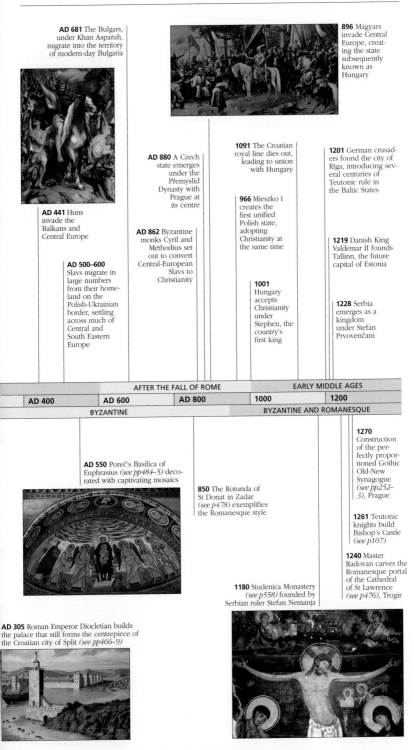

AD 681 The Bulgars, under Khan Asparuh, migrate into the territory of modern-day Bulgaria

896 Magyars invade Central Europe, creating the state subsequently known as Hungary

AD 441 Huns invade the Balkans and Central Europe

AD 500–600 Slavs migrate in large numbers from their homeland on the Polish-Ukrainian border, settling across much of Central and South Eastern Europe

AD 880 A Czech state emerges under the Přemyslid Dynasty with Prague at its centre

AD 862 Byzantine monks Cyril and Methodius set out to convert Central-European Slavs to Christianity

1091 The Croatian royal line dies out, leading to union with Hungary

966 Mieszko I creates the first unified Polish state, adopting Christianity at the same time

1001 Hungary accepts Christianity under Stephen, the country's first king

1201 German crusaders found the city of Riga, introducing several centuries of Teutonic rule in the Baltic States

1219 Danish King Valdemar II founds Tallinn, the future capital of Estonia

1228 Serbia emerges as a kingdom under Stefan Prvovenčani

AFTER THE FALL OF ROME			EARLY MIDDLE AGES	
AD 400	AD 600	AD 800	1000	1200
BYZANTINE			BYZANTINE AND ROMANESQUE	

AD 550 Poreč's Basilica of Euphrasius *(see pp484–5)* decorated with captivating mosaics

850 The Rotunda of St Donat in Zadar *(see p478)* exemplifies the Romanesque style

1270 Construction of the perfectly proportioned Gothic Old-New Synagogue *(see pp252–3)*, Prague

1261 Teutonic knights build Bishop's Castle *(see p107)*

1240 Master Radovan carves the Romanesque portal of the Cathedral of St Lawrence *(see p476)*, Trogir

1180 Studenica Monastery *(see p558)* founded by Serbian ruler Stefan Nemanja

AD 305 Roman Emperor Diocletian builds the palace that still forms the centrepiece of the Croatian city of Split *(see pp466–9)*

THE AGE OF EMPIRES

The arrival of the Ottoman Turks had a lasting impact on Europe, wiping out the nation states of the Balkans and replacing them with a multinational empire. The main challenge to the Ottomans came from the Austrian Habsburg Dynasty, which won control of Czech and Hungarian territories before expanding south and east. For centuries, the dominant force in North Eastern Europe was the Polish-Lithuanian Commonwealth, but this was ultimately toppled by Russia, the rising power in the East.

1533 Ivan IV the Terrible becomes Grand Prince of Muscovy

1349 Charles IV of Bohemia becomes Holy Roman Emperor, turning his capital Prague into a hub of politics, art and culture

1410 Polish and Lithuanian armies defeat the Teutonic knights at Grünwald

1526 Ottoman Turks defeat the Hungarians at the Battle of Mohács; the Hungarian crown falls to the Austrian Habsburg Dynasty

1415 Czech reformist theologian Jan Hus is burnt at the stake as a heretic, but his ideas inspire the development of Protestantism a century later

1282 The Habsburg Dynasty establishes its first feudal holdings in Slovene lands

1331–55 Under Stefan Dušan, Serbia becomes the leading power in the Balkans

1431 Birth of Vlad II the Impaler, who leads Wallachian resistance against Ottoman expansion

1569 Union of Lublin creates Polish-Lithuanian Commonwealth

1340 Ottoman Turks invade Thrace, gaining a foothold in Europe

1353–91 Bosnia becomes a regional power under King Tvrtko, then falls to the Ottoman Turks

1458-90 Reign of Mátyás Corvinus in Hungary

1463 The Ottomans conquer Bosnia and Herzegovina

LATE MIDDLE AGES				REFORMATION
1350	**1400**	**1450**	**1500**	**1550**
GOTHIC				RENAISSANCE

1380 Teutonic knights reconstruct Malbork Castle (see p207), creating one of the great Gothic fortresses of North Eastern Europe

1477 Veit Stoss begins work on the altarpiece of the Church of St Mary, Cracow (see p186)

1490s Berndt Notke creates the *Dance Macabre* for the Niguliste Church (see p103)

1499 John of Kastav fills St Trinity Church (see p536) with vivid late-Gothic frescoes

1420s Frescoes at the Manasija Monastery (see p558) mark the high point of Serbian religious art

1531 Construction of Gazi Husrev Bey Mosque (see p515), Sarajevo

1344 Work begins on St Vitus's Cathedral (see pp236–7), Prague's distinctive landmark

ART AND ARCHITECTURE

In Central and North Eastern Europe, imperial courts and mercantile cities imported the very latest in Gothic, Renaissance and Baroque styles. In parts of the Balkan peninsula subject to Ottoman rule, however, artistic influences came from the East, and the region was almost totally excluded from the European art world.

1552 Moscow's St Basil's Cathedral (see pp130–31) built to celebrate the victories of Ivan the Terrible

1561 Construction of Stari Most bridge (see p520) in Mostar. Destroyed in 1993, it is reconstructed in 2004

1600 Prince Michael the Brave briefly unites Wallachia, Moldavia and Transylvania to form a state corresponding to modern Romania

1878 Austria-Hungary annexes Bosnia and Herzegovina

1877–8 Russia defeats Ottoman armies in Bulgaria; establishment of independent principality of Bulgaria

1867 The Habsburg Empire is divided into Austrian and Hungarian halves, and becomes the Austro-Hungarian Empire

1721 Sweden surrenders Estonia and Latvia to Peter the Great of Russia

1683 Ottoman Turks lay siege to Vienna but are beaten back by the combined armies of Austria and Poland

1829 Serbia is formally recognized as an independent principality

1629 Estonia passes into Swedish hands

1812 Napoleon Bonaparte invades Russia but is defeated by the elements, losing most of his troops in a disastrous winter retreat

1804 First Serbian Uprising begins the process of freeing Serbia from Ottoman control

AGE OF ENLIGHTENMENT		INDUSTRIAL REVOLUTION	
1600	1650	1700	1750	1800	1850
BAROQUE		ROCOCO	NEO-CLASSICAL	REALISM AND IMPRESSIONISM

1850–70 Bulgarian architecture blossoms with styles imported from both East and West

1680s Austrian military architects begin construction of Tvrđa Fortress (*see p28*) in Osijek

1716 Vienna's sublime Karlskirche (*see p405*) built by Fischer von Elach

1885 Neo-Gothic style reaches new heights in the form of the Hungarian Parliament building (*see pp348–9*)

1703 Peter the Great founds St Petersburg

1754 Francesco Bartolomeo Rastrelli begins construction of St Petersburg's Winter Palace (*see pp150–51*)

1897 Gustav Klimt and others form the Vienna Secession in a direct challenge to the established art world

THE 20TH CENTURY TO THE PRESENT

War and revolution destroyed the multinational empires of the 19th century, and after 1918, independent nation states were re-established throughout Eastern Europe. With the onset of World War II, however, the region was first conquered by Germany, then by Soviet Russia, which imposed Communist regimes on the seized territories. Communist rule collapsed in 1989 but the transition to democracy was not smooth everywhere; Yugoslavia, in particular, was riven by conflict before the emergence of new, internationally recognized states.

1918–19 The end of World War I brings independence for Estonia, Latvia, Lithuania, Poland, Czechoslovakia and Yugoslavia

1941 Germany mounts a surprise attack on the Soviet Union

1956 An anti-Communist uprising breaks out in Hungary but is crushed by Soviet tanks

1939 Germany and the Soviet Union secretly agree to divide Poland between them, triggering World War II

1953 The death of Stalin eases political terror

1938 The Munich Agreement allows Germany to take hold of large parts of Czechoslovakia

1917 Revolution in Russia brings Lenin's Bolsheviks to power

1937–8 Stalin unleashes the Great Purge, killing an estimated 2 million citizens

1945 Collapse of Germany leaves the Soviet Union in control of Central and Eastern Europe

1914 Gavrilo Princip assassinates Austrian Archduke Franz Ferdinand in Sarajevo, sparking World War I

1924 Soviet leader Lenin dies; Stalin emerges as his successor

AGE OF IMPERIALISM				
1910	**1920**	**1930**	**1940**	**1950**
ART NOUVEAU			ART DECO AND MODERNISM	

1915 Kazimir Malevich paints his most iconic work, *The Black Square* *(see p154)*

1935–8 The Moscow Metro opens, featuring palatial stations, such as Arbatskaya and Komsomolskaya, full of mosaics and frescoes

1911 Completion of Municipal House *(see p256)* in Prague, a high point in Art Nouveau architecture

1907–11 Lithuanian painter Mikalojus Konstantinis Čiurlionis develops the quasi-mystical, Symbolist style

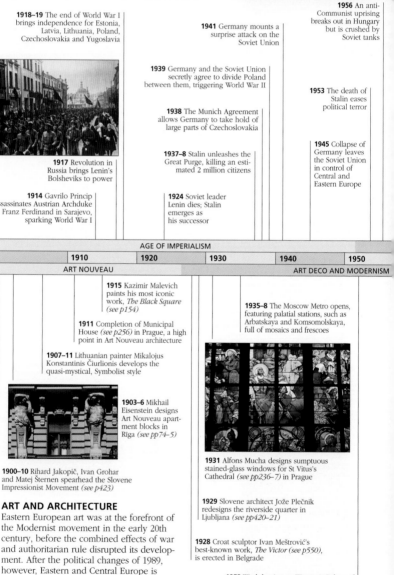

1903–6 Mikhail Eisenstein designs Art Nouveau apartment blocks in Rīga *(see pp74–5)*

1931 Alfons Mucha designs sumptuous stained-glass windows for St Vitus's Cathedral *(see pp236–7)* in Prague

1900–10 Rihard Jakopič, Ivan Grohar and Matej Šternen spearhead the Slovene Impressionist Movement *(see p423)*

1929 Slovene architect Jože Plečnik redesigns the riverside quarter in Ljubljana *(see pp420–21)*

ART AND ARCHITECTURE

Eastern European art was at the forefront of the Modernist movement in the early 20th century, before the combined effects of war and authoritarian rule disrupted its development. After the political changes of 1989, however, Eastern and Central Europe is gradually re-establishing its position at the heart of European culture.

1928 Croat sculptor Ivan Meštrović's best-known work, *The Victor (see p550)*, is erected in Belgrade

1952 Work begins on Warsaw's Palace of Culture and Science *(see p181)*, Eastern Europe's best example of Stalinist Baroque

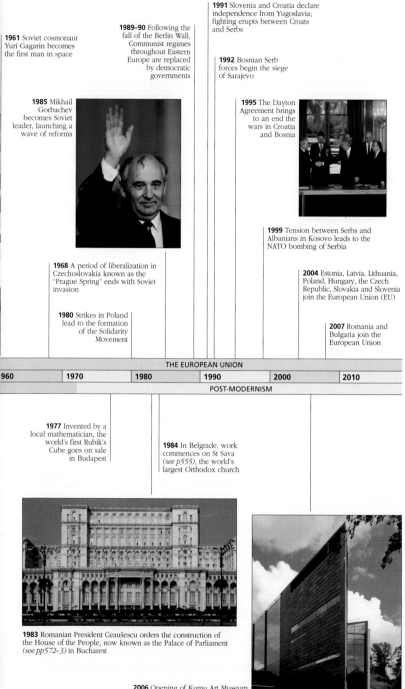

1961 Soviet cosmonaut Yuri Gagarin becomes the first man in space

1989–90 Following the fall of the Berlin Wall, Communist regimes throughout Eastern Europe are replaced by democratic governments

1991 Slovenia and Croatia declare independence from Yugoslavia; fighting erupts between Croats and Serbs

1992 Bosnian Serb forces begin the siege of Sarajevo

1985 Mikhail Gorbachev becomes Soviet leader, launching a wave of reforms

1995 The Dayton Agreement brings to an end the wars in Croatia and Bosnia

1999 Tension between Serbs and Albanians in Kosovo leads to the NATO bombing of Serbia

1968 A period of liberalization in Czechoslovakia known as the "Prague Spring" ends with Soviet invasion

2004 Estonia, Latvia, Lithuania, Poland, Hungary, the Czech Republic, Slovakia and Slovenia join the European Union (EU)

1980 Strikes in Poland lead to the formation of the Solidarity Movement

2007 Romania and Bulgaria join the European Union

THE EUROPEAN UNION

| 960 | 1970 | 1980 | 1990 | 2000 | 2010 |

POST-MODERNISM

1977 Invented by a local mathematician, the world's first Rubik's Cube goes on sale in Budapest

1984 In Belgrade, work commences on St Sava *(see p555)*, the world's largest Orthodox church

1983 Romanian President Ceaușescu orders the construction of the House of the People, now known as the Palace of Parliament *(see pp572–3)* in Bucharest

2006 Opening of Kumu Art Museum *(see p105)*, Tallinn's ultra-modern art museum, designed by Finnish architect Pekka Vapaavuori

NORTH EASTERN EUROPE

North Eastern Europe at a Glance

Long fought over by Baltic, Teutonic, Scandinavian and Slavic warlords, North Eastern Europe presents a rich palette of ancient castles, imperial cities and stately churches. Cities such as St Petersburg in Russia and Vilnius in Lithuania once ruled over extensive multinational empires, while the Latvian and Estonian capitals, Rīga and Tallinn, stood at the heart of north-European trade routes. Today the region's cities are among the fastest developing on the European continent, blending thriving urban culture with stunning landscapes and an extraordinary wealth of historic architecture.

NORTH
EASTERN
EUROPE

**EASTERN AND
CENTRAL EUROPE**

Saaremaa Island
(see pp106–107),
*the largest island in
Estonia, offers a
haunting mixture of
reed-rimmed shores
and juniper-covered
heath, in addition
to the majestic wind-
mills that are
its trademark.*

LITHUANIA
(see pp42–69)

Rundāle Palace (see pp84–5), *regarded
as Latvia's most impressive surviving
stately home, was designed by Italian
architect Francesco Bartolomeo Rastrelli
(1700–71). It features ornate rooms
decorated in the Rococo style of the
second half of the 18th century.*

Parnidis Dune *towers over the fishing village
of Nida, on the Curonian Spit (see pp62–3).
Spectacular views from the summit take in
the Baltic Sea and the Curonian Lagoon,
and stretch southwards to Kaliningrad.*

◁ **Panoramic view of Rīga on the bank of the Daugava river, Latvia**

MOSCOW AND ST PETERSBURG
(see pp118–63)

The Hermitage (see pp144–51) *houses the state rooms of the tsar's Winter Palace and has nearly three million exhibits ranging from fine arts to archaeological finds.*

St Basil's Cathedral (see pp130–31) *was built in 1555–61 for Ivan the Terrible. Pointed roofs, colourful domes and tiers of arched gables typify its stunning architectural diversity.*

ESTONIA
(see pp94–117)

LATVIA
(see pp70–93)

Gauja National Park (see pp86–7) *is one of the most attractive national parks in Latvia. Besides a compelling mix of natural landscapes and historic sites, it also offers an extensive range of outdoor activities, from canoeing to bobsledding.*

Vilnius Cathedral (see pp48–9), *is a striking Neo-Classical edifice, with huge statues of saints Casimir, Stanislaus and Helena topping the pediment. Inside, a chapel dedicated to St Casimir (1458–84), patron saint of Lithuania, is filled with stunning Baroque stuccowork and statuary.*

0 km 100
0 miles 100

LITHUANIA

The largest of the three Baltic States and one of the hidden jewels of Europe, Lithuania takes pride in its relatively undiscovered landscape of clean lakes, ancient forests and coastal dunes. The capital Vilnius, which has a UNESCO-protected Old Town, combines the romance of breathtaking Baroque architecture with the modern trappings of 21st-century Europe.

Lithuania is blessed with an unblemished natural landscape of rolling hills, lakes and rivers. The eastern half of the country is known as the "highlands" and the west as the "lowlands", even though the terrain is almost universally flat.

Following a tumultuous history, the country is forging a positive political and cultural role for itself in the expanded European Union. Many of its fine historic buildings have survived, and folk culture colours every corner of the country.

HISTORY

At the beginning of the 13th century, Lithuanian tribes, such as the Samogitia and Aukštaičiai, began to unite in the face of incursions by Germanic crusaders. In 1253, Duke Mindaugas (r. 1235–63) crowned himself king of the united tribes. However, his acceptance of Christianity enraged the Samogitians, who murdered him and reverted to paganism. In the 14th century, the Teutonic knights (German warrior-monks) returning from the Middle East joined the fight against the pagan Grand Duchy of Lithuania. In 1410, they were defeated at the Battle of Grünwald (Žalgiris) by the armies of Lithuania and Poland, which had forged an alliance by marriage in 1386. Fear of Russia led to closer ties between Lithuania and Poland and the creation of the Commonwealth

The enchanting red-brick Trakai Island Castle on Lake Galvė

◁ Pavement café along cobbled Castle Street leading to the Old Town, Vilnius

Detail from Jan Matejko's depiction of *Battle of Grünwald* (1878)

Russia, Prussia and Austria. By 1795, Poland and Lithuania had ceased to exist. Over 120 years of occupation followed, during which Russification led to the eradication of all traces of traditional Lithuania. Resistance simmered under the surface, and as World War I and the 1917 Russian Revolution destroyed the Tsarist Empire, a national council in Vilnius declared Lithuania independent on 16 February 1918. Between 1926 and 1940, under authoritarian Antanas Smetona, Lithuania enjoyed a period of growing prosperity. However, it was then occupied by the Red Army, ushering in a reign of terror defined by mass deportations and massacres that continued under the Nazis. The return of the Red Army in 1944 saw between 120,000 and 300,000 people deported to the Siberian gulags.

of the Two Nations, cemented at the Union of Lublin in 1569. When King Sigismund Augustus died without an heir, the combined position of grand duke of Lithuania and king of Poland became an elected one. The aristocracy adopted the Polish language, and Lithuanian culture was marginalized.

The 17th century was a disastrous period for Lithuania, characterized by misrule, plague and a calamitous invasion by the Russians. During the 18th century the Commonwealth gradually became a puppet state of tsarist Russia. In a series of partitions, its vast lands were divided between

In 1988, a group of intellectuals founded the Sajūdis Movement to rally popular support for demonstrations and, on 11 March 1990, Lithuania declared its independence, prompting a fierce response by Soviet troops. Freedom was finally declared in August 1991. Several years of economic hardship followed, but membership of the EU and NATO has since brought far greater prosperity.

KEY DATES IN LITHUANIAN HISTORY

AD 1236 Samogitian victory over German crusaders

1240 Duke Mindaugas unites Lithuania

1253 Duke Mindaugas crowned king

1386 Royal marriage unites Lithuania and Poland

1410 Battle of Grünwald destroys the Teutonic knights

1569 Union of Lublin creates Polish-Lithuanian Commonwealth

1655 Russian Army sacks Vilnius

1795 Final partition of the Commonwealth

1831 Rebellion against tsarist rule

1863 Lithuanian rebels persecuted by Russia

1918 Lithuania declares independence

1923 Lithuania reclaims Klaipėda

1926 President Smetona seizes power

1944 Soviets reoccupy Lithuania

1955 Partisan war against Soviet occupation dies away

1988 Sajūdis Movement founded

1990 Declaration of independence

2004 Lithuania joins NATO and becomes a member of the EU

LANGUAGE AND CULTURE

Lithuanian belongs to the Baltic family of languages. While English is commonly used as a second language, German, Russian and Polish are also widely spoken. Lithuanians celebrate a host of festivals. Most of the year's events take place in summer when the country comes alive with music, dance and food festivals.

Exploring Lithuania

With its rich history and wealth of scenic beauty, Lithuania offers many attractions. Its capital Vilnius possesses one of Europe's finest Old Towns. While Vilnius and Kaunas are the most vibrant cities, the less-visited towns and villages, with their beautiful churches and farmsteads, and the coast, with its fascinating sandy dunes and beaches, also draw visitors. Trains are cheap, but not frequent, and with few routes. The country's flat landscape makes it ideal for cycling.

SIGHTS AT A GLANCE

Curonian Spit National Park pp62–3 ❺
Kaunas pp58–9 ❸
Klaipėda pp60–61 ❹
Trakai Island Castle pp56–7 ❷
Vilnius pp46–55 ❶

View of Upper Castle across the Neris river, Vilnius

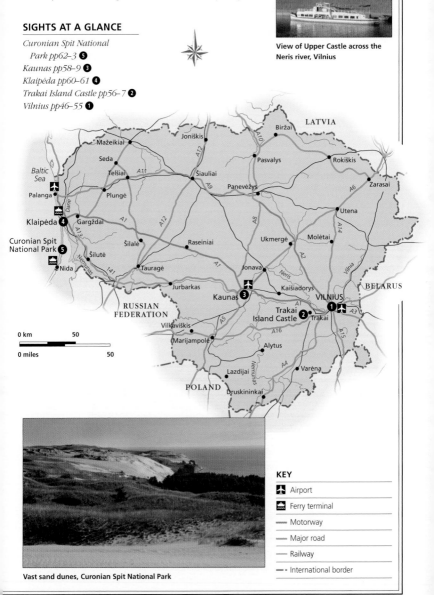

KEY

✈	Airport
⛴	Ferry terminal
—	Motorway
—	Major road
—	Railway
–·–	International border

Vast sand dunes, Curonian Spit National Park

Vilnius ❶

Whether viewed from one of the hills that overlook the Old Town or one of the many pavement cafés with tall spires rising all around, Vilnius is unmistakably a city of great beauty; it is home to six hundred thousand people. The city sustained a series of wars, invasions and fires between the early 17th and mid-18th centuries. Efforts to rebuild the city resulted in the rich offshoot of the Baroque style that is typical of Vilnius today. The Old Town, on the UNESCO World Heritage list since 1994, blends Gothic and Neo-Classical styles. The best places to begin a tour of the Old Town are Vilnius Cathedral in the north and the Gates of Dawn in the south. Vilnius University and its surrounding churches and courtyards are one of the city's finest architectural ensembles.

0 metres   200

0 yards   200

SIGHTS AT A GLANCE

Applied Arts Museum ⑤
Cathedral Square ②
Church of St Casimir ⑨
Gates of Dawn ⑩
Holocaust Museum ⑫
Lower Castle ③
The Museum of Genocide Victims ⑬
St John's Church ⑦
State Jewish Museum ⑪
Town Hall Square ⑧
Upper Castle ④
Vilnius Cathedral pp48–9 ①
Vilnius University ⑥

Outdoor cafés along a cobblestoned street, Old Town

A   B   C

GETTING AROUND

Vilnius is a compact city that can easily be explored on
foot. Walking is the best way to explore the Old Town.
Cycling is another popular way of getting around the town
centre, and the tourist office in the Old Town offers
bicycles on rent. Outlying sites can be reached by bus, but
others, located further away from the city centre, are more
easily reached by car or taxi.

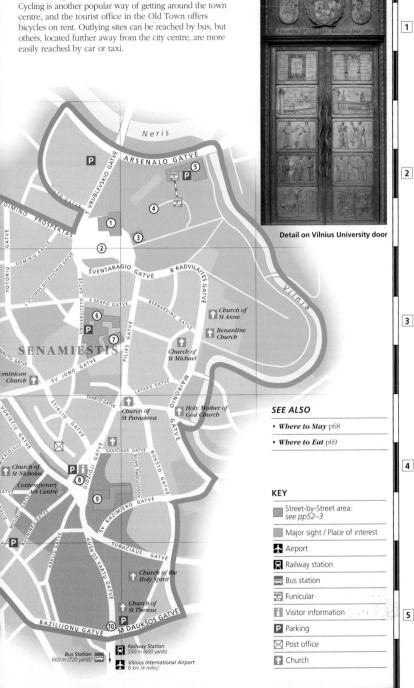

Detail on Vilnius University door

Neris

ARSENALO GATVĖ

T VRUBLEVSKIO GATVĖ

TILTO GATVĖ

GEDIMINO PROSPEKTAS

ODMINIŲ GATVĖ

TOTORIŲ GATVĖ

ŠVENTARAGIO GATVĖ

Vilnia

S SKAPO GATVĖ

B RADVILAITĖS GATVĖ

BERNARDINŲ GATVĖ

L STUOKOS GUCEVIČIAUS GATVĖ

UNIVERSITETO GATVĖ

PILIES GATVĖ

SENAMIESTIS

ŠV JONO GATVĖ

IGNOTO GATVĖ

Dominican
Church

LATAKO GATVĖ

SVARCO GATVĖ

STIKLIŲ GATVĖ

VOKIEČIŲ GATVĖ

MIKALOJAUS GATVĖ

Church of
St Nicholas

Contemporary
Art Centre

SAVIČIAUS GATVĖ

DIDŽIOJI GATVĖ

BOKŠTO GATVĖ

AUGUSTIJONŲ GATVĖ

ŠV KAZIMIERO GATVĖ

MĖSINIŲ GATVĖ

RŪDNINKŲ GATVĖ

ARKLIŲ GATVĖ

SUBAČIAUS GATVĖ

AUŠROS VARTŲ GATVĖ

BAZILIJONŲ GATVĖ

M DAUKŠOS GATVĖ

Church of
St Anne

Benardine
Church

Church of
St Michael

MAIRONIO GATVĖ

Holy Mother of
God Church

Church of
St Paraskeva

Church of the
Holy Spirit

Church of
St Theresa

Railway Station
550 m (600 yards)

Vilnius International Airport
6 km (4 miles)

Bus Station
660 m (720 yards)

SEE ALSO

- **Where to Stay** p68
- **Where to Eat** p69

KEY

	Street-by-Street area: *see pp52–3*
	Major sight / Place of interest
✈	Airport
🚉	Railway station
🚌	Bus station
🚡	Funicular
ℹ	Visitor information
P	Parking
⊠	Post office
✝	Church

D   E   F

Vilnius Cathedral ①
Vilniaus arkikatedra bazilika

Having taken various guises since it was first built as a
Christian church on the site of a pagan temple in 1251,
Vilnius Cathedral today largely dates from the late
18th century. The young architect, Laurynas Stuoka-
Gucevičius, brought the fashionable French Classicist
style to Baroque Vilnius; his idea for the cathedral
exterior and interior being a visual re-creation of a Greek
temple. Vilnius Cathedral was closed by the Soviets in
1950 and initially mooted for use as a garage for truck
repairs. In 1956, however, it opened as a picture gallery.
It was eventually returned to the Catholic Church in 1988
and reconsecrated in 1989, a year
before independence was declared.

Valavičius Chapel
*Members of the Valavičius
family were governors and
bishops of Vilnius. Their
lavish chapel was built
in the early 17th century.*

Statue of
St Helena

Stucco Sculpture
*This sculpture
depicting a bird
sacrifice can be
seen on the
tympanum of
the façade.*

Main
entrance

**Wall Painting of
the Crucifixion**
*The oldest surviving fresco
in Lithuania, dating from
the 14th century, can be
found in the crypt. It was
discovered in 1985.*

STAR FEATURES

★ St Casimir's Chapel

★ Crypt

Statue of Luke, the Evangelist
*Of the statues of the Four Evangelists
on the southern façade, the one of
Luke's appears with a bull, a symbol
of service and sacrifice.*

High Altar

The marvellously intricate tabernacle door on the High Altar, which was created in the 1620s, is fashioned from gold and silver. Two biblical scenes, the Last Supper and Christ Washing the Disciples' Feet, are beautifully depicted on the panel.

★ St Casimir's Chapel

Italian masters created this superb chapel, one of the major Baroque jewels of Vilnius, from 1623 to 1636. Its main highlights are the marble columns, magnificent stucco figures and colourful frescoes.

ST CASIMIR (1458–84)

Casimir was the second son of King Casimir IV of Poland, whose siblings became kings and queens of European states through lineage and marriage. Pious Casimir shunned the luxuries of court life and would often go to the cathedral to pray. When he died of tuber-culosis at the age of 25, it was rumoured that his cof-fin could cure the disease. A fresco in St Casimir's Chapel shows how a sick orphan, who prayed beneath the coffin, was miraculously cured.

Richly decorated altar of St Casimir's Chapel

★ Crypt

A sombre mausoleum holds the remains of two grand dukes and two wives of Sigismund Augustus (r. 1548–72), Gediminas' last descendant (r. 1316–41).

Vilnius Cathedral Belfry, Cathedral Square

Cathedral Square ②
Katedros aikštė

Map D2 & D3. 🚋 *10, 11, 33.*

The paving stones around the Cathedral Square show the outline of the wall around the Lower Castle, a defence that made Vilnius a 14th-century bastion against the crusades.

At the square's western end is the **Vilnius Cathedral Belfry**, which was originally part of the fortifications. There was also a western gate where Vilnius Cathedral stands today. The square's eastern end is dominated by a statue of the city's founder, Grand Duke Gediminas. Unveiled in 1996, it conveys his predilection for diplomacy over force. In the square's centre is a tile marked *stebuklas* (miracle), reputed to be the point from where the Baltic Way, the human chain linking Vilnius, Rīga and Tallinn in 1989, started. Locals believe that turning around on the tile three times makes wishes come true.

Lower Castle ③
Žemutinės pilis

Katedros 3a. **Map** E2. *Tel (5) 261 4063.* 🚋 *10, 11, 33.* ◯ *call in advance for timings.* 🖥 www.lvr.lt

Situated on the left bank of Neris river, the Vilnius Castle Complex consists of the Lower and Upper Castles. Vilnius Cathedral, the New Arsenal,

the Ducal Palace where the grand dukes of Lithuania resided and other buildings that stood at the foot of Castle Hill and survived the sieges of the 14th century are known as Lower Castle. In the 1520s, the palace was renovated in Renaissance style by Italian architects invited by Sigismund the Old (r. 1506–48) and his wife. Destroyed by Russians in 1802, the Ducal Palace is being rebuilt to provide Vilnius with a symbol of past glories. Once completed, the building will hold a museum devoted to the courtly culture of Lithuania's grand dukes.

Upper Castle ④
Aukštutinė pilis

Arsenalo 5. **Map** E2. *Tel (5) 261 7453.* 🚋 *10, 11, 33.* ◯ *10am–5pm Tue–Sun.* 🖥

The oldest part of the Vilnius Castle complex is the Upper Castle built atop Gediminas Hill. The western tower, the only remaining part of this complex, which once included defensive structures, is today the symbol of independent Lithuania. The viewing

platform at the top provides a panorama of the spires and rooftops of the Old Town to the south. A funicular from the courtyard of the Applied Arts Museum offers a ride to the Upper Castle.

The stone buildings of the western tower were built in 1419, and restored in the 1950s. According to legend, while on a hunting trip, Grand Duke Gediminas dreamed of an iron wolf howling from the hills in the park. This, his pagan priest said, was a sign that a fortress should be built there. As a result, wooden upper and lower castles and another one on the adjacent hill were built.

Applied Arts Museum ⑤
Taikomosios dailės muziejus

Arsenalo gatvė 3a. **Map** E2. *Tel (5) 262 8080.* ◯ *11am–6pm Tue–Sat, 11am–4pm Sun.* 🖥

The 16th-century Old Arsenal houses the Applied Arts Museum, which hosts major state-sponsored exhibitions on topics relating mainly to the history of Lithuania, the Grand Duchy and sacred art.

One of the permanent exhibitions in the museum displays Lithuanian folk art from the 17th to the 19th

Western tower, the Upper Castle's lone surviving structure

Colourful interior of Littera, with its collection of books and study material, Vilnius University

centuries, illustrating the heavy impact that Christian themes had on traditional mediums such as sculpture. The collection includes wayside wooden crosses, shrines, saints and *rūpintojėlis* (Lithuanian local representations of a weary Christ holding his head in his right hand). Particularly illuminating is the work of Vincas Svirskis (1835–1916), a prolific craftsman who carved many shrines for farmsteads and villages in the Kėdainiai and Kaunas regions.

Vilnius University ⑥

Vilniaus universitetas

Universiteto 3. **Map** D3. **Tel** (5) 268 7001. ◷ 10am–5:30pm Mon–Sat. ◪ for prior booking call (5) 268 7298. ▮ **www**.vu.lt

The oldest university in Eastern Europe, Vilnius University was founded as a Jesuit College in 1568 before becoming a school of higher education in 1579. The current campus, constructed between the 16th and 18th centuries, is a combination of different architectural styles.

Lithuania's largest university, it has 13 courtyards and multiple buildings. The most impressive of its courtyards, the Great Courtyard has open galleries dating from the 17th century, which were later lined with dedications to professors. Accessed via a passage from the western side of the Great Courtyard, the Observatory Courtyard by contrast is a serene enclosed garden from which the observatory and its zodiac symbols can be seen.

Sarbievius Courtyard, the oldest part of the campus, is located north of the Great Courtyard and at its far end, is the bookshop **Littera**. Frescoes caricaturing professors and students decorate its interior. These were painted in 1978 by Lithuanian artist Antanas Kmieliauskas.

Façade of St John's Church and adjoining bell tower

St John's Church ⑦

šv Jono bažnyčia

Universiteto 3/šv Jono 12. **Map** D3. **Tel** (5) 611 795. ◷ 10am–5pm Mon–Sat. ✝ 6pm Mon–Sat, 11am Sun.

At the southern edge of the Vilnius University campus, the impressive façade of the Church of St John the Baptist and St John the Evangelist and the nearby bell tower dominate the Great Courtyard. The original Gothic church, built here in 1426, was reconstructed in 1749 in flamboyant Baroque by Jan Krzysztof Glaubitz (1700–67). He was the most influential of Vilnius's late-Baroque architects and one of the creators of the distinct school known as Vilnius Baroque.

The magnificent structure boasts an overwhelming four-tier façade made up of clusters of columns. The church has ten imposing altars that are interconnected. These faux marble altars with Corinthian columns illuminate the otherwise austere interior. Initially, there were 22 columns, most of which were removed during further rebuilding in the 19th century. At 68 m (223 ft), the bell tower, which was given two additional tiers by Glaubitz, is considered the tallest structure in the Old Town.

Street-by-Street: Town Hall Square to the Gates of Dawn

Lithuania's distinctive Baroque architecture, known as Vilnius Baroque, can be admired in the outstanding monuments clustered around the Church of St Casimir and the Gates of Dawn. The enchanting collection of towers and sculptures was built during the 17th and 18th centuries by Italian and Polish architects and their Polish-Lithuanian noble patrons. The buildings are elegantly designed, with symmetrical façades reflecting an unmistakable Italian influence. Nonetheless, the regal atmosphere, so unique to Vilnius, distinguishes this place from similar architectural areas of other European cities.

★ Church of St Casimir
This church was the city's museum of atheism from 1963–91. The crown atop the central dome symbolizes St Casimir's royal lineage ⑨

Town Hall Square
This busy square has the impressive Town Hall as its focal point. The hall's bold Classical portico was designed by the renowned Lithuanian archi-tect, Laurynas Stuoka-Gucevičius ⑧

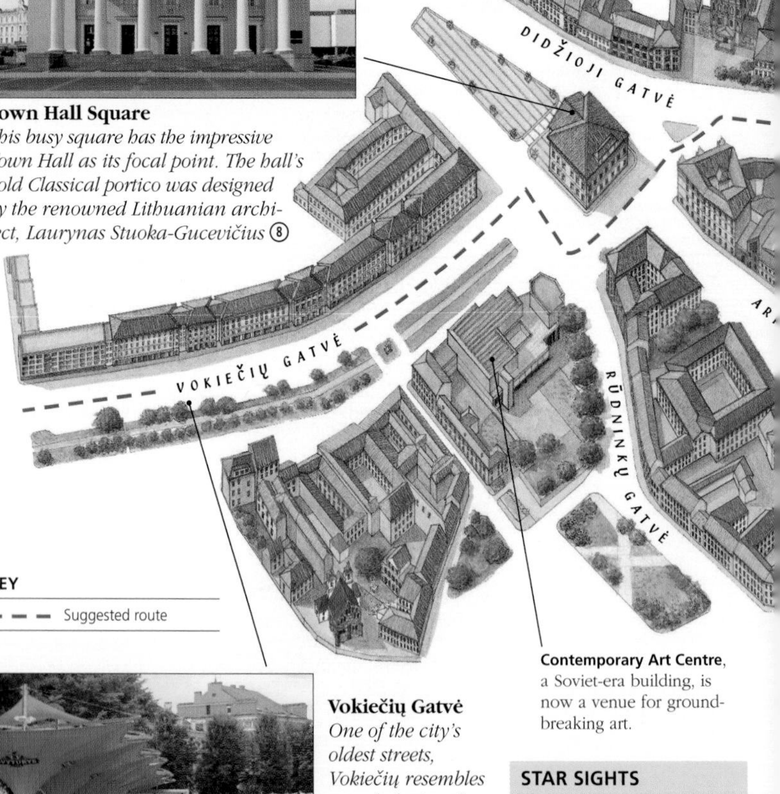

Vilnius Cathedral

DIDŽIOJI GATVĖ

VOKIEČIŲ GATVĖ

RŪDNINKŲ GATVĖ

AR...

KEY

– – – Suggested route

Vokiečių Gatvė
One of the city's oldest streets, Vokiečių resembles a park during the summer, with its outdoor cafés and a pleasant central tree-lined walkway.

Contemporary Art Centre,
a Soviet-era building, is now a venue for ground-breaking art.

STAR SIGHTS

★ Church of St Casimir

★ Church of St Theresa

★ Gates of Dawn

For hotels and restaurants in this region see pp68–9

Šv Kazimiero Gatvė

Named after St Casimir, this narrow street snakes around the back of the church towards Užupis, a district filled with cafés and art galleries.

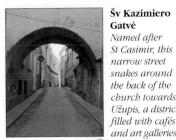

Church of the Holy Spirit

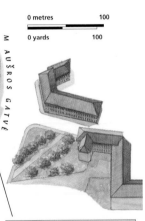

★ Church of St Theresa

Scenes from the life of St Theresa, revered for her mystical writings, adorn the vaulted nave of the church. The frescoes were painted in the late 18th century following a fire in the 17th-century church.

0 metres	100
0 yards	100

SUBAČIAUS GATVĖ

M AUŠROS GATVĖ

AUŠROS VARTŲ GATVĖ

BAZILIJONŲ GATVĖ

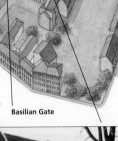

Basilian Gate

Basilian Monastery

The now dilapidated monastery complex was used as a prison to hold anti-Russian activists, including the poet Adam Mickiewicz, in the 1820s.

★ Gates of Dawn

A pilgrimage site, this gateway to the Old Town protects a silver-covered painting of the Virgin Mary, said to have miraculous powers ⑩

Nave and altar in the Church of St Casimir

Town Hall Square ⑧

Rotušės Aikštė

Didžioji 31. **Map** D4. **Town Hall**
Tel (5) 261 8007. 📅 (5) 262 6470.
🕐 8am–6pm Mon–Fri. 🎭 Kaziuko
Crafts Fair (Mar). **www**.vilnius.lt

Fully repaved in 2006, Town Hall Square was for centuries a marketplace and the centre of public life. It still bustles with activity, especially during the annual Kaziuko Crafts Fair, a festival of traditional arts and crafts marking St Casimir's Day, when stalls line the square. The main building of the square, the **Town Hall**, was earlier the site of a court; prisoners were marched from its cells to the square to be beheaded. The building was constructed at the end of the 18th century. Today, the Town Hall hosts numerous cultural and social events around the year.

Church of St Casimir ⑨

šv Kazimiero Bažnyčia

Didžioji 34. **Map** D4. **Tel** (5) 212
1715. ✝ 10:30am & 5:30pm
Mon–Fri, noon Sun.

The first Baroque church of the city, St Casimir was destroyed by fire three times after being built by the Jesuits between 1604 and 1635, prompting extensive recon-struction led by the architect, mathematician and astronomer Tomas Žebrauskas (1714–58) in the 1750s. Much of the interior was destroyed in 1812, when Napoleon's Army used the church as a granary. It became a Russian Orthodox church during the 19th cen-tury, when onion domes were added to it.

It served as a Lutheran church for the German Army during World War I, and was then returned to the Jesuits and restored in the 1920s. The central dome was rebuilt in 1942 and a crown was added. The Soviets used the church as a museum of atheism from 1963. It was reconsecrated in 1991 after heavy renovation.

Gates of Dawn ⑩

Aušros Vartai

Aušros vartų 12. **Map** D5. **Tel** (5)
212 3513. ✝ 7:30am, 9am, 10am,
5:30pm, 6:30pm Mon–Sat, 9am,
9:30am, 11am, 6:30pm Sun.

The Classical chapel of Gates of Dawn follows the centuries-old custom of having a chapel or a religious image in every gateway to safeguard a city from outside enemies and protect departing travellers. This is the only gateway from Vilnius' original defensive walls to have survived a series of attacks.

The focus of this chapel is *The Madonna of Mercy*, an image reputed to have miracle-working powers. It was painted on oak in the 1620s and encased in silver 150 years later. The miracles attributed to it were faithfully recorded by nuns at the neighbouring Carmelite convent. Hundreds of hearts of different sizes stand out on plates of silver around the painting.

The image was originally placed on the gate, in a recess, with shutters to protect it from the elements, but was shifted to a wooden chapel in the 17th century. The chapel that houses the image today dates from 1829, when it was

The Madonna of Mercy, seen through the window of the Gates of Dawn

For hotels and restaurants in this region see pp68–9

Stained-glass window at the State Jewish Museum

rebuilt to replace an earlier Baroque version. A site of pilgrimage, it was one of the first stops made by Pope John Paul II when he visited Lithuania in 1993.

State Jewish Museum ⑪
Valstybinis Vilniaus Gaono Žydų Muziejus

Pylimo 4. **Map** C3. *Tel (5) 212 7912.* ◯ *9am–1pm Mon–Fri.* 🗻 💳 *excursions of the museum & Vilnius Old Town offered.* **www**.jmuseum.lt

The hub of the city's now tiny Jewish community, this small museum displays copies of ghetto diaries and handwritten notes on the backs of cigarette packets about life in the ghetto, as well as items that remained from the museum that existed before World War II. Several objects that miraculously survived from the Great Synagogue, demolished by the Soviets, include a Ten Commandments bas-relief.

The building plays host to a newspaper in Lithuanian, English, Yiddish and Russian, *Jerusalem of Lithuania*. It is also the venue where groups, such as the Union of Former Ghetto and Concentration Camp Prisoners and the Union of Jewish War Veterans, meet.

Holocaust Museum ⑫
Holokausto Ekspozicija

Pamėnkalnio 12. **Map** B2 and C2. *Tel (5) 262 0730.* ◯ *9am–5pm Mon–Thu, 9am–4pm Fri, 10am–4pm Sun.* 🗻 💳 **www**.jmuseum.lt

Also known as the Green House, this department of the State Jewish Museum reveals some of the horrors that befell the Jews of Lithuania during World War II. A display on Jewish life before the terror unfolded is followed by maps and photographs of how and where the Holocaust was executed. There are also descriptions of the harsh life in the ghettos and eyewitness accounts of the mass killings of 100,000 people in the forests of Paneriai, outside Vilnius.

The Museum of Genocide Victims ⑬
Genocido Aukų Muziejus

Aukų 2a. **Map** B2. *Tel (5) 249 7427.* ◯ *10am–5pm Tue–Sat, 10am–3pm Sun.* 🗻 💳 🎧 **www**.genocid.lt

Also known as the KGB Museum, the Museum of Genocide Victims was opened in 1992, on the first floor of the former KGB building. In the effectively designed display area, personal stories are used to reveal the regime of terror under the Soviet occupations of 1940–41 and 1944–91. The exhibits here chronicle Soviet repression in Lithuania, the cattle-car

Holocaust Museum, annexe of the State Jewish Museum

deportations to Siberia and the futile efforts of the Forest Brothers, who fought a guerrilla-style campaign against the Soviet regime with strong support from the locals. Underground, the cells that were in use right up until the late 1980s are even more overwhelming. They include the smaller cells used in winter with no glass in their windows and the floors covered with water, as well as an execution chamber displaying, under glass, the recently exhumed remains of victims of the era.

In 1997, the museum was taken over by the Genocide and Resistance Research Centre of Lithuania, a state institution dedicated to investigating atrocities that occurred in the country during the Nazi and Soviet occupations.

Exhibition of Lithuanian partisans at the Museum of Genocide Victims

Trakai Island Castle ❷

Trakų salos pilis

Located on one of the 21 islands in Lake Galvė in the peninsula town of Trakai, the Island Castle was built as a seat of power during the reign of Vytautas the Great in the 13th century. The castle was completed just before the Grand Duchy's crushing victory over the Teutonic knights at the Battle of Grünwald. As Vilnius grew in importance, Trakai lost its significance and was destroyed by the Cossacks during the 1655 Russian invasion. In the late 19th century, the elegiac island ruins captured the imagination of poets and painters during the National Revival. Oddly, it was the Soviet authorities who, in the 1950s, sanctioned the reconstruction of this monument to Lithuania's glorious past. It was completed in 1987.

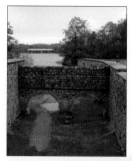

Dry moat, separating the main castle from the outer courtyard

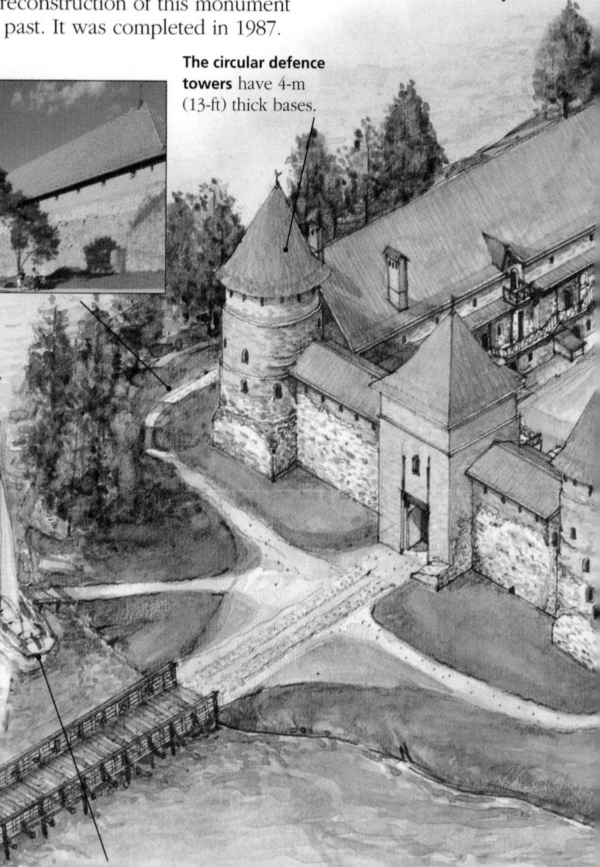

The circular defence towers have 4-m (13-ft) thick bases.

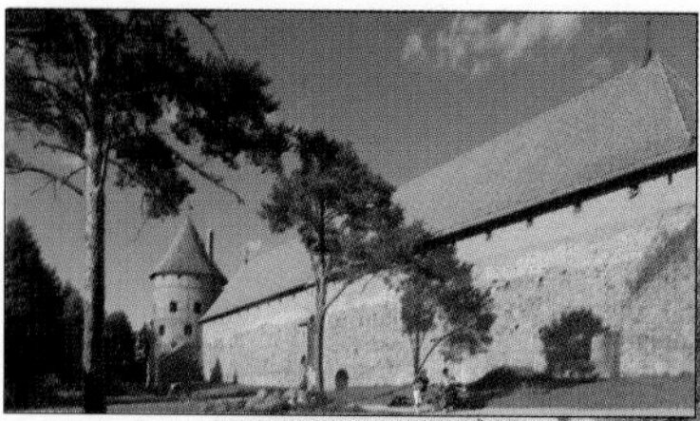

★ Lakeside Walk
One way to appreciate Trakai's idyllic lake-filled landscape and the scale of the castle's construction is to take the pretty walk that follows the shore of the island.

A wooden footbridge links Trakai to the Island Castle.

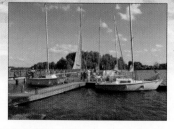

Yachts
Between May and October, yachts from the nearby Žalgiris Yacht Club are moored next to the Island Castle. They can be hired by the hour, but charges vary.

STAR SIGHTS

- ★ Lakeside Walk
- ★ History Museum

For hotels and restaurants in this region see pp68–9

Lake Galvė
This lake serves as a moat around the castle. Rowing boats and paddle boats can be hired along the quayside on the Lithuanian mainland for a spectacular view of the castle.

VISITORS' CHECKLIST

30 km (19 miles) W of Vilnius. *from Vilnius.* *from Vilnius.* Vytauto gatvė 69, (528) 51 934. **Žalgiris Yacht Club** Žemaitės gatvė 3. *Tel* (528) 52 824. **History Museum** *Tel* (528) 53 946. *May–Sep: 10am–7pm Tue–Sun; Oct–Apr: 10am–5pm Tue–Sun.* **www**.trakaimuziejus.lt

Dry moat

The Ducal Palace's keep, which is 30 m (100 ft) high, served as the residence of the grand duke.

★ History Museum
This museum showcases a wide array of weaponry as well as items found during excavations, including 16th-century tankards, tiles and coins.

THE KARAIM OF TRAKAI

A community of Turkic settlers practising a particular kind of Judaism, the Karaim, lend a distinctly exotic flavour to Trakai. Their ancestors were taken prisoners by Vytautas the Great when on a military venture to the Crimea in 1397, and they subsequently served as royal guards. The Karaim have maintained their customs and traditions. Their characteristic wooden houses, each typically with gable ends and three windows facing the street, their synagogue, or Kenesa, and the Karaim Museum are all on Karaimų gatvė, at Trakai's northern end. Their cemetery lies beside Lake Totoriskiai close to Lake Galvė.

Graves in the Karaim Cemetery, partially hidden by long grass

Kaunas ❸

Lithuania's second largest city, Kaunas stands at the confluence of the Nemunas and Neris, the country's biggest rivers. A series of disasters hindered the city's development, including invasions by the Russians (1655), Swedes (1701) and Napolean (1812). Rapid growth in the 19th century culminated in Kaunas becoming the temporary capital of newly independent Lithuania in 1919. Later, the city suffered under Nazi and Soviet occupations. Today, Kaunas is a modern city with a boulevard and a host of museums. The main historic sights are located in its well-preserved Old Town.

View of the bridge over the Nemunas river leading to the Old Town

🏛 Old Town Hall
Rotušės aikštė.
Known locally as the "White Swan" and resembling a church with its single, tiered tower, the Old Town Hall (Kauno Rotušė) has been a marriage registry office since the 1970s. It continues to be a photogenic backdrop for newlyweds. Built in the mid-16th century, it has housed magistrates and the mayor, and has been used as an ammunition store, clubhouse, fire station, theatre and a subterranean prison. Town Hall Square, where it stands, was once a busy marketplace and is still the hub of the Old Town.

🏛 Church of the Holy Trinity
Rotušės aikštė 22. **Tel** (37) 323 734.
🕂 10am Sun.
Built for a Bernardine convent in the late 1620s, this church (Šventos Trejybės bažnyčia), with its blend of Renaissance and Gothic styles and its pastel colours brightens up the northwestern corner of the Town Hall Square. The interior was redesigned just before the outbreak of World War II.

🏛 Church of St George
Papilio 9. **Tel** (37) 224 659. 🕂 6pm Mon–Fri, 10:30am Sun.
This 15th-century Gothic church (šv Jurgio bažnyčia) was destroyed twice by fire, by the Russians in the 17th century and in 1812 by Napoleon's soldiers. It was finally returned to the Bernardines in 1993.

🏰 Kaunas Castle
Pilies 17. **Tel** (37) 323 436.
⬜ 10:30am–1pm Mon–Fri.
🗝 mandatory.
The ruins of Kaunas Castle (Kauno pilis) are a reminder of its strategic location, between the rivers Neris and Nemunas. Built in the 13th century, it was damaged by the Teutonic knights in 1362. Soon after its reconstruction, the knights were defeated by Lithuanians in the Battle of Grünwald in 1410. Thereafter the castle lost its significance as a military base and was used for administrative purposes. It functioned as a prison in the 18th century, but was restored in the 1920s.

🏛 Cathedral of Sts Peter and Paul
Vilniaus 1. **Tel** (37) 324 093.
🕂 7am, 8am, 6pm daily; 9am Sat–Sun, 10:30am, noon Sun.
Several reconstructions have culminated in the Gothic and Renaissance exterior of this 15th-century cathedral (šv apaštalų Petro ir Pauliaus arkikatedra bazilika). The late-Baroque interior, however, remains largely unchanged

KEY

▭ Pedestrian zone

The elegant façade of the Old Town Hall

since 1800. The oldest painting in the cathedral, the *Suffering Mother of God*, is reputed to have miraculous powers.

🛌 Perkūnas House
Aleksoto 6. *Tel* (37) 302 994.
◯ 10am–4pm Mon–Fri, 11am–1pm Sun. 🖼
The red-brick Gothic building (Perkūno namai) was named after Perkūnas, the god of thunder. Dating from the early 1500s, it was initially a meeting house for members of the Hanseatic League. Bought by the Jesuits, the house was converted into a chapel before becoming a theatre and then a school. Later, during the Soviet period, it was used as a warehouse. It is now back with the Jesuits.

🛐 Vytautas Church
Aleksoto 3. *Tel* (37) 203 854.
🛐 6pm Tue–Thu, 10am & 6pm Sat–Sun, noon Sun.
This church (Vytauto bažnyčia) was built by Vytautas the Great after the Holy Roman Emperor decided in 1413 that the land on Nemunas river's right bank belonged to Lithuania's Grand Duchy. Used as an army storehouse by Napoleon, it was later converted to serve a Russian

The red-brick Vytautas Church, built by Vytautas the Great

congregation. After Lithuania's first independence in 1918, a reconstruction took place. In 1930, a medallion was placed in the church wall to commemorate the 500th death anniversary of Vytautas.

🛌 Laisvės Aleja
This pedestrianized street, set in the heart of modern Kaunas, is also called Freedom Avenue. A monument outside the Music Theatre at Laisvės 4 marks where Romas Kalanta, a local student, set fire to himself on 14 May 1972. His suicide sparked student protests, which were suppressed.

VISITORS' CHECKLIST

100 km (62 miles) W of Vilnius.
🏛 356,000. ✈ 🚆 🚌
ℹ Laisvės alėja 36, (37) 323 436. 🎷 International Jazz Festival (Apr). **www**.kaunas.lt

The silver-blue onion domes of the Church of St Michael dominate the street's eastern end. Built in the early 1890s, it was originally Russian Orthodox, but later served as a German Army church during World War I, and, soon after, became a Lithuanian Army church.

🏛 Mykolas Žilinskas Art Gallery
Nepriklausomybės 12. *Tel* (37) 322 788. ◯ 11am–5pm Tue–Sun. 🖼 🖼
Named after the famous art connoisseur Mykolas Žilinskas, this gallery (Mykolo Žilinskas dailės galerija) houses the valuable art collection he donated to Kaunas in the 1970s. Besides paintings and porcelain from the 16th to the 20th centuries, including *The Crucifixion* by Rubens, the gallery also includes prewar paintings and sculptures by Baltic artists.

🏛 M K Čiurlionis Art Museum
V Putvinskio 55. *Tel* (37) 229 475.
◯ 11am–5pm Tue–Sun. 🖼 🖼
Housing the paintings of the Lithuanian artist Čiurlionis, this museum (M K Čiurlionio dailės muziejus) also offers an insight into the development of art in Lithuania. It is the country's biggest art gallery, with 335,000 exhibits. Artifacts from other cultures include pieces from ancient Egypt.

🏛 Devil's Museum
V Putvinskio 64. *Tel* (37) 221 587.
◯ Oct–May: 11am–5pm Tue–Sun; Jun–Sep: 10am–5pm Tue–Sun.
🖼 🖼 🖼 🖼
This museum's (Velnių muziejus) collection of representations of devils, demons and witches from Lithuania and around the world, was brought together by avid collector Antanas Žmuidzinavičius. A sculpture of Hitler and Stalin fighting over Lithuania in a pit of bones is grim, but most of the devils are shown with humour.

KAUNAS TOWN CENTRE

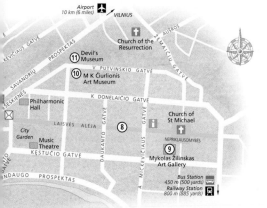

Key to Symbols *see back flap*

Klaipėda ❹

Founded in 1252 by the Livonian Order who built the city's first fortress, Klaipėda was the main trading port until 1629. The order named the city Memel after a river of the same name (Nemunas in Lithuanian). Briefly the capital of Prussia after the Napoleonic wars, Klaipėda remained an important port under Prussian control until World War I. However, in 1923, the Lithuanian Army claimed the city, renaming it Klaipėda. Despite serious damage during World War II and its status as a military-industrial centre during the Soviet years, this thriving city is Lithuania's third largest city and a major port today.

Cafés lining a pedestrian street in the Old Town

Ännchen of Tharau
Taravos anikė.
In front of the theatre in the **Theatre Square**, which is the heart of Klaipėda's Old Town, stands the statue *Ännchen of Tharau*. The statue is the focal point of the fountain dedicated to Simon Dach (1605–59), one of the city's eminent personalities. Born in Klaipėda, then known as Memel, Dach was a leading Prussian poet from the late 1630s until his death. He is well known throughout Germany for his songs, hymns and dialect poems. The statue was inspired by his poem *Ännchen of Tharau*, written in 1637.

The original statue was created in 1912, but it mysteriously vanished on the eve of World War II to make way for a statue of Adolf Hitler. On 23 March 1939, Hitler made a speech from the theatre balcony behind its original

Ännchen of Tharau in Theatre Square

location. In 1989, a replica of the original statue was placed in the middle of the fountain.

🏛 Castle Museum
Pilies 4. *Tel (46) 313 323.*
⏰ *10am–6pm Tue–Sat.* 📷
Housed in a 17th-century castle, this museum (Pilies muziejus) is one of modern Klaipėda's most recognized symbols. The castle was built on the foundations of the city's first fortress dating back to 1252. In 2002, an exhibition opened inside one of the ramparts, illustrating the development of the fortress and the city from the 13th to the 17th centuries. The exhibits include weapons, household articles, wooden tools and re-created models of the castle and the city in the 17th century. A Renaissance-era gold ring encrusted with diamonds is the highlight here.

🏛 History Museum of Lithuania Minor
Didžioji vandens 6. *Tel (46) 410 524.*
⏰ *10am–6pm Tue–Sat.* 📷
Located inside one of the Old Town's loveliest buildings, this museum (Mažosios Lietuvos istorijos muziejus) paints an illuminating picture of the earliest inhabitants of the eastern region of Lithuania Minor. Coins, maps, clothes, old photographs and models give a glimpse of the lives of the local German- and Lithuanian-speaking communities before World War II. The highlight is a collection of photographs taken during Hitler's visit in 1939.

🏛 Blacksmiths' Museum
Šaltkalvių 2a. *Tel (46) 410 526.*
⏰ *10am–6pm Tue–Sat.* 📷 📷
Black metal crosses, fences and cemetery gates are exhibited in a garden beside an old working smithy originally owned by Gustav Katzke, a metalwork artist of the early 20th century. Some of the crosses were rescued from destruction when the Sculpture Park replaced the city's main cemetery in the 1970s. Lithuania's cross-crafting tradition, in metal and in wood, was recognized by UNESCO in 2001.

Old wooden clock inside the Clock Museum

🏛 Clock Museum
Liepų 12. *Tel (46) 410 413.*
⏰ *noon–5:30pm Tue–Sat, noon–4:30pm Sun.* 📷 📷
From sundials to atomic clocks, this unique museum offers a fascinating insight into man's attempts to measure

time. The Clock Museum (Laikrodžių muziejus) was opened in 1984 inside a villa built in 1820 by John Simpson, an English merchant. Reconstructions of ancient calendars, sun, fire, water and sand clocks from around the world, and timepieces showing the changes in the faces and mechanisms of clocks dating back to the Renaissance, form the bulk of the exhibits.

The pleasant courtyard, featuring a large sundial, is a popular venue for music, dance and poetry evenings. The house next door was built by another English merchant, Mae Lean. In 1905, it was reconstructed in Art Nouveau style. The Neo-Gothic post office located close by is another striking building in the neighbourhood.

⌂ Picture Gallery and Sculpture Park

Liepų 33. *Tel (46) 410 524.*
☐ *noon–6pm Tue–Sat; noon–5pm Sun.* 🖼
The city's main state-run art gallery (Paveikslų galerija) is named after Pranas Domšaitis (1880–1965), a Lithuanian artist who was born near Königsberg and who settled in South Africa in 1949.

Heavily influenced by the Norwegian Symbolist painter Edvard Munch, Domšaitis won recognition for his art in inter-war Germany and later in South Africa. The gallery exhibits 20th-century Lithuanian art as well as a permanent exhibition of works by Domšaitis.

Situated behind the gallery, the Sculpture Park (Skulptūrų parkas) is dedicated to Martynas Mažvydas (1510–63), the author of the first Lithuanian book. Until the 1970s, the site was reserved for the city's cemetery. Spread over nearly 10 ha (25 acres), the park is dotted with abstract

VISITORS' CHECKLIST

315 km (195 miles) W of Vilnius.
🏛 187,000. ✈ 35 km (22 miles) NW of centre. 🚌
Priestočio gatvė 1. 🚌 Priestočio gatvė. ⛴ Old Castle Port, Žvejų 8, (46) 314 257; New Port, Nemuno 7, (46) 345 780.
Jun–Aug: 6:30pm–2:15am daily; Sep–May: at least hourly 6:30pm–2am. 🏛 Turgaus 7, (46) 412 186. 🎭 Klaipėda Jazz Festival (mid-Jul), Sea Festival (late Jul).

and intriguing sculptures by various artists, and new works are added to it each year.

Unique creations laid out in the Sculpture Park

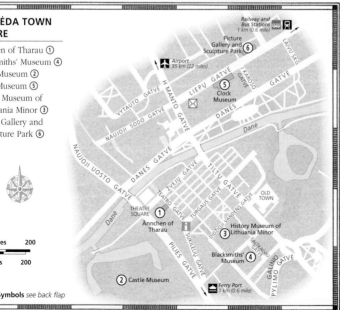

KLAIPĖDA TOWN CENTRE

Ännchen of Tharau ①
Blacksmiths' Museum ④
Castle Museum ②
Clock Museum ⑤
History Museum of
   Lithuania Minor ③
Picture Gallery and
   Sculpture Park ⑥

0 metres 200
0 yards 200

Key to Symbols *see back flap*

Curonian Spit National Park ❺
Kuršių Nerijos Nacionalinis parkas

A narrow 98-km (61-mile) strip of land on the Baltic coast, the Curonian Spit was formed 5,000 years ago. Its landscape consists largely of pine forests, dunes and sandy beaches. The park's forests are rich in wildlife such as roe deer, elk, foxes and wild boars. The dunes that tower over the village of Nida fall like cliffs into the Curonian Lagoon. Entire villages have been buried beneath the shifting sands. The Curonian Spit National Park, covering most of the spit, was created in 1991 to preserve the dunes, lagoons and surrounding area, and has been a UNESCO World Heritage Site since 2000.

KEY

☐ Curonian Spit National Park

★ Nida
The highly characteristic red-and-blue fishermen's cottages in Nida have remained unchanged for centuries. Some old weather-beaten fishing boats lie in the gardens outside the cottages.

Baltic Beach
The entire length of the spit on the side of the Baltic Sea is one long sandy beach. Areas adjacent to the villages are popular in summer, but other parts are little visited. Throughout the spit, parking is allowed only at designated parking areas.

BALTIC SEA

• Preil

★ Parnidis Dune
Looming 52 m (171 ft) above Nida, Parnidis Dune offers great views and is one of the highest points on the spit. A sundial erected here in 1995 collapsed during a storm in 1999. Only part of the sundial has been reconstructed.

Nida

Vecekrug Dune,
at 67 m (220 ft), is the highest wooded dune and can be seen from the forest trail.

★ Hill of Witches

*Comically demonic
wooden statues
lurk alongside
a path through
the pine
forest behind
Juodkrantė. The
statues were set
up by a group of
local sculptors in
the 1980s.*

Juodkrantė

VISITORS' CHECKLIST

350 km (217 miles) W of Vilnius.
🚌 Naglių 18e, Nida, (469) 52
859. ⛴ Naglių 14, Nida, (469)
51 101. Operators offer cruises
in vessels, as well as in replicas of
kurėnas (traditional fishing boats).
Visitors can explore the Dead
Dunes on the sightseeing trail of
the Nagliai Natural Reserve.
🛈 Taikos 4, Nida, (469) 52 345.
Bike rentals offered. 🚲
www.visitneringa.com

Dead Dunes

*These once-
shifting dunes are
now held in place
with vegetation and
offer a sanctuary to
birds, animals and
plants. Apart from a
scenic trail to the
Naglių Dune, the
area is out of bounds
to visitors.*

Forest Trails

*It is possible to walk or cycle the entire
length of the spit. The path takes visitors
past isolated stretches of sandy beach
and is lined with rich local flora.*

KEY

⛴	Ferry terminal
🚌	Coach station
🛈	Visitor information
🏛	Museum
🏖	Beach
══	Main road
– –	Trail
---	Ferry route

NATURAL RESERVE

Naglių
Dune

Pervalka

| 0 km | 2 |
| 0 miles | 2 |

SHIFTING DUNES

In the 17th century, when the
Curonian Spit forests were cut
down to fuel industry and
constant military campaigns,
the mountainous dunes were
released. Carried by the
Baltic winds, the sand started
to shift up to 20 m (66 ft) a
year in places, burying entire
villages. It was only in the

**Parnidis Dune seen from the
harbour at Nida**

19th century, when a vast number of trees were planted to
reforest the area, that the moving dunes were stopped.

STAR SIGHTS

★ Nida

★ Parnidis Dune

★ Hill of Witches

Practical & Travel Information

After many years of being excluded from the tourist map of Europe, Lithuania is now drawing a large number of eager visitors. Tour operators are increasing in number and offer a great variety of packages to the region. Most airlines fly to Vilnius, which has direct connections with many European cities. Lithuania is not, however, covered by Eurail or InterRail, making travelling by train from Western Europe relatively expensive.

WHEN TO VISIT

The best time to visit the country is from May to October, when the weather is generally pleasant and rarely cold. Nearly all the best festivals take place in summer, and some small museums and historic sights are only open between May and September. This is also the ideal time to explore the region's natural attractions, by visiting one of the many national parks or walking in the countryside. Autumn is often splendid in the Baltic States, but the weather can turn chilly as early as October.

DOCUMENTATION

Citizens of EU member-states, the US, Canada, Australia and New Zealand can enter Lithuania for up to 90 days in a half-year period on pre-sentation of a valid passport. Those wishing to stay beyond 90 days will need to apply for a national long-term visa or a residence permit.

Visitors from other countries should enquire about visa requirements at the relevant embassy or consulate before travelling. The official website

of the Lithuanian Ministry of Foreign Affairs offers infor-mation on visa regulations. For detailed information on entry regulations and visa costs, visitors are advised to check the official website of the **European Commission**. EU citizens are not subject to customs regulations, pro-vided they adhere to EU guidelines. All visitors should check for any customs duty or special permission required to export a cultural object before buying one.

VISITOR INFORMATION

All cities and most major towns in Lithuania have a tourist information office, which is usually located in the town centre. The coun-try's official tourism website lists all the tourist information centres across Lithuania. In the case of very small towns, the office may be situated in a museum or historic building. Tourist offices are usually open from 9am to 6pm on weekdays, but opening hours are more erratic in remote places and it is advisable to check in advance. Free brochures covering local and national

sights are available at these offices. Lithuania also has tourist offices in London, Finland, Sweden and Russia.

HEALTH AND SECURITY

Lithuania is generally a safe country to visit with instances of theft and mugging rela-tively rare. However, visitors should remain vigilant in Vilnius, particularly in and around the Old Town.

After years of underfunding *ligoninė (*Lithuanian hospitals) are in rather poor condition. Emergency treatment is free, but visitors will need to pay for medication and any subsequent medical treatment.

FACILITIES FOR THE DISABLED

Although there has been great improvement in recent years, Lithuania as a whole is not very well equipped in providing facilities for the disabled. The situation is best in Vilnius, where a large number of new buses and trolleybuses provide access for disabled people.

BANKING AND CURRENCY

Banking hours in Lithuania vary, with branches operat-ing from 8am to 5pm on weekdays. Banks in big cities open on Saturdays from 8am to 3pm or 10am to 5pm.The national currency of Lithuania is the litas, which is usually abbreviated to Lt. One litas consists of 100 centai. Foreign currency can be easily exchanged in banks or exchange bureaus. There is a wide network of ATMs across the country, most of which accept all major international credit and debit cards.

COMMUNICATIONS

Lithuania has a highly developed communications network. Mobile phone usage is high and broadband Internet access is widespread. Public payphones only accept *telefoniputka* (prepaid cards), which are available at

THE CLIMATE OF LITHUANIA

Lithuania has a temperate climate. The country usually gets its first snowfall in November. Winters are long, with temperatures dipping to -5° C (23° F). Summers generally last from mid-May to late August when temperatures average 18° C (64° F) in the capital city of Vilnius. Summer evenings are pleasant, with some short spells of rain.

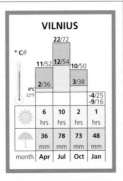

VILNIUS			
		22/72	
°C/F	11/52	12/54	10/50
	2/36		3/38
0°C 32°F			
			-4/25 -9/16
☀	6 hrs	10 hrs	2 hrs	1 hrs
☂	36 mm	78 mm	73 mm	48 mm
month	Apr	Jul	Oct	Jan

newspaper kiosks and post offices. Mobile phone users can avoid roaming costs by using local SIM cards which are available at newspaper kiosks. *Paštas* (post offices) can be found almost everywhere in the country.

ARRIVING BY AIR

Lithuania is well connected to the rest of Europe and, via major European transport hubs such as London, Copenhagen and Amsterdam, to the rest of the world. Opened in 1944, **Vilnius Airport** is the arrival point for most flights. Services at the airport include car rental offices, currency exchange, cafés and newspaper kiosks, which also sell bus tickets.

Lithuania does not have a national carrier, although Lithuania-based budget airline **Star 1** and Latvia's **airBaltic** both use Vilnius airport as a hub. The airport is also used by about 15 other airlines, including **Lufthansa**, **Finnair**, **Czech Airlines** and **Austrian Airlines**. There are connections to almost all the capitals of Western Europe as well as many cities in former Soviet republics.

Kaunas Airport has a small number of scheduled international flights, and is served by low-cost operator **RyanAir** from the UK and Ireland. **Auracom** has information on airport bus services throughout the country.

ARRIVING BY SEA

Lithuania's only commercial maritime harbour, **Klaipėda State Sea Port**, is linked by ferry to ports in Germany, Sweden and Denmark. There are connections to Kiel and Mukran in Germany, Copenhagen-Fredericia and Aabenraa-Aarhus in Denmark and Karlshamn in Sweden.

RAIL TRAVEL

The national rail network is run by **Lietuvos Geležinkeliai** (Lithuanian Railways). The main routes run from Vilnius to Šiauliai and Klaipėda; Vilnius to Visaginas, which passes Ignalina and Aukštaitija National Park; Šiauliai to Panevėžys and Rokiškis; and the speedy and regular Vilnius to Kaunas route. All train tickets must be purchased at the ticket desks in railway stations. At the larger railway stations it is possible to leave your baggage at the left luggage room for a small fee, or deposit the luggage in a self-service locker. Although the stations at Vilnius and Kaunas have been modernized, there is little emphasis on cleanliness and hygiene in other train stations.

TRAVELLING BY BUS

Lithuania has an extensive network of roads connecting the country to neighbouring

countries and there are numerous crossing points, making it fairly simple to travel by bus to or from Estonia and Latvia. There are express passenger coaches from Vilnius to Riga and Tallinn, as well as to other cities including Warsaw, Berlin, Prague, Vienna, Kaliningrad and Moscow. On the other hand, the journey from countries furthur west, such as Germany or the UK, is very long and the inconvenience is best avoided.

TRAVELLING BY CAR

Roads in Lithuania are excellent by post-Soviet era standards and present no special problems to drivers. There are no toll roads except through the Curonian Spit National Park.

Lithuanian regulations state that every car must carry a small fire extinguisher, a first-aid kit, a reflective warning triangle and reflective safety vest. It is mandatory for passengers to wear seat belts and motorists must use headlights at all times, both during the day and the night. The traffic police may not be able to speak fluent English but it can collect fines on the spot.

Driving while one is intoxicated is a punishable offence and local authorities sometimes use roadblocks and breath-analyzer tests as enforcement tools.

Shopping & Entertainment

Souvenirs and gifts in Lithuania usually consist of traditional arts and handicrafts made from locally available materials such as amber, ceramics and wood. The shops and stalls of the Old Towns in the country's larger cities, as well as in the various resorts, are flooded with offerings of this kind. A variety of entertainment is on offer in Lithuania, although, outside Vilnius the options tend to be limited. Baroque and chamber music concerts are regularly performed in churches throughout the country.

OPENING HOURS

Most shops in city centres open at 10am and stay open until 7pm. Outside the city centre, shops remain open until 9pm or even 10pm. Food shops and supermarkets that are part of larger chains often open at 8am and close late in the evening. On Saturdays, many shops open until 4pm, and some in tourist areas and larger towns and cities are open on Sundays as well.

MARKETS

The most extraordinary market in Lithuania is **Gariūnai**, located next to Vilnius's towering water-heating facility. It sells everything from inexpensive clothes, shoes, toys, toiletries and cosmetics to food, gadgets and even cars. At the southern edge of the Old Town, near the bus and train stations, is **Halės Market**, which mostly stocks fresh fruit and vegetables, cheese, meat and cakes.

TRADITIONAL CRAFTS

Lithuanian craftsmen make all manner of objects out of wood; from handcarved spatulas and spoons to grotesque masks of devils and witches. A popular religious memento is the crucifix, which is commonly made out of wood. For the musically inclined, handcarved musical instruments, such as the alluring Lithuanian *kanklės*, or zither, make ideal gifts.

The most original items of clothing on offer are made of flax. Shirts and blouses, dresses and hand-crocheted hats are all widely available.

The crafting of amber is an indisputable part of Lithuania's heritage and one to which its artisans apply great imagination. They fashion it into a wide range of objects, such as jewellery, lampshades and writing materials.

Black ceramics in the form of pots, jugs, cups and figures are among the specialities of the southern region of Lithuania, and are available throughout the country.

In Vilnius, traditional arts and crafts are most easily found along Pilies, Aušros Vartų and Didžioji streets. **Linen & Amber Studio**, a chain of gift shops, is one of the best places to find handicrafts made of flax and amber. For those interested in local textiles, a good destination is **Aukso Avis**. **Sauluva** stocks a reliable assortment of Lithuanian handicraft items made of wood, ceramic, amber and dried flowers.

FINE ART AND ANTIQUES

Vilnius offers an astonishing range of imaginative gift items in small art galleries such as **Rūtos Galerija**. Here quirky paintings, colourful plates designed with old photographs, vases with intricate patterns and decorative curios cover the gallery space. The **Artists' Union Exhibition Hall** has original artwork, hand-decorated cards and a fine range of Lithuanian and international art books, as well as works of the country's foremost sculptors, on display. The bohemian district of Užupis has a surfeit of art galleries, among which **Užupio Galerija**, selling metal and enamel pieces, is the most interesting.

FOOD AND DRINK

Traditional foods of all kinds are sold in Lithuanian shops, including *blynai* (a thin potato pancake with both sweet and savoury fillings), *spurgos* (doughnuts), smoked and steamed cheeses and a range of milk products. Smoked meats are usually sold as long, thick sausages or bound into balls. Forest berries and mushrooms can make unusual gifts, but visitors need customs clearance to carry them home. Some supermarkets have cafés offering a traditional Lithuanian meal of *cepelinai* (potato dumplings) as well as *kugelis* (baked potato pudding) and *vėdarai* (potato sausage).

Local favourites, such as *starka* (aged vodka), or *trejos devynerios* (herbal panacea), should not be missed. The best of the many varieties of *degtinė* (vodka) include Lithuania's excellent gold-topped vodkas, while the company Alita makes a popular brand of brandy. Švyturys Premium Pils and the Švyturys Ekstra Draught are both very fine bottled beers.

NIGHTLIFE

Though a little quieter than other European capitals, Vilnius has an abundance of bars and clubs featuring a variety of music genres and both local and international DJs. **Gravity**, located inside a Soviet-era bomb shelter, attracts the best DJs, while the uproarious **Bix** is for heavy metal fans. A little more central are **Paparazzi**, popular for its friendly atmosphere and wide range of cocktails, and **Pabo Latino**, specializing in Latin beats. **Žaltvykslė** hosts a number of live bands.

Club life is not limited to the capital. Klaipėda has an increasingly lively nightlife, with crowds flocking to the popular **Pabo Latino**. Some of the new bars in the Old Town even have casinos and restaurants. Kaunas has a mix of classy bars such as **Skliautai** in the Old Town and the hip and swinging club **Siena**, frequented by the young.

THEATRE

Lithuanians are passionate about theatre. Productions by Oskaras Koršunovas and Eimuntas Nekrošius are highly recommended. The **Lithuanian National Drama Theatre** and the more avant-garde **State Small Theatre of Vilnius** provide pre-recorded English translations for some performances. The **Klaipėda State Drama Theatre**, which dates from 1819, is the most famous theatre outside Vilnius.

LIVE MUSIC

With a small but fanatical following, jazz forms an inextricable part of the Lithuanian lifestyle. The **Holiday Inn Vilnius** hosts some excellent jazz performances and both Vilnius and Kaunas have brilliant jazz festivals. **Kurpiai** in Klaipėda is best known for its jazz and blues concerts.

Several outstanding Lithuanian rock and pop performers play regularly at atmospheric venues such as **Tamsta Club**, **Brodvėjus** and the **Forum Palace** in Vilnius. International artistes tend to play at the modern **Siemens Arena** or the less pretentious **Utenos Entertainment Centre**.

Folk festivals are often organized in the premises of Vilnius University.

CLASSICAL MUSIC, OPERA AND BALLET

Vilnius has a good classical music scene. Both the **National Philharmonic** and the **Congress Palace** hold superb concerts. The innovative choreography of the **Anželika Cholina Dance** Theatre is popular with locals and visitors alike. The famous **National Opera & Ballet Theatre** is often packed to capacity. Theatres in Klaipėda and Kaunas organize regular classical music concerts and opera performances.

MUSIC FESTIVALS

Several music festivals have grown in popularity over the years. The magnificent Baroque Pažaislis Monastery complex, near Kaunas, forms the backdrop to the annual **Pažaislis Music Festival**. The **Edvard Grieg and M K Čiurlionis Festival**, hosted in Kaunas each spring, features classical music concerts. The **Muzikinis Pajūris** (Musical Seaside) festival of opera and symphony takes place every summer in Klaipėda.

DIRECTORY

MARKETS

Gariūnai
Vilnius–Kaunas Highway.

Halės Market
Pylimo and Bazilijonų street corner, Vilnius.

TRADITIONAL CRAFTS

Aukso Avis
Savičiaus 10, Vilnius.
Tel (5) 261 0421.

Linen & Amber Studio
Stiklių 3, Vilnius.
Tel (5) 261 0213.
www.lgstudija.lt
(One of several branches.)

Sauluva
Literatų 3 & Šv Mykolo 4, Vilnius. *Tel (5) 212 1227.*
www.sauluva.lt

FINE ART AND ANTIQUES

Artists' Union Exhibition Hall
Vokiečių 2, Vilnius.
Tel (5) 261 9516.
www.galerija-lds.lt

Rūtos Galerija
Vokiečių 28, Vilnius.
Tel (5) 231 4537.

Užupio Galerija
Užupio 3–I, Vilnius.
Tel (5) 231 2318.

NIGHTLIFE

Bix
Etmonų 6, Vilnius.
Tel (5) 262 7791.

Gravity
Jasinskio 16, Vilnius.
Tel (5) 249 7966.

Pabo Latino
Trakų 3, Vilnius.
Tel (5) 262 1045;
Žvejų 4, Klaipėda.
Tel (46) 403 040.

Paparazzi
Totorių 3, Vilnius.
Tel (5) 212 0135.

Siena
Laisvės 93, Kaunas.
Tel (37) 424 424.

Skliautai
Aušros Vartų 11, Kaunas.
Tel (37) 224 112.

Žaltvykslė
Pilies 11, Vilnius.
Tel (5) 268 7173.

THEATRE

Klaipėda State Drama Theatre
Manto 45, Klaipėda.
Tel (46) 314 453.
www.kldteatras.lt

Lithuanian National Drama Theatre
Gedimino 4, Vilnius.
Tel (5) 262 1593.
www.teatras.lt

State Small Theatre of Vilnius
Gedimino 22, Vilnius.
Tel (5) 249 9869.
www.vmt.lt

LIVE MUSIC

Brodvėjus
Vokiečių 4, Vilnius.
Tel (5) 210 7208.
www.brodvejus.lt

Forum Palace
Konstitucijos 26, Vilnius.
Tel (5) 263 6666.
www.forumpalace.lt

Holiday Inn Vilnius
Šeimyniškių 1, Vilnius.
Tel (5) 210 3000.
www.holidayInnvilnius.lt

Kurpiai
Kurpių 1a, Klaipėda.
Tel (46) 410 555.

Siemens Arena
Ozo 14, Vilnius.
Tel (5) 247 7576.
www.siemens-arena.lt

Tamsta Club
Subačiaus 11, Vilnius.
Tel (5) 212 1185.
www.tamstaclub.lt

Utenos Entertainment Centre
Ažuolyno 9, Vilnius.
Tel (5) 242 4444.

CLASSICAL MUSIC, OPERA AND BALLET

Anželika Cholina Dance Theatre
Šimulionio 4–103, Vilnius.
Tel (5) 6883 4181.

Congress Palace
Vilnius 6–14, Vilnius.
Tel (5) 261 8828.

National Opera & Ballet Theatre
Vienuolio 1, Vilnius.
Tel (5) 262 0727.

National Philharmonic
Aušros Vartų 5, Vilnius.
Tel (5) 266 5216.
www.filharmonija.lt

MUSIC FESTIVALS

Edvard Grieg and M K Čiurlionis Festival
www.kaunofilharmonija.lt

Muzikinis Pajūris
www.muzikinis-teatras.lt

Pažaislis Music Festival
www.pazaislis.lt

Where to Stay in Lithuania

Hotels in Lithuania share a classification code with Scandinavian countries, which has helped to improve standards throughout the industry. However, it is advisable to run a check on the establishment, as some smaller hotels, particularly those converted from Soviet-era buildings, may not live up to expectations.

PRICE CATEGORIES
Price categories are for a standard double room per night in high season, including tax and service charges. Breakfast is included, unless otherwise specified.

Ⓛ Under 150 Lt
ⓁⓁ 150–300 Lt
ⓁⓁⓁ 300–450 Lt
ⓁⓁⓁⓁ 450–600 Lt
ⓁⓁⓁⓁⓁ Over 600 Lt

VILNIUS

Litinterp
Ⓟ Ⓖ — Ⓛ

Bernardinų 712, 01124 **Tel** *(5) 212 3850* **Fax** *212 3559* **Rooms** *16* — **Map** *E3*

Boasting a prime spot close to the Church of St Anne, this hotel offers perhaps the smallest and most inexpensive rooms in the Old Town. However, it is a peaceful spot to spend a night. The rooms are well equipped, with refrigerator, tea- and coffee-making facilities and phone. Some rooms have en suite bathrooms. **www.litinterp.com**

Dvaras
Ⓟ ⓘ ≋ ▤ Ⓖ — ⓁⓁⓁ

Tilto 3, 01101 **Tel** *(5) 210 7370* **Fax** *272 6210* **Rooms** *8* — **Map** *D2*

A classy guesthouse close to Vilnius Cathedral *(see pp48–9)*, Dvaras means "manor house". However, the interiors resemble a richly designed country cottage, with wooden floors, thick carpets and elegant furnishings. Excellent meals are served in a cosy but little-visited cellar restaurant. **www.dvaras.lt**

Narutis
ⓘ ≋ ▤ Ⓖ — ⓁⓁⓁⓁ

Pilies 24, 01123 **Tel** *(5) 212 2894* **Fax** *262 2882* **Rooms** *50* — **Map** *E3*

Each plush room here is individually decorated in luscious colours. French designer Anne Toulous chose soft, noise-absorbing carpets for the rooms and corridors and unique frescoes, wall paintings, original 16th-century beamed ceilings and Gothic vaults add to the charm. Two suites even have a *hammam* and Jacuzzi. **www.narutis.com**

Relais & Châteaux Stikliai
ⓘ ≋ ▤ Ⓖ — ⓁⓁⓁⓁⓁ

Gaono 7, 01131 **Tel** *(5) 264 9595* **Fax** *212 3870* **Rooms** *44* — **Map** *D4*

This opulent five-star hotel on one of the Old Town's most charming narrow streets simply exudes elegance. The rooms boast beautiful upholstery in rich fabrics and luxurious en suite bathrooms. This is where royalty and stars come to stay, particularly in the breathtaking King Mindaugas Suite. **www.stikliaihotel.lt**

REST OF LITHUANIA

CURONIAN SPIT NATIONAL PARK Ąžuolynas
Ⓟ ⓘ ≋ — ⓁⓁ

L Rėzos 54, Juodkrantė, 93101 **Tel** *(469) 53 310* **Fax** *(469) 53 316* **Rooms** *79*

Perhaps the closest thing to a resort hotel on the Curonian Spit *(see pp62–3)*, Ąžuolynas, directly facing the lagoon, has a swimming pool and waterslide for families to enjoy. It also has a Turkish bath, tennis court and fitness centre. A heath path over the dunes leads to the Baltic Sea. **www.hotelazuolynas.lt**

KAUNAS Best Western Santakos
Ⓟ ⓘ ≋ ▤ — ⓁⓁⓁⓁ

J Gruodžio 21, 44293 **Tel** *(37) 302 702* **Fax** *(37) 330 2700* **Rooms** *92*

Set in an elegant, historic red-brick building in the heart of the Old Town, this four-star hotel offers quality experience. The wonderful interiors and cosy rooms are matched by the excellent service and facilities. The in-house restaurant is among the best in Kaunas and serves artfully garnished dishes amidst a Persian-themed ambience. **www.santaka.lt**

KLAIPĖDA Radisson SAS Klaipėda
Ⓟ ⓘ ▤ Ⓖ — ⓁⓁⓁⓁ

Šaulių 28, 92231 **Tel** *(46) 490 800* **Fax** *(46) 490 815* **Rooms** *74*

With rooms decorated in 19th-century New England maritime style, Radisson SAS Klaipėda sets high standards. Free Wi-Fi, a top-notch restaurant and a cocktail bar, as well as a steam bath and superbly equipped fitness studio complete the package. **www.klaipeda.radissonsas.com**

TRAKAI Akmeninė Rezidencija
Ⓟ ⓘ — ⓁⓁ

Bražuolės Village, 21100 **Tel** *(528) 30 544* **Fax** *(528) 25 186* **Rooms** *10*

This rustic-style hotel, a complex of five hotel rooms and five villas, is a divine getaway with great views of the Trakai Island Castle *(see pp56–7)*. It offers cosy accommodation with lakeside Russian baths and top-quality dining. Water sports are available in summer, while in winter the lake turns into a giant ice-skating rink. **www.akmeninuezeiga.lt**

Map References *see map of Vilnius pp46–7*

Where to Eat in Lithuania

Traditional Baltic cooking is hearty and filling, designed to satisfy one's appetite after hard physical labour. Meat is integral to Lithuanian cuisine, although there is an increasing choice of vegetarian dishes on offer in most restaurants. Vilnius has a wide range of places to eat offering a good selection of local and international cuisine.

PRICE CATEGORIES
Based on the price per person of a three-course meal with half a bottle of wine, including cover charge, service and tax.
Ⓛ Under 55 Lt
ⓁⓁ 55–65 Lt
ⓁⓁⓁ 65–75 Lt
ⓁⓁⓁⓁ 75–85 Lt
ⓁⓁⓁⓁⓁ Over 85 Lt

VILNIUS

Čili Kaimas
Vokiečių 8 **Tel** (5) 231 2536 — **Map** D4

Offering Lithuanian food in a vast barn-style venue complete with farming implements and a tree growing up through the middle, Čili Kaimas is loud, kitsch and hugely popular. Two menu options are provided, one offering better food at higher prices. The vodka snacks followed by pig's trotters and stuffed intestines are highly recommended.

Sonnets
Bernardinų 8/8 **Tel** (5) 266 5885 — **Map** E3

Exuding elegance, Sonnets is housed in the Shakespeare Boutique Hotel. Seating ranges from snug sofas by the bar and fine-dining tables in the library to tables out on the less formal balcony. The menu includes unusual names such as "Three Musketeers" and "Toreador". Its signature dish is "Aleksandr", a mix of chesnuts, Gorgonzola and fig.

Medininkai
Aušros Vartų 8 **Tel** (5) 266 0771 — **Map** D5

This restaurant at the Europa Royale Vilnius has an atmospheric courtyard for summer dining and an evocative cellar for use in chillier weather. The chef likes to call her dishes Lithuanian fusion, but in reality Medininkai serves international cuisine with a certain panache. Service can sometimes seem slow.

Brasserie Astorija
Didžioji 35/2 **Tel** (5) 212 0110 — **Map** D4

One of the classiest restaurants in Vilnius, Brasserie Astorija is at the Radisson SAS Astorija. The chef promotes the use of fresh, healthy ingredients in his cooking and every course is a delight, especially the seafood. The wine list is exceptional and service is excellent. The glass vestibule is great for people-watching.

REST OF LITHUANIA

CURONIAN SPIT NATIONAL PARK Vella Bianca
Rėzos 1a, Juodkrantė **Tel** (469) 50 013

One of the finest restaurants on the Curonian Spit, with panoramic views of the lagoon and Juodkrantė harbour, Vella Bianca boasts excellent Italian cuisine, including desserts, and a range of fine wines. As befitting its location, it presents fabulous seafood creations, although its meat, pasta and home-made pizza dishes are also superb.

KAUNAS Bernelių Užeiga
Valančiaus 9 **Tel** (37) 200 913

Generous helpings of authentic Lithuanian food are served in this restaurant, located within the confines of Kaunas's Old Town (see p58). The 18th-century building is a protected monument. The interior evokes a country tavern while the exterior, in gaudy purple peppered with bright red flowers, makes it hard to miss.

KLAIPĖDA Petit Marseille
Žvejų 4a **Tel** (46) 430 472

Reflecting the same winning characteristics as Saint Germain, its partner restaurant in Vilnius, the Petit Marseille features a wonderful selection of French food and wine, delicious cheeses and satisfying desserts. The Old Town location and outdoor seating by the Danė river add to the charm, making it a relaxing dining spot.

TRAKAI Senoji Kibininė
Karaimų 65 **Tel** (528) 55 865

The first Karaim eating house in Trakai, this barn has been in existence for several years. Very informal, it is hugely popular considering the fact that there are only two items on the menu: kibinai (pastries) and čenakai (stewed cabbage hotpot). Guests should try both, accompanied by beer in summer and vodka at other times.

Key to Symbols see back cover flap

LATVIA

L ying between Lihuania and Estonia, Latvia is characterized by delightful forests and lakes, fascinating historical towns and dynamic cities, which are, by and large, under-explored. By contrast, the country's exciting capital, Rīga, draws hordes of Western Europeans all year round. The largest city in the Baltic region, Rīga revels in its cultural treasures and hedonistic nightlife.

Latvia's strategic geographical position prompted its more powerful neighbours to gain control over the region and largely decided the course of its history. A short period of self-determination in the early 20th century ended with occupation first by Nazi Germany and then by Soviet Russia. Independence was not restored until 1991. Nonetheless, a distinctive Latvian culture survived, assimilating foreign influences and still retaining a strong connection with nature. While still coming to terms with the legacies of the 20th century, today the country has a new confidence. Its historic cities have been restored, while rural areas are being developed for ecotourism.

HISTORY

Latvia's history is traditionally considered to begin with the advent of the Teutonic knights in 1201. Looking for conquests and converts in a pagan land, these German warrior-monks conquered Latvia and founded Rīga, which grew into an important centre for trade between the Baltic region and Western Europe. The beneficiaries of this growth were the Germans, while the Latvians were dispossessed and forced to become serfs.

The early 16th century saw Protestantism declared as the state religion. However, in 1561, Catholicism was established when Poland conquered Latvia during the

Bank of the Gauja river below Eagle Cliff, Gauja National Park

◁ Renaissance-style façade of the House of Blackheads, Rīga

Independence Day celebrations, Rīga, 1933

Livonian Wars. The clash between the Protestant Swedes and Catholic Poles resulted in Swedish rule in northern Latvia for much of the 17th century. In 1710, during the Great Northern War, the Swedes surrendered Rīga to Peter the Great of Russia, ushering in 200 years of stability.

When World War I broke out in 1914, Latvia became the main battleground between Germany and Russia. The Allied victory in 1918 forced the German troops to withdraw and Latvia was declared an independent nation. Despite the constantly changing governments that ruled until 1934, much was achieved during this period of independence. However, progress came to a halt with the Soviet invasion on 17 June 1940, which saw Latvians of influence either executed or deported to Siberia. The Germans invaded a year later, with brutal consequences for the Jewish community.

The Soviets returned to eastern Latvia and Rīga as "liberators" in the autumn of 1944. Further deportations were carried out, and Russian numbers swelled, posing a serious threat to Latvian culture.

In 1988, new political groups began to emerge. The most forceful of these, the Popular Front of Latvia (PLF), demanded full independence and won the elections in 1990, provoking clashes with Soviet forces. Moscow's conservative Communists staged a coup against President Mikhail Gorbachev in August 1991, but it collapsed and Latvia finally found itself free. Since then governments have come and gone, but the beginning of the 21st century saw the effective integration of Latvia into Western Europe, particularly with its entry into the European Union in 2004.

KEY DATES IN LATVIAN HISTORY

AD 1201 Rīga founded by Albrecht of Buxthoeven

1282 Rīga joins a trading confederation of German port cities and merchants' associations

1372 German replaces Latin as official language

1561 Latvia occupied by Poland

1629 Sweden colonizes Latvia

1710 Riga conquered by Peter the Great of Russia

1822 First Latvian newspaper printed

1850s National Awakening Movement formed

1905 Socialist revolution demands independence

1914 German occupation of Latvia begins

1918 Formal declaration of Latvian independence

1920 The Soviet Union recognizes Latvia's independence

1940 First Soviet occupation of Latvia

1941 Occupation by Nazi Germany

1944–91 Second Soviet occupation of Latvia

1988 Pro-independence Popular Front is formed

1991 Latvian independence re-established

2004 Latvia joins NATO and the EU

2007 Valdis Zatlers sworn in as president

LANGUAGE AND CULTURE

Latvian is the official language of the people, although a sizeable Russian-speaking minority also exists.

Echoes of Latvia's pagan past remain to this day, most obviously in the celebration of Midsummer. The Latvian calendar is punctuated by festivities which mark the passing of seasons; many folk rituals are incorporated into Christian celebrations.

Exploring Latvia

Latvia is extremely visitor friendly. At its heart lies
Rīga, the largest and most cosmopolitan city in the
Baltic States. Strategically positioned on the Gulf
of Rīga, it has a long history as a thriving mercantile
centre. Beyond the capital, western Latvia enchants
with its contrasts – dense forests and fertile plains,
lively cities such as Liepāja and sleepy rural towns.
Eastern Latvia, meanwhile, boasts some of the
country's most popular attractions, such as the Gauja
National Park. Most places of interest are connected
by regular trains and buses, although public transport
is less reliable for getting off the beaten track. Renting
a vehicle is a good way to get around the country on
a short trip.

Boats moored at a sailing club,
Jūrmala

SIGHTS AT A GLANCE

Cēsis **8**

Gauja National Park pp86–7 **7**

Jūrmala **2**

Kuldīga **3**

Liepāja **4**

Rīga pp74–81 **1**

Rundāle Palace pp84–5 **5**

Sigulda **6**

The Marble Hall in Rundāle Palace

| 0 km | 50 |
| 0 miles | 50 |

KEY

✈ Airport

⛴ Ferry terminal

— Motorway

— Major road

— Railway

– ‑ International border

Rīga ●

For many centuries Rīga was largely contained within the city walls on the bank of the Daugava river. Now known as the Old Town, this area contains most of the city's sites of interest. The main route through the tangle of picturesque streets and squares is Kaļķu iela, leading from the Stone Bridge (Akmens tilts) to Brīvības bulvāris and the Freedom Monument. When the city walls were removed in the mid-19th century, the space was developed into a ring of boulevards and parks. The main train and bus stations lie on the southeastern edge of this ring. To the north is the late 19th- and 20th-century extension of the city known as the Centre (Centrs), which includes some of Rīga's most impressive Art Nouveau architecture. Today the city is home to about seven hundred thousand residents.

SEE ALSO

- *Where to Stay* p92
- *Where to Eat* p93

Sculpture outside the entrance to
St Peter's Church

GETTING AROUND

The best way to get around the Old Town is on foot: parking is expensive and there is no public transport available. The main Art Nouveau district is within walking distance of the Old Town, while a network of trams and buses provides access to far-flung attractions. Taxis are also abundant on Town Hall Square (Rātslaukums). The main tourist information office here can offer advice on guided tours.

| 0 metres | 200 |
| 0 yards | 200 |

GREATER RĪGA

Kišecers

RĪGA

Priedaine

Lake Jugla

Ūlupji

Ulbroka

Riga International Airport

Daugava

Baloži

0 km   5

0 miles   5

KEY

Area of the main map

DZIRNAVU IELA

ALDEMĀRA IELA

ELIZABETES IELA

SKOLAS IELA

⓫

ESPLANĀDE

BĀZNĪCAS IELA

BRĪVĪBAS GATVE

Orthodox Cathedral ✝

AKA BULVĀRIS

DZIRNAVU IELA

P

VĀRIS

TĒRBATAS IELA

MERĶEĻA IELA

ELIZABETES IELA

⊠

Freedom Monument

VERMANES PARK

ĪBAS ULVĀRIS

RAIŅA BULVĀRIS

K BARONA IELA

ASPAZIJAS BULVĀRIS

⊠

DZENES IELA

VAINU IELA

EJU IELA

Rīga Central Railway Station 100 m (109 yards) 🚉

JANVĀRA IELA

Autoosta (Main Bus Station) 300 m (328 yards)

KEY

Street-by-Street area: see pp78–9

Major sight / Place of interest

✈ Airport

🚉 Railway station

⛴ Ferry terminal

🚌 Bus station

ℹ Visitor information

P Parking

⊠ Post office

✝ Church

▬ Major road

▬ Minor road

— Railway

SIGHTS AT A GLANCE

Dome Cathedral ①
House of Blackheads ⑧
Latvian Ethnographic Open-
    Air Museum ⑫
Museum of Decorative Arts
    and Design ⑩
Museum of Jews in Latvia ⑪
Museum of the Occupation
    of Latvia ⑦
Museum of Rīga's History
    and Navigation ②
Powder Tower ⑥
Rīga Castle ③
St James's Cathedral ④
St Peter's Church ⑨
Swedish Gate ⑤

D   E   F

1   2   3   4   5

Impressive cross-vaulted gallery of the Dome Cathedral

Dome Cathedral ①
Doma baznīca

Doma laukums 1. **Map** B3.
Tel 6721 3213. ☐ May–Sep:
9am–6pm Sat–Tue, Thu, 9am–5pm
Wed & Fri; Oct–Apr: 10am–5pm
daily. ☐ for special events. ☒ ✝
10am Sun. **www**.doms.lv

Founded as St Mary's by
Bishop Albert von
Buxhoevden in 1211, the
cathedral became one of the
city's three seats of power
along with the Town Hall and
Rīga Castle. It gained its
current name from the German
word *dom* (cathedral) during
the Reformation. The cathedral
looks as if it has sunk, but in
fact the land around it has
been raised to keep out flood-
water from the Daugava river.
  One of the largest places of
worship in the region, the
cathedral has been altered
over the years and its bulky
structure exhibits a variety of
styles. The altar alcove and
the east wing crossing are
Romanesque, with a cross-
vaulted ceiling and rows of
semi-circular windows.
Simpler Neo-Gothic
additions are
characterized by
pointed arches,
large windows
and lierne vault-
ing, while the
eastern pediment
and the steeple are
in 18th-century
Baroque style. The
portal was added in
the 19th century, followed by
an Art Nouveau vestibule in
the 20th century. Most of the

interior's decor was destroyed
during the Reformation, and it
is now very plain, except for
the tombs of merchants and
the 19th-century stained glass.
The woodwork of the
17th-century pulpit is ornate,
however, as is the organ case,
which is Mannerist with
Baroque and Rococo additions.
The organ was built in
Germany in 1884. In the
summer it is possible to visit
the cross-vaulted gallery of
the Dome, the Romanesque
cloister and courtyard.

Museum of Rīga's History and Navigation ②
Rīga's vēstures un
kuģniecības muzejs

Palasta iela 4. **Map** B3. **Tel** 6721
1358. ☐ May–Sep: 11am–5pm daily;
Oct–May: 11am–5pm Wed–Sun. ☐
Mon & Tue. ☒ ✔ **www**.rigamuz.Lv

Founded in 1773, this museum
is the oldest in Rīga. Housed
in an impressive building with
tiled stoves and stained-
glass windows, it
is also one of the
city's most interest-
ing museums.
The exhibition
on navigation
covers the mari-
time history of the
city up until World
War I, and includes
several large models
of ships and material
on Krišjānis Valdemārs (1825–
91), a key figure of the
Latvian National Awakening.

**Model ship at the
Museum of Rīga's
History and Navigation**

Other rooms cover everything
from prehistory to independence, with emphasis on the
mid-19th to mid-20th cen-
turies. Highlights from the
Middle Ages include the
*Madonna on a Crescent
Moon*, a sculpture of the
patroness of the Great Guild
(a union of Rīga merchants),
which was taken to Germany
during World War II and *Big
Kristaps*, a large 16th-century
statue of St Christopher.

Rīga Castle ③
Rīgas pils

Pils laukums 3. **Map** B3. **Museum
of Foreign Art Tel** 6722 6467.
☐ 11am–5pm Tue–Sun. ☒ ✔
www.amm.lv **History Museum
of Latvia Tel** 6722 1357. ☐ 11am–
5pm Wed–Sun. ☒ ✔

The city's original Livonian
Order castle was destroyed by
Rīga's citizens during a war
against the Order lasting from
1297 to 1330. After losing, the
townspeople were forced to
build a new castle on the
present site just outside the
city. Continuing quarrels
resulted in the Master of the
Order leaving the capital, but
Rīga Castle was destroyed by
the citizens once more in
1484. They were defeated
again and the next castle the
townspeople were compelled
to build forms the core of the
current structure and was the
headquarters of the Livonian
Order until 1561. As well as

**Changing of the guard outside Rīga
Castle in the Old Town**

being the official residence of Latvia's president, the building now houses two museums. Exhibits at the **Museum of Foreign Art** (Ārzemju mākslas muzejs) begin with copies of Egyptian and Greek statues, and continue with a collection of paintings. Most visitors will also enjoy a tour of the **History Museum of Latvia** (Latvijas vēstures muzejs). The exhibits take in religious sculpture, traditional regional costumes and consumer goods from the first period of independence in 1920. There are also rooms decorated in various styles including Biedermeier and Art Nouveau.

Entrance to the 13th-century St James's Cathedral

St James's Cathedral ④
šv Jēkaba katedrāle

Jekaba iela 9. **Map** B3. **Tel** 6732 6419. ⬜ Oct–May: 7am–6pm; May–Oct: 7am–7pm. 🕀 daily.

Sited outside the old city walls, St James's was built in 1225 to serve the surrounding villages. The church was renowned for having its bell hanging from a cupola, which is still visible on the southern side, although the bell has gone. It was rung to signal that an execution was taking place in the city, although another story insists that it was heard when unfaithful women passed by the church. The structure has been renovated several times and, today it is the seat of Rīga's Catholic archbishop.

Swedish Gate ⑤
Zviedru vārti

Between Torņa iela & Aldaru iela. **Map** C2.

The sole remnant of eight city gates, the Swedish Gate was built in 1698 during a period of Swedish rule in Rīga. It runs through the ground floor of the house at Torņa 11, and legend has it that the gate was created illegally by a wealthy merchant to give him direct access to his warehouse. More likely, it was built for the use of the soldiers stationed at St James's Barracks. Today, the gate provides access between the popular strip of shops and bars on Torņa iela and the quieter, but pleasant, Aldaru iela. Newly-married couples include the gate on their tour of the city, as passing through it is said to bring good luck.

Powder Tower ⑥
Pulvertornis

Smilšu iela 20. **Map** C3. **Tel** 6722 8147. ⬜ May–Sep: 10am–6pm Wed–Sun; Oct–Apr: 10am–5pm Wed–Sun. 🎟 donations. 🅿 **www**.karamuzejs.lv

The cylindrical Powder Tower is all that remains from a total of 18 towers that were once part of the city's defences. Its 14th-century foundations are among the oldest in the city, but the rest of the structure dates from 1650, when it was rebuilt after being destroyed by the Swedish Army in 1621. The 2.5-m (8-ft) thick walls were intended to protect the gunpowder stored inside, after which the tower was named. Nine Russian cannonballs remain embedded in the walls as proof of its strength.

The tower was bought by a German student fraternity at the end of the 19th century, and in 1919, it housed a military museum reflecting on the then-recent fight for independence as well as on World War I. The annexe building was constructed from 1937 to 1940, but the Soviet occupation meant that it did not fulfil its function until several

Swedish Gate, built through the ground floor of an old house

decades later. From 1957, the tower housed the Museum of the Revolution in the Soviet Republic of Latvia.

The tower and the annexe are now home to the **Latvian War Museum** (Latvigas kara muzejs). While the oldest exhibit – part of a cannon discovered during the 1930s – dates from the 15th century, the museum concentrates on 20th-century warfare. World War I is covered with displays of weapons, uniforms and propaganda posters. Other rooms examine the role of Latvians in the Russian Revolution, the Latvian War of Independence, World War II and the Soviet occupation. Recent additions include a collection of 360 models of military machinery.

The Powder Tower, home to the Latvian War Museum, Rīga

Street-by-Street: Around Town Hall Square

The Blackheads' patron

Until a local government reform in 1877, the Town Hall Square (Rātslaukums) was Rīga's administrative centre. Built in 1334, the Town Hall was one of three pillars of power alongside Dome Cathedral and Rīga Castle, representing the interests of the city's residents. The square functioned as a marketplace and a site where festivals were held and executions carried out. The impressive step-gabled House of Blackheads has been completely rebuilt, while the Town Hall is a modern building behind a Neo-Classical façade. At the square's edge is a Soviet-era building housing the Museum of the Occupation of Latvia.

A roadside café in summer in the courtyard of St John's Church

KEY

– – – Suggested route

Town Hall

Town Hall Square
Many of the square's elaborate buildings, destroyed by the Russians after World War II, have benefited from a restoration project tied to the city's 800th anniversary in 2001.

KAĻĶU IELA

KAĻĶU IELA

GRĒCINIEKU IELA

Statue of Roland
A legendary medieval figure and one of Charlemagne's knights, Roland became a symbol of the independence of cities from the local nobility.

Museum of the Occupation of Latvia

★ House of Blackheads
Damaged by bombing in 1941, the ornate building was restored to its former glory during the 1990s ⑧

STAR SIGHTS

★ House of Blackheads

★ Museum of the Occupation of Latvia

★ St Peter's Church

★ Museum of the Occupation of Latvia
This incongruous slab of concrete houses a chilling and detailed testament to the suffering of Latvians during the Soviet and Nazi occupations in the 20th century ⑦

Konventa Sēta
The Convent Courtyard has been renovated and is now home to shops, galleries and a porcelain museum.

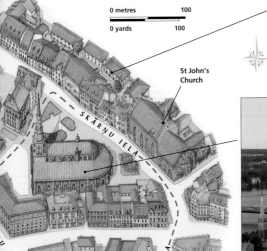

St John's Church

SKĀRŅU IELA

MĀRSTAĻU IELA

★ St Peter's Church
This striking building has been destroyed and rebuilt several times over since its original 13th-century incarnation ⑨

Photography Museum traces the development of photography from 1839 to 1941 through photographs and camera equipment.

Mentzendorff House
Constructed in 1695 to house an apothecary, this building is now a museum devoted to the life of Rīga's merchant class in the 17th and 18th centuries.

Dannenstern House was the largest dwelling in 17th-century Rīga.

0 metres 100
0 yards 100

Textile artwork on display at the Museum of Decorative Arts and Design

Museum of the Occupation of Latvia ⑦

Latvijas okupācijas muzejs

Strēlnieku laukums 1. **Map** C4.
Tel 6721 2715. ☐ May–Sep:
11am–6pm daily; Oct–Apr:
11am–5pm Tue–Sun. 🖼 donations.
🖼 🖼 www.occupationmuseum.lv

This Soviet-era structure was built to house a museum in honour of the Latvian Riflemen, but since 1993 it has provided an account of the suffering of Latvians at the hands of Nazi Germany in World War II and under the Soviets. The collection includes eyewitness accounts and photographs of deportations and political represssion.

House of Blackheads ⑧

Melngalvju nams

Rātslaukums 6. **Map** C4.
Tel 6704 4300. 🖬 Schwab House.
☐ 11am–5pm Tue–Sun. 🖼 🖼
🖼 🖼

The House of Blackheads was originally built in 1334 for the city's guilds, after the Livonian Order seized the existing guild buildings. Over time, a guild of unmarried foreign merchants, the Blackheads, became the sole occupants. Their name derives from their patron, St Maurice, and they were known for their riotous parties. The building was devastated by bombing in 1941 and the Soviet authorities demolished the remnants seven years later; the current

structure dates from 1999. Rooms that are open to the public include the Grand Hall and a concert hall.

St Peter's Church ⑨

Pēterbaznīca

Skārņu iela 19. **Map** C4. **Tel** 6722 9426. ☐ 10am–6pm Tue–Sun. 🖼 tower only. 🖼 except tower. www.peterbaznica.lv

First mentioned in 1209, St Peter's Church was largely built by the Livs, Finnic people who settled along the Gulf of Rīga some 5,000 years ago. None of the original wooden church remains, although parts of the walls date from the 13th century. The church, which had become Lutheran in 1523, was damaged by fire in 1721, when Peter the Great is said to have headed the failed efforts to rescue it. The church's steeple has been rebuilt many times. Reaching a height of 123 m (403 ft), it provides excellent views across the city.

Stone figure outside the entrance of St Peter's Church

Museum of Decorative Arts and Design ⑩

Dekoratīvās mākslas un dizaina muzejs

Skārņu iela 10/20. **Map** C3.
Tel 6722 7833. ☐ 11am–5pm
Tue–Sun. 🖼 🖼 🖼
www.dlmm.lv

This museum is housed in the former St George's Church, Rīga's oldest surviving stone building. It was constructed as the chapel for Rīga's original Livonian Order castle in 1208, and became a separate church after the castle was destroyed in 1297. After the Reformation it was used as a warehouse.

The museum gives an overview of decorative arts from the 1890s to the present day. The ground floor hosts temporary exhibitions, while the first floor, covering the 1890s to the 1960s, is the most interesting part of the main collection. Highlights include a vast selection of painted ceramics and carpet designs by local graphic artist Jūlijs Madernieks (1870–1955).

Museum of Jews in Latvia ⑪

Muzejs Ebreji Latvijā

Skolas iela 6. **Map** D1. **Tel** 6728
3484. ☐ noon–5pm Mon–Thu, Sun.
🖼 donations.

Housed inside a Jewish cultural centre, this museum is based around the collections of two Holocaust survivors, Zalman Elelson and Marģers Vestermanis, which tell the story of the Jewish community in Latvia. Beginning with the first records of Jews in the 16th century, it progresses to photographs of early 20th-century family life. The focus, however, is on the horrific years of Nazi occupation. The museum has images of the Holocaust, including footage of the massacre of Jews on Liepāja Beach. A guidebook to Rīga's Jewish sites is available which lists the places from where the once-vibrant community was erased.

Latvian Ethnographic Open-Air Museum ⑫
Latvijas etnogrāfiskais brīvdabas muzejs

Occupying 86 ha (213 acres) of woodland on the shores of Lake Jugla on the city's eastern edge, this site includes over 118 homesteads, churches, windmills and other structures from across Latvia. Founded in 1924, the site is organized according to Latvia's administrative regions – Vidzeme, Kurzeme, Zemgale and Latgale – drawing attention to variations in building design and living arrangements in different parts of the country. With craftspeople working on site during the summer, and many buildings containing everyday artifacts, the museum offers an insight into 19th-century rural life.

VISITORS' CHECKLIST

Brīvbas Gatve 440. **Map** F1.
Tel 6799 4106. 🚌 1, 19, 28.
◻ May–Sep: 10am–5pm daily;
Dec–Feb: 10am–5pm Wed–Sun.
🎫 ♿ ⛪ Sun (Usma Church).
www.brivdabasmuzejs.lv.

Dutch Windmill
Built in 1890, this windmill, from Latgale, has a movable "cap" including sails, a shaft and a gear wheel.

Vidzeme Spinning Wheel-Maker's Homestead

★ Kurzeme Peasants' Homestead
This wooden building with a reed-thatched roof is typical of 19th-century rural architecture in southwest Kurzeme.

Zemgale Peasants' Homestead includes a dwelling-house, a bathhouse and a granary.

Handicrafts
Handicraft displays include traditional wickerwork.

★ Usma Church
Most wooden churches were replaced by stone buildings in the 19th century, making this a rare example.

Entrance

Kurzeme Fishermen's Village

| 0 metres | 100 |
| 0 yards | 100 |

STAR SIGHTS

★ Kurzeme Peasants' Homestead

★ Usma Church

Old Believers' House
Located in a Latgale village, the house exhibits a loom for weaving and a samovar used to boil water for tea.

Jūrmala ❷

20 km (12 miles) W of Rīga.
🏠 *56,000.* 🚇 *from Rīga.* ℹ️ *Lienes iela 5 Majori, 6714 7900.*

Literally meaning "seaside" in Latvian, Jūrmala is an attractive stretch of beaches, small towns and pine forests alongside the Gulf of Rīga. During the 19th century, the area became famous for its medicinal mud and sulphur-rich spring water. Jūrmala soon grew into a popular resort and it became fashionable to own a summer-house here. These wooden houses still dot the area, standing alongside upmarket spas and modern guesthouses. Strict building regulations have helped preserve these 19th-century wooden summer houses and restrict further construction in the area.

Forming the heart of Jūrmala is the pedestrianized strip of Jomas iela in the town of Majori. Lining the street are several outdoor cafés, shops, restaurants and hotels, including the Historicist-style Hotel Majori, built in 1925.

To the east of Majori, in Dzintari town, is the **Exhibition of Antique Machinery**, which displays a popular collection of old cars and radio sets.

Located west of Majori, in Dubulti town, **Aspazija House** is the last home of one of Latvia's most famous poets, Elza Rozenberga (1865–1943), who wrote under the pen name "Aspazija". She was the wife of Jānis Rainis, considered

One of Jūrmala's many popular beaches

Latvia's national poet by many. Now a branch of the Jūrmala Town Museum, the house has an interesting collection of manuscripts and photographs related to the couple.

🏛 Exhibition of Antique Machinery
Turaidas iela 11, Dzintari. *Tel 2926 3329.* ⬜ *May–Sep: noon–7pm Wed–Sun.*

🏛 Aspazija House
Meierovica prosp 20, Dubulti. *Tel 6776 9445.* ⬜ *11am–5pm Tue–Sun.* 🖼

Kuldīga ❸

150 km (93 miles) W of Rīga.
🏠 *14,000.* 🚇 🚌 *Baznīcas iela 5, 6332 2259.* 🎭 *Town Festival (mid-Jul).* **www**.kuldiga.lv

With a well-preserved Old Town and an attractive location alongside the Venta river, Kuldīga is one of Latvia's most alluring provincial towns. It was founded in 1242 by the Livonian Order, who chose the site to capitalize on the river and land route linking Prussia with the lower Daugava valley.

In the 16th century, Kuldīga's castle was one of the residences of Duke Gothard Kettler and the town traded with Rīga and Jelgava. The streets near the attractive Old Town Hall Square, running alongside the Alekšupīte river, feature 17th- and 18th-century timber buildings. The Old Town also has a couple of

fine churches: St Catherine's (šv Katrīnas baznīca) and the Holy Trinity (šv Trisvienības Katoļu baznīca). A short walk from Kuldīga is the **Venta Waterfall** (Ventas rumba), the widest in Europe. Close by is a 164-m (538-ft) long brick bridge, one of Europe's longest. Overlooking the Venta river is **Kuldīga District Museum** (Kuldīgas novada muzejs), best known for its collection of playing cards.

Environs

The **Riežupe Sand Caves** (Riežupes smilšu alas), 4 km (2 miles) north of Kuldīga, form the longest cave system in Latvia. A quarter of the 2-km (1-mile) site is open to visitors.

🏛 Kuldīga District Museum
Pils iela 5. *Tel 6332 2364.* ⬜ *11am–5pm Tue–Sun.* 🖼

Venta Waterfall, stretching the width of the Venta river, Kuldīga

White-and-blue exterior of Aspazija House, Jūrmala

Liepāja ❹

Although Liepāja was officially declared a town in 1625, it expanded only in the early 19th century. The deepening of the ice-free port and the building of a railway link were followed, in 1890, by the foundation of a Russian naval port at the nearby town of Karosta. Today, Liepāja is Latvia's third largest city and boasts a vibrant cultural life. It is dotted with many interesting sights, most of which are located in its historic core. Many of the city's older buildings have been extensively restored.

🏛 Liepāja Museum

Kūrmājas prospekts 16/18. **Tel** 6342 2327. ☐ 10am–6pm Wed, Thu, Sat, Sun, 11am–7pm Fri.
www.liepajasmuzejs.lv

Set in a sculpture garden, the Liepāja Museum (Liepājas muzejs) is housed in an ornate early 20th-century building with an impressive galleried hall. The displays trace local history, with exhibits including the heads of stone cherubs from St Anne's Basilica, a series of pewter drinking vessels topped by human figures and the traditional costumes of the southern region of Kurzeme. The museum also includes a reconstruction of the workshop of the sculptor Mikelis Pankoks (1894–1983), who vanished in 1944 and was presumed dead. He had fled the country incognito, and ended his days in a Swiss mental hospital.

Wooden sculpture, Liepāja Museum

🚌 Liepāja Beach

The long, sandy Liepāja Beach (Liepājas pludmale), with its prestigious EU Blue Flag, is separated from the Old Town by the wooded Seaside Park (Jūrmalas parka). The nearby streets are lined with elegant timber buildings in the Art Nouveau style, many of which have been restored.

🏠 St Joseph's Cathedral

Rakstvežu iela 13. **Tel** 6342 9775.
Decorated inside with scenes from the Bible, St Joseph's Cathedral (šv Jāzepa katedrāle) attained its current towering form in the 19th century. The congregation needed a larger church but had no land on which to build, so they expanded the existing building upwards.

🏛 Occupation Museum

K Ukstiņa iela 7/9. **Tel** 6342 0274. ☐ 10am–6pm Wed, Thu, Sat, Sun, 11am–7pm Fri. 🅿

The Occupation Museum (Okupāciju režīmos) offers an absorbing account of the city's treatment at the hands of Nazi Germany and the Soviet Union, with notes available in English. Exhibits include photographs of people deported en masse by the Soviets in June 1941, everyday objects that were left behind and an account of the killing of the city's Jews and other "undesirables". At the end, is a display about the events leading up to independence. The offices of the Popular Front, which was based in the building, have been left intact. Rooms upstairs house a unique exhibition of antique photographic equipment.

🏠 St Anne's Basilica

Veidenbauma iela 1. **Tel** 6342 3384.
First documented in 1508, the current Neo-Gothic structure of St Anne's Basilica (šv Annas baznīca) dates from the end of the 19th century. The interior is dominated by a huge Baroque altar, carved in 1697. The altar painting depicts the Passion of Christ in three panels – with the Crucifixion at the bottom, the wrapping of his body in the centre and the Ascension at the top.

House of Craftsmen

Bāriņu 33. **Tel** 6342 3286.
☐ 9am–5pm Mon–Fri. 🅿 🖥
With a wide variety of fine handicrafts on sale, the House of Craftsmen (Amatnieku namiņš) is a place where one can watch skilled artisans at work. The world's longest amber necklace, 123 m (404 ft) long and weighing 60 kg (132 lb), is also on display along with photographs documenting its creation.

🏠 Holy Trinity Church

Baznīcas 1. **Tel** 2943 8050.
☐ 10am–4pm daily. 🎵 donations.
Organ recital (call for timings).
The modest exterior of the mid-18th-century Holy Trinity Church (Svētās Trīsvienības baznīca) belies one of the finest church interiors in the Baltic region, adorned with gilt detailing and wood-carvings. The church's organ, built in 1773, was the world's largest until 1912.

Beautifully carved Baroque altar, St Anne's Basilica, Liepāja

Rundāle Palace ➎
Rundāles pils

Designed by Francesco Bartolomeo Rastrelli, Rundāle Palace is one of the finest in the region. Work began in 1736 on a Baroque summer residence for Ernst Johann Biron, but was left unfinished when he was exiled. After Biron's return, the interiors were renovated in Rococo style. Biron's son removed most of the embellishments when he left in 1795, when Courland was annexed by Russia. Damaged in the 20th century restoration began in 1972, and is still in progress. The rooms have served as government offices, an elementary school and a granary.

Detail, Rose Room
Rococo touches such as fake marble, silver detailing and floral motifs adorn the room.

Marble Hall was used as a school gym in the 20th century.

Duke's Reception Room

★ Duke's Bedroom
This room was the focal point of Biron's private apartments, which occupied the central block of the palace.

Rose Room

The Corner Room
The Corner Room, appointed in the Russian Neo-Classical style, reflects the taste of Count Zubov, who lived in the palace after Courland was absorbed into the Russian Empire.

Grand Gallery was where the guests would dine before dancing in the White Hall. Wall paintings were uncovered during restoration.

★ Gold Hall
The initials of the palace's owner, "EJ", can be seen amidst the ornate gilt scrolls. The hall has magnificent chandeliers and ceiling decoration.

STAR FEATURES

★ Duke's Bedroom

★ Gold Hall

★ White Hall

For hotels and restaurants in this region see pp92–3

VISITORS' CHECKLIST

42 km (26 miles) SW of Rīga.
Tel 6396 2274. 🚌 *from Bauska.*
🕐 *10am–6pm daily.* 📷 🎫 *call
in advance for excursions and
events.* 🚻 www.rundale.net
The gardens 🕐 *May–Oct:
10am–7pm daily; Nov–Apr:
10am–5pm daily.*

Formal French-style gardens, re-created from the original plans

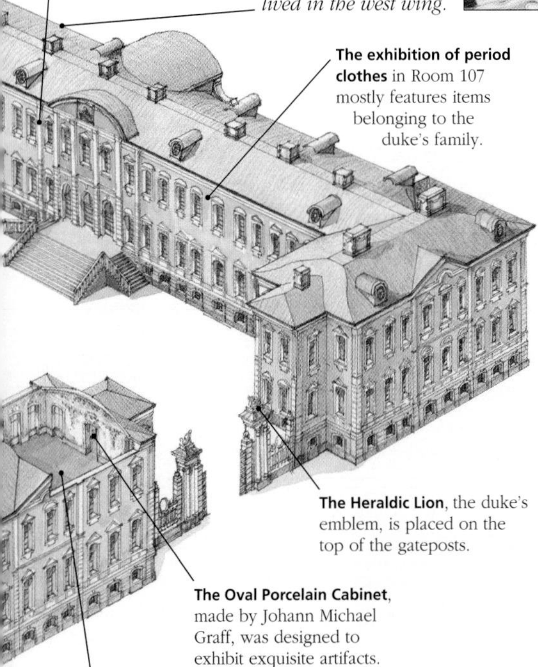

**Old photos of the
Palace in Jelgava** are
one of the many
exhibits displayed in
the palace complex.

Duchess's Boudoir
*The duchess could rest and
receive visitors during the day in
her splendidly decorated
boudoir, which has now
been restored. The duchess
and other family members
lived in the west wing.*

**The exhibition of period
clothes** in Room 107
mostly features items
belonging to the
duke's family.

ERNST JOHANN BIRON

The son of a minor
landlord, Ernst Johann
Biron was asked to leave
the academy in Königsberg
(present-day Kaliningrad in
Russia) for bad behaviour.
Failing to establish himself
in the Russian court, he
returned to Jelgava, a town
in the Zemgale region,
and became close to the
Duchess of Courland,
Anna Ivanovna. In 1730,
Anna became empress of
Russia, and three years
later Biron was appointed
Duke of Courland. After
his patron died in 1740,
Biron was sent into exile,
returning only in 1763. A
year later, Catherine II
made him duke once more
but he abdicated in 1769
in favour of his son Peter.

The Heraldic Lion, the duke's
emblem, is placed on the
top of the gateposts.

The Oval Porcelain Cabinet,
made by Johann Michael
Graff, was designed to
exhibit exquisite artifacts.

★ White Hall
*This ballroom boasts
a parquet floor and
lavish stuccowork
by German sculptor
Johann Michael
Graff. The restrained
colour scheme gives
the room its name.*

**Duke of Courland, Ernst
Johann Biron (1690–1772)**

Sigulda ❻

50 km (31 miles) NE of Rīga.
🏃 15,000. 🚆 from Rīga. 🚌 from
Rīga. 🛈 Valdemāra iela 1a, 6797
1335. www.sigulda.lv

A pretty town situated in the scenic woodland of Gauja National Park, Sigulda is a centre for outdoor activities and is often described as the Switzerland of the Vidzeme region. After the Brotherhood of the Sword subdued the Liv population in 1207, they gave the right bank of the Gauja river to the Bishop of Rīga and built their own castle on the left bank. The Brotherhood, renamed the Livonian Order, lost the town to the Poles in 1562, and it passed between the Poles and Swedes for 150

Ruins of the castle built by the Brotherhood of the Sword, Sigulda

years, until it was taken by Russia in the Great Northern War (1700–21). The castle ruins are tucked away behind the 19th-century **New Castle** (Jaunā pils), which now houses city council offices and a restaurant.

Close by is a Lutheran church and an impressive viewpoint called **Artists' Hill** (Gleznotāju kalns). Paths run through the woodland to Satzele Castle Mound, once a Liv fortress, and Peter's Cave on the bank of the Vējupīte river.

Gauja National Park ❼
Gauja nacionālā parka

Latvia's first national park was established in 1973, stretching for about 100 km (62 miles) along the Gauja River valley. Almost half of the park is forested, and it is home to about 900 plant, 149 bird and 48 mammal species. Boating and canoeing are great ways to see the caves, cliffs and ravines carved out by the river since the glaciers receded 12,000 years ago. In addition to its natural attractions, the area has some of Latvia's most fascinating historic sites, and been attracting visitors to its trails since the 19th century.

KEY

☐ Gauja National Park

Turaida Museum Reserve
The reserve comprises the extensively restored Turaida Castle, which houses historical exhibitions, and the grounds, with the outbuildings and a sculpture park.

0 km   5
0 miles   5

Sigulda offers a rare chance
to experience the thrill of
a world-class bobsleigh run
at a reasonable price.

Cēsis 🔞

90 km (56 miles) NE of Rīga.
🏘 *18,000.* 🚉 *from Rīga.* 🚌 *from Rīga.* ℹ️ *Pils laukums 9, 6412 1815.* **www**.cesis.lv.

One of Latvia's oldest towns, Cēsis has winding streets lined with attractive wooden and stone buildings. It became a member of the Hanseatic League in 1383 and grew into an important trading centre. The town served as the headquarters of the Brotherhood of the Sword, and later the Livonian Order, for much of the period between 1237 and 1561. In 1577, Ivan the Terrible took Cēsis. Further damage was inflicted during the Great Northern War and Cēsis also witnessed fierce fighting during

Row of wooden and stone houses in the Old Town, Cēsis

the War of Independence (1918–20). The Cēsis castle complex is the town's major attraction. Visitors are given builders' helmets and lanterns for the tour of the 15th- to 16th-century towers of the

13th-century Old Castle. The pink New Castle, built in 1777, is home to the **Museum of Art and History** (Cēsu vēstures un mākslas muzejs). The highlight is the well-presented "Treasures of Cēsis" exhibition. Cēsis Exhibition House (Cēsu izstāžu nams), a renovated 18th-century coach house, stands on the square in front of the New Castle.

To the north, the Castle Park is a popular place to relax in the summer. Other attractions include the 19th-century Cēsis Brewery, although the beer is now brewed outside the town.

Museum of Art and History
Pils laukums 9. 🖼 *includes access to the Old and New Castles.*

Cēsis
Once the seat of the German crusaders, Cēsis is a romantic town with a lakeside park.

VISITORS' CHECKLIST

40 km (25 miles) NE of Rīga. 🚉 *from Rīga.* 🚌 ℹ️ *Gauja National Park Visitors' Centre, Baznicas iela 7, Sigulda, 6797 4006.* 🖼 *guided canoe trips organized by Campo in Rīga (2922 2339) and Makars in Sigulda (2924 4948).* 🏕 **www**.gnp.gov.lv

Raiskums   Cīrulīši

Āraiši

Kārļi   Drabeši

ujasmala

Līgatne   Leņķi

Augšligatne

Lake Āraiši
The remains of a rudimentary fortress were found on the lake bed. A lakeside reconstruction re-creates life here in the 9th and 10th centuries.

Zvārte Rock, a 35-m (115-ft) high sandstone outcrop, boasts excellent views. It is locally believed to be a haunt of witches and demons.

Līgatne Education and Recreation Centre
This centre hosts wildlife, such as brown bears and European bison. Its footpaths and motorable tracks wind past the spacious animal enclosures.

KEY

🚉	Railway station
ℹ️	Visitor information
🚠	Cable car
🏕	Campsite
☆	Viewpoint
▬	Major road
═	Minor road
─	Other road
—	Railway
- -	Park boundary

Practical & Travel Information

Latvia offers a wealth of historic sights and cultural activities as well as stunning natural beauty. In recent years there has been a rapid increase in the number of European cities directly linked to Rīga, due mainly to the arrival of low-cost carriers which have raised the capital's profile as a destination for weekend breaks. For those who wish to avoid air travel, there are several sea routes from Scandinavia and Germany, besides comfortable trains and coaches. Travelling by car is also perfectly feasible.

WHEN TO VISIT

The best time to visit Latvia is from May to October, when the weather is pleasantly warm and the days are longer. July and August are the warmest months and can also be the wettest. Winter is cold and dark with very few daylight hours, making it difficult for outdoor excursions. March, when the snow thaws, and November and December, when it starts to fall, are also best avoided.

DOCUMENTATION

Citizens of EU member-states, the US, Canada, Australia and New Zealand, only need a valid passport for entry into Latvia for a period of up to 90 days in a half-year period. Those wishing to stay beyond 90 days will need to apply for a national long-term visa or a residence permit. Visitors from other countries should enquire at their local Latvian embassy or consulate for visa requirements before travelling. The official website of the Latvian Ministry of Foreign Affairs offers information on visa regulations. EU citizens are not subject to customs regulations, provided they adhere to EU guidelines. Visitors should check for any customs duty or special permission required to export a cultural object before buying it. For detailed information on these guidelines, entrance regulations and visa charges, it is advisable to visit the official website of the European Commission.

VISITOR INFORMATION

Practically every town and city in Latvia has a tourist office staffed by friendly English-speaking locals. These offices provide information about the major cities and towns, as well as on accommodation, entertainment venues, restaurants and historic sights. The tourist office in Rīga provides helpful city guides, free maps, brochures and regional tourism information.

Most offices are open from 9am to 6pm on weekdays and for shorter hours on Saturdays; some are also open on Sundays. In remote places, opening hours are more erratic. The Latvian Tourism Development Agency is the official tourism agency; its website lists all the tourist offices in the country. Information on tourism offices that represent this agency abroad can also be found on the website.

HEALTH AND SECURITY

Hospitals in Latvia are in a rather poor condition, so although emergency treatment is free, it is best to visit private hospitals even for general ailments. Pharmacies are usually open from 8am to 7 or 8pm on weekdays and until 3 or 4pm on Saturdays. Rīga has a few 24-hour pharmacies.

Latvia is a safe country in which to travel, with very rare instances of theft and mugging. However, it is best to remain vigilant and to avoid carrying luxury items.

FACILITIES FOR THE DISABLED

In recent years public awareness about the needs of the disabled has improved significantly in Latvia. Most upmarket hotels and restaurants in the country take such needs into consideration, although public transport in Rīga has only a limited number of buses which provide wheelchair access.

BANKING AND CURRENCY

Introduced in 1993, the monetary unit of Latvia is the lat or Ls, which is divided into 100 santīms. Although most foreign currency can be exchanged at banks, exchange bureaus and upmarket hotels, euros and dollars are preferred. Traveller's cheques are accepted only in upmarket hotels and major banks. There is a wide network of ATMs, mostly in the major towns and cities. Banks are generally open from 9am to 6pm on weekdays and 10am to 3pm on Sundays.

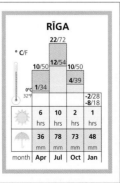

THE CLIMATE OF LATVIA

Latvia experiences a short summer, with July and August being the warmest months and subject to thunderstorms. Between May and September temperatures average between 14° C (57° F) and 22° C (72° F). Winter, between November and March, is extremely cold with temperatures rarely going above 4° C (39° F) and frequently dipping to freezing conditions.

RĪGA

	Apr	Jul	Oct	Jan
° C/F	10/50	22/72	10/50	
	1/34	12/54	4/39	
				-2/28
				-8/18
☀ hrs	6	10	2	1
☂ mm	36	78	73	48

COMMUNICATIONS

Latvia's telephone and postal networks are both reliable and efficient. Post offices provide a range of services at competitive postal rates. Payphone booths accept pre-paid phone cards, available at kiosks, post offices and supermarkets. Internet facilities are excellent in Rīga and most cafés and hotels have Wi-Fi access.

ARRIVING BY AIR

The majority of passengers arrive at **Rīga International Airport**, which is now connected to most European cities. The country's national carrier, **airBaltic**, was established in 1995 and offers some very affordable flights. Rīga is also served by other major airlines including **KLM**, **Aer Lingus**, **Lufthansa** and **Finnair**. Several low-cost carriers, such as **easyJet** from Berlin and **RyanAir** from Ireland and the UK, have also started services to the country.

There are few direct flights to Latvia from the US, New Zealand, Canada or Australia. Visitors from outside Europe usually need to change flights in London, Stockholm, Helsinki or Copenhagen.

ARRIVING BY SEA

Travelling by ferry takes longer than air travel, although crossing the Baltic Sea has its own appeal. Ferries operated by **Lisco** link the German port of Lübeck to Rīga, while **Tallink** connects Rīga to Stockholm (Sweden). Rīga's main **Ferry Terminal** can be reached by trams 5, 7 or 9 from the main bus terminal or outside the National Opera. **Terrabalt** connects Liepāja to Karlshamn (Sweden) and Rostock (Germany). Ventspils is served by **Scandlines** to Nynashamn (Sweden), Rostock and Karlshamn, and by **SSC Ferries** to Saaremaa Island (Estonia). The **Latvian Coast** website offers information.

RAIL TRAVEL

The main railway station in Rīga is **Central Railway Station**, located southeast of the Old Town. From here international rail routes head east towards Moscow, Vitebsk, Odessa and St Petersburg. The most comfortable way to travel on most routes is by *kupeja* (four-bunk compartment). However, there are more luxurious two-bunk compartments on the trains serving Moscow.

TRAVELLING BY COACH

One of the best ways to travel between the three Baltic capitals is by coach. This costs less than travelling by air, although the difference is negligible, except during the peak season. International carriers such as **Ecolines** and **Nordeka** run services between Rīga and several other European cities. Rīga's main bus terminal, **Autoosta**, is five minutes south of the Old Town.

TRAVELLING BY CAR

Since 2007, under the Schengen Agreement, there are no longer border controls between the Baltic States. Nevertheless, busy border crossings can take up to 20 minutes to negotiate. It is essential to carry the vehicle's registration document, a valid third-party insurance policy and either a European driving licence or an International Driving Permit. Vehicles must be in roadworthy condition and it is compulsory to have a first-aid kit, fire extinguisher and hazard-warning triangle. From December to March, winter tyres must be used, and drivers should fit spiked tyres between September and April.

DIRECTORY

DOCUMENTATION
www.am.gov.lv
www.ec.europa.eu

VISITOR INFORMATION
www.latviatourism.lv

EMBASSIES AND CONSULATES

Australia
Lienes iela 28, Rīga.
Tel 6722 4251.

Canada
Baznīcas iela 20/22, Rīga.
Tel 6781 3945.

France
Raina bulvāris 9, Rīga.
Tel 6703 6600.

United Kingdom
J Alunana iela 5, Rīga.
Tel 6777 4700.

United States
Raiņa bulvāris 7, Rīga.
Tel 6703 6200.

EMERGENCY NUMBERS

Ambulance
Tel 03.

Fire.
Tel 01.

Police
Tel 02.

ARRIVING BY AIR

Aer Lingus
www.aerlingus.com

airBaltic
www.airbaltic.com.

easyJet
www.easyjet.com

Finnair
www.finnair.com

KLM
www.klm.com

Lufthansa
www.lufthansa.com

RyanAir
www.ryanair.com

Rīga International Airport
www.riga-airport.com

ARRIVING BY SEA

Ferry Terminal
www.freeportofriga.lv

Latvian Coast
www.latviancoast.lv

Lisco
www.lisco.lt

Scandlines
www.scandlines.lt

SSC Ferries
www.slkferries.ee

Terrabalt
www.terrabalt.lv

Tallink
www.tallink.com

RAIL TRAVEL

Central Railway Station
www.ldz.lv

TRAVELLING BY COACH

Autoosta
www.autoosta.lv

Ecolines
www.ecolines.ee

Nordeka
www.nordeka.lv

Shopping & Entertainment

Numerous shopping centres have opened throughout Latvia since 1991, although Rīga undoubtedly has the largest range of shopping options. This is particularly true when it comes to items likely to be of interest to visitors, although outside the capital it is usually possible to find typical handicrafts such as amber jewellery and embroidered knitwear. Latvia's major cultural events are also concentrated in Rīga, although the dynamic festival calendar provides plenty of reasons to explore other parts of the country. The city is also renowned for its energetic nightlife; clubs range from small and hip to huge and mainstream, and stay open throughout the night.

OPENING HOURS

Most shops in Latvia open around 10am. Small shops close around 6 or 7pm, while bigger malls and shopping centres usually stay open until 10pm. Many small shops remain closed on Sundays.

MARKETS

Most Latvian towns have regular or even daily markets, although they are rarely aimed at visitors and are most useful for everyday food shopping. Housed in five huge zeppelin hangars, Rīga's **Central Market** has most of its indoor space dedicated to food, while the stalls and kiosks outside sell CDs, clothes and electrical goods. Also of interest is the covered outdoor antiques and organic food market on the second and fourth Sunday of each month at Berga Bazārs.

Beyond the capital, markets such as the covered market hall in Liepāja, a throwback to the Soviet era, are very atmospheric. In the summer months, markets in Jūrmala sell souvenirs as well as fresh produce.

HANDICRAFTS

Traditional Latvian handicrafts include handmade linen, amber jewellery, woodwork and knitwear embroidered with popular Latvian folk symbols. Motifs from nature, such as the sun, stars or trees, are commonly used among the repertoire of geometric designs found on many handcrafted goods. There are numerous souvenir shops in Rīga's Old Town stocking items such as linen and wooden toys. More authentic and unusual gifts can be found in **Grieži**, which also holds craft demonstrations. **Tine** boasts a wide range of souvenirs, while **Sāmsalas Kalēji** specializes in metalwork. Some shops also sell Russian goods such as *matryoshka* – wooden dolls of various sizes which are placed one inside the other. Outside Rīga, a good place to find handicrafts is the branch of **Tornis** in the tower of Turaida Castle in Gauja National Park *(see pp86–7)*.

ART AND ANTIQUES

Antique shops in Latvia are well worth exploring. A licence, which is available at most shops, is usually required before genuine antiques can be exported. Rīga has a fine selection, including the upmarket **Doma Antikvariāts**, the busy **Retro A** and **Volmar**.

The best places to buy art are commercial art galleries. There are many galleries in Rīga and the tourist information office can provide an up-to-date list. **Māksla XO** is one of the most highly regarded, while **Art Nouveau Rīga**, a leading souvenir shop, offers attractive reproductions.

AMBER

Amber jewellery is a popular Latvian souvenir, readily available in tourist areas and in some museum shops. Rīga has dozens of specialist shops such as **A&E**, **Dzintara Muzejs** and **Dzintara Galerija**. There are also several general souvenir shops selling more affordable items. However, buyers should be aware that not all amber on sale is genuine. Visitors spending a large sum of money on amber objects should ask for a certificate of authenticity.

FOOD AND DRINK

Laima chocolate is among the country's most popular buys, and the brand has a dedicated store in Rīga. Its upmarket rival, **Emihls Gustavs Chocolate**, has stores all over the city.

Another common gift is Rīga Black Balsam, a herbal liqueur taken neat or in cocktails. **Latvijas Balzams** is among the best places to buy it. Beer also makes a good gift. There are many varieties of traditional honey available in the **Latvijas Bite** shops, owned by the Latvian Association of Beekeepers.

NIGHTLIFE

With a wide range of bars and clubs, Rīga has a swinging nightlife. **Skyline Bar** in the Reval Hotel Latvija is a favourite, while **Rīgas Balzāms** is a popular place to try the eponymous drink in various cocktails. **I Love You** attracts a youthful local crowd, while **Sapņu Fabrika** offers rock to world music. The best-known nightclub, **Pulkvedim Nevienis Neraksta**, draws a young and stylish clientele. Larger venues, such as **Club Essential** and the submarine-themed **Nautilus**, feature DJs on the weekend. Casinos with gaming tables include the **Tobago Casino Club** and **Casino Aladins**.

Outside the capital city, **Latvia's 1st Rock Café** and **Fontaine Palace**, both in Liepāja, are worth visiting.

MUSIC, THEATRE AND DANCE

Rīga has a thriving live-music scene. Major international artists perform at the **Arēna Rīga**. Local bands play at a host of smaller venues – **Kaļķu Vārti**, noted for booking some of the country's top artists; **Depo**, which features alternative music; **Sapņu Fabrika**, which offers a range of genres; and **Četri Balti Krekli**, with Latvian music. The best blues venues in Rīga are the **Bites Blūza Klubs**, **Hamlets** and **Carpe Diem** restaurant. The summer sees performances on Liepāja's open-air stage **Pūt Vējiņi**.

Some of the best classical music concerts take place at annual events such as the International Early Music Festival in Rundāle Palace *(see pp84–5)*. **Saulkrasti Jazz Festival** and the **International Music Festival** in Rīga are also important events. **Ave Sol** also hosts small classical concerts.

The **Latvian National Opera** is the venue for world-class performances of opera and ballet. The **Latvian National Theatre**, the **Dailes Theatre**, the **New Rīga Theatre** and the **Russian Drama Theatre** are some of the best places to see theatre in Latvian or Russian. The **Liepāja Theatre** in Liepāja

produces expansive theatrical works. Rīga's most important theatre festival, **Homo Novus**, concentrates on experimental theatre and dance.

The **Latvian Music Information Centre** provides details of performances across the country. Bookings can be made at the venue or through ticket agencies such as **Biļešu Paradīze**. Tickets can also be booked online on the **Latvian Culture Vortal**, which has a nationwide calendar.

DIRECTORY

MARKETS

Central Market
Negu Street 7, Rīga.
Tel 6722 9985.

HANDICRAFTS

Grieži
Mazā miesnieku iela1.
Rīga. *Tel* 6750 7236.

Sāmsalas Kalēji
Laipu iela 6, Rīga.
Tel 6722 4496.

Tine
Vaļņu iela2, Rīga.
Tel 6721 6728.

ART AND ANTIQUES

Art Nouveau Rīga
Strēlnieku 9, Laipu 8, Rīga.
Tel 2836 7112.

Doma Antikvariāts
Doma laukums 1a, Rīga.
Tel 6781 4401.
www.antikvariats.lv

Māksla XO
Skārņu 8, Rīga.
Tel 2948 2098.

Retro A
Tallinas 54, Rīga.
Tel 6731 5306.

Volmar
Šķūņu 6, Rīga.
Tel 6721 4278.

AMBER

A&E
Jauniela 17, Rīga.
Tel 6722 3200.

Dzintara Galerija
Torņa iela 4, Rīga.
Tel 6732 5157.

Dzintara Muzejs
Kalēju iela 9/11, Rīga.
Tel 6708 7545.

FOOD AND DRINK

Emihls Gustavs Chocolate
Aspazijas bulvāris 24, Rīga.
www.sokolade.lv

Laima
Ģertrūdes iela 6, Rīga.
www.laima.lv

Latvijas Balzams
Audēju iela 8, Rīga.
Tel 6722 8814.

Latvijas Bite
Ģertrūdes iela 13, Rīga.
Tel 6727 9495.

NIGHTLIFE

Casino Aladins
Dzirnavu iela 57, Rīga.
Tel 2929 6060.

Club Essential
Skolas iela 2, Rīga.
Tel 6724 2289.
www.essential.lv

Fontaine Palace
Dzirnavu iela 4, Liepāja.
Tel 6348 8510.
www.fontainepalace.lv

I Love You
Aldaru iela 9, Rīga.
Tel 6722 5304.
www.iloveyou.lv

Latvia's 1st Rock Café
Stendera 18/20, Liepāja.
Tel 6348 1555.
www.pablo.lv

Nautilus
Kungu iela 8, Rīga.
Tel 6781 4455.
www.nautilus.lv

Pulkvedim Neviens Neraksta
Peldu iela 26–28, Rīga.
Tel 6721 3886.
www.pulkvedis.lv

Rīgas Balzāms
Torņa iela 4, Rīga.
Tel 6721 4494.

Sapņu Fabrika
Lāčplēša 101, Rīga.
Tel 6722 9045.
www.sapnufabrika.lv

Skyline Bar
Reval Hotel Latvija,
Elizabetes iela 55, Rīga.
Tel 6777 2222.

Tobago Casino Club
Aspāzijas bulvāris 22, Rīga.
Tel 6722 5411.

MUSIC, THEATRE AND DANCE

Arēna Rīga
Skanstes iela 21, Rīga.
www.arenariga.com

Ave Sol
Valdemāra Iela 5, Rīga.
Tel 6704 3631

Biļešu Paradīze
www.bilesuparadize.lv

Bites Blūza Klubs
Dzirnavu iela 34a, Rīga.
www.bluesclub.lv

Carpe Diem
Meistaru iela 10–12, Rīga.
www.carpediem.lv

Četri Balti Krekli
Vecpilsētas iela 12, Rīga.

Dailes Theatre
Brīvības iela 75, Rīga.
www.dailesteatris.lv

Depo
Vaļņu iela 32, Rīga.
www.klubsdepo.lv

Hamlets
Jāņa sēta 5, Rīga.
Tel 6722 9938

Homo Novus
www.theatre.lv

International Music Festival
www.rigasritmi.lv

Kaļķu Vārti
Kaļķu iela 11a, Rīga.
www.kalkuvarti.lv

Latvian Culture Vortal
www.kultura.lv/en/

Latvian Music Information Centre
www.lmic.lv

Latvian National Opera
Aspāzijas bulvāris 3, Rīga.
www.opera.lv

Latvian National Theatre
Kronvalda bulvāris 2, Rīga.
www.teatris.lv

Liepāja Theatre
Teatra iela 4, Liepāja.
Tel 6340 7811.
www.liepajasteatris.lv

New Rīga Theatre
Lāčplēša iela 25, Rīga.
www.jrt.lv

Pūt Vējiņi
Peldu iela 57, Liepāja.
Tel 6342 4479.

Russian Drama Theatre
Kaļķu iela 16, Rīga.
www.trd.lv

Saulkrasti Jazz Festival
www.saulkrastijazz.lv

Where to Stay in Latvia

Latvia has a wide range of accommodation options from luxury hotels to inexpensive hostels. The elaborate network of establishments extends to smaller towns and the countryside, where it is very easy to find a place to stay for the night. Booking is convenient as even the smallest guesthouses have their own websites.

PRICE CATEGORIES
Price categories are for a standard double room per night in high season, including tax and service charges. Breakfast is not included, unless specified.

Ⓛ Under 30 Ls
ⓁⓁ 30–60 Ls
ⓁⓁⓁ 60–90 Ls
ⓁⓁⓁⓁ 90–150 Ls
ⓁⓁⓁⓁⓁ Over 150 Ls

RĪGA

Radi un Draugi   🅸🅸   ⓁⓁ

Mārstaļu iela 1/3, LV-1050 **Tel** *6782 0200* **Fax** *6782 0202* **Rooms** *76*   **Map** *C4*

An excellent budget choice in the centre of the Old Town, this popular hotel should be booked well in advance. Owned by British-Latvians, this is a no-frills place with basic but comfortable and clean rooms. The name means "friends and family", something which the helpful staff take to heart. Breakfast is included. **www.draugi.lv**

Grand Palace   🅸🅸🅸🅸   ⓁⓁⓁⓁ

Pils 12, LV-1050 **Tel** *6704 4000* **Fax** *6704 4004* **Rooms** *56*   **Map** *B3*

A classy option popular with celebrities, this hotel has two acclaimed restaurants, a sauna, gym and a cosy lobby bar with antler chandeliers. Bedrooms are elegantly decorated in blue, white and gold and equipped with Wi-Fi, minibar, safe and pay TV. Bathrooms have tubs and heated floors. **www.schlossle-hotels.com**

Metropole   🅸🅸   ⓁⓁⓁⓁ

Aspazijas bulvāris 36/38, LV-1050 **Tel** *6722 5411* **Fax** *6721 6140* **Rooms** *86*   **Map** *D3*

Open since 1871, this is the elder statesman of Rīga's hotel scene. It is conveniently located on the edge of the Old Town, although street-facing rooms can be noisy. The Scandinavian-style rooms come equipped with wireless Internet and minibar. Facilities include a gym, sauna and business centre. Breakfast is included. **www.metropole.lv**

FURTHER AFIELD Homestay   🅿🅿   Ⓛ

Stokholmas iela 1, LV-1014 **Tel** *6755 3016* **Rooms** *4*

Located in the upmarket Mežaparks district, a 20-minute tram ride from the Old Town, Homestay is well worth the journey. The owners, a Latvian and a New Zealander, are very attentive towards their guests. The rooms are cosy and the breakfast is excellent. **www.homestay.lv**

REST OF LATVIA

GAUJA NATIONAL PARK Spa Hotel Ezeri   🅿🅸🅸🅸🅸   ⓁⓁ

Sigulda pagasts, Sigulda, LV-2150 **Tel** *6797 3009* **Fax** *6797 3880* **Rooms** *30*

This modern hotel, influenced by Scandinavian design, features a lot of wood. The spa centre includes indoor and outdoor pools, saunas and aromatherapy baths and offers a range of massages. The restaurant, with a pleasant terrace for summer dining, serves modern European cuisine. Breakfast is included. **www.hotelezeri.lv**

JŪRMALA Jūrmala Spa   🅿🅸🅸🅸🅸🅸🅸   ⓁⓁⓁⓁ

Jomas iela 47/49, LV-2015 **Tel** *6778 4415* **Fax** *6778 4411* **Rooms** *190*

This renovated Soviet-era block is a welcome addition to the hotel scene in Jūrmala. The style is retro-chic, with extensive use of natural materials, including stone in the bathrooms. The spa facilities are excellent and medical consultations are available. Breakfast is included. **www.hoteljurmala.com**

LIEPĀJA Libava   🅿🅸🅸   ⓁⓁ

Vecā ostmala 29, LV-3401 **Tel** *6342 5318* **Fax** *6342 5319* **Rooms** *7*

From the spacious lobby to the immaculate bedrooms, this canal-side hotel provides an affordable slice of luxury. Guests can take advantage of a discount at the basement spa with Jacuzzi, relax on leather sofas in the conservatory, or try the restaurant's adventurous menu. There is a working pier alongside the hotel. **www.libava.lv**

RUNDĀLE Baltā Māja   🅿🅿🅸   Ⓛ

Pilsrundāle, LV-3921 **Tel** *6396 2140* **Rooms** *8*

Located in the restored servants' quarters of Rundāle Palace *(see pp84–5)*, this hotel retains plenty of original features such as paved floors and tiled stoves. Most rooms have shared bathrooms, although one is en suite. High-quality home-cooked Latvian dishes are served in the cosy restaurant. **www.kalpumaja.lv**

Map References *see map of Rīga pp74–5*

Where to Eat in Latvia

There has been a considerable rise in the diversity and standards of restaurants in Latvia, although Rīga offers the best variety of eating places. Good food is an integral part of the culture and the abundance of traditional-style restaurants in the country attests to the pride that Latvians take in their national cuisine.

PRICE CATEGORIES
Based on the price per person of a three-course meal with half a bottle of wine, including cover charge, service and tax.
Ⓛ Under 10 Ls
ⓁⓁ 10–20 Ls
ⓁⓁⓁ 20–30 Ls
ⓁⓁⓁⓁ 30–40 Ls
ⓁⓁⓁⓁⓁ Over 40 Ls

RĪGA

Ķiploku Krogs ⓁⓁⓁ

Jēkaba 3/5, LV-1050 **Tel** *6721 1451* **Map** *C3*

True to its name, Ķiploku Krogs, which means "garlic bar", features garlic in almost every dish, including the ice cream – the menu even labels those dishes that do not contain any. The results are less gimmicky than might be expected, with some very exciting choices.

Palete ⓁⓁⓁⓁ

Gleznotāju iela 12/14, LV-1050 **Tel** *6721 6037* **Map** *D3*

A favourite with both visitors and local people, this cosy restaurant in the Vecriga hotel serves an eclectic international menu ranging from Cajun to Italian. There is something to suit most tastes, but seafood is a speciality. An open fireplace in winter adds to its old-world charm.

Vincent's ⓁⓁⓁⓁⓁ

Elizabetes iela 19, LV-1000 **Tel** *6733 2830* **Map** *E2*

With celebrity chef Mārtiņš Rītiņš at the helm, Vincent's has been a staple on Rīga's restaurant scene since it opened in 1994 and it continues to attract foreign dignitaries and celebrities who pass through the city. Adventurous international dishes are offered alongside classy versions of traditional Latvian fare.

FURTHER AFIELD LIDO Atpūtas Centrs ⓁⓁ

Krasta iela 76, LV-1019 **Tel** *6750 4420*

Part of the LIDO chain of recreation centres, this massive log cabin with an amusement park, ice-skating rink and live folk music is a tourist attraction in its own right. The buffet boasts over 500 dishes, including traditional Latvian fare. There is also a sit-down restaurant and a large beer hall.

REST OF LATVIA

GAUJA NATIONAL PARK Aparjods ⓁⓁⓁ

Ventas iela 1a, Sigulda, LV-2150 **Tel** *6797 4414*

Themed on a farmhouse, Aparjods has a warm interior decorated with sepia photographs and cane and wood furnishings. Besides traditional Latvian cuisine, it also serves more unusual European dishes, such as snails. It is popular despite its location outside the town centre.

JŪRMALA Villa Joma ⓁⓁⓁⓁ

Jomas iela 90, LV-2015 **Tel** *6777 1999*

This pastel-coloured restaurant is bright and airy, and considered to be among the best eateries in Jūrmala. The menu is helpfully displayed outside and includes international favourites such as tuna carpaccio and breast of Barbary duck. Cocktails are served at the bar.

KULDĪGA Stenders ⓁⓁ

Liepājas iela 3, LV-3301 **Tel** *6332 2703*

Housed on the first floor of a former granary, Stenders offers an array of standard Latvian dishes and is very popular locally for its signature pancakes. The cosy open-air terrace offers beautiful views of the city, particularly appealing on a summer's day. Local DJs entertain on Friday and Saturday nights.

LIEPĀJA Ilze Ⓛ

Graudu iela 23, LV-3401 **Tel** *6342 3814*

This brick-lined cellar restaurant with arched vaulting and romantic lighting is very popular with locals. It serves standard Latvian cuisine along with more exotic fare such as chicken wasabi or calamari, at reasonable prices. There is live music every evening.

Key to Symbols *see back cover flap*

ESTONIA

*P*resenting a heady mix of medieval heritage and technological advancement, Estonia has rebuilt itself in the post-Soviet era, adapting to the demands of the modern world while preserving a distinct cultural identity. With its rich historic architecture, natural landscapes and dynamic culture, the country makes a significant impression on the ever-growing number of visitors that it attracts.

Estonia's tumultuous history has resulted from its geographical position as a crossroads between Eastern and Western Europe. With Russia dominating its eastern border, Scandinavia surrounding it to the north and west and the other two Baltic States to its south, Estonia was considered a prize strategic asset among the regional powers through the centuries.

After regaining independence from the Soviet Union in 1991, Estonia was left severely dilapidated. But persistent reforms by successive governments have helped to stabilize the economy. Although the rural areas still lag behind the cities in raising living standards, Estonia has grown into a major travel destination. Its pristine islands and traditional villages are as alluring as its capital Tallinn, a pulsating city with a medieval Old Town.

HISTORY

Historical references to Estonia date from the early 13th century, when the Teutonic knights arrived, introducing a new social order in which the Germans dominated for several centuries. A bitter struggle ensued that saw the destruction of Estonia's pagan culture and its replacement by a harsh feudal system. The Danes were also involved, taking control of northern Estonia before being pushed out by the Teutonic knights.

A group of Estonian folk dancers performing in traditional costume during a local festival

◁ Glorious view of Tallinn with St Olav's spire towering above the city

The 16th century saw Estonia as the major battleground between Russia and Sweden in the Livonian Wars (1558–82). By 1629, the country was in Swedish hands. The Swedes achieved much over the next 50 years, including the introduction of schools and the establishment of Tartu University. Later, however, the Swedish kings seized German-owned estates, incurring the wrath of the Germans, who turned to Russia's Peter the Great for help. In 1709, Peter defeated the Swedish King Charles XII, which consigned the country to tsarist rule for the next 200 years.

Depiction of the Siege of Narva, Livonian Wars

During World War I (1914–18), the prospect of Estonian independence seemed bleak. However, the 1917 Revolution that ended the tsarist regime in Russia encouraged Estonia to declare independence in February 1918, in Pärnu. Political stability proved difficult to establish, however; there were 20 coalition governments between 1919 and 1933. In 1934, a prominent nationalist politician, Konstantin Päts, staged a coup.

He continued to rule until the Soviet invasion on 16 June 1940, which brought a brutal end to independent Estonia. The German invasion, which came a year later, was seen by many in Estonia as a liberation. In September 1944, the Red Army returned to Estonia, forcing the Nazis to surrender, and subjecting the country to almost five decades of Soviet rule.

From the 1960s, Estonia's link with the non-Soviet world began to grow. At the time of the collapse of the USSR in 1991, Estonians were better prepared for a capitalist economy than any of the other Soviet republics. Thirteen years after independence, entry into the EU in 2004 and NATO has further strengthened the economy.

KEY DATES IN ESTONIAN HISTORY

1208 Germans capture Otepää in southern Estonia

1219 Danes seize Tallinn

1227 Germans conquer all of Estonia

1558–83 Northern Estonia comes under Swedish rule, southern Estonia under Polish rule

1629 Estonia passes into Swedish hands

1709 Great Northern War between Charles XII of Sweden and Peter the Great results in Russian victory

1885 Russification of the Baltics begins

1918 Declaration of Estonian independence signed; Germany loses World War I

1920 Treaty of Tartu confirms Estonia's independence

1939 Molotov-Ribbentrop Pact puts Estonia under the influence of the USSR

1940 Soviet occupation begins

1944 Return of Soviet forces; Stalinist era begins

1953 Stalin dies

1991 Estonia declares independence

2004 Estonia joins NATO and the EU

2007 World's first national Internet election held

LANGUAGE AND CULTURE

In general, Estonians are more strongly influenced by Scandinavian culture than by that of their Baltic neighbours. Finns and Estonians also share close linguistic links through the Finno-Ugric language family. The most important aspects of Estonian culture are distinctly pagan in origin, such as the Midsummer festival Jaanipaev (John's Day), characterized by drinking, dancing and revelry. Folk culture is central to national identity, and the All Estonian Song Festival, held every five years since 1869, remains an iconic occasion for the nation.

Exploring Estonia

Estonia offers an irresistible blend of cultural heritage and natural beauty. Walking is an ideal way to explore the country's historic towns. Highlights include the capital Tallinn, with its lovely Old Town dotted with church spires and fascinating museums, picturesque Pärnu, with its elegant 19th-century villas and long sandy beach, and the charming university town of Tartu. The best way of getting around the country is by road, as most sights are within a few hours' drive of each other. A well-developed bus system links all the major towns and cities. Estonia's largest island, Saaremaa, is well connected to the mainland by ferry.

View towards the Baltic Sea from St Olav's Church, Tallinn

SIGHTS AT A GLANCE

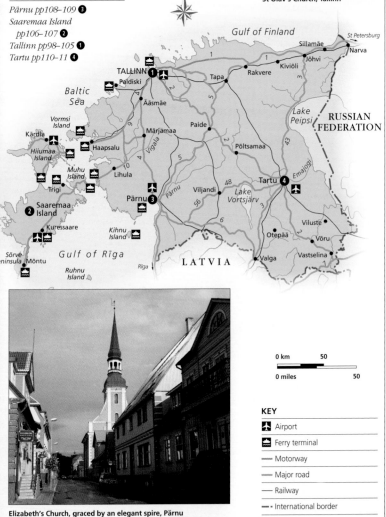

Gulf of Finland

St Petersburg

Sillamäe

Narva

Jõhvi

Kiviõli

TALLINN

Paldiski

Rakvere

Tapa

Baltic Sea

Ääsmäe

Lake Peipsi

RUSSIAN FEDERATION

Vormsi Island

Märjamaa

Paide

Kärdla

Hiiumaa Island

Haapsalu

Põltsamaa

Vigala

Muhu Island

Lihula

Tartu

Emajõgi

Trigi

Viljandi

Lake Võrtsjärv

Saaremaa Island

Pärnu

Kuressaare

Kihnu Island

Viluste

Sõrve Peninsula

Möntu

Gulf of Rīga

Ruhnu Island

Riga

LATVIA

Otepää

Võru

Valga

Vastselina

Elizabeth's Church, graced by an elegant spire, Pärnu

0 km 50

0 miles 50

KEY

✈ Airport

⛴ Ferry terminal

— Motorway

— Major road

— Railway

–·– International border

Tallinn ❶

Founded by the Danes at the beginning of the 13th century, Tallinn was for ages known by its Teutonic name, Reval. The city flourished in the 14th and 15th centuries, when it was one of the leading members of the powerful Hanseatic League. The brilliantly restored Old Town, a UNESCO World Heritage Site since 1991, is a living monument to this golden period of Tallinn's history. The vast majority of sights in the city are concentrated in and around Town Hall Square (Raekoja plats) and Toompea, in the medieval Old Town. Its winding cobbled streets are dotted with elegant back alleys, courtyards and spired churches, as well as fascinating museums that present the city's historic and cultural traditions. An architectural wonder, Tallinn has grown into a dynamic, chic and exciting city over the years, with a population of about four hundred thousand people.

| 0 metres | 200 |
| 0 yards | 200 |

SIGHTS AT A GLANCE

Alexander Nevsky Cathedral ⑪
Dominican Monastery ④
Great Guild Hall ③
Estonian Museum of Applied
  Art and Design ⑦
Fat Margaret Tower ⑨
Holy Spirit Church ②
House of Blackheads ⑥
Kadriorg Palace ⑫
Niguliste Church ⑤
St Olav's Church ⑧
Toompea Castle ⑩
Town Hall ①

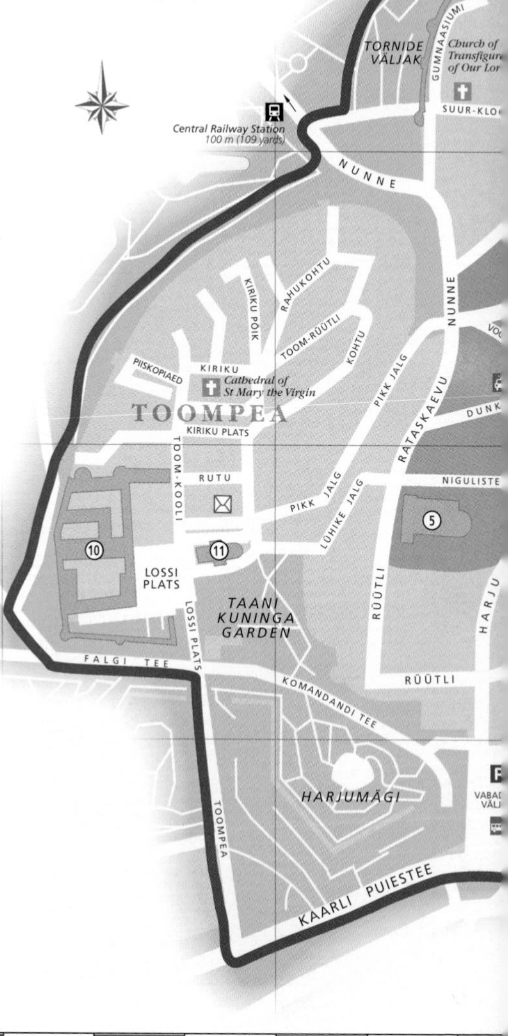

KEY

▨	Street-by-Street area: *see pp100–101*
▨	Major sight / Place of interest
✈	Airport
🚉	Railway station
⛴	Ferry terminal
🚓	Police station
ℹ	Visitor information
🅿	Parking
⊠	Post office
✝	Church
▬	Motorway
▬	Major road
—	Railway

TORNIDE VÄLJAK

Church of Transfiguration of Our Lord

SUUR-KLO

Central Railway Station
100 m (109 yards)

NUNNE

NUNNE

RAMUKOHTU

KIRIKU PÕIK

TOOM-RÜÜTLI

KOHTU

PIKK JALG

RATASKAEVU

DUNK

PIISKOPIAED

KIRIKU

Cathedral of
St Mary the Virgin

TOOMPEA

KIRIKU PLATS

TOOM-KOOLI

RUTU

PIKK JALG

LÜHIKE JALG

NIGULISTE

⑩

LOSSI PLATS

⑪

⑤

TAANI KUNINGA GARDEN

LOSSI PLATS

RÜÜTLI

HARJU

FALGI TEE

KOMANDANDI TEE

RÜÜTLI

HARJUMÄGI

TOOMPEA

KAARLI PUIESTEE

VABAD VÄLI

| A | B | C |

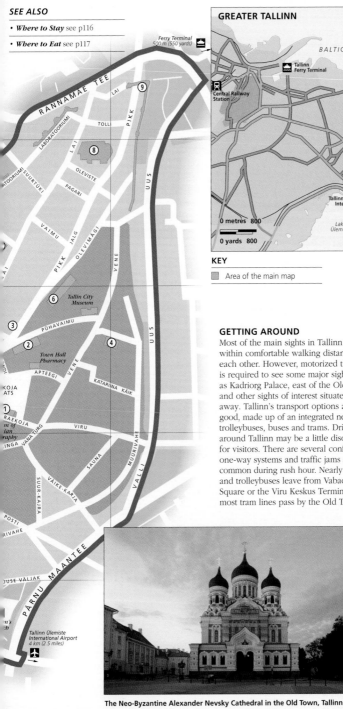

SEE ALSO

- **Where to Stay** see p116
- **Where to Eat** see p117

Ferry Terminal
500 m (550 yards)

RANNAMÄE TEE

LAI

PIKK

TOLL

9

LABORATOORIUMI

LAI

8

TOORIUMI SUURTÜKI

OLEVISTE

PAGARI

UUS

VAIMU

JALG

OLEVIMÄGI

PIKK

VENE

6 Tallin City
Museum

3

PÜHAVAIMU

UUS

2

4

Town Hall
Pharmacy

VENE

APTEEGI

KATARIINA KÄIK

KOJA
ATS

1

RAEKOJA

m of
ian
graphy

VIRU

INGA VANATURG

SAUNA

MÜÜRIVAHE

VÄIKE-KARJA

VALLI

SUUR-KAIRA

POSTI

RIVAHE

USE VÄLJAK

PÄRNU MAANTEE

n's
:b

Tallinn Ülemiste
International Airport
4 km (2.5 miles)

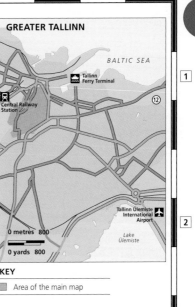

GREATER TALLINN

BALTIC SEA

1

Tallinn
Ferry Terminal

Central Railway
Station

12

2

Tallinn Ülemiste
International
Airport

Lake
Ülemiste

0 metres   800

0 yards   800

KEY

Area of the main map

GETTING AROUND

Most of the main sights in Tallinn are within comfortable walking distance of each other. However, motorized transport is required to see some major sights, such as Kadriorg Palace, east of the Old Town, and other sights of interest situated further away. Tallinn's transport options are very good, made up of an integrated network of trolleybuses, buses and trams. Driving around Tallinn may be a little disorienting for visitors. There are several confusing one-way systems and traffic jams are common during rush hour. Nearly all buses and trolleybuses leave from Vabaduse Square or the Viru Keskus Terminal, while most tram lines pass by the Old Town.

The Neo-Byzantine Alexander Nevsky Cathedral in the Old Town, Tallinn

D   E   F

Street-by-Street: Around Town Hall Square

Medieval carving, outside a gallery

In the heart of Tallinn's Old Town, the magnificent Town Hall Square has for centuries served as a marketplace. Gently sloping, the cobblestoned square is surrounded by a ring of elegantly designed medieval buildings. The early 14th-century Town Hall is northern Europe's only surviving late-Gothic town hall. A meeting point for locals and visitors, the square captures the essence of the Old Town. In summer, it is filled with open-air cafés and restaurant tables.

Busy market in Town Hall Square, seen from the Town Hall tower

House of Blackheads was the meeting place for the Brotherhood of Blackheads ⑥

Tallinn City Museum
Housed in a medieval merchants' house, this museum presents Tallinn's history through a variety of fascinating exhibits and artifacts.

PIKK

PÜHAVAIMU

KINGA RAE

VOORIME

★ **Town Hall Pharmacy**
Worth a visit just for its impressive interior, this long-running pharmacy also has a charming little museum displaying old curiosities.

KEY

 Suggested route

STAR SIGHTS

★ Town Hall Pharmacy

★ Town Hall

Holy Spirit Church
Regarded as one of Tallinn's most attractive churches, this splendidly preserved structure is a treasure trove of medieval and Renaissance features ②

Dominican Monastery
Among Tallinn's oldest buildings, the monastery complex also includes an atmospheric museum which has some beautiful stone carvings ④

Viru Street
One of the most famous in the Old Town, this busy street is packed with a variety of restaurants, bars, cafés and shops.

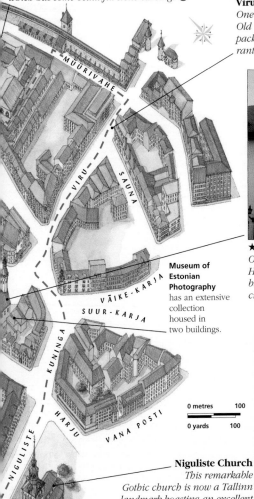

MÜÜRIVAHE

VIRU

SAUNA

Museum of Estonian Photography has an extensive collection housed in two buildings.

VÄIKE-KARJA

SUUR-KARJA

KUNINGA

HARJU

VANA POSTI

NIGULISTE

JÜTLI

0 metres	100
0 yards	100

★ Town Hall
Occupying pride of place in Town Hall Square, this imposing Gothic building has been the focus of civic life since the Middle Ages ①

Niguliste Church
This remarkable Gothic church is now a Tallinn landmark boasting an excellent museum of religious art. The church holds organ recitals every weekend ⑤

Outdoor tables of the cafés around Town Hall Square

Town Hall ①
Tallinna raekoda

Raekoja plats 1. **Map** D3. **Tel** 645 7900. 🚌 5, 40. 🚋 1, 2, 3, 4. 🕐 Jul–Aug: 10am–4pm Mon–Sat (by appointment). 🏛 🎥 💻 www.tallinn.ee/raekoda

One of the most revered symbols of Tallinn, the Town Hall dates back to 1404. Its high-pitched roof is supported by two tall gables and a late-Renaissance spire crowns the slender octagonal tower. The windows and crenellated parapet complete the building's impressive appearance. Inside the building, it is possible to see the Citizens' Hall and the Council Hall, although most visitors head straight for the tower and the 115-step ascent to the top. Facing the Town Hall is the Town Hall Square (see pp100–101), with a vaulted arcade running along its north façade. Small cafés put out tables here in summer.

Holy Spirit Church ②
Pühavaimu kirik

Pühavaimu 2. **Map** D3. **Tel** 644 1487. 🚌 5, 40. 🚋 1, 2, 3, 4. 🕐 May–Sep: 9am–5pm Mon–Sat; Oct–Apr: 10am–3pm Mon–Sat. 🏛 ✝ 3pm (in English). www.eelk.ee/tallinna.puhavaimu

Considered one of the most beautiful churches in Tallinn, the Gothic building of the Holy Spirit Church served as the Town Hall chapel before

being converted into a church. Its whitewashed exterior includes the oldest public clock in Tallinn, with carvings dating from 1684. The stepped gable is topped by a striking Baroque tower. The spire was nearly destroyed by fire in 2002, but was restored within a year. Inside, the church is a treasure trove of religious artifacts and architecture, from the magnificently intricate Baroque pews to the Renaissance-era pulpit. The sublime altar triptych, *The Descent of the Holy Ghost* (1483), by Berndt Notke, is the main highlight. The church has a special place in Estonian history, as the first sermons in Estonian were delivered here in 1535 following the Reformation.

Clock at Holy Spirit Church

Great Guild Hall ③
Suurgildi hoone

Pikk jalg 17. **Map** D3. **Tel** 641 1630. 🚌 5, 40. 🚋 1, 2, 3, 4. 🕐 11am–6pm Thu–Tue. 🏛 🎥
Estonian History Museum 🕐 Mar–Oct: 11am–6pm Wed–Sun; Nov–Feb: 11am–5pm www.eam.ee

One of the most important buildings in medieval Tallinn, the Great Guild Hall was constructed in 1417. It was owned by a powerful union of wealthy merchants and was mainly used as a gathering place for the members of the Great Guild. The starting as well as the end point of most festive processions of Tallinn, it was sometimes also rented out for wedding parties and court sessions.

The late-Gothic building has retained its original appearance through the centuries, although the windows were remodelled in the 1890s. The Great Guild Hall's majestic interior provides the perfect setting for a branch of the **Estonian History Museum**. The museum's collection of historical artifacts covers Estonian history from the Stone Age to the mid-19th century in fine detail. The exhibits, which include everything from jewellery to weaponry, are accompanied by explanatory texts in Estonian, Russian and English.

Altar of the Holy Spirit Church, Old Town

A passageway in the medieval Dominican Monastery

Dominican Monastery ④
Dominiiklaste klooster

Vene 16/18. **Map** D3. **Tel** 515 5489. 🚌 5, 40. 🚊 1, 2, 3, 4. 🕐 May–Sep: 10am–6pm daily. Private tours are available year round. 🖼 🎥 tour offered to the monastery's inner chambers through the cloister. 🏛 **Dominican Monastery Museum** 🕐 mid-May –mid-Sep: 10am–6pm daily. 🖼 **www.**kloostri.ee

Founded by Dominican monks in 1246, this monastery was a renowned centre of learning and thrived until the Reformation riots broke out in 1524. The Lutherans destroyed the monastery and forced the monks into exile. In 1531, a fire damaged most of the desecrated St Catherine's Church, the monastery's south wing.

After suffering neglect for four centuries, the ruined monastery was renovated in 1954. Today a serene cloister, its atmospheric passageways and a pretty inner garden draw visitors.

The star attraction, however, is the excellent **Dominican Monastery Museum**, with Estonia's largest collection of medieval and Renaissance stone carvings created by local stonemasons. One of the prominent works, a decorative relief of an angel on a triangular slab, is attributed to Hans von Aken, the popular 16th-century German Mannerist painter. The collection also includes carved 14th-century tombstones.

Niguliste Church ⑤
Niguliste kirik

Niguliste 3. **Map** C4. **Tel** 631 4330. 🚌 5, 40. 🕐 10am–5pm Wed–Fri. 🖼 tickets available until 4:30pm (call 644 9903 for bookings). 🎥 book in advance; extra charges for guided tours (up to 35 persons) in a foreign language. **www.**ekm.ee

Dedicated to St Nicholas, Niguliste Church was built in the 13th century, although nearly all that remains today is from the 15th century. Most of Tallinn's medieval artworks were destroyed in the Reformation riots of 1524. However, according to legend, Niguliste Church escaped being ransacked due to the laudable efforts of the church warden, who sealed the door with melted lead. The church was restored during Soviet times after being damaged by Soviet air raids in World War II and since then has served as a museum.

Today, the building houses Tallinn's most impressive collection of medieval religious artworks. These include the detailed altarpiece, painted in 1482 by Herman Rode of Lübeck, showing scenes from the life of St Nicholas, as well as the beheading of St George, and *Dance Macabre*, a 15th-century frieze by the German painter and sculptor Bernt Notke, considered the church's finest object. Unfortunately only a fragment of the

Exterior of Niguliste Church, one of Tallinn's medieval treasures

Ornate front door of the Renaissance House of Blackheads

magnificent 30-m (98-ft) original remains. Organ and choral concerts are regularly held here at weekends.

House of Blackheads ⑥
Mustpeade maja

Pikk 26. **Map** D3. **Tel** 631 3199. 🚌 5, 40. 🚊 1, 2, 3, 4. 🕐 only for chamber music concerts (call for timings) or by appointment. **www.**mustpeademaja.ee

This 15th-century Renaissance building was the meeting place of the Brotherhood of Blackheads, an association of unmarried merchants and shipowners who could join the more powerful Great Guild upon marriage. The unusual name was inspired by the North African St Maurice, the organization's patron saint, whose image can be seen on the ornate front door of the building.

Unlike their counterparts in Rīga, the Tallinn Blackheads were obliged to defend the city in times of strife and proved themselves especially formidable adversaries during the Livonian Wars *(see p96)*. However, in general, it seems that the wealthy Blackheads lived somewhat leisurely and hedonistic lives. The association survived until the Soviet invasion in 1940. Today, the House of Blackheads regularly hosts chamber music concerts in its elegant main hall.

Estonian Museum of Applied Art and Design ⑦

Eesti tarbekunsti ja disainimuuseum

Lai 17. **Map** D2. **Tel** 627 4600.
🚌 3. 🚋 1, 2. ⏱ 11am–6pm Wed–Sun. 🎫 🌐 www.etdm.ee

Housed in a converted 17th-century granary, the Estonian Museum of Applied Art and Design features the best in Estonian design from the early 20th century to the present day. The vast selection of exhibits is a splendid example of the nation's pride in applied arts. Many of the exhibits meld Scandinavian-style refinement with subtle Baltic irony to excellent effect. The furniture is especially eye-catching and a delight for art collectors. There are also some fine pieces of porcelain, dating from the 1930s to the 60s by Adamson-Eric, one of the key figures of 20th-century Estonian art.

Since the museum opened in 1980 it has done a formidable job of promoting Estonian design at home and abroad. Be sure to pick up a copy of the map, which highlights some notable examples of Estonian design around Tallinn.

St Olav's Church ⑧

Oleviste kirik

Lai 50. **Map** D2. **Tel** 641 2241.
🚌 3. 🚋 1, 2. ⏱ Apr–Oct: 10am–6pm daily. 🎫 ✝ www.oleviste.ee

The 124-m (407-ft) spire of St Olav's Church is a major Tallinn landmark and the church holds a proud place in local history. Legend says that Tallinners wanted to build the tallest spire in the world to attract merchant ships and a complete stranger promised to help them. In return he wanted the people of the city to guess his name. When the church was nearing completion, the city fathers sent a spy to his home and found out his

The soaring spire of St Olav's Church looking out over the Baltic Sea

name. As he was fixing the cross they called out "Olev" and he lost his balance and fell. In fact, the name of the church was a homage to King Olav II of Norway. The 159-m (522-ft) tall spire made the church the tallest building in the world in 1500 until a lightning strike burned it down in 1625. The church was struck by lightning six more times and burned down twice between 1625 and 1820. The original 16th-century structure of the church was renovated in the 19th century. St Olav's has an impressive vaulted ceiling and the church tower has a platform that offers breathtaking vistas of the city. The exterior rear wall features an elaborately carved 15th-century tombstone.

Detail of stone carving on the rear of St Olav's Church

Metal ship replica on the entrance wall, Estonian Maritime Museum

Fat Margaret Tower ⑨

Paks Margareeta

Pikk 70. **Map** E1. **Tel** 641 1408.
🚌 3. 🚋 1, 2. ⏱ 10am–6pm Wed–Sun. 🎫 📷 call in advance.
🏛 **Estonian Maritime Museum**
⏱ 10am–6pm Wed–Sun. 🎫
www.meremuuseum.ee

This 16th-century tower's evocative name derives from the fact that it was the largest part of the city's fortifications, with 4-m (13-ft) thick walls. It was originally built to defend the harbour as well as to impress visitors arriving by sea. From the top of the tower, there are good views of the Old Town and Tallinn's harbour and bay. Later, the tower was modified into a prison and was the scene of an outbreak of violence during the 1917 Revolution, when the prison guards were murdered by a mob of workers, soldiers and sailors. Fat Margaret Tower houses the **Estonian Maritime Museum**, a curious collection of nautical paraphernalia spread out over four storeys. The exhibits include a fascinating insight into ship-building and historical accounts of the country's harbours. There is also a scale model of the *Estonia*, the car and passenger ferry that sank between Tallinn and Stockholm in 1994. Nearby is a granite tablet with the names of the 852 people who died on board.

Toompea Castle ⑩
Toompea loss

Lossi plats 1a. **Map** B4. *Tel 631 6357.* 🚊 *3, 4.* ⬤ *10am–4pm Mon–Fri.* 📷 *call in advance.* ♿ 🚫 **www.**riigikogu.ee

The unassuming pink façade of Toompea Castle belies the history behind this vital seat of power. The castle now houses the Riigikogu (Estonia's Parliament), but for some 700 years it belonged to various occupying foreign powers. In the 9th century, a wooden fortress stood on the site, which was conquered by the Danes in 1219, who then constructed the stone fortifications around the hill, much of which still survives. The architecturally diverse castle complex features the 50-m (164-ft) Pikk Hermann Tower, above which flies the Estonian flag. The unique-looking Riigikogu, which was built in 1922, is situated in the castle courtyard. Toompea was a town in itself enjoying its own rights and privileges until 1878, when it was merged with the rest of Tallinn below.

Alexander Nevsky Cathedral ⑪
Aleksander Nevski katedraal

Lossi plats 10. **Map** B4. *Tel 644 3484.* 🚊 *3, 4.* ⬤ *8am–7pm daily.* 🚫 📷 **www.**orthodox.ee

The imposing Alexander Nevsky Cathedral was built between 1894 and 1900, under

The manicured ornamental garden of Kadriorg Palace

orders from Tsar Alexander III. As intended, the Neo-Byzantine edifice dominates Castle Square (Lossi Plats) with its towering onion domes and golden crosses. A number of icons, mosaics and the bell for the tower were carried all the way from St Petersburg.

Legend has it that the cathedral was built on the grave of the Estonian folk hero Kalev. However, it is named after the sainted Russian Duke Alexander Nevsky (1219–63), who defeated the Livonian knights on the banks of Lake Peipsi in 1242 and conquered a great part of Estonia. Disliked by many Estonians as a symbol of the Russification policies of Alexander III, it was due to be demolished in 1924, but the controversial plan was never carried out.

The extravagant altar is made up of a dazzling display of icons, while the sheer scale of the cathedral's interior is equally impressive.

Kadriorg Palace ⑫
Kadrioru loss

Weizenbergi 37. **Map** F1. *Tel 606 6400.* ⬤ *May–Sep: 10am–5pm Tue–Sun; Oct–Apr: 10am–5pm Wed–Sun.* 📷 📷 ♿ 🖼 📷 **www.**ekm.ee

Built in 1718 under orders from the Russian Tsar Peter the Great, this palace was meant to serve as a summer residence for the imperial family. The palace was named Kadriorg – which means Catherine's Valley in Estonian – to honour his wife, Empress Catherine. Designed by the famous Italian master architect Nicola Michetti, it was built in Baroque style and made to look like an Italian villa. The main attraction of the palace, however, is the astonishingly ornate Great Hall, which ranks among the finest examples of Baroque exuberance in North Eastern Europe.

Kadriorg Palace today houses the **Museum of Foreign Art** which has an excellent collection of European paintings and sculpture. The palace is also used as a venue for lectures and theatre performances.

Just behind the palace, in the kitchen building, is the **Mikkel Museum** which has some 600 works of foreign art, including a selection of European, Chinese and Russian paintings, donated by Johannes Mikkel (1907–2006). Also worth a visit is the magnificently designed **Kumu Art Museum** near the palace. It is one of the five branches of the Art Museum of Estonia.

The austere façade of Toompea Castle

Saaremaa Island ❷

The largest island in Estonia, Saaremaa is the jewel of its archipelago. The capital, Kuressaare, is strikingly picturesque, and its relatively tranquil atmosphere makes it an ideal base from which to explore the island. Sareema has a lot to offer in terms of things to see and do, but its extraordinary natural beauty is the real attraction and the reason why so many people feel compelled to return here. The breathtaking landscape of Vilsandi National Park and the abundance of old churches and fascinating historical relics that dot the island are just some of the highlights.

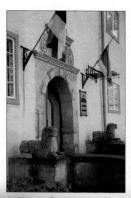

Art Nouveau lion statues outside the information centre, Kuressaare

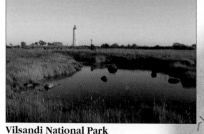

Vilsandi National Park
Known for its awe-inspiring landscapes, unspoilt islets and bird sanctuaries, this park was established in 1993 to preserve the ecology of Estonia's coastal areas.

Kihelkonna Church, a splendid 13th-century place of worship, has an impressive steeple that was added in 1897.

TAGAMÕISA PENINSULA
Vilsandi Island
78
Mustj
Kihelkonna
Karla
Lümanda
Saime
GULF
RĪG
77
Sõrve Peninsula
Mõntu
Sääre
0 km 10
0 miles 10

Sõrve Peninsula can be explored on a bicycle or by car, and has spectacular scenery unparalled by any other area on the island.

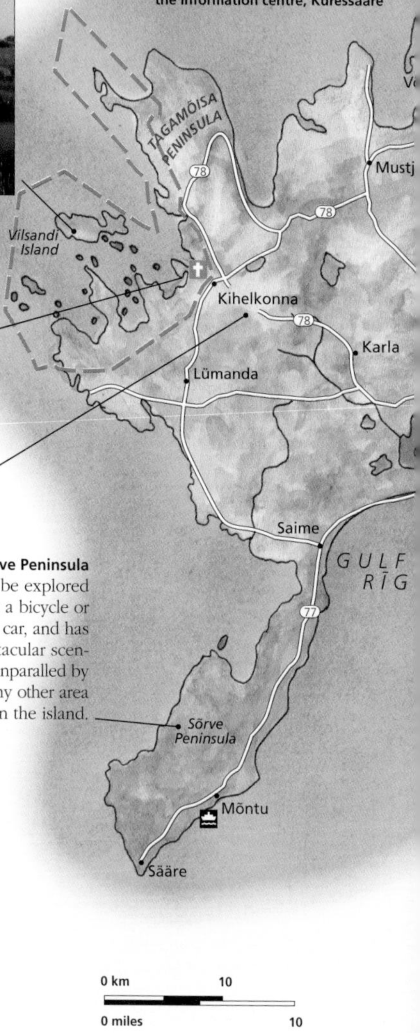

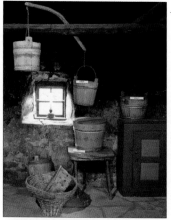

Mihkli Farm Museum
This museum has one of the most authentic displays of rural architecture and traditional lifestyles in Estonia. Many of the buildings here were built between 1827 and 1856.

For hotels and restaurants in this region see pp116–17

Angla Windmills
Standing along the main road from Kuressaare to Leisi, the five remaining wooden windmills at Angla are an iconic symbol of Saaremaa Island. In the mid-19th century there were 800 functional windmills on the island.

VISITORS' CHECKLIST

220 km (137 miles) SW of Tallinn. ✈ *Kuressaare.*
🚌 *from Tallinn, Tartu & Pärnu to Kuressaare.* ⛴ *from Virtsu to Kuivastu, Hiiumaa Island to Triigi & Roomassaare to Ruhnu,* (372) 14204. ℹ *Tallinna 2, Kuressaare,* 453 3120. ◯ *May–Sep: 9am–7pm Mon–Fri, 10am–4pm Sat, Sun; Oct–Apr: 9am–5pm Mon–Fri, 10am–4pm Sat, Sun.*
🖥 www.saaremaa.ee

Kaarma Church, which dates from the 13th century, has a striking 15th-century pulpit.

Karja Church
The medieval church is best known for its elaborate stone carvings, which include a relief of the Crucifixion above the side door and some remarkable figures inside depicting saints.

Bishop's Castle
The most important landmark in Kuressaare, the castle has a powerful defence tower and a slender watchtower, both unique features of the architecture of the Teutonic Order. Inside is the Saaremaa Regional Museum.

KEY

✈	Airport
⛴	Ferry terminal
ℹ	Visitor information
✝	Church
▬	Major road
═	Minor road
---	Ferry route
‑ ‑	Park boundary

Pärnu

Often referred to as Estonia's summer capital, Pärnu has historic buildings, pastel-coloured wooden houses and elegant late 19th-century villas set along leafy streets. With an ultra-modern concert hall and theatre, the town also has a noteworthy cultural scene. All the main sights are within walking distance from the town centre and the Old Town is centred around the pedestrianized Rüütli Street.

Wooden door carving

However, Pärnu's main draw is its beautiful beach where Estonians flock throughout the summer, transforming the town into a thriving holiday spot.

🏛 Town Hall
Uus 4/Nikolai 3.
The elegant Neo-Classical building that is now the Town Hall (Raekoja) was erected in 1797 as a wealthy merchant's residence. In 1819, the structure was altered to serve as the house for the town's governor and, in 1839, it took on its current function as Pärnu's Town Hall. What makes it worth visiting is the magnificent Art Nouveau extension built in 1911. Its brooding dark exterior is in total contrast to the bright yellow façade of the original structure and provides a fascinating juxtaposition of two radically different architectural styles.

🔒 Elizabeth's Church
Nikolai 22. **Tel** 443 1381. ⬜ Jun–Aug: noon–6pm daily; Sep–May: 10am–4pm Mon–Fri. 🔓
www.eliisabet.ee
An excellent example of local Baroque architecture, this church (Eliisabeti kirik) has an elegant ochre exterior and a maroon spire towering above the surrounding narrow side streets. It was founded specifically as a Lutheran church in 1747 by the Russian Empress Elizabeth (1709–61). Today, it serves as the largest Protestant place of worship in Pärnu.

The wood-panelled interior is refined and understated, but all the more impressive for it. The church's spire was built by Johann Heinrich Wülbern, who also constructed Rīga's St Peter's Church. Elizabeth's Church is also renowned for its organ, one of the best in Estonia, built in 1929 by H Kolbe of Rīga.

Green domes and yellow walls of St Catherine's Church

🔒 St Catherine's Church
Vee 16. **Tel** 444 3198. ⬜ 9am–5pm daily. 🔓
Built in 1768 for the Pärnu garrison during the reign of Catherine the Great, St Catherine's (Ekateriina kirik) is arguably the finest example of a Baroque-style church in Estonia. With bottle-green domes and lemon-yellow walls, the church boasts an elegant exterior and opulent

interior. Intended as an architectural showpiece, St Catherine's had a significant influence on Orthodox churches throughout the region.

🏛 Pärnu Concert Hall
Aida 4. **Tel** 445 5800. ⬜
11am–8pm daily (box office).
📷 ♿ 🚻 www.concert.ee
Completed in 2002, the Pärnu Concert Hall (kontserdimaja) is a source of great pride for the local people. Designed by three architects – K Koov, K Nõmm and H Grossschmidt – the curvaceous glass and steel building is a strong example of modern Estonian architecture. Its seashell-like shape was intended to symbolize Pärnu's status as a coastal town. The multifunctional building mostly hosts theatre performances and concerts, although it also houses an art gallery and a music school.

🏛 Tallinn Gate
Mere puiestee.
The only trace of the 17th-century ramparts that protected Pärnu at one time, Tallinn Gate (Tallinna värav) still offers a fascinating glimpse of the once impressive fortifications. Until 1710, when Swedish rule came to an end, it was known as Gustav's Gate, named after King Gustav II Adolph of Sweden. Today, the gate's only function is to provide an elegant portal between the Old Town and the area leading to the sea. The cobblestoned passageway offers a relaxed walk.

Tallinn Gate, sole remainder of Pärnu's 17th-century ramparts

For hotels and restaurants in this region see pp116–17

Art Nouveau carving on the façade of Ammende Villa

🏨 Ammende Villa

Mere puiestee 7. *Tel* 447 3888.
🕚 *noon–11pm daily.*
www.ammende.ee
Built in 1905 by a wealthy local merchant for the wedding party of his beloved daughter, Ammende Villa is one of the most impressive examples of Art Nouveau architecture in Estonia. Over the years, it has served as a casino, a health establishment and a library, before two Estonian businessmen renovated it and converted it into a luxury hotel *(see p116)*. The villa is located a short walk from the sea and the Old Town.

🏛 Lydia Koidula Museum

J V Jannseni 37. *Tel* 443 3313.
🔵 *May–Aug: 10am–5pm Tue–Sat; Sep–Apr: 10am–5pm Tue–Sun.* 🔊
📷 *call in advance.* **www**.pernau.ee
Situated a short walk across the Pärnu river, the Lydia Koidula Museum provides a moving testimony to one of Estonia's most revered poets. The museum, which was established in 1945, is situated in the building where her father, Johann Valdemar Jannsen, ran a primary school from 1857 to 1863. The highlight of the museum is a reconstruction of the bedroom where the 43-year old Koidula died of cancer in 1886 in the Russian naval base of Kronstadt. Although very little of Lydia Koidula's work is available in English, the museum offers insight into 19th-century Estonian literature.

VISITORS' CHECKLIST

128 km (80 miles) S of Tallinn.
🏘 44,000. ✈ 5 km (3 miles) N of centre. 🚌 Riia mnt 116. 🚆 Pikk tänav. 🚌 ℹ Rüütli 16, 447 3000. 🎬 Pärnu Film Festival (Jul), Oistrakh Festival (Jul).

LYDIA KOIDULA (1843–86)

Lydia Emilia Florentine Jannsen was a highly influential figure in Estonian history. Although convention forced her to write anonymously under the pseudonym Koidula, meaning "of the dawn", her poetry was ecstatically received. Her *My Country is My Love* became the unofficial national anthem during Soviet times. Some critics believe that Koidula's finest writing was her passionate correspondence with the writer Friedrich Reinhold Kreutzwald, although his wife eventually put an end to it. Koidula married a Latvian doctor whose work took them to Kronstadt in the Gulf of Finland, where she later died, pining for her country to the very end.

Lydia Koidula, Estonia's beloved writer and poet

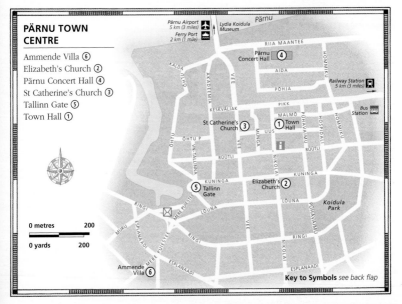

PÄRNU TOWN CENTRE

Ammende Villa ⑥
Elizabeth's Church ②
Pärnu Concert Hall ④
St Catherine's Church ③
Tallinn Gate ⑤
Town Hall ①

0 metres   200
0 yards   200

Key to Symbols *see back flap*

Tartu ❹

Home to the venerable Tartu University, the town is frequently referred to as the intellectual capital of Estonia. The university was founded in 1632 by King Gustav II Adolph of Sweden *(see p108)* and has played a major role in Estonian history ever since. With the second largest population in Estonia, Tartu has a thriving cultural scene and exciting nightlife, and makes a convenient base from which to explore the southeast of the country.

Statue of King Gustav II Adolph

Town Hall Square, with the Kissing Students Fountain in the centre

🏛 Town Hall Square

Tartu's historic centre is set around this square (Raekoja plats), with the Emajõgi river to the east and Toomemägi hill just behind. Overlooking it from the top is the Town Hall, in front of which stands the **Kissing Students Fountain**

erected in 1998. Most of the square's original medieval architecture burned down in the Great Fire of 1775, and today, the gently sloping cobblestoned square is distinctly Neo-Classical, a look that is in sync with the rest of the city centre.

🏛 Tartu University Main Building

Ülikooli 18. **Tel** 737 5100. ☐ 11am–5pm Mon–Fri. 🎦 📷 🕭 www.ut.ee

Completed in 1809, Tartu University Main Building (Tartu ülikooli peahoone), with its impressive Art Museum, is one of Estonia's finest Neo-Classical buildings. The first students registered in this university in 1632 making this only the second in the province of Swedish Livonia. The original graffiti by the students on the walls makes for amusing reading.

⛪ St John's Church

Jaani 5. **Tel** 744 2229. ☐ May–Sep: 10am–6pm Tue–Sat, 10am–1pm Sun. 🎦 🕭 www.eelk.ee/tartu.jaani

Dating from 1330, this church (Jaani kirik) was severely damaged by bombing during World War II. Despite extensive renovations and the addition of a new spire in 1999, the church remains one of Northern Europe's best examples of brick Gothic architecture. Hundreds of elaborate terracotta figures, dating from the Middle Ages, adorn its interior and exterior. Originally there were more than 1,000 such figures but some have been destroyed over time.

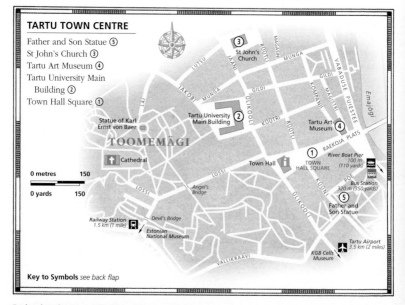

TARTU TOWN CENTRE

Father and Son Statue ⑤
St John's Church ③
Tartu Art Museum ④
Tartu University Main Building ②
Town Hall Square ①

Statue of Karl Ernst von Baer
TOOMEMÄGI
Cathedral
Tartu University Main Building ②
Tartu Art Museum ④
RAEKOJA PLATS
Town Hall ① TOWN HALL SQUARE
River Boat Pier 100 m (110 yards)
Bus Station 320 m (350 yards)
Father and Son Statue ⑤

0 metres   150
0 yards   150

Angel's Bridge
Railway Station 1.5 km (1 mile)
Devil's Bridge
Estonian National Museum
KGB Cells Museum
Tartu Airport 3.5 km (2 miles)

Key to Symbols see back flap

Leaning building in which the Tartu Art Museum is housed

🏛 Tartu Art Museum

Raekoja plats 108. **Tel** 744 1080. ⭘ 11am–6pm Wed–Sun. 🖼 free on Fri. 🎫 call in advance. ⬛ www.muuseum.ee

Housing one of the finest collections in the country, Tartu Art Museum (Tartu kunstimuuseum) features the works of prominent Estonian artists such as Elmar Kits (1913–72), Ülo Sooster (1924–70) and Marko Mäetamm (b. 1965). A thorough and captivating overview of Estonian painting, sculpture and drawing, which spans the 19th century through to the present, is also provided. The museum's building conspicuously leans to one side and belonged to the famous Russian Field Marshal Barclay de Tolly, who successfully led the Russian Army against Napoleon in 1812.

Father and Son Statue

Küüni (close to Poe).

Originally planned for Tallinn, this delightful little statue by Ülo Õun (1940–88) was conceived in 1977. It was cast in bronze in 1987, purchased by the Tartu town government in 2001 and finally unveiled on Children's Day (1 June) in 2004. The father figure is modelled after the sculptor, and the child after his son Kristjan, when he was around one-and-a-half years old. Interestingly, both father and son are proportionately equal in this highly unusual and extremely poignant monument.

🏛 KGB Cells Museum

Riia 15b. **Tel** 746 1717. ⭘ 11am–4pm Tue–Sat. 🖼 🎫 www.linnamuuseum.tartu.ee

Situated in the basement of the regional headquarters of the former KGB/NKVD, the KGB Cells Museum (KGB kongid) is a grim testimony to the nightmare of the Soviet occupation. Some of the former cells have been turned into exhibition spaces, while others have been restored to their original condition to provide a picture of what so many Estonians suffered under the Soviet regime. Much attention is paid to the mass deportations that took place between 1940 and 1949, including the official plans to carry them out. There are gut-wrenching artifacts from the Gulags, the notorious correction camps where thousands of Estonians died.

A desk in the KGB Cells Museum, with Stalin's portrait on the wall

🏛 Estonian National Museum

Kuperjanovi 9. **Tel** 742 1311. ⭘ 11am–6pm Tue–Sun. 🖼 free on Fri. 🎫 call in advance. 🅰 ⬛ 🛈 www.erm.ee

Estonia's most important ethnological centre, the Estonian National Museum (Eesti rahva muuseum) boasts over one million artifacts collected over the last 100 years. Dedicated to the great Estonian folklorist and linguist Jakob Hurt (1839–1907), the museum highlights Estonian and other Finno-Ugric cultures, and its collection covers every imaginable aspect of life in this country. From chairs made of gnarled birch wood to warped wooden beer tankards, the displayed objects eloquently attest to a way of life that seems quaintly anachronistic in modern times.

In addition, there are vast photographic and documental archives and a collection of costumes, including a punk jacket (c. 1982–85). The museum occasionally holds temporary exhibitions that encompass themes from furniture to photography.

KARL ERNST VON BAER (1792–1876)

A Baltic-German biologist, Karl Ernst von Baer was one of the founders of embryology. His pioneering work in this area was recognized by Darwin, although Baer himself was extremely critical of the Theory of Evolution. Baer studied at Tartu University and later taught at Königsberg and the St Petersburg Academy of Sciences, before living out his last years in Tartu. A statue of him sitting pensively atop a large plinth has pride of place on Toomemägi. A rather endearing tradition takes place every year, on the eve of St Philip's Day (1 May), when Tartu University students wash Baer's bronze hair.

Statue of Karl Ernst von Baer on Toomemägi

Practical & Travel Information

Estonia has a well-developed network of visitor
information centres, even in small towns. There is an
abundance of useful literature to help visitors get the
best out of their trip. Several major international carriers
from many European cities provide links to Estonia's
capital, Tallinn. The country is also well served by both
domestic and international ferries, with regular services
to Tallinn and the popular island of Saaremaa.

WHEN TO VISIT

The best time to visit Estonia is
from May to September when
it is pleasantly warm. July
and August are the warmest
months. Winter, between
October and March, is cold,
dark and damp but very
atmospheric when forests
are laden with snow. January,
the coldest month, is best
avoided, as is the rainy month
of April, when the snow melts
and turns sludgy.

DOCUMENTATION

Citizens of EU member-states,
the US, Canada, Australia and
New Zealand can enter
Estonia for a period of up to
90 days in a half-year period
on presentation of a valid passport. Those wishing to stay
beyond 90 days will need to
apply for a national long-term
visa or a residence permit.
Visitors from other countries
should enquire at their local
Estonian embassy or consulate
to check visa requirements
before travelling. The official
website of the Estonian
Ministry of Foreign Affairs
offers information on visa regulations. EU citizens are not
subject to customs regulations,

provided they adhere to EU
guidelines. All visitors should
check for any customs duty or
special permission required to
export a cultural object, before
buying it. For detailed information on all these guidelines,
entrance regulations and visa
charges, it is advisable to visit
the official website of the
European Commission.

VISITOR INFORMATION

The network of information
centres in the country is supported by an equally advanced
structure of tourism websites.
Most towns have a tourist
information office located in
or close to the town square.
There are no tourist offices at
the land borders or at Tallinn
airport but there is one at the
Tallinn harbour. Offices are
generally open from 9am to
6pm on weekdays and for
shorter hours on Saturdays;
many are also open on
Sundays. The staff is friendly
and speak English. Free brochures listing local sights and
events are available at these
offices, which also sell maps
and guidebooks. Estonia's
official tourism website has a
list of all the tourist information
offices in the country.

HEALTH AND SECURITY

Estonian *haigla* (hospitals)
tend to be in poor condition.
Private clinics exist in all major
cities and are a better option
for non-emergency treatment.
EU citizens with an EHIC card
are entitled to free treatment.
Visitors are also advised to
drink bottled mineral water
rather than tap water.

Using common sense is the
best way to ensure personal
safety. Visitors should never
accept drinks from strangers
and avoid disreputable-
looking nightclubs. It is wise
not to carry any luxury items.

FACILITIES FOR THE DISABLED

Although there has been a
significant improvement in
recent years, Estonia is not
very well equipped in providing facilities for the
disabled. In Tallinn, there are
several steep winding cobblestoned streets. Trolleybuses,
trams and trains do not
provide wheelchair access
and only a few buses do.

BANKING AND CURRENCY

In Estonia, banks are usually
open from Monday to Friday
between 9am and 6pm. Major
banks stay open on Saturdays
from 9am to 2pm. Exchange
bureaus are widespread and
have better exchange rates
than hotels. ATMs are found
everywhere, including petrol
stations. Estonia's monetary
unit is the kroon (EEK),
translated as crown, and is
divided into 100 sentis.

COMMUNICATIONS

Estonia's communications
infrastructure is very efficient.
All phone lines are digital,
ensuring high-quality connections. Mobile phone usage is
particularly high. The post
offices offer a range of express
delivery options. Internet
access is limited in provinces.

ARRIVING BY AIR

The sleek-looking **Lennart
Meri Tallinn Airport** is the
main Estonian airport with

THE CLIMATE OF ESTONIA

From May to September
there is little risk of cold
weather, but winters are
freezing, with temperatures
dipping to -12° C (10° F).
Rain comes in brief, sharp
outburst throughout the year.
Days are short in December
and January, with 18 hours
of darkness, but between
March and October, the long
12-hour days are excellent for
outdoor activities.

TALLINN

	month	Apr	Jul	Oct	Jan
°C/F	high	7/61	20/75	10/61	-10/14
	low	0/46	12/63	4/48	
				4/39	
☀		6 hrs	10 hrs	2 hrs	1 hrs
☂		31 mm	68 mm	68 mm	39 mm

0°C 32°F

regular scheduled flights. In recent years the airport has become a regional hub, serviced by approximately 15 airlines including major carriers such as **Finnair**, **airBaltic**, **Lufthansa** and **KLM**.

Founded in 1991, **Estonian Air** is the country's national carrier. Based in Tallinn, it offers a good standard of service in both business and economy class. The airline has direct links with several major European destinations as well as many Estonian cities and islands. Visitors from outside Europe need to catch a connecting flight from cities such as London, Copenhagen, Helsinki or Stockholm.

As a consequence of the EU "open-skies" policy, which was implemented in 2004, several economical carriers, such as **easyJet**, now provide daily flights to Tallinn from London.

ARRIVING BY SEA

Estonia is very well served by ferry, with Tallinn's **Passenger Port** (*reisisadam*) handling about 7 million passengers a year. The main line **Tallink** has routes to Helsinki (Finland), Rostock (Germany) and Stockholm (Sweden), while other carriers such as **Viking Line** and **Eckerö Line**

are accessible from Helsinki and Stockholm. Travellers from Helsinki are spoilt for choice, with a range of catamarans, ferries and even a hydrofoil making the crossing at regular intervals. The Passenger Port is within walking distance of Tallinn's Old Town and a taxi ride should cost between 50 and 75 krooni. Tallinn also features on an increasing number of Baltic Sea cruise itineraries, although these normally only allow for a day's stopover.

RAIL TRAVEL

Tallinn's main railway station, **Balti Jaam**, is a short walk away from the Old Town. The only international links are a nightly train to Moscow, and an irregular service to St Petersburg. Tickets should be pre-booked, since Russian visa specifications insist on dates of entry and exit. The Rail Baltica route is due to link Tallinn with Rīga and Vilnius by 2013.

TRAVELLING BY COACH

International coach routes to Estonia are provided by **Eurolines** and **Ecolines**, which operate connections between Tallinn and Berlin, Munich, Kaliningrad, Warsaw and

St Petersburg, among others. International coaches arrive at the **Tallinn Bus Station** (*bussijaam*). From there, it is a short taxi ride into the city centre, or one can catch tram number 2 or 4, or bus number 17, 17a or 23. Passengers travelling to Tallinn by bus from Rīga or Vilnius can get off at the more central Viru väljak bus stop. There are also limited international coach connections with Pärnu and Tartu. The coach network is efficiently run and cheap, and services are clearly posted in bus stations.

TRAVELLING BY CAR

Since 2007, when the Baltic States agreed to the Schengen Agreement (under which systematic border controls were abolished between Schengen countries), there are no border restrictions for Schengen visa holders. Crossing the border from Latvia is easy, especially for EU passport holders. The border crossing with Russia is slower and border guards are likely to scrutinize one's documents. Visitors bringing their own car into Estonia are required to show the Vehicle Registration document, an international driving permit and a valid Green Card insurance policy.

DIRECTORY

DOCUMENTATION

www.vm.ee
www.ec.europa.eu

VISITOR INFORMATION

www.visitestonia.com

EMBASSIES

Canada
Toomkooli 13, Tallinn.
Tel 627 3311.
www.canada.ee

United States
Kentmanni 20, Tallinn.
Tel 668 8100.
www.usemb.ee

United Kingdom
Wismari 6, Tallinn.
Tel 667 4700.
www.britishembassy.ee

EMERGENCY NUMBERS

Ambulance
Tel 112.

Fire
Tel 112.

Police
Tel 112.

ARRIVING BY AIR

airBaltic
www.airbaltic.com

easyJet
www.easyjet.com

Estonian Air
www.estonian-air.ee

Finnair
www.finnair.com

KLM

www.klm.com

Lennart Meri Tallinn Airport
Tel 605 8888.
www.tallinn-airport.ee

Lufthansa
www.lufthansa.com

ARRIVING BY SEA

Eckerö Line
www.eckeroline.fi

Passenger Port
Sadama 25, Tallinn.
Tel 631 8550.
www.portoftallinn.com

Tallink
www.tallink.ee

Viking Line
www.vikingline.fi

RAIL TRAVEL

Balti Jaam
Toompuiestee 37,
Tallinn.
Tel 3721 447.
www.baltijaam.ee

ARRIVING BY COACH

Ecolines
www.ecolines.ee

Eurolines
www.eurolines.ee

Tallinn Bus Station
Lastekodu 46,
Tallinn.
Tel 3721 2550.

Shopping & Entertainment

Traditional handicrafts and souvenirs can be found all over Estonia. There are plenty of stores and market stalls that specialize in art, antiques, jewellery and knick-knacks, and Tallinn's Old Town is one of the best places in the capital for gift shopping and souvenir hunting. The country also has an eclectic entertainment scene. The larger towns and cities such as Tartu and Pärnu have a crowded cultural calendar as well as a splendid nightlife. Tallinn's many classical music and opera performances are a major draw.

OPENING HOURS

Most shops are generally open from 10am to 6 or 7pm on weekdays, from 10am to 4pm on Saturdays, and are closed on Sundays. Shopping centres usually open from 10am to 8 or 9pm daily. In small towns and villages, opening hours are more erratic at weekends, with many shops staying closed or only opening for half a day. Grocery stores normally keep longer hours. However, there are several 24-hour convenience stores in Tallinn.

MARKETS

Just about every Estonian town has a *turg* (market), although they often sell only fruit, vegetables, household goods and everyday items. Tallinn's main market, the open-air Central Market, offers a glimpse into the everyday life of the city's inhabitants. The market selling knitwear at the corner of Viru and Müürivahe Streets covers a stretch of the Old Town wall and is a great place to find a gift. Uus Käsitööturg, a popular stall in this market, has a good selection of traditional handicrafts and souvenirs. The Christmas Market in Town Hall Square *(see pp100–1)*, which runs through December, features everything from knitwear to marzipan.

HANDICRAFTS

Towns and villages are good places to find local specialities, including textiles, ceramics and ornaments. Marble is used to make carved ashtrays, and pestles and mortars. The use of dolomite, a translucent

mineral, is unique to Saaremaa Island *(see pp106–107)*. Pärnu *(see pp108–109)* is known for its handwoven linen.

Tallinn abounds with a variety of handicrafts. Wooden toys and utensils are common, as are traditionally woven rugs with beautiful and elaborate patterns and a wide range of ceramics. **Bogapott**, an exclusive ceramics studio, and **Galerii Kaks**, with its wide range of textiles, are worthy of a visit. **Nukupood** stocks handmade toys as well as dolls in traditional folk costumes. In **Katariina Gild**, craftsmen can be seen at work on handicrafts, jewellery and ceramics. **A-Galerii** has a great selection of local handmade jewellery.

ART AND ANTIQUES

Tallinn's contemporary art scene offers plenty of galleries and small shops that stock a variety of attractive oil paintings, graphic art, sculpture, textiles and off-beat ceramics. **Navitrolla Galerii** sells both originals and prints. The city also has many antique stores, selling everything from Soviet-era paraphernalia to exorbitantly priced Russian icons. Special permission is needed to take some objects out of the country, so check with the shop's manager before buying. With stunning bronze items, silverware and crystalware, **Reval Antiik** and **Shifara Art & Antiques**, are among Tallinn's best antique stores.

FOOD AND DRINK

Estonian food products can be bought in any supermarket. Rye bread is a local staple, as are sprats, smoked fish and

cheese. Try **Kaubamaja** and **Stockmann**, two of the country's largest department stores, for variety. Chocolate-lovers should try the brand Kalev, Estonia's oldest confectionary producer and, in Tallinn, the handmade delicacies at **Anneli Viik**. There are also numerous bakeries selling delicious pastries and cakes.

Estonia's national drink is a sweet brown liqueur called Vana Tallinn, but in terms of consumption, beer is the most popular tipple. Saku Original, Tartu Alexander and A Le Coq are all popular brands. Locally made as well as quality imported vodka is cheaper here than in other European countries. Saare Dzinn, a gin flavoured with berries from the Estonian islands, is good too. **Liviko**, one of Estonia's leading alcohol producers, has stores all over Tallinn.

NIGHTLIFE

Tallinn's Old Town is packed with bars and pubs of every size and description. There are several popular Irish and English-style pubs, including **Molly Malone's** and **Scotland Yard**, as well as stylish lounge bars such as **Déjà Vu** and the extravagant **Lounge 24**. There are also a number of quieter, cosier pubs scattered around the Old Town. **Hell Hunt**, contrary to its name, is a relaxing spot for a chat and a drink. Most of the good clubs are situated in or within walking distance of the Old Town. Many, such as **Bonnie and Clyde**, are equally popular with locals and visitors. **Club Privé** and **BonBon** are the most exclusive hangouts, while serious clubbers can try the port-side **Oscar**.

Elsewhere, Tartu has an impressive range of lively places. One of the best-known nightclubs is **Atlantis**, while the most exclusive is **Illusion**. Another favourite is the **Maailm**. Occasional live performances take place at the **Genialistide Klubi**.

Pärnu also has an active nightlife. **Lime Lounge** is a stylish place for a drink, while **Postipoiss** is a restaurant-cum-pub with frequent live music.

Among the clubs, **Mirage** is often packed while **Bravo** is the slickest.

MUSIC, THEATRE AND DANCE

Lovers of live music are spoilt for choice in Tallinn. **Café Amigo** attracts the biggest local rock, pop and blues bands. **Von Krahl Baar** is one of the best places in the city to experience the local alternative scene, while **Rock Café** offers everything from blues to funk. **No99** hosts jazz concerts on Fridays and Saturdays.

Estonia has an outstanding tradition of classical music. Tallinn's **National Symphony Orchestra** regularly puts on sell-out performances.

Concerts also take place in churches and in the **Estonian Music Academy**. **Kanuti Gildi Saal** usually hosts the best of contemporary Estonian and international dance.

The best place for serious theatre lovers is the **Von Krahl Theatre** (though English translations are rare) and the **Tallinn Linnateater**, which specializes in contemporary works.

In Tartu, the main concert venue, **Vanemuine**, stages theatre, classical music, ballet and other shows while in Pärnu, the town's Concert Hall hosts a wide range of concerts and music events.

Eesti Muusikafestivalid has a list of nationwide music festivals and *The Baltic Times* and *In Your Pocket* offer

information on arts and entertainment. Bookings for cultural events can be made at the venue or through ticketing agencies such as **Piletilevi**.

FOLK FESTIVALS

A major part of Estonia's cultural life revolves around folk festivals. Among the most important, the **Folkloorifestival** in Võru, is one of the biggest, while the **Hiiu Folk Festival** in Hiiumaa has a particularly authentic ambience created by its rustic setting. The splendid **Narva Historic Festival** involves a re-enactment of the Great Northern War, while Obinitsa hosts several festivals celebrating Setu culture.

DIRECTORY

HANDICRAFTS

A-Galerii
Hobusepea 8, Tallinn.
Tel 646 4101.

Bogapott
Pikk jalg 9, Tallinn.
Tel 631 3181.

Galerii Kaks
Lühike jalg 1, Tallinn.
Tel 641 8308.

Katariina Gild
Vene 12, Tallinn.
Tel 644 5365.

Nukupood
Raekoja plats 18, Tallinn.
Tel 644 3058.

ART AND ANTIQUES

Navitrolla Galerii
Pikk tanav 36, Tallinn.
Tel 631 3716.

Reval Antiik
Harju 13, Tallinn.
Tel 644 0747.

Shifara Art & Antiques
Vana-posti 7, Tallinn.
Tel 644 3536.

FOOD AND DRINK

Anneli Viik
Pikk 30, Tallinn.
Tel 644 4530.

Kaubamaja
Gonsiori 2, Tallinn.
Tel 667 3100.

Liviko
Mere pst 6, Tallinn.
Tel 683 7745.

Stockmann
Liivalaia 53, Tallinn.
Tel 633 9539.

NIGHTLIFE

Atlantis
Narva mnt 2, Tartu.
Tel 738 5485.

BonBon
Mere pst 6e, Tallinn.
Tel 661 6080.

Bonnie and Clyde
Olümpia Hotel, Liivalaia 33, Tallinn. *Tel 631 5333.*

Bravo
Hommiku 3, Pärnu.
Tel 5344 3887.

Club Privé
Harju 6, Tallinn.
Tel 631 0545.

Déjà Vu
Sauna 1, Tallinn.
Tel 645 0044.

Genialistide Klubi
Lai 37, Tartu.
Tel 5348 5530.

Hell Hunt
Pikk 39, Tallinn.
Tel 681 8333.

Illusion
Raatuse 97, Tartu.
Tel 742 4341.

Lime Lounge
Hommiku 17, Pärnu.
Tel 449 2190.

Lounge 24
Radisson Hotel, Rävala pst 3, Tallinn. *Tel 682 3424.*

Maailm
Rüütli 12, Tartu.
Tel 742 9099.

Mirage
Rüütli 40, Pärnu.
Tel 447 2404.

Molly Malone's
Mündi 2, Tallinn.
Tel 631 3016.

Oscar
Sadama 6, Tallinn.
Tel 661 4721.

Postipoiss
Vee 12, Pärnu.
Tel 446 4864.

Scotland Yard
Mere pst 6e, Tallinn.
Tel 653 5190.

MUSIC, THEATRE AND DANCE

Café Amigo
Hotel Viru, Viru väljak 4, Tallinn. *Tel 680 9380.*
www.amigo.ee

Eesti Muusikafestivalid
www.festivals.ee

Estonian Music Academy
Rävala 16, Tallinn. *Tel 667 5700.* www.ema.edu.ee

Kanuti Gildi Saal
Pikk 20, Tallinn. *Tel 646 4704.* www.saal.ee

National Symphony Orchestra
www.erso.ee

No99
Sakala 3, Tallinn.
Tel 668 8798.

Piletilevi
www.piletilevi.ee

Rock Café
Tartu mnt. 80d, Tallinn.
Tel 681 0878.
www.rockcafe.ee

Tallinn Linnateater
Lai 23, Tallinn.
Tel 665 0800.
www.linnateater.ee

Vanemuine
Vanemuise 6, Tartu.
Tel 744 0165.
www.vanemuine.ee

Von Krahl Baar
Rataskaevu 10/12, Tallinn.
Tel 626 9090.
www.vonkrahl.ee

Von Krahl Theatre
Rataskaevu 10, Tallinn.
Tel 626 9090.
www.vonkrahl.ee

FOLK FESTIVALS

Folkloorifestival
www.werro.ee

Hiiu Folk Festival
www.hiiufolk.ee

Narva Historic Festival
www.narvamuseum.ee

Where to Stay in Estonia

From luxury hotels and city-centre hostels to rural guesthouses, Estonia offers an extensive range of accommodation. Although there is an abundance of good-quality mid-range and budget options in the capital city of Tallinn, it is advisable to book well in advance, between April and September.

PRICE CATEGORIES
Price categories are for a standard double room per night in high season, including tax and service charges. Breakfast is included, unless otherwise specified.

Ⓚ Under 600 EEK
ⓀⓀ 600–900 EEK
ⓀⓀⓀ 900–1,200 EEK
ⓀⓀⓀⓀ 1,200–1,500 EEK
ⓀⓀⓀⓀⓀ Over 1,500 EEK

TALLINN

Hotel G9
P   ⓀⓀ
Gonsiori 9, 10117 **Tel** *626 7100* **Fax** *626 7100* **Rooms** *23*   **Map** *F1*

Located on the third floor of an office building, Hotel G9 offers decent, strikingly decorated rooms at good rates. Services are limited and there is no catering on site. However, it is only a 5-minute walk from the Old Town *(see pp100-1)* and is close to several restaurants, theatres, bars and casinos. **www.hotelg9.ee**

OldHouse Guesthouse
P   ⓀⓀ
Uus 22, 10111 **Tel** *641 1464* **Fax** *641 1664* **Rooms** *6*   **Map** *E2*

Well located in the Old Town, this excellent-value guesthouse has unusually nice rooms for this price range. There is a fine-dining room with a fireplace and the kitchen is open to guests for self-catering. The owners also have apartments for rent. Free parking is available. **www.oldhouse.ee**

Pirita Cloister Guesthouse
🍽 P 🚻   ⓀⓀⓀ
Merivalja 18, 11911 **Tel** *605 5000* **Fax** *640 5006* **Rooms** *20*   **Map** *F1*

Just 7 km (4 miles) from the city centre, this award-winning modern guesthouse lies close to the beach. All the rooms have an Internet connection and showers. Lunch and dinner have to be arranged in advance. Discounts are available from September to May.

Uniquestay
P 🍴 🖥 🚻   ⓀⓀⓀⓀ
Toompuiestee 23, 10137 **Tel** *660 0700* **Fax** *661 6176* **Rooms** *77*   **Map** *F1*

This elegant limestone building was built as a residence for a German baron. Its interior is warm and stylish, and the so-called Zen rooms and apartments come with NASA-designed gravity-free chairs. All rooms have flat-screen computers and digital safes. **www.uniquestay.com**

Schlössle
P 🍴 🖥 🚻   ⓀⓀⓀⓀⓀ
Pühavaimu 13/15, 10123 **Tel** *699 7700* **Fax** *699 7777* **Rooms** *24*   **Map** *D3*

This award-winning hotel fully deserves its five stars. The lavishly furnished rooms perfectly complement the splendid medieval-style interior, while the romantic restaurant is outstanding. Facilities include 24-hour room service, babysitting, limousine hire and a private sauna and massage service. **www.schlossle-hotels.com**

REST OF ESTONIA

PÄRNU Ammende Villa
P 🍴   ⓀⓀⓀⓀⓀ
Mere pst 7, 80010 **Tel** *447 3888* **Fax** *447 3887* **Rooms** *24*

A glorious Art Nouveau house, Ammende Villa *(see p109)* has been converted into a luxury hotel. The rooms are beautifully furnished in authentic period style, while the service is second to none. The hotel is close to the beach and a short walk from the Old Town. Car hire is available. **www.ammende.ee**

SAAREMAA ISLAND Georg Ots Spa Hotel
P 🍴 🏊 🖥 🚻   ⓀⓀⓀⓀⓀ
Tori 2, Kuressaare, 93815 **Tel** *455 0000* **Fax** *455 0001* **Rooms** *91*

The interior of this award-winning hotel is minimalist, yet remains warm and intimate. The swimming pool is a masterpiece of design and an excellent range of spa and beauty treatments is on offer as well as a great dining experience. The hotel is also close to all the main sights in Kuressaare. **www.gospa.ee**

TARTU Draakon
P 🍴 🖥 🚻   ⓀⓀⓀⓀ
Raekoja plats 4, 51003 **Tel** *744 2045* **Fax** *742 3000* **Rooms** *41*

Located right on Town Hall Square *(see p110)*, Draakon is a plush hotel mainly catering to businessmen and high-end visitors. All rooms have Internet connection, and suites come with their own saunas. There is an elegant Baroque-style restaurant and an atmospheric medieval-style beer cellar-restaurant. **www.draakon.ee/eng**

Where to Eat in Estonia

Estonia offers an impressive choice of dining options. Although traditional food is popular, visitors can sample everything from eclectic international cuisine to quality pizzas. An authentic Baltic meal may not be particularly subtle, but it is extremely tasty and portions are usually generous. Smoking is banned in restaurants and bars.

PRICE CATEGORIES
Based on the price per person of a three-course meal with half a bottle of wine, including cover charge, service and tax.

Ⓚ Under 100 EEK
ⓀⓀ 100–200 EEK
ⓀⓀⓀ 200–300 EEK
ⓀⓀⓀⓀ 300–400 EEK
ⓀⓀⓀⓀⓀ Over 400 EEK

TALLINN

African Kitchen
ⒶⓉⓋⓎ   ⓀⓀ

Uus 34, 10111 **Tel** 644 2555   **Map** E2

This restaurant's vibrant and lively interior is matched by the excellent food, which is the most authentic African cuisine in the Baltic States. African Kitchen is a hip, fun place to eat, with an impressively diverse menu of fresh, spicy and exotic fare.

Olde Hansa
ⒶⓉⓋⓎ   ⓀⓀⓀ

Vana turg 1, 10140 **Tel** 627 9020   **Map** D4

A tourist attraction in its own right, Olde Hansa is an immensely enjoyable experience. Huge traditional dishes are served by waiters in medieval costumes in a candlelit setting, while an ensemble plays live traditional music. The menu is reputed to be based on carefully researched recipes from medieval times.

Bocca
ⓋⓎ   ⓀⓀⓀⓀ

Olevimägi 9, 10123 **Tel** 641 2610   **Map** D2

Sleek and minimalist, Bocca is a favourite with Tallinn's trendy crowd. The suitably stylish menu includes some excellent pasta and fillet dishes, along with delicacies such as ravioli stuffed with lemon and cinnamon-flavoured ricotta and grilled lamb with herbs and blackberry sauce. The lighting is wonderfully atmospheric.

Gloria
ⒶⓉⓎ   ⓀⓀⓀⓀ

Müürivahe 2 **Tel** 644 6950   **Map** C4

Opened in 1937, Gloria has a very stylish 1930s European interior decorated with Art Nouveau originals and artifacts from the private collection of the owner, Dimitri Demjanov. Service is attentive, and customers can enjoy fantastic wine from Gloria's own cellar as well as Cuban cigars.

Three Sisters Restaurant
ⓉⓋⓎ   ⓀⓀⓀⓀⓀ

Pikk 71/Tolli 2, 10133 **Tel** 630 6300   **Map** E1

One of the most luxurious restaurants in Tallinn, Three Sisters simply oozes opulence. The food is excellent and can be enjoyed on the terrace or in the charming courtyard in summer, while the wine cellar stores over 300 wines. The private Angels Room has an 18th-century ceiling fresco.

REST OF ESTONIA

PÄRNU Postipoiss
♿ⒶⓉ   ⓀⓀ

Vee 12, 80011 **Tel** 446 4864

This restaurant offers an authentic taste of Russia, with everything from *blini* (pancakes) and *pelmeni* (dumplings) to *solianka* (Russian beef soup), and decent home-made beer to wash it down. Weekend nights are usually very lively, belying the quaint, rustic interior.

SAAREMAA ISLAND Grand Rose Spa Hotel
⬛♿ⓋⓎ   ⓀⓀⓀⓀ

Tallinna 15, 93811 **Tel** 666 7000

This hotel's cosy cellar-restaurant is one of the best places to eat on the island. Its partitioned rooms and arched brick ceiling provide an intimate setting, and there is an atmospheric, medieval-style feel to the place. The excellent menu includes some local Saaremaa specialities.

TARTU Kalinka
ⒶⓉⓋ   ⓀⓀⓀ

Ülikooli 10, 51003 **Tel** 730 5997

This establishment offers authentic Russian and Slavic cuisine in a friendly tavern-style setting. All the staple Russian classics are on the menu, which features several dishes named after Russian presidents – Putin Soljanka, for example. **www.tavernkalinka.ee**

Key to Symbols *see back cover flap*

MOSCOW AND ST PETERSBURG

*F*rom her 12th-century origins as an obscure defensive outpost, Moscow has come to govern one sixth of the globe. The story of her rise is laced with glory and setbacks, including the two centuries when St Petersburg was the capital of Russia and Moscow lived as a dignified dowager. Today, both cities symbolize the "New Russia".

The Russian Federation, or Russia as it is commonly known, stretches from the Baltic to the Pacific and is the world's largest country. Moscow, the capital, lies at the heart of European Russia, while St Petersburg is situated at its northwest corner. Till the end of 1991, Russia was part of the Soviet Union, but Mikhail Gorbachev's policies of glasnost (openness) and perestroika (restructuring) led to changes that saw the end of the USSR. There have been social problems over the years, however the standard of living is improving. Today, Russia is a member of the CIS, a commonwealth of former Soviet republics.

HISTORY

First mentioned in the *Ipatievskaya Chronicles* of 1147, when Kiev was the capital of Russia, Moscow has endured wars, revolutions and drastic social changes. Over four centuries it was transformed from an isolated kremlin (fortress), built in 1156, into a thriving capital. Ironically, Moscow's pre-eminence in Russia came about as a result of the 250-year domination by the Mongols, who invaded in 1137. In the 14th century they chose Moscow's grand prince, Ivan I, to collect tribute from subjugated principalities. However, this sealed their fate and they were defeated in the

The ornate interior of the Church on Spilled Blood, St Petersburg

◁ Monument to Minin and Pozharskiy near St Basil's Cathedral in Red Square, Moscow

Painting of Lenin leading the Russian Revolution, 1917

Battle of Kulikovo (1380), and the Russian nation was reborn. During the long reign of Ivan III the Great (r. 1462–1505), Moscow's prestige increased and continued under his grandson Ivan the Terrible (r. 1533–84), the first to be called "Tsar of All the Russias". Yet, his reign ended in disaster, leading to the so-called Time of Troubles. To end this strife, in 1613, Moscow's citizens chose Mikhail Romanov to be tsar, thus initiating the 300-year Romanov rule. His grandson, Peter the Great, transformed medieval Russia into a modern European state.

He built the city of St Petersburg and declared it the capital in 1712. For most of the 18th century Russia was ruled by women, of whom the most significant was Catherine II.

Napoleon's unsuccessful invasion of Moscow in 1812 and his defeat turned Russia into a major European power. Towards the end of the century, however, the country was on the verge of breakdown. Economic unrest and the urgent need for social reform led to the 1905 Revolution. The outbreak of World War I brought about a surge of patriotism, but wartime losses provoked a series of strikes, the tsar's abdication and the establishment of a provisional government. This was the signal for exiled revolutionaries, such as Vladimir Ilyich Lenin, to organize an uprising in October 1917, heralding more than 70 years of Soviet rule. In 1918, Moscow was reinstated as the capital of the country.

The Germans invaded the Soviet Union in 1941, subjecting St Petersburg (then Leningrad) to a 900-day siege, but Moscow was never taken; Hitler had underestimated both the harshness of the Russian winter and the willingness of the people to fight.

The USSR ceased to exist in 1991. Since then, Russia has tried to reinvent itself as a modern democratic nation. Vladimir Putin succeeded Boris Yeltsin as president in 2000. In 2008, after two terms as president, Putin became prime minister.

KEY DATES IN RUSSIAN HISTORY

863 Missionaries Cyril and Methodius create the Cyrillic alphabet

1147 Moscow is founded

1380 Mongols defeated at the Battle of Kulikovo

1613 Mikhail Romanov becomes first tsar of the Romanov Dynasty

1682 Peter the Great ascends the throne

1703 St Petersburg is founded

1712 Seat of government moves to St Petersburg

1762 Catherine II seizes the throne

1812 Napoleon invades Moscow but has to retreat

1861 Emancipation of serfs

1906 Inauguration of the Duma (parliament)

1917 The Russian Revolution

1918 Civil War starts. Capital moves to Moscow

1953 Death of Stalin

1991 Dissolution of the USSR

1955 Warsaw Pact is established

2000 Putin becomes President of Russia

2008 Medvedev elected president of Russia

LANGUAGE AND CULTURE

Russian is the official language of the people of Moscow and St Petersburg and Cyrillic is the alphabet used. Classical music is the central theme of a large number of festivals attracting performers from all over the world. Christmas masquerades and the Spas Yablochni Medovy harvest celebration are some of the folk festivals.

Exploring Moscow and St Petersburg

The city of Moscow offers a wide variety of sights, ranging from the historic and architectural treasures enclosed within the walls of the Kremlin, to galleries housing spectacular collections of Russian and Western art. Public transport in Moscow is abundant and efficient and an ideal way to explore the city. St Petersburg's short history is reflected in many of its museums such as the Hermitage, which displays Catherine the Great's fine art collection. The most enjoyable way to get around St Petersburg is on foot.

Engraved doors in St Isaac's Cathedral, St Petersburg

SIGHTS AT A GLANCE

Moscow pp122–37 **1**
St Petersburg pp138–55 **2**

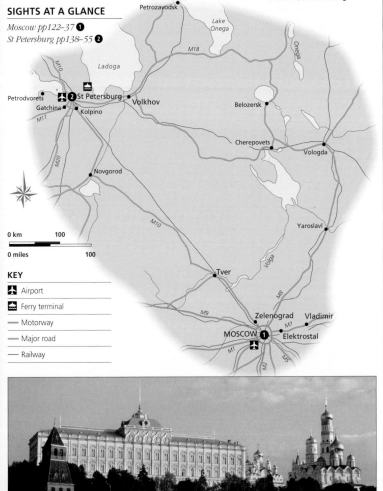

KEY

✈ Airport

⛴ Ferry terminal

— Motorway

— Major road

— Railway

Great Kremlin Palace viewed from the Kremlin embankment, Moscow

Moscow ➊

With a population of over ten million, the Russian capital is now a place where past and present combine to captivate and charm. Most of Moscow's sights are situated in the city centre, within the area bounded by the Garden Ring (Sadovoye Koltso) and the Boulevard Ring (Bulvarnoye Koltso). From the gleaming onion domes of its churches to the graves of Soviet heroes, reminders of the city's past appear in almost every corner. At the heart of the city lies the Kremlin – a source of wealth and power that has dominated Russian life for over 800 years – comprising an impressive complex of buildings from the 15th to the 20th centuries.

Sixteenth-century frescoes in the Cathedral of the Assumption

SIGHTS AT A GLANCE

Cathedral of Christ
  the Redeemer ⑮
Cathedral of the Annunciation ⑤
Cathedral of the Archangel ④
Cathedral of the Assumption ③
Gorky Park ⑰
GUM ⑪
Ivan the Great Bell Tower ②
Lenin Mausoleum ⑨
Melnikov House ⑫
Novodevichiy Convent ⑱
Pushkin House-Museum ⑬
Pushkin Museum of
  Fine Arts ⑭
Red Square ⑧
Resurrection Gate ⑦
St Basil's Cathedral pp130–31 ⑩
State Armoury ⑥
Tretyakov Gallery pp136–7 ⑯
Trinity Tower ①

Ivan the Great Bell Tower, with the Tsar Bell in the foreground

SEE ALSO

• *Where to Stay* pp160–61

• *Where to Eat* pp162–3

GETTING AROUND

Moscow's centre is quite spread out and not easily covered on foot. However, the area within the Boulevard Ring contains many sights and is good for walking. The city's vast metro network is the most reliable way of getting around, and trolley-buses are a good option in the city centre. Taxis are the most flexible, but the most expensive way of getting around. River cruises are pleasant and pass several major sites of interest.

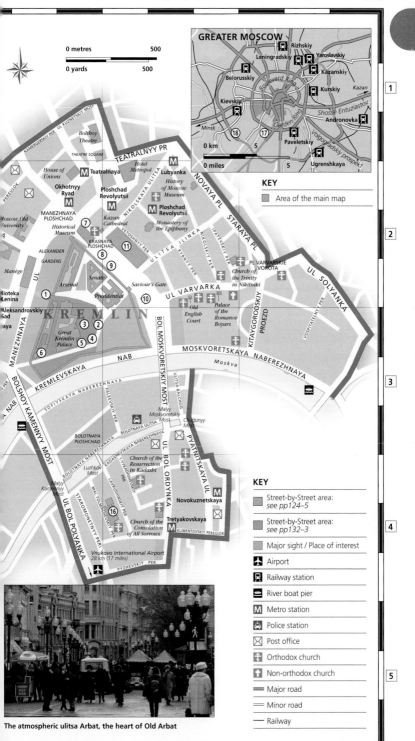

0 metres 500
0 yards 500

GREATER MOSCOW

Rizhskiy
Leningradskiy
Yaroslavskiy
Belorusskiy
Kazanskiy
Kurskiy
Kievskiy
Boulevard Ring
Minsk
Garden Ring
Kazan
Shosse Entuziastov
Andronovka
18
17
Paveletskiy
Volgogradskiy prospekt
Ugreshskaya

0 km 5
0 miles 5

KEY

- Area of the main map

Bolshoy
Theatre
THEATRE SQUARE
TEATRALNYY PR
House of
Unions
Teatralnaya
Hotel
Metropol
Lubyanka
Okhotnyy
Ryad
Ploshchad
Revolyutsii
History
of Moscow
Museum
NOVAYA PL
STARAYA PL
Moscow Old
University
MANEZHNAYA
PLOSHCHAD
Historical
Museum
Kazan
Cathedral
Ploshchad
Revolyutsii
Monastery of
the Epiphany
ULITSA ILINKA
ALEXANDER
GARDENS
KRASNAYA
PLOSHCHAD
PL VARVARSKIE
VOROTA
Church
of the Trinity
in Nikitniki
UL SOLYANKA
Manège
Arsenal
Senate
Presidential
Saviour's Gate
UL VARVARKA
Old
English
Court
Palace
of the
Romanov
Boyars
KITAYGORODSKIY
PROEZD
Biblioteka
Lenina
KREMLIN
Great
Kremlin
Palace
Presidential
MANEZHNAYA
Aleksandrovskiy
Sad
BOLSHOY KAMENNYY MOST
KREMLEVSKAYA
NAB
BOL MOSKVORETSKIY MOST
Moskva
MOSKVORETSKAYA NABEREZHNAYA
SOFIYSKAYA NABEREZHNAYA
BOLOTNAYA
PLOSHCHAD
Luzhkov
Most
Malyy
Moskvoretskiy
Most
Chugunyy
Most
ULITSA BALCHUG
PYATNITSKAYA UL
Malyy
Kamennyy
Most
UL BOL POLYANKA
BOLOTNAYA ULITSA
Church of the
Resurrection
in Kadashi
UL BOL ORDYNKA
Novokuznetskaya
Church of the
Consolation
of All Sorrows
Tretyakovskaya
KLIMENTOVSKIY PEREULOK
Vnukovo International Airport
28 km (17 miles)
PYZHEVSKIY PER
UL BOL POLYANKA
STAROMONETNYY PER

KEY

	Street-by-Street area: see pp124–5
	Street-by-Street area: see pp132–3
	Major sight / Place of interest
✈	Airport
🚆	Railway station
⛴	River boat pier
M	Metro station
🚓	Police station
⊠	Post office
✚	Orthodox church
✝	Non-orthodox church
—	Major road
—	Minor road
—	Railway

The atmospheric ulitsa Arbat, the heart of Old Arbat

D E F

Street-by-Street: The Kremlin

The Kremlin is home to the Russian president and the
seat of his administration. As a result less than half of it is
accessible to the public, but highlights including the State
Armoury, the Patriarch's Palace and the churches in Cathedral
Square (Ivanovskaya ploshchad) are open to visitors. Christians
have worshipped on this site for more than eight centuries,
but their early stone churches were demolished in the 1470s
to make way for the present magnificent ensemble of cathedrals. In imperial times, these were the setting for great state
occasions such as coronations, baptisms and burials.

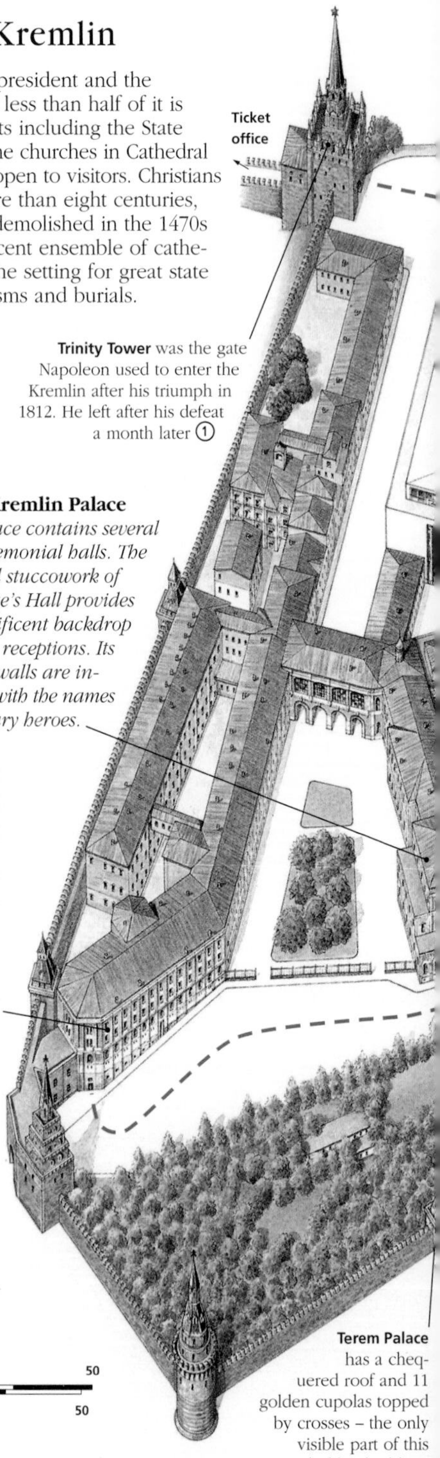

Ticket office

Trinity Tower was the gate
Napoleon used to enter the
Kremlin after his triumph in
1812. He left after his defeat
a month later ①

Great Kremlin Palace
*The palace contains several
vast ceremonial halls. The
splendid stuccowork of
St George's Hall provides
a magnificent backdrop
for state receptions. Its
marble walls are in-
scribed with the names
of military heroes.*

★ State Armoury
*The State Armoury was designed to
complement the Great Kremlin Palace.
Constructed in the 19th century, it is
now a museum. It houses the imperial
collections of decorative and applied
art and the State Diamond Fund* ⑥

KEY

– – – Suggested route

STAR SIGHTS

★ State Armoury

★ Cathedral of
the Assumption

0 metres 50

0 yards 50

Terem Palace
has a cheq-
uered roof and 11
golden cupolas topped
by crosses – the only
visible part of this
hidden building.

Patriarch's Palace
An imposing palace, rebuilt for Patriarch Nikon between 1652 and 1666, now houses the Museum of 17th-century Life and Applied Art.

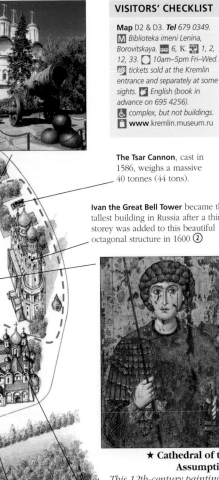

The Tsar Cannon, cast in 1586, weighs a massive 40 tonnes (44 tons).

Ivan the Great Bell Tower became the tallest building in Russia after a third storey was added to this beautiful octagonal structure in 1600 ②

★ **Cathedral of the Assumption**
This 12th-century painting of St George the Warrior is one of the oldest surviving Russian icons. It forms part of the iconostasis in the cathedral's richly decorated interior ③

Cathedral Square

Faceted Palace was constructed by two Italian architects, Marco Ruffo and Pietro Solario, between 1485 and 1491.

Cathedral of the Archangel has many elaborate tombs including that of Tsarevich Dmitry, son of Ivan the Terrible, who died as a child in 1591 ④

Cathedral of the Annunciation
Frescoes cover the walls and ceiling of this cathedral. In the dome above the iconostasis is a painting of Christ Pantocrator, above tiers of pictures of angels, prophets and patriarchs ⑤

The striking red-brick Trinity Tower, with its contrasting conical spire

Trinity Tower ①

Троицкая башня
Troitskaya bashnya

The Kremlin. **Map** D2.

This tower takes its name from the Trinity Monastery of St Sergius, which once ran a mission nearby. The tower's Trinity Gate used to be the entrance for patriarchs and the tsars' wives and daughters. It is one of the only two towers – the other being Borovitskaya Tower, to the southwest – of the Kremlin walls' 19 towers that admit visitors into the complex.

At 76 m (249 ft), the seven-storey Trinity Tower is the Kremlin's tallest. It was built between 1495 and 1499 and in 1516 it was linked by a bridge over the Neglinnaya river to the Kutafya Tower. The river now runs underground and the Kutafya Tower is the sole survivor of the circle of towers that were originally built to defend the Kremlin walls.

In September 1812, Napoleon triumphantly marched his army into the Kremlin through the Trinity Gate. They left just a month later when Muscovites set fire to their city and fled, leaving the French Army without shelter or provisions.

Ivan the Great Bell Tower ②

Колокольня Ивана Великого
Kolokolnya Ivana Velikovo

The Kremlin. **Map** D3.

Built to a design by Marco Bon Friazin, the 16th-century bell tower takes its name from the Church of St Ivan Climacus, which stood on the site in the 14th century. The "Great" in its name is derived from the height of the tower. In 1600 it became the tallest building in Moscow when Tsar Boris Godunov added a third storey, extending it to 81m (266 ft). The 16th-century four-storey Assumption Belfry was built beside the bell tower by Petrok Maliy. It holds 21 bells, the largest of which is the 64-tonne (71-tons) Assumption Bell. A museum on the first floor displays the story of the Kremlin. The annexe next to the belfry was commissioned in 1642 by Patriarch Filaret. Outside the bell tower is the **Tsar Bell**. The largest in the world, it weighs over 200 tonnes (221 tons). When it fell from the tower and shattered in a fire in 1701, the fragments were used in a bell ordered by Tsarina Anna. This bell was still in its casting pit when the Kremlin caught fire in 1737. As a result, a large piece broke off as water was poured over the bell.

Frescoes on the entrance to the Cathedral of the Assumption

Cathedral of the Assumption ③

Успенский собор
Uspenskiy sobor

The Kremlin. **Map** D3.

From the early 14th century, the Cathedral of the Assumption was Moscow's most important church, where princes were crowned and the metropolitans and patriarchs of the Orthodox church buried. In the 1470s, Ivan the Great decided to build a more imposing cathedral and summoned Italian architect Aristotele Fioravanti to Moscow. Inspired by the spirit of the Renaissance, the cathedral is a spacious masterpiece. It houses superb iconostasis and frescoes, including *Scenes from the Life of Metropolitan*

The Tsar Bell, with the hole left by the section that broke off

Peter by the famous 15th-century artist, Dionysius, painted on the southern wall of the cathedral.

Cathedral of the Archangel ④

Архангельский собор
Arkhangelskiy sobor

The Kremlin. **Map** D3.

This was the last of the great cathedrals to be built in the Kremlin. Commissioned by Ivan III and designed by Aleviz Novy in 1505, it is a combination of early-Russian and Renaissance architecture.

This site was the burial place for Moscow's princes and tsars from 1340. The tombs of the tsars, white stone sarcophagi with bronze covers inscribed in Old Slavonic, are in the nave. The tsars, with the exception of Peter II, who died in 1730, were no longer buried here after the capital was moved to St Petersburg in 1712. The walls, pillars and domes of the cathedral are covered with spectacular frescoes painted by a team of artists led by Semen Ushakov, the head of the icon workshop in the State Armoury.

There are more than 60 full-length portraits of Russian rulers and a few striking images of the Archangel Michael, the protector of the rulers of early Moscow. The cathedral's four-tiered iconostasis was constructed between 1680 and 1681, but the Icon of the Archangel Michael on the lowest tier dates from the 14th century.

Cathedral of the Annunciation ⑤

Благовещенский собор
Blagoveshchenskiy sobor

The Kremlin. **Map** D3.

Unlike the other cathedrals in the Kremlin, which were created by Italian architects, the Cathedral of the Annunciation is a wholly Russian affair. Commissioned by Ivan III in 1484 as a royal

Tiers of frescoes on the central cupola of the Cathedral of the Archangel

chapel, it stands beside the Faceted Palace, which is all that remains of a large palace built for Ivan III. The cathedral, built by architects from Pskov, had three domes and open galleries on all sides but, after a fire in 1547, the corner chapels were added and the galleries enclosed. On the south façade is the Groznenskiy Porch, added by Ivan the Terrible *(see p120)* when he contravened church law by marrying for the fourth time in 1572. Barred from attending religious services, he could only watch through a grille in the porch.

The interior of the cathedral is painted with frescoes. The artwork around the iconostasis was painted in 1508 by the monk Feodosius, son of the icon painter Dionysius. The warm colours of the frescoes create an atmosphere of intimacy and the vertical thrust of the pillars draws the eye

The Cathedral of the Annunciation, crowned by golden onion domes

upwards to the cupola and its awe-inspiring painting of Christ Pantocrator. Three of the greatest masters of icon painting in Russia contributed to the iconostasis. Theophanes the Greek painted the images of Christ, the Virgin and the Archangel Gabriel in the Deesis Tier, while the Icon of the Archangel Michael on this tier is attributed to Andrey Rublev. Several of the icons in the Festival Tier were also painted by Rublev. Most of the other icons in this tier are the work of Prokhor Gorodetskiy.

State Armoury ⑥

Оружейная палата
Oruzheinaya palata

The Kremlin. **Map** D3.

The collection of the State Armoury represents the wealth accumulated by Russian princes and tsars over many centuries. The first written mention of a state armoury occurs in 1508, but there were forges in the Kremlin as early as the 13th century. Later, gold- and silver-smiths, workshops producing icons and embroidery, and the Office of the Royal Stables all moved into the Kremlin. The original armoury was demolished in 1960 to make way for the State Kremlin Palace. The current State Armoury was built as a museum by Tsar Nicholas I (r. 1825–55). It was designed by Konstantin Ton in 1844 and completed in 1851. It is home to the State Diamond Fund.

Resurrection Gate ⑦

Воскресенские ворота
Voskresenskie vorota

Krasnaya ploshchad. **Map** D2.
M *Okhotnyy Ryad, Ploshchad Revolyutsii.*

Rebuilt in 1995, this gateway, with its red twin towers topped by green tent spires, is an exact copy of the original completed on this site in 1680. The first gateway was demolished in 1931 on Stalin's orders. There are mosaic icons on the gate, one of which depicts Moscow's patron saint, St George, slaying a dragon.

Within the gateway is the equally colourful **Chapel of the Iverian Virgin**, originally built in the late 18th century to house an icon. Whenever the tsar came to Moscow, he would visit this shrine before entering the Kremlin *(see pp124–5)*. Visitors should try to see the gate at night, when it is impressively lit up.

The vast expanse of Red Square, with the Historical Museum at the far end

Resurrection Gate, housing the Chapel of the Iverian Virgin

Red Square ⑧

Красная площадь
Krasnaya ploshchad

Map E2. **M** *Ploshchad Revolyutsii, Okhotnyy Ryad.* **Historical Museum**
Tel 692 4019. ◯ *11am–6pm Mon, Wed–Sat, 11am–8pm Sun.* ▨ ▣
♿ ▣

Towards the end of the 15th century, Ivan III gave orders for houses in front of the Kremlin to be cleared to make way for this square. It

originally served as a market, locally called the *torg*, but the wooden stalls burnt down so often that the area later became popularly known as Fire Square. The current name dates from the 17th century and is derived from the Russian word *krasnyy*, which originally meant "beautiful" but later came to denote "red". The association between the colour red and Communism is coincidental.

Red Square, which is almost 500 m (1,600 ft) in length, was also the setting for public announcements and executions. At its southern end, in front of St Basil's Cathedral *(see pp130–31)*, there is a small circular dais. Called **Lobnoe Mesto**, this is the platform from which the tsars and patriarchs would address the people. In 1606 the first "False Dmitry", a usurper of the throne, was killed by a hostile crowd. His body was finally left at Lobnoe Mesto. Six years later, a second pretender to the throne, who like the first "False Dmitry" was backed by Poland, took power. He was expelled from the Kremlin by an army led by the Russian heroes Dmitriy Pozharskiy and Kuzma Minin, who proclaimed Russia's deliverance at Lobnoe Mesto. In 1818, a statue was erected in their honour which now stands in front of St Basil's.

Red Square has also long been a stage for pageants and processions. Before the 1917 Revolution, the patriarch would ride a horse dressed like a donkey through Saviour's Gate to St Basil's

each Palm Sunday to commemorate Christ's entry into Jerusalem. Religious processions were abolished in the Communist era. Military parades took their place and were staged each year on May Day and on the anniversary of the Revolution. Rows of grim-faced Soviet leaders observed them from outside the Lenin Mausoleum. They, in turn, would be keenly studied by professional kremlinologists in the West trying to work out the current pecking order.

Today, the square is used for a variety of concerts, firework displays and cultural events. The red-brick building facing St Basil's Cathedral was constructed by Vladimir Sherwood in 1883 in the Russian-Revival style. It houses the **Historical Museum**, which boasts over four million exhibits covering the rise and expansion of the Russian state. In front of the

Lobnoe Mesto, the platform from which the tsars would speak

museum on Manezhnaya ploshchad is a statue of Marshal Georgiy Zhukov, one of the heroes of World War II. This statue, sculpted by Vyacheslav Klykov (1939–2006), was unveiled in 1995 to mark the 50th anniversary of the end of World War II.

Lenin Mausoleum ⑨

Мавзолей В.И. Ленина
Mavzoley V.I. Lenina

Krasnaya ploshchad. **Map** E2.
Tel 623 5527. Ⓜ *Ploshchad Revolyutsii, Okhotnyy Ryad.* ◯ *10am–1pm Tue–Thu, Sat–Sun.* ⌀

Following Lenin's death in 1924, and against his wishes, it was decided to preserve the former Soviet leader's body for posterity. The body was embalmed and placed in a temporary wooden mausoleum in Red Square. Once it became clear that the embalming process had worked, Soviet architect Aleksey Shchusev designed the current mausoleum as a pyramid of cubes cut from red granite and black labradorite.

Paying one's respects to Lenin's remains was once akin to a religious experience, and queues used to trail all over Red Square. In 1993, however, the goose-stepping guard of honour was replaced by a lone militiaman and now the mausoleum attracts mostly tourists. There are rumours that Lenin's body will soon be moved elsewhere or buried.

Behind the mausoleum, at the foot of the Kremlin Wall, are the graves of other famous Communists. They include Lenin's successors, Joseph Stalin, who at one time was laid beside Lenin in the mausoleum, Leonid Brezhnev and Yuriy Andropov. Lenin's wife and sister are also buried here, as are the first man in space, Yuriy Gagarin, writer Maxim Gorky and American journalist John Reed. The latter was honoured as the author of *Ten Days that Shook the World*, published in 1919, an account of the October Revolution, when Bolshevik forces took control of St Petersburg.

Lenin Mausoleum, just outside the walls of the Kremlin

St Basil's Cathedral ⑩

Собор Василия Блаженного
Sobor Vasiliya Blazhennovo

See pp130–31.

GUM ⑪

ГУМ
GUM

Krasnaya ploshchad 3. **Map** E2.
Tel 788 4343. Ⓜ *Ploshchad Revolyutsii, Okhotnyy Ryad.* ◯ *10am–10pm daily.* ♿ **www.**gum.ru

Before the 1917 Revolution, this building was known as the Upper Trading Rows after the covered market that used to stand on the site. In fact,

lines of stalls used to run all the way from here to the Moskva river. GUM has three separate arcades, which are still called "lines". The store's name, Gosudarstvennyy Universalnyy Magazin, dates from its nationalization in 1921. The glass-roofed structure is considered the largest department store in Russia. The building was designed by Aleksandr Pomerantsev between 1889 and 1893 in the fashionable Russian-Revival style. Its archways, wrought-iron railings and stuccoed galleries inside are especially impressive when sunlight streams through the glass roof.

There were once more than 1,000 shops located in GUM, selling goods ranging from furs and silks to items of everyday use such as candles. For a period, however, during the rule of Stalin starting from 1924 and ending only with his death in 1953, GUM's shops were requisitioned as offices. Nowadays, Western brands such as Benetton, Estée Lauder and Christian Dior dominate the prestigious ground floor along with a variety of Western-style cafés and restaurants, and even a bank's branch.

The glass-roofed interior of Russia's largest department store, GUM

St Basil's Cathedral ⑩

Собор Василия Блаженного
Sobor Vasiliya Blazhennovo

Bell Tower

Chapel of the Trinity

Detail, Chapel of the Entry of Christ into Jerusalem

Commissioned by Ivan the Terrible to mark the capture of the Mongol stronghold of Kazan in 1552 and completed in 1561, this cathedral is reputed to have been designed by Postnik Yakovlev. According to legend, Ivan had him blinded so he could never design anything as exquisite again. Officially, it was called the Cathedral of the Intercession since the final siege of Kazan began on the Feast of the Intercession of the Virgin. However, it gets its popular name from the "holy fool" Basil the Blessed whose remains are interred here. Its design was inspired by Russian timber architecture and is a riot of gables, roofs and domes.

★ Domes

Destroyed by fire in 1583, these multi-faceted onion domes replaced the original helmet-shaped cupolas. The domes have been colourfully painted since 1670, but at one time St Basil's was white with golden domes.

Chapel of St Cyprian

This is one of eight main chapels com-memorating the campaigns of Ivan the Terrible against the town of Kazan, east of Moscow. It is dedicated to St Cyprian.

MININ AND POZHARSKIY

This statue by Ivan Martos depicts two heroes from the Time of Troubles (1598–1613), Kuzma Minin and Prince Dmitriy Pozharskiy who raised a force to defeat the invading Poles in 1612. The stat-ue was erected in 1818 and originally placed in the centre of the Red Square facing the Kremlin. It was moved in front of St Basil's during the Soviet era.

Monument to Minin and Prince Pozharskiy

The Chapel of St Basil

Entrance to the cathedral

Chapel of the Three Patriarchs

STAR FEATURES

★ Domes

★ Main Iconostasis

★ Gallery

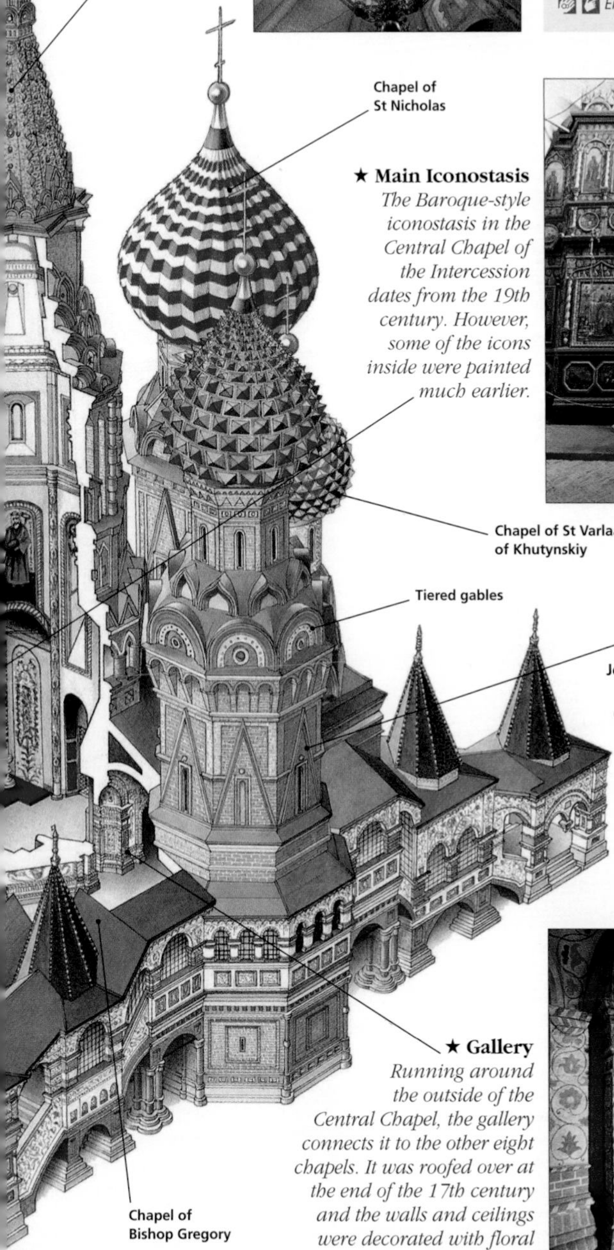

Central Chapel of the Intercession
Light floods in through the windows of the 61-m (200-ft) high tent-roofed central church.

VISITORS' CHECKLIST

Krasnaya ploshchad 2. **Map** E2.
Tel 698 3304. Ⓜ *Okhotnyy Ryad, Ploschad Revolyutsii.* 🚌 25. 🚋 8. 🕆 *religious hols.*
🕐 *May–Nov: 11am–6pm Wed–Mon; Dec–Apr: 11am–5pm daily.*
📷 👍 *English.* **www**.shm.ru

Chapel of St Nicholas

★ Main Iconostasis
The Baroque-style iconostasis in the Central Chapel of the Intercession dates from the 19th century. However, some of the icons inside were painted much earlier.

Chapel of St Varlaam of Khutynskiy

Tiered gables

The Chapel of the Entry of Christ into Jerusalem was used as a ceremonial entrance during the annual Palm Sunday procession. On this day the patriarch rode from the Kremlin to St Basil's Cathedral on a horse dressed up to look like a donkey.

Chapel of Bishop Gregory

★ Gallery
Running around the outside of the Central Chapel, the gallery connects it to the other eight chapels. It was roofed over at the end of the 17th century and the walls and ceilings were decorated with floral tiles in the late 18th century.

Street-by-Street: Old Arbat

In the 19th century, Old Arbat was the haunt of artists, musicians, poets, writers and intellectuals. Some of their homes have been preserved and opened as museums, and are among the district's many houses of that era that have been restored and painted in pastel shades of blue, green and ochre. At the heart of Old Arbat is the pedestrianized ulitsa Arbat. It is lined with antique shops, boutiques, souvenir stalls, pavement cafés and a variety of restaurants – from pizzerias and hamburger joints to traditional Russian pubs. Today, pavement artists, buskers and street poets give it a renewed bohemian atmosphere.

Spaso House
is a grand Neo-Classical mansion. It has been the residence of the US ambassador since 1933.

This small garden
contains a statue of Alexander Pushkin.

Novyy Arbat ↑

★ Pushkin House-Museum
The poet Alexander Pushkin lived here just after his marriage in 1831. The interior of the house has been carefully renovated ⑬

PEREULOK KAMENNOY SLOBODY

SPASOPESK PEREULOK

KARMANITSKIY PEREULOK

Ulitsa Arbat
This 19th-century street was pedestrianized in 1985. Its lively shops, restaurants and cafés are now popular with Muscovites and visitors to the city alike.

DENEZHNYY PEREULOK

Bely House-Museum
Andrei Bely, best known for two works – a novel, Petersburg, *and his memoirs – lived in this flat for the first 26 years of his life. It is now a museum and the exhibits on display include this photo of Bely with his wife and his fascinating Symbolist illustration,* Line of Life.

Georgian Centre

The Foreign Ministry
is one of the seven Stalinist-Gothic skyscrapers in Moscow.

Spasopeskovskiy Pereulok

On one side of this lane is the 18th-century Church of the Saviour on the Sands. It overlooks a secluded square and garden, a reminder that the Arbat was at that time a genteel suburb.

BOLSHOY NIKOLOPESKOVSKIY PEREULOK

Arbat Square

ULITSA ARBAT

KALOSHIN PEREULOK

Pushkin Museum of Fine Arts

★ Skryabin House-Museum

This apartment has been preserved as it was between 1912 and 1915 when experimental composer Aleksandr Skryabin (1872–1915) lived here. The furniture in the rooms is Style Moderne and the lighting is dim, since Skryabin disliked direct light.

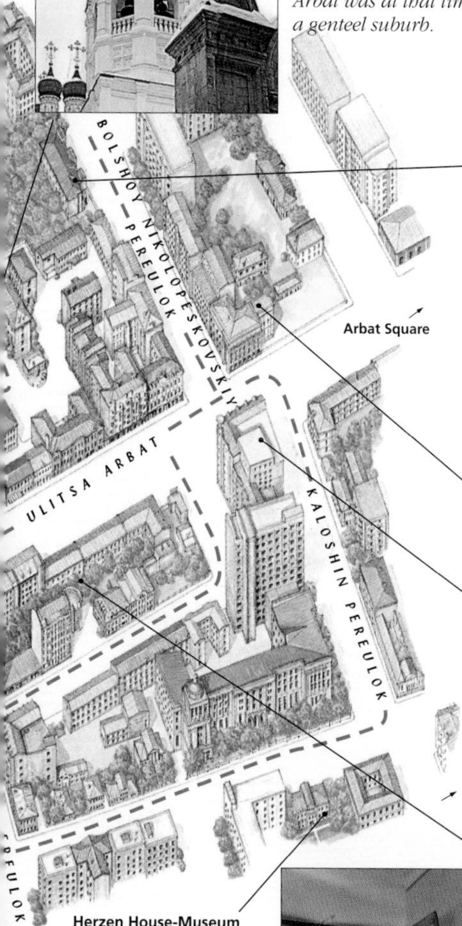

The Vakhtangov Theatre was established here in 1921 by Yevgeniy Vakhtangov, one of Moscow's leading theatre directors. The current theatre building dates from 1947.

Pre-Revolution apartments, designed for wealthy Muscovites, are decorated with fanciful turrets and sculptures of knights.

0 metres 100
0 yards 100

KEY

— — — Suggested route

Herzen House-Museum was the home of the radical writer Aleksandr Herzen from 1843 to 1846.

STAR SIGHTS

★ Pushkin House-Museum

★ Skryabin House-Museum

Melnikov House

Built in the 1920s by Constructivist architect Konstantin Melnikov, who lived here until his death in 1974, this unusual cylindrical house is now dwarfed by the apartments on ulitsa Arbat ⑫

Melnikov House ⑫

Дом Мельникова
Dom Melnikova

Krivoarbatskiy pereulok 10. **Map** B3.
Ⓜ *Smolenskaya*.

This unique house was designed by Konstantin Melnikov (1890–1974), one of Russia's greatest Constructivist architects, in 1927. Made from brick overlaid with white stucco, the house consists of two interlocking cylinders. These are studded with rows of hexagonal windows, creating a curious honeycomb effect. A spiral staircase rises through the space where the cylinders overlap, linking the light, airy living spaces.

Melnikov's house was built for his family, but it was also to have been a prototype for future housing developments. However, his career was blighted when Stalin encouraged architects towards a new monumental style. In spite of this, Melnikov was one of the very few allowed to live in a privately built dwelling in central Moscow. His son, Viktor, had a studio in the house until his death in 2006.

Viktor Melnikov's light-filled art studio in the Melnikov House

Pushkin House-Museum ⑬

Музей-квартира А.С. Пушкина
Muzey-kvartira A.S. Pushkina

Ulitsa Arbat 53. **Map** B3. **Tel** 241
2246. Ⓜ *Smolenskaya*. ◯ *10am–
6pm Wed–Sun, 10am–9pm Thu.* 🚫 🅲 *English (book in advance)*.

Alexander Pushkin rented this elegant, blue and white Empire-style flat for the first three months of his marriage

to society beauty Natalya Goncharova. They were married in the Church of the Great Ascension on Bolshaya Nikitskaya ulitsa in February 1831. However, by May 1831 Pushkin had tired of Moscow, and the couple moved to St Petersburg, where a tragic fate awaited him. Gossip began to claim that Pushkin's brother-in-law, a French officer called d'Anthès, was making advances to Natalya. Upon receiving letters calling him "Grand Master to the Order of Cuckolds", Pushkin challenged d'Anthès to a duel, dying of his wounds two days later.

The ground floor exhibition gives an idea of what the city would have been like when Pushkin was growing up, before the Great Fire of 1812. Among the prints, lithographs and watercolours there are some unusual wax figures of a serf orchestra that belonged to the Goncharova family.

Pushkin and Natalya lived on the first floor. There are very few personal possessions here, although the poet's writing bureau and some family portraits are displayed. The atmosphere resembles a shrine more than a museum, an indication of the special place Pushkin has in the hearts of Russians.

Pushkin Museum of Fine Arts ⑭

Музей изобразительных искусств имени АС Пушкина
Muzey izobrazitelnykh iskusstv imeni A.S. Pushkina

Ulitsa Volkhonka 12. **Map** C3.
Tel 697 9578. Ⓜ *Kropotkinskaya.*
🚎 *1,2,16, 33.* ◯ *10am–7pm Tue–
Sun.* 🅲 🅲 🅿 🅲 *English.*
www.museum.ru/gmii

Founded in 1898, the Pushkin Museum of Fine Arts houses several excellent French Impressionist and Post-Impressionist paintings. These reflect the tastes of many private collectors, whose holdings were nationalized by the Soviet government. The most important of these belong to two outstanding connoisseurs, Sergey Shchukin

A portrait of Pushkin's wife, Natalya Goncharova

and Ivan Morozov. Shchukin had over 220 paintings by French artists, including Cezanne, and had also championed Matisse and Picasso when they were relatively unknown. Morozov also collected these two painters along with pictures by Renoir, Van Gogh and Gauguin. Highlights include *Nude* by Renoir, *The Great Buddha* by Gauguin and *Goldfish* by Matisse.

Following the collapse of the Soviet Union, the curators admitted that they had countless works of art hidden away for ideological reasons. Some of these are now on display, including paintings by Russian-born artists Vasily Kandinsky and Marc Chagall. There is an enviable collection of Old Masters and art from ancient civilizations, such as the Treasure of Troy display, with gold artifacts excavated from the famous city in the 1870s.

Cathedral of Christ the Redeemer ⑮

Храм Христа Спасителя
Khram Khrista Spasitelya

Ulitsa Volkhonka 15. **Map** C4.
Ⓜ *Kropotkinskaya*.

Rebuilding this cathedral, blown up on Stalin's orders in 1931, was the most ambitious construction project by the enterprising mayor of Moscow, Yuriy Luzhkov. The basic structure of the new cathedral was built between 1994 and 1997. Before this, the site was

Cathedral of Christ the Redeemer, rebuilt in the 1990s at huge cost

miles. With a floor area of 9,000 sq m (97,000 sq ft), it could accommodate more than 10,000 worshippers.

Tretyakov Gallery ⑯

Третьяковская галерея
Tretyakovskaya Galereya

See pp136–7.

Gorky Park ⑰

Парк культуры и отдыха
имени М. Горького
Park Kultury i otdykha imeni
M. Gorkovo

Krymskiy val 9. **Map** F1. **Tel** 237 0707. Ⓜ *Park Kultury, Oktyabrskaya.* ⬜ *10am–10pm daily (pleasure park open May–Oct).*

Moscow's most famous park is named in honour of the writer Maxim Gorky (1868–1936) and extends for more than 120 ha (297 acres) along the Moskva river. Opened in 1928 as the Park of Culture and Rest, it incorporates the Golitsyn Gardens, laid out by Matvey Kazakov (1738–1812) in the late 18th century, and a 19th-century pleasure park.

During the Soviet era, loudspeakers across the park delivered speeches by Communist leaders. The park was immortalized in the opening scenes of Michael Apted's film *Gorky Park*. However, due to the tense political climate of 1983, the

Five-tier iconostasis in the cathedral of Novodevichiy Convent

film was shot in Finland. Today, the highlights include fairground rides, woodland walks, boating lakes, a 10,000-seat outdoor theatre and, in winter, an ice rink.

Novodevichiy Convent ⑱

Новодевичий монастырь
Novodevichiy monastyr

Novodevichiy proezd 1. **Map** E1. **Tel** 246 8526. Ⓜ *Sportivnaya.* 🚌 *64, 132.* 🚊 *5, 15.* ⬜ *10am–5:30pm Wed–Mon.* 📷 *book in advance.* ♿ *grounds only.*

Considered one of the most beautiful of the semi-circle of fortified religious institutions to the south of Moscow, Novodevichiy Convent was founded by Basil III in 1524 to commemorate the capture of Smolensk from the Lithuanians. The Cathedral of the Virgin of Smolensk was built at this time though the five-tier iconostasis, frescoes and onion domes were added in the 17th century. Most of the other buildings were also added in the late 17th century by Peter the Great's half-sister, the Regent Sophia. In 1812, Napoleon's troops tried to blow up the convent but, according to one story, it was saved by the nuns. The cemetery here is the final resting place of several famous Russians, such as the writer Nikolai Gogol and the composer Dmitry Shostakovich.

used as a swimming pool. The rebuilding project was controversial from the start, on the grounds of taste and cost. In 1995 a presidential decree declared that no public money should be spent on it. Funds were to come via donations from the public, the Russian Church and foreign donors. Much of the US$200 million spent, however, came from the state budget, at a time when Muscovites were suffering extreme poverty.

The original cathedral was built to commemorate the deliverance of Moscow from Napoleon's Grande Armée in 1812. Begun in 1839, but not completed until 1883, it was designed by Konstantin Ton, who also designed the State Armoury. The cathedral was Moscow's tallest building then, the gilded dome rising to a height of 103 m (338 ft) and dominating the skyline for

Outdoor ice-skating in Gorky Park, a popular activity in the winter months

Tretyakov Gallery ⑯

Третьяковская галерея
Tretyakovskaya galereya

The gallery was founded in 1856 by Pavel Tretyakov, a wealthy merchant, who presented it to the city in 1892. It continued to expand after the Revolution as numerous private collections were nationalized. Today it has the largest collection of Russian art in the world – with more than 100,000 works on display. The building has a striking façade, with a bas-relief of St George and the dragon at its centre. A new wing was added in 1930. Many of the early 20th-century works are now in the New Tretyakov Gallery, an annexe to the main building.

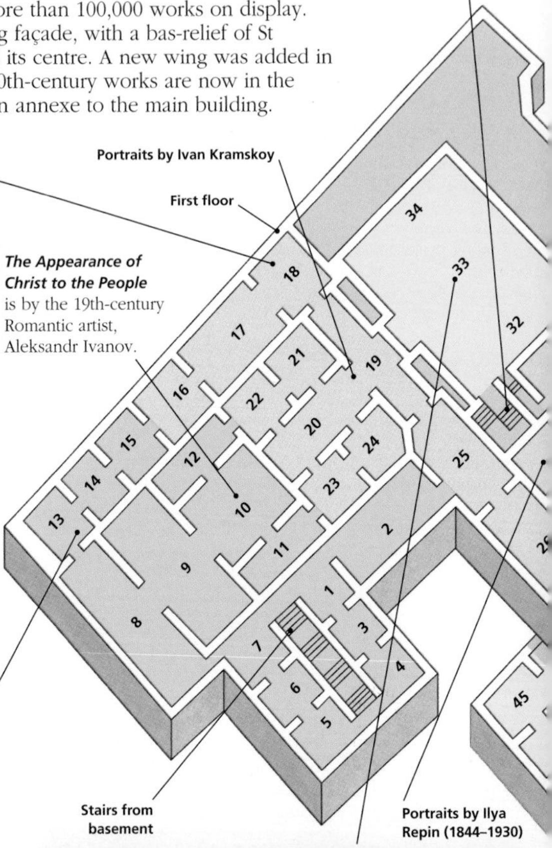
Stairs down to ground floor
Portraits by Ivan Kramskoy
First floor
Stairs from basement
Portraits by Ilya Repin (1844–1930)
1
2
3
4
5
6
7
8
9
10
11
12
13
14
15
16
17
18
19
20
21
22
23
24
25
32
33
34
45

The Appearance of Christ to the People is by the 19th-century Romantic artist, Aleksandr Ivanov.

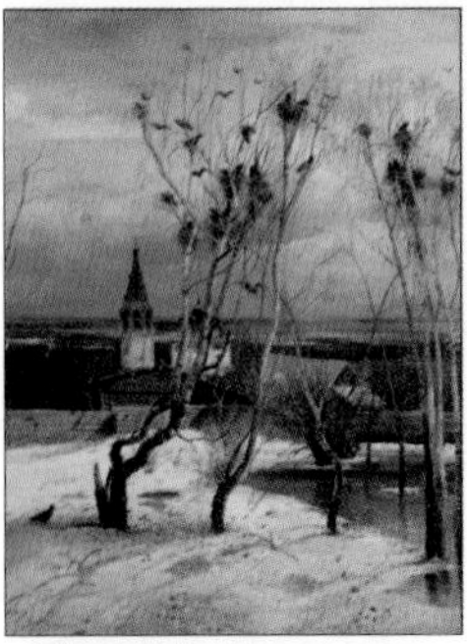

The Rooks Have Come (1871)
This bleak winter scene by Aleksey Savrasov contains a message of hope – rooks are taken by Russians as a sign of the coming spring.

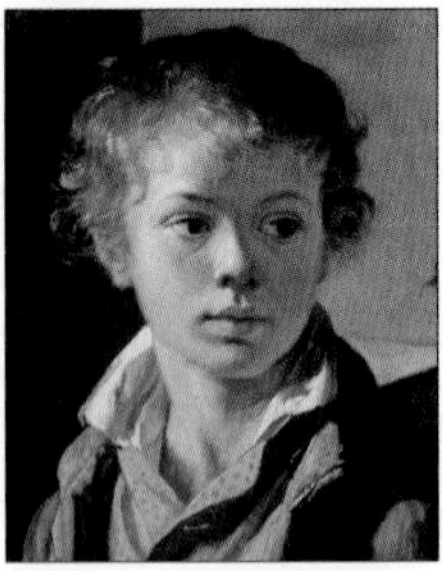

Portrait of Arseny Tropinin, the Artist's Son (c. 1818)
This portrait is by Vasiliy Tropinin, who was a serf for 47 years before gaining freedom and finding success.

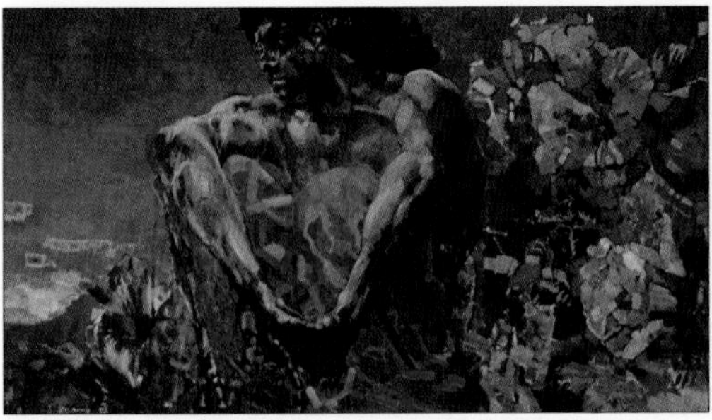

★ **Demon Seated** (1890)
This is one of several innovative paintings by Mikhail Vrubel, who adopted a new, strikingly modern style. They are inspired by Mikhail Lermontov's Symbolist poem, The Demon *(1839), with which Vrubel became obsessed.*

STAR EXHIBITS

★ Demon Seated

★ The Trinity

For hotels and restaurants in this region see pp160–61 and pp162–3

Religious Procession in Kursk Province (1880–83)
*Ilya Repin, a socially committed artist, painted this to
contrast the religious devotion of the peasants with the
cold hypocrisy of the rich.*

VISITORS' CHECKLIST

Lavrushinskiy Pereulok 10. **Map**
E4. **Tel** 951 1362. M Tretyakovskaya. 🚌 6, K, 25. 🚎 1, 4, 8,
33, 62. 🕐 10am–6:30pm Tue–
Sun. 🎫 📷 Eng. 🎧 Eng. 🔌 🚻
📷 📱 www.tretyakovgallery.ru

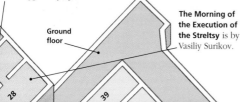

**The Morning of
the Execution of
the Streltsy** is by
Vasiliy Surikov.

Ground
floor

28

39

38

41

37

36

42

40

35

61

60

55

54

53

52

51

50

56

62

59

57

58

Exit

Main entrance

Russian
jewellery

★ **The Trinity** (1420s)
*This beautiful icon was
painted by Andrey Rublev
for the Trinity Monastery
of St Sergius, where he
had been a novice
monk. He dedicated
it to the monastery's
founder, St Sergius
of Radonezh.*

GALLERY GUIDE

*There are 62 rooms on two
main floors. Visitors first go
to the basement ticket office,
then head to the first floor.
Paintings are hung in rooms
1–54: visitors come down to
the ground floor after viewing
room 34. Rooms 56–62 contain
ancient Russian art; room 55
features collections of jewellery,
precious stones and icons.*

Main Façade
*The gallery's façade was
designed in 1902 by
Viktor Vasnetsov. An
example of the Russian-
Revival style, it has a
frieze inspired by
medieval manuscripts.*

KEY

▢	18th and early 19th centuries
▢	Second half of the 19th century
▢	Late 19th and early 20th centuries
▢	Drawings and watercolours of the 18th–20th centuries
▢	Icons and jewellery
▢	Non-exhibition space

St Petersburg ❷

Once Russia's capital and known as its "Window
on the West", St Petersburg was built on the
marshy lands where the Neva river joins the Gulf
of Finland. With a population of just under five
million, it is Russia's second largest city. The
southern bank of the Neva, Palace Embankment,
is lined with glorious palaces. To the east is
Gostinyy Dvor, the commercial hub of the city,
with bars and restaurants lining Nevskiy Prospekt.
To the west lies Sennaya Ploshchad, combining
tree-lined canals with decrepit reminders of the
19th-century life decribed in Fyodor Dostoevsky's
novels. Vasilevskiy Ostrov, the city's largest
island, celebrates St Petersburg's naval heritage
with its scholarly institutions and museums.
Petrogradskaya, to the north, is dominated by
the Peter and Paul Fortress.

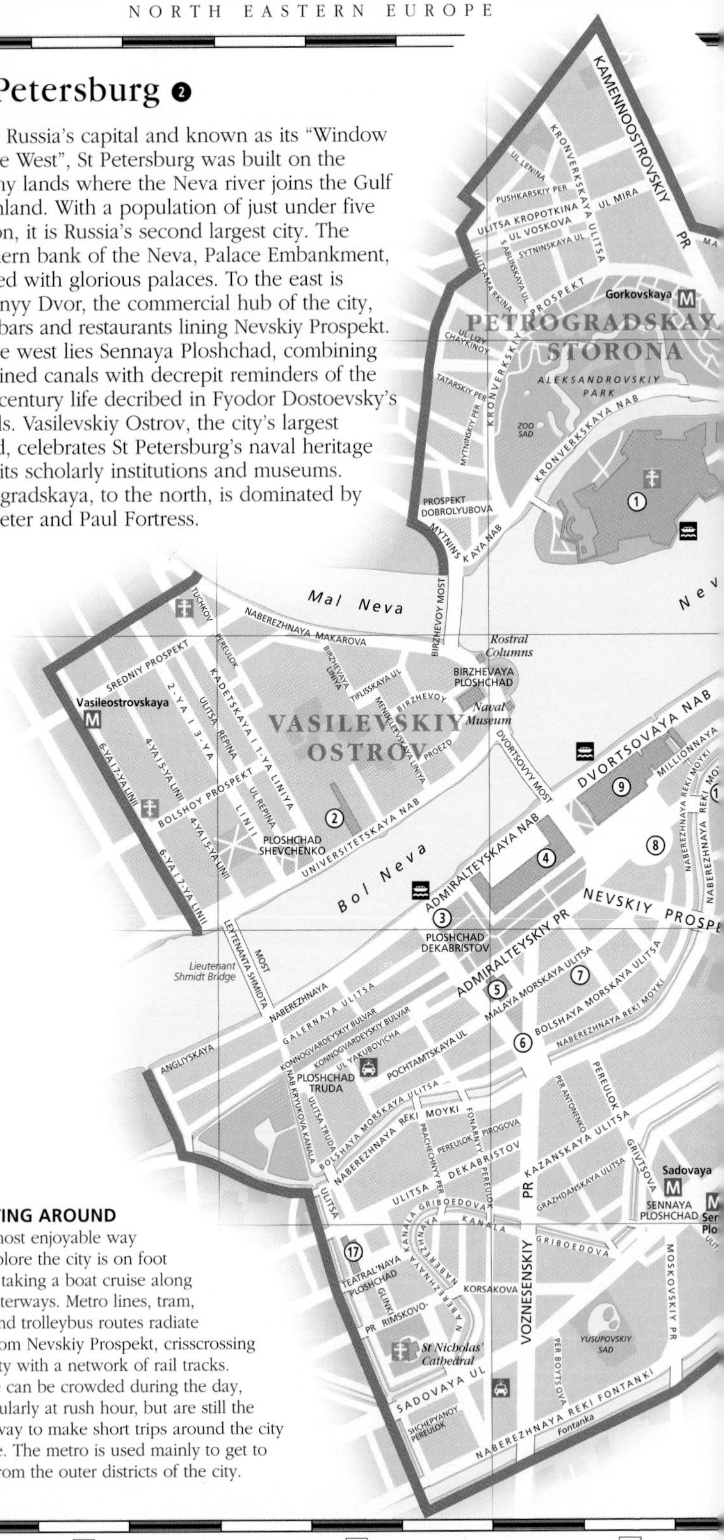

GETTING AROUND

The most enjoyable way
to explore the city is on foot
or by taking a boat cruise along
its waterways. Metro lines, tram,
bus and trolleybus routes radiate
out from Nevskiy Prospekt, crisscrossing
the city with a network of rail tracks.
These can be crowded during the day,
particularly at rush hour, but are still the
best way to make short trips around the city
centre. The metro is used mainly to get to
and from the outer districts of the city.

SIGHTS AT A GLANCE

Arts Square ⑮
Church on Spilled Blood ⑬
Malaya Morskaya Ulitsa ⑦
Mariinskiy Theatre ⑰
Menshikov Palace ②
Nevskiy Prospekt ⑯
Palace Square ⑧
*Peter and Paul Fortress
pp140–41* ①

Pushkin House-Museum ⑫
Russian Museum ⑭
St Isaac's Cathedral ⑤
St Isaac's Square ⑥
Summer Garden ⑪
Summer Palace ⑩
The Admiralty ④
The Bronze Horseman ③
The Hermitage pp144–51 ⑨

SEE ALSO

• *Where to Stay* pp160–61

• *Where to Eat* pp162–3

KEY

▓	Major sight / Place of interest
🚢	River boat pier
Ⓜ	Metro station
🚓	Police station
✚	Orthodox church

View of the city and the gilded spire of the Admiralty

Peter and Paul Fortress ①

Петропавловская крепость
Petropavlovskaya krepost

The building of the Peter and Paul Fortress, ordered on 27 May 1703 by Peter the Great, is considered to mark the founding of St Petersburg. First built in wood it was later replaced in stone by Domenico Trezzini between 1706 and 1740. Its history is gruesome, since hundreds of forced labourers died while building the fortress and its bastions were later used to guard and torture many political prisoners. The prison cells are open to the public, along with a couple of museums and the magnificent cathedral, which houses the tombs of the Romanovs.

The Archives of the War Ministry occupy the site of the "Secret House", a prison for political criminals in the 18th and 19th centuries.

↑ **Artillery Museum**

0 metres   100
0 yards   100

Trubetskoy Bastion
From 1872 to 1921, the dark, damp, solitary-confinement cells in this bastion served as a grim prison for enemies of the state.

The Mint, founded in 1724, still produces ceremonial coins, medals and badges.

The Beach
During summer, the beach is full of sunbathers. In winter, it is the haunt of "The Walruses", a group of people who break through the ice to dip into the waters beneath.

The Naryshkin Bastion is where the noon cannon is fired. The tradition began in 1873, stopped after the Revolution and was resumed in 1957.

Neva Gate is also known as "Death Gateway".

Commandant's House
For 150 years this attractive Baroque house was the scene of interrogations and trials of political prisoners. It now houses a museum with a ground-floor exhibition on medieval settlements in the region.

STAR SIGHT

★ Cathedral of SS Peter and Paul

★ Cathedral of SS Peter and Paul

This magnificent cathedral was designed by Domenico Trezzini in 1712. Within is the iconostasis, a masterpiece of gilded woodcarvings, designed by Ivan Zarudnyy and executed by Moscow craftsmen in the 1720s.

The Boat House is now a ticket office and souvenir shop.

VISITORS' CHECKLIST

Petropavlovskaya krepost.
Map C2. **Tel** *232 9454.*
M *Gorkovskaya.* 🖼 🗹 English.
Trubetskoy Bastion ◯
10am–6pm Thu–Mon, 11am–
5pm Tue. **Commandant's**
House ◯ *10am–6pm Thu–Mon,*
11am–5pm Tue. **Cathedral**
◯ *10am–6pm Thu–Mon,*
11am–5pm Tue. **Engineer's**
House ◯ *11am–6pm Thu–*
Mon, 11am–5pm Tue.

The Grand Ducal burial vault is the last resting place of several grand dukes shot by the Bolsheviks in 1919 and of Grand Duke Vladimir who died in exile.

Golovkin Bastion

St Peter's Gate

Completed in 1718, this ornate Baroque structure features the Romanov double eagle with an emblem of St George and the dragon.

Ivan Gate, in the outer wall, was constructed between 1731 and 1740.

Kamennoostrovskiy Prospekt, Gorkovskaya Metro and Trinity Bridge

Statue of Peter the Great by Mikhail Chemiakin (1991).

Peter I Bastion

Engineer's House

This building, dating from 1748–9, houses temporary exhibitions of artifacts used in everyday life in St Petersburg before the Revolution.

Ochre-painted southern façade of Prince Menshikov's 18th-century palace

Menshikov Palace ②

Меншиковский дворец
Menshikovskiy dvorets

Universitetskaya naberezhnaya 15. **Map** B3. **Tel** (812) 323 1112. ▇ 7, 47, K-47, K-128, K-209, K-147, K-187. ▇ 1, 10. ▇ 1, 11. ◯ 10:30am– 6pm Tue–Sat, 10:30am– 5pm Sun. ▓ ▓ compulsory (English, French, German available).

Completed in 1720, this Baroque palace, was one of the earliest stone buildings in St Petersburg. It was designed by Giovanni Fontana and Gottfried Schädel for Prince Menshikov, friend and advisor to Peter the Great. Menshikov entertained here, often on behalf of Peter the Great, who adopted the palace as a pied-à-terre. Now a branch of the Hermitage (see pp144–51), it houses exhibitions on early 18th-century Russian culture, revealing the extent to which the court was influenced by Western tastes. Peter and Menshikov often received guests in the Walnut Study. The Great Hall decorated in gold is where balls and banquets were held. Upstairs, rooms are decorated with 17th-century Dutch engravings of Leyden, Utrecht and Cracow.

The Bronze Horseman ③

Медный Всадник
Mednyy Vsadnik

Ploshchad Dekabristov. **Map** B3. ▇ 3, 10, 22, 27. ▇ 5, 22.

The statue of Peter the Great, known as The Bronze Horseman after Pushkin's famous poem, was unveiled in Decembrists' Square (Ploshchad Dekabristov) in 1782, as a tribute from Catherine the Great. The French sculptor, Etienne Falconet, spent over 12 years overseeing the project. The pedestal weighs 1,625 tonnes (1,791 tons) and was hewn from a block of granite, which was hauled from the Gulf of Finland. It bears the inscription "To Peter I from Catherine II" in Latin and Russian. A serpent, beneath the horse's hooves, symbolizes treason.

The Bronze Horseman, Tribute to Peter the Great

The Admiralty ④

Адмиралтейство
Admiralteystvo

Admiralteyskaya naberezhnaya 2. **Map** C3. ▇ 7, 10, K-228, K-187, K-209. ▇ 1, 5, 7, 10, 17, 22.

Built as a shipyard between 1704 and 1711 by Peter the Great, the Admiralty's purpose was to gain access to the sea and dominance over Sweden. Rebuilt in 1806 by architect Andrey Zakharov, The façade, adorned with sculptures, documents the glory of the Russian fleet. Zakharov retained some of the original features, including the spire, which he recast in the Neo-Classical style.

St Isaac's Cathedral ⑤

Исаакиевский собор
Isaakievskiy sobor

Isaakievskaya ploshad 1. **Map** C4. **Tel** (812) 315 9732. ▇ 3, 10, 22, 27, K-169, K-190, K-289. ▇ 5, 22. ◯ 10am–11pm Thu–Tue; Oct–Apr: 11am–7pm.

One of the world's largest cathedrals, St Isaac's, was designed in 1818 by architect Auguste de Montferrand. The engineering operation needed to erect the cathedral was, at the time, of an almost unprecedented scale. Opened in 1858, it was designated a museum of atheism during the Soviet era. Officially still a museum today, the church is filled with hundreds of impressive 19th century works of art. The gilded dome, adorned with angels, offers views accross the city. Inside, ringed by gilded stucco mouldings and white marble, the ceiling is decorated with a painting of the Virgin in Majesty (1847) by Karl Bryullov. The iconostasis has three rows of icons that surround the royal doors. Pyotr Klodt's sculpture, Christ in Majesty (1859), rests above the doors while splendid malachite and lapis lazuli columns frame the pretty iconostasis.

St Isaac's Square ⑥

Исаакиевская площадь
Isaakievskaya ploshchad

Map C4. ▇ 3, 10, 22, 27. ▇ 5, 22.

Dominated by St Isaac's Cathedral, this square was created during the reign of

Tower and spire of the Admiralty, built between 1806 and 1823

For hotels and restaurants in this region see pp160–61 and pp162–3

St Isaac's Cathedral and the statue of Nicholas I, St Isaac's Square

Nicholas I (r. 1825–55), although a few of its earlier buildings date from the 18th century. The monument to Nicholas I at its centre was designed by Montferrand. Erected in 1859 and sculpted by Pyotr Klodt, it depicts the tsar in the uniform of one of Russia's most prestigious regiments, the Kavalergardskiy guards. The pedestal is embellished with allegorical sculptures of his daughters and wife, who represent faith, wisdom, justice and might.

To the west lies the Myatlev House, a Neo-Classical mansion dating from the 1760s. French encyclopedist, Denis Diderot, stayed here between 1773 and 1774. In the 1920s it became the premises of the State Institute of Artistic Culture where some of Russia's most influential avant-garde artists including Kazimir Malevich and Vladimir Tatlin worked. The former German embassy, designed by Peter Behrens, lies alongside. The southern end of the square is dominated by the Mariinskiy Palace which now houses the city hall.

Malaya Morskaya Ulitsa ⑦

Малая Морская улица
Malaya morskaya ulitsa

Map C4. 🚌 3, 10, 22, 27. 🚎 5, 22.

Malaya Morskaya ulitsa was recently renamed ulitsa Gogolya after the great writer, Nikolai Gogol, who lived at No. 17 between 1833 and 1836. It was here that Gogol wrote *The Diary of a Madman* and *The Nose*, two biting satires on the archetypal Petersburg bureaucrat. The composer, Pyotr Tchaikovsky, died in the apartment at No. 13 shortly after the completion of his *Pathétique* symphony in 1893. It is believed that he committed suicide, after an alleged homosexual affair.

Novelist Fyodor Dostoevsky lived in No. 23. He was arrested here for his participation in the socialist Petrashevsky circle. Today, the street continues to exude a 19th-century feel despite the many shops and businesses.

Palace Square ⑧

Дворцовая площадь
Dvortsovaya ploshchad

Map C3. 🚌 7, 10, K-47, K-169, K-190, K-209, K-228. 🚎 1, 7, 10.

The Palace Square has played a unique role in Russian history. It was the setting for military parades before the Revolution. In January 1905, it was the scene of the massacre of "Bloody Sunday", when gathered troops fired on thousands of unarmed demonstrators. Then, on 7 November 1917, Lenin's Bolshevik supporters secured the Revolution by attacking the Winter Palace *(see pp150–51)* from the square. It still remains a popular venue for political meetings, rallies and events such as rock concerts.

The resplendent square is the work of the architect Carlo Rossi, the city's last great exponents of Neo-Classicism. On the southern side of the square is Rossi's magnificent **General Staff Building**, the headquarters of the Russian Army. The two graceful, curving wings – the eastern one now a branch of the Hermitage – are connected by a double arch leading to Bolshaya Morskaya ulitsa. The arch is crowned by the sculpture, *Victory in her Chariot* (1829). To the eastern side of this ensemble is the Guards Headquarters, designed by Aleksandr Bryullov in the 19th century. To the west lies The Admiralty. The **Alexander Column** in the centre of the square is dedicated to Tsar Alexander I for his role in the triumph over Napoleon. On the pedestal are inscribed the words "To Alexander I, from a grateful Russia". The red granite pillar is balanced by its 600-tonne (661-tons) weight, making it the largest free-standing monument in the world. The column, designed by Montferrand, was erected between 1830 and 1834. It is topped by a bronze angel, and together they stand 47 m (154 ft) high.

The Alexander Column and the General Staff Building, Palace Square

The Hermitage ⑨

Эрмитаж
Ermitazh

One of the most famous museums in the world, the Hermitage occupies a grand ensemble of buildings. The most impressive is the Winter Palace (see pp150–51), to which Catherine the Great added the more intimate Small Hermitage. In the 18th century, she built the Large Hermitage to house her collection of art. The Theatre was built in the 18th century, the New Hermitage between 1839 and 1851. The New and Large Hermitages were opened by Nicholas I in 1852 as a museum. From 1918 to 1939 the Winter Palace was incorporated into the museum. The Neo-Classical General Staff Building was added in the late 1990s. Mid- and late-19th-century collections are being moved there.

The New Hermitage was designed by Leo von Klenze to form a coherent part of the Large Hermitage. It is the only purpose-built museum within the whole complex.

Court ministries were located here until the 1880s.

Atlantes
Ten 5-m (16-ft) tall granite Atlantes hold up what used to be the public entrance to the Hermitage museum from 1852 until after the Revolution.

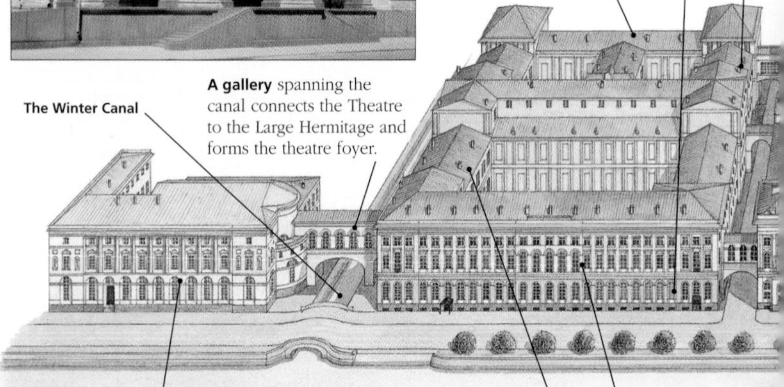

The Winter Canal

A gallery spanning the canal connects the Theatre to the Large Hermitage and forms the theatre foyer.

The Large Hermitage was designed by Yuriy Velten to house Catherine's paintings.

Theatre
During Catherine's reign, there were regular performances held in Quarenghi's theatre. Today, it hosts exhibitions and concerts.

★ **Raphael Loggias**
Catherine was so impressed by engravings of Raphael's frescoes in the Vatican that in 1787 she commissioned copies to be made on canvas.

STAR FEATURES

★ Raphael Loggias

★ Pavilion Hall

★ Winter Palace State Rooms

Hanging Gardens
This unusual, raised garden is decorated with statues and fountains. During the Siege of Leningrad in 1941, Hermitage curators grew vegetables here.

VISITORS' CHECKLIST

Dvortsovaya ploschad 2. **Map** C3. **Tel** (812) 710 9079. 7, 10, K-141, K-187, K-209, K-228, K-252. 1, 7, 10. 10:30am–6pm Tue–Sat, 10:30am–5pm Sun. (last admission one hour before closing). English (571 8446).

The Small Hermitage, built between 1764 and 1775, by Vallin de la Mothe and Yuriy Velten, served as Catherine's retreat from the bustle of the court.

Winter Palace Façade
Rastrelli embellished the palace façades with 400 columns and 16 different window designs.

Palace Square

Main entrance via courtyard

General Staff Building

River Neva adds to the grandeur of the Hermitage, which is situated on its banks.

The Winter Palace was the official residence of the imperial family until the 1917 Revolution.

★ Pavilion Hall
Andrey Stakenschneider's white marble and gold hall replaced Catherine's original interior. The hall houses Englishman James Cox's famous Peacock Clock, which was once owned by Catherine's secret lover, Prince Grigory Potemkin.

★ Winter Palace State Rooms
The tsars spared no expense in decorating rooms such as the Hall of St George. These rooms were not intended for private life, but were used for state ceremonies.

The Hermitage Collections

Catherine the Great purchased some of Western Europe's best collections between 1764 and 1774, acquiring over 2,500 paintings, 10,000 carved gems, 10,000 drawings and a vast amount of silver and porcelain with which to adorn her palaces. None of her successors matched the quantity of her remarkable purchases. After the Revolution, the nationalization of both royal and private property brought more paintings and works of applied art, making the Hermitage one of the world's leading museums.

The Knights' Hall is used for displays of armour and weapons from the former imperial arsenal.

Stairs to ground floor

Skylight rooms

Raphael Loggias (see p144)

First floor

The Gallery of Ancient Painting is decorated with scenes from ancient literature. It houses a display of 19th-century European sculpture.

The Litta Madonna (c. 1491)
One of two works by Leonardo da Vinci here, this was much admired by his contemporaries.

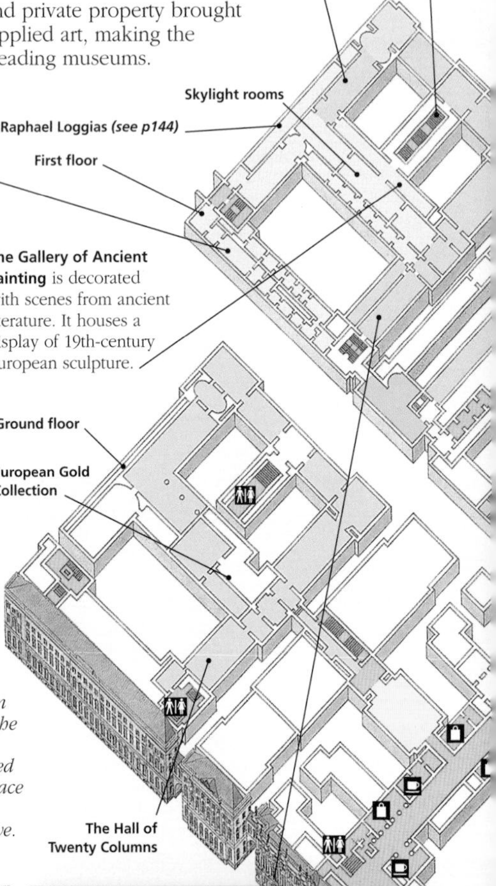

Ground floor

European Gold Collection

GALLERY GUIDE

Individual visitors enter via Palace Square, then cross the main court-yard; group tours use other entrances by arrangement. Visitors can start with the interiors of the Winter Palace State Rooms on the first floor to get an overview of the museum. Nineteenth- and 20th-century European Art is best reached by either of the staircases on the Palace Square side of the Winter Palace. However, some collections may move.

The Hall of Twenty Columns

★ Abraham's Sacrifice (1635)
In the 1630s Rembrandt painted religious scenes in a High Baroque style, using dramatic and striking gestures rather than detail to convey his message.

Main entrance

STAR EXHIBITS

★ Abraham's Sacrifice

★ Ea Haere Ia Oe

★ La Danse

Ticket Office

Entrance for tours and guided groups

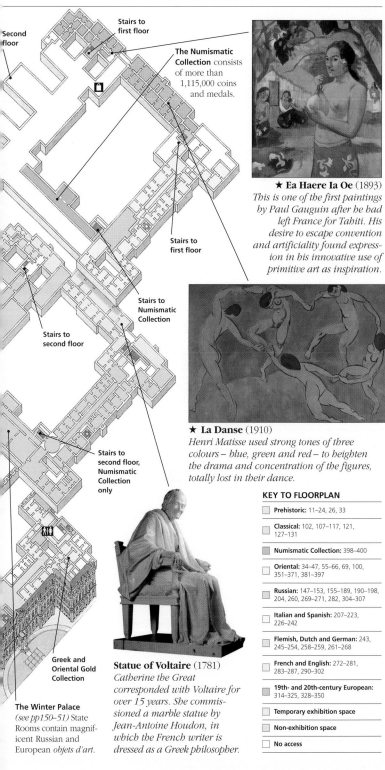

Second floor

Stairs to first floor

The Numismatic Collection consists of more than 1,115,000 coins and medals.

Stairs to first floor

Stairs to Numismatic Collection

Stairs to second floor

Stairs to second floor, Numismatic Collection only

Greek and Oriental Gold Collection

The Winter Palace *(see pp150–51)* State Rooms contain magnificent Russian and European *objets d'art*.

★ **Ea Haere Ia Oe** (1893)
This is one of the first paintings by Paul Gauguin after he had left France for Tahiti. His desire to escape convention and artificiality found expression in his innovative use of primitive art as inspiration.

★ **La Danse** (1910)
Henri Matisse used strong tones of three colours – blue, green and red – to heighten the drama and concentration of the figures, totally lost in their dance.

Statue of Voltaire (1781)
Catherine the Great corresponded with Voltaire for over 15 years. She commissioned a marble statue by Jean-Antoine Houdon, in which the French writer is dressed as a Greek philosopher.

KEY TO FLOORPLAN

- Prehistoric: 11–24, 26, 33
- Classical: 102, 107–117, 121, 127–131
- Numismatic Collection: 398–400
- Oriental: 34–47, 55–66, 69, 100, 351–371, 381–397
- Russian: 147–153, 155–189, 190–198, 204, 260, 269–271, 282, 304–307
- Italian and Spanish: 207–223, 226–242
- Flemish, Dutch and German: 243, 245–254, 258–259, 261–268
- French and English: 272–281, 283–287, 290–302
- 19th- and 20th-century European: 314–325, 328–350
- Temporary exhibition space
- Non-exhibition space
- No access

Exploring the Hermitage Collections

It is not possible to absorb the Hermitage's encyclopedic collection in one or even two visits. Whether it be Scythian gold, antique vases and cameos, or Iranian silver, every room has something that catches the eye. The furniture, applied art, portraits and rich clothing of the imperial family make up the Russian section, which also includes the superb state rooms. The collection of European paintings was put together largely according to the personal taste of the imperial family while most of the 19th- and 20th-century European art, notably the Impressionists, Matisse and Picasso, came from private collections after the Revolution.

Eigth-century fresco of a wounded warrior from Tajikistan

Comb with a naturalistic scene of Scythians in battle

PREHISTORIC ART

Prehistoric artifacts found all over the former Russian Empire include pots, arrow heads and sculptures from Palaeolithic sites nearly 24,000 years old, as well as gold items from the time of the Scythian nomads living in the 7th–3rd centuries BC. Peter the Great's Siberian collection and the European Gold Collection showcase gold objects. Greek masters worked for the Scythians, and from the Dnepr region comes a late 5th-century decorative comb. Unusually well-preserved items from 2,500-year-old burial sites, uncovered during excavations in the Altai between 1927 and 1949, are also on display.

CLASSICAL ART

The Graeco-Roman marble sculptures range from the famous Tauride Venus of the 3rd century BC to Roman portrait busts. The smaller objects, however, are the real pride and joy of the Classical department. The collection of red-figured Attic vases from the 6th–4th centuries BC is

unequalled anywhere in the world, while the tiny terracotta figurines from Tanagra, dating back to the 4th and 3rd centuries BC, are exquisite. Other stunning exhibits include the 10,000 carved gems collected by Catherine the Great, the Gonzaga Cameo, presented to Tsar Alexander I, and intricate 5th-century gold jewellery made by Athenian craftsmen.

Third-century BC Gonzaga Cameo, made in Alexandria

ORIENTAL ART

This selection of artifacts covers a wide range of cultures from ancient Egypt and Assyria, through Byzantium, India, Iran, China and Japan, to the marvels of Uzbekistan and Tajikistan. The most complete sections are where excavations were conducted by the Hermitage, mainly in China and Mongolia before the Revolution, and in Central Asia during the Soviet period. An array of objects, ranging from Buddhist sculptures, fabrics, paintings, utensils, traditional Persian miniatures and carpets are on display, along with some marvellous

8th-century frescoes from Uzbekistan and Tajikistan. Rare Mughal jewelled vessels, Iranian weapons and Chinese gold objects are displayed in the Greek and Oriental Gold Collection.

RUSSIAN ART

Although major Russian works of art were transferred to the Russian Museum (see p154) in 1898, everything else that had belonged to the imperial family was nationalized after the Revolution. Later, the department also began acquiring medieval Russian art, including icons and church utensils.

The tsars from Peter the Great onwards invited foreign craftsmen and artists to train locals. Peter studied with them and his fascination for practical things is reflected in his large collection of sundials, instruments and wood-turning lathes, which includes the universal sundial by Master John Rowley. Russian artists were soon combining traditional art forms with European skills to create intricate marvels. The gunsmiths of Tula, located south of Moscow, perfected their technique to such an extent that they began producing unique furniture in steel inlaid with gilded bronze. The state interiors are the pride of the Russian department, revealing the work of Russian and foreign craftsmen from the mid-18th to the early 20th century. The discovery of stone deposits led to rooms filled with malachite and marble.

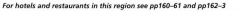

ITALIAN AND SPANISH ART

The fine display of Italian art begins with some early works revealing the rise of the Renaissance in the 14th and 15th centuries. The merits of the later Florentine and Venetian schools can be seen in the masterpieces by da Vinci, Michelangelo, Titian and Raphael, while the Baroque style is represented by the vast canvases of Luca Giordano and other artists. Elegant sculptures by Antonio Canova stand in the Gallery of Ancient Painting.

The Spanish collection is more modest, but Spain's greatest painters can all be seen, from El Greco's *The Apostles Peter and Paul*, to Ribera, Murillo, and Zurbarán with *St Lawrence*. The portrait of a courtier, *Count Olivares*, (c. 1640) by Velázquez, contrasts with a much earlier genre scene of a peasant's breakfast (1617–18).

FLEMISH, DUTCH AND GERMAN ART

The small collection of early paintings from the Netherlands includes a *Madonna and Child* (1430s) by the Master of Flemalle. Over 40 works by Rubens cover religious subjects and scenes from Classical mythology, as well as landscapes and portraits. The Dutch section is rich in Rembrandts. Among the many small-genre paintings is Gerard Terborch's *Glass of Lemonade* from the mid-17th century, in which all the usual elements of a genre scene are imbued with psychological tension and heavy symbolism.

In the German collection, it is the works of Lucas Cranach the Elder which captivate the viewer. His *Venus and Cupid* (1509), the stylish *Portrait of a Woman in a Hat* (1526) and the tender *Virgin and Child Beneath an Apple Tree* reveal the varied aspects of his talent.

FRENCH AND ENGLISH ART

French art was *de rigeur* for collectors in the 18th century. Major artists of the 17th century, including Louis Le Nain and the two brilliant and contrasting painters Claude Lorrain and Nicolas Poussin, are well represented. Antoine Watteau's *Embarrassing Proposal* (c. 1716), *Stolen Kiss* (1780s) by Jean Honoré Fragonard and François Boucher's far-from-virtuous heroines represent the more wicked side of 18th-century taste, but Catherine the Great preferred didactic or instructional works. She also patronized sculptors and English artists. Catherine purchased works by Etienne-Maurice Falconet, Jean-Antoine Houdon, Sir Godfrey Kneller

Stolen Kiss (1780s), by French artist Jean Honoré

and Sir Joshua Reynolds. However, her most daring purchase was of works by the still largely unknown Joseph Wright of Derby. *The Iron Forge* (1773) is a masterpiece of artificial lighting, but *Firework Display at the Castel Sant'Angelo* (1774–5) is a truly romantic fiery spectacle. She provided much work for English cabinet-makers and carvers of cameos and was one of Wedgwood's most prestigious clients, ordering the famous Green Frog Service.

19TH- AND 20TH-CENTURY EUROPEAN ART

Although the royal family did not patronize the new movements in art in the 19th century, there were far-sighted private individuals whose collections were nationalized and entered the Hermitage after the 1917 Revolution. The Barbizon school is well represented by works from Camille Corot and French Romanticism by two richly-coloured Moroccan scenes of the 1850s by Delacroix. Nicholas I acquired works by the German Romantic painter Caspar David Friedrich. Collectors Sergey Shchukin and Ivan Morozov brought the museum its fine array of Impressionist and Post-Impressionist paintings including pieces by Monet, Renoir and Pissarro and several pastels by Degas. Works by Van Gogh, such as his *Women of Arles* (1888), and those by Gauguin, Cézanne, Matisse and Picasso show the changes in colour and technique introduced over a period of time. The bold innovation of Picasso's Cubist period of 1907–12 fills a whole room.

Women of Arles (1888), painted by Vincent Van Gogh

The Winter Palace

Зимний дворец
Zimnii dvorets

The existing Winter Palace, built between 1754 and 1762, is a great example of Russian Baroque. Created for Tsarina Elizabeth, this opulent winter residence was the finest achievement of Bartolomeo Rastrelli. Though the exterior has changed little, the interiors were largely restored after a fire gutted the palace in 1837. After the assassination of Alexander II in 1881, the imperial family rarely lived here. During World War I a field hospital was set up in the Nicholas Hall and other state rooms. In July 1917, the provisional government took the palace as its headquarters, which led to its storming by the Bolsheviks.

The 1812 Gallery has portraits of Russian military heroes of the Napoleonic Wars, most by English artist George Dawe.

The Armorial Hall, with its vast gilded columns, covers over 800 sq m (8,600 sq ft). Hospital beds were set up in this cavernous room during World War I.

★ **Small Throne Room**
Dedicated in 1833 to the memory of Peter the Great, this room houses a silver-gilt English throne, made in 1731.

The Field Marshals' Hall was the reception room where the devastating fire broke out in 1837.

The Hall of St George has monolithic columns and wall facings of Italian Carrara marble.

The Nicholas Hall, the largest room in the palace, was always used for the first ball of the season.

North façade overlooking the Neva river

★ **Main Staircase**
This vast, sweeping staircase was Rastrelli's masterpiece. It was from here that the imperial family watched the Epiphany ceremony of baptism in the Neva river, which celebrated Christ's baptism in the Jordan.

★ **Malachite Room**
Over 2 tonnes (2 tons) of ornamental stone was used in this room, which is decorated with malachite columns and vases, gilded doors and ceiling, and rich parquet flooring.

Alexander Hall
Architect Aleksandr Bryullov employed a mixture of Gothic vaulting and Neo-Classical stucco bas-reliefs of military themes in this reception room of 1837.

BARTOLOMEO RASTRELLI (1700–71)

The Italian architect Bartolomeo Rastrelli came to Russia with his father in 1716 to work for Peter the Great. His rich Baroque style became very fashionable and he was appointed Chief Court Architect in 1738. During Elizabeth's reign, Rastrelli designed several buildings, including his magnum opus, the Winter Palace, the dazzling Palace of Tsarskoe Selo and the fine Smolnyy Convent, all in areas around St Petersburg. Unlike Elizabeth, Catherine the Great preferred Classical simplicity and Rastrelli retired in 1763, after she came to power.

Bartolomeo Rastrelli

The French Rooms, designed by Bryullov in 1839, house a collection of 18th-century French art.

The White Hall was decorated for the wedding of Alexander II in 1841.

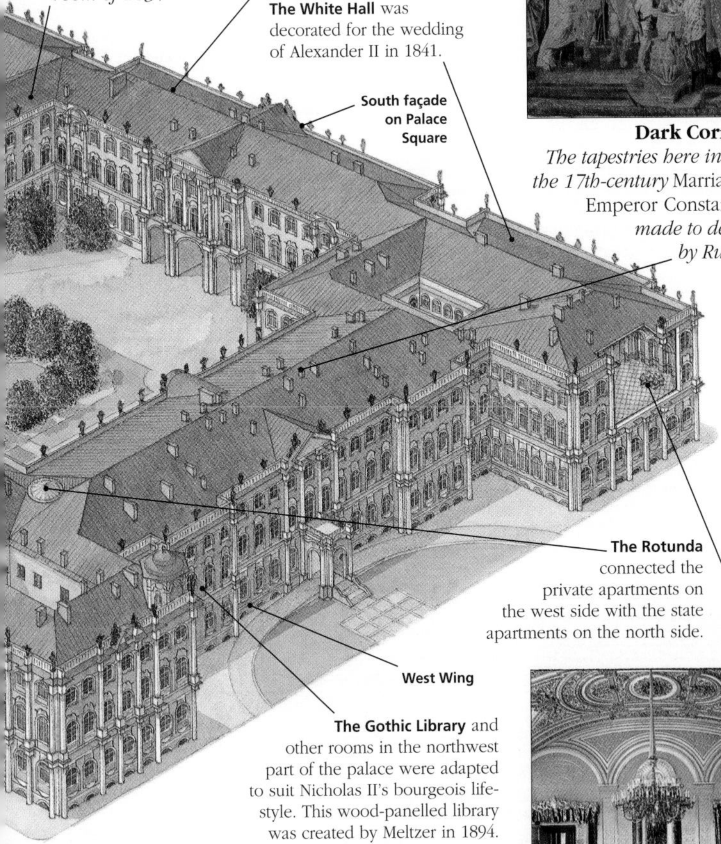

South façade on Palace Square

Dark Corridor
The tapestries here include the 17th-century Marriage of Emperor Constantine, made to designs by Rubens.

The Rotunda connected the private apartments on the west side with the state apartments on the north side.

West Wing

The Gothic Library and other rooms in the northwest part of the palace were adapted to suit Nicholas II's bourgeois life-style. This wood-panelled library was created by Meltzer in 1894.

STAR FEATURES

★ Small Throne Room

★ Main Staircase

★ Malachite Room

The Gold Drawing Room
Created in the 1850s, this room was decorated in the 1870s with all-over gilding of walls and ceiling. It houses a display of Western European carved gems.

Summer Palace ⑩

Летний дворец
Letniy dvorets

Naberezhnaya Kutuzova. **Map** D2.
Tel 314 0374. ▦ 46, 49. ☐ *May–
Nov: 10am–6pm Wed–Mon.* ◑ *last
Mon of each month.* ▨ ✎

Built for Peter the Great, the
modest two-storey Summer
Palace is the oldest stone
building in the city. Designed
in the Dutch style by
Domenico Trezzini, it was
completed in 1714. The
Prussian sculptor Andreas
Schlüter created the delightful
maritime bas-reliefs as an
allegorical commentary on
Russia's naval triumphs under
Peter the Great's stewardship.
   Grander than his
wooden cabin, located on
Petrogradskaya across the
Neva river, Peter's second St
Petersburg residence is still by
no means comparable to the
magnificent palaces built by
his successors. On the ground
floor, the reception room has
portraits of the tsar and his
ministers and contains Peter's
oak Admiralty Chair. The
tsar's bedroom has its original four-poster bed with a
coverlet of Chinese silk, and
an 18th-century ceiling fresco
showing the triumph of
Morpheus, the god of sleep.
Next door is the turnery that
contains some original Russian
lathes as well as a carved
wooden meteorological
instrument, designed in
Dresden in 1714.

The remarkable stove in the Summer Palace's tiled kitchen

The palace boasted the city's
first plumbing system with
water piped directly into the
kitchen. The original black
marble sink can still be seen,
along with the beautifully
tiled kitchen stove and an
array of early 18th-century
cooking utensils. The kitchen
opens onto the exquisite
dining room, imaginatively
refurbished to convey an
atmosphere of domesticity.
It was used only for small
family gatherings since major
banquets were held at the
Menshikov Palace *(see p142)*.
   A lavish suite on the first
floor was used by Peter's second wife, Catherine, while the
throne in the aptly named
Throne Room is ornamented
with Nereides and other sea
deities. The glass cupboards
in the Green Room once
displayed Peter's lovely collection of curiosa before it was
moved to the Kunstkammer
on Vasilevskiy Ostrov.

Summer Garden ⑪

Летний сад
Letniy sad

Letniy Sad. **Map** D3. ▦ 46, 49.
▨ 3. ☐ *May–Sep: 10am–10pm
daily; 10 Oct–31 Mar: 10am–6pm
daily.* ◑ *Apr.* ♿ ▣

In 1704, Peter the Great
commissioned this beautiful
garden, which was among the
first in the city. Designed by a
Frenchman in the style of
Versailles, the allées were
planted with imported elms
and oaks and adorned with
fountains, pavilions and some
250 Italian statues dating from
the 17th and 18th centuries.
A flood in 1777 destroyed
most of the Summer Garden,
and the English-style garden,
which exists today, is largely
the result of Catherine the
Great's tastes. A splendid
feature is the fine filigree iron
grille along the Neva
embankment, created by
architects Yuriy Velten and
Pyotr Yegorov.
   For a century the Summer
Garden was an exclusive
preserve of the nobility. When
the garden was opened to the
public by Nicholas I, two Neo-
Classical pavilions, the Tea
House and the Coffee House,
were erected overlooking the
Fontanka. These are now
used for temporary art exhibitions by local artists. Nearby,
the bronze statue of Ivan
Krylov, Russia's most famous
writer of fables, is a favourite
with children. Sculpted in
1854 by Pyotr Klodt, with
charming bas-reliefs on the
pedestal, it depicts animals
from Krylov's fables.

Ivan Krylov's statue amidst autumn foliage in the Summer Garden

For hotels and restaurants in this region see pp160–61 and pp162–3

Pushkin House-Museum ⑫

Музей-квартира А. С. Пушкина
Muzey-kvartira A.S. Pushkina

Naberezhnaya reki Moyki 12.
Map C3. *Tel* 571 3531.
⬚ 10:30am–6pm Wed–Mon.
⬤ last Fri of each month. 🖼 📷
www.museumpushkin.ru

Pushkin was born in Moscow in 1799 *(see p134)*, but spent many years of his life in St Petersburg. From the autumn of 1836 until his death in 1837, Pushkin lived in this fairly opulent apartment overlooking the Moyka, with his wife Natalya and other family members. It was here that he bled to death after his fateful duel with d'Anthès.

Some half a dozen rooms on the first floor have been refurbished in the Empire style of the period. The most evocative is Pushkin's study, which is arranged exactly as it was when he died. On the writing table is an ivory paper knife given to the poet by his sister, a bronze handbell and an inkstand. Embellished with the figure of an Ethiopian boy, the inkstand is a reminder of Pushkin's great grandfather, Abram Hannibal. Bought as a slave in Constantinople in 1706, Hannibal served as a general under Peter the Great and was the inspiration for Pushkin's unfinished novel *The Negro of Peter the Great*.

On the wall in front of Pushkin's desk is a Turkish sabre presented to him in the Caucasus, where he had been exiled in 1820. It was there

Mosaic tympanum at the Church on Spilled Blood

that he began his most famous work, *Eugene Onegin*, a novel in verse written between 1823 and 1830. The apartment's most impressive feature is the poet's library, which contains more than 4,500 volumes in a staggering 14 European and Oriental languages. Among these are works by Byron, Shakespeare and Dante.

Church on Spilled Blood ⑬

Храм Спаса-на-Крови
Khram Spasa-na-Krovi

Naberezhnaya Kanala Griboedovazb.
Map D3. *Tel* 315 1636. Ⓜ Gostinyy Dvor, Nevskiy Prospekt. ⬚ May–Sep: 10am–11pm Thu–Tue; Oct–Apr: 11am–7pm Thu–Tue. 🖼 📷
www.cathedral.ru

Also called the Resurrection Church of Our Saviour, this church was built on the spot where Tsar Alexander I was assassinated on 1 March 1881. In 1883, his successor, Alexander III, launched a competition for a permanent memorial. The winning design, favoured by the tsar himself, was by Alfred Parland and Ignatiy Malyshev. The Russian Revival style of the exterior provides a dramatic contrast to the Neo-Classical and Baroque architecture which dominates the centre of St Petersburg. The foundation stone was laid in 1883.

A riot of colour, the overall effect of the church is created by the imaginative juxtaposition of materials. Mosaic panels showing scenes from the New Testament adorn the exterior.

They were based on designs by artists such as Viktor Vasnetsov and Mikhail Nesterov. The 144 mosaic coats of arms on the bell tower represent the regions, towns and provinces of the Russian Empire. They were intended to reflect the grief shared by all Russians in the wake of Alexander II's assassination. The perimeter of the lower wall has 20 dark-red plaques made of Norwegian granite, which illustrate key events of the 25-year reign of Alexander II.

Inside, more than 20 types of minerals, including jasper, rhodonite, porphyry and Italian marble are lavished on the mosaics of the iconostasis, icon cases, canopy and floor. The interior reopened in 1998 after more than 20 years of restoration work.

Colourful exterior of the Church on Spilled Blood

Personal effects in Pushkin's study, Pushkin House-Museum

Russian Museum, in the Neo-Classical Mikhaylovskiy Palace

Russian Museum ⑭

Русский Музей
Russkiy Muzey

Inzhenernaya ulitsa 4. **Map** D3.
Tel 595 4248. Ⓜ *Nevskiy Prospekt,*
Gostinyy Dvor. 🚌 *3, 7, 22, 27,*
K-128, K-129, K-169, K-187, K-228.
🚃 *1, 5, 7, 10, 22.* ◯ *10am–5pm*
Mon, 10am–6pm Wed–Sun (last
ticket an hour before closing). 🎟
☑ *English.* 🎧 *English.* ♿ *call for*
details. 🖥 🎦 *www.*rusmuseum.ru

Housing one of the greatest
collections of Russian art, the
Russian Museum was opened
to the public for the first time
in 1898. When the museum
was nationalized after the
1917 Revolution, art was
transferred to it from palaces,
churches and private col-
lections. The museum is
housed in the Mikhaylovskiy
Palace, one of Carlo Rossi's
finest Neo-Classical creations,
which was built between
1819 and 1825 for Grand
Duke Mikhail Pavlovich.

The chronologically
arranged exhibition starts
on the first floor. The exhibition continues on the ground
floor of the main building and
Rossi Wing, then the first floor
of the Benois Wing, which
was added between 1913
and 1919. The museum's
exhibits range from 12th–17th
century Russian icons to
avant-garde painting by
Kandinsky and Malevich.
Highlights of the exhibition
are the works of Russia's
first-known portrait painters,
Ivan Nikitin and Andrey
Matveev and the brooding
canvases of 19th- and
20th-century artist Mikhail
Vrubel, who combined
Russian themes with an
international outlook. Other
leading artists, including Marc
Chagall, El Lissitskiy and
Alexander Rodchenko, are
also well represented in the
museum. Exhibitions are
changed regularly.

The museum also has a
selection of folk art, which
is wonderfully diverse and
includes painted ceramics
and exquisitely embroi-
dered textiles.

Arts Square ⑮

Площадь Искусств
Ploshchad Iskusstv

Map D3. Ⓜ *Nevskiy Prospekt,*
Gostinyy Dvor.

Several of the city's leading
cultural institutions are
located on this imposing Neo-
Classical square; hence its
name. The attractive square
was designed by Carlo Rossi in
the early 19th century.
Opposite the Russian Museum
is the Great Hall of the St
Petersburg Philharmonia, also
called the Shostakovich Hall.
The Philharmonic Orchestra
has been based here since
the 1920s. Among the works
that premiered here were
Beethoven's *Missa Solemnis*
in 1824 and *Pathétique* by
Tchaikovsky in 1893. On the
square's western side is the
Mikhailovsky Theatre. In the
centre of the square is a
sculpture of one of Russia's
greatest literary figures,
Alexander Pushkin.

Nevskiy Prospekt ⑯

Невский проспект
Nevskiy prospekt

Map C3. Ⓜ *Nevskiy Prospekt,*
Gostinyy Dvor.

Russia's most famous street,
Nevskiy prospekt, is also
St Petersburg's main thoroughfare. In the 1830s, the novelist
Nikolai Gogol declared with
pride: "There is nothing finer
than Nevskiy Avenue...in
St Petersburg it is everything...
is there anything more gay,
more brilliant, more resplendent than this beautiful street
of our capital?" Not much has
changed as the street's
intrinsic "all-powerful" atmosphere still prevails today.

Laid out in the early days of
the city, it was first known
as the Great Perspective
Road, and ran 5 km (3 miles)
from the Admiralty *(see*
p142) to the Alexander
Nevsky Monastery. In spite
of roaming wolves and

**Pushkin's statue located in the
centre of Arts Square**

uncontrollable flooding from the Neva, which made the avenue navigable in 1721, fine mansions, such as the Stroganov Palace, soon started to appear. Shops and bazaars, catering for the nobility, and inns for travelling merchants followed. By the mid-18th century the avenue had become the place to meet for gossip, business and pleasure.

Many of the city's sights are close to the stretch between the Admiralty and Anichkov Bridge. Some of the best shops (see pp158–9) can be found around Gostinyy dvor and Passazh arcade. Nevskiy prospekt also offers a wealth of cultural interest: the Small Philharmonia Concert Hall, the Russian National Library, Beloselskiy-Belozerskiy Palace and a wide variety of museums, theatres, churches, including the Church of St Catherine, shops, cinemas and eateries.

One of Russia's most important cultural institutions, the Mariinskiy Theatre

View along the bustle of Nevskiy prospekt, the hub of St Petersburg

Mariinskiy Theatre ⑰

Мариинский театр
Mariinskiy teatr

Teatralnaya ploshchad 1. **Map** B5. **Tel** 326 4141. 🚌 3, 22, 27. 🚊 5, 22. 🌐 🚪 ♿ www.mariinski.ru

Often still known internationally by its Soviet title, the Kirov, this theatre was originally named after Tsarina Maria Alexandrovna, Alexander II's wife, and has now reverted to its first name. Erected in 1860 by the architect who designed Moscow's Bolshoy Theatre, Albert Kavos, it stands on the site of an earlier theatre that was destroyed by fire. Between 1883 and 1896, Viktor Schröter remodelled the Neo-Renaissance façade and added most of the ornamental detail. The pale blue and gold auditorium, where so many illustrious dancers have made their debuts, creates a dazzling impression. Its architectural decoration of twisted columns, atlantes, cherubs and cameo medallions has remained unchanged since the theatre's completion, and the imperial eagles have been restored to the royal box. The ceiling fresco of dancing girls and cupids by Italian artist Enrico Franchioli dates from c. 1856, while the superb stage curtain was added during Russian ballet's golden age in 1914. Equally remarkable is the glittering foyer, decorated with fluted pilasters, bas-reliefs of Russian composers and mirrored doors. One of the country's leading opera houses, this theatre was where most of Russia's great 19th-century operas premiered. These include Mussorgsky's *Boris Godunov* (1874), Tchaikovsky's *Queen of Spades* (1890) and Shostakovich's controversial opera *Lady Macbeth of Mtsensk* (1934).

THE BALLETS RUSSES

The legendary touring company that revolutionized ballet between 1909 and 1929 was the brainchild of the impresario and art critic Sergey Diaghilev (1872–1929). His choreographer Mikhail Fokine shared his vision of a spectacle that would fuse music, ballet and decor in a seamless artistic whole. Diaghilev had the pick of the dancers from Mariinskiy Theatre and, in 1909, he took his Ballets Russes to Paris. His company had a remarkable impact on the contemporary art world. The ballets of Fokine, in particular, prepared audiences for greater innovation and experimentation. Exciting contributions from costume and set designers Léon Bakst and Alexandre Benois, the composer Igor Stravinsky and the dancers Vaslaw Nijinsky, Anna Pavlova and Tamara Karsavina all played a part in expanding artistic frontiers. After Diaghilev's death in 1929, the Ballets Russes fragmented, but its ethos and traditions have been preserved in many of today's leading companies.

An early 20th-century Ballets Russes programme

Practical & Travel Information

Moscow is not as difficult for visitors to find their way around as it may seem at first. Although tourist facilities are fairly basic, there is an excellent metro system, and passers-by and people working in hotels, restaurants and shops will usually be helpful. In St Petersburg, conventional tourist offices do not exist and information points are often concentrated in hotels and other areas frequented by foreigners. In recent times the city has started putting up English signs pointing out major sights and shops. However, it is a good idea for visitors to familiarize themselves with the Cyrillic alphabet in order to decipher signs.

WHEN TO VISIT

The best time to visit Moscow and St Petersburg is during the peak tourist season that lasts from May to late August. Winters in Moscow are bitterly cold and best avoided. January is a good time to visit St Petersburg, when the days are sunny.

DOCUMENTATION

Visitors from almost all countries, including the Baltic States, will need a visa to visit Moscow and St Petersburg. Only citizens of the other CIS member-states are exempt. Independent tourist visa applications must be supported with appropriate documentation as well as proof of pre-booked hotel accommodation or an invitation (visa support) from a tour company, business or private individual in Russia. Anyone intending to reside in Russia for longer than three months is advised to register with their own embassy or consulate in Moscow. Officially, all foreigners are supposed to register with **OVIR**, the Visa and Registration Department, within three days of their arrival; hotels do this for their guests.

All visitors have to fill out a customs declaration form on arrival. Valuables such as jewellery and computers should be declared on entry, otherwise duty may be payable.

VISITOR INFORMATION

There are no conventional tourist information offices in Moscow or St Petersburg, so hotels are the main source of guidance for visitors. Upmarket hotels in Moscow are the most helpful. Smaller hotels have a service bureau offering similar services, but advice can be indifferent.

Cosmos, **Neva Travel Company** and the **MIR Travel Company** in St Petersburg provide tourist assistance including information on booking accommodation and entertainment options.

HEALTH AND SECURITY

Most hotels have their own doctor, and this should be the first port of call for anyone who falls ill. There are several companies, notably the **European Medical Centre** and the **American Medical Centre** in Moscow, and **MEDEM** and **Euromed** in St Petersburg, which deal with medical emergencies. Medical insurance, however, is essential.

Despite media reports worldwide about the activities of the mafia, Moscow and St Petersburg are relatively safe cities. Petty crime should be the only concern for visitors, and even this can be avoided with the usual precautions. It is advisable to make copies of your passport and visa, and to make a note of traveller's cheque and credit card numbers.

BANKING AND CURRENCY

The official currency of Moscow and St Petersburg is the rouble. Roubles cannot be obtained outside Russia, but there are numerous exchange bureaus all over Moscow, including at the airports. Banks are open from 9am to 6pm and accept a variety of currencies and credit cards as well as traveller's cheques.

COMMUNICATIONS

Russia's phone system has rapidly been brought up to date, with direct dialling worldwide. Blue Comstar satellite phone boxes are installed at airports, in business centres,

---

THE CLIMATE OF MOSCOW AND ST PETERSBURG

Moscow experiences warm summers with temperatures reaching 23° C (73° F). Winters are long and cold with temperatures dropping as low as −16° C (3° F). In St Petersburg, summers are mild at 20° C (68° F), while winters are less bitter than in Moscow, with temperatures down to −13° C (9° F).

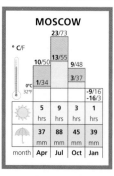

MOSCOW

°C/F	Apr	Jul	Oct	Jan
	10/50	23/73	9/48	
	1/34	13/55	3/37	
0°C 32°F				−9/16
				−16/3
☀	5 hrs	9 hrs	3 hrs	1 hrs
☂	37 mm	88 mm	45 mm	39 mm
month	Apr	Jul	Oct	Jan

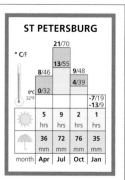

ST PETERSBURG

°C/F	Apr	Jul	Oct	Jan
	8/46	21/70	9/48	
	0/32	13/55	4/39	
0°C 32°F				−7/19
				−13/9
☀	5 hrs	9 hrs	2 hrs	1 hrs
☂	36 mm	72 mm	76 mm	35 mm
month	Apr	Jul	Oct	Jan

most hotel foyers and some restaurants. These accept credit cards or phone cards, which are sold in most major hotels, restaurants and clubs, but calls are expensive.

Moscow's **Main Post Office** and St Petersburg's **Westpost** and **Post International** offer ordinary, express, courier and poste restante services.

ARRIVING BY AIR

There is a reasonable choice of flights to Moscow from the UK. **British Airways**, **Aeroflot** and **Transaero** operate direct flights, while **SAS**, **KLM** and **Austrian Airlines** run flights via various destinations. The international terminal is **Domodedovo**. Transaero and Aeroflot operate flights from the US, Australia and Canada. Transaero is considered a good alternative to Aeroflot.

Direct flights from the UK to St Petersburg run daily on British Airways and three days a week on **Rossiya**, while those from Ireland, Canada, South Africa, Australasia and the US are limited. The international **Pulkovo Airport**, although modernized, is basic.

ARRIVING BY SEA

Arriving by boat can be one of the most exciting ways to approach St Petersburg. However, ferries and cruises operate irregularly, so it is best to check with a travel agent for details. Ferries from Scandinavia usually dock at the **Maritime Passenger Terminal**. Trolleybus No. 10 and bus No. 7 run from here to the centre or, heading in the other direction, to Primorskaya metro station.

Luxury cruise ships from the US, London and elsewhere arrive at St Petersburg's cargo port, 5 km (3 miles) southwest of the centre. Ships have their own coaches to carry tourists into town and back.

RAIL TRAVEL

Rail is a relatively inexpensive way to travel within Russia. Moscow can be reached by train from Paris, Brussels, Berlin and several other European capitals, while St Petersburg is connected to Moscow, Helsinki and London. Travellers should be prepared for a lengthy wait at the

Russian border while all of the train's wheels are changed to fit the wider Russian tracks.

TRAVELLING BY COACH

It is possible to get to Moscow by coach, but it is usually only worth it if visitors are travelling from a neighbouring country or are on a tight budget. There are coach routes to Moscow from the Czech Republic, Poland, Hungary and Slovakia. **Finnord** coaches offer a more affordable alternative to trains.

TRAVELLING BETWEEN MOSCOW AND ST PETERSBURG

The most popular form of transport between the two cities is the train, of which there are ten or more a day. Prices vary according to the class of the train – the Red Arrow being the most expensive – and the choice of seat.

Regular commercial flights run by Aeroflot, Pulkovo and Transaero also connect the two cities. Prices are modest and tickets are available from the airport or the Central Air Communication Agency.

DIRECTORY

DOCUMENTATION

www.petersburgcity.com

OVIR
Tel (499) 238 6400.

VISITOR INFORMATION

Cosmos
Tel (812) 327 7256.
www.cosmos-dmc.ru

MIR Travel Company
Tel (812) 325 7122.
www.mir-travel.com

Neva Travel Company
www.nevatravel.ru

EMBASSIES

Australia
www.russia.embassy.gov.au

Canada
www.canadaeuropa.gc.ca/russia

Ireland
Tel (495) 937 5911.

New Zealand
www.nzembassy.msk.ru

United Kingdom
www.ukinrussia.fco.gov.uk/en/

United States
www.usembassy.ru

EMERGENCY NUMBERS

Ambulance
Tel 03, 112.

Fire
Tel 01, 112.

Police
Tel 02, 112.

HEALTH AND SECURITY

American Medical Centre
Tel (495) 933 7700.

Euromed
Tel (812) 327 0301.

European Medical Centre
Tel (495) 933 6655.

MEDEM
www.medem.ru

COMMUNICATIONS

Main Post Office
Malaya Dmitrovka 29, Moscow.
Tel (495) 733 9073.

Post International
Tel (812) 570 4472.

Westpost
Nevskiy prospekt 86, St Petersburg.
Tel (812) 275 0784.

ARRIVING BY AIR

Aeroflot
www.aeroflot.ru

Austrian Airlines
www.aua.com

British Airways
www.britishairways.com

Domodedovo
Tel (495) 933 6666.

KLM
www.klm.com

Pulkovo Airport
www.pulkovoairport.ru

Rossiya
Tel (812) 647 0647.
www.rossiya-airlines.com

SAS
www.sas-airlines.com

Transaero
www.transaero.ru

ARRIVING BY SEA

Maritime Passenger Terminal
Tel (812) 322 6052.

RAIL TRAVEL

www.rzd.ru

TRAVELLING BY COACH

Finnord
Tel (812) 314 8951.

Shopping & Entertainment

It is easy to find interesting and beautiful souvenirs in Moscow and St Petersburg. A wide range of goods is available, from enamelled badges to hand-painted Palekh boxes and samovars. Traditional crafts were encouraged by the state in the former Soviet Union and many items are still made by artisans using age-old methods. Moscow and St Petersburg also offer an impressive and varied choice of entertainment, from theatre, opera and ballet to lively nightlife venues. St Petersburg has many rock and jazz clubs, bars, art cafés, discos, nightclubs and casinos. Moscow's street performers are additional attractions.

OPENING HOURS

Shops in Moscow and St Petersburg usually open from 10am to 7pm. In Moscow, shops are open all day on Saturdays, and for shorter hours on Sundays. In St Petersburg, department stores and other large shops remain open on Sundays; smaller places may close at weekends in summer.

MARKETS

The markets in Moscow and St Petersburg cater more to the daily needs of locals than to visitors. However, there are a number of souvenir and flea markets. **Izmaylovo Market** in Moscow has all the usual souvenirs on sale, including Soviet memorabilia and painted Russian *matryoshka* dolls.

The official souvenir market in St Petersburg, near the Church on Spilled Blood (*see p153*), sells the best and cheapest selection of *matryoshka* dolls. Visitors are also likely to find handmade chess sets, watches, fur hats, old cameras and military paraphernalia.

HANDICRAFTS

Handmade goods are cheaper in Moscow and St Petersburg than in the West, and they make interesting souvenirs to take home. The best places to shop in Moscow are Izmaylovo Market and the souvenir shops on ulitsa Arbat. Elsewhere in the city, a good range of arts and crafts is available at **Russkiy Uzory**. For more unusual souvenirs, **Dom Farfora** sells hand-painted tea sets and Russian crystal and the **Salon of the Moscow Cultural Fund** offers samovars, old lamps and sculptures.

In St Petersburg, there are good gifts to be found in the **Souvenir Market** and **Gostinyy Dvor**. Local porcelain is available in the **Imperial Porcelain Factory**.

ART AND ANTIQUES

Both Moscow and St Petersburg have a host of treasure-filled art and antique shops worth exploring. Ulitsa Arbat, in Moscow, has many of the best antique shops. **Serebryaniy Ryad** offers a good selection of icons, silver, jewellery and china, while **Ivantsarevich** has a variety of interesting Soviet porcelain. **The Foreign Book Store**, though principally a bookshop, also sells furniture, china and lamps.

Most shops in St Petersburg are very expensive, but **Tertia** is an exception, with readily exportable items to suit all pockets. The **Antique Centre** is a veritable treasure trove. It is worth visiting **Anna Nova** or **S.P.A.S.** to see the paintings on sale. The **Union of Artists** has exhibitions by local artists, while the **Pushkinskaya 10** artists' colony stages shows at weekends, some with works for sale.

FOOD AND DRINK

Russia is the best place in the world to buy vodka and caviar. Caviar should not be bought in the street and it is advisable to buy it in tins rather than in jars. Popular vodkas such as Stolichnaya and Moskovskaya are available in supermarkets such as **Sedmoi Kontinent**.

Gostinyy Dvor and **Passazh** are the most central and reliable places for both vodka and caviar in St Petersburg. For something sweet, the **Krupskaya Fabrika** chocolate factory has long been famous across the Soviet Union, while the **Chocolate Museum** sells novelties such as famous buildings crafted in chocolate.

NIGHTLIFE

Nightlife in Moscow is booming. For mainstream pop and disco, there are large clubs in Moscow such as **Zona**. Foreign DJs often perform at **Propaganda** and **Fabrique**. House music is blended with more up-tempo Latin beats at **Karma Bar**, while **Kult** offers more urban grooves. **Na Lesnitse** and **Slava** cater to the "new-rich", with prices and cover charges to match.

St Petersburg's nightclubs offer mostly techno and mainstream pop. **Metro** plays house, techno and Russian dance music. **Havana Club** has Latin evenings, but also plays house and pop, while **Tribunal** is purely mainstream. Smaller, more diverse clubs, such as the underground **Griboedov**, are still very much of the alternative culture trend, playing a variety of the latest hits from Europe.

MUSIC, THEATRE AND DANCE

In Moscow, many famous foreign acts, as well as the best in local talent, play at clubs such as **Music Town** and **Sixteen Tons**. The **Tchaikovsky Concert Hall** and the **Moscow Conservatory** stand out among the classical music venues, while opera and ballet are performed at the **Bolshoy Theatre**. The city's theatre scene is vibrant and the **Taganka Theatre** and **Mossoviet Theatre** are among the city's best, staging excellent productions of Russian classics.

The **Moscow Arts Theatre**, the **Lenkom Theatre** and **Malyy Theatre** stage musicals and plays by contemporary Russian writers, while performances at the **Gypsy Theatre** consist of gypsy dancing and singing.

In St Petersburg, gig venues include **Pyatnitsa**, which features punk bands. The **Great Hall of the Philharmonia**, the **Small Hall of the Philharmonia** and the **Academic Capella** are the historic venues that are used for classical concerts.

Opera and ballet are performed at the **Mikhailovsky Theatre**. The **Mariinskiy Theatre** is the epitome of the best in Russian ballet and opera while the **Alexandriinskiy Theatre** is the oldest in Russia.

DIRECTORY

MARKETS

Izmaylovo Market
Izmaylovskoe Shosse, Moscow.

HANDICRAFTS

Dom Farfora
Leninskiy prospekt 36, Moscow.
Tel (499) 137 6023.

Gostinyy Dvor
Nevskiy prospekt 35, St Petersburg.
Tel (812) 710 5408.

Imperial Porcelain Factory
151 Obukhovskoy Oborony prospekt, St Petersburg.
Tel (812) 560 8544.

Russkiy Uzory
Ul Petrovka 16, Moscow.
Tel (495) 923 1883.

Salon of the Moscow Cultural Fund
Pyatnitskaya ul 16, Moscow.
Tel (495) 951 3302.

Souvenir Market
Naberezhnaya Kanala Griboedova, St Petersburg.

ART AND ANTIQUES

Anna Nova
Ul Zhukovskovo 28, St Petersburg.
Tel (812) 275 9762.

Antique Centre
3-ya Sovetskaya ul 36/5, St Petersburg.
Tel (812) 327 8271.

The Foreign Book Store
Malaya Nikitskaya ul 16/5, Moscow.
Tel (495) 290 4082.

Ivantsarevich
Ul Arbat 4, Moscow.
Tel (495) 291 7444.

Pushkinskaya 10
Ligovskiy prospekt 53, St Petersburg.
Tel (812) 764 5371.

Serebryaniy Ryad
Arbat 18, Moscow.
Tel (495) 691 7308.

S.P.A.S.
Naberezhnaya Reki Moyki 93, St Petersburg.
Tel (812) 571 4260.

Tertia
Italyanskaya ul 5, St Petersburg.
Tel (812) 710 5568.

Union of Artists
Bolshaya Morskaya ul 38, St Petersburg.
Tel (812) 314 3060.

FOOD AND DRINK

Chocolate Museum
Nevskiy prospekt 17, St Petersburg.
Tel (812) 315 1348.

Krupskaya Fabrika
Ul Vosstaniya 15, St Petersburg. *Tel (812) 346 5532.*

Passazh
Nevskiy prospekt 48, St Petersburg.
Tel (812) 571 1426.

Sedmoi Kontinent
Bolshaya Gruzinskaya ul 63, Moscow.
Tel (495) 721 3874.

NIGHTLIFE

Griboedov
Voronezhskaya ul 2A, St Petersburg.
Tel (812) 764 4355.

Havana Club
Moskovskiy pr 21, St Petersburg.
Tel (812) 259 1155.

Fabrique
Sadovnicheskaya ul 33, Moscow.
Tel (495) 953 6576.

Karma Bar
Pushechnaya ul 3, Moscow.
Tel (495) 624 5633.

Kult
Ul Yauzskaya 5, Moscow.
Tel (495) 917 5706.

Metro
Ligovskiy prospekt 174.
Tel (812) 766 0204.

Na Lesnitse
2nd Smolenskiy prospekt 1/4, Moscow.
Tel (495) 921 1989.

Propaganda
Bolshoy Zlatoustinskiy prospekt 7, Moscow.
Tel (495) 624 5732.

Slava
Shosse Entuziastov 58, Moscow.
Tel (495) 672 3333.

Tribunal
Pl Dekabristov 1, St Petersburg.
Tel (812) 311 1690.

Zona
Leninskaya Sloboda 19, Moscow.
Tel (495) 675 6975.

MUSIC, THEATRE AND DANCE

Academic Capella
Nab Reki Moyki 20, St Petersburg.
Tel (812) 314 1058.

Alexandriinskiy Theatre
Ploshchad Ostrovskovo 2, St Petersburg.
Tel (812) 710 4103.

Bolshoy Theatre
Teatralnaya pl 1, *Tel (495) 250 7317* (Moscow).

Nab Reki Fontanki 65, *Tel (812) 310 9242* (St Petersburg).

Great Hall of the Philharmonia
Mikhaylovskaya ul 2, St Petersburg
Tel (812) 710 4257.

Gypsy Theatre
Leningradskiy prospekt 32/2, Moscow.
Tel (495) 251 8522.

Lenkom Theatre
Ul Malaya Dmitrovka 6, Moscow.
Tel (495) 699 0708.

Malyy Theatre
Ul Rubinsteyna 18, St Petersburg.
Tel (812) 713 2078.

Mariinskiy Theatre
Teatralnaya pl 1, St Petersburg.
Tel (812) 326 4141.

Mikhailovsky Theatre
Pl Iskusstv 1, St Petersburg.
Tel (812) 595 4305.

Moscow Conservatory
Bolshaya Nikitskaya Ul 13/6, Moscow.
Tel (495) 629 9401.

Moscow Arts Theatre
Kamergerskiy Pereulok 3, Moscow.
Tel (495) 629 8760.

Mossoviet Theatre
Bolshaya Sadovaya 16, Moscow.
Tel (495) 699 2035.

Music Town
B Dmitrovka 1, Moscow.
Tel (495) 937 5419.

Pyatnitsa
Moskovskiy prospekt 10–12, St Petersburg.
Tel (812) 310 2317.

Sixteen Tons
Presnenskiy Val 6, Moscow.
Tel (495) 253 5300.

Small Hall of the Philharmonia
Nevskiy prospekt 30, St Petersburg.
Tel (812) 571 8333.

Taganka Theatre
Zemlyanoy Val 76, Moscow.
Tel (495) 915 1015.

Tchaikovsky Concert Hall
Triumfalnaya ploshchad 4/31, Moscow.
Tel (495) 299 3681.

Where to Stay in Moscow and St Petersburg

The hotel situation in Moscow and St Peterburg has improved over the years. However, expansion seems to have taken place at the top end of the market in Moscow, while in St Petersburg many mini-hotels and luxury hotels have opened in outstanding locations.

PRICE CATEGORIES
Price categories are for a double room per night in high season, including tax and service charges. Breakfast is not included, unless specified. Prices for St Petersburg are within brackets.

⑤ under $125 (under $100)
⑤⑤ $125–$250 ($100–$175)
⑤⑤⑤ $250–$375 ($175–$250)
⑤⑤⑤⑤ $375–$500 ($250–$325)
⑤⑤⑤⑤⑤ over $500 (over $325)

MOSCOW

Hilton Moscow Leningradskaya   ⑤
Ulitsa Kalanchevskaya 21/40 **Tel** *(495) 627 5550* **Fax** *(495) 627 5551* **Rooms** *329*   **Map** *F1*

Designed by architect L Polyakov in 1954, this hotel is one of the most famous in the city and offers a unique combination of style and modern technology. Rooms on the top floors offer panoramic views of the city and the hotel is just 15 minutes from the Red Square by metro. **www.hilton.com**

Tourist   ⑤
Ulitsa Selkokhozyaystvennaya 17/2 **Tel** *(495) 785 6075* **Fax** *(495) 181 0158* **Rooms** *450*   **Map** *F1*

This hotel has been a popular venue for visiting athletes since it opened in 1955. The complex unites five separate hotels, the best being Building 5. Rooms are basic but clean. A true Soviet experience offering unrivalled value for money. **www.hotelturist.ru**

Sovietsky   ⑤⑤
Leningradskiy prospekt 32/2 **Tel** *(495) 960 2000* **Fax** *(495) 250 8003* **Rooms** *100*   **Map** *F1*

Built in Stalinist style, the Sovietsky is wonderfully grandiose, with a restaurant in a spectacular mirrored hall. The bedrooms are large, with high moulded ceilings, wooden floors and period furniture; the bathrooms can be a bit untidy. The hotel is a 15-20 minute drive from the city centre. **www.sovietsky.ru**

Golden Ring   ⑤⑤⑤
Smolenskaya ulitsa 5 **Tel** *(495) 725 0100* **Fax** *(495) 725 0101* **Rooms** *293*   **Map** *F1*

The Golden Ring was built in 1970 and refurbished in 1998. Convenient for the centre, its rooms are proportionate and well equipped, with good access for disabled visitors. A wide range of cuisine, including Russian, Alsace and Japanese, is served in the hotel's restaurants. **www.hotel-goldenring.ru**

Le Meridien Country Club   ⑤⑤⑤⑤
Nakhabino, Krasnogorsky District **Tel** *(495) 926 5911* **Fax** *(495) 926 5921* **Rooms** *131*   **Map** *F1*

Just 45 minutes from the city centre, this hotel offers a luxurious retreat from the urban sprawl. It primarily caters to golfing enthusiasts, boasting Russia's only 18-hole championship course (home to the Russian Open). The Country Club here is a favourite weekend retreat for the city's elite. **www.lemeridien.com**

Swissôtel Krasnye Holmy   ⑤⑤⑤⑤
Kosmodamianskaya naberezhnaya 52/6 **Tel** *(495) 787 9800* **Fax** *(495) 787 9898* **Rooms** *233*   **Map** *F1*

Located on the edge of the centre, the Swissôtel is new to the Moscow hotel scene, but is considered to be one of the city's best. The two restaurants are excellent, as are the business facilities. The modern rooms are well equipped and the view from the upper floors is stunning; the building is 34-storeys high. **www.moscow.swissotel.com**

Ararat Park Hyatt   ⑤⑤⑤⑤⑤
Neglinnaya ulitsa 4 **Tel** *(495) 783 1234* **Fax** *(495) 783 1235* **Rooms** *216*   **Map** *F1*

Conveniently located in the city centre, the Ararat boasts a wonderful view of the Bolshoy Theatre and the Kremlin *(see pp124–5)* from its terrace. Elegant yet relaxed, it has large, understated rooms. The hotel's atrium is a marvel of glass and chrome. **www.moscow.park.hyatt.com**

Metropol   ⑤⑤⑤⑤⑤
Teatralnyy proezd 1/4 **Tel** *(499) 501 7800* **Fax** *(499) 501 7810* **Rooms** *363*   **Map** *E2*

The Metropol is a wonderful example of Style Moderne from the turn of the 20th century. Its spectacular interior is adorned with mosaics, golden chandeliers and stained glass and many of the rooms are similarly lavish. The hotel restaurant is lit by great rings of lamps on long gilded stalks. **www.metropol-moscow.ru**

National   ⑤⑤⑤⑤⑤
Mokhovaya ulitsa 15/1 **Tel** *(495) 258 7000* **Fax** *(495) 258 7100* **Rooms** *231*   **Map** *D2*

Renovated in the early 1990s, the National has firmly established itself as one of Moscow's top luxury hotels. The pricier rooms contain antique furniture and rugs. Rooms get smaller and less impressive the higher up they are, and the Kremlin view comes at a premium. **www.national.ru**

Map References see map of Moscow pp122–3 and St Petersburg pp138–9

FURTHER AFIELD Budapest

Petrovskie linii ulitsa 2/18 **Tel** *(495) 924 8820* **Fax** *(495) 921 5290* **Rooms** *116*

Located on a quiet street off ulitsa Petrovka, close to the Bolshoy Theatre *(see p159)*, the Budapest was built in 1876. The rooms are bright and clean, with sparse furnishings, although the communal parts have an unkempt air. The bar resembles an English pub, while the restaurant serves traditional Russian food. **www.hotel-budapesht.ru**

ST PETERSBURG

Comfort

Bolshaya Morskaya ulitsa 25 **Tel** *(812) 570 6700* **Fax** *(812) 570 6700* **Rooms** *14*   **Map** *C4*

Despite limited facilities, the Comfort offers excellent value for money by virtue of its helpful staff and unbeatable location at the heart of the historic centre, which is packed with restaurants. Rooms are spacious and elegantly furnished. Cots are available. Good for business travellers. **www.comfort-hotel.spb.ru**

Prestige Hotel

3-ya liniya 52, Vasilevskiy ostrov **Tel** *(812) 328 5011* **Fax** *(812) 328 4228* **Rooms** *10*   **Map** *A3*

This is a modern hotel, set in a restored 19th-century building on a residential street on Vasilevskiy Ostrov, just a short walk away from the Strelka and the sights, and the shops and bustling atmosphere around Vasileostrovskaya metro station. There is no lift, but there are few floors. **www.prestige-hotels.com**

Shelfort

3-ya liniya 26, Vasilevskiy ostrov **Tel** *(812) 328 0555* **Fax** *(812) 323 5154* **Rooms** *15*   **Map** *A3*

Set on a quiet residential street a short walk from the Strelka, the Shelfort has plain interiors with beautifully restored tiled stoves. Two luxury suites have fireplaces; one also has a balcony. The hotel does not have a lift, but consists of ground and first floors only; wheelchair users can request a room on the ground floor. **www.shelfort.ru**

Casa Leto

Bolshaya Morskaya ulitsa 34 **Tel** *(812) 600 1069* **Fax** *(812) 314 6639* **Rooms** *5*   **Map** *C4*

Run by an Italian-Russian couple, this tiny establishment is arguably the best of St Petersburg's mini-hotels. It boasts light-filled rooms, many complimentary extras and a superb central location. Personal services include business support and tour and ticket bookings. **www.casaleto.com**

Angleterre

Bolshaya Morskaya ulitsa 39 **Tel** *(812) 494 5666* **Fax** *(812) 494 5125* **Rooms** *193*   **Map** *C4*

The stylishly refurbished Angleterre is the sister hotel to the slightly superior Astoria next door, whose facilities it shares. There is a nightclub and a casino, and a rather good lunchtime brasserie. The superb central location on St Isaac's Square is within walking distance of the Hermitage *(see pp144–51)* and Nevskiy prospekt. **www.angleterrehotel.com**

Astoria

Isaakievskaya pl, Bolshaya Morskaya ulitsa 39 **Tel** *(812) 494 5750* **Fax** *(812) 494 5059* **Rooms** *223*   **Map** *C4*

Fully renovated in 2002, the Astoria's historic interior has the calm and grace of a hotel with a history. Rooms at the front offer outstanding views over St Isaac's Cathedral and Square, and along the Moyka river. Those who cannot afford, or choose not to stay here, may come here for tea in the downstairs lounge. **www.thehotelastoria.com**

Grand Hotel Europe

Mikhaylovskaya ulitsa 1/7 **Tel** *(812) 329 6000* **Fax** *(812) 329 6002* **Rooms** *301*   **Map** *D4*

The Grand Hotel Europe's location just off Nevskiy Prospekt is close to the city's main sights. It has historic interiors and a wonderful, airy mezzanine café serving coffee and sumptuous cakes to visitors after an exhausting day's sightseeing. **www.grandhoteleurope.com**

Renaissance St Petersburg Baltic

Pochtamtskaya ulitsa 4a **Tel** *(812) 380 4000* **Fax** *(812) 380 4001* **Rooms** *102*   **Map** *B4*

This elegant establishment has been decorated on the theme of "historic St Petersburg", blending old-fashioned materials with modern design. Some rooms offer views over St Isaac's Square, and the area is very quiet. Despite its luxury status, with one of the best fitness suites in the city, the hotel maintains a cosy feel. **www.marriot.com/ledbr**

FURTHER AFIELD German Club

Gastello ulitsa 20 **Tel** *(812) 371 5104* **Fax** *(812) 371 5690* **Rooms** *16*

One of the city's first "mini-hotels", the German Club is modest but cosy, and set in a quiet location, a short walk from Moskovskaya metro station. Staff is very friendly and numerous extra personalized services are on offer, from arranging guided tours and tickets to simple advice on where to go and what to do. **www.hotelgermanclub.com**

FURTHER AFIELD Brothers Karamazov

Sotsialisticheskaya ulitsa 11a **Tel** *(812) 335 1185* **Fax** *(812) 335 1186* **Rooms** *28*

Located at the heart of Dostoyevsky country, this hotel lies near the apartment (now a museum) where he wrote *The Brothers Karamazov*. Each room is named after a heroine in one of the author's works. Opened in 2004, the hotel is airy and bright, decorated mainly in white and cream. **www.karamazovhotel.ru**

Key to Symbols *see back cover flap*

Where to Eat in Moscow and St Petersburg

Visitors to Moscow and St Petersburg will have little trouble finding a place to match both appetite and budget. All the major cuisines are represented, including Russian, European and Asian, as well as regional dishes from Georgia, Armenia and other former Soviet republics.

PRICE CATEGORIES
Based on the price per person of a three-course meal with half a bottle of wine, including cover charge, service and tax. Prices for St Petersburg are within brackets.

⑤ under $45 (under $25)
⑤⑤ $45–$55 ($25–$40)
⑤⑤⑤ $55–$65 ($40–$60)
⑤⑤⑤⑤ $65–$75 ($60–$80)
⑤⑤⑤⑤⑤ over $75 (over $80)

MOSCOW

Maki Café
Glinishchevskiy pereulok 3 **Tel** *(495) 692 9731*   V   ⑤
Map *F1*

Maki Café offers an eclectic menu and a tasteful minimalist interior of exposed concrete and polished metal. Guests can enjoy Japanese, French, Italian and Russian dishes. Located on a quiet street just off Tverskaya ulitsa, the restaurant is reasonably priced and the food here is of good quality. Booking is recommended at weekends.

Rus'
Ulitsa Arbat 12 **Tel** *(495) 691 9626*   ⑤
Map *B3*

Built in the style of a log cabin, the Rus' has a traditional Russian menu including such delicacies as solyanka (fish soup) and black caviar. Although it lacks a non-smoking area, the ventilator is effective. The Rus' is equally popular with Russian politicians and celebrities.

Champagne Café
Bolshaya Nikitskaya ulitsa 12 **Tel** *(495) 629 5325*   ⑤⑤
Map *F1*

Set in Venetian-style halls with stained-glass windows, the Champagne Café offers an extensive list of wines and champagnes, as well as a fusion menu of Italian, French and other European dishes, including well-prepared seafood. There is live music on Thursdays and Fridays.

Cutty Sark
Novinskiy bulvar 12 **Tel** *(495) 202 1312*   V   ⑤⑤⑤
Map *F1*

Located fairly close to the New Arbat, Cutty Sark is a seafood restaurant designed to resemble an ocean-going yacht. It serves fresh seafood from all over the world, and has separate sushi and oyster bars and a good selection of wines. The service is attentive, and there is a special VIP cigar room.

Polo Club
Ulitsa Petrovka 11/20 **Tel** *(495) 937 1024*   ⑤⑤⑤
Map *F1*

Conveniently located for the Kremlin *(see pp124–5)* and Red Square *(see p128)*, the Polo Club is a steak house with an enviable reputation. Situated on the second floor of the Marriott Royal Aurora Hotel, it has a good seafood menu and a large selection of desserts as well. The international wine list is extensive and well chosen.

Simple Pleasures
Ulitsa Sretenka 22/1 **Tel** *(495) 607 1521*   V   ⑤⑤⑤
Map *F1*

Simple Pleasures has elegant minimalist decor, including a room with an open fireplace. Its eclectic menu ranges from Mediterranean to South American, taking in French and Spanish cuisine along the way. There is an exhaustive, if unspectacular, wine list, and live music in the evenings – usually unobtrusive blues.

Godunov
Teatralnaya ploshchad 5 **Tel** *(495) 698 4480*   V   ⑤⑤⑤⑤
Map *F1*

Once part of the Zaikonospassky Monastery near the Kremlin, and built under the rule of Boris Godunov (regent of Russia from 1584–98), the Godunov serves excellent *borscht* and other rich soups, delicious game, *pirozhki* (meat pies) and a good choice of vegetarian main dishes. There is traditional Russian entertainment in the evenings.

Blue Elephant
Novinskiy Bulvar 31 **Tel** *(495) 580 7756*   V   ⑤⑤⑤⑤⑤
Map *F1*

Thai food is not abundant in Moscow, but the Blue Elephant, an exclusive international chain, is certainly the best option in the city. Prices are high for even the set menu and vegetarian options. Soups and appetizers are excellent and service is good.

Central House of Writers
Povarskaya ulitsa 50 **Tel** *(495) 691 1515*   V   ⑤⑤⑤⑤⑤
Map *F1*

This former exclusive Soviet writers' haunt features carved-oak decor, fireplaces, piano entertainment and a medley of delicious Russian and European dishes prepared by Russian and Italian chefs. The restaurant has an atmosphere unlike any other and is well worth a visit, especially for devotees of Russian literature.

Map References *see map of Moscow pp122–3 and St Petersburg pp138–9*

Praga

☐ Ⓥ ☐ ⑤⑤⑤⑤⑤

Ulitsa Arbat 2/1 **Tel** *(495) 690 6171*

Map *B3*

Located right between the New and Old Arbats, Praga is one of the most famous restaurants in the city, featuring Russian, Japanese, European, Caucasian and Brazilian cuisine. A special historical menu is available with dishes made according to tsarist recipes, such as dressed sturgeon.

ST PETERSBURG

Senat Bar

☐ ☐ ☐ Ⓥ ⑤

Galernaya ulitsa 1 **Tel** *(812) 314 9253*

Map *B4*

Senat is known both for its elegant Russian and European menu and for its "imperial" decor, featuring portraits and busts of tsars and 19th-century antiques. Despite the fact that women are present and there is dancing in the evenings, the mood is masculine, with lots of business diners – some doing deals, others just relaxing.

Literary Café

☐ ☐ ☐ Ⓥ ⑤

Nevskiy prospekt 18 **Tel** *(812) 312 6057*

Map *D4*

This is the former Wolff and Beranger Café, from which the idolized Russian poet Alexander Pushkin set off for his fatal duel. The venue retains its popularity with tourists and lovers of Russian literature, though the appeal of eating here is more historical than gastronomical. Traditional, rather heavy dishes are served, with lots of meat in rich sauces.

Caravan

☐ Ⓥ ⑤⑤

Voznesenskiy prospekt 46 **Tel** *(812) 310 5678*

Map *C5*

Caravan serves an unusual combination of dishes from the republics of Georgia, Azerbaijan and Uzbekistan, and is famous for its Georgian *shashlyk* (kebabs) and Uzbek *chebureki* (folded pastry pockets stuffed with ground beef, and tasty sauces). The staff bake their own bread in a clay oven. It attracts more locals than tourists.

Spoon

☐ Ⓥ ☐ ⑤⑤

Bolshaya Morskaya ulitsa 13 **Tel** *(812) 999 9191*

Map *B4*

Despite being extremely fashionable, Spoon manages to keep its profile and its prices low. Famous local faces might be spotted settled in the cosy armchairs on almost any night of the week. Light European cuisine is served in a relaxed café-style atmosphere. A rare combination of style and substance.

Austeria

☐ ⑤⑤⑤

Peter and Paul Fortress **Tel** *(812) 230 0369*

Map *C2*

Located right by Peter and Paul Fortress *(see pp140–41),* Austeria is the ideal spot for visitors to take a break for refreshments while visiting nearby places of interest. The interior reflects Peter the Great's favourite Dutch style, in line with the Fortress Cathedral, while the menu comprises traditional Russian dishes.

Caviar Bar and Restaurant

☐ ☐ ☐ ☐ ⑤⑤⑤⑤

Grand Hotel Europe, Mikhaylovskaya ulitsa 1/7 **Tel** *(812) 329 6651*

Map *D3*

Open only in the evenings, this bar-restaurant has the most elegant and varied ways of serving caviar and fish in town. Try caviar in quail's egg, salmon marinated in vodka, or one of the Russian regional dishes served as monthly specials. The interior is tiny with a small fountain, resembling a grotto in an 18th-century park.

L'Europe

☐ ☐ ☐ Ⓥ ☐ ⑤⑤⑤⑤

Grand Hotel Europe, Mikhaylovskaya ulitsa 1/7 **Tel** *(812) 329 6630*

Map *D3*

This cavernous, Art-Nouveau hall with its stained-glass ceiling is not a recreation of St Petersburg's glorious past, but the real thing, beautifully restored. The food is first-class European – lobster soup, steak tartare – but it also hosts other special events and festivals of Russian cuisine. Sunday brunch attracts many local Russians.

New Island

☐ ⑤⑤⑤⑤⑤

Rumyantsevskiy Spusk, Universitetskaya Naberezhnaya 15 **Tel** *(812) 320 2100*

Map *B3*

This floating restaurant, much loved by the powerful, has played host to Bush, Putin and Chirac. In winter the boat is reserved for banquets, but from late spring to autumn it sails four times daily. Visitors can eat caviar and *blini* (Russian pancakes) as the boat sails past the Winter Palace towards the Smolnyy, where it turns back to its moorings.

FURTHER AFIELD Matrosskaya Tishina

☐ ⑤⑤⑤

Ulitsa Marata 54/34 **Tel** *(812) 764 4413*

The advertisement for this restaurant reads "fish fashion", and indeed it is. Inside are parts of a real trawler; aquariums stuffed with live lobsters, oysters, crayfish and sea scallops, and just the right wines to wash them down. None of the fish or seafood is frozen – everything is delivered fresh and kept cool on ice.

FURTHER AFIELD Aquarel

☐ ☐ ☐ ⑤⑤⑤⑤⑤

Near Birzhevoy Bridge, Dobrolyubova prospekt 14A **Tel** *(812) 320 8600*

This is the city's most fashionable and most expensive hi-tech fusion restaurant, with modern, luxurious decor. Effectively a glass box, it sits on a pontoon on the Neva river, and offers great views. The Aquarel itself is situated on the first floor but one floor up the prices are nearly halved in the associated Italian bistro called Aquarellissimo.

Key to Symbols *see back cover flap*

CENTRAL
EASTERN EUROPE

Central Eastern Europe at a Glance

At the geographical heart of mainland Europe, Hungary, Poland and the Czech Republic have witnessed a huge surge in visitor numbers since the end of Communism in the late 1980s and early 1990s. Major cities such as Budapest, Cracow and Prague have been painstakingly restored after the ravages of two world wars and offer a stunning variety of art, historic architecture and rich culture. The region is also abundant in natural attractions, with forest-cloaked mountains in the northern reaches of the Czech and Slovak republics, the farmstead-dotted flatlands of the eastern Hungarian plain, and the dramatic Tatra Mountains. Despite fast-growing tourism, the unique cultural identity of these once little-known countries remains well preserved.

CENTRAL EASTERN EUROPE

EASTERN AND CENTRAL EUROPE

České Švýcarsko (see pp266–7), *otherwise known as "Bohemian Switzerland", in the Czech Republic, is an area of extraordinary sandstone formations, with weathered pillars of rock towering above dense green forests. The landscape is best characterized by Pravčicka Brána – the largest natural rock bridge in Central Europe.*

CZECH REPUBLIC
(see pp226–29)

VIENNA
(see pp398–409)

Vienna (see pp398–409), *the capital of Austria, is a beautiful city with a rich architectural heritage, exquisite art collecions and an illustrious musical tradition. Its Naturhistorisches Museum (see p403) has one of the finest collections of its kind in Europe. The star attraction is its much-visited dinosaur hall.*

◁ View of the Bridge Tower from Charles Bridge at dawn, Prague

zyński Palace
e p205)

POLAND
(see pp168–225)

SLOVAKIA
(see pp296–331)

HUNGARY
(see pp332–397)

Cracow (see pp182–97), *in southern Poland, has historic monuments spanning hundreds of years, and has been declared a UNESCO World Heritage Site. Its most impressive building, the Cloth Hall (see p185), dominates the Main Market Square. Dating from the 16th century, it is a lively example of Renaissance architecture.*

Tatra Mountains (see pp316–17), *the most spectacular mountain ranges in Slovakia, are among the highest in Central Europe, with several peaks above 2,500 m (8,202 ft).*

Pécs (see pp374–5), *Hungary's finest town, after Budapest, is famous for its architectural legacy, ranging from Roman tombstones and Ottoman mosques to medieval fortifications and Baroque churches. The highlight is St Peter's Cathedral (see p374), an imposing Neo-Romanesque structure in the heart of the town.*

km   100

miles   100

POLAND

*L*ocated between Russia and Germany, Poland has always been a fiercely contested land. Released from the Eastern Bloc in 1989, the country is now developing rapidly, as seen in the cities of Warsaw, Cracow, Gdańsk and Wrocław. Monuments attest to a stormy history, but Poland is famed for its virtues, especially the generosity of its people and the excellence of its vodka.

Poland has an extremely varied landscape. Alpine scenery predominates in the Tatra Mountains to the south, while the north is dominated by lakes. The country's inhabitants, who number almost 39 million, all but constitute a single ethnic group, with minorities accounting for less than 4 per cent of the population. The largest minorities are Germans, who are concentrated mainly around the city of Opole in Silesia, and Belarusians and Ukrainians, who inhabit the east of the country. The majority of Poles are Catholic, but large regions of the country, such as Cieszyn in Silesia, have a substantial Protestant population. In the east there are also many Orthodox Christians.

HISTORY

The origins of the Polish nation go back to the 10th century, when Slav tribes living in the area of Gniezno united under the Piast Dynasty, which ruled Poland until 1370. Mieszko I (c. 922–92) converted to Christianity in 966, thus bringing his kingdom into Christian Europe, and made Poznań the seat of Poland's first bishopric. After this dynasty died out, the great Lithuanian Grand Duke Jagiełło took the Polish throne and founded a new dynasty. The Treaty of Krewo in 1385 initiated a long process of consolidation between Poland and Lithuania, culminating in 1569 with the signing of the Union of Lublin and the

The imposing Stalinist Neo-Baroque Palace of Culture and Science, Warsaw

◁ Rolling fields at the foot of the Tatra Mountains

Solidarity demonstrators at a mass rally in 1987

formation of the Commonwealth of the Two Nations (Rzeczpospolita Obojga Narodów). In 1572, the Jagiełłonian Dynasty ended, after which the Polish authorities introduced elective kings, with the nobility having the right to vote. The 17th century was dominated by wars with Sweden, Russia and the Ottoman Empire, and although the country survived, it was considerably weakened, and its period of dominance was over. In 1795, the republic was partitioned by Russia, Prussia and Austria, and was wiped off the map for more than 100 years. Attempts to wrest independence by insurrection were unsuccessful, and Poland did not regain its sovereignty until 1918. The arduous process of rebuilding and uniting the nation was still incomplete when, at the outbreak of World War II, a six-year period of German and Soviet occupation began. The price that Poland paid was very high: millions of people were murdered, including virtually the entire Jewish population. The country suffered devastation and huge territorial losses, which were only partly compensated by the Allies' decision to move the border westwards.

After the war, the Soviet Union subjugated Poland, but the socialist economy proved ineffective. The formation of Solidarity (Solidarność), the first Independent Autonomous Trades Union, in 1980, led by Lech Wałęsa, accelerated the pace of change. This was completed when Poland regained its freedom after the June 1989 elections. In 1999, Poland became a member of NATO, and in 2004 it joined the European Union (EU).

KEY DATES IN POLISH HISTORY

AD 966 Adoption of Christianity under Mieszko I

1025 Coronation of Bolesław the Brave, first king of Poland

1320 The unification of the Polish state

1385 Poland and Lithuania agree on dynastic union under the Treaty of Krewo

1569 The Union of Lublin creates the Polish-Lithuanian Commonwealth of the Two Nations

1596 The capital moves from Cracow to Warsaw

1655 Beginning of the "Deluge" (the Swedish occupation); it ends in 1660

1772–1918 Poland divided three times between Russia, Prussia and Austria. The final partition (1795) is made after a Polish uprising led by Tadeusz Kościuszko

1918 Poland regains independence

1939 Invasion by German, then Soviet forces

1940 Auschwitz-Birkenau concentration camp established; over one and a half million Poles and Jews are gassed here during the war

1945 Communist government takes control

1980 Solidarity formed, led by Lech Wałęsa

1989 First free postwar elections are held. Lech Wałęsa wins the presidency by a landslide

1999 Poland joins NATO

2004 Poland becomes a member of the EU

2010 President Lech Kaczynski and 96 others killed in air crash; Poland goes to polls

LANGUAGE AND CULTURE

Polish is a West Slavic language closely related to Slovak and Czech. Many of its words are borrowed from Latin, although German, Italian and English words are also common.

The legacy of more than 100 years of partition rule is still visible in Poland's cultural landscape. Russian, Prussian and Austrian administrations left their mark not only on architecture, but also on the customs and outlook of the people. The Poles have a deep reverence for religious symbols and rituals, and the presence of the church can be seen everywhere, either in the form of Baroque shrines or in images of the Black Madonna.

Exploring Poland

Bordering the Baltic Sea, Poland is one of the largest countries of Central Europe. Warsaw, its capital, is in the centre of the country and is an ideal base for visiting other cities, such as Cracow, the ancient royal capital; Gdańsk, the Hanseatic city and Poznań, one of the oldest Polish cities. Declared a World Heritage Site in 1978, Cracow, with a host of historical monuments, is one of the most beautiful cities in Europe.

SIGHTS AT A GLANCE

Cracow pp182–97 **2**
Gdańsk pp208–213 **9**
Malbork **7**
Poznań pp202–205 **4**
Raczyński Palace **5**
Sopot **8**

Toruń pp206–207 **6**
Warsaw pp172–81 **1**
Wrocław pp198–201 **3**

Zygmunt Chapel at Cracow Cathedral, Cracow

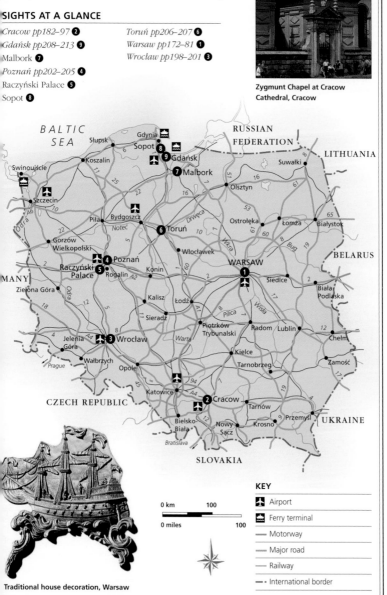

KEY

✈	Airport
⛴	Ferry terminal
—	Motorway
—	Major road
—	Railway
–·	International border

0 km 100
0 miles 100

Traditional house decoration, Warsaw

Warsaw ●

Warsaw is believed to have been founded in the late
13th century, when Duke Bolesław of Mazovia built a
castle here overlooking the Vistula river. It became
capital of Poland in 1596, making it one of Europe's
youngest capital cities, with a population of nearly
two million. Most places of interest are located in
the historic centre, the geographical heart of the city,
which has now been declared a UNESCO World
Heritage Site. The Old Town (Stare Miasto), partially
surrounded by medieval walls, is the oldest district
in Warsaw. Next to it is the more recent New Town
(Nowe Miasto), which became a separate urban
entity in 1408. Almost completely destroyed during
the war, the reconstruction of these two districts was
an undertaking on a scale unprecedented in the
whole of Europe. Today, they are the most popular
tourist destinations in Warsaw.

| 0 metres | 500 |
| 0 yards | 500 |

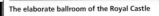

The elaborate ballroom of the Royal Castle

SIGHTS AT A GLANCE

Cathedral of St John ③
Krakowskie Przedmieście pp178–9 ⑧
Monument to the Warsaw Uprising ⑤
Monument to the Heroes of the Ghetto ⑩
National Museum ⑭
Old Town Market Square ④
Pac Palace ⑨
Palace of Culture and Science ⑬
Pawiak Prison ⑫
Royal Castle ②
St Hyacinth Church ⑥
Ulica Freta ⑦
Umschlagplatz Monument ⑪
Zygmunt's Column ①

KEY

▧	Street-by-Street area: *see pp174–5*
▧	Street-by-Street area: *see pp178–9*
▧	Major sight / Place of interest
🚊	Railway station
Ⓜ	Metro station
🛈	Visitor information
🅿	Parking
🚓	Police station
✚	Church
✡	Synagogue
▨	Pedestrian zone

A   B   C

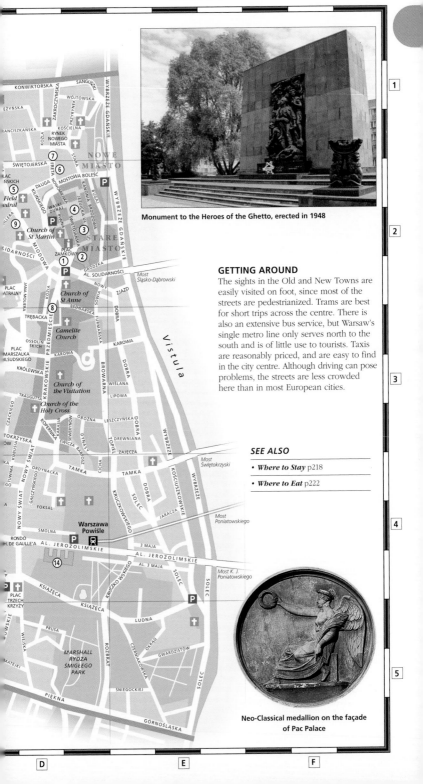

Monument to the Heroes of the Ghetto, erected in 1948

GETTING AROUND

The sights in the Old and New Towns are easily visited on foot, since most of the streets are pedestrianized. Trams are best for short trips across the centre. There is also an extensive bus service, but Warsaw's single metro line only serves north to the south and is of little use to tourists. Taxis are reasonably priced, and are easy to find in the city centre. Although driving can pose problems, the streets are less crowded here than in most European cities.

SEE ALSO

- *Where to Stay* p218
- *Where to Eat* p222

Neo-Classical medallion on the façade of Pac Palace

Street-by-Street: The Old Town

The oldest district in Warsaw, the Old Town is, today, one of the most attractive places in the city. Partially surrounded by medieval walls, it was almost completely destroyed during World War II but reconstructed on a scale unprecedented in Europe. The pride of the historic Old Town is the Old Town Square (Rynek Starego Miasta), surrounded by townhouses, also rebuilt after World War II. Of great interest here are the Cathedral of St John and the Royal Castle. On the square and in nearby streets, especially Piwna, there are many restaurants and bars that are reputed to be the best in Warsaw.

Church of St Martin
This modern crucifix incorporates a fragment of a figure of Christ that was burnt during the 1944 Warsaw Uprising.

★ Cathedral of St John
After suffering damage during World War II, the cathedral was rebuilt in the Gothic style ③

Jesuit Church, a Baroque-Mannerist sanctuary of Our Lady of Mercy, the patron saint of Warsaw, was rebuilt after World War II.

Zygmunt's Column is the oldest secular monument in Warsaw ①

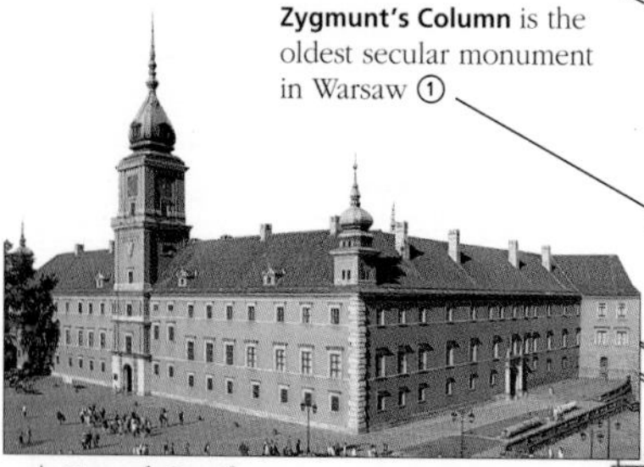

★ Royal Castle
This former royal residence, rebuilt in the 1970s, is today the symbol of Polish independence ②

The Palace Under the Tin Roof
Built in 1720, this palace was the first in Warsaw to have a tin, rather than tiled, roof.

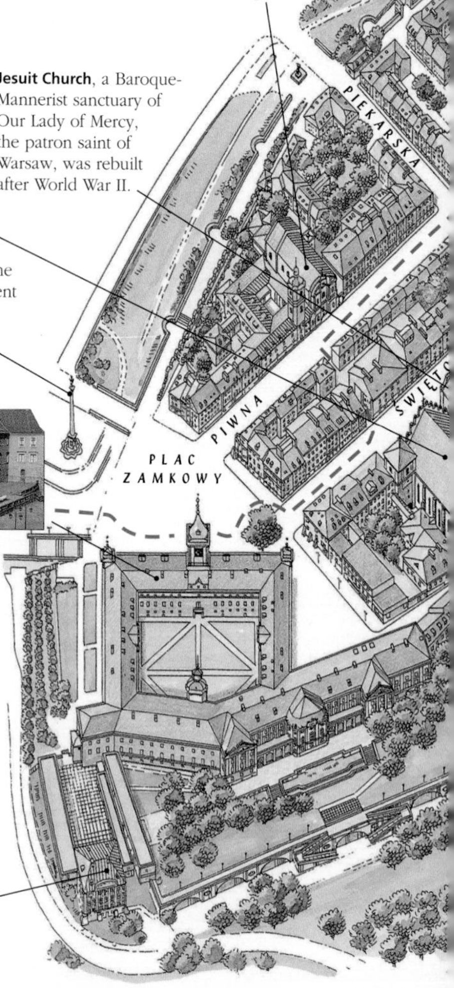

PIEKARSKA

ŚWIĘ

PIWNA

PLAC ZAMKOWY

Barbican and City Walls
This impressive brick fortification, constructed between the 14th and 16th centuries, once protected the northern approach to the city.

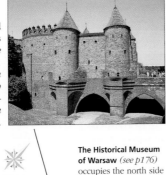

The Historical Museum of Warsaw *(see p176)* occupies the north side of Old Town Square.

Statue of Zygmunt III Waza at the top of Zygmunt's Column

Zygmunt's Column ①
Kolumna Króla Zygmunta

Plac Zamkowy. **Map** D2. 🚌 *100, 116, 175, 178, 180, 195, 222, 503, N44 (on-request stop night bus).* 🚊 *13, 23, 26, 32.*

Placed in the centre of Plac Zamkowy, King Zygmunt's Column is the oldest secular statue in Warsaw. It was erected in 1644 by Zygmunt III Waza's son, Władysław IV. This monument, which stands 22 m (72 ft) high, consists of a striking Corinthian granite column supported on a tall plinth and topped by a bronze statue of the ruler, who is depicted with a cross in his left hand and a sword in his right. The figure was created by Clemente Molli, and the monument was designed by Augustyn Locci the Elder and Constantino Tencalla, two Italian architects working for the king. The monument glorifies the ruler in a manner which had until then been reserved for saints and other religious figures. Despite repeated damage and repairs, the statue retains its original appearance. However, the column on which it stands has already been replaced twice. An older, fractured shaft can be seen on the terrace near the south façade of the Palace Under the Tin Roof.

★ Old Town Square
One of the most beautiful sights of Warsaw, this square pulsates with life until late in the evening ④

Statue of the Mermaid

0 metres   100
0 yards   100

KEY

Suggested route

STAR SIGHTS

★ Cathedral of St John

★ Royal Castle

★ Old Town Square

A painting on display in the Senators' Room, Royal Castle

Royal Castle ②

Zamek Królewski

Plac Zamkowy 4. **Map** D2. *Tel* (022) 355 5170. 🚌 100, 116, 175, 178, 180, 195, 222, 503, N44. 🚋 13, 23, 26, 32. ◯ 10am–4pm Tue–Sat, 11am–4pm Sun. 🎧 free on Sun.

Warsaw's Royal Castle stands on the site of an original castle built here by the Mazovian dukes in the 14th century. It was transformed between 1598 and 1619 by King Zygmunt III Waza, who asked Italian architects to restyle the castle into a polygon. The king chose this castle as his royal residence in 1596, after the *Sejm* (Parliament) had moved here from Cracow in 1569. In the 18th century, King Augustus III remodelled the east wing in Baroque style and King Stanisław August Poniatowski added a library. In 1939, the castle was burnt, and then blown up by the Nazis in 1944. Funded by public donations, it was reconstructed between 1971 and 1988.

The castle's fascinating interiors are the result of its dual role: being a royal residence as well as the seat of Parliament. It houses royal apartments as well as the Chamber of Deputies and the Senate. Some of the woodwork and stucco is original, as are many of the furnishings and much of the art. The coats of arms of all the administrative regions of the country are depicted on the walls. Among the paintings are 18th-century works by Bellotto and Bacciarelli. The Lanckoroński Gallery, on the second floor, has a collection of paintings including two by Rembrandt – *Portrait of a Young Woman* and *Scholar at his Desk*.

Cathedral of St John ③

katedra św Jana

Świętojańska 8. **Map** D2. *Tel* (022) 831 0289. 🚌 116, 175, 178, 180, 195, 222, 503. 🚋 13, 23, 26, 32. ◯ 10am–noon, 4–6pm daily. www.katedra.mkw.pl

Completed in the early 15th century, Cathedral of St John was originally a parish church. Gaining collegiate status in 1406, it was not until 1798 that it became a cathedral. The coronation of Poland's last king, Stanisław August Poniatowski, in 1764, and the swearing of an oath by the deputies of the *Sejm* to uphold the 1791 Constitution took place here.

After World War II, various elaborate 19th-century additions were removed from the façade, and the cathedral was restored to its Mazovian Gothic style. The interior features religious art, richly carved wooden stalls and ornate tombs, including those of Gabriel Narutowicz (1865–1922), Poland's first president, assassinated two days after taking office, and Nobel Prize-winning novelist Henryk

Baryczkowski Crucifix

Sienkiewicz (1846–1916). In a chapel founded by the Baryczka family hangs a 16th-century crucifix, which is credited with several miracles.

Old Town Market Square ④

Rynek Starego Miasta

Map D2. 🚌 116, 175, 180, 195, 503. 🚋 13, 23, 26, 32. **Historical Museum of Warsaw** *Tel* (022) 635 1625. ◯ 11am–6pm Tue, Thu, 10am–3:30pm Wed, Fri, 10:30am–4:30pm Sat–Sun. ● Mon, pub hols & one weekend a month. 🎧 free on Sun. ▣ **Note:** *A 20-min English-language film about Warsaw is screened at noon daily.*

Painstakingly restored after World War II, the Old Town Market Square was the centre of Warsaw public life until the 19th century, when the focus of the growing, modern city moved. The tall, ornate, and colourful houses, which lend the square its unique character, were built by wealthy merchants in the 17th century.

The houses on one side form the **Historical Museum of Warsaw** (Muzeum Historyczne m st Warszawy). This displays the city's history through paintings, photographs, sculpture and archaeological finds. There is also a film show, with footage of the Nazis' systematic destruction of Warsaw in 1944. Today, café tables and stalls line the square, and horse-drawn carriages offer tours of the Old Town.

The Historical Museum of Warsaw in the Old Town Square

The sombre Monument to the Warsaw Uprising

Monument to the Warsaw Uprising ⑤

Pomnik Powstania Warszawskiego

pl. Krasińskich. **Map** D2. 🚌 *116, 178, 180, 222, 503, N44.* 🚌 *15, 18, 35, 36.*

This monument, unveiled in 1989, commemorates the heroes of the 1944 Warsaw Uprising. It consists of sculptures by Wincenty Kućma placed in an architectural setting by Jacek Budyń. The sculptures show soldiers – one group defending the barricades, the other going down into the sewers, which were used by the insurgents to move around during the uprising. The entrance to one such sewer can be seen nearby.

It was in front of this monument, during the 50th anniversary celebrations of the event, that the then president of Germany, Roman Herzog, apologized to the Polish nation for the Third Reich's unleashing of World War II and the bloody suppression of the Warsaw Uprising.

St Hyacinth Church ⑥

Kościół św Jacka

ul. Freta 10. **Map** D2. *Tel (022) 635 4700.* 🚌 *116, 178, 180, 222, 503, N44.* 🕙 *7am–5pm daily.* 🔔 *mass.*

At the beginning of the 17th century, while the Jesuits were building a Baroque church in the Old Town, the Dominicans started work on a Gothic chancel for St Hyacinth Church. They returned to the Gothic style partly because of the

conservatism of Mazovian buildings and partly in an attempt to endow the church with the appearance of age. This was done to create an illusion of the age-old traditions of the order – which had in fact only been set up in Warsaw in 1603. When work was interrupted by a plague that raged in Warsaw in 1625, the few remaining monks listened to confessions and gave communion through openings drilled in the doors. The work was completed in

Façade of the St Hyacinth Church seen from ulica Freta

1639. The largest monastery in Warsaw was constructed next to it. Features inside the church, which was rebuilt after World War II, include vaulting above the aisles, a Gothic chancel decorated with stuccowork of the Lublin type and 17th-century tombstones. The Baroque tomb of Adam and Małgorzata Kotowski, by the Dutch architect Tylman van Gameren, is also noteworthy. The domed chapel in which it stands is decorated with portraits of the donors, who became prosperous and were ennobled despite their humble origins.

Ulica Freta ⑦

Map D1 & D2. 🚌 *116, 178, 180, 222, 503, N44.* **Maria Skłodowska-Curie Museum** *Tel (022) 831 8092.* 🕙 *8:30am–4pm Tue, 9:30am–4pm Wed–Fri, 10am–4pm Sat, 10am–3pm Sun.* 🈺 🎟

The main road in the New Town, ulica Freta developed along a section of the old route leading from Old Warsaw to Zakroczym, which is to the northeast of the city. At the end of the 1300s, buildings began to appear along it, and in the 15th century it came within the precincts of New Warsaw (Nowa Warszawa).

Several antique shops and cafés line this street. The house at No. 15, where Marie Curie was born, is now the **Maria Skłodowska-Curie Museum** (Maria Skłodowska-Curie Muzeum) dedicated to her. Films about her life and the history of chemistry are presented to groups on request.

MARIA SKŁODOWSKA-CURIE (1867–1934)

Maria Skłodowska was 24 years old when she left Warsaw to study in Paris. Within a decade she had become famous as the co-discoverer of radioactivity. Together with her husband, Pierre Curie, she discovered the elements radium and polonium. She was awarded the Nobel Prize twice: the first time in 1903, when she won the prize for physics jointly with her husband – becoming the first woman Nobel laureate – and the second in 1911 for chemistry.

Marie Curie, the famous physicist

Street-by-Street: Krakowskie Przedmieście ⑧

Rebuilt after World War II, Krakowskie Przedmieście is one of the most beautiful streets in Warsaw. Lined with trees, green squares and statues of distinguished Poles, the street is dominated by several palaces such as the Presidential Palace (Namiestnikowski Palac). Some of these now house government departments. On weekdays, this is one of the liveliest streets, as two great institutions of higher education – the University of Warsaw and the Academy of Fine Arts – are situated here. Numerous restaurants, bars and cafés line the street.

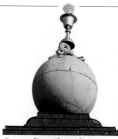

Carmelite Church
This Baroque church was built for the order of the Discalced Carmelites between 1661 and 1682.

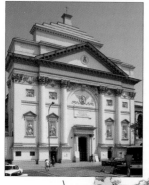

★ Church of St Anne
This Gothic church was built for the Bernardine Order in the second half of the 15th century. The Neo-Classical façade was a later addition.

Presidential Palace was rebuilt in the Neo-Classical style for the tsar's governor. It is now the president's residence.

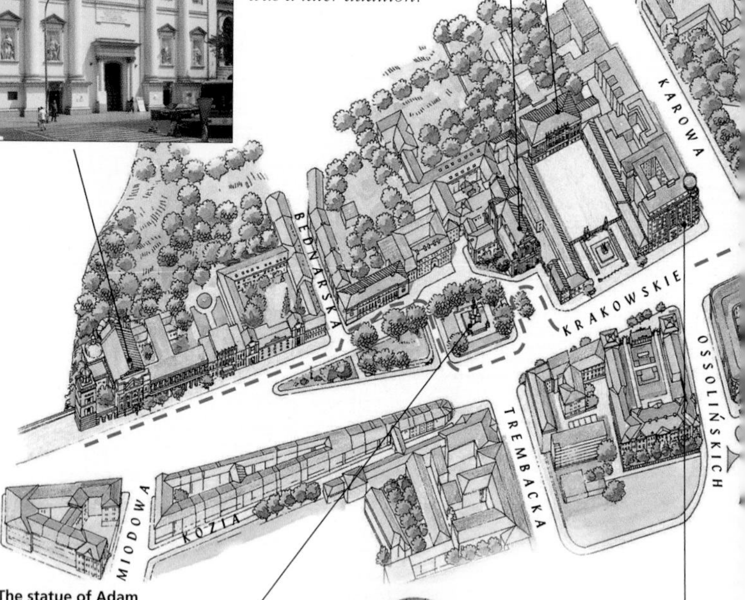

The statue of Adam Mickiewicz, the Romantic poet, was unveiled in 1898 on the centenary of his birth.

STAR SIGHTS

- ★ Church of St Anne
- ★ Church of the Holy Cross
- ★ University of Warsaw

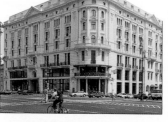

Hotel Bristol
This hotel, which overlooks the Presidential Palace, is the most luxurious, as well as the most expensive hotel in Warsaw.

For hotels and restaurants in this region see pp218–21 and pp222–5

Church of the Visitation
Also known as the Church of St Joseph, this is one of the few churches in Warsaw that was not destroyed during World War II. Its interior features remain intact.

Statue of Nicolaus Copernicus, the Polish astronomer, was removed by the Germans for scrap during World War II but was later returned to its original site.

VISITORS' CHECKLIST

Map D2 & 3. ▦ E-1, E-2, E-3, 100, 111, 116,122, 125, 160, 170, 172, 174, 175, 180, 190, 192, 195, 222, 303, 307, 403, 460, 495, 495, 503. ▦ 13, 26, 32, 46. **Church of St Anne Tel** (022) 826 8991. ⬜ 6:30am–7:30pm Mon–Sat, 8am–10:30pm Sun. ◼ mass. **Church of the Holy Cross Tel** (022) 556 8820. ⬜ 9am–5pm, daily. **University of Warsaw Tel** (022) 552 0000.

0 metres   100

0 yards   100

Staszic Palace, built between 1820 and 1823 in the late Neo-Classical style, now houses the Polish Academy of Sciences.

Academy of Fine Arts

★ **Church of the Holy Cross**
This church has urns containing the hearts of composer Frédéric Chopin and novelist Władysław Reymont, awarded the Nobel Prize in 1924.

★ **University of Warsaw**
The university is the largest educational institution in Poland but only some of the faculties are situated at its main site on Krakowskie Przedmieście.

KEY

– – – Suggested route

Nineteenth-century Gothic interior of the Pac Palace

Pac Palace ⑨
Pałac Paca

ul. Miodowa 15. **Map** D2. *Tel (022)
634 9600.* 🚌 *100, 116, 175, 180,
195.* ⬜ *occasionally.*

This Baroque palace, formerly
the residence of the Radziwiłł
family, was designed and built
between 1681 and 1697 by
Dutch-born architect Tylman
van Gameren. One of the
palace's 19th-century owners,
Ludwik Pac, commissioned
the architect Henryk Marconi
to redesign it; work was completed in 1828. The interiors
were decorated in the Gothic,
Renaissance, Greek and
Moorish styles, and the façade
remodelled in the Palladian
manner. The palace gate was
modelled on a triumphal arch
and adorned with Classical
bas-relief sculptures – the

**Detail from the Monument to the
Heroes of the Ghetto**

work of Ludwik Kaufman,
a pupil of the celebrated
Italian Neo-Classical sculptor
Antonio Canova. Today, the
palace houses the Ministry
of Health.

Monument to the Heroes of the Ghetto ⑩
Pomnik Bohaterów Getta

ul. Zamenhofa. **Map** C1. 🚌 *107,
111, 180.*

The city of Warsaw still lay in
ruins when the Monument to
the Heroes of the Ghetto was
erected in 1948. Created by the
sculptor Natan Rapaport and
the architect Marek Suzin, it
symbolizes the heroic defiance
of the Ghetto Uprising of 1943,
which was planned not as a
bid for liberty but as an honourable way to die. The daring
revolt lasted for one month.

Reliefs on the monument
depict men, women and children struggling to flee the burning ghetto, together with a
procession of Jews being driven to death camps under the
threat of Nazi bayonets.

On 7 December 1970, Willy
Brandt, the then chancellor of
West Germany, knelt in front
of this monument, to pay
homage to the murdered victims. Today, people come
here from all over the world
to remember the heroes. A
new museum, **Museum of
the History of Polish Jews**
(Muzeum Historii Żydów
Polskich) is being built close
to the monument, within the
former ghetto area of the city.

Between the Monument to
the Heroes of the Ghetto and
the Umschlagplatz Monument
runs the **Path of Remembrance**,
opened in 1988. It is marked
by a series of 16 granite blocks
bearing inscriptions in Polish,
Hebrew and Yiddish. The
nearby Bunker Monument, on
the site where the Uprising
commanders blew themselves
up, has been specially marked.
Each block is dedicated to the
450,000 Jews murdered in the
Warsaw Ghetto between 1940
and 1943, to the heroes of the
Ghetto Uprising of 1943 and
to certain key individuals
from that time.

Umschlagplatz Monument ⑪
Pomnik na Umschlagplatz

ul. Stawki. **Map** C1. 🚌 *100,
157, 303, 307.* 🚋 *16, 17, 19, 33,
35, 36, 41.*

Unveiled in 1988, the
Umschlagplatz Monument
marks the site of a former
railway siding on ulica Dzika.
It was from here that some
300,000 Jews from the Warsaw
Ghetto and elsewhere were
loaded onto cattle trucks and
dispatched to extermination
camps. Among them was
Janusz Korczak, Polish-Jewish
author and pediatrician, and
his group of Jewish orphans.
Living conditions in the ghetto
were indescribably inhumane,
and by 1942 over 100,000 of
the inhabitants had died. The
monument, on which the
architect Hanna Szmalenberg
and the sculptor Władysław
Klamerus collaborated, is made
of blocks of black-and-white
marble bearing the names of
hundreds of Warsaw's Jews.

**One of the granite blocks marking
the Path of Remembrance**

Pawiak Prison ⑫
Więzienie Pawiak

ul. Dzielna 24/26. **Map** C2. **Tel** (022)
831 9289. ▦ 170, 500, 510. ▦ 16,
17, 19, 33. ◯ 9am–4pm Tue, Sat,
9am–5pm Wed, 10am–5pm Fri;
10am–4pm Sun. ● Mon, Thu.
▦ ▦ ▦

Built between 1829 and 1835
by Polish architect Henryk
Marconi, this prison was initially used as a transfer camp
during the 1863 Uprising for
political prisoners to be deported to Siberia. Pawiak got its
name from ulica Pawia, the
street where it was located.
The prison became notorious
during the Nazi occupation,
when it was used to imprison
Jews and Poles arrested by the
Germans. Many of those who
were at the prison were either
executed, tortured or sent to
concentration camps.

Blown up by the Germans
in 1944, the prison was partially reconstructed to house
this poignant museum. The
opening of the museum in
1965 was a hugely, emotional
event, attracting crowds of former inmates and their families.

**Tree with obituary notices in
front of Pawiak Prison**

Palace of Culture
and Science ⑬
Palac Kultury i Nauki

pl. Defilad 1. **Map** C4. **Tel** (022) 656
7600. ▦ several routes. ▦ 2, 7, 8,
9, 18, 21, 22, 24, 25, 35, 36. Ⓜ
Centrum. **Viewing Terrace** ◯
9am–6pm daily. ▦ www.pkin.pl

This monolithic building –
a gift for the people of
Warsaw from the nations of

**The 30-storey high Palace of Culture
and Science**

the USSR – was built between
1952 and 1955 to the designs
of Russian architect, Lev
Rudniev. The palace resembles
Moscow's Socialist Realist
tower blocks, and although
it has only 30 storeys, with its
spire it is 231 m (757 ft) high.
Its volume is over 800,000
cubic m (28 million cubic ft)
and it contains 40 million
bricks. It is said to incorporate various architectural and
decorative elements requisitioned from Poland's historic
stately homes. At the time, this
monument to "the spirit of
invention and social progress"
was the second tallest building in Europe. Despite the
passage of time, this symbol
of Soviet domination still
provokes extreme reactions
from people, ranging from
admiration to demands for
its demolition.

However, since the end
of Soviet rule, the building's
role has changed. The tower
now provides office space
and the Congress Hall is used
for concerts and festivals. The
palace remains a cultural
centre in other ways, with
the Theatre of Dramatic Art,
a cinema, puppet theatre,
technology museum and a
sports complex. It also offers
the best view of Warsaw from
its **Viewing Terrace**.

National Museum ⑭
Muzeum Narodowe

al. Jerozolimskie 3. **Map** D4. **Tel**
(022) 629 3093. ▦ E-5, 111, 117,
158, 517, 521. ▦ 7, 8, 9, 21, 22,
24, 25. ◯ 10am–5pm Tue, Wed,
10am–5pm Thu, noon–9pm Fri,
noon–6pm Sat, Sun. ● Mon, pub
hols. ▦ free Sat. **Military Museum**
Tel (022) 629 5271. ◯ 10am–5pm
Wed, 10am–4pm Thu–Sun. ▦ ▦
▦ ▦ ▦ ▦ www.mnw.art.pl

Originally established in 1862
as the Fine Arts Museum, the
National Museum was created
in 1916. Despite wartime
losses, today it has a large collection of works of art covering
all periods from antiquity to
modern times. The collections
are arranged over three floors.
On the ground floor are the
Galleries of Ancient Art, with
their displays of Egyptian,
Greek and Roman artifacts,
the Faras Collection and the
Gallery of Medieval Art. The
first floor houses a collection
of Polish art which includes
two paintings – Jan Matejko's
Battle of Grünwald (1878)
and the *Polish Hamlet*, a
portrait of the aristocrat and
politician Aleksander
Wielopolski, painted by Jacek
Malczewski in 1903 in the style
of the Polish Symbolist school.
The foreign art collection is
displayed on the first and
second floors and includes
the *Virgin and Child* (c. 1465)
by Sandro Botticelli and *The
Raising of Lazarus* (1643) by
Carel Fabritius, a pupil of
Rembrandt. In the build-
ing's east wing, the **Military
Museum**, illustrates the history
of Polish firearms and armour.

**Tenth-century fresco of St Anne,
National Museum**

Cracow ❷

For nearly six centuries, Cracow was the capital of Poland and the country's largest city. Polish rulers resided at Wawel Royal Castle until the court and parliament moved to Warsaw in 1596. Even then, Cracow continued to be regarded as the nation's spiritual heart and rulers were still crowned and buried in the cathedral on Wawel Hill. Most places of interest are located in its fairly compact historic centre. A good place to start is Wawel Hill with its imposing castle and Gothic cathedral. North of Wawel Hill lies the Old Town, with an attractive market square, the Church of St Mary and the picturesque Cloth Hall. To the south of the hill is the Kazimierz district, with its preserved Jewish quarter. Today, the city has seven hundred and fifty thousand inhabitants, and in recent years many buildings and monuments have been restored to their former glory.

SIGHTS AT A GLANCE

Auschwitz pp194–7 ⑭
Cathedral Museum ⑨
Church of Sts Peter and Paul ⑥
Church of St Mary pp186–7 ④
City Hall Tower ②
Cloth Hall ①
Cracow Cathedral pp190–91 ⑪
Czartoryski Museum ⑤
Fortifications on the Wawel ⑧
Kazimierz District pp192–3 ⑬
"Lost Wawel" Exhibition ⑩
Stanisław Wyspiański Museum ⑦
Ulica Floriańska ③
Wawel Royal Castle ⑫

The lavishly decorated high altar, Cracow Cathedral

BASZTOW
J. DUNAJEWSKIEGO
ŚW. MARKA
PIJARSKA
PLAC SZCZEPAŃSKI
SŁAWKOWSKA
Cultural Information Centre
SZCZEPAŃSKI
SZEWSKA
⑦
JAGIELLOŃSKA
Church of St Anne
ŚW. ANNY
Collegium Maius
WIŚLNA
GOŁĘBIA
PODWALE
RYNEK GŁÓWNY
①
②
St Barbara's
St Adalbert's Church
PL.
BRACKA
FRANCISZKAŃSKA
Franciscan Church
DOMIN
GRODZKA
F. STRASZEWSKIEGO
POSELSKA
PLANTY
KANONICZA
Church of St Andrew
Church of St
P
PODZAMCZE
⑧
ŚW. IDZIEGO
⑪
⑫
⑨
⑩
BERNARDYŃSKA
Church of the Bernardines
P
SMOCZA
KOLETEK
SUKIENNICZA
J. DIETLA
Most Grunwaldzki
Vistula
Paulite Church

A　　　B　　　C

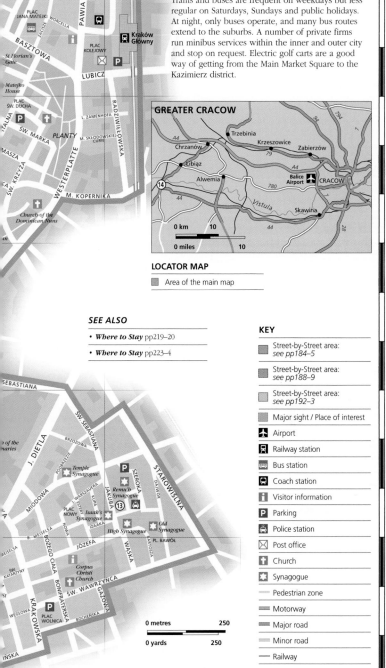

GETTING AROUND

Central Cracow is small and compact, making it
easy to get around on foot or by public transport.
Trams and buses are frequent on weekdays but less
regular on Saturdays, Sundays and public holidays.
At night, only buses operate, and many bus routes
extend to the suburbs. A number of private firms
run minibus services within the inner and outer city
and stop on request. Electric golf carts are a good
way of getting from the Main Market Square to the
Kazimierz district.

GREATER CRACOW

Trzebinia
Krzeszowice
Zabierzów
Chrzanów
Libiąz
Alwernia
Balice Airport
CRACOW
Vistula
Skawina

0 km   10

0 miles   10

LOCATOR MAP

☐ Area of the main map

SEE ALSO

• **Where to Stay** pp219–20

• **Where to Stay** pp223–4

KEY

☐	Street-by-Street area: *see pp184–5*
☐	Street-by-Street area: *see pp188–9*
☐	Street-by-Street area: *see pp192–3*
	Major sight / Place of interest
✈	Airport
🚉	Railway station
🚌	Bus station
🚍	Coach station
ℹ	Visitor information
P	Parking
🚓	Police station
⊠	Post office
✝	Church
✡	Synagogue
	Pedestrian zone
▬	Motorway
▬	Major road
═	Minor road
—	Railway

Street-by-Street: Main Market Square

The huge Main Market Square (Rynek Główny) was laid out when Cracow received its new municipal charter in 1257. One of the largest squares in Europe, it brims with life all year round. In summer, pedestrians negotiate the maze of café tables that fill the lively square, along with a host of shops, antique dealers, restaurants, bars and clubs. There are also numerous interesting museums, galleries and historic sights, including some splendid Renaissance and Baroque houses and mansions.

★ **Church of St Mary**
The façade of this church, with its two impressive towers, is one of the finest Gothic structures in Poland ④

Ulica Floriańska is one of the busiest streets in Cracow ③

★ **Cloth Hall**
This beautiful Renaissance building replaced an earlier Gothic market hall. The upper floor houses a branch of the National Museum ①

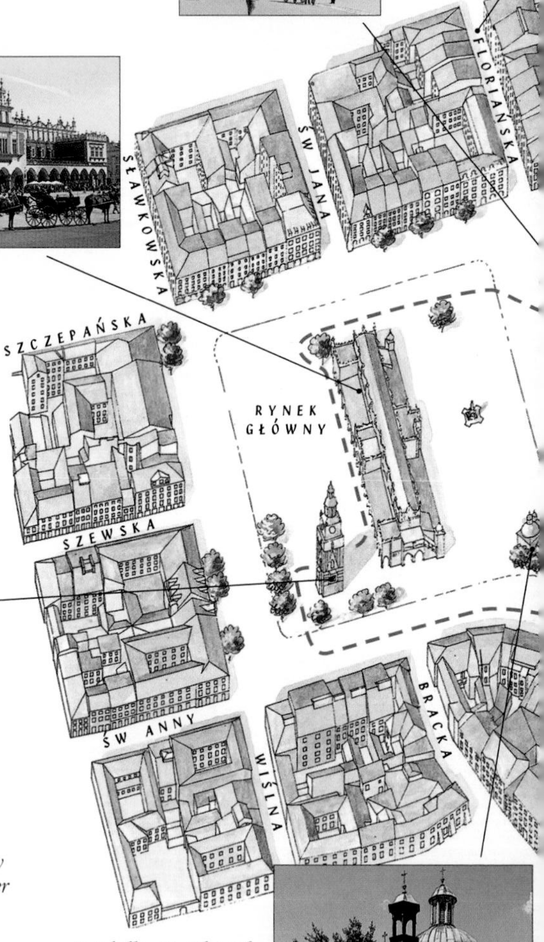

City Hall Tower
The Gothic tower is the only remaining part of the former City Hall. A café has been opened in the basement ②

St Adalbert's Church
This is a small but splendid Romanesque church. It predates the planning of the vast Main Market Square and is all now but lost in it.

SŁAWKOWSKA

SW JANA

FLORIAŃSKA

SZCZEPAŃSKA

RYNEK GŁÓWNY

SZEWSKA

BRACKA

SW ANNY

WIŚLNA

STAR SIGHTS

★ Cloth Hall

★ Church of St Mary

Church of St Barbara
Dating from the late 14th century, this church contains many treasures, including a 15th-century Gothic pietà. It was the principal Polish church in Cracow during Austrian rule.

Merchant's House, also known as "At a Sign of the Lizard", gets its name from the relief of lizards carved in stone above the main portal. It is now a pub and cultural centre.

0 metres 50

0 yards 50

KEY

– – – Suggested route

Frenzy, by Władysław Podkowiński, Cloth Hall

Cloth Hall ①
Sukiennice

Rynek Główny 1/3. **Map** C2.
🚊 *103, 124, 152, 502.* 🚋 *3, 4, 5, 13, 14, 15, 18, 19.* **Musuem of 19th Century Art** *Tel* (012) 422 1166. ⬜ *call ahead or check website for opening hours.* 🖼 www.muzeum.krakow.pl

Set in the centre of the Main Market Square, the Cloth Hall replaced an earlier Gothic trade hall dating from the late 14th century. Destroyed in a fire then rebuilt by Giovanni Maria Padovano, it owes part of its present appearance to Tomasz Pryliński's Romantic-style restoration between 1875 and 1879. Today, the ground floor is filled with a selection of souvenir shops and cafés. The **Musuem of 19th Century Art**, a branch of the National Museum, is located on the upper floor. It has a collection of 19th-century paintings by renowned artists, including Jan Matejko and Henryk Siemiradzki.

City Hall Tower ②
Wieża Ratuszowa

Rynek Główny 1. **Map** C2. 🚊 *103, 124, 152, 502.* 🚋 *3, 4, 5, 13, 14, 15, 18, 19.* **Historical Museum** *Tel* (012) 619 2318. ⬜ *Apr–Oct: 10:30am–6pm daily.* ⬤ *1, 3 May & 15 Aug.* 🖼

The Gothic tower, crowned by a Baroque cupola, which dominates the Main Market Square is the only remaining vestige of the City Hall, built in the 14th century and pulled down in the 19th century. Today, it houses a branch of the **Historical Museum**. Aspects of the city's history can be seen in the Museum of the History of the Market, in the crypt of the neighbouring St Adalbert's Church.

Ulica Floriańska ③

Map D2. 🚊 *103, 124, 179, 192, 424, 502.* 🚋 *1, 7, 8, 18, 36, 38.* **Matejko House** *Tel* (012) 422 5926. ⬜ *10am–6pm Tue–Sat, 10am–4pm Sun.* ⬤ *Mon.* 🖼 *free on Thu.* 🎫 **Jama Michalika** ⬜ *9am–10pm Sun–Thu, 9am–11pm Fri, Sat.*

This charming street in the Old Town is full of restaurants, cafés and shops. It leads from the Main Market Square to the **Florian Gate** and was once part of the Royal Route, along which rulers would ride on their way from Warsaw to their coronation in Cracow.

Matejko House (Dom Matejki), at No. 41, is the birthplace of the painter Jan Matejko. He spent most of his life here. On display is a collection of his paintings and his studio, full of artist's materials.

A little further on, at No. 45, is **Jama Michalika**, a café that was very fashionable in the late 19th to early 20th centuries. The fine Art Nouveau decor by Karol Frycz can still be seen. The Florian Gate at the end of the street is one of the few surviving remnants of the city's medieval fortifications, along with a section of the city wall.

Medieval Florian Gate at the end of ulica Floriańska

Church of St Mary ④
Kościół Mariacka

The imposing Church of St Mary was
built by the citizens of Cracow to rival
the Cracow Cathedral on Wawel Hill
(see pp188–9). Construction began
in 1355, and continued until the
mid-15th century; the lower tower
was not completed until the early
16th century. Inside, Neo-Gothic
paintings cover the walls. This
great basilica, with its rows of side
chapels, contains an exceptional
number of works of art.

★ **Crucifix**
*The large sand-
stone crucifix
by Veit Stoss is
a fine example
of 15th-cen-
tury sculpture.*

Hejnał Tower
*The famous trumpet
call – the Hejnał – is
sounded hourly from
the watchtower. As per
legend, the call is
unfinished, in mem-
ory of a medieval
trumpeter, shot
while sounding
the alarm. The
Hejnał is broad-
cast live on
Polish radio
daily at noon.*

**Main
entrance**

Baroque Porch
*The exuberant pentagonal
porch was built in the mid-
18th century to a design by
Francesco Placidi.*

Ciborium
*This intricately constructed
ciborium in the form of a
Renaissance church was
made by Giovanni Maria
Padovano around 1552.*

STAR FEATURES

★ Crucifix

★ Altar of the Virgin

Gothic stained-
glass window

★ **Altar of the Virgin**
Carved by sculptor Veit Stoss
between 1477 and 1489,
this great Gothic polyptych
altarpiece is 12 m (39 ft)
long and 11 m (36 ft) high.

Visitors'
entrance

Leonardo da Vinci's *Lady with an
Ermine*, Czartoryski Museum

Czartoryski
Museum ⑤
Muzeum Książąt
Czartoryskich

ul. św Jana 19. **Map** D1. *Tel (012)*
422 5566. 🚌 *124, 152, 424, 502,*
512. 🚋 *2, 4, 5, 12, 13, 14, 15, 24.*
⏰ *closed for renovations, call to
check.* 🎫 *free on Sun for permanent
exhibitions.* 🎫

This museum has one of
Poland's most varied art
collections. Assembled in
Puławy at the end of the 18th
century by Princess Izabella
Czartoryska, it was the private
collection of the Czartoryski
family. The collection was
later taken to Paris and then
to Cracow, where it was put
on public view. It includes
examples of handicrafts, but
most significant are the paintings – among them are
Leonardo da Vinci's *Lady with
an Ermine* (c. 1485) and
Rembrandt's *Landscape with
Good Samaritan* (1638).

Church of Sts
Peter and Paul ⑥
Kościół św Piotra i
św Pawła

ul. Grodzka 52a. **Map** C3. *Tel (012)*
422 6573. 🚋 *1, 6, 7, 8, 10, 12, 18.*
⏰ *9am–7pm Mon–Sat, 1:30–5:30pm
Sun.* 🎫

This twin-domed church is
one of the most beautiful
examples of early-Baroque
architecture in Poland. It
was built for the Jesuits
after their arrival in Cracow

in the 1580s, but after a
structural disaster in 1605, the
church was almost completely
rebuilt to the designs of an
unknown architect.

The church is enclosed by
railings topped with the figures
of the apostles dating between
1715 and 1722. The interior
contains fine stuccowork by
Giovanni Battista Falconi. The
high altar and organ screen,
designed by Kacper Bażanka,
are also noteworthy. Among
the many funerary monu-
ments the 17th-century marble
tomb of Bishop Andrzej
Tomicki is most striking.
Standing in front of the church
is the statue of Piotr Skarga, a
Jesuit preacher and champion
of the Counter-Reformation,
erected in 2001. He died in
1612 and was buried in the
crypt below the high altar.

Baroque façade of the Jesuit
Church of Sts Peter and Paul

Stanisław
Wyspiański
Museum ⑦
Muzeum Stanisława
Wyspiańskiego

ul. Szczepańska 11. **Map** C2.
Tel (012) 422 7021. 🚌 *124,*
152, 424, 502, 512. 🚋 *2, 4, 8*
12, 13, 14, 15, 24. ⏰ *10am–
6pm Wed–Sat, 10am–4pm Sun.*
🎫 *free on Sun.* 🎫

This museum, devoted
to Cracow's foremost Art
Noveau artist, Stanisław
Wyspiański, was established
in the 1980s. Exhibits of
interest here include stage
designs, textiles, pastels
and portraits of friends
and family. The stained-
glass windows he produced
for the Franciscan church
display his ingenuity.

Street-by-Street: The Wawel

In about 1038 Kazimierz the Restorer made the citadel on Wawel Hill the seat of Polish political power. In the 16th century the Jagiellonian rulers transformed the Gothic castle into a magnificent Renaissance palace. Once the site of coronations and royal burials, the cathedral is regarded as a shrine by Poles. The Wawel Royal Castle beside it is a symbol of national identity.

★ Wawel Royal Castle
Once home to the Jagiellonian kings, the Wawel Royal Castle has survived without major damage. It incorporates the walls of older Gothic buildings ⑫

Fortifications on the Wawel have been demolished and renewed several times since the Middle Ages – right up to the 20th century ⑧

Monument of Tadeusz Kościuszko

★ Cracow Cathedral
The Gothic cathedral, lined with royal burial chapels from different ages, has some extraordinarily valuable furnishings ⑪

Cathedral Museum
On display are religious and royal regalia from the cathedral treasury, including the magnificent robe of Stanisław August Poniatowski (see p176) ⑨

STAR SIGHTS

★ Cracow Cathedral

★ Wawel Royal Castle

0 metres 50
0 yards 50

The Crown Treasury and Armoury situated in the historic Gothic rooms of the castle were used for storing the Polish coronation insignia and Crown Jewels. Memorabilia of the Polish monarchs and objects from the former treasury are also on display here.

Senatorial Tower

"Lost Wawel" Exhibition displays various finds from archaeological excavations on the Wawel Hill ⑩

Sandomierz Tower

Thieves' Tower

Fortified walls

KEY

--- Suggested route

Fortifications on the Wawel ⑧
Fortyfikacje, Mury Obronne

Wawel. **Map** C4. 🚋 *8, 10, 18, 36, 38, 40.*

The Wawel Hill was fortified from early times but today only fragments of the oldest Gothic fortifications remain. However, three towers raised in the second half of the 15th century still survive – the Senatorial Tower, the Thieves' Tower and the Sandomierz Tower. Of the fortifications dating between the 16th and 17th centuries the most interesting is the Vasa Gate. The monument to the national hero Tadeusz Kościuszko, leader of the failed insurrection of 1794, on the Władysław Bastion is another highlight. The Wawel continued to play a defensive role into the 19th century, and a system of fortifications dating between the late 18th and mid-19th centuries can still be seen.

Sandomierz Tower, one of three towers of the Wawel fortifications

Cathedral Museum ⑨
Muzeum Katedralne

Wawel 3. **Map** C4. **Tel** *(012) 422 5155.* 🚋 *3, 6, 8, 10, 18, 40.* ⭘ *Oct–Mar: 9am–4pm Mon–Sat; Apr–Sep: 9am–5pm Mon–Sat.* ⬤ *1 Jan, Easter, 15 Aug & 25 Dec.* 📷

This museum is located in buildings near the cathedral and contains a valuable collection of pieces from the cathedral treasury. Among the finest liturgical vessels and vestments is the chasuble of Bishop Piotr Kmita, which

Embroidered hood of Bishop Trzebicki's cope, Cathedral Museum

dates from 1504 and has quilted embroidery depicting scenes from St Stanisław's life. Some fascinating pieces of royal memorabilia are also on display at the museum.

"Lost Wawel" Exhibition ⑩
Wawel Zaginiony

Wawel 5. **Map** C4. **Tel** *(012) 422 5155.* 🚋 *3, 6, 8, 10, 18, 40.* ⭘ *Apr–Oct: 9:30am–5pm Tue–Fri, 9:30am–1pm Mon, 11am–4pm Sat–Sun; Nov–Mar: 9:30am–4pm Tue–Sat, 10am–4pm Sun.* 📷 *free Nov–Mar: Sun; Apr–Oct: Mon.* **www**.wawel.krakow.pl

For anyone interested in archaeology, this exhibition is a real delight. The display charts the development of the Wawel over a long period of time, and includes a virtual image of the Wawel buildings as they existed in the early Middle Ages, archaeological finds from Wawel Hill and a partially reconstructed early Romanesque chapel dedicated to the Blessed Virgin. Built at the turn of the 11th century, the chapel was discovered during research work in 1917.

Chapel of the Blessed Virgin, part of the "Lost Wawel" exhibition

Cracow Cathedral ⑪
Królewska Katedra na Wawelu

The Cracow Cathedral, which stands on the Wawel *(see pp188–9)*, is one of the most important churches in Poland. Before the present cathedral was erected (1320–64), two churches stood on the site. The cathedral has many features, including a series of chapels founded by bishops of which the most beautiful is the Renaissance Zygmunt Chapel. There are royal tombs in the cathedral and the Crypt of St Leonard, a remnant of the Romanesque Cathedral of St Wacław.

The top of the clock tower is decorated with statues of saints.

Zygmunt Bell
Constructed in 1520, this is the largest bell in Poland. Weighing almost 11 tonnes (24,251 lbs), it has a diameter of over 2 m (6 ft).

Main entrance

★ Tomb of Kazimierz the Jagiełłonian
Completed in 1492, this royal tomb in the Chapel of the Holy Cross is one of the last commissions that the German sculptor Veit Stoss fulfilled in Poland.

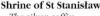

Shrine of St Stanisław
The silver coffin containing the relics of St Stanisław, the bishop of Cracow to whom the cathedral is dedicated, was built between 1669 and 1671 by Pieter van der Rennen, a goldsmith from Gdańsk.

STAR FEATURES

★ Tomb of Kazimierz the Jagiellonian

★ Zygmunt Chapel

Stalls
The early Baroque oak stalls in the chancel were built around 1620.

High Altar

VISITORS' CHECKLIST

Wawel 3. **Map** C4. *Tel (012) 422 5155.* 🚌 *103, 502.* 🚃 *3, 6, 8, 10, 18, 40.* ○ *Apr–Sep: 9am–5pm Mon–Sat, 12:30–5pm Sun; Oct–Mar: 9am–4pm Mon–Sat, 12:30–4pm Sun.* 🏛 *Royal Tombs & Zygmunt Bell.* 🚻 ♿

★ **Zygmunt Chapel**
The chapel with the tombs of the last two Jagiellonian kings is the jewel of Italian Renaissance art in Poland. The tomb of Zygmunt I the Old was made by Bartolomeo Berrecci after 1530, while that of Zygmunt August was built between 1574 and 1575 by Santi Gucci.

Room in the Hen's Foot Tower, Wawel Royal Castle

Wawel Royal Castle ⑫

Zamek Królewski na Wawelu

Wawel Hill. **Map** C4. *Tel (012) 422 1697.* 🚌 *103, 502.* 🚃 *3, 6, 8, 10, 18, 40.* ○ *Nov–Mar: 9:30am–4pm Tue–Sat; Apr–Oct: 9:30am–noon Mon, 9:30am–5pm Tue, Fri, 11am–6pm Sat, Sun.* 🏛 *Apr–Oct: free on Mon; Nov–Mar: Sun.* 🚻 *Royal Private Apartments.*

One of Central Europe's most magnificent Renaissance residences, the Wawel Royal Castle was built for King Zygmunt I the Old, the penultimate ruler of the Jagiellonian Dynasty. The four-winged palace, built between 1502 and 1536, incorporated the remains of a 14th-century building that stood on the site. Italian architects Francisco Fiorentino and Bartolomeo Berrecci designed and constructed it. One of the highlights of the castle is the impressive Renaissance-style courtyard that was built in the 16th century. The rooms in the **Hen's Foot Tower** are among the most beautiful in the castle. The tower was rebuilt after it was damaged by fire in the 16th and 17th centuries.

After the royal court was transferred from Cracow to Warsaw, the palace fell into neglect, and during the era of the partitions it served as barracks. At the beginning of the 20th century, the castle was given to the city of Cracow, which started a restoration programme and turned it into a museum.

Royal Tombs
These Baroque sarcophagi were made for members of the royal Vasa Dynasty. The cathedral is the final resting place of most of the Polish kings, as well as national heroes such as Tadeusz Kościuszko (see p189) and several revered poets.

Street-by-Street: Kazimierz District ⑬

Narrow streets lined with low buildings make up the district
of Kazimierz. Founded in 1335 by Kazimierz the Great, it
soon developed a thriving Jewish population. Czech and
German refugees came here to join Jews displaced from
Cracow in the late 15th century, and the area bears
witness to centuries of co-existence between Jews and
Poles. The Jewish quarter, located in the district's
eastern part, was concentrated around Szeroka
ulica, later known as New Square. Many synagogues, bathhouses and cemeteries were established and Kazimierz became a centre of Judaic
culture and learning. During World War II,
much of the quarter was destroyed in the
Nazi invasion, but recently many galleries,
cafés and bars have opened here.

Temple Synagogue
*The decoration of this synagogue,
built in the Neo-Renaissance style,
was influenced by Moorish art.*

KEY

– – – Suggested route

JEWISH TOMBS

The signs carved on Jewish tombs have
symbolic value. The grave of a rabbi is
indicated by hands joined in prayer.
Those of Levites are distinguished by
basins and jugs for the ritual ablution of
hands. Three interlaced snakes feature on
the grave of a physician, and a crown of
knowledge on that of a learned man. A
lion or a six-pointed Star of David signifies
a descendant of Judah.

0 metres   50

0 yards   50

Intricately carved symbolic motifs on Jewish tombs

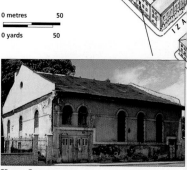

Kupa Synagogue
*Built in the 17th century, this synagogue,
financed by the Kahal, the municipality
of Kazimierz, was also used for non-
religious purposes. It has recently been
converted into a Jewish cultural centre.*

★ Remu'h Cemetery

This evocative Jewish cemetery contains a Wailing Wall which commemorates the tragic fate met by Cracow's Jews during World War II.

Bath *(mikvah)*   **Poper Synagogue**

Remu'h Synagogue

This synagogue is dedicated to Rabbi Remu'h, who was reputed to be a miracle worker. His grave is still venerated by Jewish pilgrims.

DAJWÓR

SZEROKA

JÓZEFA   BARTOZA

Synagogue on the Hill

Isaak's Synagogue was built as a foundation of Isaak Jakubowicz, a Jewish elder.

High Synagogue

Designed in Gothic style, the High Synagogue is one of Cracow's most attractive synagogues.

STAR SIGHTS

★ Remu'h Cemetery

★ Old Synagogue

★ Old Synagogue

Although destroyed by the Nazis, Poland's oldest synagogue has been painstakingly restored. This menorah is among its many treasures.

Auschwitz I ⑭
Oświęcim

For most people, Auschwitz represents the ultimate horror of the Holocaust. The Nazis began the first mass transportation of European Jews to Auschwitz in 1942 and it soon became the centre of extermination. Over the next three years, more than one and a half million people, a quarter of those who died in the Holocaust, were killed at Auschwitz and the neighbouring Birkenau camp (see pp196–7), also known as Auschwitz II. Today, Auschwitz is a UNESCO World Heritage Site and the camp has been preserved as a poignant memorial. The prison blocks have been turned into a museum charting the history of the camps and of persecution in Poland.

Exhibitions
The daily horrors of life in the camp are displayed in some of the barracks.

THE CAMP

Auschwitz I opened in 1940 on the site of former Polish Army barracks. Originally built to incarcerate only Polish political prisoners, further buildings were added in the spring of 1941 as the number of prisoners drastically increased. Camp administration was also based here.

Gas Chambers and Crematoria
The entire Auschwitz complex had seven gas chambers and five crematoria. Four of the gas chambers were in Birkenau but the first was at Auschwitz, operating from 1941.

Guard house and office of the camp supervisor

THE TWO CAMPS

Although part of the same camp complex, Auschwitz and Birkenau are in fact 3 km (2 miles) apart. The small Polish town of Oświęcim was commandeered by the Nazis and renamed Auschwitz. Birkenau was opened in March 1942 in the village of Brzezinka, where the residents were evicted to make way for the camp. There were an additional 47 sub-camps in the surrounding area.

Aerial view of Auschwitz I and Birkenau taken by the Allies in 1944

"Arbeit Macht Frei" Entrance
The infamous words above the entrance to Auschwitz translate as "Work makes you free". This was certainly not the case for the prisoners transported here, who were often worked to death.

The "Wall of Death"
This is a reconstruction of the wall near Block 11 used for summary executions carried out by a firing squad. It now serves as a place of remembrance.

Block 11, the central jail, was where the first experiments with gas were carried out in 1941.

VISITORS' CHECKLIST

75 km (50 miles) W of Cracow.
Map E2. 🚌 to Oświęcim, then
🚌 24, 25, 26, 27, 28, 29. ⏰
Dec–Feb: 8am–3pm; Mar & Nov:
8am–4pm; Apr & Oct: 8am–5pm;
May & Sep: 8am–6pm; Jun–Aug:
8am–7pm. ● 1 Jan, Easter Day,
25 Dec. 📷 call in advance, fee
applies. **Note**: Shuttle bus to
Birkenau runs hourly; leaving
from the Information Centre.
www.auschwitz.org.pl

Store containing the poison, Zyklon B, used to kill prisoners.

Maksymilian Kolbe
This Franciscan priest who, was later canonized, chose to die to save another inmate's life here. He was given death by starvation.

Camp kitchen

Information Centre for visitors

Roll Call Square
Roll call took place up to three times a day and could last for hours. Eventually, due to the large number of prisoners, roll call was taken in front of individual barracks.

TIMELINE

1939 On 1 Sep, Hitler invades Poland	**1940** First deportation of German Jews into Nazi-occupied Poland	**1941** Hitler reported to have ordered the "Final Solution"	**1942** First section of Birkenau camp completed	**1944** As the Soviet Army closes in on Auschwitz, the SS begin destroying all evidence of the camp	**1945** 27 Jan, Soviet soldiers liberate the few remaining prisoners at Auschwitz
1939	**1940**	**1941**	**1942**	**1943**	**1944**	**1945**
1940 Oświęcim chosen as the site of the Nazis' new concentration camp	**1941** Himmler makes first visit to Auschwitz and orders its expansion	**1941** First gas chamber goes into operation	**1942** Beginning of mass deportation to Auschwitz	**1943** Four gas chambers built for mass murder **1945** 18 Jan, 56,000 prisoners evacuated on "Death March"	**1945** 7 May, Germany finally surrenders to the Allies

Auschwitz II–Birkenau
Oświęcim-Brzezinka

Birkenau was primarily a place of execution. Over one million people were killed in its four gas chambers, 98 per cent of whom were Jewish. Victims included Poles, Russian prisoners of war, gypsies and Czech, Yugoslav, French, Austrian and German citizens. Birkenau was also an enormous concentration camp, housing 90,000 slave labourers by mid-1944 and providing labour for many of the factories and farms of southwestern, Nazi-occupied Poland. The gas chambers were quickly destroyed by the Nazis shortly before the Soviet Army liberated the camp in January 1945.

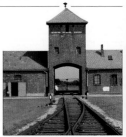

Hell's Gate
In 1944, the numbers arriving at the camp began to increase dramatically. A railway line was extended into the camp. The entrance gate through which the trains passed was known as "Hell's Gate".

Visiting Birkenau
There is little left of the camp today; its main purpose is for remembrance. Most visitors come to pay their respects at the Monument to the Victims of the Camp, on the site of the gas chambers.

Gas chamber and crematorium

The Unloading Ramp
This was possibly the most terrifying part of the camp. It was here that SS officers separated the men from the women and children, and the SS doctors declared who was fit for work. Those declared unfit were taken immediately to their death.

Towers and barbed wire isolated the camps from the outside world.

Women's Barracks
The conditions in the living quarters at the camps were terrible. With little or no sanitation, poor nutrition and no medical care, diseases such as typhus and cholera spread rapidly. This image shows the women's barracks at Birkenau shortly after liberation.

For hotels and restaurants in this region see pp218–21 and pp222–5

Kanada
This was the nickname of the barracks where property stolen from prisoners was stored. It was the preferred place to work at Auschwitz II-Birkenau as it offered opportunities for inmates to pilfer items to barter for food or medicine later.

The Sauna
New arrivals selected for work were deloused and disinfected in this building, which became known as the "sauna". Periodic disinfection of existing prisoners was also carried out here.

Area of expansion, nicknamed "Mexico", was never completed.

The Ash Pond
Tonnes of ash – the remains of hundreds of thousands of Auschwitz victims – were dumped in ponds and troughs dug around the outskirts of the camp.

THE CAMP RECONSTRUCTION

In 1944, Birkenau had more than 90,000 prisoners, the majority of whom were exterminated. It was the largest concentration camp in Nazi-occupied Europe. From the unloading ramp to the gas chambers, the crematoria to the ash dumping grounds, the whole process of murder was carried out systematically and on a huge scale. This reconstruction shows the camp at its peak in 1944, when as many as 5,000 people were killed every day.

Men's barracks, with about 500 to 600 people living in each building.

Hell's Gate

THE LIBERATION OF THE CAMPS

With the war all but lost, in mid-January 1945 the Nazi authorities gave the order for all the camps to be destroyed. However, only a part of Birkenau could be destroyed before the collapse of the German Army. Between 17 and 21 January, more than 56,000 inmates were evacuated by the Nazis and forced to march west, but many died en route. When the Soviet Army entered the camps on 27 January 1945, they found just 7,000 survivors.

Survivors of Auschwitz II-Birkenau, filmed by Soviet troops

Wrocław ❸

Emblem of the Golden Deer House, Main Market Square

The beautiful city of Wrocław bears the stamp of several cultures. It was founded by Duke Vratislav of Bohemia in the 10th century and a Polish bishopric was established here in AD 1000. Later it became the capital of the Duchy of Silesian Piasts, and then came under Czech rule in 1335. In 1526, with the whole Czech state, it was incorporated into the Habsburg Empire, and in 1741 was transferred to Prussian rule. The fierce defence that German forces put up here at the end of World War II left almost three quarters of Wrocław in ruins but the city has now been painstakingly reconstructed.

Baroque *pietá* in the University Church of the Blessed Name of Jesus

Ostrów Tumski
Cathedral of St John the Baptist
pl. Katedralay 18. ☐ *10am–4pm Mon–Sat, 2pm–4pm Sun.*
www.katedra.archidiecezja.wroc.pl
Once an island in the Odra river, Ostrów Tumski is where the history of Wrocław began. In the 19th century, the northern arm of the Odra was filled in and Tumski ceased to be an island. Ostrów Tumski's principal landmark, the **Cathedral of St John the Baptist** (Katedra św Jana Chrzciciela), has a fine interior despite having suffered the ravages of World War II. Other highlights include the two-tiered Church of the Holy Cross, established in 1288 by Henry IV, the Pious and the Archdiocesan Museum, a rich repository of Gothic art built between 1519 and 1527. A walk through the narrow streets can be followed by a visit to the Botanical Gardens.

🏛 Wrocław University
pl. Uniwersytecki 1. **Tel** *(071) 375 2618.* **Assembly Hall** ☐ *10am–3:30pm Mon, Tue, Thu, 11am–5pm Fri–Sun.* 📷
Established as an academy by Emperor Leopold I in 1702, Wrocław University (Uniwersytet Wrocławski) was given its current status in 1811. The university has produced eight Nobel laureates including the nuclear physicist Max Born. Since 1945 it has been a Polish centre of learning.
  The highlight of this Baroque building is the **Assembly Hall** (Aula Leopoldina) whose interior includes stuccowork, gilding by Franz Josef Mangoldt and paintings by Christoph

Handke glorifying Wisdom, Knowledge and Science, and the founders of the academy.

The richly ornamented interior of Wrocław University's Assembly Hall

University Church Blessed Name
Wrocław University
Arsenal
Church of St Barbara
Współczesny Theatre
Church of St Elizabeth ⑫
Town Hall ⑪
University Library
Royal Palace ⑬
PLAC WOLNOŚCI
Church of Sts Wenceslas, Stanisław and Dorothy ⑭
Dolnośląska Opera Hause
Airport 11 km (7 miles)

0 metres 200
0 yards 200

CENTRAL WROCŁAW

🔒 University Church of the Blessed Name of Jesus

pl. Uniwersytecki 1. **Tel** (071) 343 6382. 🔒

Built for the Jesuits in 1689–98, this church (Uniwersytecki Kościoł Najświętszego Imienia Jesuza) exemplifies Silesian Baroque church architecture. The interior was built by Krzysztof Tausch in 1722–34. The vaulting was decorated by the Viennese artist Johann Michael Rottmayer in 1704–6.

The Gothic Church of St Vincent with Hochberg Chapel in front

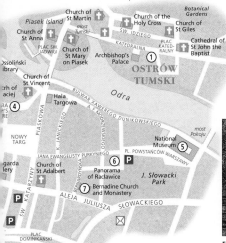

Key to Symbols see back flap

🏛 Nankiera Bishop's Square

The buildings in this square (Plac Biskupa Nankiera) date from various periods. The Gothic **Church of St Vincent** (Kościoł św Wincentego), at No. 5, was erected in the 13th to 15th centuries. At No. 16, the 17th-century Baroque monastery, Old Order of St Clare, now hosts a post elementary school.

The group of Baroque monastic buildings at No. 16 also encloses the small

including the tombstone of Henry IV the Good, dating from 1300. The first floor has a 16th- and 17th-century painting collection, including works by the Silesian artist Michael Willmann (1630–1706) and wooden sculptures by Thomas Weissfeldt (1630–1712). The second floor is devoted to contemporary works by Polish artists.

Façade of the National Museum

13th-century **Church of St Clare** (Kościoł św Klary). The church, used by the Piasts as a mausoleum, still contains Gothic Ducal tombs. Next door, at No. 17, is the Gothic **Church of St Maciej** (Kościoł św Macieja), which was once owned by the Knights Hospitallers of the Red Star. The pavilion of the gallery at No. 8, on the opposite side of the square, contains the 13th-century walls of the **House of the Nuns of Trebnica** (dom sióstr trebnica), the oldest surviving secular building in the city.

🏛 National Museum

pl. Powstańców Warszawy 5. **Tel** (071) 343 8839. 🕙 10am–4pm Wed, Fri, 9am–4pm Thu, 11am–7pm Sat, 11am–5pm Sun. 🎫 free on Sat, limited availability. **www**.mnwr.art.pl

The ground floor of the National Museum (Muzeum Narodowe) contains examples of Silesian and Gothic art,

Panorama of Racławice

ul. Purkyniego 11. **Tel** (071) 344 2344. 🕙 winter: 9am–4pm Tue–Sun; summer: 9am–5pm daily. 🎫 🚻

The Panorama of Racławice (Panorama Racławicka) depicts the Battle of Racławice of 4 April 1794, when the Poles defeated the Russians. It is 120 m (400 ft) long and 15 m (46 ft) high and took artists Wojciech Kossak and Jan Styka nine months to paint. Unveiled in 1894 in Lviv, in Ukraine, it was brought to Poland in 1946 and was put on display in Wrocław in 1985.

Rotunda containing the Panorama of Racławice

Wrocław: Old Town

For those who enjoy exploring on foot, the Old Town (Stare Miasto) of Wrocław is a delightful place. The restored buildings located around the large Main Market Square have been given over to an assortment of bars, restaurants and cafés with alfresco seating, while the nearby churches contain a wealth of religious art and ecclesiastical furnishings. The impressive Gothic Town Hall has a finely decorated interior. On summer evenings, this bustling square comes alive as locals as well as visitors gather here, some to gossip and exchange news, others to attend the concerts and many cultural events that are held in the square.

The façade of the House of the Seven Electors, Main Market Square

Late-Gothic portal of the Bernadine Church and Monastery

🛈 Bernadine Church and Monastery

ul. Bernardyńska 5. **Architecture Museum Tel** (071) 344 8278.
🕐 10am–4pm Tue, Wed, Fri, Sat, noon–6pm Thu, 11am–5pm Sun. 🖼 free on Wed. **www**.ma.wroc.pl
This impressive group of monastic buildings (Kościół i Klasztor pobernardyński) was constructed by Bernadine monks between 1463 and 1502. Rebuilt from their wartime ruins, they now house the **Architecture Museum** (Muzeum Architektury). The monastery is of interest for its late-Gothic cloisters and the Church of St Bernard of Siena, a towering Gothic basilica with a typically Baroque gable.

🛈 St Mary Magdalene's Church

ul. św Marii Magdaleny. **Tel** (071) 344 1904. 🕐 9am–noon, 4–6pm daily.
The great Gothic St Mary Magdalene's Church (Kościół św Marii Magdaleny) was erected between 1330 and

the mid-15th century, incorporating the walls of a 13th-century church that had previously stood on the site. Inside the basilica is a Gothic stone tabernacle, a Renaissance pulpit made between 1579 and 1581 by Friedrich Gross and tombstones of various periods. The portal on the north side is a superb example of late 12th-century Romanesque sculpture. It was taken from a demolished Benedictine monastery in Olbina and added in 1546. The tympanum, depicting the Dormition of the Virgin, is now on display in the National Museum (see p199).

Relief, St Mary Magdalene's Church

🏛 Kameleon Store

ul. Szewska 6–7.
The Kameleon Store (Dom Handlowy Kameleon) is an unusual building on the corner of ulica Szewska and ulica Oławska. It was built by the German architect Erich Mendelsohn as a retail store for Rudolf Petersdorf between 1927 and 1928. Its semicircular bay, formed of rows of windows, juts out dramatically. Nearby, at the intersection of ulica Łaciarska and Ofiar Oświęcimskich, an office building built between 1912 and 1913

by renowned architect Hans Poelzig is another interesting example of Modernist architecture.

🏛 Main Market Square

Rynek.
Wrocław's Main Market Square is the second largest in Poland, after the one in Cracow. In the centre stand the Town Hall and a group of buildings separated by alleys. The houses around the square date from the Renaissance to the 20th century. Some still have their original 14th- and 15th-century Gothic vaults. The west side of the square is the most attractive with the late-Baroque **House of the Golden Sun**, at No. 6, built in 1727 by Johann Lucas von Hildebrandt, as well as the **House of the Seven Electors**, its paintwork dating from 1672. Also to the south is **Under the Griffins** (Pod Gryfami), at No. 2, built between 1587 and 1589. It has a galleried interior courtyard. On the east side, at No. 31 and No. 32, is **Feniks Store** of 1904 and, at No. 41, **Under the Golden Dog** (Pod Złotym Psem), a rebuilt town house of 1713. The north side was reconstructed after World War II. Just off the corner of the Main Market Square, in front of the Church of St Elizabeth (Kościół św Elżbiety), are two small acolytes' houses, the Renaissance Jaś of around 1564, and the 18th-century Baroque Małgosia.

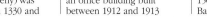

🏛 Town Hall

ul. Sukiennice 14/15. **Museum of City Art** 🕙 *11am–5pm Wed–Sat, 10am–6pm Sun.* 📷 **www.muzeum.miejskie.wroclaw.pl**

Wrocław's Town Hall (Muzeum Miejskie Wrocławia) is one of the most important examples of Gothic architecture in Eastern and Central Europe. Its present appearance is the result of extensive rebuilding that took place between 1470 and 1510.

The building's southern façade was embellished with Neo-Gothic stone carvings around 1871. Inside are impressive vaulted halls, the largest being the triple-aisled Grand Hall on the ground floor that served as an important venue for public meetings and receptions. There are also a number of late-Gothic and Renaissance doorways. The building also houses the **Museum of City Art** (Muzeum Sztuki Mieszczańskiej).

A plaque outside the entrance to the Town Hall commemorates the prominent poet and writer Aleksander Fredro (1793–1876), who acquired fame with his comedies about the Polish upper classes. The plaque was made in 1879 by Leonard Marconi and transferred to Wrocław from Lviv in 1956.

Gothic gables of the east façade of the Town Hall

🔒 Church of St Elizabeth

ul. św Elżbiety. **Tel** *(071) 343 1638.* 🕙 *8am–6pm Mon–Sat, 1–6pm Sun.*

The tower dominating the Main Market Square is that of the Church of St Elizabeth (Kościół św Elżbiety), one of the largest churches in Wrocław. The Gothic basilica was built in the 14th century on the site of an earlier church. However, the tower was not completed until 1482. It became a Protestant church in 1525 and has been a garrison church since 1946.

The church suffered damage from a succession of wars and accidents. A fire in 1976 destroyed the roof and the fine Baroque organ. Fortunately, more than 350 epitaphs and tombstones have survived, forming a display of Silesian stone-carving from Gothic to Neo-Classical periods.

Church of St Elizabeth with Jaś and Małgosia, acolytes' houses

🏛 Royal Palace

ul. Kazimierza Wielkiego 35. **Archaeology Museum** ul. Cieszyńskiego 9. **Tel** *(071) 347 1696.* 🕙 *11am–5pm Wed–Sat, 11am–6pm Sun.* 📷 **Ethnographic Museum** ul. Traugutta 111/113. **Tel** *(071) 344 3313.* 🕙 *10am–4pm Tue, Wed, Fri–Sun, 9am–4pm Thu.* 📷 *free on Sat.*

This Baroque palace (Pałac Królewski) with Classical details, enclosed by a court of annexes, was built in 1719. After 1750, when Wrocław was under Prussian rule, it became a residence for the Prussian kings. On the side facing Plac Wolności, only a side gallery remains of the Neo-Renaissance palace built between 1843 and 1846.

The Royal Palace contains two interesting collections: the **Archaeology Museum** and **Ethnographic Museum**, the latter illustrating Silesian art and folk history, including a large collection of dolls in traditional garments.

Church of Sts Wenceslas, Stanisław and Dorothy

🔒 Church of Sts Wenceslas, Stanisław and Dorothy

ul. Świdnicka. **Tel** *(071) 343 2721.*

Dedicated to three saints, the Czech St Wenceslas, the Polish St Stanisław and the German St Dorothy, this Franciscan church (Kościół św Wacława, Stanisława i Doroty) was built in 1351 to strengthen relations between Wrocław's three nationalities.

The church's unusually narrow interior is Gothic. The beautiful Rococo tombstone of Gottfried von Spaetgen (c. 1725–1753) stands in the nave.

THE OSSOLINEUM

The National Ossoliński Institute was founded by Count Józef Maksymilian Ossoliński (1748–1829) in Vienna in 1817. In 1827 it moved to Lwów (later Lviv), where it assembled collections of manuscripts, prints, etchings and drawings, promoted scientific research and engaged in publishing. After World War II, most of the collections were transferred to the National Museum *(see p199)* in Wrocław, while the manuscripts were housed in the Baroque monastery of the Knights Hospitallers of the Red Star in Wrocław.

The Baroque monastery that houses the Ossolineum

Poznań ❹

Poznań is the capital of Wielkopolska, a historical region in west-central Poland, and is its largest city. A stronghold by the name of Polan stood here in the 8th century and it became the capital of the emerging Polish state in the 10th century. It was declared the seat of the first bishopric in Poland in 968. Today, Poznań is Poland's second financial centre after Warsaw and a centre of commerce. Annual trade fairs have been held here since 1921. The city has many historic buildings, the finest of which are its cathedral and those in the Old Town (Stare Miasto). A visit to the late 19th-century quarter is also worth a visit.

ground floors of the buildings around the square are filled by banks, cafés and restaurants.

From spring to autumn, the square bustles with life; local artists display their paintings, and the outdoor cafés are permanently busy. The square also serves as a venue for cultural events. Some of the houses here were destroyed during the battles for Poznań in 1945 and were rebuilt after

Interior of the Church of the Most Sacred Heart of Jesus

🔒 Church of the Most Sacred Heart of Jesus
ul. Szewska 18. *Tel (061) 852 5076/853 3359.*

This magnificent church (Kościół Serca Jezusowego), built in the 13th century, is the oldest in the Old Town. It was a Dominican church until 1920, when it was passed to the Jesuits. During the German occupation in World War II, a repository was set up here for Polish books removed from the libraries in Poznań.

🔒 Church of Sts Mary Magdalene and Stanisław
ul. Gołębia 1. *Tel (061) 852 6950.*

Construction work on this Baroque church (Kościół św Marii Magdaleny i św Stanisław), began in 1651 and continued for more than 50 years. Several architects, craftsmen and artists, including Tomasso Poncino, Jan Catenaci and Bartołomiej Wąsowski, had a role in the project.

The most impressive aspect of the church is its monolithic interior. Gigantic columns lead towards the high altar, which

was designed and constructed in 1727 by Pompeo Ferrari. Over this is a painting illustrating a legendary episode from the life of St Stanisław. Then a bishop, he was accused by the Polish King Bolesław III Wrymouth (1085–1138) of not paying for a village he had incorporated into his territory. In order to prove his innocence, St Stanisław resurrected the deceased former owner of the land to testify on his behalf.

The Baroque buildings of a former Jesuit monastery and college stand close to the church, built for the brotherhood between 1701 and 1733. Today, they are used by the city council for secular purposes.

🏛 Old Town Square
The Old Town Square (Stary Rynek) is the heart of the Old Town. It is surrounded by town houses with colourful façades, among which stands the Renaissance Old Town Hall. The centrepiece of the square is the Baroque Proserpine Fountain of 1766, depicting the abduction of the ancient Roman goddess of fertility, Proserpine. Nearby, a 20th-century fountain commemorates 18th-century Catholic settlers from Bamberg, in southern Germany. The

World War II, but others escaped any serious damage. They include Mielżyński Palace, which dates from 1796–8, and Działyński Palace, both in Neo-Classical style.

🏛 Old Town Hall
Stary Rynek 1. **Historical Museum of Poznań** *Tel (061) 856 8193.*
⭕ 9am–3pm Tue–Thu, noon–9pm Fri, 11am–6pm Sat, Sun. 🎟 free on Sat. **www**.mnp.art.pl
Poznań's Old Town Hall (Ratusz) is one of the finest municipal buildings in Europe. It was built between

POZNAŃ CITY CENTRE

Archdiocese Museum ⑪
Church of the Most Sacred
  Heart of Jesus ①
Church of Sts Mary Magdalene
  and Stanisław ②
Działyński Palace ⑤
National Museum ⑦
Old Town Hall ④
Old Town Square ③
Ostrów Tumski ⑩
Poznań Cathedral ⑫
Przemysław Castle ⑥
Raczyński Library ⑧
St Adalbert's Hill ⑨

1550 and 1560 by the Italian architect Giovanni Battista di Quadro. The façade has three tiers of arcades, topped by a grand attic and a large tower, and decorated with portraits of the kings of Poland. The clock tower is an attraction in its own right. At noon each day, two clockwork goats emerge from doors 12 times to butt heads. The building now houses the **Historical Museum of Poznań** (Muzeum Historii Miasta Poznania). The Renaissance Hall on the first floor is lavishly decorated to reflect the affluence of the city's municipal leaders. The coffered ceiling is covered with an intricate series of paintings.

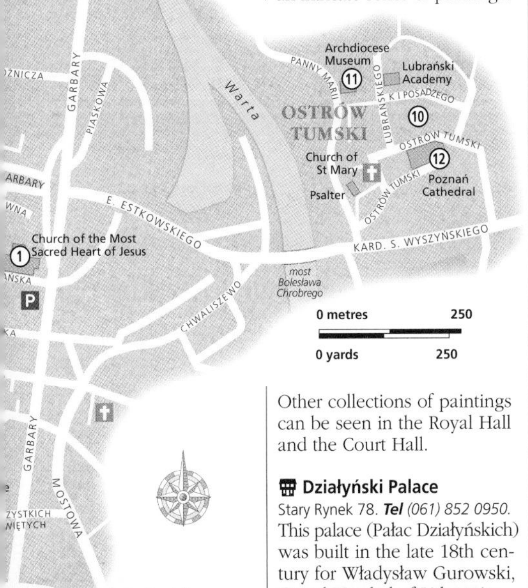

[Map of Poznań city centre showing numbered locations including Archdiocese Museum ⑪, Lubrański Academy ⑩, OSTRÓW TUMSKI, Church of St Mary, Psalter, Poznań Cathedral ⑫, Church of the Most Sacred Heart of Jesus ①, most Bolesława Chrobrego, streets: NOCNA, GARBARY, PASKOWA, ŻNICZA, ARBARY, WNA, INSKA, KA, GARBARY, MOSTOWA, ZYSTKICH MIĘTYCH, E. ESTKOWSKIEGO, CHWALISZEWO, KARD. S. WYSZYŃSKIEGO, PANNY MARII, LUBRAŃSKIEGO, K. POSADZEGO, OSTRÓW TUMSKI, Warta]

0 metres 250
0 yards   250

Key to Symbols *see back flap*

Other collections of paintings can be seen in the Royal Hall and the Court Hall.

🏛 Działyński Palace
Stary Rynek 78. **Tel** (061) 852 0950.
This palace (Pałac Działyńskich) was built in the late 18th century for Władysław Gurowski, Grand Marshal of Lithuania.

VISITORS' CHECKLIST

319 km (175 miles) W of
Warsaw. 🚂 560,000.
✈ 7 km (4 miles) W of centre.
🚉 Dworzec Główny ul.
Dworcowa 1. 🛈 Stary Rynek
59, (061) 852 6156.
🎭 Poznań International Trade
Fair (all year). 🎭 Malta
International Theatre Festival
(Jun). **www**.poznan.pl

**Façade of the magnificent
Działyński Palace**

The Neo-Classical façade is crowned with a large eagle and set with figures of Roman soldiers made by Anton Höhne between 1785 and 1787. The columned Red Room is worth a visit. The building is now used as a library, theatre and concert hall.

⚜ Przemysław Castle
Góra Przemysła 1. **Applied Arts
Museum Tel** (061) 856 8186.
🕐 9am–3pm Tue–Thu, noon–9pm
Fri, 11am–6pm Sat & Sun. 🎟 free
on Sat. **www**.mnp.art.pl
Little remains of the castle (Zamek Przemysława) built by Przemysław II in the 13th century, once the largest in Poland. The reconstructed castle that now stands on the site houses the **Applied Arts Museum** (Muzeum Sztuk Użytkowych), which holds a collection of everyday objects, decorative artifacts and religious items dating from the Middle Ages to the present. The Baroque Franciscan Church on ulica Góra Przemysła dates from the early 18th century. Frescoes by the Franciscan painter Adam Swach decorate the nave.

Poznań's colourful Old Market Square

🏛 National Museum

al. Marcinkowskiego 9. *Tel (061)*
852 5969. ☐ *9am–3pm Tue–Thu,*
noon–9pm Fri, 11am–6pm Sat & Sun.
📷 *free on Sat.* **www**.mnp.art.pl

The National Museum
(Muzeum Narodowe) is
housed in what was originally
the Prussian Friedrich Museum
a Neo-Renaissance building
from 1900–1903. Its collections
of Polish paintings are among
the best in the country. They
include medieval art of the
12th to the 16th centuries and
17th- to 18th-century coffin
portraits. Canvases by Jacek
Malczewski are the best examples of painting by the Young
Poland Movement. The Gallery
of European Art contains
works from various collections,
including those belonging to
Atanazy Raczyński, brother of
Count Edward Raczyński. The
most outstanding paintings are
those by Dutch and Flemish
artists including Joos van Cleve
and Quentin Massys. Italian,
French and Spanish painters
are also represented.

🏛 Raczyński Library

pl. Wolności 19. *Tel (061) 852
9442.* ☐ *9am–7pm Mon–Fri.*
www.bracz.edu.pl

Architecturally, Raczyński
Library (Biblioteka Raczyński)
is one of the most distinguished buildings in the city.
Its columned façade combines
grandeur with elegance, and
it cannot be compared with
any other building in Poznań.
The idea for a library was

**Statue of Hygeia, Greek goddess of
health, the Raczyński Library**

initiated by Count Edward
Raczyński in 1829. The aim
of this visionary aristocrat
was to turn Poznań into a
"New Athens". The library
was to be a centre of culture.
Although the library's architect
is unknown, it is thought
to have been built by the
French architects and
designers Charles Percier
and Pierre Fontaine.

A seated statue of Hygeia,
the ancient Greek goddess
of health, with the features
of Konstancja z Potockich,
Edward Raczyński's wife,
was installed in front of the
library in 1906.

St Adalbert's Hill

This hill (Wzgórze św
Wojciecha) is believed to
be the spot where 1,000
years ago, St Adalbert gave
a sermon before setting off

on his campaign to evangelize
the Prussians. On the summit,
two churches face each other
across a small square. One
is the Discalced Carmelites'
Church of St Joseph, built by
Cristoforo Bonadura the Elder
and Jan Catenaci between 1658
and 1667. It contains the tomb
of Mikołaj Jan Skrzetuski
on whom novelist Henryk
Sienkiewicz based the hero
of his historical saga *With
Fire and Sword (Ogniem i
Mieczem).* The other is
the Gothic Church of
St Adalbert, forming a
pantheon with the same
function as the Pauline
Church on the Rock in
Cracow. The crypt contains
the remains of eminent
local figures, including Józef
Wybicki, who wrote the
Polish national anthem.

Ostrów Tumski

The oldest part of Poznań,
Ostrów Tumski was the site of
one of the first capital cities of
the Polish state in the 10th
century. Today, it is dominated by the Gothic towers of
Poznań Cathedral, which contains many fine works of art.
Near the cathedral stands the
small Gothic **Church of
St Mary** (Kościół Najświętszej
Marii Panny), which was built
between 1431 and 1448 for
Bishop Andrzej Bniński by
Hanusz Prusz, a pupil of the
prominent late medieval
architect Heinrich Brunsberg.
Down the road from the

The Neo-Renaissance façade of the National Museum

For hotels and restaurants in this region see pp218–21 and pp222–5

church is the **Lubrański Academy**, the first institute of higher education to be established in Poznań. Founded in 1518 by Bishop Jan Lubrański, it acquired its greatest renown in the early 16th century. Among its alumni was Jan Struś, a physician during the Polish Renaissance.

In the gardens on the other side of ulica Kl Podsadzego stand a number of charming houses, one of which holds the collections of the **Archdiocese Museum**. The late Gothic **Psalter**, built around 1520 by Bishop Lubrański, is distinguished for its stepped and recessed gables.

🏛 Archdiocese Museum

ul. Lubrańskiego 1. **Tel** (061) 852 6195. ⬜ 10am–5pm Tue–Fri, 9am–3pm Sat. ⬤ public hols. 🖼 🎫
The outstanding collection of religious art on display in the Archdiocese Museum (Muzeum Archidiecezjalne) includes medieval painting and sculpture, pieces of Gothic embroidery and some fine *kontusz* (silk sashes). The most important pieces are the *Madonna of Ołobok*, a Gothic-Romanesque statue dating from around 1310–29, and a fascinating group of coffin portraits, painted on metal plates.

🛐 Poznań Cathedral

Ostrów Tumski 17. **Tel** (061) 852 9642. ⬜ Mar–Oct: 9am–6pm Mon–Sat, 2–6pm Sun; Nov–Feb: 9am–4pm Mon–Sat, 2–6pm Sun.
In 966, shortly after Poland adopted Christianity, a pre-Romanesque basilica was built on this site and Poland's first rulers were buried here. Between 1034 and 1038, the basilica was destroyed during pagan uprisings, but it was rebuilt in the Romanesque style. It was remodelled in the Gothic and Baroque periods, and after suffering war damage was restored to its Gothic form. Vestiges of the pre-Romanesque and Romanesque churches can be seen in the crypt. Among the highlights of the interior is Golden Chapel, built between 1834 and 1841. Here lie the tombs of two of Poland's first rulers, Mieszko I and Bolesław II the Bold,

whose statues were carved by Chrystian Rauch. The 16th-century tomb of Bishop Benedykt Izdbieński is the work of Jan Michałowicz of Urzędow, the celebrated sculptor of the Polish Renaissance.

Monument to the Victims of June 1956

🏯 Former Kaiser District

After the Second Partition of Poland in 1793, Poznań came under Prussian rule. In the second half of the 19th century, Prussia heightened its policy of Germanization in the region. One of its instruments was the German Union of the Eastern Marches (Deutscher Ostmarkenverein), which the Poles called the "Hakata" colonization commission from the acronym of the initials of its founders. When the city's ring of 19th-century fortifications was demolished, a decision was made to use the space for government buildings.

Designed by German town planner Josef Stübben, the buildings were built between 1903 and 1914 and today stand amidst gardens, avenues and the royal academy. Dominating the scene is the Kaiserhaus Castle by Franz Schwechten, although little survives of its original splendour. Renamed the Zamek, it now houses the Zamek Cultural Centre. The **Monument to the Victims of June 1956**, which stands beside it in Plac Mickiewicza, takes the form of two large crosses. It was unveiled in 1981 to commemorate the victims of the Poznań's Workers' Uprising in 1956.

Raczyński Palace ❺
Palac Raczyńskich

330 km (205 miles) W of Warsaw. **Palace Museum Tel** (061) 813 8030. ⬜ Nov–Apr: 10am–4pm Tue–Sat, 10am–6pm Sun; May to Oct: 10am–6pm Tue–Sun. ⬤ Mon. 🖼 free on Sat. 🎫 www.free.art.pl/rogalin

Located in the village of Rogalin, Raczyński Palace is one of the most magnificent buildings in the region. The seat of many Polish nobles, it was begun around 1770 for Kazimierz Raczyński, Palatine of Wielkopolska and Grand Marshal of the Crown.

Although designed in the Baroque style, architectural ornamentation was abandoned during construction. The main building, however, retains its late Baroque solidity. Between 1782 and 1783, colonnades were added and complemented by annexes in the classic Palladian style. A drawing room and grand staircase designed by royal architect Jan Chrystian Kamsetzer were added between 1788 and 1789. A pavilion built between 1909 and 1912 contains a collection of Polish and European paintings dating from about 1850 to the early 20th century, including works by Jacek Malczewski and Jan Matejko.

The grounds contain formal gardens as well as one of the largest areas of protected oak woodland in Europe. The palace's Mausoleum Chapel, designed in the style of a Classical temple, contains the tombs of members of the Raczyński family.

Protected oak trees, Raczyński Palace grounds

Toruń

Founded by the Teutonic knights in 1233, Toruń quickly became a major centre of trade. In 1454, when its citizens rebelled against the knights' rule, it passed to the kings of Poland. Famous as the birthplace of the astronomer Nicolaus Copernicus (1473–1543), the city is also renowned for its architecture. Picturesquely situated on the banks of the Vistula river, the Old Town of Toruń retains its medieval street plan, and has a rare calm, since most of the streets are closed to traffic.

The elaborate east end of the Gothic St Mary's Church

🎭 Wilam Horzyca Theatre
pl. Teatralny 1. *Tel (056) 622 5222.*
This delightful theatre, in the Art Nouveau style with Neo-Baroque elements, was built in 1904 by the Viennese architects Ferdinand Fellner and Hermann Helmer. The Kontakt Theatre Festival, held here each year, brings together performers from all over Europe drawing a large number of enthusiastic audiences to its performances.

⛪ St Mary's Church
ul. Marii Panny. *Tel (056) 622 2603.*
The Gothic St Mary's Church (Kościół Mariacki) was built for Franciscan monks between 1270 and 1300. It has a richly ornamented east gable. Late 14th-century wall paintings are in the southern aisle, while in the northern aisle is a 16th-century Mannerist organ loft, the oldest in Poland. By the presbytery is the mausoleum of Anna Vasa, sister of Zygmunt III, made in 1636. Although of royal blood, she could not be buried at Wawel Royal Castle *(see p191)* as she was of the Protestant faith.

🏛 Old Market Square
The Old Market Square (Stary Rynek) is the heart of the historic district. The centrepiece is the Town Hall. On the south side, at No. 7, is the Meissner Palace, built in 1739 for Jakob Meissner, the mayor of Toruń, and given a Neo-Classical façade in 1798. To the east, Star House built in 1697, has an ornamented façade. In the square stands a monument to Nicolaus Copernicus, made by Friedrich Tiecek in 1853, and a fountain with the figure of a raftsman.

🏛 Town Hall
Rynek Staromiejski 1. **Regional Museum** *Tel (056) 622 7038.* ◻ *Oct–Apr: 10am–4pm, Tue–Sun; May–Sep: 10am–6pm, Tue–Sun.* ● *Mon.* 🎫 *(ground floor free on Wed).* **Tower** ◻ *May–Oct: 10am–7pm.* 🎫
The Town Hall (Ratusz) was built between 1391 and 1399 as a two-storey edifice. In the 17th century, architect Antonis van Opbergen added the third floor and gave the building its Mannerist appearance. It now houses the **Regional Museum** of Gothic art and its **Tower** commands fine views.

A room in the 15th-century Copernicus House

🏛 Copernicus House
ul. Kopernika 15/17. *Tel (056) 622 6748.* ◻ *Jan–Apr: 10am–4pm daily; May–Sep: 10am–6pm daily; Oct–Dec: 10am–4pm daily.* 🎫
These two neighbouring Gothic town houses from the 15th century are outstanding examples of Hanseatic merchants' houses. The painted façades and fine carving of the arched gables bear witness to the city's former wealth. The house at No. 17 was where Mikołaj Kopernik, Copernicus's father, lived. Although it may not be the one in which the astronomer Copernicus was born, it is now a museum (Muzeum Kopernika).

🏛 Crooked Tower
ul. Pod Krzywą Wieżą 1.
One of Toruń's greatest attractions, this tower (Krzywa Wieża) is part of the town's old fortification system, and was probably built in the first half of the 14th century. Although it leans significantly from the perpendicular, the floors that were added later

St Mary's Church, as viewed from the top of the Town Hall Tower

are perfectly level – so that
beer glasses in the pub that it
now houses can be set down.

♠ Castle of the Teutonic Knights
ul. Przedzamcze 3.
Little more than ruins remain
of the castle that the Teutonic
Knights began building in
Toruń during the 13th century.
Before the castle was built at
Malbork, Toruń was the
knights' capital. The castle
was extended in the 14th
century, however, it was
destroyed in 1454 when
the people rose in rebellion
against the knights. Only the
latrine tower – a tower over-
hanging a stream that acted as
a sewer – was left standing,
although part of the cellars
and cloisters still survive.

The Gothic house that was
built on the site in 1489, probably with materials scavenged
from the castle, was the meeting house of the Brotherhood
of St George.

♛ New Market Square
The New Town emerged as a
separate civic entity in 1264.
Although it does not have as
many historic buildings as the
Old Town, it has a lively
atmosphere. In summer, the
Market Square (Rynek
Nowomiejski) is filled with
fruit and vegetable stalls. In
the centre is a former
Protestant church, built in
1824, probably by the German
architect Karl Friedrich
Schinkel. It has been converted into a gallery of
contemporary art. Fine houses,
some with ornate façades
like that of the Baroque
house at No. 17 surround the
square. On the corner of
ulica Królowej Jadwigi is the
Golden Lion pharmacy, originating in the 15th century.

Malbork Castle, the great fortress on the Nogat river

Malbork ⑦

316 km (196 miles) NW of Warsaw.
40,000. ul. Dworkowa
17, (055) 612 1000. summer.
www.zamek.malbork.pl

Malbork, the castle of the
Teutonic knights, was begun
in the 13th century. In 1309, it
was made the capital of an
independent state established
by that order. The first major
phase of building was the
Assembly Castle, a fortified
monastery later known as the
Upper Castle. The Middle
Castle was built after 1310,
and includes the Palace of
the Grand Master, a structure
almost without equal in medieval Europe, built between
1382 and 1399 by Konrad
Zöllner von Rotenstein (c.
1335–90), the 23rd Grand
Master of the Teutonic Order.
The Summer Refectory and
Winter Refectory are alongside. The Upper Castle's inner
courtyard is surrounded by
slender Gothic arches with

Towering granite central column,
Summer Refectory, Malbork

triangular vaulting. The
partly reconstructed farm
buildings in the Lower Castle,
abutting the former Chapel of
St Lawrence, have been converted into a hotel.

Sopot ⑧

394 km (245 miles) NW of Warsaw.
43,000. ul.
Dworcowa 4, (058) 550 3783.
International Festival of Song
(Aug). www.sopot.pl

The most popular resort town
on the Baltic coast, Sopot was
established as a sea-bathing
centre in 1824 by Jean
Georges Haffner, a physician
in the Napoleonic Army. Since
the 17th century, Sopot has
been favoured by the wealthy
burghers of Gdańsk for their
mansions. In the interwar
years, it attracted some of the
richest people in Europe.
The pier is a continuation
of the main street, colloquially known as Monciak.
Considered the longest pier in
Europe, it is 512 m (1,680 ft)
long with a bench running all
the way around it. Filled with
bars and restaurants, the pier
is a pleasant place to enjoy a
beer and the sea air. Visitors
also flock to the Art Deco
Sofitel Grand Hotel (see p221),
built between 1924 and 1927,
which overlooks the beach.

In the hills behind the
town is the Opera in the
Woods (Opera Leśna), built
in 1909 and the venue for the
International Festival of Song.
Founded in 1961, this was
once regarded as Eastern
Europe's answer to the
Eurovision Song Contest.

Gdańsk ⑨

Among the finest cities of northern Europe, Gdańsk has a history that goes back more than 1,000 years. One of the wealthiest cities in Poland, it was completely destroyed during World War II, but a postwar rebuilding programme has restored many of its grand buildings. Most of the historic buildings are located along the pedestrianized ulica Długa and Long Market (Długi Targ) in the city centre. Despite severe war damage, the Old Town (Stare Miasto) retains a handful of churches, the most remarkable of which is the medieval Church of St Mary, dating back to the 14th century.

The Upland Gate, part of the fortifications of 1571–6

GETTING AROUND

Vehicle access to the historic part of the Old Town is restricted. The city centre can be reached by taking a bus or tram to the Main Station (Gdańsk Główny), the Upland Gate (Brama Wyżynna) or Podwale Przedmiejskie, and continuing on foot from there. Buses, trams or the urban railway (SKM) serve the outlying parts of the city.

0 metres   200

0 yards   200

SEE ALSO

• *Where to Stay* p220

• *Where to Eat* p224

SIGHTS AT A GLANCE

Artus Court ⑩
Central Maritime Museum ⑪
Church of St Catherine ④
Church of St Mary ⑥
Gdańsk Crane ⑤
Great Armoury ⑦
Great Mill ③
Main Town Hall ⑨

Monument to the Fallen
  Shipyard Workers ①
National Museum ⑫
Old Town Hall ②
Uphagen House ⑧

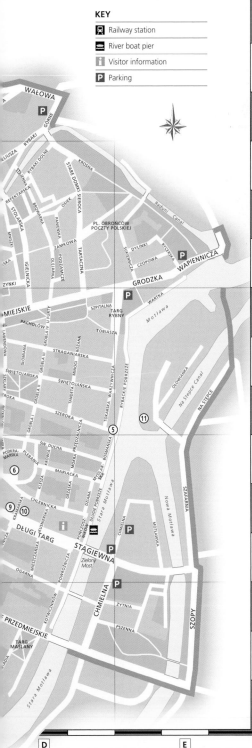

KEY

🚉 Railway station

🚢 River boat pier

ℹ️ Visitor information

🅿️ Parking

Monument to the Fallen Shipyard Workers ①

Pomnik Poległych Stoczniowców

plac Solidarności. **Map** C1.

This monument was built a few months after the Gdańsk Shipyard workers' strike of 1980 and the creation of the first Independent Solidarity Trades Union *(see p170)*. Erected in honour of the shipyard workers who were killed during the first strike and demonstrations of December 1970, it stands 30 m (100 ft) from the spot where the first three victims fell. Its three stainless steel crosses, 42 m (130 ft) high, were intended both as a warning against such tragedies in the future, and as a symbol of hope and remembrance. The monument was designed by the shipyard workers along with a group of artists including Bogdan Pietruszka, Robert Pepliński, Wiesław Szyślak and Elżbieta Szczodrowska. It was built by a team of shipyard workers. In the 1980s, the cross was the rallying point for Solidarity demonstrations.

The towering Monument to the Fallen Shipyard Workers

The impressive façade of Great Mill

Old Town Hall ②
Ratusz Starego Miastsa

ul. Korzenna 33/35. **Map** C3.
Tel (058) 301 1051.

Built by Antonis van
Opbergen between 1587
and 1595, the Old Town Hall
is an outstanding example of
Dutch Mannerist architecture.
A compact building with no
distinctive ornamentation,
it is equipped with a strong
defence tower. The stone
doorway was probably made
by artist Willem van der
Meer at the end of the 16th
century. Beneath each bracket
are two distorted masks
personifying Vice, and two
smiling, chubby masks,
representing Virtue.

Even though very little is
left of the original decorative
scheme of 1595, the paintings,
sculptures and furniture within
the Town Hall are fascinating.
Of particular interest is the
painted ceiling in one of the
rooms by Hermann Hahn,
a 17th-century artist from
Pomerania. It was removed
from a house at ulica Długa
39 and transferred to this
building some time after
1900. The theme of the ceiling paintings are allegorical:
the central one depicts The
Lord's Blessing and the Polish
King Zygmunt III also appears
in the painting. Today, the
building houses the Baltic Sea

Culture Centre (Nadbałtyckie
Centrum Kultury). The main
room on the ground floor
houses a changing series of
exhibitions devoted to local,
regional, cultural and historical
themes. In the main hall is the
bronze figure of Jan Hevelius,
a Polish astronomer and
city councillor.

Great Mill ③
Wielki Młyn

ul. Wielkie Młyny 16. **Map** C2.
☐ 10am–6pm Mon–Fri, 10am–1pm
Sat.

The seven-storey Great Mill is
regarded as one of the largest
industrial buildings in medieval Europe. Construction
began during the rule of the
Teutonic knights, who seized
the town in 1308, and was
completed around 1350. Built
in brick, it is crowned by a
tall and steeply pitched roof.
The mill consisted of a two-
storey bakery with a chimney
set against its gable that
reached the height of its roof.
Also part of the mill were 12,
later 18, large poles to which
millstones were attached for
grinding various types of grain.
The mill was destroyed by fire
in 1945, but was restored after
World War II. This remarkably
old edifice has now been
converted into a modern shopping centre although traces of
the original building still exist.

Church of St Catherine ④
Kościół św Katarzyny

ul. Profesorska 3. **Map** C2.
Tel (058) 301 1595.

The Church of St Catherine,
or "Katy" as locals call it, was
built between 1227 and 1239
by the dukes of Gdańsk-
Pomerania. Regarded as the
oldest and most important
parish church in the Old
Town, it underwent major
rebuilding in the 14th century.

The 76-m (250-ft) high
Baroque tower of the church
was added in 1486. It also
houses an impressive 49-bell
carillon. A major landmark,
the tower was demolished in
1944 and then rebuilt. It is
well worth climbing to the
top of the tower; the effort
is rewarded by wonderful
views of the city. The presbytery on the east side
of the church has a fine
late-Gothic gable. Most of
the Gothic, Baroque and
Mannerist furnishings that the
church once contained were
pillaged or destroyed in 1945
at the end of World War II.
The most notable surviving
pieces are paintings by Anton
Möller and Izaak van den
Blocke, the Baroque memo-
rials to various townspeople
and the tombstone of the
Polish astronomer Jan
Hevelius and his family,
dating from 1659.

**Gothic tower of the Church
of St Catherine**

Iconic Gdańsk Crane, a unique medieval structure

Gdańsk Crane ⑤
Żuraw

ul. Szeroka 67/68. **Map** D3.
Central Maritime Museum
Tel (058) 301 6938. ⬚ 10am–4pm Tue–Sun (Jul & Aug: to 6:30pm).
📧 www.cmm.pl

One of the city's iconic buildings, the Gdańsk Crane was built in the 14th century and renovated between 1442 and 1444. Its present appearance combines the functions of a city gate and a port crane.

The crane, a huge wooden structure, is set between two circular brick towers. It was operated by men working the huge treadmills within, and was capable of lifting weights of up to 2 tonnes (2 tons) to a height of 27 m (90 ft). It was originally used not only to load and unload goods but also to fit masts to ships. The Gdańsk Crane was destroyed by fire in 1945. As part of the rebuilding programme after World War II, it was repaired and reconstructed together with its internal mechanism. It is now part of the collection of the **Central Maritime Museum** (see p213). The Crane Tower looks out over ulica Długie Pobrzeże, which runs alongside the Motława river. The tower, once known as the Long Bridge, was originally a wooden footbridge that functioned as a quay where ships from all over the world were moored. Today, yachts offering trips around the port of Gdańsk are moored here.

Church of St Mary ⑥
Kościół Mariacki

ul. Podkramarska 5. **Map** D4.
Tel (058) 301 3982. ⬚ 9am–6pm daily (5pm in winter). **Tower** ⬚ opening hours vary, call in advance.
📧 www.bazylikamariacka.pl

The Church of St Mary is the largest medieval brick-built church in Europe. Building work began in 1343 and took 150 years to complete. The final stage of construction, involving the 100-m (325-ft) long nave, was carried out by Henryk Hetzel. From 1529 to 1945, when it was destroyed, it was a Protestant church. Like many other parts of Gdańsk, it was rebuilt after World War II. The interior has Gothic, Mannerist and Baroque furnishings. It also contains several memorial tablets to prominent local families. The Tablet of the Ten Commandments (1480–90) depicts each of the commandments in two scenes, illustrating obedience to and disregard of the laws. The Tablet of Charity, an ornate panel made in 1607 by Anton Möller, was used to encourage churchgoers to be generous. The memorial tablet dedicated to Valentyn von Karnitz of around 1590, has many Dutch Mannerist features. The centre painting depicts the biblical tale of the Lamentation of Abel.

The church has a number of unique features, including the Gothic sacrarium, which is

Finely decorated façade of the monumental Great Armoury

Anton Möller's decorative Tablet of Charity, Church of St Mary

in the shape of an open work tower, decorated with pinnacles and over 8 m (26 ft) high. Also notable is the 15th-century *Madonna of Gdańsk*, by an unknown artist, in the church's Chapel of St Anne. Another attraction is the Astronomical Clock made by Hans Durunger between 1464 and 1470. It shows the hour and also the days, dates of moveable feasts and phases of the moon. At noon, a procession of figures representing Adam and Eve, the Apostles, the Three Kings and Death appears. The church's 402 steps leading to its 82-m (270-ft) high **Tower**, offers panoramic views of the city.

Great Armoury ⑦
Wielka Zbrojownia

ul. Targ Węglowy 6. **Map** C3.
Academy of Fine Arts
www.asp.gda.pl

One of the finest examples of the Dutch Mannerist style in Gdańsk, the Great Armoury was built, probably to plans by Antonis van Opbergen in collaboration with architect Jan Strakowski, between 1600 and 1609. Today, the ground floor of the former weapons and ammunition store is filled with shops, while the upper storeys are occupied by the **Academy of Fine Arts**. The building has a façade with 17th-century decorative carvings by Wilhelm Barth.

The ornate Rococo doorway of Uphagen House

Uphagen House ⑧
Dom Uphagena

ul. Długa 12. **Map** C4. *Tel* (058) 301 2371. ☐ 10am–3pm Tue,10am–4pm Wed–Sat, 11am–4pm Sun. 🗞 *free on Tue.* **www.**mhmg.gda.pl

The house that originally stood here was acquired by Johann Uphagen, a town councillor, in 1775. He had it demolished, and a new residence was built in its place. The architect Johann Benjamin Dreyer completed the project in 1787. The result was an attractive building combining Baroque, Rococo and early Neo-Classical features. The sole ornamentation of the restrained façade is the Rococo decoration to the door, which is inscribed with the initial "A", for Abigail, the owner's wife.

Main Town Hall ⑨
Ratusz Głównego Miasta

ul. Długa 46/47. **Map** D4. **Museum of the History of Gdańsk** *Tel* (058) 767 9100. ☐ noon–6pm Tue–Fri, 10am–4pm Sat, 11am–4pm Sun. 🗞 *free on Sun.* **www.**mhmg.gda.pl

The city's first Town Hall was built after 1298 on the orders of Świętopełk II, Duke of Gdańsk-Pomerania. It functioned as an office of the Hanseatic League, a union of trading cities from the Baltic States to the North Sea.
Work on the current building began in 1327. A tower was added between 1486 and 1488,

during one of several phases of rebuilding. After a fire in 1556, the Gothic structure was remodelled in the Mannerist style. The interior was lavishly decorated from 1593–1608 by prominent painters and craftsmen of the day, including Hans Vredeman de Vries, Izaak van den Blocke and Simon Herle. Their combined genius produced one of the finest town halls in all of northern Europe, proof of the city's wealth and power. It also served as a royal residence.
The highlight of the Town Hall is the Red Room, which was once the Great Council Chamber. The Renaissance fireplace is by Willem van der Meer and the centrepiece of the ceiling paintings, the *Apotheosis of Gdańsk* (1608), by Izaak van den Blocke.
After it was destroyed in 1945, it was rebuilt and many furnishings were reconstructed. It now houses the **Museum of the History of Gdańsk**.

Artus Court ⑩
Dwór Artusa

ul. Długi Targ 44. **Map** D4. ☐ 10am–3pm Tue, 10am–4pm Wed–Sat, 11am–4pm Sun. 🗞 *free on Tue.* 📷 🚫

Originally established in the 14th century, Artus Court was a meeting place for the wealthy burghers of Gdańsk, who were inspired by the chivalrous traditions of King Arthur and the knights of the Round Table. Similar fraternities were set up throughout Europe, and they were

St George killing the Dragon (1485) carving in Artus's Court

particularly fashionable in the cities of the Hanseatic League. Visitors came to discuss the issues of the day and to enjoy the unlimited supply of fine beer that was served there.
The original building was destroyed by fire in 1477 and reconstructed by 1481. Its rear elevation preserves the building's original Gothic style, but the façade was rebuilt twice – first in 1552 and again from 1616–17 by the architect and sculptor Abraham van den Blocke (1572–1628). Despite wartime destruction, reconstruction has succeeded in re-creating something of the court's historic atmosphere. One of the highlights of the interior is the intricately decorated 12-m (40-ft) high, 16th-century Renaissance tiled stove. The furnishings were changed several times, funded mainly by individual fraternities, who would gather for meetings on benches along the walls of the court.

The Red Room in the Main Town Hall

Central Maritime Museum ⑪

Centralne Muzeum Morskie

ul. Ołowianka 9–13. **Map** E3.
Tel (058) 301 8611. ▦ 106, 111,
138. ◯ 10am–6pm Tue–Sun (to
4pm winter). 📷 **www**.cmm.pl

In the 17th century, Poland
strove to be "master of the
Baltic Sea" and her seafarers
were dedicated to maintaining
the country's maritime
presence. The themes of
the displays in the Central
Maritime Museum are Gdańsk's
seafaring traditions and
navigation on the Vistula
river. Exhibits include a
reconstruction of scenes from
a sailor's life aboard the
Swedish ship *Solen*, sunk at
the Battle of Oliwa in 1627
and raised from the seabed in
the Gulf of Gdańsk in 1970.

The museum consists of
buildings on both sides of the
Motława river. The two sections are connected by a ferry
that goes from one
bank to another at
regular intervals. On
the west bank is the
Gdańsk Crane *(see
p211)*. Period
Gdańsk, a reconstruc-
tion of a merchant's
office in the Harbour Town
Life exhibition, is one of the
highlights here. The
adjoining Sklad
Kolonialny contains
an interesting col-
lection of boats from distant
parts of the world. The main
museum is in a series of grain
houses on the east bank. The
naval weapons on display here
include 17th-century Polish
cannons, as well as ones taken
from the Swedish warship
Solen. The exhibits in the adjacent granaries are dedicated to
the naval presence of Poland
and Gdańsk from the Middle
Ages to the present day. The
waxwork exhibition here, *Poles
on the World's Seas*, depicts the
lives of Polish sailors. *Sołdek*,
the first Polish ocean-going
ship to be constructed after
World War II, was built in the
Gdańsk Shipyard. It is permanently anchored in Motława
river and its holds are now
used for exhibitions.

**The Griffin's Talons
on display in the
National Museum**

Sołdek, used as an exhibition space by the Central Maritime Museum

National Museum ⑫

Muzeum Narodowe

ul. Toruńska 1. **Map** C5. **Tel** (058)
301 6804. ▦ 106, 111, 112, 120,
121, 138, 166, 178, 186. 🚋 8, 13.
◯ 10am–5pm Tue–Sun; Oct–Apr:
9am–4pm Tue–Fri, 10am–5pm Sat,
Sun. 📷 free on Fri.
www.muzeum.narodowe.gda.pl

The National Museum is
laid out in a former Gothic
Franciscan monastery from
1422–1522. It was set up
due to the efforts of Rudolf
Freitag, a lecturer at the
Royal School of Fine Arts, in
1872. It was closed
during World War II
and was reopened
as the City Museum
after the war. The
impressive museum
was also known
as the Pomeranian
Museum till 1952
before being ele-
vated to the rank of a National
Museum in 1972. The museum
contains a wealth of artifacts,
from wrought-iron grilles to
sculpture, painting, ceramics,
gold jewellery, goldwork,
metalwork and furniture.
Exhibits are spread over
three floors. Gothic art and
gold jewellery are displayed
on the ground floor and
paintings on the first.
The upper floor holds
temporary exhibitions.

The museum's most prized
piece is *The Last Judgement*,
by the Flemish painter Hans
Memling (c. 1430–94). The
central panel of the triptych
depicts the Last Judgement,
while the panel on the left
represents the Gates of
Heaven and the one on
the right hand portrays the
Torments of Hell. In 1473,
it was plundered by privateers
from Gdańsk from a ship
bound for Italy. Other fascinating exhibits are *The Griffin's
Talons*, a 15th century bison-
horn cup belonging to a
sailing fraternity, and the
Longcase Clock. This Rococo
clock, made in around 1750,
is decorated with scenes
from the biblical story of
Tobias and the Raising of
the Copper Snake.

The Last Judgement (1467) by Hans Memling, National Museum

Practical & Travel Information

Since the fall of Communism in 1989, tourism in Poland has greatly increased. Foreign visitors are drawn to the country for its history, folk culture, great architecture and unique scenic beauty. The quality of service has improved, especially in banks. New hotels have sprung up, many of which are cheaper than those in Western Europe. The best-equipped hotels and restaurants are, however, expensive.

WHEN TO VISIT

The best time to travel to Poland is late spring or early autumn, when temperatures are usually pleasantly warm and the coastal, lakeside and mountain resorts are not too crowded. The big cities, by contrast are noticeably quieter in summer; this is also when theatres close for the holiday season. However, other events such as festivals take place during summer. After the summer season, many guesthouses, hotels, clubs and restaurants in coastal resorts and other popular lakeside spots close. The skiing season runs from the end of November to mid-March.

DOCUMENTATION

Citizens of all European Union (EU) countries, Canada, New Zealand and Australia can stay in Poland without a visa for up to 90 days. Beyond that, it is necessary to apply for a residence permit. Visitors of other nationalities should contact the Polish Embassy in their respective country for entry requirements.

VISITOR INFORMATION

Information centres can be found in most towns and cities. Travel agencies such as **Orbis** can advise on tickets, trains and accommodation. Information is also available at train stations. Hotel employees are often very helpful.

HEALTH AND SECURITY

Citizens of the EU and the European Economic Area (EEA) are entitled to free medical treatment in Poland provided they have their European Health Insurance Card (EHIC). For citizens of other countries, transport to hospitals is provided free of charge in case of emergencies, but treatment of serious health problems may incur a fee. Visitors are advised to take out full medical insurance before arriving and always carry policy documents and passport for identification at the hospital during medical emergencies. An ambulance service is available 24 hours a day from any private clinic.

Polish cities suffer from the same security problems and crime as most European capitals, so visitors should stay alert for petty thefts and pickpockets. They should take extra care of their belongings in busy railway stations, especially in Warsaw. Theft in overnight trains is an increasing menace so it is important to keep compartment doors locked.

BANKING AND CURRENCY

The official Polish currency is the złoty, which is divided into 100 groszy. Money can be changed at *kantor* (exchange bureaus), many of which offer better rates than banks. Most banks will cash traveller's cheques, although the transactions are time consuming. The majority of banks are open from 8am to 6pm. ATMs can be found in most towns and cities and accept most international credit cards.

COMMUNICATIONS

The most inexpensive way to make international calls is on pre-paid phone cards, which can be bought at most kiosks. Another option is to call from one of the phone-card-operated machines. For long-distance calls, rates are highest between 8am and 6pm. Local calls are cheapest from 10pm to 6am. Poczta Polska, the Polish post office, is open from 8am to 8pm on weekdays. GSM mobile phones have coverage all over Poland; it is best to buy a pre-paid SIM card from local operators. There are also Internet cafés and free WiFi areas all over the country, but connections outside the capital tend to be slow.

FACILITIES FOR THE DISABLED

Poland has a poor record for providing for disabled people but this is changing rapidly. All renovated and new public buildings have ramps or lifts built into them, and special taxis are also available. Nevertheless, many traditional sites of interest may still be poorly equipped. For general advice or information about sites, contact the **Disabled People's National Council**.

THE CLIMATE OF POLAND

Poland's climate is influenced by cold polar air from Scandinavia and sub-tropical air from the south. Polar-continental fronts dominate in winter, bringing crisp, frosty weather and snow. Winters in the north can be particularly cold. In contrast, late summer and autumn (the most popular times to visit) offer plenty of warm sunny days.

WARSAW

month	Apr	Jul	Oct	Jan
°C/F	12/54	23/75	13/55	0/32
	3/37	15/59	5/41	-6/21
hrs	5 hrs	7 hrs	4 hrs	2 hrs
mm	37 mm	96 mm	38 mm	27 mm

ARRIVING BY AIR

International flights from some 50 cities in 30 countries arrive in Warsaw. The airports at Gdańsk, Katowice, Szczecin, Poznań, Wrocław, and Cracow also have international flights, linking Poland with Western Europe as well as Bucharest, Budapest, Prague, Sofia and the capitals of the former Soviet Bloc. Some 25 airlines, including British Airways, Air France, SAS (Scandinavia) and Lufthansa (Germany), operate from Warsaw Okęcie Airport, which also has direct connections with Canada, the US, Israel and Thailand. Most cities including Cracow and Gdańsk, are served by budget airlines such as RyanAir, easyJet and Wizzair.

RAIL TRAVEL

Poland is covered by a dense network of railway lines. International train services run between all major Polish and European cities. The journeys by fast train from Warsaw to Prague and Berlin take just 6 and 9 hours respectively. Most big cities are connected by express lines. The Polish Rail Network (PKP) operates a range of trains, out of which InterCity, EuroCity and express trains are the fastest and are usually punctual. InterCity trains are the most comfortable and expensive, but also serve snacks on board. Both EuroCity and InterCity trains have special compartments for women with children and the disabled. Ordinary trains, such as Osobowy and Tanie Linie Kolejowe, are reasonable. Express trains and sleeping cars are expensive. Tickets can be booked through InterCity's website. The official website Rozklad offers information on timetables and fares.

Suburban routes are served by electric trains, some of which are open-plan, double-decker carriages. Tickets can be booked at railway stations. The main station in the capital is Warsaw Central.

TRAVELLING BY BUS

Polish Motor Transport, Polska Komunikacja Samochodowa (PKS), serves most of Poland's long-distance routes.

Local buses are sometimes the only means of getting to smaller towns and villages. These services are generally efficient, although before 8am and in the afternoon, they may be crowded. Tickets are usually bought in advance from the bus station's *kasa* (ticket offices).

TRAVELLING BY CAR

There are very few motorways, and those that exist are generally in poor condition. An exception is the Cracow–Katowice Highway.

When driving, always carry your passport, car insurance, Green Card, licence and, if applicable, rental contract. If using a foreign car, the international symbol of its country of origin must be displayed. Seat belts need to be fastened at all times; use of mobile phones while driving is illegal. Follow speed limits and switch on headlights even during the day. All the major international car rental companies, including Avis and Hertz, operate out of Warsaw and Cracow.

ARRIVING BY FERRY

Poland's main port is the Gdańsk Ferry Terminal and ships from Scandinavian countries dock here. There are ferries between Gdynia's port and Kaelskrona, Sweden. Information can be found through the agency Orbis.

DIRECTORY

DOCUMENTATION

www.visitpoland.com

EMBASSIES

Australia
Ul. Nowogrodzka 11, Warsaw. *Tel* (022) 521 3444. www.poland. embassy.gov.au

Canada
Ul. Matejki 1/5, Warsaw. *Tel* (022) 584 3100. www.canada.pl

New Zealand
Al.Ujazdowskie 51, Warsaw. *Tel* (022) 521 0521. www. nzembassy.com

United Kingdom
Al. Róż 1, Warsaw. *Tel* (022) 311 0000. www.britishembassy.pl

United States
Al Ujazdowskie 29/31, Warsaw. *Tel* (022) 504 2000. www.poland. usembassy.gov

VISITOR INFORMATION

Orbis
www.orbis.pl

EMERGENCY

Ambulance, Fire and Police
Tel 999.

Road Emergencies
Tel 981.

FACILITIES FOR THE DISABLED

Disabled People's National Council
Ul Zamenhofa 8, Warsaw. *Tel* (022) 831 4040.

ARRIVING BY AIR

Air France
www.airfrance.com

British Airways
www.britishairways.com

easyJet
www.easyjet.com

Lufthansa
www.lufthansa.com

RyanAir
www.ryanair.com

SAS
www.flysas.com

Wizzair
www.wizzair.com

Warsaw Okęcie Airport
Tel (022) 650 4220.

RAIL TRAVEL

EuroCity
www.eurocity.pl

InterCity
www.intercity.com.pl

Rozklad
www.irozklad-pkp.pl

Warsaw Central
Tel (022) 511 6003.

TRAVELLING BY CAR

Avis
Tel (012) 629 6108.
www.avis.pl

Hertz
Tel (012) 429 6262.
www.hertz.com.pl

ARRIVING BY FERRY

Gdańsk Ferry Terminal
Tel (058) 343 1887.

Shopping & Entertainment

Poland is a great place to pick up memorable souvenirs. These range from handicrafts to beautiful silver and amber jewellery, and hand-embroidered tablecloths, porcelain and ceramic items. Thick, hand-knitted woollen sweaters and ornamented leather slippers can be found in local markets around the country. Vodka, the national drink, is available in various flavours. The country has a vibrant cultural life and there are plenty of jazz clubs, nightclubs, casinos, theatres, opera venues, cinemas and concert halls in all the big cities. In summer, many smaller resorts host folk music festivals or jousting tournaments.

OPENING HOURS

Shops are open from 10am to 6pm Monday to Friday and 10am to 2pm on Saturdays. In the larger cities, shops usually close at 7pm, with most of the department stores staying open for an extra hour until 8pm. All shops are closed on public holidays, with the exception of some pharma-cies and food shops.

MARKETS AND MALLS

The majority of Poles buy fruit, vegetables and delica-tessen products from markets such as **Stary Kleparz** in Cracow and **Hala Targowa** in Gdańsk. Household goods and fashionable clothes are increasingly sold in big shopping malls situated just outside city centres. Among the largest malls are **Złote Tarasy**, next to Warsaw's central station, and **Galeria Krakowska** near Cracow's main station.

ART AND CRAFTS

Many visitors to Poland return home with contempo-rary paintings, prints and posters, which are available at very reasonable prices. Paintings on glass, with tradi-tional or modern designs, are sold in many galleries around the country. Galleries in Warsaw include **Zapiecek** and **Art Gallery ZPAP** (Union of Polish Artists and Designers), while in Cracow there is **Kociol Artystyczny**. The range of folk art and handicrafts in Poland is truly impressive and almost every region has its own speciality. Painted Easter eggs and Christmas tree ornaments are distinctive examples of folk art. All these items, as well as hand-woven tapestries, embroi-dered tablecloths and doilies and leather goods are sold in outlets of the **Cepelia** chain found in Warsaw and other big cities.

ANTIQUES

In most towns throughout Poland, antiques and collect-ables are sold in *Desa* (auction houses) shops. In Wrocław, **Antykwariat Daes** also sells antique products.

GIFTS AND SOUVENIRS

Some of the best Polish souvenirs are porcelain and pottery products. The most renowned make is Ćmielów porcelain, which is available all over the country. Traditional ceramics are also popular, especially the white and navy-blue crockery decorated with circles and small stylized flowers. **Bolesławiec** and Cepelia are good places to find them. Also worth shopping for is Poland's high-quality modern glass and traditional cut glass or crystal. A variety of designs is available, hand-cut on perfectly transparent glass.

JEWELLERY

Silver jewellery is a speciality of Polish craftsmen. It is rela-tively cheap and comes in a variety of sophisticated, mod-ern designs. Amber jewellery is also extremely popular. This is sold at a range of outlets, but to avoid the risk of buying a fake it is best to go to an established shop. Most Polish amber comes from the Gulf of Gdańsk, and the Old Town of Gdańsk has several reliable outlets, including **M&M** and **Nord Amber Gallery**.

FOOD AND DRINK

A good souvenir from Poland could be a jar of dried ceps (porcini mushrooms), honey, smoked eel or dried sausage. The best places to buy such items are bazaars and markets such as Hala Mirowska near Plac Mirowski in Warsaw, Stary Kleparz in Cracow, Plac Wielkopolski in Poznań or in the market halls of Wrocław and Gdańsk. Polish sweets are of a high quality, and chocolates made by the Warsaw firm **Wedel** and the Cracow firm **Wawel** are particularly esteemed. Polish liquor is internationally renow-ned, especially the pure vodka which is available in a bewil-dering array of varieties. Another popular spirit is *zubrówka*, a vodka with an unusual herbal flavour. Polish mead is equally distinctive. Made with honey according to traditional recipes, it is the accompaniment to dessert.

NIGHTLIFE

Warsaw is a major nightlife destination with a host of clubs offering live music or DJ-driven dance events. **Hybrydy** has been hosting a well-balanced mixture of gigs and club nights for over 45 years. Cracow is bursting with nightlife activity with a host of characterful bars and clubs grouped around the main square. Elsewhere, Poznań's Przemysław Castle's boiler room makes for a unique jazz venue, the **Blue Note Club**.

In Your Pocket guide provides up-to-date listings on their website.

THEATRE

Poland has over 80 theatres scattered across its cities. In Warsaw, the most popular theatre is the **Ateneum**, which specializes in comedy shows. The **Teatr Żydowski** (Jewish Theatre) presents spectacles in Yiddish and is the only such place in the country. In Cracow, **Teatr Stary** is considered one of the country's best theatres. In Warsaw, information about advance booking for cultural events can be found at **Kasy ZASP**. In Cracow, tickets can be bought in advance at the **Cultural Information Centre**. Local tourist information offices can also provide information on shows and booking procedures.

MUSICALS, OPERA AND BALLET

Musicals, opera and ballet can provide the best form of entertainment even for those who do not speak Polish. Operettas and musicals are performed at **Opera i Operetka** in Cracow and at **Roma** in Warsaw. For opera-lovers, the productions of the **Great Theatre** (Teatr Wielki) in Warsaw are

recommended. There are also opera houses in Gdańsk, Wrocław, Poznań and Cracow. Poland's two best ballet companies perform in the Teatr Wielki in Warsaw and Poznań.

CLASSICAL AND FOLK MUSIC

There are over 20 classical orchestras in Poland and they perform in almost all of its big cities. Particularly renowned are the **National Philharmonic Orchestra** (Filharmonia Narodowa) in Warsaw, the **Filharmonia Baltycka** in Gdańsk and the **Poznań Philharmonia**, which performs in the University Hall. Classical music shows are held in museums, churches and palaces throughout the year. In the rest of the country, many bands perform the traditional folk music of individual regions, but it can be difficult to track down their concerts. The best chance of seeing them is at various music festivals in the summer. Many folk groups also

perform in concerts organized by hotels or tourist agencies. Tickets can be bought from the Cultural Information Centre.

FESTIVALS

Poland hosts several local and international festivals. A major theatre festival is the Malta International Drama Festival, held from late June to early July in the streets and theatres of Poznań. In Warsaw, the Garden Theatres Competition runs throughout the summer. Opera festivals, such as the Mozart Festival in Warsaw, and Poznan's ballet festivals are also popular. For those interested in religious music, the Wratislava Cantans are held in September in Wrocław. Jazz festivals are also quite renowned in Poland and major events include the Warsaw Jazz Jamboree, Jazz on the Oder in Wrocław (May) and Jazz All Souls' Day in Cracow (early November).

DIRECTORY

MARKETS AND MALLS

Galeria Krakowska
ul. Pawia 5, Cracow.
Tel (012) 428 9900.

Hala Targowa
ul. Pańska, Gdańsk.

Stary Kleparz
Rynek Kleparski, Cracow.

Złote Tarasy
ul. Złota 59, Warsaw.
Tel (022) 222 2200

ART AND CRAFTS

Art Gallery ZPAP
ul. Krakowskie
Pzedmieście 15/17,
Warsaw.
Tel (022) 827 6414.

Cepelia
www.cepelia.pl

Kociol Artystyczny
ul. Mikolajska 6, Cracow.
Tel (012) 292 0029.

Zapiecek
ul. Zapiecek 1, Warsaw.
Tel (022) 831 9918.

ANTIQUES

Antykwariat Daes
pl. Kosciuszki 15,
Wrocław.
Tel (071) 344 7280.

GIFTS AND SOUVENIRS

Bolesławiec
ul. Prosta 2/14, Warsaw.
Tel (022) 624 8480.

JEWELLERY

M&M
ul. Dlugie Pobrzeże 1,
Gdańsk.
Tel (058) 346 2717.

Nord Amber Gallery
ul. Mariacka 44, Gdańsk.
Tel (058) 301 4131.

FOOD AND DRINK

Wedel
ul. Szpitalna 8, Warsaw.
Tel (022) 827 2916.

Wawel
Rynek Glowny 33, Cracow.
Tel (012) 423 1247.

NIGHTLIFE

Blue Note Club
www.bluenote.Poznań.pl

Hybrydy
www.hybrydy.com.pl

In Your Pocket
www.inyourpocket.com

THEATRE

Ateneum
ul. Jaracza 2, Warsaw.
Tel (022) 625 7330.

Cultural Information Centre
ul. św Jana 2, Cracow.
www.karnet.
krakow2000.pl

Kasy ZASP
Al Jerozolimskie 25,
Warsaw.
Tel (022) 621 9454.

Great Theatre
pl. Szczepanski 1, Cracow.
Tel (012) 422 4040.

Teatr Żydowski
pl. Grzybowski 12/16,
Warsaw.
Tel (022) 620 6281.

MUSICALS, OPERA AND BALLET

Opera i Operetka
ul. Lubicz 48, Cracow.
Tel (012) 628 7071.

Roma
ul. Nowogrodzka 49,
Warsaw.
Tel (022) 628 0360.

Teatr Wielki
pl. Tatralny 1, Warsaw.
Tel (022) 692 0200.

CLASSICAL AND FOLK MUSIC

Filharmonia Baltycka
ul. Olowianka 1, Gdańsk.
Tel (058) 320 6262.

National Philharmonic Orchestra
ul. Sienkiewicza 10,
Warsaw. *Tel (022)
551 7128.*

Poznań Philharmonia
ul. św Marcin 81, Poznań.
Tel (061) 852 4708.

Where to Stay in Poland

Poland has experienced a big improvement in hotel standards in recent years. New luxury accommodation has been built and many existing hotels have been modernized. Across the country, several manor houses and historic buildings have been converted into small resorts. In Warsaw, good, moderately priced hotels are scarce.

PRICE CATEGORIES
Price categories are for a standard double room with bathroom per night in high season, including tax and service charges.

ⓩ under 270 zloty
ⓩⓩ 270–400 zloty
ⓩⓩⓩ 400–600 zloty
ⓩⓩⓩⓩ 600–800 zloty
ⓩⓩⓩⓩⓩ over 800 zloty

WARSAW

Nathan's Villa Hostel
ⓩ
ul. Piękna 24–26, 00549 **Tel** *(022) 622 2946* **Fax** *(022) 622 2946* **Rooms** *10*   **Map** *C5*

Warsaw's best-loved hostel boasts brand-new dormitories, modern fittings and a quiet courtyard setting. Facilities on offer include fast Internet access, a fully equipped kitchen and daily laundry service. A range of private rooms has been added for those who prefer not to share a dormitory. **www.nathansvilla.com**

Oki Doki
P | ⓩ
pl. Dąbrowskiego 3, 00057 **Tel** *(022) 826 5112* **Fax** *(022) 826 8357* **Rooms** *37*   **Map** *C3*

Rooms inside this Socialist-era building are decorated courtesy of local thrift stores and artists, and they come with names such as Raspberry Thicket and House of the Cat. The bar promises to serve the cheapest beer in Warsaw. A fully equipped kitchen is also available. **www.okidoki.pl**

Ibis Stare Miasto
P ⑪ 🖩 | ⓩⓩ
ul. Muranowska 2, 00209 **Tel** *(022) 310 1000* **Fax** *(022) 310 1010* **Rooms** *333*   **Map** *C1*

Located close to the Old Town and Royal Castle *(see p176)*, Ibis is an ideal base from which to explore the Polish capital. The rooms, with pastel-coloured walls, are cozy, spacious and comfortable. One of the best deals in the city, this is often fully booked, so it is advisable to reserve in advance. **www.ibishotel.com**

Sofitel Victoria
P ⑪ 🏊 📺 🖩 ♿ | ⓩⓩ
ul. Królewska 11 **Tel** *(022) 624 0800* **Fax** *(022) 620 2629* **Rooms** *126*   **Map** *C3*

Located in the heart of Warsaw and facing the sprawling Saxon Garden, the Sofitel Victoria is a luxurious hotel with well-furnished rooms containing wooden tables and chairs, and comfortable beds. The two restaurants in the hotel serve Polish and French cuisine. Cheaper rates are available for longer stays. **www.sofitel.com**

InterContinental
P ⑪ 🏊 📺 🖩 | ⓩⓩⓩⓩ
ul. Emilii Plater 49, 00125 **Tel** *(022) 328 8888* **Fax** *(022) 328 8889* **Rooms** *326*   **Map** *C4*

This five-star hotel is one of the tallest buildings in the capital. Immaculate rooms in ultra-modern style offer Internet access and cable TV. The star attraction, however, is the swimming pool, gym and spa located on the 43rd and 44th floors. **www.warsaw.intercontinental.com**

Le Royal Meridien-Bristol
P ⑪ 🏊 📺 🖩 | ⓩⓩⓩⓩ
ul. Krakowskie Przedmieście 42/44, 00325 **Tel** *(022) 551 1000* **Fax** *(023) 625 2577* **Rooms** *205*   **Map** *D3*

A sumptuous Art Nouveau-building and, arguably, the most famous hotel in Poland: the guest list spans regents to rock stars. Rooms combine a prewar aesthetic with 21st-century gadgetry, and the hotel has won countless awards for excellence. Its Sunday brunches are renowned across the city. **www.lemeridien-bristol.com**

Mercure Fryderyk Chopin
P ⑪ 📺 🖩 | ⓩⓩⓩⓩ
al. Jana Pawla II 22, 00133 **Tel** *(022) 528 0300* **Fax** *(022) 528 0303* **Rooms** *250*   **Map** *C3*

This modern and stylish glass-fronted hotel is located close to the Palace of Culture and Science *(see p181)*. Bright, multi-coloured rooms have air conditioning, Internet access, minibar and cable TV. A jazz trio plays three times a week in the bar. Most of the places of interest are within easy walking distance from the hotel. **www.mercure.com**

Radisson BLU Centrum
P ⑪ 🏊 📺 🖩 | ⓩⓩⓩⓩ
ul. Grzybowska 24, 00132 **Tel** *(022) 321 8888* **Fax** *(022) 321 8889* **Rooms** *311*   **Map** *C3*

In the heart of Warsaw's financial quarter, the Radisson is a chic five-star hotel. The hotel's modern façade conceals rooms designed in three distinct styles: maritime, Scandinavian and Italian. Amenities include TV, minibar, a writing desk and coffee-making facilities. **www.radissonblu.com**

Residence St Andrew's Palace
P ⑪ | ⓩⓩⓩⓩ
ul. Chmielna 30, 00020 **Tel** *(022) 826 4660* **Fax** *(022) 826 9635* **Rooms** *24*   **Map** *C4*

Luxury apartments available for short- and long-term stays inside a building renovated to its prewar 1900s glory. Overlooking a central courtyard, the apartments have fully equipped kitchens and separate living rooms, complete with a minibar, sound system and cable TV. Housekeeping services are also provided. **www.residence.com.pl**

Map References *see map of Warsaw pp172–3 and Cracow pp182–3*

REST OF POLAND

CRACOW Abel

ul. Józefa 30, 31056 **Tel** *(012) 411 8736* **Fax** *(012) 411 8736* **Rooms** *15*　　　　**Map** D5

While the rooms at this adorably eclectic hotel are not large, what they lack in size they more than make up for in character. Each one is furnished individually and has an en suite bathroom (sometimes just with a shower) and TV. Not all rooms have air conditioning. **www.hotelabel.pl**

CRACOW Trecius

ul. św Tomasza 18, 31020 **Tel** *(012) 421 2521* **Fax** *(012) 426 8730* **Rooms** *6*　　　　**Map** D2

Each room in this much-renovated 13th-century house is decorated in a fabulous, unique way. They all have showers (but not baths) as well as amenities such as satellite TV. While prices are cheap for the location, breakfast is not included, and smoking is not allowed in any of the rooms. **www.trecius.krakow.pl**

CRACOW Royal

ul. św Gertrudy 26/29, 31048 **Tel** *(012) 421 3500* **Fax** *(012) 421 5857* **Rooms** *120*　　　　**Map** D3

Located in the heart of the Old Town in Planty Park, the elegant Royal is a classic example of 19th-century Art Nouveau architecture. It is split into one-star and two-star sections and offers relatively basic amenities; rooms are en suite and have TV. **www.royal.com.pl**

CRACOW Wit Stwosz

ul. Mikołajska 28, 31027 **Tel** *(012) 429 6026* **Fax** *(012) 429 6139* **Rooms** *17*　　　　**Map** D2

Close to Main Market Square, this hotel is owned by the Church of St Mary and offers generously sized but sparsely furnished rooms. All have bathrooms with showers and TV. The best ones are those in the attic, with kylights and high, sloping ceilings. **www.wit-stwosz.com.pl**

CRACOW Hotel Francuski

ul. Pijarska 13 **Tel** *(012) 627 3777* **Fax** *(012) 627 3700* **Rooms** *42*　　　　**Map** C1

Each and every room in this luxurious hotel is graced with antique furniture, and the location close to the Main Market Square makes it the perfect option for those looking for a relaxed and pampered stay in Cracow. There is a car park to the rear of the hotel; a rare luxury in this city. **www.orbis.pl**

CRACOW Pollera

ul. Szpitalna 30, 31024 **Tel** *(012) 422 1044* **Fax** *(012) 422 1389* **Rooms** *42*　　　　**Map** D2

An Art Nouveau gem in the heart of the Old Town, Pollera was founded by entrepreneur Kasper Poller in 1834. During World War II, the Germans fell in love with the place and forbade anyone else (except the staff) from entering. The rooms are elegantly decorated and there is also a restaurant on site. **www.pollera.com.pl**

CRACOW Elektor

ul. Szpitalna 28, 31024 **Tel** *(012) 423 2317* **Fax** *(012) 423 2327* **Rooms** *21*　　　　**Map** D2

The Elektor is regarded as the city's best hotel. The comfortable rooms are richly furnished; some with wooden ceilings and regal upholstery. Service is exceptional. High-profile guests have included Prince and Princess Takamodo of Japan, King Harald V of Norway and Grand Duke Jean of Luxembourg. **www.hotelelektor.com.pl**

CRACOW Grand Hotel Cracow

ul. Sławkowska 5/7 **Tel** *(012) 424 0800* **Fax** *(012) 421 8360* **Rooms** *62*　　　　**Map** C1 & 2

For more than a century, this hotel has offered the very best in comfort and service. Housed in a restored palace, the suites are regally furnished with antique furniture, wooden beams and paintings. The hotel has one grand restaurant, a café and a bar. **www.grand.pl**

CRACOW Sheraton

ul. Powiśle 7, 31101 **Tel** *(012) 662 1000* **Fax** *(012) 662 1100* **Rooms** *232*　　　　**Map** E2

The atrium at the Sheraton is one of the modern wonders of Cracow, all glass and marble, colonnades and fountains. The highest standards are to be expected, with high-speed Internet and 24-hour room service. It also offers outstanding dining and entertainment. **www.sheraton.com/krakow**

FURTHER AFIELD CRACOW Batory

ul. Sołtyka 19, 31529 **Tel** *(012) 294 3030* **Fax** *(012) 294 3033* **Rooms** *29*

Close to the Jewish district, Batory is a family-run hotel with a homely atmosphere. Rooms are warmly decorated with pastel-coloured walls and comfortable furniture. Amenities include TV, en suite bathrooms (some just with shower), lockers and Internet access. The in-house restaurant specializes in Polish cuisine. **www.hotelbatory.pl**

FURTHER AFIELD CRACOW Fortuna

ul. Czapskich 5, 31110 **Tel** *(012) 422 3143* **Fax** *(012) 411 0806* **Rooms** *25*

A historic hotel, Fortuna is set in a charming building with flowering plants beneath its windows. The bright rooms are larger than usual for this type of building, and the bathrooms are also well sized. Its restaurant offers delicious Polish cuisine. Parking is available but must be booked in advance. **www.hotel-fortuna.com.pl**

Key to Symbols *see back cover flap*

FURTHER AFIELD CRACOW Pugetòw

P 11 目   ⓩⓩⓩ

ul. Starowiślna 15a, 31038 **Tel** *(012) 432 4950* **Fax** *(012) 378 9325* **Rooms** *7*

Set in one of the loveliest houses in Cracow, this "art hotel" has original oil paintings lining the walls and beautiful little porticoes. The elegant rooms feature grand furnishings, giving them a regal touch. Reservations should be made several months in advance. **www.donimirski.com/hotel_pugetow**

GDAŃSK Królewski

P 11   ⓩⓩⓩ

ul. Olowianka 1, 80751 **Tel** *(058) 326 1111* **Fax** *(058) 326 1110* **Rooms** *30*   **Map** *E3*

Overlooking the Motława river, this hotel is set inside a former granary, next door to the Central Maritime Museum *(see p213)*. The rooms are smartly decorated with comfortable furniture and soft lighting. Facilities include TV, Internet and telephone. Guests should consider booking one of the loft suites. **www.hotelkrolewski.pl**

GDAŃSK Szydłowski

11 Y 目   ⓩⓩⓩ

ul. Grunwaldzka 114, 80244 **Tel** *(058) 345 7040* **Fax** *(058) 344 3877* **Rooms** *35*   **Map** *F4*

Located in the suburb of Wrzeszcz, the Szydłowski is the best hotel within easy reach of Gdańsk's airport. Rooms are furnished to an unremarkable three-star standard, although the hotel is notable for being the lodging of choice for locally born German author Günter Grass. **www.szydlowski.pl**

GDAŃSK Wolne Miasto

P 11   ⓩⓩⓩ

ul. św Ducha 2, 80834 **Tel** *(058) 322 2442* **Fax** *(058) 322 2447* **Rooms** *43*   **Map** *D4*

A row of reconstructed tenement buildings hides this interesting Old Town hotel. Rooms capture the spirit of prewar Danzig with sepia photographs of the city in its heyday, while simultaneously boasting 21st-century amenities such as plasma screens and card keys. The restaurant is one of the most innovative in Gdańsk. **www.hotelwm.pl**

GDAŃSK Dwór Oliwski

P 11 ≋ Y 目   ⓩⓩⓩⓩ

ul. Bytowska 4, 80328 **Tel** *(058) 554 7000* **Fax** *(058) 554 7010* **Rooms** *70*   **Map** *F4*

Housed in a beautiful 17th-century manor house between Gdańsk and Sopot, this luxury hotel is hemmed in by carefully tended gardens. The spacious rooms are furnished elegantly with snug sofas and include a minibar, TV and Internet connection. The hotel even has a Presidential Suite. **www.dwor-oliwski.com.pl**

GDAŃSK Hanza

P 11 目   ⓩⓩⓩⓩ

ul. Tokarska 6, 80888 **Tel** *(058) 305 3427* **Fax** *(058) 305 3386* **Rooms** *60*   **Map** *D3*

Located in the heart of Gdańsk's historic quarter, the façade of this riverfront hotel has been designed to fit in seamlessly with the surrounding burgher houses. Inside, all the rooms are modern and aesthetically designed using dark, polished woods; all are equipped with the latest facilities. **www.hotelhanza.pl**

GDAŃSK Podewils

P 11 Y 目   ⓩⓩⓩⓩ

ul. Szafarnia 2, 80755 **Tel** *(058) 300 9560* **Fax** *(058) 300 9570* **Rooms** *10*   **Map** *E4*

A Baroque-style mansion with views overlooking Gdańsk's small marina. The lobby filled with antiques and oil paintings evokes the atmosphere of a private residence, while the upstairs rooms offer luxuries such as DVD players and Jacuzzi tubs. Dining at the restaurant is justly regarded as an unmissable experience. **www.podewils.pl**

GDAŃSK Holiday Inn

P 11 Y 目   ⓩⓩⓩⓩⓩ

ul. Podwale Grodzkie 9, 80895 **Tel** *(058) 300 6000* **Fax** *(058) 300 6003* **Rooms** *143*   **Map** *C2*

This squat modern building faces the train station, with the Old Town just minutes away on foot. The international Holiday Inn standard is impeccably observed, with generous-sized rooms, well-trained staff and all the facilities associated with such a respected hotel chain. **www.Gdańsk.globalhotels.pl**

MALBORK Stary Malbork

11 P   ⓩⓩ

ul. 17 Marca 26-27, 82200 **Tel** *(055) 647 2400* **Fax** *(055) 647 2412* **Rooms** *31*

This Art Nouveau, green-coloured hotel is made up of two former townhouses dating from the 19th century. It has since been renovated and converted into a three-star gem of a hotel. Rooms are spacious and catch the sun in the mornings. It also boasts a small bar, restaurant and cosy fireplace. **www.hotelstarymalbork.com.pl**

POZNAŃ Domina Prestige

P 11 目   ⓩⓩⓩ

ul. św Marcina 2, 61803 **Tel** *(061) 859 0590* **Fax** *(061) 859 0591* **Rooms** *41*

The best accommodation option in Poznań, Domina Prestige provides luxury serviced apartments on the border of the Old Town. Rooms are modern and pleasant with TV, Internet access, a fully equipped kitchen and even bathrobes. Daily housekeeping. **www.dominahotels.com**

POZNAŃ Vivaldi

P 11 ≋ Y 目   ⓩⓩⓩ

ul. Winogrady 9, 61663 **Tel** *(061) 858 8100* **Fax** *(061) 852 2977* **Rooms** *48*

An upmarket hotel with a wide range of rooms to pick from: rattan-furnished doubles to luxury suites decorated with striped walls and cream leather seating. The swimming pool is little larger than a bathtub, but this hotel has charm aplenty as well as friendly, dedicated staff. **www.vivaldi.pl**

SOPOT Monte Cassino de Luxe

P   ⓩⓩ

ul. Bohaterów Monte Cassino 50, 81759 **Tel** *(058) 555 7777* **Fax** *(058) 555 7778* **Rooms** *5*

As the name suggests, this is top-quality accommodation at surprisingly low prices. Beautifully designed rooms boast DVD players, flat-screen TVs and classical furnishings. It is also just a stone's throw from Sopot's main street. Advance bookings are recommended. **www.sopothotel.pl**

Map References *see map of Cracow pp182–3 and Gdańsk pp208–209*

SOPOT Villa Sedan

P 11

ul. Pulaskiego 18/20, 81762 **Tel** *(058) 555 0980* **Fax** *(058) 551 0617* **Rooms** *21*

In the heart of Sopot, Villa Sedan has the atmosphere of a boutique pension and is very good value. Housed in a rambling building, its rooms have a personal touch, with wrought-iron beds and wooden floors. The loft suite makes for a particularly memorable stay. **www.sedan.pl**

SOPOT Haffner

P 11 ≌ 🖵 📋

ul. Haffnera 59, 81715 **Tel** *(058) 550 9999* **Fax** *(058) 550 9800* **Rooms** *106*

Located by the beach, this modern structure houses some of the finest guestrooms in Sopot. Decorated in crisp, modern style, their suites boast two telephone lines, dressing gowns and plush lounge areas with padded leather sofas. Other features include a state-of-the-art spa and swimming pool. **www.hotelhaffner.pl**

SOPOT Villa Baltica

P 11 🖵 📋

ul. Emilii Plater 1, 81777 **Tel** *(058) 555 2800* **Fax** *(058) 555 2801* **Rooms** *33*

This former orphanage now boasts chic cream-coloured rooms (some with views of the sea) and sparkling bath-rooms. The restaurant, in a hexagonal dining room attached to the hotel, is in a class of its own. The downstairs spa offers a full range of luxury beauty treatments. **www.villabaltica.com**

SOPOT Sofitel Grand

ul. Powstańców Warszawy 12/14, 81718 **Tel** *(058) 520 6000* **Fax** *(058) 520 6099* **Rooms** *127*

The Grand is positioned right on the seashore, with Sopot's 19th-century pier to one side. The hotel's recent acquisition by the Sofitel group has seen it fully renovated, with rooms decorated in a splendid Art Deco style to evoke the interwar years, when Sopot was known as a millionaires' playground. **www.orbis.pl**

TORUŃ Mercure-Helios

P 11

ul. Kraszewskiego 1/3, 87100 **Tel** *(056) 619 6550* **Fax** *(056) 622 1964* **Rooms** *110*

Originally built in the 1960s, the Mercure-Helios is undergoing a timely revamp, ridding itself of its reputation as a hotel stuck in a Communist-era time warp. Though still unlikely to win awards for charm, it does meet all the criteria for a pleasant stay. **www.orbis.pl**

WROCŁAW Bugatti

P 11

ul. Kosmonautów 328, 54041 **Tel** *(071) 349 3523* **Fax** *(071) 349 1426* **Rooms** *20*

Located on the city limits, this 100-year-old villa is ideal for visitors who prefer to stay removed from the bustle of the city. Interiors are grand, especially the dining hall with its magnificent chandeliers. Rooms are brightly painted but still relaxing. There is a golf course nearby. **www.hotelbugatti.pl**

WROCŁAW Dwór Polski

P 11

ul. Kiełbaśnicza 2, 50108 **Tel** *(071) 372 3415* **Fax** *(071) 372 5829* **Rooms** *28*

This historic hotel in the centre has numerous legends attached to it; apparently, Poland's King Sigismund once held covert meetings here with his future wife. Gloomy corridors lead to decent rooms, many of which have been spruced up, though the hotel has been eclipsed by more modern rivals. **www.dworpolski.Wrocław.pl**

WROCŁAW Patio

P 11

ul. Kiełbaśnicza 24, 50110 **Tel** *(071) 375 0400* **Fax** *(071) 343 9149* **Rooms** *50*

This small, modern hotel with a historic façade offers decent mid-range rooms grouped around a covered atrium that doubles as a shopping centre. Rooms have high-speed Internet access and are decorated with creamy walls and the occasional artificial plant; some have original exposed brickwork. **www.hotelpatio.pl**

WROCŁAW Art Hotel

P 11 🖵 📋

ul. Kiełbaśnicza 20, 50110 **Tel** *(071) 787 7100* **Fax** *(071) 342 3929* **Rooms** *80*

A Neo-Gothic façade hides a modern hotel with luxury trimmings and rooms geared towards both business and pleasure. Situated on one of Wrocław's most engaging streets, the Art Hotel is the closest the city comes to a boutique hotel, while the Wraclawia restaurant, in the vaulted cellars, offers a classy menu. **www.arthotel.pl**

WROCŁAW Park Plaza

P 11 🖵 📋

ul. Drobnera 11/13, 50257 **Tel** *(071) 320 8400* **Fax** *(071) 320 8459* **Rooms** *177*

A large hotel on the banks of the Odra river, the Park Plaza has rooms overlooking Wrocław's grand Old Town. The modern rooms serve their purpose but are short on character; however, the hotel's popularity with the business community means that excellent discounts can be found at weekends. **www.parkplaza.pl**

WROCŁAW Qubus Hotel

P 11 ≌ 🖵 📋

ul. św Marii Magdaleny 2, 50103 **Tel** *(071) 797 9800* **Fax** *(071) 341 0920* **Rooms** *83*

This luxurious hotel stands in the shadow of the St Mary Magdalene's Church. Rooms feature all the modern amenities that one would expect at this level; the Presidential Suite is one of the finest splurges in town. The hotel's restaurant serves both Polish and European dishes. **www.qubushotel.com**

WROCŁAW Radisson BLU

P 11 🖵 📋

ul. Purkyniego 10, 50156 **Tel** *(071) 375 0000* **Fax** *(071) 375 0010* **Rooms** *162*

Located near Dominikanski Square, the Radisson is surrounded by a park and has brilliant views of the Odra river. Rooms have a chic, modern edge, and the restaurant stands out as a top dining experience. Wrocław's biggest tourist attraction, the monumental painting known as the Panorama of Racławice, is closeby. **www.radissonblu.com**

Key to Price Guide *see p218* **Key to Symbols** *see back cover flap*

Where to Eat in Poland

Polish food has undergone a change of image lately with the opening of a new generation of restaurants all over the country. Many take pride in offering a modern take on traditional specialities such as *pierogi* (ravioli) and dumplings. Good restaurants are plentiful in Warsaw and Cracow, but watch out for high prices in the more touristy areas.

PRICE CATEGORIES
Based on the price per person of a three-course meal, including cover charge, service and tax.

ⓩ under 50 zloty
ⓩⓩ 50–70 zloty
ⓩⓩⓩ 70–90 zloty
ⓩⓩⓩⓩ 90–110 zloty
ⓩⓩⓩⓩⓩ over 110 zloty

WARSAW

Kompania Piwna Podwale 25
ⓩ
ul. Podwale 25, 00261 **Tel** *(022) 635 6314*
Map D2

An Old Town gem with a courtyard designed to resemble a Central European town square, and an interior filled with wooden benches and drinking slogans on the walls. Heaps of meat and potatoes are served on wooden boards by staff in traditional dress. One of the few low-budget success stories in town.

Jajo
ⓩⓩ
ul. Zgoda 3, 00018 **Tel** *(022) 826 4493*
Map C4

Literally meaning "egg", Jajo is a fashionable spot with hip lighting and great music, attracting a young crowd. The menu specializes in spaghetti and has won fans across the city, but other continental bites are available too. This place doubles as a bar and has excellent wines.

Adler
ⓩⓩⓩ
ul. Mokotowska 69, 00-530 **Tel** *(022) 628 7384*
Map D5

Decked out with baskets of dried flowers and the odd *pickelhaube* (spiked helmet), Adler embodies the atmosphere of a Bavarian beer hall, with staff in ethnic costume rushing around delivering gigantic portions of pig's neck and *schnitzel* (fried meat coated in bread crumbs).

Galeria Bali & Buddha Club
ⓩⓩⓩ
ul. Jasna 22, 00054 **Tel** *(022) 828 6771*
Map C3

This is fusion food at top-tier prices, though the quality more than justifies the bill. The Buddha Club brings Indonesia to the table with dishes such as stir-fried beef in oyster sauce and fried lobster in coconut crumbs. Everything is for sale here, from the cutlery to the gold-plated statue of Buddha that sits peacefully inside.

India Curry
ⓩⓩⓩ
ul. Żurawia 22, 00515 **Tel** *(022) 438 9350*
Map D4

Indian food has not travelled well to Poland, with many chefs choosing to cook only the mildest of curries. India Curry, however, gets everything right – from its menu, which goes beyond the mainstream dishes, to the tasteful interiors, which include a bubbling fountain. Those on a budget will enjoy the lunch deals.

Kuchnia Kwai
ⓩⓩⓩ
ul. Marszałkowska 64, 00-544 **Tel** *(022) 621 2181*
Map C3&4

Relatively new, Kuchnia Kwai is a hit with the local media and expat community. Fusion food with Korean and Thai influences is served in a clean room decorated with Oriental sculptures and pictures of the People's Army. After your meal, be sure to pay a visit to Bar Below downstairs, the drinking den of choice for visitors in Warsaw.

Papaya
ⓩⓩⓩ
ul. Foksal 16, 00372 **Tel** *(022) 826 4851*
Map D4

A great addition to Warsaw's booming fusion scene, Papaya features a tepanyaki grill and dishes such as kobe sirloin, and tuna steak with Thai basil and shrimps. The white colour scheme contributes to a hip, urbane atmosphere that attracts a flashy crowd. Expect a heavy bill.

Sakana Sushi Bar
ⓩⓩⓩ
ul. Moliera 4/6, 0007 **Tel** *(022) 826 5958*
Map D3

Warsaw is sushi-crazy, and Sakana is the best of the dozens of sushi restaurants to be found across town. Food drifts by on paper boats, while a fashion-conscious clientele sits around the circular dining area. It is definitely on the small side, so be prepared to wait for a seat during the lunch-hour rush.

U Fukiera
ⓩⓩⓩⓩⓩ
Rynek Starego Miasta 27, 00275 **Tel** *(022) 831 1013*
Map D2

Its main-square location and a guest list that includes world leaders and royalty speak volumes for U Fukiera's reputation and prices. Set inside a beautiful network of chambers, the interiors alone are worth a visit, while the menu focuses on Polish classics cooked with ingenuity. The summer courtyard provides starlit dining at its finest.

Map References *see map of Warsaw pp172–3 and Cracow pp182–3*

REST OF POLAND

CRACOW Green Way

ul. Mikołajska 14, 31027 **Tel** *(012) 431 1027*

Map D2

Part of a Poland-wide chain, this relatively expensive vegetarian fast-food bar has a few tables at the back where diners can enjoy their meat-free snacks in relative comfort. The food is less than adventurous, but with vegetarian options thin on the ground in this city, the queues at lunchtime can be annoyingly long.

CRACOW Klezmer Hois

ul. Szeroka 6, 31053 **Tel** *(012) 411 1245*

Map E4

While Klezmer Hois is bold enough to admit that it has no rabbinical certificate of supervision (the Kashrut), it does keep strict standards, and all dishes are kosher, not to mention great value. Enjoy Sabbath soup, shubaha herring and Sephardic salads alongside meaty treats such as stuffed goose neck.

CRACOW La Bodega

ul. Sławkowska 12, 31014 **Tel** *(012) 425 4981*

Map C2

At Cracow's best tapas bar, the food is not seen as something that merely gets in the way of the wine. In fact, a wide variety of bite-size portions is available and, if visitors order it right, they can eat well for a fairly good price. The wine list is what brings people to this location; it is truly outstanding, with something for every pocket.

CRACOW Pierogarnia

ul. Sławkowska 32, 31014 **Tel** *(012) 422 7495*

Map C1 & 2

No visitor to Cracow should leave the city without tasting the Polish speciality *pierogi* (ravioli), and Pierogarnia is about the best place in town to do so. These tasty treats can be eaten as a snack or as part of a larger meal, and fillings are innumerable. The restaurant also serves other Polish delicacies.

CRACOW Sukiennice

Rynek Główny 1/3, 31042 **Tel** *(012) 422 2468*

Map C2

Set under the colonnades of a fantastic building, the terrace of this trendy venue on Main Market Square is packed out in summer, with live bands performing impromptu sets to delighted diners. If the weather is inclement, head inside, where elegant tables, soft lighting and simple fusion dishes make this a romantic place for a light meal.

CRACOW Chimera

ul. św Anny 3, 31011 **Tel** *(012) 429 5126*

Map C2

Traditional Polish dishes, including roast pork and lamb, are served on the ground floor of this restaurant, while the salad bar in the basement serves light, healthy food and a wide selection of vegetarian options. Specialities are the home-made fruit liqueurs.

CRACOW Wentzl

Rynek Główny 19, 31008 **Tel** *(012) 429 5712*

Map C2

Local merchant John Wentzl opened a restaurant here in 1792, and today it is one of the best eateries in the city. The high ceilings, polished oak floors and outstanding service complement the menu, which is dominated by Czech, Slovak and Hungarian specialities. The wine list takes in France, Austria and Spain as well as Chile and South Africa.

CRACOW Balaton

ul. Grodzka 37, 31001 **Tel** *(012) 422 0469*

Map C3

The less-than-salubrious setting is redeemed by a delicious menu of specialities from Hungary. Try the Hungarian national dish, goulash, or spicy sausages. Paprika features in most dishes, so those who prefer their food mild need to mention that to the waiter. Reservations are necessary, since Balaton fills up early most evenings.

CRACOW Pod Aniołami

ul. Grodzka 35, 31001 **Tel** *(012) 421 3999*

Map C3

This restaurant is located in medieval cellars decorated with a selection of historical objects. The menu features traditional Polish dishes, in particular delicacies from the highlands. Try *oszczypki* (a special kind of cheese prepared by Polish highlanders) or *żurek* (soup made with rye flour).

CRACOW Farina

ul. św. Marka 16, 31017 **Tel** *(012) 422 1680*

Map D2

In this simple, uncluttered restaurant, the bare, highly polished wooden floors and whitewashed walls serve to focus the diner's attention on the excellent menu. A successful mix of Polish and Italian dishes, including plenty of seafood, brings in scores of locals and visitors alike. Reservations are necessary in the evenings.

CRACOW Cyrano de Bergerac

ul. Sławkowska 26, 31014 **Tel** *(012) 411 7288*

Map C1

Prices here may seem high, but the diners who reserve tables weeks in advance don't seem to mind. This is a world-class French restaurant occupying two elegant rooms, with a quiet patio used in the summer months. The food is exquisite, cooked under the auspices of masterchef Pierre Gallard. Try the *garbure soupe béarnaise*, a soup made with goose.

Key to Symbols *see back cover flap*

FURTHER AFIELD CRACOW The Olive

ul. Powiśle 7, 31-101 **Tel** (012) 662 1660

As expensive as any restaurant in Cracow, the Sheraton's showpiece is an award-winning eaterie famed for its high-class Mediterranean cuisine. There is a particularly good selection of seafood and fish dishes, and the wine list is pitch-perfect. A glass roof makes dining here in winter a particularly pleasurable experience.

GDAŃSK Tawerna Mestwin
ul. Straganiarska 21/22, 80837 **Tel** (058) 301 7882   **Map** D3

Time stands still in Tawerna Mestwin, a restaurant serving traditional Kashubian cuisine, with an emphasis on tasty hunks of meat. Staffed by an elderly, friendly team, it is crammed with so many local arts and crafts it could be mistaken for an ethnographic museum. Excellent fare at low prices.

GDAŃSK Kubicki
ul. Wartka 5, 80841 **Tel** (058) 301 0050   **Map** E3

Founded in 1919, this legendary restaurant is still in the hands of the same family. The interiors are full of interesting old furniture, while the food is typical of traditional Polish port cities, with a good selection of starters and an excellently prepared fried trout. Be sure to leave some room for the delicious cheesecake.

GDAŃSK Pierogarnia u Dzika
ul. Piwna 59/60, 80-831 **Tel** (058) 305 2676   **Map** C4

Boar pelts and animal heads cheer up a peach-coloured interior, but design issues should be overlooked by anyone who appreciates good, inexpensive food. As the name suggests, *pierogi* (stuffed pasta) are the speciality here, and there is a vast collection of fillings to choose from: meat and cabbage to seasonal offerings such as fresh fruit.

GDAŃSK Pod Lososiem

ul. Szeroka 52/54, 80835 **Tel** (058) 301 7652   **Map** C3

This opulent restaurant has hosted luminaries such as George Bush Sr and Pope John Paul II. The name means "under the salmon", and grilled salmon is, indeed, the house speciality, though guests should also keep an eye out for the game dishes. This historic building originally housed the first Goldwasser vodka distillery in the city.

GDAŃSK Restauracja w Palacu Opatów
ul. Cystersów 18, 80333 **Tel** (058) 524 5699   **Map** xx

In the shadow of the Oliwa Cathedral is this wonderful restaurant, offering fine dining at its best. A maître d' escorts diners to their table, laid out in one of three rooms elegantly decorated in the style of an aristocrat's retreat. The menu changes with each season. The blini with caviar are perfect for small appetites.

FURTHER AFIELD GDAŃSK Chata Chlopska

ul. Gielguda 4, 80207 **Tel** (058) 524 0095

Locals flock to this thatched lodge, which is just outside the fringes of the Old Town, to feast on vast portions of meat and hoist their beers in the air. The rustic decor makes an enjoyable change from downtown Gdańsk's more formal eateries, and the menu serves as a great whistle-stop tour of traditional Polish cuisine.

FURTHER AFIELD GDAŃSK Kresowa

ul. Ogama 12, 80826 **Tel** (058) 301 6653

Highly recommended, this restaurant is located in the Old Town, next to the shipyard where the anti-Communist party Solidarnośc was born. The excellent menu borrows literally from the culinary traditions of Poland, Russia, Lithuania and Armenia, and dishes are served by waiters dressed in traditional costumes.

FURTHER AFIELD GDAŃSK VNS
al. Grunwaldzka 82 (4th floor, Manhattan Shopping Centre), 80244 **Tel** (058) 767 7900

Shopping-mall dining has been completely reinvented with VNS. Forget about stopping for a fast-food burger, this is a class act with a designer look generated by skylights, a piano stage and a minimalist interior. The menu would not be out of place in any international restaurant; dishes such as duck in honey are divine.

MALBORK Zamkowa
ul. Staroscinnska 14, 82200 **Tel** (055) 272 2738

This large restaurant is located in the rebuilt wings of Malbork Castle's outbuildings, and it has a knightly theme. The menu serves up traditional Polish cuisine, including a dish called "Castle Soup" – in essence a beef goulash, accompanied by olives and capers. It is a good spot to regenerate after a day spent touring the castle.

POZNAŃ Bee Jay's
Stary Rynek 87, 61772 **Tel** (061) 853 1115

Bee Jay's boasts a main-square location and a truly eclectic menu. Burgers can be found on one page, Mexican on the next, and Indian on the following one. Perhaps more surprising is that the ethnic food is pretty good – a real bonus in a gastronomically conservative town. Big-screen live sports make for a lively atmosphere.

POZNAŃ Brovaria
Stary Rynek 73/74, 61772 **Tel** (061) 858 6868

Brovaria is a hotel, restaurant and microbrewery all under one roof, each of which wins praise for excellence. The chic restaurant offers beautifully presented dishes such as veal stuffed with chicken and veal mousse. Finish off with cocktails at the impressive steel-and-glass bar.

Map References *see map of Cracow pp182–3 and Gdańsk pp208–209*

SOPOT Image

ul. Grunwaldzka 8, 81777 **Tel** *(058) 550 7576*

The eccentric interior of this restaurant in Sopot's city centre, is decorated with scenes from the *Kama Sutra*. Diners come here to enjoy the Mediterranean dishes such as beef carpaccio with capers, as well as traditional Polish specialities, such as sour rye soup with mushrooms. The wine list covers all of the world's main wine-producing regions.

SOPOT Rucola

ul. Poniatowskiego 8, 81777 **Tel** *(058) 551 5046*

Located in the basement of the Museum of Sopot, this restaurant is an attractive space with black-and-white ceiling and linen-covered seating. It is especially renowned for its Mediterranean dishes, although a small selection of Polish dishes is on offer too. Try the lemon soup.

SOPOT Klub Wieloryb

ul. Podjazd 2, 81805 **Tel** *(058) 551 5722*

Ring the doorbell to enter and then take your time to admire Klub Wieloryb's grotto-like interior. Submarine engines, grotesque sculptures and other decorative oddities will leave your mind spinning. The menu is French-influenced and a meal here will prove to be one of the best in the region.

SOPOT Villa Baltica

ul. Emilii Plater 1, 81777 **Tel** *(058) 555 2800*

This stand-out restaurant, a short walk from the beach, is attached to the luxurious hotel of the same name. It comes with a fresh cream colour scheme, interesting pieces of modern art and soft music playing in the background. The menu ranges from light snacks to more substantial dishes, such as boar.

SOPOT Rozmaryn

ul. Ogrodowa 8, 81759 **Tel** *(058) 551 1104*

Within a charming cottage-style building, Rozmaryn has a disappointingly dull interior, but that should act as no deterrent to diners. This is said to be the best Italian restaurant in the region, and rightly so. The menu changes each month, and the seafood, especially the fish soup, is renowned across the town.

TORUŃ Gromada

ul. Żeglarska 10/14, 87100 **Tel** *(056) 622 6060*

Despite its rather outdated image, this hotel-restaurant offers some very good food. The menu revolves around typical Polish cuisine, including tripe and *żurek* soup. The potato dumplings served in *czernina* (soup made with duck blood and chicken broth) is particularly impressive.

WROCŁAW Abrams' Tower

ul. Kraińskiego 14, 50-153 **Tel** *(071) 725 6652*

In the past one may had to travel to Warsaw to enjoy Mexican food, but the arrival of Abrams' Tower means that this is no longer the case. Indeed, this restaurant looks set on changing the conservative dining habits of the locals. The owners stress that this is Mexican food prepared Californian-style, inside the trendy interior of a medieval tower.

WROCŁAW Art Restauracja i Kawiarnia

ul. Kiełbaśnicza 20, 50110 **Tel** *(071) 787 7102*

The Art Hotel is one of the best in town, so it comes as no surprise that such quality extends to the kitchen. Descend to the basement to enter a vaulted brick cellar decorated with murals of city scenes. The menu changes with the seasons and sees the chef experimenting with recipes from all over Europe.

WROCŁAW Sakana

ul. Odrzańska 17/1a, 50-113 **Tel** *(071) 343 3710*

This restaurant is owned by the same team behind the best sushi stop in the capital. Wrocław's version of Sakana is equally good, the only difference being that this venture is actually larger that the Warsaw branch. Once more, the food floats around a circular bar on paper boats, eagerly consumed by a young and fashionable crowd.

WROCŁAW Spiż

Rynek Ratusz 2, 50106 **Tel** *(071) 344 7225*

Spiż is split into two rooms: a microbrewery with huge copper vats and a formal dining room. The service is not fast, but patience is rewarded with outstanding home-brewed beer and tempting dishes such as Argentinian beef and saddle of lamb, as well as Polish choices. The restaurant section is popular with an older crowd.

WROCŁAW Splendido

ul. Swidnicka 53, 50030 **Tel** *(071) 344 7777*

Cluttered with exposed beams, flowers and lampshades, this is one of Wrocław's best choices, provided one is willing to part with the cash. The menu is a collection of Mediterranean dishes, among which the seafood is especially noteworthy, with a superb sea bass prepared in balsamic sauce. The exclusive Vulevu Club is found in the basement.

WROCŁAW Piano Bar Casablanca

ul. Wlodkowica 8a, 50072 **Tel** *(071) 344 7817*

One of the most revered restaurants in town (and popular with local celebrities), the Piano Bar Casablanca is decorated with North African rugs and framed pictures of Humphrey Bogart. The garden area feels a world away from the frantic flutter of central Wrocław, and the menu offers both local and Mediterranean dishes.

Key to Price Guide *see p222* **Key to Symbols** *see back cover flap*

CZECH REPUBLIC

The Czech Republic is one of Europe's youngest states. In the years after World War II, foreign visitors to what was then Czechoslovakia, rarely ventured further than the capital, Prague. Today, the country's beautifully preserved medieval towns, palaces and castles, which were neglected during the Communist era, are attracting an ever-increasing number of visitors.

Landlocked in Central Europe, the Czech Republic is divided into two regions – Bohemia and Moravia. Rolling plains and lush, pine-clad mountains, dotted with medieval châteaux and 19th-century spa resorts characterize the landscape of southern and western Bohemia. However, much of northern Bohemia has been given over to mining and other heavy industries, with devastating effects on the local environment. Moravia has orchards and vineyards in the south, and a broad industrial belt in the north of the region. Prague, Bohemia's largest city and the capital of the Czech Republic, is a thriving cultural and commercial centre. Its wealth of great architecture, spanning over 1,000 years, has withstood the ravages of two world wars in the last century.

HISTORY

From 500 BC, the area now known as the Czech Republic was settled by Celtic tribes, who were later joined by Germanic peoples. The first Slavs, the forefathers of the Czechs, came to the region around AD 500. Struggles for supremacy led to the emergence of a ruling dynasty, the Přemyslids, at the start of the 9th century. The Přemyslids were involved in many family feuds and in 935 Prince Wenceslas was murdered by his brother, Boleslav. Later canonized, Wenceslas became Bohemia's best-known patron saint.

Ruins of a castle on top of a hill, a common sight in the Czech Republic

◁ Grand interior of the Strahov Monastery, Prague

The reign of Holy Roman Emperor Charles IV in the 14th century heralded a Golden Age for Bohemia. Charles chose Prague as his imperial residence and founded many institutions there, including Central Europe's first university.

In the early 15th century, Central Europe lived in fear of an incredible fighting force – the Hussites, followers of the reformer Jan Hus, who attacked the corrupt practices of the Catholic church. Hus's execution in 1415 led to the Hussite Wars.

Engraving showing the reformer Jan Hus being burnt at the stake

At the start of the 16th century, the Austrian Habsburgs took over the region and went on to rule for almost 400 years. Religious turmoil led, in 1618, to the Protestant revolt and the Thirty Years' War. The 19th century saw a period of Czech national revival and the burgeoning of civic pride. However, it was not until 1918 and the collapse of the Habsburg Empire that the independent republic of Czechoslovakia was declared. World War II brought German occupation, followed by four decades of Communism. In 1968, a programme of liberal reforms (the Prague Spring) was introduced, but it was swiftly quashed by Soviet leaders. The overthrow of Communism did not come until November 1989, when a protest rally against police brutality led to the Velvet Revolution – a series of mass demonstrations and strikes that resulted in the resignation of the existing regime. In 1993, the peaceful division of Czechoslovakia resulted in the creation of two independent states – Slovakia and the Czech Republic.

KEY DATES IN CZECH HISTORY

500 BC Celts settle in Bohemia and Moravia. Joined by Germanic tribes in 1st century AD

AD 500–600 Slavs settle in the region

870 Přemyslids build Prague Castle

1333 Charles IV makes Prague his home, marking the start of the city's Golden Age

1415 Jan Hus executed for heresy; start of the Hussite Wars

1526 Habsburg rule begins with Ferdinand I

1583 Accession of Habsburg Emperor Rudolf II

1618 Protestant revolt leads to the Thirty Years' War

1627 Beginning of Counter-Reformation committee in Prague

1916 Czechoslovak National Council created in Paris

1918 Foundation of Czechoslovakia

1948 Communist Party assumes power

1989 Year of the Velvet Revolution; Communist regime finally overthrown

1993 Czechoslovakia ceases to exist; creation of the new Czech Republic

2004 Czech Republic joins the EU

2007 New centre-right coalition forms a government

LANGUAGE AND CULTURE

Under the Habsburgs, Czech identity was largely suppressed and the Czech language became little more than a dialect. In the 19th century, however, Austrian rule relaxed, and the Czechs began rediscovering their own culture. Czech was re-established as an official language, thanks to the historian František Palacký, who also wrote the first history of the Czech nation.

Since the Golden Age of the 14th century, Prague has prided itself on its reputation as a flourishing cultural centre. In the early 20th century, the city hosted a Cubist movement that rivalled the one in Paris. The Czech Republic has also produced writers, artists and musicians of world renown.

Exploring the Czech Republic

One of Europe's most beautiful capital cities, Prague is the highlight of a visit to the Czech Republic. However, the Bohemian countryside is home to dozens of well-preserved castles and historic towns such as České Budějovice. Most of these sights can be visited on a day-trip from Prague, and are easily reached by good public transport. Slightly further afield, Český Krumlov merits at least a couple of days' exploration.

SIGHTS AT A GLANCE

Beautifully restored house,
Český Krumlov

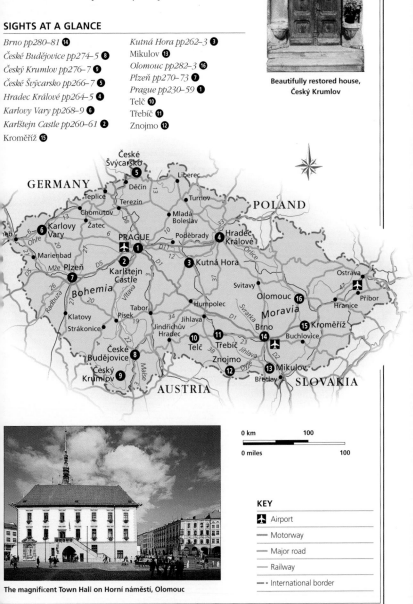

KEY

✈ Airport

— Motorway

— Major road

— Railway

-·- International border

The magnificent Town Hall on Horní náměstí, Olomouc

Prague ❶

The capital of the Czech Republic, Prague has a population of just over one million. In the late Middle Ages, during the reign of Charles IV, Prague's position at the crossroads of Europe led it to evolve into a magnificent city, larger than Paris or London. In the 16th century, it was taken over by the Austrian Habsburgs, who built many of the Baroque palaces and gardens that delight visitors today. Some of these now house important museums. The fascinating Jewish Quarter has a handful of synagogues and a cemetery that remarkably survived the Nazi occupation. Despite neglect under Communist rule, the historic centre of the city has been preserved, making Prague one of the most beautiful and interesting of all European capitals.

The Three Fiddles, an old house sign in Nerudova ulice

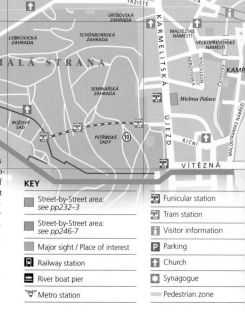

GETTING AROUND

The historic centre of Prague covers a relatively small area and is best explored on foot. Prague's subway, or metro, is the fastest way of getting to other parts of the city. It has three lines, A, B and C, and 54 stations. Line A covers the majority of the city centre. There is an efficient network of buses and trams. Trams operate during the night as well. Routes 14, 17 and 22 pass many major sights on both banks of the Vltava. While the metro and trams serve the city centre, buses are used to reach the suburbs.

KEY

	Street-by-Street area: see pp232–3
	Street-by-Street area: see pp246–7
	Major sight / Place of interest
🚉	Railway station
⛴	River boat pier
Ⓜ	Metro station
🚡	Funicular station
🚋	Tram station
ℹ	Visitor information
P	Parking
✝	Church
✡	Synagogue
	Pedestrian zone

SIGHTS AT A GLANCE

SEE ALSO

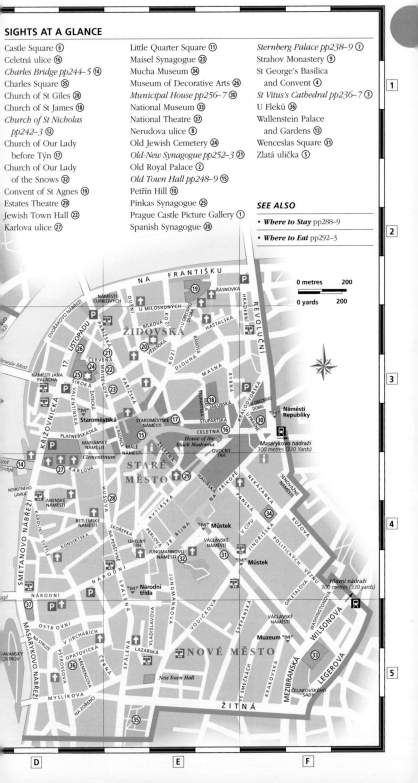

Street-by-Street: Prague Castle

The history of Prague began with the foundation of Prague Castle in the 9th century. Despite fires and invasions, the castle has retained churches, chapels and towers from every period of its history, from the Gothic splendour of St Vitus's Cathedral *(see pp236–7)* to the 16th-century Renaissance additions. The courtyards date from 1753–75, when the whole area was rebuilt in the late-Baroque and Neo-Classical styles. The castle became the seat of the Czechoslovak president in 1918 and the current president of the Czech Republic has an office here.

★ **St Vitus's Cathedral**
This relief in the Gothic St Vitus's Cathedral decorates the Golden Portal ③

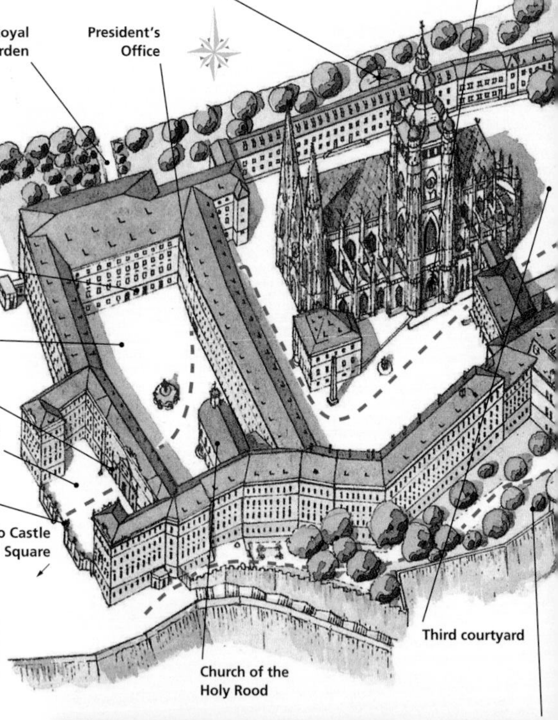

The Powder Tower, used in the past for storing gunpowder and as a bell foundry, is now a museum.

Gothic reliquary of St George's arm in St Vitus's Cathedral

Prague Castle Picture Gallery Renaissance and Baroque paintings hang in the restored stables of the castle ①

To Royal Garden

President's Office

Second courtyard

Matthias Gate

First courtyard

To Castle Square

Third courtyard

Church of the Holy Rood

Castle Gates
The gates of the castle are crowned by copies of 18th-century statues called Fighting Giants *by Ignaz Platzer.*

South Gardens
Here 18th-century statues stand along the old ramparts.

★ St George's Basilica
The superb vaulted chapel of the royal Bohemian martyr St Ludmila is decorated with 16th-century paintings ④

★ Zlatá Ulička
The picturesque artisans' cottages along the inside of the castle wall were built in the late 16th century for the castle's guards and gunners ⑤

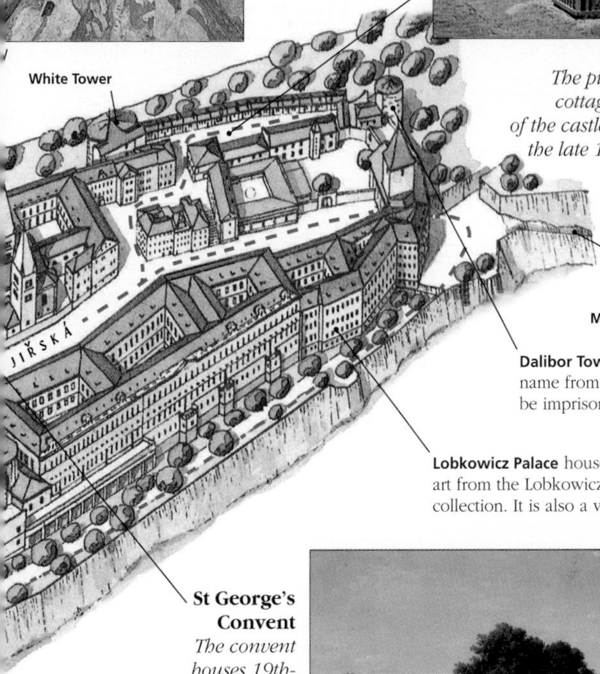

White Tower

Old Castle steps down to Malostranská Metro

Dalibor Tower takes its name from the first man to be imprisoned in it.

JIRSKÁ

Lobkowicz Palace houses works of art from the Lobkowicz family's private collection. It is also a venue for concerts.

St George's Convent
The convent houses 19th-century Czech art such as a piece titled Summer Countryside with Chapel *by Adolf Kosárek* ④

| 0 metres | 60 |
| 0 yards | 60 |

★ Old Royal Palace
The uniform exterior of the palace conceals many Gothic and Renaissance halls. Coats of arms cover the walls and ceiling of the Room of the New Land Rolls ②

STAR SIGHTS

★ St Vitus's Cathedral

★ St George's Basilica

★ Zlatá Ulička

★ Old Royal Palace

KEY

— — — Suggested route

Rib vaulting in the Vladislav Hall, Old Royal Palace

Prague Castle Picture Gallery ①
Obrazárna pražského hradu

Prague Castle, second courtyard.
Map B3. **Tel** 224 373 531. 🚇 22.
🚋 *Malostranská, Hradčanská.*
◯ *Apr–Oct: 9am–6pm daily; Nov–Mar: 9am–4pm daily.* 🎫 ♿
www.obrazarna-hradu.cz

This gallery was created in Prague Castle in 1965 to display, among other works, what remains of the great art collection of the Habsburg Emperor Rudolph II (r. 1576–1612). Though many works of art were looted by the occupying Swedish Army in 1648, some fine paintings remain, including works by artists Hans von Aachen and Bartolomeus Spranger. Paintings from the 16th to the 18th centuries make up the bulk of the gallery's collection. Highlights include Rubens's *The Assembly of the Olympic Gods,* featuring Venus and Jupiter, Tintoretto's *Flagellation of Christ* and Titian's *The Toilet of a Young Lady.* Master Theodoric, Paolo Veronese and the Czech Baroque artists Jan Kupecký and Petr Brandl are among the other painters represented. The sculptures include a bust of Rudolph II by Adriaen Vries.

Visitors can also see the remains of the castle's first church, the 9th-century Church of Our Lady, believed to have been built by Prince Bořivoj, the first Přemyslid prince to be baptized a Christian.

Old Royal Palace ②
Starý královský palác

Prague Castle, third courtyard.
Map B3. **Tel** 224 373 102.
🚇 22. 🚋 *Malostranská, Hradčanská.* ◯ *Apr–Oct: 9am–6pm daily; Nov–Mar: 9am–4pm daily.* 🎫 ♿ 📷 **www**.hrad.cz

From the time Prague Castle was first fortified in the 11th century, the Old Royal Palace was the seat of a long line of Bohemian kings.

The vast palace complex consists of three different architectural layers. A Romanesque palace, built around 1135, forms the basement of the present structure. Over the next 200 years, two further palaces were built above this – the first by Přemysl Otakar II in 1253, and the second by Charles IV in 1340. On the top floor is the massive Gothic Vladislav Hall, with

Titian's *The Toilet of a Young Lady* in Prague Castle Picture Gallery

its splendid rib vaulting. Designed for King Vladislav Jagiello, it was completed in 1502. The Rider's Staircase, just off the hall, is a flight of steps with a magnificent Gothic rib-vaulting ceiling. It was used by knights on horseback to get to jousting contests.

Under Habsburg rule, the palace housed government offices, courts and the old Bohemian parliament. The Bohemian Chancellery, the former royal offices of the Habsburgs, is the site of famous 1618 defenestration, In 1619 the Bohemian nobles deposed Emperor Ferdinand II as king of Bohemia, electing in his place Frederick of the Palatinate. This led to the first major battle of the Thirty Years' War *(see p228).*

St Vitus's Cathedral ③

See pp236–7.

St George's Basilica and Convent ④
Bazilika a klášter sv Jiří

Jiřská náměstí. **Map** B3. **Tel** 224 373 368. 🚇 22. 🚋 *Malostranská, Hradčanská.* ◯ *Apr–Oct: 9am–6pm daily; Nov–Mar 9am–4pm daily.* 🎫 ♿ 📷 **Concerts** ◯ *Apr–Sep: call for timings.* **www**.hrad.cz

St George's Basilica was founded by Prince Vratislav in 920 and is the best preserved Romanesque church in Prague. The huge twin towers and austere interior have been restored to give an idea of the church's original appearance.

The interior contains the 10th-century tomb of Vratislav I, located opposite the presbytery. Also buried in the church are Prince Boleslav II, who died in 992, and Princess Ludmila (grandmother of St Wenceslas), who was murdered in 921 and is revered as the first Bohemian saint. Her 14th-century tombstone is located in the Gothic side chapel. Other points of interest include a rare early

13th-century painting, *New Jerusalem*, in the choir vault. The double staircase to the chancel is a remarkable late-Baroque addition and now provides a perfect stage for chamber music concerts. Outside, the south portal of the church features a 16th-century relief depicting St George and the dragon.

The adjacent former Benedictine nunnery is the oldest convent building in Bohemia. It was founded in 973 by Princess Mlada, sister of Boleslav II. Throughout the Middle Ages, the convent and St George's Basilica formed the heart of the castle complex. Rebuilt several times, the convent and its religious functions finally ceased in 1782.

Today, the convent holds the National Gallery's collection of 19th-century Czech art. The collection features fine examples by artists such as Jan Kupecký, Petr Brandl, Bartolomeus Spranger, Matthias Braun and Ferdinand Brokof.

Zlatá Ulička ⑤

Map C3. 📷 22. Ⓜ *Malostranská, Hradčanská.* 📷

Named after the goldsmiths who lived here in the 17th century, Golden Lane (Zlatá ulička) is one of the prettiest lanes in Prague. One side of the lane is lined with tiny, brightly painted houses built right into the arches of the castle walls. These were constructed in the late 16th century for Rudolph II's 24 castle guards. A century later, the goldsmiths moved in and modified the buildings.

Picturesque 16th-century cottages in Zlatá ulička

However, by the 19th century the area had degenerated into a slum and was populated by Prague's poor and the criminal communities. In the 1950s, all the remaining residents were moved and the area was restored to something like its original state. Most of the houses were converted into shops selling books, Bohemian glass and other souvenirs for visitors, who now flock to this narrow lane.

Despite the street's name, Rudolph II's alchemists never produced gold here. Their laboratories were in Vikářská, the lane between St Vitus's Cathedral and the Powder Tower (Mihulka).

Zlatá ulička has, however, been home to well-known writers such as Franz Kafka *(see p31)*, who stayed at No. 22 with his sister around 1916–17 and Jaroslav Seifert, the Nobel Prize-winning Czech poet.

Castle Square ⑥

Hradčanské náměstí

Map B3. 📷 22. Ⓜ *Malostranská, Hradčanská.* **Schwarzenberg Palace Tel** *224 810 758.* ⏰ *10am–6pm Tue–Sun.* **www.ngprague.cz**

The vast, grand square in front of Prague Castle was once lined with workshops and artisans' houses, but after the devastating fire of 1541, they were replaced by a series of imposing palaces. These were built by Czech and foreign noblemen, eager to live close to the court of the Habsburgs. On the south side stands the 16th-century **Schwarzenberg Palace** (Schwarzenberský palác), a beautiful Renaissance building with graceful attics and magnificent *sgraffito* that gives the impression that the façade is clad in Italian-style diamond-point stonework. The western end of the square is taken up by the Thun-Hohenstein Palace (Thun-Hohenšteinský palác), built between 1689 and 1691 and crowned with statues by Ferdinand Brokof. To the north lies the Archbishop's Palace (Arcibiskupský palác), a 16th-century building with a Rococo façade in pink and white, added in the 1760s. The Renaissance Martinic Palace (Martinický palác), at the corner of Castle Square, has *sgraffito* depicting scenes from the Bible. Its high terrace provides views of the city.

Schwarzenberg Palace in Castle Square, notable for its *sgraffito* decoration

St Vitus's Cathedral ③
chrám sv Víta

Work began on St Vitus's Cathedral, Prague's
most distinctive landmark, in 1344. Architect
Peter Parler was largely responsible for the
grandiose Gothic design, though the building
was not completed for another 600 years.
The cathedral contains the tomb of Good
King Wenceslas and some fine works of art
including an exquisite Alfons Mucha window.

**Window by
Alfons Mucha**
*The beautiful
glass window
was painted by
Alfons Mucha in
Czech Art
Nouveau style.*

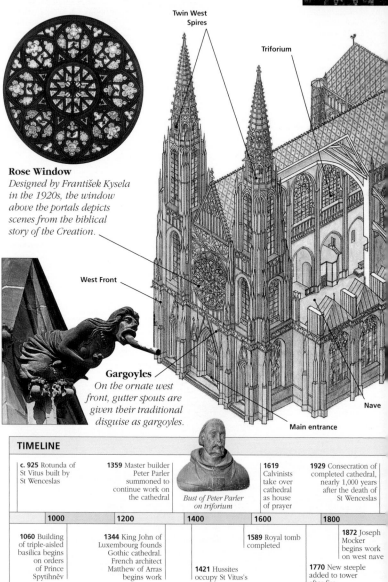

Twin West
Spires

Triforium

Rose Window
*Designed by František Kysela
in the 1920s, the window
above the portals depicts
scenes from the biblical
story of the Creation.*

West Front

Gargoyles
*On the ornate west
front, gutter spouts are
given their traditional
disguise as gargoyles.*

Nave

Main entrance

TIMELINE

c. 925 Rotunda of St Vitus built by St Wenceslas	**1359** Master builder Peter Parler summoned to continue work on the cathedral	*Bust of Peter Parler on triforium*	**1619** Calvinists take over cathedral as house of prayer	**1929** Consecration of completed cathedral, nearly 1,000 years after the death of St Wenceslas
1000	**1200**	**1400**	**1600**	**1800**
1060 Building of triple-aisled basilica begins on orders of Prince Spytihněv	**1344** King John of Luxembourg founds Gothic cathedral. French architect Matthew of Arras begins work	**1421** Hussites occupy St Vitus's	**1589** Royal tomb completed	**1770** New steeple added to tower after fire · **1872** Joseph Mocker begins work on west nave

★ Flying Buttresses
The slender buttresses that surround the exterior of the nave and chancel, supporting the vaulted interior, are richly decorated.

VISITORS' CHECKLIST

Prague Castle, third courtyard. **Map** B3. *22 to Prague Castle.* *Hradčanská, Malostranská.* **Cathedral** *Mar–Oct: 9am–5pm Mon–Sat, 12pm–5pm Sun; Nov–Feb: 9am–4pm Mon–Sat, 12pm–4pm Sun.* **Bell tower** *Apr–Oct: 9am–4pm daily.*
www.hrad.cz

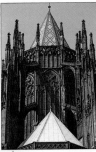

The Renaissance bell tower is capped with a Baroque "helmet".
Chancel
To Old Royal Palace
The tomb of St Wenceslas is connected to an altar, decorated with semi-precious stones.

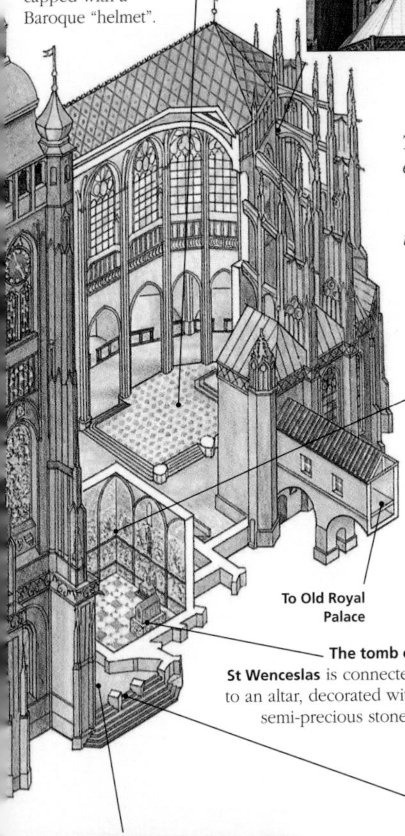

★ Chapel of St Wenceslas
This opulent, jewel-studded chapel, home to the saint's tomb, is the highlight of a visit to St Vitus's Cathedral. This bronze ring hangs on the chapel's north portal.

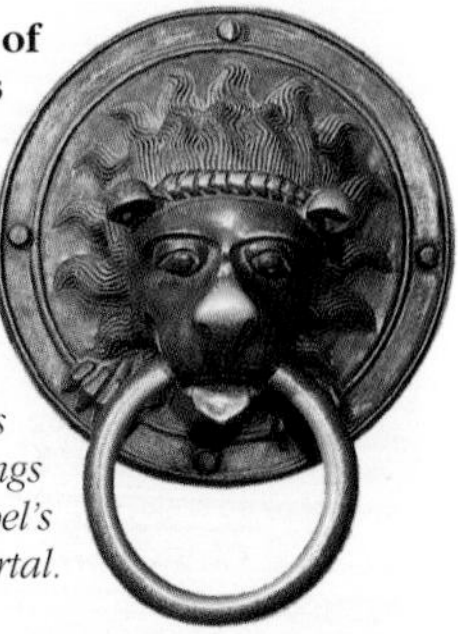

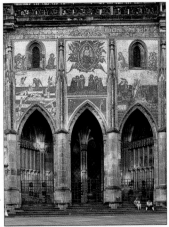

★ Golden Portal
Until the 19th century, this was the main cathedral entrance and it is still used on special occasions. Above it is a mosaic of The Last Judgment *by 14th-century Venetian craftsmen.*

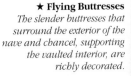

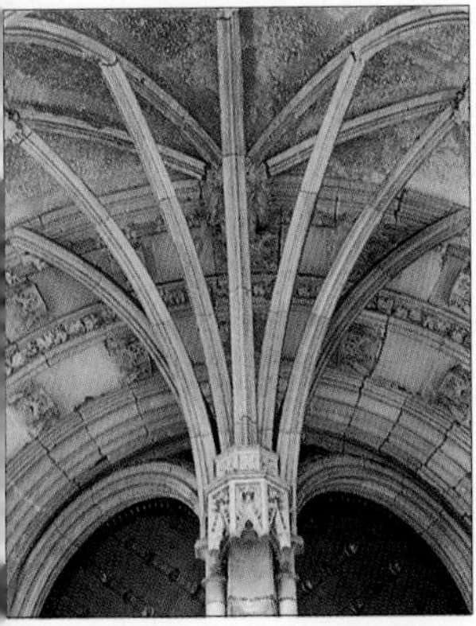

Gothic Vaulting
The skills of architect Peter Parler are clearly seen in the delicate fans of ribbing that support the three Gothic arches of the Golden Portal.

STAR FEATURES

- ★ Flying Buttresses
- ★ Chapel of St Wenceslas
- ★ Golden Portal

Sternberg Palace ⑦

šternberský palác

The 18th-century Sternberg Palace has been home to the National Gallery's collection of European art since 1949. Franz Josef Sternberg founded the Society of Patriotic Friends of the Arts in Bohemia in 1796. Fellow noblemen would lend their finest sculptures and pictures to the society, which had its headquarters in the Sternberg Palace. The Baroque building has a superb range of works by Old Masters.

The Lamentation of Christ (1408)
The sculptural figures make this one of the finest paintings by Lorenzo Monaco.

Cardinal Cesi's Garden in Rome (1548)
Henrick van Cleve's painting provides a valuable image of a Renaissance collection of antiquities.

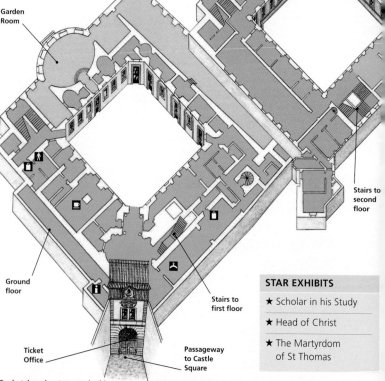

First floor

Garden Room

Stairs to second floor

Ground floor

Stairs to first floor

Ticket Office

Passageway to Castle Square

STAR EXHIBITS

★ Scholar in his Study

★ Head of Christ

★ The Martyrdom of St Thomas

★ Scholar in his Study (1634)
Rembrandt used keenly observed detail to convey wisdom in the face of the old scholar.

Chinese Cabinet

The Garden of Eden (1618)
Roelandt Savery studied the animals in the menagerie of Rudolph II. He liked to include them in his biblical and mythological works.

Second floor

Stairs down to other floors and exit

★ Head of Christ
Painted by El Greco in the 1590s, this portrait emphasizes the humanity of Christ. At the same time the curious square halo gives the painting the qualities of an ancient icon.

★ The Martyrdom of St Thomas (1636)
This magnificent work is by Peter Paul Rubens, a Flemish Baroque painter from the 17th century.

VISITORS' CHECKLIST

Hradčanské náměstí 15. **Map** B3. *Tel* 233 090 570. 22, 23. Malostranská, Hradčanská. 10am–6pm Tue–Sun. last guided tour at 5pm. www.ngprague.cz

GALLERY GUIDE
The gallery is arranged on three floors around the central courtyard of the palace. The ground floor, reached from the courtyard, houses German and Austrian art from the 15th to 19th centuries. The stairs to the upper floors are opposite the ticket office. The first and the second floors have works of art from various European countries.

KEY
- German and Austrian Art 1400–1800
- Flemish and Dutch Art 1400–1600
- Italian Art 1400–1500
- Roman Art
- Flemish and Dutch Art 1600–1800
- French Art 1600–1800
- Icons, Classical and Ancient Art
- Venice 1700–1800 and Goya
- Spanish Art 1600–1800
- Naples and Venice 1600–1700
- Italian Art 1500–1600
- Non-exhibition space

Nerudova Ulice ⑧

Map B3. 🚋 *12, 20, 22.*
Ⓜ *Malostranská.*

A picturesque narrow street
leading up to Prague Castle,
Nerudova ulice is bustling,
noisy and crowded by day, but
becomes deserted at night –
over time, souvenir shops and
offices have replaced the ordinary residents. The street is
named after the poet and journalist Jan Neruda, who wrote
many stories set in this part of
Prague. He lived in the house
called At the Two Suns (No.
47) between 1845 and 1857.

Until the introduction of
house numbers in 1770, the
city's dwellings were distinguished by signs. Nerudova
ulice's houses have a splendid
selection of these, featuring
symbols, emblems and heraldic beasts made of stone,
stucco or metal, painted or
carved. They often indicate a
profession or special interest
of the former occupants.

Proceeding up Nerudova's
steep slope, those of particular
interest include the Red Eagle
(No. 6), the Three Fiddles (No.
12), the Old Pharmacy Museum (No. 32) and the Golden
Horseshoe (No. 34). There are
also many Baroque buildings,
most of which have become
embassies. Among them are
the Thun-Hohenstein Palace
(No. 20, now the Italian
Embassy), whose entrance is
framed by an imposing portal
with two spread-wing eagles
by Matthias Braun, and
Morzin Palace (No. 5, the
Romanian Embassy). The
façade of the latter has two
vast statues of Moors (a pun
on the name Morzin) supporting the semicircular balcony
on the first floor sculpted by
Ferdinand
Brokof. Another
impressive
façade is that
of the Church
of Our Lady
of Unceasing Succour
(Kostel Panny
Marie v
neutuchajícím
pomoc v nouzi), the church
of the Theatines, an order
founded during the
Counter-Reformation.

The magnificent Philosophical Hall, within the Strahov Monastery

**Sign of Jan Neruda's house,
47 Nerudova Street**

Strahov
Monastery ⑨
Strahovský klášter

Královská Kanonie Premonstrátů na
Strahové, Strahovské nádvoří 1/132,
Strahovská. **Map** A4. **Tel** *233 107
711.* 🚋 *22, 23.* ◯ *9am–noon,
12:30–5pm daily.* **Church of Our
Lady**, **Philosophical Hall**,
Theological Hall, **Picture Gallery**
◯ *9am–noon, 1–5pm daily.* ●
Easter Sun, 25 Dec. 📷 🚻 📷
www.strahovskyklaster.cz

When it was founded by
Vladislav II in 1140 to serve
an austere religious order, the
Premonstratensians, Strahov
rivalled Prague Castle (see
pp232–3) in size. Burnt down
in the 13th cen-
tury, then rebuilt,
it acquired its
present Baroque
form in the 18th
century. In 1783,
during the reign of
Joseph II, the
monastery man-
aged to escape
dissolution by declaring itself
an educational establishment,
citing its vast library. The
monks were finally driven out

in 1950 by the Communists.
After the Velvet Revolution
(1989), the monastery resumed
its original function, and
monks can sometimes be seen
going about their business.

The abbey courtyard is
entered via a Baroque gateway sporting a statue of St
Norbert, the founder of the
Premonstratensian Order. The
main monastery church is the
Church of Our Lady
(Nanebevzetí Panny Marie),
featuring statues by Johan
Anton Quitainer on its façade.
The restored Baroque interior
dazzles with opulence.
Besides the magnificent altars
and furnishings, the frescoes
are particularly striking,
covering the ceiling and walls
above the arcades.

Inside the monastery, the
two Baroque libraries are
among the most beautiful in
Europe. The first of these, the
Philosophical Hall (Filosofický
sál) was built to house the
books and bookcases from
Louca monastery in Moravia,
dissolved by Joseph II. The
vault is decorated with a 1782
fresco depicting mankind's
quest for truth. The second
library is the **Theological Hall**

Teologický sál), dating from the 16th century. It is equally impressive, with a number of 17th-century astronomical globes and frescoes. The **Picture Gallery** (Obrazárna), in the nearby 17th-century Church of St Roch, is one of the finest art galleries in Prague, focusing on the interpretation of the works of masters such as Dali and Chagall.

Petřín Hill ⑩
Petřínské sady

Map B4. 🚋 6, 9, 12, 20, 22, then take the funicular railway from Újezd.

Petřín Hill, to the west of Little Quarter (Malá Strana), is the highest of Prague's nine hills at 61 m (200 ft). A path winds up its slopes, offering fine views of Prague, but visitors can also take the funicular from Újezd, which lies to the south of Little Quarter. At the top, there are many paths to explore and several attractions, including a version of the Eiffel Tower (Rozhledna), built in 1891 as a tribute to the city's strong cultural and political links with Paris at that time. A mini Gothic castle (Bludiště), containing a hall of distorting mirrors, is particularly popular with children.

Little Quarter Square ⑪
Malostranské náměstí

Map C3. 🚋 12, 20, 22. Ⓜ Malostranská.

This sloping square, busy with trams and people stopping for a drink or a bite to eat, has been the centre of activity in Little Quarter since its foundation in 1257. It began as a marketplace in the outer bailey of Prague Castle. Most of the houses here have a medieval core, but all were rebuilt during the Baroque and Renaissance periods.

The square is dominated by the Church of St Nicholas, regarded as the best example of High Baroque in the city. Opposite the church is the vast Neo-Classical façade of Lichtenstein Palace. Other

Baroque Church of St Nicholas in Little Quarter Square

important buildings include the Town Hall, with its fine Renaissance façade, and Sternberg Palace, built on the site of the outbreak of the 1541 fire, which destroyed most of the district.

Church of St Nicholas ⑫

See pp242–3.

Wallenstein Palace and Gardens ⑬
Valdštejnská palác a zahrada

Valdštejnské náměstí 4. **Map** C3. 🚋 12, 18, 20, 22. Ⓜ Malostranská. **Tel** 257 075 707. **Palace** ◻ 10am–4pm Sat & Sun (subject to change). ♿ from Valdštejnske. ◘. **Gardens** ◻ Apr, May, Sep & Oct: 7:30am–6pm Mon–Fri; Jun–Aug: 7:30am–7pm Mon–Fri, 10am–6pm Sat & Sun. ♿ from Valdštejnské náměstí. ▣ www.senat.cz

The first important secular building of the Baroque era in Prague, the Wallenstein Palace

stands as a monument to the ambitions of military chief Albrecht von Wallenstein. His string of victories over the Protestants in the Thirty Years' War made him vital to Emperor Ferdinand II. When Wallenstein started to covet the crown of Bohemia and also dared to negotiate with the enemy, he was assassinated on the emperor's orders.

Wallenstein spent only 12 months in the palace that he had built for himself between 1620 and 1630. It was designed by Italian architect Andrea Spezza. The main hall has a ceiling fresco of Wallenstein himself, portrayed as Mars, the god of war, riding in a triumphal chariot. Today, the palace is home to the Czech Senate. The restored gardens are laid out as they were when Wallenstein dined in the huge garden pavilion that looks out over the Fountain of Venus (1599) and rows of bronze statues.

Fountain of Venus in front of the Wallenstein Palace

ALBRECHT VON WALLENSTEIN

Wallenstein, politician and commander

Albrecht von Wallenstein (Valdštein) was born in Bohemia in 1583. He studied in Italy and later converted to Catholicism. He joined Rudolph II's Army and rose in prominence to lead the imperial armies in Europe. During the Thirty Years' War he had several victories over the Protestants. In 1630, he negotiated secretly with the Protestants and then joined them. For this, he was killed in 1634 by mercenaries acting on Emperor Ferdinand II's orders.

Church of St Nicholas ⑫
Kostel sv Mikuláše

The Church of St Nicholas divides and dominates the
two sections of Little Quarter Square. Construction
began in 1703 and the last touches were put to the
glorious frescoed nave in 1761. It is recognized as the
masterpiece of father-and-son architects Christoph
and Kilian Ignaz Dientzenhofer, Prague's greatest
exponents of High Baroque, though neither lived
to see the church's completion. The statues, frescoes
and paintings inside are by leading Baroque artists
and include the fine *Passion Cycle* (1673) by Karel
Škréta. Renovation in the 1950s dealt with the
damage caused by 200 years of leaky cladding.

Altar Paintings
The side chapels hold
many works of art. This
painting of St Michael is
by Francesco Solimena.

★ Pulpit
*Dating from 1765,
the ornate pulpit by
Richard and Peter
Prachner is lavishly
adorned with
golden cherubs.*

Baroque Organ
*A fresco of St Cecilia watches
over the superb organ, built
in 1746 by Tomáš Schwarz.
There were originally three
Schwarz organs here.*

Entrance
from the west
side of Little
Quarter Square

**Chapel of
St Anne**

**Chapel of
St Catherine**

STAR FEATURES

★ Pulpit

★ Dome Fresco

★ Statues of the Eastern
Church Fathers

Façade
*St Paul, by John Frederick Kohl,
is one of the statues that grace the
curving façade. It was completed in
1710 by Christoph Dientzenhofer,
who was influenced by Italian
architects Borromini and Guarini.*

The dome was completed by Kilian Ignaz Dientzenhofer in 1751, shortly before his death.

The belfry, added between 1751 and 1756, was the last part to be built. Visitors can climb up to admire the view.

VISITORS' CHECKLIST

Malostranské náměstí. **Map** C3.
Tel 257 534 215. 🚋 12, 20, 22
to Malostranské náměstí.
Ⓜ Malostranská. ⬜ Mar–Oct:
9am–5pm daily; Nov–Feb: 9am–
4pm daily. ⬛ ⬛ ⬛ ⬛
Concerts www.psalterium.cz

★ Dome Fresco
Franz Palko's superb fresco, The Celebration of the Holy Trinity *(1752–3), fills the 70-m (230-ft) high dome.*

High Altar
A copper statue of St Nicholas by Ignaz Platzer (1717–87) surmounts the high altar. Below it, the painting of St Joseph is by Johann Lukas Kracker.

★ Statues of the Eastern Church Fathers
The impressive statues of the church fathers, which stand at the four corners of the crossing, are the work of Ignaz Platzer.

THE DIENTZENHOFER FAMILY

Christoph Dientzenhofer (1655–1722) came from a family of Bavarian master builders. His son Kilian Ignaz (1689–1751) was born in Prague and educated at the Jesuit Clementinum. Together, they were responsible for the greatest treasures of Jesuit-influenced Prague Baroque architecture. The Church of St Nicholas, their last work, was completed by Kilian's son-in-law, Anselmo Lurago.

Kilian Ignaz Dientzenhofer

Charles Bridge ⑭
Karlův most

Prague's most familiar monument was built by Peter Parler *(see p236)* for Charles IV in 1357 after the Judith Bridge was destroyed by floods. It connects the Old Town (Staré Město) with the Little Quarter (Malá Strana) and was the only bridge across the Vltava until 1741.

STAR SIGHTS

★ St Luitgard

★ St John Nepomuk

★ Staré Město Bridge Tower

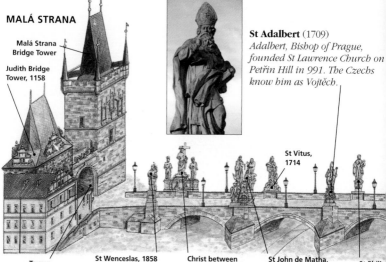

MALÁ STRANA

Malá Strana Bridge Tower

Judith Bridge Tower, 1158

Tower entrance

St Wenceslas, 1858

Christ between St Cosmas and St Damian, 1709

St Vitus, 1714

St John de Matha, St Felix de Valois and the Blessed Ivan, 1714

St Philip Benizi, 1714

St Adalbert (1709)
Adalbert, Bishop of Prague, founded St Lawrence Church on Petřín Hill in 991. The Czechs know him as Vojtěch.

STARÉ MĚSTO

Thirty Years' War
In the last hours of this war, Staré Město was saved from the Swedish Army. The truce was signed in the middle of the bridge in 1648.

St Cyril and S[t] Methodius (1[...])
The saints are widely acknowledged [...] the two who in[tro]duced Christia[nity] to the region.

St Norbert, St Wenceslas and St Sigismund, 1853

St Christopher, 1857

St Anne, 1707

St Francis Borgia, 1710

St John the Baptist, 1857

St Francis Xavier

St Joseph, 18[...]

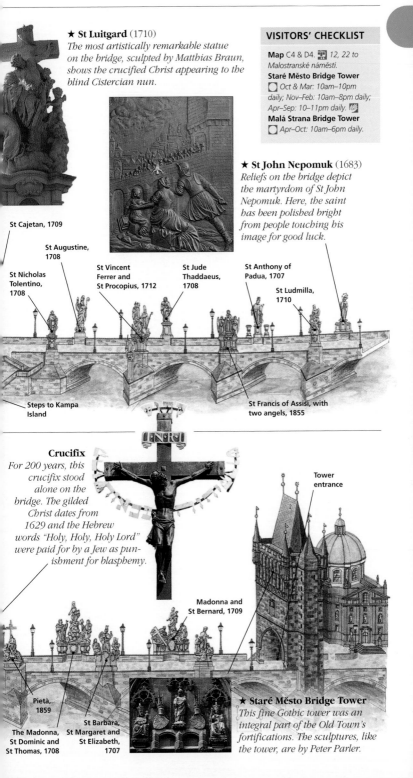

★ St Luitgard (1710)
The most artistically remarkable statue on the bridge, sculpted by Matthias Braun, shows the crucified Christ appearing to the blind Cistercian nun.

VISITORS' CHECKLIST

Map C4 & D4. 🚊 *12, 22 to Malostranské náměstí.*
Staré Město Bridge Tower
☐ *Oct & Mar: 10am–10pm daily; Nov–Feb: 10am–8pm daily; Apr–Sep: 10–11pm daily.* 🖾
Malá Strana Bridge Tower
☐ *Apr–Oct: 10am–6pm daily.*

★ St John Nepomuk (1683)
Reliefs on the bridge depict the martyrdom of St John Nepomuk. Here, the saint has been polished bright from people touching his image for good luck.

St Cajetan, 1709

St Augustine, 1708

St Nicholas Tolentino, 1708

St Vincent Ferrer and St Procopius 1712

St Jude Thaddaeus, 1708

St Anthony of Padua, 1707

St Ludmilla, 1710

Steps to Kampa Island

St Francis of Assisi, with two angels, 1855

Crucifix
For 200 years, this crucifix stood alone on the bridge. The gilded Christ dates from 1629 and the Hebrew words "Holy, Holy, Holy Lord" were paid for by a Jew as punishment for blasphemy.

Tower entrance

Madonna and St Bernard, 1709

Pietà, 1859

St Barbara, St Margaret and St Elizabeth, 1707

The Madonna, St Dominic and St Thomas, 1708

★ Staré Město Bridge Tower
This fine Gothic tower was an integral part of the Old Town's fortifications. The sculptures, like the tower, are by Peter Parler.

Street-by-Street: Old Town

In the 11th century, the settlements around Prague Castle (see pp232–3) grew manifold and the Old Town (Staré Město) was created. Free of traffic and ringed with historic buildings, the Old Town Square (Staroměstské náměstí) ranks among the finest public spaces in any city. In summer, café tables spill out on to the cobblestoned streets, and the area draws visitors in droves. Prague's colourful history comes to life in the buildings around the square.

Church of Our Lady before Týn
The church's Gothic steeples are the Old Town's most distinctive landmark ⑰

Kinský Palace
The palace, built by Kilian Ignaz Dientzenhofer, has a stucco façade crowned with statues of the four elements.

Church of St Nicholas

The Jan Hus Monument was erected in 1915 on the 500th anniversary of Jan Hus's (see p228) burning at the stake.

STAROMĚSTSKÉ NÁMĚSTÍ

MALÉ NÁMĚSTÍ

ŽELEZNÁ

The Štorch House
Based on designs by Mikoláš Aleš, the façade has a painting of St Wenceslas on horseback.

The Štorch House

The House at the Two Golden Bears has a carved Renaissance portal which is the finest of its kind in Prague.

KEY

– – – Suggested route

STAR SIGHTS

★ Old Town Hall

★ Municipal House

★ **Old Town Hall**
Located in the Old Town Square, the Town Hall's famous astronomical clock dates from the early 1400s. A procession of wooden statues moves at the top of the clock every hour ⑮

Church of St James
Made in the 15th century, this wooden pietà can be seen on the main altar of the church ⑱

★ Municipal House
A popular concert venue, this Art Nouveau building has an interior adorned with allegories of civic virtues by Alfons Mucha ㉚

Powder Gate, a much-restored Gothic gate, is a relic of the time when there was a royal palace located here, at the entrance to the Old Town.

Týn courtyard

JAKUBSKÁ

ŠTUPARTSKÁ

U PRAŠNÉ

CELETNÁ

OVOCNÝ TRH

House of the Black Madonna

Estates Theatre featured in Miloš Forman's 1984 film, *Amadeus* ㉙

The Carolinum
This was the heart of the university founded by Charles IV in 1348. A carved Oriel window projects from the oldest surviving part.

Celetná Ulice
This ornamental Baroque plaque is the emblem of the House at the Black Sun, on the famous Celetná ulice ⑯

| 0 metres | 100 |
| 0 yards | 100 |

Old Town Hall ⑮
Staroměstská radnice

One of the most striking buildings in Prague, the Old Town Hall was established in 1338 by King John of Luxemburg. Over the centuries, several nearby houses were knocked together as the Town Hall expanded, and it now consists of a row of colourful Gothic and Renaissance buildings. Most of these have been restored after damage inflicted by the Nazis in 1945. The 69-m (228-ft) high tower offers a great view.

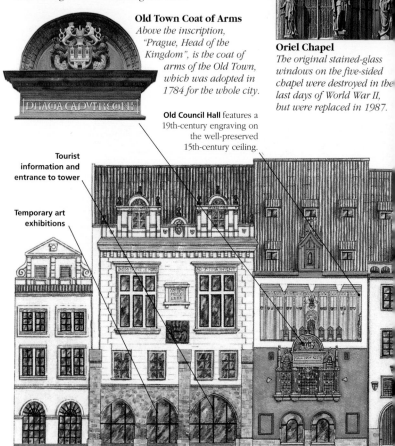

Old Town Coat of Arms
Above the inscription, "Prague, Head of the Kingdom", is the coat of arms of the Old Town, which was adopted in 1784 for the whole city.

Oriel Chapel
The original stained-glass windows on the five-sided chapel were destroyed in the last days of World War II, but were replaced in 1987.

Old Council Hall features a 19th-century engraving on the well-preserved 15th-century ceiling.

Tourist information and entrance to tower

Temporary art exhibitions

EXECUTIONS IN THE OLD TOWN SQUARE

A bronze tablet below the Oriel Chapel records the names of the 27 Protestant leaders who were executed here by order of Emperor Ferdinand II on 21 June 1621. This was the result of Czech's humiliating defeat at the Battle of the White Mountain, which was the first battle of the Thirty Years' War in 1620. It led to the emigration of Protestants unwilling to give up their faith, a Counter-Reformation drive by the Catholic Church and a campaign of Germanization.

An illustration depicting the execution of the Protestant leaders

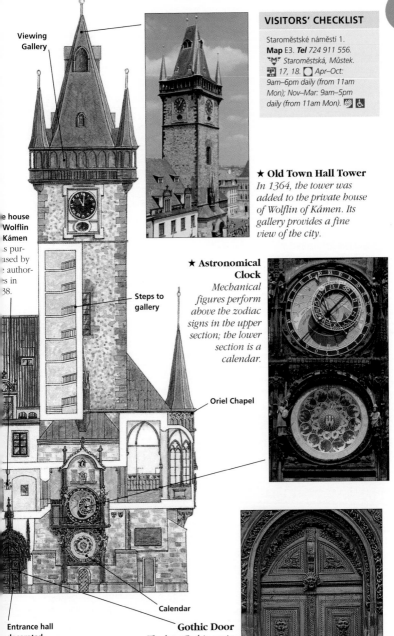

Viewing Gallery

e house
Wolflin
Kámen
s pur-
ased by
e author-
es in
38.

Steps to gallery

Oriel Chapel

Calendar

Entrance hall decorated with mosaics

★ **Old Town Hall Tower**
*In 1364, the tower was
added to the private house
of Wolflin of Kámen. Its
gallery provides a fine
view of the city.*

★ **Astronomical Clock**
*Mechanical
figures perform
above the zodiac
signs in the upper
section; the lower
section is a
calendar.*

Gothic Door
*The late-Gothic main
entrance to the Town
Hall and tower was
carved by Matthias
Rejsek. The entrance
hall is filled with wall
mosaics after designs by
the Czech painter
Mikoláš Aleš.*

STAR FEATURES

★ Old Town Hall Tower

★ Astronomical Clock

Celetná Ulice ⑯

Map E3. Ⓜ *Náměstí Republiky,
Můstek.* **House of the Black
Madonna** *Tel 224 211 746.*
🅾 *10am–6pm Tue–Fri.* 🖼 ♿ 🖵

One of the oldest streets in
Prague, Celetná ulice follows
an old trading route from eastern Bohemia. Its name comes
from the plaited bread rolls
that were first baked here in
the Middle Ages. In the 14th
century, it gained prestige as
a section of the Royal Route
which linked the Royal Court
and Prague Castle via Old
Town Square; it was used for
coronation processions.

Most of the houses along
Celetná ulice date from the
Middle Ages. The foundations
of Romanesque and Gothic
buildings can be seen in
some of the cellars, but the
majority, with their striking
signs, are the result of
Baroque remodellings. At
No. 34, the **House of the
Black Madonna** (Dům U
Černé Matky Boží), is an
exception, being a splendid
example of Cubist architecture, designed by Josef Gočár
in 1912. The distinctive
polychrome figure of
the Madonna with
Child comes from an
earlier house that stood
on this site. The build-
ing is home to an
interesting collection of
Czech Cubist paintings,
sculptures, furniture
and architectural
plans. The 1759
Pachts' Palace,
across the street, has
a balcony that rests
on the shoulders of four
miners and soldiers sculpted
by Ignaz Platzer.

The most impressive
example of Baroque architecture is the Hrzánský Palace at
No. 558, whose façade features busts, gargoyles and
stuccoes, as well as a portal
with caryatids. A popular
venue for state dinners, the
palace has been visited by
numerous important heads
of state. Today, most of
Celetná's shops veer towards
the chic side of the Czech
market, making it a popular
place for shopping.

*Statue, House of
the Black Madonna*

**Towering nave of the Church of Our
Lady before Týn**

Church of Our Lady
before Týn ⑰
Kostel matky boží před
týnem

Staroměstské náměstí 604. **Map** E3.
Tel 602 457 200. Ⓜ *Můstek,
Staroměstská.* 🅾 *10am–1pm, 3–5pm
Tue–Sat, 9am–12pm, 8pm–10pm Sun.*
⚫ *Mon.* 🖼 🚫 🕇

Dominating the Old Town
Square are the multiple
steeples of this historic church,
a source of Czech national
pride. The present
Gothic building was
started in 1365 and soon
became associated with
the reform movement in
Bohemia. From the early
15th century until 1620,
Týn was regarded as the
main Hussite church in
Prague. It was taken
over by the Jesuits in
the 17th century and
they were responsible
for the Baroque renovation
inside, which jars with the

Gothic style of the original
church. On the northern side
is an entrance portal, built in
1390, decorated with scenes
of the Christ's Passion. The
interior has several notable
features, including Gothic
sculptures of *Calvary*, a
pewter font and a 15th-century
Gothic pulpit. The Danish
astronomer Tycho Brahe
(1546–1601), court astronomer
to Rudolf II, is buried here.

Church of
St James ⑱
Kostel sv jakuba

Malá Štupartská. **Map** E3. *Tel 224
828 816.* Ⓜ *Můstek, Náměstí
Republiky.* 🅾 *10am–noon,
2–3:45pm Mon & Sat.* 🕇

This attractive Baroque
church was originally the
Gothic presbytery of a
Minorite monastery. The
order, a branch of the
Franciscans, was invited to
Prague by King Wenceslas I
in 1232. The Baroque reconstruction occurred after a fire
in 1689, allegedly started by
agents of French king Louis
XIV. More than 20 side altars
were added, decorated with
works by painters such as Jan
Jiří Heinsch and Petr Brandl.

The tomb of Count Vratislav
of Mitrovice, designed by
Johann Bernhard Fischer
von Erlach and with sculptures by Maximilian Brokof of
Prague, is the most beautiful
Baroque tomb in Bohemia.
The count is believed to have
been buried alive by accident;
his corpse was later found
sitting up in the tomb. There
is an equally macabre tale
regarding a 400-year-old

Baroque organ in the Church of St James

For hotels and restaurants in this region see pp288–91 and pp292–5

century: the Master of the Vyšší Brod Altar and Master Theodoric. The latter's splendid series of panels for Charles IV's chapel at Karlštejn Castle *(see pp260–61)* are the unmissable works in the gallery. These larger-than-life portraits of saints and church fathers are full of intense expression and rich colours. Other interesting works include moving *Crucifixion* from Prague's Na Slovanech Monastery, 14th-century panels by the Master of Třeboň, and an anonymous sculpture of the Madonna and Child, much influenced by the famous Krumlov *Madonna*, now in a museum in Vienna.

The early 16th century is represented with works by the Master of Litoměřice. These include a Holy Trinity triptych and the stunning *Visitation of the Virgin Mary*.

Třeboň altarpiece, Convent of St Agnes

mummified forearm to be found hanging on the right side of the church entrance. According to legend, when a thief tried to steal the jewels from the Madonna on the high altar, the Virgin grabbed his arm and held on so tightly that it had to be cut off.

The acoustics in the lengthy nave are excellent and concerts are often held here. The splendid organ dates from 1702.

Convent of St Agnes ⑲
Klášter sv anežky české

U Milosrdných 17. **Map** E2. **Tel** 224 810 628. 🚊 17 to Law Faculty *(Právnická fakulta)*, 5, 8, 14 to Dlouhá třída. 🚌 133 to Řásnovka. Ⓜ Staroměstská, Náměstí Republiky. ◻ 10am–6pm Tue–Sun. 📷 🎦 ♿ 📷 www.ngprague.cz

The Convent of the Poor Clares, founded by Princess Agnes in 1234, was one of the first Gothic buildings in Bohemia. It functioned as a convent until 1782, when the Order was dissolved by Joseph II.

Following a painstaking restoration, the premises now houses a magnificent collection of medieval art belonging to Prague's National Gallery. Among its most precious exhibits are works by two Czech artists of the 14th

Spanish Synagogue ⑳
Španělská synagóga

Vězeňská 1. **Map** E3. **Tel** 224 810 628. 🚊 17, 18. 🚌 133 to Řásnovka ulice. Ⓜ Staroměstská. ◻ Apr–Oct: 9am–6pm Sun–Fri; Nov–Mar: 9am–4:30pm Sun–Fri. ◻ Jewish hols. ♿ www.jewishmuseum.cz

This is the site of Prague's first synagogue, known as the Old School (Stará škola). In the 11th century, the Old School was the centre of the Sephardic Jewish community; they lived strictly apart from the Ashkenazi Jews, who were concentrated around the Old-New Synagogue *(see pp252–3)*. The present Moorish building dates from the second half of the 19th century. The ornate exterior gives way to an even more fantastically decorative and gilded interior. The rich stucco decorations are reminiscent of the Alhambra palace in Spain, hence the name. Once closed to the public, the Spanish Synagogue is now home to an interesting permanent exhibition dedicated to the history of Prague's Jews of Bohemia, from the time of the 1848 Jewish emancipation.

Old-New Synagogue ㉑

See pp252–3.

Jewish Town Hall ㉒
Židovská radnice

Maiselova 18. **Map** E3. **Tel** 222 319 002. 🚌 133. 🚊 17, 18. Ⓜ Staroměstská. ◻ to the public. 📷

At the core of this attractive pink and white building is the original Jewish Town Hall, built between 1570 and 1577 by the rich mayor, Mordechai Maisel. This is one of the few buildings to survive the Holocaust. It acquired its flowery late-Baroque image in 1763 and further alterations were made in the early 20th century.

Permission for constructing the belfry, a small wooden clock tower with a distinctive green steeple, was granted by Ferdinand III. It has a clock on each of its four sides, one of which has Hebrew figures. Since Hebrew reads from right to left, it turns in an anticlockwise direction. The building now houses a popular kosher restaurant.

Belfry of the Jewish Town Hall, with its two clocks in view

Old-New Synagogue ㉑
Staronová synagóga

Built around 1270, this is the oldest synagogue in Europe and one of the earliest Gothic buildings in Prague. The synagogue has survived fires, the slum clearances of the 19th century and many Jewish pogroms. Residents of the Jewish Quarter have often had to seek refuge within its walls and it is still the religious centre for Prague's Jews. It was originally called the New Synagogue until another synagogue, which was later destroyed, was built nearby.

Right-hand Nave
The glow from the chandeliers provides light for worshippers, who sit in the seats lining the walls.

Fourteenth-century stepped brick gable

★ Jewish Standard
The historic banner of Prague's Jews is decorated with a Star of David, within which is depicted the hat that had to be worn by Jews in the 14th century.

These windows formed part of the 18th-century extensions built to allow women a view of the service.

Candlestick holder

The cantor's platform (*bima*) is surrounded by a Gothic wrought-iron grille.

Entrance

★ Five-rib Vaulting
Two massive octagonal pillars inside the hall support the five-rib vaults: one rib was added to the traditional four ribs.

Entrance Portal
The tympanum above the door in the south vestibule is decorated with bunches of grapes and vine leaves.

East Façade
The east and west façades possess an austerity that is in contrast with the Gothic interior.

The tympanum above the Ark is decorated with 13th-century leaf carvings.

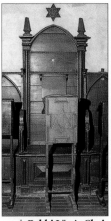

★ Rabbi Löw's Chair
A Star of David marks the chair of the Chief Rabbi, placed where Rabbi Löw once sat. A 16th-century scholar, he was Prague's most revered Jewish sage.

The interior is dim since the small windows do not allow much light in.

The Ark
This is the holiest place in the synagogue as it holds the sacred scrolls of the Torah (the five books of Moses) and of the books of the Prophets.

STAR FEATURES

★ Jewish Standard

★ Five-rib Vaulting

★ Rabbi Löw's Chair

Exterior of Maisel Synagogue, rebuilt in Gothic style

Maisel Synagogue ㉓
Maiselova synagóga

Maiselova 10. **Map** E3. 🚊 Staroměstská. 🚌 133. 🕐 Apr–Oct: 9am–6pm Sun–Fri; Nov–Mar: 9am–4:30pm Sun–Fri. ⬤ Jewish hols. 📷 🚻 www.jewishmuseum.cz

When it was first built, in the late 16th century, Maisel Synagogue was a private house of prayer for use by mayor Mordechai Maisel and his family. It was the most richly decorated synagogue in the city. Maisel, who made a fortune lending money to Rudolph II, funded the extensive Renaissance recon-struction of the ghetto.

The original building was destroyed in a fire that also devastated the Jewish Town Hall in 1689, and a new syn-agogue was built in its place. Its present Gothic aspect dates from the early 20th cen-tury. The synagogue now houses a superb collection of Jewish silver and other metal-work dating from Renaissance times. It includes early exam-ples of items used in the Jewish service, such as Torah crowns and finials, used to decorate the rollers which hold the text of the Torah, shields (hung on the mantle draped over the Torah) and pointers (used by readers to follow the text). Most of these treasures were brought to Prague by the Nazis from synagogues all over Bohemia and Moravia.

Old Jewish Cemetery
Starý židovský hřbitov

Široká 3. **Map** D3. *Tel 222 317 191
(reservations); 222 711 511 (Jewish
Museum).* 🚊 *17, 18.* Ⓜ️
Staroměstská. ⭕ *Apr–Oct: 9am–6pm
Sun–Fri; Nov–Mar: 9am–4:30pm Sun–
Fri (last adm 30 mins before closing).*
🎞️ ♿ www.jewishmuseum.cz

Founded in 1478, this historic
site was, for over 300 years,
the only burial ground permitted to Jews. An estimated
100,000 people are believed to
have been buried here; due to
lack of space they were buried
on top of each other, up to 12
layers deep. Today, over
12,000 gravestones exist in this
cemetery. The last burial took
place in 1787.

From the late 16th century
onwards, the tombstones were
decorated with symbols denot-
ing the background, family
name or profession of the
deceased. The tomb of writer
and astronomer David Gan
(1541–1613) is adorned with
symbols representing his name
– a Star of David and a goose.

The most visited tomb in the
cemetery is that of Rabbi Löw,
a 16th-century philosopher

and scholar who was believed
to possess magical powers
(see p253). Visitors place a
pebble on his grave as a
mark of respect. Elsewhere,
fragments of 14th-century
Gothic tombstones can be
seen embedded in the wall,
bought from an older Jewish
cemetery in Staré Město.

Near the entrance to the
cemetery stands the Klausen
Synagogue. It has a rich display of religious objects in its
fine, barrel-vaulted interior.

Pinkas Synagogue ㉕
Pinkasova synagóga

Široká 3. **Map** E3. *Tel 222 326 660.*
🚊 *133.* 🚋 *17, 18.* Ⓜ️
Staroměstská. ⭕ *Apr–Oct: 9am–6pm
Sun–Fri; Nov–Mar: 9am–4:30pm.* 🎞️
♿ 📷 www.jewishmuseum.cz

Regarded as the second oldest
synagogue in Prague, Pinkas
Synagogue was founded in
1479 by Rabbi Pinkas and
expanded in 1535 by his great-
nephew Aaron Meshulam
Horowitz. Since then, it has
been rebuilt several times.
Excavations have revealed
fascinating relics of life in the
medieval ghetto, including a

**Stained-glass window inside the
Museum of Decorative Arts**

mikva (ritual bath). The core
of the present building is a hall
with Gothic vaulting. The gallery for women was added in
the early 17th century.

The synagogue now serves
as a memorial to all the Jewish
Czechoslovak citizens who
were imprisoned in the Terezín
concentration camp and later
deported to various Nazi extermination camps. The names
of the 77,297 Czech Jews who
went missing during the
Holocaust are inscribed on the
walls. There is also a haunting
display of children's drawings
from the Terezín camp.

Museum of Decorative Arts ㉖
Uměleckoprůmyslové
muzeum

17 listopadu 2. **Map** D3. *Tel 251
093 111.* 🚊 *133.* 🚋 *17, 18.*
Ⓜ️ *Staroměstská.* ⭕ *10am–6pm
Wed–Sun, 10am–7pm Tue.* 🎞️ 📷
🖥️ www.upm.cz

The museum's collection of
glass is one of the largest in
the world, but space con-
straints mean that only a
fraction of it is on display.
Pride of place goes to the
Bohemian glass, of which
there are many fine Baroque
and 19th- and 20th-century
pieces. Other exhibits include
Meissen porcelain, Gobelin
tapestries, costumes, textiles,
photographs and some
exquisite furniture.

View across the Old Jewish Cemetery to the Klausen Synagogue

For hotels and restaurants in this region see pp288–91 and pp292–5

Karlova Ulice ㉗

Map D3. Ⓜ️ *Staroměstská.*

Dating back to the 12th century, this narrow, winding street was part of the Royal Route, along which coronation processions passed on the way to Prague Castle *(see pp232–3)*. Many original Gothic and Renaissance houses remain, although most have been converted into shops to attract tourists.

A café at No. 18, in the House at the Golden Snake, was established in 1714 by an Armenian, Deodatus Damajan, who handed out slanderous pamphlets from here. It is now a restaurant. Also noteworthy is At the Golden Well at No. 3, which has a magnificent Baroque façade and stucco reliefs of saints including St Roch and St Sebastian, who are believed to offer protection against plague.

Church of St Giles ㉘

Kostel sv Jiljí

Husova. **Map** E3. **Tel** *224 220 235.* 🚋 *6, 9, 17, 18, 22.* Ⓜ️ *Národní třída.* ☐ *by appt.* ✝️

Despite a beautiful Gothic portal on its south side, the inside of this church is essentially Baroque. Founded in 1371 on the site of a Romanesque church, it became a Hussite parish church in 1420. Following the Protestant defeat in 1620, Ferdinand II gave the church

Baroque sculpture of an angel on the altar, Church of St Giles

to the Dominicans, who built a huge friary on its southern side. The monks were evicted in the Communist era, but they have since been able to return.

The vaults are decorated with stunning frescoes by the painter Václav Vavřinec Reiner, who is buried in the nave. The main fresco, a glorification of the Dominicans, shows St Dominic and his friars helping the pope defend the Catholic Church from non-believers.

Estates Theatre ㉙

Stavovské divadlo

Ovocný trh 1. **Map** E4. **Tel** *224 901 448.* Ⓜ️ *Můstek.* ☐ *for prior booking call 224 902 231.* ♿ **www**.narodni-divadlo.cz

Built in 1783 by the German-speaking Count Nostitz Rieneck, the Estates Theatre is one of the finest examples of Classical elegance in Prague. Its white, gold and blue auditorium resembles a luxury chocolate box. Until 1920, the main language used

on stage was German, with occasional performances given in Czech or Italian.

The theatre is renowned for its premieres of operas by Mozart. On 29 October 1787, the public was treated to the world premiere of *Don Giovanni*, with the composer himself conducting from the piano. Acknowledging the connection between Mozart and the theatre, the interior was used by Miloš Forman in his famous Oscar-winning film *Amadeus* (1984).

In 1834, the theatre witnessed the first performance of *Fidlovačka,* a comic opera by Josef Kajetán Tyl. One of its songs, *Kde domov můj?* "Where is My Home?", later became the Czech national anthem. More than a century later, in the spirit of the national revival, the theatre was renamed after Tyl, though it has since reverted to its original name.

The Carolinum, opposite, is the core of Prague University, founded by Charles IV. In the 15th and 16th centuries, the university led the movement to reform the church.

Estates Theatre, a mecca for Mozart fans

Municipal House ㉚
Obecní dům

Prague's most prominent Art Nouveau building
was built between 1905 and 1911 on the site
of the former royal palace. On 28 October 1918,
the Municipal House was the scene of the proc-
lamation of the new independent state of
Czechoslovakia. The flamboyant interior, decorated with works by leading Czech artists,
including Alfons Mucha, is well worth visiting.
It includes Prague's top concert venue, as well
as other smaller halls, a restaurant and café.

★ Mayor's Salon
*This splendid room has furniture
by J Krejčuk and murals depicting
Czech heroes by Alfons Mucha –
a Czech master of Art Nouveau.*

★ Mosaic by Karel Špillar
*The façade has a vast semicircular
mosaic depicting* Homage to Prague
by noted artist Karel Špillar.

The Glass Dome towers above
Hollar's Hall, a circular room
next to the exhibition rooms.

Shops

Main Hall
*Lifts in the main hall have
beautiful Art Nouveau
details and ornaments.*

STAR FEATURES

★ Mayor's Salon

★ Mosaic by Karel
Špillar

★ Smetana Hall

★ Smetana Hall
*The auditorium, seating 1,500, is occasionally
used as a ballroom. The box to the left of the
stage is reserved for the president of the
Republic, the one to the right, for the Mayor.*

Side Portal
Here, caryatids and cherubs demonstrate the Art Nouveau era's love of classical motifs.

VISITORS' CHECKLIST

Náměstí Republiky 5.
Map F3. **Tel** 222 002 101. 5, 8, 14. Náměstí Republiky.
Gallery only during exhibitions: 10am– 7pm daily. by arrangement.

Decorative Detail
The Mayor's Salon has this delightful detail in one of its columns.

Figures seen on all sides of the building are by Czech artists who combined historic and Classical symbols with modern motifs.

Bronze statue of St Wenceslas, Wenceslas Square

Magnificent glass dome

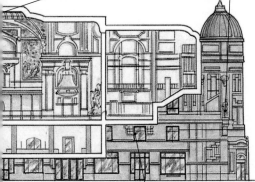

The wing
facing U Obecního Domu ulice includes four dining rooms with original panelling, mirrors and clocks.

Decorative Elements
Lavish stucco decoration covers all sides of the Municipal House; including floral motifs typical of the Art Nouveau style.

Wenceslas Square ㉛
Václavské náměstí

3, 9, 14, 24. **Map** E4. Můstek, Muzeum.

Originally a horse market, today Wenceslas Square remains an important commercial centre. The square has witnessed many key events. It was here that the student Jan Palach burnt himself to death in 1969 in protest against the Soviet-led invasion of 1968, and in November 1989, a protest rally against police brutality led to the Velvet Revolution and the overthrow of Communism *(see p228)*.

At one end of the square is the National Museum, which was completed in 1890. In front of the museum is a huge equestrian statue of St Wenceslas by the late sculptor Josef Myslbek, erected in 1912. At the foot of the pedestal there are statues of Czech patron saints. A memorial near the statue commemorates the victims of the former regime.

Walking down the square from the monument, there are several buildings of interest. To the left, down a passage, is Lucerna Palace, built in the early 20th century by Václav Havel, father of the former Czech president. It is now a shopping and entertainment complex. On the opposite side of the square is the Art Nouveau Grand Hotel Europa.

Church of Our Lady of the Snows ㉜

Kostel Panny Marie Sněžné

Jungmannovo náměstí 18. **Map** E4.
Tel 224 490 350. Můstek.
9am–7pm daily.

Founded in 1347 by Charles IV to mark his coronation, this remarkable church was once regarded as one of the great landmarks of Wenceslas Square *(see p257)*. According to legend, the church owes its name to a 4th-century miracle in Rome, when the Virgin Mary appeared to the pope in a dream telling him to build a church on the spot where snow fell in August. Charles IV envisaged the church to be over 100 m (330 ft) long, but it was never completed. The building that exists today was the presbytery of the projected church.

The church had a checkered history. It suffered damage in the Hussite Wars *(see p228)* and was left to decay until 1603, when it was restored by the Franciscans. The intricate net vaulting of the ceiling dates from this period. Most of the interior decoration is in Baroque style, including the splendid three-tiered gold-and-black altar, crowded with statues of saints.

National Museum ㉝

Národní muzeum

Václavské náměstí 68. **Map** F5.
Tel 224 497 111. Muzeum.
10am–6pm daily, 10am–8pm
Sat. first Tue of month.
www.nm.cz

The vast and magnificent Neo-Renaissance building at one end of Wenceslas Square houses the National Museum. Designed by Bohemian architect Josef Schulz as a triumphal affirmation of the Czech National Revival, the museum was completed in 1890. On closer inspection of the façade, there are visible pockmarks left by shells from Warsaw Pact tanks used during the invasion of Prague in 1968. The entrance is reached by a ramp flanked by allegorical statues; seated by the door are the figures of History and Nature. In front there is a fountain symbolizing the Czech nation and the Czech rivers.

Inside, a monumental staircase lit by grand brass candelabras leads to the Pantheon, a dome-topped hall. This contains statues and busts of the most prominent figures in Czech political,

The lavishly decorated staircase in the National Museum

intellectual and artistic life. The vast room, with windows overlooking Wenceslas Square, has four huge paintings by Czech artists Václav Brožík and František Ženíšek. The exquisite gilt-framed glass cupola overhead fills the space with light.

While the rich marbled decoration is impressive, it overwhelms the museum's displays, which are devoted mainly to mineralogy – including one of Europe's largest collections of rocks – archaeology, anthropology, numismatics and natural history. Temporary exhibitions are sometimes held on the ground floor. However, the museum is due to close in 2011 for renovation.

Mucha Museum ㉞

Muchovo muzeum

Panská 7. **Map** F4. **Tel** 224 216
415. 3, 5, 9, 14, 24, 26.
Můstek, Náměstí Republiky.
10am–6pm daily.
www.mucha.cz

The 18th-century Kaunicky Palace is home to the Mucha Museum, dedicated to Alfons Mucha (1860–1939), the Czech master of Art Nouveau. The exhibits include personal memorabilia, paintings, drawings, photographs – some taken by Mucha – and also a documentary film. The artist's time spent in Paris is well documented. During summer, the museum's central courtyard is converted into a café.

The towering Church of Our Lady of the Snows

Charles Square ㉟
Karlovo náměstí

Map E5. 🚊 *3, 4, 6, 10, 14, 16, 18, 22, 24.* 🚋 *Karlovo náměstí.*

In the southern part of New Town, built around Wenceslas Square and Senovážné Square, lies Prague's biggest square, Charles Square. The public garden in the square was laid out in the mid 19th-century and offers a peaceful and welcome retreat. The statues in the park are of various figures from Czech history.

Charles Square was created when Charles IV was establishing Nové Město in 1348. Built at its centre was a wooden tower, where the coronation jewels were put on display once a year. In 1382, the tower was replaced by a chapel. It was from here that, in 1437, the historic document informing the Czechs about the concessions granted to the Hussites by the pope was read out for the first time.

Until the 19th century, the square was used mainly as a cattle market and for selling firewood and coal. On its north side stands the New Town Hall, one of Prague's finest Gothic buildings, embellished with steep, triangular gables. On the south side is the magnificent **Church of St Ignatius**, built by Italian architect Carlo Lurago in the 1660s. The superb façade is topped by a statue of the church's patron saint, St Ignatius of Loyola. At the time, the

A spectacular ceiling fresco inside the National Theatre

church's rules allowed only Christ and the Virgin Mary to be represented in this fashion, but the Jesuits succeeded in obtaining an exemption from the Pope on this occasion. Inside, the profusion of gilt is truly dazzling.

U Fleků ㊱

Křemencova 11. **Map** D5. 🚊 *6, 18, 22.* 🚋 *Národní třída, Karlovo náměstí.* **Tel** *224 934 019.* **www**.ufleku.cz

A short walk northwest of Charles Square is one of the most famous beer halls in Prague, U Fleků. Records indicate that beer was brewed here as early as 1459. The owners of this archetypal beer hall have kept up the tradition of brewing; the present brewery, the smallest in the capital, produces and serves a special strong, dark beer, sold exclusively on the premises.

National Theatre ㊲
Národní Divadlo

Národní 2. **Map** D5. **Tel** *224 901 448.* 🚊 *17, 18, 22 to Národní Divadlo.* 🚋 *Národní třída.* **Auditorium Tel** *221 714 152.* ⭕ *Sat & Sun for tours.* 🎦 🎫 *8:30–11am.* ♿ **www**.narodni divadlo.cz

This gold-crested theatre is a cherished symbol of the Czech cultural revival. The original Neo-Renaissance building was designed by Czech architect Josef Zítek

and construction began in 1868. Just days before the official opening it was completely destroyed by fire. Josef Schulz was given the job of rebuilding the theatre and all the best Czech artists of the period contributed towards its lavish decoration. During the late 1970s and early 80s, the theatre underwent restoration and the New Stage (Nová Scena) was built.

The beautiful **Auditorium** has an elaborately painted ceiling by František Ženíšek, adorned with allegorical figures representing the arts. Equally impressive are the gold and red stage curtains. There is also a stunning ceiling fresco in the theatre's lobby. The final part of a triptych, painted by František Ženíšek in 1878, depicts the golden age of Czech art.

The theatre's vivid sky-blue roof is covered with stars and is believed to represent the sky – the summit all artists should aim for.

U Fleků, Prague's finest and best known beer hall

Stately façade of the National Theatre on the Vltava river

Karlštejn Castle ❷
hrad Karlštejn

This Gothic castle is one of the most visited historic sites in the country. It was built for the Holy Roman Emperor Charles IV in 1348 as a royal residence and a treasury where the imperial insignia and crown jewels as well as documents, works of art and holy relics were stored. In the 16th century, Karlštejn was remodelled in the Renaissance style. The castle was restored in the 19th century by Josef Mocker, who returned the building to its original appearance.

Grand Tower

★ **Holy Cross Chapel**
The walls of the Holy Cross Chapel are hung with a unique collection of 129 portraits of saints and monarchs – the work of Master Theodoric, court painter to Charles IV.

Voršilka Tower
The Voršilka Tower was once the castle's main entrance. Now the entrance is via the gate below the tower, and along the former moat.

The first floor of the Grand Tower features two rooms, which in the 19th century were turned into a museum with a collection of paintings of Karlštejn and other castles.

The Well Tower
The Well Tower is situated at the lowest point of the castle complex. Inside is an old wooden treadwheel for hauling water, which was operated by two people.

STAR FEATURES

★ Holy Cross Chapel

★ Church of St Mary

★ Church of St Mary

One of the paintings in the Church of St Mary depicts Charles IV receiving two thorns from the crown of Jesus from the French dauphin, Charles.

VISITORS' CHECKLIST

25 km (16 miles) SW of Prague. **Tel** *311 681 695.* from Prague. *Státní hrad, 311 681 617.* Mar–Nov: Tue–Sun. interiors. **Holy Cross Chapel** Jun–Oct: Tue–Sun. **www**.hradkarlstejn.cz

St Catherine's Chapel

Used as a place of meditation by Charles IV, this tiny chapel has walls that are richly decorated with paintings and semi-precious stones.

Madonna Statue

The 14th-century marble statue of the Madonna, in the royal bedchamber, belonged to King Charles IV.

The Imperial Palace's first floor was used by courtiers; the second by the emperor for private and official functions.

Vassals' Hall of the Imperial Palace

A striking feature of the Vassals' Hall is the late-Gothic altarpiece from St Palmatius's Church in the village of Budňany at the foot of Karlštejn Castle.

Kutná Hora ❸

A rich source of silver between the 13th and 18th centuries, Kutná Hora was the second most important town in Bohemia, after Prague. Its wealth funded many beautiful buildings, including St Barbara's Cathedral (sv Barbora); the Italian Court (Vlašský Dvůr), which housed the royal mint and later the Town Hall; the 14th-century Church of St James (sv Jakub) and the 15th-century Stone House (Kamenný Dům). Since 1995 the historic centre of Kutná Hora has been on the UNESCO Cultural Heritage List. Located to the northeast of the centre is the suburb of Sedlec, home to an extraordinary ossuary where bones accumulated over centuries were put together by carver František Rint in 1870 to form crosses, a coat of arms and a chandelier.

Cathedral's Front Façade
In 1388, German architect Peter Parler planned this five-aisled building, with three tented spires.

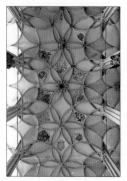

★ Vault
The central nave, with its magnificent geometric vaulted ceiling, was designed in the early 16th century by Benedikt Ried. It incorporates coats of arms from local crafts guilds.

Organ
The Baroque organ case dating from 1740–60 hides a much newer mechanism installed in the early 20th century by local organ maker Jan Tuček.

ST BARBARA'S CATHEDRAL

Dedicated to the patron saint of miners, St Barbara's Cathedral is one of Europe's most spectacular Gothic churches. Both the interior and exterior are richly ornamented, and the huge windows ensure it is filled with light. Many of the side chapels are decorated with interesting frescoes, some of which depict miners at work and men striking coins in the mint, reflecting the sources of the town's wealth.

STAR FEATURES

★ Vault

★ High Altar

Pulpit

The pulpit dating from 1655 is decorated with four stone reliefs, depicting the four Evangelists, produced in 1566 by Master Leopold.

VISITORS' CHECKLIST

70 km (45 miles) E of Prague.
🚲 21,000. 🚆 🚌 from Prague.
ℹ Palackého náměstí, 327 512 378. **Cathedral** ⬜ Nov–Mar: 10am–4pm Tue–Sun; Apr, Oct: 9am–4pm Tue–Sun; May–Sep: 9am–5:30pm Tue–Sun. 📷
www.kutnahora.cz

Oak Stalls

The late 15th-century stalls, originally designed for St Vitus's Cathedral in Prague, feature Gothic spired canopies and carved balustrades.

Stained-glass Window

The Art Nouveau stained-glass windows designed by František Urban were added in the early 20th century.

★ High Altar

The central scene of the Neo-Gothic high altar (1901–5), a replica of the original, depicts the Last Supper.

Balustrade

The stone balustrade of the presbytery includes the initials of King Vladislav Jagiello ("W") and his son Ludwig ("L").

Hradec Králové

Located at the confluence of the Labe and Orlice rivers, Hradec Králové is one of the most beautiful towns in Bohemia. It first appeared in historical records in 1225 and later became an important Hussite and then Counter-Reformation centre. In the 20th century, the town acquired a new face when architects Jan Kotěra and Josef Gočár built many Modernist structures outside the medieval centre. The New Town (Nové Město) was developed between 1920 and 1930 by the two architects.

Old Town Hall and White Tower in Big Square

🏛 Big Square

The historic sights of the Old Town (Staré Město) are clustered around its former market square (Velké náměstí). One of the most opulent buildings here is the Old Town Hall (radnice). This Gothic edifice, erected before 1418, was remodelled in the late 16th century in the Renaissance style and the two clock towers were added in 1786. The hall served as a prison during the late 16th century.

On the southern side of the square stands the Bishop's Palace, one of the town's finest Baroque buildings. It was designed by Giovanni Santini, a Bohemian architect of Italian origin who also created its magnificent entrance portal. Adjacent is the small-scale Baroque Špulak House (Dům U Špuláků). It was remodelled in 1750 by local architect F Kermer. The 20-m (66-ft) column in the square was erected in 1717 in thanksgiving for sparing the town from the plague of the previous year. The monument is probably by sculptor and

architect GB Bullo. Adjoining the square to the northeast is the medieval Small Square (Malé náměstí).

Relief from the house opposite the cathedral

🔒 Cathedral of the Holy Ghost

Velké náměstí.
This Gothic cathedral (Katedrála sv Ducha), founded in 1307, is proof of the town's wealth. In 1424, the church was the temporary burial site of Jan Žižka, leader of the Hussite movement. Striking features of its plain interior are the late-Gothic, 15th-century high altar, and in the south aisle, the Baroque altarpiece with a painting of St Anthony by Petr Brandl. The pewter baptismal font, dating from 1406, is one of the oldest in Bohemia.

🏛 White Tower

Franušova 1. **Tel** 495 513 966.
⬜ Apr–Sep: 9am–noon, 1–5pm daily.
The 72-m (235-ft) tall Renaissance belfry next to the cathedral was erected in 1589. The white stone used as the building material gave the structure its name White Tower (Bílá věž), though the stone is now grey. The replacement clock fitted in 1829 can be misleading – the small hand points to the minutes and the large one to the hours.

🔒 Church of the Assumption of the Virgin Mary

Velké náměstí.
This church (Kostel Nanebevzetí Panny Marie) was built for the Jesuit Order by Carlo Lurago in the mid-17th century. A century later, the church burned down and only the chapel of St Ignatius Loyola, with its wall paintings and a picture by Petr Brandl of the glorification of the saint, was spared. The present façade, with its two towers, dates from 1857. The former Jesuit College, the long building to the right of the church, dates from the late 17th century.

🏛 Modern Art Gallery

Velké náměstí 139/140. **Tel** 495 514 893. ⬜ 9am–noon, 1–6pm Tue–Sun. 📷 www.galeriehk.cz
The striking five-storey Art Nouveau building of the Modern Art Gallery (Galerie

Interior of the Church of the Assumption of the Virgin Mary

Impressive entrance hall of the Modern Art Gallery

moderního umění) was designed in 1912 by Osvald Polívka. Inside is an extensive collection of works by the finest Czech artists, including Jan Zrzavý, Jan Preisler, Josef Váchal, Václav Špála, Josef Čapek and Jiří Kolář.

Former Synagogue
Československé armády.
This distinctive building (synagoga) has a magnificent dome overlaid with sheet copper. It was completed in 1905 to a design by Václav Weinzettel, in the Art Nouveau style, with some Oriental elements. Apart from the prayer hall it also included the domestic quarters of the rabbi, the shammash and the caretaker; there was also a

meeting room and space for the archives. The building served the Jewish community until World War II. After 1960 it was acquired and renovated by the Hradec Králové Research Library, and it remains a library today.

East Bohemia's Regional Museum
Eliščino nábřeží 465. **Tel** 495 514 624.
🕙 9am–5pm Tue–Sun. 📷 🛆
www.muzeumhk.cz
The building of East Bohemia's Regional Museum (Krajské muzeum východních Čech) is one of the prime examples of Bohemian Modernism. It was built between 1909 and 1912 to a design by Jan Kotěra. Inside, are some interesting exhibits – in particular, a scale model of the town from 1865, complete with all of its fortifications.

VISITORS' CHECKLIST

116 km (72 miles) E of Prague.
🚄 100,000. 🚉 Pouchovská
153. 🚌 Pouchovská 153.
🚏 Velké náměstí 165, 495 512
462. 🎭 Folklore Festival (early
Jun), International Jazz Festival
(Oct). **www**.ic-hk.cz

Prague Bridge
The 60-m (200-ft) long bridge (Pražský most) was designed by Jan Kotěra in 1910. It replaced the oldest bridge in Hradec Králové, dating from 1796. Between 1910 and 1912, Kotěra added four pavilions to house shops. The architect also gave it distinctive fairy lighting and masts with the town's emblem. The bridge leads into the section of the New Town across the Labe.

View of the Labe river from the Prague Bridge

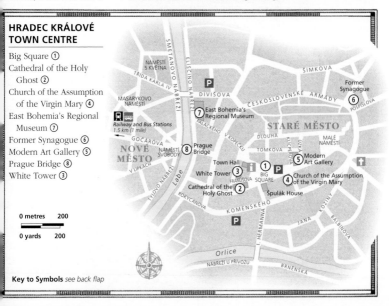

HRADEC KRÁLOVÉ TOWN CENTRE

Big Square ①
Cathedral of the Holy Ghost ②
Church of the Assumption of the Virgin Mary ④
East Bohemia's Regional Museum ⑦
Former Synagogue ⑥
Modern Art Gallery ⑤
Prague Bridge ⑧
White Tower ③

0 metres 200
0 yards 200

Key to Symbols see back flap

České Švýcarsko ❺

**Information sign
on a hiking trail**

Famous for its extraordinary
natural beauty, České Švýcarsko
is a landscape of forests and
fantastically shaped sandstone
rocks, criss-crossed by gorges
and ravines. Attracting visitors as
early as the 19th century, a section
of the region was designated a
national park in 2000. Spread over
an area of 79 sq km (30 sq miles) the geological
park contains some of the area's most spectacular
natural treasures and is a haven for wildlife.

Pravčicka Brána
*This is the largest natural
rock bridge in Central Europe,
at 26 m (85 ft) long, 7–8 m
(25 ft) wide, and rising to a
height of 16 m (52 ft).*

A hiking trail from Mezní
Louka leads to the stone
bridge of Pravčická brána,
6.5 km (4 miles) away.
From here, hikers can
continue for another
2.5 km (2 miles) on the
same trail to Hřensko.

Falcon's Nest
*This small castle, by the
Pravčicka Brána, belonged to
the Clary-Aldringen
family. It now
houses a
restaurant and
the National
Park Museum.*

Labe

0 km 1
0 miles 1

Hřensko
Děčín
12 km (7 miles)

Mezní Louka

Mezná

Kamenice

Kameni
Strá

Tichá Soutěska
*Known as the "quiet gorge", this
section of Kamenice Gorge
stretches for 960 m (3,150 ft).*

Kamenice Gorge
*This narrow gorge
runs between
vertical walls of
rocks, 50–150 m
(165–500 ft) high.
Boat trips go up-
or downstream. The
footpath along its
banks was built in
the 19th century
by Italian workers.*

Wildlife in the National Park

České Švýcarsko National Park is home to a range of animal species including the European beaver, river otter and lynx, which settled here in the 1930s, and the Alpine chamois, introduced in 1907.

VISITORS' CHECKLIST

144 km (89 miles) N of Prague.
🚃 from Děčín. ℹ️ Hřensko 82,
412 554 286. **www**.pbrana.cz
National Park Museum
Falcon's Nest. **Tel** 604 238 209.
🕐 Apr–Oct: 10am–6pm daily;
Nov–Mar: 10am–4pm daily.

Trails

A network of clearly signposted hiking and cycling trails covers the entire area of the park.

Sokolí vrch
▲
486 m
(1,594 ft)

Doubice

Ostroh
🌼▲
484 m
(1,588 ft)

Jetřichovické Range

Jetřichovice

Rynartice

Šaunštejn

This high rock platform, which was once the site of the small Šaunštejn Castle, can be reached by a series of vertical stepladders.

Jetřichovice

This scenic village, whose timber houses provide accommodation to many walkers, makes a good base for forays into the Jetřichovické Range.

KEY

🚉	Railway
🌼	Viewpoint
▲	Peak
ℹ️	Visitor information
══	Road
- -	Trail

Karlovy Vary ❻

World famous for its mineral springs, the town of Karlovy Vary was founded by Charles IV in the mid-14th century. Legend has it that he discovered it when his dog fell into a hot spring (*vary* means "hot spring") when out hunting. Since the 18th century, the rich and the famous have flocked here to take the waters. All the springs, the historic colonnades and architectural sights are located along the Teplá river. The town is also known for its porcelain and for Moser glassware.

The lovely wooden Market Colonnade and Castle Tower

🛁 Imperial Baths
Mariánskolázeňska 2.
The Imperial Baths (Císařské lázně), looking more like a theatre than a medical establishment, was once the most opulent structure in Karlovy Vary. Built between 1892 and 1895, it features a Neo-Renaissance façade and Art Nouveau decorations.

🏛 Karlovy Vary Museum
Nová louka 23. **Tel** 353 226 252.
◻ 9am–noon, 1–5pm Wed–Sun. 📷
The museum (Karlovarské Muzeum), established in 1853, has collections relating to the region's history and its natural environment; also on display are glass and porcelain items and handicrafts. Besides permanent displays, there are also topical exhibitions organized throughout the year.

🎭 Karlovy Vary Theatre
Divadelni náměstí 21.
Tel 353 225 801.
The Karlovy Vary Theatre (Městské divadlo), built between 1884 and 1886, is the work of Viennese architects Ferdinand Fellner and Hermann Helmer, who designed many theatre buildings all over Europe. It is worth stepping inside to see the grand interior decor, which includes paintings by Gustav Klimt, his brother Ernst and Franz Matsche. A collective work of all three 19th-century artists is the stage curtain, on which they painted their joint self-portrait. Following many years of reconstruction, the theatre was opened again in 1999.

🔒 Church of St Mary Magdalene
Kostelní náměstí.
Dating from 1732, and among the best work of the Bohemian architect Kilian Ignaz Dientzenhofer, this church (Kostel sv Máří Magdalény) is one of the finest examples of Baroque architecture in the region.

The single-aisled church with an oval floor plan has an impressively spacious interior with fine decor. The high altar features an image of Mary Magdalene from 1752. It is flanked by Jakob Eberle's 1759 sculptures of Saints Augustine, Jerome, Peter and Paul. It is also worth taking a closer look at the lavishly decorated side altars, the dome and the splendid galleries high up. The wavy façade of the church, with two towers, features a semi-circular stairway.

Detail above Karlovy Vary Theatre entrance

🛁 Market Colonnade
Lázeňská. **Tel** 353 362 100.
This lovely white wooden colonnade (Tržni kolonáda), designed in Swiss style by architects Ferdinand Fellner and Hermann Helmer, was built between 1883 and 1884 on the site of a former Town Hall, which was demolished in 1879.

The colonnade contains two springs. Between 1991 and 1992 it underwent a thorough reconstruction, although it has retained its original appearance.

SPA RESORTS

Clustered in the western part of the country, spa resorts began to emerge and flourish in the 18th century. Crowds of patients and prominent figures visited spas, initially to take medicinal baths, and later to drink spring waters in truly exclusive company and opulent surroundings. During the Communist era, spa cures were open to all who needed them, and spa treatments remain popular in the Czech Republic today. The spa towns continue to attract numerous German, Austrian and Russian visitors, and during the past 20 years many have been restored to their former glory.

Karlovy Vary in 1891

For hotels and restaurants in this region see pp288–91 and pp292–5

Columns of the Mill Spring Colonnade

🏛 **Mill Spring Colonnade**

Mlýnské nábřeží.

Built between 1871 and
1881 by architect Josef Zítek,
creator of the National Theatre
(*see p259*) in Prague, the Mill
Spring Colonnade (Mlýnská
kolonáda) is the largest of
the town's colonnades, and
one of its most opulent.

The Neo-Renaissance gallery,
132-m (430-ft) long and
13-m (43-ft) wide, has a coffered ceiling resting on 124
columns with Corinthian capitals. Inside are five springs,
with water temperature
exceeding 50° C (120° F).
Statues at each end represent
the 12 months of the year.

🏛 **Park Spring Colonnade**

Dvořákovy sady.

Right at the centre of town,
stands Park Spring Colonnade
(Sadová kolonáda), a beautiful painted wrought-iron
structure made of columns

decorated with sculptures,
terminating in two pavilions.
The colonnade was designed
by Ferdinand Fellner and
Hermann Helmer between
1880 and 1881. It is located in
the Dvořákovy sady gardens.

Gilded domes of the Church of
Sts Peter and Paul

⛪ **Church of Sts Peter
and Paul**

Krále jiřího. ⏰ 10am–5pm daily.

This church (Kostel sv Petra a
Pavela) was built between
1893 and 1897 by architect
G Wiedermann, and is among
the world's largest Russian
Orthodox churches. It was
built for the Russian aristocracy, who flocked to Karlovy
Vary in the 19th century.

⛰ **Diana Viewpoint**

Funicular. ⏰ Jun–Sep: 9:15am–
6:45pm; Nov, Dec, Feb, Mar:
9:15–4:45pm; Apr, May, Oct:
9:15–5:45pm.

Behind the Grand Hotel Pupp
(*see p291*), at the southern
end of Stará Louka, is the
lower station of the funicular,
which runs to the top of the
Hill of Friendship. Built in
1912, the funicular rises
167 m (550 ft). At the top
is the Diana Viewpoint
(rozhledna Diana), providing
a great view over the resort.

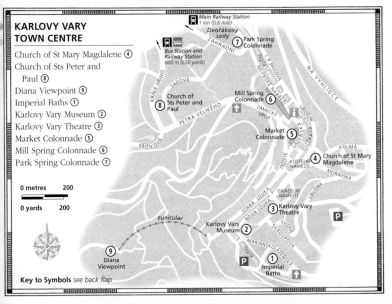

KARLOVY VARY TOWN CENTRE

Key to Symbols see back flap

Plzeň **⑦**

West Bohemia's capital was established in 1295 by Wenceslas II at the crossroads of the main trading routes between Saxony, Bohemia and Bavaria. Today, the city is famous for its two main industries – Pilsner Urquell beer, produced here since 1842, and the large Škoda factory that has made armaments and cars since the late 19th century. Most of Plzeň's historic sites, including the Republic Square (Náměstí Republiky) and the Town Hall, are found on the left bank of the Radbuza.

Plague Column on Náměstí Republiky

🏰 Republic Square

The market square of Plzeň, (Náměstí Republiky) is one of the largest in the Czech Republic, covering an area of 2.5 ha (6.5 acres). Standing at its centre is the Cathedral of St Bartholomew. The square is fringed by a number of beautiful houses, with the best-preserved along the southern side. Particularly striking is the Red Heart House (U cerveneho srdce), built in 1894 and sporting magnificent *sgraffito*, a popular style of wall decor. Painted by Mikuláš Aleš, it shows two mounted knights in full tournament gear. The Archdeanery (Arciděkanství) is located on the west side of the square. A market is held in the square every Friday.

A statue on Cisařský dům

🏰 Cathedral of St Bartholomew
See pp272–3.

🏛 Town Hall
Náměstí Republiky. ◯ *8am–6pm daily.*
The lovely Renaissance Town Hall (Stará radnice) was designed by Italian architect Giovanni de Statio. This four-storey edifice with its spectacular gables was built between 1554 and 1559. The interesting *sgraffito* decorations on the façade are the work of J Koul, produced between 1907 and 1912. Standing in front of the Town Hall is the Plague Column built in 1681. It was erected in thanksgiving for the fact that the plague epidemic suffered at that time was only mild.

🏛 Imperial House
Náměstí Republiky 41.
Located to the left of the Town Hall, this Renaissance edifice (Cisařský Dům), dating from 1606, played host to Emperor Rudolph II twice. Today, it houses the tourist information office. The adjacent, Pechlátowský House (Pechlátowský dům) was created by combining two Renaissance buildings and adding a Neo-Classical façade to them.

🔷 Great Synagogue
Sady Pětatřicátníků 11.
Tel 377 235 749. ◯ Apr–Oct: 10am–6pm Sun–Fri.
🔶 *Jewish festivals.*
The world's third largest sacred Jewish building, after the synagogues in Jerusalem and Budapest (see p353), the Great Synagogue (Velká synagóga) was built

in the 1890s. It was funded by donations from the Plzeň Jewish community. Its architect, Rudolf Štech, designed it in a Moorish-Romanesque style. The synagogue could accommodate 2,000 worshippers, and, the high balcony, intended for women, could take up to 800 people. After World War II, the building and its furnishings, including the unique organ located above the Torah, suffered gradual deterioration. In 1998, it was reopened after restoration.

Onion-domed twin towers of the Great Synagogue

🔷 Tyl Theatre
Smetanovy sady 16. **Tel** 378 038 128.
This theatre (divaldo JK Tyla) is named after Josef Kajetan Tyl, Czech playwright and novelist, and a champion of national culture in the 19th century. This Neo-Classical-style building was erected in 1902 and, like the National Theatre (see p259) in Prague, its design was intended to symbolize and reinforce Czech patriotism. The figures on the theatre's façade are allegories of opera and drama. The beautiful stage curtain was painted by Augustin Němejc.

🏰 Franciscan Monastery and Church of the Assumption
Františkánská.
This early-Gothic monastery (Františkánský klášter s kostelem Nanebevzetí) is one of the oldest buildings in the city. Off the lovely cloisters is the 13th-century Chapel of

rescoes in the Franciscan Monastery

t Barbara; the chapel is
ecorated with frescoes from
round 1460. The monastery's
Church of the Assumption has
main altarpiece painting of
he Annunciation, a copy of
tubens's work. The Gothic
Madonna, below the painting,
s from the late 14th century.

Museum of West Bohemia

Kopeckého sady 2. **Tel** 378 370 110.
☐ 10am–6pm Tue– Sun.
www.zcm.cz

This museum (Západočeské
muzeum) is in a Neo-Baroque
building with a grand Art
Nouveau interior dating from
1898. The reliefs on the
staircase and the Art Nouveau
library furnishings are impressive. Exhibits include the

armoury of Charles IV, and a
glass and porcelain collection
in the vast, stately Jubilee Hall.

**Beautiful façade of the Museum of
West Bohemia**

🏛 Brewery Museum

Veleslavínova 6. **Tel** 377 235 574.
☐ Jan–Mar: 10am–5pm daily;
Apr–Dec: 10am–6pm daily.
Appropriately housed in an
old malt house, this museum
(Pivovarské muzeum) traces
the history of brewing in
Plzeň with a fascinating range
of beer-related exhibits.

🍺 Pilsner Urquell Brewery

U Prazdroje 7. **Tel** 377 062 888.
☐ Jan–Mar: 10am–5pm daily;
Apr–Dec: 10am–6pm daily.
The opulent brewery building,
with its imposing empire-
style gate, is a 1917 work
of the architect H Zapala.
The attractions here – besides
tasting Pilsner Urquell
(Plzeňský Prazdroj) beer –
include the chance to explore
the interesting 10-km (6-mile)
long cellars, used between
1838 and 1930 to store
the fermenting brew.

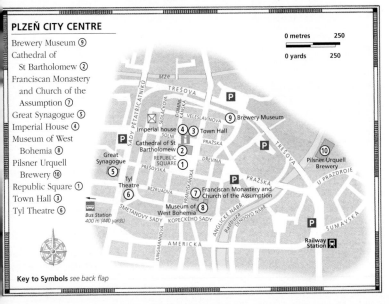

PLZEŇ CITY CENTRE

Brewery Museum ⑨
Cathedral of
St Bartholomew ②
Franciscan Monastery
and Church of the
Assumption ⑦
Great Synagogue ⑤
Imperial House ④
Museum of West
Bohemia ⑧
Pilsner Urquell
Brewery ⑩
Republic Square ①
Town Hall ③
Tyl Theatre ⑥

0 metres 250
0 yards 250

Key to Symbols see back flap

Plzeň: Cathedral of St Bartholomew
Chrám sv Bartoloměje

The Gothic Cathedral of St Bartholomew dominates Plzeň's Market Square *(see p270)* from its position in the centre. Its 102-m (335-ft) spire can be seen from all over the city, and was used in the 19th century by the imperial land surveyors in laying out transport routes around Plzeň. Construction of the church started in the late 13th century and continued until 1480. The Sternberg Chapel, adjoining the south wall of the presbytery, is an early 16th-century addition featuring an unusual keystone at the centre of the vault and Renaissance paintings.

★ Cathedral Tower
Originally the cathedral had two towers. One collapsed when struck by lightning in 1525.

Sculptures in the Cathedral
The church houses a large number of sculptures, including the figures of Saints Barbara, Katherine and Wenceslas, on the pillars of the main nave.

This small tower is over the main nave.

The tower has a balcony at the top, which is open to the public.

Stained-Glass Windows
The striking elongated stained-glass windows in the aisles and the presbytery, which provide the church interior with beautiful light, were fitted in the early 20th century.

STAR FEATURES

★ Cathedral Tower

★ Plzeň Madonna

★ Sternberg Chapel

Main door

Pulpit
The sandstone Gothic pulpit as well as the grand traceried canopy above it, date from around 1360, the same period as the rood arch figures.

★ Plzeň Madonna
The statue of the Virgin Mary set at the centre of the main altarpiece dates from around 1390 and is an outstanding example of the International Gothic style.

The presbytery
was given its
present form
around 1360.

Pendant Boss, Sternberg Chapel
This unusual hanging keystone in the vault of the chapel is a unique late-Gothic detail.

★ Sternberg Chapel
The Sternberg family founded this chapel in the early 16th century. It has a beautiful altar and marvellous Renaisssance paintings.

Entrance

Rood Arch
Standing on the beam of the rood arch are figures in a Calvary scene. The crucifix was made in the 1470s by the Bohemian Master of Plzeň.

České Budějovice ❽

Founded in 1265, the town of České Budějovice had two magnificent churches and mighty town walls from as early as the 13th and 14th centuries. Spared by the Thirty Years' War, it was destroyed by the Great Fire of 1641. Today, the town is the political and commercial capital of southern Bohemia and is renowned for its Budvar Brewery. The town's well-preserved historic centre has maintained its original layout, with a central square and surrounding streets in a grid pattern.

České Budějovice's Town Square, one of Europe's largest squares

🏛 Town Square

The Town Square (Náměstí Přemysla Otakara II) bears the name of the town's founder, Přemysl Otakar II. Measuring 133 m (436 ft) on each side, the square is surrounded by arcaded houses, built mostly during the Middle Ages, that now have Baroque and Renaissance façades because of the numerous alterations made by their German owners. At the square's centre stands Samson's Fountain, built in 1727, with a sculpture of Samson and the lion. Made by Josef Dietrich, it was for some time the only source of water for the town's population. The cobblestones were laid in 1934 in distinctive square pattern.

🏛 Town Hall

Náměstí Přemysla Otakara II. *Tel 386 801 413.* ◻ Jul & Aug: 10am, 2pm, 4pm Mon–Fri, 10am, 2pm Sat, Sun; May, Jun, Sep: 2pm daily. 🈁 ◻
The southwest corner of the Town Square is occupied by the Baroque three-towered, white-and-blue Town Hall

Coat of arms on the Town Hall

(radnice) built by Antonio Martinelli between 1727 and 1730 to replace a Renaissance building. Allegorical statues of Justice, Providence, Wisdom and Honesty stand on the roof. On top of the tallest tower is a statue of the Czech lion, and on the left side is the medieval standard ell measure (the forearm), used when measuring cloth. The Debating Hall features *The Judgement of Solomon* (1730) by Jan Adam Schöpf.

🅰 Dominican Monastery and Church of the Sacrifice of the Virgin

Piaristické náměstí. ◻ 10am–5pm daily.
This former monastery (Kostel Obětování Panny Marie) was built at the same time as the founding of České Budějovice in 1265 and was altered by Peter Parler in the 14th century. Inside the monastery's church, cross-rib

vaulting can be seen. The furnishing is mostly Neo-Gothic, but there is also a spectacular Rococo pulpit dating from 1759, and 17th-century organs. The Gothic cloister also has two original tracery windows that are fine examples of medieval stonemasonry work.
The large stone amphibian carved on the side wall by the church entrance, is a reminder of the local legend about the creature. It was believed to have been guarding a treasure that was hidden here, and had tried to prevent the construction of the church.

🏛 Butchers' Market

Krajinská 13.
The Renaissance Butchers' Market (Masné krámy) is now home to one of the most famous restaurants, Masné krámy, in České Budějovice. The building has three stone masks and the year of its construction, 1531, on its façade.

🏛 Black Tower

U Černé věže. *Tel 386 801 413.* ◻ Apr–Jun, Sep, Oct: noon–6pm Tue–Sun; Jul, Aug: 10am–6pm daily. 🈁
The Gothic-Renaissance Black Tower (Černá věž), dating from 1577, stands next to St Nicholas's Cathedral. It formerly served as a belfry and the town's observation tower. In 1723, two bells were placed in the belfry; a third bell, Budvar, was added in 1995. It was presented to the town by the nearby Budvar brewery. Visitors get a fine view of

The three-towered façade of the Town Hall

For hotels and restaurants in this region see pp288–91 and pp292–5

Black Tower with Samson's Fountain in the foreground

the town after climbing the 225 winding stairs to the top at a height of 72 m (236 ft).

St Nicholas's Cathedral
U Černé věže.
On a small plot at the northeastern corner of the Town Square is St Nicholas's Cathedral (Chrám sv Mikuláše). This triple-aisled edifice started as a church in the 13th century. The original Gothic building burnt down in 1641 and was rebuilt a few years later in the Baroque style. The pulpit, a painting in the south chapel *Death of the Virgin Mary*

(1740) and the main altarpiece (1791) by Leopold Huber are truly fascinating.

South Bohemia Museum
Dukelská 1. **Tel** 387 929 311.
☐ 9am–5pm Tue–Sun.
www.muzeumcb.cz
Established in 1887, this museum (Jihočeské muzeum) is the oldest of its kind in the region. It houses a natural science collection, regional exhibits and 16th–18th century art.

Iron Maiden
Zátkovo nábřeží.
Iron Maiden (Železná Panna), erected in the 14th century, was once a prison and torture chamber. The tower is named

The 14th-century Iron Maiden, standing on the bank of the Malše

after the instrument of torture (and death) that was used here, the shape of which resembled a woman.

Motorcycle Museum
Piaristické náměstí. **Tel** 387 200 849. ☐ Mar–Oct: 10am–6pm Tue–Sun.
The Motorcycle Museum (Motocyklové muzeum) housed in the former Salt House has numerous well-preserved old Czech machines and some Harley-Davidsons.

Environs
Located 1km (0.6 mile) north of the centre is the state-owned **Budvar Brewery**, (Budějovický Budvar) where beer has been made since the 19th century. Visits can be arranged directly or via the tourist information office.

Budvar Brewery
Karolíny Světlé 4. **Tel** 387 705 347.
☐ 9am–4pm daily (by appt).

VISITORS' CHECKLIST

156 km (97 miles) S of Prague.
🚶 100,000. 🚌 Novohradská
393. 🚏 Žižkova 32.
ℹ️ Náměstí Přemysla Otakara
II 2, 386 801 413. 🎭 City
Hall Summer Festival (Jul–Aug).
www.c-budejovice.cz

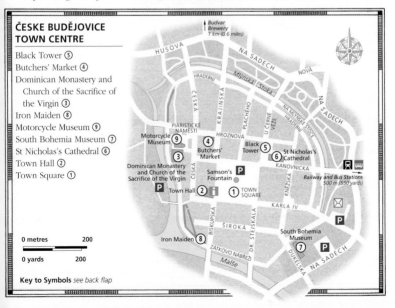

ČESKÉ BUDĚJOVICE TOWN CENTRE

Black Tower ⑤
Butchers' Market ④
Dominican Monastery and Church of the Sacrifice of the Virgin ③
Iron Maiden ⑧
Motorcycle Museum ⑨
South Bohemia Museum ⑦
St Nicholas's Cathedral ⑥
Town Hall ②
Town Square ①

0 metres 200
0 yards 200

Key to Symbols see back flap

Budvar Brewery 1 km (0.6 miles)
HUSOVA
NA SADECH
NOVA
HRADEBNÍ
Mlýnská Stoka
NA SADECH
ČESKÁ
KRAJINSKÁ
PLACHÉHO
U ČERNÉ VĚŽE
HRADEBNÍ
NA MLÝNSKÉ STOCE
PIARISTICKÉ NÁMĚSTÍ
Motorcycle Museum ⑨
HROZNOVA
④ Butchers' Market
Black Tower ⑤
⑥ St Nicholas's Cathedral
③
Dominican Monastery and Church of the Sacrifice of the Virgin
ČESKÁ
Samson's Fountain
KANOVNICKÁ
Railway and Bus Stations 500 m (550 yards)
Town Hall ②
① TOWN SQUARE
KNĚŽSKÁ
BISKUPSKÁ
ŠIROKÁ
DR STEJSKALA
KARLA IV
Iron Maiden ⑧
ZÁTKOVO NÁBŘEŽÍ
Malše
South Bohemia Museum ⑦
DUKELSKÁ
NA SADECH

Český Krumlov ❾

A well-preserved medieval town, Český Krumlov is one of the most visited places in the Czech Republic. Founded in the 13th century, it belonged to the Rožmberk Dynasty between 1302 and 1611. It was added to the UNESCO World Cultural Heritage List in 1992. The historic town centre is situated on the rocky banks of the sharply meandering Vltava river. The Inner Town (Vnitřní Město), with its market square, Town Hall and Church of St Vitus, is located on the right bank.

⛪ Egon Schiele Centre

Široká 71. **Tel** 380 704 011. ◐
10am–6pm. ● Mon. 📷 ♿ 🚻 🏠

A former brewery building, not far from Concord Square, this centre (Egon Schiele Centrum) now houses a gallery devoted to Austrian artist Egon Schiele (1890–1918), who lived in Český Krumlov in 1911. On display are water-colours and drawings, including several famous male and female nudes which in Schiele's day caused a scandal. He was driven out of the town for employing young local girls to pose for him. There are also temporary exhibitions of contemporary works on display.

Coat of arms on the Town Hall

🏛 Concord Square

The most imposing building in this market square (Náměstí Svornosti) is the Town Hall (radnice). It was created in the mid-15th century by combining two Gothic houses. The Marian Plague Column at the centre of the square was erected in 1716 as a thanks-giving for sparing the town from an outbreak of plague in 1682. Matthäus Jäckel, a Prague sculptor, placed a statue of the Madonna at the top of the column. At the foot of the column, in one of the niches, is a figure of St Roch, the saint invoked for protection against this disease.

⛪ Church of St Vitus

ulice Horní.

The Church of St Vitus (Chrám sv Víta) provides a visual counterbalance to the lofty tower of the Krumlov Castle. Dating from the early 15th century, and built on the site of an earlier church, this triple-aisled Gothic edifice has one of the oldest examples of net vaulting in Europe. The sanctuary by the north wall of the presbytery is a splendid example of stonemasonry dating from about 1500. The early-Baroque high altar, made between 1673 and 1683, has paintings depicting St Vitus and the coronation of the Virgin Mary. The late-Gothic porch has an unusual vault in the shape of octagonal stars. Gothic wall paintings dating from 1430 including *St Elizabeth with a beggar, St Katherine, The Crucifixion, St Veronica* and *Mary Magdalene* can be seen on the north wall of the side aisle. The church once housed the *Krumlov Madonna* (1390), regarded by many as the finest example of the International Gothic style. It is now displayed in the Art History Museum in Vienna. Its 15th-century replica can be seen in the National Gallery in Prague.

The imposing nave of the Church of St Vitus

🏛 Ulice Horní

Regional Museum ◐ May–Sep: 10am–5pm daily; Oct–Apr: 9am–4pm Tue–Fri; 1–4pm Sat, Sun.

Located off the market square, ulice Horní was once terminated by a town gate that was demolished in 1839. At No. 159 is the chaplaincy that was built between 1514 and 1520, with a beautiful Gothic gable and Renaissance window jambs. At No. 155 is the former prelature, built in the 14th century and remod-elled several times since. Adjoining it is the former Jesuit College at No. 154, designed by Baldassare Maggi and now a hotel. At No. 152, the **Regional Museum** (Regionální muzeum) has on display a fascinating scale model of the town in 1800.

🏛 Latrán

The old quarter of Latrán was once a village inhabited by craftsmen and merchants, who provided services for the

Part of the façade of the former Jesuit College in ulice Horní

The arcaded bridge linking Krumlov Castle with Castle Theatre

♣ Krumlov Castle

Zámek 59. **Tel** *380 704 711.* ⬜ *Apr–Sep: 9am–5pm Tue–Sun (Jun–Aug: to 6pm).* ⬜ ⬜ *2 routes.* ⬜ **Castle Theatre Tel** *380 704 721.* ⬜ *May–Oct: 10am–4pm (every hour, last adm 3pm) Tue–Sun.*

This castle (Státní hrad a zámek Český Krumlov) is second only to Prague Castle in terms of its size with a total of 300 rooms. The most breathtaking are the Rožmberk Rooms, completed in 1576, with wooden vaults and Renaissance wall frescoes. The Hall of Masks, which is decorated with some extraordinary trompe-l'oeil paintings depicting carnival scenes. A 17th-century tiered bridge (Plášťovy most), complete with

VISITORS' CHECKLIST

177 km (110 miles) S of Prague.
🚶 *14,000.* 🚆 *TŘ Míru.*
🚌 *Objižď' Kova.* 🛈 *Náměstí Svornosti 2, 380 704 622.*
📅 *Five-Petalled Rose Festival (mid-Jun), International Music Festival (mid-Jul–Aug).*
www.ckrumlov.info

statues, links the Upper Castle with **Castle Theatre** (Zámecké divadlo). Built in 1767, the theatre has a well-preserved interior, costumes and stage machinery. It was refurbished in the 20th century and offers a glimpse of theatrical life in the 18th century.

Entrance to the Minorite Monastery in Latrán

Krumlov Castle. It is linked to the Inner Town by a bridge over the Vltava river.

All that remains today of the former village is a complex of late-Gothic and Baroque buildings, including the Minorite Monastery, the Convent of the Poor Clares and a church. The entire complex was linked with the castle by a covered walkway running over Latrán. Close by is the Renaissance Budějovice Gate, the only one left of the eight original town gates. It was built between 1598 and 1602 by the Italian architect Dominik Cometta.

ČESKÝ KRUMLOV TOWN CENTRE

Church of St Vitus ③
Concord Square ②
Egon Schiele Centre ①
Krumlov Castle ⑥
Latrán ⑤
Ulice Horní ④

0 metres 100
0 yards 100

Key to Symbols *see back flap*

Telč ⑩

161 km (100 miles) SE of Prague.
🏠 6,000. 🚇 🚌 ℹ️ *Náměstí Zachariáše z Hradce 10, 567 112 407.* **www**.telc-etc.cz

The turning point for Telč came in 1530, when a fire devastated the town. Lord Zachariáš, the governor of Moravia, brought in Italian master builders and architects to rebuild the town's castle. In the end, they rebuilt almost all the houses in the Renaissance style, endowing the town with a striking architectural uniformity that has survived to this day. Telč was added to the UNESCO List in 1992.

The Main Square (Náměstí Zachariáše z Hradce), is lined with pastel-coloured houses with a breathtaking variety of gables and pediments, some 250 years old. At the narrow western end of the square is the **Telč Chateau** (Zámek telč), a Renaissance building devised by Lord Zachariáš. Inside, the highlights are the rooms with stunning coffered ceilings, such as the Knight's Chambers. It also has a fine collection of arms and porcelain.

Modern Telč is separated from the Old Town by two fishponds, which almost surround the tiny historic centre.

⛪ Telč Chateau
Tel 567 243 943. ◻ *Apr–Oct: 9am–12pm, 1–4pm Tue–Sun; May–Sep: 9am–12pm, 1–5pm Tue–Sun.* 🎟️ 🎫 **www**.zamek-telc.cz

Telč Chateau seen beyond the town's fishponds

Třebíč ⑪

163 km (101 miles) SE of Prague.
🏠 41,000. 🚇 🚌 ℹ️ *Karlovo náměstí 53, 568 847 070.*
www.trebic.cz

The industrial town of Třebíč is best known for the **Basilica of St Procopius** (Bazilika sv Prokopa) and its historic Jewish quarter. The church once belonged to a monastery, founded in 1101 by the Czech Royal Dynasty, the Přemyslids. It was transformed into a castle in the 1600s. The 13th-century church was restored in the Baroque period but retains its Romanesque portal, with floral and geometric patterns. Notable features include the rosette window in the apse and the unusual "dwarfs' gallery" running outside. The enormous crypt features 50 columns, each with a different capital. The restored Jewish quarter,

Zámostí, between the Jihlava river and Hrádek Hill, is on UNESCO's World Heritage List. Třebíč's Jewish population peaked at the end of the 18th century but subsequently dwindled due to the impact of the Holocaust. With many original buildings intact, the quarter is evocative of the old ghetto. In particular, the colourful Leopold Pokorný ulice and richly frescoed Rear/New Synagogue (Zadní/Nová synagóga) are worth a visit.

⛪ Basilica of St Procopius
Zámek 1. Tel 568 610 022. ◻ *daily.* 🎟️ 🎫 *(book in advance).*

Znojmo ⑫

205 km (128 miles) SE of Prague.
🏠 36,000. 🚇 🚌 ℹ️ *Obroková 10, 515 222 552.* **www**.znojmocity.cz

Above the Dyje river lies Znojmo, one of Moravia's oldest towns, with a network of small streets at its heart. The best of its historic sights is the Romanesque Rotunda of St Catherine (sv Kateřiny), located inside the **Znojmo Castle** (Znojemský hrad), which has striking frescoes and portraits of Přemyslid princes. A large part of the castle is now a brewery. The lane of Velka Mikulasska leads to the Gothic Cathedral of St Nicholas (sv Mikuláš), which has a globe-shaped Baroque pulpit.

⛪ Znojmo Castle
Přemyslouců 8. *Tel 515 222 311.* ◻ *Apr: 9am–5pm Sat & Sun; May–Sep: 9am–5pm Tue–Sun.* 🎟️ ♿ *limited access.*

Panoramic view of Znojmo, one of Moravia's oldest towns

Mikulov ⑬

251 km (156 miles) SE of Prague.
🏠 *8,000.* 🚉 🚌 ℹ *Náměstí 1, 519
510 899.* **www**.mikulov.cz

Built on a hillside close to
the Austrian border east of
Znojmo, Mikulov is a picture-
postcard town with delightful
streets and some fine
Renaissance and Baroque
houses. **Mikulov Castle** (zámek
Mikulov), originally 13th-cen-
tury but much altered, was
used by the Gestapo, the
secret state police of Nazi
Germany, to hoard confis-
cated art objects. It was burnt
down in the final days of
World War II. Rebuilt in the
1950s, it now houses the local
museum and has a large collection of portraits of
Habsburg royalty and car-
dinals. It also has fine vaults,
which were used for centuries
to store locally made wine.

In the mid-19th century
Mikulov was home to the
second largest Jewish community in the Czech region.
Its once thriving Jewish
quarter, with a renovated
16th-century synagogue, lies to
the west of the castle. Round
the corner on Brněnská ulice,
a rugged path leads to a medieval Jewish cemetery which
has over 4,000 graves and
finely carved marble tombstones dating back to 1605.

🏰 **Mikulov Castle**
Zámek 1. **Tel** *519 309 019.*
⬜ *Apr, Oct: 9am–4pm Tue–Sun;
Jul, Aug: 9am–6pm Tue–Sun; May,
Jun, Sep: 9am–5pm Tue–Sun.* 📷
www.rmm.cz

Sumptuous furnishings in the Imperial Room, Archbishop's Palace, Kroměříž

Brno ⑭

See pp280–81.

Kroměříž ⑮

271 km (169 miles) SE of Prague.
🏠 *30,000.* 🚉 🚌

The historic town of Kroměříž,
with its lovely gardens and
architecturally appealing
buildings, has survived the
Communist period relatively
unscathed. The main square,
Velké náměstí, has been carefully restored and is one of
the prettiest in Moravia. The
main attraction, just north of
the square, is the magnificent
UNESCO-listed **Archbishop's
Palace** (Arcibiskupský zámek),
the seat of the Bishops of
Olomouc between the
12th and the 19th centuries.
This vast Baroque fortress has
some splendidly furnished
rooms and houses the
impressive art collection

of the Liechtenstein family,
with works by Titian, Van
Dyck, Veronese and Cranach.

Among the highlights is the
Assembly Hall, where talks
were once held by the exiled
Austrian Imperial Parliament
from 1848–9, during which
they drafted a new constitution. The Imperial Room
includes portraits of Franz
Joseph I, who went hunting
here with Tsar Alexander III.
Their trophies can be seen
in the Hunting Hall. Above
the main entrance, the Vassals'
Hall (Mansky sál) has a
magnificent ceiling fresco
(1759) by the Viennese
artist F A Mauelbertsch, while
the library houses 90,000
volumes dating from the
16th and 17th centuries.

🏰 **Archbishop's Palace**
Sněouní náměstí 1. **Tel** *573 502
011.* ⬜ *Apr, Oct: 9am–4pm Sat &
Sun; May, Jun, Sep: 9am–5pm Tue–
Sun; Jul, Aug: 9am–6pm Tue–Sun
(or by appt).* 📷 🎫 *2 routes.*

Mikulov Castle, set above the red rooftops of the pretty town of Mikulov

Brno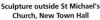

The second largest city in the Czech Republic, Brno occupies the site of what was in the 9th century the main settlement in the Great Moravian Empire. Located on the confluence of the Svitava and Svratka rivers, the city developed at the foot of Petrov Hill. In 1641 it became the new capital of Moravia but did not develop significantly until the 19th century. World War II devastated the city and despite being totally rebuilt, Brno has never quite regained its former lustre. However, its buoyant theatre life and numerous museums have made Brno a major cultural centre. The city's Old Town is focused around two squares – Zelný trh and Náměstí Svobody.

Sculptures by Anton Pilgram on the Old Town Hall's doorway

View of the Cathedral of Sts Peter and Paul

🔒 Cathedral of Sts Peter and Paul

Petrov Hill. ⏰ 8:15am–6:15pm Mon–Sat, 7am–6:30pm Sun. 🔋

This cathedral (Katedrála sv Petra a Pavla) was built on the site where Brno's first castle probably stood in the 11th and 12th centuries. Originally Romanesque, the church acquired a Gothic appearance in the 1200s, but countless subsequent alterations eventually obliterated its original shape. It was restored to its Gothic form in the late 1800s. Of great interest inside is the crypt of the original church.

🔒 Church of the Holy Cross

Kapucínské náměstí. 5.
Crypt ⏰ 9am–noon, 2–4pm Tue–Sat (also May–Sep: Mon), 11–11:45am, 2–4:30pm Sun.

The austere façade of the Church of the Holy Cross (Kostel sv Kříže), near the foot of Petrov Hill, is typical of Capuchin churches elsewhere in Europe. The rather macabre attraction of the church are the mummified monks in the **Crypt**.

🏛 Zelný Square

This square (Zelný trh), meaning cabbage market, has served as a vegetable market for the locals since the Middle Ages, and has retained its original, sloping shape. Its main adornment is the Parnassus Fountain. Made to a design by Fischer von Erlach in the 1690s, it combines the best traits of Baroque naturalism, trompe-l'oeil and theatrics. Among the buildings around the square is the home of the Reduta theatre. This is the oldest theatre building in Brno. The Dietrichstein Palace (Ditrichšteinský palác), built in 1700 at the square's southern end, is

Sculpture outside St Michael's Church, New Town Hall

home to the Moravian National Museum, devoted to Brno's early history.

🏛 Old Town Hall

Radnická 8. ⏰ Apr–Sep: 10am–6pm daily; Oct–Mar: 8am–6pm Mon–Fri, 9am–5pm Sat & Sun.

Just off Zelný trh, the Old Town Hall (Stará radnice) is the oldest secular building in Brno, dating from 1240. In 1510, a doorway was cut into the tower on Radnická and framed by a superb Gothic portal. This work by Anton Pilgram is decorated at the lower level with figures of knights and, above, with statues of the city's aldermen. At the centre is the allegorical figure of Blind Justice. The main tourist office is located here.

🏛 New Town Hall

Dominikánské náměstí.
Tel 542 171 111.

The New Town Hall (Nová radnice), the seat of the city council, dates mainly from the 1700s. It was built inside a former Dominican monastery; the Dominican **St Michael's Church** stands nearby. Gothic cloisters survive inside the Town Hall.

🏛 Freedom Square

Brno's main square (Náměstí Svobody) buzzes with life – its restaurants and cafés being popular meeting places. The architecture around the square spans 400 years. Its finest buildings include the Schwartz

House (Schwarzův palác), with a 16th-century façade decorated with *sgraffito*, and the 20th-century House of the Four Mamlases (Dům u Čtyř Mamlasů), whose four comical Atlas figures strain to support the building. The chief landmark is the Plague Column.

⛫ Moravian Gallery
Husova 18. **Tel** 532 169 111. ☐ *10am–6pm Wed, Fri–Sun, 10am–7pm Thu.* 🎟
The Moravian Gallery (Moravská Galerie) is spread over three premises. The most unusual collection is at the UPM (Uměleckoprůmyslové Muzeum) at Husova 14, dedicated to the applied arts. The exhibits include superb late 19th-century furniture and Art Nouveau glassware.

♠ Špilberk
Špilberk. **Tel** 542 123 613. **Dungeons** ☐ *Jul, Aug: 9am–5pm Tue–Sun.* 🎟 www.spilberk.com
A hilltop castle was built on this site by the Moravians in the 13th century, but Špilberk gained the status of a royal residence only

400 years later, when it was transformed into a mighty Baroque fortress. Its **Dungeons**, a maze of dark subterranean corridors, were transformed, during the reign of Emperor Joseph II, into a series of gruesome prisons. These prisons were later used by the Nazis. Displays inside relate to Brno and the castle.

⛪ Augustinian Monastery
Mendlovo náměstí. **Tel** 543 424 010. **Museum** ☐ *10am–6pm Tue–Sun (to 5pm Nov–Mar).* 🎟 ♿
The Augustinian monastery (Augustiniánský klášter) has a fine Gothic church, but it is famous above all as the place where Gregor Mendel (1822–84) discovered and formulated his theory of genetics. A **Museum**, known as the Mendelianum and dedicated to his work, is located in the monastery's west wing.

Brno's Freedom Square, with its Baroque Plague Column

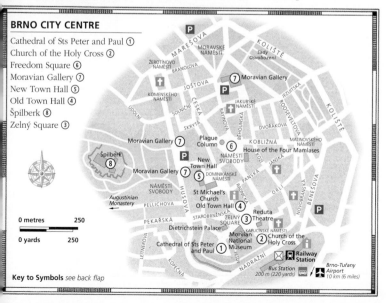

BRNO CITY CENTRE

Cathedral of Sts Peter and Paul ①
Church of the Holy Cross ②
Freedom Square ⑥
Moravian Gallery ⑦
New Town Hall ⑤
Old Town Hall ④
Špilberk ⑧
Zelný Square ③

0 metres   250
0 yards   250

Key to Symbols see back flap

Olomouc ⑯

According to legend, Olomouc, one of Moravia's oldest towns, was founded by Julius Caesar. However, it did not actually come into existence until the 7th century, when it grew into a major power centre. In 1063 it was made a bishopric and in 1187, the capital of Moravia; from 1655 it became a military stronghold. Today, Olomouc is a prosperous and vibrant university town. The oldest part of the historic town centre, surrounded by a ring of parks, is centred on the Main Square (Horní náměstí). This part of the town is fascinating to explore for its lively atmosphere and beautiful religious buildings.

Stained-glass window, Church of St Maurice

🔒 Church of St Maurice

Úzká. ◻ 8am Mon–Sat, 7:30am, 9am & 10:30am Sun. 🔳 **Tower** ◻ May–Oct: 9am–5pm Mon–Sat, noon–5pm Sun.

The 15th-century Church of St Maurice (sv Mořice), with two asymmetrical towers, resembles a medieval fortress. Outside, it has a highly unusual architectural detail in the form of an external staircase enclosed within a round cage. The Gothic interior is impressive, with stained-glass windows and a vast 1505 wall painting. It also houses the largest organ in Central Europe, made by organ maker Michael Engler, in 1745. The church's **Tower** provides panoramic views of the Main Square.

Top of the Holy Trinity Column

🏛 Main Square

The Main Square (Horní náměstí) has at its centre the grand 13th-century **Town Hall** (radnice), which was greatly extended in the 15th century, when it acquired an exquisite astronomical clock. A finely vaulted Gothic Debating Hall and a chapel dedicated to St Jerome were also added during the renovation.

The huge Holy Trinity Column (sousoší Nejsvětější Trojice) in front of the Town Hall was added to the UNESCO World Heritage List in 2000. This unique example of Baroque sculpture was erected between 1716 and 1717. Its three tiers are decorated with historical figures and saints and crowned by figures representing the Holy Trinity. Olomouc has seven fountains, three of which are located in this square. The largest of them, made by local architect Jan J Schauberger in 1725, is the **Caesar Fountain**, sporting an equestrian statue of Gaius Julius Caesar, the legendary founder of the town. The other two are the Arion Fountain, depicting the ancient poet Arion, and the Hercules Fountain, portraying the famed Greek hero holding a white eagle – the official symbol of the town.

🔒 Church of St Michael

Žerotinovo náměstí. ◻ 10am–noon, 2:30–3:30pm Wed, 2:30–3:30pm Fri.

The Dominicans, who arrived in Olomouc in about 1240, soon began to build a monastery and the Church of St Michael (sv Michala) on the town's most elevated site. In the 14th and 15th centuries it was destroyed by fire, and in the 17th century it suffered damage during the Thirty Years' War. Between 1673 and 1699 it was rebuilt in Baroque style by the architect Giovanni Pietro Tencalla, who designed the first three-domed edifice in Moravia. Most of the furnishings, including the organs, date from the Baroque period. In 1829, the main façade of the building was decorated with fine statues of the Virgin Mary and Christ, produced by Ondřej Zahner.

Sculptures in the cloister of the Church of St Michael

🔒 St Jan Sarkander Chapel

Na Hradě. **Tel** 603 282 975.

This chapel (sv Jana Sarkandera) is a Neo-Baroque building designed by E Sochor between 1909 and 1912. Dedicated to Jan Sarkander, a 17th-century preacher who was canonized by Pope John Paul II in 1995, it was erected on the site of the town prison.

🔒 Church of Our Lady of the Snows

Denisova.

Built between 1712 and 1722 by Olomouc Jesuits, this church (Panny Marie Sněžné) served, until 1778,

Sculptures on the dome of St Jan Sarkander Chapel

as the university church. In recent years it has undergone a thorough restoration. The main features of its façade are the monumental portal including four columns and a balustraded balcony. The lavishly decorated interior includes superb Baroque paintings.

🏛 Olomouc Art Museum

Denisova 47. **Tel** 585 514 111. ☐ 10am–6pm Tue–Sun. 🗟

This art gallery (muzeum umění) is located in a modernized historic building. It has a wide collection of paintings by Italian artists ranging from the 14th century onwards, as well as an excellent collection of 20th-century Czech works.

🏛 St Wenceslas Cathedral

Václavské náměstí.

Not many traces remain of the Romanesque church that was originally built on this site in 1107. The present church (sv Václav) was a result of the initiative of Archbishop Bedřich Fürstenberg, who ordered its reconstruction between 1883 and 1892 in Neo-Gothic style.

Decorative motifs on the pillars inside St Wenceslas Cathedral

⛪ Přemyslid Palace

Václavské náměstí. **Tel** 585 514 111. ☐ May–Sep: 10am–6pm Tue–Sun. **Olomouc Archdiocesan Museum** ☐ Tue–Sun. 🗟

This palace (Přemyslovský palác) is one of Olomouc's most picturesque buildings. It was built after 1126 by Bishop Jindřich Zdík and was one of the most excellent works of residential architecture in Europe. The bishop's rooms, with their carved Romanesque windows and columns, are considered to be the best in the country. The **Olomouc Archdiocesan Museum** was opened here in 2006, with some fine paintings collected by the Olomouc bishops. The building also houses the Mozarteum concert hall.

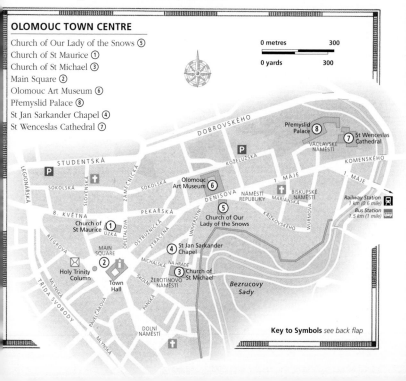

OLOMOUC TOWN CENTRE

Church of Our Lady of the Snows ⑤
Church of St Maurice ①
Church of St Michael ③
Main Square ②
Olomouc Art Museum ⑥
Přemyslid Palace ⑧
St Jan Sarkander Chapel ④
St Wenceslas Cathedral ⑦

0 metres 300
0 yards 300

Key to Symbols see back flap

Practical & Travel Information

Since the Velvet Revolution of 1989 *(see p228)*, the Czech Republic has become far more open to visitors. The country has responded well to the huge influx of tourists, and facilities such as communications, public transport, banks and information centres have improved considerably. Travelling by train is a great way to explore the country at leisure, although buses tend to be cheaper and faster. Remote places are most easily visited by car.

WHEN TO VISIT

The best time to visit the country is between May and September. During these months the warm weather makes for pleasant outdoor excursions such as camping and mountain trekking. The busiest months are August and September, although Prague can also be very crowded in June. While the main sights are often packed at these times, the crowds lend a festive atmosphere, which can make a visit all the more enjoyable. Late September is a good time to visit Moravia to catch the grape harvest season. Many sights are closed between the end of October and the beginning of April.

DOCUMENTATION

Citizens of EU countries do not need a visa to travel to the Czech Republic; they are simply required to carry a passport that is valid for at least 6 months, or an ID card. EU, New Zealand, Australian and US citizens need a valid passport to enter the country and can stay for up to 90 days. UK citizens are entitled to stay for up to 180 days without a visa. For more information, consult the nearest Czech Embassy or the Foreign Affairs Ministry's website.

VISITOR INFORMATION

The Czech Republic has a very efficient network of tourist information offices, which can be found in almost every town, village and resort. They are usually run by the local council and are open from 9am to 5pm (7pm in Prague). Many employ English-speaking staff and offer a variety of English-language publications, maps and guides. The **Prague Information Service (PIS)** is the best source of tourist information for visitors to the capital. It has three offices in the city centre, providing information in English, German and Czech.

HEALTH AND SECURITY

There is a reasonable standard of health care in the Czech Republic. EU nationals are entitled to receive free medical treatment, but in all other cases medical help has to be paid for. It is advisable to take out travel insurance to cover any medical costs incurred abroad. For prescription and non-prescription medicines, it is advisable to visit a *lékárna* (pharmacy). Pharmacies are found in large towns and are open on weekdays from 8am until 6pm, and on Saturdays until 2pm.

Violent crime against tourists is rare in the Czech Republic. The main problem, especially in Prague, is petty theft from cars, hotel rooms and pockets. Visitors are advised to carry their passports with them and to keep a photocopy.

FACILITIES FOR THE DISABLED

Despite some improvements, the country is not very easy for disabled travellers to negotiate. In Prague, however, hotels, restaurants and historic sights have made efforts to improve access. A number of railway stations, trains and some of the capital's metro stations now provide wheelchair access. Disabled travellers seeking advice on transport, accommodation and sight-seeing tours should contact the **Prague Organization of Wheelchair Users**.

BANKING AND CURRENC

The Czech unit of currency is the Czech crown (Kč). Banking hours are generally 9am to 5pm Monday to Friday with some branches closing for lunch. Private exchange bureaus add higher commission charges, and the rate of exchange is often much less favourable than that offered by banks. Traveller's cheques can only be changed in banks. Credit cards are becoming more widely accepted.

COMMUNICATIONS

Telephone and postal service in the Czech Republic are very efficient. Every town and village has a post office and public telephones.

THE CLIMATE OF THE CZECH REPUBLIC

The Czech Republic enjoys long, warm days in summer, the hottest months being June, July and August. Winter can be bitterly cold, with temperatures often dropping below freezing; heavy snow is not uncommon. The wettest months are October and November, but frequent, light showers occur in the summer months as well.

PRAGUE

°C/F	Apr	Jul	Oct	Jan
high	12/54	23/73	12/54	0/32
	3/37	13/55	5/41	-5/23
sun (hrs)	6	8	4	2
rain (mm)	27	68	33	18
month	Apr	Jul	Oct	Jan

Card-operated public phone booths are found all over the country. *Telefonní karta* (phone cards) are available at post offices and newsstands. International calls can be made from public phones, post offices or hotels, although the latter option is expensive. Most post offices are open from 8am to 6pm, Monday to Friday, and on Saturday morning. *Známky* (stamps) can be purchased at most newsstands as well as post offices. All towns have at least one Internet café. Many hotels also offer Internet access.

ARRIVING BY AIR

The country's biggest air transport hub for both international and domestic flights is Prague's **Ruzyně Airport**, which is about 20 km (12 miles) from the city centre. The main Czech carrier is **Czech Airlines (ČSA)**, although Prague is also served by most major European airlines as well as a number of low-cost carriers, including **easyJet**, **Ryanair** and **Wizzair** from the UK and Ireland.

Those travelling from Australia, New Zealand and Canada will need to fly to another European capital and take a connecting flight to

Prague. A number of carriers, including **Lufthansa**, operate flights from the US via another European city.

Čedaz runs an inexpensive minibus service from Prague's Ruzyně Airport to the city centre. Taxis are also available from the airport to Prague.

RAIL TRAVEL

Prague is connected by rail to all the major capitals of Europe. Nearly all international trains arrive at and depart from Hlavní Nádraží, the city's biggest and busiest station.

The rail network is run by Czech Railways, **České Dráhy (ČD)**, which operates two types of domestic routes. Express trains *(rychlík)* stop only at major towns and cities and it is best to reserve a *místenka* (seat) on these. Slower, cheaper trains, or *osobní*, stop at every station and run on local routes. Czech railway stations are well equipped. Detailed information on train services, fares and timetables is available on the ČD website.

TRAVELLING BY BUS

Travelling by bus between Prague and other European cities is significantly less

expensive than rail or air travel. It is advisable, especially in summer, to book well in advance. **Eurolines** is one of the main operators of international bus routes to Prague.

Within the Czech Republic, there is an extensive network of inter-city bus routes operated by a variety of national and regional companies. Travelling by bus is cheaper than by train, and is faster.

The main bus terminal in Prague is Florenc Station, which serves all international and domestic routes.

TRAVELLING BY CAR

Well-maintained roads and long sections of motorway make driving one of the best methods of exploring the country. Visitors driving on Czech roads must carry a valid International Driving Permit and an ID card. To travel on the motorways, visitors are required to purchase a *dálniční známka* (tax disc). These are valid for either 10 days or a month and are available from post offices and petrol stations.

Most of the major car rental firms, including **Avis** and **Budget**, have offices in Prague and at Ruzyně Airport, but hiring is relatively expensive.

DIRECTORY

DOCUMENTATION
www.mzv.cz

VISITOR INFORMATION
www.czechcentres.cz

Prague Information Service
Na příkopě 20, Prague.
Tel 221 714 444.
www.pis.cz

EMBASSIES

Australia
Klimentská 10, Prague.
Tel 296 578 350.

Canada
Muchova 6, Prague.
Tel 272 101 800.
www.canada.cz

New Zealand
Dykova 19, Prague.
Tel 222 514 672.

United Kingdom
Thunovská 14, Prague.
Tel 257 402 111.
www.britain.cz

United States
Tržiště 15, Prague.
Tel 257 022 000.
www.usembassy.cz

EMERGENCY NUMBERS

Ambulance
Tel 112.

Fire
Tel 112.

Police
Tel 112.

FACILITIES FOR THE DISABLED

Prague Organization of Wheelchair Users
Benediktská 6, Prague.
Tel 224 826 078.
www. pov.oz

ARRIVING BY AIR

Czech Airlines (CSA)
www.csa.cz

easyJet
www.easyjet.com

Lufthansa
www.lufthansa.com

Ruzyně Airport
www.prg.aero

Ryanair
www.ryanair.com

Wizzair
www.wizzair.com

RAIL TRAVEL

České Dráhy (ČD)
Nábřeží ludvíka svobody 12, Prague. **Tel** 972 211 111. www.cd.cz

TRAVELLING BY BUS

Eurolines
www.eurolines.co.uk

TRAVELLING BY CAR

Avis
Klimentská 46, Prague.
Tel 221 851 225.
www.avis.cz

Budget
Ruzyně Airport, Prague.
Tel 220 560 443.
www.budget.cz

Shopping & Entertainment

Shopping in the Czech Republic is undergoing great changes, with malls springing up in towns and international chains opening branches. In Prague an eclectic range of Western goods is on offer, as well as typical Czech products such as crystal, wooden toys, antiques and Czech gemstones, particularly garnets. The country also offers a wide variety of entertainment with something for every taste. Those looking for nightlife will get the most from Prague, with its scores of nightclubs, theatres and music venues. Outside Prague, most towns and cities have a lively cultural scene. Many towns organize rock concerts featuring local and international artists.

OPENING HOURS

Most shops are open from 9am to 5pm, Monday to Friday; shopping centres and supermarkets stay open for longer. Small shops may close for an hour at lunchtime. On Saturdays shops close at 1 or 2pm, with large shopping centres remaining open until 8pm. On Sundays only large shopping centres and selected food stores open for business, and in small towns and villages all shops remain closed, or open for just a few hours in the morning.

MARKETS

Prague has several famous markets. Its Christmas and Easter markets in the Old Town Square and Wenceslas Square (see p257) are filled with festive and traditional goods. There are also two permanent markets. The central, open-air **Havel Market** sells fruit and vegetables as well as toys and ceramics; it is open all year round. The indoor **Holešovice Market** sells consumer goods and is also open year round.

Outside Prague there are local markets in most towns and cities selling produce and crafts.

GLASS AND CERAMICS

Bohemia is famous for its high-quality lead, crystal and ornamental glass and almost every town has a shop specializing in glass and crystalware. The Staré Město quarter (see pp246–7) in Prague has scores of them with **Erpet**, **Dana-Bohemia**, **Moser** and **Parcela Plus** among the best known. Interesting souvenirs include gilded and hand-painted crystal wine glasses and traditional earthenware beer tankards decorated with the Czech brewery logo.

HANDICRAFTS

Czech craftsmen have kept up the tradition of making handicrafts and the range of souvenirs on offer includes ceramics, wooden vessels and toys. The largest selection of such goods can be found at local markets, but gift and souvenir shops may also stock some interesting items.

ANTIQUES

The Czech Republic is rich in antiques. During the 1990s specialist antique shops, called *starožitnosti*, opened and are now to be found in almost every town. Some of the well-known dealers in Prague's Old Town include **Alma Mahler Antique**, **Dorotheum** and **Starožitnosti Uhlíř**, stocking antique furniture, paintings and porcelain. The prices are often more reasonable than in Western Europe.

FOOD AND DRINK

Czech chocolates are famous worldwide, and range from boxed chocolates to *tyčinky* (bars) and wafers. Spa hotels and speciality shops often sell spa wafers. The country is also known for producing excellent cheese. Try the long strings of smoked cheese available in delicatessens, or *olomoucke rožki*, an oval cheese with a distinct flavour. Department stores, found in almost every large town, are a good bet for food shopping.

The famous Czech beers Pilsner Urquell (*Plzensky Prazdroj*) and Budvar, which make excellent presents, can be bought in almost every food store. Czech vodkas, including the famous Becherovka, are also available throughout the country. Absinthe and *slivovice* (plum brandy) are other popular Czech spirits. As for wine, those from southern Moravia are the country's finest and are well worth taking back home. In Prague, a good selection of alcoholic drinks is available in the **Jan Paukert Delicatessen and Wine Bar**.

CINEMA

There are cinemas throughout the country, even in small towns. One of the biggest multiplexes in Prague is the **Cinema City Flora** complex. The annual International Film Festival is the largest Czech cinema event, held in late June and early July in Karlovy Vary (see pp268–9).

CLASSICAL MUSIC, THEATRE AND OPERA

Classical music has a long tradition in the Czech Republic and the country has produced some well-known composers, including Bedřich Smetana, Antonín Dvořák, Leoš Janáček and Bohuslav Martinů. Their works figure in the repertoires of local orchestras all year round. Although most orchestras and concert halls close over the summer holiday season, this is when numerous classical music concerts are staged in churches, castles and palaces. Many churches in Prague and several other large cities organize concerts of Baroque music year round. The **Rudolfinum** in Prague is home to the Czech Philharmonic Orchestra, while the Prague Symphony Orchestra is based at the **Municipal House** (see pp256–7).

Brno also *(see pp280–81)* has an active classical music scene with the **National Theatre** being another superb venue for concerts.

Theatre has played an important role in the cultural development of the Czech Republic. Most large towns have a theatre, often a historic building with a beautiful interior. Prague's **National Theatre** is the city's main drama venue, but there are many mainstream and fringe theatres, such as the **Laterna Magika** and the **Komedie Theatre**, both of which stage more avant-garde productions. Tickets for the National Theatre can be purchased on the Internet, with group tickets to the most popular performances available well in advance.

As a rule, theatres display the plays that are currently in their repertoire on the front of the building. Few productions outside Prague are performed in English. During the 20th century, opera became popular in Prague and there are now two major opera companies in the city: the **State Opera** and the **Estates Theatre**. Both stage first-class operas and ballets. The State Opera presents all its performances in the language in which they are written, usually Italian.

MUSIC FESTIVALS

Czech music festivals are one of the country's greatest attractions for music lovers. Of these the most famous is the **Prague Spring International Music Festival**. Prague Castle also stages **Strings of Autumn**, a traditional music festival held from October to December.

NIGHTLIFE

Every large Czech town has a music club, although Prague naturally has the greatest number. The best-known cultural centre in the capital is the **Palace Akropolis** complex, including a theatre, concert hall, exhibition space, café and restaurant.

It attracts many world music artists. **Agharta Jazz Centrum** is Prague's best jazz club. **Malostranská Beseda** is a venue for more traditional rock, jazz, blues, country and folk music. There are a number of rock venues, generally small clubs and cafés, which host a variety of groups; the **Rock Café** is among the most popular. Prague also has a lively gay and lesbian scene; **Valentino** is one of the most popular gay bars.

Most cities and larger towns have venues with live music at night, mainly performed by local bands and musicians. Techno and dance is very popular throughout the country.

Information on events in Prague can be found in the weekly English-language *Prague Post*. Other sources of information are the leaflets and posters in the local area. For information on gigs and clubs outside Prague, check the posters around town.

DIRECTORY

MARKETS

Havel Market
Havelská, Prague.

Holešovice Market
Holešovice, Prague.

GLASS AND CERAMICS

Dana-Bohemia
Národní 43, Prague.
Tel 224 214 655.

Erpet
Staroměstské náměstí 27, Prague.
Tel 224 229 755.

Moser
Na Příkopě 12, Prague.
Tel 224 211 293.

Parcela Plus
Malé náměstí 6, Prague.
Tel 224 228 459.

ANTIQUES

Alma Mahler Antique
Valentinská 7, Prague.
Tel 222 325 865.

Dorotheum
Ovocný trh 2, Prague.
Tel 224 222 001.

Starožitnosti Uhlíř
Mikulandská 8, Prague.
Tel 224 930 572.

FOOD AND DRINK

Jan Paukert Delicatessen and Wine Bar
Národní 17, Prague.
Tel 224 222 615.

CINEMA

Cinema City Flora
Vinohradská, Prague.
Tel 255 741 002.
www.cinemacity.cz

CLASSICAL MUSIC, THEATRE AND OPERA

Estates Theatre
Ovocný trh 1, Prague.
Tel 224 901 448.
www.narodni-divadlo.cz

Komedie Theatre
Jungmannova 1, Prague.
Tel 224 222 734.
www.divadlokomedie.cz

Laterna Magika
Národní 4, Prague.
Tel 224 931 482.

Municipal House
Náměstí Republiky 5, Prague. *Tel 222 002 101.*
www.obecnidum.cz

National Theatre
Dvořákova 11, Brno.
Tel 542 158 111.
www.ndbrno.cz

National Theatre
Národní 2, Prague.
Tel 224 901 448.
www.nationaltheatre.cz

Rudolfinum
Alšovo Nábřeží 12, Prague.
Tel 227 059 227. **www**.
ceskefilharmonie.cz

State Opera
Wilsonova 4, Prague.
Tel 224 227 266.
www.opera.cz

MUSIC FESTIVALS

Prague Spring International Music Festival
www.praguespring.cz

Strings of Autumn
www.strunypodzimu.cz

NIGHTLIFE

Agharta Jazz Centrum
Železná 16, Prague.
Tel 222 211 275.
www.agharta.cz

Malostranská Beseda
Malostranské náměstí 21, Prague.
Tel 257 532 092.

Palace Akropolis
Kubelíkova 27, Prague.
Tel 296 330 913.
www.palacakropolis.cz

Rock Café
Národní 20, Prague.
Tel 224 933 947.
www.rockcafe.cz

Valentino
Vinohradská 40, Prague.
Tel 222 513 491.
www.club-valentino.cz

Where to Stay in the Czech Republic

The Czech Republic has a variety of accommodation to choose from at a range of prices. The top-range hotels are as good as any in Europe but often just as expensive. In Prague, especially, budget options are scarce. However, finding a place to stay in a town or village is not difficult.

PRICE CATEGORIES
Price categories are for a standard double room with bathroom per night in high season, including breakfast, tax and service charges.

Ⓚ under 3,000Kč
ⓀⓀ 3,000–4,500Kč
ⓀⓀⓀ 4,500–6,000Kč
ⓀⓀⓀⓀ 6,000–8,000Kč
ⓀⓀⓀⓀⓀ over 8,000Kč

PRAGUE

Pension Březina
Ⓟ ⑪ ▤   Ⓚ

Legerova 41, Praha 2 **Tel** *224 266 779* **Fax** *224 266 777* **Rooms** *35*   **Map** *F5*

This run-down building houses a wonderful bed-and-breakfast establishment. The rooms are simple and modern, many facing a small garden at the back, and some have exposed wooden beams. It also has two suites, ideal for families. Breakfast is served in a small dining room. **www.brezina.cz**

Cloister Inn
Ⓟ ⑪ ▤   ⓀⓀ

Konviktská 14, Praha 1 **Tel** *224 211 020* **Fax** *224 210 800* **Rooms** *75*   **Map** *D4*

This modern hotel, close to the Charles Bridge (*see pp244–5*), offers large, comfortably furnished rooms with attached bathrooms. Breakfast is served in a spacious dining room while tea and coffee are available all day. There is free Internet access for guests in the lobby. **www.cloister-inn.com**

Pension Dientzenhofer
Ⓟ ♿   ⓀⓀ

Nosticova 2, Praha 1 **Tel** *257 311 319* **Fax** *257 320 888* **Rooms** *9*   **Map** *C4*

Located only a few minutes' walk from the Charles Bridge, this well-kept pension was the birthplace of Baroque architect Kilian Ignaz Dientzenhofer. The rooms are comfortable with en-suite bathrooms, satellite TV and minibar. Guests can make use of a small terrace. **www.dientzenhofer.cz**

Sax
⑪ ▤   ⓀⓀ

Jánský vršek 3, Praha 1 **Tel** *257 531 268* **Fax** *257 534 101* **Rooms** *22*   **Map** *B3*

Situated close to Prague Castle (*see pp232–3*), this Neo-Classical hotel is ideal for those who wish to be the first to arrive in the morning in Hradčany. The rooms are simply furnished, with windows facing the spectacular glass-roofed inner atrium. **www.sax.cz**

Betlem Club
Ⓟ   ⓀⓀⓀ

Betlémské náměstí 9, Praha 1 **Tel** *222 221 574* **Fax** *222 220 580* **Rooms** *21*   **Map** *D4*

Close to the Old Town Square (*see pp246–7*), this hotel is housed in a pretty medieval, pastel-green building in Betlémské Square. The rooms are small but well furnished and have attached bathrooms. Rebuilt many times, the house has a fascinating history and still has its original cellar. **www.betlemclub.cz**

Domus Henrici
Ⓟ ⑪ ▤   ⓀⓀⓀ

Loretánská 11, Praha 1 **Tel** *220 511 369* **Fax** *220 511 502* **Rooms** *8*   **Map** *A3*

Part of the Hidden Places hotel group, Domus Henrici is about as close to the Prague Castle as one can get, so visitors will love the location. Rooms are enormous and tastefully decorated. An excellent buffet breakfast is served on the terrace in the summer. **www.hidden-places.com**

U Brány
Ⓟ ⑪ ▤   ⓀⓀⓀ

Nerudova 21, Praha 1 **Tel** *257 212 029* **Fax** *257 212 758* **Rooms** *17*   **Map** *B3*

One of the best hotels in Prague, U Brány is always fully occupied during high season, so it is best to book well in advance. The rooms, comprising two-, three- and four-room suites, are elegantly furnished, and the bathrooms are fantastic. Facilities include satellite TV and minibar. **www.ubrany.cz**

U Zlatého Stromu
Ⓟ ⑪   ⓀⓀⓀ

Karlova 6, Praha 1 **Tel** *222 220 441* **Fax** *222 220 441* **Rooms** *22*   **Map** *D4*

Housed in a historic building, the rooms of the U Zlatého Stromu are small but have plenty of character. All the furnishings are tasteful, including the lovely wood-beamed ceilings. Some windows face the courtyard while others overlook the busy streets. **www.zlatystrom.cz**

Bellagio
⑪ ▤   ⓀⓀⓀⓀ

Klimentská 30 **Tel** *222 314 350* **Fax** *222 312 708* **Rooms** *76*   **Map** *E3*

This lovely hotel, pastel-pink on the outside, offers tastefully furnished rooms, large and small, with fair-sized bathrooms. All rooms are equipped with free Wi-Fi Internet access. The hotel bar is one of the most fashionable in Prague, and its restaurant Isabella is equally popular. **www.bellagiohotel.cz**

Map References *see map of Prague pp230–231*

iskupský Dům (Bishop's House)

P ‖ ⊗⊗⊗⊗

ražického náměstí 6, Praha 1 **Tel** 257 533 833 **Fax** 257 531 840 **Rooms** 45

Map C3

ully restored in 1990, this hotel occupies a 16th-century building facing the historic Royal Route through the
ty. The rooms are simple and comfortably furnished. Those on the upper floor feature exceptionally high
eilings with wood beams and delightful nooks. **www.hotelbishopshouse.com**

ům U Červeného Lva (Red Lion)

P ‖ ⊗⊗⊗⊗

erudova 41, Praha 1 **Tel** 257 533 832 **Fax** 257 535 131 **Rooms** 21

Map B3

Vith its lovely views over the Royal Route, Prague Castle and Petřín Hill (see p241), this former burgher's house is
uperbly located. Its rich interiors include painted Renaissance ceilings, original period furniture and parquet floors.
also has a traditional beerhall. **www.hotelredlion.com**

rand Hotel Praha

‖ ▤ ⊗⊗⊗⊗

taroměstské náměstí 22, Praha 1 **Tel** 221 632 556 **Fax** 221 632 558 **Rooms** 31

Map E3

ue to its excellent location by the Old Town Square, the Grand Hotel Praha proves quite popular with visitors,
o it is advisable to book well in advance. The large rooms and suites have simple, classic furnishings, but meet
odern requirements. Breakfasts are served in the historic U Orloje restaurant. **www.grandhotelpraha.cz**

berty

P ‖ 📺 ▤ ⊗⊗⊗⊗

8 Října 11, Praha 1 **Tel** 224 239 598 **Fax** 224 237 694 **Rooms** 32

Map E4

tuated in the centre of Prague, understated elegance and modern comfort are the hallmarks of this pleasant
otel. Rooms are spacious, with attached bathrooms and service is efficient. The hotel's health club, Relax, offers
tness facilities, massage and a solarium. **www.hotelliberty.cz**

Metamorphis

P ‖ ▤ ⊗⊗⊗⊗

lalá Štupartská 5, Praha 1 **Tel** 221 771 011 **Fax** 221 771 099 **Rooms** 24

Map E3

ocated at the heart of the Staré Město (see pp246–7), in the Týn courtyard, Metamorphis occupies a venerable
d house. It offers large rooms with pleasant bathrooms; some have antique furniture. The hotel's restaurant
erves delicious pizzas. **www.metamorphis.cz**

even Days

P ‖ 📺 ▤ ⊗⊗⊗⊗

tná 46, Praha 2 **Tel** 222 923 111 **Fax** 222 923 222 **Rooms** 50

Map F5

ocated in the centre of the Nové Město, this marvellous Neo-Classical building has spacious rooms with excellent
rnishings. All rooms are equipped with a wireless Internet connection and TV. A sauna and whirlpool are also
vailable for a small charge. **www.hotelsevendays.cz**

ria

P ‖ 📺 ▤ ⊗⊗⊗⊗

žiště 9, Praha 1 **Tel** 225 334 111 **Fax** 225 334 666 **Rooms** 52

Map B3

this charming, unusual hotel, the rooms are not very large, but each one is furnished in a style inspired by a
fferent musical legend, such as "Dizzy" Gillespie, Puccini or Mozart. The hotel offers live music in its Winter
arden as well as a music library and a music salon with a fireplace. **www.ariahotel.net**

offmeister

P ‖ 📺 ▤ ⊗⊗⊗⊗⊗

od Bruskou 7, Praha 1 **Tel** 251 017 111 **Fax** 251 017 120 **Rooms** 37

Map C2

ocated halfway up the hill leading to Chodkov, this high-class hotel, close to Prague Castle has a spa and
tness club. Its large rooms are flamboyantly furnished using colourful fabrics, and offer magnificent views
ver the Vltava river. **www.hoffmeister.cz**

ařiž

P ‖ ⊗⊗⊗⊗

Obecního Domu 1, Praha 1 **Tel** 222 195 195 **Fax** 224 225 475 **Rooms** 86

Map F3

his Neo-Gothic building, with a number of Art Nouveau elements, was built by the celebrated architect Jan
ejrych and was declared a historic monument in 1984. The rooms have been refurbished to meet international
andards and everything is in pristine condition. **www.hotel-paris.cz**

adisson SAS Alcron

P ‖ 🏊 📺 ▤ ⊗⊗⊗⊗

těpánská 40, Praha 1 **Tel** 222 820 000 **Fax** 222 820 100 **Rooms** 211

Map E5

his large, luxurious hotel is located in a superbly restored 1930s building near Wenceslas Square. The rooms and
uites are spacious and comfortable with high ceilings and classic period furnishings. The upper floors provide
agnificent views. **www.radissonblu.com**

avoy

P ‖ 📺 🏋 ▤ ⊗⊗⊗⊗⊗

eplerova 6, Praha 1 **Tel** 224 302 430 **Fax** 224 302 128 **Rooms** 61

Map A3

modern, deluxe hotel, the Savoy occupies a splendid, elegant building with an Art Nouveau façade. The large,
xurious suites and rooms have the biggest bathrooms in Prague, and the hotel prides itself on its service.
menities include a library and a fitness centre. **www.hotel-savoy.cz**

entana

‖ ▤ ⊗⊗⊗⊗⊗

eletná 7, Praha 1 **Tel** 221 776 600 **Fax** 221 776 603 **Rooms** 29

Map E3

ocated in the centre of the Staré Město, this classic Prague hotel has imaginatively furnished rooms with four-
oster beds. The reception is boldly Art Deco in style. Extensive breakfasts are served in the library with a view
ver the Church of Our Lady before Týn (see p250). **www.ventana-hotel.net**

Key to Symbols see back cover flap

REST OF THE CZECH REPUBLIC

BRNO Amphone

Třída Kapitána Jaroše 29, 602 00 **Tel** *545 428 310* **Fax** *545 428 311* **Rooms** *54*

Set in a quiet street at the centre of Brno, the Amphone occupies a restored 19th-century townhouse. In addition to small but well-equipped double rooms, it also has a small apartment available. Facilities include billiards, table tennis and a sauna. The hotel offers excellent food. **www.amphone.cz**

BRNO Holiday Inn Brno

Křižkovského 20, 603 00 **Tel** *543 122 111* **Fax** *543 246 990* **Rooms** *202*

Situated near the trade fair complex towards the centre of Brno, this hotel has won numerous awards for its high-quality service. The large rooms, decorated in red and yellow, are well equipped and comfortable. The Prominent restaurant has an open kitchen. There is also a hotel brasserie. **www.hibrno.cz**

BRNO Hotel Voroněž 1

Křižkovského 47, 603 73 **Tel** *543 141 111* **Fax** *543 212 002* **Rooms** *75*

This four-star hotel, modernized in 2002, has the region's largest business centre and provides excellent service. Rooms and suites are of the highest standards and have attached bathrooms. There is a whisky bar with live music every evening. **www.voronez.cz**

ČESKÉ BUDĚJOVICE Hotel U Solné Brány

Radniční 11, 370 01 **Tel** *386 354 121* **Fax** *386 354 120* **Rooms** *12*

Located in the centre of České Budějovice, this hotel's rooms have balconies or terraces attached, as well as bathrooms. The restaurant offers a wide selection of dishes, including superb local fish and game, and a good choice of Moravian wines. **www.hotelusolnebrany.cz**

ČESKÉ BUDĚJOVICE Grand Hotel Zvon

Náměstí Přemysla Otakara II 28, 370 01 **Tel** *381 601 601* **Fax** *381 601 605* **Rooms** *70*

Occupying three historic buildings in the Town Square, this hotel dates back to the 16th century. The main reception area features some beautiful paintings and a 17th-century hand-carved ceiling. Rooms are spacious and well furnished and the hotel also has three restaurants. **www.hotel-zvon.cz**

ČESKÝ KRUMLOV Leonardo

Soukenická 33, 381 01 **Tel** *380 725 911* **Fax** *380 725 910* **Rooms** *11*

Situated in a historic building dating from 1582, the Leonardo is centrally located near the main square. A cosy, recently refurbished hotel, it features lovely wooden ceilings and a Baroque staircase. The price includes breakfast, which is served in a large dining room. **www.hotel-leonardo.cz**

ČESKÝ KRUMLOV Pension Rosa

Linecká 54, 381 01 **Tel** *723 854 195* **Fax** *380 712 318* **Rooms** *17*

Located on the edge of the historic town centre, this small, comfortable pension in a pink Baroque building is still within easy reach of the main sights. It offers luxury rooms fitted with satellite TV and en suite bathrooms. Pets are also allowed. **www.pension-rosa.cz**

ČESKÝ KRUMLOV Zlatý Anděl

Náměstí Svornosti 11, 381 01 **Tel** *380 712 310* **Fax** *380 712 927* **Rooms** *36*

Housed in a Baroque building opposite the Town Hall, this magnificent hotel perfectly combines tradition with modernity. All rooms, with en suite bathrooms, satellite TV and minibar, are of a very high standard. The hotel has two restaurants, a cocktail bar, a café and a grill. **www.hotelzlatyandel.cz**

HRADEC KRÁLOVÉ Nové Adalbertinum

Velké náměstí 32, 500 01 **Tel** *495 063 111* **Fax** *495 063 405* **Rooms** *35*

A well-appointed pension with a restaurant, Nové Adalbertinum is housed in a historic Baroque building in Hradec Králové's Old Town square. Rooms are clean and simply furnished with bathroom, TV and telephone. Nearby is a large car park, where hotel guests may leave their vehicles. **www.naveadalbertinum.cz**

HRADEC KRÁLOVÉ U Královny Elišky

Malé náměstí 117, 500 03 **Tel** *495 518 052* **Fax** *495 518 872* **Rooms** *35*

In the historic town centre, this hotel occupies two burghers' houses dating from the 14th century. Although the buildings have been modernized, the old cellars and vaulted ceilings have been left untouched. Rooms are luxuriously furnished and the wine bar features live music. **www.hotel-ukralovnyelisky.info**

KARLOVY VARY Hotel Kavalerie

T G Masaryka 43, 360 01 **Tel** *353 229 613* **Fax** *353 236 171* **Rooms** *5*

Located in the centre of a pedestrianized zone in a peaceful district of Karlovy Vary, this hotel is within easy reach of the bus and train stations. It has large, bright rooms with pleasant decor and comfortable beds, and the hotel restaurant offers home cooking and outdoor seating. **www.kavalerie.cz**

Key to Price Guide *see p288* **Key to Symbols** *see back cover flap*

KARLOVY VARY Grand Hotel Pupp
P 11 ≋ 🎭 🖼 🗏   ⓚⓚⓚⓚⓚ

Mírové náměstí 2, 360 91 **Tel** *353 109 111* **Fax** *353 224 032* **Rooms** *112*

One of the most famous Czech hotels, the Grand Hotel Pupp dates back to the early 18th century. Besides its luxuriously furnished rooms with minibar, satellite TV, safe and dazzling bathrooms, it also has a restaurant, a casino, an impressive concert hall with Neo-Baroque interiors, and a fabulous spa centre. **www.pupp.cz**

KROMĚŘÍŽ Pension Excellent
P 11   ⓚ

Riegrovo náměstí 7 **Tel/Fax** *573 333 023* **Rooms** *12*

Located in the historic centre of Kroměříž, the Pension Excellent guesthouse is housed in a beautiful old building. The comfortable rooms have satellite TV and there is a lovely terrace and a restaurant serving traditional Czech cuisine. Facilities include a sauna and free Internet access. **www.excellent.tunker.com**

KUTNÁ HORA Hotel U Zvonu
P 11   ⓚ

Zvonařská Č.P. 286, 284 01 **Tel** *327 511 516* **Fax** *327 516 571* **Rooms** *7*

A small, congenial place located within the Old Town, close to the town square and the bus station, Hotel U Zvonu occupies a lovely 18th-century Baroque building. All rooms have en suite facilities, and there is a pleasant restaurant. **www.uzvonu.cz**

KUTNÁ HORA U Vlašského Dvora
11   ⓚ

28. Října 511, 284 01 **Tel** *327 514 618* **Fax** *327 514 627* **Rooms** *10*

A snug hotel in a historic 15th-century building, U Vlašského Dvora is situated in the medieval town centre, with a park, swimming pool and several tennis courts nearby. Well-appointed rooms have views over the towers and steeples of the Old Town. The hotel also has a good restaurant. **www.vlasskydvur.cz**

MIKULOV Réva
P 11   ⓚ

Česká 2, 692 01 **Tel/Fax** *519 512 076* **Rooms** *20*

Situated in the centre of the town, the Réva has rooms and a summer terrrace overlooking the spectacular Mikulov Castle. The restaurant offers a wide selection of Czech dishes and local wines as well as Italian cuisine; pizzas are a speciality. **www.hotelreva.cz**

OLOMOUC Arigone
P 11   ⓚ

Univerzitní 20, 771 00 **Tel** *585 232 351* **Fax** *585 232 350* **Rooms** *14*

This small, stylish hotel in the centre of Olomouc occupies a historic building and owes its name to the Italian painter Francesco Arigone, who owned it in the 18th century. Remains of the original Romanesque stone masonry can still be seen inside. It has a popular restaurant on two levels, and a bar. **www.arigone.cz**

OLOMOUC Hotel Gemo
P 11 🎭   ⓚⓚ

Pavelčakova 22, 772 00 **Tel** *585 222 115* **Fax** *585 231 730* **Rooms** *34*

Housed in a 13th-century building, Hotel Gemo's interior decor was designed by the famous Czech painter Kristian Kodet. Art Nouveau-style wooden furniture, handmade carpets and paintings by Moravian artists all contribute to an unforgettable atmosphere. The restaurant is excellent. **www.hotel-gemo.cz**

PLZEŇ Hotel Continental
P 11 🎭   ⓚ

Zbrojnická 8, 310 16 **Tel** *377 235 292* **Fax** *377 221 746* **Rooms** *85*

Located in the historic centre of Plzeň, Hotel Continental originally dates from 1895. Fully modernized in 1991, its elegant rooms have themed decor such as the sea, old Paris or London. Its former guests include celebrities such as Marlene Dietrich and John Malkovich. **www.hotelcontinental.cz**

PLZEŇ Parkhotel Plzeň
P 11 ≋ 🎭   ⓚⓚ

U Borského parku 31, 320 04 **Tel** *378 772 977* **Fax** *378 772 978* **Rooms** *72*

Opened in 2004, this hotel is in a beautiful area of Borský Park and offers comfortable, luxuriously furnished rooms. Italian food is served in the romantic Emporio restaurant, and there is an excellent wine bar. A golf driving range is attached to the hotel, with facilities to hire equipment. **www.parkhotel-plzen.cz**

TELČ Hotel Na hrázi
P 11 &   ⓚ

Na hrázi 78, 588 56 **Tel** *567 213 150* **Fax** *567 213 151* **Rooms** *13*

Beautifully located between the lakes that surround the Old Town of Telč, this hotel has well furnished and comfortable rooms equipped with satellite TV. The hotel terrace and guest room balconies offer magnificent views over the town. **www.nahrazi.cz**

TŘEBÍČ Grand Hotel
P 11 ≋ 🎭   ⓚ

Karlovo náměstí 5, 674 01 **Tel** *568 848 560* **Fax** *568 848 563* **Rooms** *67*

Located in the town centre, this modern hotel offers simply furnished rooms with pale wooden floors. Amenities include a sauna, bowling alley and fitness club. Local specialities and a good selection of wines are on offer at the hotel restaurant. **www.hotel-trebic.cz**

ZNOJMO Hotel Morava
P 11   ⓚ

Horní náměstí 16, 669 01 **Tel** *515 224 147* **Fax** *515 224 147* **Rooms** *10*

Situated in the Old Town Square in Znojmo, in a historic house, the Morava offers spacious rooms, all individually furnished. The restaurant has an appealing menu, and the cellar wine bar provides an opportunity to sample many local wines. **www.hotel-morava-znojmo.cz**

Where to Eat in the Czech Republic

New restaurants are opening all the time as a result of the thriving tourist industry. Many continue to serve local dishes as well as international cuisine, and compared to Western Europe, eating out is inexpensive. Czech beer is world famous and makes an excellent accompaniment.

PRICE CATEGORIES
Based on the price per person of a three-course meal with half a bottle of wine, including cover charge, service and tax.

Ⓚ under 250 Kč
ⓀⓀ 250–450 Kč
ⓀⓀⓀ 450–650 Kč
ⓀⓀⓀⓀ over 650 Kč

PRAGUE

ABA Restaurant, Bar and Night Club
Ⓚ

Žitná 4, Praha 2 **Tel** *222 232 315* — **Map** *E5*

The ABA has a welcoming interior of brick walls, graceful arches and original candelabra. The feeling of comfort is further boosted by the food – steaks, sirloin, fish, salads and delicious apple pie for dessert – as well as a good selection of beers and wines. Large parties often make for a lively atmosphere.

Bohemia Bagel
Ⓚ

Masná 2, Praha 1 **Tel** *224 812 560* — **Map** *E3*

The best breakfast deal in Prague is available until late in the morning at this busy bagel shop and café. High-speed Internet connections are also on offer at reasonable rates. It has become so popular that a second Bohemia Bagel has now opened across the Vltava, at Ujezd 16.

Klub Architektů
ⓀⓀ

Betlémské náměstí 5A, Praha 1 **Tel** *224 401 214* — **Map** *D4*

This hidden gem is tucked away in a warren of tunnels and arches and can be reached through a courtyard near the Bethlehem Chapel. For an inexpensive Prague eatery the servings are hearty, and the menu includes an interesting vegetarian section.

Orange Moon
ⓀⓀ

Rámová 5, Praha 3 **Tel** *222 325 119* — **Map** *E3*

Immensely popular, Orange Moon serves Thai, Indian and Burmese food. Spicy dishes are especially marked with a red pepper rating on the menu, but there are also some unmarked dishes for those who prefer milder flavours. The restaurant's specialities are the duck red curry with basil, spicy Burmese chicken curry and phad Thai tofu.

Restaurace Století
ⓀⓀ

Karoliny Světlé 21, Praha 1 **Tel** *222 220 008* — **Map** *D4*

Arched ceilings, sepia prints and old Chinese porcelain evoke a gentle ambience in this warm, friendly restaurant. The names of the dishes are inspired by famous figures of yesteryear, for example: a Louis Armstrong (pork medallions with peanut and orange curry sauce), or an Al Capone (roast chicken leg with hot salsa and papaya).

U Pinkasů
ⓀⓀ

Jungmannovo náměstí 16, Praha 1 **Tel** *221 111 150* — **Map** *E4*

This inexpensive, good-quality beer hall has been here since 1843. It is arranged on three levels: the basement houses a traditional beer hall, the ground floor is a bar serving light meals and snacks and above it is a traditional restaurant. The place is popular, particularly during the lunch hour. The food is simple yet tasty.

Chez Marcel
ⓀⓀⓀⓀ

Haštalská 12, Praha 1 **Tel** *222 315 676* — **Map** *E3*

Chez Marcel brings a touch of France to the centre of Prague. Its tables spill on to a quiet square, encouraging executives and students alike to come for reasonably priced regional plats du jour and to linger for steak au poivre, fresh mussels and the best chips in town.

Cicala
ⓀⓀⓀ

Žitná 43, Praha 1 **Tel** *222 210 375.* — **Map** *F5*

The owner is an Italian who does not speak English and has only a rudimentary knowledge of Czech. This is the most genuine Italian restaurant in Prague, the walls hung with photos of the best dishes, which taste like "mamma's food". Its *zuppa di cozze* (mussel soup) is the tastiest in the city.

Da Nico Wine Bar and Restaurant
ⓀⓀⓀ

Dlouhá 21, Praha 1 **Tel** *222 311 807* — **Map** *E3*

Da Nico serves mouthwatering Italian cuisine, including pizza, pasta dishes and risotto, and offers one of the best selections of Italian wines in the Czech Republic (over 300). Its cosy interior and efficient staff make it ideal for both romantic trysts and business meetings.

Map References *see map of Prague pp230–31*

Mount Steak

Josefská 1, Praha 1 **Tel** *257 532 652*

Map C3

A great place for meat-lovers, this restaurant offers an enormous choice of over 60 types of steak, from classic beef to wild boar, kangaroo, shark and ostrich meat. All meats are roasted, fried or grilled according to the customer's request and are served with potatoes and vegetables. A large and tempting selection of salads is also on offer.

Nebozízek

Petřínské sady 411, Praha 1 **Tel** *257 315 329.*

Map B4

In spring and summer, the particularly popular feature of this famous restaurant in Petřín Park is its patio with a magnificent view over Prague. The interior is snug and elegant. The menu includes seafood, steaks, Chinese food and Czech cuisine. Specialities are mouthwatering desserts such as stuffed pear with ricotta cheese mousse.

U Fleků

Křemencova 11, Praha 1 **Tel** *224 934 019*

Map D5

This is a combination of restaurant, pub and brewery *(see p259)* set in a maze of rooms resembling a network of caverns; it is said that some of them date from 1499. The brewery was founded in the early 20th century. Book in advance for the restaurant, which serves robust Czech pub fare.

Zahrada v opeře

Legerova 75, Praha 1 **Tel** *224 239 685*

Map F5

The "Garden at the Opera" lies between the National Museum *(see p258)* and the State Opera. It has a sophisticated menu, which includes imaginative salads, and the decor is modern. Outstanding value for money, it makes a perfect gourmet dinner choice before or after a night at the opera.

David

Tržiště 21, Praha 1 **Tel** *257 533 109*

Map B3

David can only be reached along a steep cobbled lane, but is well worth the climb. The gourmet set lunch of traditional Czech specialities, including duck and rabbit, is a two- to three-hour affair. The restaurant also offers an interesting international selection of wines. Booking is essential.

El Gaucho

Na příkopě 13, Praha 1 **Tel** *234 076 322*

Map E4

El Gaucho is a surprisingly genuine Argentinian restaurant. The food is hearty and plentiful and steaks are cooked on an authentic "Asado" grill. Waiters are dressed as gauchos, and there is a good choice of South American wines.

Kamenný Most

Smetanovo Nábřeží 195, Praha 1 **Tel** *224 097 100*

Map D4

A visit to this restaurant is an unforgettable experience, due to its stunning views of the Charles Bridge *(see pp244–5)*. It serves modern and traditional Czech and international cuisine and has a great wine list. There is also a live music bar and an Irish pub.

Mlýnec

Novotného Lávka 9, Praha 1 **Tel** *221 082 208*

Map D4

The chef at Mlýnec, Marek Purkart, is the first in the Czech Republic to be awarded the Michelin Bibendum three times, so diners here can expect the best food at the highest prices. Well-prepared traditional Czech cuisine is on offer, such as crisp roasted duck served with white and red cabbage and fine Karlovy Vary dumplings.

Peklo

Strahovské Nádvoří 1, Praha 1 **Tel** *220 516 652*

Map A3

The name of this upmarket, underground restaurant translates as "Hell". It is located within the Strahov Monastery complex *(see p240–41)*, which belongs to the Order of Premonstratensians, who have been keeping wine in their cellars since the 14th century. It offers Czech and international cuisine and a wide selection of wines.

Pravda

Pařížská 17, Praha 1 **Tel** *222 326 203*

Map E3

A stylishly decorated restaurant offering superb service, the Pravda will tempt the adventurous with its beautifully presented Asian and Scandinavian-inspired fare. This includes relatively expensive seafood dishes such as Cajun crayfish and poached cod, along with excellent puddings.

Staroměstská

Staroměstské náměstí 19, Praha 1 **Tel** *224 232 534*

Map E3

Housed in a medieval building on Staroměstské náměstí, this much-loved inn is famous for its classic Czech cuisine and Pilsner beer. The menu includes steaks, salads and home-made desserts. It is possible to dine outside during the summer months, enjoying spectacular views over the square.

U Malířů

Maltézské náměstí 11, Praha 1 **Tel** *257 530 318*

Map C4

There has been a restaurant on this spot since 1543, and even then U Malířů received high acclaim: Emperor Rudolph II's food tasters awarded it three royal stars. Expect the highest quality traditional and contemporary French cuisine, including a pricey châteaubriand. The elegant decor is still worthy of royal guests.

Key to Symbols *see back cover flap*

REST OF THE CZECH REPUBLIC

BRNO Restaurant Bugatti

*Lidická 14, 659 89 **Tel** 541 321 207*

The modern decor of this hotel-restaurant has a striking gold-and-blue colour scheme. Particularly recommended are the *carpaccio* (dish of raw meat or fish), Peking soup, breast of duck in saffron sauce with wild mushrooms and hot apple pie with vanilla cream and blueberries.

BRNO U Minoritů

*Orlí 17, 602 00 **Tel** 542 215 614*

A stylish restaurant in the Old Town *(see p280)*, U Minoritů is housed in a building of an old Minorite monastery established in 1230. The rooms are decorated with Baroque sculptures. The themed menu gives its dishes ecclesiastical names, and includes Bohemian delicacies and vegetarian choices. Moravian wines are also on offer.

ČESKÉ BUDĚJOVICE Hotel U Solné Brány

*Radniční 11, 370 01 **Tel** 386 354 121*

The interior of this modern hotel-restaurant is adorned with tapestries and paintings. It serves international cuisine with strong French accents. Specialities include onion soup with cheese, roast halibut with rosemary and hot raspberries with raspberry ice cream.

ČESKÉ BUDĚJOVICE U Rytíře

*Náměstí Premysla Otakara II č 33, 370 01 **Tel** 386 358 151*

Located in Town Square, this restaurant has a medieval-themed decor and menu and offers a large selection of traditional Bohemian cuisine, delicious fish and sumptuous home-made desserts. A good choice of Bohemian and Moravian wines is also on offer.

ČESKÝ KRUMLOV Restaurant Don Julius

*Náměstí Svornosti 11, 381 01 **Tel** 380 712 310*

Don Julius sports a witty, unconventional interior with an open hearth and walls decorated with a relief of the market square. Among a large selection of Bohemian and international dishes, it is worth trying the tomatoes stuffed with cheese salad, potato soup, Wiener Schnitzel and the tart with berries and whipped cream.

ČESKÝ KRUMLOV Le Jardin

*Latran 77, 381 01 **Tel** 380 720 109*

The solemn atmosphere of this restaurant with monastery vaults creates a lasting impression. Modern Czech cuisine is recommended here, with dishes such as roast duck leg with champagne cabbage, lobster bisque and sea bass with grilled vegetables.

HRADEC KRÁLOVÉ Satchmo

*Dlouhá 96, 500 02 **Tel** 495 514 590*

Situated between the two town squares in Hradec Králové's Old Town, this elegant restaurant has a cellar wine bar with a large selection of Moravian wines. In addition to Bohemian and European cuisine, including a great variety of fish dishes, it serves the best coffee in town and hosts live jazz performances. Closed on Sundays.

HRADEC KRÁLOVÉ U Královny Elišky

*Malé náměstí 117, 500 02 **Tel** 495 518 052*

The idiosyncratic interior of this hotel-restaurant, with brick-arched ceilings, is simple yet cosy. The menu has something for everyone, from carpaccio of salmon with herbs and soup with meat and dumplings to trout fried in butter, and fruits in dry sparkling wine.

KARLOVY VARY Restaurant Dvořák

*Slovenská 2, 360 01 **Tel** 353 102 119*

Restaurant Dvořák has a modern, cosy interior decorated in warm colours. Specializing in Bohemian and international cuisine, interesting options on the menu include tuna and soy salad, roast rabbit with spring vegetables and chocolate tart with orange and banana ice cream.

KARLOVY VARY Grand Restaurant Pupp

*Mírové náměstí 2, 360 91 **Tel** 353 109 111*

This delightful restaurant is located in the world-famous Grand Hotel Pupp *(see p291)*, with stylish decor featuring stucco wall decorations and soft furnishings. Highlights include smoked fish served with balsamic sauce, salmon cream soup, and roasted sea fish with jasmine rice, pepper and saffron.

KARLŠTEJN Koruna Restaurant

*Karlštejn 13, 267 18 **Tel** 311 681 465*

A pleasant hotel-restaurant furnished in traditional style, Koruna offers Bohemian dishes that are not particularly sophisticated but very tasty. Especially good are the scrambled eggs with caviar, onion soup, mixed grill with chips or rice and blueberry tart.

Key to Price Guide *see p292* **Key to Symbols** *see back cover flap*

KARLŠTEJN Restaurant U Karla IV

Karlštejn 173, 267 18 **Tel** *311 513 496*

This restaurant stands only a few paces from the walls of Karlštejn Castle *(see pp260–61)*. It has three rooms and three terraces, as well as a beer-garden with a grill. The cuisine is traditional Bohemian including fish, poultry and grills. It also hosts knights' tournaments and traditional dance performances.

KROMĚŘÍŽ Bouček Hotel Restaurant

Velké náměstí 108, 767 01 **Tel** *573 338 100*

Situated in the historic town centre, Bouček serves Bohemian and international cuisine. A large selection of wines is also available. In summer there are tables outside in the arcaded hotel entrance with a wonderful view of Kroměříž's main square. Live music and dancing on Fridays and Saturdays.

KUTNÁ HORA U Vlašského Dvora

28 Října 511, 284 01 **Tel** *327 514 618*

Located on the ground floor of the hotel of the same name, this pleasant restaurant serves excellent Czech and French cuisine. It also has a good choice of Moravian wines. A garden with a grill opens at the back of the hotel in the summer, and there is also sunny outdoor seating at the front.

KUTNÁ HORA U Zvonu

Zvonařská 286, 284 01 **Tel** *327 511 516*

Housed in a small hotel in the town centre, this exquisite restaurant specializes in Bohemian cuisine, but also serves a choice of international dishes. An extensive list of local and foreign wines is also on offer. The decor is plain and slightly rustic.

OLOMOUC Caesar

Horní náměstí-Radnice, 771 00 **Tel** *585 229 287*

Situated in Gothic rooms inside the historic Town Hall, alongside an interesting commercial gallery, this restaurant-café serves top-notch Italian cuisine and a large selection of alcoholic drinks, coffee and other beverages. The café garden overlooks Olomouc's Main Square.

OLOMOUC Hotel Gemo

Pavelčákova 22, 772 00 **Tel** *585 222 115*

Set in the Hotel Gemo, the interior of the restaurant is modern yet cosy, with Art Nouveau elements. The excellent food is varied and superbly flavoured; among the dishes are vegetables with mozzarella, basil and olive oil, cream of mushroom soup, salmon fillet in cream sauce with pasta and baked vanilla ice cream.

PLZEŇ Parkhotel Plzeň, Emporio Restaurant

U Borského Parku 31, 320 04 **Tel** *378 772 977*

A warm, homely atmosphere has been achieved here through carefully selected furniture and decor, which matches the style of the cooking: simple, yet delicious. Specialities include chicken salad in mustard mayonnaise, bread filled with traditional home-made Bohemian potato soup, chicken breast with courgettes, and gingerbread.

PLZEŇ Hotel Central

Náměstí Republiky 33, 301 00 **Tel** *377 226 757*

This modern, spacious restaurant is one of the most popular in town. Highlights from the extensive menu are the home-made pâté, hunter's soup with beans and sausage, venison roulade cooked in wine, fried potato dumplings and baked ice cream with chocolate and cream.

TELČ Restaurace U Zachariáše

Náměstí Zachariáše Z Hradce 33 **Tel** *567 243 672*

Located in the town square, this spacious, airy indoor restaurant has a high ceiling and fills two rooms. In the summer there is outdoor seating as well, which offers views of the square. Both Bohemian and European dishes are on the menu, and the wine list features plenty of Moravian wines.

TŘEBÍČ Restaurace Fantazie

Modřínova 599, Třebíč-Hajek **Tel** *568 827 261*

Set in an amusement centre, this spacious restaurant is ideal for families and groups, with indoor billiards and mini-golf. Steaks and pizzas feature on the menu as well as the chef's specialities: pork, ribs and tuna steak, cooked with garlic.

TŘEBÍČ Grand Hotel

Karlovo náměstí 5, 674 01 **Tel** *568 848 560*

Situated in the town centre, the Grand Hotel restaurant serves sumptuous Bohemian cuisine in a stylish modern setting. Special events are also hosted, from interesting Moravian evenings with cask wine tasting to samplings of traditional local food.

ZNOJMO Hradní Restaurace

Hradní 1, 669 02 **Tel** *515 228 164*

Situated in the Gothic surroundings of Znojmo Castle *(see p278)*, the menu at this stylish restaurant is dominated by Bohemian cuisine, specializing in grilled and spit-roasted fare. In spring and summer, visitors can sit outside and enjoy historical vignettes played out in the castle's front courtyard.

SLOVAKIA

A province of the kingdom of Hungary for nine centuries and part of Czechoslovakia for 70 years, Slovakia has had a tumultuous past. It gained independence in 1993 and is now one of Europe's youngest countries. With diverse topography, beautifully preserved architecture and rich folk culture, the country holds great appeal to visitors.

Landlocked at the heart of Central Europe, Slovakia combines a dynamic economy with a wealth of natural assets – mountains, lakes, unspoilt valleys and spectacular ice caves. Beautiful churches ranging, from the Romanesque to Art Nouveau, are a feature of its towns and cities, while numerous castles and ruined fortresses stand testimony to the region's turbulent history. Slovakia, nevertheless, remains a relatively little-known country, with few visitors.

HISTORY

During the 5th and 6th centuries the Slavs arrived in the Danube Lowlands, but they were later conquered by the nomadic Avars. In 795 the Avars were beaten by Charlemagne (r. 742–814), at the head of an alliance of Franks and Moravians. This cleared the way for the establishment of two Slavic principalities, out of which grew the Great Moravian Empire. By 885, this incorporated parts of present-day Slovakia, Germany and Poland, as well as Bohemia and Moravia. The Moravian Empire was destroyed in the 9th century by the invading Magyars, who took control of the Danube Lowlands, including much of modern-day Slovakia. From this period the Czechs and Slovaks were exposed to different cultural and political influences. In 1025, the

A vintage tourist bus in Bratislava's Old Town

◁ Breathtaking view of the Tatra Mountains, central Slovakia

Slovak Lands became part of the kingdom of Hungary. The turning point in Slovakia's history came with the Battle of Mohács (1526), when the invading Ottoman Army crushed the forces of King Louis II Jagiełło, then ruler of Hungary and the Czech lands. Slovakia came under Habsburg rule and due to its position between Christian Europe and the Muslim Ottoman Empire, it was repeatedly ravaged by raids and military campaigns. Homegrown troubles also surfaced, thanks to the Reformation and resistance to the Habsburgs' centralist policies. The enlightenment reforms of the 18th century resulted in the codification of the Slovak language and the stirrings of nationalism. By 1848, revolutions had broken out all over Europe, including the Habsburg Empire. The leader of the Slovak Nationalist Movement, L'udovit Štur, demanded self-determination for Slovakia in vain. After suppressing the revolution, Emperor Franz Joseph II restored absolute monarchy. The situation worsened after the creation of the Austro-Hungarian Empire in 1867,

Hungarians entering former Czech territory

when Slovakia was placed in the Hungarian-ruled half of the monarchy. Slovak politicians forged links with Czech activists and, in 1918, the Czechoslovak Republic was declared. Czech politicians rejected Slovakia's bid for autonomy, however, steadfastly promulgating the concept of a single country. When Hitler took the Sudetenland in 1938, the Slovaks declared independence, but the country became little more than a Nazi puppet state. The democratic state of Czechoslovakia was reborn in 1945, only to fall under the control of the Communist Party three years later. Not until the Velvet Revolution of 1989 was the Communist government finally overthrown. On 1 January 1993, the sovereign Slovak Republic was proclaimed, and its position within the international community was confirmed when, in 2004, Slovakia joined NATO and the European Union.

KEY DATES IN SLOVAKIAN HISTORY

5th–6th centuries Slav tribes colonize Danube Lowlands

833 Foundation of the Great Moravian Empire

1000 St Stephen crowned king of Hungary

1241–42 Mongol invasion

1536 Bratislava (Pressburg) becomes capital of the kingdom of Hungary

1683 Ottoman Turks defeated at the Battle of Vienna

1840s L'udovit Štur becomes leader of the Slovak Nationalist Movement

1867 Creation of Austro-Hungary Monarchy

1918 Czechs and Slovaks proclaim the creation of Czechoslovakia

1938 Parliament proclaims the Slovak Republic

1944 Slovak National Uprising

1948 Communists take control of Czechoslovakia

1993 Creation of the Slovak Republic

2004 Slovakia joins NATO and becomes an EU member

2007 Slovakia signs the Schengen Agreement

LANGUAGE AND CULTURE

Slovakian is the official language of Slovakia, although there is a sizeable Hungarian minority in the south. There is a full calendar of cultural events and folk festivals are one of the country's main attractions. Slovakia is also rich in religious traditions: Catholic feasts are celebrated throughout the country while Orthodox rituals are mainly observed in the east.

Exploring Slovakia

Slovakia surprises visitors with its diverse scenery and cultural wealth. The majority of the historic sights in the capital city of Bratislava can be found in its compact Old Town centre. Western Slovakia boasts the city of Trnava, with its many magnificent Gothic, Renaissance, Basque and Neo-Classical buildings. Central Slovakia, regarded as the country's true heart, is primarily a mountainous region, encompassing the High Tatra Mountains. Eastern Slovakia's towns of Spiš and Levoča are treasure-houses of the country's history, while Košice enjoys a well-deserved reputation as its cultural centre. The country's well-developed network of public transport can be used for exploring the region.

Tablet in the Church of
St James, Levoča

SIGHTS AT A GLANCE

KEY

✈	Airport
—	Motorway
—	Major road
—	Railway
–∙–	International border

Snow-clad peaks in the Tatra Mountains

Bratislava ❶

Founded by the Celts in the 2nd century BC, Bratislava is Slovakia's administrative centre and has long been the focus of the country's social and cultural life. It became the capital of Slovakia in 1993. Today, with a population of 4 million, it is the country's largest city. Most of the historic sights are located in the Old Town centre on the left bank of the Danube (Dunaj) river. Some of the finest buildings, such as the Mirbach Palace and the Old Town Hall, can be seen around Franciscan Square (Františkánské námestie). West of the town centre, Bratislava Castle offers fantastic views over the city.

Detail of the elegant altarpiece in St Anne's Chapel, St Martin's Cathedral

SIGHTS AT A GLANCE

Bratislava Castle ⑥
Devín Castle ⑬
Franciscan Church ③
House at the Good
  Shepherd ⑦
Michael's Gate ⑤
Mirbach Palace ④
New Bridge ⑫
Old Town Hall ①
Primate's Palace ②
Red Stone Castle ⑭
Reduta ⑩

Slovak National Gallery ⑪
Slovak National Theatre ⑨
St Martin's Cathedral
  pp306–307 ⑧

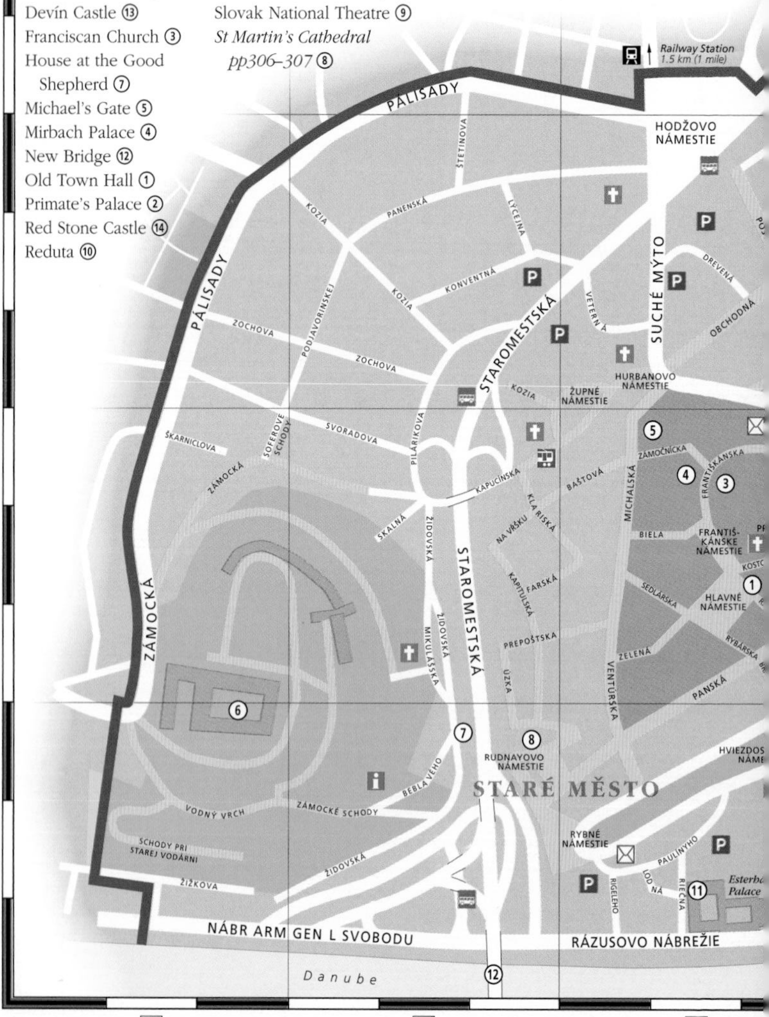

Railway Station
1.5 km (1 mile)

GETTING AROUND

The historic centre of Bratislava is mostly pedestrianized, so the best way to explore it is on foot. For longer trips within the city and into its environs, there is a quick and efficient network of buses, trams and trolleybuses. These also run at intervals throughout the night, starting from námestie SNP. Drivers should be aware that it can be difficult to get a parking space, and that leaving a car illegally parked could incur a heavy fine. From April to October ferries and sightseeing boats operate from a jetty on the Danube at Fajnorovo Nábrežie.

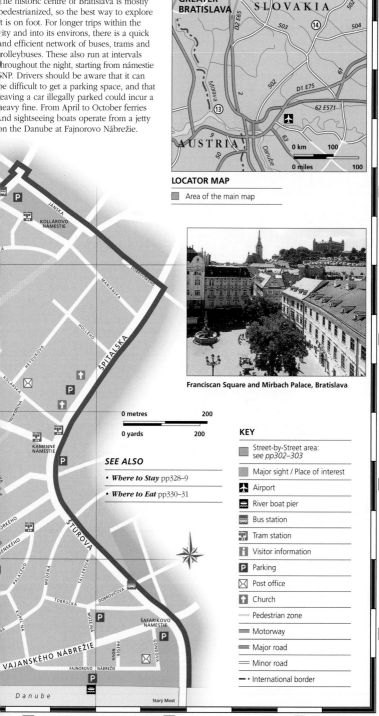

GREATER BRATISLAVA

LOCATOR MAP

Area of the main map

Franciscan Square and Mirbach Palace, Bratislava

0 metres 200

0 yards 200

SEE ALSO

• *Where to Stay* pp328–9

• *Where to Eat* pp330–31

KEY

	Street-by-Street area: see pp302–303
	Major sight / Place of interest
✈	Airport
	River boat pier
	Bus station
	Tram station
ℹ	Visitor information
P	Parking
⊠	Post office
✝	Church
	Pedestrian zone
	Motorway
	Major road
	Minor road
–·–	International border

Street-by-Street: Old Town

The centre of Bratislava's historic Old Town (Staré Město) consists of two interlinked squares: Hlavné námestie and Františkánské námestie. The first has the distinctive Old Town Hall. This square also lay along the coronation route of the Hungarian kings, now marked by golden crowns embedded in the pavement. The pride of Františkánské námestie, apart from its lovely trees, is the Marian Column, erected in 1657. With attractive cafés, both squares are popular meeting places.

Michael's Gate
This is the only gate that remains from the medieval fortifications. In the 18th century it was topped with a statue of the Archangel Michael ⑤

Mirbach Palace
One of Bratislava's finest architectural relics, this Rococo palace now houses the City Gallery ④

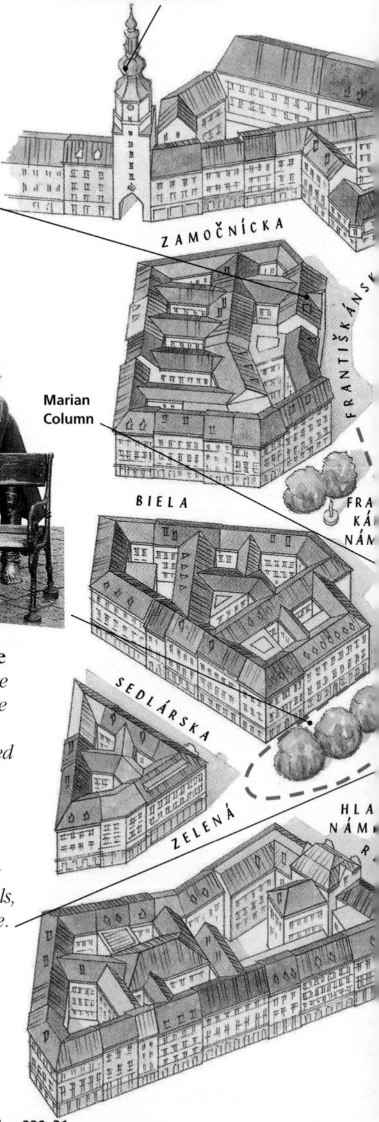

Statue of Napoleon's Soldier
This is one of several life-sized figures in the Old Town. Others include a photo-grapher and a worker poking his head out of a manhole.

Marian Column

ZAMOČNÍCKA

BIELA

SEDLÁRSKA

ZELENÁ

FRANTIŠKÁNSK

FRA
KÁ
NÁM

HLA
NÁM

Hlavné Námestie
At the centre of the main square is the 1572 Maximilian Fountain, designed by Andreas Luttringer, from where Roland, a medieval French knight adopted as patron by the locals, surveys the square.

STAR SIGHTS

★ Franciscan Church

★ Primate's Palace

★ Franciscan Church
Bratislava's oldest religious building, the Franciscan Church was erected in the 13th century. Remodelled several times, it acquired its Baroque form in the 18th century ③

★ Primate's Palace
One of the city's finest Neo-Classical structures, this palace was built between 1778 and 1781 by architect Melchior Hefele for Archbishop Josef Batthyány, the head of the Hungarian church ②

The Jesuit Church was built between 1636 and 1638 by Protestants. Its greatest treasure is its pulpit by L'udovit Gode.

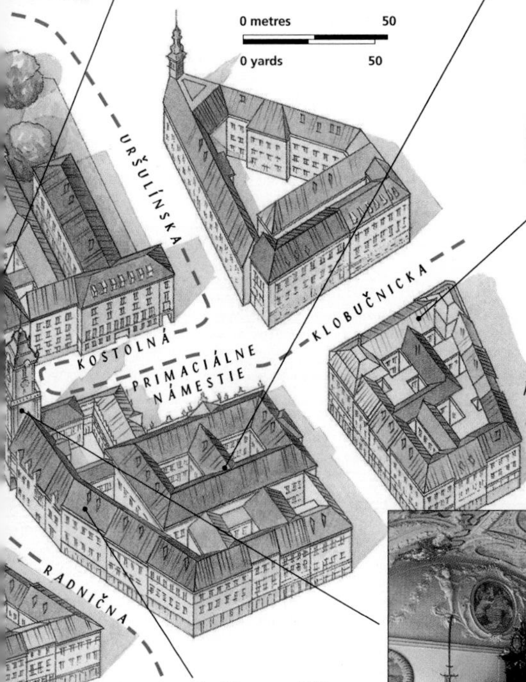

0 metres 50
0 yards 50

URŠULÍNSKA
KOSTOLNÁ
PRIMACIÁLNE NÁMESTIE
KLOBUČNICKA
RADNIČNÁ

Museum of Music
The birthplace of Johann Nepomuk Hummel, a celebrated composer and pianist, this Renaissance house has displays about his life and works, as well as the history of music in Bratislava.

The Museum of Wine Production, part of the City Museum, displays wooden grape presses that are over 200 years old.

Old Town Hall
Remodelled and rebuilt many times since the 13th century, the Old Town Hall is now home to the impressive City Museum, which houses exhibits related to the history of Slovakia ①

KEY
— — Suggested route

Old Town Hall ①
Stará Radnica

Hlavné námestie. **Map** C4.
City Museum *Tel (02) 5920 5130.*
⬜ *10am–5pm Tue–Fri, 11am–6pm
Sat & Sun.* ♿

The charming Old Town Hall, in Hlavné námestie, was created in the 15th century by combining a number of residential houses. At the turn of the 16th century, it was rebuilt in the Renaissance style. In the 18th century, its much older corner tower was remodelled in Baroque style; excellent views can be had from the top. On the lower section of the tower is a plaque marking the level of flood waters recorded in February 1850. Higher up, to the left of the Gothic window, is another historical relic – a cannonball embedded in the wall during the 1809 siege of Bratislava by Napoleon's Army. It is worth taking a look at the unusual colourful roof of the building on the side of Primaciálne námestie.

The Town Hall houses the popular **City Museum** (Mestské múzeum). Displayed within its splendid vaulted interiors are exhibits associated with the history of Bratislava, including an unusual collection of 17th–19th century painted shooting targets.

Opposite the Town Hall stands the Jesuit Church of the Holy Saviour. It was built between 1636 and 1638 for Bratislava's Protestant community, which explains its plain façade. Its Baroque furnishings include a richly decorated black and gold Rococo pulpit with gilded tassles.

An ornate fountain in the courtyard at the Primate's Palace

Primate's Palace ②
Primaciálny Palác

Primaciálne námestie 1. **Map** C4.
Tel (02) 5935 6394. ⬜ *10am–5pm
Tue–Sun.* ♿

The most beautiful palace in Bratislava, Primate's Palace was built between 1778 and 1781 to a design by architect Melchior Hefele, for Jozef Batthyány, the primate of Hungary and archbishop of Esztergom.
Its lovely Neo-Classical pink-and-gold façade features a magnificent pediment that is crowned with the archbishop's coat of arms and topped with a giant-sized cardinal's hat. The figures of angels on the façade hold the letters I and C, a reference to the motto in the cardinal's coat of

**Statue in the
Franciscan Church**

arms – Iusticia (Justice) and Clementia (Mercy). The palace, now the seat of the town's mayor, is partly open to the public. The most opulent room is the Hall of Mirrors, where in 1805, the Peace Treaty of Pressburg was signed between Napoleon and Francis I, after the French victory at the Battle of Austerlitz. Other first-floor rooms are occupied by a branch of the Municipal Gallery, with a modest collection of paintings and six unique English tapestries dating from 1632, depicting the love story of Hero and Leander. The strikingly bright tapestries were discovered in a hidden compartment during building works in the early 20th century.

Franciscan Church ③
Františkánský Kostol

Primaciálne námestie. **Map** C4.
⬜ *10:30am–5pm Mon–Fri.*

The oldest religious building in Bratislava stands behind an inconspicuous Baroque façade. Built in the 13th century, the church was consecrated in 1297 in the presence of King Andrew II. Subsequent remodelling obliterated its original Gothic form, but it is still possible to see the medieval rib vaulting above the presbytery. Particularly impressive is the two-tier 14th-century chapel of St John the Evangelist. During coronation pageants, the church was used for knighting ceremonies, in which the new monarch appointed Knights of the Golden Spur. This prestigious honour was bestowed on those who distinguished themselves through feats of bravery.

The church's elaborate furnishings, mainly Baroque in style, date from the 17th and 18th centuries. The 15th-century Pietà, in a side altar, is a highlight.

Imposing façade of Bratislava's eclectic Old Town Hall

Mirbach Palace ④
Mirbachov Palác

Františkánske námestie 11. **Map** C4.
City Gallery *Tel* (02) 5443 1556.
◯ 11am–6pm Tue–Sun. 🖫
www.gmb.sk

The Rococo Mirbach Palace, opposite the Franciscan Church, has a beautiful façade with stuccoes and a triangular pediment. The building was erected between 1768 and 1770 by a rich brewer, Martin Spech. Its subsequent owner, Count Karol Nyary, ordered his family crest to be placed in the tympanum. The last owner, Emil Mirbach, bequeathed the building to the city.

Now an art gallery, the palace currently holds the main collection of Bratislava's **City Gallery** (Galéria mesta Bratislavy), including examples of 17th- and 18th-century Baroque paintings. Two of the first-floor halls have walls almost entirely covered with colourful 18th-century engravings set in wood panelling.

Michael's Gate ⑤
Michalská Brána

Michalská ulica 24. **Map** C4.
Museum of Weapons and Town Fortifications *Tel* (02) 5443 3044.
◯ Oct–Apr: 9:30am–4:30pm Tue–Sun; May–Sep: 10am–5pm Mon–Fri, 11am–6pm Sat & Sun. 🖫

Built in the first half of the 14th century, Michael's Gate is the only surviving gateway to the medieval city. In the 18th

Michael's Gate with its striking Baroque cupola

Bratislava Castle perched above the Danube river

century, its Gothic tower was raised to its present height of 51 m (167 ft) by the addition of a Baroque cupola, and the statue of the Archangel Michael on top. The tower now houses the captivating **Museum of Weapons and Town Fortifications** (múzeum zbraní a mestského opevnenia), which throws light on the history and fortifications of the town.

The viewing terrace affords a stunning panorama of the city and beyond. Next to the gate stands Bratislava's oldest pharmacy, the Baroque At the Red Lobster (U červeného raka).

Bratislava Castle ⑥
Bratislavský hrad

Bratislavský hrad. **Map** A5. **Slovak National Museum** *Tel* (02) 5441 1444. ◯ 9am–5pm Tue–Fri, 10am–6pm Sat & Sun (last adm 45 mins before closing). 🖫
www.bratislava-hrad.sk

The Bratislava Castle, first mentioned in 907, is perched on a large, rocky hill above the scenic Danube. It was strategically located at the crossing of ancient trade routes including the ancient Amber Route. Fortified in the 11th and 12th centuries, the castle was rebuilt in Gothic style in the 15th century, and between 1552 and 1560 remodelled into a superb Renaissance residence. Between 1750 and 1760 it acquired beautiful Rococo furnishings. In 1811, the castle burnt down; it was rebuilt in the 1950s. Inside there are several sections of the **Slovak**

National Museum (Slovenské národne múzeum). The largest collections are from the Slovak History Museum (Slovenské Historické múzeum), including furniture, clocks and folk artifacts. In the Treasury of Slovakia (Klenoty davnej minulosti Slovenska) stands the tiny *Venus of Moravany*, a fertility figure carved from a mammoth tusk about 25,000 years ago. The Music Museum (Hudobné múzeum) displays scores, recordings and some fascinating folk instruments.

House at the Good Shepherd ⑦
Dom U Dobrého Pastiera

Židovska 1. **Map** B5. **Tel** (02) 5441 1940. **Museum of Clocks** ◯ 10am–5pm Mon–Fri, 11am–5pm Sat & Sun.

One of the city's finest examples of Rococo architecture can be seen at the House at the Good Shepherd, named after the statue of the Good Shepherd on its corner. Built between 1760 and 1765, it is one of the few remaining 18th century houses in the area. It is colloquially referred to as the "house like an iron", because of its tall, flat wedge shape, dictated by the plot on which it was erected. It is believed to be the narrowest building in Europe, and contains only one room on each floor. Inside is the **Museum of Clocks** (múzeum hodín), a branch of the City Museum located in the Old Town Hall. The exhibits date from the 17th to the 20th centuries and are mostly the works of Bratislava's clockmakers.

St Martin's Cathedral ⑧

Dóm šv Martina

This imposing Gothic edifice, with a wide nave flanked by two aisles, was built in 1452 on the site of an earlier 14th-century Romanesque church. Between 1563 and 1830, 11 Hungarian kings and 8 queens were crowned in the cathedral. From here it is possible to walk the former coronation route through the Old Town by following a series of golden crowns embedded in the pavement. In the 19th century, the church was rebuilt in Neo-Gothic style by architect Jozef Lippert and its interior refurbished along more purist lines.

Structure of the Cathedral
Vibrations from heavy traffic on the road to New Bridge (see p308) have damaged the cathedral, which often has to undergo restoration.

Presbytery
After completing the hall the builders realized that the section by the altar was too small, and added a presbytery with a fine net vault. The coat of arms on the vault is that of the Hungarian King Mátyás Corvinus (see p333).

★ Sculpture of St Martin
Originally made for the main altar, this statue of St Martin (1734) by sculptor Georg Raphael Donner depicts St Martin in Hungarian dress, cutting his cloak to share it with a beggar.

St Anne's Chapel

Chapel of St John the Almsgiver
In 1732 Georg Raphael Donner built the side chapel of St John the Almsgiver at the request of Archbishop Esterházy.

STAR FEATURES

★ Sculpture of St Martin

★ Altar of St Anne's Chapel

For hotels and restaurants in this region see pp328–9 and pp330–31

The tower, 85 m (280 ft) tall, is topped by a slender cupola and a gold-plated replica of the Hungarian crown; a reminder that the cathedral was once the venue for coronations.

Interior
In the late 19th century the Baroque furnishings were replaced with Neo-Gothic ones and the main altar, along with its angels paying homage to St Martin, was removed.

Stained-Glass Windows
The stained glass in the presbytery dates from the second half of the 19th century and was mostly produced by the Viennese company, K Geyling.

The Chapel of the Czech queen, Sophia, and the Canons' Chapel are adjacent to the sacristy under the tower.

★ Altar of St Anne's Chapel
The central section of the ornate altarpiece in St Anne's Chapel depicts the scene of the Crucifixion of Christ.

Main portal with Neo-Gothic vestibule

Impressive façade of the Neo-Renaissance Slovak National Theatre

Slovak National Theatre ⑨
Slovenské Národné Divadlo

Hviezdoslavovo námestie 1. **Map** C5.
Tel (02) 2047 2298. ⬚ 8am–
5:30pm Mon–Fri, 9am–1pm Sat.
www.snd.sk

The Neo-Renaissance Slovak
National Theatre, on the east
side of Hviezdoslavovo
námestie, was built between
1884 and 1886 by Viennese
architects Ferdinand Fellner
and Hermann Helmer, who
specialized in theatres. The
façade is decorated with busts
of Goethe and Shakespeare,
among others. At the centre
of the tympanum is a sculptural group including the
muse of comedy, Thalia.
The theatre stages performances of ballet and opera,
and attending one of these
is the only way to see the
interior. In front of the theatre
is a fountain made in 1880
by sculptor V Tilger. It depicts
the Trojan youth Ganymede
flying on the back of Zeus,
who is disguised in the form
of an eagle.

Reduta ⑩

Palackého 2. **Map** C5. **Tel** (02) 2047
5233. ⬚ 1–7pm Mon, Tue, Thu, Fri;
8am–2pm Wed. **www**.filharm.sk

Near the Slovak National
Theatre stands the imposing
building of the Reduta. Built
between 1913 and 1918, with
a grand lobby and staircase, it

used to stage social and
artistic events, symphony
concerts and theatre performances. Today the Reduta
is home to the Slovak
Philharmonic, and every
autumn it is the venue for the
Bratislava Music Festival. A
section of the building, on the
side of Mostova ulica, houses
a casino and a restaurant.

**The Reduta, home to the acclaimed
Slovak Philharmonic**

Slovak National Gallery ⑪
Slovenská Národná Galéria

Riečna 1. **Map** C5. **Tel** (02) 5443
4587. ⬚ 10am–5:30pm Tue–Sun.
⬛ 21 & 24 Apr, 1 & 8 May. ⬚ ⬚
www.sng.sk

Established in 1948, the Slovak
National Gallery occupies a
building that was created by
combining two structures –
the four-wing 18th-century
Baroque naval barracks,

designed by G Martinelli and
F Hildebrandt, and architect
V Dĕdeček's house. In 1990,
the gallery's collections were
also placed in the neighbouring Neo-Renaissance Esterházy
Palace. Designed by I Feigler
Jr and built between 1870 and
1876, Esterházy Palace is
reminiscent of an Italian
Renaissance town palace. On
the ground floor is the legendary Berlinka Café, one of the
most popular cafés in the city.
The gallery boasts a number
of works of art. The finest are
the 13th- and 14th-century
Slovak art collections, including altarpieces and statues
from churches in the Spiš
region in eastern Slovakia.
The most compelling works
in the Baroque section are
those by sculptor Franz
Xaver Messerschmidt.
Modern Slovak art is also
well represented, with models
of buildings, photographs,
ceramics, jewellery and posters giving an eclectic overview
of the country's creative output over the last 100 years.
As well as Slovak artists,
the collection includes works
by a number of acclaimed
foreign artists including
Rubens, Caravaggio, Manet
and Picasso.

New Bridge ⑫
Nový Most

Staromestská. **Map** B5.

Also known as the Bridge of
the Slovak National Uprising
(SNP), this steel construction
was built between 1967 and
1972. It officially opened on
26 August 1972, as the second
bridge over the Danube. This
feat of engineering is sus-
pended from one pylon on
the south bank of the
Danube. The sheer size
of this single, open suspen-
sion bridge is impressive; it
is 431 m (1,414 ft) high
and weighs 7,537 tonnes
(8,308 tons). At the top
of the pylon is a restaurant,
whose saucer-like shape is
reminiscent of the Starship
Enterprise from *Star Trek*.
From here there are beautiful
sweeping views of the city
on the north bank, and of

the vast housing estates of Petržalka on the south. Built by Communists, this estate houses more than 150,000 of the city's inhabitants.

The construction of New Bridge and the Staromestská Highway, which cuts through the city and over the bridge, involved the complete destruction of the former Jewish quarter at the foot of Bratislava Castle *(see p305)*.

Devín Castle ⑬
Zámok Devín

8 km (5 miles) W of Bratislava. **Map** F1. *Tel* (02) 6573 0105. 🚌 *28, 29.* 🚢 *from Central Bratislava.* ⬜ *10am–5pm Tue–Fri, 11am–6pm Sat & Sun.* 🎫

At the confluence of the Morava and the Danube rivers lie the ruins of Devín Castle, perched on a high rock. The rock was once the site of a Celtic settlement. Later, the Romans built a fortress here and in the 9th century, Prince Rastislav, king of Great Moravia between 846 and 870, chose it for his stronghold. It changed hands many times until 1809, when it was blown up by the French Army during

Coat of arms from the well in the courtyard of Red Stone Castle

the Napoleonic Wars. In the 19th century, during the period of national rebirth, the castle became a symbol in the shaping of Slovak national identity, promoted by Ľudovít Štúr, the leader of the Slovak Nationalist Movement *(see p298)*.

During the 1980s the castle area, separated from Austria by the Danube, was closed to the public. Now, it is a popular recreational spot for Bratislavans. One section of the castle has been reconstructed, and features the remains of a Roman fortress and an archaeological museum.

Red Stone Castle ⑭
hrad Červený Kameň

155 km (96 miles) N of Bratislava. **Map** F1. *Tel* (033) 690 5803. 🚌 ⬜ *Nov–Feb: 9:30am–3:30pm daily; Apr–Aug: 9am–5pm daily; Sep & Oct: 9am–4pm daily (till 5pm Sat & Sun).* 🎫 📷 🖥 www.hradcervenykamen.sk

The remarkable Red Stone Castle is regarded as one of the best-preserved castles in Slovakia. A mighty edifice with four corner towers, it was acquired in the 16th century by a German banking family, the Fuggers. Anton Fugger, one of the richest men in 16th-century Europe, converted the original 13th-century fort into a Renaissance castle. When the Pálffy family took it over in 1580, they converted it into a Baroque residence.

The castle's interior includes finely preserved porcelain and furnishings while the castle chapel has lavishly decorated walls and marble altars. An unusual feature is the 1656 *sala terrena*, an artificial grotto with trompe-l'oeil paintings and stuccoes. The castle also houses collections from the Slovak National Museum, including a gallery of paintings with portraits of the Habsburgs and Pálffy family members.

Environs
Častá, about 1 km (0.6 mile) east of Red Stone Castle, has been a centre of wine-making for centuries and several cellars offer tastings. Its 15th-century Gothic Church of St Imre has interesting medieval paintings.

The ruins of Devín Castle, high above the Danube river

Trnava ❷

One of Slovakia's oldest towns, Trnava was granted town privileges in 1238. In the 16th and 17th centuries, it was the seat of the Hungarian primate and the headquarters of the Church of Hungary. Known as the "Slovak Rome", the town acquired numerous churches and monasteries. The historic town centre is enclosed within old walls, forming an almost complete square. The main Holy Trinity Square is at its heart. The chief attraction of the town are its religious buildings and relaxed ambience.

🏛 Holy Trinity Square

The town's main square, Trojičné námestie, sports the lofty Municipal Tower dating from 1574, with a viewing gallery and a cupola crowned with a golden statue of Our Lady. There is also an 18th-century Plague Column. Close by is the 1831 **Municipal Theatre** (Trnavské divadlo), the oldest theatre building in Slovakia. Just north of the square, the **Holy Trinity Church** (now known as Jesuitský kostol in Slovakian) was built in the early 18th century by the Trinitarian monks. It has been used by the Jesuits since 1853. To the west of the square is the single-towered **Church of St Jacob** (šv Jakub), built in 1640 and given a Baroque remodelling in 1712.

Plague Column, Holy Trinity Square

present shape after a fire in 1676. They are still not identical; the southern tower is slightly narrower. Inside, the main attraction is the octagonal chapel of the Virgin Mary, added in 1741 to the left aisle of the church. It contains the miraculous picture of the Trnava Madonna, which is particularly revered in Slovakia. The gilded Renaissance-Baroque main altarpiece dates from 1639. Built into the side walls of the chapels are a number of interesting Renaissance and Baroque tombstones.

🏛 St Nicholas's Square

This spindle-shaped square (námestie šv Mikuláša) by the old city walls was the focus of the town in the Middle Ages. At its centre is the 1731 Baroque column of St Joseph, surrounded by

Baroque column of St Joseph, St Nicholas's Square

chapter buildings. Among these is the **Archbishop's Palace** (Arcibiskupský palác), built by the Italian masters Pietro and Antonio Spazzi in 1562. During the 16th and 17th centuries, this Renaissance edifice was the seat of the Hungarian primates, whose residence in Esztergom had been appropriated by the Ottomans. It was also the headquarters of the Church of Hungary at the height of the Ottoman threat. The archbishops went back to Esztergom in 1820, but a Slovak archbishopric was re-established here in 1990.

🏛 Cathedral of St John the Baptist
See pp312–13.

🏛 Church of St Nicholas
Námestie sv Mikuláša. 🛈
The twin towers of the Church of St Nicholas (šv Mikuláš), with their distinctive bell-shaped cupolas, are one of Trnava's chief landmarks. The church, dedicated to the patron saint of merchants, was built in the 11th century. The original structure was demolished in the 14th century to make way for the new Gothic church built between 1380 and 1421. Its outside walls are supported by mighty buttresses, particularly imposing in the presbytery. The towers, initially of unequal size, were given their

The twin towers of Church of St Nicholas's

🏛 Music Museum
M S Trnavského 5. **Tel** *(033) 551 4421.* ⬜ *9am–5pm Tue–Fri, 11am–5pm Sat & Sun.* 📷
The Music Museum (Dom hudby) occupies a building called Dom hudby, which used to be the home of one of Trnava's most famous citizens – the composer Mikulas Schneider Trnavský (1881–1958). It displays objects and mementos associated with the musician and serves as a concert venue.

🏛 Synagogue
Halenárska 2. **Tel** *(033) 551 4657.* ⬜ *10am–noon, 1–5pm Tue–Fri, 1–6pm Sat & Sun.* 📷 www.snm.sk
This imposing edifice in Byzantine-Moorish style was built in the 19th century to a design by Viennese architect Jakub Gartner. Today, it

ouses a centre of modern
rt and the Museum of Jewish
.ulture, and is also used as
n exhibition and concert
all. Standing in front of
he Synagogue (Synagoga) is
 black marble monument,
esigned by architect Artur
zalatnai-Slatinský, dedicated
› the memory of Trnava's
:ws, who were murdered in
.e Holocaust.

ineteenth-century synagogue in
yzantine-Moorish style

▣ Museum of West Slovakia
luzejné námestie 3. **Tel** (033) 551
9 14. ☐ 8am–5pm Tue–Fri,
1am–5pm Sat & Sun. 🗟
)ne of the biggest in the
ountry, the Museum of West
lovakia (Západoslovenské

múzeum) is housed in the
13th-century convent next to
the Church of the Assumption
of the Virgin Mary.

Following administrative
restructuring of the empire's
institutions carried out during
the reign of Joseph II in the
late 18th century, the building
became a military hospital,
and later, a warehouse. In
1954 it became a museum,
with the aim of continuing
Trnava's museum traditions.

The collections, spread
over two floors, include
archaeological discoveries, an
exhibition of religious art,
ethnography, natural history
displays and eight rooms of
folk ceramics as well as a
unique collection of bells.

🔒 Church of the Assumption of the Virgin Mary
Muzejné námestie. 🚩
The Order of the Poor Clares
settled in Trnava during the
Middle Ages. This church
(Nanebovzatia Panny Márie)
was built for the nuns in the
13th century as an aisleless
Romanesque structure.
Following a fire in the
17th-century it was extended
and remodelled in the
Baroque style. Original
features of the interior include
the early 18th-century high
altar and three side altars.

VISITORS' CHECKLIST

46 km (28 miles) NE of
Bratislava. 🏠 68,300.
🚆 Kollárova. 🚌 Stanična.
🛈 Trojičné námestie 1, (033)
323 6440. 🎭 Lumen (early
May), Dobrofest International
Music Festival (late Aug)
www.trnava.sk

**Interior of the Church of the
Assumption of the Virgin Mary**

🔒 Church of St Helen
Dolné Bašty. 🚩
Trnava's oldest church, šv
Helena, dates from the 14th
century. Adjoining its north
façade is the original tower
with Gothic windows. There
are statues of saints above
the portal.

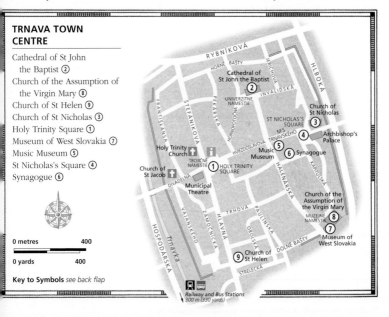

**TRNAVA TOWN
CENTRE**

Cathedral of St John
  the Baptist ②
Church of the Assumption of
  the Virgin Mary ⑧
Church of St Helen ⑨
Church of St Nicholas ③
Holy Trinity Square ①
Museum of West Slovakia ⑦
Music Museum ⑤
St Nicholas's Square ④
Synagogue ⑥

0 metres   400
0 yards   400

Key to Symbols see back flap

Trnava: Cathedral of St John the Baptist
Katedrálny Chrám šv Jána Krstiteľa

The first monumental Baroque structure in Slovakia and one of the largest and most impressive religious buildings, the Cathedral of St John the Baptist was constructed between 1629 and 1637. The building, intended as a church for the Jesuit-run university, was founded by Count Miklós Esterházy. It has an ornamented Italianate interior with oval frescoes and wooden altarpieces. From 1777, when the university was moved to Buda in Hungary, the church was used by war veterans.

Main Façade
The impressive twin towered façade, divided by protruding cornices, is decorated with statues of various saints, including Sts Joachim, Anna, and Elizabeth.

Pilasters
decorate the façade.

Main Portal
The inscription in Latin above the entrance refers to Count Miklós Esterházy, the cathedral's founder.

Interior
The walls, windows and vault are decorated with stucco ornamentation – figurative, floral and geo-metric – by artists Giovanni Rossi and Tornini.

Main entrance

Figures of the apostles
fill the niches on the south side of the church.

St John's Pulpit
This Baroque pulpit, decorated with figures depicting the Fathers of the Church, was built by artisans B Kniling and V Stadler in 1640.

VISITORS' CHECKLIST

Univerzitne námestie. **Tel** (033) 551 4586. ☐ May–Sep: 8am–noon, 2–5pm & 30 min before each mass. ✝ 7:30am daily, 9:30 & 11:30am Sun. ☑

★ The High Altar
This lavish Baroque gilded wooden altarpiece (1640) depicts the scene of Christ's baptism.

Ornate Door
Above the richly carved wooden door leading to the sacristy is an ornate metal grille with gilded elements.

★ Vaulted Ceiling
Paintings on the arched vaulting of the presbytery ceiling depict scenes from the life of St John the Baptist.

STAR FEATURES

★ The High Altar

★ Vaulted Ceiling

Bojnice Castle ❸
Zámok Bojnice

Originally built in the 12th century, the romantic Bojnice Castle is one of Slovakia's greatest attractions. In the 13th century, it passed into the hands of the most powerful Hungarian warlord of the time, Matúš Čák. In 1527, the Thurzo family converted the castle into a comfortable Renaissance residence and in the 19th century, its last owner, Count Ján Pálffy, remodelled it into a stately residence resembling the Gothic castles of France's Loire Valley.

Pálffy's Tomb
The chapel crypt contains the impressive Neo-Romanesque marble sarcophagus of the castle's last owner, Ján Pálffy.

Chapel
The chapel, with its stuccoed and painted vault, was built in the 17th century, in a former bastion.

★ **Golden Hall**
The hall's spectacular vault, made of pine and covered with gold leaf, was modelled on the interior of the Venetian Academy of Fine Arts.

Music Room
The present Music Room was once Count Ján Pálffy's bedroom. It now houses a beautiful piano made in Vienna in 1884.

The Castle Courtyards are used in summer to host medieval tournaments and falconry shows.

Castle Grounds

Bojnice is located in a large park with many rare species of trees, including what is claimed to be the oldest lime tree in Slovakia. In summer, various events are staged in the grounds.

VISITORS' CHECKLIST

181 km (123 miles) NE of Bratislava. **Tel** (046) 543 0535. 🚆 🚌 from Bratislava. ⏰ May–Sep: 9am–5pm Tue–Sun; Oct–Apr: 10am–3pm Tue–Sun; Jun–Sep daily. 🎫 🔦 night tours available. **www**.bojnicecastle.sk

Central Castle

The rooms of the Central Castle are furnished in Gothic style. The top floor is the Knights' Hall, with 14- to 17th-century weapons.

Neo-Gothic Gallery

Entrance Tower and Gate

Well in the Fourth Courtyard

Standing in the smallest of the castle's courtyards, this decorative well was once linked to an old thermal spring. Its ornate grille was made in 1895.

STAR FEATURES

★ Golden Hall

★ Bojnice Altarpiece

★ Bojnice Altarpiece

The altarpiece, painted by Italian painter Nardo di Cione, is the only complete surviving work by the artist. Painted in the mid-14th century, using tempera paint on a wooden panel, it is the most important piece from Ján Pálffy's collection.

Narodna Street, leading to the market square in Banská Bystrica

Banská Bystrica ❹

208 km (130 miles) NE of Bratislava.
🚶 82,100. 🚉 🚌 🛈 Námestie SNP
14, (048) 415 5085.

One of the oldest towns in Slovakia, Banská Bystrica (Neusohl) was granted royal privileges associated with the mining of gold, silver and copper in 1255. In 1944 it became the centre of the Slovak National Uprising (Slovenské národné povstanie).

The historic sights are concentrated along the pedestrianized Dolna, the large market square námestie SNP, and Horna. The central square is flanked by buildings of the old castle complex. Of these, the parish **Church of Our Lady** (Nanebovzatia Panny Márie), begun in 1255 and rebuilt in 1761, has magnificent Baroque furnishings. Its greatest treasures are the Gothic Altar of St Barbara, and the Side Altar, which contains a fine 15th-century Gothic triptych of St Mary Magdalene. The castle complex also includes the Church of the Holy Cross, the Matthias House and the Town Hall as well as remnants of the old fortifications. Nearby, the striking concrete **SNP Museum** (SNP múzeum) is dedicated to Slovak history, with particular emphasis on the 1944 Uprising against the Nazis and the fate of Slovak Jews.

🏛 **Church of Our Lady**
Námestie Š Moyzesa. **Tel** (048) 412 4531. ⬜ during mass. 🚫

🏛 **SNP Museum**
Námestie SNP. **Tel** (048) 412 3258. ⬜ May–Sep: 9am–6pm daily; Oct–Apr: 9am–4pm daily. 🎦 📷

Tatra Mountains ❺

Logo of the Tatra National Park

Slovakia's Northern Tatra Mountains consist of three ranges: the Western Tatras (Západné Tatry), the High Tatras (Vysoké Tatry) and the small area of Eastern Tatras (Belianské Tatry), a protected reserve that is closed to the public. All of them are within the Tatra National Park. The most spectacular range, the High Tatras, is a major draw for hikers.

View from Around Zuberec
The village of Zuberec, at the mouth of the Roháčska Valley, offers magnificent views of Roháče, the start of the Western Tatras.

Habovka

Oso,
▲ 1,68
(5,5.

Zuberec

ROHAČE

❄

▲
Salatín
2,050 m
(6,726 ft)

584

Baranec
2,184 m ▲
(7,165 ft)

Jalovecký p.

Smrečianka

Brobrovec

Liptovský Mikuláš
This town, set in a valley surrounded by peaks, is an interesting and convenient base for the Low Tatras.

Liptovský
Mikuláš

18

D1

Váh

Prouba

Liptovský
Hrádok

Banská Bystrica
75 km (47 miles

Liptovský Hrádok
This town is famous for its ruined 14th-century castle, later extended into a Renaissance palace. The palace now houses an Ethnography Museum dating from the 19th century.

For hotels and restaurants in this region see pp328–9 and pp330–31

Gerlachovský Štít
The highest peak of the Tatras range, the 2,654-m (8,707-ft) high Gerlachovský Štít can only be climbed with the help of a professional guide.

VISITORS' CHECKLIST

339 km (210 miles) NE of Bratislava. ✈ Poprad-Tatry. 🚋 from Poprad to Tatranská Lomnica, Starý Smokovec, Štrbské Pleso. 🛈 Starý Smokovec, (052) 442 3440. ⏱ 8:30am–4pm Mon–Fri, 8am–1pm Sat; May–Sep: daily. **www**.tanap.org

Lomnický Štít
The second highest peak, at 2,632 m (8,635 ft), it is accessible by cable car.

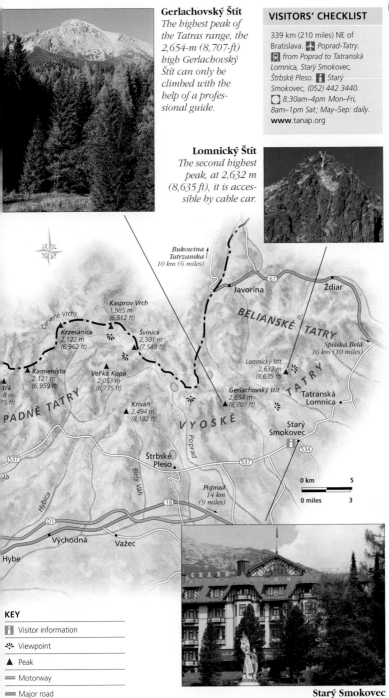

Bukowina Tatrzanska
10 km (6 miles)

Javorina

Ždiar

67

BELIANSKE TATRY

Červené Vrchy

Kasprov Vrch
1,985 m
(6,512 ft)

Krzesanica
2,122 m
(6,962 ft)

Švinica
2,301 m
(7,549 ft)

Spišská Belá
16 km (10 miles)

Kamienista
2,121 m
(6,959 ft)

Veľká Kopa
2,053 m
(6,735 ft)

Lomnický štít
2,632 m
(8,635 ft)

Tatranská
Lomnica

PADNÉ TATRY

trá
8 m
5 ft)

Kriváň
2,494 m
(8,182 ft)

VYOSKÉ

Gerlachovský štít
2,654 m
(8,707 ft)

TATRY

537

Štrbské
Pleso

Biely Váh

Poprad

Starý
Smokovec

534

Poprad
14 km
(9 miles)

537

elá

Hybica

0 km 5
0 miles 3

D1

18

Východná

Važec

Hybe

KEY

🛈 Visitor information

🔆 Viewpoint

▲ Peak

▬ Motorway

▬ Major road

═ Minor road

▪ ▪ International border

Starý Smokovec
This attractive spa complex has several hotels, pensions and restaurants that blend well with their woodland surroundings.

The striking Renaissance Thurzo House in the old centre of Levoča

Levoča ⑥

396 km (246 miles) NE of Bratislava.
🏘 *14,000.* 🚉 🚌 ℹ *Námestie Majstra Pavla 58, (053) 451 3763.*
www.levoca.sk

The former capital of the Spiš region, a historic province populated by Saxon settlers, Levoča is situated between the High Tatras and the Slovenské Rudohorie Mountains. The town has a well-preserved historic centre, full of magnificent Gothic, Baroque, Renaissance and Neo-Classical buildings. Its main square, námestie Majstra Pavla, features the Gothic **Church of St James** (šv Jakub), containing a set of 18 altarpieces and a splendid collection of medieval and Renaissance sacred art. The main altarpiece, 18.6 m (61 ft) high, is the world's tallest Gothic altar. The tall statues of the Madonna, St James and St John the Evangelist are by Master Pavol of Levoča, an outstanding sculptor of the late-Gothic period. To the south of the church lies the former **Town Hall**.

The most striking historic houses around the main square are the **Thurzo House** (Thurzov dom), crowned with a Renaissance attic, and the **House of Master Pavol of Levoča**, now a museum devoted to the sculptor's life and works. At the edge of the historic district, the 14th-century **Old Minorites' Church** (Starý kláštor minoritov) has a dazzling Baroque interior.

🏛 House of Master Pavol of Levoča
Námestie Majstra Pavla 20.
Tel (053) 451 3496. ⏺ daily (by appt Mon). 📷

Levoča:Town Hall
Radnica

One of Levoča's most distinguished buildings, the Town Hall was erected in 1550 in Gothic style, replacing an earlier building that had been destroyed by fire. In the early 17th century it was remodelled along Renaissance lines. The bell tower dates from 1656–61, with Baroque decorations added in the 18th century. The Neo-Classical pediments were added in the 19th century. The Town Hall is still used for civic functions, and it also houses the main branch of the Spiš Museum on the first floor, with exhibits on regional history.

★ **Arcades**
The original Town Hall did not have any galleries. The two-tier arcades were added to the central part of the building in 1615.

CAGE OF DISGRACE

The infamous 16th-century Cage of Disgrace

The wrought-iron cage by the south wall of the Town Hall is the 16th-century Cage of Disgrace, in which women who had committed minor crimes were locked up and put on public display. It used to stand in a park belonging to the Probstner family, who gave it to the town in 1933.

Town's Coat of Arms
The town's striking coat of arms consists of a red shield with a double cross supported by two lions.

Main Hall
The main hall's vaulted ceiling bears witness to the Gothic origin of the Town Hall.

VISITORS' CHECKLIST

Námestie Majstra Pavla. *Tel* (053) 451 2449. ◯ 9am–5pm daily. **Spiš Museum** ◯ 9am–5pm daily. ✆ www.snm.sk

★ Council Chamber
In 1998, this room was used for a summit meeting between the presidents of 11 European countries, including Slovakia, Poland, Czech Republic, Hungary, Romania, Bulgaria and Slovenia.

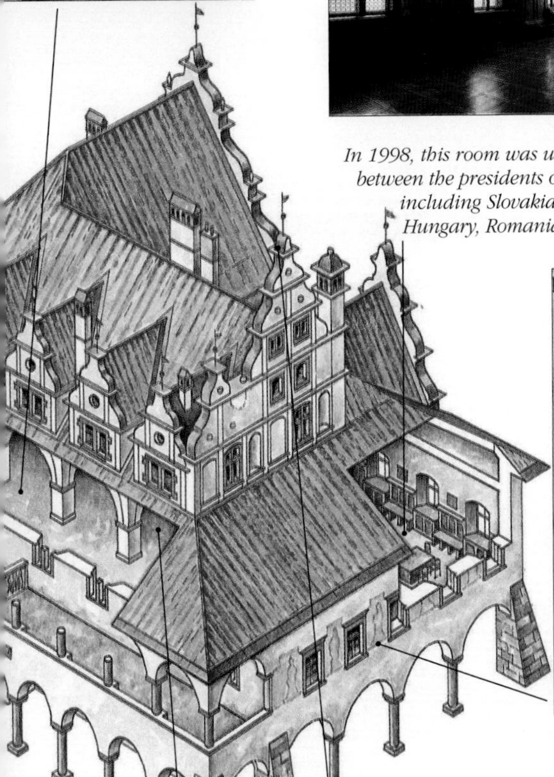

PRVDENTIA EST VIRTVS ACCVRATE RESPICIENS ID QVOD IN VNA QVAQVE ACTIONE DECET.

★ Wall Paintings
The impressive Renaissance wall paintings on the south elevation of the building depict the civic virtues of restraint, courage, justice and patience.

Coat of arms

The Neo-Classical pediments date from the 19th century.

The Spiš Museum, on the first floor, contains several important historical artifacts as well as an exhibition on the town's history.

Corner column buttresses were added in the 19th century to protect the arches from structural failure.

STAR FEATURES

★ Arcades

★ Council Chamber

★ Wall Paintings

Impressive Church of the Holy Spirit in Žehra near Spišská Kapitula

Spišská Kapitula ❼

400 km (249 miles) NE of Bratislava.

The walled, one-street town of Spišská Kapitula is located on a ridge, west of Spišské Podhradie. Since 1776 it has been the seat of the Spiš bishopric and the ecclesiastical capital of the Spiš region. Dominating the town is the late-Romanesque, twin-towered **St Martin's Cathedral**, (katedrála šv Martina) dating from 1245–75, with two Romanesque portals and the statue of a white lion at the entrance. The interior has unique medieval frescoes in the central nave. The interesting burial chapel of the Zápolya family, by the south wall, dates from the 15th century. Further along the street stand the imposing Baroque Bishop's Palace with a clock tower, and a row of Gothic canon houses. Spišská Kapitula has been on the UNESCO World Cultural Heritage list since 1993.

Environs
The village of **Žehra** lies 6 km (4 miles) southeast of Spišská Kapitula. It features the historic UNESCO-protected 13th-century Romanesque Church of the Holy Spirit (šv Duch), a white building with a tower and a bell, topped with onion-shaped wooden cupolas. Inside, 13th–15th-century frescoes cover the presbytery and a wall of the nave, and there is a 13th-century stone font.

> 🛈 **St Martin's Cathedral**
> ⏲ 10am–5:30pm Mon–Sat, Sun 11am–5:30pm.

Spiš Castle ❽
Spišský hrad

The ruins of Spiš Castle are part of a historic complex, along with the small town of Spišské Podhradie (*podhradie* means "below the castle") and Spišská Kapitula to the northwest; all three are on the UNESCO World Cultural Heritage list. Spiš Castle was the administrative capital of the Spiš region, a historic province populated by Saxon settlers. Its oldest parts date from between the 11th and 12th centuries. In 1780, the castle burned down, but it is now gradually being restored. Most impressive from a distance, it is nonetheless worth a visit for its spectacular views.

Fortress
Occupying an area of 4 ha (10 acres), Spiš Castle is the remains of the largest fortress complex in Central Europe. In the 17th century it had 2,000 inhabitants.

Gate
The entrance gate leads to a vast lower courtyard, nearly 300 m (985 ft) long and 115 m (380 ft) wide.

★ Castle Chapel
Six wooden statues of saints adorn the interior of the 15th-century Gothic chapel of the Zápolya family. The chapel was completely renovated in 2003.

VISITORS' CHECKLIST

405 km (252 miles) NE of
Bratislava. **Tel** *(053) 454 1336.*
🚌 🚐 *from Spišské Podhradie.*
⭕ *mid-Mar–Apr: 9am–5pm
daily; May–Sep: 9am–7pm daily;
Oct: 10am–4:30pm daily.* 🔲
www.spisskyhrad.sk

Walls
The Zápolya family, who owned the castle in the 15th and 16th centuries, had the defensive walls rebuilt, reinforced and equipped with new gun positions.

★ Upper Castle
Situated at the highest point on the hill, the Upper Castle, with its Romanesque palace and tower, was built in the 14th century. Burnt down in 1780, it was not rebuilt.

Kruchová Tower,
dating from the first half of the 12th century, was used as a residence and observation point.

★ Museum
A section of the chapel has been given over to a small exhibition devoted to the archaeology and history of Spiš Castle, and to a collection of historic arms and armour.

STAR SIGHTS

★ Castle Chapel

★ Upper Castle

★ Museum

Tournaments
During summer, colourful historical pageants and tournaments are held in the castle courtyards, featuring men dressed as knights.

Košice

**Košice's coat
of arms**

Slovakia's second largest city, Košice has roots reaching back to the 12th century. At the crossroads of major trade routes, it was granted the same town privileges as the then capital of Hungary, Buda, in 1347. In 1369, King Louis the Great gave the town its coat of arms, making it the first town in Europe to receive this by royal decree. Due to its proximity to the Hungarian border, Košice has always had a large Hungarian population. The most interesting sights in the city are clustered within its large and superbly restored historic centre.

The Plague Column and beautiful houses in Hlavná

🏛 Hlavná

This lovely avenue, full of shops and cafés, makes for an enjoyable stroll. The most striking of its buildings are the Gothic Levoča House (Levočský dom) and the Old Town Hall, its façade decorated with sculptures of ancient heroes by Anton Kraus (1705–1752). Built between 1722 and 1723, the Plague Column is Košice's most beautiful piece of Baroque sculpture.

The Singing Fountain in front of the ornate State Theatre

🏛 State Theatre

Hlavná 58. **Tel** (055) 622 1231.
🕐 performances only. **www**.sdke.sk
The imposing building of the State Theatre (Štátné divadlo) was built between 1897 and 1899, to a design by Hungarian architect Adolf Lang. Its lofty dome is topped with the torch-bearing figure of Dawn. The interior, with its beautiful auditorium and lyre-shape floor plan, features a magnificent ceiling with paintings of scenes from Shakespeare's works. The foyer and the rest of the theatre are richly decorated with stuccoes.

🏛 Singing Fountain

Hlavné námestie.
In the square between the theatre and St Elizabeth's Cathedral is the Singing Fountain (Spievajúca fontána), which spouts water to music. At night, the pearly jets are lit up by coloured lights that change with the rhythm of the music. The fountain is at the centre of a narrow water channel that runs the length of the square.

🏛 Urban Tower

Hlavná. **Tel** (055) 832 4576.
🕐 noon–4pm Tue–Sun.
The 14th-century Urban Tower (Urbanova veža) is dedicated to St Urban, the patron saint of viniculture, as wine production has always been a source of Košice's wealth. St Urban's bell was cast in 1557 and installed inside the tower; the tower itself was remodelled in Renaissance style in 1628.

⛪ St Elizabeth's Cathedral

Hlavná 28. **Tel** (055) 622 1555.
🕐 9am–5pm, daily. 🔲
The largest church in Slovakia, St Elizabeth's Cathedral (Dóm šv Alžbety) dominates the main square. Begun in 1378, the church is an achievement of the popular European Gothic style. The main, western façade was meant to have two towers, but by 1477 only one had been built. In 1508 work was completed on the beautifully vaulted presbytery. Not until 1775 was the second tower of the cathedral built, topped with an impressive Rococo copper cupola.

The present form of the church is the result of the intricate reconstruction that began in the late 19th century, when it was restored to its former appearance, close to the original design. Inside, the spectacular main altarpiece has 48 panels. The relief work over the north and west doors is also impressive.

**Detail from St
Elizabeth's Cathedral**

⛪ St Michael's Chapel

Hlavná 26. 🕐 9am–5pm, daily. 🔲
The chapel of St Michael (šv Michal) was built in the 14th century, on the site of a cemetery south of St Elizabeth's Cathedral. The lower section of the building served as an ossuary, while the upper section was used to celebrate masses for the souls of the dead. During the 16th

For hotels and restaurants in this region see pp328–9 and pp330–31

century, the chapel was converted into a storehouse for weapons and ammunition when the Turkish threatened to invade. In the early 20th century, 17 old tombstones from the cemetery were built into the chapel walls. Highlights of the interior include the altarpiece depicting St Michael the Archangel, the lovely stone tabernacle, and above the sacristy door, the oldest coat of arms of Košice.

Bas-relief from the Jesuit Church's façade

✦ Former Synagogue
Puškinova.

The Former Synagogue was built between 1926 and 1927. In 1992, a bronze memorial plaque was added to the front of the building to commemorate over 12,000 Jews who were taken from Košice to concentration camps in 1944.

⚌ Executioner's Bastion
Hrnčiarska 7. ◯ *9am–5pm Tue–Sat.*

The bastion (Katova bašta) takes its name from a nearby house, which was once the home of the city's hangman. This semicircular structure was built around 1500 and served defense purposes, with eight cannon chambers set in

its walls. The lower section of the bastion is reinforced with slanting buttresses.

⛪ Jesuit Church
Junction of Hlavná & Univerzitna.

One of the finest remaining Baroque structures in the city, this church (Univerzitný kostol šv Trojice) was built in 1681 by the Jesuit order. Its austere, early-Baroque façade, bearing traces of the Renaissance style, hides a lavishly furnished interior, which includes a 17th-century pulpit and stalls and a 19th-century main altar. The central nave and side chapels are beautifully decorated with magnificent trompe l'oeil paintings.

▥ East Slovak Museum
námestie Maratónu Mieru 2. **Tel** *(055) 622 1361.* ◯ *9am–5pm Tue–Sat, 9am–1pm Sun.* ▨

One of Slovakia's oldest museums, the East Slovak Museum (Východoslovenské múzeum) was established in 1872 as the Upper Hungary Museum. Its vast collections, numbering half a million exhibits, are displayed in an early 20th-century Neo-Renaissance building.

VISITORS' CHECKLIST

445 km (277 miles) NE of Bratislava. 🏠 *240,000.*
✈ 6 km (4 miles) SE of centre. 🚉 Staničné námestie.
🚌 Staničné námestie.
🛈 Hlavná 59, (055) 625 8888.
www.kosice.sk

The impressive façade is decorated with the town's coat of arms and carved figures of Perseus and Vulcan. The museum's greatest attraction is the "golden treasure of Košice" – a huge find of nearly 3,000 gold coins dating from the 15th to the 17th centuries.

The Neo-Renaissance building housing the East Slovak Museum

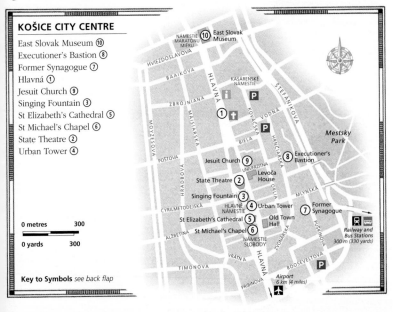

KOŠICE CITY CENTRE

East Slovak Museum ⑩
Executioner's Bastion ⑧
Former Synagogue ⑦
Hlavná ①
Jesuit Church ⑨
Singing Fountain ③
St Elizabeth's Cathedral ⑤
St Michael's Chapel ⑥
State Theatre ②
Urban Tower ④

0 metres 300
0 yards 300

Key to Symbols *see back flap*

East Slovak Museum ⑩
Jesuit Church ⑨
State Theatre ②
Singing Fountain ③
Urban Tower ④
St Elizabeth's Cathedral ⑤
St Michael's Chapel ⑥
Executioner's Bastion ⑧
Levoča House
Old Town Hall
Former Synagogue ⑦

Railway and Bus Stations 300 m (330 yards)

Airport 6 km (4 miles)

Mestsky Park

Practical & Travel Information

Slovakia is a visitor-friendly destination. Numerous historic sights, good roads, efficient internal transport, tasty local food and a wide choice of accommodation options have contributed to the steadily growing number of visitors to the country. A good network of tourist information offices, found in almost every town and village, also helps to provide invaluable information and assistance to travellers.

WHEN TO VISIT

Slovakia can be visited throughout the year. Spring and autumn are a good time for nature enthusiasts to visit – ideal for mountain hikes, bike tours and cave exploration. Summertime is excellent for swimming in the numerous pools and bathing centres, and indulging in water sports on its many artificial lakes. In winter, Slovakia tempts visitors with its excellent ski slopes as well as more unusual attractions such as swimming in outdoor thermal pools.

DOCUMENTATION

Nationals of EU countries may enter Slovakia on presenting a valid passport or ID card, but if they intend to stay in the country for more than 90 days, they are required to report to the police and apply for a resident's permit. Australian, New Zealand, US, Canadian and Japanese citizens can stay in the country without a visa for a period of 90 days.

Foreigners entering the country have to carry €50, or the equivalent in any convertible currency, in the form of traveller's cheques, cash or credit cards, for each day of their intended stay (children up to the age of 16 need half this amount). This rule is, however, applied to EU citizens only in exceptional circumstances. The sum may be reduced on presentation of documents confirming advance payment for some services, such as hotel bookings or car hire.

Customs regulations do not apply to visitors from within the EU as long as they stay within the EU guidelines for personal use.

VISITOR INFORMATION

Local tourist information centres provide details on accommodation and the region's attractions, as well as popular cultural and sporting events. The most reliable information can be obtained from the **Asociácia Informačných Centier Slovenska** (AICES) affiliated offices. Many places also have their own information centres providing similar services. These may also sell parking permits and local discount cards to tourists and exchange foreign currency. In some of these centres (although very few) it is even possible to book accommodation. The **Bratislavská Informačná Služba** (BIS) in Bratislava is specifically set up to help visitors, providing maps and booking information.

However, almost none of the maps, guidebooks and information brochures that can be obtained from tourist information offices are free of charge; the best visitors can hope to be given for free are a few pamphlets.

Tourist information offices are usually open from 9am to 5pm, although some of them close for an hour at lunchtime. On Saturdays many offices close at 1pm and many remain closed on Sundays. The staff usually speak English and German.

HEALTH AND SECURITY

In emergencies and life-threatening situations, EU nationals with an EHIC (European Health Insurance Card) are entitled to free medical treatment, but in all other cases, hospitalization or medical help has to be paid for. *Lekareň* (pharmacies) can be found in all towns and villages and are open from 8am to 6pm. Large towns also have 24-hour pharmacies.

Visitors to Slovakia do not require any immunizations or vaccinations. Drinking water is safe but mineral water is also widely available.

In Slovakia, crime directed at visitors remains relatively rare. Slovaks would usually prefer to resolve disagreements by way of negotiation rather than open confrontation. The best way for visitors to protect themselves against losing documents, cash or other valuables is for them to take a few basic precautions, particularly in crowded places.

FACILITIES FOR THE DISABLED

Facilities for the disabled are limited in Slovakia, although buildings are gradually being adapted to their needs. Most trains have

---

THE CLIMATE OF SLOVAKIA

Slovakia has a continental climate with fairly hot summers and cold winters. Temperatures in summer, between June and August, can reach 20° C (68° F), and fall to -2° C (28° F) in winter, between November and February. Spring and autumn usually experience pleasant and mild weather.

BRATISLAVA

°C/F	Apr	Jul	Oct	Jan
high	16/61	23/73	15/59	
		16/61		
low	6/43		7/45	2/36
				-3/27
sunshine (hrs)	7 hrs	9 hrs	5 hrs	2 hrs
rainfall (mm)	42 mm	73 mm	54 mm	43 mm
month	Apr	Jul	Oct	Jan

0°C / 32°F

wheelchair access to at least one carriage, but it is often difficult to get through the station to reach the carriage.

BANKING AND CURRENCY

The national currency of Slovakia is the euro. Most Slovak banks are open from 8am to 5pm and accept traveller's cheques, which can also be cashed in exchange bureaus. An increasing number of services and retail outlets now accept credit card payments. It is easy to find a bank for exchanging or withdrawing money in towns and tourist resorts. The most common are branches of large banks such as **Slovenská Sporiteľňa**, **VÚB** and **Tatra Banka**. Slovak banks are generally open from 8am to 5pm.

COMMUNICATIONS

Slovak telephone and postal services are widely available and efficient and are usually open from 8am to 5pm. Public phones are mostly in good working order, and making a local or international call is fairly easy. Payphones in Slovakia are both coin- and card-operated. The service is

quick and efficient, but not all public telephones allow international calls. Those that do not allow outgoing calls to international and mobile numbers are marked with an orange sticker. Post offices can be found in all towns and larger villages. A poste restante service is available in the main post office in every major town and city.

ARRIVING BY AIR

Bratislava's **M R Štefánika Airport** is served by airlines from all over Europe, but the most popular are **Air Slovakia**, **Czech Airlines**, **Austrian Airlines**, **RyanAir**, **Aeroflot**, **Lufthansa** and **KLM**. Visitors to southern Slovakia can fly to Vienna's **Schwechat International Airport**, less than 50 km (30 miles) from the border, while those heading for northern Slovakia can consider taking a flight to Cracow in Poland, which is closer than Bratislava, and head south from there.

Low-cost airlines offer a good range of deals on flights to Prague, Brno, Bratislava and Cracow in Poland, and the number of routes is steadily increasing.

Bratislava's airport is 12 km (7 miles) from the city centre. Vienna's airport also operates a bus service to Bratislava.

RAIL TRAVEL

Trains in Slovakia are run by **ŽSR** (Želenice Slovenskej Republiky). Travelling by train is more comfortable than by coach, but it should be stressed that standard fares on international train routes are usually very high – so travelling by air might not cost much more. Discounted fares may be available on advance bookings or with concessions. The main train station in Slovakia is the **Bratislava Main Train Station**.

TRAVELLING BY COACH

Visitors can travel to Slovakia by coaches operated by international carriers. These run scheduled services between **Autobusová Stanica Bratislava** and major European cities. Travelling by coach is generally less expensive than by air, but it may be less comfortable, and takes much longer. The coaches on international routes are well equipped with air conditioning.

DIRECTORY

DOCUMENTATION

www.slovakia.org
www.ec.europa.eu

VISITOR INFORMATION

www.slovakia.travel

Asociácia Informačných Centier Slovenska
www.aices.sk

Bratislavská Informačná Služba
www.bkis.sk

EMBASSIES

United Kingdom
Panská 16, 814 99,
Bratislava.
Tel (02) 5998 2000.

United States
Hviezdoslavovo námestie 4, 811 02, Bratislava.
Tel (02) 5443 3338.

EMERGENCY NUMBERS

Ambulance
Tel 155, 112.

Fire
Tel 150, 112.

Police
Tel 158, 112.

BANKING AND CURRENCY

Slovenská Sporiteľňa
Suché Mýto 6, Bratislava.
www.slsp.sk

Tatra Banka
Hodžovo námestie 3,
Bratislava.
www.tatrabanka.sk

VÚB
Mlynské Nivy, 1829 90,
Bratislava. www.vub.sk

ARRIVING BY AIR

Air Slovakia
www.airslovakia.sk

Aeroflot
www.aeroflot.ru

Austrian Airlines
www.aua.com

Czech Airlines
www.czechairlines.com

KLM
www.klm.com

Lufthansa
www.lufthansa.com

M R Štefánika Airport
www.letiskobratislava.sk

RyanAir
www.ryanair.com

Schwechat International Airport
www.viennaairport.com

RAIL TRAVEL

Bratislava Main Train Station
Predstaničné námestie 1,
Bratislava.
Tel (02) 5341 3173.

ŽSR
www.zsr.sk

TRAVELLING BY COACH

Autobusová Stanica Bratislava
Mlynské Nivy 31,
821 09, Bratislava.
Tel (972) 222 222.
www.slovaklines.sk

Shopping & Entertainment

Shops in Slovakia range from small local outlets and stalls in bazaars and markets to department stores and supermarkets belonging to large international chains. The country is famed for its handcrafted goods such as traditional clothing, tablecloths, lace, wooden or china figurines, sculptures, ceramics and paintings. Slovakia also has wide-ranging cultural entertainment that should satisfy most visitors. There are scores of theatres, cinemas, clubs, concert halls, art galleries and museums. Visitors can catch world-class artistes in larger cities, or traditional folk festivals in provincial areas.

OPENING HOURS

Shops in Slovakia are generally open from 9am to 6pm, although some food stores open as early as 6am and do not close until 8 or 9pm. Some shops are open on Saturdays and Sundays, usually till 1pm. Many close for lunch, which lasts from noon till 1pm, or longer.

MARKETS

In many Slovak towns and villages the traditional market day is Saturday. This is the best opportunity to buy fresh local fruit, vegetables and meat. The most famous weekly produce market takes place in Hlavné námestie and Františkánské námestie *(see pp302–303)*, the twin central market squares in Bratislava.

Slovak markets are also a great place to taste local delicacies, such as *lokša* (potato pancakes) and *langoš* (fried garlic cakes) and sample local wines.

HANDICRAFTS

Slovakia is rich in culture and traditions, most of which have been carefully preserved by the conscientious people.

Typical crafts include handmade dolls dressed in traditional costume, embroidered tablecloths, carved wooden figurines, painted Easter eggs, dolls made of dried corn leaves or wire, and secular or religious paintings on glass, wood or ceramic. Slovak artists are also renowned for their woodcarvings, mostly depicting saints and nativity

figures. Hand-carved nativity scenes are quite expensive but make superb and unique souvenirs that last for decades. Traditional crafts and art products can be bought relatively easily in larger towns and tourist resorts at shops such as **U Žofky** in Bratislava, or **Kora** in Bojnice. **UL'UV Stores** (Centre for Folk Art Production) is a chain of stores specializing in Slovak handicrafts that has branches in Bratislava, Banská Bystrica and Trnava.

ART AND ANTIQUES

Slovakia is renowned for its colourful ceramicware. Majolica from Modra (western Slovakia) is sold in most towns, although the best selection is available in **Benekit v.o.s.**, **Corvus**, **Folk – Folk** and **LÚČ Vydavateľské Družstvo** in Bratislava.

Starožitnosti (antique shops) are found in most towns, and there are many interesting items that can be picked up for a good bargain. **Hubová** in Bratislava also offers a wide array of antiques.

FOOD AND DRINK

Shops sell a variety of traditional local food products, including a varied and delicious range of cheeses and a wide variety of wines, beers and spirits.

Sheep cheeses to try include *brynza*, smoked *oštiepky* and steamed *pařenice*. Those who enjoy good liquor might like to bring home a few bottles of local wine, liqueurs, the famous plum brandy *slivovice* or cognac. They are all

relatively inexpensive. The bottled Slovak Zlatý bažant beer is excellent.

NIGHTLIFE

Bratislava pulsates with life around the clock. From April until early October countless outdoor bars and music venues spring up around the city. The focus of social life in the evenings is the bars and pubs in Korzo, on the outskirts of the Old Town. Visitors interested in partying can venture into a fashionable discotheque or visit one of the capital's music clubs housed, for example, in post-Communist nuclear shelters. The flourishing nightlife is encouraged by the relatively low prices of drinks.

The best-known and most popular clubs and discos in Bratislava include: **17's Bar** and **Harley Davidson** for rock, **Café Kút** for reggae, **Jazz Café** for jazz, **Cirkus Barok**, which is situated on a boat, **Flamenco** for Latino disco and **Laverna Klub** for disco.

Nightlife is not limited to the capital city – those who enjoy spending their time in clubs can also find something to their liking in Košice, Trnava and in the foothills of the Tatras, although the entertainment on offer is rather modest compared with that in Bratislava. Inevitably, Bratislava offers the most vibrant gay and lesbian nightlife. Two established gay clubs there are **D4** and **Apollon Gay Club**.

MUSIC AND THEATRE

The main establishments associated with classical music, opera and ballet have their homes in the capital, Bratislava. The **Slovak Philharmonic Orchestra** is housed in the Neo-Baroque Reduta *(see p308)* building, while the country's best opera and ballet theatre is the **Slovak National Theatre**.

Of the 24 national theatres in Slovakia, a few, such as the **Hungarian Theatre** and **Romany Theatre** in Košice, give performances in foreign languages, however, there are not many performances in nglish. The contemporary **storka Theatre** in Bratislava marvelous. Other theatres here include **Radošin Naive heatre**, **GUnaGU** and **T.O.K.A.**. Slovakia also hosts number of international theatre festivals, including the iennial **Bábkarska Bystrica** (festival of puppet theatres) Banská Bystrica, and aulkiar, a popular mime now, held in the **Aréna Mime Theatre** in Bratislava. Numerous music events nd festivals also take place throughout Slovakia. The most prominent are the **Bratislava Music Festival** and **Bratislava**

Jazz Days, both held in the autumn. The best-known Slovak festival of popular music is Bratislava Lyre, which was one of the flagship national entertainment events under Communist rule, and is now a nationwide song festival. The Jewish folklore music group **Pressburger Klezmer Band** often perform in festivals.

The free English-language weekly *The Slovak Spectator* and the monthly magazine *What's on – Bratislava & Slovakia* are a good source of information about the events in the capital and around the country, and contain some

good reviews. Visitors are advised to visit tourist offices for latest information.

FOLK FESTIVALS

Most folk festivals take place in summer. The **Eurofolklor International Folklore Festival** in Banská Bystrica, and the **International Historic Fencing Festival** in Spiš Castle *(see pp320–21)*, draw the biggest crowds. The Košice **Days of Traditional Folk Music** is a series of concerts, dance performances and discussions held in a number of venues across the town.

DIRECTORY

HANDICRAFTS

Kora
Hurbanovo námestie 46, 972 01 Bojnice.
Tel (04) 6541 2495.

U Žofky
Michalská 5, 811 01 Bratislava.
Tel (02) 5443 1994.

UL'UV Stores
Main store:
Obchodná 64, 816 11 Bratislava.
Tel (02) 5273 1351.

Other branches:
Dolná 14, 974 01 Banská Bystrica. *Tel (04) 8412 3657.*

Hlavná 5, 917 00 Trnava.
Tel (03) 3551 3684.
www.uluv.sk

ART AND ANTIQUES

Benekit v.o.s.
Gorkého 15, 811 01 Bratislava. *Tel (02) 5443 4029.*

Corvus
Europalia 24, 945 01 Komárno, Bratislava.
Tel (02) 9035 72125.

Hubová
Zochova 1013/8, 026 01 Dolný Kubín, Bratislava.
Tel (09) 0556 6116.

Folk – Folk
Obchodná 24, 811 01 Bratislava.
Tel (02) 5443 4874.

LÚČ Vydavatelské Družstvo
Špitalská 7, 813 59 Bratislava.
Tel (02) 6042 1233.

NIGHTLIFE

17's Bar
Hviezdoslavovo námestie 17, 811 22 Bratislava.
Tel (09) 0363 7038.

Apollon Gay Club
Panenská 24, 820 00 Bratislava.
Tel (02) 9154 8031.
www.apollon-gay-club.sk

Café Kút
Zámočnícka 11, 811 03 Bratislava.
Tel (02) 5443 4957.

Cirkus Barok
Rázusovo Nábrežie 2, 811 02 Bratislava.
Tel (02) 5464 2091.

D4
Jedlíkova 9, 811 06 Bratislava.

Flamenco
Štefánikova 14, 811 05 Bratislava.
Tel (02) 9056 1290.

Harley Davidson
Rebarborová 1, 821 07 Bratislava.
Tel (02) 4319 1094.

Jazz Café
Ventúrska 5, 811 01 Bratislava.
Tel (02) 5443 4661.
www.jazz-cafe.sk

Laverna Klub
Laurinská 19, 811 02 Bratislava. *Tel (02) 5443 3165.*

MUSIC AND THEATRE

Aréna Mime Theatre
Viedenská Cesta 10, 851 01 Bratislava.
Tel (02) 6720 2557.

Astorka Theatre
Suché Mýto 17, 811 03 Bratislava. *Tel (02) 5443 2093.*

Bábkarska Bystrica
Marionet's Festival
www.BDNR.sk

Bratislava Jazz Days
www.bjd.sk

Bratislava Music Festival
Michalská 10, 811 03 Bratislava.
Tel (02) 5443 0378.
www.bhsfestival.sk

GUnaGU
Na Františkánskom námestie 7, Bratislava.
Tel (02) 5443 3335.

Hungarian Theatre
Thalia Mojmirova 3, 04001 Košice.
Tel (055) 622 5866.
www.thaliaszinhaz.sk

Pressburger Klezmer Band
www.klezmer.sk

Radošin Naive Theatre
Škultétyho 5, 831 04 Bratislava.
Tel (02) 5556 3508.

Romany Theatre
Stefanikova 4, 040 01 Košice. *Tel (055) 622 4980.* www.romathan.sk

Slovak National Theatre
Gorkého 4, 811 02 Bratislava. *Tel (02) 5443 3083.* www.snd.sk

Slovak Philharmonic Orchestra
Palackého 2, 811 02 Bratislava. *Tel (02) 5920 8233.* www.filharm.sk

S.T.O.K.A.
Pribinova 1, P.O.Box 235, 810 00 Bratislava.
Tel (09) 0521 1031.

FOLK FESTIVALS

Days of Traditional Folk Music
www.cassovia.sk

Eurofolklor International Folklore Festival
www.sosbb.sk

International Historic Fencing Festival
www.spisskyhrad.sk

Where to Stay in Slovakia

Finding accommodation in Slovakia is unlikely to be a problem, even in small villages. Large towns, popular resorts and tourist regions offer a variety of options for all budgets – from large international chains and smart luxury hotels set in historic buildings, to humble hostels and lodges.

PRICE CATEGORIES
Price categories are for a double room per night in high season, including breakfast, tax and service charges.

€ under 65 euros
€€ 65–130 euros
€€€ 130–200 euros
€€€€ 200–265 euros
€€€€€ over 265 euros

BRATISLAVA

Botel Marina
€€   Map A5

Nábrežie arm gen L. Svobodu, 811 02 **Tel** *(02) 5464 1804* **Fax** *(02) 5464 1771* **Rooms** *32*

This four-star hotel is attractively located on a boat moored off the left bank of the Danube, under Bratislava Castle *(see p305)*. It offers comfortable cabins and suites with air conditioning, Internet access and a minibar. There is a nightclub on board. **www.botelmarina.sk**

Devin
€€€   Map C5

Riečna 4, 811 02 **Tel** *(02) 5998 5111* **Fax** *(02) 5443 0858* **Rooms** *94*

Devin is located in the historic centre of Bratislava, on the banks of the Danube. The comfortable rooms are furnished in wood and other natural materials, and have state-of-the-art facilities as well as views of the Danube and the castle. The hotel also plays host to heads of government during state visits. **www.hoteldevin.sk**

Radisson SAS Carlton Hotel
€€€   Map C5

Hviezdoslavovo námestie 3, 811 02 **Tel** *(02) 5939 0000* **Fax** *(02) 5939 0010* **Rooms** *168*

Situated in the heart of town, near the Slovak National Theatre *(see p308)*, the Carlton is housed in an imposing building. Each floor is dedicated to a famous composer and one suite is named after Maria Theresa, the first woman to rule the Habsburg Empire. The Mirror Bar serves fantastic cocktails. **www.bratislava.radissonsas.com**

Danube
€€€€   Map B5

Rybné námestie 1, 813 38 **Tel** *(02) 5934 0000* **Fax** *(02) 5441 4311* **Rooms** *276*

This is a top-class hotel in the heart of Bratislava's Old Town *(see pp302–303)*, with a splendid view over the Danube and the castle. It offers air-conditioned rooms with all facilities, a restaurant and bar, excellent service and a friendly atmosphere, all of which contribute to a truly enjoyable stay. **www.hoteldanube.com**

Marrol's
€€€€   Map D5

Tobrucká 4, 811 02 **Tel** *(02) 5778 4600* **Fax** *(02) 5778 4601* **Rooms** *42*

At once modern and retro, this is one of the city's most exclusive hotels, situated close to the Old Bridge (Starý Most). It offers a range of beautiful rooms and three spectacular suites, and organizes numerous events to entertain guests. It also has a private taxi service. **www.marrols.sk**

FURTHER AFIELD Echo
€

Prešovská 39, 821 08 **Tel** *(02) 5556 9170* **Fax** *(02) 5556 9174* **Rooms** *34*

This hotel is situated on the eastern edge of the city centre. All the rooms are clean, comfortable and have satellite TV, telephone and an en suite bathroom. The lobby has free Wi-Fi access. The hotel's restaurant serves breakfast, lunch and dinner. The cuisine served is Italian and duck is the chef's speciality. **www.hotelecho.sk**

FURTHER AFIELD Turist
€

Ondavská 5, 822 05 **Tel** *(02) 5557 2789* **Fax** *(02) 5557 3180* **Rooms** *99*

About 2 km (1 mile) from the historic town centre, this hotel offers plain yet comfortable rooms at reasonable prices. All rooms have balconies; some even have their own refrigerators. There are also many amenities nearby, including a park, swimming pool, skating rink and bowling alley. **www.turist.sk**

FURTHER AFIELD Sorea
€€

Kráľovské údolie 6, 811 02 **Tel** *(02) 5441 4442* **Fax** *(02) 5441 1017* **Rooms** *39*

Standing to the west of the castle, surrounded by greenery, this hotel is a 10-minute walk from the city centre. Belonging to the Slovak Sorea chain, it offers modern, well-kept rooms and a breakfast bar. The Vitalcentre spa offers a sauna, massage facilities and a range of individual treatments. **www.sorea.sk**

FURTHER AFIELD Apartmánový Hotel Residence Sulekova
€€€

Šulekova 20, 811 06 **Tel** *(02) 5441 9383* **Fax** *(02) 5441 9388* **Rooms** *32*

The only hotel of its kind in Bratislava, this place offers beautifully fitted apartments with modern decor, complete with kitchen and minibar. Part of the Ma Maison chain, which operates hotels in the capital cities in Central Europe, there are special discounts for visitors planning to stay for extended periods. **www.residence-sulekova.com**

Map References *see map of Bratislava pp300–301*

FURTHER AFIELD Best Western Hotel West

Česta na Kamzik, 833 29 **Tel** *(02) 5478 8692* **Fax** *(02) 5477 7781* **Rooms** *49*

The hotel stands in a forested area northwest of the city, close to the mountains. Since 1999 it has been part of the international Best Western chain, which guarantees a high standard of service. The rooms are luxuriously furnished. The somewhat imposing in-house restaurant serves a wide variety of dishes. **www.hotel-west.sk**

REST OF SLOVAKIA

BANSKÁ BYSTRICA Hotel Lux

Nám Slobody 2, 974 00 **Tel** *(048) 414 4141* **Fax** *(048) 414 3853* **Rooms** *141*

Situated in the town centre, this modern, high-rise hotel has been in business for many years and offers pleasant rooms and excellent, professional service. The restaurant serves a wide selection of Slovak and international dishes, with the option of dining out on a terrace in summer. **www.hotellux.sk**

BANSKÁ BYSTRICA Horský Hotel Šachtička

Šachtička, 974 01 **Tel** *(048) 414 1911* **Fax** *(048) 414 5670* **Rooms** *47*

The hotel has both rooms and apartments and is set amidst beautiful mountain scenery, in the Tatras, about 10 km (6 miles) from Banská Bystrica. It has a restaurant offering Slovak and international cuisine as well as a swimming pool, sauna, massage tub and fitness centre. **www.sachticka.sk**

BOJNICE Hotel Pod Zámkom

Hurbanovo námestie 2, 972 01 **Tel** *(046) 518 5100* **Fax** *(046) 540 2582* **Rooms** *67*

Standing in the town centre by the castle walls, Hotel Pod Zámkom (under the castle) belongs to the European Wellness chain. A variety of pleasantly furnished rooms are available and the hotel prides itself on its excellent service. **www.hotelpodzamkom.sk**

BOJNICE Kaskáda

Jánošíková 1301/24, 972 01 **Tel** *(046) 518 3010* **Fax** *(046) 540 2793* **Rooms** *70*

This is a modern hotel with an Aquacentre boasting a pool, hydro-massage, sauna and solarium. The comfortable rooms and apartments offer satellite TV, Internet connection and a minibar. The popular restaurant, Kontesa de Jean Ville, serves international and Slovak cuisine, accompanied by top-quality wines. **www.kaskada.sk**

KOŠICE Best Western Hotel Teledom

Timonova 27, 040 01 **Tel** *(055) 327 4401* **Fax** *(055) 327 4444* **Rooms** *20*

This three-star hotel and conference centre is located in the southwest part of the Old Town. The rooms are well equipped and decorated in muted colours. Air-conditioned suites are also available, some of them intended for non-smokers. **www.hotel.teledom.sk**

KOŠICE Dália

Löfflerova 1, 040 01 **Tel** *(055) 632 5949* **Fax** *(055) 633 1717* **Rooms** *11*

Located to the east of the Old Town, this hotel is aimed at visitors who favour a quiet, family atmosphere. Attractive, tastefully furnished rooms create a feeling of total comfort. The Dália restaurant offers a wide selection of vegetarian dishes along with Slovak and international dishes. There is also a sauna. **www.hoteldalia.sk**

KOŠICE Hotel Ambassador

Hlavná 101, 040 01 **Tel** *(055) 720 3720* **Fax** *(055) 720 3727* **Rooms** *14*

At the centre of Košice, the Ambassador is a modern hotel offering simple and comfortably furnished rooms and suites. All have en suite bathrooms, satellite TV, video, Wi-Fi and refrigerators. In summer, a popular café with outdoor seating opens on Košice's atmospheric main street. **www.abba.sk**

LEVOČA Arkáda

Námestie Majstra Pavla 26, 054 01 **Tel** *(053) 451 2372* **Fax** *(053) 451 2255* **Rooms** *32*

Set in Levoča's historic town square *(see p318)*, the Arkáda is housed in an imposing Gothic building. The hotel was modernized in the 1990s. All the rooms in the hotel are bright and airy and have en suite bathrooms. **www.arkada.sk**

TRNAVA Penzion U MaMi

Jeruzalemská 3, 917 01 **Tel** *(033) 535 4216* **Fax** *(033) 535 4217* **Rooms** *14*

Situated in a peaceful street close to the Archbishop's Palace and Church of St Nicholas *(see p310)*, this hotel has 11 en suite rooms and three suites, all comfortably furnished. The restaurant is open only to residents. The fitness centre can be used free of charge by guests. **www.penzionumami.sk**

TRNAVA Dream

Kapitulská 12, 917 01 **Tel** *(033) 592 4111* **Fax** *(033) 592 4115* **Rooms** *23*

The Dream is attractively located in a smartly painted historic building, offering stylishly furnished rooms and suites with air conditioning and Internet access. The restaurant offers a large selection of Slovak and international cuisine, plus a good choice of wines. **www.hoteldream.sk**

Key to Symbols *see back cover flap*

Where to Eat in Slovakia

The standard of eating places in Slovakia has improved significantly in recent years. Many new restaurants are appearing, often serving modern versions of traditional Slovak dishes, or very hearty soups. Slovaks enjoy eating out and visitors will find that traditional eateries and pubs are usually busy and welcoming.

PRICE CATEGORIES
Based on the price per person of a three-course meal with half a bottle of wine, including cover charge, service and tax.

€ under 7 euros
€€ 7–20 euros
€€€ 20–35 euros
€€€€ over 35 euros

BRATISLAVA

Bagel & Coffee Story   €
Štúrova 13, 811 02 **Tel** *(02) 5263 1656*   **Map** E5

A classic American-style restaurant, this place offers bagel sandwiches with a variety of fillings, including French, Italian and vegetarian salads and a fantastic selection of drinks ranging from cappuccinos, lattes and flavoured coffees to milkshakes and fresh juices. Several other branches are spread across the city.

Chez David   €€
Zámocká 13, 811 01 **Tel** *(02) 5441 3824*   **Map** A4

Near Bratislava Castle *(see p305)*, Chez David is a well-established kosher restaurant, specializing in cuisine from Europe and Israel, though there are dishes from other parts of the world, too. It serves kosher wines and organizes regular performances of Jewish music.

Slovenská Reštaurácia   €€
Hviezdoslavovo námestie 20, 811 02 **Tel** *(02) 5443 4883*   **Map** C5

Located near the National Theatre and Opera House, Slovenská Reštaurácia has won many awards for its contemporary and traditional Slovak cuisine, which includes a variety of creamy meat as well as potato dishes. It also has an extensive wine list.

Mezzo-Mezzo   €€€
Rybárska Brána 9, 811 01 **Tel** *(02) 5443 4393*   **Map** C4

A modern restaurant near the Slovenská Reštaurácia, Mezzo-Mezzo focuses on meat dishes, fish and spaghetti. Visitors should try the grilled octopus, served with toasted baguette and salsa. A soothing decor and attentive service make this a good place to enjoy an expansive evening meal. Breakfast is also served.

Tempus Fugit   €€€
Sedlárska 5, 811 01 **Tel** *(02) 5441 4357*   **Map** C4

Attractively located in a 14th-century Gothic building in the Old Town, this restaurant's leisurely charm belies its name, literally "time flies". The menu is contemporary and includes dishes such as roast suckling-pig and smoked salmon with avocado and crayfish. Cigars are also available.

Francúzska reštaurácia   €€€€
Riečna 4, 811 02 **Tel** *(02) 5998 5852*   **Map** C5

This French restaurant in the Devin Hotel *(see p328)* is very popular with locals and visitors alike for its international cuisine. Highlights include breast of duck in orange served with home-made pasta. Quality French and Slovak wines add to its appeal.

Le Monde   €€€€
Rybárská Brána 8, 811 01 **Tel** *(02) 5441 5411*   **Map** C4

Occupying a historic house, this restaurant and bar specializes in French cuisine, but also serves fare from Asia, Central Europe, Scandinavia and the Mediterranean. Main courses include classic game, duck and steak dishes, and there is a mouth-watering selection of desserts.

Romeo e Giulietta   €€€€
Rybné námestie 1, 813 38 **Tel** *(02) 5934 0812*   **Map** B5

In the Danube hotel *(see p328)*, Romeo e Giulietta is run by native Italians. It offers all types of pasta and risotto, grilled lamb and delicious tiramisu in a relaxed and quiet atmosphere. Its wine cellar is well stocked with Italian as well as Slovak wines. Closed on Sunday for lunch and dinner.

FURTHER AFIELD Caribic's   €€
Žižková 1/A, 811 02 **Tel** *(02) 5441 8334*

Located at the foot of Bratislava Castle, this restaurant is unusual in offering Caribbean cuisine, dominated by fish and seafood. Highlights include fish baked in banana leaf, salmon steak tartare with sesame oil and steamed fresh crayfish.

Map References *see map of Bratislava pp300–301*

FURTHER AFIELD Preégo

...inská 4, 811 08 **Tel** *(02) 5262 5702*

...is award-winning restaurant and café, with modern interior decor and international cuisine, grows ever more ...pular. The chef's specialities include beef steak with spinach, and salmon steak in cream sauce with prawns, ...I and white wine.

FURTHER AFIELD Traja Mušketieri €€

...ádkovičova 7, 811 04 **Tel** *(02) 5443 0019*

...med after the novel by noted French writer Alexander Dumas, the Three Musketeers restaurant is decorated in ...uis XIV style. The menu gives names of dishes straight from the era of the Sun King, such as valet Mousqueton's ...ultry pâté with prunes and pistachios; or Koketa – roast chicken breasts in sesame oil.

FURTHER AFIELD Poľovinka reštuarácia sv Huberta €€€

...ulovo námestie 1, 821 08 **Tel** *(02) 5596 8550*

...ne of the best of its kind in Slovakia, this huntsman-style restaurant in the Apollo Hotel is decorated with ...merous hunting trophies. The menu dominated by game (venison, pheasant and wild boar) also features a ...I list of the best Slovak and Moravian wines. The staff are friendly.

EST OF SLOVAKIA

BANSKÁ BYSTRICA Hotel Šachtička ©

...chtičky 34, 974 01 **Tel** *(048) 414 1911*

...cated in the attractive winter sports centre in Banská Bystrica, the huge windows here offer superb views over ...e surrounding wooded mountain slopes. The restaurant serves Slovak and international cuisine and has a Gypsy ...nd playing most nights.

BANSKÁ BYSTRICA Hotel Dixon €€

...ermová 32, 974 04 **Tel** *(048) 413 0808*

...hotel-cum-restaurant located close to the winter sports complex, this is an excellent venue for business meetings ...d banquets offering both Slovak and international cuisine at reasonable prices. Although the restaurant is large, ...warm colours and softly lit interiors create an intimate atmosphere.

BANSKÁ BYSTRICA Lux €€€

...ámestie Slobody 2, 974 00 **Tel** *(048) 4144 14145*

...x is located in the hotel of the same name in the town centre, with attractive views over the Old Town. The menu ...cludes a wide range of vegetarian options, alongside dishes such as Côte d'Azur duck breast in orange sauce, ...ef, veal and pork and home-made desserts.

KOŠICE 12 Apoštolov €€

...ováčska 51, 040 01 **Tel** *(055) 729 5105*

...cated in Košice's Old Town in a 14th-century burgher's house, 12 Apoštolov (Twelve Apostles) has been ...business since 1910. It has a snug interior and an extensive menu and wine list, featuring both Slovak and foreign ...fferings. The chef's specialities include breast of duck with almonds and orange salsa and turkey roulade.

KOŠICE Krčma Letna €€

...tná 1, 040 01 **Tel** *(055) 633 3405*

...is is one of the best restaurants in Košice for traditional Slovak cuisine, supplemented by international dishes. ...ouse specials include breast of duck with pineapple sauce, beans and potatoes, and foie gras with Cumberland ...uce. It offers as many as 180 Slovak and French wines.

KOŠICE Monte Bianco €€

...ováčska 11, 040 01 **Tel** *(055) 625 2145*

...n Italian restaurant in the town centre, Monte Bianco can claim a pleasant atmosphere and efficient service as ...ell as a large selection of Italian dishes and wines. The panna cotta and other Italian desserts are highly recom-...ended. In summer visitors can sit outdoors on an attractive terrace.

KOŠICE Uhorsky Dvor €€€

...očná 10, 040 01 **Tel** *(055) 728 8493*

...ošice has a large Hungarian community and this restaurant offers the best of their cuisine. The dining room is ...ecorated in traditional folk-Hungarian style; there is also a beer-hall serving grilled meats. Chicken legs cooked in ...ark beer with dry plums and bacon go down well with locals and visitors alike. Vegetarian dishes are also available.

LEVOČA Reštaurácia u 3 apoštolov €€

...ámestie Majstra Pavla 11, 054 01 **Tel** *(053) 451 2302*

...is is an elegant restaurant located in Levoča's historic town centre. It offers extremely well-prepared dishes ...presenting traditional Slovak cuisine, including a large selection of fish at reasonable prices, and vegetarian dishes. ...is is a good place to sample local staples such *bryndzové halušky* (cheesy gnocchi) and spicy spiš sausages.

Key to Symbols *see back cover flap*

HUNGARY

*U*niquely in Central Europe, Hungary is peopled by descendants of Magyars, a race from Central Asia who settled here in the 9th century. In recent times, the country has fought against Ottoman, German, Austrian and Soviet occupiers, yet its indigenous culture remains intact. In 1989 Hungary became the first Eastern Bloc country to embrace Western-style democracy.

Hungary has a varied landscape, with forests and mountains dominating the north and a vast plain covering the rest of the country. The Tisza river and its tributaries shape the eastern regions, while the west has Lake Balaton, one of the largest lakes in Europe. The mighty Danube flows through the heart of the country, bisecting the capital, Budapest, where one-fifth of the population lives.

HISTORY

In AD 100 the Romans established the town of Aquincum near modern-day Budapest, and ruled the area, then called Pannonia, for three centuries. They withdrew completely following the arrival of the Huns in the early 5th century. After the death of Attila the Hun in 453, the area was ruled by the Goths, the Lombards and the Avars. The ancestors of the modern Hungarians, the Magyars, migrated from the Urals in 896, under the leadership of Prince Árpád, whose dynasty lasted until 1301, when King András III died without leaving an heir. The throne then passed to a series of foreign kings, but the country flourished, and during the reign of Mátyás Corvinus (r. 1458–90) it became the greatest monarchy in Central Europe. The Ottomans won a major victory at the Battle of Mohács in 1526. They returned to capture Buda in 1541, which became the capital of

View from Castle Hill across the Danube, with the Parliament visible beyond Elizabeth Bridge, Budapest

The grand Széchenyi Baths in Városliget, Budapest

Ottoman Hungary. To quell their advance, the Austrians, under Ferdinand of Habsburg, occupied western Hungary, while the central plains stayed under Ottoman control; the eastern region, including Transylvania, became a semi-autonomous land, tied to the Ottomans. Christian armies led by the Habsburgs finally defeated the Ottomans in 1686. Economic prosperity came with Austrian rule, but nationalism was suppressed, which led to a major uprising in 1848. After crushing the rebellion, Emperor Franz Joseph I sought to unite the two nations, and so created the Dual Monarchy of Austro-Hungary in 1867. Following World War I, the Habsburg Empire was dismantled, and

Mátyás Corvinus,
King of Hungary

Hungary lost two-thirds of its territor to the "successor states" of Yugoslavi Czechoslovakia and Romania. It was regain these territories th Hungary backed German in World War II, but in 194 Budapest was occupied the Soviets. The subseque Communist rule was rutl lessly upheld, most visib in 1956 when demon strations were crushed Soviet tanks. Nevertheles free elections took plac in 1989, resulting i victory for the democra opposition. Since then, th country has invested in tourism, whic is now a major source of income.

LANGUAGE AND CULTURE

Modern Hungarian derives from language originally spoken by th Finno-Ugric tribes of the Ural

Exploring Hungary

Located in the heart of Central Europe, Budapest is the perfect base for exploring Hungary. Szentendre, with its Serbian religious art, is a short drive north. Pécs, a treasure trove of European history, lies to the south, while the popular town of Eger in the wine-producing area is to the east. The country has an excellent rail network and fares are low while the road infrastructure has expanded in recent years.

SIGHTS AT A GLANCE

olk dancers performing at a wine festival, Tihany

KEY DATES IN HUNGARIAN HISTORY

c. AD 100 Romans establish Aquincum

c. 410 Huns overrun the region

896 Magyar tribes arrive

1001 Coronation of Stephen I (István), Hungary's first king

1300s Angevin rule begins

1458–90 Reign of Mátyás Corvinus

1526 Ottomans win the Battle of Mohács

1526–41 Ottomans conquer Buda three times

1541 Start of Ottoman rule

1686 Habsburg troops enter Buda, ending Turkish rule in Hungary

1848 Hungarian Nationalist Uprising

1867 Compromise with Austria gives Hungary independence in internal affairs

1873 Buda and Pest become Budapest

1918 With the break-up of the Austro-Hungarian Empire, Hungary gains independence after nearly 400 years of foreign rule

1941 Hungary enters World War II

1945 Soviet Army takes Budapest

1956 The Soviet suppresses a nationalist uprising

1989 Hungary proclaimed a democratic republic

2004 Hungary becomes a member of the EU

raditional peasant culture was all but destroyed in the 20th century, but folk ongs and dances still survive. Musically, the country has produced everal famous composers, including ranz Liszt and Béla Bartók, while in terature, powerful voices include Tibor Déry and István Örkény. Hungary is lso known for its beer and meat-based lishes, the latter spiced with paprika, he country's most famous export.

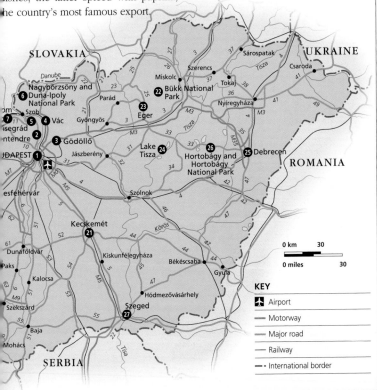

KEY

Airport

Motorway

Major road

Railway

International border

Budapest ●

Budapest was founded in 1873 after the unification of three separate towns – Buda and Obuda on the west bank of the Danube, and Pest on the east. All three towns developed in the second half of the 12th century; Buda became the seat of Hungary's rulers in 1247. A period of Turkish rule from 1541 to 1686 left few traces, except for the city's wonderful bathhouses. Now home to two million people, Budapest is considered one of the most beautiful cities in Europe. Most of the historic sights lie along the banks of the Danube, including the Neo-Classical Parliament, Neo-Gothic Mátyás Church and the Hungarian National Museum.

0 metres   50●
0 yards   500

SIGHTS AT A GLANCE

Budapest History
  Museum ②
Gellért Hill
  see pp344–7 ⑥
Great Synagogue ⑰
Heroes' Square ⑲
Holy Trinity Square ④
Hungarian National
  Gallery ①
Hungarian National
  Museum ⑯
Inner City Parish Church ⑬
Jewish Quarter ⑱
Margaret Island ㉔
Mátyás Church see pp342–3 ⑤
Mátyás Fountain ③
Museum of Applied Arts ⑮
Museum of Fine Arts ⑳
Parliament see pp348–9 ⑦
Roosevelt Square ⑧
State Opera House ⑩
St Stephen's Basilica ⑨
Széchenyi Baths ㉒
University Church ⑭
Váci Utca ⑫
Vajdahunyad Castle ㉓
Városliget ㉑
Vigadó Square ⑪

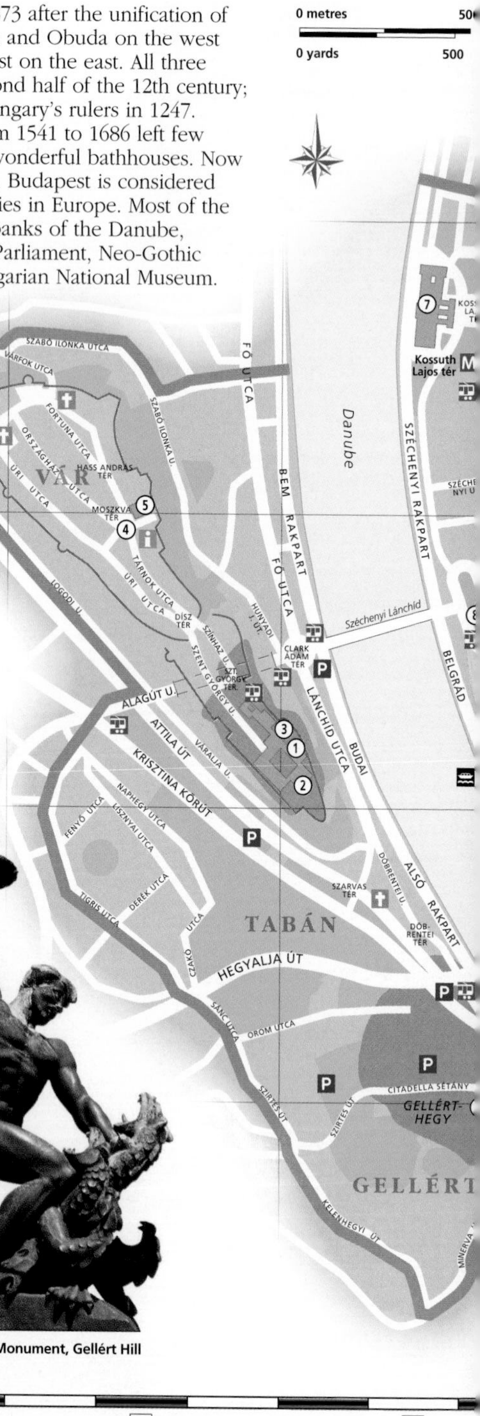

Sculpture at the foot of Liberation Monument, Gellért Hill

GETTING AROUND

The best way to take in Budapest's fascinating architecture is on foot. Most sights of interest are centrally located and easily reached by trolleybus, rail or tram. Trams are a particularly efficient way of getting around as they avoid road traffic and run at frequent intervals. Three lines – yellow M1, red M2, blue M3 – serve the Pest area.

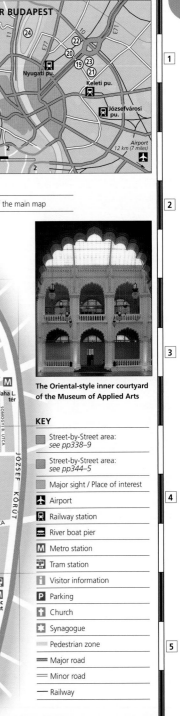

GREATER BUDAPEST

Nyugati pu.

Déli-pu.

Keleti pu.

Józsefvárosi pu.

Airport
12 km (7 miles)

0 km   2

0 miles   2

KEY

Area of the main map

The Oriental-style inner courtyard of the Museum of Applied Arts

KEY

Street-by-Street area:
see pp338–9

Street-by-Street area:
see pp344–5

Major sight / Place of interest

✈ Airport

🚉 Railway station

River boat pier

M Metro station

🚊 Tram station

ℹ Visitor information

P Parking

✝ Church

✡ Synagogue

Pedestrian zone

Major road

Minor road

Railway

SEE ALSO

- *Where to Stay* pp390–91

- *Where to Eat* pp394–5

Street-by-Street: The Royal Palace

The Royal Palace has experienced many incarnations
over the centuries. Even now it is not known exactly
where, in the 13th century, King Béla IV began
building his castle, though it is thought to be near
the site of Mátyás Church *(see pp342–3)*. The Holy
Roman Emperor Sigismund of Luxembourg built a
Gothic palace on the present site, from which today's
castle began to evolve. After the Ottoman occupation,
the Habsburgs built a monumental palace here in the
18th century. The current form dates from the
rebuilding of the 19th-century palace after
its destruction in February 1945. During the
renovation, the remains of the 15th-century
Gothic palace were exposed and archaeologists decided to showcase the defensive
walls and royal chambers in the reconstruction.

Sándor Palace

Ornamental Gateway
*Dating from 1903, this
gateway leads to the
Habsburg Steps and
the Royal Palace.
Nearby, a bronze
sculpture of the
mythical turul bird
guards the palace.*

★ **Mátyás Fountain**
*In the northern courtyard of the Royal
Palace stands the Mátyás Fountain. It
was designed by Alajos Stróbl in 1904
and depicts King Mátyás Corvinus and
his beloved Ilonka* ③

Lion Gate
*This gate, leading to the
rear courtyard of the
palace, gets its name
from the four lions
that watch over it.
These sculptures were
designed by János
Fadrusz in 1901.*

TIMELINE

	1255 First written document, a letter by King Béla IV, refers to building a fortified castle	**c. 1400** Sigismund of Luxembourg builds an ambitious Gothic palace on this site	**1541** After capturing Buda, the Ottomans use the Royal Palace to stable horses and store gunpowder	**1719** The building of a small palace begins on the ruins of the old palace, to a design by Hölbling and Fortunato de Prati	**1881** Architect Miklós Ybl begins a programme to rebuild and expand the palace
1200	**1400**		**1600**		**1800**
	c. 1356 Louis I builds a royal castle on the southern slopes of Castle Hill		**1686** The assault by Habsburg soldiers leaves the palace completely razed to the ground	**1849** The Royal Palace is destroyed again, during an unsuccessful attack by Hungarian insurgents	Turul *bird*
	1458 A Renaissance palace evolves under King Mátyás		**1749** Maria Theresa builds a vast palace comprising 203 chambers		

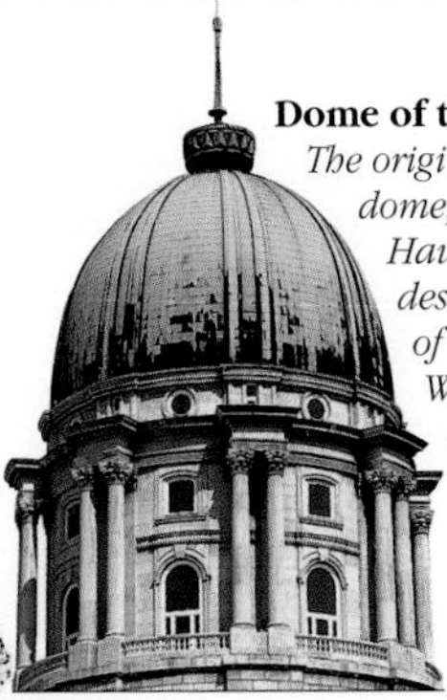

Dome of the Royal Palace
The original Neo-Baroque dome, designed by Alajos Hauszmann, was destroyed in the razing of the palace during World War II; it was later rebuilt in Neo-Classical style.

Statue of Prince Eugene of Savoy
Unveiled in 1900, this statue by József Róna commemorates the 1697 Battle of Zenta, which was a turning point in the Turkish War. The bas-reliefs on the base depict scenes from the battle.

0 metres 50
0 yards 50

★ Hungarian National Gallery
Works of art illustrating Hungary's turbulent history are displayed here. Periods of both foreign domination and patriotic home rule are brought to life through the gallery's extensive collection ①

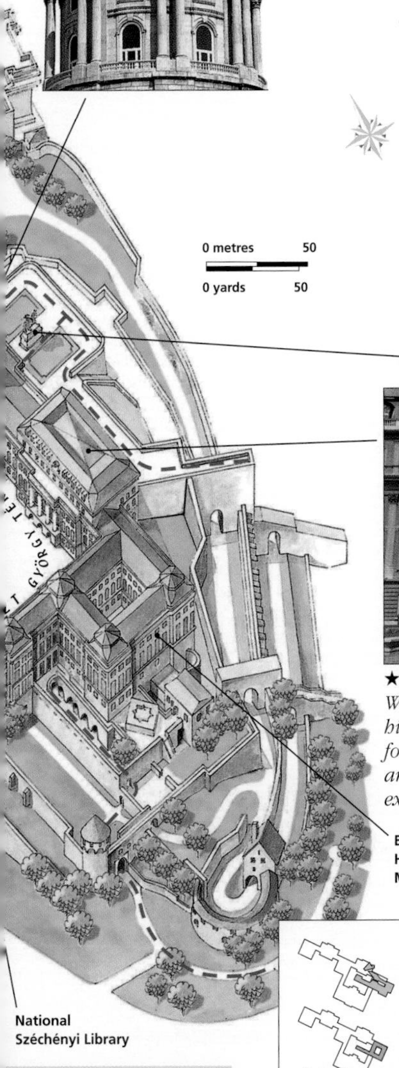

Budapest
History
Museum ②

KEY

– – – Suggested route

National
Széchényi Library

STAR FEATURES

★ Mátyás Fountain

★ Hungarian
National Gallery

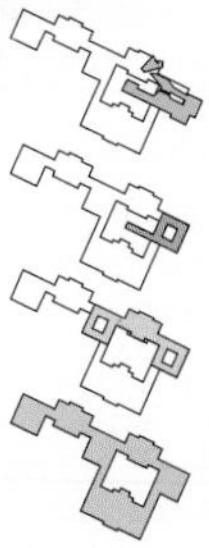

BUILDING THE ROYAL PALACE

In the early 15th century, a Gothic Royal Palace was built on the site. This was rebuilt in the Renaissance style by King Mátyás in 1458. After the Ottoman occupation, it was razed and built on a smaller scale. The palace was further developed by Queen Maria Theresa and was rebuilt again after World War II, to a design conceived in 1905.

■ 15th century	■ 1749
■ 1719	■ 1905

The Visitation (1506) by Master MS,
Hungarian National Gallery

Hungarian National Gallery ①

Magyar Nemzeti Galéria

Royal Palace, Szent György tér 2.
Map C3. **Tel** (01) 439 7325. ▥ 5,
16, 78, Várbusz. ◯ 10am–6pm
Tue–Sun. 🖾 🖪 to arrange for an
English-speaking guide call (01) 439
7326. 🖵 🛋 www.mng.hu

Established in 1957, the
Hungarian National Gallery
houses a comprehensive
collection of Hungarian art
from medieval times to the
20th century. Gathered by
various groups and institutions since 1839, these works
were previously exhibited
at the Hungarian National
Museum *(see p352)* and the
Museum of Fine Arts *(see
p354)*. The collection was
moved to the Royal Palace
(see pp338–9) in 1975.

The gallery houses six
permanent exhibitions, comprising the most valuable
and critically acclaimed
Hungarian art in the world.
Highlights include religious
artifacts spanning several
centuries, Gothic altarpieces
as well as Renaissance and
Baroque art.

The collection is spread
over three floors. On the
ground floor are early stone
and Gothic exhibits, including
sculptural and architectural
fragments discovered during
the reconstruction of the Royal
Palace. Among the star exhibits are a carved stone head
of King Béla III, from c. 1200,
the *Madonna of Bártfa*

(1465–70) and the *Madonna
of Toporc* (c. 1420). Originally
crafted for a church in Spiš
(now part of Slovakia), it is
a fine example of medieval
wood sculpture in the
Gothic style.

Late-Gothic, Renaissance,
Baroque and 19th-century
artifacts share the first floor.
The Visitation (1506) by
Master MS, a fragment of
a folding altarpiece from a
church in modern-day
Slovakia, is a delightful example of late-Gothic Hungarian
art. Several works by Mihály
Munkácsy, widely regarded as
Hungary's greatest artist, show
the development of 19th-
century historicist art and the
influence of Impressionism.
The Woman Bathing (1901),
by Károly Lotz, better known
for his frescoes, is one of the
best examples of Neo-Classical
painting in Hungary. The
painting reflects Lotz's fascination with the work of the
French painter Ingres.
Another impressive work of
art is the elaborately decorated
folding St Anne altarpiece (c.
1520) from Kisszeben.

Works from the 20th century,
including paintings and exhibits from the Art Nouveau era
as well as the Expressionist,
Surrealist and avant-garde
movements, are all showcased
on the second floor. Those
by painter Tivadar Kosztka
Csontváry give a unique,
idiosyncratic vision of the
world. Temporary exhibits are
housed on the third floor.

Budapest History Museum ②

Budapesti Történeti
Múzeum

Royal Palace, Szent György tér 2.
Map C3. **Tel** (01) 487 8800. ▥ 5,
16, 78, Várbusz. ◯ 16 May–15 Sep:
10am–6pm daily; 16 Sep–Oct & Mar–
15 May: 10am–6pm Wed–Mon;
Nov–Feb: 10am–4pm Wed–Mon. 🖾
🖪 www.btm.hu

The Budapest History
Museum, also known as Castle
Museum, holds an interesting
collection of artifacts relating
to the city's development.

The Royal Palace was
damaged during World War I
and during its reconstruction,
chambers dating from the
Middle Ages were uncovered
in the south wing. These
remarkable rooms, including
a prison cell and a chapel,
have been recreated in the
basement and provide an
insight into the character of a
much earlier castle within
today's Habsburg recon-
struction. They now house an
exhibition on the palace's
medieval history, with
weapons, seals and other
early artifacts.

The museum also has an
interesting display on
Budapest in the Middle Ages,
illustrating the evolution of the
town from its Roman origins
to a 13th-century settlement,
and one on Budapest in modern times tracing the city's history from 1686 to the present.

Fifteenth-century majolica floor, Budapest History Museum

Buda's Old Town Hall, crowned with an onion-shaped dome, on Holy Trinity Square

Mátyás Fountain ③
Mátyás Kút

Royal Palace. **Map** C3. 🚌 5, 16, 78, Várbusz.

The ornate fountain in the northernmost courtyard of the Royal Palace was designed by Hungarian sculptor and artist, Alajos Stróbl in 1904. Decorated with bronze sculptures, this flamboyant fountain is dedicated to the great Renaissance king, Mátyás Corvinus who is the subject of many popular legends and fables.

The design of the bronze figures takes its theme from a 19th-century ballad by the poet Mihály Vörösmarty (1800–55). According to the legend, King Mátyás met a peasant girl, Ilonka, while on a hunting expedition. The two fell in love but their love was doomed. This representation shows the king dressed as a hunter, standing proudly with his kill. He is accompanied by his chief hunter and several hunting dogs in the central part of the fountain. Below the columns on the left, is the statue of Galeotto Marzio, an Italian court poet, with a hawk in his hand. The striking figure of the young Ilonka, with a doe, is below the columns on the right. In keeping with the romantic reputation of King

Mátyás, a new tradition is gaining popularity with visitors, who throw coins into the fountain in the belief that this will ensure their safe return to Budapest in the future.

Statue of King Mátyás with his hunting trophy, Mátyás Fountain

Holy Trinity Square ④
Szentháromság tér

Map B3. 🚌 Várbusz from Moszkva tér.

This square, located close to the Royal Palace, is the central point of the Old Town. It takes its name from the Baroque Holy Trinity Column in the middle of the square, which was originally sculpted by Philipp Ungleich between

1710 and 1713 and restored in 1967. The column was commissioned by the Buda Council after the outbreak of the second plague in the city. It commemorates the dead of two outbreaks of the plague, which struck the inhabitants of Buda in 1691 and 1709. The pedestal of the column is decorated with bas-reliefs by Anton Hörger depicting the horrific fate Buda's citizens suffered during those epidemics. Further up the ornate column are statues of holy figures, while at the summit is a superb composition of the figures of the Holy Trinity. The central section of the column is decorated with beautiful angelic figures surrounded by clouds.

Buda's Old Town Hall, a large Baroque building with two courtyards, was also built on the square at the beginning of the 18th century. It was designed by the 17th-century imperial court architect, Venerio Ceresola, whose architectural scheme incorporated the remains of medieval houses. In the 18th century an east wing was built and bay windows and a stone balustrade with Rococo urns, by Mátyás Nepauer, were also added. The corner niche, opposite Mátyás Church, houses a small statue of the Greek goddess Pallas Athene by Carlo Adami.

Mátyás Church ⑤

Mátyás templom

The Parish Church of Our Lady Mary was built on this site between the 13th and 15th centuries. Some of the architectural style dates from the reign of Sigismund of Luxembourg, but the church was named after King Mátyás Corvinus, one of the greatest Hungarian rulers. Much of the original detail was lost when the Ottomans converted the church into the Great Mosque in 1541. The liberation of Buda saw the church almost totally destroyed, but it was rebuilt in the Baroque style by the Franciscan friars. It sustained further damage in 1723 but was restored in the Neo-Gothic style between 1873 and 1896 by the architect Frigyes Schulek. The crypt houses the Museum of Ecclesiastical Art.

Rose Window
Architect Frigyes Schulek faithfully reproduced in stone, the medieval stained-glass window to its original Gothic style.

Béla Tower
Named after the church's founder, King Béla IV, this tower has retained several of its original Gothic features.

★ Baroque Madonna
According to legend, the original statue was set into a wall of the church during the Ottoman occpation. When the church was destroyed in 1686, the statue miraculously appeared. The Ottomans took this as an omen of defeat.

Main Portal
Below the arches of the west entrance is an impressive 19th-century bas-relief by sculptor Lajos Lantai showing the Madonna and Child seated between two angels.

STAR FEATURES

★ Baroque Madonna

★ Tomb of King Béla III and Anne de Châtillon

★ Mary Portal

★ Tomb of King Béla III and Anne de Châtillon

The remains of this royal couple were transferred from Székesfehérvár Cathedral to Mátyás Church in 1860. They lie beneath an ornamental stone canopy in the Trinity Chapel.

VISITORS' CHECKLIST

Szentháromság tér 2. **Map** B2.
Tel (01) 489 0716. Várbusz.
9am–5pm Mon–Fri, 9am–
noon Sat, 1–5pm Sun.
Museum 9am–5pm Sun–Fri.

The roof is decorated with multicoloured glazed tiles.

Pulpit
The richly decorated pulpit of the church includes the intricately carved stone figures of the four Holy Fathers of the Church and the four Evangelists.

The main altar, created by Frigyes Schulek, was based on Gothic triptychs.

Stained-Glass Windows
This beautiful 19th-century stained glass depicting Christ the Lamb, is from one of the three arched windows on the south elevation.

★ Mary Portal
This depiction of the Assumption of the Blessed Virgin Mary is the most magnificent example of Gothic stone carving in Hungary. Frigyes Schulek reconstructed the portal from fragments.

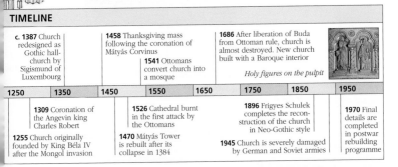

TIMELINE

c. 1387 Church redesigned as Gothic hall-church by Sigismund of Luxembourg	**1458** Thanksgiving mass following the coronation of Mátyás Corvinus	**1686** After liberation of Buda from Ottoman rule, church is almost destroyed. New church built with a Baroque interior		
	1541 Ottomans convert church into a mosque	*Holy figures on the pulpit*		

1250	1350	1450	1550	1650	1750	1850	1950

1309 Coronation of the Angevin king Charles Robert

1255 Church originally founded by King Béla IV after the Mongol invasion

1526 Cathedral burnt in the first attack by the Ottomans

1470 Mátyás Tower is rebuilt after its collapse in 1384

1896 Frigyes Schulek completes the reconstruction of the church in Neo-Gothic style

1945 Church is severely damaged by German and Soviet armies

1970 Final details are completed in postwar rebuilding programme

Street-by-Street: Gellért Hill ⑥

Rising steeply beside the Danube, Gellért Hill is one of the city's most attractive areas. It is named after Bishop Gellért, who converted the pagan Magyars to Christianity at the behest of King Stephen (István), the first king of Hungary. In the 11th century, Prince Vata, brother of King Stephen, incited a heathen rebellion here that resulted in the death of the bishop. Under the Ottomans, a stronghold was built on the hill to protect Buda, and in 1851, the Habsburgs placed their own intimidating Citadel at the summit. It was not until the end of the 19th century that Gellért Hill became a venue for picnickers. In 1967, the area around the Citadel was made into an attractive park.

Queen Elizabeth Monument
Close to the entrance of Elizabeth Bridge stands this statue of Habsburg Emperor Franz Joseph's wife, Elizabeth, who was popular with the Hungarians.

Elizabeth Bridge

Gellert Hill's reservoir

HEGYALIA ÚT

★ Statue of St Gellért
The statue of Bishop Gellért, blessing the city with his uplifted cross, overlooks Elizabeth Bridge. He is regarded as the patron saint of Budapest.

Citadel
Once a spot that inspired terror, the Citadel now hosts a hotel, restaurant and wine bar, where people can relax and enjoy the splendid view.

KEY

– – – Suggested route

Liberation Monument
Designed by Hungarian sculptor Zsigmond Strobl, the monument commemorates the liberation of Budapest by the Soviet Army in 1945.

STAR SIGHTS

★ Statue of St Gellért

★ Gellért Hotel and Baths Complex

For hotels and restaurants in this area see pp390–93 and pp394–7

Rudas Baths, with decorative Ottoman cupolas, are famous Turkish baths that date from the 16th century.

Observation Terraces
The observation terraces on Gellért Hill offer spectacular views of the southern part of Buda and the whole of Pest.

THE RESERVOIR
To supply the capital with drinking water, in 1978, a new reservoir was built near Uránia Observatory to the northwest of Gellért Hill. The surface of the reservoir is covered over and provides a point from which to observe the Royal Palace (*see pp338–9*) to the north. A sculpture by Márta Lesenyei decorates the structure.

Sculpture by Márta Lesenyei on Gellért Hill's reservoir

Rock Church
This church was established in 1926 in a holy grotto. Under the Communists, the Pauline Order of monks was forced to abandon the church, but it was reopened in 1989.

★ Gellért Hotel and Baths Complex
One of a number of bath complexes built at the beginning of the 20th century, this impressive spa hotel (see pp346–7), with its thermal pool, was built to exploit the natural hot springs here.

SZENT GELLÉRT RAKPART

Liberty Bridge

| 0 metres | 500 |
| 0 yards | 500 |

Gellért Hotel and Baths Complex
Gellért Szálló és Fürdo

Stained-glass window by Bózó Stanisits

Located at the foot of Gellért Hill, this hotel and spa was built between 1912 and 1918 in the Modernist Art Nouveau style by architects Ármin Hegedűs, Artúr Sebestyén and Izidor Sterk. The earliest reference to the existence of healing waters at this spot dates from the 13th century. During the reign of King András II in the Middle Ages, a hospital stood on the site. Baths built here by the Ottomans were mentioned by the renowned 17th-century Turkish travel writer, Evliya Çelebi. Destroyed during World War II, the hotel was later rebuilt and modernized. Today it also houses several restaurants and cafés. The baths complex includes an institute of water therapy, set within Art-Nouveau-era interiors, but with modern facilities.

Outdoor Wave Pool
Built in 1927, this swimming pool with a wave mechanism is situated at the back of the complex, providing a view of Gellért Hill.

★ **Baths**
Two separate baths, one for men and another for women, are identically arranged. In each there are three plunge pools – with water at different temperatures – a sauna and a steam bath.

Balconies
The balconies fronting the hotel rooms have fanciful Art Nouveau balustrades decorated with lyre and bird motifs.

★ **Entrance Hall**
Like the baths, the interior of the hotel has kept its original Art Nouveau decor, with elaborate mosaics, stained-glass windows and statues.

For hotels and restaurants in this area see pp390–93 and pp394–7

Sun Terraces
Situated in the sunniest spot, these terraces are a popular place for drying off in summer.

VISITORS' CHECKLIST

Szent Gellért tér. *Tel (01) 889 5500.* 🚌 7, 7A, 86. 🚋 18, 19, 47, 49. ⚙ ⊘ 🚻 ▭ ▢
Baths Kelenhegyi út.
⏰ 6am–8pm daily. 📷 ⚙ ⊘
www.danubiusgroup.com

Hot pool with medicinal spa water

Eastern-Style Towers
The towers and turrets of the hotel were designed in characteristically Oriental cylindrical form.

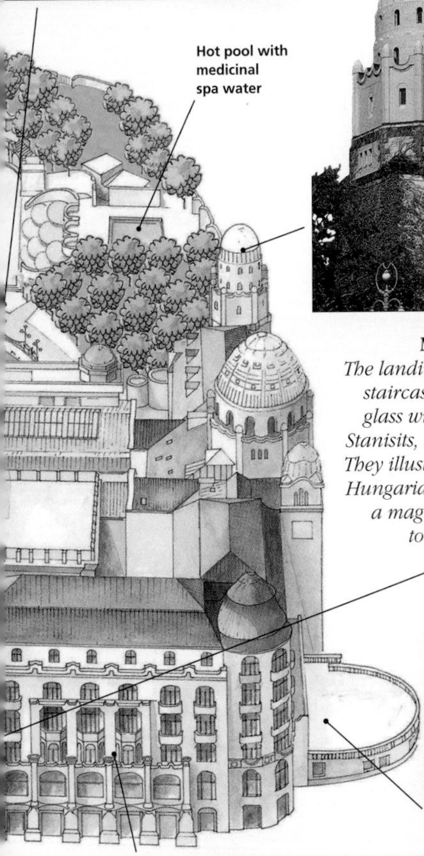

Main Staircase
The landings of the main staircase have stained-glass windows by Bozó Stanisits, added in 1933. They illustrate an ancient Hungarian legend about a magic stag, referred to in the poetry of János Arany.

Restaurant Terrace
This first-floor terrace offers diners a pretty view of Budapest. The ground and first floors of the hotel house a total of four cafés and restaurants.

★ Main Façade
Behind the hotel's façade are attractive recreational facilities and a health spa that is also open to non-guests. The entrance to the baths is around to the right from the main entrance, on Kelenhegyi út.

STAR FEATURES

★ Baths

★ Entrance Hall

★ Main Façade

Parliament ⑦
Parlamentnek

One of the pair of lions at the main entrance

The largest building in the country, Hungary's Parliament has become a symbol of Budapest. A competition, held to choose its design, was won by Hungarian architect Imre Steindl, who based his plans on the Houses of Parliament in London, built by Charles Barry in the mid-19th century. Steindl's Neo-Gothic masterpiece, constructed between 1885 and 1904, is 96 m (315 ft) high and has 691 rooms.

Lateral View
The magnificent dome marks the central point of the Parliament building. Although the façade is elaborately Neo-Gothic, the ground plan follows Baroque conventions.

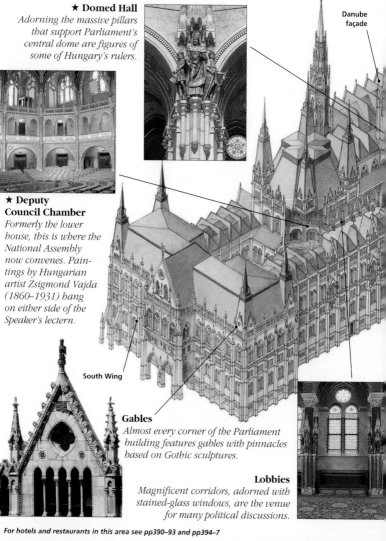

★ Domed Hall
Adorning the massive pillars that support Parliament's central dome are figures of some of Hungary's rulers.

Danube façade

★ Deputy Council Chamber
Formerly the lower house, this is where the National Assembly now convenes. Paintings by Hungarian artist Zsigmond Vajda (1860–1931) hang on either side of the Speaker's lectern.

South Wing

Gables
Almost every corner of the Parliament building features gables with pinnacles based on Gothic sculptures.

Lobbies
Magnificent corridors, adorned with stained-glass windows, are the venue for many political discussions.

Dome
The ceiling of the 96-m (315-ft) high dome is covered in an intricate design of Neo-Gothic gilding combined with heraldic decoration.

VISITORS' CHECKLIST

Kossuth Lajos tér. **Map** C2. *Tel* (01) 441 4000. 70, 78. 2, 2A. Kossuth tér. non-EU. English 10am, noon, 2pm. www.parlament.hu

Tapestry Hall
This room, on the Danube side of the Domed Hall, has a tapestry depicting Prince Árpád with seven Magyar leaders under his command, as he signs a peace treaty and takes an oath.

North Wing

Old Upper House Hall
This vast hall is virtually a mirror image of the Deputy Council Chamber. Both halls have public galleries running around a horseshoe-shaped interior.

The Royal Insignia, excluding the Coronation Mantle *(see p352)*, are kept in the Domed Hall.

The main entrance on Kossuth Lajos tér

Main Staircase
The best contemporary artists were invited to decorate the Parliament's interior. The sumptuous main staircase features ceiling frescoes by painter Károly Lotz and sculptures by György Kiss.

STAR FEATURES

★ Domed Hall

★ Deputy Council Chamber

Roosevelt Square ⑧
Roosevelt tér

Map C3. 🚋 16. 🚎 2.

Known by different names
over the years – Unloading
Square and Franz Joseph
Square among others –
Roosevelt Square received its
current title in 1947. It leads
into the Pest side of the **Chain
Bridge**, the city's first permanent bridge over the Danube
river. A major feat of engineering, the bridge was
designed by Englishman
William Tierney Clark and
built by the Scot, Adam Clark,
between 1839 and 1849.

At the beginning of the
20th century, the square was
lined with hotels, the Diana
Baths and the Lloyd Palace,
designed by József Hild. The
only building from the 19th
century still standing today
is the Hungarian Academy
of Sciences. All other
buildings were demolished
and replaced by the Gresham
Palace and the Bank of
Hungary, on the corner of
József Attila utca. There is a
statue to Baron József Eötvös,
a reformer of public
education, in front of the
InterContinental Budapest.

In the centre of the square
are monuments to two
famous politicians: Count
István Széchenyi, the leading
social and political reformer
of his age, and Ferenc Deák,
who was instrumental in the
Compromise of 1867, which
led to the Dual Monarchy of
Austria-Hungary.

St Stephen's Basilica ⑨
Szent István Bazilika

Szent István tér. **Map** D3. **Tel** (01)
317 2859. M Deák Ferenc tér.
🕐 9am–5pm Mon–Sat, 2–5pm Sun.
🖼 ♿ ✝

Dedicated to St Stephen
(István), the first Hungarian
Christian king, this church was
designed by József Hild in the
Neo-Classical style, using a
Greek cross floor plan.
Construction began in 1851
and was taken over in 1867
by the great Hungarian

**Impressive exterior of the
St Stephen's Basilica**

architect, Miklós Ybl. He
added the Neo-Renaissance
dome after the original collapsed in 1868. József Kauser
completed the church in 1905.
It received the title of Basilica
Minor in 1938, the 900th anniversary of St Stephen's death.

A marble statue of the saint
stands on the main altar, and
scenes from his life are depicted behind it. A painting to
the right of the main entrance
shows St Stephen, who was
left without an heir, dedica-
ting Hungary to the Virgin
Mary. His mummified forearm
is kept in the Chapel of the
Holy Right Hand.

The outer colonnade at the
back of the church has the
figures of the 12 Apostles.
The dome is decorated with
superb mosaics by Károly
Lotz and it reaches 96 m

(315 ft) and is visible all over
Budapest. The basilica has
two towers, one of which
houses a bell weighing 9
tonnes (10 tons). This was
funded by German Catholics
to compensate for the loss of
the original bell, which was
looted by the Nazis in 1944.

State Opera House ⑩
Magyar Állami Operaház

Andrássy út 22. **Map** D2. **Tel** (01)
331 2550, 353 0170 (box office).
M Opera. 🖼 📷 3pm & 4pm daily.
♿ ✉ 📷 www.opera.hu

Opened in September 1884,
the State Opera House was
built to rival those in Paris,
Vienna and Dresden. Its
beautiful architecture and
interior decor were the life's
work of architect Miklós Ybl.

The façade celebrates
musical themes, with statues
of Hungary's most prominent
composers, including Ferenc
Liszt. The interior contains
ornamentation by Hungarian
artists, including Alajos Strobl
and Károly Lotz.

The opulence of the foyer,
with its chandeliers and
vaulted ceilings, is echoed
in the grandeur of the sweeping main staircase and the
three-storey auditorium.
During its lifetime, the opera
house has seen some influential musical directors,
including Ferenc Erkel, composer of the Hungarian opera
Bánk Bán, Gustav Mahler and
Otto Klemperer.

The imposing façade of the State Opera House

Vigadó Square ⑪
Vigadó tér

Map C3. 🚋 2.

The square is dominated by the Vigadó Concert Hall, with its mix of eclectic forms. Built to designs by architect Frigyes Feszl between 1859 and 1864, it replaced an earlier building destroyed by fire during the uprising of 1848–9. The façade has arched windows and includes features such as folk motifs, dancers on columns and busts of former monarchs, rulers and other Hungarian personalities. An old Hungarian coat of arms is also visible in the centre.

The Budapest Marriott Hotel, located on one side of the square, was designed by József Finta in 1969. It was one of the first modern hotels to be built in the city.

On the Danube promenade is a statue of a childlike figure on the railings, *Little Princess*, by László Marton. Vigadó Square also has craft stalls, cafés and restaurants.

Váci Utca ⑫

Map D4. Ⓜ Ferenciek tere.

Once two separate streets which were joined at the beginning of the 18th century, the two ends of Váci utca still have distinct characters.

Today, part of the southern section is open to traffic, but the northern end is pedestrianized and has long been a popular commercial centre. Most of the buildings lining the street date from the 19th and early 20th centuries, although new banks, modern department stores and shopping arcades have now sprung up along the street among the older original buildings.

The street has a number of famous buildings, notable for their architecture or for their place in local history. Philantia, an Art-Nouveau-style florist's shop opened in 1905, now occupies part of the Neo-Classical block at No. 9, built in 1840 by József Hild. The same block also houses

Thonet House, with Zsolnay tile decoration, Váci Utca

the Pest Theatre, which stages classic plays by Russian playwright Anton Chekhov, among others. The building was once occupied by the "Inn of the Seven Electors" which had a large ballroom and concert hall, and it was here that a 12-year-old Ferenc (Franz) Liszt performed in 1823.

Built by Ödön Lechner and Gyula Pártos, the Thonet House, at No. 11, is most notable for the Zsolnay tiles from Pécs *(see pp374–5)* that adorn its façade. The oldest building on Váci utca, No. 13, was built in 1805. In contrast, the Post-Modern Fontana department store at No. 16 was constructed in 1984. Outside there is a bronze fountain with a figure of the Greek god Hermes, dating from the mid-19th century.

The Nádor Hotel once stood at No. 20 and featured a statue of Archduke Palatine József. Today, the Taverna Hotel, designed by József Finta and opened in 1987, stands here. It has a popular coffee shop.

In a side street off Váci utca, at No. 13 Régiposta utca, stands a Modernist-style building. An unusual sight in the city, this striking Bauhaus-influenced building dates from 1937 and is by Lajos Kozma.

Inner City Parish Church ⑬
Belvárosi Plébánia Templom

Március 15 tér 2. **Map** D4. **Tel** *(01) 318 3108.* Ⓜ *Ferenciek tere.* ⏰ *9am–7pm daily.* 🚻

Built in the 11th century, this is the oldest building in Pest. It was first established during the reign of St Stephen, on the burial site of the martyred St Gellért, who played a major role in converting Hungary to Christianity. In the 12th century it was replaced by a Romanesque church of which a wall fragment remains in the façade of the South Tower.

In the 14th century, it became a large Gothic structure and subsequently a mosque – a small prayer niche, a reminder of the Ottoman occupation, can be seen beside the altar.

Crest of Pest, Inner City Parish Church

Damaged by the Great Fire of 1723, the church was partly rebuilt in the Baroque style by György Paur between 1725 and 1739. The interior also contains Neo-Classical elements by János Hild, as well as some 20th-century works such as the main altar, which replaced the original in 1948. The altar was painted by Károly Antal and Pál Molnár. On the south side of the church is a tabernacle bearing the Crest of Pest.

The Baroque nave of the Inner City Parish Church

Magnificent sculptures decorating the pulpit in the University Church

University Church ⑭
Egyetemi templom

Papnövelde utca 7. **Map** D4.
Tel (01) 318 0555. Ⓜ Kálvin tér.
⬤ 7am–7pm daily.

This single-aisle church, built between 1725 and 1742, is considered one of the most impressive Baroque churches in Budapest. It is believed to have been designed by local architect András Mayerhoffer and the tower was added in 1771. The church was built for the Pauline Order, which was founded by Canon Euzebiusz in 1263; it was the only religious order to be founded in Hungary.

The superb exterior features a tympanum and a row of pilasters that divide the façade. Figures of St Paul and St Anthony flank the emblem of the Pauline Order, which crowns the exterior. The carved-wood interior of the main vestibule is also worth seeing.

Inside the church, a row of side chapels stand behind unusual marble pilasters. In 1776, Bohemian artist Johann Bergl painted the vaulted ceiling with frescoes depicting scenes from the life of Mary, though these are now in poor condition. The main altar dates from 1746, and the carved statues behind it are

the work of József Hebenstreit. Above it is a copy of the famous Polish painting *The Black Madonna of Częstochowa* (c. 1720). The balustrade of the organ loft, the confessionals and the carved pulpit are the work of the Pauline monks.

Museum of Applied Arts ⑮
Iparművészeti múzeum

Üllői út 33–7. **Map** E5. **Tel** (01) 456 5100. Ⓜ Ferenc körút. ⬤ 10am–5:45pm Tue–Sun. 🎫 🔲 🔲 www.imm.hu

Opened in 1896 by Emperor Franz Joseph I as part of the Millennium Celebrations, this museum is housed within an outstanding Art Nouveau building designed by Gyula Pártos (1845–1916) and Ödön Lechner (1845–1914). The exterior incorporates elements inspired by the Orient as well as the Zsolnay ceramics characteristic of Lechner's work. Damaged in 1945 and again in 1956, the building was recently restored to its original magnificence.

The building is set around a glorious, arcaded courtyard, surrounded by cloisters and designed in an Indian-Oriental style. The museum, established in 1872, comprises many superb examples of arts and crafts workmanship.

Among the permanent collections are furniture from the 14th to the 20th centuries, including fine French pieces,

A 17th-century dress in the Museum of Applied Arts

Thonet bentwood furniture, and a large collection of ceramics. The fine metalwork collection comprises watches, jewellery and other items made by foreign and Hungaraian craftsmen. The textiles section includes silks from the 13th and 14th centuries and also traces the history of traditional lacemaking.

The museum holds regular temporary exhibitions. The library, dating from 1872, contains around 50,000 books, making it one of the largest in Hungary.

Gothic painting of *Saint Martin of Tours*, Hungarian National Museum

Hungarian National Museum ⑯
Magyar Nemzeti múzeum

Múzeum körút 14–16. **Map** E4. **Tel** (01) 338 2122 (327 7773 for English). 🚌 9, 15. 🚊 47, 49. Ⓜ Kálvin tér, Astória. ⬤ 10am–6pm Tue–Sun. 🎫 🔲 🔲 www.hnm.hu

Housed in a Neo-Classical edifice built by Mihály Pollack, the Hungarian National Museum was founded in 1802. It was started when Count Ferenc Széchényi bequeathed his collection of coins, books and documents to the nation. The museum's expanding collection of art spans from the 11th century to the present day and offers the richest source of art and artifacts relating to the country's history.

Among the star exhibits are a textile masterpiece made of Byzantine silk, which became the Coronation Mantle in the 12th century, a 6th-century BC figure of a Golden Stag and a 13th-century golden funeral crown, discovered on Margaret Island (*see p355*).

Great Synagogue ⑰
Zsinagóga

Dohány utca 2. **Map** E3. **Tel** (01) 342 8949. Ⓜ Astoria. 🚊 74. **Jewish Museum** ◯ Mar–Oct: 10am–6pm Mon–Thu & Sun, 10am–3pm Fri; Nov–Feb: 10am–3pm Mon–Thu & Sun, 10am–2pm Fri. 🅰 🅲

The Great Synagogue is the largest in Europe. Built in a Byzantine-Moorish style between 1854 and 1859 by the Viennese architect Ludwig Förster, it has three naves and, in accordance with Orthodox tradition, separate galleries for women. Together the naves and galleries can accommodate up to 3,000 worshippers. Some features, such as the position of the reading platform, reflect elements of Judaic reform. The interior has valuable decorative fittings, such as those on the Ark of the Law, by Frigyes

A large rose window is flanked by two richly decorated towers crowned by distinctive onion domes.

A Hebrew inscription from the second book of Moses is set under the rose window.

The façade has white and red bricks and intricately designed ceramic friezes.

Feszl. In 1931, a **Jewish Museum** was established here with a vast collection of historical relics, devotional items and everyday objects, from ancient Rome to the present day. These include the book of Chevra Kadisha from 1792. There is also a Holocaust Memorial Room.

Jewish Quarter ⑱
Zsidó Negyed

Király utca, Rumbach Sebestyén utca, Dohány utca & Akácfa utca. **Map** E3. Ⓜ Deák Ferenc tér.

Jews first came to Hungary in the 13th century, initially settling in Buda and Óbuda and, later, in the 19th century, establishing a larger community outside the Pest city boundary. In the late 19th century, three synagogues were built and many Jewish shops and workshops were established. Kosher businesses were a common feature of the

area. The Jewish community became well integrated into Hungarian society until, in 1941, a series of anti-Semitic laws were passed. In 1944, a ghetto was created in the area around the Great Synagogue and the deportation of thousands of Jews to camps, including Auschwitz (see pp194–7), was implemented. In total, 600,000 Hungarian Jews were victims of the Holocaust. A plaque on the Orthodox Synagogue in Rumbach utca commemorates the thousands of Jews sent from Budapest. Today, the Jewish Quarter is recovering its pre-ghetto character, and shops are being rebuilt.

Heroes' Square ⑲
Hősök tér

Király utca, Rumbach Sebestyén utca, Dohány utca & Akácfa utca. **Map** F1. Ⓜ Hősök tere.

Heroes' Square is a relic of a proud age in Hungary's history – it was here that the Millennium Celebrations opened in 1896. This marked a

Millennium Monument, Heroes' Square

high point in the development of Budapest and in the history of the Austro-Hungarian monarchy. The city underwent a huge programme of modernization, with the construction of hundreds of civic buildings and palaces as well as the introduction of gas lighting and Europe's first underground transport system. The square is surrounded by monuments including the Museum of Fine Arts, the Széchenyi Baths and the Vajdahunyad Castle (see p355) built in Városliget.

Dominating the square is the **Millennium Monument**, featuring statues of prominent Hungarian leaders. The famous Statue of Anonymous (1903), by Miklós Ligeti, stands in front of the castle.

Detail of the Orthodox Synagogue, Jewish Quarter

Magnificently decorated ceiling at the Museum of Fine Arts

Museum of Fine Arts ⑳
Szépművészeti Múzeum

Dózsa György út 41. **Map** F1.
Tel (01) 469 7100. 4, 20, 30,
105. 75, 79. Hősök tere.
10am–6pm Tue–Sun.
www.szepmuveszeti.hu

The origins of the Museum of Fine Arts date from 1870, when the state bought a spectacular collection of paintings from the aristocratic Esterházy family. The museum's collection was further enriched by donations and acquisitions. In 1906, it moved to its present location, a Neo-Classical building with Italian Renaissance influences, designed by Hungarian architects Albert Schickedanz and Fülöp Herzog. The tympanum crowning the portico is supported by eight Corinthian columns. It depicts the Battle of the Centaurs and Lapiths, and is copied from the Temple of Zeus at Olympia, Greece.

The museum's collection encompasses a wide range of art from antiquity to the 20th century. Among the Egyptian artifacts, most of which were unearthed by Hungarian archaeologists during 19th century excavations, the collection of bronze figures from the New Kingdom of Ptolemy is the most fascinating.

The collection of Greek vases is the highlight of the classical artifacts, along with the famous Grimani jug, which dates from the 5th century BC. In the sculpture gallery, a small bronze figure by Leonardo da Vinci stands out, while the rich collection of Dutch and Flemish art features the sublime *St John the Baptist's Sermon* (1566), by Pieter Bruegel the Elder. There are Italian and Spanish works, including some by Raphael, El Greco and Goya and drawings and graphics by one of the best-known German painters, Albrecht Dürer. Also on view are stunning 19th- and 20th-century works by Pablo Picasso as well as gems by French Impressionists.

Városliget ㉑
Városliget

Városliget. **Map** F1. Hősök tere, Széchenyi Fürdő.

Városliget, also known as City Park, was once an area of marshland used as a royal hunting ground. Drained and planted during the reign of Queen Maria Theresa, the park was laid out in the English style in the late 19th century. Városliget was the centre for the Millennium Celebrations in 1896, when the Museum of Fine Arts, Vajdahunyad Castle and the Heroes' Square Monument *(see p353)* were built. Among its attractions is a lake, Varosligetito, which serves as an ice rink in winter and a boating lake in summer. The park is also home to the Széchenyi Baths, Budapest's zoo and the 110-year-old Gundel Restaurant.

Széchenyi Baths ㉒
Széchenyi Strandfürdő

Állatkerti körút 11. **Map** F1.
72. **Tel** (01) 363 3210.
Széchenyi fürdő. **Swimming Pool** 6am–10pm daily.
Thermal Pool 6am–7pm daily.
www.spasbudapest.hu

The largest complex of spa baths in Europe, Széchenyi Baths also has the deepest and hottest baths in Budapest; the water here reaches the surface at a temperature of about 75° C (180° F). The spa, housed in an attractive Neo-Baroque building by Gyözö Czigler and Ede Dvorzsák, was constructed between 1909 and 1913. At the main entrance stands a statue of geologist Vilmos Zsigmondy, who discovered a hot spring here while drilling a well in 1879. In 1926, three open-air swimming pools were added; these are popular throughout the year due to the heat of the water. The springs are known for their alleged healing properties and are recommended for treating rheumatism, disorders of the nervous system, joints and muscles.

An outdoor pool at Széchenyi Baths

Vajdahunyad Castle ㉓

Vajdahunyad Vára

Városliget. **Map** F1. *Tel (01) 363 1973.* 🚃 *70, 72, 75, 79.* 🚌 *4, 20, 30.* Ⓜ *Széchenyi fürdő.* **Museum of Agriculture** *Tel (01) 422 0765.* ⭕ *mid-Mar–mid-Oct: 10am–5pm Tue–Sun; mid-Oct–mid-Mar: 10am–4pm Tue–Sun.* 📷 🎫 ♿ www.mmgm.hu

Located at the edge of the lake in Városliget, this fairytale castle is a complex consisting of several buildings reflecting various architectural styles. Designed by architect Ignác Alpár for the Millennium Celebrations in 1896, it illustrates the history of architecture in Hungary. Originally intended as temporary exhibition pavilions, the castle proved so popular with the public that, between 1904 and 1906, it was rebuilt using brick to create a more permanent structure.

The pavilions are grouped chronologically in style, with individual styles linked to give the impression of a single, cohesive design. Each one uses authentic details copied from Hungary's most important historic buildings, or is the interpretation of a style inspired by a specific architect of that period. The medieval period, often considered a glorious time in Hungary's history, is emphasized, while the controversial Habsburg era is not. The Romanesque complex features a copy of the portal from a rural village as well as a monastic cloister and palace.

The details on the Gothic pavilion stem from castles such as that in Segesvár, now in Romania. The famous Austrian architect Josef Emanuel Fischer von Erlach *(see p402)* inspired the Renaissance and Baroque complex. The façade copies part of the Bakócz chapel in the lovely Esztergom Basilica *(see pp360)*.

The popular **Museum of Agriculture**, in the Baroque section, has interesting exhibits on wine-making, cattle-breeding, hunting and fishing.

The delightful Japanese Garden, Margaret Island

Margaret Island ㉔

Margitsz viget

Margitsziget. **Map** F1. 🚌 *26 from Nyugati Station.*

Inhabited as far back as Roman times, Margaret Island is a tranquil oasis in the middle of the Danube river. The 2.5-km (1.5-mile) long island was also known as the Island of Rabbits, as it served as a popular hunting ground for medieval kings. Monks, too, were drawn to its peaceful setting. During Ottoman rule it was used as a harem. In the 1200s, Princess Margaret (1242–70), daughter of King Béla IV after whom the island is named, spent most of her life as a recluse in a convent here. It has been open to the public since 1869.

Today, Margaret Island still offers the perfect escape after sightseeing in the busy city. Besides its lovely green spaces, swimming pools and playgrounds, notable attractions include the Centenary Monument, a unique water tower and a serene Japanese Garden. Designed by István Kiss, the Centenary Monument was erected in 1973 to celebrate a century of the merger of the cities of Buda, Pest and Óbuda. At the centre of the island, the 57-m (187-ft) high water tower, built in 1911, offers great views from its lookout gallery. The relaxing Japanese Garden, one of three lovely land-scaped parks, features a wide range of flora as well as rock gardens, ponds, waterfalls and playgrounds.

Gothic and Renaissance sections of Vajdahunyad Castle, seen across the lake in Városliget

Szentendre ❷

With its Baroque architecture, Orthodox churches, cobbled streets and riverside setting, Szentendre makes for an idyllic visit. It is also known for its museums, which document the history of the region. Originally founded by the Romans in the 4th century, the town was settled by Serbian refugees in the 14th century. They fled here first from the Ottoman Turks after the Battle of Kosovo in 1389, and again after the Battle of Belgrade in 1690, ushering in a period of great prosperity. In the 1920s, many Serbs moved away to be replaced by artists who were attracted by the town's air and light. It remains popular with them today.

Entrance to the fascinating Charles Ferenczy Museum

🏛 Fő Square
Szentendre Gallery *Tel* (026) 310 244. ☐ 9am–5pm Tue–Sun. 🖼
János Kmetty Memorial Museum *Tel* (026) 310 244. ☐ 9am–5pm Tue–Sun. 🖼 🖼 🖼

At the heart of Szentendre lies the bustling Fő Square (Fő tér), which is packed with hawkers and street artists in summer. A wrought-iron cross was raised here in 1763 by the survivors of the last major outbreak of bubonic plague.

On the Danube side of the square is the Orthodox Blagoveštenska Church, built between 1752 and 1754 and designed by András Mayerhoffer (1690–1771). Its elegantly curved balcony and tall, split-level belfry are fine examples of late-Baroque simplicity. Inside, frescoes of the Roman emperor, Constantine, a fine choir and a colourful iconostasis depicting the Annunciation vie for attention.

Opposite the church is the **Szentendre Gallery**, featuring the work of local artists. The building was originally a terrace formed by six

identical merchants' houses; it was converted into a gallery in 1987.

Opposite, in an early-19th-century Saxon-style house, is the **János Kmetty Memorial Museum**, devoted to the life and works of the painter János Kmetty (1889–1975), a pioneering Cubist who lived here for 45 years.

🏛 Charles Ferenczy Museum
Fő tér 6. *Tel* (026) 310 790. ☐ 9am–5pm Tue–Sun. 🖼 🖼 🖼

This art museum (Károly Ferenczy muzeum), north-east of the Blagoveštenska Church, houses the work of Hungarian Impressionist painter Károly Ferenczy (1862–1917), who lived in Szentendre between 1889 and 1906. Rooms here also display the works of his wife, painter Olga Fialka, and their three children: a painter, a sculptor and a weaver.

Although most of Ferenczy's best works are on display at the Hungarian National Gallery *(see p340)*, the lucid and comic *Acrobats* (1912) and his serene *Portrait of*

Mrs Sándor Ernst (1916) can be seen here. The museum's fine arts collection has some 8,000 works by local artists.

🏛 Templom Square
Czóbel Museum *Tel* (026) 310 244. ☐ 9am–5pm Wed–Sun. 🖼 🖼 🖼

This walled square (Templom tér), at the top of a hill above Fő Square, stands on the site of the original Roman fort of Ulcisia. The square was the centre of the town in the Middle Ages and is popular today for the views it offers of the streets below.

The Catholic church in the middle of the square was first built in Romanesque style in the 14th century and reno-vated in Baroque style in the 18th century. A few original features remain, including the sundial on the right-hand side

Opposite the church is a charming building housing the **Czóbel Museum**. It is dedicated to painter Béla Czóbel, famous for his land-scapes and nudes. He lived in Szentendre from 1946 until his death in 1976.

🔒 Belgrade Church and Museum of Serbian Orthodox Ecclesiastical Art
Pátriárka utca 5. *Tel* (026) 312 399. ☐ *May–Sep:* 10am–6pm Tue–Sun; *Oct–Dec, Mar–Apr:* 10am–4pm Tue–Sun; *Jan–Feb:* 10am–4pm Fri–Sun. 🖼 🖼

Constructed by Serbs but often known as the Greek Church, the Belgrade Church (Szerb Ortodox Egyházművészeti Gyűjtemény, Könyvtár és Levéltár) is the Hungarian seat of the Serbian Orthodox Patriarch, and is therefore,

Monument and pretty colourful houses in Fő Square

officially a cathedral. Built between 1756 and 1764, it is a sublime mix of Baroque and Rococo styles, its clock tower topped by a tall spire. Inside, it contains icons of Orthodox saints by Vasili Ostoic and a red marble altar.

In the garden outside the church, the Museum of Serbian Orthodox Ecclesiastical Art has around 2,000 icons, vestments, treasures and art objects brought here in the last 150 years after the closure of their original host churches.

Icons of Orthodox saints in the Belgrade Church

🏛 Bogdányi Utca
Imre Ámos/Margit Anna Museum ⬭ 9am–5pm Tue–Sun; Jun–Aug: 9am–7pm Fri–Sun. 🇬 🇫 ♿

Winding its way north from Fő Square, Bogdányi utca is a lively thoroughfare lined with historical buildings, and packed with many shops, stalls and portrait painters.

The **Imre Ámos/Margit Anna Museum** at No. 10 commemorates the life and works of well-known painters Imre Ámos and Margit Anna, who married in 1936, and moved to Szentendre in 1937. Ámos, a Jew, was taken to a labour camp in Vojvodina in 1940, where he continued to paint. He was deported to Germany in 1944, where he died, probably in a concentration camp. His wife Margit lived until 1991. Her Cubist paintings are on the ground floor, while Ámos's works, including his account of life in the camp, are displayed on the first floor.

A wine barrel sign in Bogdányi utca

VISITORS' CHECKLIST

25 km (16 miles) N of Budapest. 🚍 22,000. 🚊 Dunakanyar körút (HEV). 🚌 🚗 Dunakanyar körút. 🚢 Dunakorzó (summer only). 🛈 Tourinform, Dumtsa Jenő utca 22, (026) 317 965. 🎭 Serb Folk Festival (19 Aug).

A cross on the corner of Bogdányi utca and Lázár tér stands where the body of the legendary Serb ruler Prince Lázár once lay in a church. He was killed by a traitor at the Battle of Kosovo Polje in 1389. His body was taken back to Serbia in the 1800s, and the church was later destroyed in a fire.

Built between 1741 and 1746, Preobraženska Church, is another fine Baroque Serbian Orthodox church. It is also famous for the annual Serb Folk Festival that takes place here on 19 August.

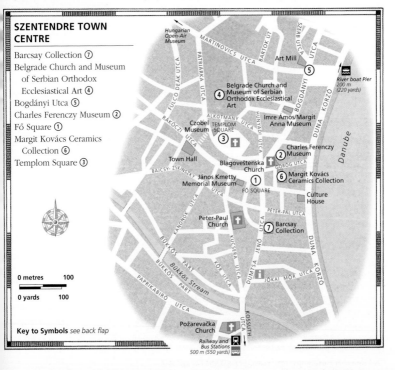

SZENTENDRE TOWN CENTRE

Barcsay Collection ⑦
Belgrade Church and Museum of Serbian Orthodox Ecclesiastical Art ④
Bogdányi Utca ⑤
Charles Ferenczy Museum ②
Fő Square ①
Margit Kovács Ceramics Collection ⑥
Templom Square ③

0 metres   100
0 yards   100

Key to Symbols see back flap

🏛 Margit Kovács Ceramics Collection

Vastagh György utca 1. **Tel** *(026) 310 244.* ⬜ *9am–5pm Tue–Sun.*
🖼 ♿

This striking 18th-century building (Kovács Margit Kerámiagyűjtemény) was originally a salt storage facility, and later became a vicarage for the Blagoveštenska Church. Since 1973 it has been devoted to the work of ceramic artist Margit Kovács (1902–77). Kovács attended Budapest's School of Applied Arts before learning the fundamentals of pottery in the workshop of artist Herta Bücher in Vienna. She developed her skills further in the State School for Applied Arts in Munich before returning to Hungary. *Nursing* (1948) is an example of Kovács's obsession with the Madonna, a common theme in many of her early works, while the *Bread Cutter* (1962) is a witty satire on the idealized peasant woman from a feminist perspective.

Plaque, Margit Kovács Ceramics Collection

🏛 Barcsay Collection

Dumtsa Jenő utca 10. **Tel** *(026) 310 244.* ⬜ *Mid-Mar–Sep: Tue–Sun 9am–5pm; Oct–mid-Mar: Wed–Sun 1–5pm.* 🖼

Barcsay Collection (Barcsay Gyűjtemény), located in a 19th-century Saxon house, is dedicated to Jenő Barcsay (1900–88), who settled in Szentendre in 1926 after studying art in Budapest and Paris. Regarded as the first Hungarian Constructivist, he strongly influenced his contemporaries. His finest works, including *Landscape at Szentendre* (1934) and *Street at Szentendre* (1932), are displayed here.

🏛 Hungarian Open-Air Museum

Sztaravodai út. **Tel** *(026) 502 500.* 🚌 *7.* ⬜ *Apr–Nov: 9am–5pm Tue–Sun.* 🖼 📷 ♿ **www**.skanzen.hu

Hungary's largest and best open-air village museum (Szabadtéri Néprajzi Múzeum) is 4 km (2 miles) from Szentendre. The museum, opened in 1967, is spread over 55 ha (136 acres) and features a reconstructed village from each of Hungary's five historic regions. Each of the villages is complete and self-contained, comprising houses, churches, schools, mills, wine presses, forges and stables. In particular, it is worth seeing the three huge outdoor ovens in the village of the Great Plain, brought to the museum from the village of Kisbodak; the roadside crucifixes in the central Transdanubian village; and the flintstone walls of the Bakony region houses.

All the buildings in the museum are open to the public, and some are working museums, with artisans demonstrating traditional skills from pottery to wine-making. Special courses in traditional skills are also on offer at various times of the year.

The façade of the Baroque Royal Palace at Gödöllő

Gödöllő ❸

35 km (22 miles) NE of Budapest. 🚉 *29,000.* 🚃 *HÉV from Budapest.* 🛈 *Tourinform, Királyi Kastély, (028) 415 402.*

Once the summer residence of the Habsburgs, Gödöllő is most famous for the **Royal Palace**, built in 1741. The enchanting Baroque palace was commissioned by the flamboyant aristocrat Antal Grassalkovich I and designed by Andras Meyerhoffer. Home to a long line of Hungarian rulers from Emperor Franz Joseph to Admiral Horthy, the palace has been restored to its full glory. Elegant rooms and extravagant furnishings offer a glimpse into the lives of the rulers who lived here.

The oldest building in the town, dating from 1661, was once the home of local landowner Ferenc Hamvay. Today, it houses the excellent **Gödöllő Town Museum**. Besides displays that tell the story of the town and its greatest patron, Antal Grassalkovich, there is an exhibition focusing on the works of the Gödöllő Artists' Colony, a group of artists active between 1901 and 1920, who pursued ideals of communal rural living.

🏛 Royal Palace

Királyi Kastély. **Tel** *(028) 410 124.* ⬜ *Apr–Oct: 10am–6pm daily; Non–Mar: 10am–5pm Tue–Sun.* 🖼 📷 🔲 🏠 📷

🏛 Gödöllő Town Museum

Szabadság tér 5. **Tel** *(028) 422 003.* ⬜ *10am–6pm Tue–Sun.* 🖼 📷 *Hungarian only.*

A thatched building in the Hungarian Open-Air Museum

Vác ❹

40 km (25 miles) N of Budapest.
🚂 33,000. 🚉 from Budapest.
🚌 from Budapest. 🛈 Tourinform,
Március 15 tér 17, (027) 316 160.
🕒 daily, behind Március 15 tér.

Founded in the year 1000,
Vác is situated on the eastern
bank of the Danube river.
The town was rebuilt in the
late 17th century after being
destroyed by war. Its central
square, around Március 15 tér,
dates from the 18th century
and was a thriving marketplace until 1951. The market
itself survives, although it is
now hidden behind the Town
Hall, a Baroque masterpiece
from 1680. The superb
façade, with two Corinthian
half-columns guarding the
entrance, is adorned with an
intricate wrought-iron
balcony. The Sisters of Charity
Chapel and Hospital, built in
the 17th century and still a
functioning hospital to this
day, is located next door.

On the southern side of the
square stands the **Dominican
Church of Our Lady of Victory**,
the construction of which
began in 1699. Due to the War
of Independence, however,
work on the interior only
began in 1755. As a result the
façade is sober, while the interior is rich in Rococo artwork.

At the northernmost end of
the Old Town, on Köztársaság
út, stands the only triumphal
arch in Hungary. This was
built in 1764, ostensibly to
honour Queen Maria Theresa.

Visegrád ❺

40 km (25 miles) N of Budapest.
🚂 1,700. 🚉 from Budapest. 🚌
from Budapest. 🚌 from Budapest,
Esztergom; from Szentendre (summer
only). **www**.visegrad.hu

Set on the narrowest stretch
of the Danube, the village of
Visegrád is a popular tourist
destination that is dominated
by its spectacular ruined citadel. Built in the 13th century
by King Béla IV (1206–70),
this was once one of the finest
royal palaces in Hungary.
The massive outer walls are
still intact, and offer superb

The Dominican Church in Vác, with
its rich Rococo ornamentation

views. Halfway down the hill,
in the Solomon Tower, is the
fascinating **Mátyás Király
Museum**, a collection of items
excavated from the ruins of
the **Royal Palace**.

Built by King Béla IV
at the same time as
the citadel, this
lovely palace was
renovated two
centuries later
by King Mátyás
Corvinus (r. 1458–90),
in magnificent
Renaissance style. It
fell into dereliction
in the 16th century
after the Turkish inva-
sion and was then
buried in a mud
slide. The ruins
were not rediscov-
ered until 1934,
when excavations took place.

**Signpost in Duna-Ipoly
National Park**

🏛 **Mátyás Király Museum**
Salamon-Torony utca. **Tel** (026)
597 010. 🕒 May–Oct: 9am–5pm
Tue–Sun. 🎫

🏛 **Royal Palace**
Fő utca 23. **Tel** (026) 398 026.
🕒 9am–5pm Tue–Sun. 🎫 📷

Nagybörzsöny and Duna-Ipoly National Park ❻

72 km (45 miles) N of Budapest.
🚌 from Szob (to Nagybörzsöny).
www.dinpi.hu

Home to the fine 14th-century
stone Romanesque Church of
St Stephen, a working mid-
19th-century water mill (open
to the public) and a mining
museum, Nagybörzsöny is
best known as the gateway
to the Duna-Ipoly National
Park, one of the largest in the
country. The Buda Hill caves
and the Sas-hegy nature trail
outside Budapest are also
within the park's borders.

The park is home to
more than 70 protected
plants and more than half of
Hungary's native bird species,
including black and white-
backed woodpeckers.

A narrow-gauge railway
runs at weekends from
Nagybörzsöny to
Nagyirtás across the
Börzsöny Hills, from
where well-marked
hiking trails fan
out across the
park. There is also
a long trail starting
from the town of
Nagybörzsöny itself,
leading up to Nagy
Hideg Hegy peak,
which offers views
across to Slovakia.

A second narrow-gauge
railway, from Kismaros to
Királyrét, opens up the
southern part of the park.
There are hiking trails from
Királyrét across the hills,
and on to Nógrád, where
there is a spectacular castle
in ruins.

The magnificent ruins of the citadel, towering over Visegrád

Esztergom ❼

Esztergom is the seat of the Archbishop of Hungary and the most sacred city in the country. St Stephen, Hungary's first king, was baptized in the city and crowned here on Christmas Day in the year AD 1000. Almost completely destroyed by the Mongol invasion 250 years later, the city was gradually rebuilt during the 18th and 19th centuries. Although it is dominated by the huge Esztergom Basilica, the city has much to offer besides its mighty cathedral, including the remains of a 10th-century castle, a picturesque Old Town, the fascinating Danube Museum and Hungary's finest collection of ecclesiastical art.

⛪ Esztergom Basilica

Szent István tér 1. *Tel (033) 402 354.*
⏰ *Mar–Sep: 7am–6pm daily; Oct–Feb: 7am–5pm Tue–Sun.* 🎧 📷 ♿
📷 *treasury, crypt.* 🚻
Rising above the Danube, its bright blue cupola visible from afar, Esztergom Basilica (Esztergomi bazilika) has been a symbol of Hungary for a millennium, since St Stephen was crowned here. Hungary's largest cathedral, the present structure dates from the 19th century and was built over a 47-year period from 1822 to 1869. Its interior has a copy of Titian's *Assumption of the Virgin* (1853–4), the largest single-canvas painting in the world. Other highlights include the Treasury, which holds the country's most valuable collection of liturgical and royal art.

⛪ Royal Palace and Castle Museum

Szent István tér 1. *Tel (033) 402 354.*
⏰ *9am–5pm Tue–Sun.* 🎧 📷
Opposite the Basilica stands the Royal Palace (Vár), parts of which date back to the 10th century. From 1256 it

served as the palace of Esztergom's Archbishops until it was sacked during the Ottoman invasion. Much of the palace survived, and is open today as the Castle Museum (Vármúzeum). The only way to see it is on a guided tour, which takes in the study of King Mátyás's tutor, with Renaissance-style ceiling frescoes, and the 12th-century Royal Chapel, with an original rose window and 13th-century portraits of the Apostles.

To the south and north are well-preserved remains of the ramparts and steps back into the town. The Esztergom Castle Festival takes place in the palace grounds.

⛪ Víziváros

Berényi utca.
A district of mainly Baroque buildings, Víziváros (Watertown), has narrow streets, single-storey houses and tiny well-kept gardens. The area was developed during the regeneration of Esztergom after the

withdrawal of the Ottomans. Víziváros Parish Church, consecrated by Jesuits in 1728, is a perfect example of the Baroque architecture of the time, with its rounded façade and high nave. The twin spires were added in the middle of the 19th century. The Baroque interior was lost during World War II. A bridge behind the church leads to the island of Prímás Sziget, from where another bridge crosses the river into Slovakia.

The intricately carved Lord's Coffin of Garamszentbenedek

🏛 Christian Museum

Mindszenty tér 2. *Tel (033) 413 880.*
⏰ *Mar–Oct: 10am–6pm Tue–Sun; Nov–Feb: 11am–3pm Tue–Sun.* 🎧 📷
The Roman Catholic Primate of All Hungary, János Simor, moved into this grand Neo-Renaissance palace after it was completed in 1882 and immediately opened the palace and its vast collection of paintings, including works by early Italian Renaissance artists Migazzi and Bertinelli, to the public. The building has been a dedicated museum (Keresztény múzeum) since 1924, and its collection of church art, bolstered by many subsequent purchases, is now the finest in Hungary. Tamás Koloszvári's *Ascension* (1427), is considered the most outstanding example of Hungarian Gothic art.

The splendid, wheeled Lord's Coffin of Garamszentbenedek (1480), now in Slovakia, decorated with carved figures

View of the imposing Esztergom Basilica

For hotels and restaurants in this region see pp390–93 and pp394–7

s used in Easter processions.
Though called a coffin, its
purpose has always been
symbolic; it is believed not
to contain any human remains.
The room devoted to altarpieces, some of which are
700 years old, is stunning
in its colour and historical
import. Besides the picture
gallery, there are equally
superb sculpture and
icon galleries.

🏛 Bálint Balassa Museum

Mindszenty tér 5. **Tel** (033) 500 175.
⬜ May–Oct: 9am–5pm Tue–Sun;
Nov–Apr: 9am–5pm Wed–Sun.
🈂 📷 Hungarian only.
www.balassamuzeum.hu

Named after a Renaissance
poet who died in 1594 while
fighting the Turks, the Bálint
Balassa Museum (Bálint
Balassa múzeum) focuses
primarily on life in Esztergom
during the Middle Ages and
the Ottoman era. It also
includes some archaeological
finds from the Royal Palace.

The two-storey museum
building, with its huge, tunnel-
like entrance, dates from
1860 and was originally a
boys' school.

**The Danube Museum, devoted to
the famous river**

🏛 Danube Museum and
Lower Esztergom

Kölcsey utca 2. **Tel** (033) 500 250.
⬜ May–Oct: 10am–6pm Wed–Mon;
Nov–Dec, Feb–Apr: 10am–4pm
Wed–Mon. 📷 ♿
www.dunamuzeum.hu

The role of the Danube in the
history and development of
Esztergom is given due importance in this excellent museum
(Duna múzeum) close to the
city centre. The building itself
is a gem, originally built in
Baroque style in the 18th
century and fully renovated in
1973, when the museum

moved here from its previous
location. The museum
houses all sorts of hydraulic
equipment from the 20th
century, as well as exhibits
devoted to damming the
Danube and navigation.
There is a collection of engineering tools, as well as a
history of water management
since Roman times. There are
several hands-on displays
aimed at children.

A five-minute walk south
along Vörösmarty utca leads
to Széchenyi tér, centre of the
Lower Town and surrounded
on all sides by a mixture of
Baroque and Neo-Classical
houses, many of which are
now cafés. Its focal point is
the Town Hall, an immacu-
lately preserved Rococo
building from 1729.

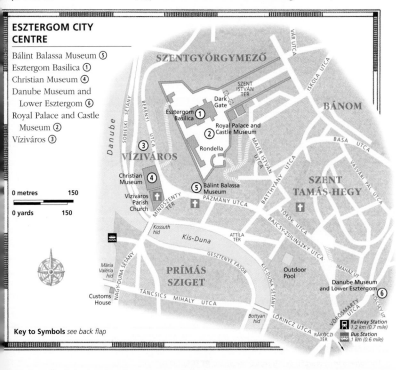

**ESZTERGOM CITY
CENTRE**

0 metres   150
0 yards   150

Key to Symbols see back flap

Railway Station
1.2 km (0.7 mile)
Bus Station
1 km (0.6 mile)

Székesfehérvár ❽

60 km (37 miles) SW of Budapest.
🏠 105,000. 🚃 from Budapest.
🚌 from Budapest. 🚗 Piac tér.
ℹ️ Tourinform, Városház tér 1,
(022) 537 261. 🚗 Piac tér, daily.

Settled by the Magyar chieftan
Arpad in the 9th century,
Székesfehérvár was the first
permanent settlement on the
Székesferhérvár plain. Arpad's
descendants, Prince Geza and
St Stephen, erected a castle
and a vast basilica respectively.
The walled city that grew
around them was the site of
Hungary's Diet, or Parliament,
until the Turkish occupation
in 1543. Although much of the
city was destroyed in World
War II, the Old Town was
spared, and its cobbled streets
are packed with historically
and religiously signifi-
cant buildings.

On the main square,
Városház tér, the
Baroque **Bishop's
Palace**, designed by
Jakob Riedler, was
built in 1801 using
stone from the Royal
Basilica. Across the
square, behind the
18th-century Town
Hall, is the 15th-
century St Anne's
Chapel, the only
part of the medieval
city to have survived the
Ottoman occupation. Behind
it is **St Stephen's Cathedral**,
founded by Bela IV, where
parts of the original Hungarian
coronation ceremony once
took place. Renovated in
Baroque style, the entrance

Pannonhalma Abbey's great library housing ancient manuscripts

features statues of St Stephen,
Laszlo and Imre. The **Carmelite
Monastery** features colourful,
dramatic frescoes by Viennese
artist Franz Anton
Maulbertsch, while the
18th-century altar
fresco in the
Cistercian Church
was painted by local
artists. Opposite this
stands the Black Eagle
Pharmacy Museum,
adorned with hun-
dreds of old medi-
cine bottles and an
amazing frescoed
ceiling. The town's
most visited site,
however, is the **Bory
Castle**, built by Jeno Bory
(1879–1959). Part Roman
forum, part Gothic castle, it
houses sculptures and artworks by Bory and his wife.

**Entrance to
St Stephen's Cathedral**

Pannonhalma Abbey ❾
Pannonhalmi Főapátság

100 km (62 miles) W of Budapest.
Tel (096) 570 191. 🚃 🚌
Abbey & Arboretum ⭕ 22 Mar–
Apr & Oct: 9am–4pm Tue–Sun; May–
Sep: 9am–5pm daily; Nov–21 Mar:
10am–3pm Tue–Sun. **Library**
Tel (096) 570 142. 🎦 🗹 ♿
🎦 Abbey 🚻 🛍️

The story of Pannonhalma
Abbey is as old as Hungary
itself. A UNESCO World
Heritage Site since 1996, there
has been an abbey here since
1002, the same year St Stephen
brought Christianity to the

Magyars. The original
abbey burnt down in 1137,
and was replaced with a
Romanesque construction that
itself was superseded by the
late-Romanesque basilica still
in existence today. The
Western Tower, added in
1832, is one of the abbey's
most prominent features.

The basilica's main portal
of receding arches is one of
the most important surviving
examples of a *porta speciosa*
extant in Hungary. Though
now hemmed in by extension
to the complex, it is an outstanding example of its kind –
an ornamental portal held in
red marble with rich wood
carvings. Inside, the stained-
glass window, added in 1860,
depicts the popular Roman
Catholic saint, Martin of Tours,
who was born at Szombathely
in western Hungary.

The Neo-Classical **Library**
holds 330,000 volumes, including the Tihany Manuscript, the
earliest written Hungarian text.
On the far side of the basilica
Our Lady's Chapel has three
Baroque altars and a tiny
organ. All the abbey's monks
are buried here. The abbey
also houses a treasury that
is home to a rich collection
of ecclesiastical art and
historical artifacts. The
abbey's Benedictine grammar
school, founded in 1802, is
one of the finest in Hungary.
The abbey's **Arboretum**, on
the eastern slope, is the site
of hundreds of rare tree and
shrub species that have
grown wild in its grounds.

**Stunning 18th-century Town Hall
in Székesfehérvár**

Győr ⑩

20 km (74 miles) W of Budapest.
125,000. from Budapest.
from Budapest. Tourinform,
rpád utca 32, (096) 311 771.
ily flower market, Arany János
ca. Győr Spring Festival (Mar).

ocated halfway between
udapest and Vienna, where
e Danube, Rába and Rábca
vers meet, Győr has long
een a place where empires
et, and clashed. During the
ttoman Wars it became home
the most impregnable fort-
ss in Hungary. Today it is a
odern, vibrant city, full of
onuments that tell of its
ventful past.

Founded in the 11th century,
yőr Cathedral was rebuilt in
othic style between 1257
nd 1267; its Baroque interior
ates from after the Ottoman
eriod, when the altarpieces
nd superb frescoes by Franz
nton Maulbertsch were
dded. It houses the remains
f St Laszlo, one of Hungary's
ost sacred relics, and a mira-
ilous painting of the Virgin
ary, one of its most signi-
cant pilgrimage sites.

The imposing **Bishop's
alace**, next door, saw most
f its fortifications added in
e 16th century, to keep out
e Ottomans. Nearby, the
iocesan Treasury and Library
nd Lapidary houses a trea-
ure trove of manuscripts and
urgical items, including an
uminated manuscript once
elonging to King Mátyás.

Up Apaca utca to the
orth, the Margit Kovács
xhibition houses a vast

yőr's Bishop's Palace, built as a
efence against Ottoman invaders

Magnificent interiors of a bedroom in the Esterházy Palace in Fertőd

collection of ceramics by
Hungary's leading 20th-cen-
tury abstract sculptor, while
to the south, Szechényi tér,
once the city's market place,
is ringed by splendid buildings, many of which now
house museums.

Fertőd ⑪

184 km (114 miles) W of Budapest.
3,400. from Szombathely.
from Sopron. Tourinform,
Joseph Haydn utca 3, (099) 370 544.
Haydn Festival (Jun–Sep).

The small town of Fertőd
was created in 1950, when
two former estates belonging
to the Esterházy family, Süttör
and Esterháza, were merged.
For three centuries the
Esterházy family was one of
the richest and most powerful
in Hungary. They flourished
under the Habsburgs, under
whom family members served
in a variety of political and
military offices.

Originally constructed as
a hunting lodge in 1720, the
Esterházy Palace is the result
of vast extensions by architect
Melchior Hefel in the 1770s.

The Neo-Baroque French
gardens were laid out at the
same time, though these were
remodelled along English
ideas of garden design at the
beginning of the 20th century.

The palace is approached
through a grand wrought-
iron entrance gate, with its
Rococo-stone-vase separating
columns. Although the palace
was badly damaged during
World War II, the main ball-
rooms and drawing rooms
have been restored to
their glorious best, filled
with priceless French furniture, Venetian mirrors and
Flemish tapestries.

Joseph Haydn's presence
at the palace, from 1766 to
1790, is celebrated by the
annual Haydn Festival, with
concerts showcasing the
Austrian composer's work.
The emphasis is on his chamber music, which is performed by outstanding musicians
in the Grand Gallery and the
beautiful gardens.

🎹 Esterházy Palace
Joseph Haydn utca 2.
Tel (099) 537 640. Nov–Mar:
10am–4pm Fri–Sun; Apr–Oct:
10am–6pm daily.

Fertő-Hanság National Park ⑫

Fertő-Hanság Nemzeti Park Igazgatósága

195 km (121 miles) W of Budapest. 🚆 from Sopron, Győr. 🚌 from Zalaegerszeg. 🛈 Rév-Kócsagvár, Sarród (Park Administration), (099) 537 620. 🗓 ♿ www.ferto hansag.hu

Located in northwest Hungary near the Austria-Hungary border, the Fertő-Hanság National Park, set around Lake Fertő, was once one of the most heavily guarded sections of the Iron Curtain. Now a designated nature reserve, it is regarded as one of Europe's most significant water habitats and was included on UNESCO's list of World Heritage Sites in 2001.

Lake Fertő is shallow – in most places less than 1-m (3-ft) deep – and is famous for its vast expanse of tall reeds. Its main sources of water are rainfall and two streams. More than 200 species of birds nest here, including the Hungarian ibis, spoonbill, heron and egret, and there are also numerous rare plant species.

With the eastern Alps as its backdrop, the lake is encircled by one of Europe's best cycle paths, which takes in superb scenery in both Hungary and Austria. Favourable, frequent winds also make the lake a popular place for sailing, while the shallow waters are regarded as good swimming spots.

Frozen Lake Fertő in the picturesque Fertő-Hanság National Park

The main resort on the Hungarian side, Fertőrákos, is popular both as a sailing spot and for its grassy beaches and attractive nature walks.

Many parts of the park can only be visited with a special permit or on organized guided tours. Information about visits and tours is available from the park's administration office in the small village of Sarród, located southwest of the park.

The Firewatch Tower, a striking landmark in Sopron

Sopron ⑬

209 km (130 miles) W of Budapest. 👥 56,000. 🚆 from Győr, Vienna. 🚌 from Győr. 🚉 🛈 Tourinform, Liszt Ferenc utca 1, (099) 517 560. 🏛 Csarnok utca, daily. 🎭 Early Music Days (Jun), Sopron Festival Weeks (Jun–Jul), Volt Pop Festival (Jul), Sopron Jazz (Sep), Christmas Market (Dec).

A border town of the Pannonia province, Sopron is regarded as one of Hungary's most attractive towns. Its proximity to Austria is evident in the street signs and shops with German-speaking staff that dominate the town. The country's oldest cultural centre, Sopron has remains of Roman edifices, and city walls as well as grand medieval buildings, including both churches and a synagogue. Among its

other attractions are a Pharmacy Museum and an outstanding art collection.

The town is built around the magnificent Belváros – the Inner Town. Centred around Fő tér, an impressive central square that acts as a focal point, Belváros contains most of the town's main sights. Built between 1861 and 1864, the former Ursuline Convent houses a fine collection of ecclesiastical art, owned and managed by Sopron's Catholic Convent. Most of the items on display date from the Baroque period but there is also a collection from the early 1800s. Sopron's largest church, the **Benedictine Church**, on Fő tér, was built by Franciscan monks in 1280 and displays remnants of medieval frescoes. It is also known as the Goat Church, as it is believed that a goatherd financed it from the treasure found by his flock. Opposite the Benedictine Church, the Storno House is a grand house built in the 1400s, which was home to King Mátyás between 1482 and 1483. Originally a Renaissance building, it was remodelled in the Baroque style in 1720. It displays a collection of art and period furniture.

Sopron also has a wealth of fine Art Nouveau architecture including the **Firewatch Tower** from where superb views unfold. In 1921, the towns-people voted to stay in Hungary, rather than join Austria and the Gate of Loyalty, at the foot of the tower, was added in 1928 to honour the result of that plebiscite. Also worth visiting is the medieval Synagogue, one of the oldest in Europe, believed to have been built around 1300. Abandoned in 1526, when the Jews were expelled from the town, many of its original features remain intact, including a replica of the Ark of the Covenant.

🔒 **Benedictine Church**
Templom utca 1, Fő tér. **Tel** (099) 523 768. ◯ 9am–5pm daily. 🖼 ♿

🏰 **Firewatch Tower**
Fő tér. ◯ May–Aug: 10am–8pm Tue–Sun; Apr, Sep–Oct: 10am–6pm Tue–Sun. 🖼

Kőszeg ⑭

19 km (136 miles) W of Budapest.
12,000. from Szombathely.
from Sopron. Tourinform,
Jurisics tér 7, (094) 563 120.

Nestled in lowland hills just
minutes from the Austrian
border, Kőszeg is a small, quiet
town. Spared during World
War II, it is regarded as one of
the prettiest towns in the
region. The town preserves
the memory of Captain Miklós
Jurisics, who led the
Hungarians against the
Turks. Its main
square, castle and
museum are named
after him. **Jurisics
Castle** is on the site
where Miklós
Jurisics and 450
soldiers held
Turkish forces at
bay for 25 days in
August 1532; the bells
of the town toll
every day at 11am
in his honour. A fire
destroyed parts of the castle
in 1777; however, the interior
arcades were built after the
blaze. The Castle Museum has
displays on the town's history,
including various depictions
of the siege. In the heart of
Kőszeg's Old Town stands the
elegant Miklós Jurisics tér,
surrounded by churches and
museums. The impressive
entrance to the square, the
Heroes' Gate, was erected to

**Crest above the gate
to Jurisics Castle**

commemorate the 400th
anniversary of the Turkish
siege. The **Jurisics Museum**
has a fine collecton of memorabilia belonging to the
artisans and tradesmen who
inhabited the town. Set in a
Baroque house on Jurisics
tér, the **Golden Unicorn
Pharmaceutical Museum**, contains a superb late 18th-century
wooden apothecary counter
with old medicine bottles.
Nearby, the Gothic **Church of
St James**, completed in 1407,
but reconstructed in the 18th
century, has served
Jesuit, Protestant and
Roman Catholic con-
gregations. Inside, the
faded frescoes by an
unknown artist por-
traying the Magi
date from 1403. An
original statue of
the Madonna from
the Gothic period is
also noteworthy. Built
between 1892 and
1894 to designs by
Austrian architect
Otto Kott, the fantastical Neo-
Gothic **Jesus's Heart Church**,
on Fő tér, is famous for its
stained-glass altar windows
depicting Sts Stephen, Imre
and Elizabeth.

Sárvár ⑮

212 km (132 miles) W of Budapest.
16,000. from Szombathely.
from Szombathely. Tourinform,
Várkerület 33, (095) 520 178.

Located on the banks of the
Rába river, this town was
originally the site of Roman
and Celt fortifi-
cations. Sárvár,
(mud castle),
derives its name
from the castle of
mud that was built
here by the Magyars
in the 10th century.
The Sárvár Castle
that now attracts
visitors is, how-
ever, a distant rela-
tion to its muddy
ancestor, having
been built in the
16th century. Its
illustrious patrons
were the Nádasdy
family, who bought

**Superb frescoes depicting battle
scenes, Sárvár Castle**

the town in 1534. Patriarch
Tamás Nádasdy brought in
Italian architects to create a
genuine Renaissance masterpiece. This, with various
additions including a palatial
interior, has remained intact to
the present day. Much of the
castle is devoted to the captivating **Ferenc Nádasdy
Museum**, which has exhibitions on the history of the
family and the town, regional
folk art and period furniture.
Highlights include two series
of frescoes: 17th-century works
showing the Hungarians in
battle with the Turks, and
scenes from the Old Testament
painted by artist István
Dorffmaister in 1769.

In 1961, the search for oil
led to the discovery of hot
springs in Sárvár. Since then
the development of spas has
added to the town's appeal as
a tourist destination. The
famous **Sárvár Spa and
Wellness Centre** has grown to
become one of the largest and
most modern bath complexes
in Hungary. It comprises
indoor and outdoor pools,
leisure and splash pools, a
sauna and a treatment centre
offering various therapies.

🏛 **Ferenc Nádasdy Museum**
Várkerület 1. **Tel** (095) 320 158.
⏰ 9am–5pm Tue–Sun.
Hungarian only.

💧 **Sárvár Spa and Wellness
Centre**
Vadkert utca 1. **Tel** (095) 523 600.
⏰ 8am–10pm daily.

Heroes' Gate in Miklós Jurisics Square, Kőszeg

Veszprém ⑯

The site of the nation's first bishopric, and for centuries the seat of the Queen of Hungary's household, Veszprém is one of Hungary's great historic towns. It was all but razed by the Turks as they fled Hungary in the 1600s. Spread over five hills, the most picturesque part of the city is its Castle District (Vár), with its delightful mixture of medieval and Baroque buildings. The twin towers of St Michael's Cathedral, visible from afar, are a symbol of Veszprém. Many sights are at the top of long staircases or at the end of steep, cobbled streets. Down below, the lower city also offers some fine Baroque architecture, great museums and quaint streets.

Dazzling golden interior of St Michael's Cathedral

🔒 St Michael's Cathedral

Vár utca 27. **Tel** (088) 426 088.
◯ May–Oct: 10am–5:30pm.
There was a church here as early as 1001, when St Stephen created a bishopric, but the cathedral's (Szent Mihály Érseki Székesegyház) present appearance dates back to 1908, when it was extensively rebuilt in Neo-Romanesque style. Remains of earlier styles include the Gothic undercroft and the crypt's vaulting, both from 1380. The towers were built in 1723, and many older features of the cathedral have recently been restored.

🔒 Gizella Chapel

Vár utca 18. **Tel** (088) 426 088.
◯ May–Oct: 10am–5pm Tue–Sun.
This 13th-century Gothic chapel (Gizella Kápolna) commemorates the life of Gizella, wife of Stephen and first queen of Hungary. The chapel was lost and only rediscovered in the 1760s, during building work. It retains original Byzantine frescoes of the apostles on its walls.

🏛 Archbishop's Palace

Vár utca 16–18. **Tel** (088) 426 088.
◯ May–Oct: 10am–5pm Tue–Sun
(only a few rooms are open to the public).
Veszprém's finest building, this (Érseki Palota) is a brilliant example of Baroque design by Jakab Fellner, built in 1764 with his trademark rounded four-columned loggia. Used to house the archbishop's archive, it also has a fine collection of Baroque furniture and frescoes.

🏛 Castle Gate and Museum

Vár utca. **Tel** (088) 426 088.
Museum ◯ Apr–Sep: 9am–3pm daily.
Although it looks medieval, this gate (Várkapu) is a replica of the original castle gate that was built in 1938 to commemorate the Hungarian dead of World War I. The tower affords good views of the city from the top.

🏛 Óváros Square

Óváros tér.
Veszprém's former market square, Óváros Square (Óváros tér) is surrounded by some fine houses, many of which have been turned into cafés. The Pósa House at No. 3 was built for a local merchant, Endre Pósa, in 1783. Its showy decoration, especially the two cherubs below the roof, was intended to offset the linearity of the building. The contours of the Art Nouveau house next door are gentler. Opposite is the Neo-Classical **Town Hall**, built in 1896 as church offices, but renovated and converted in 1990. Behind the Town Hall, up a flight of stairs, is Lenke Kiss's fountain *Girl with a Jug*, affectionately known as "Zsuzsi" by locals.

A late-Art Nouveau stained-glass window in the Petőfi Theatre

🎭 Petőfi Theatre

Óváry Ferenc utca 2. **Tel** (088) 424 235. 🌐 www.petofiszinhaz.hu
This late-Art Nouveau municipal theatre building, set in well-kept gardens, is named after revolutionary playwright and poet Sándor Petőfi. The theatre (Petőfi Színház) was designed in 1908 by István Medgyaszay, who studied in Vienna. It has intricate folk motifs on the façade, typical of the later Art Nouveau buildings.

Façade of the Neo-Classical Town Hall, built in 1896

Laczkó Dezső Museum

rzsébet Sétány 1. **Tel** (088) 564 330.
Mar–Oct: 10am–6pm Tue–Sun;
Nov–Feb: noon–4pm Tue–Sun.

Designed by the local architect
stván Medgyaszay, the
County Museum (Laczkó
Dezső múzeum) was opened
n 1922. It displays local arti-
acts and folk costumes dating
back to Celtic times. Most of
the collection was donated by
local Piarist monks, after
whose leader, Laczkó Dezső,
the museum was named. It
also housed Hungary's first
public library, still a leading
research facility.

Bakony Regional Folk House

rzsébet Sétány 3. **Tel** (088) 564 330.
May–Oct: 10am–6pm Tue–Sun.

Hungary's first ethnographic
museum, the Bakony House
Bakonyi Ház) was created in
1935, and modelled on the
9th-century houses of a
nearby town. The house is
built on high foundations
and has a covered terrace.
A staircase leads to a single
door. Inside, items on show
date to 1700.

**St István Viaduct, designed by the
Hungarian architect Róbert Folly**

St István Viaduct

Szent István völgyhíd.
Stretching over the Fejes
valley, from Dózsa György
utca to the St László Church,
the St István Viaduct
(Szent István
Völgyhíd) was
built in 1938, a
major engineering
achievement at the time.
Designed by a
Hungarian, Róbert Folly,
it rises 50 m (164 ft)
above the Séd river
at its highest point.
It offers magnificent
views of the castle and
the Bakony Mountains
to the north.

VISITORS' CHECKLIST

110 km (68 miles) SW of
Budapest. 60,000.
90 km (56 miles) S of centre.
Jutási út. Piac tér.
Piac tér, Szabadság tér.
Tourinform, Vár utca 4
(088) 404 548. Gizella
Art Days (May).

Veszprém Zoo

Kittenberger Kálmán út 15–17.
Tel (088) 566 140. May–Sep:
9am–6pm daily; Apr, Oct: 9am–5pm
daily; Mar, Nov: 9am–4pm daily; Dec–
Feb: 9am–3:30pm daily.
www.zoo.hu/veszprem
Hungary's best zoo
(Kittenberger Kálmán
Növény És Vadaspark) is
named after 19th-century
biologist and natural historian
Kálmán Kittenberger
(1881–1958).
Spread over 13 ha
(32 acres) in the
lovely Fejes valley,
it is home to 120
species, including
Sumatran tigers,
Kamchatka bears
and wonderful
exotic birds.

**A giraffe in
Veszprém Zoo**

VESZPRÉM CITY CENTRE

0 metres   200

0 yards   200

Benedek Hill
PATAK TÉR
ÚRKÚT UTCA
Gizella Museum
① St Michael's Cathedral
② Gizella Chapel
③ Archbishop's Palace
St István Viaduct and Veszprém Zoo
DEÁK FERENC UTCA
Séd
VÁR UTCA
FÉNYES U.
VÖGYIKÚT UTCA
CSERHÁT UTCA
Railway Station 2 km (1.2 miles)
Bus Station
④ Castle Gate and Museum
Town Hall
THOLDY UTCA
BUHIM UTCA
CSAPLÁR JÁNOS UTCA
Covered Market
Firetower
Pósa House
⑤ ÓVÁROS SQUARE
RÁCKÓ U.
JÓKAI MÓR UTCA
FESTŐ UTCA
RÁNOLDER JÁNOS TÉR
HORGOS UTCA
VÁS UTCA
VIRÁG UTCA
KOSSUTH LAJOS UTCA
JUTÁSI ÚT
BEM UTCA
DÓZSA GYÖRGY ÚT
TOBORZÓ UTCA
ÓVÁRI FERENC UTCA
SZABADSÁG TÉR
BRUSZNYAI UTCA
BUDAPEST
BUDAPEST ÚT
⑥ Petőfi Theatre
County Hall
MEGYEHÁZ TÉR
KORKÁZ UCTA
ISKOLA UTCA
New Library
ERZSÉBET TÉR
ERZSÉBET SÉTÁNY
Laczkó Dezső Museum ⑦
⑧ Bakony Regional Folk House
MÁRTIROK UTCA

KEY

Pedestrian zone

Key to Symbols see back flap

Marina in Siófok, departure point for pleasure cruises and water sports

Siófok ⑰

88 km (54 miles) SW of Budapest.
🏠 *23,000.* 🚉 🚌 *from Budapest.*
⛴ *from Balatonalmádi, Tihany.*
ℹ️ *Tourinform, Víztorony, Szabadság tér (084) 310 117.* 🎭 *Golden Cockle Folklore Festival (Jul).*
www.siofoktourism.com

The largest and liveliest resort on Lake Balaton's southern coast, Siófok stretches along the shore for 17 km (11 miles). It is popular with weekenders from Budapest, many of whom have holiday homes here. The main attraction is the beach. It is split into two parts – Golden Shore (Aranypart) to the north, and Silver Shore (Ezüstpart) to the south – by the Sió canal, which was originally built by the Romans in AD 276. Like all of Lake Balaton's resorts, Siófok offers mainly grass beaches. The resort's marina is at the head of the canal, from where pleasure cruisers and ferries depart for the nearby Tihany Peninsula, Hungary's first conservation area. The port is a good place to hire sailing boats, and to organize a variety of other water sports.

On summer evenings, Siófok comes alive with tens of thousands of young people looking for a good time in the resort's innumerable bars, discos and nightclubs, many of which are in the open air. Visitors looking for a quiet night may prefer to go to one of the smaller resorts along the coast.

Lake Balaton Tour ⑱

Spread over an area of 596 sq km (230 sq miles), Lake Balaton is the largest freshwater lake in Central Europe. It is often referred to as Budapest-on-Sea and attracts thousands of holidaymakers every summer. Most of the southern side of the lake is very shallow, with an average depth of just 4 m (13 ft), and the waters are fairly warm, making this the most popular shore with bathers and families. The southern shore is, therefore, the most developed, with sandy beaches and a wide choice of accommodation.

Kis-Balaton ⑪
The Kis-Balaton Nature Reserve at the mouth of the Zala river covers an area of 40 sq km (15 sq miles). It is home to many rare plants and animals.

Balatonberény ⑩
One of the first resorts on the lake to become popular, Balatonberény retains a late-19th-century charm, most apparent in its delightful lakeside cottages and rural houses.

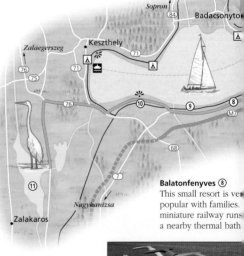

Balatonfenyves ⑧
This small resort is very popular with families. A miniature railway runs to a nearby thermal bath.

Balatonmáriafürdő ⑨
This lively resort attracts water sports enthusiasts and those looking for a good range of bars and restaurants.

For hotels and restaurants in this region see pp390–93 and pp394–7

Zamárdi ①
A world away from noisy Siófok, Zamárdi is home to some fine thatched cottages, including this arcaded house on Fő utca, now the village's museum.

Balatonföldvár ②
This town owes its name to Iron Age fortifications called *földvár*, remains of which can still be seen. The village's leafy promenade is generally considered the finest on the south shore.

Kőröshegy ③
A short detour south of Balatonföldvár is Kőröshegy, with a well-preserved Gothic fortified church dating from 1460.

Balatonszemes ④
This quiet resort has a Postal and Carriage Museum. Its tree-lined streets are ideal for a stroll and there is an aquapark nearby.

```
0 km          10
0 miles     5
```

KEY

🚢	Ferry terminal
Ⓐ	Campsite
☀	Viewpoint
▬	Motorway
▬▬	Motorway under construction
▬	Tour route
=	Minor road
—	Railway
---	Ferry route

Somogyvár ⑤
Somogyvár is well worth the detour south from Buzsák – the impressive ruins of the Benedictine monastery here date back to the 11th century.

Buzsák ⑥
The Living Museum of Arts and Crafts at Buzsák is the best place around Balaton to learn about the traditions of the lake and its people. Fine cloth, pottery and garments are still made here.

Fonyód ⑦
Unremarkable as a resort, Fonyód sits at the foot of the largest hill on the southern shore, the 233-m (764-ft) high Várhegy, an extinct volcano.

Keszthely ⑲

Keszthely is the oldest and largest of the towns that line the shores of Lake Balaton (*see pp368–9*). Many of its elegant streets evocatively preserve the small-town atmosphere of the 19th century, when it was the property of the Festetics family. Their Baroque family seat, Festetics Palace (*see pp372–3*), is one of Hungary's finest stately homes. The town possesses one of the lake's few sandy beaches and serves as Balaton's cultural hub, hosting the annual Balaton Festival. Since the conversion in 2006 of a nearby former Soviet airfield into the FlyBalaton Airport, Keszthely is transforming itself into one of the most visited places in Hungary.

Town Hall, one of many attractive buildings on Fő Square

🏛 Fő Square and Town Hall
Fő tér.

At the heart of Keszthely is the bustling Fő Square (Fő tér), dominated on its northern side by the attractive late-Baroque, pastel-pink Town Hall (Polgármesteri Hivatal). This was built in 1790, although the façade was extensively remodelled in the 1850s. Erected earlier, in 1770, the Baroque Trinity Column, in the centre of the square, looks its best in early summer when it is surrounded by bedding flowers of every colour.

🔒 Franciscan Church
Fő tér 5. **Tel** *(083) 314 271.*

This grand building, towering over the southern side of the square, is the Franciscan Church and former monastery (Magyarok Nagyasszonya Templom), built in the 14th century. Its tall Neo-Gothic tower with a 10-m (33-ft) spire was added in the 18th century. The crypt holds the tomb of György Festetics (*see p373*),

the patriarch of the Festetics family and uncle of István Széchenyi, one of Hungary's social and political reformers.

The church was originally built in Gothic style using stone taken from an old Roman settlement nearby.

Stained-glass window in the Franciscan Church

During restoration work in 1974, remains of captivating 14th- and 15th-century frescoes were discovered. Lost during the Ottoman occupation, when the church served as a fortress and was connected to Lake Balaton by a canal, these represent the largest collection of Gothic frescoes remaining in Hungary. The fine rose window above the eastern portal is also an original 14th-century feature.

🏛 Kossuth Utca

Keszthely's main thoroughfare was built to allow the Festetics family easy access from their castle to the lake. Undoubtedly the widest street in the older part of the town, it is lined with some fine houses. The oldest, at No. 22, is the birthplace of the Hungarian-Jewish pianist Karl Goldmark. With its porticos and covered upper-level loggia, the house has a Mediterranean feel. Just behind, in a leafy courtyard, is Keszthely's well-preserved Neo-Renaissance synagogue. Originally dating from 1780, it was entirely rebuilt between 1851 and 1852.

🏛 Balaton Museum

Múzeum utca 2. **Tel** *(083) 312 351.*
◐ *May–Oct: 10am–6pm Tue–Sun; Nov–Apr: 9am–5pm Tue–Sat.* 🎫 ♿

The mustard-yellow Neo-Baroque Balaton Museum (Balatoni múzeum) building was erected in the 1920s to a design by Dénes Györgyi, and is worth seeing in its own right.

The exhibitions inside are equally interesting and include a fascinating look at life around Lake Balaton in pre-Roman times. There are displays showing the development of fishing on the lake as well as a more sombre display explaining the effects of pollution on life in the lake. Models of sailing ships, streamers and paddleboats that once traversed the lake are also on view.

There is also a collection of outstanding Roman stoneware from the region and an original milestone from Aquincum, a Roman town 69 km (43 miles) from

Excavated fishing equipment on display at the Balaton Museum

VISITORS' CHECKLIST

187 km (116 miles) SW of
Budapest. ₪ *10,000.*
✈ *10 km (6 miles) S of centre.*
🚉 *Kazinczy utca.* 🚌 *Kazinczy
utca.* 🚌 *Kazinczy utca.*
ℹ *Tourinform, Kossuth utca 28,
(083) 314 144.* 🎭 *Balaton
Festival (May), Helikon Chamber
Music Festival (May).*
www.*keszthely.hu*

Keszthely, whose remains
were excavated at the end
of the 19th century.

🏛 Georgikon Farm Museum

Bercsényi Miklós utca 65–7. *Tel (083)
311 563.* ☐ *May–Oct: 10am–5pm
Mon–Sat, 10am–6pm Sun.* 🈂 🈂
Hungarian and German only. ♿
Europe's first Academy of
Agriculture was set up here
by György Festetics in 1797. It
was converted into a museum
(Georgikon Majormúzeum) in
1972, and exhibitions focus
on the history of Hungarian
agriculture from Celtic times
to the present day. There are
separate displays on wine
production in the Balaton

area and domestic farming
in southern Transdanubia,
a region along the border
between Hungary and Austria.
A selection of antique agricultural equipment ranges
from Bronze Age tools to
steam ploughs, including
an early motor tractor.

🏛 Doll and Waxwork Museum

Kossuth Lajos utca 11. *Tel (083) 318
855.* ☐ *10am–6pm Mon–Sun.* 🈂
This museum (Történelmi
Panoptikum) is actually three
museums in one. The first
contains a collection of 700
porcelain dolls. Each doll
wears the traditional costume

of a particular Hungarian
village, and was handmade
there. The dolls are complemented by a display of local
village architecture, with more
than 200 scale models,
including houses, stables and
churches. The second part of
the museum holds waxworks,
featuring 500 life-size figures
of eminent Hungarians, from
Prince Árpád to Imre Nagy.

The third section is a
7-m (23-ft) long model of
Hungary's Parliament, which
was made by Ilona Miskei
from more than four million
sea-snail shells.

🎠 Festetics Palace

See pp372–3.

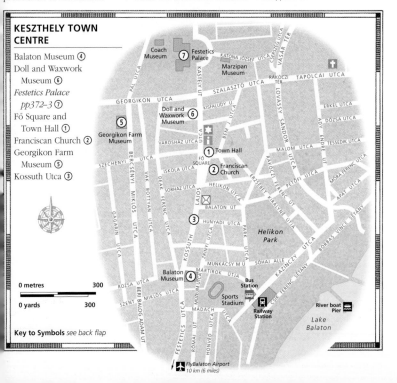

KESZTHELY TOWN CENTRE

Balaton Museum ④
Doll and Waxwork
  Museum ⑥
Festetics Palace
* pp372–3* ⑦
Fő Square and
  Town Hall ①
Franciscan Church ②
Georgikon Farm
  Museum ⑤
Kossuth Utca ③

0 metres   300
0 yards   300

Key to Symbols *see back flap*

Keszthely: Festetics Palace
Festetics Palota

Originally the home of the Festetics family, the stately Neo-Baroque Festetics Palace is the magnum opus of little-known architect Viktor Rumpelmayer, who redesigned the palace in the 1880s. It was requisitioned by the Soviet Army in 1944. Today, the palace houses the Helikon Palace Museum, which is a popular day trip from Lake Balaton *(see p368–9)*. More than half of the palace's 101 rooms are open to the public, and feature fine examples of exotic art, furniture and arms gathered on the family's many foreign expeditions. The palace is famous for its 100,000-volume library and its fine English gardens, which cover over 42 ha (104 acres).

★ Baroque Tower
This Neo-Baroque façade is based on the French stately homes of the same era. The central tower's dome, however, evokes an earlier Baroque style.

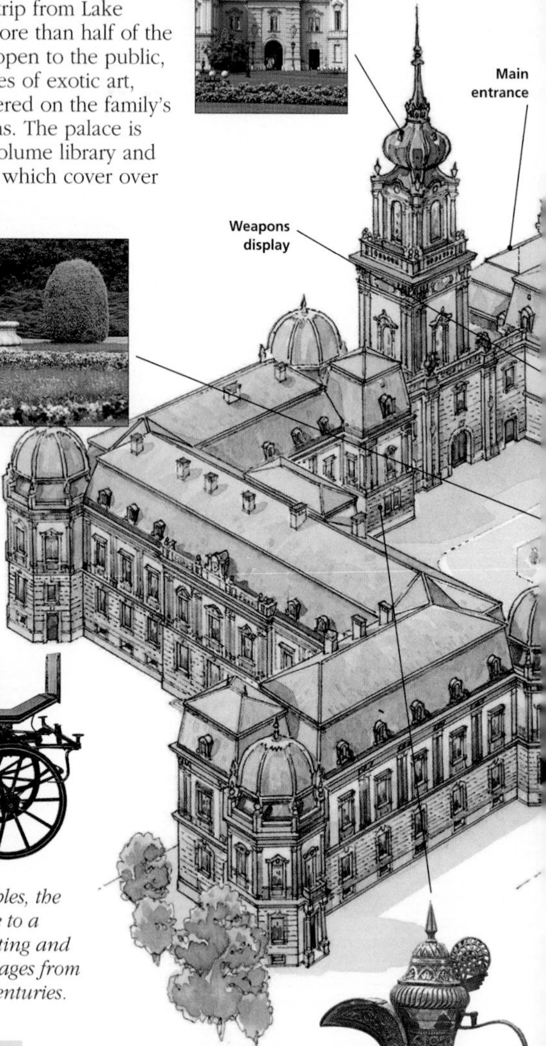

Main entrance

Weapons display

English Gardens
English stately homes were the inspiration for the beautiful palace gardens. These were laid out by the English landscape artist Edward Miller.

Carriage Museum
In the palace's former stables, the Carriage Museum is home to a priceless collection of hunting and parade coaches and carriages from the 18th and early 19th centuries.

STAR FEATURES

★ Baroque Tower

★ Mirror Room

★ Library

The World of Islam
The Festetics family filled the mansion with treasures brought back from their travels to North Africa and the Middle East. The collection has been enhanced with loans from the Tareq Rajab Museum, Kuwait.

★ Mirror Room
Adorned with Venetian mirrors and English furniture, the striking Mirror Room, also known as the Main Hall, regularly hosts chamber music concerts and operettas.

VISITORS' CHECKLIST

Kastély utca 1, Keszthely.
Tel *(083) 314 194.* 🚌 🚃 🚗
ℹ️ *Tourinform, Kossuth Lajos utca 28, (083) 314 144.* ⏰ *Sep–May: 10am–5pm Tue–Sun; Jun: 9am–5pm Tue–Sun; Jul–Aug: 9am–6pm daily.* 📷 📹 ♿ 🖵
📷 **Note:** *fee payable for photography & video cameras.*
www.helikonkastely.hu

Each room is decorated in a different colour scheme and features priceless artifacts.

Chapel
The small, private Festetics Chapel was built in the 1880s, when the extent of the palace was considerably expanded.

★ Library
The Rococo Helikon Library holds over 100,000 volumes on its oak shelves. Hungary's literary elite gathered here in the 19th century.

Portrait Gallery
Beautiful portraits of almost every member of the Festetics family, as well as prominent members of Hungarian and Viennese society, line the palace's walls.

GYÖRGY FESTETICS

A polymath who combined a love for agriculture and the arts with the progressive ideals of the Enlightenment, György Festetics (1755–1819) was the grandson of Kristóf Festetics, who had been given the Helikon Estate in 1743 by the Habsburgs. György is best known for founding Europe's first agricultural college, the Georgikon *(see p371)* at Keszthely in 1797. A great explorer, he went on to become a generous patron of the arts and organized poetry and music festivals at the palace.

Statue of György Festetics

Pécs ⓴

Cosmopolitan Pécs calls itself "Hungary's Mediterranean city", as the sun shines here for more than 200 days a year. Many of the city's streets also have an Oriental feel to them. Pécs was founded by the Romans, who called the place Sopianae, in the 3rd century AD. It served as the capital of Valeria Province and was an early centre of Roman Christianity – as evidenced by the 4th-century tombs on Apáca utca. It was the Ottoman Turks, however, 1,000 years later, who left the deepest marks on the city's landscape. Széchenyi tér, the bustling heart of the city, is dominated by the former Gazi Kasim Pasha mosque, the largest surviving original Islamic construction in Hungary. The city also boasts excellent galleries, museums and great examples of Islamic architecture.

Impressive sculpture outside the Modern Hungarian Gallery

🏛 St Peter's Cathedral and Bishops' Palace

Dóm tér. *Tel (072) 513 050.* ◯ mid-Apr–mid-Oct: 9am–5pm Tue–Sat, 1–5pm Sun; mid-Oct–mid-Apr: 10am–4pm Tue–Sat, 1–4pm Sun. 🎫 🚻

The historic centre of Pécs, Dóm tér, is dominated by St Peter's Cathedral (Szent Péter Székesegyház), first built as a Neo-Romanesque church in 1009 when St Stephen made Pécs a bishopric. The original church, which burnt down in 1064, was replaced by a Baroque cathedral built over nearly 200 years. Badly damaged by the Mongols, it was almost entirely rebuilt as a Gothic church in the 15th century. The current edifice dates from 1891, and is the work of Viennese architect Friedrich Schmidt. The interior is impressive, especially the frescoes in the chapel by Károly Lotz and the reliefs

in the crypt by György Zala. A bronze statue of Janos Pannonius, a leading humanist, stands in front of the cathedral.

Opposite is the deep red, 19th-century Neo-Renaissance Bishops' Palace (Püspöki Palota). It has a statue of Hungary's most prominent musician Franz Liszt in a raincoat, on the southern balcony. The palace is home to one of Hungary's largest libraries.

🏛 Modern Hungarian Gallery

Káptalan utca 4. *Tel (072) 540 040.* ◯ May–Oct: 10am–6pm Tue–Sat, 10am–4pm Sun; Nov–Apr: 10am–4pm Tue–Sun. 🎫 ✍ 🎫 🚻

One of the finest collections of 20th-century Hungarian art in the country, this gallery (Modern Magyarképtár) features works by every major artist of the age, including József Rippl-Rónai, Lajos Gulácsy and Farkas Molnár. In the garden there is a

collection of large granite statues by Budapest-born sculptor Pierre Szekely, who lived and died in France.

🏛 Csontváry Museum

Janus Pannonius utca 11. *Tel (072) 310 544.* ◯ 10am–6pm Tue–Sun. ✍ 🎫 🚻

A tortured soul and former pharmacist turned artist, Tivadar Kosztka Csontváry (1853–1919) produced most of his work between 1903 and 1909, after which he moved to Naples. Most of Kosztka Csontváry's masterpieces, including the startling *View of the Dead Sea from the Temple Square in Jerusalem* (1905), have been on display in this Neo-Renaissance building since 1973.

🏛 Apáca Utca and Early Christian Mausoleum

Christian Burial Site Apáca utca 14. *Tel (072) 312 719.* ◯ by appt only; book in advance. ✍ 🎫
Early Christian Mausoleum Szent István tér 4. ◯ 10am–6pm Tue–Sun. ✍ 🎫

Four graves at Apáca utca 14, all from AD 390, mark one of the earliest Christian burial sites in Europe. The bodies are buried under a chapel, and not in sarcophagi. Nearby, the **Early Christian Mausoleum** (Ókeresztény Mauzóleum), below an excavated chapel, is even older, dating from AD 275. It is decorated with biblical frescoes. These and two further burial chambers at Pécs were declared UNESCO World Heritage Sites in 2000.

St Peter's Cathedral, with its distinctive corner towers

🏛 Archaeological Museum

Széchenyi tér 12. **Tel** *(072) 312 719.*
◯ *May–Oct: 10am–2pm Tue–Sat;*
Nov–Apr: 10am–3pm Mon–Fri by
appt only. ♿

This 18th-century building
(Régészeti múzeum) was
converted into a museum in
1922. The highlight is the
story of Pécs in Roman times.
The museum also features
artifacts left behind by Goths,
Huns, Tatars and Visigoths
and a bust of Marcus Aurelius.

🏛 Gazi Kasim Pasha Mosque/ Inner City Parish Church

Széchenyi tér. **Tel** *(072) 321 976.*
◯ *mid-Apr–mid-Oct: 10am–4pm*
Mon–Sat; mid-Oct–mid-Apr: 10am–
noon Mon–Sat. 📷 ♿

Built in 1579 for Gazi Kasim
Pasha, this lovely mosque
(Gazi Kasim Pasha Dzámi/
Belvárosi Templom) was the
largest in Hungary, and
remains its most important
Ottoman monument.

Converted into a Christian
church in the late 1600s,
calligraphy at the entrance
and a prayer niche are
reminders of its origins.

🏯 Király Utca

Largely pedestrianized, Király
utca is an architectural showcase. Art Nouveau façades
can be seen at No. 5 –
Palatinus hotel *(see p392)* –
as well as at Nos. 8, 10, 19
and the National Theatre.
The St Pauline Church at
No. 44 is in Baroque style.

✡ Synagogue

Kossuth tér. ◯ *10am–5pm Sun–Fri.*
📷 ♿

This grand Neo-Renaissance
synagogue (Zsinagóga), built
in the 1860s, indicates the high
standing that the 5,000-strong
Jewish community had in
Pécs society. They lived in
Pécs until 1944, when the
anti-Semitic Arrow
Cross government
sent them to camps
in Auschwitz *(see
pp194–7).* A mem-
orial commemo-
rates those who
were killed.
Services take
place in the
smaller prayer
hall at the side.

**Façade of Pécs
Synagogue**

VISITORS' CHECKLIST

202 km (126 miles) SW of
Budapest. 🏠 *156,000.*
🚉 *Indóház tér.* 🚌
🚉 *Zólyom utca, Széchenyi tér.*
ℹ *Tourinform, Széchenyi tér 9,
(072) 213 315.* 🎭 *Spring
Festival (last two weeks Mar),
Pécs Cultural Festival (first week
Sep).* **www**.baranyatour.hu

🏛 Jakovali Hassan Mosque

Rákóczi út. 2. **Tel** *(072) 313 853.*
◯ *Apr–Sep: 10am–6pm Mon,
Tue, Thu–Sun.* 📷 📷

This 16th-century mosque
(Jakovali Hassan Dzámi) was
converted into a Catholic
church in 1714, but its 23-m
(75-ft) high minaret
remains intact.
Since 1975 it has
been a museum
documenting the
Ottoman occupa-
tion of Pécs. Many
exhibits were don-
ated by the Turkish
government as a
mark of friendship
in the 1990s.

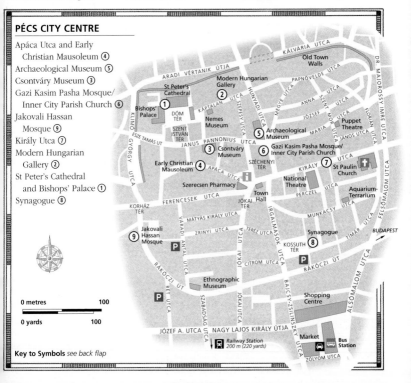

PÉCS CITY CENTRE

0 metres   100
0 yards   100

Key to Symbols *see back flap*

Kecskemét ㉑

Logo of the Zwack distillery

The city of Kecskemét dates back to 1368, though little remains from that era. Kecskemét benefited from self-government during Ottoman rule, and the Habsburgs encouraged the development of agriculture in the region, which is often called the "Garden of Hungary". The local plums are the source of a delicious brandy.

An earthquake in June 1911 shook the city, but the outstanding Baroque and Art Nouveau city centre was mercifully spared. Home to some great museums, Kecskemét is a superb place to explore.

🔒 Piarist Church and School

Jókai tér. **Church** ◯ 11am–2pm daily.

The Piarists were a relatively progressive and scientific Catholic Order founded in Rome in 1597 by St Joseph Calasanctius. They arrived in Kecskemét in 1715 and founded the school on Jókai tér. The present school building (Rendház), however, was built in the late 1940s. The Baroque church (Piarista Templom) opposite the school was erected between 1729 and 1765, to designs by Andras Mayerhoffer. St Calasanctius is represented by one of four statues in front of the building, alongside the Virgin Mary and St Stephen and St László.

🏛 Ornamental Palace

Rákóczi utca 1. **Tel** (076) 480 776. ◯ 10am–5pm Tue–Sat, 1:30–5pm Sun. 🖼 ♿

This masterpiece (Cifra Palota), completed in 1902, was the work of architect Géza Markus. An art gallery since World War II, the palace holds over 10,000 works and

The Art Nouveau Ornamental Palace

exhibitions on the Art Nouveau architects Tóth and Glücks. The green and orange tiled roof is outstanding.

🏛 Hungarian Photography Museum

Katona József tér 12. **Tel** (076) 483 221. ◯ 10am–5pm Wed–Sun. 🖼 ♿ **www**.fotomuzeum.hu

This museum (Magyar Fotográfiai múzeum), is housed in a former synagogue that retains many of its original features. The museum displays the works of every great Hungarian photographer, including André Kertész and László Moholy-Nagy. There are regular exhibitions by international artists. A photography bookshop is attached to the museum.

🏛 József Katona Theatre and Holy Trinity Monument

Katona József tér 5. **Tel** (076) 501 170. ◯ during performances only. ♿ Ø

Resembling a jewellery box, this theatre (Katona József Színház) was the creation of Austrian architects Ferdinand Fellner and Hermann Helmer. Completed in 1896, it was named after playwright József Katona. It is worth attending a performance to see the ceiling alone. The superb Holy Trinity Monument (Szentharomság Szobor) in front of the theatre was erected after the end of the most recent outbreak of plague, in 1742.

🔒 Great Catholic Church

Nagytemplom

Kossuth tér 2. ◯ 9am–7pm daily; spire and viewing platform summer only. 🖼 ♿

The gigantic Great Catholic Church was built in 1772–96. Its spire rises to 73 m (240 ft), offering superb views. The Baroque exterior features statues and reliefs of figures from Hungarian history. Grand steps lead to the pulpit in an otherwise plain interior.

Room in the Museum of Medicinal and Pharmaceutical History

🏛 Museum of Medicinal and Pharmaceutical History

Kölcsey utca 3. **Tel** (076) 329 964. ◯ May–Oct: 10am–2pm Tue–Sun. 🖼 ♿

Although this museum (Orvos És Gyógyszerészettörténeti Kiállítás) houses only a small collection, consisting mainly of colourful old medicine bottles, intricate old surgical instruments, a weighing chair and various reference works, it is worth a visit if only to see the superb building, which was once a pharmacy.

🏛 Museum of Hungarian Naïve Art

Gáspár András utca 11. **Tel** (076) 324 767. ◯ Mar–Oct: 10am–5pm Tue–Sun; Nov–Feb: by appt only. 🖼 ✏

This charming museum (Magyar Naiv Művészek Múzeuma) is devoted to local Naïve artists who produced some stunning work. Unique in Hungary, the museum provides a thorough survey of the genre. There are more than 2,500 exhibits, with the collection of small animal sculptures, a special highlight.

For hotels and restaurants in the region see pp390–93 and pp394–7

Mechanical toys in the Toy Museum and Workshop

🏛 Szórakaténusz Toy Museum and Workshop

Gáspár András körát 11. **Tel** (076) 481 469. ☐ Mar–Oct: 10am–5pm Tue–Sun; Nov–Feb: by appt only. 🔖 🖸

Next to the Museum of Hungarian Naïve Art is this children's paradise, housed in a specially built wooden building (Szórakaténusz Játékmúzeum És Műhely). There is a wide array of Hungarian toys from the 18th century to the present, with dolls and wooden toys taking pride of place. Among them are some relatively clumsy mechanical toys that were considered state of the art in the 1950s. There are also interactive toy workshops for children during summer.

🏛 Zwack Fruit Brandy Distillery and Exhibition

Matkói utca 2. **Tel** (076) 487 711. ☐ Mon–Fri, by appt only. 🔖 🖸 compulsory.

Zwack Unicum Company is the Hungarian market leader in plum brandy, and its factory offers a fascinating insight into the world of alcohol distillation. Visitors can see how the brandy is made – before tasting it – and learn about the life of the Zwack family. The plant is open only to group tours; Tourinform provides information on where and when to join one.

🏛 Museum of Applied Folk Art

Serfőző utca 19. **Tel** (076) 327 203. ☐ 10am–5pm Tue–Sat. ☐ 17 Dec– 10 Jan. 🔖 🖸 Hungarian only. ♿

This vast and enchanting building (Népi Iparművészeti múzeum) and garden, formerly a brewery for nearly 200 years, is a fascinating place to visit. Opened to the public in 1984 as the Museum of Popular Folk Art, the permanent collection expanded now covers woodcarving, pottery, embroidery and weaving. Visitors can access on-site workshops to watch the artisans at work and then try embroidering a waistcoat or tablecloth themselves; an interactive kitchen produces local specialities in traditional ovens. However, the workshops and kitchen are open only on selected days in the summer.

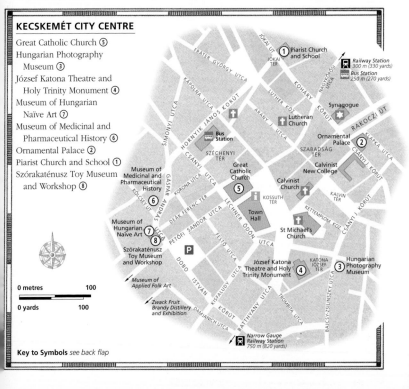

KECSKEMÉT CITY CENTRE

Great Catholic Church ⑤
Hungarian Photography Museum ③
József Katona Theatre and Holy Trinity Monument ④
Museum of Hungarian Naïve Art ⑦
Museum of Medicinal and Pharmaceutical History ⑥
Ornamental Palace ②
Piarist Church and School ①
Szórakaténusz Toy Museum and Workshop ⑧

0 metres 100
0 yards 100

Key to Symbols see back flap

Bükk National Park ㉒
Bükki Nemzeti Park

Since 1977, most of the Bükk Mountain region in northern Hungary has been classified as a national park. It extends from Eger *(see pp380–81)* in the south to Mályinka, 61 km (38 miles) to the north. An area of outstanding natural beauty, Bükk, meaning "beech", is renowned for its beech forests and steep cliffs, riddled with more than 800 caves. There is some skiing in winter at Felső-Borovnyák, but the main activities are hiking and climbing. Routes of all grades and lengths criss-cross the range, linking the main towns in the region.

Lipizzaners in Szilvásvárad Horse Museum
The famous Lipizzaner horses were brought here from Lipica, in Slovenia, in the 16th century.

Fátyol Waterfall
Staggered limestone steps make this 17-m (56-ft) long waterfall one of the most attractive in Hungary. The steps grow a little every year as the water deposits more lime.

Romanesque Bélapátfalva, erected by Cistercian monks in the 1200s, is the best preserved abbey in Hungary.

The Szalajka Narrow Gauge Railway runs along the entire length of the Szalajka Valley during summer.

Vineyards in Felsőtárkány
The pretty town of Felsőtárkány, surrounded by vineyards and parks, is one of the best gateways to Bükk National Park.

Climbing on Felső-Borovnyák

The steep, high cliffs of the Bükk offer challenging rock-climbing experiences for even the most experienced climbers.

VISITORS' CHECKLIST

143 km (89 miles) NE of Budapest. to Eger, Miskolc, Lillafüred, Szilvásvárad. Tourinform Eger, Bajcsy-Zsilinszky tér 9, (036) 517 715; Tourinform Miskolc, Varoshaz tér 13, (046) 350 425. **Anna Cave** Apr 1–Oct 15: 10am–5pm daily; Oct 16–Mar 31: scheduled visits only. **Subalyuk Cave** Apr–Oct: 10am–4pm daily. www.bnpi.hu

Mályinka

KIS-FENSÍK

Garadna

Újmassa

2505

Ómassa

Hámori-tó

Hámor

István-lápa Cave

Tűzköves
895 m (2,936 ft)

Lillafüred

2505

BÜKK-FENSÍK

Bükkszentlászló
Stará Huta

Miskolc
10 km (6 miles)

Rejtek

Bükkszentkereszt
Nová Huta

2505

Répáshuta

Nagybodzás
668 m (2,192 ft)

Magás-tető
664 m (2,178 ft)

Hajnoczy Cave

Bükkzsérc

Cserépfalu

Anna Cave

Six interconnected caves are accessible via a series of natural limestone staircases.

Bükk Mountains

The Bükk region is renowned for its clean air. The highest peak in the mountains is Istállós-kő.

Subalyuk Cave

Traces of Palaeolithic Man have been found in this cave, making it one of the oldest known dwellings in Europe.

KEY

	Railway station
	Viewpoint
∩	Cave
▲	Peak
	Major road
	Other road
	Railway
- -	Trail

0 km 3

0 miles 3

Eger ⑳

Situated off the main road from Budapest to the east of Hungary, Eger is a sleepy, provincial town dominated by its castle *(see pp382–3)* and the legend of the great siege of 1552. Eger has been rebuilt twice, almost from scratch, by the church. After destruction by the Mongols in 1241, it was reconstructed with money from the Minorite and Franciscan Orders. After the withdrawal of the Ottomans in 1687, the local bishopric revived the town by commissioning many of the Baroque masterpieces that remain today, including the cathedral, the Lyceum and the Bishop's Palace. Nowadays, Eger is also known for its Bull's Blood wine *(see p383)* and its university.

🔓 Eger Cathedral

Pyrker János tér 1. **Tel** *(036) 515 725.* ◯ *8am–8pm daily.* ♿ ✝

The second largest church in Hungary, Eger Cathedral (Főszékesegyház – Szent János Apostol És Evangélista Szent Mihály Főangyal) is the most astonishing sight in the town, though its mixture of Neo-Classical and Neo-Romanesque styles, in bright yellow, may not be to everyone's taste. It was built between 1831 and 1837 to a design by the architect József Hild, who would later design the even larger and more stunning basilica at Esztergom *(see p360)*.

The cathedral is unique in Hungary, with a cupola, which at 40 m (131 ft) is shorter than the two western towers, which measure 44 m (144 ft). At the other end of the building, three gargantuan statues loom over the colonnaded Neo-Classical façade. These represent Faith, Hope and Charity, and were the work of the Italian sculptor Marco Casagrande. The cathedral's interior is sombre, brightened primarily by Viennese artist Johann Kracker's ceiling frescoes of the *Kingdom of Heaven* on the inside of the cupola. The cathedral is also home to Hungary's largest organ, which is played every Sunday after morning mass at 12:45pm.

🏛 Bishop's Palace

Széchenyi utca 1. **Tel** *(036) 517 589.* ◯ *9am–5pm Tue–Sat.*

The second element of central Eger's ecclesiastical architectural triumvirate is the former Bishop's Palace (Római Katolikus Érseki Palota). It was built in Baroque style to the designs of 18th-century architect Jakab Kellner and completed in 1766.

The palace houses the Ecclesiastical Collection of the Eger Bishopric, and the coronation cloak of Habsburg Empress Maria Theresa among other priceless objects.

🏛 Lyceum

Eszterházy Károly tér 1. **Tel** *(036) 520 400.* ◯ *9:30am–1pm Sat–Sun.* 🖼 🚻 ♿

Founded in 1765 by Bishop Károly Eszterházy as a Catholic university, this university (Líceum, Eszterházy Károly Főiskola) was relegated to the ranks of a lyceum by the imperial authorities who opposed the idea of a church university. The highlight is the library, which holds over 150,000 volumes, including the first book ever printed in Hungary, in 1473. The library boasts Johann Kracker's fresco of 132 figures, depicting the meeting of the Council of Trent (1545–63). The tower is Hungary's leading centre of astronomy, with a collection of astronomical items and a 19th-century camera obscura.

Façade of the Lyceum, built as a Catholic university

🏛 Kossuth Lajos Utca

The wide boulevard of Kossuth Lajos utca has long been home to Eger's most important administrative and ecclesiastical buildings. At No. 4 is the Vice-Provost's Palace, a pastel-shaded Rococo mansion with a façade of hewn stone dating from 1758. On the same side of the street, at No. 14, is the Franciscan Church and Monastery, a single-nave church built in 1738 on the ruins of a mosque.

Opposite, at No. 9, is the Baroque County Hall, completed in 1758. It is famed for the two grand wrought-iron gates, crafted by the blacksmith Henrik Fazola (1730–79), who moved to Eger from Germany to take the city's waters. He is also

The sombre interior of Eger Cathedral, brightened by ceiling frescoes

Aerial view of Kossuth Lajos utca, Eger's most sought-after address

responsible for most of the ironwork that typifies many of the buildings on Kossuth Lajos utca, as well as the famous Hungarian National Gallery *(see p340)* in Budapest and Festetics Palace in Keszthely *(see pp372–3)*.

🏛 Minorite Church

Dobó István tér

Set against the background of the open spaces of Dobó István tér, the ornate exterior of the former Minorite Church (Szent Antonius Minorita Templom) has more aesthetic appeal than the cathedral.

The rounded, tiered façade and twin towers were designed by Bohemian architect Kilian Ignaz Dientzenhofer, but the church was not completed until 1773. It is dedicated to St Anthony of Padova and scenes from the saint's life feature in the ceiling frescoes painted by Márton Raindl. St Anthony is also depicted alongside the Virgin Mary on the altar, in a painting by Johann Kracker.

Main façade of the former Minorite Church, built in the 18th century

VISITORS' CHECKLIST

137 km (85 miles) NE of Budapest. ⚐ 56,000. 🚃 Vasút utca. 🚌 Pyrker János tér. 🚌 Dobó István tér 9. 🛈 Tourinform, Bajcsy-Zsilinszky tér 9, (036) 517 715. 🛒 Dobó István tér, daily.

🕌 Minaret

Knézich Károly utca. ⚐ Apr–Oct: 10am–6pm daily. 🎫

A relic of the Ottoman regime, Eger's minaret (Minaret) is a classic of its genre. Sleek and perfectly symmetrical, the 14-sided sandstone tower rises on an incline to its needle-like point, 40 m (131 ft) above the street. It is topped with a crescent moon and a cross. Closed for 150 years after the mosque next to it was demolished in 1841, the 17th-century minaret is now open to visitors and offers fine views of the city to those prepared to climb the 97 steps up to the balcony.

⚔ Eger Castle

See pp382–3.

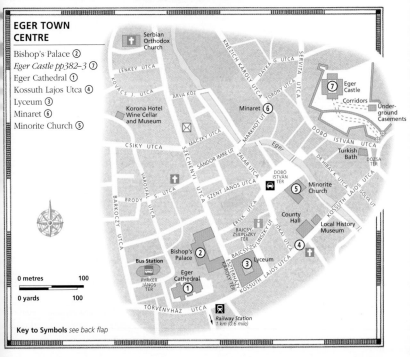

0 metres 100
0 yards 100

Key to Symbols see back flap

Eger: Eger Castle
Eger Vár

The site of a legendary siege against the invading Ottomans, Eger Castle is an imposing edifice. Entered by a tiny gate set into 3-m (10-ft) thick walls with the menacing upper fortress in the background, it was here, in 1552, that the greatest rearguard action in Hungarian military history was carried out. The castle, defended by a garrison of just 2,000 soldiers and ably assisted by the women of the town, held out against a formidable Ottoman force five times that size for six weeks. The Ottomans eventually retreated, but took the castle 44 years later, only for much of it to be destroyed in 1702 by the Habsburgs.

★ Bishop's Palace
The names of all those who defended the castle in 1552 are engraved in a marble tablet in the main hall.

Fold Bastion Waxworks
A great collection of lifelike wax figures, displayed over three levels of the bastion, recreates scenes from the siege.

Art Gallery
The Art Gallery hosts an unrivalled collection of Hungarian Baroque paintings and sculptures, including this bas-relief above the entrance.

Round Tower

Ticket Office

Dobó Bastion
The bastions and walls were fortified from the mid-1500s under István Dobó, who led the defenders during the siege.

STAR FEATURES

★ Bishop's Palace

★ Ruins of Romanesque Cathedral

★ Underground Corridors

For hotels and restaurants in this region see pp390–93 and pp394–7

★ Ruins of Romanesque Cathedral
Among the ruins of a 10th-century baptistry in the inner courtyard stands the grave of Eger's first bishop, Buldus.

★ Underground Corridors
Castle Hill is a warren of underground chambers and paths, dug by the Ottomans in order to attack the castle from below. Some 200 m (656 ft) are open to the public.

Three Crosses Hill

Tomb of Gárdonyi

Main entrance

Cannon Hill

Ippolito Gate and Bornemissza Bastion
This striking castle gate is named after an Italian cardinal, Ippolito d'Este, who became the Archbishop of Esztergom.

BULL'S BLOOD WINE

Bull's Blood of Eger is Hungary's most celebrated wine. Comparable to the Bordeaux wines of France, Bull's Blood is robust and fruity, made of a mix of Cabernet Sauvignon, Merlot and Cabernet Franc grapes. During the Siege of Eger, copious amounts of the wine were drunk by the defending soldiers, and word was put about that their bravery was based on the blood of bulls that had been added to the wine. The stories were almost certainly false, but they impressed the superstitious Ottomans, and played a minor role in their defeat and retreat.

Hungary's Bull's Blood wine

Lake Tisza ❷❹

Tisza-tó

199 km (124 miles) E of Budapest. 🚆 *from Debrecen.* 🚌 *from Debrecen.*

Although it is considered one of the natural wonders of Hungary, Lake Tisza is, in fact, an artificial lake. It was created in the early 1970s, when the Tisza river was dammed for the irrigation of the Great Plain, which covers about 56 per cent of the country. Covering 127 sq km (49 sq miles), the lake is second in size only to Lake Balaton (see p368–9), and is increasingly challenging its famous neighbour as the summer holiday destination of choice. Most of the northern part of the lake is a protected nature reserve. Much loved by bird-watchers, the reserve is accessible only with a guide. Almost 200 species can be seen here, including peregrine falcons, which enjoy the microclimate generated by the lake waters.

Peregrine falcons at Lake Tisza

The largest resort on Lake Tisza is the bustling town of **Tiszafüred**, which has many grass beaches, boat launches and one of Hungary's oldest regional museums, **Pál Kiss House Museum**. Housed in a Neo-Classical villa, the museum was founded in 1877 and displays painted furniture, pottery and an archaeology exhibition with Roman coins and mosaics. Named after Pál Kiss, a general in the revolution of 1848, it is also a major bird-watching centre.

The family-oriented resort of Kisköre is home to the lake's best beaches. The town of **Tiszaderzs**, set back from the shores of the lake, has a 13th-century Romanesque church rebuilt in the 1600s and an 18th-century Baroque Reformed Church. South of Tiszaderzs, the water park at **Abádszalók** is one of the lake's most popular attractions. It is also known for water sports. On the western shore, the village of Sarud, has many 18th- and 19th-century thatched cottages as well as a great shallow beach. North of Sarud rowing boats are available for hire at the village of Poroszló and there is also a nature trail that meanders around the surrounding countryside.

🏛 **Pál Kiss House Museum**
Tel (059) 352 106. ⏰ 9am–noon, 1–5pm Tue–Sat.

Abádszalók
ℹ (059) 535 346.

Debrecen ❷❺

220 km (137 miles) E of Budapest. 🏘 200,000. 🚆 *from Budapest.* 🚌 *from Budapest.* 🚉 *Railway Station, Múzeum utca.* ℹ *Tourinform, Piac utca 20, (052) 412 250.* 🚆 *daily.* 🎉 *Spring Festival (Mar), Jazz Days (Mar), Summer Theatre (Aug), Flower Carnival (Aug).* **www**.debrecen.hu

Famous for its Calvinist Reformed College and Calvinist Church, the pretty town of Debrecen is Hungary's second largest. It has always been an important market

Imposing Great Reformed Church and fountain, Debrecen

town and, during the revolution of 1848, it served as Hungary's capital. Today it is celebrated for its grand thermal bath complex and excellent university.

Debrecen's defining landmark, the **Great Reformed Church**, towers above the town from the top of its main street, Piac utca. Built between 1819 and 1823, on the site of an earlier church to designs by Mihaly Pechy, this is where Hungary's parliament met between 1848 and 1849, and where its secession from the Habsburg Empire was declared. Across the square is the Civis Aranybika Hotel (see p392), an Art Nouveau masterpiece designed by Alfred Hajos, Hungary's first Olympic champion. Piac utca leads into the central square, Kalvin tér, which is home to the **Calvinist Reformed College**, founded by Dominican monks in 1538. Rebuilt twice, the present building was designed by Mihaly Pechy. It was in the Oratory here that Hungary's provisional parliament met in 1944 while Budapest was under siege.

Nearby stands the excellent **Deri Museum**, built between 1926 and 1928, to house local industrialist Frigyes Deri's art collection. It has a rich collection of antiquities from Egypt and Ancient Greece as well as displays on Debrecen's history, ethnography and art.

Debrecen's famous thermal bath complex lies just north of the centre, with an extensive range of pools and baths and a vast water-therapy treatment centre.

The popular water park at Abádszalók, Lake Tisza

Hortobágy and Hortobágy National Park ㉖

Hortobágyi Nemzeti Park

183 km (114 miles) E of Budapest.
Pásztormúzeum, Petőfi tér 1, Hortobágy, (052) 589 321.
Hortobágy National Park Tel (052) 589 170. ☐ 8am–4pm daily. ♿ 🚻 ☐ ☐ **www**.hnp.hu

Established in 1973, this was the first national park in Hungary and remains the largest, stretching over 820 sq km (317 sq miles) from Lake Tisza to Debrecen. It was added to UNESCO's World Heritage List in 1999. The vast plain, known locally as the *puszta*, meaning "emptiness", is the nesting site of as many as 152 bird species, including great bustards, herons, storks and spoonbills. Up to 342 different bird species have been spotted here in migration, including tens of thousands of screeching cranes, which can be seen in late September.

The park is also home to cattle, horses, buffalo, and Hungarian long-haired sheep, which continue to be herded by semi-nomadic farmers as they have been for centuries.

The 300-year-old **Hortobágy Máta Stud Farm** riding centre, located inside the park, is Hungary's best. It organizes riding performances by the *Csikós* (Hungarian cowboys), as well as riding lessons for visitors throughout summer.

While much of Hortobágy National Park is open to visitors all year round, some parts have limited access. The park's administration and visitors' centre is in the tiny but charming village of Hortobágy itself.

Here, the 17th-century Hortobágy Csárda restaurant serves Hungary's national dish, goulash (gulyásleves), which originated in the *puszta*. A small **Shepherds' Museum** (Pásztormúzeum) offers a fascinating insight into the life of the *puszta* shepherd.

The unique Nine-Arch Bridge (Kilenclyukú Híd), built between 1827 and 1833 to designs by Ferenc Povolny, crosses the Hortobágy river and once formed part of the main road from Budapest to Debrecen.

Hortobágy Máta Stud Farm
Czinege J utca 1, Hortobágy.
Tel (052) 369 092. ☐ 8am–8pm daily. ♿ 🐎 *riding lessons.*

🏛 **Shepherds' Museum**
Petőfi tér 1, Hortobágy. **Tel** (052) 589 321. ☐ Mar–Apr: 10am–4pm daily; May–Sep: 9am–6pm daily; Oct–Dec: 10am–2pm daily. ● Jan–Feb. ♿

Szeged ㉗

170 km (105 miles) SE of Budapest.
🚶 97,000. 🚌 from Budapest.
🚏 🚃 Roosevelt tér. **Tourinform, Dugonics tér 2, (062) 488 690.**
🎭 Szeged Open Air Theatre Festival (mid-Jul–Sep). **www**.szeged portal.hu

The fourth largest city in the country, Szeged straddles the Tisza river less than 20 km (12 miles) from the point where Hungary, Serbia and Romania meet. Completely destroyed by the spring floods in 1879, Szeged was entirely

Twin-towered Neo-Romanesque Votive Church, Szeged

remodelled and its avenues, squares and variety of architectural styles are testimony to enlightened town planning. Today, the city is an important centre for the salami and paprika trades.

Constructed between 1913 and 1930, the grand Neo-Romanesque **Votive Church** on Dom tér contains several ornate frescoes and the third largest organ in Europe. In front of it stands the Demetrius Tower, built between the 12th and 13th centuries, while behind it is the single-towered Serbian Orthodox Church. Founded by Serb immigrants in the 1700s, it contains a magnificent iconostasis engraved in pear wood.

To the west, beyond the university, are two notable Art Nouveau buildings. The elaborate **Reok Palace**, was designed by Ede Magyar Oszadszki for local merchant Istvan Reok in 1907. In the Jewish Quarter, the New Synagogue, built between 1900 and 1903, has a grand dome and a marble tabernacle covered with gold leaf.

Szechenyi tér, has a pond commemorating the devastating 1879 flood. Further away is the Neo-Baroque **National Theatre** on Déak Ferenc utca, which stages ballets, opera and performances by the Philharmonic Orchestra. The Old Synagogue, in the Jewish Quarter, bears a plaque displaying the level of the flood waters. The Art Nouveau-style New Synagogue, built between 1900 and 1903, has a grand dome with a marble tabernacle covered with gold leaf.

A pair of storks in Hortobágy National Park, Hortobágy

Practical & Travel Information

In recent years, tourism has become an important part of the Hungarian national economy and as a result there have been vast improvements in communications, banking facilities and public transport. The biggest problem visitors face is the formidable language barrier. However, staff at many tourist offices, hotels and major attractions speak English or German.

WHEN TO VISIT

The best time to visit Hungary is between April and the end of June, and from the middle of August until October. July is usually hot and Budapest can become quite uncomfortable, although away from the capital the heat is less severe. From November until March, many museums have shorter opening hours and may close altogether.

DOCUMENTATION

Citizens of the US, Canada, Australia, New Zealand, and the European Union (EU) simply require a valid passport to visit Hungary for up to 90 days. For more information about visas and extended visits, visitors should check the website of the Hungarian Ministry of Foreign Affairs.

VISITOR INFORMATION

Visitors can obtain various information leaflets and maps from the **Hungarian National Tourist Office**, which has branches worldwide.

Within Hungary, there are tourist information offices in most large towns. In Budapest, visitors can get advice on sightseeing, accommodation and cultural events from the offices of **Tourinform Budapest**. The official website also provides brochures and maps, all of which can be downloaded for free in various formats. The **BTH Tourinform** sells entry tickets to most major attractions in Budapest and organizes specialist tours.

The Budapest Card entitles card holders, along with one child under 14, to unlimited use of the city's public transport system, free entry to 60 museums, the zoo and the funfair, a 50 per cent discount on guided tours and 10–20 per cent discount on selected cultural events and restaurants.

HEALTH AND SECURITY

Hungary has long been a world leader in medical research and development. No special vaccinations are required to visit the country. However, visitors with allergy problems and breathing difficulties who intend to visit Budapest should be aware of the summer smog conditions, which are particularly acute in Pest. Those with heart ailments should seek medical advice before using Hungary's thermal baths. For minor ailments, it is advisable to visit a *patika* or *gyógyszertár* (pharmacy). If the nearest store is closed, it usually displays a list of 24-hour emergency pharmacies.

Hungary has a relatively low crime rate. However, as in most cities that attract a large number of visitors, pickpockets operate in Budapest, targeting crowded metro stations, buses and shopping malls.

FACILITIES FOR THE DISABLED

The country's transport system, museums and other major attractions are gradually being renovated to make them wheelchair-friendly, although access problems can still occur. Those seeking advice on transport and sightseeing tours for the disabled should contact the **Hungarian Disabled Association**.

BANKING AND CURRENCY

The Hungarian currency is the forint (HUF or Ft). Banks are open from 8am to 5pm, Monday to Friday and closed on weekends; exchange bureaus and ATMs, however, remain open all week. Since banks and exchange bureaus offer the best rates, it is always advisable to change money there.

Credit cards are more widely accepted now than before, but are still not as commonly used as elsewhere in Europe, so it is a good idea to carry sufficient cash.

COMMUNICATIONS

The Hungarian telephone system used to be notoriously bad, but improvements are now slowly being made. Phone cards, which are available from tobacconists, post offices, petrol stations and newspaper kiosks, are the best option when using public phones, although some booths still accept coins.

Post offices are open from 8am to 6pm Monday to Friday and on Saturday

---

THE CLIMATE OF HUNGARY

Hungary enjoys some of the best weather in Europe, with an average of eight hours of sunshine a day in summer. June, July and August are the hottest months. In winter, temperatures can fall well below freezing point and there may also be snow. The country has comparatively low rainfall. June usually gets the most rain, while autumn is the driest season.

BUDAPEST

° C/F	24/75		
	17/63	16/61	16/61
	7/45		7/45
0°C 32°F			1/34
			-4/25

	7 hrs	10 hrs	5 hrs	2 hrs
	45 mm	56 mm	57 mm	37 mm
month	Apr	Jul	Oct	Jan

nornings. Visitors should
e prepared to wait as service
s slow and there are often
ong queues.

ARRIVING BY AIR

Budapest's international
irport is **Ferihegy Airport**,
ocated 16 km (10 miles)
rom the city centre. **British
Airways** and **Malév**, the
Hungarian national airline,
each operate three daily
cheduled flights from
ondon. Many low-cost
irlines also operate daily
lights from London. Malév
lso runs direct scheduled
lights between New York's
FK airport and Budapest.
Other major airlines flying
rom the US and Canada to
Hungary include **Air France**,
Britsh Airways, **KLM**,
ufthansa and **Northwest
Airlines**, although services
entail a transfer or touch
lown at another European
ity. Many low-cost airlines
lso operate daily flights from
ondon. The Airport Minibus
huttle takes passengers from

the airport to any address in
the capital. Taxis are also a
quick and comfortable way
of getting into the city.

RAIL TRAVEL

The Hungarian national rail
network is efficient, reliable
and punctual. Budapest has
direct rail links to 25 other
capital cities, with **Keleti Pu
Station** handling the majority
of international traffic. High-
speed trains to Vienna, the
main communications hub
for Western Europe, depart
every 3 hours approximately
and take about 2 hours,
25 minutes to get there.
    Almost all trains within
Hungary are operated by
Magyar Államvasutak (MÁV),
a state-owned company that
offers excellent value for
money. There are different
types of local trains, each
categorized according to its
speed: *személy* (slow), *sebes*
(speedy) or *gyors* (fast). There
are also modern Intercity
services between Budapest
and the larger cities. A number

of concessionary fares are
available for those planning
extensive rail travel within the
country. **European Rail Passes
(Eurail)** are also valid.

TRAVELLING BY BUS

Buses to all European
destinations depart from
Népliget Station. Within
Hungary, the state-owned
Volánbusz company operates
an extensive network of buses
to most cities and towns.

TRAVELLING BY CAR

Although the government
has recently invested in a
new motorway network, many
towns are still only connected
by single-lane roads. To hire a
car, visitors should be aged 21
or over and they must have
held a valid driving license for
at least a year. An international
driving licence is also useful.
Most of the international car
hire firms have offices at the
airport in Budapest, and rentals
can also be arranged through
travel agencies and at hotels.

DIRECTORY

DOCUMENTATION

www.mfa.gov.hu

VISITOR INFORMATION

BTH Tourinform
Liszt Ferenc tér 11,
Budapest. *Tel (01) 322
4098.*

**Hungarian National
Tourist Office**
www.tourinform.hu

**Tourinform
Budapest**
Sütő utca 2, Budapest.
Tel (01) 438 8080.
www.tourinform.hu

EMBASSIES

Australia
1126 Királyhágó tér 8–9,
Budapest. *Tel (01) 457
9777.* www.australia.hu

Canada
1027 Ganz út
12–14, Budapest.
Tel (01) 392 3360.
www.canadaeuropa.gc.
ca/hungary

United Kingdom
1051 Harmincad
utca 6, Budapest.
Tel (01) 266 2888.
www.britishembassy.hu

United States
1054 Szabadság tér
12, Budapest.
Tel (01) 429 6360.
www.usembassy.hu

EMERGENCY NUMBERS

Ambulance
Tel 104.

Fire
Tel 105.

Police
Tel 107.

FACILITIES FOR THE DISABLED

**Hungarian Disabled
Association**
1032 San Marco utca 76,
Budapest. *Tel (01) 388
2388.* www.meosz.hu

ARRIVING BY AIR

Air France
Tel (01) 483 8800
(Hungary). *Tel 800 237
2747* (US).

British Airways
Tel (01) 411 5555
(Hungary). *Tel 0845 773
3377* (UK). *Tel 877 428
2228* (US).

Ferihegy Airport
Tel (01) 296 9696.

KLM
Tel (01) 373 7737
(Hungary). *Tel 800 374
7747* (US).

Lufthansa
Tel (01) 411 9900
(Hungary). *Tel 800 645
3880* (US).

Malév
Tel (01) 235 3222
(Hungary). *Tel 800 223
6884* (US).

Northwest Airlines
Tel (01) 325 5037
(Hungary). *Tel 800 225
2525* (US).

RAIL TRAVEL

**European Rail
Passes (Eurail)**
www.raileurope.com

Keleti Pu Station
Kerepesi út 2/6, Budapest
Tel (01) 313 6835.
www.elvira.mav-start.hu

**Magyar
Államvasutak (MÁV)**
Andrassy út 35, Budapest.
Tel (01) 371 9449.
www.mav.hu

TRAVELLING BY BUS

Népliget Station
Üllői út 131, Budapest.
Tel (01) 219 8080.

Volánbusz
Üllői út 131, Budapest.
Tel (01) 219 8063
(reservations).
www.volanbusz.hu

Shopping & Entertainment

Shopping in Hungary has changed dramatically in recent years. The choice of places to shop ranges from small, family-owned shops selling inimitable trinkets and luxuries to flea markets packed with the bizarre and the beautiful. Souvenir hunters are spoilt for choice and those looking for something typically Hungarian have a variety of Zsolnay porcelain, vintage Tokaji wine and paprika to choose from. The range of cultural events and entertainment is also richly varied. Even the smallest of towns has its own orchestra, dance company and theatre.

OPENING HOURS

Shops in Budapest are open from 9am to 6pm Monday to Friday and 9am to 1pm on Saturday. Many stay open until 8 or 9pm on Thursday. In the rest of the country an increasing number of shops and outlets remain open on Saturdays and Sundays. Supermarkets are open seven days a week, until 8pm. Shops are also open on public holidays with the exception of Christmas and New Year's Day.

MARKETS

Markets are an essential aspect of life in Budapest. The most spectacular are the cavernous late 19th-century market halls dotted around the city, of which the largest is the three-level **Central Market Hall** (Nagy Vásárcsarnok) on Fővám tér. This is open from 7am to 6pm Monday to Friday and 7am to 1pm on Saturday.

Many other cities also organize open-air craft and folk art markets. The Debrecen city craft fair is held during August in Kossuth tér.

FOLK ART

Hungarian folk art items such as embroidered peasant blouses and wooden carvings are still made in many rural areas, and many are sold in the capital. These can be found at flea markets around Parliament *(see pp348–9)*. Handmade items are available at **Folkart Kézművesház** and machine-made products at **Folkart Centrum**. Other local goods worth looking out for include carpets, especially rugs

with plain, naïve designs and wooden toys including soldiers in Habsburg-era uniforms.

PORCELAIN, CRYSTAL AND ANTIQUES

Hungary has a long tradition of producing high-quality porcelain, with the **Herend** and **Zsolnay** names carrying a worldwide reputation. Herend porcelain is famous for its decorative and colourful designs; the factory shop in the small town of Herend, north of Lake Balaton, stocks a small selection. The Zsolnay porcelain factory has a shop located in Pécs. Ajka crystal, made near the town of Veszprém has been recognized as Hungary's finest for more than 150 years. **Ajka Crystal** in Budapest is a good place to pick up this excellent work of art. Antique shops in Budapest are concentrated in the Vár and Víziváros areas and are good places to purchase domestic items from the 18th and 19th centuries. The tiny shop **Moró Antik** specializes in 18th-century weapons, while the **Nagyházi Gallery** sells everything from jewellery to furniture.

FOOD AND DRINK

Paprika – as a condiment – can be bought in all colours and varieties. Along with a wide variety of spicy salamis, it is available in many supermarkets and smaller delicatessens scattered all around the country. Cheese is another popular delicacy. The best sort is smoked, such as *sonkás*, an excellent cheese flavoured with ham. Visitors wishing to buy – and sample –

Hungary's regional wines, including the golden Tokaji, should head for either **Borház** or the **House of Hungarian Wines** in Budapest, both of which stock a superb selection from all over the country. Locally made apricot and plum liqueurs and *palinka* (brandy) can be purchased in Budapest at **House of Palinka**.

CINEMA

Most major Hungarian cities have a multiplex cinema housed within the main shopping centre. Almost all foreign films are dubbed and subtitled in Hungarian, allowing cinema-goers to choose which version they prefer. Non-Hungarian speakers should opt for the *angol nyelvű* (English soundtrack) version.

MUSIC, OPERA AND DANCE

The **Ferenc Liszt Academy of Music** in Budapest is one of Europe's finest classical music venues. The **Palace of Art** is a recent addition among the capital's music venues, while organ or choral music are performed at **Mátyás Church** *(see pp342–3)* and **St Stephen's Basilica** *(see p350)*. The standard of opera in Budapest is very high. Both the **State Opera House** *(see p350)* and the **Erkel Theatre** have a mainly classical repertoire. For jazz, the best place in the capital is the **Jazz Garden** restaurant, which hosts live performances in summer. Famous names in rock and pop play at the modern **Papp László Budapest SportArena**. For live rock, the party boat **A38** and **Fat Mo's** are also popular.

Elsewhere in the country, Veszprém is known for its music and small-scale chamber concerts in the Castle District courtyard, the highlight of all summer visits here. Pécs also has a rich cultural heritage, with renowned opera and dance companies, as well as the Pannon Philharmonic Orchestra, all of which perform at the **Pécs National Theatre**. The best way of securing a seat for concerts at the Ferenc Liszt Academy of Music or major opera productions is via the **Cultur-Comfort Central Ticket Office** based in Budapest.

Tickets for plays and concerts can be purchased in advance from the box office at the relevant venue.

MUSIC FESTIVALS

Music festivals – from Baroque to jazz – feature regularly on the international arts calendar. Prominent events include the annual **Debrecen Jazz Festival** and the **Sopron Early Music Days**. For fans of rock and pop, the biggest event is the three-day **Sziget Festival** held in August.

NIGHTLIFE

There are plenty of buzzing nightspots in Budapest. Some of the favourites include **Szóda**, a big, brash disco with two dance floors and train-inspired decor, and **Dokk**, a superb venue notable for its top DJs and cutting-edge music.

Outside the capital, the university cities of Szeged and Győr are among the liveliest, with a wide range of pubs and clubs. Győr's **Vigadó Pince Pub** has live bands most nights, while the **Mister Bigg Pub** stays open until the early hours. In Veszprém, the **Expresszó Club** is the busiest venue, while the **Mythos Music Club** features live acts

or international DJs on weekends. During the summer almost all of Lake Balaton's resorts thump to the beat of Euro-pop. Siófok's **Palace Disco** is one of the country's largest, only a 15-minute walk out of the town centre. A little more sophisticated is the north Balaton resort of Balatonfüred, where the **Macho Pub** and **Atrium Music Club** pull in the crowds.

The country is also home to a number of classy casinos attracting gamblers from all over Europe and the Middle East. Those in Győr and Sopron are housed in glorious historical buildings. Most casinos stay open 24-hours and require visitors to dress smartly.

DIRECTORY

MARKETS

Central Market Hall
Vámház körút 1–3
Fővám tér, Budapest.
Tel (01) 366 3300.

FOLK ART

Folkart Centrum
Váci út 58, Budapest.
Tel (01) 318 5840.

Folkart Kézművesház
Régposta út 12, Budapest.
Tel (01) 318 5143.

PORCELAIN, CRYSTAL AND ANTIQUES

Ajka Crystal
Jozsef Attila 7, Budapest.
Tel (01) 317 8133.

Herend
Andrásst út 16, Budapest.
Tel (01) 374 0006.

Moró Antik
Falk Miksa út 13,
Budapest.
Tel (01) 311 0814.

Nagyházi Gallery
Balaton út 8, Budapest.
Tel (01) 475 6000.

Zsolnay
Kecskeméti út 14,
Budapest.
Tel (01) 318 2643.

FOOD AND DRINK

Borház
Jókai tér 7, Budapest.
Tel (01) 317 5919.

House of Hungarian Wines
Szentháromság tér 6,
Budapest.
Tel (01) 212 1032.

House of Palinka
Rákóczi út 17, Budapest.
Tel (01) 338 4219.

MUSIC, OPERA AND DANCE

A38
Pázmány Péter Sétány
3–11, Budapest.
Tel (01) 464 3940.

Cultur-Comfort Central Ticket Office
Paulay Ede út 31,
Budapest.
Tel (01) 322 0000.

Erkel Theatre
Köztársaság tér 30,
Budapest.
Tel (01) 333 0540.

Fat Mo's
Nyáry Pál út 11, Budapest.
Tel (01) 267 3199.

Ferenc Liszt Academy of Music
Liszt Ferenc tér 8,
Budapest.
Tel (01) 462 4600.

Jazz Garden
Veres Pálné út 44,
Budapest.
Tel (01) 266 7364.

Mátyás Church
Szentháromság tér 2.
Tel (01) 355 5657.

Palace of Art
Komor Marcell út 1,
Budapest.
Tel (01) 555 3300.

Papp László Budapest SportArena
Stefánia út 2, Budapest.
Tel (01) 555 5515.

Pécs National Theatre
Preczel Miklós út 17, Pécs.
Tel (072) 51 2660.

St Stephen's Basilica
Szent István tér 2,
Budapest.
Tel (01) 318 9159.

State Opera House
Andrássy út 22, Budapest.
Tel (01) 332 7914.

MUSIC FESTIVALS

Debrecen Jazz Festival
www.debrecen.hu

Sopron Early Music Days
www.prokultura.hu

Sziget Festival
www.szigetfestival.com

NIGHTLIFE

Atrium Music Club
Blaha út 7–9,
Balatonfüred.
Tel (087) 343 229.

Dokk
Hajogyari Sziget 122,
Budapest.
Tel 0630 535 2747.

Expresszó Club
Brusznyai út 2, Veszprém.
Tel (020) 940 2772.

Macho Pub
Vasút út 4, Balatonfüred.
Tel (087) 342 969.

Mister Bigg Pub
Fehérvári út 11, Győr.
Tel (096) 413 622.

Mythos Music Club
Szabadsag tér 1,
Veszprém.

Palace Disco
Deák Ferenc Sétány 2,
Siófok. *Tel (084) 350 698.*

Szóda
Wesselnyi utca 18,
Budapest.
Tel (01) 461 0007.

Vigadó Pince Pub
Kisfaludy út 2, Győr.
Tel (096) 296 2964.

Where to Stay in Hungary

Visitors to Hungary can choose from everything between top-class chain hotels and family-run pensions and hostels. In Budapest, the budget-conscious can take advantage of the weekend reductions offered by many hotels in the low season. Outside the capital most towns have one or two imperial-era hotels as well as a number of pensions.

PRICE CATEGORIES
Price categories are for a standard double room with bathroom per night in high season, including breakfast, tax and service charges.

ⓗ Under 15,000 HUF
ⓗⓗ 15,000–25,000 HUF
ⓗⓗⓗ 25,000–35,000 HUF
ⓗⓗⓗⓗ 35,000–50,000 HUF
ⓗⓗⓗⓗⓗ Over 50,000 HUF

BUDAPEST

Citadella
Citadella sétány, 1118 **Tel** (01) 466 5794 **Fax** (01) 386 0505 **Rooms** 14   🚭 P   ⓗ   **Map** C5

This lovely hostel-style hotel occupies the casements of the Citadel on Gellért Hill *(see pp344–5)*. It offers reasonably priced double and multiple-occupancy rooms. A popular wine bar, restaurant and nightclub are all located within the Citadella complex. **www.citadella.hu**

Best Western Orion
Döbrentei út 13, 1013 **Tel** (01) 356 8583 **Fax** (01) 375 5418 **Rooms** 30   P 🍴 &   ⓗⓗ   **Map** C4

This pleasant hotel offers clean but plainly decorated rooms with en suite bathrooms, air conditioning and colour televisions. A small restaurant serves a good range of inexpensive Hungarian and international cuisine. Service is efficient. **www.bestwestern.com**

Kulturinnov
Szentháromság tér 6, 1014 **Tel** (01) 224 8102 **Fax** (01) 375 1886 **Rooms** 16   P 🍴   ⓗⓗ   **Map** B2

Situated in the heart of Budapest's Vár area, the Kulturinnov is a simple, reasonably priced hotel. There is no excessive luxury here but the rooms are spacious and have en suite facilities. Occupying a magnificent Neo-Gothic edifice, it makes a good choice for visitors. **www.mka.hu**

Leo Panzió
Kossuth Lajos út 2/a, 1053 **Tel** (01) 266 9041 **Fax** (01) 266 9042 **Rooms** 14   🍴 📺 &   ⓗⓗ   **Map** D4

This superb pension is located in the very heart of the city and offers decent accommodation at reasonable prices. All rooms have private bathrooms with a shower and TV, and provide excellent views of the lively streets below. A good buffet breakfast is also included. **www.leopanzio.hu**

Astoria
Kossuth Lajos út 19–21, 1053 **Tel** (01) 889 6000 **Fax** (01) 889 6091 **Rooms** 130   🍴 📺 & ♿   ⓗⓗⓗ   **Map** D4

Designed in the Art Noveau style, the Astoria has been refurbished to recreate its original interior. The bedrooms are spacious and luxurious and the lovely breakfast room is designed in Neo-Baroque style. Even for visitors not staying at the hotel, it is worth visiting the café to see the beautiful interior. **www.danubiusgroup.com/astoria**

Burg
Szentháromság tér 7, 1014 **Tel** (01) 212 0269 **Fax** (01) 212 3970 **Rooms** 26   P 🍴 & ♿   ⓗⓗⓗ   **Map** B2

Located opposite Mátyás Church *(see pp342–3)* in Vár, the Burg provides comfortable and well-furnished rooms with en suite bathrooms. Several rooms provide magnificent views of the church. Some of the rooms are on the small side but levels of comfort and service are reassuringly high. **www.burghotelbudapest.com**

Cotton House
Jókai út 26, 1066 **Tel** (01) 354 2600 **Fax** (01) 354 1341 **Rooms** 18   🍴 📺 🍴 &   ⓗⓗⓗ   **Map** D2

An atmospheric hotel Cotton House offers some of the best decorated rooms in Hungary. Luxurious and classy, it particularly appeals to couples and music fans. All the rooms are named – and decorated – in honour of famous personalities from the stage or silver screen. **www.cottonhouse.hu**

Danubius Hotel Gellért
Szent Gellért tér 1, 1111 **Tel** (01) 889 5500 **Fax** (01) 889 5505 **Rooms** 233   P 🍴 ♨ 📺 & ♿   ⓗⓗⓗ   **Map** D5

This legendary spa hotel has both indoor and outdoor pools that provide a congenial environment in which to relax. The hotel has a bar, a café and a nightclub along with several banquet halls. Massages and other spa treatments are also available. **www.danubiusgroup.com/gellert**

K + K Opera
Révay út 24, 1065 **Tel** (01) 269 0222 **Fax** (01) 269 0230 **Rooms** 205   P 🍴 📺 & ♿   ⓗⓗⓗⓗ   **Map** D3

Located close to the State Opera House *(see p350)*, this hotel boasts a splendid façade and offers comfortable accommodation in modern, clean and incredibly spacious rooms. It also features a café, pub, bar and secure parking. A full buffet breakfast is also included. **www.kkhotels.com**

Map References *see map of Budapest pp336–7*

Radisson SAS Béke

Teréz körút 43, 1067 **Tel** *(01) 889 3900* **Fax** *(01) 889 3915* **Rooms** *247*
Map *D2*

Recently restored, this fine hotel has a beautiful façade with striking mosaics. All rooms are equipped with high-speed Internet access and satellite TV. The hotel's restaurants serve European and local delicacies while the Zsolnay Café offers the chance to sip tea and coffee from stunning Zsolnay porcelain. **www.danubiusgroup.com/beke**

Four Seasons Gresham Palace

Roosevelt tér 5–6, 1051 **Tel** *(01) 268 6000* **Fax** *(01) 268 5000* **Rooms** *179*
Map *C3*

Derelict for more than 50 years, the Gresham Palace has now been fully restored to count itself among the best hotels in Central Europe. The lobby is a tourist attraction in itself and the hotel's restaurants are among the city's finest. Service is also excellent. **www.fourseasons.com**

Sofitel Budapest Chain Bridge

Roosevelt tér 2, 1051 **Tel** *(01) 266 1234* **Fax** *(01) 266 9101* **Rooms** *349*
Map *C3*

Located close to the Danube, most of the Sofitel's rooms have terrific views of Vár and the Pest skyline. Rooms are decorated in warm colours and have flat-screen TVs. The hotel's stylish restaurants serve international and Hungarian cuisine. Souvenir boutiques and the Las Vegas Casino are on the ground floor. **www.sofitel.com**

Corinthia Grand Hotel Royal

Erzsébet krt 43–49, 1073 **Tel** *(01) 479 4000* **Fax** *(01) 479 4333* **Rooms** *414*
Map *E3*

Behind its distinguished façade, the former Grand Hotel Royal has been transformed into the modern and elegant Corinthia Grand Hotel Royal. The lobby is exquisite, setting the tone for the stunning and luxurious guest rooms, all of which are furnished in mahogany. **www.corinthiahotels.com**

Hilton

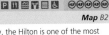

Hess Andrástér 1–3, 1014 **Tel** *(01) 889 6600* **Fax** *(01) 889 6644* **Rooms** *322*
Map *B2*

Housed in a building incorporating parts of a Gothic church and a Jesuit monastery, the Hilton is one of the most luxurious hotels in Budapest. Located in the heart of Vár, with magnificent views over the Danube and the Pest cityscape, the high prices are more than justified. **www.budapest.hilton.com**

Kempinski Corvinus

Erzsébet tér 7–8, 1051 **Tel** *(01) 429 3777* **Fax** *(01) 429 4777* **Rooms** *369*
Map *D3*

This exclusive hotel often welcomes heads of state and other notable personalities. The spacious and luxuriously furnished rooms are relaxing, providing a perfect mix of tradition and modernity. It has excellent fitness facilities, a pool, two restaurants and a pub. **www.kempinski-budapest.com**

Le Meridien Budapest

Erzsébet tér 9–10, 1050 **Tel** *(01) 429 5500* **Fax** *(01) 429 5555* **Rooms** *218*
Map *D3*

Housed in the centrally located and tastefully renovated Adria Palace, Le Meridien is an elegantly furnished hotel, with even its standard rooms larger than most rooms in the city. The fitness centre is one of Budapest's best, complete with a plunge-pool and Jacuzzi. **www.budapest.lemeridien.com**

FURTHER AFIELD City Hotel Ring

Szent István körút 22, 1137 **Tel** *(01) 340 5450* **Fax** *(01) 340 4884* **Rooms** *39*

Located a few minutes from the Parliament *(see pp80–81)*, the charming City Hotel Ring provides clean rooms decorated in neutral shades at reasonable rates. Although the hotel does not have a restaurant, it does have a cheerful breakfast room. **www.taverna.hu**

FURTHER AFIELD Mercure Budapest City Center

Váci út 20, 1052 **Tel** *(01) 485 3100* **Fax** *(01) 485 3111* **Rooms** *230*

The delightful Mercure Budapest city centre offers elegant rooms amidst the noise and bustle of the busy commercial district. All suites come equipped with Jacuzzis and saunas. The hotel's café, on the ground floor, is famous for its pastries. **www.accorhotels.com**

FURTHER AFIELD Mercure Nemzeti

József körút 4, 1088 **Tel** *(01) 477 2000* **Fax** *(01) 477 2001* **Rooms** *76*

Built at the end of the 19th century, this wonderful Art Deco-style hotel features a magnificent grand staircase. The rooms are comfortable, with those facing the courtyard particularly pleasant. The Art Nouveau-style restaurant offers delicious food. **www.accorhotels.com**

FURTHER AFIELD Andrássy Hotel

Andrássy út 111, 1063 **Tel** *(01) 462 2100* **Fax** *(01) 322 9445* **Rooms** *69*

Elegance and charm dominate this boutique hotel. Built in Bauhaus style, it provides beautiful Mediterranean-style rooms and an excellent restaurant. Located on one of the most prestigious streets in Budapest, several luxury shops, cafés and historical monuments are nearby. **www.andrassyhotel.com**

FURTHER AFIELD Hilton Budapest WestEnd

Váci út 1–3 (inside WestEnd City Centre), 1069 **Tel** *(01) 288 5500* **Fax** *(01) 288 5588* **Rooms** *230*

Situated next to the WestEnd shopping centre, the Hilton Budapest has a charming rooftop garden with the usual Hilton mix of modernity, efficiency, class and outstanding service. Facilities include wireless Internet access. **www.hilton.co.uk/budapestwestend**

Key to Symbols *see back cover flap*

REST OF HUNGARY

DEBRECEN Best Western Kálvin

Kálvin tér 4, 4026 **Tel** *(052) 418 522* **Fax** *(052) 525 301* **Rooms** *66*

This is one of the most popular hotels in Debrecen. Most rooms are equipped with baths as well as showers and have excellent views of the Great Reformed Church and Kalvin tér. Guests also have access to the swimming pool and sauna of the Civis Aranybika hotel across the square. **www.bestwestern.com**

DEBRECEN Civis Aranybika

Piac utca 11–15, 4025 **Tel** *(052) 508 600* **Fax** *(052) 421 834* **Rooms** *205*

With an exquisite Art Nouveau-style façade, the Civis Aranybika was once considered to be one of the best hotels in the country and still offers reasonably priced accommodation. There is a large swimming pool and a good ice-cream parlour on the ground floor. The buffet breakfast is outstanding. **www.civishotels.hu**

EGER Panorama

Dr Hibay Károly utca 2, 3300 **Tel** *(036) 412 886* **Fax** *(036) 410 136* **Rooms** *38*

Set halfway between Eger Castle *(see pp382–3)* and the city centre, this elegant hotel has modern and bright interiors, spacious rooms and a fine restaurant with a terrace. There is also a spa centre with a sauna, whirlpool and a steam room.

ESZTERGOM Esztergom

Prímás-sziget, Helischer J utca, 2500 **Tel** *(033) 412 555* **Fax** *(033) 412 853* **Rooms** *36*

This hotel is well located near the basilica, and reasonably priced. The colourful rooms are comfortable and well furnished, while the 1960's style common areas are well kept and spacious. Staff is helpful and service is excellent. **www.hotel-esztergom.hu**

FERTŐD Esterházy Palace

Joseph Haydn U 2, 9431 **Tel** *(099) 537 649* **Rooms** *21*

The surroundings of the magnificent Esterházy Palace, a budget hotel, are second to none and make a stay here worthwhile. Even though the rooms are not furnished with period pieces, simply being able to come back here after a day's sightseeing is reason enough. Advance booking is advised.

GYŐR Klastrom

Zechmeister utca 1, 9021 **Tel** *(096) 516 910* **Fax** *(096) 327 030* **Rooms** *40*

Located in the heart of Old Győr, this former monastery has been wonderfully renovated; the monks' cells have been converted into rather spartan but elegant and comfortable rooms. The Baroque former library, now the most amazing conference room in Hungary, is also worth seeing. **www.klastrom.hu**

KECSKEMÉT Aranyhomok

Kossuth tér 3, 6000 **Tel** *(076) 503 730* **Fax** *(076) 503 731* **Rooms** *111*

Located on Kossuth tér, the wonderful Aranyhomok hotel provides spacious rooms with comfortable beds and bathrooms with both bath and shower. Guests and non-guests alike can also take advantage of the hotel's health centre, steam bath and fitness room. **www.hotelaranyhomok.hu**

KESZTHELY Kakadu

Pázmány Péter utca 14, 8360 **Tel** *(083) 312 042* **Fax** *(083) 510 736* **Rooms** *34*

The elegant, well-furnished rooms of the Kakadu are set in two connected buildings close to Lake Balaton. There is a small but pleasant swimming pool and a rooftop sunbathing terrace. The hotel also offers a full range of health services including mud treatments and specialist massages. **www.castrum-group.hu**

KESZTHELY Helikon

Balatonpart 5, 8360 **Tel** *(083) 889 600* **Fax** *(083) 889 609* **Rooms** *232*

Located on the lake shore, the splendid Helikon provides plush rooms offering fantastic views either across the lake or over the town. There is also a little jetty at the end of a pier from where guests can hire sailing boats and pedaloes. **www.danubiushotels.com/helikon**

KŐSZEG Arany Strucc

Várkör utca 124, 9730 **Tel** *(094) 360 323* **Fax** *(094) 563 330* **Rooms** *15*

Housed in a gorgeous Baroque house dating from the late 17th century, the Arany Strucc is one of Hungary's oldest hotels. Behind the façade, the interior design is rather garish, but the rooms are reasonably priced and have glorious high ceilings. Guests are advised to book well in advance in summer. **www.aranystrucc.hu**

PÉCS Palatinus

Király utca 5, 7621 **Tel** *(072) 889 400* **Fax** *(02) 889 438* **Rooms** *94*

A mix of Art Nouveau and Art Deco styles, the façade and lobby of this hotel are tourist attractions in themselves. In addition, the hotel boasts sumptuous rooms and a first-class location on the elegant Király utca. Sauna, solarium and steam bath are located in the basement. **www.danubiushotels.com/palatinus**

Key to Price Guide *see p390* **Key to Symbols** *see back cover flap*

PÉCS Patria

Rákóczi út 3, 7626 **Tel** *(072) 889 500* **Fax** *(02) 889 506* **Rooms** *116*

The wonderfully designed Patria is a Modernist masterpiece. The rooms are bright and colourful with TV, minibar, Internet access and decent-sized bathrooms. There is a fine terrace and café on the first floor overlooking the hotel's courtyard. **www.danubiushotels.com/patria**

SÁRVAR Vitalmed

Vadkert utca 1, 9600 **Tel** *(095) 523 700* **Fax** *(095) 523 707* **Rooms** *26*

The Vitalmed hotel's out-of-the-way location southwest of the city centre means that visitors can enjoy luxury at a terrific price. The rooms are spacious, the beds are extremely comfortable, and the breakfast is excellent. Guests also have free access to the spa facilities next door. **www.vitalmedhotel.hu**

SIÓFOK Park

Batthyány út 7, 8600 **Tel** *(084) 310 539* **Fax** *(084) 310 539* **Rooms** *60*

Set back from the lake in a garden setting, the Park hotel is peaceful and quiet. The rooms are spacious and comfortable, if somewhat bare, and Internet connection is provided. There is a good outdoor restaurant with a barbecue in the evenings. **www.parkhotel.hu**

SIÓFOK Janus Atrium

Fő út 93–5, 8600 **Tel** *(084) 312 546* **Fax** *(084) 312 432* **Rooms** *26*

Situated in the centre of Siófok, this boutique hotel provides individually designed rooms with themes ranging from Japanese to Gothic to Gustav Klimt; the "1001 Nights Suite" is the best and most over-the-top. The hotel's delightful café serves delicious cakes and sandwiches. **www.janushotel.hu**

SOPRON Best Western Pannonia

Várkerület 75, 9400 **Tel** *(099) 312 180* **Fax** *(099) 340 766* **Rooms** *62*

The oldest hotel in Sopron, the Pannonia was opened in 1893. Built to a design by architect Móric Hintertraeger, its Neo-Classical façade is matched by a wonderful colonnaded dining room and stunning common areas. The rooms fall short of genuine luxury, but are nevertheless well equipped. **www.pannoniahotel.com**

SOPRON Wollner

Templom út 20, 9400 **Tel** *(099) 524 400* **Fax** *(099) 524 401* **Rooms** *18*

Originally a Baroque house dating from 1715, the Wollner was remodelled in Neo-Classical style in the 19th century and given its current façade after World War II. The rooms are spacious and furnished with antiques and fine art. **www.wollner.hu**

SZEGED Forras

Szent-Györgyi Albert út 16–24, 6721 **Tel** *(062) 566 466* **Fax** *(062) 566 468* **Rooms** *177*

This good-value hotel offers a wide range of services including an indoor swimming pool, a good restaurant and beautiful gardens. Guests are permitted free entrance to Szeged's main thermal bath complex, which has some of the best water slides in Hungary. **www.hunguesthotels.hu**

SZÉKESFEHÉRVÁR Novotel

Ady Endre 19–21, 8000 **Tel** *(022) 534 300* **Fax** *(022) 534 350* **Rooms** *96*

Located on the outskirts of the historic part of Székesfehérvár, the Novotel is both modern and convenient, with spacious, well-furnished rooms of typical Novotel standard. There is a vast fitness complex including a children's pool and the hotel restaurant is well priced. **www.accor.hu**

SZENTENDRE Villa Vitae

Ady Endre út 26, 2000 **Tel** *(026) 318 342* **Rooms** *9*

Located just a short drive from central Szentendre, this splendid villa is set in lush surroundings with immaculate gardens. The rooms are spacious and superbly furnished, but the highlight is the great, cave-like plunge-pool in the cellar. There is also a sauna and an outdoor pool. **www.villavitae.hu**

VESZPRÉM Oliva Pension

Buhim út 14–16, 8200 **Tel** *(088) 551 900* **Rooms** *11*

The legendary Oliva Pension is as renowned for its restaurant as for its rooms. Accommodation is spacious and luxurious, in modern, brightly furnished rooms with Internet access. A sumptuous breakfast is also provided. **www.oliva.hu**

VESZPRÉM Villa Medici

Kittenberger K út 11, 8200 **Tel** *(088) 590 070* **Fax** *(088) 590 070* **Rooms** *26*

Located close to Veszprém's famous viaduct, Villa Medici is, in every way, exquisite. The rooms are elegantly furnished and have to be seen to be believed, while the suites are worth the extra cost. The restaurant is one of the city's best while the swimming pool and tiled Turkish bath are delightful. **www.villamedici.hu**

VISEGRÁD Honti

Fő út 66, 2025 **Tel** *(026) 398 120* **Fax** *(026) 397 274* **Rooms** *30*

A lovely villa with a sloping roof and large balconies, the Honti is a good choice for budget travellers. Almost every room has a terrific view and visitors should note that this is one of Hungary's few pet-friendly hostelries. The rooms have TV, minibar and en suite bathrooms. **www.hotelhonti.hu**

Where to Eat in Hungary

Hungary has a long tradition of hospitality and culinary excellence. Budapest especially is home to some of Central Europe's most historic restaurants. Yet eating out remains a relatively low-cost experience and a number of outlets serve snacks round the clock. There are also some excellent cafés and patisseries.

PRICE CATEGORIES
Based on the price per person of a three-course meal with half a bottle of wine, including cover charge, service and tax.

Ⓕ Under 3,000 HUF
ⒻⒻ 3,000–4,000 HUF
ⒻⒻⒻ 4,000–5,000 HUF
ⒻⒻⒻⒻ 5,000–6,000 HUF
ⒻⒻⒻⒻⒻ Over 6,000 HUF

BUDAPEST

BohémTanya

Paulay Ede út 6 **Tel** (01) 268 1453   **Map** E2

For any visitor looking for reasonably priced, hearty Hungarian food in pleasant surroundings, the BohémTanya is a good choice. Diners are seated in wooden alcoves large enough for eight; when the restaurant is busy they may be asked to share their table with others.

Hanna Ortodoxkóser Étterem

Dob út 35 **Tel** (01) 342 1072   **Map** E3

This simple kosher eatery in the courtyard of the Orthodox Synagogue (see p353) serves traditional Jewish dishes and kosher wines. Opening hours are from 8am to 4pm, except on Friday and the Sabbath, when it also opens in the evenings. Sabbath meals need to be paid for either the day before or the day after.

Picasso Point

Hajós út 31 **Tel** (01) 312 1727   **Map** D2

Just a short way from the State Opera House (see p350), Picasso Point is a café and restaurant serving delicious bistro food and pizzas, and superb cakes. Food is served all day but this spot is especially popular in the evenings as a bar and café. There is also a nightclub in the cellar.

Belvárosi Lugas Étterem

Bajcsy-Zsilinszky út 15/a **Tel** (01) 302 5393   **Map** D2

Well-made, hearty dishes served in a simple yet appealing atmosphere make this place a favourite with locals. Informal and relaxed, it offers excellent food at reasonable prices, especially the daily specials, which are chalked up on a blackboard; the sumptuous soups are popular. In summer tables are set up outside on the pavement.

Café Kör

Sas út 17 **Tel** (01) 311 0053   **Map** D3

Booking is recommended at this popular, good-value bistro, which serves fine salads and Hungarian/European-inspired dishes, with vegetarian food made to order. A wide selection of Hungarian wines hints at the origins of this café, which began as a wine bar.

Tabáni Kakas Vendéglő

Attila út 27 **Tel** (01) 225 0478   **Map** D3

Poultry dishes are a speciality at this small restaurant with a family atmosphere. Goose and duck feature in soups, and main courses include goose breast with bread dumplings and vegetable sauce. There is no shortage of foie gras and a good selection of after-dinner ports at low prices. Live folk music in the evenings.

Vak Varjú

Paulay Ede út 7 **Tel** (01) 268 0888   **Map** E2

This restaurant provides superb views from enormous windows that open out on to one of Budapest's busiest streets. Well laid out with an attractive raised section and a spacious area for non-smokers, it has a lively atmosphere and an extensive menu featuring contemporary international cuisine. Live jazz is performed several evenings a week.

Articsóka

Zichy Jenő út 17 **Tel** (01) 302 7757   **Map** D2

The wonderfully bright and breezy Articsóka is decorated with hanging baskets, pastel-coloured paintwork and quality contemporary art. The Mediterranean cuisine on offer – with a good vegetarian selection – is both prepared and presented with flair. It comes highly recommended.

Pierrot Café Restaurant

Fortuna út 14 **Tel** (01) 375 6971   **Map** B2

This popular place opened as a private café during Communist times. Although it now faces stiff competition, the charming atmosphere keeps a loyal crowd coming. It has been redesigned, but the original, elegant interior still has a cosy café feel. Live piano music is played in the evening and all day at weekends. Highly recommended.

Map References see map of Budapest pp336–7

Sir Lancelot Lovagi Étterem

Podmaniczky út 14 **Tel** *(01) 302 4456* **Map** *D2*

At this excellent restaurant Renaissance-inspired dishes are served by staff in period costumes. Dishes are sumptuous and portions substantial; diners rarely manage to finish them. Renaissance-era music is played in the evenings. Booking is advised, especially on weekends.

Soul Café & Restaurant

Ráday út 11–13 **Tel** *(01) 217 6986* **Map** *E4*

This once gloomy street now thrives with cafés, restaurants and shops, including this intimate restaurant with its pleasant, relaxed atmosphere. Well-prepared and tasty international cuisine is served alongside Hungarian standards. There are plenty of options for vegetarians.

Baraka

Andrássy út 111 **Tel** *(01) 483 1355* **Map** *D3*

Located in the Andrássy Hotel, the trendy Baraka serves fine, French-inspired food, much of it genuinely inventive. The wine list is excellent and tempting and, provided one avoids the imported wines, meals work out to be relatively reasonable. Booking should be made in advance.

Carmel Étterem

Kazinczy út 31 **Tel** *(01) 342 4585* **Map** *E3*

This legendary, non-kosher Hungarian-Jewish cellar restaurant is always crowded with locals and visitors enjoying its famed *sólet* (Jewish bean stew) with smoked goose. The restaurant serves some fine wines. Reservations are recommended, especially at weekends.

Kárpátia Étterem És Söröző

Ferenciek Tere 7–8 **Tel** *(01) 317 3596* **Map** *D4*

First opened in 1877, the Kárpátia Étterem És Söröző offers Hungarian cuisine, hospitality and imperial elegance at its best. Set in beautifully decorated surroundings, the beer hall shares the premises and serves the same dishes at lower prices. Gypsy music is played in the evenings. Reservations are advised.

Mare Croaticum

Nagymező út 49 (Entrance on Weiner Leo út) **Tel** *(01) 311 7345* **Map** *D2*

Croatia is famous for its fish, and the Mare Croaticum does its homeland proud by serving only the freshest catch, along with a good selection of tangy Croatian white wines. There is a wide variety of good, non-fish dishes on the menu too, but the delicacies from the sea are the main attraction.

Marquis de Salade

Hajós út 43 **Tel** *(01) 302 4086* **Map** *D2*

The Marquis offers an extensive menu of dishes from around the world, from interesting lamb dishes from Azerbaijan and Georgia to basic Hungarian fare such as goulash. It is good value, and vegetarians have plenty to choose from. Staff is efficient and the service impeccable.

Pest Buda Vendéglő

Fortuna út 3 **Tel** *(01) 212 5880* **Map** *B2*

A small, elegant restaurant in a listed building, the Pest Buda Vendéglő is part of a former underground cave system with arcades along its walls and plenty of space for its popular and extensive Hungarian and international wine cellar. The menu is interesting and the cooking is excellent.

Alabárdos Étterem

Országház út 2 **Tel** *(01) 356 0851* **Map** *B2*

Set in an outstanding Gothic building, the Alabárdos Étterem serves Hungarian cuisine from old, pre-paprika times. This is a truly exclusive place – everything from the service to the atmosphere exudes class, and the prices are as expensive as anywhere in the city. Evening guitar music adds to the candle-lit ambience.

Búsuló Juhász Étterem

Kelenhegyi út 58 **Tel** *(01) 209 1649* **Map** *C5*

There are spectacular views from this traditional Hungarian restaurant on the western slopes of Gellért Hill *(see pp344–5)*. Lighter versions of Hungarian specialities will satisfy those who do not favour much paprika. There is also pleasant gypsy music in the evenings.

Fekete Holló

Országház út 10 **Tel** *(01) 356 2367* **Map** *B2*

Located on Vár, this is a little gem of a traditional Hungarian restaurant, where the kitsch medieval decor fails to detract from the excellent food. All the Hungarian favourites are on the menu, although there is little choice for vegetarians. Service can be slow because the place is usually full.

Maligan

Kossuth Lajos út 38 **Tel** *(01) 240 9010* **Map** *D4*

A superb wine bar and bistro, the Maligan serves classic Hungarian cuisine with plenty of goose dishes and other game such as pheasant and duck. Prices are reasonable and the service is superb, with the staff knowledgeable about both the food and wine on offer.

Key to Symbols *see back cover flap*

REST OF HUNGARY

DEBRECEN Trendo

Piac út 11–15 **Tel** *(020) 286 2860*

A real treasure, the Trendo restaurant provides an extensive menu of Italian pasta dishes and also plenty in the way of paprika-flavoured Hungarian stews. A great wine list and a friendly host, who makes a point of visiting every table, also help to make this one of the best restaurants in Hungary.

EGER Tulipánkert Vendéglő

Szépasszonyvölgy út 47 **Tel** *(036) 412 533*

A short drive southwest of Eger on Szépasszonyvölgy, this simple but idyllic restaurant has a terrace, garden and wine cellar offering great Hungarian wines alongside superb cuisine. In summer a gypsy band creates a lively atmosphere as the barbecue sizzles with fine local pork and sausages.

ESZTERGOM Csülök Csárda

Batthyány út 9 **Tel** *(033) 412 420*

A short walk down Majer út, the popular Csülök Csárda is worth seeking for its good if unadventurous Hungarian cuisine at decent prices. Its specialities include baked or boiled pork knuckle and catfish in paprika sauce. The wine list is, in fact, better than that of its more famous neighbour, Primás Prince – a favourite among visitors to Esztergom.

FERTŐD Gránátos

Bartók Béla utca 1 **Tel** *(099) 370 944*

When in Fertőd there are few places better to enjoy a good meal than the colonnaded terrace at Gránátos. The menu is simple but portions are generous and the quality of food is excellent. A coffee on the terrace, in the shadow of the Esterházy Palace *(see p363)*, is equally enjoyable.

GYŐR Belgian Beer Café

Árpád út 34 **Tel** *(096) 889 460*

The Royal Belgian Beer Café on the ground floor of Győr's Raba hotel is a delightful place to eat, drink and relax. Diners will find long wooden tables, a fine selection of Belgian beers, good food and a terrific atmosphere in the evenings. The small terrace fills up on summer evenings, when booking is advised.

GYŐR La Maréda

Apáca út 4 **Tel** *(096) 510 980*

Although the building dates from 1617, dining in this plush and opulent restaurant is like stepping into a scene from the 19th century. Imperial charm lines the walls in the form of stucco reliefs, while fine cigars and wines complement the enjoyable Hungarian cuisine.

KECSKEMÉT Kecskeméti Csárda és Borház

Kölcsey út 7 **Tel** *(076) 488 686*

A short walk from the central square, this is one of the best traditional Hungarian restaurants in the country and certainly the best on the southern Great Plain. The food is outstanding and the expert chefs are always keen to push the boundaries of Puszta cuisine. Game is a speciality, but it comes at a price.

KESZTHELY Hungaria Gösser

Kossuth Lajos utca 35 **Tel** *(083) 312 265*

On the pedestrianized part of Kossuth Lajos utca and the corner of Fő tér, this superb and popular restaurant is in a wonderful, renovated Art Nouveau house, complete with stained-glass windows. The reasonably priced food is traditional Hungarian with a modern twist. Booking is advisable.

KŐSZEG Taverna Florian

Várkör 59 **Tel** *(094) 563 072*

Set in a quiet location just a short walk from the heart of Kőszeg, this splendid bright red house is four venues in one. There is a wine cellar, a dining cellar, an elegant ground-floor restaurant and a garden and street café. Diners can expect excellent Italian-influenced food and friendly service.

PÉCS Cellárium

Hunyadi János út 2 **Tel** *(072) 314 453*

Housed in catacombs that allegedly provided shelter from attacking Ottomans, the Cellárium offers delicious local specialities alongside classic dishes, including a number of choices for vegetarians. There is live music most weekend evenings – reservations are essential for weekends.

PÉCS Aranykacsa

Teréz út 4 **Tel** *(072) 518 860*

The Aranykacsa (Golden Duck) serves tasty Hungarian food in a traditional setting within its ground floor restaurant and outside on a pleasant terrace, while downstairs a lively bar and music venue stays open till the early hours. As one might expect, given its name, local game is the speciality.

Key to Price Guide *see p394* **Key to Symbols** *see back cover flap*

SÁRVÁR Várkapu

Várkerület 5 **Tel** *(095) 320 475*

This yellow pension is a charming spot in which to sample high-quality and ground-breaking Hungarian cuisine. Every month a gala evening is held when the chef is given the freedom to create new masterpieces. There is a good selection of classic dishes, all of which are best enjoyed on the little terrace complete with picket fence.

SIÓFOK Fogas

Fő út 184 **Tel** *(084) 311 405*

Housed in Siófok's former post office, the Fogas specializes in fish freshly caught from Lake Balaton *(see p368–9)*. There is also a selection of meat dishes and a very good children's menu. Tempting pastries are made daily on the premises. Fogas also serves a good selection of wines.

SIÓFOK Piroska

Balatonszéplak-Felső 7 **Tel** *(084) 350 683*

This superb traditional Hungarian restaurant is decorated with folk art, with painted scenes of Siófok's past in place of windows. Tables are set around a vast open hearth. Try the extra-hot goulash accompanied by Balaton wines from the outstanding wine list. Open March to December.

SOPRON Wollner

Templom út 20 **Tel** *(099) 524 400*

In a gorgeous Neo-Baroque house in the heart of Old Sopron, the Wollner hotel is home to some of the city's best food. There are two dining options – the wine cellar downstairs and the courtyard terrace at the back. Both have the same excellent-value menu featuring traditional Hungarian dishes. The hotel also holds wine-tasting events.

SOPRON Vadászkurt Vendéglő

Udvarnoki út 6 **Tel** *(099) 314 385*

This is a truly outstanding restaurant with one of the best wine lists in the country. Everything about the place exudes luxury, from the polished parquet floors to the superb garden terrace. Refined dishes include goats' cheese from Őrség served with olives and garlic on toast.

SZEGED Fehértói Halászcsárda

Budapesti út 4 **Tel** *(062) 555 960*

Located a short distance from Szeged, this restaurant is bright and atmospheric. Fish soup is the signature dish among a number of regional specialities. The restaurant is set around a vast attractive courtyard and its cellar has a very good selection of wines from southern Hungary.

SZÉKESFEHÉRVÁR Belgian Beer Café

Szent Istvan 14 **Tel** *(022) 507 585*

Besides an outstanding selection of Belgian beers, the long menu at the Belgian Beer Café features a number of traditional Belgian dishes, including mussels and sausages. The interior, which features wood panelling and sturdy stiff-backed chairs, successfully conjures up the atmosphere of a 19th-century café.

SZENTENDRE Aranysárkány

Alkotmány út 1/a **Tel** *(026) 301 479*

The Aranysárkány (Golden Dragon) offers high-quality local dishes with game taking pride of place. There is goose, venison and even fried pigeon on the menu, all cooked in an open kitchen. The prices are reasonable, but patrons are advised to choose their wine carefully if they are on a budget.

SZENTENDRE Nemzeti Bormuzeum es Labirintus Étterem

Bogdányi út 10 **Tel** *(026) 317 054*

This outstanding restaurant in the cellars of Szentendre's National Wine Museum offers a great selection of traditional Hungarian food, including venison, all served with equally worthy wines. There is also a small room on the ground floor for larger groups, and a small but sublime terrace.

VÁC MoMo

Timár út 9 **Tel** *(027) 306 607*

The best place to eat in Vác is also a perfect spot to relax in the large garden and terrace that form one of the town's most popular meeting places. The food is excellent, with inventive dishes such as pork filled with seasoned feta cheese, served with a Greek salad. Prices are relatively high but well worth it.

VESZPRÉM Oliva

Buhim út 14–16 **Tel** *(088) 561 900*

Renovated in 2000, this high-class restaurant is the best in town and serves meat-heavy Hungarian staples as well as a melange of dishes from far and wide – New Zealand green clams, for example. In summer there's a barbecue in the garden as well as regular jazz evenings.

VISEGRÁD Renaissance

Fő tér 11 **Tel** *(026) 398 081*

There are few good restaurants in Visegrád, but the Renaissance is one of the better establishments. It is a medieval-themed restaurant, with all diners seated at long or round tables and issued with paper crowns. Substantial meat portions are served along with wine from huge jugs. Jousting performances take place in the courtyard.

VIENNA

Originally a Celtic settlement, Vienna's location on the edge of the Hungarian plains made it vulnerable to attacks, and Barbarian invasions reduced the town to ruins by the early 5th century. In the 10th century, the German Babenberg Dynasty acquired Vienna and it became a major trading centre. Later, in the 13th century, Vienna came under the control of the prosperous Habsburgs, who remained in power until 1918. In the 16th century, the threat of Ottoman invasion hindered its progress, and it was not until 1683, with the final defeat of the Ottoman Turks, that Vienna was able to flourish. In the mid-19th century, the city's defences were demolished and the Ringstrasse, a wide circular boulevard, was built, linking new political and cultural institutions. Today, Vienna is an architectural delight, with its magnificent palaces, imposing churches and world-class museums. The city's rich cultural scene and vibrant nightlife add to its appeal.

SIGHTS AT A GLANCE

GETTING AROUND

Vienna's city centre is easily explored on foot. Trams 1 and 2 take visitors around the Ringstrasse, past many of the important sights. *Fiakers* (horse-drawn carriages) are a novel way to get around. Hopper buses serve the city centre while larger buses run to the outer suburbs, which are also served by the U-Bahn (subway) service. The Badner Bahn, a tram line, also connects major sights.

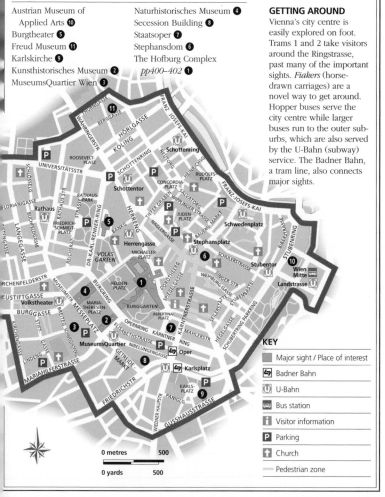

KEY

▮	Major sight / Place of interest
🚋	Badner Bahn
Ⓤ	U-Bahn
🚌	Bus station
ℹ	Visitor information
P	Parking
✚	Church
—	Pedestrian zone

0 metres 500
0 yards 500

◁ Baroque high altar showing the martyrdom of St Stephen, Stephansdom

The Hofburg Complex ●

What began as a small fortress in 1275 grew over the centuries into a vast palace, the Hofburg. It was the seat of Austrian power for over six centuries, and successive rulers were all anxious to leave their mark. The various buildings range in style from Gothic to late 19th-century Neo-Renaissance. The Hofburg is particularly impressive when seen from Heldenplatz. This is one of Vienna's most lively areas, both by day and at night, when the rooms of the palace serve as a theatre and concert halls.

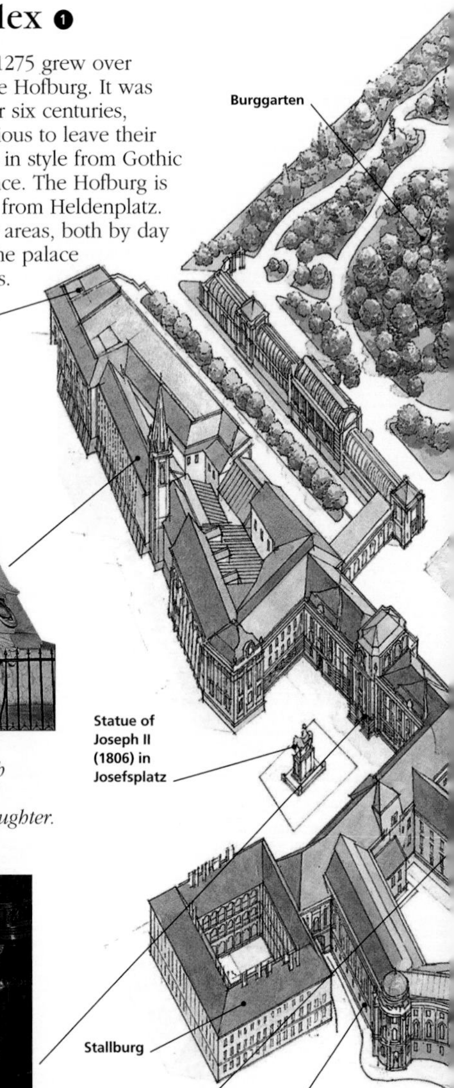

Burggarten

Albertina, built in 1781, now houses one of the finest collections of graphic art in Europe.

★ Augustinerkirche
The Habsburgs' former parish church houses the late 18th-century tomb of Maria Christina, Maria Theresa's daughter.

Statue of Joseph II (1806) in Josefsplatz

Prunksaal
The showpiece of the Austrian National Library is the grand, wood-paneled Prunksaal, or Hall of Honor.

Stallburg

Schatzkammer (the treasury) is housed in the Alte Burg.

Michaelertor is the gate through which visitors reach the older parts of the palace.

STAR SIGHTS

★ Augustinerkirche

★ Spanish Riding School

★ State Apartments

★ Spanish Riding School
The gracious interior of the riding school is lined with 46 columns and adorned with elaborate plasterwork, chandeliers and a coffered ceiling.

For hotels and restaurants in this region see pp408–409

Mozart Memorial *(1896)*
*Viktor Tilgner's statue of
the composer stands just
inside the entrance to
the Ringstrasse.*

VISITORS' CHECKLIST

Michaelerkuppel, Hofburg
Complex. **Tel** (01) 533 7570.
Ⓤ *Stephansplatz, Herrengasse,
Volkstheater.* 🚌 *2A, 3A.*
🚋 *D, J, 1.* ☐ *Sep–Jun:
9am–5:30pm daily; Jul &
Aug: 9am–6pm daily.*
www.hofburg-wien.at

The Burgtor, or outer gate,
was built to a design by
Peter Nobile between
1821 and 1824.

Neue Burg
*The last wing of
Hofburg, was built
just before the out-
break of World War I,
during the final days
of the monarchy.*

Volksgarten

**Monument to Eugene
of Savoy (1865)**

Heldenplatz

Schweizertor
*This 16th-century
gateway leads to the
Schweizerhof, the oldest part
of the Hofburg, originally a
stronghold with four towers.*

Hofburgkapelle, the
Hofburg chapel,
is where the famous
Vienna Boys'
Choir performs.

★ State Apartments
*The table in the state banqueting
hall is laid as it used to be during
the latter part of the reign of
Franz Joseph I (1848–1916).*

Exploring the Hofburg Complex

The vast Hofburg complex contains the former
imperial apartments and treasuries (Schatzkammer)
of the Habsburgs, several museums, a chapel, a church,
the Austrian National Library, the Winter Riding
School and the offices of the president of Austria.
The entrance to the imperial apartments and treasuries
is through the Michaelertor on Michaelerplatz.

*Elisabeth of Bavaria, Empress of
Austria (1865) by Winterhalter*

Neue Burg
Heldenplatz. **Tel** *(01) 5252 4484.*
⬚ *10am–6pm Wed–Mon.* ⬤ *1 Jan,
6 Apr, 25 May, 2 Nov.* 🖼
www.khm.at
The massive curved building,
Neue Burg, was added to the
Hofburg between 1881 and
1913. The Ephesus Museum
houses archaeological finds
from Ephesus, while pianos
that belonged to Haydn,
Schubert and Beethoven are
kept in the musical instruments
museum – the Sammlung alter
Musikinstrumente. The collection of weapons in the Hofjagd
und Rüstkammer is one of the
finest in Europe. There is also
a fine ethnological collection,
the Museum für Völkerkunde,
as well as art collections from
the Kunsthistorisches Museum.

Augustinerkirche
Augustinerstrasse 3. **Tel** *(01) 5330
9470.* **www**.augustinerkirche.at
The church has one of the
city's best-preserved 14th-cen-
tury Gothic interiors. The
Loreto Chapel here has a
series of silver urns that contain the hearts of the Habsburg
family. The church is also
celebrated for its music, with
masses by Schubert or Haydn
performed here on Sundays.

State Apartments
Michaelerkuppel-Feststiege.
Tel *(01) 533 7570.* ⬚ *Sep–Jun:
9am–5pm daily; Jul & Aug: 9am–6pm
daily.* 🖼 🔲 *Sat & Sun.*
The State Apartments
(Kaiserappartements) in the
Reichkanzleitrakt (1726–30)
and the Amalienburg (1575)
include the rooms occupied by
Franz Joseph I from 1857 to
1916, those of Empress
Elisabeth from 1854 to 1898
and those where Czar
Alexander I lived during the
Congress of Vienna in 1815.

Spanish Riding School
Tel *(01) 533 9031.* ⬚ *for
performances.* ⬤ *pub hols.* 🖼
♿ *some areas.*
The Spanish Riding School is
believed to have been founded
by the Habsburgs in 1572 to
cultivate the classic skills of
haute école horsemanship.
Today, 80-minute shows take
place in the building known
as the Spanish Riding School,
built between 1729 and 1735,
to a design by Josef Emanuel
Fischer von Erlach.

Schatzkammer
Schweizerhof. **Tel** *(01) 525 240.*
⬚ *10am–6pm Wed–Mon.* ⬤ *pub
hols.* 🖼 ♿
Sacred and secular treasures
amassed during centuries of
Habsburg rule are displayed in

*Tenth-century crown of the Holy
Roman Empire, Schatzkammer*

21 rooms known as the
treasuries (Schatzkammer).
They include relics of the
Holy Roman Empire, the
crown jewels and liturgical
objects of the imperial court.
Visitors can also admire the
dazzling gold, silver and porcelain that were once used
at state banquets.

Hofburgkapelle
Schweizerhof. **Tel** *(01) 533 9927.*
⬚ *11am–3pm Mon–Thu, 11am–1pm
Fri.* ⬤ *pub hols.* 🖼 **Vienna Boys'
Choir** *Jan–Jun & Sep–Dec: 9:15am
Sun (book by phone).* 🖼
Originally built in 1296, the
Hofburgkapelle was renovated
in 1440s by Friedrich III; it
contains Gothic statues in can-
opied niches. Every Sunday,
visitors can hear performances
by the renowned Vienna Boys'
Choir (Wiener Sängerknaben).

Burggarten and Volksgarten
Burgring/Opernring/Dr-Karl-Renner-
Ring. ⬚ *daily.*
Some of the space left around
the Hofburg after Napoleon's
invasion was transformed by
the Habsburgs into gardens.
The Volksgarten opened in
1820, but the Burggarten
remained the palace's
private garden until 1918.

Ornamental pond in the Volksgarten, with Burgtheater in the background

Hunters in the Snow (1565) by Pieter Bruegel the Elder

centres in the world. It houses a diverse range of facilities from art museums to venues for film, theatre, architecture, dance and new media.

The complex includes **KUNSTHALLE wien**, Vienna's main showcase for international and contemporary art exhibitions. It focuses on transdisciplinary work, including photography and film, as well as modern-art retrospectives. To the left of Kunsthalle is the **Leopold Museum**, home to over 5,000 works of Austrian art of which the highlights are major works by Gustav Klimt and the world's largest Egon Schiele collection. The **Museum of Modern Art Ludwig Foundation Vienna (MUMOK)** contains one of the largest European collections of modern art ranging from Pop Art to Viennese Actionism.

Kunsthistorisches Museum ❷

Maria Theresien-Platz. *Tel (01) 52524 4025.* 🚇 D, J, 1, 2. 🚌 2A, 57A. Ⓣ *Volkstheater, MuseumsQuartier.* ⏰ *10am–6pm Tue, Wed, Fri–Sun; 10am–9pm Thu.* 🎫 🎧 ♿ www.khm.at

Built in the style of the Italian Renaissance, the Museum of Art History houses a collection amassed over the centuries by generations of Habsburg monarchs. The public was given access to these art treasures when the museum opened in 1891 in Ringstrasse, built to designs by Karl von Hasenauer (1833–94) and Gottfried Semper (1809–79). The museum's lavish interior complements its exhibits perfectly and attracts more than a million people each year.

The collection focuses on Old Masters from the 15th to the 18th centuries. Due to links between the Habsburgs and the Netherlands, Flemish art is also well represented. Highlights are about half the surviving works by Pieter Bruegel the Elder, including his *The Tower of Babel* and most of the cycle of *The Seasons*, all from the mid-16th century. Among the other outstanding works are Dutch paintings from genre scenes of great charm to magnificent landscapes. *The Artist's Studio* (1665), an enigmatic allegorical painting by Vermeer (1632–75), is believed by some to be a self-portrait of the artist at

work. The most interesting Spanish works are by Velasquez (1599–1660), who immortalized the eight-year-old Margarita Teresa, the future wife of Emperor Leopold I (1640–1705), in *Infanta* (1659).

Schiele's *Kneeling Female Nude*, (1917) MuseumsQuartier Wien

MuseumsQuartier Wien ❸

Museumsplatz 1. *Tel (01) 523 5881.* 🚇 1, 2, 49, D, J. 🚌 2A, 48A. Ⓣ *MuseumsQuartier, Volkstheater.* **Visitor Centre** ⏰ *10am–7pm daily.* www.mqw.at. **KUNSTHALLE wien** ⏰ *10am–7pm Fri–Wed, 10am–10pm Thu.* 🎫 ♿ **Leopold Museum** ⏰ *10am–6pm Fri–Mon, Wed, 10am–9pm Thu.* ⏺ *Tue, pub hols.* 🎫 **Museum of Modern Art Ludwig Foundation Vienna** ⏰ *10am–6pm Tue, Wed, Fri–Sun, 10am–9pm Thu.* ⏺ *Mon, 24–25 Dec.*

Once home to the imperial stables and carriage houses, the MuseumsQuartier Wien is one of the largest cultural

Naturhistorisches Museum ❹

Maria Theresien-Platz. *Tel (01) 52177.* 🚇 1, 2, 46, 49, D. 🚌 2A, 48A. Ⓣ *Volkstheater.* ⏰ *9am–6:30pm Thu–Mon, 9am–9pm Wed.* ⏺ *1 Jan, 1 May, 1 Nov, 25 Dec.* 🎫 ♿ 💻 📷 www.nhm-wien.ac.at

Almost a mirror image of the Kunsthistorisches Museum, the Natural History Museum was designed by the same architects and opened in 1889. Both were built under the reign of Franz Joseph I.

The Natural History Museum is home to one of the richest and most wide-ranging collections in the world. It includes archaeological, anthropological, mineralogical, zoological and geological displays. Besides casts of dinosaur skeletons, it also has the world's oldest collection of meteorites. It also includes prehistoric sculptures, Bronze Age items and extinct birds and mammals as well as Europe's most comprehensive exhibition of gems. The archaeological section includes the celebrated *Venus of Willendorf*, a 25,000-year-old Paleolithic fertility figurine.

Splendid grand staircases gracing the side wings of the Burgtheater

Burgtheater ❺

Dr Karl-Lueger-Ring 2. *Tel* (01)
5144 4140. 🚊 *1, 2, D.*
Ⓤ *Schottentor.* ⬜ *Sep–Jun:
9am–6pm Mon–Fri, 9am–noon
Sat (tickets).* 🎧 📷 *3pm daily.*
🦽 www.burgtheater.at

The impressive Burgtheater is
one of the most prestigious
stages in the German-
speaking world. The original
theatre, built under Maria
Theresa's reign, was replaced
in 1888 by the present Italian
Renaissance-style building by
architects Karl von Hasenauer
and Gottfried Semper. It
closed for refurbishment in
1897 after it was discovered
that several seats had no view
of the stage. A bomb devastated the building at the end
of World War II, leaving
only the side wings containing the grand staircases intact.
It has since been restored to
wide acclaim.

Stephansdom ❻

Stephansplatz 1. *Tel* (01) 51552
3526. 🚌 *1A, 2A.* Ⓤ *Stephansplatz.*
⬜ *6am–10pm daily.* 🎧 📷 *9am,
1pm Mon–Sat, 1pm Sun &
pub hols.* 🎧 🦽 🎵 *Organ
concerts May–Nov: 7pm Wed.*
www.stephanskirche.at

The Stephansdom, with its
magnificent glazed-tile roof, is
the heart and soul of Vienna.
A church has stood on the site
for over 800 years, but all that
remains of the original 13th-
century Romanesque structure

are the Heathen Towers and
Giant's Doorway. Severely
damaged during World War II,
the cathedral was later
restored to its former glory.
Its interior contains an
impressive collection of art
spanning several centuries.
Highlights are the Braoque
high altar and Pilgram's
pulpit, decorated with portraits of the Four Fathers of
the Church. The 15th-century,
137-m (450-ft) Steffl or
South Spire, is the striking
symbol of the city.

Staatsoper ❼

Opernring 2. *Tel* (01) 51444 2250.
🚌 *59A.* 🚊 *1, 2, D, J.* Ⓤ *Karlsplatz.*
www.wiener-staatsoper.at

Vienna's Opera House, the
Staatsoper, was the first of
the grand Ringstrasse

Superb sculptures adorn Singer
Gate, Stephansdom

buildings to be completed.
It opened on 25 May 1869,
to the strains of Mozart's
Don Giovanni. Built in Neo-
Renaissance style, the
Staatsoper did not appeal to
Emperor Franz Joseph, who
compared it to a "railway
station" leading Eduard van
der Nüll, its Austrian architect,
to commit suicide. Yet, when
the Opera House was hit by a
bomb in 1945 and largely
destroyed, the event was seen
as a symbolic blow to the city.

With a new state-of-the-
art auditorium and stage,
the Opera House reopened
on 5 November 1955, with a
performance of Beethoven's
Fidelio. Gustav Mahler,
Richard Strauss and Herbert
von Karajan are among the
illustrious composers who
have conducted here. Each
year, on the last Thursday
of Carnival, the stage is
extended to create a vast
dance floor for the Vienna
Opera Ball.

The imposing façade of Vienna's
Opera House, Staatsoper

Secession
Building ❽

Friedrichstrasse 12. *Tel* (01) 587
5307. 🚌 *59A.* Ⓤ *Karlsplatz.*
⬜ *10am–6pm Tue, Wed,
Fri–Sun, 10am–8pm Thu.* 🎧
www.secession.at

Designed by Joseph Maria
Olbrich in 1898, the unusual
Secession Building was a
showcase for the Secession
movement's artists such as
Gustav Klimt, Kolo Moser and
Otto Wagner. The almost
windowless building, with its
filigree globe of entwined
laurel leaves on the roof, is a
squat cube with four towers.

Golden filigree dome adorning the Secession Building

The motto of the founders, on the façade, states: "To every Age its Art, to Art its Freedom".

The Secession Building's best-known exhibit is Klimt's *Beethoven Frieze*. This 34-m (110-ft) painting is regarded as one of the masterpieces of Viennese Art Nouveau. Designed in 1902 and covering three walls, it shows interrelated groups of figures thought to be a commentary on Beethoven's *Ninth Symphony*.

Karlskirche ❾

Karlsplatz 8. *Tel* (01) 505 6294.
🚌 4A. 🚋 1, 2, 71, D, J.
Ⓤ Karlsplatz. ◯ 9am–12:30pm,
1–6pm Mon–Thu, Sat, 12–5:45pm
Fri, Sun. 🅿 📷 **www**.karlskirche.at

During Vienna's plague epidemic of 1713, Emperor Karl VI vowed that as soon as the city was delivered from its plight he would build a church dedicated to St Charles Borromeo (1538–84), a former archbishop and patron saint of plague victims. He announced a competition to design the church, which was won by Johann Bernhard Fischer von Erlach's (1656–1723), architect of many of Vienna's finest buildings. His eclectic Baroque masterpiece has a gigantic Neo-Classical dome and portico borrowed from classical Greek and Roman architecture, flanked by two minaret-like towers.

One of the most striking features is the frescoes in the cupola painted by

Johann Michael Rottmayr between 1725 and 1730, depicting the *Apotheosis of St Charles Borromeo*. It was the painter's last commission. Others include the typically Baroque high altar featuring a stucco relief by Albert Camesina, which shows St Charles Borromeo being taken to heaven on a cloud filled with angels and putti, and the Two intricate columns, inspired by Trajan's Column in Rome. These feature scenes from the life of the saint, illustrating his qualities of steadfastness and courage.

Stucco relief on the Baroque high altar, Karlskirche

Austrian Museum of Applied Arts ❿

Stubenring 5. *Tel* (01) 711 360.
🚋 1, 2. 🚌 1A, 74A. Ⓤ Stubentor,
Landstrae. Ⓢ Wien Mitte. ◯ 10am–
midnight Tue, 10am–6pm Wed–Sun.
🅿 free on Sat. **www**.mak.at

The Austrian Museum of Applied Arts (Museum für angewandte Kunst or MAK), founded in 1864, was the first of its kind in Europe and exercised a strong influence on the development of the applied arts for some time.

The renovated museum acts both as a showcase for Austrian decorative arts and as a repository for fine objects from around the world. Originally founded in 1864 as a museum of art and industry, it expanded and diversified over the years to

include objects representing new artistic movements. The permanent collection, presented according to periods from the Gothic to the present, includes world famous works by the Wiener Werkstätte, an arts and crafts cooperative workshop from 1870 to 1956. Furniture, textiles, glassware, and fine Renaissance jewellery are also on display. A number of rooms are devoted to the Art Nouveau period.

Freud Museum ⓫

Berggasse 19. *Tel* (01) 319 1596.
🚌 37, 38, 40, 41, 42, D. 🚌 40A.
Ⓤ Schottentor, Schottenring.
◯ 9am–5pm daily. 🅿
www.freud-museum.at

Berggasse No. 19, a typical 20th-century Viennese town house, is now one of the city's most famous addresses. The father of psychoanalysis, Sigmund Freud (1856–1939), lived, worked and received patients here from 1891 till 1938, when he was forced to leave the city, where he had lived almost all his life, by the Nazis. Although abandoned by Freud in a hurry, the flat still preserves an intimate atmosphere with most of his belongings still in place.

The room in which Freud received patients is on the mezzanine floor. There are at least 420 items of memorabilia on display, including his letters and books. His frayed hat and travel trunk can be seen in the small, dark lobby. A cabinet contains some archaeological objects collected by Freud. The world-famous couch is now in the Freud Museum in London.

Beautifully restored patients' waiting room in the Freud Museum

Practical & Travel Information

Vienna is well equipped for both winter and summer tourism. The public transport system is clean, efficient and easy to use and banking and currency exchange facilities are widely available in the city. The official language is German but English is widely spoken throughout the city.

DOCUMENTATION

Citizens of the US, Canada, Australia and New Zealand need just a passport to visit Vienna. No visa is required for visitors who intend to stay for three months or less. Most European Union (EU) citizens require only a valid identity card to enter the country.

VISITOR INFORMATION

Austria has a wide network of local tourist offices. In Vienna, the **Wiener Tourismusverband** (Vienna Tourist Board) is very helpful, especially with regard to forthcoming events and booking accommodation.

Visitors can also plan their trip to Vienna by contacting travel agencies or the representatives of **Österreich Werbung** (the Austrian National Tourist Office) in their native country. For information on cheap accommodation, youth hostels and tickets for concerts, the multilingual staff at **Jugendinformation Wien** (Vienna Youth Information Office) can provide assistance and leaflets.

HEALTH AND SECURITY

Hospitals in Vienna are of a high standard. In case of medical emergencies, visitors should call an ambulance or the local doctor on call. For minor ailments or injuries, it is best to go to a pharmacy. All pharmacies are marked with a distinctive red "A" sign, and when closed, display the address of the nearest open one.

Although visitors are unlikely to encounter any violence in Vienna, it is always advisable to be cautious when out walking. The police and emergency services are easy to contact if the need arises.

BANKING AND CURRENCY

The official currency of Austria is the euro. Banks are the best place to change money and are open Monday to Friday from 8am to 12:30pm and from 1:30 to 3pm. Some, generally those at main train stations and airports, stay open longer and do not close for lunch. Major credit cards are accepted at large stores, hotels and restaurants, but visitors are advised to carry some cash as well. However, traveller's cheques are the safest way to carry large sums of money and can be exchanged in most banks in Vienna. *Bankomats* or ATMs are found everywhere in the city, even railway stations and airports; most are closed after midnight.

COMMUNICATIONS

The telecommunications network in Vienna is run by **Telekom Austria**. Calls are among the most expensive in Europe. Public phones are coin- or card-operated and visitors can buy phone cards from post offices and news-agents. The postal service in the city is very reliable and post offices are open Monday to Friday between 8am and noon and 2 and 6pm.

FACILITIES FOR THE DISABLED

Public awareness of the needs of the disabled is growing in Austria. Wiener Tourismusverband has a good online information service with details of wheelchair access points at tourist sights, hotels and public toilets.

ARRIVING BY AIR

Vienna's **Schwechat International Airport** is 19 km (12 miles) from the city centre. There are direct flights from the United States on

DIRECTORY

VISITOR INFORMATION	Canada	Police	RyanAir
	Tel (01) 531 383 000.	*Tel 133.*	www.ryanair.com
Jugendinformation Wien	www.kanada.at	**COMMUNICATIONS**	**Schwechat International Airport**
www.infoup.at	**United Kingdom**		
	Tel (01) 716 130.	**Telekom Austria**	www.viennaairport.com
Österreich Werbung	www.britishembassy.at	www.telekom.at	
www.austriatourism.com	**United States**	**ARRIVING BY AIR**	**RAIL TRAVEL**
Wiener Tourismusverband	*Tel (01) 313 39.*	**Austrian Airlines**	**Rail Enquiry**
www.wien.info	www.usembassy.at	www.aua.com	www.oebb.at
EMBASSIES	**EMERGENCY NUMBERS**	**British Airways**	**ARRIVING BY COACH**
Australia	**Ambulance**	www.britishairways.com	**Busterminal Erdberg**
Tel (01) 506 740. www. australian-embassy.at	*Tel 144.*	**Delta Airlines**	Erdbergstrasse 200A.
	Fire	www.delta.com	**Eurolines**
	Tel 122.	**Lauda Air**	www.eurolines.com
		www.laudaair.com	

Delta Airlines from New York and Orlando. **Austrian Airlines** flies from New York, Chicago and Washington, while **Lauda Air** operates from Miami. There are several flights a day from Gatwick and Heathrow airports in London. **British Airways** and **RyanAir** also offer regular flights to Vienna.

RAIL TRAVEL

Vienna's most important train stations for international travel are Westbahnhof, which serves Western European destinations, and Südbahnhof which serves destinations to the east. Südbahnhof will be partially closed for long-term renovation, during which Wien-Meidling Station in the west of the city will handle a large proportion of international

---

THE CLIMATE OF VIENNA

Summers (May–August) in Vienna are warm but not too hot with average temperatures of 25° C (77° F) between June and August. Spring (March–April) and autumn (September–October) are very pleasant. Winters (November–March) are very cold with regular snow. Temperatures usually dip to as low as -4° C (25° F).

VIENNA			
°C/F	23/74		
	15/59 15/59	14/57	
	6/43	7/45	
0°C 32°F			1/34
			-4/25
☀ 6 hrs	9 hrs	4 hrs	2 hrs
☂ 45 mm	84 mm	56 mm	39 mm
month Apr	Jul	Oct	Jan

---

trains. Information about train schedules are available on the official website.

ARRIVING BY COACH

International coach services arrive at **Busterminal Erdberg**

in the east of the city, right beside the U3 Erdberg underground station. The Old Town is a short six-stop journey from here. **Eurolines** operates daily services from Busterminal Erdberg to most Eastern European cities.

Shopping & Entertainment

Shopping in Vienna can be expensive, but it is a good place to buy traditional goods such as Loden coats, porcelain and glass. Famous for its coffee shops, Christmas markets, world-class opera and orchestras, Vienna is also the centre of entertainment in Austria.

FOOD AND DRINK

Austria is justly famous for its cakes and pastries. Visitors should try the buttery *advent stollen* (Christmas cake), stuffed with fruit and nuts and dusted with icing sugar, available from the **Meinl am Graben** delicatessen. Specialist chocolate shops such as **Altmann & Kühne** are also worth a visit, both for the chocolates and their unusual packaging.

SOUVENIRS

Petit-point embroidery, which adorns elegant handbags, powder compacts and similar articles, is a Viennese speciality. A wide range of these goods is available at **Petit Point** and **Maria Stransky**. *Trachten* (Austrian costumes) shops sell typical hats, pretty children's dresses, jackets and blouses. **Rasper & Söhne** is the best place for glassware.

THEATRE AND MUSIC

Viennese theatre enjoys a high reputation and the **Burgtheater** *(see p404)* is the city's leading venue. The **Volkstheater** puts on modern plays while the **Theater an der Wien** produces lavish musicals.

At the **Staatsoper** *(see p404)*, operas are normally performed in the original language whereas at most other theatres, they are sung in German. The principal venues for classical music are the **Musikverein** and the concert halls of **Konzerthaus**. The city supports two great orchestras, the Wiener Philharmoniker and the Wiener Symphoniker. Seasonal events include the **Vienna Festival** in May and June, and the Klangbogen Wien in July and August, held at the Theater an der Wien. Seasonal opera, drama and concert performances take place throughout the city in late July and August.

DIRECTORY

FOOD AND DRINK

Altmann & Kühne
Tel (01) 533 0927.
www.feinspitz.com

Meinl am Graben
Tel (01) 532 3334.
www.meinlamgraben.at

SOUVENIRS

Maria Stransky
Tel (01) 533 6098.
www.maria-stransky.at

Petit Point
Tel (01) 512 4886.

Rasper & Söhne
Tel (01) 534 33.

THEATRE AND MUSIC

Burgtheater
www.burgtheater.at

Konzerthaus
www.konzerthaus.at

Musikverein
www.musikverein.at

Staatsoper
www.staatsoper.at

Theater an der Wien
www.theater-wien.at

Vienna Festival
www.festwochen.at

Volkstheater
www.volkstheater.at

Where to Stay in Vienna

With more than 500 hotels and pensions, Vienna offers accommodation to suit everyone. It has some of Europe's grandest hotels as well as numerous boarding houses and self-catering lodgings. Hotels are generally larger and better equipped than pensions, which tend to be bed-and-breakfast establishments.

PRICE CATEGORIES
Price categories are for a standard double room with bathroom per night in high season, including tax and service charges.
€ Under 75 euros
€€ 75–110 euros
€€€ 110–145 euros
€€€€ 145–200 euros
€€€€€ over 200 euros

VIENNA

Neuer Markt   🍴   €

Seilergasse 9, 1010 **Tel** *(01) 512 2316* **Fax** *(01) 513 9105* **Rooms** *37*

First opened in the 1920s, Neuer Markt is a cosy Viennese-style pension with dusty-rose-coloured furnishings and friendly and personal service. For visitors staying longer than seven nights, the pension provides a free pick-up service from the airport or train station upon arrival. **www.hotelpension.at**

Aviano   €€

Marco d'Avianogasse 1, 1010 **Tel** *(01) 512 8330* **Fax** *(01) 512 8330* **Rooms** *17*

Located near the Staatsoper *(see p404)*, this four-star pension has a friendly, welcoming atmosphere with cheerful, well-decorated rooms. Service is very good and the staff can help organize sightseeing tours and tickets to concerts. Good value for money. **www.secrethomes.at**

Post   🅿 🍴 ▤ ♿   €€

Fleischmarkt 24, 1010 **Tel** *(01) 515 830* **Fax** *(01) 5158 3808* **Rooms** *107*

Located on the site of a former inn patronized by Mozart, Richard Wagner and Friedrich Nietzsche, this traditional hotel has rooms in contemporary style. There are also business rooms with broadband Internet access, and a restaurant. **www.hotel-post-wien.at**

Arenberg   ▤   €€€€

Stubenring 2, 1010 **Tel** *(01) 512 5291* **Fax** *(01) 513 9356* **Rooms** *22*

Located on the Ringstrasse, the Arenberg is an elegant establishment with charming and comfortable bedrooms that are traditionally decorated. The bathrooms are modern and clean. The hotel also provides several economical weekend packages. **www.arenberg.at**

Mailberger Hof   🍴   €€€€

Annagasse 7, 1010 **Tel** *(01) 512 0641* **Fax** *(01) 512 0641* **Rooms** *40*

A family-run hotel near the Staatsoper and Stephansdom *(see p404)*, Mailberger Hof occupies a Baroque palace comprising two merged Gothic houses and is a protected building. A wide stone staircase leads to the spacious, tastefully furnished bedrooms. Visitors can dine in the striking vaulted restaurant. **www.mailbergerhof.at**

Wandl   ▤   €€€€

Peterplatz 9, 1010 **Tel** *(01) 534 550* **Fax** *(01) 534 5577* **Rooms** *138*

Located near the Stephansdom, this charming, old-fashioned hotel has been in the same family for generations. Fine stuccoes feature in the covered courtyard, which serves as a breakfast room, as well as in some of the bedrooms. Other rooms are simpler, but large, and have parquet floors. **www.hotel-wandl.com**

Astoria   🍴 ▤   €€€€€

Kärntner Strasse 32–34, 1015 **Tel** *(01) 515 77* **Fax** *(01) 515 77 582* **Rooms** *118*

A hotel since 1912 and located near the Staatsoper, Astoria boasts a panelled Art Nouveau foyer leading to a grand dining room on the first floor. The splendid rooms are spacious and traditionally furnished, often with period decor. Some have their own brass letterboxes. **www.austria-trend.at**

Kaiserin Elisabeth   ▤   €€€€€

Weihburggasse 3, 1010 **Tel** *(01) 512 26* **Fax** *(01) 515 267* **Rooms** *63*

This elegant hotel, named after the indomitable Habsburg empress, is located just off Stephansplatz. In the 1800s it played host to many famous musicians such as Wagner and Liszt. The *fin-de-siècle*-style bedrooms are smart, and Persian rugs decorate the public rooms. **www.kaiserinelisabeth.at**

Palais Coburg Hotel Residenz   🅿 🍴 🛏 📺 ♿ ▤   €€€€€

Coburgbastei 4, 1010 **Tel** *(01) 518 180* **Fax** *(01) 518 18100* **Rooms** *35*

This 19th-century former Saxe-Coburg-Gotha palace was renovated in 2003 and is now a luxury Relais and Chateaux hotel. There are 35 elegant suites, some traditional, others contemporary, as well as a unique rooftop spa and two fine restaurants. It has one of Europe's finest wine collections. **www.palaiscoburg.at**

Where to Eat in Vienna

The staples of Vienna's cuisine are assimilated from the cooking traditions of the Habsburg Empire. The range of gastronomy is vast – from gourmet nouvelle cuisine to booths selling sausages and beer on street corners. Mealtimes here are flexible and in the city centre visitors will be able to find hot meals until midnight.

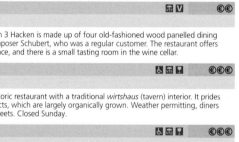

PRICE CATEGORIES
Based on the price per person of a three-course meal with half a bottle of wine, including cover charge, service and tax.

€ Under 20 euros
€€ 20–30 euros
€€€ 30–40 euros
€€€€ 40–50 euros
€€€€€ over 50 euros

VIENNA

Glacis Beisl

€

MuseumsQuartier, Zugang Breitegasse 4, 1070 **Tel** *(01) 526 5660*

Located in the museum district, this is a moderately priced restaurant that has a huge aquarium at the entrance. Popular with tourists, it offers carefully chosen dishes featuring meat, dumplings, pasta and fish. It has a shady summer garden for fine weather as well as an enclosed winter garden. Open daily till 2am.

Steman

€€

Otto/Bauer Gasse 7, 1060 **Tel** *(01) 597 8509*

This is a comfortable and homely guesthouse retaining many period features. Diners eat family-style at long tables surrounded by panelled wood and old oil paintings. The Viennese dishes have won favourable comment in the local press. Closed Saturday and Sunday.

Zu den 3 Hacken

€€

Singerstrasse 28, 1010 **Tel** *(01) 512 5895*

Reputed to be Vienna's oldest tavern, Zu den 3 Hacken is made up of four old-fashioned wood panelled dining rooms, one of which is dedicated to the composer Schubert, who was a regular customer. The restaurant offers classic Viennese cooking in a friendly ambience, and there is a small tasting room in the wine cellar.

Ofenloch

€€€

Kurrentgasse 8, 1010 **Tel** *(01) 533 8844*

Classic Viennese dishes are served in this historic restaurant with a traditional *wirtshaus* (tavern) interior. It prides itself on using only the very best local products, which are largely organically grown. Weather permitting, diners can eat outside on one of Vienna's oldest streets. Closed Sunday.

Plachutta

€€€

Wollzeile 38, 1010 **Tel** *(01) 512 1577*

The Plachutta restaurants are dedicated to keeping Viennese traditional cooking alive, using classic ingredients and methods. This is the flagship restaurant of the chain and the unrivalled headquarters of Austria's famous *tafelspitz* dish of boiled beef. Open daily until midnight.

Wrenkh

€€€

Bauernmarkt 10, 1010 **Tel** *(01) 533 1526*

Famous for years as Vienna's premier vegetarian restaurant, Wrenkh now serves chicken and fish as well, although tofu still figures prominently on the menu. Its unique "happy cuisine" philosophy aims to take the seriousness out of haute cuisine, and is demonstrated in cooking workshops open to the public. Closed Sunday.

Do & Co

€€€€

Stephansplatz 12, 1010 **Tel** *(01) 533 3969*

A Viennese institution and part of a catering empire, Do & Co is on the 7th floor of a high-rise building and has a striking view of the Stephansdom. Excellent international and regional dishes are served, with kebabs among the specialities. Reservations are required.

Drei Husaren

€€€€

Weihburggasse 4, 1010 **Tel** *(01) 512 1092*

Touted as Vienna's oldest luxury restaurant, Drei Husaren offers fine Viennese cuisine in an environment fit for a Habsburg. Meat, fish and other fare is prepared and served with style. The Drei Husaren Torte, a special cake made to the restaurant's own secret recipe, is recommended for dessert. Reservations are advised.

Meinl am Graben

€€€€€

Graben 19, 1010 **Tel** *(01) 532 3334 6000*

Meinl is the biggest food name in Austria. The restaurant is one of the best in the country, and is applauded for its creativity and superb presentation. The downstairs wine bar always has 30 wine varieties to taste and the café with attached garden offers unlimited blends of coffee beans.

SOUTH EASTERN EUROPE

South Eastern Europe at a Glance

One of the most diverse areas of the European continent, South Eastern Europe is where the cultural traditions of Central Europe, the Mediterranean and the Balkans come together. So it is not uncommon to see Catholic churches, Orthodox monasteries and Muslim holy sites rubbing shoulders. The region's island-scattered Adriatic coast and the golden-hued sands of Romania and Bulgaria offer ample opportunities to relax on the beach. Inland, rugged mountain regions, rich in wildflowers and woodland, provide the perfect backdrop for exhilarating hikes.

EASTERN AND CENTRAL EUROPE

SOUTH EASTERN EUROPE

Mount Triglav (see pp436–7), *the highest peak in Slovenia, stands at the heart of a national park filled with jagged summits, evergreen woodland and glacier-carved lakes.*

SLOVENIA *(see pp414–449)*

CROATIA *(see pp450–507)*

BOSNIA AND HERZEGOV *(see pp508–525)*

Zagreb (see pp486–7), *capital of Croatia and an important regional cultural centre, boasts a fine collection of museums and galleries and a year-round supply of top-quality music and theatre.*

Jajce (see pp518–19), *the medieval Bosnian capital, is a picturesque hilltop town famous for its thundering waterfall and water-powered mills.*

MONTE *(see pp5*

Ostrog Monastery (see pp536–7), *one of the highlights of Montenegro, is a popular pilgrimage site. Its painted rock churches are among the most beautiful religious buildings in the Balkans.*

◁ **Magnificent view of the town of Kotor, Montenegro**

Peleş Castle (see pp582–3) *is nestled in the Transylvanian Alps. Its fairy tale spires and turrets reflect the romantic tastes of its high-living first resident, German-born King Carol I of Romania.*

0 km   100

0 miles   100

ROMANIA
(see pp566–599)

SERBIA
pp544–565)

BULGARIA
(see pp600–641)

Sofia (see pp604–605), *capital of Bulgaria, is rich in Roman remains, medieval treasures and Orthodox churches. The cavernous Neo-Byzantine Aleksandûr Nevski Memorial Church serves as the city's graceful centrepiece.*

Belgrade (see pp548–9), *the Serbian capital, centres on the sprawling Kalemegdan Fortress, overlooking the Danube river. With its crumbling bastions built by former conquerors, it is now a tranquil park laced with flowerbeds and tree-shaded promenades.*

SLOVENIA

espite being one of Europe's smallest nations, Slovenia offers magnificently varied scenery and splendid architecture. Since 1991, it has re-established itself as a major holiday destination for outdoor pursuits, high-quality health spas and ski resorts. Economic growth has helped sustain tourism, and the lively people make Slovenia a welcoming place to visit.

Few countries in South Eastern Europe pack as much variety into such a small geographical area as Slovenia. The landscape changes swiftly between the Alps and limestone plateaus, dense forests and Mediterranean coastline, all within a very short distance of each other. At the heart of the country is Ljubljana, a city combining graceful architecture with an exuberant lifestyle.

The population is relatively homogenous with 83 per cent of its two million inhabitants ethnically Slovene. Small but significant minorities include Albanians, Bosnians, Croats and Serbs, who came to live and work in Slovenia during the Yugoslav period.

HISTORY

The Slovene nation has its origins in the great migrations of the 6th century, when Slav tribes from the Carpathian basin settled in the Drava and Sava valleys. A Slav tribal state known as Carantania came into existence in the territory of present-day Slovenia and southern Austria, but this soon came under the control of more powerful German-speaking rulers.

In the medieval period, the country was governed by feudal landowners, including the Babenbergs, the Spannheims and the Counts of Celje. Ultimate authority was also wielded at various times by Hungarian kings, German emperors

Pavement café on Old Square, Ljubljana's oldest medieval square

◁ The exquisite Church of the Assumption, Lake Bled

Guards carrying Tito's coffin at his funeral in 1980

and the Austrian Habsburg family, who established control over most of Slovenia by the 15th century. Around the same time, the Ottoman Turks mounted attacks deep into Central Europe, turning Slovenia into the front line in the region's defence.

Throughout the Habsburg period, the predominant language was German, with Slovene spoken only among the peasantry. However, a brief period of French rule (1809–1813) introduced Slovene-language schooling and a new generation of educated Slovenes rose to promote national culture. Following the collapse of the Habsburg Empire in 1918, Slovenia entered the newly created kingdom of Serbs, Croats and Slovenes, later renamed Yugoslavia. This multi-ethnic state was invaded by Hitler in April 1941 and Slovenia was divided between Nazi Germany and Fascist Italy. After World War II, Slovenia became a federal republic within a reconstituted, Communist-ruled Yugoslavia. The Yugoslav Federation functioned successfully under the leadership of President Tito. With the death of Tito and the onset of economic problems however, the union began to disintegrate.

Slovenia declared independence from Yugoslavia on 25 June 1991. The Ten Day War (27 June–6 July) with Yugoslavia followed, in which the Yugoslav People's Army was outmanoeuvred by Slovenia's defence forces. Slovenia went on to establish itself as one of the economic and political successes of the new Europe, joining NATO and the European Union in 2004.

KEY DATES IN SLOVENIAN HISTORY

AD 591 Slavs arrive in the upper Drava region

1282 The Habsburg Dynasty establishes its first feudal holdings in Slovene lands

1573 Peasant Uprising ends with the defeat of the rebels and bloody retribution by the nobility

1813 A brief period of Napoleonic rule is followed by a return to Habsburg control

1918 Slovenia joins other south Slav peoples to form the kingdom of Serbs, Croats and Slovenes

1921 Vidovdan Constitution establishes a constitutional monarchy; Belgrade is the capital

1938 Josip Broz Tito appointed leader of the Communist Party of Yugoslavia

1941 Slovenia divided between Fascist Italy, Nazi Germany and Miklós Horthy's Hungary

1974 The 1974 Constitution gives each republic greater responsibility for its internal affairs

1980 Yugoslavia enters a period of crisis following the death of Tito

1991 Slovenia declares independence from Yugoslavia

2004 Slovenia joins NATO

2007 Euro introduced in Slovenia

LANGUAGE AND CULTURE

Modern Slovene belongs to the Slavic family of languages and is closely related to Croatian and Serbian. Centuries of Austrian rule has left a profound imprint on the language and many colloquial expressions are of German origin. The Austrian influence also extended to architecture, with Alpine farmhouses and onion-domed churches scattered across parts of the country. Slovenia was predominantly a peasant country until the early 20th century and folk music and village festivals are still an integral part of national life. During the 1970s and 80s, Slovenia emerged as a centre of contemporary art and popular music and Slovenian culture retains a modern outlook.

Exploring Slovenia

A delightful destination in its own right, Ljubljana is also a good base from which to explore the rest of the country. The city lies at the centre of Slovenia's road and rail network and many regional attractions are within a couple of hours' drive. To the north are the grand Julian Alps, towering above Lakes Bled and Bohinj. To the west, routes cross the cave-studded karst region before descending towards the coast, characterized by Venetian-style architecture and lush vegetation.

Traditional Alpine farmhouses along a stream, Lake Bohinj

SIGHTS AT A GLANCE

0 km   40

0 miles   40

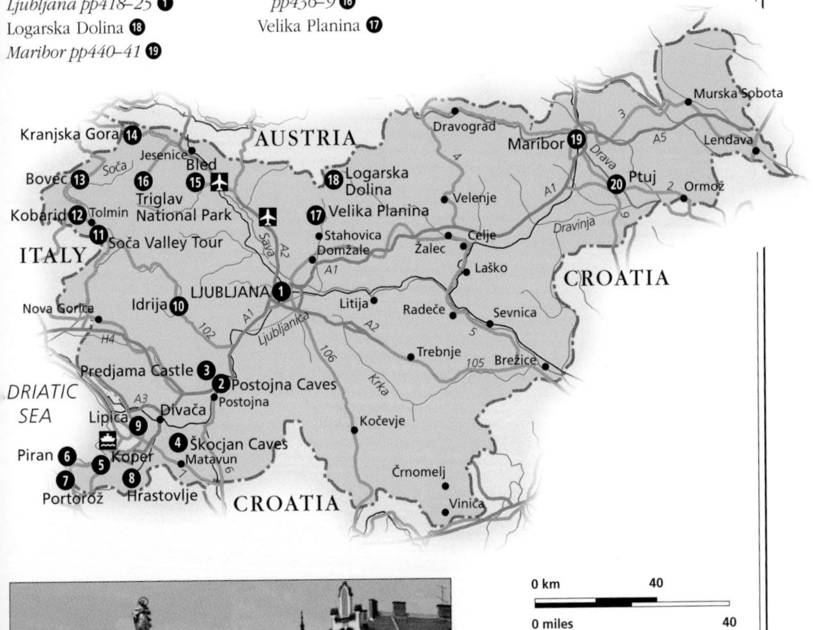

KEY

✈ Airport

⛴ Ferry terminal

— Highway

— Major road

— Railway

—·— International border

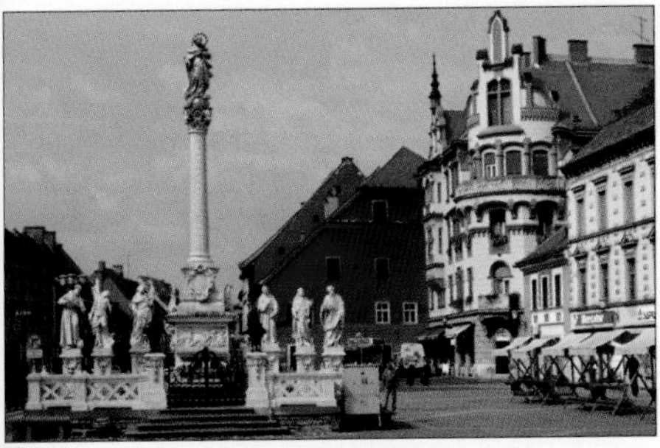

The Plague Column in the town of Maribor

Ljubljana

Slovenia's capital, Ljubljana, began life as the Roman colony of Emona, a major trading centre that was sacked by the Huns in AD 452. Reoccupied by Slavs in the 7th century, the focus of the settlement was moved to the east bank of the Ljubljanica river, where both Ljubljana Castle and the Old Town are located today. With a population of two hundred and eighty thousand, it is one of Europe's smallest capital cities. The Prešeren Square (Prešernov trg) is a good base from which to explore the main sights. On the right bank of the river is the fascinating Old Town (Stari Grad), with its Baroque architecture and several ancient churches. Important museums and galleries, such as the Modern Gallery and National Gallery, as well as the sprawling Tivoli Park, are located on the left bank.

SIGHTS AT A GLANCE

Ljubljana Castle ①
Market ③
Modern Gallery ⑦
National Gallery ⑤
National Museum ⑧
National and University
  Library ⑨
Plečnik House ⑩
Prešeren Square ④
St Nicholas's Cathedral ②
Tivoli Park ⑥

SEE ALSO

• *Where to Stay* p446

• *Where to Eat* pp448–9

KEY

▨	Street-by-Street area: *see pp420–21*
▨	Major sight / Place of interest
🚆	Railway station
🚌	Bus station
🚡	Funicular station
ℹ	Visitor information
🅿	Parking
⊠	Post office
✝	Church
▬	Pedestrian zone

Sequin Castle

TIVOLI PARK

Tivoli Castle

JAKOPIČEVO SPREHAJALIŠČE

TIVOLS

The Triple Bridge spanning the Ljubljanica river, designed by leading architect Jože Plečnik

A   B   C

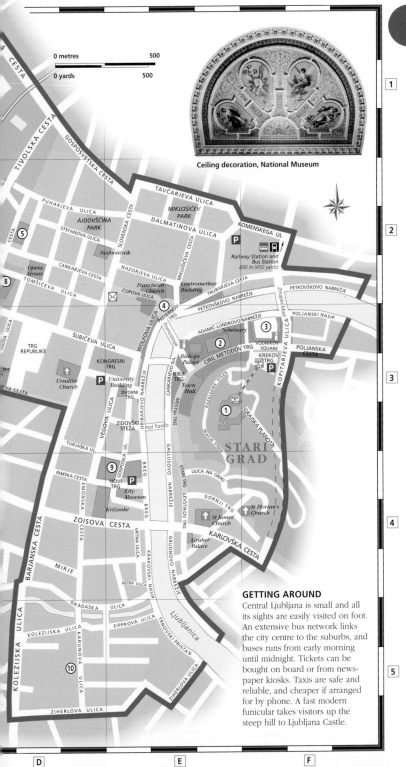

0 metres   500

0 yards   500

Ceiling decoration, National Museum

TIVOLSKA CESTA

CESTA

GOSPOSVETSKA CESTA

PUHARJEVA ULICA

AJDOVŠČINA PARK

SLOVENSKA CESTA

STEFANOVA ULICA

Neboličnik

CESTA

Operni House

CANKARJEVA CESTA

TOMŠIČEVA ULICA

Franciscan Church
ČOPOVA ULICA

TAVČARJEVA ULICA

MIKLOŠIČEV PARK

DALMATINOVA ULICA

KOMENSKEGA UL

NAZORJEVA ULICA

MIKLOŠIČEVA CESTA

Centromerkur Building

TRUBARJEVA ULICA

Railway Station and Bus Station
400 m (450 yards)

PETKOVŠKOVO NABREŽJE

ŠUBIČEVA ULICA

WOLFOVA ULICA

PREŠERNOV TRG

Tromostovje

PETKOVŠKOVO NABREŽJE

ADAMIČ-LUNDROVO NABREŽJE

Seminary

POLJANSKI NASIP

Streliška ulica

ULICA

TRG REPUBLIKE

Ursuline Church

CESTA

KONGRESNI TRG

University Building

VEGOVA ULICA

DVORNI TRG

HRIBARJEVO NABREŽJE

CANKARJEVO NA

Bishops Palace

RIBJI TRG

Town Hall

CIRIL METODOV TRG

MESTNI TRG

VODNIKOV SQUARE

STRITARJEVA ULICA

KREKOV TRG

KOPITARJEVA ULICA

POLJANSKA CESTA

ZIDOVSKI STEZA

Pod Trančo

ŽIDOVSKA STEZA

GALUSOVO NABREŽJE

MAČJA STEZA

RAZGLEDNA STEZA

GRAJSKA PLANOTA

STARI GRAD

TURJAŠKA UL.

RIMSKA CESTA

EMONSKA

GOSPOSKA UL.

NOVI TRG

City Museum

Križanke

BREG

BREG

STARI TRG

LEVSTIKOV TRG

ULICA NA GRAD

GORNJI TRG

St James' Church

St Florian's Church

ZOISOVA CESTA

BARJANSKA CESTA

EMONSKA CESTA

MIRJE

VRTNA ULICA

KRAKOVSKI NASIP

GRUDNOVO NABREŽJE

Gruber Palace

KARLOVŠKA CESTA

REČNA ULICA

GRADAŠKA ULICA

KOLEZIJSKA ULICA

KOLEZIJSKA ULICA

KARUNOVA ULICA

EIPPROVA ULICA

TRNOVSKI PRISTAN

Ljubljanica

ŽIHERLOVA ULICA

ŽIHERLOVA ULICA

GETTING AROUND

Central Ljubljana is small and all
its sights are easily visited on foot.
An extensive bus network links
the city centre to the suburbs, and
buses runs from early morning
until midnight. Tickets can be
bought on board or from newspaper kiosks. Taxis are safe and
reliable, and cheaper if arranged
for by phone. A fast modern
funicular takes visitors up the
steep hill to Ljubljana Castle.

1

2

3

4

5

D   E   F

Street-by-Street: Ljubljana Old Town

Located between the medieval castle and the leafy banks of the Ljubljanica river, Ljubljana's Old Town contains one of the best-preserved ensembles of Baroque buildings in South Eastern Europe. Arcaded 18th-century houses, domed churches and fountain-studded piazzas add to its elegant character. Narrow cobbled alleys such as Stari trg and Mestni trg, lined these days with swanky cafés and upmarket shops, provide a vibrant introduction to the Slovene capital.

★ Market
Ljubljana's lively outdoor market is known for its fresh herbs and dried mushrooms alongside every kind of local produce ③

St Nicholas's Cathedral
The cathedral's bronze doors, decorated with scenes from the history of Christianity in Slovenia, were created in 1996 to commemorate the visit of Pope John Paul II to Ljubljana ②

Statue of Valentin Vodnik

VODNIKOV SQUARE

ADAMIČ-LUNDROVO NABREŽJE

The Market Colonnade, an elongated pavilion built by architect Jože Plečnik in 1939, houses food shops and a fish market.

The Triple Bridge (Tromostovje) was designed for pedestrians by Jože Plečnik in 1932 as part of the renovation of the riverbank area.

KEY

– – – Suggested route

Franciscan Church of the Annunciation
Ljubljana's most attractive Baroque church, with a single nave and two rows of lateral chapels, contains a splendid 18th-century altar by Italian sculptor Francesco Robba, richly adorned with spiral columns and figurines.

The Prešeren Statue, one of Ljubljana's best-known landmarks, honours Romantic poet and national icon France Prešeren.

A **funicular railway** from Krekov Square transports visitors to the wooded Castle Hill.

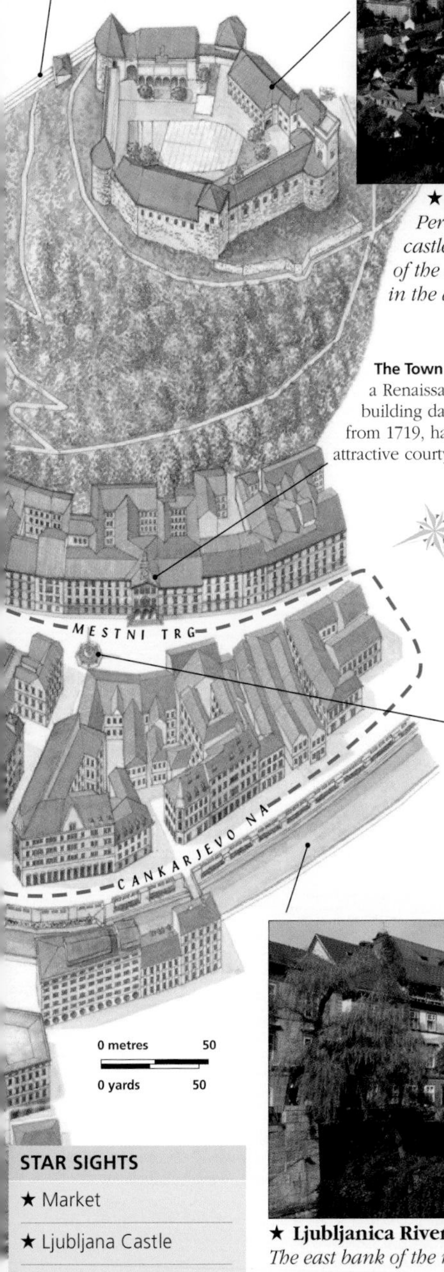

★ **Ljubljana Castle**
Perched high above the Old Town, the castle's clock tower provides a great view of the city with the Karavanke Mountains in the distance ①

The Town Hall, a Renaissance building dating from 1719, has an attractive courtyard.

MESTNI TRG

CANKARJEVO NA

Fountain of the Three Rivers of Carniola
Completed in 1751, Francesco Robba's Fountain of the Three Rivers symbolizes the three main rivers of Slovenia.

0 metres 50

0 yards 50

★ **Ljubljanica Riverbank**
The east bank of the river is lined with willow trees, orange- and red-roofed townhouses and fabulous terrace cafés and restaurants.

STAR SIGHTS

★ Market

★ Ljubljana Castle

★ Ljubljanica Riverbank

Exterior of St Nicholas's Cathedral, dominated by its twin towers

Ljubljana Castle ①
Ljubljanski grad

Grajska planota 1. **Map** E3.
Tel *(01) 306 4293.* ◻ *May–Sep:*
9am–10pm daily; Oct–Apr: 10am–
9pm daily. **Virtual Museum**
◻ *10am–6pm daily.* 🎫

Looming above the Old Town, Ljubljana Castle dates from the 11th century when the Spannheims adopted the city as their feudal power base. Following Ljubljana's absorption by Austria in 1355, the castle became the property of the Habsburg family. It went on to serve as army barracks, a refuge for the poor and a prison. Now an immaculate building with manicured

A section of Ljubljana's medieval castle, high above the Old Town

lawns, the castle has several points of interest grouped around its irregular courtyard. Built in 1848 to serve as a viewing platform, the spectacular **Clock Tower** provides a wonderful view of the city, with the Karavanke Mountains visible to the north.

On the western side of the courtyard, the remarkable 15th-century Gothic **Chapel of St George** has a ceiling decorated with the coats of arms of the Carniola province's leading feudal families. The nearby **Virtual Museum** (Virtualni muzej) showcases the history of the city through an impressive 20-minute audio-visual presentation.

St Nicholas's Cathedral ②
Stolnica sv Nikolaja

Dolničarjeva ulica. **Map** E3.
Tel *(01) 231 0684.* ◻ *6am–noon*
& 3–7pm daily.

Built on the site of an earlier church by leading Jesuit architect Andrea Pozzo in 1707, this Baroque cathedral is dedicated to St Nicholas, patron saint of fishermen and sailors. The cathedral's exterior has two doors, built for Pope John Paul II's visit in 1996, each decorated with expressive bronze reliefs. The west door is adorned with scenes from the history of Slovene Christianity; it portrays the baptism of the Slovene nation at the bottom,

with Pope John Paul II shown peering from a window at the top. The south door depicts the tall mitred profiles of six of Slovenia's 20th-century bishops, praying at the tomb of Christ.

Inside, the cathedral has a rich sequence of side chapels and a nave dominated by an Illusionist ceiling painting of the Crucifixion by Giulio Quaglio (1610–58).

Down a side street brightened by flower stalls is the 18th-century portal of Ljubljana's seminary, framed by a pair of titans carved by Andrea Pozzo. The seminary's library is decorated with frescoes by Quaglio and can be visited by contacting the Ljubljana tourist information office in advance *(see p442).*

Local produce in Ljubljana's bustling Market

Market ③
Glavna tržnica

Adamič-Lundrovo nabrežje. **Map** F3.
◻ *Nov–Mar: 8am–3pm Mon–Sat;*
Apr–Oct: 8am–5pm Mon–Sat.

The northern end of Ljubljana's Old Town has long been the site of the city's large and lively market. Running along the curving bank of the Ljubljanica river is the Market Colonnade, a Classical-inspired structure built by Jože Plečnik in 1942 to provide shelter for a row of delicatessen stalls. Built into the riverbank itself, the colonnade's lower storey is home to a fish market filled with glistening heaps of octopus, squid and lobster from the Adriatic Sea. The lower storey also has a simple seafood snack bar and an arcaded terrace looking out on to the river.

Outside the colonnade are stalls selling souvenirs, herbs and speciality foods. Just east of this area is the main fruit and vegetable section of the market, where trestle tables fill the broad expanse of Vodnikov Square. Presiding over the southern end of the square is a statue of Valentin Vodnik, the famous priest and poet whose works helped to shape the modern Slovene language.

Marking the eastern end of the market is the Dragon's Bridge (Zmajski most), named after the personable bronze dragons – a traditional symbol of the city – adorning each of its four corners. Built to mark the 60th birthday of Austrian Emperor Franz Josef in 1901, the bridge also features a row of ornate Art Nouveau lampposts.

Statue of Romantic poet France Prešeren, Prešeren Square

Dragon sculpture, Dragon's Bridge, Market

Prešeren Square ④
Prešernov trg

Map E2 & 3.

Standing at the junction between Ljubljana's Old Town and the 19th-century districts on the west bank of the Ljubljanica river, Prešeren Square is the symbolic heart of the city. It is named in honour of France Prešeren, the Romantic poet whose patriotic verses were central to the development of a Slovene national conscious-ness. Prešeren is commemo-rated by a monument in the centre of the square, portray-ing the poet with a book in hand, accompanied by a muse. Opposite the statue is the Franciscan Church, con-taining a fine 18th-century high altar by famous Italian sculptor Francesco Robba.

Around the square are some of the finest Art Nouveau struc-tures in Ljubljana. On the

northeastern corner, the **Centromerkur Building**, top-ped by a statue of Mercury, the Roman god of commerce, was built as a department store in 1903. On the opposite side of the square is the angular **Hauptman House**, decorated with multicol-oured tiles. Just behind the house, the building at Wolfova No. 4 fea-tures a relief of the 19th-century beauty Julija Primic, peering from a first-floor window. Primic was the object of France Prešeren's unrequited love and the inspiration behind many of his poems.

A short walk north along Miklošičeva cesta leads to the most vivacious of Ljubljana's buildings, the Cooperative Bank built by architect Ivan Vurnik in 1922. Covered in bright red, yellow and blue chevrons, it is a unique mixture of Art Deco and folk art influences.

National Gallery ⑤
Narodna galerija

Prešernova 24. **Map** D2. *Tel* (01) 241 5418. ⬜ 10am–6pm Tue–Sun. 🖼 ⬡ ⬚ ⬛ www.ng-slo.si

Slovenia's national art collection occupies an ele-gant 19th-century building with stucco ceilings and ornate chandeliers. A modern annexe was added in 2001. At the junction of the two buildings is a tall atrium holding Francesco Robba's original Fountain of the Three Rivers of Carniola, completed in 1751, symbolizing the meeting of the Sava, Krka and Ljubljanica rivers. The fountain initially stood in the Old Town, but was replaced by a replica in 2006.

The gallery's Slovene collection is particularly rich in Gothic statuary; highlights include a 13th-century Madonna on Solomon's Throne, carved by the little-known Master of the Solčava Maria. There is also an out-standing collection of work by Slovene Impressionists such as Rihard Jakopič, Matija Jama and Matej Sternen, whose canvases exalt the Slovene landscape and its peasantry in the years before World War I.

The European galleries contain an impressive cross-section of Flemish still life and genre paintings, a rich collection of Baroque altar pieces, and Max Reichlich's early 16th-century carving *Killenberg Triptych*, in which the Virgin Mary and St Anne nurse the infant Jesus.

Superb interior of Slovenia's National Gallery

The green expanses of Ljubljana's Tivoli Park

Tivoli Park ⑥
Park Tivoli

Celovska cesta. **Map** C1 & C2.
◻ Nov–Mar: 8am–3pm Mon–Sat;
Apr–Oct: 8am–5pm Mon–Sat.
International Graphic Arts Centre
Tivolski grad. **Tel** (01) 241 3800.
◻ 11am–6pm Wed–Sun. 🖼
www.mglc-lj.si. **National Museum
of Contemporary History**
Celovška cesta 23. **Tel** (01) 300
9610. ◻ 10am–6pm daily.
🖼 **www**.muzej-nz.si. **Cankar
Memorial Room** Cankarjev vrh 1.
Tel (01) 241 2506. ◻ Apr–Oct:
11am–6pm Sat & Sun. ◗ Nov–
Mar. 🖼

To the west of the National
Gallery (see p423) stretches
Tivoli Park, a well-tended
expanse of lawns and trees
much loved by locals and visitors alike. The park's main avenue, Jakopičevo sprehajališče,
is lined with display stands
that regularly show art and
photography exhibitions. At
the end of the avenue stands
Tivoli Castle (Tivolski grad),
an 18th-century villa that
now houses the excellent
**International Graphic Arts
Centre** (Mednarodni grafični
likovni centre). As well as
organizing the Ljubljana
Biennale of Graphic Arts, held
in autumn every odd-num-
bered year, the centre also
hosts exhibitions of posters,
prints and drawings.
   On the northern edge of the
park is the stately Baroque
Sequin Castle (Cekinov grad),
housing the **National Museum
of Contemporary History**

(Muzej novejše zgodovine
Slovenije). The museum chronicles the history of 20th-cen-
tury Slovenia in multimedia
form, using film footage to
bring each period to life.
   Rising above the western
end of the park is a series
of wooded hills, including
the 391-m (1,283-ft) high
Rožnik Hill, a popular destination for hikers. Reached
by a network of well-sign-
posted tracks, the hill is
topped by the Church of St
Mary's Visitation. Downhill
from the church is the Pri
Matiji Inn, once the home
of famous novelist Ivan
Cankar (1876–1918). The
nearby **Cankar Memorial
Room** (Spominska soba
Ivana Cankarja) displays
his writing desk and personal possessions.

**Magnificent staircase decorated
with sculptures, National Museum**

Modern Gallery ⑦
Moderna galerija

Tomšičeva 14. **Map** D2. **Tel** (01) 241
6800. ◻ 10am–6pm Tue–Sun.
www.mg-lj.si

The interesting Modern
Gallery contains the national
collection of 20th-century
art, along with paintings
and sculptures from several
other former Yugoslav
republics. Slovenia was at
the forefront of modernism
in the years following World
War I and the movement
is represented here by the
Constructivist works of artist
Avgust Černigoj and his poet
collaborator Srečko Kosovel.
More fascinating still is the
work of the contemporary
group Irwin, who mix
avant-garde art and extreme
political symbolism to
create a series of ironic
statements on the nature
of national identity.

National Museum ⑧
Narodni muzej

Prešernova 3. **Map** D2.
◻ 10am–6pm Tue–Sun. 🖼
🏛 **www**.narmuz-lj.si

The National Museum actually
comprises two museums: a
small but spectacular archaeological collection in one wing
and a natural history collection
in the other. Housed since
1888 in the grand Rudolfinum
building, the museum features
an impressive staircase overlooked by beautiful frescoes
of cavorting muses.
   The ground floor contains
an extensive collection of
expressively carved funerary
monuments from the Roman
settlement of Emona, together
with a gilded bronze statue of
a young male aristocrat.
Ancient Egypt is represented
by an intriguing 6th-century
BC coffin of the priest Isahta,
decorated with brightly
painted hieroglyphs.
   The upstairs galleries
display Stone Age pottery,
Copper Age vessels and
implements from the Ljubljana
marshes, along with Celtic
weaponry and jewellery. The
most valued item on display

is the Vače Situla, a 30-cm (12-inch) high bronze bucket from the 6th century BC that once served as a ritual drinking vessel. Its outer surface has stunning frieze-like reliefs depicting a parade of horsemen, a drinking party and a line of antelope-like animals being stalked by a big cat.

The natural history collection features an ancient mammoth skeleton found near Kamnik and a 200-million-year-old fossilized fish skeleton discovered near Triglav National Park *(see pp436–9)* as well as a large collection of minerals.

Plečnik House, residence of Slovenia's most influential architect

National and University Library ⑨

Narodna in univerzitetna knjižnica

Turjaška 1. **Map** E4. **Tel** *(01) 200 1188.* ◻ *8am–8pm Mon–Fri, 9am–2pm Sat.* ◪ ◻

Set back from the west bank of the Ljubljanica river on the site of a former palace, the National and University Library is considered to be the masterpiece of Jože Plečnik, the architect responsible for the appearance of modern Ljubljana.

Completed in 1940, the landmark building is typical of Plečnik's work, combining the straight lines popular in the architecture of the period with inspired decorative details. The exterior is a

Detail of library door handle

patchwork of different hues, mixing grey hunks of Slovene granite with terracotta-coloured brickwork. Inside, a dark stairway of polished black limestone leads to the brightly lit first floor reading rooms, symbolizing the transition from ignorance to knowledge. The exquisite doorknobs, table lamps and chandeliers were all designed by Plečnik himself, fusing Art Deco with folk-influenced motifs to create a highly personalized style.

Immediately south of the library is **Križanke**, a medieval monastery complex renovated by Plečnik and turned into an outdoor concert venue. A major venue for rock concerts in summer, Križanke also hosts several classical music events as part of the popular Ljubljana Summer Festival *(see p444)*, held between July and August every year.

Plečnik House ⑩

Plečnikova hiša

Karunova 4. **Map** D5. **Tel** *(01) 280 1600.* ◻ *10am–6pm Tue–Thu, 9am–3pm Sat.* ◪ ◪ **www.**aml.si

Present-day Ljubljana would be unimaginable without the work of Jože Plečnik, the architect and town planner responsible for the Triple Bridge, Market Colonnade *(see pp420)* and the Ljubljanica riverbank area, as well as the National and University Library. Plečnik's work was in many ways a precursor of Post-Modernism, combining pure forms of modern architectural style with ornamental details drawn from Egypt, Classical Greece and Central European folk art.

The house where Plečnik lived from 1921 until his death in 1957 exemplifies his extraordinary commitment to the world of architecture. With each room having its own design scheme, the house now serves as an intimate and absorbing museum of his work. Visitors can view the sunny, cylindrical annexe he built to serve as a work space, filled with furniture he designed himself. Most of his original plans, photographs and models of his major works are preserved here. Most famous among his unfinished projects is the Slovene Acropolis, a monumental parliament building originally intended for Ljubljana's Castle Hill.

Aerial view of the imposing National and University Library

Postojna Caves ❷
Postojnske jame

Slovenia's most popular natural attraction, Postojna Caves constitute the longest subterranean system in the country, with over 20 km (12 miles) of chambers and tunnels. They were formed by the seeping waters of the Pivka river and its tributaries, which carved out several levels of underground galleries over a period of roughly three million years. The caves were first opened to visitors in 1819, with Austrian Emperor Francis I as the guest of honour. The site currently receives just under half a million people a year, making it one of the most visited natural attractions in Europe. Inside, magnificent formations of stalactites and stalagmites seem to stretch endlessly in all directions.

Visitors outside the main entrance to Postojna Caves

Tracks and Walkways
Guided tours, lasting 90 minutes, begin with visitors riding an electric train into the heart of the caves, before embarking on a walking tour through a series of halls encrusted with intricate rock formations.

Russian Bridge
Built by Russian prisoners during World War I, the Russian Bridge leads to the Macaroni Hall, which is covered with stunning pure-white stalactites.

Stalactites, formed by constantly dripping water, hang from the ceiling of the caves.

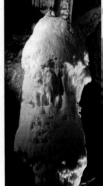

STAR SIGHTS
★ The Diamond
★ White Passage
★ Concert Hall

★ The Diamond
This huge stalagmite, also called "Brilliant", on account of its dazzling white surface and peculiar shape, is one of the highlights of the spectacular Winter Chamber.

Big Mountain
This 45-m (147-ft) high rocky mound was created when the ceiling collapsed.

VISITORS' CHECKLIST

53 km (33 miles) S of Ljubljana. 🚌 *from Ljubljana.* 🚋 *from Ljubljana.* 🛈 *Jamska Cesta 9, Postojna, (05) 720 1610.* **www.** tdpostojna.si. ⬜ *July & Aug: tours hourly 9am–6pm; May, Jun & Sep: tours hourly 9am–5pm; Apr & Oct: tours at 10am, noon, 2pm & 4pm; Jan–Mar, Nov–Dec: tours at 10am, noon & 3pm.* 📷🎫⏸🏪♿ **www.**postojna-jama.si

The Vivarium
The caves are the natural habitat of this rare worm-like amphibian, known as the human fish. It can be seen in the Vivarium, where visitors can learn about species of the underground world.

★ White Passage
One among a series of chambers collectively known as Beautiful Caves, the White Passage is crammed with impressive stalagmites and stalactites.

Predjama Castle, built into a natural rock arch on a hill slope

Predjama Castle ❸
Predjamski grad

50 km (31 miles) S of Ljubljana. 🚌 *from Ljubljana.* ⬜ *Jan–Mar, Nov–Dec: 10am–4pm; Apr & Oct: 10am–5pm; May, Jun & Sep: 9am–6pm; Jul & Aug: 9am–7pm.* 📷 🏪 📷 *Erasmus Jousting Tournament (Aug).* **www.**turizem-kras.si

There are few fortresses more dramatically situated than Predjama Castle, which stands halfway up a hillside at the mouth of a cave. The site was fortified as early as the 13th century. However, most of what remains today is the result of a 16th-century renovation by the then owner Ivan Kobencl.

The castle museum has several fascinating rooms containing period furnishings and weaponry. Several exhibits recall its 15th-century owner Erazem Lueger, a Robin Hood figure who, according to legend, was killed by a cannon ball that hit the castle. Inside the chapel is a delicately carved Gothic pietá dating from 1420.

Steep passageways descend into the **Cave** below the castle, an interesting, atmospheric underground chamber that can be visited only by guided tour.

⛰ **Cave**
📷🎫 *May–Sep: 11am, 1pm, 3pm & 5pm daily.* **www.**turizem-kras.si

★ Concert Hall
Visitors finally emerge into the Concert Hall, a vast space where orchestral performances are occasionally held, before returning by train to the cave entrance.

Škocjan Caves ❹
Škocjanska jama

80 km (51 miles) SW of Ljubljana.
🚊 *from Divača.* 🚌 ℹ️ *Matavun,
(05) 708 2110.* ⏰ *call in advance.*
📷 📹 🔲 🏪 www.park
skocjanske-jame.si

Located in rolling countryside just outside the town of Divača, the Škocjan Caves are one of Slovenia's most spectacular karst features and a UNESCO World Heritage Site. The labyrinthine complex of passages and collapsed valleys is believed to be the world's largest network of subterranean chambers and remains only partially explored to this day. About half of the 5 km (3 miles) of underground passageways are open to the public, accessible by a 90-minute guided tour. Tickets are available at the tourist information centre in the village of Matavun, a short distance from the cave entrance. Highlights of the tour include the 15-m (49-ft) long stalactites of the Great Hall and the underwater river in the canyon-like Murmuring Cave. The temperature underground is a constant 12° C (53° F), so warm clothing is recommended.

Koper ❺

120 km (75 miles) SW of Ljubljana.
🏘️ 24,000. 🚊 🚌 ⛴️ ℹ️ *Titov trg
3, (305) 664 6403.* www.koper.si

Now Slovenia's main port, Koper started off as a small Roman settlement known as Goat Island (Insula Caprea). It became a major trading

Main altar of the Cathedral of Mary's Assumption, Koper

centre under the Venetian Empire (1278–1797), leaving its attractive Old Town rich in Venetian-influenced architecture. Koper was home to a largely Italian-speaking community until it became part of Slovenia in 1954; the town still bears traces of its Italian heritage, with bilingual street signs and many locals speaking both languages.

Central Koper is an enjoyable warren of narrow, pedestrian-only streets, most of which meet at Tito Square (Titov trg). Its most enduring symbol, the **Praetorian Palace** (Pretorska palača), is a striking example of Venetian Gothic architecture with fancy tooth-like crenellations. Embedded in the façade are several coats of arms belonging to distinguished families from Koper. Opposite the palace

Stair detail, Praetorian Palace

stands the town loggia, with a beautifully proportioned ground floor arcade. Also on the square is the 12th-century **Cathedral of Mary's Assumption** (Stolna cerkev Marijinega vnebovzetja), which contains the ornate medieval sarcophagus of local protector St Nazarius behind the main altar. On the right side of the transept is an animated *Madonna with Child on the Throne and Saints* attributed to the Venetian painter Carpaccio (1460–1526), who is believed to have lived in Koper for a time. Behind the cathedral is a 12th-century rotunda that originally served as the baptistry, bearing a faded relief of St John the Baptist above the door.

A short walk west of Tito Square, the **Regional Museum** (Pokrajinski muzej) houses a rich collection of archaeological finds and medieval stonework. East of the square, the **Ethnographic Collection** (Etnološka zbirka) fills a restored Gothic house with a display of domestic utensils, farmers' tools and local costumes.

🏛️ **Regional Museum**
Kidričeva 6. **Tel** (05) 663 3570.
⏰ *9am–1pm & 6–9pm Tue–Sun.* 📷

🏛️ **Ethnographic Collection**
Gramšijev trg 4. **Tel** (05) 663 3586.
⏰ *9am–1pm & 6–9pm Tue–Sun.* 📷

Piran ❻

124 km (77 miles) SW of Ljubljana.
🏘️ 4,600. 🚌 ℹ️ *Tartinijev trg, (05)
673 4440.* www.portoroz.si

A jumble of pastel-coloured houses on a small peninsula, Piran is coastal Slovenia's most charming town. The town centres around Tartini Square (Tartinijev trg), named after local violinist and composer Giuseppe Tartini (1692–1770); Antonio dal Zotto's statue of Tartini occupies the centre. The most striking building on the square is the 14th-century wine-red Venetian House

Breathtaking stalactites in one of Škocjan Caves's chambers

Panoramic view of the coastal town of Piran, centred on the Tartini Square

(Benečanka hiša), with delicate Gothic windows and balustraded balconies. Nearby, St Peter's Church (Cerkev sv Petra) contains a 14th-century crucifix that shows Jesus on a fork-shaped cross, thought to symbolize the Tree of Life. Tucked away in a small plaza behind the church, **Tartini House** (Tartinijeva hiša) honours the composer with a collection of heirlooms, including one of his violins. Uphill from the square, narrow streets wind towards St George's Cathedral (Stolna cerkev sv Jurja), a single-nave structure paired with a Venetian-style campanile. The small Parish Museum (Župnijski muzej) displays the church silverware, including an 18th-century statuette of St George studded with semi-precious stones. To the west of Tartini Square, the **Aquarium** (Akvarij) has a selection of fish and

crustaceans indigenous to the Adriatic Sea. On the opposite side of the harbour, the **Sergej Mašera Maritime Museum** (Pomorski muzej Sergaj Mašera) recounts the history of Piran as a trading town.

🏛 **Tartini House**
Tartinijev trg. *Tel* (05) 663 3570.
⬜ Jun–Aug: 9am–noon & 6–9pm daily; Sep–May: 11am–noon & 5–6pm daily. 📷

Aquarium
Kidričevo nabrežje 4. *Tel* (05) 673 2572. ⬜ mid-Jun to mid-Sep: 9am–10pm daily; mid-Sep to mid-Jun: 10am–noon & 2–7pm daily. 📷

🏛 **Sergej Mašera Maritime Museum**
Cankarjevo nabrežje 4. *Tel* (05) 671 0040. ⬜ Sep–Jun: Tue–Sun 9am–5pm; Jul–Aug: Tue–Sun 9am–noon & 5–9pm.
www.pommuz-pi.si

Portorož ❼

122 km (76 miles) SW of Ljubljana.
🏘 3,100. 🚌 ℹ Obala 16, (05) 674 8260. www.portoroz.si

Strung along the sun-bathed sweep of Piran Bay, Portorož is Slovenia's biggest beach resort. Apart from the grand Habsburg-era hotel – the Kempinski Hotel built in 1911 – most of the modern cafés, hotels and casinos bordering the palm-lined main boulevard date from the post-World War II period.
Portorož is a popular spa resort busy throughout the year thanks to a warm microclimate and the therapeutic qualities of the seawater. The large crescent beach, with its seaside park, has tennis and volleyball courts.

Hrastovlje ❽

104 km (65 miles) SW of Ljubljana.
🏘 120. 🚉

Located in the arid hills above the coast, the rustic village of Hrastovlje is home to one of Slovenia's most outstanding medieval treasures. Crowning a hillock slightly apart from the rest of the village is the Romanesque **Holy Trinity Church** (Cerkev sv Trojice), its interior covered from floor to ceiling with dazzling frescoes painted by local artist John of Kastav in 1490. The most famous of the friezes is the *Dance of Death* on the southern wall, in which a group of skeletons leads people old and young, rich and poor alike, towards the grave. Many other scenes feature stories from the Bible. The main characters are clad in 15th-century attire, providing an insight into the lifestyle of late-medieval Slovenia.

🔒 **Holy Trinity Church**
Hrastovlje 6275. *Tel* (05) 664 6403 (Koper Tourist Office).
⬜ 8am–noon & 1–5pm daily, call in advance. 📷

Multistorey hotels along the tree-lined waterfront in Piran

The stone tower and walls of Holy Trinity Church, Hrastovlje

Lipica ❾

86 km (53 miles) SW of Postojna.
🏛 *120*. 🚗 🚃 www.lipica.org

Located near the Italian border
in the hills above Trieste, the
village of Lipica is synony-
mous with the Lipizzaner
horses bred here since 1580.
Established by the Habsburg
Archduke Charles of Styria,
the **Lipica Stud Farm** crossed
Arab horses with local steeds,
resulting in the uniquely
graceful white Lipizzaner.
The breed found favour with
the prestigious Spanish Riding
School *(see pp400–401)* in
Vienna and has been considered an aristocrat in the
equine world ever since.

Tours of the stables allow
visitors to see the horses
at close quarters, while the
Classical Riding School stages
shows in which the horses
perform complex routines.

Horse and carriage trips
can be arranged between
April and October and it is
also possible to book riding
sessions provided reservations
are made in advance. The
stable complex also contains
an art gallery devoted to
August Černigoj (1898–1985),
the avant-garde painter who
spent his final years in Lipica.

Lipica Stud Farm
Lipica 5. *Tel (05) 739 1580.*
☐ *Jan–Mar & Nov–Dec:*
10am–3pm Tue–Sun; Apr–Jun
& Sep–Oct: 9am–5pm Mon–Fri,
9am–6pm Sat & Sun; Jul & Aug:
9am–6pm daily. 🎞 🎦 *tours*
of the Lipica stables take place
on the hour. **Classical Riding**
School ☐ *Apr–Oct: 3pm Tue,*
Fri & Sun. 🍴 🖥 📷
www.lipica.org

The colourful walls of Gewerkenegg Castle, Idrija

Idrija ❿

70 km (44 miles) W of Ljubljana.
🏛 *6,500*. 🚃 *from Bovec.*
🛈 *Vodnikova 3, (05) 374 3916.*
www.idrija-turizem.si

One of the largest mercury
mining centres in the world,
Idrija once provided 13 per
cent of the global output. Since
active mining came to a halt
in 2008, the town has begun
to develop into a major centre
of industrial heritage tourism.

The best way to get a feel
of Idrija's mining past is to
take the tour of **Anthony's**
Shaft (Antoniev gred), a network of tunnels excavated in
1500. The tour starts with a
video presentation about the
history of the mine. Visitors
are then led down the shaft,
where mining techniques of
the past are demonstrated.
The **Town Museum** (Mesni
muzej), housed in the 16th-
century Gewerkenegg Castle,
contains an exhibition on
mining history as well as an

interesting display on Idrija
lace-making – a household
industry. Several industrial
monuments are located
around the town centre. The
pavilion at St Francis' Shaft
(Jašek Frančiške gred) contains a display of mining machinery, while the reconstructed
19th-century Miner's House
(Rudarska hiša) shows how
miners' families used to live.

Environs
Some 25 km (16 miles) north
of Idrija is the **Franja Partisan**
Hospital, a timber-built
field hospital used by Slovene
resistance fighters during
World War II. Active from
December 1943 until the
end of the war, the hospital
under restoration was
damaged by floods in 2007.

🏛 Anthony's Shaft
Kosovelova 3. *Tel (05) 377 1142.*
🎞 🎦 *10am & 3pm Sat & Sun.*

🏛 Town Museum
Prelovčeva 9. *Tel (05) 372 6600.*
☐ *9am–6pm Mon–Fri.* 🎞 📷

Portraits of World War I heroes in the
Kobarid Museum *(see p432)*

THE SOČA FRONT (ISONZO FRONT)
During World War I, Italy declared war on Austria-
Hungary in 1915, believing that victory would lead
to territorial gains in the northern Adriatic Sea. The
Soča Front, extending from north of Bovec through
Kobarid to north of Trieste, Italy, served as the front
line for almost three years. The Austrians used the
mountainous terrain to their advantage, hurling back
12 successive Italian offensives. In 1917, the Italians
were forced to retreat in the 12th battle, known as
the Battle of Caporetto. Memories of the Soča Front
are poignant for the Slovenes, who fought and died
alongside Croats and Czechs, in defence of an
Austro-Hungarian Empire that collapsed in 1918.

Soča Valley Tour ⑪

Famous for its turquoise Alpine waters, the
Soča river, also known by its Italian name,
Isonzo, rises in the Triglav National Park *(see
pp436–9)* and flows south towards the Gulf
of Trieste. The Soča valley has many typical
features of the Slovene karst, including waterfalls, limestone gorges and rock formations.
Several monuments recall the battles of World
War I, when Italian and Austro-Hungarian
forces fought for control of the valley.

TIPS FOR DRIVERS

Starting point: Bovec.
Highway number 203 from
Bovec to Kobarid, and number
102 from Kobarid to Tomlin, runs
alongside the Soča river.
Length: 40 km (25 miles).
Stopping-off points: There are
several restaurants along the
route, especially in Kobarid;
most serve traditional cuisine.

Boka Waterfall ②
This tumbling waterfall in the hills
west of Bovec is a popular
tourist spot.

Bovec ①
The main town of the northern Soča valley,
Bovec is Slovenia's leading resort for
adventure sports.

0 km		5
0 miles		5

Kobarid ③
The town of Kobarid witnessed
the bloodiest battles of World War
I. The town museum documents
the suffering of the soldiers.

Tolmin ④
The museum in Tolmin sheds light
on the costumes, trades and
lifestyles of the valley's inhabitants.

KEY

ℹ️	Information
☆	View point
▬	Tour route
═	Other road
—	Railway
▬▪	International border

Tolminka Gorge ⑤
Northeast of Tolmin lies the steep Tolminka gorge,
with a walking route running precariously above. The
Tolmin–Čadrg road crosses the gorge at the
Devil's Bridge (Hudičev most).

Interior of the fascinating Kobarid Museum, Kobarid

Kobarid ⑫

118 km (73 miles) NW of Ljubljana.
🏛 *4,500.* 🚆 *from Ljubljana.*
ℹ *Gregorčičeva 8, (05) 380 0490.*
www.lto-sotocje.si

A pleasant town characterized
by a mix of Alpine and
Italianate architecture,
Kobarid (Caporetto in Italian)
is famous as the site of the
Battle of Caporetto *(see p430)*,
which saw Austro-Hungarian
and German units rout their
way through Italian lines in
1917. The **Kobarid Museum**
(Kobariŝk muzej) poignantly
documents the battle through
a 20-minute film and mock-up
trenches. The museum's Black
Room conveys the horrors of
war through an alarming series
of photographs.

East of the town centre lies
Charnel House, a memorial
for fallen Italian soldiers. It
was opened in 1938, with
Mussolini in attendance, when
much of western Slovenia
belonged to Italy. Inside the
huge ossuary are the remains
of soldiers killed on the Soča
Front. The nearby Church of St

Anthony, set on three tiers of
arcaded octagonal platforms,
dominates the landscape of
the lower Soča valley *(see
p431)*. A walking route heads
north from the Charnel House
on to the surrounding hillsides,
where World War I trench
positions can still be seen.

🏛 **Kobarid Museum**
Gregorčičeva 10. **Tel** (05) 389 0000.
⬜ *Apr–Sep: 9am–6pm Mon–Fri,
9am–7pm Sat & Sun; Oct–Mar:
10am–5pm Mon–Fri, 9am–6pm Sat
& Sun.* 📷 ♿ www.kobariski-
muzej.si

Bovec ⑬

130 km (81 miles) NW of Ljubljana.
🏛 *3,400.* 🚆 ℹ *Trg Golobarskih
Žrtev, (05) 389 6444.* **www**.bovec.si

Nestling on the eastern side
of the Triglav massif, Bovec
occupies the broad plain
formed by the confluence of
the Koritnica and Soča rivers.

A flourishing skiing and
hiking resort, it is connected
to the nearby Kanin Moun-
tains by cable car. The stretch
of the Soča river to the south
and west of Bovec is regarded
as prime white-water terrain,
with numerous travel agencies
offering kayaking and canoeing trips during the high season from April to September.
However, the most popular
attraction in these parts is the
breathtaking **Boka Waterfall**,
which tumbles from the karst
some 6 km (4 miles) southwest of Bovec, and is reached
by a walking trail.

Kranjska Gora ⑭

85 km (53 miles) NW of Ljubljana.
🏛 *5,500.* 🚆 *from Jesenice.*
ℹ *Ticarjeva 2, (04) 580 9440.*
www.kranjska-gora.si

Set in the mountain-fringed
Upper Sava valley, the Alpine
town of Kranjska Gora is
Slovenia's premier winter holiday resort. Most of the skiing
trails are located on the slopes
of the 1,555-m (5,102-ft) high
Vitranc Mountain, southwest
of the town. There are also
ski slopes at Podkoren resort,
3 km (2 miles) up the valley.

Located alongside the lovely
parish church is **Liznjek House**,
Kranjska Gora's main urban
attraction. A beautiful balconied 18th-century building,
it was the property of a
wealthy local farmer and once
served as a country inn.

SKIING

The mountains of northern and western Slovenia provide
a wealth of winter sports opportunities. The season runs
from mid-December to late March and almost all ski centres are equipped with snowmobiles. The largest resort,
Kranjska Gora, has 30 km
(19 miles) of ski trails. The
Mariborsko Pohorje resort,
outside Maribor *(see p440)*,
is Slovenia's largest ski
area, with a wide range
of intermediate runs and
good facilities. Another
favourite is Mount Vogel,
accessible by cable car
from Lake Bohinj *(see
pp438–9)*. Several ski centres can be visited on a day-
trip from Velika Planina.

**Winter sports enthusiasts skiing on
the slopes of Velika Planina**

**The evocative Charnel House
in Kobarid**

The world's highest ski jump at Planica, Kranjska Gora

Inside is a wonderful display of folk crafts and traditional furnishings including wooden beds, wardrobes, folk-painted trousseau chests and grandfather clocks painted with bright floral designs.

In summer, Kranjska Gora is a popular base for hiking in Triglav National Park *(see pp436–9)*. Starting at Mojstrana, 13 km (8 miles) east of Kranjska Gora, the Triglavska Bistrica walking trail runs up the ruggedly beautiful Vrata valley before reaching the forbidding north face of Mount Triglav, Slovenia's highest mountain.

For visitors wishing to explore the area by car, Kranjska Gora stands at the intersection of several scenic mountain routes. North of the town, a road winds dramatically across the Würzen pass towards the city of Villach in Austria. To the south are the hairpin bends of the Vršič pass, high among the peaks of Triglav National Park. A major feat of engineering, the road over the pass was built by Russian Prisoners of War during World War I, to send supplies to Habsburg armies defending the Soča Front.

To the west of Kranjska Gora lies Planica valley, the site of the world's highest ski jump. Built in 1935, it is a powerful symbol of Slovene prowess in winter sports and annually hosts the famous ski-jumping World Cup.

Bled ⑮

See pp434–5.

Triglav National Park ⑯

See pp436–9.

Velika Planina ⑰

30 km (19 miles) NE of Ljubljana.
🚡 www.velikaplanina.si

Literally meaning "Big Mountain", Velika Planina is one of the most popular destinations in the Kamnik Alps. Reached by cable car from the Kamniška Bistrica valley, at 1,666 m (5,466 ft) it is a relatively smooth mountain, covered in highland pastures where dairy herds graze during the summer. Scattered across the mountain are wooden huts topped by broad shingle roofs and surrounded by wooden stockades. A unique form of traditional architecture, they were built by local shepherds as seasonal sleeping quarters.

In winter, Velika Planina is a popular out-of-town destination for skiers, offering a choice of downhill and cross-country runs. It is also busy during summer, when its well-marked paths become busy with hikers. Many choose to walk up the mountain without taking the cable car, an exhilarating hike that begins in the village of Stahovica.

Logarska Dolina ⑱

100 km (62 miles) NE of Ljubljana. 🚌 *from Ljubljana.*
www.logarska-dolina.si

Hidden away on the northern side of the Kamnik Alps, the Logarska Dolina valley is one of the most beautiful spots in northern Slovenia. It is a typical example of a glacier-carved valley, with a level green valley floor dotted with dairy farms and steep sides where dense forests give way to bare cliffs. The relatively isolated valley can be entered via the village of **Solčava**, which is accessed by road from the regional centre of Velenje, a mining town located 50 km (31 miles) northeast of Ljubljana. Solčava itself is famous for the splendid 13th-century Solčava Madonna, a Romanesque statuette housed in the local parish church.

About 2 km (1 mile) beyond Solčava is the starting point of the Logarska Dolina hiking route, which runs for 6 km (4 miles) along the valley floor to reach the charming Rinka Waterfall, surrounded by grizzled grey mountain peaks.

Running parallel to Logarska Dolina to the west is **Matkov Kot**, another stunning glacial valley. The main target for hikers here is the famous Matk's Tub (Matkov Škaf), a dramatic circular hollow gouged out of bare rock by a seasonal waterfall.

Distinctive conical, shingled wooden huts on Velika Planina

Bled ⑮

With its placid lake, fairy tale island church, clifftop castle and girdle of grey mountains, Bled has become a visual trademark for the Slovene tourist industry. Although it emerged as a popular spa resort in the mid-19th century, Bled's key attractions today consist of boat trips to the island church and excursions into the Alpine surroundings. Offering plenty of good hotels, Bled also makes a good base for exploring nearby places of interest such as the enchanting Lake Bohinj and Triglav National Park *(see pp436–9)*. In winter, buses connect Bled with the skiing and snowboarding centre at Mount Vogel, near Lake Bohinj.

Boats moored on the forested lakeshore, Bled

🐟 Lake Bled

Just over 2 km (1 mile) long, 2 km (1 mile) wide and 30 m (98 ft) deep, Lake Bled (Blejsko jezero) fills a hollow gouged out by retreating glaciers towards the end of the last Ice Age. With wooded hills surrounding the lake and Alpine peaks in the distance, it is nothing less than truly entrancing. The best way to soak in the landscape is to walk along the asphalt path which leads right around the lake, a circuit that takes about an hour to complete. The most stunning views are from the western end, with the church spire on Bled Island set against the stupendous backdrop of the snow-capped Karavanke Alps.

On the southern shore of the lake, visitors can stop by the gardens of Vila Bled *(see p447)*, built for Yugoslav strongman Josip Broz Tito in 1947 and now converted into an upmarket hotel.

⚓ Bled Castle

***Tel** (04) 572 9782.* ☐ *8am–6pm, daily.* 🎟 🍴 🖥 📷 **www**.blejski-grad.si

Dramatically located on a sheer cliff overlooking the lake's eastern end, Bled Castle (Blejski grad) began as the 11th-century stronghold of the Bishops of Brixen, who ruled over the area until 1803. Rebuilt by various owners over the years, the castle now houses an absorbing museum and a restaurant. The former features an imaginative audio-visual display, detailing both the history of the castle and the development of tourism in the region. Replicas of historical costumes recall the Slavs who first settled in the area in the 6th century, while a natural history section exhibits the 5th-century skeleton of an elk. The wine cellar and herb gallery are also worth a visit.

Outside, the castle terrace commands an outstanding view, with the lake directly below and the Karavanke mountain range looming in the distance.

Bled Island

☐ *Nov–Mar: 9am–4pm daily.* 🎟 📷 **www**.blejskiotok.si

Perched atop the hummock-shaped Bled Island (Blejski otok), the creamy-ochre Church of the Assumption (Cerkev Marijinega vnebovzetja) occupies a site that has been sacred for centuries.

The island initially served pagan Slavs as a shrine, inspiring a famous episode in France Prešeren's epic poem "Baptism on the Savica" ("Krst pri Savici"), in which the Slovene prince, Črtomir, falls in love with the beautiful Bogomila, daughter of the island shrine's guardian.

After the region's conversion to Christianity, the island became a focus of Catholic pilgrimage. It has been associated with the cult of the Virgin Mary since the early Middle Ages, when a wooden chapel stood on the site of the current church. Pilgrimages boomed during the Baroque

Bled Castle, perched on a rock above the town

Church of the Assumption on Bled Island

boat (*pletna*). Visitors disembark at the bottom of a 99-step staircase, which leads to the front door of the church. Inside are the fragmentary remains of some 15th-century frescoes illustrating the lives of the Virgin Mary and Jesus Christ.

Hanging from a small tower above the nave is the 15th-century Wishing Bell, which was presented to the church by a wealthy pilgrim whose prayers had been answered. Among the various legends surrounding it, it is believed that the original bell sank in a shipwreck and had to be replaced by one donated by the Pope. It is also believed that those who ring the bell to honour the Blessed Virgin will have their wishes granted.

People used to walk across the ice to the church during harsh winters, although due to changes in the climate, ice is a rare occurrence nowadays.

era, when the church was expanded and redecorated. Today, the island remains a popular place for pilgrimages on the Marian feast days, notably the Ascension and the Birth of the Virgin. These are traditionally all-night affairs with participants arriving late in the evening and celebrating mass at 4am. The island is open to visitors throughout the year and can be reached either by motor launch or by traditional canopied rowing

VISITORS' CHECKLIST

53 km (34 miles) NW of Ljubljana. 🏙 10,900. 🚊 Lesce-Bled. 🚉 Bled Jezero. 🚌 🚐 🛈 Cesta svobode 10, (04) 574 1122. 🎭 Bled Days (Jul), Ascension (Aug 15) & Birth of the Virgin (Sep 8). **www**.bled.si

Vintgar Gorge

Tel (04) 572 5266. ◯ Apr–Oct: 8am–7pm daily. 🎫 🛈
Located 4 km (2 miles) north of Bled, Vintgar gorge (Soteska Vintgar) is a 2-km (1-mile) long ravine carved by the rushing waters of the Radovna river. In 1893, the locals decided to construct wooden walkways and galleries to make the ravine accessible to visitors, turning it into a major attraction. Visiting the gorge is an exhilarating experience as the trail winds its way beneath sheer cliffs, passing gurgling rapids and whirlpools on the way. The walkway culminates at the 16-m (52-ft) high Šum Waterfall, which marks the northern end of the gorge. The waterfall is at its most impressive in spring, when it throws up clouds of steam.

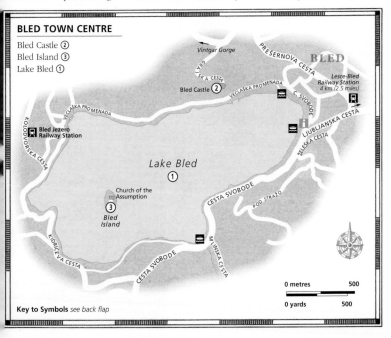

BLED TOWN CENTRE

Bled Castle ②
Bled Island ③
Lake Bled ①

Vintgar Gorge

PREŠERNOVA CESTA

BLED

GRAD

SK A CESTA

Bled Castle ②

VEČLAŠKA PROMENADA

Lesce-Bled Railway Station 4 km (2.5 miles)

C. SVOBODE

VEČLAŠKA PROMENADA

🚉 Bled Jezero Railway Station

LJUBLJANSKA CESTA

KOLODVORSKA CESTA

ŽELEŠKA CESTA

Lake Bled ①

Church of the Assumption

③
Bled Island

CESTA SVOBODE

POD STRAŽO

KIDRIČEVA CESTA

CESTA SVOBODE

MLINSKA CESTA

| 0 metres | 500 |
| 0 yards | 500 |

Key to Symbols *see back flap*

Triglav National Park ⑯
Triglavski narodni park

Established in 1961, Slovenia's only national park is
centred on the country's highest mountain, the 2,864-m
(9,396-ft) high Mount Triglav. Starkly beautiful outcrops of
bare limestone characterize the higher altitudes of the park,
while its lower reaches encompass forests of spruce and
beech, which are home to a fantastic range of flora and
fauna. An outstanding network of picturesque trails, valleys,
deep blue lakes and peaks makes Triglav National Park
one of the most visited places in the country.

Vršič Pass, a spectacular
mountain road cutting
through the heart of
the park, features an
exhilarating sequence of
hairpin bends.

ITALY

Kra

TAMAR VALLEY

PLANICA VALLEY

Vršič

Strmec

Log Pod
Mangartom

MLINARIC
GORGE

Trenta

Zgornja
Bavšica

Soča

Kršovec

206

TRENTA VALLEY

Soča

Gr
La

Pristava
Lepena

Bla

k
1,520 m (4,9

LOWER BOHINJ MC

Krn
2,182 m
(7,159 ft)

Tolm
Ra

Alpinium Juliana
*This lush botanical garden
on the southern approaches
of the Vršič Pass showcases the
diverse flora of the Slovene Alps.
About 600 botanical species can
be found here.*

Soča Trail
*This 20-km (12-mile) long trail runs along
the Soča river as it carves its way through
the pine-fringed Trenta valley to the tiny
hamlet of Kršovec.*

| 0 km | 5 |
| 0 miles | 5 |

Valley of the Triglav Lakes
*This sequence of seven glacial lakes,
surrounded by boulders and spruce
trees, constitutes one of the park's
most captivating sights.*

Vrata Valley
A classic glacial valley on the northern side of Mount Triglav, Vrata valley is overlooked by towering limestone rock formations.

VISITORS' CHECKLIST

60 km (37 miles) NW of Ljubljana. from Bled.
Bled *Ljubljanska cesta 27, (386) 578 0200;* **Trenta** *Na Logu, (386) 5388 9330;* **Zgornja Radovna** *Pocar Farm, Zgornja Radovna 25, (386) 578 0200.* on *Lake Bohinj and in Bled and Kranjska Gora, just outside the park.*
www.tnp.si

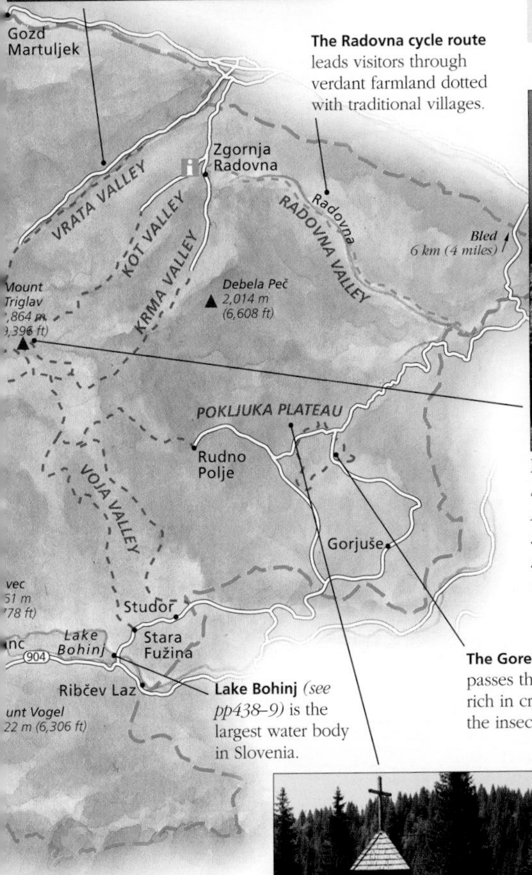

The Radovna cycle route leads visitors through verdant farmland dotted with traditional villages.

Gozd Martuljek

VRATA VALLEY

Zgornja Radovna

KOT VALLEY

KRMA VALLEY

RADOVNA VALLEY

Radovna

Bled 6 km (4 miles)

Mount Triglav ,864 m ,396 ft)

Debela Peč ▲ 2,014 m (6,608 ft)

POKLJUKA PLATEAU

VOJA VALLEY

Rudno Polje

Gorjuše

vec 51 m 78 ft)

Studor

inc

Lake Bohinj

Stara Fužina

(904)

Ribčev Laz

unt Vogel 22 m (6,306 ft)

Lake Bohinj *(see pp438–9)* is the largest water body in Slovenia.

Mount Triglav
Slovenia's highest peak, Mount Triglav is a national symbol; its three-peaked silhouette appears on the national flag.

The Goreljek Peat-Bog Nature Trail passes through unspoilt wetlands, rich in cranberries, bilberries and the insect-devouring sundew plant.

KEY

Visitor information
▲ Peak
= Minor road
- - Walking trail
- - Cycle route
- - Park boundary
-·- International border

Pokljuka Plateau
This unspoilt area of pine forests and pastures is crisscrossed by nature trails. The highlight is the Pokljuka Gorge, which burrows through the plateau's northern flanks.

Triglav National Park: Lake Bohinj

Tucked into the southeastern corner of Triglav National
Park, Lake Bohinj is a beautiful expanse of water, fed
by clear mountain streams and with high mountains on
almost all sides. Surrounded by some of Slovenia's best-
preserved rustic villages, it is ideal for swimming and
kayaking and an excellent base from which to explore
the region's hiking trails. In winter, Mount Vogel, to the
south of the lake, is a popular spot for skiing and
snowboarding, while the frozen lake provides a great
opportunity for ice skating.

**Visitors canoeing near Ribčev Laz,
at the eastern end of Lake Bohinj**

Slap Savica
*A popular walking trail west from
Ukanc leads to Slap Savica, a pair of
waterfalls surrounded by high cliffs.
Their waters feed the Sava river,
which flows southeast to meet the
Danube at Belgrade in Serbia.*

*Slap Savica
1.5 km (1 mile)*

Savica

A World War I Cemetery
holds the graves of
about 300 soldiers
buried between 1915
and 1917.

UKANC

**The cable car
to Mount Vogel**
begins from the
southern shores
of Bohinj.

*Mount Vogel
1.5 km (1 mile)*

Ukanc
*The small village of Ukanc, at the
lake's western end, has pebbly
beaches and is surrounded by the
peaks of Pršivec and Komna.*

Mount Vogel
*At an altitude of 1,800 m (5,906 ft), Mount
Vogel is a paradise for skiers in winter and
hikers in summer. The cable car from the
shores of Lake Bohinj ascends to a plateau
from where there are breathtaking views of
the Triglav massif to the north.*

For hotels and restaurants in this region see pp446–7 and pp448–9

Stara Fužina
With charming Alpine farmhouses, Stara Fužina is one
of the best-preserved traditional villages in western
Slovenia. The 13th-century St Paul's Church, in the
outskirts of the village, is also worth a visit.

| 0 metres | 500 |
| 0 yards | 500 |

Lake Bohinj

STARA FUŽINA

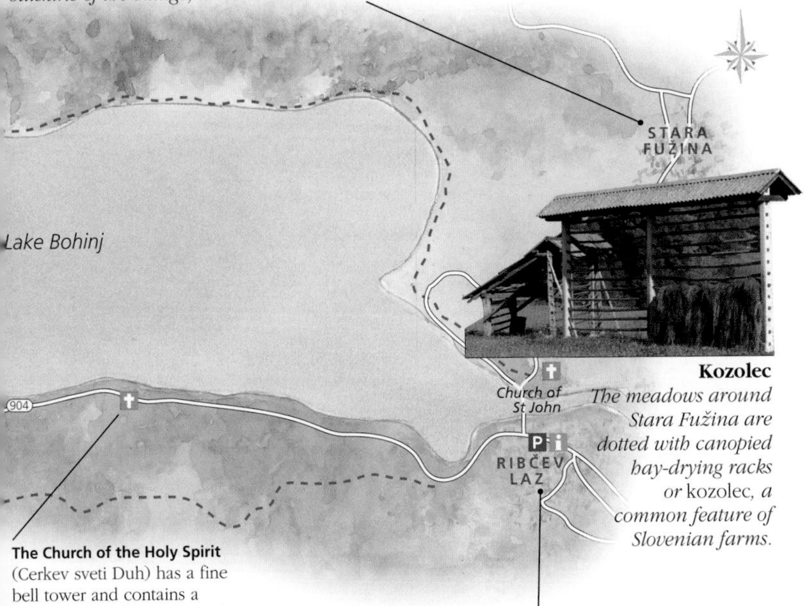

Kozolec
*The meadows around
Stara Fužina are
dotted with canopied
hay-drying racks
or* kozolec, *a
common feature of
Slovenian farms.*

Church of
St John

🅿 🛈
**RIBČEV
LAZ**

The Church of the Holy Spirit
(Cerkev sveti Duh) has a fine
bell tower and contains a
number of notable 15th- and
16th-century frescoes.

KEY

🛈 Visitor information

🅿 Parking

✝ Church

⊞ Cemetery

🚡 Cable car

🅰 Campsite

═══ Minor road

- - Trail

★ Ribčev Laz
*The main settlement at the eastern end of Lake Bohinj,
Ribčev Laz is famous for its dainty parish Church of St John
(sveti Janez), which contains some late-Gothic frescoes.*

Maribor ⑲

Baroque statue

Slovenia's second largest city, Maribor occupies a strategic location on the Drava river. Settled by Slavs in the early Middle Ages, the city became an important trading centre. However, with the expansion of the Ottoman Empire, it turned into a border fortress and trade declined. The city's fortunes improved with the construction of the Vienna–Trieste railway in 1846. Today, it has a mix of old and new architecture; the riverside quarter of Lent has the most attractive Baroque buildings.

bell tower was added in 1601. The interior decorations date mostly from the Baroque period, although some exquisitely carved medieval stone stalls remain in the choir. A chapel to the left of the main altar is dedicated to Bishop Anton Slomšek, who promoted the Slovenian language at a time when Maribor was ruled by a German-speaking elite.

Ornate west wing façade of the 15th-century Maribor Castle

♣ Maribor Castle and Regional Museum

Grajska 2. **Tel** (02) 228 3551.
⬜ 9am–4pm Tue–Sat, 9am–2pm Sun. 🖳 **www**.pmuzej-mb.si
Dominating the northern end of Castle Square (Grajski trg), Maribor Castle (Mariborski grad) was built in 1478 to protect Maribor from Ottoman attacks. Once the Turkish threat receded, the castle became an aristocratic residence. Today, it is home to the Regional Museum (Pokrajinski muzej), which displays folk costumes, military uniforms, furniture spanning several eras and Gothic and Baroque religious art. The building's 18th-century Rococo staircase, adorned with statues, is remarkable.

♠ Cathedral of St John the Baptist

Slomškov trg. **Tel** (386) 2251 8432.
⬜ dawn–dusk daily.
Just southwest of the castle, Maribor's medieval cathedral (Stolna Cerkev sv Jana Krstnika) is predominantly Gothic in style, although a characterful Renaissance

▥ Main Square

The town's long, rectangular Main Square (Glavni trg) took shape in the 13th century, when Maribor was emerging as a major commercial centre in the region. On its northern side is the Town Hall (Rotovž),

Baroque Plague Column on the Maribor's Main Square

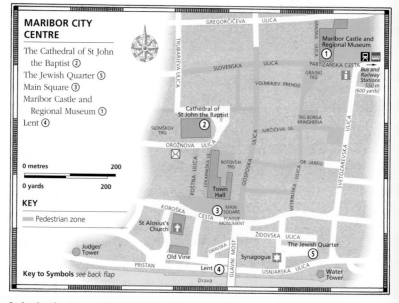

MARIBOR CITY CENTRE

```
0 metres          200
0 yards           200
```

KEY

▬ Pedestrian zone

Key to Symbols see back flap

Map labels:
GREGORČIČEVA ULICA
TRUBARJEVA ULICA
SLOVENSKA ULICA
GRAŠKA ULICA
Maribor Castle and Regional Museum ①
PARTIZANSKA CESTA
Bus and Railway Stations 550 m (600 yards)
GRAJSKI TRG
VOLMERJEV PREHOD
Cathedral of St John the Baptist ②
SLOMŠKOV TRG
OROŽNOVA ULICA
POŠTNA ULICA
LEKARNIŠKA UL.
TRG BORISA KRAIGHERIA
JURČIČEVA UL.
GOSPOSKA ULICA
VETRINJSKA ULICA
OB JARKU
SVETOZAREVSKA ULICA
ROTOVŠKI TRG
Town Hall
MAIN SQUARE ③
KOROŠKA CESTA
PLAGUE MONUMENT
St Alosius's Church
ŽIDOVSKA ULICA
The Jewish Quarter ⑤
DRAVSKA
Judges' Tower
PRISTAN
Old Vine
Lent ④
GLAVNI MOST
Synagogue
USNJARSKA ULICA
Water Tower
Drava

Old Vine adorning the Drava
riverfront in the Lent quarter

with an onion-domed clock
tower and an arcaded
Renaissance courtyard at the
back. In the centre of the
square is an ornate Baroque
Plague Column (Kužno
znamenje), raised in 1743
to commemorate the Great
Plague of the 17th century.

🏛 Lent

Downhill from the city centre
is the charming riverside
quarter of Lent, which was
once a busy port from where
rafts laden with local timber began their journey
south along the Drava and
Danube rivers.

Today, Lent is a bustling
neighbourhood, its well-
preserved Baroque houses
home to modern art galleries,
cafés and bars. Growing
along the façade of one of
the waterfront houses is the

VISITORS' CHECKLIST

133 km (83 miles) NE of
Ljubljana. 🚶 91,000 🚊 from
Ljubljana, Vienna or Zagreb. 🚌
from Ljubljana. 🛈 Partizanska
cesta 6, (02) 234 6611.

famous 400-year-old Old
Vine (Stara trta), believed
to be the oldest vine in the
world. Marking Lent's western
boundary is the **Judges' Tower**
(Sodni stolp), a barrel-shaped
medieval structure with a
curious mansard roof. To
the east is the rather peculiar
16th-century **Water Tower**
(Vodni stolp) featuring a
pentagonal ground plan
and a tall, tapering roof.

🏛 The Jewish Quarter

Židovska 4. **Tel** (02) 252 7836.
🕙 8am–4pm Mon–Fri, 9am–2pm
Sun. 🌐 www.pmuzej-mb.si
Standing on a terrace
immediately inland from
the Water Tower is the Jews'
Tower (Židovski četrt), a
quadrangular red-brick
structure attached to a short
stretch of the surviving city
wall. The narrow lanes beside
the tower were once home
to Maribor's Jewish community, who were an important
presence in the city from the
13th century until their extermination by the Nazis during
World War II. The beautifully
restored 14th-century
Synagogue (Sinagoga) now
houses an exhibition devoted
to local Jewish heritage.

Period furnishings at the Regional
Museum, Ptuj Castle

Ptuj ⑳

135 km (84 miles) NE of Ljubljana.
🚶 11, 000. 🚊 🚌 🛈 Slovenski
trg 5, (02) 779 6011. 🎭 Ptuj
Carnival (late Feb/early Mar).
www.ptuj-tourism.si

Set on the banks of the Drava
river, the charming rural town
of Ptuj is one of the oldest
in Slovenia. During the Roman
period, it served as a legionary
base and the centre of local
trade. Ptuj's most revered
sight is the 2nd-century
Orpheus Monument (Orfejev
spomenik), the carved tombstone of a Roman adminis-
trator, which depicts the scene
of Orpheus playing the lyre
and taming a group of wild
animals. This stands on
Slovenski Square (Slovenski
trg), in the town centre.
Slightly uphill from the monument, **St George's Church**
(Cerkev sv Jurij) is a treasure
trove of Gothic religious art,
with a famous statue of
St George near the main
entrance. The grand attraction
of the town, however, is the
fortified **Ptuj Castle** (Ptujski
grad), dating from the 10th
century. Expanded several
times, the most important
renovation occurred under
Walter Leslie, Baron of
Balquhane, in the 1650s. The
castle is now home to the
Regional Museum, which
boasts an extensive archaeological collection, furniture
acquired through the ages and
a section on local ethnography.

⌂ Ptuj Castle

Tel (02) 778 8780. 🕙 May–mid-
Oct: 9am–6pm daily; mid-Oct–Apr:
9am–5pm Tue–Sun. 🌐 🖥

Water Tower on the banks of the calm Drava river, Maribor

Practical & Travel Information

With Slovenia's popularity as a holiday destination growing rapidly, standards in the travel industry there have improved greatly. Slovenia is one of the better-developed countries in South Eastern Europe and travelling is a pleasant experience. The extensive road network is in good condition and public transport is efficient and well organized. The country also has a modern communications network, making it easy to keep in touch by telephone, post or Internet. Many young Slovenes speak fluent English, and Italian and German are also widely spoken.

WHEN TO VISIT

Slovenia's vibrant capital city, Ljubljana, is a year-round destination. Elsewhere in the country, April to October is the best time to visit as many museums and tourist attractions have restricted opening hours, or close altogether, for the rest of the year. July and August can be hot in lowland areas and along the coast, but in other parts of the country, cool Alpine breezes create the perfect conditions for summer hiking.

Mountain resorts are at their liveliest during the winter skiing season, which lasts from mid-December until March.

DOCUMENTATION

Citizens of the European Union (EU) can enter Slovenia on presentation of a valid identity card. Citizens of the US, Canada, Australia and New Zealand require a valid passport to visit Slovenia and can stay for up to 90 days. The official website of the **Slovene National Tourist Office** offers guidance on visa regulations and extended visits.

VISITOR INFORMATION

The **Slovene Tourist Information Centre** provides brochures and information leaflets on tours and transportation. The **Ljubljana Tourist Information Centre** also maintains a website in English. Most towns have their own information centres. The staff, most of whom speak English, are usually proficient in several foreign languages and helpful in providing information on accommodation and events.

HEALTH AND SECURITY

High standards of hygiene and health care are maintained in Slovenia and no special vaccinations are required for a visit to the country. Most town centres have a pharmacy (*lekarna*) with trained staff, most of whom speak English. These are open from 8am to 7pm, Monday to Friday, and for a few hours on Saturday mornings. In Ljubljana, there are pharmacies that stay open all night.

Slovenia has a very low crime rate and is considered extremely safe. The threat posed by petty thieves and pickpockets is relatively minor, but visitors should still be on their guard, particularly in crowded buses and busy shopping centres.

BANKING AND CURRENCY

Banks are open from 8:30am to 5pm, Monday to Friday and from 8:30 to 11am on Saturday mornings. Credit cards are widely accepted and ATMs are easy to find throughout the country. On January 1 2007, Slovenia officially adopted the euro. It is advisable to exchange foreign currency at banks and bureaus rather than hotels as they offer better exchange rates.

COMMUNICATIONS

Postal and telephone services in Slovenia are problem free. Public phones use *telekartice* (phone cards), which can be purchased from post offices, tobacco shops and newspaper kiosks. However, for long distance and international calls it is best to go to the post office. The Slovene postal service is well developed. Post offices are open from 8am to 7pm, Monday to Friday and from 8am to 1pm on Saturdays. Internet cafés are common in several city centres and most hotels now offer Wi-Fi Internet connection to guests.

FACILITIES FOR THE DISABLED

There has been a significant improvement in recent years with regard to the needs of the disabled traveller. The **Paraplegics Association of Slovenia** gives advice on the facilities available. Public transport offers wheelchair facilities while ramps feature in an increasing number of train stations. High-end

THE CLIMATE OF SLOVENIA

Slovenia has a Continental climate characterized by warm, dry summers and fairly cold winters. In summer, daytime temperatures reach 20° C to 25° C (68° F to 77° F). The weather is best from May to September, when the days are warm and the nights cool. January is the coldest month with temperatures frequently falling below freezing point.

LJUBLJANA

month	Apr	Jul	Oct	Jan
°C/F	15/59	22/72 14/57	15/59	
	4/39		6/43	2/36
				-4/25
(sun) hrs	5	8	3	2
(rain) mm	98	113	151	88

hotels have at least one room equipped for wheelchair users, however, this is less common in the lower-category hotels.

ARRIVING BY AIR

The easiest way to reach Slovenia is to fly. The Slovene national airline, **Adria Airways**, has direct scheduled flights from London's Gatwick Airport to the **Ljubljana Airport** at Brnik, situated 26 km (16 miles) north of the capital. In addition, budget airline **easyJet** flies several times a week from London's Stansted airport to Ljubljana. There are no direct flights from the US and Canada to Slovenia, but there are several one-stop options involving a change of flight in Amsterdam, Frankfurt or London. A regular bus service runs daily from the Brnik airport to Ljubljana bus station until around 8pm. A privately operated minibus shuttle service is also available, which runs till slightly later.

RAIL TRAVEL

The Slovene railways run a smooth service. Ljubljana stands at the centre of the rail network, offering fast and punctual services to destinations such as Maribor, Postojna, Koper, Ptuj and Bled. Mountainous areas such as the Triglav National Park (see pp436–9) and the Soča valley (see p431) are not served by train; however, they are well connected by bus.

Within Slovenia, trains fall into three categories. The InterCity Slovenia (ICS) trains currently serve the Ljubljana–Maribor route. InterCity (IC) trains offer a relatively speedy connection between major towns, while P (potniški), or "passenger" trains, are the slowest, stopping at every station en route. Some of the older potniški trains have hard seats and no air conditioning; however, standards of comfort on all other trains are very good.

Ljubljana is a good starting point for onward travel to Central Europe, with daily trains from the **Ljubljana Train Station** to Vienna, Budapest, Zagreb and Belgrade.

TRAVELLING BY BUS

The **Ljubljana Bus Station** serves most destinations in Slovenia. Major towns and cities have frequent departures, although smaller destinations may only have one or two buses a day. Timetable information regarding bus services is available on the bus station's website.

Buses are comfortable and ticket prices reasonable. International services also run daily to Belgrade and Sarajevo.

TRAVELLING BY CAR

Slovenia's well-surfaced roads are uncrowded and well signposted. In order to drive here each vehicle must display a windscreen sticker or vinjeta (vignette), which can be bought from petrol stations and newspaper kiosks. A six-month vignette for a car costs €35.

Ljubljana's central location means that a drive from here to anywhere else in the country can be completed in two hours or less. Two-lane highways run southwest from Ljubljana to the Adriatic coast, and east to Maribor.

Note that mountain roads, especially the Predel pass and the Vršič pass in the Triglav National Park, may be closed in winter due to harsh weather conditions.

DIRECTORY

DOCUMENTATION

Slovene National Tourist Office
www.slovenia.info

VISITOR INFORMATION

Free telephone information line
Tel 080 1900.

Ljubljana Tourist Information Centre
Stritarjeva 2, Ljubljana.
Tel (01) 306 1215.
www.ljubljana-tourism.si

Slovene Tourist Information Centre
Krekov trg 10, Ljubljana.
Tel (01) 306 4575.
www.slovenia.info

EMBASSIES

Australia
Železna cesta 14.
Ljubljana.
Tel (01) 234 8675.
www.dfat.gov.au

Canada
trg republike 3, Ljubljana.
Tel (01) 252 4444.

United Kingdom
trg Republike 3, Ljubljana.
Tel (01) 200 3910.
www.ukinslovenia.fco.
gov.uk

United States
Prešernova 31, Ljubljana.
Tel (01) 200 5500.
www.slovenia.usembassy.
gov

EMERGENCY NUMBERS

Ambulance
Tel 112.

Fire
Tel 112.

Police
Tel 133.

FACILITIES FOR THE DISABLED

Paraplegics Association of Slovenia
Štihova 14, Ljubljana.
Tel (01) 432 7138. www.
zveza-paraplegikov.si

ARRIVING BY AIR

Adria Airways
Tel 080 1300 (Slovenia),
(020) 7734 4630 (UK).
www.adria.si

easyJet
www.easyjet.com

Ljubljana Airport
Brnik. Tel (04) 206 198.
www.lju-airport.si

RAIL TRAVEL

Ljubljana Train Station
trg osvobodilne fronte.
Tel (01) 291 3332.
www.slo-zeleznice.si

TRAVELLING BY BUS

Ljubljana Bus Station
trg osvobodilne fronte,
Ljubljana.
Tel (090) 934 230.
www.ap-ljubljana.si

Shopping & Entertainment

Slovenia has a lively and varied shopping culture that embraces old-style outdoor markets as well as modern malls. A wide range of handmade goods is available including crystal, black pottery and fine lace. Food items are also of particularly high quality. As for entertainment, the Slovenes are outgoing people. They enjoy spending time in the country's cafés and bars and the capital city, Ljubljana, has a vibrant clubbing scene. Theatres and concert venues can be found in all the country's cities. Several interesting local events, such as excellent traditional music and art festivals are also held in most big cities and towns.

OPENING HOURS

Shops are mostly open from 8am to 7pm Monday to Friday and from 8am to 2pm on Saturday. Only a handful of food stores stay open on Saturday afternoons and Sundays.

MARKETS

The area around Ljubljana's Slovenska cesta offers the most choice in the way of high-street shops and department stores, while the nearby Old Town is the best place for luxury goods, gifts and souvenirs. At the northern end of the Old Town, Ljubljana's colourful main market offers a variety of fresh fruit and vegetables as well as delicatessen products, dried herbs and craft items. The Sunday morning antiques and bric-a-brac market on the Ljubljanica riverbank is full of potential discoveries. Most towns have their own markets selling fruits, vegetables and home-cured meats.

CRAFTS AND SOUVENIRS

Slovenia is renowned for its traditional handicrafts. Quality crystal from the town of Rogaška in the east of the country can be found at **Galerija Rogaška** in Ljubljana's Old Town. The delightfully intricate lace made by the women of Idrija is available at **Galerija Idrijske Čipke**, also in the Old Town. An especially typical form of folk art is the decoration of beehives with scenes depicting village life or wild animals. Painted boards displaying beehive motifs and black pottery are exhibited in museums, but are also sold in most souvenir shops, including **Etnogalerija Skrina** in Ljubljana.

Lavishly illustrated books on Slovene architecture, the natural landscape and folk traditions are sold at bookshops. **Mladinska Knjiga Konzorcij** in Ljubljana is one of the bigger outlets where these books can be purchased.

FOOD AND DRINK

Many of Slovenia's delicatessen products make ideal gifts, with *pršut* (home-cured ham) of the karst region topping the list. Other gourmet delights include *klobase* (farmhouse sausages), *med* (honey) and *bučno olje* (pumpkin seed oil).

Most food shops and supermarkets stock a wide selection of Slovene wines. Alongside excellent Merlots, Sauvignons and Rieslings, there are a handful of outstanding indigenous wines: the dry white šipon from eastern Slovenia; rich red teran from the karst region; and the gentler red refošk from the coast. Strong *viljamovka* (Williams pear brandy), the splendid *brinjevec* (Juniper brandy) and delicious *slivovka* (plum brandy) are among the most popular local spirits.

PUBS AND BARS

Most places in Slovenia have a downtown area with cafés and bars. The Old Town in Ljubljana and the Lent riverside area in Maribor are two of the liveliest places for bar hopping. Clubbing and live music are major features of Ljubljana's nightlife, although venues change from one year to the next. Fans of live rock should head to **Metelkova Mesto**, a former Yugoslav Army barracks that has been taken over by several alternative cultural organizations and transformed into a nest of bar and club venues.

CLASSICAL MUSIC

Slovenia offers a diverse musical repertoire. The **Slovene National Theatre, Opera and Ballet** and the **Slovene Filharmonic** are among the best of their kind in Central Europe.

Located in the heart of Ljubljana, **Cankarjev Dom** can claim to be one of Europe's finest cultural venues frequently hosting top international performances. Tickets for concerts are available from the box offices of the venues themselves.

FESTIVALS

Festivals form an integral part of Slovenian cultural life. The popular **Ljubljana Summer Festival** embraces classical music, jazz, opera and folk and usually takes place from July to mid-September.

Other well-known annual festivals include **Druga Godba**, featuring ethnic music from around the world, which takes place in Ljubljana during May. Tickets for both the Summer Festival and Druga Godba can be obtained from the Ljubljana Summer Festival box office opposite the Križanke concert venue. The noted **Lent Festival**, which covers everything from pop to classical music on outdoor riverside stages, takes place in Maribor from late June to early July.

Slovenia also has firmly rooted seasonal traditions, as evidenced by its famous Pust Festival. Held in February each year, this is regarded as the most famous of Slovenia's pre-Lent carnivals and involves riotous displays of masked revelry.

Sports Activities

Dominated by one of Europe's most stunning mountain ranges, the Julian Alps, Slovenia is an excellent outdoor destination and a major centre for activity holidays. The country's picturesque mountains, beautiful rivers and lakes offer unlimited opportunities to indulge in a wide range of adventure sports including hiking and skiing, whitewater rafting or kayaking in the Soča valley *(see p431)* and cycling through the majestic hills of Dolenjska. The Slovene coast offers some of the best windsurfing in Europe while scuba diving and sailing are also popular.

HIKING

Hiking has been a popular pursuit in Slovenia for well over a century and a half. There is a wide variety of trails to suit the recreational rambler as well as the serious mountain climber, and routes are well kept with frequent signposts. Hiking maps are widely available and there is an established network of mountain huts offering refuge to the long-distance trekker.

CYCLING

The popularity of cycling has grown in recent years. Slovenia's varied topography presents endless opportunities for cyclists. There is a broad range of well-marked mountain biking trails in the north and west of the country including the mountain trails in Triglav National Park *(see pp436–9)*. There are also several well-organized recreational routes in the lowlands.

Cycling is permitted on all roads except motorways. Local tourist information centres are well equipped to advise visitors regarding cycling routes. Mountain bikes are available for hire in the main resort centres.

RAFTING

Slovenia offers various water sports, from boating for relaxation to adrenaline-inducing white water descents over steep waterfalls and rapids. The fast flowing Alpine rivers are perfect for rafting, canoeing and kayaking, with numerous agencies offering trips on the Soča river. Among these are **Maya**, **Soča Rafting** and **Bled Rafting** in the towns of Tolmin, Bovec and Bled respectively. The same agencies also arrange adventure sports such as canyoning and bungee jumping.

SKIING

In winter, visitors flock to Slovenia's wonderful ski slopes. Snowboarding and downhill skiing are popular in the Alpine parts of Slovenia. Kranjska Gora and Mariborsko Pohorje are the largest and best-equipped ski resorts, although there are several smaller destinations to choose from, many of which are only an hour's drive from the capital, Ljubljana. Since Slovenia's split from Yugoslavia in 1991, many Slovenes have achieved tremendous success in winter sports. The most notable event in the Slovenian sporting calendar is the World Ski-Jumping Championships, held in Planica in March.

Other winter pleasures include snowmobile rides – in Kranjska Gora – and organized sled runs outside the ski centres. Depending on the weather, the ski season usually lasts from December to March.

DIRECTORY

CRAFTS AND SOUVENIRS

Etnogalerija Skrina
Breg 8, Ljubljana. **Tel** (01) 425 5161. **www**.skrina.si

Galerija Idrijske Čipke
Mestni trg 17, Ljubljana. **Tel** (01) 425 0051. **www**.idrija-lace.com

Galerija Rogaška
Mestni trg 22, Ljubljana. **Tel** (01) 241 2701. **www**.steklarna-rogaska.si

Mladinska Knjiga Konzorcij
Slovenska cesta 29, Ljubljana. **Tel** (01) 241 4761. **www**.mladinska.com

FOOD AND DRINK

Čokoladnica Cukrček
Mestni trg 11, Ljubljana. **Tel** (01) 421 0453. **www**.cukrcek.si

Kraševka
Ciril Metodov trg 10, Ljubljana. **Tel** (01) 232 1445. **www**.krasevka.si

PUBS AND BARS

Metelkova Mesto
Metelkova cesta, Ljubljana. **www**.metelkova.org

CLASSICAL MUSIC

Cankarjev Dom
trg republike, Ljubljana. **Tel** (01) 241 7100. **www**.cd-cc.si

Slovene Filharmonic
Kongresni trg 10, Ljubljana. **Tel** (01) 241 0800. **www**.filharmonija.si

Slovene National Theatre, Opera and Ballet
Cankarjeva 11/1, Ljubljana. **Tel** (01) 241 1700. **www**.opera.si, **www**.balet.si

FESTIVALS

Druga Godba
Ljubljana. **Tel** (01) 430 8260. **www**.drugagodba.si

Lent Festival
Maribor. **Tel** (02) 229 4000. **www**.lent.slovenija.net

Ljubljana Summer Festival
Ljubljana. **Tel** (01) 241 6026. **www**.ljubljanafestival.si

RAFTING

Bled Rafting
Hrastova 2, Bled. **Tel** (04) 167 8008. **www**.bled-rafting.si

Maya
Padlih borcev 1, Tolmin. **Tel** (05) 380 0530. **www**.maya.si

Soča Rafting
trg Golobarskih žrtev 14, Bovec. **Tel** (05) 389 6200. **www**.socarafting.si

Where to Stay in Slovenia

Slovenia offers a range of accommodation, from luxurious hotels to family-run pensions. For those travelling on a budget, there are several bed and breakfast inns. It is advisable to reserve ahead during the high season, especially in the capital, Ljubljana, and in popular ski resorts such as Kranjska Gora (see pp432–3).

PRICE CATEGORIES
Price categories are for a standard double room per night in high season, including tax and service charges. Breakfast is not included, unless specified.

€ Under 50 euros
€€ 50–70 euros
€€€ 70–100 euros
€€€€ 100–150 euros
€€€€€ Over 150 euros

LJUBLJANA

Vila Veselova   P   €€

*Veselova 14, 1000 **Tel** (01) 5992 6721 **Rooms** 8*   **Map** D3

This grand 19th-century villa on the edge of Tivoli Park (see p424) conceals a simple but intimate hostel-cum-pension. Guests can choose between self-contained doubles, or six- to eight- bed dormitories, some of which have en suite facilities in the hallway. Free Internet access. **www.v-v.si**

Antiq Hotel   P ▤   €€€

*Gornji trg 3, 1000 **Tel** (01) 421 3560 **Fax** (01) 421 3565 **Rooms** 16*   **Map** E4

Located in the heart of the Old Town, this boutique hotel has rooms ranging from snug doubles with shared facilities to regular-sized rooms with en suite bathrooms. There is also a split-level four-person apartment which would suit those travelling as a group. **www.antiqhotel.si**

Maček   €€€

*Krojaška 5, 1000 **Tel** (01) 425 3791 **Rooms** 5*   **Map** E3

Situated right in the middle of the city centre and on the banks of the scenic Ljubljanica river, Maček is an informal bed and breakfast. The hotel offers bright and cheerful bedrooms with laminated floors above its popular café-bar. Wireless Internet is provided. **www.sobe-macek.si**

Allegro   ▤   €€€€

*Gornji trg 6, 1000 **Tel** (059) 119 620 **Fax** (059) 119 620 **Rooms** 12*   **Map** E4

A small and intimate bed and breakfast in one of Ljubljana's most picturesque corners, occupying a recently renovated house of medieval origin. Rooms feature warm colours, boldly patterned wallpaper and fancy textiles. Breakfast is served in an atmospheric vaulted cellar and there is Wi-Fi coverage. **www.allegrohotel.si**

City Hotel   P ⁞⁞   €€€€

*Dalmatinova 15, 1000 **Tel** (01) 239 0000 **Fax** (01) 239 0001 **Rooms** 200*   **Map** E2

The City Hotel is handily located midway between the Old Town and the train and bus stations. The spacious rooms are attractively decorated in red and cream along contemporary lines and equipped with modern features such as flat-screen TVs. Wireless Internet is also available. **www.cityhotel.si**

Prenočišče Slamič   P   €€€€

*Keršnikova 1, 1000 **Tel** (01) 433 8233 **Fax** (01) 433 8022 **Rooms** 10*   **Map** E2

This homely pension-style place is situated between the main shopping area and Tivoli Park. Tastefully decorated rooms each have a minibar and free Internet access. There are doubles as well as suites to accommodate three or four guests. Breakfast is served in the Kavačaj café located next door. **www.slamic.si**

Grand Hotel Union   P ⁞⁞   €€€€€

*Miklošičeva 1, 1000 **Tel** (01) 308 1270 **Fax** (01) 308 1015 **Rooms** 327*   **Map** E2

A glorious Art Nouveau property near the Tromostovje bridge, this hotel offers spacious rooms in the main building and contemporary-style rooms aimed at business visitors in the modern annexe. There are on-site cafés and restaurants, including Smrekarjev Hram, serving some of Ljubljana's best international cuisine. **www.gh-union.si**

Slon   ⁞⁞   €€€€€

*Slovenska cesta 34, 1000 **Tel** (01) 470 1100 **Fax** (01) 251 7164 **Rooms** 171*   **Map** E2

Located a short distance from the Old Town, Slon offers fully equipped rooms with Internet facilities. Habsburg Emperor Maximilian II once stayed at an inn on this site together with an elephant (slon in Slovene) presented to him by the king of Portugal; hence the hotel's name. **www.hotelslon.com**

FURTHER AFIELD Hostel Celica   P ⁞⁞ ▤   €€

*Metelkova 8, 1000 **Tel** (01) 230 9700 **Fax** (01) 230 9714 **Rooms** 20*

A classic among Europe's hostels for its distinct interiors, Celica (The Cell) is housed in a former Yugoslav military police station. Each room has been designed with a different theme and double rooms as well as bunk-bed dormitories are available. A popular hostel, so advance booking is recommended. **www.hostelcelica.com**

Map References see map of Ljubljana pp418–19

REST OF SLOVENIA

BLED Kompas

 €€€€

Cankarjeva 2, 4260 **Tel** *(04) 620 5100* **Fax** *(04) 578 2499* **Rooms** *107*

Within walking distance of Bled's lakefront, cafés and shops, the Kompas is an ideal resort-hotel offering
a wealth of facilities under one roof. The rooms are decorated in warm colours and come with TV, minibar and
Internet access. It also has a swimming pool, squash courts, saunas and a solarium. **www.kompashotel.com**

BLED Vila Bled

€€€€€

Cesta svobode 26, 4260 **Tel** *(04) 575 3710* **Fax** *(04) 575 3711* **Rooms** *31*

Now a luxury hotel, Vila Bled was once the private holiday residence of President Tito. The rooms incorporate
wooden furnishings alongside contemporary features such as modern bathrooms. There is a sauna and Turkish
steam bath on site and the hotel's gardens provide wonderful views of Lake Bled. **www.vila-bled.com**

KOBARID Hvala

€€€€

Trg svobode 1, 5222 **Tel** *(05) 389 9300* **Fax** *(05) 388 5322* **Rooms** *31*

Located in the heart of Kobarid, Hvala is a family-run hotel with en suite rooms. The hotel is a good base from
which to explore the World War I battlefields of the Soča Front *(see p430)*. Being situated in a popular fly-fishing
area close to the Soča river, the hotel sells fishing licences and equipment. **www.hotel-hvala.si**

KRANJSKA GORA Kotnik

€€€

Borovška cesta 75, 4280 **Tel** *(04) 588 1564* **Fax** *(04) 588 1859* **Rooms** *15*

A classy family-run hotel with friendly staff, Kotnik has tastefully decorated rooms with all the essential amenities,
Internet facilities and minibar. A couple of triples and quadruples are available for families. The popular Pizzeria
Pino restaurant is part of the hotel. **www.hotel-kotnik.si**

LAKE BOHINJ Bellevue

 €€€

Ribčev Laz, 4265 **Tel** *(04) 572 3331* **Fax** *(04) 572 3684* **Rooms** *59*

The Bellevue is located on a wooded hill above the village of Ribčev Laz, on the eastern shores of Lake Bohinj
(see pp438–9). In winter, a ski bus connects the hotel to the ski slopes at Vogel. The hotel library is named after
the crime writer Agatha Christie, who stayed here in 1967. All rooms are en suite. **www.hoteli-bohinj.si**

LAKE BOHINJ Zlatorog

 €€€€

Ukanc 65, 4265 **Tel** *(04) 572 3381* **Fax** *(04) 723 384* **Rooms** *84*

A former hunting lodge at the peaceful western end of Lake Bohinj, Zlatorog has played host to dignitaries
such as President Tito, Leonid Brezhnev and Willy Brandt. Enjoying close proximity to Bohinj's pebbly beaches,
the hotel offers snug rooms as well as wireless Internet and bike hire. **www.hoteli-bohinj.si**

MARIBOR Orel/Hotel Uni

€€€€

Volkmerjev prehod 7, 2000 **Tel** *(02) 250 6700* **Fax** *(02) 251 8497* **Rooms** *71*

Ideally located in the heart of Maribor's pedestrian zone, this combined hotel and hostel offers two types of
accommodation under one roof. Choose between three-star hotel rooms with TV, minibar and Internet access
or plainly decorated doubles and triples in the hostel section. All rooms are en suite. **www.termemb.si**

PIRAN Tartini

 €€€€

Tartinijev trg 15, 6330 **Tel** *(05) 671 1000* **Fax** *(05) 671 1665* **Rooms** *43*

A medium-sized hotel on Piran's Italianate main square, Tartini offers en suite rooms decorated in bold colours
with contemporary furnishings. A balconied room on the hotel's western side provides spectacular views of
the sea, while the penthouse suite comes with a roof terrace. **www.hotel-tartini-piran.com**

PORTOROŽ Riviera

 €€€€€

Obala 33, 6320 **Tel** *(05) 692 6020* **Fax** *(05) 692 9003* **Rooms** *176*

The Riviera is the best equipped of the many four-star hotels along Portorož's seafront. On-site spa facilities
lend it the air of a self-contained health resort. Spacious bedrooms come with decent-sized bathrooms, most
with full-sized tubs. Sea-facing rooms are slightly more expensive. **www.lifeclass.net**

PTUJ Kurent

€

Osojnikova 9, 2250 **Tel** *(02) 771 0814* **Fax** *(02) 771 0815* **Rooms** *6*

A well-organized hostel next door to Ptuj's tourist information centre and within easy walking distance of the
bus and train stations, Kurent offers cosy double rooms with or without showers or six-person dormitories with
bunk beds. Breakfast is included and the hotel also provides Internet access and scooter hire.

PTUJ Mitra

 €€€

Prešernova 6, 2250 **Tel** *(02) 787 7455* **Fax** *(02) 787 7459* **Rooms** *29*

A stone's throw away from Ptuj's famous Orpheus Monument *(see p441)*, this restored 19th-century townhouse
contains en suite rooms furnished in Art Nouveau and Neo-Classical styles. Facilities include a wellness centre
equipped with a sauna and Turkish steam bath. **www.hotel-mitra.si**

Key to Symbols *see back cover flap*

Where to Eat in Slovenia

Slovenia offers a variety of restaurants to suit most budgets. *Restavracija* is the standard word for a restaurant, although in the countryside visitors are likely to come across a *gostilna*, a traditional inn, which serves both as an eatery and a local pub. Home-grown, organic food is appreciated and most restaurants use local ingredients.

PRICE CATEGORIES
Based on the price per person of a three-course meal with half a bottle of wine, including cover charge, service and tax.

€ Under 20 euros
€€ 20–30 euros
€€€ 30–50 euros
€€€€ 50–80 euros
€€€€€ Over 80 euros

LJUBLJANA

Ajdovo Zrno
€
Trubarjeva cesta 7, 1000 **Tel** *(01) 690 468* **Map** *E2*

Located in a courtyard only a few steps away from the central Prešeren Square, Ajdovo Zrno is the perfect spot for a quick healthy meal while sightseeing. A clean and bright self-service canteen, it offers a choice of vegetarian-only dishes and fresh salads. Closed on Saturdays and Sundays.

Čajna Hiša Cha
€
Stari trg 3, 1000 **Tel** *(01) 252 7010* **Map** *E4*

This attractive tea-house in the heart of the Old Town is the ideal place to relax over afternoon tea, with a choice of speciality brews on offer. The place also has a good selection of sandwiches and salads. The adjoining shop here sells a variety of leaf teas from around the world. Closed on Sundays.

Figovec
€€€
Gosposvetska 1, 1000 **Tel** *(01) 426 4410* **Map** *D2*

Situated on one of central Ljubljana's most prominent street corners, this charming, old-fashioned restaurant is renowned for its horsemeat – served as a starter in the form of carpaccio and as a main course foal fillet. Mainstream meat dishes on offer include *wiener schnitzel* (veal coated in breadcrumbs) and spicy goulashes.

Gostilna As
€€€
Čopova 5/A, 1000 **Tel** *(01) 425 8822* **Map** *E3*

This chic venue, Gostilna As has long been a favourite among local gourmets, offering a blend of Mediterranean and Central European cuisine and using local ingredients. The adjoining lounge serves affordable pastas and salads alongside an impressive range of cocktails.

Le Petit Café
€€€
Trg francoske revolucije 4, 1000 **Tel** *(01) 251 2575* **Map** *D4*

An enduringly popular French-style café with a large – and frequently crowded – terrace, Le Petit Café looks out towards Jože Plečnik's Illyrian Monument. Popular for fresh pastries and croissants, there is also plenty in the way of more substantial meals, with salads and pastas predominating.

River House
€€€
Gallusovo nabrežje 31, 1000 **Tel** *(01) 425 4090* **Map** *E4*

This combined restaurant and lounge-bar enjoys an enviable location, with its outdoor terrace overlooking the Ljubljanica river. Pasta dishes and Mediterranean salads share space on the menu with traditional Slovene meat and fish dishes. It is also a popular late-night venue with DJs performing on weekend evenings.

Šestica
€€€
Slovenska cesta 40, 1000 **Tel** *(01) 242 0850* **Map** *E2*

A highly popular restaurant, Šestica has an attractive garden courtyard. The menu covers most regions of Slovenia, from goulash from the plains of eastern Slovenia to squid and grilled fish from the coast. The *prekmurska gibanica* (poppy-seed-and-custard cake) makes for an outstanding dessert. Closed on Sundays.

Sokol
€€€
Ciril Metodov trg 18, 1000 **Tel** *(01) 439 6855* **Map** *E3*

Occupying a warren of rooms in the Old Town, Sokol predominantly serves hearty pork and steak dishes. The menu also includes game, freshwater fish and east Slovene specialities such as *telečja obara* (a paprika-rich veal stew). The in-house beer comes in both light and dark versions.

Špajza
€€€
Gornji trg 28, 1000 **Tel** *(01) 425 3094* **Map** *E4*

Situated uphill from the Old Town on the peaceful Gornji Square, Špajza has a homely, soothing ambience and is decorated with classy bric-a-brac. The menu includes fresh fish from the Adriatic as well as inland Slovenian classics such as breast of duck, horsemeat fillets and game.

Map References *see map of Ljubljana pp418–19*

Zlata Ribica
Cankarjevo nabrežje 5–7, 1000 **Tel** *(01) 241 2680*

€€€

Map E3

Occupying a historic riverside building, Zlata Ribica, or the Little Goldfish, is a pleasant spot to sample a traditional Slovene menu of grilled fish. Adriatic *brodet* (fish soup) and treats from inland Slovenia such as *štrukli* (baked cheese dumplings), hearty pork and game dishes are also available. The lunch menus are very affordable.

REST OF SLOVENIA

BLED Okarina
Ljubljanska cesta 8, 4260 **Tel** *(04) 574 1458*

€€

A high-quality fusion restaurant, Okarina has an off-beat interior with quirky paintings lining one wall and Indian textiles on the other. The menu spans Adriatic seafood, Balkan-style grilled meats and spicy Indian dishes with several vegetarian options. There is also a good selection of Slovene wines.

IDRIJA Kos
Tomšičeva 4, 5280 **Tel** *(05) 372 2030*

€€

This family-owned pub-restaurant serves Slovene staples such as grilled sausage, veal cutlets and freshwater fish. Its signature dish *idrijski žlikrofi* (ravioli stuffed with potato or mushrooms) is usually served with either roasted pork or goulash. Closed on Sundays.

KOBARID Hiša Franko
Staro Selo 1, 5222 **Tel** *(05) 389 4120*

€€€€

This restaurant 5 km (3 miles) west of Kobarid has established itself as a cult destination for creative cuisine. The imaginative menu features fish and game as the main ingredients, garnished with organic vegetables; there is also a good selection of Italian and Slovene wines. Closed on Mondays.

KOBARID Kotlar
Trg svobode 11, 5222 **Tel** *(05) 389 1110*

€€€€

A family-run restaurant just off the town square, Kotlar features a boat-shaped bar at one end of the dining room. Adriatic seafood is the main attraction, with squid, lobster and shellfish dominating the menu. Known for its speciality dessert *kobariški štruklji* (dumplings with walnut filling). Closed on Tuesdays and Wednesdays.

KRANJSKA GORA Miklič
Vitranška 13, 4280 **Tel** *(04) 588 1635*

€€€

This highly regarded hotel-restaurant near the ski trails offers an eclectic menu of meat, game and seafood. Grilled Adriatic fish is served with *blitva* (spinach-like greens) from Dalmatia. Other local specialities include pasta dishes dressed with Istrian truffles. A rich selection of Slovene wines complements the tasty meals.

MARIBOR Gril Ranca
Dravska 10, 2000 **Tel** *(02) 252 5550*

€

The Gril Ranca's Balkan-styled grilled meats are not strictly Slovenian but extremely popular with local diners. Favourites include *čevapčiči* (grilled minced-meat rissoles), *pljeskavice* (hamburger-style patties) and *vešalice* grilled pork skewers). The beautiful riverside location is an added attraction.

PIRAN Čakola
Partizanska 2, 6330

€€

A cosy café-bar on a picturesque Mediterranean square, Čakola has a unique interior with its modern lounge bar set in a 19th-century living room. A popular pub, it also offers speciality teas, fresh sandwiches and platters of cold meats including home-cured *pršut* (smoked ham).

PIRAN Neptun
Župančičeva 7, 6330 **Tel** *(05) 673 4111*

€€€

A seafood restaurant, Neptun is located in a quiet street a few steps away from the main square and there are few better places in Piran to sample expertly grilled fresh Adriatic fish. There is also a good choice of squid, scampi and lobster. Closed on Tuesdays.

PTUJ Amadeus
Prešernova 36, 2250 **Tel** *(02) 771 7051*

€€€

This centrally located restaurant and bar specializes in *štruklji* (cheesy dumpling-style pastries), a traditional staple of Slovene cuisine. The menu also offers plenty of mainstream veal and pork dishes, alongside traditional treats such as *žganci* (a buckwheat-based crumble) served with chopped liver.

PTUJ Gostilna Ribič
Dravska 9, 2250 **Tel** *(02) 749 0635*

€€€

Situated just outside central Ptuj, Ribič is a traditional riverside inn with a big outdoor terrace. The menu offers a good choice of freshwater fish and seafood as well as plenty of seasonal specials, notably game. The dessert menu includes sumptuous cakes. Closed on Mondays.

Key to Symbols *see back cover flap*

CROATIA

*S*ituated between Eastern and Western Europe, Croatia has long served both as a land of passage and a point of contact between different worlds and cultures. Though small, it has great ethnic, historical and architectural diversity as well as a variety of landscapes. The beautiful Adriatic coast is an outstanding attraction and the largely unspoilt interior has great rural charm.

Croatia forms a meeting point between the Mediterranean Central Europe and the Balkans. The north of the country has a Viennese look; while to the west, the Adriatic coast boasts a great deal of Italian-style architecture. The 1991–5 war which followed the break-up of Yugoslavia had a disastrous effect on Croatia's economy but the country is regaining its reputation as a popular holiday destination.

HISTORY

Croatia has been home to human civilization since the Neolithic era. Illyrian tribal states established themselves throughout the region during the 1st millennium BC. They were, however, no match for the Romans, who conquered present-day Croatia in the 2nd century BC.

Slav tribes, including the Croats, settled in South Eastern Europe from the early 6th century onwards. Croats on the Adriatic coast accepted the rule of Byzantium, which had inherited Roman possessions in Eastern Europe. Croats living inland carved out an independent territory of their own. In the 9th century, invading Hungarians were thrown back by Croatian rulers strengthening their hold over northern and eastern Croatia. Over the next 200 years, the Croats extended their territories towards the Adriatic, allowing a Christian Slav culture to flourish.

Ruins of the Roman Amphitheatre in Pula, dating from the 3rd century AD

◁ Turquoise lakes and waterfalls in Plitvice Lakes National Park

Marshal Josip Tito, the first president of Yugoslavia

The last Croatian king died childless in 1091, and the crown was claimed by the Hungarians. Hungarian monarchs ruled over Croatia until 1526, when their armies were destroyed by the Ottoman Turks. Croatia turned to the Habsburg Empire for protection, and became a front line state in the Habsburgs' wars against the Ottomans.

The Ottoman threat had receded by the 19th century, and patriotic Croats began to demand political and cultural autonomy from the Habsburgs. These calls were left unanswered until the end of World War I, when the Habsburgs were defeated and began to disintegrate. Croatia declared its independence in October 1918, and entered into a political union with the neighbouring kingdom of Serbia, creating the kingdom of Serbs, Croats and Slovenes. The kingdom was renamed Yugoslavia in 1929. However, the Croats and Serbs could not agree on how power was to be shared in the new state, and Yugoslavia remained an unstable unit with frequent political crises.

Yugoslavia was invaded by Germany and Italy in 1941, breaking up the country and re-establishing Croatia as a pro-Nazi puppet state. Resistance to the Nazis was led by the partisan movement created by local Communist leader Josip Broz Tito. At the end of World War II, Tito re-established Yugoslavia as a Communist federation composed of six equal republics. Following Tito's death in 1980, tensions between Yugoslavia's republics re-emerged, leading to a disintegration of central authority. Slovenia and Croatia declared their independence in 1991. Serbs living in Croatia launched a rebellion, supported by the Yugoslav People's Army. Fighting continued for four years, and was finally brought to an end by Croatian military victories in August 1995. Croatia has since developed into a modern European democracy, becoming a member of the EU in 2004 and of NATO in 2009.

KEY DATES IN CROATIAN HISTORY

1200 BC Illyrian settlement in the Balkans

229 BC The Roman Army destroys Illyrian forts, and rules Illyria for the next three centuries

AD 7 Croats settle in Pannonia and Dalmatia

899 Hungarians enter the Balkans but are pushed back by the Croats

901 Prince Tomislav defeats the Hungarians and forces them beyond Sava river

1091 Hungarian King Ladislas seizes the Croatian crown

1526 Hungary is defeated by the Ottomans; Croatia turns to the Habsburg Empire for support

1918 Croatia proclaims independence after the fall of the Habsburg Empire

1945 The Yugoslav Federal State is founded with Croatia, Serbia, Macedonia, Montenegro, Slovenia and Bosnia and Herzegovina as members

1980 Yugoslavia's President Tito dies, leaving the state without a firm leader

1991 Croatia declares independence; Serb forces occupy large parts of the country

1995 Croatian forces recapture occupied territory

2009 Croatia joins NATO

LANGUAGE AND CULTURE

The official language of Croatia is Croatian, although many dialects are spoken in its regions. Croatia is a devoutly Catholic country and colourful religious festivals take place throughout the year. During the summer, traditional songs and dances are performed at folk festivals.

Exploring Croatia

Croatia is a fascinating country made up of a wide variety of landscapes. Its capital, Zagreb, is a delight, dotted with galleries and museums. The country's coast and islands are spectacular, with the national parks preserving its natural charm. The rest of Croatia features rolling fields and hills covered with vineyards. The country also benefits from an efficient transport system with excellent connections between the mainland and the islands.

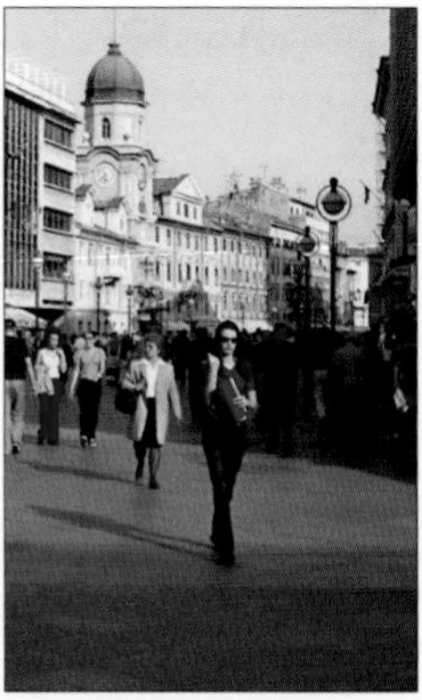

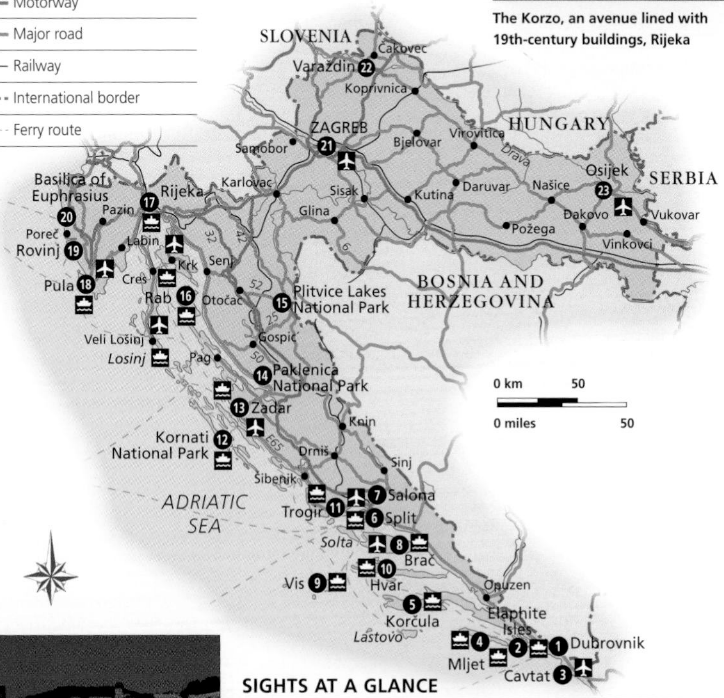

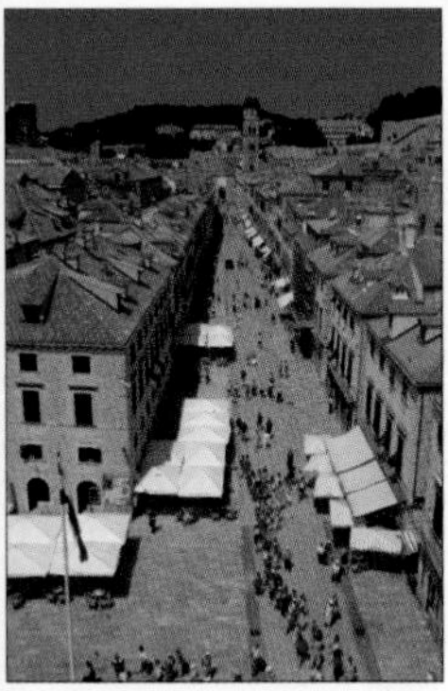

The Korzo, an avenue lined with 19th-century buildings, Rijeka

KEY

- Airport
- Ferry terminal
- Motorway
- Major road
- Railway
- International border
- Ferry route

Pedestrianized street in Dubrovnik's Old Town

SIGHTS AT A GLANCE

Basilica of Euphrasius pp484–5 20
Brač 8
Cavtat 3
Dubrovnik pp454–60 1
Elaphite Isles 2
Hvar pp474–5 10
Korčula pp464–5 5
Kornati National Park 12
Mljet pp462–3 4
Osijek pp496–7 23
Paklenica National Park 14
Plitvice Lakes National Park pp480–81 15
Pula 18
Rab 16
Rijeka 17
Rovinj 19
Salona pp470–71 7
Split pp466–9 6
Trogir pp476–7 11
Varaždin pp494–5 22
Vis 9
Zadar 13
Zagreb pp486–93 21

Dubrovnik ❶

Located on the Adriatic coast, the city of Dubrovnik is renowned for the beauty of its monuments and its magnificent walls. It was founded by refugees from Roman Epidaurum, now Cavtat *(see p461)*, in the 7th century. Dubrovnik (or island of Ragusa as it was called) came under Byzantine, Venetian and then Hungarian suzerainty, although by the late 14th century, it was a de facto self-governing city-state. In the 15th and 16th centuries, its fleet exceeded 500 ships. Artistically it flourished, and its wealth increased due to its privileged access to the trade routes of the Ottoman Empire. Much of the Old Town centre dates from the rebuilding that took place after the earthquake of 1667. A UNESCO World Heritage Site, Dubrovnik has been restored to its former glory after the seige in the 1990s by Serb and Montenegrin forces.

The Big Fountain of Onofrio, dating from 1438–44

A superb view from the impressive city walls

🚾 Walls

Access to the walls near the Franciscan Monastery in Poljana Paška Miličevića, the large square behind Pile Gate. 🗓 *(020) 324 641.*
◯ *summer: 9am–7pm daily; winter: 10am–3pm.* 🖼

A symbol of Dubrovnik, the walls (Gradske Zidine) offer splendid views from their parapets. They were built in the 10th century, with modifications completed in the 13th century, and then reinforced over the years by architects such as Michelozzo Michelozzi (1396–1472), Juraj Dalmatinac (c. 1400–73) and Antonio Ferramolino (c. 1490–1550).

The walls and ramparts are 1,940 m (6,363 ft) long and reach a height of 25 m (82 ft) in some parts. Those facing inland are up to 6 m (20 ft) wide and strengthened by an outer wall with ten semi-circular bastions. Other towers and the Fort of St John defend the section facing the Adriatic Sea and the Old Port. Completing the

defences to the east and west of the city are two fortresses, the Revelin and the Lovrijenac.

🚾 Pile Gate

The main entrance to the old fortified centre is through the imposing Pile Gate (Gradska Vrata Pile). The stone bridge leading to the gate dates from 1537, and

Pile Gate, leading to the Old Town

crosses a moat which is now a garden. The gate is a strong defensive structure built on different levels. Above the ogival arch stands a statue of St Blaise, the patron saint of Dubrovnik, by Ivan Meštrović *(see p491).* Between the inner and outer walls is a Gothic portal.

🚾 Big Fountain of Onofrio

In the square which opens out immediately beyond the Pile Gate is the Big Fountain of Onofrio (Velika Onofrijeva Fontana), one of the best-known monuments in the city. It was built between 1438 and 1444 by the Neapolitan architect, Onofrio della Cava, who was responsible for designing the city's water supply system. He decided to draw water from the Dubrovačka river for this purpose. The fountain once had two storeys, but the upper level was destroyed in the earthquake of 1667, which killed thousands of people and destroyed countless buildings. Tucked between the city walls and the Franciscan Monastery, opposite the fountain, is the **Church of St Saviour** (sv Spas), built after an earlier earthquake of 1520. Its façade is an example of Venetian-Dalmatian Renaissance architecture.

⛪ Franciscan Monastery

Stradun 2. **Tel** (020) 321 410.
◯ summer: 9am–6pm daily; winter:
by appointment. **Franciscan
Museum** ◯ Apr–Oct: 9am–6pm
daily; Nov–Mar: 9am–5pm. 🌀
Construction of the Franciscan
Monastery (Franjevački
Samostan) began in 1317 and
was completed in the following century. It was almost
entirely rebuilt after the
earthquake in 1667. However,
the Venetian Gothic south
door, dating from 1499, along
with a 15th-century marble
pulpit and the cloister,
escaped undamaged.

One side of the cloister
leads to the Pharmacy (Stara
Ljekarna), in use since 1317,
lined with shelves of alembics,
measuring apparatus and jars.
The capitular room of the
monastery is home to the
Franciscan Museum (Muzej
Franjevačkog Samostana), with
religious art, pharmaceutical
instruments and a library.

**Stradun, the busy main street
of Dubrovnik**

🚋 Stradun

The wide street that crosses
the city from east to west
between two city gates is
known as Stradun or Placa.
It was constructed in the 12th
century by filling in the marshy
channel which separated the
island of Ragusa from the
mainland. The street was

VISITORS' CHECKLIST

600 km (375 miles) SE of Zagreb.
🏙 30,000. ✈ 20 km (12 miles)
NE of centre. 🚌 Obala Pape
Ivana Pavla 11. 🚆 Svetog
Dominika. 🛈 Local: Cvijete
Zuzorić 1, (020) 324 999;
Regional: (020) 324 999.
🎭 Festival of Dubrovnik (Jul–
Aug). **www**.tzdubrovnik.hr

paved in 1468 and stone
houses were built after the
earthquake of 1667. Today, its
lively shops and cafés are popular with locals and visitors.

🚋 Minčeta Tower

The most visited of the
walls' defensive structures,
this tower (Tvrđava Minčeta)
was designed by Michelozzo
Michelozzi in 1461 and completed by Juraj Dalmatinac in
1464. The semi-circular tower
is crowned by a second tower
with embrasures at the top.

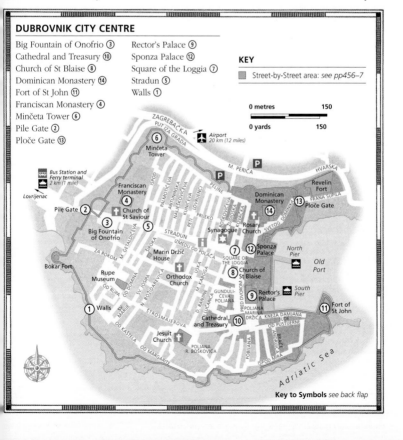

DUBROVNIK CITY CENTRE

Big Fountain of Onofrio ③
Cathedral and Treasury ⑩
Church of St Blaise ⑧
Dominican Monastery ⑭
Fort of St John ⑪
Franciscan Monastery ④
Minčeta Tower ⑥
Pile Gate ②
Ploče Gate ⑬

Rector's Palace ⑨
Sponza Palace ⑫
Square of the Loggia ⑦
Stradun ⑤
Walls ①

KEY

▨ Street-by-Street area: see pp456–7

0 metres   150
0 yards   150

Street-by-Street: Old Town

In 1991, the peaceful city of Dubrovnik was the target of heavy shelling by Serb and Montenegrin troops. This period saw some of the most significant symbols of Dalmatian culture badly damaged. The war also sent the city's economy, especially tourism, into decline. Only after the Erdut Agreement of 1995 did life begin

Ornate knocker on the door of the Rector's Palace

to return to normal. UNESCO and the European Union set up a special commission for the reconstruction of the city and the damage was repaired in a remarkably short period of time. Dubrovnik has now regained much of its former splendour and tourism is flourishing once again. Besides its magnificent walls, the city has several churches, monasteries and museums that throw light on an eventful history.

★ **Rector's Palace**
Considered the political centre of the city, this originally served as the rector's residence and now houses the city's history museum.

★ **Cathedral Treasury**
The provenance of the objects here demonstrates Dubrovnik's trading relations with the principal cities of the Mediterranean. With artifacts from the Byzantine, Middle Eastern, Apulian and Venetian schools, it features gold and enamel objects as well as paintings by great artists.

LUČARICA GUNDULIĆEVA POLJANA

PRED DVORO

POLJANA MARINA DRŽIĆA

KNEZA DAMJANA JUD

KEY

– – – Suggested route

View of Dubrovnik
Spectacular views of the entire city can be seen from the beautiful coast about 2 km (1 mile) to the south, where there is a car park.

The Church of St Blaise, originally a 16th-century church, was redesigned in the 18th century by Marino Groppelli.

Sponza Palace
Built in the 16th century, this palace features Renaissance arches and Venetian Gothic windows. A Latin inscription in the courtyard refers to the public scales that once stood here. Today, it houses the State Archives.

★ Dominican Monastery
Since its foundation in 1315, the monastery has played a leading role in the cultural activities of the city. Important sculptors and architects played a part in its construction.

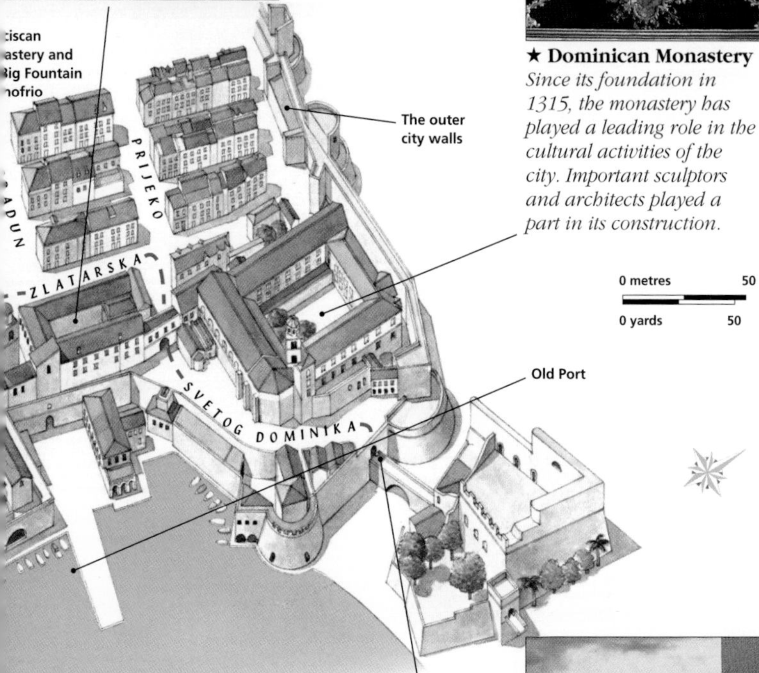

ciscan
astery and
Big Fountain
nofrio

The outer
city walls

PRIJEKO

ADUN

ZLATARSKA

SVETOG DOMINIKA

Old Port

0 metres	50
0 yards	50

Ploče Gate
Next to the Dominican Monastery is the Ploče Gate, which leads to the suburb of Ploče. From there goods arrived from, and were sent to, every port in the Mediterranean.

Fort of St John
This imposing fortress was one of many bulwarks built to make the city impregnable. It now houses an interesting museum devoted to the city's maritime past.

STAR SIGHTS

★ Rector's Palace

★ Cathedral Treasury

★ Dominican Monastery

🏛 Square of the Loggia
Luža.

The political and economic heart of Dubrovnik, the Square of the Loggia is situated at the eastern end of Stradun and surrounded by important buildings.

On the eastern side of the square is a delightful Clock Tower (Gradski Zvonik), which was restored in 1929. The nearby **Loggia of the Bell**, with four bells, dates from 1463. The bells were rung to alert the citizens whenever danger threatened. Next to this stands the Main Guard House, rebuilt in 1706, after the earthquake of 1667. It has a large Baroque doorway and, on the first floor, Gothic mullioned windows, reminiscent of the earlier building constructed on this site in the late 15th century.

Today, the square is a popular meeting place, particularly around Orlando's Column, which was built by Croatian sculptor Antonio Ragusino in 1418.

🔒 Church of St Blaise
Luža. **Tel** *(020) 323 887.*
🕐 *8am–noon & 4:30–7pm daily.*
The pretty Church of St Blaise (Crkva sv Vlaha) was rebuilt at the beginning of the 18th century according to a 17th-century design and contains many Baroque works of art.

On the main altar stands a 15th-century statue of St Blaise, the patron saint of Dubrovnik. It depicts the saint holding a model of the city in the Middle Ages.

The 18th-century Baroque façade of the Church of St Blaise

Rector's Palace, the administrative centre of Dubrovnik

🏛 Rector's Palace
Pred Dvorom 1. **Tel** *(020) 323 904.*
🕐 *summer: 9am–6pm daily;*
winter: 9am–2pm daily. 📷
For centuries, the Rector's Palace (Knežev Dvor) was the political and administrative centre of Ragusa *(see p454)*. It housed the Upper Council, as well as the rector's quarters and rooms for diplomatic meetings and audiences. The official building, including the arches and loggias in the internal courtyard, was designed by Onofrio della Cava in 1435. The portico, by Petar Martinov from Milan, was added in 1465. The Gothic works are by the 15th-century architect and sculptor Juraj Dalmatinac. Concerts are held in the courtyard during the Festival of Dubrovnik.

The rooms of the palace house the interesting **Museum of Dubrovnik** (Dubrovački Muzej), which offers an overview of the city's history through furniture, costumes and paintings by Venetian and Dalmatian artists. It also houses the famous "Dubrovnik arm", a unit of measurement, and coins from 1305 to 1803.

Over 15,000 works are on display, documenting major periods of artistic and commercial vitality in the city. There are numerous uniforms, once worn by the governors and nobles. Also of interest are the portraits of illustrious personalities who were born or lived in Dubrovnik, whose histories are narrated through commemorative medals and heraldic coats of arms.

Among the paintings are the 16th-century *Venus and Adonis* by Paris Bordon and *Baptism of Christ* (1509) by Mihajlo

Hamzić. Next door is the Neo-Renaissance **Town Hall** (Općina), designed and built by Emilio Vecchietti in 1863. It is also home to Gradska Kavana, a charming café, and the prestigious Civic Theatre.

Impressive dome of Dubrovnik's Baroque Cathedral

🔒 Cathedral and Treasury
Kneza Damjana Jude 1.
🕐 *Apr–Oct: 8am–5pm Mon–Sat, 11am–5pm Sun; Nov–Mar: 8am–noon & 3–5pm Mon–Sat, 11am–noon, 3–5pm Sun.*
Cathedral Treasury Tel *(020) 323 459.* 📷
The elegant Cathedral (Velika Gospa) was built after the earthquake of 1667, following designs by Italian architects Andrea Buffalini and Paolo Andreotti. Inside, there are three aisles enclosed by three apses. Paintings by Italian and Dalmatian artists from the 16th and 18th centuries

decorate the side altars, while the *Assumption* (c. 1513) by Titian dominates the main altar. Alongside the church is the Cathedral Treasury (Riznica Katedrale), famous for its collection of about 200 reliquaries. It includes the arm of St Blaise, which dates from the 13th century, and the Holy Cross, which contains a fragment of the cross on which Jesus is said to have been crucified. The tondo *Virgin of the Chair* (c. 1513) is thought to have been painted by Raphael and is a copy of the masterpiece which is now in Florence.

The treasury also has an extraordinary collection of sacred objects in gold, including a pitcher and basin with decoration showing the flora and fauna of Dubrovnik.

⚓ Fort of St John

Maritime Museum *Tel* (020) 323 904. ⬭ Apr–Oct: 9am–6pm Tue–Sun; Nov–Mar: 9am–4pm Tue–Sun. 🖼 **Aquarium** *Tel* (020) 323 978. ⬭ Jun–Sep: 9am–7pm daily; Oct–May: 9am–6pm Mon–Sat. 🖼

The imposing Fort of St John (Tvrđa sv Ivana) was once the city harbour's main defence, a part of a chain that stretched from here to the Tower of St Luke (Kula sv Luke), along the walls.

The upper areas of the fort house the **Maritime Museum** (Pomorski muzej), where the seafaring history of the city is told through displays of

Sponza Palace and Clock Tower

model ships, prints, diaries and portraits. On the lower level is an **Aquarium** (Akvarij) with an assortment of Mediterranean marine life, including sea horses. At the top is the circular Bokar Fort (Tvrđava Bokar), built by Michelozzo Michelozzi.

⛪ Sponza Palace

Tel (020) 321 032. ⬭ 8am–3:30pm Mon–Fri, 8am–2pm Sat.

To the left of the Square of the Loggia stands the splendid Sponza Palace (Palača Sponza), remodelled between 1516 and 1522. It has an elegantly sculpted Renaissance loggia on the ground floor, a Venetian Gothic three-mullioned window on the first floor – evidence of its 14th-century origins – and a statue of St Blaise on the upper floor. Once the city's

custom house, it was the Mint in the 14th century and now houses the State Archives.

⛪ Ploče Gate

Luža.

To the northeast of the Sponza Palace is the Ploče Gate (Vrata Od Ploča), which faces a small port and is preceded by the polygonal Asimov Tower. Dating from the 1300s, the gate is a complex structure with a double defence system, reached by a stone bridge. A moat separates it from the **Revelin Fort** (Tvrđava Revelin). Designed in 1538 by Antonio Ferramolino, the fort was the last of the defences to be built. Based on a pentagonal ground-plan, it has walls enclosing three large rooms and a terrace. Such was its strength that the city's art treasures were brought here for safe keeping during times of trouble.

Dubrovnik's tiled roofs as seen from Ploče Gate

Church of St Dominic, in the Dominican Monastery

🔒 Dominican Monastery

sv Dominika 4. *Tel (020) 321 423.*
⬜ *May–Oct: 9am–6pm daily;*
Nov–Apr: 9am–5pm daily. 🎟

Located in the eastern part of Dubrovnik, near the Ploče Gate, the Dominican Monastery (Dominikanski Samostan) was first built in 1315, but it soon became clear that because of the size of the complex, the city walls would have to be enlarged. The monastery was later rebuilt after the earthquake of 1667.

A long flight of steps with a stone balustrade leads up to the church. The elaborate door, by Bonino of Milan, is decorated with a Romanesque statue of St Dominic. The interior has a wide single nave; hanging from the central arch is a splendid gilded panel – *Crucifix and Symbols of the Evangelists* – by 14th-century painter Paolo Veneziano.

The various rooms of the monastery, arranged around a superb 15th-century Gothic Renaissance cloister by sculptor Maso di Bartolomeo, house the **Dominican Museum** (muzej Dominikanskog Samostana). It contains an extraordinary collection of works of art from the Dubrovnik school, including a beautiful triptych and an Annunciation by Niccolò Ragusino, from the 16th century. There

are also works of art from the Venetian school, including *St Blaise*, *St Mary Magdalene*, and *the Angel Tobias and the Purchaser* by Titian, as well as precious reliquaries and objects in gold and silver.

Environs
The serene island of **Lokrum**, 700 m (2,296 ft) across the water from Dubrovnik, is a nature reserve set up to protect the exotic plants found there. Its scenic beauty makes it a popular tourist destination.

The first inhabitants of the island were the Benedictines, who founded an abbey here in 1023. This was rebuilt in the 14th century but destroyed by the 1667

Statue of Neptune overlooking the pond in Trsteno's arboretum

earthquake. In 1859, the Habsburg Archduke Maximilian (1832–67) built a palace here and renovated the cloister, which later became the Natural History Museum. The fort, built by the French in 1808, provides sweep-ing views of the island.

In **Trsteno**, 20 km (12 miles) northwest of Dubrovnik, is an arboretum. Begun in 1502, it is in a park surround-ing a villa built by a noble, Ivan Gučetić (1451–1502), and has the typical layout of a Renaissance garden, with grottoes and ruins. In the middle of the park is an attractive lily pond, filled with fish and over-looked by an impressive statue of the god Neptune. Above the park beside the main road are two huge plane trees, thought to be over 400 years old.

Elaphite Isles ❷

3 km (2 miles) N of Dubrovnik.
🚶 *2,000.* 🚌 ⛴ *from Dubrovnik*
ℹ *(020) 324 222.*

The beautiful Elaphite Isles (Elafitski Otoci) were named after the fallow deer said to roam here by the natural historian Pliny the Elder (AD 23–79). The islands became a part of the Dubrovnik Republic in the 14th century. Only three of them are inhabited – **Šipan**, **Lopud** and **Koločep** – while Jakljan is devoted to farming. The islands are characterized by woods of maritime pines and cypresses, beautiful beaches and bays frequented by pleasure boats. They have long been popular with the aristocracy of Dubrovnik, who built villas here. Many of the churches date from the pre-Romanesque per-iod, although few remain intact. Some islands had monasteries, which were suppressed with the arrival of French troops in 1808.

The island nearest to Dubrovnik, Koločep, has been a popular summer retreat since the 16th century. A large part of

Aerial view of Šipan, the largest of the Elaphite Isles

the island is covered in subtropical undergrowth and maritime pines. The churches of St Anthony and St Nicholas have pre-Romanesque origins, while the Parish Church dates from the 15th century.

Lopud, covering 4.6 sq km (1.7 sq miles), has a fertile valley sheltered from the cold winds by two ranges of hills. Most of the inhabitants live in the village of Lopud, strung around a wide, curving bay. The Franciscan Monastery dates from 1483. The monastery church, St Mary of the Rocks (sv Marija od Špilica), contains several works of art including a polyptych (1520) by Pietro di Giovanni, triptychs by Nikola Božidarević and by Girolamo di Santacroce depicting the Virgin and Child and a carved choir from the 15th century.

In the southeast of the island, **Šunj** draws visitors to its sandy beach, but its church is also worth visiting for many intriguing works of art, including a painting by Venetian artist Palma il Giovane and a polyptych by Matej Junčić.

The largest of the Elaphite Isles, Šipan, covering 15 sq km (6 sq miles), has just two settlements, Šipanska Luka and Sudurad. Šipanska Luka has the pre-Romanesque Church of St Michael and the ruins of a Benedictine monastery, while the village of Sudurad has the ruins of a bishop's palace and a castle.

Cavtat ❸

20 km (12 miles) S of Dubrovnik
🏘 1,900. 🚌 from Dubrovnik.
🚢 🛈 Tiha 3, (020) 479 025.
📅 Summer in Cavtat, Gospa od Cavtata (5 Aug).
www.tzcavtat-konavle.hr

The pretty coastal town of Cavtat is the Croatian name for Civitas Vetus, the site of the ancient Roman town of Epidaurum, destroyed in the 7th century by the Avars. Occasional excavations have revealed the remains of a theatre, several tombs and also parts of a road. The present-day village attracts visitors for the beauty of the area, its beaches, luxuriant vegetation and interesting

monuments. Much of Cavtat's charm is encapsulated in the Old Town located behind the waterfront. The 16th-century Count's Palace houses the impressive Baltazar Bogišić collection. It was assembled and donated by Bogišić (1834–1908), a cultural activist and jurist of the 19th century who spent a lifetime promoting literature and learning. Several books from Bogišić's collection are displayed here. The works of well-known painter Vlaho Bukovac (1855–1922) are also displayed inside the palace, including his depiction of the local carnival celebrations in 1901.

At the end of the seafront stand the Church of St Blaise (sv Vlaho) and a Franciscan monastery, both dating from the end of the 15th century. On the hilltop is the **Račić Mausoleum**, built by Ivan Meštrović (*see p491*) for a local ship-owning family in 1922. The Byzantine-inspired domed structure is decorated with Greek angels and ornate gargoyles. Eagles and Neo-Assyrian winged lambs adorn the elaborate cupola.

A pair of fine shingle and sandy beaches lie about 1 km (0.6 miles) east of the town centre in an area known as Žal, literally meaning "beach". Visitors throng the beaches in spring and summer.

A panoramic view of the seafront and port of Cavtat

Mljet ❹

The island of Mljet, called Melita by the Romans and Meleda by the Venetians, covers an area of 98 sq km (37 sq miles). It is mountainous, with two limestone depressions in which there are two saltwater lakes linked by a channel. In Roman times, Mljet was a holiday resort for the wealthy of Salona (see pp470–71), who built villas here. In 1151, Duke Desa, Grand Prefect of Zahumlje, in Herzegovina, gave the island to the Benedictines of Pulsano in Gargano, Italy, who founded a monastery here. Two centuries later, Stjepan, Governor of Bosnia, gave it to Dubrovnik (see pp454–60). In 1960, the western end, which covers an area of 31 sq km (12 sq miles) and is entirely forested, was declared a national park.

Roman Palatium
Near Polače lie the ruins of a Roman settlement named Palatium. It includes the remains of a large villa and an early Christian basilica.

Pomena
Govedari
Polače
MLJET NATIONAL PARK
Kozarica
Soline
Blato

Monastery of St Mary
In the centre of Veliko Jezero is a small island with a 12th-century Benedictine monastery, remodelled in the 1500s. It features colourful altarpieces carved from local stone.

Veliko Jezero
Covering about 145 ha (358 acres) Veliko Jezero (Big Lake) reaches a depth of 46 m (150 ft). A channel links the lake to the sea and another links it to a smaller lake, Malo Jezero.

Mljet National Park
The national park was created to save the forest of Aleppo pine and Holm oak. In the 19th century, mongooses were introduced to kill snakes; they still live in the forests.

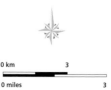

0 km   3
0 miles   3

VISITORS' CHECKLIST

70 km (44 miles) W of Dubrovnik. 1,300. *from Dubrovnik.* **Mljet National Park** *Govedari Pristanište 2, (020) 744 041.*
www.np-mljet.hr
***Note**: The park can be visited on foot or by bicycle following the trails. Boats must be authorized – call information office for details.*

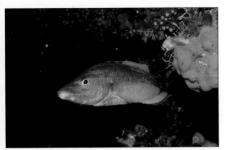

Marine Life
Dozens of species of fish, including grouper, inhabit the underwater ravines and caves along the coast. The endangered monk seal, protected in these waters, is highly valued.

The village of Babino Polje was founded around the middle of the 10th century by a group of refugees from the mainland. The governor's residence was built in 1554, when the island became part of the Republic of Ragusa, now Dubrovnik.

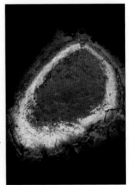

Uninhabited Islands
Nature is left undisturbed on these islands, with woods of pine, Holm oak and oak stretching down to the rocky shore.

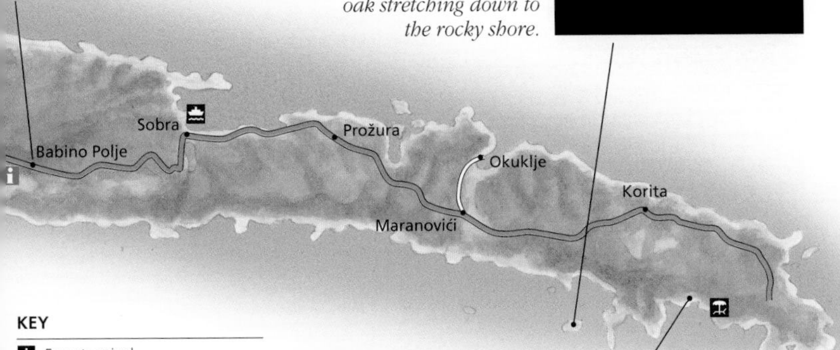

Sobra
Babino Polje
Prožura
Okuklje
Korita
Maranovići

KEY

- Ferry terminal
- Visitor information
- Beach with facilities
- Major road
- Minor road
- Park boundary

Saplunara lies at the southernmost tip of the island. It boasts the most beautiful beach in the area and has been declared a nature reserve for its greenery and lush vegetation.

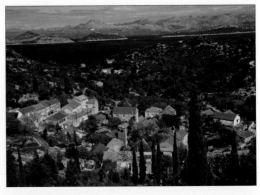

Fishing Villages
The island's ancient stone villages are inhabited mainly by farmers and fishermen. Along with the delightful bays and surrounding coves, these villages are lovely places to visit and spend time.

Korčula ❺

At a length of 47 km (29 miles), Korčula is one of the largest islands in the Adriatic Sea. Mountains run the length of the island, reaching an altitude of 560 m (1,837 ft) at their peak, and dense forests of Aleppo pine, cypress and oak are found all over. Inhabited since prehistoric times, the island was named Korkyra Melaina by the Greeks. After AD 1000, it was fought over by Venice and the Croat

Gothic relief in All Saints' Church

kings, and later by the Genoese and the Ottoman Turks. In the 1298 naval battle between Genoa and Venice, the Genoese captured Marco Polo said to be a native of the island. Today, Korčula is a popular holiday spot for its beaches, scenic villages and the eponymous town.

Land Gate, the main entrance to Korčula's Old Town

Korčula Town

This enchanting town is perched on a peninsula and surrounded by strong 13th-century walls, which were reinforced with towers and bastions by the Venetians after 1420. The **Land Gate** (Kopnena Vrata), the main entrance to the Old Town, was fortified by a huge tower, which overlooked a canal dug by the Venetians

to isolate the town. Narrow streets branching off the main road were designed to lessen the impact of the strong Bora wind common in this area.

Facing the central square, Strossmayerov Square, is the 13th-century **Cathedral of St Mark** (Katedrala sv Marka), built in pale, honey-coloured stone. The skill of Korčula's sculptors and stone masons is evident in its ornate door.

On the left stands an imposing bell tower, while inside the church are large columns with elaborately decorated capitals and several important sculptures, including the tomb of Bishop Toma Malumbra. The paintings include Venetian artist Tintoretto's impressive *St Mark with St Jerome and St Bartholomew* (1550). On a wall are trophies recalling the Battle of Lepanto of 1571.

Next to the cathedral, in the Bishop's Palace, now the Abbot's House, is the **Abbey Treasury** (Opatska Riznica). It is particularly known for its Dalmatian and Venetian art, including a polyptych by Blaž of Trogir, two altar paintings by Pellegrino of San Daniele, a Sacred Conversation and an Annunciation by Titian and *Portrait of a Man* by Vittore Carpaccio. To the left of the cathedral, a door by Bonino of Milan decorates the Gothic Church of St Peter (sv Petar). Facing the church are the Gothic Arneri Palace and the 16th-century Renaissance Gabriellis Palace. The latter has been the **Civic Museum** (Gradski muzej) since 1957 and contains documents on Korčula's seafaring history, an interesting archaeological section covering the period from prehistoric to Roman times and other works of art.

Along the seafront is the All Saints' Church (Svi Sveti), built in 1301 and remodelled in the Baroque style; it belongs to the oldest brotherhood on the island. Inside is an 18th-century wooden *Pietà* by the Austrian artist George Raphael Donner, and a 15th-century polyptych by Blaž of Trogir. In the nearby quarters of the brotherhood

KEY

Proizd

📧 Ferry terminal

ℹ️ Visitor information

🏖️ Beach with facilities

▬▬ Major road

══ Minor road

--- Ferry route

Hvar
41 km (25 miles)

Vela Luka

Prigradica

Potirna

Blato

Prižba

Brna

The beautiful rocky coastline of Korčula

is the **Icon Gallery** (Galerija Ikona), famous for its collection of Byzantine icons from the 13th to the 15th centuries. Outside the walls are the Church and Monastery of St Nicholas (sv Nikola), from the 15th century, with paintings by Italian artists.

🏛 Abbey Treasury
trg sv Marka. 🛈 (020) 715 701. ⏲ call for information. 🈺

🏛 Civic Museum
trg sv Marka. **Tel** (020) 711 420. ⏲ Jun–Sep: 10am–9pm Mon–Sat; Oct–May: 10am–2pm Mon–Sat, by appointment on Sun.

🏛 Icon Gallery
trg Svih Svetih. 🛈 (020) 711 306, (091) 593 1281. ⏲ summer: 10am–2pm & 5–8pm Mon–Sat; Winter & Sun: by appointment.

Lumbarda
Thought to have been founded by Greeks, the village of Lumbarda lies 6 km (4 miles) southeast of Korčula town. In the 16th century, it became a holiday resort for the nobles of Korčula. Some inscriptions

from the Greek period are now kept in the Archaeological Museum of Zagreb (see p493). Today, the village is one of the centres of production for Grk, a liqueur-like, white wine made from grapes of the same name. The nearby beaches are famous for their golden sands.

Blato
The central square of the village of Blato, towards the western end of the island, has an 18th-century Baroque loggia, the **Arneri Castle**, where the Civic Museum documenting local history is being developed, and **All Saints' Church** (Svi Sveti), of medieval origin. Enlarged and rebuilt in the 17th century, the church has an altarpiece of the *Virgin with Child and Saints* (1540) on the main altar by Girolamo di Santacroce and, in the chapel, the relics of the local focus of veneration, the martyr St Vincenza. The cemetery church of the Holy Cross and that of St Jerome date from

the 14th century. Every April, the central square plays host to the folk festival of the Kumpanija, dedicated to the patron saint, St Vincenza, which is celebrated with songs and music.

Vela Luka
Situated about 45 km (28 miles) west of Korčula town is Vela Luka, known as "the oldest and the newest town", because it was built at the beginning of the 19th century on the Neolithic site of Vela Spilja. One of the largest towns on the island, it has a number of industries that coexist with attractive bays and islands. The surrounding hills shelter the town from the winds from the north and south. Vela Luka is also the main port on the island and there are regular ferry services to Split (see pp466–9).

Town of Korčula, on a peninsula on the northeast coast of the island

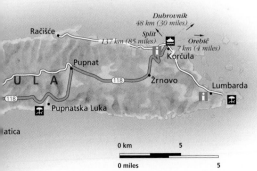

Račišće — Dubrovnik 48 km (30 miles) / Split 137 km (85 miles) — Orebić 7 km (4 miles) — Korčula — Pupnat — 118 — Žrnovo — Lumbarda — ULA — 118 — Pupnatska Luka — atica

0 km 5
0 miles 5

Split ⑥

Detail of Papalić Palace

Built on the remains of an imperial Roman palace, Split is a fascinating and vibrant Mediterranean city, featuring palm-lined avenues and bustling pavement cafés. At its heart is the Palace of Diocletian, a 3rd-century structure that was abandoned by the Romans before being settled by sanctuary-seeking locals. Adapted to the needs of a growing city, the palace area is nowadays a labyrinth of atmospheric alleyways with exciting architectural discoveries at every corner. During the Middle Ages, a steadily growing Slav population turned Split into a centre of Croatian language and culture. Almost four centuries of Venetian rule (1409–1797) filled the city with Italianate art and architecture. During the 20th century, Split became the biggest ferry terminal on the Adriatic, and remains the main gateway to Croatia's seductively beautiful islands.

View of the port and the seafront in Split

🏛 Palace of Diocletian
See pp468–9.

🏛 Braće Radića Square
This medieval square (trg Braće Radić) is on the south-west corner of the Palace of Diocletian. The tall **Hrvoje's Tower** (Hrvojeva Kula) is the only evidence of the imposing castle built here by the Venetians in the second half of the 15th century to strengthen the city's sea-facing defences. Built on an octagonal groundplan, it stands on the southern side of the square.

On the northern side of the square is the Baroque **Milesi Palace**, from the 17th century, and at its centre is a striking bronze statue dedicated to Marko Marulić (1450–1524), the writer and

scholar who composed the first epic poem in the Croatian language. His statue, by sculptor Ivan Meštrović, is inscribed with verses by another famous Croatian poet, Tin Ujević.

The 15th-century Hrvoje's Tower on Braće Radića Square

🏛 People's Square
The busy People's Square (Narodni trg/Pjaca) was Split's centre of business and administration during the 15th century, and the nobility erected prestigious buildings here. Examples include the Venetian Gothic Cambi Palace and the Renaissance **Town Hall** (Vijećnica), built in the first half of the 15th century, which has a loggia with three arches on the ground floor and a Gothic window on the upper floor.

🔒 Church of St Francis
trg Republike. 🛈 *(021) 348 600.*
⬜ *by appt.*
The pretty Church of St Francis (sv Frane) has been rebuilt in recent times, but the Romanesque-Gothic cloister, with thin columns enclosing a flower garden, is original.

The church, with mainly Baroque furnishings, has a 15th-century crucifix by Blaž Jurjev Trogiranin (c. 1412–48). It also houses the tombs of the city's illustrious citizens, including that of Archdeacon Toma, the first Dalmatian historian, writer Marko Marulić and the well-known composer Ivan Lukačić.

🏛 Museum of Croatian Archaeological Monuments
Šetalište Ivana Meštrovića 18.
Tel *(021) 358 420.* ⬜ *Jul–Sep: 9am–1pm & 5–9pm Mon–Fri, 9am–2pm Sat; Oct–Jun: 9am–4pm Mon–Fri, 9am–2pm Sat.* 🖼
www.mhas-split.hr
Set up in 1975, this museum (muzej Hrvatskih Arheoloških Spomenika) houses finds from the area around Split dating from the early Middle Ages. The collection also includes the works of early Croat sculptors, from AD 800. The stone fragments, salvaged from castles and churches, consist mainly of tombs, capitals, altar fronts, ciboria and windows. Highlights include Prince Višeslav's 9th-century hexagonal baptismal font and the striking 10th-century sarcophagus of Queen Jelena discovered in Solin, near the ancient Roman city of Salona *(see pp470–71).*

preserves the artist's apartments. Further down the road is the **Kaštelet**, a 17th-century residence that belonged to the Capogrosso-Kavanjin family and was bought by Meštrović in 1932 to set up an exhibition hall. It can be visited with the same ticket. He also built a church here to exhibit a series of reliefs.

🏛 Archaeological Museum

Zrinsko Frankopanska 25.
Tel *(021) 329 340.* ⬜ *May–Sep: 8am–2pm & 4pm–8pm Mon–Sat; Oct–Apr: 8am–2pm & 4pm–8pm Mon–Fri, 8am–2pm Sat.* 🖼 ⬜ ♿
Considered Croatia's oldest museum, the Archaeological Museum (Arheološki muzej) was founded in 1820 and moved to its present location in 1914. It contains a fine collection of finds from the Roman, early Christian and medieval periods that are exhibited in rotation. Of particular interest are the finds from the ruins of Salona including sculptures, capitals, sarcophagi, jewellery, coins and small objects in glazed terracotta and ceramic.

Distant Chords *(1918) by Ivan Meštrović, Meštrović Gallery*

🏛 Meštrović Gallery

Šetalište Ivana Meštrovića 46.
Tel *(021) 340 800.* ⬜ *May–Sep: 9am–7pm Tue–Sun; Oct–Apr: 9am–4pm Tue–Sat, 10am–3pm Sun.* 🖼
Regarded as one of the most important sculptors of the 20th century, Ivan Meštrović *(see p491)* himself designed the Meštrović Gallery (Galerija Meštrović) building, which was his residence in the early 1930s. His sculptures decorate the garden and the interior and part of the building still

VISITORS' CHECKLIST

210 km (131 miles) NW of Dubrovnik. 🏠 220,000. ✈ 20 km (12 miles) N of centre. 🚌 Obala kneza Domagoja. 🚍 Obala kneza Domagoja. ⛴ Jadrolinija. 🛈 trg Republike 2, (021) 345 606. 🎉 St Domnius Feast (7 May), Summer Festival (Jul–Aug), Festival of New Film and Video (Sep–Oct).
www.visitsplit.com

🏞 Marjan Peninsula

Rising to the west of central Split is the Marjan Peninsula, a hilly, densely wooded area crisscrossed by attractive footpaths. The best way to reach Marjan is to walk through the Varos district immediately west of the Old Town, taking a flight of steps which gradually ascends Marjan's flanks. Near the top, fine views of Split's port, along with the islands of Brač *(see p472)* and Hvar *(see pp474–5)* to the south are clearly visible. Near the summit of Marjan is a small zoo. Paths along the southern edge of the peninsula lead past a sequence of medieval chapels.

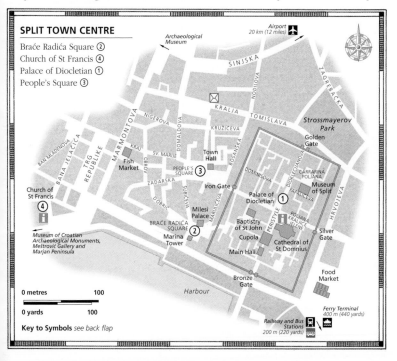

SPLIT TOWN CENTRE

Braće Radića Square ②
Church of St Francis ④
Palace of Diocletian ①
People's Square ③

Archaeological Museum

Airport
20 km (12 miles) ✈

SINJSKA

ZAGREBAČKA

KRALJA

NODILOVA

TOMISLAVA

Strossmayerov Park

NIGEROVA

KRUŽIĆEVA

MARMONTOVA

DOMALDOVA

BOSANKA

Golden Gate

BAN MLADENOVA

TRG REPUBLIKE

BANA JELAČIĆA

KRAJ

SV. MARIJE

OBROV

Fish Market

Town Hall

PEOPLE'S SQUARE ③

DOMINISOVA

DIOKLECIJANOVA

CARRARINA POLJANA

Museum of Split

Church of St Francis ④

ZADARSKA

DOBRIC

SUBIĆEVA

Iron Gate

MARULIĆEVA

Palace of Diocletian ①

PERISTYLE

PAPALIĆEVA

POLJANA KRALJICE JELENE

HRVOJEVA

Silver Gate

Milesi Palace

BRAĆE RADIĆA SQUARE ②

Baptistry of St John

Cathedral of St Domnius

Museum of Croatian Archaeological Monuments, Meštrović Gallery and Marjan Peninsula

Marina Tower

Cupola

Main Hall

Bronze Gate

Food Market

0 metres 100
0 yards 100

Harbour

Ferry Terminal
400 m (440 yards)

Railway and Bus Stations
200 m (220 yards)

Key to Symbols *see back flap*

Split: Palace of Diocletian
Dioklecijanova palača

Split's main attraction is the Old Town centre, a fantastic
architectural jumble built on what remains of the once-
magnificent Palace of Diocletian, now a World Heritage
Site. Believed to be a native of Salona, Diocletian became
emperor of Rome in 284. After governing for 20 years, he
retired from public life and in 305 moved into the palace
in the bay of Split. The corners of the palace were marked
by four square towers. Four further towers were set along
each of the north, east and south sides, while the side
facing the sea had a loggia with arches. After Diocletian's
death, the palace was used as an administrative centre
and also housed the governor's residence. In 615, refugees from Salona found shelter here after the destruction
of their city by the Avars.

**Iron Gate and the
Clock Tower**
*The best preserved gate
leads to the Church of Our
Lady of the Belfry, with a
12th-century bell tower
next to it.*

★ Temple of Jupiter
*Consecrated in the 6th century,
the Temple of Jupiter had an
atrium with six columns, while
the main building had a coffered
vault resting on a crypt. In the
early Middle Ages, it was
turned into the Baptistry
of St John.*

Temple of Cybele

**The Temples of
Venus and Cybele**
were circular
outside and
had a hexagonal
ground plan
inside. A colon-
naded corridor
ran around
the outside.

Bronze Gate

★ Peristyle
*Near the crossroads where the Cardo and
Decumanus intersected, the peristyle gave
access to the sacred area of the palace. On
one side were the temples of Venus and
Cybele and, further back, that of Jupiter,
now the Baptistry of St John.*

STAR FEATURES

★ Temple of Jupiter

★ Peristyle

★ Cathedral of
St Domnius

Golden Gate
The main entrance to the palace, the Golden Gate, facing Salona (see pp470–71), was the most imposing of the gates, with twin towers and numerous decorations.

(see pp470–71)

Diocletian's Emblem
After reorganizing the empire, Emperor Diocletian sought the spiritual unification of its citizens. The state religion, personified by the emperor, grew steadily in importance and temples were constructed bearing his image.

The Cardo was the main street of the complex.

The Silver or Eastern Gate was a simpler version of the Golden Gate.

RECONSTRUCTION OF DIOCLETIAN'S PALACE

The spectacular palace, shown here in its original form, was laid out in the same way as a Roman military camp. It was 215-m (705-ft) long and 180-m (590-ft) wide and was enclosed by very thick walls, at times 28-m (92-ft) high. The four-sided stronghold was reinforced with towers on the north, east and west sides. There is a gate on each side, connected by two roads corresponding to the Roman Cardo and Decumanus.

The Decumanus, a transverse path, divided the complex into two halves.

★ **Cathedral of St Domnius**
Originally Emperor Diocletian's mausoleum, the cathedral was consecrated in the 7th century when the sarcophagus containing the emperor's body was removed. The superb interior features Roman columns and fine Romanesque carvings.

Salona ⓻

Detail of the Tusculum

The ancient town of Salona, 5 km (3 miles) from Split, is famous for its Roman ruins, scattered among meadows, olive groves and vineyards. The name Salona derives from the salt works in the area, the Latin for salt being *sal*. Originally an Illyrian settlement, it later came under Greek control, but only became an important centre when the Romans built a town next to the Greek city. Under the rule of Augustus, it became a Roman colony called Martia Julia Salonae, and in due course was made capital of the Dalmatian province. In the 1st century AD, the Romans built theatres, temples, town walls, towers and an amphitheatre, and Salona became the richest and most populous town in the mid-Adriatic. In 614, it was destroyed by the Avars and Slavs; the buildings were stripped and the stone used for new structures.

Main road leading to Salona

Ruins of the town walls and triangular tower

Exploring Salona

At the end of the 19th century, excavations began to bring to light the buried remains of this ancient settlement. The work revealed that the town had two districts dating from different periods: the original, Old Town (Urbs Vetus) and a later part which dates from the Augustan-era (Urbs Nova Occidentalis and Urbs Nova Orientalis). The excavations have uncovered only a part of the layout of the **Outer Walls**, which were frequently reinforced over the centuries. However, the foundations and the remains of the towers, with triangular or rectangular bases, are still visible.

The tour usually begins from the site closest to the entrance, the **Necropolis of Manastirine**, a burial area just outside the walls, north of the town. In the 4th century, a religious building was constructed here to house the relics of the Salonian saints, victims of Emperor Diocletian's persecution of Christians. The ruins of the necropolis and the basilica are well preserved.

Located near Manastirine is the **Tusculum**, a villa with interesting sculptures embedded in the walls and the garden. It was built for the distinguished archaeologist Frane Bulić (1846–1934) to enable him to study the ruins of Salona. A scholar and director of the Archaeological Museum *(see p467)* in Split, Bulić devoted much of his life to

researching the ancient city. The building is now a small museum, but the most interesting finds are now housed in the Archaeological Museum in Split.

Further on is the richest area of ruins with the foundations of baths, the **Caesarea Gate** and early-Christian basilicas. The **Baths** were built in the 1st century when the town became the capital of the province of Dalmatia. In the early Christian period, the buildings were probably transformed into religious buildings such as those in the **Bishop's Complex** in the northeastern part of ancient Salona. This comprised basilicas, a baptistry and the bishop's residence. Before Christianity became widespread, several early Christian martyrs were slayed here, including St Domnius, (patron saint of Split) and Sts Venantius and Anastasius.

The foundations of two basilicas have been excavated: the Urban Basilica,

Excavated remains of the Necropolis of Manastirine

The Basilica Urbana in the Bishop's Complex

and Honorius's Basilica, which had a Greek cross plan. This is also the site of what remains of the impressive Caesarea Gate, which features arches flanked by two octagonal towers, displaying the advanced building techniques used by the Romans in the imperial era.

Moving west along the walls, visitors reach the **Necropolis of Kapljuč**, another early Christian burial site, and then the imposing ruins of the **Amphitheatre**, in the western most part of the settlement.

The amphitheatre, in brick, was probably covered in stone and stood in the newer part of the town on the northwest edge of the Old Town (Urbs Vetus) close to the walls. According to historians, it could seat 20,000 people. The foundations and a part of the lower tribune have been excavated and the discovery of a network of underground channels has led to the theory that simulated naval battles were held in the arena. The amphitheatre's construction

date was controversial for a long time, but it has now been dated to the second half of the 2nd century AD. From the amphitheatre, another path leads to the **Theatre** at the edge of the Old Town. This was built in the first half of the 1st century AD and part of the stage and the foundations of the stalls have been excavated. Next to the theatre is the **Forum**, the political and commercial heart of the town. Unlike the forum in Zadar (see p478), the paving was dismantled and only the foundations remain. In the Roman era, some of the most important buildings stood around the Forum, which began to be built in the 1st century AD and were subsequently modified.

The best preserved Roman construction of ancient Salona is the aqueduct, built to bring

VISITORS' CHECKLIST

255 km (158 miles) NE of Dubrovnik. *from Split.* (021) 210 048. **Ruins** *summer: 7am–7pm; winter: call to check opening times.* www.solin-info.com

water from the Jadro river to the town, and extended during the reign of Diocletian to reach his palace (see pp468–9) in Split. Repair work was carried out at the end of the 19th century and the southern part of the aqueduct is still in use. Alongside the walls it is possible to see some parts of the aqueduct – more evidence of the great skill of Roman civil engineers.

From the theatre, visitors return to the Necropolis of Manastirine. North of this stands the **Necropolis of Marusinac**, built outside the ancient town around the tomb of St Anastasius.

The Amphitheatre, of which only a part of the lower tribune remains

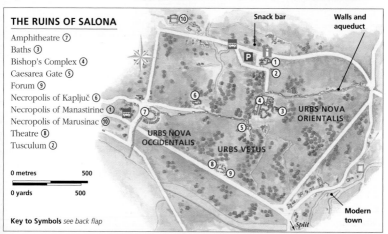

THE RUINS OF SALONA

Amphitheatre ⑦
Baths ③
Bishop's Complex ④
Caesarea Gate ⑤
Forum ⑨
Necropolis of Kapljuč ⑥
Necropolis of Manastirine ①
Necropolis of Marusinac ⑩
Theatre ⑧
Tusculum ②

0 metres   500
0 yards   500

Key to Symbols see back flap

Brač ⑧

175 km (109 miles) NW of Dubrovnik. 🏘 14,000. ✈ 🚌 🚢 to Supetar from Split. **Supetar** 🛈 trg P Jakšića 17, (021) 630 551. **Bol** 🛈 Uz Pjacu 4, (021) 635 638. **www**.bol.hr

The third largest island in the Adriatic, Brač has an interesting geological structure. In some areas, the limestone hills have sinkholes and are cut by deep ravines and gorges. In others a white, hard stone prevails, which has been quarried since ancient times. Extensive woods cover some parts of the island, while other parts are cultivated.

Although Brač has always been inhabited, it was first ruled by Salona (see pp470–71) and the rich Salonians built villas and sought refuge here when their town was attacked by the Avars. It was later ruled by Split (see pp466–9). However, both Split and Brač came under Byzantine and then Venetian rule (1420–1797).

Ferries departing from Split on the mainland dock to the Old Town of **Supetar**, which has some good beaches. **Škrip** is probably the site of the first settlement on the island and the presumed birthplace of Helen, mother of Emperor Constantine, the first Christian Roman emperor. The church and a painting by Palma il Giovane (see p474) on its main altar are dedicated to Helen. A fortified house in Škrip is home to the **Brač Museum**, which displays archaeological finds from the area.

Zlatni Rat, Bol's famous beach which changes with the seasons

To the southwest lies **Milna**, which was founded at the beginning of the 18th century and faces a sheltered bay. The exterior of the Church of the Annunciation of Mary (Gospa od Blagovijesti) is Baroque, with a Rococo interior. In the centre of the island, **Nerežišća** was Brac's main town for a long period. The governor's palace, the loggia and a pedestal with the lion of St Mark are signs of its former status.

The major attraction at **Bol**, on the southern coast, is its famous long beach, Zlatni Rat, meaning Golden Horn – a triangular spit of shingle which reaches out into the sea and changes shape with the seasonal winds. It is a popular spot for windsurfing. A Dominican monastery, founded in 1475, stands on a headland at the edge of the village. The beautiful church here is decorated with paintings, including a *Virgin with Saints*

(1563) attributed to Tintoretto. A rich treasury includes liturgical objects. From Bol, visitors can make the 2-hour climb up the 778-m (2,552-ft) high **Vidova Gora**, one of the highest peaks in the Dalmatian islands, near which a fortified monastery, Samostan Blaca, clings to the rocks. In **Pučišća**, to the northeast, quarrymen can be seen at work and the old Roman quarries can also be visited. Similarly charming is **Sumartin**, further east, which was founded by refugees from the coastal region of Makarska, when they fled the Turks in 1645. There is a fine Franciscan monastery, the foundations

The town of Pučišća on the island of Brač

KEY

🛫 Airport

🚢 Ferry terminal

🛈 Visitor information

🏖 Beach with facilities

▲ Peak

━━ Major road

══ Minor road

--- Ferry route

ŠOLTA — Split 17 km (11 miles) — Maslinica — Grohote — Stomorska (111)

Split 18 km (11 miles) — Supetar — Škrip — Nerežišća — Milna (114) — **BRAČ** — Vidova Gora 778 m (2,552 ft) ▲ — Bol (115) — Pučišća — Povlja — Selca — Sumartin — Makarska 14 km (9 miles) (113)

0 km — 10
0 miles — 10

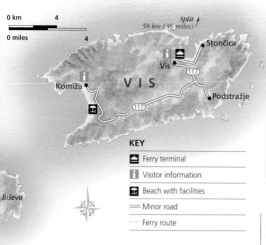

KEY

⛴	Ferry terminal
ℹ	Visitor information
🏖	Beach with facilities
═══	Minor road
- - -	Ferry route

The façade of the Church of Our Lady of Spilica, Vis

of which were laid by the poet Andrija Kačić Miošić (1704–60).

Environs
The long island of **Šolta**, to the northwest of Brač, was a holiday resort for the nobility of Roman Salona. After the attack on Salona in 614, some of the refugees fled and established villages. It was later abandoned in favour of Split and left uninhabited for over a century due to frequent Turkish raids. Traces of defence towers can be seen, as well as the ruins of Roman villas.

🏛 Brač Museum
Škrip. **ℹ** *(021) 646 325.*
☐ *summer: 8am–8pm Mon–Sat; winter: by appt.*

Vis ❾

220 km (137 miles) NW of Dubrovnik. **👥** *4,300.* **⛴** *from Split.*
ℹ *Šetalište Stare Isse 2, (021) 717 017.* **Komiža** **ℹ** *(021) 713 455.*

Further out to sea than the other Dalmatian islands, Vis was a military base until 1989 and closed to tourism. Now gradually being rediscovered by intrepid travellers, it has a jagged coastline with beaches, and an inland mountain chain with Mount Hum reaching a height of 587 m (1,925 ft).

The island was chosen by Dionysios of Syracuse as a base for Greek domination of the Adriatic. The Greeks founded the town of Issa here. The island was later ruled by the Romans, the Byzantines

and, from 1420, the Venetians. Vis played a key role during World War II – in 1944, Marshal Tito used it as a base for partisan military operations.

The main town of **Vis** has Venetian Gothic buildings and the Renaissance church of Our Lady of Spilica (Gospa od Spilica), with a painting by Girolamo di Santacroce (1516–84). In the town of **Komiža**, on the western coast, there is a tower built by the Venetians.

Environs
The island of **Biševo**, to the southwest of Vis, has a Blue Grotto (Modra Spilja), where, at midday, the water takes on beautiful colours. Day-trips by boat depart from Komiža in the mornings. The ruins of a monastery, built around AD 1000, can be seen; it resisted raids by pirates and Saracens for 200 years.

Beautiful coastline near Komiža, on the island of Vis

Hvar ⑩

Art treasures, a mild climate, good beaches and fields of scented lavender make this island one of the gems of the Adriatic. Limestone hills form the central ridge. Hvar's story begins in the 4th century BC when Greeks from Paros founded Pharos and Dimos, present-day towns of Stari Grad and Hvar. Traces have been left by the Romans, the Byzantines, the Croatian sovereigns and the Venetians, who ruled from 1278 until 1797. After 1420, defences were built, and the capital was moved from Pharos to Hvar. In 1886, under Austria-Hungary, the Hvar Hygienic Society began to promote the town as a health resort. Crucially for Croatian literature, Hvar was the native island of Renaissance poets Hannibal Lucić and Petar Hektorović, both of whom wrote lyrically about the people and landscapes of the Adriatic.

Main square of Hvar, with the Cathedral of St Stephen

A peaceful bay on the island of Hvar

Hvar Town

This beautiful town is one of the most visited on the eastern coast of the Adriatic Sea, thanks to the treasures within its 13th-century walls. During Venetian rule, local nobles and governors decided to make the town a safe harbour for the fleets going to, or returning from, the Orient. They also transferred the bishopric and built monasteries there.

Hvar has a long tradition of art and culture. It is home to one of the first theatres ever built in Europe. The town was also the birthplace of the Renaissance poet Hanibal Lucić (c. 1485–1553) and the playwright Martin Benetović (c. 1550–1607).

The town's most important buildings stand on three sides of the main square, the fourth side is open to the sea. The Renaissance **Cathedral of St Stephen** (Katedrala sv Stjepana) has a trefoil pediment and a 17th-century bell tower standing to one side. The interior contains many works of art including *Virgin and Saints* (1627) by Palma il Giovane (1544– 1628), *pietà* (c. 1520) by Juan Boschetus, *Virgin with Saints* (1692) by Domenico Uberti and a fine 16th-century wooden choir.

The Clock Tower, the civic Loggia below and **Hektorović Palace** (Hektorovićeva Palača), recognizable by the beautiful Venetian Gothic mullioned window, all date from the 15th century.

On the south side of the square is the **Arsenal**, which dates from the late 16th century. A theatre was built on the first floor in 1612. This was the first "public theatre" in the Balkans; people of all classes could come and watch performances here, regardless of their social standing.

Outside the walls of the Old Town are the **Franciscan Monastery** (Franjevački Samostan), dating from 1461, and the Church of Our Lady of Charity (Gospa od Milosti), with a relief on the façade by Nikola Firentinac. Inside are *St Francis receiving the Stigmata* and *St Diego* by Palma il Giovane, three polyptychs by Francesco da Santacroce, *Christ on the*

For hotels and restaurants in this region see pp502–505 and pp506–507

Lavender growing wild on the island of Hvar

VISITORS' CHECKLIST

165 km (103 miles) NW of
Dubrovnik. 11,500.
from Split & Jadrolinija.
trg Svetog Stjepana,
021) 741 059. **Stari Grad**
from Split; Jadrolinija.
Nova Riva 2, (021) 765
763. **Sućuraj** from
Drvenik. (021) 717 288.
www.tzhvar.hr

Cross by Leandro da Bassano, and six scenes inspired by the Passion of Christ by Martin Benetović.

There are also many works of art in the rooms facing the cloister. The painter of the *Last Supper* in the refectory is unknown. The 16th-century Španjola fort and early 19th century Napoleon fort both offer splendid views of the town.

The cloister of the Franciscan Monastery, outside Hvar

Stari Grad

This town was originally called Pharos and was founded by the Greeks in the 4th century BC. Remains of the town can be seen in Ciklopska Ulica. Around Pod Dolom are the ruins of a Roman villa with mosaic floors.

Stari Grad lies at the end of a long bay and the key sights are situated around the main square. Facing the square are the 17th-century Church of St Stephen (sv Stjepan) and the

Baroque Biankini Palace (Palača Biankini), the home of an archaeological collection.

The heart of the town is dominated by Kaštel Tvrdalj, the fortified residence of Petar Hektorović (1487–1572), which houses an Ethnographic Collection and has a seawater fishpond. Hektorović, a poet, built the fort in around 1520. He was the author of the poem "Fishing and Fishermen's Conversation" (*Ribanje i ribarsko prigovaranje*) in which he describes a fishing trip around the islands of Hvar, Brač *(see p472)* and Šolta.

The **Dominican Monastery** (Dominikanski Samostan) was founded in 1482. It was rebuilt and fortified after destruction by the Turks and has a rich library and a collection of paintings. The town also has an International School of Painting and Sculpture.

🏛 Dominican Monastery
Tel *(021) 765 442.* ☐ *Jun–Sep: 10am–noon & 4–8pm; Oct–May: by appt.*

Kaštel Tvrdalj, Stari Grad

Vrboska

The road leading to this small village is a marvellous sight in June when the surrounding fields are covered with lavender. Vrboska is home to the 16th-century Church of St Mary (sv Marija), fortified in 1575 to provide shelter for villagers in the event of a siege. The Baroque Church of St Lawrence (sv Lovro) has a polyptych (c. 1570) on the main altar by Paolo Veronese and a *Virgin of the Rosary* by Leandro da Bassano.

Sućuraj

Lying in a sheltered bay at the eastern tip of the island is the village of Sućuraj with the remains of a castle built by the Venetians in around 1630.

Environs

To the west of the island are the **Pakleni Islands**. Facing the town of Hvar, these islands are uninhabited and mostly wooded. Their name derives from the *paklina* (resin) that was once extracted from the pines and used to waterproof boats. During the summer, boat trips to the islands depart from Hvar. The nearest island, Jerolim, is given over to naturism.

The island of **Šćedro**, off the south coast of Hvar, is covered in pines and maquis. Illyrian tombs and parts of a Roman villa have been found here.

KEY

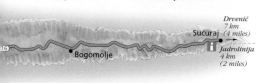

Drvenić 7 km (4 miles)
Sućuraj
Jadrolinija 4 km (2 miles)
Bogomolje

⛴	Ferry terminal
ℹ	Visitor information
🏖	Beach with facilities
▬	Major road
═	Minor road
---	Ferry route

Trogir ⑪

Set on an island joined to the mainland by a bridge, Trogir is one of the jewels of the Dalmatian coast. The Greeks of Issa, now Vis (see p473), first settled here in 380 BC, when they founded the fortified town of Tragyrion, which became Tragurium under the Romans in AD 78. In 1123, Trogir was attacked and destroyed by the Saracens and abandoned by the surviving inhabitants. It revived again 70 years later and a period of extraordinary artistic growth ensued, first under the kings of Hungary and later under Venetian rule. Trogir's buildings display a profusion of architectural styles, evidence of its earlier prosperity and cultural past. In 1997, it was listed as a UNESCO World Heritage Site.

The picturesque seafront at Trogir

⊞ Land Gate
Hrvatskih Mučenika.
Rebuilt in the 16th century, the Land Gate (Sjeverna Vrata) was made from a tall doorway in pale rusticated stone, with grooves that once supported a drawbridge. On the cornice above the arch is the Lion of St Mark and, above that, on a pedestal, stands a statue of the St John of Trogir (sv Ivan Trogirski), one of the town's patron saints.

�fiↂ Civic Museum
Gradska Vrata 4. **Tel** (021) 881 406.
☐ Jul–Aug: 9am–9pm daily; Sep–Jun: call in advance. 🎨 🗖 🚫
Through the Land Gate is the lovely Baroque Garagnin Fanfogna Palace, now the Civic Museum (Muzej Grada Trogira), with 18th century furnishings. On display are interesting archaeological collections, books, documents, drawings and antique clothes linked to the town's history.

⊞ Stafileo Palace
Matije Gupca 20. ● to the public.
Built in the late 15th century, the Stafileo Palace (Palača Stafileo) has a series of five windows in Venetian Gothic style on each of its two floors, their openings framed by pillars and carved arches. Around the arches are reliefs of flowers and leaves. The design is attributed to the school of Juraj Dalmatinac (see p458), who worked for many years in Trogir.

⊞ Čipiko Palace
Gradska ulica. ● to the public, except courtyard.
An inscription indicates 1457 as the year of completion of the Čipiko Palace (Palača Čipiko), built for Trogir's most illustrious family. Over a Renaissance doorway, distinguished by its columns, is a shell decoration above a finely worked cornice. The first floor has a beautiful mullioned window with a balustrade in stone; the second floor is similarly designed but lacks the balustrade. A second door, opening onto a side street, has a complex structure with two sculpted lions holding a coat of arms. They are flanked by sculptures of angels.

🔒 Cathedral of St Lawrence
trg Ivana Pavla II. **Tel** (091) 531 4754. ☐ mid May–Oct: 9am–7pm; Nov–mid May: by appt.
This opulent Cathedral of St Lawrence (Katedrala sv Lovre) stands on the site of an ancient church destroyed by the Saracens. Construction began in 1193, but was prolonged for decades. Its most spectacular feature is the west door, decorated with carved reliefs executed by local stonemason Master Radovan in 1240. His delightful frieze, filled with plants and animals, depicts the changing of the seasons. Inside, there is an octagonal pulpit from the 13th century and a ciborium on the main altar with sculptures depicting the Annunciation.
To the right of the cathedral stands a 14th-century Venetian Gothic bell tower, rebuilt when Trogir became part of the Venetian territory.

⊞ Town Hall
trg Ivana Pavla II.
On the eastern side of John Paul II Square (trg Ivana Pavla II) stands the impressive Town Hall (Gradska Vijećnica), originating in the 15th century. It has three storeys with open arches and a mullioned window with a balustrade on the upper floor; the façade is decorated with coats of arms. The pretty porticoed courtyard is open to the public.

Exterior of the Čipiko Palace, built for Trogir's most illustrious family

⊞ Loggia and Clock Tower
trg Ivana Pavla II.

On the southern side of the square is the striking town Loggia (Gradska Loža); its roof is supported by six columns with Roman capitals and dates from the 14th century. On the wall are two splendid reliefs – *Justice* (1471) by Nikola Firentinac, and *Ban Berislavić* (1950) by Ivan Meštrović. The Clock Tower, to the left of the Loggia, supports a pavilion dome salvaged in 1447.

⚐ Church of St John the Baptist
trg Ivana Pavla II. ⚫ for restoration.

The Romanesque Church of St John the Baptist (sv Ivan Krstitelj), built in the 13th century, is the pantheon of the powerful Čipiko family. The church is home to an art gallery (Pinacoteca) with collections of medieval illuminated manuscripts, ornaments, paintings and gold pieces from various churches. However, the collection is currently in the Museum of Sacred Art near the cathedral, while the church undergoes retoration.

⚐ Church of St Nicholas
Gradska ulica 2. *Tel* (021) 881 631. ⚫ for restoration; call in advance.

The Church of St Nicholas (sv Nikola) and Benedictine convent date from the 11th century, but were rebuilt in the 16th century. The convent now houses the Zbirka Umjetnina Kairos, an art collection that includes the *Kairos*, a relief of Greek origin dating from the 1st century BC, a Gothic crucifix and a Romanesque statue of *The Virgin with Child*.

⊞ Kamerlengo Castle and St Mark's Tower
Hrvatskog Proleća.

In the southwest corner of the island stands Kamerlengo Castle (Kaštel Kamerlengo), at one time the residence of the Venetian governor. Built in around 1430, it stands facing the sea. It was once connected to St Mark's Tower (Kula Svetog Marka), also built by the Venetians in 1470 for defence; artillery was installed at the top of the castle for defence purposes.

Imposing St Mark's Tower, built for defence in 1470

VISITORS' CHECKLIST

240 km (150 miles) NW of Dubrovnik. 11,000. 7 km (5 miles) N of centre. Jadranska Magistrala. Obala Bana Berislavića. trg Ivana Pavla II 1, (021) 881 412. Trogir Summer Festival (Jun–Aug).

TROGIR TOWN CENTRE

Airport 7 km (5 miles)
JADRANSKA MAGISTRALA
Market
Bus Station
BLAŽA JURJEVA TROGIRANINA
Land Gate ①
Civic Museum ②
GRADSKA
RADOVANOVA TRG
SUBICEVA
HRVATSKIH MUČENIKA
Čipiko Palace ④
⑤ Cathedral of St Lawrence
TRG IVANA PAVLA II
Stafileo Palace ③
MATIJE GUPCA
Loggia and Clock Tower ⑦
⑥ Town Hall
⑧ Church of St John the Baptist
SINJSKA
AUGUSTINA KAŽOTIĆA
MORNARSKA
OBROV
IVANA DUKNOVIĆA
GRADSKA UL.
⑩ St Mark's Tower
HRVATSKOG PROLEĆA 1971
MATICE HRVATSKE
Walls
VUKOVARSKA
Church of St Dominic
Church of St Nicholas ⑨
Marmont's Gloriette
Kamerlengo Castle ⑩
OBALA BANA BERISLAVIĆA
OBALA BANA BERISLAVIĆA

0 metres 100
0 yards 100

Key to Symbols *see back flap*

Kornati National Park ⑫

Nacionalni Park Kornati

340 km (213 miles) NW of Dubrovnik. 🚢 *from Biograd, Murter, Primošten, Rogoznica, Vodice, Zadar.* 🛈 *Butina 2, (022) 435 740.* 🖳 www.kornati.hr

The Zadar Archipelago is made up of more than 300 islands surrounded by crystal-clear waters. In 1980, the southern part of the archipelago was designated as Kornati National Park. It is 36 km (22 miles) long and 6 km (4 miles) wide and is made up of 89 islands of white stone, which about 20,000 years ago were the peaks of a mountain chain. These include Kornat (for which the National Park is named), Piškera, Lavsa, Mana, Katina and the southern part of Dugi Otok, along with dozens of rocky outcrops. Nearly all are uninhabited and have little or no vegetation. Today, they belong to the people of the small island of Murter, who bought these islands around the end of the 19th century for grazing sheep. The park was set up to protect the waters, to allow marine life to flourish and to stop people from building on the islands. With around 350 plant and 300 animal species, it is a popular destination with scuba divers and sailors. To conserve this diversity, fishing is prohibited in the park's waters. The best way to visit it is by a sailing boat, and there are also organized day-trips from Zadar and Murter, Biograd, Vodice, Primošten and Rogoznica.

Aerial view of the spectacular islands of Kornati National Park

Zadar ⑬

360 km (225 miles) NW of Dubrovnik. 🏙 *73,000.* ✈ 🚍 *from Zagreb.* 🚌 *from Rijeka, Split, Zagreb.* 🚢 *Jadrolinija.* 🛈 **City** *Mihe Klaica 5, (023) 316 166.* **Regional** *sv Leopolda Mandića 1, (023) 315 316, 315 107.* 🎭 *Musical evenings at St Donat (Jul & Aug), Summer Theatre.* www.tzzadar.hr

Set on a narrow peninsula on the Adriatic coast, Zadar's present layout dates back to Roman rule when it became an important *municipium*, and a port for the trading of timber and wine. It later enjoyed a spell of prosperity under Venetian rule, when many of its churches and palaces were built. Today, its proximity to the Zadar Archipelago has turned it into a major ferry

Imposing exterior of the Church of St Donat, Zadar

port. The centre of public life is the People's Square – a business district and the site of political debate, it has been the heart of the town since medieval times. Further away is Green Square (Zeleni trg), where the main square of the ancient Roman city of Jadera once stood. Little remains of the Forum that once stood here since much of the original stone from the Forum found its way into the adjacent 9th-century **Church of St Donat** named after its foun-der Bishop Donat. One of the finest examples of Byzantine architecture, it has a circular groundplan and a women's gallery. It has not been used as a church since 1797, but concerts are often held here.

The superb Romanesque **Cathedral of St Anastasia** is another attraction of the Forum. The interior contains fine Venetian carvings in the 15th-century wooden choir stalls. Beneath the ciborium lies the sarcophagus of St Anastasia, dating from the 9th century. The bell tower that stands to one side of the cathedral, was completed in the 19th century by architect Thomas G Jackson. Housed in a building near the Forum is the **Archeological Museum**. The museum's collections date from

KEY

🚢 Ferry terminal

🏖 Beach with facilities

🔭 Viewpoint

- - Trail

- - Park boundary

Sali
Dugi Otok
Telašćica *Mala Proversa* *Katina*
Svršata
KORNATI *Lučica*
Vrulje
NATIONAL *Kornat*
Mana
Piškera
PARK *Smokvica*
Lavsa
Kurba Vela

0 km   5

0 miles   5

prehistory to recent times and come from the entire Zadar area and the islands. Nearby stands the **Church of St Mary**, built in 1066. Behind its Renaissance façade is a triple- aisled interior with a women's gallery. The monastery next door is now the Museum of Sacred Art, with gold pieces, paintings and statues, including a polyptych (1487) by the Italian artist, Vittore Carpaccio.

🏛 **Church of St Donat**
Forum. 🛈 *Archaeological Museum, (023) 250 516.* ⬜ *summer: 9am–8pm, daily; winter: by appt only.* 📷

🏛 **Cathedral of St Anastasia**
Forum. *Tel (023) 251 708.* ⬜ *summer: 8am–6:30pm Mon–Fri, 8am–noon Sat; winter: 8am–noon & 5pm–6:30 pm Mon–Fri.*

Paklenica National Park ⑭

Nacionalni Park Paklenica

370 km (231 miles) NE of Dubrovnik. 🚌 *from Zadar.* 🛈 *Starigrad Paklenica, (023) 369 202.* ⬜ *May–Sep: 6:30am–8pm daily; Mar, Apr, Oct: 7am–7pm daily; Nov–Feb: 8am–3pm Mon–Thu, 7am–5pm Fri–Sun.* 📷 **www.**paklenica.hr

Situated in the Velebit massif, Paklenica National Park was founded in 1949. The entire Velebit massif chain is nearly 150 km (93 miles) long. The terrain is made up of

Striking Renaissance façade of the Church of St Mary, Zadar

limestone karst with many sink holes and plateaus separated by deep fissures. In 1978, UNESCO listed Velebit as a biological reserve with the aim of protecting this wildlife haven, which hosts 2,700 plant species and colonies of large birds of prey. The *kukovi* – rock formations sculpted by wind and water – are also protected.

The park itself covers an area of 36 sq km (14 sq miles), and is formed by two gorges, Big Paklenica (Velika Paklenica) and Small Paklenica (Mala Paklenica), which cut into the limestone mountains. Parts of the canyon walls are more than 400 m (1,312 ft) tall. High up, birds of prey make their nests in a habitat ideal for breeding. Golden eagles, vultures and even peregrine falcons can be spotted, while in the forests there are bears, wild

boars, foxes and hares. The bare rock faces of Velika Paklenica are popular with rock climbers. The rock is pierced by numerous caves, but they are not easily accessible. Only the Manita Cave is open to visitors, when accompanied by a guide. However, deep within the walls of the canyon is an extensive network of underground tunnels built by the Yugoslav Army. These are currently being renovated for use as galleries and exhibition areas.

Hiking and mountain biking are popular activities. A path in the valley penetrates far into the interior of the park to a cliff edge, which offers magnificent views of the wooded Vaganski Vrh, the highest peak in the Velebit chain. In summer, visitors can stay overnight in the mountain hut, on the banks of the Velika Paklenica creek.

One of the forested paths leading to Paklenica National Park

Plitvice Lakes National Park ⑮

Nacionalni Park Plitvička Jezera

The picturesque Plitvice Lakes National Park, in the heart of Croatia, was founded in 1949. This area of 300 sq km (115 sq miles), covered in lakes and forest, has been on the UNESCO World Heritage Site since 1979. It is particularly known for its spectacular water-falls. There are 16 lakes within the park, each offering eye-catching scenery; visitors can explore by following the paths along the shores or by using footbridges. There are no towns or villages in the reserve, only hotels. Electric buses take people to the starting points of the trails and to the hotels. The largest lake can be toured by electric boat.

A charming shepherd's hut located by the lake shore

| 0 metres | 500 |
| 0 yards | 500 |

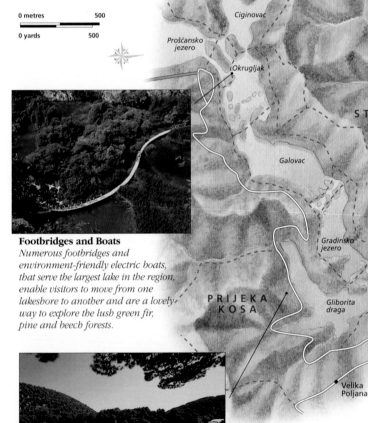

Footbridges and Boats
Numerous footbridges and environment-friendly electric boats, that serve the largest lake in the region, enable visitors to move from one lakeshore to another and are a lovely way to explore the lush green fir, pine and beech forests.

Ciginovac

Prošćansko jezero

Okrugljak

STUBI

Galovac

Gradinsko jezero

PRIJEKA KOSA

Gliborita draga

Velika Poljana

Dense Forests
The forests alongside the waters are home to some of the largest European species of animal, including wolves, lynx, foxes, wild boars, bears, roebucks, wild cats, otters and badgers.

For hotels and restaurants in this region see pp502–505 and pp506–507

Flora
The park flora ranges from waterlilies on the lakes to forests of gigantic trees. The rich undergrowth is also a source of food for the park's wildlife.

VISITORS' CHECKLIST

460 km (288 miles) NW of Dubrovnik. 🚌 from Zagreb. 🚹 Scientific Research Center, (053) 751 001. ☐ Apr–Oct: 8am–sunset daily; Nov–Mar: 9am–sunset daily. 🎫 🚸 ♿ partly. www.np-plitvicka-jezera.hr

Waterfalls
Signposted routes direct visitors to walk behind the waterfalls to watch the rushing water as it cascades from above.

Plitvice

🚢

Draga
Matijaševac

Zagreb
161 km (100 miles)

Jezero
Kozjak

Gavanovac

Zagreb
160 km
(99 miles)

ℹ️

🅿️

Entrance 1

E71

Dubrovnik
460 km (288 miles)

Special routes are taken by the park's electric buses to take visitors around the area.

KEY

🚢	Electric boat
ℹ️	Visitor information
🅿️	Parking
▬	Major road
═	Minor road
- -	Trail
- - -	Boat route

View of the Korana River
The lakes drain into the Korana river, one of Croatia's cleanest waterways. The long-winding river flows between steep cliffs amidst spectacular scenery, and is a popular place for kayak and raft trips.

View of the beautiful town of Rab with its four striking bell towers

Rab ⑯

460 km (288 miles) NW of
Dubrovnik. 🏘 9,000. ⛴ from
Rijeka & Zagreb. ⛴ from Rijeka &
Zadar. 🛈 trg Municipium Arba 8,
(051) 724 064. 🎭 Tournament
of Rab (May 9), Musical Evenings,
Church of the Holy Cross (Jun–Sep).
www.tzg-rab.hr

The Kvarner Gulf region,
home to the enticing island of
Rab, lies parallel to the Velebit
massif. With its sandy beaches
and mild climate, the island is
a popular holiday destination.
The main town, Rab, which
gives its name to the island,
became a bishopric in the
early Christian period and
was inhabited by Slavic people in the 6th century. The
town came under Venetian
rule between 1409 and 1797
and has some fine examples
of Venetian architecture,
including its four famous bell
towers which make it look
like a ship. The Sea Gate, a
tower from the 14th century,

leads to the town square.
The heart of Rab, the square,
is graced by the 13th-century
Romanesque **Prince's Palace**,
which was later rebuilt in
Renaissance style with
mullioned windows. In the
courtyard are some Roman
and medieval remains.

The town has many
monastic buildings. Among
them, the fine Romanesque
Cathedral of St Mary the Great
has a stunning façade of
pink and white stone with a
sculpted *Deposition* by Petar
Trogiranin above the portal.
Inside is a beautiful font,
made by the same sculptor
in 1497. At a height of 70 m
(230 ft), the cathedral's
13th-century bell tower is
the tallest on the island.

Northwest of Rab, set on
a long bay, the village of
Kampor is famous for the
Church of St Bernard, which
contains superb panels.
Further north, at the end of
a rocky peninsula, is the village of Lopar, popular for its
beaches and leisure facilities.

Rijeka ⑰

620 km (388 miles) NW of
Dubrovnik. 🏘 168,000. ✈
🚆 from Zagreb. 🚌 from Pula,
Zadar & Zagreb. ⛴ from Riva,
Verdijeva, Jadrolinija Riva.
🛈 Korzo 33, (051) 335 882.
🎭 Rijeka Carnival (Feb & Mar),
Rijeka's Summer Nights Arts
Festival (Jun–Jul).

Once the Roman city of
Tarsatica, Rijeka came under
the Habsburgs in 1466 and
was declared a free town
in 1719. Today Rijeka is one
of Croatia's main ports and a
key rail and road junction.

The Korzo, a broad avenue
running south of the Old
Town, is the heart of the
city and lined with majestic
19th-century buildings.
Halfway along stands the
domed Civic Tower, deco-
rated with the coat of arms
of the city. In the Old Town
is the **Cathedral of St Vitus**.
Built at the top of a hill
between 1638 and 1742,
the interior features a
Gothic crucifix from the
13th century on the main
altar. To the west stands
the late 19th-century
Governor's Palace, which
since 1955 has housed the
**Maritime and Historical
Museum of Croatia**. Founded
in 1876, the museum docu-
ments the history of navigation through a collection of
seafaring equipment from
the 17th and 18th centuries.
East of the cathedral lies
Tito Square, from where
561 steps lead up to the
Sanctuary of Our Lady of
Trsat, a church and a monastery built by Martin Frankopan.
According to legend, parts
of the Holy House of Mary
of Nazareth were brought
here in 1291, before being
transferred to Italy. To compensate the local people for
this loss, Pope Urban V
donated a *Virgin with Child*
in 1367. Painted by St Luke,
it now stands on the main
altar. Opposite the church
is Trsat Castle, built by the
Romans to defend Tarsatica,
parts of which are intact.

In February and March each
year, Rijeka hosts Croatia's
largest carnival celebrations.

The Sea Gate, one of the many
entrances into Rab town

Gothic crucifix in the Cathedral
of St Vitus, Rijeka

The Temple of Romae and Augustus, a jewel of Roman architecture, Pula

Pula ⑱

720 km (450 miles) NW of Dubrovnik. 🚶 63,000. ✈ 🚌 from Zagreb. 🚌 from Poreč, Rovinj & Zagreb. 🚢 from Zadar. 🛈 Forum 3, (052) 212 987. 🎭 Music events in Arena, Pula Amphitheatre (summer), Croatian Film Festival (summer). **www**.pulainfo.hr

The hisoric town of Pula is best known for its magnificent monuments from the Roman era, when it was a colony known as Pietas Julia. It was destroyed by an East-Germanic tribe, the Ostrogoths, but began to flourish again when it became the main base for the Byzantine fleet in the 6th and 7th centuries. In 1150, it came under Venetian rule and in 1856, Austria made it the base for its fleet. Pula continues to be one of the most important naval bases in Croatia and is also now an important university town.

The **Pula Amphitheatre** is the town's star attraction. Regarded as one of the sixth largest Roman amphitheatres in the world, it once seated 23,000 spectators. Originally built by Emperor Claudius, it was expanded by Emperor Vespasian in AD 79 for gladiator fights. Today, it is a popular venue for concerts ranging from opera to rock as well as an annual film festival.

To the south of the amphitheatre, two gates mark the entrance to the heart of the town. The single-arched **Gate of Hercules**, with a carving of the head of Hercules at the top, was built in the 1st century BC and is the oldest

and best-preserved Roman monument in the town. Just north, towards the harbour, the later Twin Gate, with an ornate frieze, leads to the Archaeological Museum. On display are finds from Pula and the surrounding area, with collections from Prehistoric times to the Middle Ages. Roman antiquities and architectural remains from medieval times are the other items on exhibit.

In the southeast of the town stands the **Arch of Sergii**, also known as the Golden Gate. It was erected in the 1st century BC to honour three brothers who held important positions in the Roman Empire. Its frieze has a bas-relief depicting a chariot pulled by horses.

Headless statue, Archaeological Museum

Rovinj ⑲

700 km (438 miles) NW of Dubrovnik. 🚶 13,000. ✈ 🚌 from Pula, Poreč, Rijeka & Zagreb. 🛈 Obala P Budicina 12, (052) 811 566. 🎭 Grisia, International Art Exhibition (2nd Sun Aug); Patron St Euphemia's Day (16 Sep). **www**.tzgrovinj.hr

Originally a port built by the Romans, the pleasant town of Rovinj is situated on what was formerly an island. The strait separating it from the coast was filled in 1763, after which the town expanded on to the mainland. Rovinj was ruled by the Byzantines and Franks, from 1283 until 1797, and then passed into Venetian

hands. The remains of a wall dating back to the Middle Ages can still be seen. In the square in front of the pier is Balbi's Arch, an ancient city gate, as well as a striking late Renaissance clock tower. A loggia dating from 1680 is now the **Civic Museum**, housing 18th-century art from the Venetian school and works by modern Croatian artists.

Dominating the town from its hilltop location is the 18th-century **Cathedral**, dedicated to the third-century martyr St Euphemia. Originating in early Christian times, it was rebuilt in 1736. The saint's remains are preserved in a Roman sarcophagus in the apse of the triple-aisled church. The adjacent bell tower is over 62 m (200 ft) high and was modelled on that of San Marco in Venice. It is crowned by a copper statue of St Euphemia. Along the waterfront, the interesting Institute of Marine Biology, founded in the late 19th century, houses one of the oldest aquariums in Europe.

To the south of the town lies Zlatni Rt, an attractive park planted with cedars and cypresses and fringed by rocky beaches.

🏛 **Civic Museum**
trg M Tita 11. **Tel** (052) 816 720. 🕐 summer: 10am–2pm & 6–10pm Tue–Fri, 10am–2pm & 7–10pm Sat & Sun; winter: 10am–1pm Tue–Sat.

The port-town of Rovinj, dominated by the cathedral and its bell tower

Basilica of Euphrasius ⑳
Eufrazijeva Bazilika

A mosaic in the apse

Located in the town of Poreč, this 6th-century church is a Byzantine master-piece decorated with mosaics on a gold background. It was built for Bishop Euphrasius between 539 and 553 by expanding the existing 4th-century Oratory of St Maurus Martyr, patron saint of Poreč.

Although the building has undergone many alterations over the centuries, some of the original floor mosaics survive. In December 1997, the basilica was added to the UNESCO World Heritage Site. Classical concerts are held in the church from July to September.

★ Ciborium
Dominating the presbytery is a beautiful 13th-century ciborium supported by four marble columns. The canopy is decorated with mosaics.

★ Apse Mosaics
Mosaics from the 6th century cover the apse. Christ and the Apostles are depicted on the arch, while the Virgin appears on the vault enthroned with child and two angels. Bishop Euphrasius himself is shown with a model of the basilica.

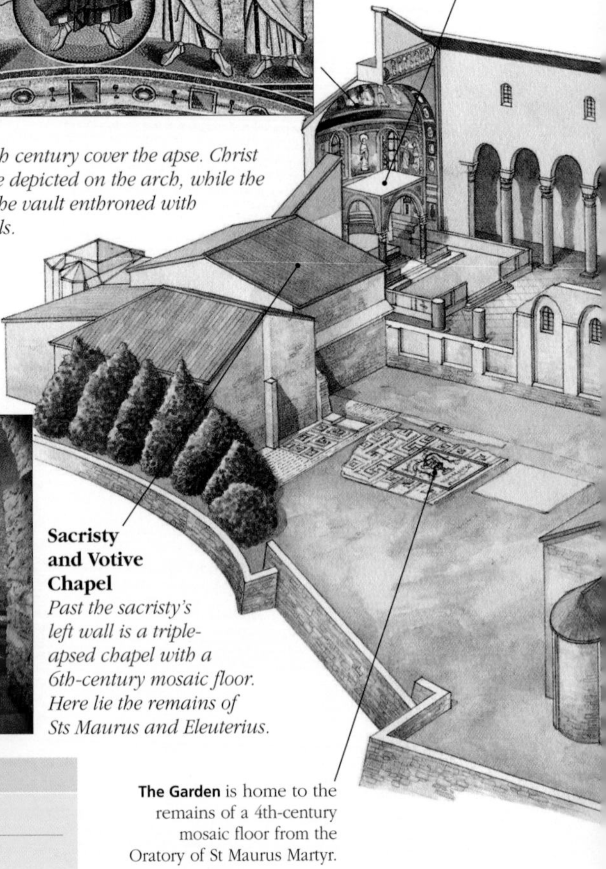

Sacristy and Votive Chapel
Past the sacristy's left wall is a triple-apsed chapel with a 6th-century mosaic floor. Here lie the remains of Sts Maurus and Eleuterius.

STAR FEATURES

★ Ciborium

★ Apse Mosaics

The Garden is home to the remains of a 4th-century mosaic floor from the Oratory of St Maurus Martyr.

Interior

The entrance leads to a large basilica with a central nave and two side aisles. The 18 Greek marble columns have carved capitals featuring animals, some of Byzantine origin and others Romanesque. All bear the monogram of Euphrasius.

VISITORS' CHECKLIST

710 km (444 miles) NE of Durbovnik. *Tel* (052) 431 595. from Rovinj, Pula & Zagreb. Zagrebačka 9, Poreč, (052) 451 458. Jun–Aug: 9am–7pm daily; Apr–May & Sep–Nov: 10am–2pm.

Bell tower

Baptistry

This octagonal building dates from the 6th century. In the centre is a baptismal font and there are also fragments of mosaics. To the rear is a 16th-century bell tower.

The Bishop's Residence, a triple-aisled building dating from the 6th century, now houses paintings by Antonio da Bassano, Palma il Giovane and a polyptych by Antonio Vivarini.

Atrium

The church atrium is composed of a square portico with two columns on each side. Medieval tombstones and archaeological finds are displayed here.

Zagreb ㉑

Croatia's capital since 1991, Zagreb is the heart of the
political, economic and cultural life of the country. With
a population of seven hundred and eighty thousand, it
is also Croatia's largest city. Zagreb is divided into two
parts: the Old Town (Gornji grad or Upper Town), which
includes the two districts of Gradec and Kaptol, and the
modern area (Donji grad or Lower Town). The Upper
Town is home to the main centres of religious, political
and administrative power. The Lower Town developed
after 1830 around a U-shaped series of parks and open
spaces known as the "green horseshoe", and the major
museums, including the Mimara Museum and Gallery of
Old Masters, are all located here, as well as the Croatian
National Theatre. Around Governor Jelačić Square (trg
Bana Jelačića), where the Upper and Lower towns meet,
there are plenty of lively cafés with summer terraces.

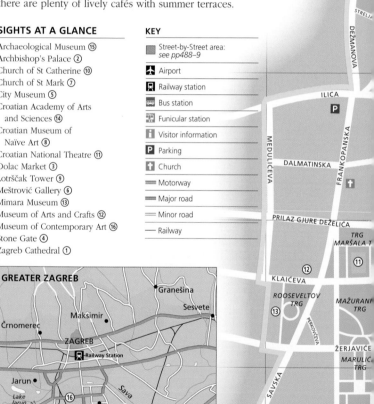

Mary with Child,
Church of St Mark

SIGHTS AT A GLANCE

Archaeological Museum ⑮
Archbishop's Palace ②
Church of St Catherine ⑩
Church of St Mark ⑦
City Museum ⑤
Croatian Academy of Arts
  and Sciences ⑭
Croatian Museum of
  Naïve Art ⑧
Croatian National Theatre ⑪
Dolac Market ③
Lotrščak Tower ⑨
Meštrović Gallery ⑥
Mimara Museum ⑬
Museum of Arts and Crafts ⑫
Museum of Contemporary Art ⑯
Stone Gate ④
Zagreb Cathedral ①

KEY

Street-by-Street area: *see pp488–9*

✈ Airport
🚉 Railway station
🚌 Bus station
🚡 Funicular station
ℹ Visitor information
🅿 Parking
✝ Church
━ Motorway
━ Major road
━ Minor road
━ Railway

GREATER ZAGREB

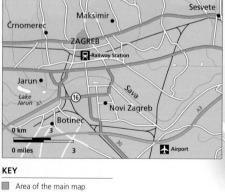

Granešina · Sesvete · Maksimir · Črnomerec · ZAGREB · Railway Station · Jarun · Lake Jarun · Botinec · Sava · Novi Zagreb · Airport

0 km 3
0 miles 3

KEY

Area of the main map

A B C

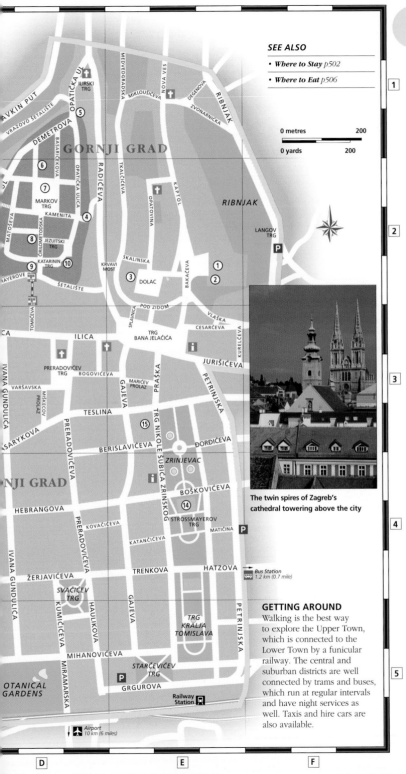

SEE ALSO
- **Where to Stay** p502
- **Where to Eat** p506

| 1 |

0 metres   200

0 yards   200

AVKIN PUT

VRAZOVO ŠETALIŠTE

DEMETROVA

OPATIČKA UL.

JURSKI TRG

MEDVEDGRADSKA

MIKLOUŠIĆEVA

NOVA VES

DEGENOVA

RIBNJAK

ZVONARNIČKA

GORNJI GRAD

BASARIČEKOVA

OPATIČKA ULICA

RADIĆEVA

TKALČIĆEVA

OPATOVINA

KAPTOL

RIBNJAK

MARKOV TRG

KAMENITA

MATOŠEVA

CIRILOMETODSKA

JEZUITSKI TRG

KATARININ TRG

MAYEROVE

ŠETALIŠTE

KRVAVI MOST

SKALINSKA

DOLAC

BAKAČEVA

LANGOV TRG

| 2 |

TOMIĆEVA

POD ZIDOM

ŠPAJNIČA

VLAŠKA

CESARČEVA

KURELČEVA

CA

ILICA

TRG BANA JELAČIĆA

JURIŠIĆEVA

| 3 |

PRERADOVIĆEV TRG

BOGOVIĆEVA

GAJEVA

MARIČEV PROLAZ

PRAŠKA

PETRINJSKA

VARŠAVSKA

IVANA GUNDULIĆA

MISKECOV PROLAZ

SARYKOVA

PRERADOVIĆEVA

TESLINA

BERISLAVIĆEVA

TRG NIKOLE ŠUBIĆA ZRINSKOG

ĐORĐIĆEVA

The twin spires of Zagreb's cathedral towering above the city

NJI GRAD

HEBRANGOVA

PRERADOVIĆEVA

KOVAČIĆEVA

ZRINJEVAC

BOŠKOVIĆEVA

STROSSMAYEROV TRG

MATIČINA

| 4 |

IVANA GUNDULIĆA

ŽERJAVIĆEVA

KATANČIĆEVA

TRENKOVA

HATZOVA

PETRINJSKA

Bus Station
1.2 km (0.7 mile)

SVAČIĆEV TRG

KUMIČIĆEVA

HAULIKOVA

GAJEVA

TRG KRALJA TOMISLAVA

GETTING AROUND

Walking is the best way to explore the Upper Town, which is connected to the Lower Town by a funicular railway. The central and suburban districts are well connected by trams and buses, which run at regular intervals and have night services as well. Taxis and hire cars are also available.

MIHANOVIĆEVA

STARČEVIĆEV TRG

GRGUROVA

OTANICAL GARDENS

MIRAMARSKA

Railway Station

| 5 |

Airport
10 km (6 miles)

| D | E | F |

Street-by-Street: the Upper Town

Pietà by Ivan Meštrović

In the Upper Town (Gornji grad) there are various institutions that have played a significant part in the history of the city and of Croatia. They now house the political and cultural centres of the country: the presidency of the republic, the parliament, the State Audit Court and several government ministries. All of these buildings were restored, repaired or rebuilt after the devastating earthquake of 1880. Some of the ancient noble palaces have been converted into museums. There are also three interesting churches: the ancient Church of St Mark, the Baroque Church of St Catherine, built by the Jesuits, and the Church of Sts Cyril and Methodius. The daily signal to close the city gates was rung from the medieval Lotrščak Tower.

The Natural History Museum, created from three collections, houses most of the finds from Krapina, which date human presence in Croatia back to the Palaeolithic era.

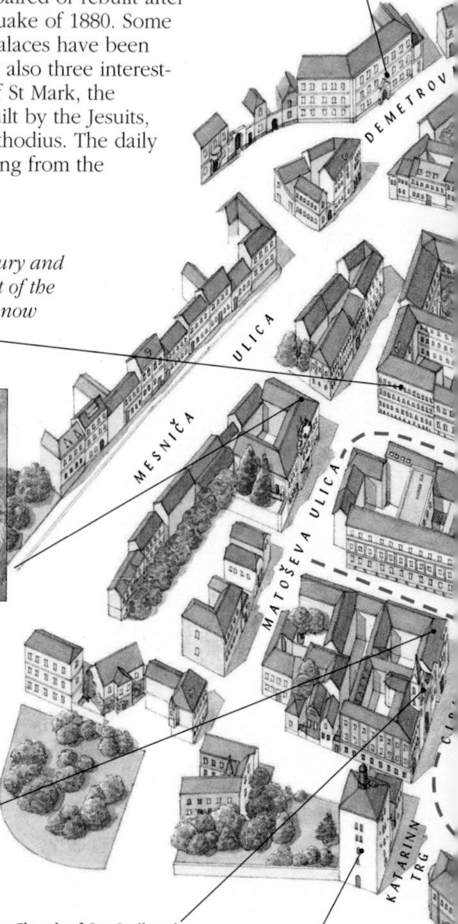

Ban's Palace
The building dates from the 17th century and was built after the city became the seat of the Ban, Governor of Croatia, in 1621. It now houses the presidency of the republic.

Croatian Historical Museum
This museum, housed in the splendid Vojković-Oršić Palace, hosts seasonal exhibitions devoted to various aspects of the nation's history.

★ The Croatian Museum of Naïve Art
Over 1,500 works of Naïve art by the founders and followers of the Hlebine school are held here ⑧

The Church of Sts Cyril and Methodius was designed in the early 19th-century by Bartol Felbinger. This Byzantine-style church serves Croatia's Ukrainian community and has a splendid iconostasis.

Lotrščak Tower
At noon every day a cannon is fired from this tower, which dates from the 12th century ⑨

KEY

– – – Suggested route

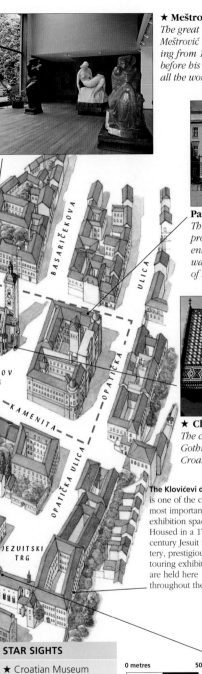

★ Meštrović Gallery
The great Croatian sculptor Ivan Meštrović lived in this 18th-century building from 1922 to 1941. About ten years before his death, he donated his home and all the works of art in it to the state ⑥

Parliament Building
This building dates from 1910, when the provincial administration offices were enlarged. The independence of Croatia was proclaimed from the central window of the building in 1918.

★ Church of St Mark
The coloured tiles on the roof of this fine Gothic church form the coats of arms of Croatia, Dalmatia, Slavonia and Zagreb ⑦

The Klovićevi dvori
is one of the city's most important art exhibition spaces. Housed in a 17th-century Jesuit monastery, prestigious touring exhibitions are held here throughout the year.

Church of St Catherine
Built on the site of an ancient Dominican church, this is the city's most fascinating Baroque building ⑩

STAR SIGHTS

★ Croatian Museum of Naïve Art

★ Meštrović Gallery

★ Church of St Mark

| 0 metres | 50 |
| 0 yards | 50 |

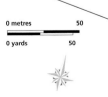

Awe-inspiring central nave of Zagreb Cathedral

Zagreb Cathedral ①
Katedrala

Kaptol. **Map** E2. *Tel (01) 481 4727.* ☐ *10am–5pm Mon–Sat, 1–5pm Sun.*

Dedicated to the Assumption and the Blessed Virgin Mary, Zagreb's cathedral is the city's most recognizable landmark. Despite its 11th-century origins, the cathedral owes its present appearance to the reconstruction carried out by Austrian architect Friedrich von Schmidt and Hermann Bollé following the earthquake of 1880.

The imposing Neo-Gothic façade is topped by a slender pair of 105-m (345-ft) high

Intricate detail on a pillar inside Zagreb Cathedral

spires. The lofty interior contains a string of Neo-Gothic altars and some impressive earlier tombstones, notably the fine Baroque plaque honouring the warrior-aristocrat Toma Bakac Erdödy. Behind the altar is an effigy of Cardinal Alojzije Stepinac, who was persecuted by the Communist regime and subsequently beatified by Pope John Paul II.

Archbishop's Palace ②
Nadbiskupska palača

Kaptol. **Map** E2. ◑ *to the public.*

The complex of buildings that forms the Archbishop's Palace encloses three sides of Cathedral Square. It incorporates three of five round towers and one square tower, which were built from 1469 onwards as defence against Ottoman attacks. The present palace dates from 1730, when several buildings were linked and unified by a single, imposing Baroque façade.

In the square in front of the palace stands a fountain crowned by a statue of Mary with four angels, by Viennese sculptor Dominik Fernkorn, in around 1850.

The former moat east of the palace has now been converted into the Ribnjak Park, with various statues, including one called *Modesty* by Antun Augustinčić. A leafy area ideal for strolling, the park also includes a couple of popular cafés.

Dolac Market ③

Dolac. **Map** E2. *Tel (01) 481 4959.*

Overlooking Governor Jelačić Square (trg bana Jelačića) and west of Zagreb Cathedral is this picturesque market, which has held this spot since 1930. Local farmers display their colourful produce, while fresh fish from the Adriatic is sold from a pavilion in the market's northwestern corner. Dominating the plaza above Dolac Market is a sculptural ensemble by Vanja Radauš featuring Petrica Kerempuh, a fictional character who figures strongly in Croatian literature.

On the western side of the market is the **Church of St Mary** (Crkva sv Marija), a 14th-century church rebuilt in Baroque style in 1740. Inside is a fine collection of marble altars by 18th-century Slovene stonemason Franjo Rottman.

Stone Gate ④
Kamenita vrata

Kamenita. **Map** D2.

West of Dolac Market, the streets ascend towards Gradec, a well-preserved old quarter, that was once surrounded by defensive walls. Gradec's only surviving gate is the Stone Gate, a 13th-century structure that houses one of the city's most venerated shrines. According to popular belief, a painting of the Virgin Mary, which hangs inside the gate,

Baroque façade of the elegant Archbishop's Palace

Sculptures in the garden of the Meštrović Gallery

miraculously survived a fire in 1731. The painting became the centre of a popular cult, and Zagreb folk still come here to light candles and offer prayers.

On the other side of the gate, on the corner of Habdelićeva and Kamenita, stands **Ljekarna Aligheri**, a pharmacy that has been in existence since 1350. The pharmacy was named after the previous owner, Nicolò Alighieri, great-grandson of Italian poet Dante Aligheri.

City Museum ⑤
Muzej grada Zagreba

Opatička ulica 20. **Map** D1. **Tel** (01) 485 1364. ☐ 10am–6pm Tue, Wed & Fri, 10am–10pm Thu, 11am–7pm Sat, 10am–2pm Sun. 🖼 🎫 by appt. ♿ 🎥 **www**.mgz.hr

Three historic buildings – the Convent of the Nuns of St Clare from around 1650, a 12th-century tower and a granary from the 17th century – combine to form the City Museum. Its 12 collections, consisting of 4,500 objects on permanent display, illustrate the history and culture of Zagreb from its origins to the present day. The exhibits include maps, paintings and views of the city, standards, flags, military uniforms and archaeological finds. Many items were donated by the city's famous citizens, including actress Tilla Durieux, composer Ivan Zajc, musician Rudolf Matz, the soprano Milka Trnina and architect

Viktor Kovačić. On the same street as the museum stands the 19th-century **Ilirska Dvorana Palace**, which houses part of the Croatian Academy of Arts and Sciences. The 19th-century Paravić Palace, with wrought-iron gates, is now the Institute of Historical Studies.

Statues of saints from the main portal of the convent, City Museum

Meštrović Gallery ⑥
Atelje Meštrović

Mletačka 8. **Map** D2. **Tel** (01) 485 1123. ☐ 10am–6pm Tue–Fri, 10am–2pm Sat & Sun. 🖼

This 17th century gallery building was modernized by sculptor Ivan Meštrović and was his residence between 1922 and 1942. It now belongs to the Meštrović Foundation, which also owns the gallery and the Kaštelet in Split *(see pp467)* as well as Meštrović's mausoleum, and houses a collection of Meštrović's work. There are almost 300 works on display, including copies of *History of Croatia, Deposition* and *Woman in Agony*.

Church of St Mark ⑦
Crkva sv Marko

Markov trg. **Map** D2. **Tel** (01) 485 1611. ☐ call in advance.

Now the Upper Town's parish church, the Church of St Mark was first mentioned in 1256, when King Bela IV granted permission to hold a fair in front of the church. On the south side of the church is a Gothic portal carved by Ivan Parler between 1364 and 1377. Surrounding the portal are 15 niches containing statues of Jesus, Mary, St Mark and the 12 apostles. The tiles of the church roof portray the coats of arms of Croatia and the city of Zagreb.

IVAN MEŠTROVIĆ

Born in 1883, Ivan Meštrović (1883–1962) is regarded as one of the most important sculptors of the 20th century. He studied sculpture in Zagreb and Vienna before he established himself in Paris in 1907. He worked in various cities, including Split – where he created many of the works now on display in the Meštrović Gallery – and Zagreb. After World War II, he taught at universities in the US, where he died in 1962. He was buried in the mausoleum in Otavice that he designed for himself and his family.

The 20th-century sculptor Ivan Meštrović

Woodcutters (1959) by Ivan Generalić, Croatian Museum of Naïve Art

Croatian Museum of Naïve Art ⑧

Hrvatski muzej naivne umjetnosti

Ćirilometodska ulica 3. **Map** D2. **Tel** (01) 485 1911. ☐ 10am–6pm Tue–Fri, 10am–1pm Sat & Sun. 🈺 🎫 ☐ www.hmnu.org

Since 1994, this 19th-century building, with its Neo-Baroque façade, has housed works from an exhibition of Naïve painters that opened in Zagreb in 1952. Inspired by peasant craft traditions, the paintings are characterized by the use of vivid colour and a strong feeling for narrative. There are paintings by the founders of the Naïve trend, including Ivan Generalić and Mirko Virius; some new works by the Hlebine School of Painting, which originated in the village of Hlebine near the Hungarian border; and works by artists such as Ivan Rabuzin from other regions.

Lotrščak Tower ⑨

Kula Lotrščak

Strossmayerove šetalište. **Map** D2. **Tel** (01) 485 1768. ☐ Apr–Oct: 11am–7pm Tue–Fri, 2–7pm Sat & Sun. 🈺

Dating from the 13th century, the captivating Lotrščak Tower, or Burglars' Tower, is one of the oldest buildings in Zagreb and a remnant of its fortifications. Since the middle of the 19th century, the city's inhabitants have set their clocks at noon by the sound of a cannon fired from this tower, a

practice begun in 1877 to coordinate the city's bell-ringers. Today, the tower houses an art gallery and a gift shop. It is worth climbing the spiral staircase up to the terrace for fine views over the red-tiled roofs of the city.

Church of St Catherine ⑩

Crkva sv Katarina

Katarinin trg. **Map** D2. **Tel** (01) 485 1950. ☐ 8am–8pm daily.

Considered to be one of the most beautiful religious buildings in Zagreb, the Church of St Catherine was built by Jesuits around 1630 on the site of a Dominican building. The white façade has a doorway with four niches for statues and six prominent pilasters. Above is a niche with a statue of the Virgin Mary. The single-nave church has one of the most striking Baroque interiors

in Croatia. Of particular interest are the stucco reliefs covering the walls and ceiling made by Antonio Quadrio. On the ceiling is a medallion depicting *Scenes of the Life of St Catherine* by Franc Jelovšek, while the main altar, dating from 1762, has *St Catherine among the Alexandrian Philosophers and Writers*, by Kristof Andrej Jelovšek.

Croatian National Theatre ⑪

Hrvatsko narodno kazalište

trg maršala Tita 15. **Map** C4. **Tel** (01) 482 8532. ☐ for performances only. 🌑 Mon, 1 Jan, Easter, 1 May, 1 Nov, 25–26 Dec. www.hnk.hr

The Croatian National Theatre stands in the square that marks the beginning of a U-shaped series of parks and squares called the "green horseshoe", the design of engineer Milan Lenuci. Completed in 1895, the theatre was designed by the architects Hermann Helmer and Ferdinand Fellner and is a blend of Neo-Baroque and Rococo styles.

The richly decorated interior is famous for the stage curtain, which features a patriotic scene entitled *The Croatian Renewal* by painter Vlaho Bukovac. In front of the theatre stands a masterpiece by sculptor Ivan Meštrović (*see p491*) called *The Well of Life*, depicting a group of bronze figures huddled around a well.

Stately exterior of the Neo-Baroque Croatian National Theatre

The Bather (1868) by Renoir in the Mimara Museum

Museum of Arts and Crafts ⑫

Muzej za umjetnost i obrt

trg maršala Tita. **Map** C4. *Tel* (01) 488 2111. ☐ 10am–7pm Tue, Wed, Fri & Sat, 10am–10pm Thu, 10am–2pm Sun. ▣ ▣ www.muo.hr

This elegant 19th-century building contains the finest collection of applied art in the country, with an extensive display of furniture throughout the ages. Many of the exhibits are by graduates of the Zagreb School of Applied Arts, which has been turning out talented ceramicists, glass-makers and graphic designers since its establishment in 1882. An outstanding collection of photography and poster art is also on display.

Mimara Museum ⑬

Muzej Mimara

Rooseveltov trg 5. **Map** C4. *Tel* (01) 482 8100. ☐ Oct–Jun: 10am–5pm Tue, Wed, Fri & Sat, 10am–2pm Sun; Jul–Sep: 10am–7pm Tue–Fri, 10am–5pm Sat, 10am–2pm Sun. ● Mon. ▣ ▣ ▣

In 1972, Ante Topić Mimara, a businessman who was also a collector, painter and restorer, donated his extensive collections to the city of Zagreb, and the Mimara Museum was set up for their display. The museum is housed in a Neo-Renaissance building built by the German architects Ludwig and Hülsner in 1895. The ground floor contains

archaeological finds, Oriental carpets and Ming vases. The first floor concentrates on applied art and religious sculpture, including some fine medieval statues. On the top floor, a wide-ranging collection of paintings takes in Byzantine icons, a Rembrandt, a Rubens, a Renoir and some delightful still lifes by Manet.

Croatian Academy of Arts and Sciences ⑭

Galerija starih majstora

trg Nikole Šubića Zrinskog 11. **Map** E4. *Tel* (01) 489 5117. ☐ 10am–1pm & 5–7pm Tue, 10am–1pm Wed–Sun. ▣ ▣ ▣

In 1876, Bishop Strossmayer of Đakovo, one of the proponents of the pan-Slav movement, had this building constructed to house the Yugoslav Academy of Arts and Sciences. Earlier called the Gallery of Old Masters and Sciences, the building contains one of the country's finest picture collections, most of which was donated by Strossmayer himself. The collection features Renaissance art including canvases by Tintoretto and El Greco. In the entrance hall is the 11th-century Baška tablet, bearing one of the oldest-known inscriptions in the Glagolitic script. Glagolitic was used by medieval rulers until it was replaced by the Roman alphabet.

St Sebastian, Croatian Academy of Arts and Sciences

Susanna and the Old Men, Croatian Academy of Arts and Sciences

Archaeological Museum ⑮

Arheološki muzej

trg Nikole Šubića Zrinskog 19. **Map** E3. *Tel* (01) 487 3101. ☐ 10am–5pm Tue–Fri (until 8pm Thu), 10am–1pm Sat–Sun. ▣ ▣ by appt. ☐ www.amz.hr

The Neo-Classical Vraniczany-Hafner Palace has housed this museum since 1945. It contains artifacts from all over Croatia, ranging from prehistoric finds to Greek vases and medieval Croatian jewellery. One of the most captivating objects on display is the Vučedol Dove, a three-legged pouring vessel in the shape of a bird which dates from the Copper Age (c. 2500 BC). Discovered near Vukovar, it is regarded as the emblem of the museum. Among the Egyptian mummies on display is the so-called Zagreb Mummy, dating from the 3rd century BC.

Museum of Contemporary Art ⑯

Muzej suvremene umjetnosti

Avenija Dubrovnik 17. **Map** A5. *Tel* (01) 605 2700. ▣ 14. ☐ 11am–7pm Tue–Sun, 11am–10pm Thu. ▣ ▣ ▣ ▣ ▣ ▣ www.msu.hr

A major centre of avant-garde art in the years following 1945, the museum, which opened in 2009, showcases contemporary Croatian art. Highlights include abstract canvases by painters Ivan Picelj, Aleksandar Srnec and Julije Knifer and conceptualist pieces by Mladen Stilinović, Tomislav Gotovac and Vlado Martek. International acquisitions include artist Carsten Höller's toboggan slides. The building is in itself an attraction, displaying both moving images and abstract light displays on its façade at night.

Varaždin ❷

Door detail, Church of the Assumption

Although traces of the Neolithic Age and the Roman period have been identified around Varaždin Castle, the first documented mention of the town of Varaždin was in 1181, when King Bela III (r. 1172–96) confirmed the rights of the Zagreb Curia to the thermal spas in the area. In 1209, it was declared a free town by King Andrew II (r. 1205–35) and began to develop as a trading centre. From the 16th century onwards, Varaždin was a border fortress defending Habsburg territories from the Ottoman Turks, and the Croatian Parliament began to meet here in 1756. In 1776, a huge fire caused widespread destruction, but left many churches and palaces standing. Today, Varaždin is one of the best-preserved towns in Croatia.

View of Varaždin Castle, home to the Civic Museum

🏛 Varaždin Castle and Civic Museum

Strossmayerovo šetalište 7. *Tel (042) 658 754.* ⬜ *Apr–Sep: 10am–6pm Tue–Sun; Oct–Mar: 10am–5pm Tue–Fri, 10am–1pm Sat & Sun.* 🖼 📷 🚫

Varaždin Castle (Stari grad i Gradski muzej) has origins in the 12th century, and was rebuilt between the 14th and 19th centuries when an Ottoman attack was imminent. The stout round bastions built at this time are still an impressive sight. The castle was remodelled in the 1560s, when Italian architect Domenico dell'Allio created a Renaissance structure with a beautiful arcaded courtyard. The castle's present look dates from the time of the powerful Erdödy counts, who added bastions and a moat. Now the Civic Museum, it houses collections of weapons, porcelain, handicrafts and an 18th-century pharmacy. Ruins of the wall and the Lisak Tower, to the east of the castle, are the only remaining evidence of the ancient walls.

🏛 Gallery of Old and Modern Masters

Stančićev trg 3. *Tel (042) 214 172.* ⬜ *Apr–Sep: 10am–6pm Tue–Sun; Oct–Mar: 10am–5pm Tue–Sun.* 🖼 *by appt.* 🚫

The gallery (Galerija Starih i Novih Majstora) has a large collection of works from all over Europe, particularly landscapes by Flemish and Italian artists as well as portraits by German and Dutch painters.

🏛 Tomislav Square

Town Hall trg kralja Tomislava 1. *Tel (042) 402 508.* ⬜ *by appt.* **Drašković Palace** trg kralja Tomislava 3. 🔵 *to the public.*

The charming Tomislav Square (trg kralja Tomislava) is the heart of the town. Facing the square is the **Town Hall** (Gradska Vijećnica), one of the oldest buildings in Varaždin. Built in the 15th century in Gothic style, it has since been altered and a clock tower added. It was a private house until 1523, when its owner Prince George of Brandenburg gave it to the town to serve as

the Town Hall. It is guarded in summer by the Purgars, the traditional town guard, who wear 19th-century uniforms and bearskin hats.

To the east of the square stands **Drašković Palace** (Palača Drašković), built in the late 17th century with a Rococo façade. The Croat Parliament met here between 1756 and 1776. Opposite stands the Renaissance Ritz House, one of the oldest in the town; the date of construction, 1540, is engraved on its doorway.

🔒 Cathedral of the Assumption

Pavlinska ulica 4. *Tel (042) 210 688.* ⬜ *9:30am–12:30pm & 4–7pm daily.*

The Church of the Assumption (Katedrala Uznesenja Marijina) became a cathedral in 1997. Both the church and the monastery annexed to it were built in the first half of the 17th century by the Jesuits. Later, the Pauline Order took over.

The cathedral's tall façade features pillars. The interior is in the Baroque style. The main altar occupies the width of the central nave and is a riot of gilded columns, stuccoes and engravings. At the centre is an *Assumption of the Virgin*, reminiscent of Titian's work in Venice. Baroque music concerts are held here in the evenings.

Rich Baroque altar in the Cathedral of the Assumption

🔒 Church of St John the Baptist

Franjevački trg 8. *Tel (042) 213 166.* ⬜ *8:30am–noon & 5:30–7pm daily.*

Built in 1650 in the Baroque style on the site of a 13th-century church, the Church of St John the Baptist (Crkva sv Ivan Krstitelj) has a Renaissance

Bell tower of the Church of St John the Baptist, Tomislav Square

doorway with a tympanum and statues of St Anthony of Padua and St Francis of Assisi. The interior has eight side chapels and an ornate gilded pulpit from the late 17th century. The bell tower is 54 m (177 ft) high.

In front of the church is a copy of the *Monument of Bishop Gregory of Nin* by Ivan Meštrović. The adjacent former pharmacy has many works of art, among them some allegorical frescoes by the 18th-century painter Ivan Ranger.

🏛 Herzer Palace

Franjevački trg 6. ⬭ *Apr–Sep: 10am–6pm Tue–Sun; Oct–Mar: 10am–5pm Tue–Fri, 10am–1pm Sat & Sun.* **Entomological Museum** *Tel (042) 658 760.*

Built at the end of the 18th century, the Herzer Palace (Palača Herzer) has housed the **Entomological Museum** (Entomološki Odjel Gradskog muzeja) since 1954. The museum was founded by entomologist Franjo Košćec, who, in 1959, donated his own natural history collection to the town. It also hosts occasional themed exhibitions.

🏛 Church of the Holy Trinity

Kapucinski trg 7. *Tel (042) 213 550.* ⬭ *9am–noon & 6–7pm Mon–Sat, Sun before and after mass.*

The Church of the Holy Trinity (Crkva Presvetog Trojstvo) dates from the early 18th century and houses Baroque paintings, furnishings by local masters and an organ with figures of angels playing instruments. The neighbouring monastery is famous for its library, containing manuscripts, parchments and incunabula and some of the oldest documents written in Kajkavski (ancient Croatian).

VISITORS' CHECKLIST

90 km (56 miles) NE of Zagreb. 🚶 *42,000.* 🚉 *Frane Supila.* 🚌 *Kolodvorska 17.* 🛈 *Ivana Padovca 3, (042) 210 987.* 🎭 *Varaždin Baroque evenings (Sep–Oct), Špancirfest (late Aug).* **www**.spancirfest.com **www**.tourism-varazdin.hr

🎭 National Theatre

Ulica Augusta Cesarca 1. *Tel (042) 214 688.* ⬭ *for performances only.*

Built by Hermann Helmer in 1873, the National Theatre (Narodno Kazalište) is one of the main cultural centres in the town. During summer and autumn, theatregoers from all over Europe come to attend the performances here.

🏛 Municipal Cemetery

Hallerova aleja. ⬭ *Feb: 7am–6pm; Mar & Oct: 7am–7pm; Apr & Sep: 7am–8pm; May–Aug:7am–9pm; Nov–Jan: 7am–5pm.*

To the west of the castle, this cemetery (Gradsko groblje) is a public garden as well as a place of rest. It was laid out in the early 20th century by cemetery keeper, Herman Haller.

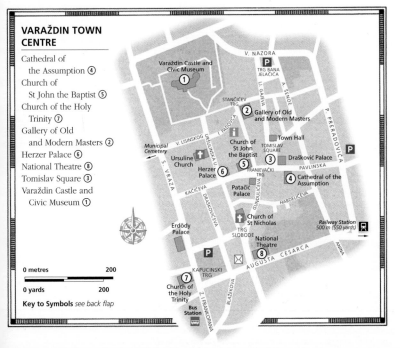

VARAŽDIN TOWN CENTRE

Cathedral of
  the Assumption ④
Church of
  St John the Baptist ⑤
Church of the Holy
  Trinity ⑦
Gallery of Old
  and Modern Masters ②
Herzer Palace ⑥
National Theatre ⑧
Tomislav Square ③
Varaždin Castle and
  Civic Museum ①

0 metres   200
0 yards   200

Key to Symbols *see back flap*

Osijek ㉓

The capital of Slavonia, Osijek sits in the middle of a fertile plain. The city developed in 1786 with the merger of three districts: the Fort (Tvrđa), Lower Town (Donji grad) and Upper Town (Gornji grad). Due to its position on the Drava river, Osijek has always played a strategic role. In 1991, after the declaration of independence by Croatia, the city was bombed by Yugoslav forces and much of the old centre was damaged. Osijek never fell, and emerged from the war to become a prosperous centre. Trvđa, the fortified centre, escaped serious damage during the war and has preserved much of its Baroque architecture. The Upper Town, meanwhile, presents Osijek's modern face with bustling streets, filled with shops, bars and restaurants.

The main square, trg sv Trojstva, in the heart of Tvrđa

🏛 Museum of Slavonia

trg sv Trojstva 6, Tvrđa. **Tel** (031) 250 730. ◯ 8am–2pm Tue–Fri, 10am–1pm Sat & Sun. 🗓 🎥 🗷 🗋

On the eastern side of Tvrđa is the old Town Hall, which has housed the Museum of Slavonia (Muzej Slavonije) since 1946. There is a rich collection devoted to local folklore, including intricately embroidered traditional costumes from surrounding

Statue from Roman Mursa, Osijek Archaeological Museum

villages. Local crafts are represented with a range of painted wooden furniture. It also hosts temporary exhibitions on regional history.

🏛 Osijek Archaeological Museum

trg sv Trojstva 2, Tvrđa. **Tel** (031) 232 132. ◯ 10am–3pm Mon–Wed & Fri, 10am–3pm & 5–8pm Thu, 10am–1pm Sat & Sun. ◉ Mon. 🗓 🗷

This museum (Arheološki muzej) is housed in a restored 18th-century guardhouse on the western side of the square. It has displays of statuary and tombstones from the Roman settlement of Mursa, as well as weapons and jewellery belonging to the first Croat settlers.

🔒 Church of the Holy Cross

Franjevačka, Tvrđa. **Tel** (031) 208 177. ◯ 8am–noon & 3–8pm, daily.

Northeast of trg sv Trojstva, on the site of a sacred medieval building, stands this church (Crkva Svetog Križa), built by the Franciscans between 1709 and 1720. Inside

is a pretty statue of the Virgin Mary from the 15th century and some liturgical furnishings.

🔒 Church of St Michael

trg Jurja Križanića, Tvrđa. **Tel** (031) 208 990. ◯ before mass.

The second biggest chuch in the city, this impressive church (Crkva sv Mihovila) was built by the Jesuits in the first half of the 18th century. The Baroque façade is flanked by two bell towers, and the monastery has a splendid doorway built in 1719. Below street level, the foundations of the 16th-century Kasim-paša Mosque are still visible.

🚆 Europska Avenija

This avenue is Osijek's main thoroughfare, linking Tvrđa to the Upper Town. It is famous for the superb row of Art Nouveau houses built for local industrialists at the beginning of the 20th century. It runs through the leafy Park kralja Držislava, which contains the monumental sculpture *Soldier in the Throes of Death* (1894) by Croatian sculptor Robert Frangeš-Mihanović.

Soldier in the Throes of Death, Park kralja Držislava, Europe Avenue

🏛 Gallery of Fine Arts

Europska avenija 9. **Tel** (031) 251 280. ◯ 10am–6pm Tue–Fri, 10am–1pm Sat & Sun. 🗓 🗷 by appt. 🗷

This gallery (Galerija likovnih umjetnosti), founded in 1954, is housed in an elegant 19th-century house. There are collections of paintings from the 18th and 19th centuries, as well as works by

Splendid Neo-Gothic Church of Sts Peter and Paul

popular Croatian artists. A special setion is dedicated to works of art from the Osijek school.

🅰 Church and Monastery of St James

Kapucinska 41, Gornji grad.
Tel (031) 201 182. 🕐 *6:30am–noon, 4–8pm & by appt, daily.*
The medieval Gothic Church and Monastery of St James (Crkva i samostan sv Jakov), with a Capuchin monastery, is the oldest building in the Upper Town. In the sacristy are mid-18th-century paintings on the life of St Francis.

🅰 Church of Sts Peter and Paul

trg Marina Držića, Gornji grad.
Tel (031) 310 020. 🕐 *2–6:30pm Mon, 9am–6:30pm Tue–Fri.*
This imposing late 19th-century Neo-Gothic church (Crkva sv Petar i Pavao) is dedicated to Sts Peter and Paul. It was designed by Franz Langenberg. The 40 stained-glass windows and some sculptures are by the Viennese artist Eduard Hauser.

🎭 Croatian National Theatre

Županijska 9, Gornji grad.
Tel (031) 220 700.
Osijek has a long and rich theatre tradition. The Croatian National Theatre (Hrvatsko narodno kazalište) was built

in Moorish style in the 19th century, but was badly damaged during the bombing by Yugoslav forces in 1991. It has now been restored and stages a number of opera and drama productions from September to May.

Lavish interior of the Croatian National Theatre

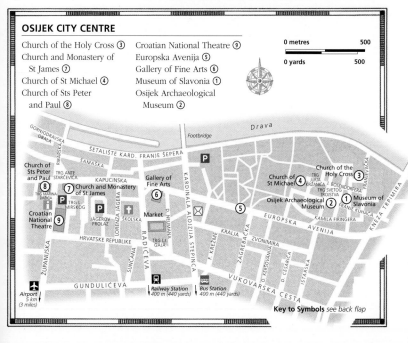

OSIJEK CITY CENTRE

Church of the Holy Cross ③
Church and Monastery of St James ⑦
Church of St Michael ④
Church of Sts Peter and Paul ⑧
Croatian National Theatre ⑨
Europska Avenija ⑤
Gallery of Fine Arts ⑥
Museum of Slavonia ①
Osijek Archaeological Museum ②

0 metres 500
0 yards 500

Key to Symbols *see back flap*

Practical & Travel Information

Croatia is a welcoming country to visit with minimal border formalities, an up-to-date transport network and a well-organized tourist information infrastructure. Modern highways ensure speedy access to the Adriatic coast, while a busy fleet of passenger ferries serves the offshore islands. Public services and tourist facilities are efficient and modern, making the country an increasingly popular holiday destination in South Eastern Europe.

WHEN TO VISIT

The most popular time to visit Croatia is in summer, during July and August. With its crystal-clear seas, islands and bays offering plenty of opportunities for exploration and swimming, the coast is a major attraction. For a quieter holiday, off-season months such as May, June or September are preferable, when the weather is still fine, resorts are not so crowded and accommodation is cheaper. Cities such as Zagreb, Dubrovnik and Split are enjoyable destinations all year round.

DOCUMENTATION

Citizens of European Union (EU) countries, the US, New Zealand, Canada and Australia may visit Croatia for up to 90 days without a visa. The **Croatian Ministry of Foreign Affairs** website provides a list of countries whose citizens require visas. All foreign visitors must register with the local police within 48 hours of arrival; this is usually arranged by hotel staff. Failure to do so may result in a penalty or even deportation from the country.

VISITOR INFORMATION

Every town and city has a tourist office, usually called the Turistički Ured, Turistička Zajednica or Turistički Informativni Centar. The staff is usually helpful and speak English. The **Croatian National Tourist Board** has offices in cities throughout the world, including London and Washington, and also runs a useful website.

Opening hours for tourist offices vary depending on the season. In July and August, the tourist offices open daily from 8am to 8pm; in May, June and September hours are shorter. In smaller towns, some tourist offices may be closed altogether between October and April.

HEALTH AND SECURITY

Croatian public health services meet the standards of those elsewhere in Europe, and in general visitors run no serious health risks. There are no endemic diseases and the most common ailments are those caused by insect bites and over-exposure to the sun. There are *bolnica* or *klinički*

centar (hospitals and clinics) in all the major towns and health centres and *ljekarna* (pharmacies) in the smaller towns. Visitors need not pay for medical services if the Health Care Convention has been signed between Croatia and their home country. This applies to most countries in the EU including the UK, Ireland and Italy. If not, visitors have to pay for treatment according to a standardized price list.

Croatia has a relatively low crime rate and violent crime is rare. If petty theft occurs, it is most likely to happen on crowded beaches during the summer season, so visitors should be vigilant in these places.

FACILITIES FOR THE DISABLED

Croatia is quite well equipped with facilities for the disabled. Most public places, including trains, buses and toilets, are wheelchair-friendly.

BANKING AND CURRENCY

The Croatian currency is the kuna. Money can be changed in banks and authorized exchange bureaus as well as post offices and tourist agencies. In cities and major towns, cash can be withdrawn from ATMs using internationally recognized cards.

COMMUNICATIONS

Public telephones are found everywhere and are operated using phone cards, which are usually sold in units of 15, 30, 50 and 100 kuna. They can be bought from news kiosks and tobacco shops.

SIM cards from local mobile network providers such as **Tele2**, **T-Mobile** and **Vipnet** are economical, but visitors should check with their own phone service providers for advice on roaming facilities within the country.

Internet facilities are widely available, and it is easy to find Internet cafés with good connections in most places.

THE CLIMATE OF CROATIA

Along the coast, the climate is typically Mediterranean, with mild winters and hot, dry summers; the Dalmatian coast is one of the sunniest parts of Europe. Inland, the weather is Continental, with hot summers and cold winters. The mountainous areas have an Alpine climate, with plenty of rain, including thunderstorms and snow in winter.

ZAGREB

°C/F	Apr	Jul	Oct	Jan
high	16/61	24/75	16/61	3/37
low	8/46	17/63	9/48	-3/27
sun (hrs)	5.5 hrs	8.8 hrs	9 hrs	3 hrs
rain (mm)	50 mm	90 mm	90 mm	30 mm
month	Apr	Jul	Oct	Jan

ARRIVING BY AIR

The national airline, **Croatia Airlines**, links Croatia's main airports with the rest of Europe. Other European airlines offering scheduled services to Croatia include **Air France**, **Lufthansa** and **Austrian Airlines**. Among the budget airlines, **Wizzair** flies direct to Zagreb from London Luton airport while **easyJet** and **RyanAir** operate summer season flights from the UK and Ireland to several cities on the Croatian coast. There are no direct flights from North America or Australasia although one or two-stop flights involving a change at a major European airport are easy to arrange.

Croatia has airports at **Zagreb**, **Split**, **Dubrovnik**, Pula, Rijeka and Zadar. All are close to their respective city centres and well connected to them by regular bus services.

ARRIVING BY SEA

Several boat companies operate between Croatia and Italy. **Jadrolinija**, the main ferry company, runs between Ancona and Split four times a week all year round. **Split Tours** also runs daily services.

RAIL TRAVEL

Croatia is well connected to the rest of Europe by rail, especially Central Europe. Visitors travelling from London to Zagreb should contact **Rail Europe** or see their website for information. Connections from other European cities include Munich, Berlin and Vienna.

Within Croatia, all the major towns and cities are linked by rail, with the exception of Dubrovnik, where there is no railway station. The hub of the Croatian railway network is in the capital Zagreb, where the head office of **Croatian Railways** is located.

TRAVELLING BY BUS

Croatia is also well linked to other countries by bus. International buses connect the country with the bordering states and also with France, Switzerland, Germany, Slovakia, Austria and Italy. Within Croatia, the bus network is comprehensive but can be expensive. Services are divided into Intercity (direct connections between the larger cities) and regional services (with connections to smaller towns and the main cities). For information, visitors can contact or check the website of the main bus station, **Autobusni Kolodvor Zagreb**.

TRAVELLING BY CAR

Travelling to Croatia by car is most popular with visitors from neighbouring countries. Those driving in Croatia need to carry a valid driving licence, the car's log book and a Green Card.

Hiring a car is relatively easy and rental agencies can be found in all the main towns and cities. It is best to hire from big companies such as **Avis** or **Hertz**, which offer competitive prices. One of the advantages of renting a car through these companies is having the option of leaving the car in a different town from the collection point.

DIRECTORY

DOCUMENTATION

Croatian Ministry of Foreign Affairs
www.mvp.hr

EMBASSIES

Australia
Kaptol Centar, Zagreb.
Tel (01) 489 1200.

Canada
Prilaz Gjure Deželića 4,
Zagreb. **Tel** (01) 488
1200.

New Zealand
Vlaška 50a, Zagreb.
Tel (01) 461 2060.

United Kingdom
1. Lučića 4, Zagreb.
Tel (01) 600 9100.

United States
Ul. Thomasa Jeffersona 2,
Zagreb. **Tel** (01) 661
2200. **www**.usembassy.hr

VISITOR INFORMATION

Croatian National Tourist Board
Iblerov trg 10/IV, Zagreb.
Tel (01) 469 9333.
www.croatia.hr

EMERGENCY NUMBERS

Ambulance
Tel 94.

Fire
Tel 93.

Police
Tel 92.

COMMUNICATIONS

Tele2
www.tele2.hr

T-Mobile
www.t-mobile.hr

Vipnet
www.vipnet.hr

ARRIVING BY AIR

Air France
www.airfrance.com

Austrian Airlines
www.aua.com

Croatia Airlines
www.croatiaairlines.hr

Dubrovnik Airport
Tel (020) 773 100.
www.airport-dubrovnik.hr

easyJet
www.easyjet.com

Lufthansa
www.lufthansa.com

RyanAir
www.ryanair.com

Split Airport
Tel (021) 203 506.
www.split-airport.hr

Wizzair
www.wizzair.com

Zagreb Airport
Pieso bb HR - 10 150,
Zagreb. **Tel** (01) 4562
170. **www**.zagreb
airport.hr

ARRIVING BY SEA

Jadrolinija
Riječki Lukobran bb,
Rijeka. **Tel** (051) 211 444.

Split Tours
www.splittours.hr

RAIL TRAVEL

Croatian Railways
Tel (060) 333 444.
www.hznet.hr

Rail Europe
Tel (08448) 484 064.
www.raileurope.co.uk

TRAVELLING BY BUS

Autobusni Kolodvor Zagreb
Tel (060) 313 333.
www.akz.hr

TRAVELLING BY CAR

Avis
www.avis.hr

Hertz
www.hertz.hr

Shopping & Entertainment

Souvenir-hunters in Croatia will be spoilt for choice, with a range of traditional crafts such as costume dolls, exquisite handmade lace and hand-painted ceramics and jewellery to choose from. Ties and fountain pens, both of which originated in Croatia, also make good purchases. A variety of accessible and engaging entertainment caters for all age groups and tastes, ranging from opera and ballet to folk music festivals and nightclubs. In summer, performances are sometimes held outdoors in places with a particularly pretty setting.

OPENING HOURS

Shops and department stores are usually open from 8am to 8pm Monday to Friday (sometimes 7am to 9pm) and from 8am to 2 or 3pm on Saturday. It should be noted that smaller shops often close at lunchtime, usually from noon to 4pm. Shops are generally closed on Sundays and holidays, although many remain open in the high season in tourist resorts.

MARKETS

The street markets of Croatia are colourful, lively places to stroll around. In Zagreb, the **Dolac** is a daily market where food is sold under bright red umbrellas. In Split, a morning market is held every day on Pazar, selling absolutely everything: fruit, vegetables, shoes, flowers, clothes and a vast assortment of souvenirs.

Bigger shopping centres are mainly found in larger towns and cities where most merchandise is sold under one roof, and usually include a department store or supermarket. In Zagreb, the busiest shopping centres are the **Importanne Centar** in the city centre and **Avenue Mall** in the southern suburb of Novi Zagreb.

HANDICRAFTS

Croatia has a long tradition of producing fine handicrafts. In Zagreb, **Valentino Moda** has an array of dolls in traditional costume, embroidered items, terracotta, ceramics and wooden objects. In Split, an assortment of souvenirs,

including objects inspired by maritime themes is available. Visitors can also find good reproductions of Roman objects in the underground area of Diocletian's Palace (see pp468–9). In Osijek, the most interesting buy are textiles, finely embroidered with gold and silver thread.

A typical Croatian craft is needlework with red geometric patterns stitched on to a white background. This characteristic design, painstakingly sewn by hand, is mostly used to decorate table linen, pillowcases and blouses. The art of lacemaking is also widely admired. A centuries-old tradition, the lace was originally used to embellish women's blouses. The patterns produced are the lace-maker's interpretation of designs that have been passed down from generation to generation. Beautiful lace can be bought in most places, but two well-known shops are **Bakina kuća** and **Includo** in Zagreb.

JEWELLERY

There is one item of jewellery that can only be found in Croatia or, more precisely, in Rijeka. This is the *morčić,* a small figurine in the form of a black Moorish character wearing a turban. It was originally produced as earrings but today tie-pins and brooches can also be found. Considered a symbol of good luck, the item is traditionally made of glazed ceramic, although precious stones may be used to decorate it on request. The best place to buy a *morčić* in Rijeka is the **Mala Galerija.**

SOUVENIRS

Three good souvenirs from Croatia are ties, fountain pens and lavender. The country can claim to have invented the tie, or cravat, which was originally a scarf used by Croatian cavalrymen to distinguish them from other soldiers during the Thirty Years' War in the 17th century. A good selection can be found in leading clothes stores in Zagreb such as **Boutique Croata** and **Heruc Galeria**. Another little-known fact is that the inventor of the fountain pen, Eduard Slavoljub Penkala, was an engineer from Zagreb. Pens are available in most department stores in the capital.

The country's best-known natural product is lavender, which is sold dried, in small bags, or as essence, in bottles. It can be found more or less all over Croatia but is particularly linked with the island of Hvar (see pp474–5).

FOOD

Among Croatia's gastronomic specialities, mustard (in traditional containers), honey and *cukarini* biscuits are particularly worth buying. Truffles from Istria and olive oil from the Dalmatian Islands are highly prized by gourmets. Another valued delicacy is *paški sir,* a mature cheese made from sheep's milk, produced on the island of Pag. Food specialities can be bought from **Zigante Tartufi** and **Natura Croatica** in Zagreb.

NIGHTLIFE

Croatia is never short of nightlife. For an all-night party, however, the capital or the coast are the best places to be. There are lots of lively bars along the pedestrianized Tkalčićeva ulica in Zagreb; while clubs like **Aquarius Club** (house and techno) and **Močvara** (alternative rock) provide plenty in the way of DJ action and live music.

Apart from Zagreb, other places have an equally lively nightlife. Rijeka has over the last 20 years seen the birth of several new bands, many performing in the cult venue **Club Palach**, named after Jan Palach, the Czech student who set fire to himself in 1968 to protest against the Soviet invasion of Czechoslovakia. Another good spot for lively alternative rock concerts is **Rock Club Uljanik**, occupying a vacant building above the shipyards in Pula.

Split features clubs with open-air terraces looking out to sea, the best of which are **O'Hara** on the seafront path and **Hemingway** near the yachting marina. The alleyways of Dubrovnik's Old Town are full of café-bars that remain lively until the early hours, while the **Latino Club Fuego** is casual and relaxed, and plays a range of music.

Hvar, one of the country's many islands, has developed a reputation as a party island. Early evening activity centres around the harbour in bar-cum-clubs such as **Carpe Diem**, where the dancers warm up before heading up the tree-covered hillside to **Veneranda**, a big old Venetian fort that has been converted into an open-air nightclub.

THEATRE, DANCE AND FESTIVALS

Although usually performed in Croatian, high-class stagings of opera and theatre are enjoyable, especially those put on by Zagreb's **Croatian National Theatre**, Rijeka's **Ivan Zajc Theatre** and Split's **National Theatre**. For a more unusual form of drama, a visit to the unique Zagreb puppet theatre, **Zagrebačko Kazalište Lutaka**, can be rewarding. They have performances almost every weekend and tickets can be bought on the spot. Information about programmes is available from the tourist information office or on posters announcing forthcoming events.

Croatia also has many traditional festivals, of which the most famous is the sword dance, enacted in Korčula's town centre twice a week throughout the summer. Any festive occasion incorporates folk dances such as the *poskočica*, where couples weave themselves into intricate configurations.

Tickets for performances can be bought in advance from an agency or at the relevant venue.

FOLK MUSIC

Croatia has a rich tradition of folk music and folk bands play all along the Adriatic, in open-air concerts and at holiday festivals. Unusual instruments to look out for are the *tamburica*, a mandolin-type instrument of Anatolian origin common in Slavonia and in the extreme east of the country, and the *citura*, a poignant-sounding type of zither (a horizontal stringed instrument). Visitors will also encounter variations on the folk theme such as *klapa* – five- to ten-part harmony singing, mainly by males – or *linđo*, the most popular dance of Dubrovnik, accompanied by a traditional instrument with three strings called a *lijerica*. The **Dubrovnik Summer Festival**, held between July and August, is not to be missed, nor any event at Pula's ancient and stunning **Pula Amphitheatre**.

DIRECTORY

MARKETS

Avenue Mall
Av Dubrovnik 16, Zagreb.
Tel (01) 364 0231.

Dolac
Tel (01) 481 4400.

Importanne Centar
Starcevicev trg, Zagreb.
Tel (01) 457 7076.

HANDICRAFTS

Bakina kuća
Strossmayerov trg 7, Zagreb.
Tel (01) 485 2525.

Includo
Pod zidom 5, Zagreb.
Tel (01) 550 9960.

Valentino Moda
trg Jelačića, Zagreb.

JEWELLERY

Mala Galerija
Uzarska 12, Rijeka.
Tel (051) 335 403.

SOUVENIRS

Boutique Croata
Prolaz Oktogon, Ilica 5, Zagreb. *Tel (01) 481 2726.*

Heruc Galeria
Ilica 26, Zagreb.
Tel (01) 483 3569.

FOOD

Natura Croatica
Preradovićeva 8, Zagreb.
Tel (01) 485 5076.

Zigante Tartufi
Vlaška 43, Zagreb.
Tel (01) 481 0358.

NIGHTLIFE

Aquarius Club
Aleja Matije Ljubeka, Jarun, Zagreb.
Tel (01) 364 0231.

Carpe Diem
Riva, Hvar.

Club Palach
Kruzna 6, Rijeka.
Tel (051) 215 063.

Hemingway

VIII. Mediteranskih igara 3, Split.
www.hemingway.hr

Latino Club Fuego
Brsalije 11, Near Pile Gate, Dubrovnik.
Tel (020) 312 070.

Močvara
Trnjanski nasip, Zagreb.
Tel (01) 615 9668.

O'Hara
Uvala Zenta 3, Split.
Tel (098) 364 262.
www.ohara.hr

Rock Club Uljanik
Dobrilina 2, Pula.
Tel (052) 217 623.

Veneranda
Gornja cesta bb, Hvar.
Tel (098) 855 151.

THEATRE, DANCE AND FESTIVALS

Croatian National Theatre
trg Maršala Tita 15, Zagreb.
Tel (01) 488 8418.

Ivan Zajc Theatre
Uljarska 1, Rijeka.
Tel (051) 355 900.

National Theatre
trg Gaje Bulata 1, Split.
Tel (021) 344 999.

Zagrebačko Kazalište Lutaka
ulica Baruna Trenka 3, Zagreb.
Tel (01) 369 5457.

FOLK MUSIC

Dubrovnik Summer Festival
www.dubrovnik-festival.hr

Pula Amphitheatre
Forum 3, Pula.
Tel (052) 219 197.

Where to Stay in Croatia

Although the tourism industry was badly affected during the war of the 1990s, it has improved in recent years and Croatia now offers a wide range of places to stay. There are many modern hotels, apartments and holiday villages, especially along the coast. Book in advance for hotels in July and August, which is the high season.

PRICE CATEGORIES

Price categories are for a standard double room per night in high season, including tax and service charges. Breakfast is included, unless otherwise specified.

ⓚ Under 500 kuna
ⓚⓚ 500–750 kuna
ⓚⓚⓚ 750–1,000 kuna
ⓚⓚⓚⓚ 1,000–1,200 kuna
ⓚⓚⓚⓚⓚ Over 1,200 kuna

ZAGREB

Hotel Jadran   P 🖾   ⓚⓚ

Vlaška 50 **Tel** *(01) 455 3777* **Fax** *(01) 461 2151* **Rooms** *48*   **Map** *E3*

Located only minutes away from Zagreb's central square, the façade of Hotel Jadran looks a little austere and some of the rooms are a bit old-fashioned, but others are fine and clean. It is advisable to check the room first before booking and to request one at the back of the hotel to minimize any street noise. **www.hup-Zagreb.hr**

Hotel Palace   P 🍴 🖾   ⓚⓚⓚⓚ

trg J J Strossmayerov 10 **Tel** *(01) 489 9600* **Fax** *(01) 481 1357* **Rooms** *123*   **Map** *E4*

Built in 1891, the Palace is the grand old lady of Zagreb's hotels. Located near the historic centre of the city, the hotel oozes old-world aristocracy. The rooms are a good size and smart with wood panels and good furniture. The communal areas are faded and veering towards old-fashioned. **www.palace.hr**

Regent Esplanade   🍴 ⛱ 🖾   ⓚⓚⓚⓚⓚ

Mihanovićeva 1 **Tel** *(01) 456 6666* **Fax** *(01) 456 6050* **Rooms** *209*   **Map** *D5*

Set in a regal building (c. 1925), the Regent Esplanade is a refined establishment with excellent service – probably the best in Zagreb. The rooms are tastefully decorated with luxurious bathrooms, while the communal areas are swathed in marble and adorned with chandeliers. It also has its own restaurants and bars. **www.regenthotels.com**

FURTHER AFIELD Central   🖾   ⓚⓚⓚ

Branimirova 3 **Tel** *(01) 484 1122* **Fax** *(01) 484 1304* **Rooms** *79*

A modern hotel close to the railway and bus station, Central is convenient for those on the move as well as sightseers. The rooms are small but fairly well furnished. Facilities include high-speed Internet, TV and stylish bathrooms. There is also a bar, though it is rather uninspiring. **www.hotel-central.hr**

FURTHER AFIELD Westin Zagreb   🍴 ⛱ 🖾   ⓚⓚⓚⓚ

Kršnjavoga 1 **Tel** *(01) 489 2000* **Fax** *(01) 489 2001* **Rooms** *378*

Once known as the Opera Hotel, Westin Zagreb is located at the very heart of the city near the major cultural and historical attractions. Rebranded and refurbished, it is now a top-notch luxury hotel within a modern building, which provides international standards of service at a good price. **www.westin.com/Zagreb**

REST OF CROATIA

BRAČ Hotel Kaštil   🍴 🖾   ⓚⓚⓚⓚ

F Radića bb, Bol **Tel** *(021) 635 995* **Fax** *(021) 635 997* **Rooms** *32*

An excellent choice for a medium-sized three-star hotel, the Hotel Kaštil is built in traditional white stone (it was once a Baroque fortress) and set peacefully by the town harbour. All the rooms and the terrace restaurant look out across the sea. The restaurant gets busy in the evening. **www.kastil.hr**

BRAČ Hotel Riu Borak   🍴 ⛱ 🖾   ⓚⓚⓚⓚⓚ

Bračka cesta 13, Bol **Tel** *(021) 306 202* **Fax** *(021) 306 215* **Rooms** *136*

A large four-star resort set amidst cypresses and pines alongside a few other major hotels. The main attraction is its location right beside Croatia's most famous beach, Zlatni Rat *(see p468)* – hence the high price – but it has been renovated and has all the facilities visitors might want. Crowded in high season. **www.bluesunhotels.com**

CAVTAT Hotel Supetar   🍴 🖾   ⓚⓚⓚ

Obala Dr A Starčevića 27 **Tel** *(020) 479 833* **Fax** *(020) 479 858* **Rooms** *28*

In an old stone house on the waterfront, with sea views and a nearby "beach" (a concrete platform with sun loungers), the Supetar is hard to beat for charm, setting and value for money, although the interior lacks imagination. The nearby pine-covered peninsula is edged with swimming places. **www.hoteli-croatia.hr/supetar**

Map References *see map of Zagreb pp486–7*

CAVTAT Croatia

Frankopanska 10 **Tel** *(020) 475 555* **Fax** *(020) 478 213* **Rooms** *158*

This supersized hotel clings to a wooded hill, almost hidden from sight. The rooms are tastefully decorated and well furnished, and it has its own private bathing ledges off the rocks into the open sea. It does not have as many facilities as visitors might expect, but it does feel quite exclusive. **www.hoteli-croatia.hr**

DUBROVNIK Hotel Sumratin

Šetalište Kralja Zvonimira 27 **Tel** *(020) 436 333* **Fax** *(020) 436 006* **Rooms** *44*

Out of town on the Lapad Peninsula, this three-storey 1922 villa with a pleasant garden, is located near the beach and is handily placed for restaurants and bars. It has been renovated recently, though its dated interior and basic facilities are still not quite enough for it to transcend its two-star status. **www.hotels-sumratin.com**

DUBROVNIK Excelsior

Frana Supila 12 **Tel** *(020) 353 353* **Fax** *(020) 353 100* **Rooms** *160*

Situated east of the city, this luxury hotel is known for attracting famous guests such as Margaret Thatcher and Queen Elizabeth. The rooms are elegant, the views fantastic and the service outstanding. There are good restaurants and a lovely terrace too. **www.hotel-excelsior.hr**

DUBROVNIK Hotel Stari Grad

Od Sigurate 4 **Tel** *(020) 322 244* **Fax** *(020) 321 256* **Rooms** *8*

A tiny boutique hotel located in the Old Town that is furnished like an aristocrat's mansion with chandeliers, rugs, mirrors and paintings. The star feature is the panoramic view from the roof terrace, where one can dine alfresco. However, light sleepers should note that the Old Town is not the quietest of places. **www.hotelstarigrad.com**

DUBROVNIK Hotel Pucić Palace

Od Puča 1 **Tel** *(020) 326 222* **Fax** *(020) 326 223* **Rooms** *17*

Opened in 2003, this five-star boutique hotel is set in an 18th-century palace overlooking the Old Town's market square (Gundulic). Very expensive, this is where high society stays and luxurious rooms with antique furniture and dark wooden beams are the norm. Good restaurants and a wine bar too. **www.thepucicpalace.com**

DUBROVNIK Vis

Masarykov put 4 **Tel** *(020) 433 540* **Fax** *(020) 437 333* **Rooms** *136*

Overlooking Lapad bay, this wide, white modern complex has all the comforts and regular hotel facilities, with views out to the open sea. Clean, modern enough and the service is good too. It might be a bit short on character but it works well on its own level. **www.hotelmaestral.com**

HVAR Amfora

Dolac bb **Tel** *(021) 750 300* **Fax** *(021) 750 301* **Rooms** *330*

This is a large hotel on the beachfront not far from Hvar town. Modern and stylish, the rooms are nicely furnished and incorporate 100 apartments. There are two pleasant restaurants with sea views (one with live music in the evenings). It also offers good tennis facilities and a diving school. **www.suncanihvar.hr**

HVAR Hotel Podstine

Podstine bb **Tel** *(021) 740 400* **Fax** *(021) 740 499* **Rooms** *40*

Just under 2 km (1 mile) southwest of Hvar town centre, this hotel is set apart in a quiet cove, surrounded by shade-giving trees, with its own private beach and soothing outdoor seaside terraces. The rooms are simple, with views out over the sea; most have balconies. **www.podstine.com**

KORČULA Korčula

Korčula **Tel** *(020) 711 078* **Fax** *(020) 711 746* **Rooms** *24*

A small and traditional-looking hotel in the centre of town with a great waterfront terrace. Built in lovely light-coloured Korčula stone, it has an old-fashioned feel about it. The hotel is not perfect by any means, but the location is unbeatable. **www.korcula-hotels.com**

OSIJEK Hotel Central

trg A Starčevića 6 **Tel** *(031) 283 399* **Fax** *(031) 283 891* **Rooms** *39*

Originally built in 1889, this medium-sized traditional hotel is set in the heart of town and caters to a discerning clientele. Rooms are good, with modern but classically-styled furniture. The common areas are cosy and exude an old-world charm. There is also a Viennese coffee house. **www.hotel-central-os.hr**

OSIJEK Hotel Waldinger

Županijska ulica 8 **Tel** *(031) 250 450* **Fax** *(031) 250 453* **Rooms** *16*

A lovely old-fashioned hotel near the centre, only a short walk from the Drava Promenade. With only 16 elegant rooms (some with Jacuzzi), it offers an intimate four-star experience. The hotel coffee shop has an excellent selection of desserts. **www.waldinger.hr**

POREČ Hotel Neptun

Obala Maršala Tita 15 **Tel** *(052) 400 800* **Fax** *(052) 431 351* **Rooms** *143*

The best hotel in town, delightfully located on the promontory looking out to sea over the harbour. It can be susceptible to noise, so it is best to take the front rooms with harbour views. Keen swimmers can take advantage of the free boat service to St Nicholas Island. **www.riviera.hr**

Key to Symbols *see back cover flap*

POREČ Parentium

Zelena Laguna **Tel** *(052) 411 500* **Fax** *(052) 451 536* **Rooms** *368*

A resort-hotel set on its own peninsula amidst shady pines – but be aware that the trees hide some of the sea views. There is a marina on one side of the promontory and some good beaches on the other. The hotel is clean, provides the usual array of facilities and offers plenty for children to do. **www.plavalaguna.hr**

POREČ Tamaris
Lanterna **Tel** *(052) 401 000* **Fax** *(052) 443 500* **Rooms** *319*

This major resort-hotel complex set about 10 km (6 miles) from Poreč enjoys a secluded setting and has a pebble beach nearby with pine trees providing shade. It is particularly good for families, offering plenty of activities such as cycling, tennis and diving. **www.riviera.hr**

PULA Hotel Omir
Serđa Dobrića 6 **Tel** *(052) 218 186* **Fax** *(052) 213 944* **Rooms** *18*

This is a tidy two-star hotel in the heart of Pula. A friendly family-run establishment, it is one of a kind, offering its own pizza restaurant and a pet shop with good deals for pampering guests' pets. The rooms are functional and fairly inexpensive. **www.hotel-omir.com**

PULA Hotel Riviera

Splitska 1 **Tel** *(052) 211 166* **Fax** *(052) 219 117* **Rooms** *65*

With a classical-columned façade in the Austro-Hungarian style, this city hotel looks grander than a one-star establishment. It has clean rooms, most of which have balconies with views of the historic centre or the waterfront. The café bar is spacious with a big terrace. Close to the Pula Amphitheatre *(see p483)*. **www.arenaturist.hr**

PULA Hotel Histria
Verudela **Tel** *(052) 590 000* **Fax** *(052) 214 175* **Rooms** *240*

Located 4 km (2 miles) outside the city, opposite Marina Veruda, this is a large, comfortable and well-equipped resort hotel with spacious, luxurious rooms. Some have balconies with panoramic views of the sea. Facilities include a casino, piano bar, yacht club, restaurant and terrace café. **www.arenaturist.hr**

PULA Hotel Valsabbion

Pješćana Uvala 1X/26 **Tel** *(052) 218 033* **Fax** *(052) 383 333* **Rooms** *10*

This is a smart, intimate, family-run boutique hotel in a seaside villa, 6 km (4 miles) south of Pula. Rooms are elegant, some with bright furnishings. Past guests include John Malkovich, Placido Domingo and Naomi Campbell. The restaurant is one of Croatia's best. **www.valsabbion.net**

RAB Padova

Banjol bb **Tel** *(051) 724 184* **Fax** *(051) 724 117* **Rooms** *175*

A large, modern hotel located across the bay from Rab's Old Town, with good sports facilities, indoor and outdoor pools and a new sauna; beauty treatments are available. It has excellent views across the water to Rab. Note that not all rooms have air conditioning. **www.imperial.hr**

RIJEKA Jadran

Šetalište XIII Divizije 46 **Tel** *(051) 216 600* **Fax** *(051) 216 458* **Rooms** *69*

The sea laps at the foundations of this monolithic building situated on the Rijeka-Split coastal road. Rooms have been refurbished and are large and well furnished; most have big windows and expansive views out over the sea (rooms overlooking the road are cheaper). Internet access is available. **www.jadran-hoteli.hr**

RIJEKA Bonavia

Dolac 4 **Tel** *(051) 357 100* **Fax** *(051) 335 969* **Rooms** *121*

Despite being 125 years old, the Bonavia appears modern. Set in the centre of town, it is business-oriented, with Internet access in every room and a variety of restaurants and bars. The rooms are very pretty and some have sea views. Service is top-notch and the hotel can arrange all sorts of tours and excursions. **www.bonavia.hr**

ROVINJ Valdaliso

Monsena bb **Tel** *(052) 805 500* **Fax** *(052) 811 541* **Rooms** *120*

A short distance around the bay from Rovinj, this hotel provides access to good pebble beaches and bathing rocks and offers a wide range of activities – sports, diving and even a painting class. Rooms are decent if lacking in flair. The hotel also has two annexes and a large camp site, so it can get busy. **www.maistra.hr**

ROVINJ Hotel Angelo D'Oro

V Svalba 38–42 **Tel** *(052) 840 502* **Fax** *(052) 840 111* **Rooms** *23*

This boutique hotel occupies a restored 17th-century palace – the period detailing adds to the atmosphere. There is a pleasant suntrap of a patio and a shady loggia or balcony to look out over the red-tiled roofs to the sea. The high quality of the service and the gourmet restaurant are matched by the prices. **www.rovinj.at**

SPLIT Hotel Jadran

Sustipanski Put 23 **Tel** *(021) 398 622* **Fax** *(021) 398 586* **Rooms** *31*

A modern hotel, a 20-minute walk from central Split, the Jadran is set on the coast with most rooms looking out to sea. Sports facilities include an Olympic-sized pool, tennis courts and sailing. A good choice, especially as the pine-covered Marjan Peninsula *(see p467)* is only a short walk away. **www.hoteljadran.hr**

SPLIT Hotel President

Starčevićeva 1 **Tel** *(021) 305 290* **Fax** *(021) 305 225* **Rooms** *73*

This is an upmarket hotel with well-furnished and well-appointed rooms. It attracts business customers, lending it a slightly corporate atmosphere, but delivers sophisticated service right in the centre of Split, and the prices are not too high either. **www.hotelpresident.hr**

SPLIT Hotel Globo

Lovretska 18 **Tel** *(021) 481 111* **Fax** *(021) 481 118* **Rooms** *25*

Spacious, refined bedrooms and four-star comforts supplemented by a similarly high quality of service offset the bland exterior and rather ordinary urban setting of Globo. It is a 15-minute walk into town and further to reach the beaches. The hotel offers bikes, cars and scooters for rent. **www.hotelglobo.com**

TROGIR Hotel Concordia

Bana Berislavica 22 **Tel** *(021) 885 400* **Fax** *(021) 885 401* **Rooms** *14*

This is an impressive 18th-century stone townhouse converted into an attractive boutique hotel in the centre of Trogir's Old Town. Most of the rooms have sea views, and though they are a little snug, in general, the hotel offers value and services beyond its two-star rating. **www.concordia-hotel.net**

TROGIR Trogirski Dvori

Kralja Trpimira 245 **Tel** *(021) 885 444* **Fax** *(021) 881 318* **Rooms** *12*

A family-run hotel, about a 10-minute walk from the centre of town and two minutes away from the nearest beach. Rooms are comfortable and all have balconies. There is a tennis court on site. The restaurant is known for its Dalmatian cuisine and Croatian wines served on a vine-shaded terrace. **www.hotel-trogirskidvori.com**

TROGIR Villa Sikaa

Obala Kralja Zvonimira 13 **Tel** *(021) 798 240* **Fax** *(021) 885 149* **Rooms** *10*

A small, boutique hotel in a 300-year-old building set on the waterfront looking across to the old island town of Trogir. Most rooms are large with decent furniture and fittings. Staff are very helpful and there is a travel agency that can arrange car and bike-hire for guests. Outstanding value. **www.vila-sikaa-r.com**

VARAŽDIN La'Gus

Varaždinberg **Tel** *(042) 652 940* **Fax** *(042) 652 944* **Rooms** *26*

Only a 15-minute drive from Varaždin, this small hotel, with a pretty vineyard setting, is a good option for those who wish to enjoy the countryside or find the hotels in town booked up. It is not terribly appealing from the road, but the rooms are pleasant and there is a large terrace at the back. **www.hotel-lagus.hr**

VARAŽDIN Pansion Garestin

Zagrebačka 34 **Tel** *(042) 214 314* **Rooms** *10*

This combination hotel-restaurant is only a few minutes walk from Varaždin's Baroque town centre. The attractive-looking building has a faux-Baroque exterior on one side with a modern rustic-style look on the other. Rooms are plain, but it has a large terrace and a restaurant with excellent food. **www.gastrocom.hr**

VIS Hotel Tamaris

Obala sv Jurja 20 **Tel** *(021) 711 350* **Fax** *(021) 711 349* **Rooms** *27*

A stately, Austro-Hungarian, 19th-century villa with characteristically high ceilings and wooden floors, right in the centre of Vis. The hotel is right beside the main quay for yachts and is perfectly placed for nearby seafood restaurants. The rooms are simply furnished and inexpensive; try to get one with a harbour view.

VIS Hotel San Giorgio

Petra Hektorovića 2 **Tel** *(021) 711 362* **Fax** *(021) 717 501* **Rooms** *35*

Located on the eastern side of town amidst a nest of cobbled streets and ancient buildings, this is an especially attractive-looking hotel. Rooms are decked out in contemporary style and come with swish modern bathrooms. Cosy and family-run, it is good value and has an excellent restaurant. **www.hotelsangiorgiovis.com**

ZADAR Hotel Donat

Majstora Radovana 7 **Tel** *(023) 206 500* **Fax** *(023) 332 065* **Rooms** *240*

This large and functional modern complex with three-star facilities has elegant rooms and stylish bathrooms. It has excellent sports facilities, including an outdoor swimming pool, but its main selling points are its reasonable prices and its position right on the beach along a lovely stretch of coastline. **www.falkensteiner.com**

ZADAR Hotel Adriana Select

Majstora Radovana 7 **Tel** *(023) 206 636* **Fax** *(023) 332 065* **Rooms** *48*

Set in an attractive 19th-century villa near the beach and restored into a so-called lifestyle hotel, this does not have rooms but rather "junior suites". The suites are clean and also have balconies. There is a good swimming pool and an excellent restaurant. **www.falkensteiner.com**

ZADAR Hotel President

Vladana Desnice 16 **Tel** *(023) 333 696* **Fax** *(023) 333 595* **Rooms** *27*

A smart hotel, verging on plush, the interior of the President is slightly over-the-top – covered in dark cherrywood and thickly draped curtains. Nevertheless it exudes calm and quality. Service is good, and the restaurant is well worth trying. It is also close to the beach. **www.hotel-president.hr**

Where to Eat in Croatia

Croatia's coastal cuisine has been influenced by the long years of Venetian rule, while inland areas reflect the tastes of Central Europe. Fresh fish, meat and vegetables are popular, as are air-dried hams called *pršut*. Prices are much lower than in Western European countries, making eating out excellent value.

PRICE CATEGORIES
Based on the price per person of a complete meal with drinks (except wine), including service (a tip is recommended).

ⓚ Under 100 kuna
ⓚⓚ 100–200 kuna
ⓚⓚⓚ 200–300 kuna
ⓚⓚⓚⓚ 300–400 kuna
ⓚⓚⓚⓚⓚ Over 400 kuna

ZAGREB

Vallis Aurea
ⓚⓚ
Tomićeva 4 **Tel** *(01) 483 1305*   **Map** *D3*

Located near the funicular, this place has a pleasantly old-fashioned interior featuring whitewashed walls and dark wood. Often busy, it serves Slavonian dishes such as *pastičada* (beef stew with prunes), *strukli* (stuffed pastries), smoked pork ribs and trout. Wines are fine and the staff are helpful.

Baltazar
 ⓚⓚⓚ
Nova Ves 4 **Tel** *(01) 466 6824*   **Map** *E1*

This is an old favourite on the Zagreb scene, just north of the St Stephen's Cathedral and justifiably acclaimed. It offers all the classic dishes, good service and a wonderful atmosphere within a traditional arched basement. On sunny days, book ahead for one of the coveted summer courtyard tables.

Paviljon
🍴🍷 ⓚⓚⓚⓚⓚ
trg Kralja Tomislava 22 **Tel** *(01) 481 3066*   **Map** *D2*

This pavilion in the park is worth visiting for the striking architecture alone, although the food and service are excellent too. An Italian-inspired menu includes beef carpaccio with grana and rocket; white truffle tagliatelle; and a Dalmatian version of saltimbocca using pork fillet, sage and *pršut* (ham).

REST OF CROATIA

BRAČ Ribarska Kućica
🍴 ⓚⓚ
Ante Starčevića, Bol **Tel** *(021) 635 033*

From the terrace here there are beautiful views out over the sea and the restaurant's own secluded beach. There is a wide choice of fish dishes as well as pizza, and a fixed price menu after 8pm every evening. The gnocchi with *pršut* in a cheese sauce is highly recommended; rather filling, but perfect after a hard day's swimming.

CAVTAT Galija
 ⓚⓚⓚ
Vuličevićeva 1 **Tel** *(020) 478 566*

Cavtat's top restaurant is located close to the main promenade on the way to the peninsula near the Franciscan Monastery. It is an old-fashioned tavern with a lovely terrace under pine trees, by the sea – all tables have linen and candles and the menu is a little more adventurous than most. Worth booking ahead, especially at weekends.

DUBROVNIK Lokanda Peskarija
🍴 ⓚ
Na Ponti **Tel** *(020) 324 750*

Located near the harbour fish market this restaurant is famous for its simple, fresh fish and seafood. The traditional wood-heavy interior provides a warm, cosy atmosphere. Food is served in traditional black pots and there is also a buzzing bar. In summer, tables are put outside. Booking in advance is advised.

DUBROVNIK Nautika
 ⓚⓚⓚⓚ
Brsalje 3 **Tel** *(020) 442 526*

One of the most elegant restaurants in the city, the Nautika offers lovely views of the walls and sea just by the Pile Gate *(see p454)*. The food, though expensive, is of a high standard. Specialities include the fish dishes. Also definitely worth trying are the grilled lobster and the *brodet* (fish stew) with polenta. Reserve ahead at weekends.

HVAR Macondo
🍴 ⓚⓚⓚ
Groda **Tel** *(021) 742 850*

Located up the hill from the main square (look for the signs), the Macondo serves sumptuous fish. Sample the marinated anchovies or sublime spaghetti with lobster; finish off with homemade *prosec* (fortified wine). The terrace is great for people-watching, and the restaurant can get busy at weekends when Hvar's glitterati flock in.

Map References *see map of Zagreb pp486–7*

KORČULA Morski Konjić

Šetalište Petra Kanavelića **Tel** *(020) 711 878*

An intimate *konoba* (fishing-themed restaurant) right on the end of the fortified peninsula. It can get busy, so be prepared to queue for the freshly cooked fish and excellent shellfish. It is plain inside with chequered tablecloths and a few nautical items; there are tables outside as well. It also stocks a wide range of good Croatian wines.

OSIJEK Bijelo Plavi

Martina Divalta 8 **Tel** *(031) 571 000*

Located near the town swimming pool and the Gradski Vrt stadium, this restaurant offers typical regional dishes such as spicy paprika-flavoured stews and freshwater fish. The interior is inviting, with simple white walls and dark wooden beams; it also has a good choice of wines.

POREČ Konoba Ulixes

Dekumanus 2 **Tel** *(052) 451 132*

Situated in the Old Town of Poreč, this small and intimate restaurant is a bit of a gem where one can try Istrian truffle dishes without breaking the bank and enjoy good fish and seafood as well. It is rustic and cosy inside, with a small sun trap of a terrace outside dotted by an olive tree or two.

PULA Milan

Stoja 4 **Tel** *(052) 210 200*

Dating back to 1967, this fine hotel-restaurant has over the years built up a list of 700 wines and also serves some marvellous fish – monkfish, sardines, cuttlefish and red mullet. Try the *lazanje sa jastogom* (creamy lobster lasagne). The decor is fairly modern and simple.

RAB Kordić

Barbat 176

Set 2 km (1 mile) along Rab's east coast, Barbat is a traditional fishing port. This comes through strongly in the cooking at the Kordić restaurant, where diners can sample locally caught spiny crab salad, whole grilled catch of the day or lobsters from the tank – simply grilled or served with fresh tomato sauce along with a glass of dry wine.

RIJEKA Municipium

trg Riječke Revolucije 5 **Tel** *(051) 213 000*

Located in a historic 19th-century building, Municipium is one of the best restaurants in Rijeka. Try the *škampi buzara* (fish in a rich garlic, tomato and Cognac sauce) or a heartier *pašticada* (beef stew with homemade gnocchi). Alongside the wide range of fish and shellfish, they also have a small selection of vegetarian dishes.

ROVINJ Veli Jože

Svetoga Križa 1 **Tel** *(052) 816 337*

This attractive restaurant serves traditional Istrian dishes such as *bakalar* (salt cod) in a white sauce or lamb stew cooked with potatoes, pasta and grilled fish – all washed down with the extremely drinkable local Malvasia white wine. There is also a good-sized terrace.

SPLIT Šumica

Put Firula 6 **Tel** *(021) 389 897*

To the east of the city in a chic part of town, this restaurant enjoys a lovely location shaded by cooling pines and overlooking the sea. Dine out on the terrace and feast on excellent fish and shellfish as well as typical grilled meats and pasta while the sun sets. Specialities also include scampi and dry white wine.

TROGIR Kamerlengo

Vukovarska 2 **Tel** *(021) 884 772*

Located in the heart of the Old Town, this restaurant has a lovely walled patio garden that also houses a wood-burning oven and a char-grill. It specializes in seafood but actually serves anything that can be roasted, grilled or barbecued. It is a little hidden down a cobbled side street, but the sign is visible.

VARAŽDIN Royal

Uska ulica 5 **Tel** *(042) 213 477*

Located in the town centre, this restaurant offers delicious food and Croatian wines. The mahogany covered interior is a bit dark but there is a bar in the basement and a small terrace. Game is a speciality with venison and wild boar on the menu along with fish – freshwater and from the coast.

VIS Villa Kaliopa

V Nazora 32 **Tel** *(021) 711 755*

This restaurant is set in the middle of the walled garden of the 16th-century Garibaldi palace, which is dotted with statues and unusual plants. Very atmospheric, it attracts a well-heeled yachting crowd and romantic couples. The food and wine are excellent, though a little expensive.

ZADAR Maestral

Ivana Mažuranića 2 **Tel** *(023) 236 186*

Situated in the marina complex on the waterfront, the Maestral provides breathtaking harbour views from the first floor up. More upmarket than an average beachside restaurant, it offers quality meat dishes – especially steaks – and of course locally caught fish. It can be busy at weekends when the shipping traffic increases.

Key to Symbols *see back cover flap*

BOSNIA AND HERZEGOVINA

*I*n the light of its tragic history in recent times, it is easy to forget that Bosnia and Herzegovina was one of the most powerful states in Europe in the Middle Ages. Although the country still wears the scars of battle, it nevertheless charms visitors with its breathtaking scenery, atmospheric medieval towns and warm, hospitable people.

Situated in the southwestern Balkans, the mountainous northern part of Bosnia has long been paired with Herzegovina, its smaller neighbour; both regions are bound by centuries of common history. Although the capital, Sarajevo, has recovered from its wartime ordeal, towns such as Mostar are yet to be fully restored, and many settlements remain abandoned. Despite the danger of landmines, it is still possible to get a flavour of the country's natural treasures, from mountains and lush forests to rivers and dramatic gorges, in the company of experienced local guides. Rafting on Bosnia's world-class rapids is especially popular.

HISTORY

The earliest evidence of human settlement in the region dates back to 12,000 BC. However, the first significant records are of the Illyrians, who occupied the western Balkans in the 6th century BC before the Romans conquered it some four centuries later. By the 6th century, attacks by Huns, Goths and Avars had weakened the Romans, and the arrival of Slavic tribes from northeast Europe further added to the region's veritable melting pot of ethnicities. The region was first ruled by the Serbs, then by the Croats, and finally by the Hungarians, before establishing itself as an independent

The pedestrianized Old town market in the capital city, Sarajevo

◁ The landmark single-arch stone bridge on the Neretva river, Mostar

Depiction of the assassination of Archduke Ferdinand

kingdom under King Tvrtko in 1377. Following Tvrtko's death in 1391, the country was absorbed into the expanding Ottoman Empire. When the Austro-Hungarians took over from the Ottomans in 1908, they sought to unite the country's ethnic and religious groups as loyal Habsburg subjects. However, this attempt at homogeneity was resisted by nationalists seeking independence from Austria, and led the radical Bosnian Serb Gavrilo Princip to assassinate the Austro-Hungarian heir Franz Ferdinand and his wife in Sarajevo in 1914. It was

this event that triggered World War I. Bosnia and Herzegovina joined the newly formed Kingdom of Serbs, Croats and Slovenes in 1918. During World War II, the Nazis established a puppet state in Croatia which grew to include Bosnia and Herzegovina. After the war, the country was reintegrated into Yugoslavia, and enjoyed a relatively peaceful and prosperous period. As the Yugoslav regime slowly collapsed throughout 1990–91, Bosnia and Herzegovina voted for independence, but despite international recognition it soon fell prey to inter-ethnic violence. The republic's largest ethnic group, the Bosnian Muslims, were challenged by ethnic Serbs and Croats who did not want to become part of an independent Bosnian state. The Bosnian Croats claimed an area of the country for themselves, while the Bosnian Serbs created Republika Srpska (the Serb Republic) within the borders of Bosnia and Herzegovina. The army of the Republika Srpska, and, to a lesser extent, the Croatian army, carried out ethnic cleansing in the form of mass exterminations and deportations. In 1995, the Dayton Agreement brought an end to the conflict. Since then, thousands of EU soldiers have maintained the peace, but despite sharing a common government, Bosnia's ethnic groups still cooperate poorly.

KEY DATES IN THE HISTORY OF BOSNIA AND HERZEGOVINA

AD 445 The region is conquered by Ostrogoths

1189 Signing of the Kulin Ban Charter trade agreement between Bosnia and Dubrovnik

1377 Bosnia becomes a kingdom under King Tvrtko I

1463 The Ottomans conquer Bosnia and Herzegovina

1908 Austria-Hungary annexes Bosnia and Herzegovina

1914 Archduke Franz Ferdinand is assassinated, sparking World War I

1918 Bosnia and Herzegovina becomes part of the kingdom of Serbs, Croats and Slovenes

1945 Bosnia and Herzegovina becomes part of a new federal Yugoslavia

1990 Collapse of Yugoslav regime

1992 Bosnia and Herzegovina is recognized as an independent country

1995 Dayton peace accord signed by Croatia, Montenegro and Bosnia and Herzegovina

2006 Constitutional amendment for EU integration rejected in Parliament

LANGUAGE AND CULTURE

There are three official languages spoken in Bosnia and Herzegovina: Bosnian, Croatian and Serbian – German is a common second language. With a multi-ethnic composition, the country's cultural heritage is truly diverse. Orthodox Christianity and Islam have combined with Austro-Hungarian and Catholic traditions to create a unique culture.

Exploring Bosnia and Herzegovina

Bosnia and Herzegovina has a wealth of fascinating towns to explore as well as stunning natural beauty. The capital, Sarajevo, is one of Europe's most lively cities, yet retains an old-world charm. To the south lies Mostar, with its atmospheric medieval centre, while to the northwest Jajce enjoys a picturesque location above two waterfalls. The country's rail network is poorly connected, but its roads are in reasonably good condition. Although most towns are served by buses, car hire provides greater flexibility.

The well-preserved medieval fortress dominating the town of Travnik

SIGHTS AT A GLANCE

KEY

✈ Airport

— Motorway

— Major Road

— Railway

–·– International border

Church of St James in the central square at Međugorje

Sarajevo ❶

Founded by the Ottoman Empire in the 15th century, the vibrant capital of Bosnia and Herzegovina was at the centre of the longest siege in modern European history. Between 1992 and 1995, it lost over 11,000 of its citizens in the Bosnian War. Today, Sarajevo is home to a population of nearly three million people and a massive reconstruction effort has returned the city to its former glory. Its bustling streets are now lined with designer boutiques, trendy bars and cafés catering to the influx of visitors, while the 16th-century Old Town (Baščaršija) offers laid-back charm. Scattered throughout the city are mosques, synagogues and Catholic and Orthodox churches, a reflection of Sarajevo's complex history and rich cultural diversity.

Sebilj Fountain in the Old Town's main market

SIGHTS AT A GLANCE

Archangel Michael and Gabriel Orthodox Church and Museum ③
Ashkenazi Synagogue ⑩
Emperor's Mosque ⑧
Franciscan Church of St Anthony ⑨
Gazi Husrev Bey Mosque ⑤
History Museum ⑬
Latin Bridge ⑦

Long Bazaar and Brusa Bazaar ⑥
National Art Gallery ⑪
National Library ②
National Museum ⑫
Old Synagogue and Jewish Museum ④
Old Town ①

KEY

🚆 Railway station
ℹ️ Visitor information
🅿️ Parking
⊠ Post office
✚ Church
C Mosque
▬ Pedestrian zone

GETTING AROUND

The compact city centre and the Old Town are easily visited on foot. The pedestrianized Ferhadija runs through the heart of the city. Efficient tram and bus services cover the whole city and are a reliable way of getting around. Taxis are plentiful and fairly inexpensive; taxi stands can be found all over the city and operate 24 hours a day.

Decorative arch, Ashkenazi Synagogue

SEE ALSO

- *Where to Stay* p524

- *Where to Eat* p525

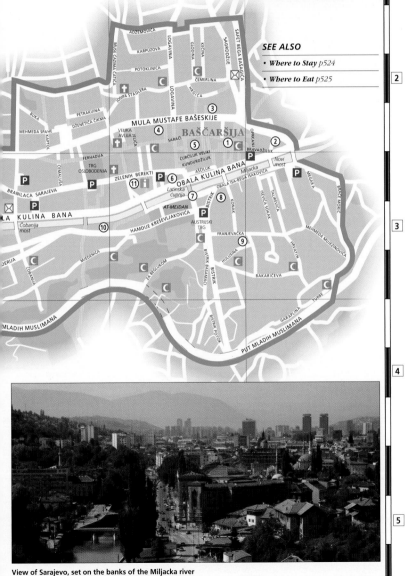

View of Sarajevo, set on the banks of the Miljacka river

The atmospheric Old Town market lined with old buildings and shops

Old Town ①
Baščaršija

Baščaršija. **Map** E2.

A labyrinth of cobbled streets, the Old Town is known as Baščaršija after its main market, which has been a trading place since the 16th century. In the centre of the market stands the Moorish-style Sebilj Fountain, built in 1753 on the orders of Mehmed Paša Kukavica, governor of Bosnia and patron of fine architecture.

Reminiscent of an Arabian souk, the market's narrow streets, lined with small shops, offer an intriguing choice of authentic souvenirs. Local cuisine can be sampled in any of the kebab shops and Turkish-style coffee houses as well as at the Morica Han *(see p525)*, an ancient Ottoman inn with a shaded courtyard.

National Library ②
Nacionalna biblioteka

Obala Kulina Bana. **Map** F2.

One of the city's most striking works of architecture, the building that once served as Sarajevo's Town Hall became the National Library after World War II. This impressive structure is one of the few edifices in the capital that has yet to be restored following the Bosnian War.

Opened in 1896, the building was originally designed to resemble a grand palace, featuring elaborate arched windows, a decorative rooftop crenellation and a first floor balcony. The Czech architect Alexander Wittek, responsible for the building's construction, visited Cairo for inspiration but committed suicide before its completion.

Although its magnificent Moorish façade survived the war relatively unscathed, the interior, which housed the National Library, was completely gutted by fire during shelling in August 1992. The library's irreplaceable repository of Bosnian written culture was almost completely destroyed.

Entrance to the Orthodox Church and Museum, marked by an icon

Archangel Michael and Gabriel Orthodox Church and Museum ③
Stara pravoslavna crkva i muzej

Mula Mustafe Bašeskije 59. **Map** E2. ⬜ *8am–5pm daily.* 📷 🎥 📷 **www**.staracrkva.org

Built below ground level and hidden behind stone walls, the Archangel Michael and Gabriel Orthodox Church is thought to rest on the foundations of a 5th-century church. However, its current appearance dates back to 1734.

The cramped interior is supported by wooden columns and dominated by a wonderful gilt iconostasis. Intricately carved, it features colourful 17th-century icons by local master painters as well as others added in 1734. Religious artworks by 19th-century artists adorn the walls.

The neighbouring museum, opened in 1890, is one of Bosnia's oldest, and displays the church's treasures in smartly renovated surroundings. Among the exhibits are 17th-century gold- and silver-plated icons by Russian, Greek and Cretan master painters, along with a rare copy of the Sarajevo *Nomocanon* (a book of church and secular laws) and valuable churchware.

Old Synagogue and Jewish Museum ④

Velika avlija i muzej jevreja

Velika Avlija bb. **Map** E2.
Tel *(033) 533 431.* 🅾 *10am–6pm Mon–Fri, 10am–1pm Sun.* 🖼
www.muzejsarajeva.ba

Built in 1850, the Old Synagogue long served as the centre of Sarajevo's vibrant Jewish community. The majority of Sarajevo's Jews were Sephardis, descended from the Jews of Spain and Portugal who were expelled from the Iberian Peninsula in the 1490s. Bosnia's Ottoman rulers gave them refuge, valuing their expertise in banking and trade.

The interior once featured arched balconies, but the building was plundered during World War II and used as a Jewish prison during the Holocaust, when Sarajevo's Jewish population of 12,000 was reduced by 85 per cent. The synagogue's restoration in 1965 was timed to coincide with the celebration of 400 years of Jewish presence in Bosnia, when it became a museum of Jewish history. It was then badly damaged after repeated shelling during the Bosnian War, but was renovated in 2003.

The museum's collections, which include some rare manuscripts, document the thriving Jewish culture in the region up until the Holocaust.

Gazi Husrev Bey Mosque ⑤

Gazi Husrev-begova džamija

Sarači 8. **Map** E2. ***Tel*** *(033) 532 144.* 🅾 *1 May–30 Sep: 9am–noon, 2:30pm–4pm & 5:30pm–7pm daily.* 🏛 **www**.vakuf-gazi.ba

Regarded as one of the finest examples of Ottoman Islamic architecture in the world, this stunning old mosque with its five-arch porch and multiple domes was commissioned in 1531 by Gazi Husrev Bey, who governed Bosnia between 1521 and 1541. Persian architect Adzem Esir Ali was

Ornate entrance to Gazi Husrev Bey Mosque

brought in to design what was to be the region's grandest mosque. This was achieved by combining a series of domes with a 45-m (148-ft) minaret, and by illuminating the interior with over 50 windows around the base of the central dome. Elaborate calligraphic quotations from the Koran adorn the walls and thick Oriental rugs, gifted by visiting rulers over the centuries, cover the floor.

The mosque's spacious courtyard is dominated by an ancient chestnut tree and contains two domed mausoleums as well as a beautiful marble fountain used by worshippers for their ritual ablutions. The mosque was, however, a key target during the Bosnian War and despite its 2-m (7-ft) thick walls suffered extensive damage from shelling, though

it has since been restored. Gazi Huzrev Bey also funded the construction of a children's religious *maktab* (school) within the complex and an advanced *madrasa* (school) opposite, with an intricately decorated arched entrance.

The administrative building to the west of the courtyard is notable for its imposing clock tower. Built in 1697, the tower measures lunar time and shows precisely when the sun sets.

Long Bazaar and Brusa Bazaar ⑥

Dugi bezistan i Brusa bezistan

Kundurdžiluk 10, Baščaršija.
Map E3. 🅾 *15 Apr–15 Oct: 10am–4pm Mon–Fri, 10am–3pm Sat.* 🖼 **www**.muzejsarajeva.ba

Sarajevo's largest covered market, the Long Bazaar was built in 1542 on the orders of Governor Gazi Husrev Bey. The massive stone structure is covered by a vaulted ceiling and once housed 52 shops selling goods imported from all over Europe and the Ottoman Empire. The bazaar lies along Kundurdžiluk Street, which also leads to the Gazi Husrev Bey Mosque commissioned by the governor 12 years earlier.

The nearby Brusa Bazaar was built in 1551 by the Ottoman General Grand Vizier Rustem for trade in Bursa silk from Turkey. Its eight cupolas and rough stone walls were damaged by shelling, but since its reconstruction it has been used as an ethnographic and historical museum.

Hand-decorated shell and mortar cases on sale in the bazaars

The historic Latin Bridge over the Miljacka river

Latin Bridge ⑦
Latinska ćuprija

Obala Kulina Bana. **Map** E3.

Before the Bosnian War drew the world's attention to Sarajevo, the city was best known for a series of events that sparked World War I. On 28 June 1914, the Bosnian Serb nationalist Gavrilo Princip assassinated Archduke Franz Ferdinand and his wife Sofia as they crossed a bridge over the Miljacka river during an official visit. Princip was considered a national hero by Bosnian Serbs, and his footsteps were marked in the pavement, a memorial was built nearby and the bridge was renamed in his honour, until the recent war when Bosnian Serbs turned against the city.

Today, there is little acknowledgement of Princip's infamous deed other than a brass plaque and an exhibition of black-and-white photographs in the adjacent Sarajevo Museum. The historic bridge has now been renamed Latin Bridge.

Emperor's Mosque ⑧
Careva džamija

Obala Isa-bega Isakovića. **Map** E3.
8am–6pm daily.

Built in 1566, during the reign of Suleiman the Magnificent, the Emperor's Mosque is one of Sarajevo's main holy sites and was enlarged in the 19th century under Sultan Abdülmedcid to accommodate the expanding congregation. The interior is decorated with simple floral motifs.

Behind the Emperor's Mosque's imposing stone walls are tranquil gardens and a pleasant courtyard centred around an intricately designed fountain, where worshippers gather for ritual ablutions before prayer.

Franciscan Church of St Anthony ⑨
Franjevački samostan Svetog ante

Franjevačka 6. **Map** E3. **Tel** (033) 236 107. 8am–6pm daily.
www.bosnasrebrena.ba

Constructed in 1912 during Austro-Hungarian rule, St Anthony's Church and the neighbouring Franciscan monastery were designed by prominent Czech architects.

Splendidly illuminated exterior of the Emperor's Mosque

The church was the last work of architect Josip Vancaš, while his colleague Karlo Panek built the monastery, which houses a superb collection of ancient religious literature and works of art.

The church's Neo-Gothic façade is dominated by its 43-m (141-ft) tower, while the interior is brightened by colourful stained-glass windows. In 2005, the Archbishop of Canterbury gave an Anglican Eucharist service here as part of an initiative to build bridges between communities of different faiths.

Ashkenazi Synagogue ⑩
Aškenaska sinagoga

Hamdije Kreševljakovića 59.
Map D3. 8am–7pm daily.

In 1959, most of the functions of the Old Synagogue (see pp515) were transferred to the Ashkenazi Synagogue, a grand Moorish-style edifice built in the early 20th century. Today, the synagogue is the main cultural and religious centre for the city's 700 remaining Jews.

National Art Gallery ⑪
Umjetnička galerija

Zelenih BereKti 8. **Map** E3.
noon–8pm Tue–Sat.

Standing opposite the leafy Alije Izetbegovića park, the eclectic National Art Gallery hosts both permanent and temporary exhibitions and occasional jazz performances. The building's façade is still pockmarked with bullet holes despite its restoration following the Bosnian War.

Founded in 1946, the gallery has over 4,500 works, including some by several prominent 20th-century Bosnian artists, paintings from the early Yugoslavian and Austro-Hungarian periods and a collection by the Swiss painter Ferdinand Hodler. The highlight of the gallery's absorbing icon collection, displayed in the central foyer,

Monolithic entrance to the History Museum

is the striking *Virgin Hodegetria*, painted by Montenegrin iconographer Tudor Vuković in 1568.

National Museum ⑫
Zemaljski muzej

Zmaja od Bosne 3. **Map** A3.
Tel *(033) 668 027.* ☐ *10am–5pm Tue–Fri, 10am–2pm Sun.* 🖾 🖬 🖪
www.zemaljskimuzej.ba

First opened in 1888 and located in its current imposing building since 1913, the National Museum is regarded as Bosnia's oldest museum.

Inside, the Archaeology Department has many exhibits from the Stone Age to the Middle Ages. The most intriguing, however, are the *stećci* (tombstones) which adorn the front garden. Bosnia's most legendary symbol, these monumental tombstones first appeared between the 12th and the 15th centuries and thousands are scattered across the country. Many are covered with engravings of animals, plants and obscure symbols linked to the region's early Slavic culture. Other highlights include the priceless Sarajevo Haggadah *(see p31)* a richly illustrated 14th-century book which includes one of the first depictions of the world as a sphere. Also on display is an array of national costumes from the 19th century in the Ethnographic Department. The Natural History collection has been depleted to a large extent as a result of damage inflicted during the Bosnian War.

History Museum ⑬
Istorijski muzej

Zmaja od Bosne 9. **Map** A3.
Tel *(033) 210 416.* ☐ *9am–4pm Tue–Fri, 9am–1pm Sat–Sun.* 🖾

The battered façade of this modernist concrete building, with its broken, weed-covered steps and bullet-scarred walls, gives an impression of abandonment that seems like a deliberate historic statement. The museum and its collection were almost completely destroyed during the devastating Bosnian War.

The building is currently open to the public, but its original collection of 400,000 artifacts has been reduced to a one-room display entitled "Bosnia and Herzegovina through the Centuries", consisting mainly of documents and old photographs. The museum's main attraction is the "Surrounded Sarajevo" presentation on the first floor, to which Sarajevans have contributed objects, photographs and documents relating to their personal experience of the war. The result is a powerful yet understated exhibition which gives an invaluable insight into the siege. The struggle for survival is illustrated through home-made weapons used to defend the city, improvised lamps to combat the lack of electricity and editions of the Sarajevo newspaper printed every day to boost people's morale.

Interior of the poignant Tunnel Museum

TUNNEL MUSEUM
The nondescript rural home of the Kolar family in Butmir, on the outskirts of Sarajevo, was the scene of the biggest clandestine supply operation during the siege. The house, which was within the free territories (land defended by Sarajevans), is now the Tunnel Museum. It is situated over the entrance to the 800-m (2,625-ft) long tunnel dug under the nearby UN-administered airport in 1993, which was the city's only constant supply route throughout the siege. The tunnel took six months of manual digging to complete and was repeatedly targeted by Bosnian Serb forces. Today, only a section of it remains, but it is enough to give an impression of the cramped and dangerous underground journey an average of 4,000 Sarajevans made daily, each carrying around 50 kg (110 lbs) of food and supplies into Sarajevo. It was also used by the first president of Bosnia and Herzegovina, Alija Izetbegović. Guided tours of the tunnel are available.

Travnik ❷

95 km (59 miles) NW of Sarajevo.
🏚 *33,000.* 🚌

Dwarfed by the lush green
mountains to which it owes its
name, Travnik is overlooked
by the medieval 15th-century
Travnik Fortress (Travnička
tvrdava). It is famous as the
birthplace of the Nobel Prize-
winning novelist Ivo Andrić,
who immortalized the town in
his book, *Bosnian Chronicle*.
The fortress and the surrounding Old Town, perched on
steep slopes with dramatic
views, were built and strengthened during the reign of
Bosnian kings in the early
15th century. In 1463, the
fortress fell to the Ottomans
(see p510), who coveted its
commanding position and
built a mosque, of which only
the minaret remains. The
interesting Archaeological and
Ethnographic Museum in the
complex presents an eclectic
display of local finds as well
as regional costumes. From
the heights of the Old Town,
the minaret of the **Many
Coloured Mosque** (Šarena
džamija) is clearly visible.
Originally constructed in 1757
and rebuilt after a fire in 1815,
the mosque stands above a
covered bazaar. Its interior is
decorated with floral patterns.

One of the best-developed
ski resorts in Bosnia,
Babanovac lies 28 km
(17 miles) north of the town,
on Mount Vlašić. The

**Detailing on the façade of the
Many Coloured Mosque, Travnik**

mountain reaches a height
of 1,943 m (6,375 ft) at
Paljenik, its highest peak. The
surrounding highlands are still
populated by shepherds but
the threat of landmines means
that hiking should not be
attempted without experi-
enced local guides.

⛰ **Travnik Fortress**
Old Town. ◯ *8am–8pm daily.*
🅿 🔓

🅲 **Many Coloured Mosque**
ulica Bosanka. ◯ *8am–7pm daily.*

Jajce ❸

137 km (85 miles) NW of Sarajevo.
🏚 *31,000.* 🚌

The town of Jajce – meaning
egg – takes its name from the
egg-shaped hill upon which

its fortified citadel was
founded in the 14th century.
It served as the capital of the
Bosnian Kingdom before
succumbing twice to the
Ottomans: first in 1463 and
again in 1527. From then on,
Jajce remained part of the
Ottoman Empire until the
Austro-Hungarians took
over in 1908.

The idyllic position of this
small town on a hillside above
the mighty Pliva Waterfalls
belies its disturbing recent
history. Before the Bosnian
War, Jajce was a peaceful
multi-ethnic town, but in May
1992, most of its Bosnian Serb
residents fled in fear of Croat
aggression. In October 1992,
the army of Republika Srpska
responded by heavily bombard-
ing the town, forcing the
Bosnian Croat and Muslim
population out. Croat forces
recaptured the town in 1995,
causing the Serb population
to flee once more. Though
much of the damage to the
town has since been repaired,
few of its original Bosnian
Serb residents have returned.

One of the town's oldest
sights is the ruined **St Mary's
Church** (Crkva sv Marije),
which dates back to the
12th century and was used
as a Franciscan monastery in
the 14th century. The last
Bosnian queen, Katerina
Kotromanić, added St Luke's
Tower to the church building
but fled with the saint's relics
when the Ottomans conquered
the region and converted the

The picturesque town of Travnik, with its towering minarets

For hotels and restaurants in this region see p524 and p525

church into a mosque. Nearby are some catacombs that were carved out in the early 1400s. It is widely believed that they were used as a chapel and crypt for the family of Duke Hrvoje Vucović, a powerful Bosnian feudal leader. Adjoining the church are the remains of a 4th-century Roman temple dedicated to the god Mithras.

Beyond the church looms Jajce's sturdy medieval **Bear Tower** (Medvjed kula). The tower, impenetrable in its day, boasted 6-m (20-ft) thick walls in places and could only be reached by a ladder. In recent years, a ground level entrance has been added. Access to the tower, the catacombs and the Roman temple can be arranged by staff at the nearby information office.

The spectacular 20-m (66-ft) high Pliva Waterfalls, below the town at the confluence of the Pliva and Vrbas rivers, are a popular attraction. The river's superb canyons make it a perfect spot for rafting.

🔒 **St Mary's Church**
Svetog Luke.

🏛 **Bear Tower**
Svetog Luke. ◻ 9am–7pm daily.
🖼 🛈 ulica Svetog Luke.

Bihać ❹

281 km (175 miles) NW of Sarajevo.
🏙 78,000. 🚌

Situated on the Una river, the picturesque town of Bihać is renowned for the pleasant fish restaurants that line its river banks. Medieval Bihać was one of the last Bosnian towns to fall into Ottoman hands, finally succumbing in 1592. After spending the next three centuries as a border fortress on the Austrian-Ottoman frontier, Bihać was absorbed into the Austro-Hungarian Empire in 1878. The town was heavily bombarded in World War II after Josip Broz Tito, who later became the president of Yugoslavia, made it the centre of his anti-Fascist movement. Bihać's majority Bosnian Muslim population

The impressive Pliva Waterfalls, set amidst lush forests below Jajce

was subjected to a three-year siege by Serbian forces between 1992 and 1995. The siege was finally broken when Croatian forces participating in Operation Storm pushed forward to join their Bosnian allies.

The **Captain's Tower** (Kapetanova kula), in the Main Square, is one of the town's few remaining medieval fortified buildings. The tower was turned into a prison when the Austro-Hungarians took control and continued to function as such until 1959; since then it has housed the Regional History Museum's well-presented collection.

Behind it stands St Anthony's Church, which was turned into the current **Fethija Mosque** by the Ottomans in the 16th century.

The lovely countryside around Bihać is notorious for being densely mined. Hiking and mountain biking trips, though possible, should not be undertaken without experienced local guides.

🏛 **Captain's Tower**
ulica 5 Korpusa 2. **Tel** (037) 229 743. ◻ Mon–Fri 10am–8pm.
🖼

🇨 **Fethija Mosque**
ulica 5 Korpusa. ◻ 7am–7pm daily.

Whitewater rafting on the rapids of the Vrbas river

RAFTING

Stunning mountain landscapes along with captivating waterfalls have made Bosnia a popular destination with adventure sports enthusiasts. The waters of the Vrbas, Drina, Tara, Una and Neretva rivers offer such an extensive range of rafting and kayaking experiences that the World Rafting Championship was held here in May 2009. The remarkable UNESCO-protected Tara river canyon, the second deepest in the world, offers some of the most intense and challenging rafting in Europe.

Mostar ❺

Located on the banks of the Neretva river, Mostar has been the political, cultural and economic cornerstone of Herzegovina since Turkish rule. Once the provincial capital of the Ottoman Empire, the town suffered more severely than any other during the Bosnian War. In 1992, it came under attack from the Yugoslav People's Army, dominated by Serbs. The Croats and Muslims joined forces to expel them, but in 1993, these two groups turned against each other and occupied opposing sides of the Neretva river, creating a racial divide that still exists. Today, the popular Old Bridge (Stari most), symbolizes Mostar's pre-war glory.

salt cellars fashioned from empty shell cases. In the heart of the Old Town is the 16th century Kriva Ćuprija, the oldest single-arch stone bridge in Mostar. The bridge was built by the Turkish architect, Cevjan Kethoda. Near Kriva are the Hamam and Tabhana Turkish baths. Severely damaged during the war, the place is still worth visiting, especially for the gorgeous views of the Neretva river and the Old Bridge from its terrace.

The narrow cobbled streets of Mostar's Old Town

🏛 Old Town

A UNESCO World Heritage Site, the historic Old Town (Stari grad) is the main attraction of Mostar with its grand Turkish houses and the Old Bridge. Ideal for a walking tour, the area can easily be explored in a day. The Kujundžiluk Bazaar, with its rambling streets of small shops and cafés, is charming, and the only reminders of the 1990s conflict are the souvenir

🏛 Old Bridge

Mostar's symbolic centrepiece, the elegant stone Old Bridge (Stari most) spans the Neretva river, connecting the two sides of the Old Town. Built by Mimar Hajruddin in the 16th century, during the reign of the Ottoman ruler Suleiman the Magnificent, the bridge reaches a maximum height of 21 m (69 ft). Despite being recognized by UNESCO as a World Heritage Site, the bridge became the focus of target practice for Croatian soldiers during the Bosnian War and was completely destroyed in November 1993. Reconstruction began soon after the war ended and the renovated bridge, which is

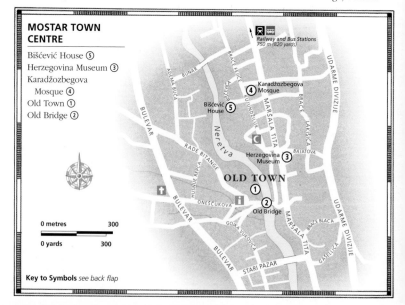

MOSTAR TOWN CENTRE

Railway and Bus Stations
750 m (820 yards)

OLD TOWN

0 metres   300

0 yards   300

Key to Symbols see back flap

an exact replica of the original, was opened to the public in July 2004.

The Old Bridge is a popular spot, especially during summer, when visitors jostle for space to catch a glimpse of daring local men who collect money from onlookers before jumping off the bridge.

Mostar's landmark Old Bridge, spanning the Neretva river

Herzegovina Museum

Bajatova 4. ***Tel*** *(036) 551 602.* *9am–2pm Mon–Fri, 10am–noon Sat.* **www**.muzejhercegovine.com

Founded in 1950, the eclectic Herzegovina Museum (Muzej Hercegovine) is housed in the residence of Džemal Bijedić, former head of the Yugoslav government. Built in an Oriental style with a porch and a courtyard, the building was established to promote the literary and cultural history of Herzegovina. It exhibits a variety of regional costumes and traditional tools alongside archaeological discoveries and a display outlining Mostar's history.

VISITORS' CHECKLIST

139 km (86 miles) SW of Sarajevo. *110,000.* *Rade Bitange 5, (036) 580 275.* **www**.visitmostar.net

Karadžozbegova Mosque

Kujundžiluk. *9am–9pm daily.*

On the eastern side of Mostar stands the most significant example of sacred Islamic architecture in Herzegovina. Built in 1557, this mosque (Karadžozbegova džamija) is typical of Ottoman architecture, with a marble fountain and an *madrasa* (Islamic school) in the courtyard. Its interior was once adorned with floral motifs, of which only fragments remain. The slender minaret offers sweeping views over Mostar and its environs.

Bišćević House

Bišćevića. *(036) 580 275.* *9am–6pm daily.*

The delightful 17th-century Bišćević House (Bišćevića kuća), is a fine example of Turkish design. Partially supported by tall stone columns, the interior of the house features segregated living quarters and period furnishings. The building enjoys a lofty position on the eastern bank of the Neretva river and offers fine views over the town.

Elegant interior of the Karadžozbegova Mosque

Statue of the Virgin Mary on Apparition Hill, Međugorje

Međugorje 6

169 km (105 miles) SW of Sarajevo. *5,000.* **www**.medjugorje.hr

The village of Međugorje, in the southern part of Herzegovina, is regarded as Bosnia's most famous Catholic pilgrimage site.

The small parish owes its reputation to a series of reported visions of the Virgin Mary. The "Queen of Peace", as locals refer to her, was initially witnessed in 1981 by six children. Crowds of eager pilgrims gathered to see the apparition, but it was only visible to the children, who were reportedly told ten secrets about the future of the planet. Today, over 20 million people have visited the site and numerous independent sightings have been recorded. However, the Vatican has never acknowledged the apparitions and dismisses the claims. A blue cross stands on the mountain, now called Apparition Hill, where the first sighting took place.

Also worth visiting is the impressive Church of St James, in the heart of the town. Completed in 1969, this is the gathering place for worshippers and holy masses are regularly held here in many languages.

Southwest of the town stands Mount Križevac, on top of which an 8-m (26-ft) high cross was planted in 1934 to commemorate the 1,900th anniversary of Christ's death.

Practical & Travel Information

Bosnians are traditionally hospitable people and will often go out of their way to help visitors. Visitor information centres with English-speaking staff are rare outside big towns. With the increasing influx of visitors, accommodation is now readily available in most towns. The country's good network of trains and buses ensures easy travel, although a lack of sleeper carriages means that overnight train journeys can be exhausting. It is most convenient to travel by car but drivers need to be aware of the danger of landmines. Hiking is also a great way to explore the countryside, but not without guides.

WHEN TO VISIT

The best time to visit Bosnia and Herzegovina is in summer, when days are warm and evenings pleasant. In general, summer is from June to September, although in Herzegovina, it begins earlier in May. Bosnia experiences severe cold winters, while in Herzegovina they are relatively mild. For skiers, the best time to visit Bosnia is from January to March.

DOCUMENTATION

All European Union (EU), US and Canadian citizens can enter Bosnia without a visa for up to 90 days, on a valid passport. Other nationalities should apply to their nearest embassy for a visa. Visitors are required to register with the police on arrival, but hotels will arrange this automatically.

VISITOR INFORMATION

Bosnia's only official tourist information offices with English-speaking staff are in Sarajevo and Mostar. The **Sarajevo Tourist Information Centre** and **Mostar Tourist Information Centre** are well equipped and have brochures covering the whole country. Smaller towns have tourist association offices, but have unreliable opening hours and staff is unlikely to speak English.

HEALTH AND SECURITY

Visitors are advised to get vaccinated against tetanus, hepatitis A, diphtheria and polio prior to travel. Public health clinics are best avoided as private clinics offer better medical care. The **Emergency Medical Service** in Sarajevo is open to visitors and has good doctors, while in Mostar, the **Clinical Hospital Mostar** also has good medical care. In case of any emergency it is advisable to contact the relevant embassy.

Crime against visitors is virtually non-existent, although visitors should be wary of pickpockets, especially in trams and trains.

FACILITIES FOR THE DISABLED

Public awareness about the needs of travellers with disabilities is poor in Bosnia and Herzegovina. Only hotels and restaurants in major towns have facilities for the disabled.

BANKING AND CURRENCY

Although the official currency is KM (2 KM is approximately 1 euro), euro notes, but not coins, are accepted as a second currency almost everywhere. Banks will usually exchange traveller's cheques and major currencies. In small towns and villages, credit cards are less likely to be accepted and ATMs are scarce, so visitors should carry enough cash for their journey.

COMMUNICATIONS

Most towns in Bosnia have at least one Internet café. Many city hotels offer free Wi-Fi to guests. Public telephones require phone cards, which are sold in post offices or newspaper kiosks.

LANDMINES

One of Bosnia's biggest safety concerns for both locals and visitors are the landmines laid during the Bosnian War, which cover an estimated four per cent of the country. Mine clearance has been ongoing since 1995, but the sheer danger of the work, combined with lack of funding and alleged misappropriation of funds, has hampered progress. Although the densely populated areas have been cleared, there is a real danger of unexploded mines in open countryside and isolated buildings. The roads have been largely cleared, but the possibility of roadside mines means that drivers should avoid pulling over on to rough or unmarked ground. Hikers should consult Sarajevo's Tourist Information Centre before setting out and are strongly advised to take a professional guide. Bosnia's **Mine Action Centre** has

THE CLIMATE OF BOSNIA AND HERZEGOVINA

The south and west of Bosnia as well as Herzegovina, has a Mediterranean climate with long, hot summers and mild, wet winters. In the north and east, much of the country has warm summers and cold winters, with snow at higher altitudes benefiting ski resorts close to Sarajevo and Mount Vlašic. Sarajevo averages 20° C (68° F) in summer and -1° C (30° F) in winter.

SARAJEVO

° C/F			
	26/79		
15/59	13/55	16/61	
5/41		6/43	3/37
0°C 32°F			-4/25

☀	5 hrs	9 hrs	4 hrs	2 hrs
☂	64 mm	71 mm	103 mm	66 mm
month	Apr	Jul	Oct	Jan

up-to-date information on the current situation, as does the **UK Foreign Office**.

ARRIVING BY AIR

Sarajevo International Airport, 12 km (7 miles) southwest of the city, is the only international airport with daily flights. It is worth noting that the airport is prone to fog in winter, which can cause flight cancellations or delays at short notice. Mostar's airport has weekly flights to Zagreb in Croatia. Since Bosnia lacks its own national carrier, Zagreb acts as a hub for Croatian Airlines to connect Sarajevo with regular flights to major European cities. **British Airways** has regular indirect flights from London to Sarajevo, while **Lufthansa**, **Malév** and **Austrian Airlines** have direct flights from Munich, Budapest and Vienna.

RAIL TRAVEL

Bosnia's rail network suffered severe damage during the Bosnian Wars. Its services are still limited and journeys are slow, as the routes tend to be circuitous. Mainline connections with neighbouring capitals have been introduced

and overnight trains run north from Sarajevo to Belgrade (10hrs) and Budapest (12hrs), and west to Zagreb (9hrs) but there are no sleeper carriages. The southern line from Sarajevo via Mostar to Ploče, in Croatia, is the country's most scenic route. Bosnia is now accessible with an InterRail ticket, but not yet with Eurail. **Sarajevo Train Station** is easily accessible from the downtown area.

TRAVELLING BY BUS

The country has a reliable bus network with daily services covering the whole country. International buses run daily from Sarajevo to Ljubljana, Kotor, Belgrade, Zagreb and Dubrovnik. Eurolines operates coaches from Sarajevo to other European cities through the Bosnian bus company **Centrotrans**. Reservations can be made through Eurolines offices abroad.

TRAVELLING BY CAR

Travelling by car is the most convenient form of transport in Bosnia. It is safe to drive all around the country, although

the usual landmine warnings about not straying off the road apply. Petrol stations are plentiful and often accept credit cards. Major car rental firms at Sarajevo Airport include **Budget** and **Thrifty**, while **Misag** and **Lami** offer slightly older cars. Those travelling in their own car will need registration documents, Green Card insurance and an EU or international driving licence. Snow chains are essential for winter travel. Drivers should ensure that they carry a dual language road map as most of the road signs in Republika Srpska – one of the two main political divisions of the country – are in Cyrillic.

OUTDOOR ACTIVITIES

Before Bosnia's natural beauty was marred by landmines, it was a paradise for hiking, mountain biking, climbing and rafting. None of these activities are now recommended without a local professional guide. Both **Green Visions** and the **Encijan Mountain Association** provide internationally qualified guides and run organized wilderness trips in areas that are clear of mines.

DIRECTORY

EMBASSIES

United Kingdom
Tina Ujevića 8, Sarajevo.
Tel (033) 282 200.

United States
Alipasina 43, Sarajevo.
Tel (033) 445 700.

VISITOR INFORMATION

Mostar Tourist Information Centre
Tel (036) 580 275.
www.visitmostar.net.
www.hercegovina.ba

Sarajevo Tourist Information Centre
Tel (033) 250 200.
www.sarajevo-tourism.com

EMERGENCY NUMBERS

Ambulance
Tel 124.

Fire
Tel 123.

Police
Tel 122.

HEALTH AND SECURITY

Clinical Hospital Mostar
Tel (036) 336 500.

Emergency Medical Service
Kolodvorska 14, Sarajevo.
Tel (033) 611 111.

LANDMINES

Mine Action Centre
www.bhmac.org

UK Foreign Office
www.fco.gov.uk

ARRIVING BY AIR

Austrian Airlines
www.aua.com

British Airways
www.britishairways.com

Lufthansa
www.lufthansa.com

Malév
www.malev.com

RAIL TRAVEL

Sarajevo Train Station
Tel (033) 655 330.

TRAVELLING BY BUS

Centrotrans
Tel (033) 464 045.
www.eurolines.ba

TRAVELLING BY CAR

Budget
Tel (033) 219 992.
www.budget.ba

Lami
Tel (061) 260 609.

Misag
Tel (033) 684 323.
www.misagbh.com

Thrifty
Tel (033) 760 645.
www.thrifty.ba

OUTDOOR ACTIVITIES

Green Visions
www.greenvisions.ba

Encijan Mountain Association
www.pkencijan.com

Where to Stay in Bosnia and Herzegovina

Except for a handful of four- and five-star hotels, the majority of the country's hotels are mid-range or inexpensive; most places are clean. Hostels and guesthouses are popular budget options, especially in Sarajevo where the busier, central establishments require advance bookings.

PRICE CATEGORIES
Price categories are for a standard double room for one night during the high season. Breakfast is included, unless otherwise specified.

ⓀⓂ Under 45 KM
ⓀⓂⓀⓂ 45–75 KM
ⓀⓂⓀⓂⓀⓂ 75–100 KM
ⓀⓂⓀⓂⓀⓂⓀⓂ 100–150 KM
ⓀⓂⓀⓂⓀⓂⓀⓂⓀⓂ Over 150 KM

SARAJEVO

Hostel Ljubičica
🏢 🖥 ⓀⓂ

ulica Mula Mustafe Baseskije 65, 71000 **Tel** *(033) 535 829* **Rooms** *200* **Map** *E2*

This reliable hostel is one of the best providers of budget accommodation in Sarajevo, and has a 24-hour agency in the Old Town. It offers a free pick-up service from bus and railway stations, kitchen facilities and free breakfast for guests, which is served in a converted medieval stable. **www.hostelljubicica.net**

Motel Šeher
🅿 🏢 🖥 ⓀⓂⓀⓂⓀⓂ

ulica Safet bega Bašagića 34, 71000 **Tel** *(033) 446 126* **Fax** *(033) 446 126* **Rooms** *8* **Map** *E2*

Occupying two floors of a renovated, traditional-style house right in the centre of the Old Town, the unpretentious Motel Šeher has clean, bright and spacious rooms. Parking is an added bonus. The in-house restaurant serves local specialties. **www.motelseher.com**

Astra
🅿 🏢 🍽 🖥 ⓀⓂⓀⓂⓀⓂⓀⓂ

ulica Zelenih Beretki 9, 71000 **Tel** *(033) 252 100* **Fax** *(033) 209 939* **Rooms** *35* **Map** *E3*

An excellent central location, combined with on-site secure parking, makes Astra one of the city's most convenient hotels. Its impressive new interior is tastefully decorated and the staff is polite and efficient. Facilities include a modern conference room, sauna and Jacuzzi. **www.hotel-astra.com.ba**

REST OF BOSNIA AND HERZEGOVINA

BIHAĆ Ada
🅿 🏢 🍽 ⓀⓂⓀⓂⓀⓂ

Orljani bb, 77000 **Tel** *(037) 318 100* **Rooms** *82*

Situated in pleasant countryside just outside Bihać, Ada's lovely riverside complex provides a quiet, relaxed atmosphere. Rooms are simply furnished, but clean and spacious. The restaurant has a lovely terrace with outdoor seating and fantastic views of the river. **www.aduna.ba**

JAJCE Stari Grad
🅿 🏢 🖥 ⓀⓂⓀⓂ

Svetog Luke 3, 70101 **Tel** *(030) 654 006* **Fax** *(030) 654 008* **Rooms** *15*

Just a short distance from the Pliva Waterfalls *(see p518)* in the centre of the Old Town, the Stari Grad is one of Jajce's oldest hotels. Photographs of the region adorn the walls and rooms are smartly furnished. Turkish and Finnish saunas give guests the opportunity to relax after a hard day's sightseeing. **www.jajcetours.com**

MOSTAR Villa Sara
🅿 🖥 ⓀⓂ

Sasarogina br 4, 88000 **Tel** *(036) 555 940* **Fax** *(036) 555 941* **Rooms** *9*

One of the country's best-run hostels, Villa Sara has bathrooms and kitchens on each of its four floors as well as a choice of dormitories or en suite double rooms. Facilities include Internet access and a laundry. Bird-lovers will appreciate the owner's bird collection on the rooftop. Breakfast is optional. **www.villasara-mostar.com**

MOSTAR Bevanda
🅿 🏢 🍽 🖥 ⓀⓂⓀⓂⓀⓂⓀⓂⓀⓂ

Stara Ilićka bb **Tel** *(036) 332 332* **Fax** *(036) 332 335* **Rooms** *33*

This sophisticated five-star hotel is centrally located and has the highest standards in town, although some may regard it as gaudy. Rooms are opulent and richly furnished with heavy wooden furniture. It also has an excellent outdoor restaurant in the well-manicured garden, surrounded by fountains. **www.hotelbevanda.com**

TRAVNIK ABA Motel
🅿 🏢 ⓀⓂⓀⓂ

ulica Sumece 166, 72270 **Tel** *(030) 511 462* **Fax** *(030) 518 185* **Rooms** *18*

Set at the foot of steep forested hills, the newly built ABA Motel is a comfortable place to stay, offering spotless rooms with shiny marble floors. Its small restaurant offers a sumptuous breakfast. The hotel has pleasant staff and the service excellent. **www.aba.ba**

Map References *see map of Sarajevo pp512–13*

Where to Eat in Bosnia and Herzegovina

Bosnia specializes in meaty dishes with little emphasis on salads or side dishes. *Ćevapi*, a kind of sausage, is a typical offering. Hotel restaurants often have a reasonable selection of international cuisine. Eastern sweets such as *baklava* can be found in most cafés.

PRICE CATEGORIES
Based on the price per person of a three-course meal with half a bottle of wine, including cover charge, service and tax.

ⓀⒺ Under 20 KM
ⓀⒺ ⓀⒺ 20–50 KM
ⓀⒺ ⓀⒺ ⓀⒺ 50–100 KM
ⓀⒺ ⓀⒺ ⓀⒺ ⓀⒺ 100–160 KM
ⓀⒺ ⓀⒺ ⓀⒺ ⓀⒺ ⓀⒺ Over 160 KM

SARAJEVO

Ćevapdžinica Željo
ulica Kundurdžiluk 19, 71000 **Tel** *(033) 447 000* — **Map** *E3*

One of the best places in town to sample the local fast-food speciality *ćevapi*, small spicy cylinders of ground lamb and beef which are grilled and then sandwiched in a *somun* (springy flat bread). The place is full of football memorabilia relating to local team Željezničar.

Sedef
ulica Ferhadija 16, 71000 **Tel** *(033) 200 588* — **Map** *D3*

Warm and atmospheric, Sedef is an excellent family-run eatery both bright and spotless; the owners are friendly and service is good. The varied menu features fresh salads, high-quality grilled meat and other traditional dishes such as *ćevapi* with *kajmak* (a cheesy-tasting cream).

Morica Han
ulica Sarači 77, 71000 **Tel** *(033) 236 119* — **Map** *E2*

One of the Old Town's most appealing restaurants, Morica Han is housed in a 16th-century Ottoman inn. Diners can sit outside in the quiet cobbled courtyard and sample dishes from a meat-heavy menu such as Sarajevo steak with cheese. Portions are large. The complex also has a lovely carpet shop.

National Restaurant
Zmaja od Bosne 4, 71000 **Tel** *(033) 288 000* — **Map** *A3*

Located on the mezzanine floor of the Holiday Inn, the National Restaurant is one of the city's best eateries, offering well-prepared traditional specialities and international dishes. The atmosphere is luxurious, with plush leather chairs and immaculate service. It also boasts an extensive wine list and a delicious selection of pastries.

REST OF BOSNIA AND HERZEGOVINA

BIHAĆ Sunce
Korpusa 5, 77000 **Tel** *(037) 310 487*

This delightful restaurant overlooking the picturesque Una river is by far the best spot to enjoy a break from sightseeing. The menu features regional specialities using freshly caught fish, a few European preparations and other popular dishes from around the country. There is often live music in the evenings.

JAJCE Stari Grad
Svetog Luke 3, 70101 **Tel** *(030) 654 006*

Housed in the hotel Stari Grad, this restaurant is a cosy spot, especially when the fire is lit in winter. The menu has an extensive choice of the area's specialties, of which Bosnian stew is particularly recommended. Over 50 wines are listed. Service is excellent.

MOSTAR Kulluk
ulica Kurluk 1, 88000 **Tel** *(036) 551 716*

Raised above street level on a cobbled terrace, Kulluk overlooks the Neretva river, with a great view of the Old Bridge. The menu is bound in old book covers and has been translated into innumerable languages; it offers the usual range of Bosnian cuisine along with a good choice of pasta dishes.

TRAVNIK Lovac
ulica Bosanka 63, 72270 **Tel** *(030) 512 774*

In the heart of the Old Town, Lovac is a small and intimate restaurant with a fireplace. Known particularly for its traditional cuisine, it offers meaty dishes including Travnik steak and Lovac Hunter's steak. A reasonable selection of Croatian and Montenegrin wine is available.

Key to Symbols *see back cover flap*

MONTENEGRO

*F*amous for its idyllic Adriatic coastline, Montenegro is enormously popular with those looking to plant beach umbrellas or moor their luxury yachts, yet this small and newly independent country has far more to offer. Venetian-flavoured, fortified towns line the coast, while national parks protect the best of its abundant and largely unspoilt natural beauty.

Montenegro's mountains have long provided a buffer between this small country and its neighbours. To the north lies Serbia; to the west, Bosnia and the coastal sliver of Croatia. However, despite an eventful and frequently war-ravaged past, Montenegro has attracted a steady flow of visitors since the 1970s. Its lush forests, glacial lakes, waterfalls and mountains offer rewarding opportunities for rafting, caving, climbing, skiing and hiking.

HISTORY

The region now known as Montenegro was settled as early as the Stone Age. However, its complex history begins in the 6th century BC

with the Illyrians. During the Illyrian Wars of the 3rd century BC, the Romans conquered much of the territory and maintained a strong presence there until the split of their empire in the 4th century AD, when the Byzantines wrested control of the region. Meanwhile, Slavic Serb and Croat tribes settled in the west and developed a Slavic state, which was recognized by the Byzantine Empire. In 1189, the Serbian ruler Stefan Nemanja conquered Montenegro – known at the time as Duklja – and renamed it Zeta. Upon the collapse of the Serbian Empire in the late 14th century, two powerful local tribes, the Balšić and the Crnojević, took control of Zeta. The Balšić held

The serpentine Crnojević river, Lake Skadar National Park

◁ A stretch of Slovenska Beach, one of Budva's most popular attractions much of the coast, while the Crnojević occupied the mountainous interior. Under threat from the advancing Ottoman Empire in the 15th century, Stefan Crnojević (r. 1451–65) forged a defensive alliance with the Venetians, who occupied mvvost of the coast. However, by 1496 much of the region had succumbed to the Ottomans. At this time Cetinje was established as capital of Crna Gora (Montenegro), the mountainous interior region. Due to the difficult terrain, the Montenegrins were left largely to their own devices, while the Ottomans focused on taking control of strategic coastal towns.

Following an unsuccessful allegiance with Russia against the Ottomans in 1710, Montenegro came under frequent attack by the Turks. Sporadic conflicts continued until 1878, when the Berlin Congress recognized it as an independent state. Allied with Serbia during World War I, Montenegro was soon occupied by Austria-Hungary. In 1918, Montenegro joined the new kingdom of Serbs,

Đukanović supporters holding his portrait, 2006 rally

Croats and Slovenes, losing much of its identity in the process. During World War II, the country was occupied first by the Italians and then the Germans, whose eventual defeat led to the creation of Tito's Federal Republic of Yugoslavia, in which Montenegro was one of six republics. Following the break up of Yugoslavia (1991–95), Montenegro sided with Serbia in attacks on Bosnia and Croatia. However, in 1996 President Mizo Đukanović began to slowly move away from Serbian tutelage, beginning the move towards full Montenegrin independence. On 26 May 2006, a referendum finally established Montenegro as a sovereign state.

KEY DATES IN MONTENEGRIN HISTORY

AD 395 Roman Empire divided into two: Serbia and Montenegro are part of Byzantine Empire

1015 Duklja develops into a Serb-controlled principality

1189 Serbian ruler Stefan Nemanja conquers Duklja and renames it Zeta

1496 Cetinje established as the capital of the interior region of Crna Gora (Montenegro)

1667 A devastating earthquake hits the Adriatic coast, destroying Kotor

1800s Prince Petar I seeks Russian support in the struggle against the Ottomans

1876–8 Montenegro wins freedom from a shrinking Ottoman Empire

1918 Montenegro joins the newly formed kingdom of Serbs, Croats and Slovenes, accepting the Serbian royal family as its new monarchs

1941 Mussolini occupies Montenegro with plans to absorb it as an Italian protectorate

2006 Montenegrins vote in a referendum for independence from Serbia

2007 Montenegro signs a membership agreement with the EU

LANGUAGE AND CULTURE

Montenegrins speak Serbo-Croatian and officially use both the Latin and Cyrillic alphabets. There is little to culturally differentiate Montenegrins from Serbians as they have been intermarrying for centuries; variations in traditions are most pronounced between the communities of the Ottoman-influenced coast and those of the interior. Right up until the last century, elaborate regional costume played an important role in the cultural life of the interior communities; it was a custom to be buried in full traditional dress. Colourful festivals are still a regular feature of Montenegrin life.

Exploring Montenegro

Montenegro is dominated by towering peaks that provide a stunning backdrop to the sparkling blue Adriatic and the sandy beaches that line the country's coastline. Its capital is the Ottoman-influenced city of Podgorica, dotted with mosques, cafés and restaurants. Among the other cities of interest is Kotor, located on Montenegro's most beautiful bay. Getting around is easy as the bus service is extensive, although sporadic inland. A railway line runs from Bar to Podgorica, and on to Belgrade.

Venetian buildings along the cobbled streets of the Old Town, Budva

SIGHTS AT A GLANCE

Bar ❸
Budva ❺
Cetinje ❿
Durmitor National Park ⓬
Herceg Novi ❼
Kotor ❽
Lake Skadar National Park ❷

Lovćen National Park ❾
Ostrog Monastery pp536–7 ⓫
Podgorica ❶
Tivat ❻
Ulcinj ❹

KEY

🛫 Airport

⚓ Ferry terminal

— Major road

— Minor road

— Railway

--- International border

0 km 25

0 miles 25

Impressive Millennium Bridge over the Morača river, Podgorica

Podgorica ❶

🏙 180,000. 🛬 🚉 🚌
ℹ️ Slobode 47, (020) 667 535.
www.podgorica.me

Podgorica initially developed as an important centre for trade; the first official mention of it was in 1326. The city thrived during medieval times but then succumbed to the Ottomans who occupied it as a defensive citadel for four centuries. In 1878, the city was integrated into Montenegro and it flourished economically and culturally for several decades. Podgorica suffered in the 20th century, however, due to intensive bombing during World War II and severe economic decline during the Yugoslav Wars in the 1990s. Today, Montenegro's capital has a handful of minor sights that can be explored in a day. The most striking structure and a symbol of 21st-century progress is the 140-m (459-ft) long Millennium Bridge (Most Milenijum) across the Morača river. The city's Old Town,

south of the Ribnica river, was almost entirely destroyed during World War II. However, some remnants of its Ottoman past remain. In the Old Town Square is the 30-m (98-ft) high 18th-century Turkish Clock Tower (Sahat Kula) while the Muslim quarter houses the renovated 16th-century Glavatovići and Osmanagića mosques.

To the north of the Ribnica river, the New Town's **City Museum** (Muzeji i galerije Podgorice) houses absorbing archaeological and ethnographic collections. Further north is the 11th-century **St George's Church** (Crkva Sv Đorđa), with frescoes depicting the life of St George. Podgorica's finest building, King Nikola's former Winter Palace contains the **Modern Art Gallery** (Centar Savremene Umjetnosti) with a collection of ethnographic art from Africa and Asia among other exhibits. Nearby is the **Orthodox Cathedral of the Resurrection of Christ**, which boasts 17 Russian bells; the largest, at 11 tonnes (12 tons), is the heaviest in the Balkans.

🏛 **City Museum**
Marka Miljanova 4. **Tel** (020) 242 543. ⏰ noon–8pm Tue–Fri, 9am–2pm Sat & Sun. 📷 🚫

⛪ **St George's Church**
ulica 19 Decembar. ⏰ 7am–8pm daily. 📷

🏛 **Modern Art Gallery**
Ljubljanska ulica BB. **Tel** (020) 225 043. ⏰ 4–9pm Mon–Fri.

⛪ **Orthodox Cathedral of the Resurrection of Christ**
ulica Georga Vašingtona.
⏰ 7:30am–7pm daily. 📷

Lake Skadar National Park ❷
Skadarsko jezero

25 km (16 miles) S of Podgorica. 🚌 from Podgorica. 🚤 Vranjina Island, close to Virpazar, (020) 879 103; Centre for Protection and Research of Birds in Montenegro, Piperska 370A, (067) 24 5006. **www**.nparkovi.co.me

Located in the Zeta Skadar valley and surrounded by picturesque mountains, the 400-sq-km (154-sq-mile) Lake Skadar is the Balkan Peninsula's largest lake and is split between Albania and Montenegro. In 1983, two-thirds of the lake on the Montenegro side was designated as a national park. The lake is fed by around 50 underwater springs and is home to about 264 bird species, such as great white herons, Caspian terns, black-headed gulls, Griffon vultures, Dalmatian pelicans and white-tailed eagles. It also has about 40 species of fish including mullet, carp, eel and chub. The northern and eastern shores of the lake are characterized by marshlands which are scattered with yellow water lilies during spring. The lake's islands are also home to many monasteries and churches, some dating back to the 11th century; there are several ruined medieval fortresses as well.

The visitors' centre in Vranjina can arrange boat trips around the park and to the monasteries as well as fishing permits. It also offers general information on Montenegro's national parks.

Dalmatian pelican, Lake Skadar

The magnificent Lake Skadar National Park, home to numerous species of flora and fauna

For hotels and restaurants in this region see pp541–2 and p543

Bar ❸

70 km (43 miles) S of Podgorica.
🏠 *16,000.* 🚃 🚌 ⛴ 🛈 *Obala 13 Jul bb, (030) 312 912.*
www.bar.me

The beautiful coastal town of Bar is the country's only international port, with ferries from Greece and Italy docking every day.

However, the star attraction is the Old Town (Stari Bar), situated 4 km (2 miles) inland on a rocky plateau at the foot of Mount Rumija. Founded in the 6th century, the town was ruled by Byzantines, Serbs and Venetians before becoming part of the Ottoman Empire from 1571 to 1878. It was gradually abandoned in the early 20th century after being destroyed during the War of Liberation (1878) and suffering two catastrophic explosions in 1882 and 1912. Archaeological and restoration work begun in the 1950s was set back by another earthquake in 1979 which again devastated the Old Town.

Today, many of the Old Town's buildings and sections of its walls have been restored and are used as a summer venue for cultural events. The 12th-century St George's Church was built upon the ruins of the 9th-century St Theodor's Church and was once the Old Town's largest cathedral. The Ottomans rebuilt it as a mosque in the 17th century, but today only its foundations remain. Also worth visiting is the restored Church of St Venerada, used for music recitals, and the old Bishop's Palace, which houses a small museum of the Old Town history.

A more comprehensive museum collection can be found in the **Homeland Museum** (Zavičajni muzej) on the seafront in the New Town (Novi Bar). It is located in the 19th-century summer residence of King Nikola, who used the mansion to receive guests from abroad. The town is also famous for its numerous olive trees. According to legend, locals were unable to marry until they had planted at least ten olive trees. One, in particular, is believed to be over 2,000 years old and can be found near the Old Town.

🏛 **Homeland Museum**
Šetalište Kralje Nikole. **Tel** *(030) 314 079.* ⬜ *9am–2pm & 6pm–8pm daily.* 📷 🔌

The 2,000-year-old olive tree near Bar's Old Town

Ulcinj ❹

95 km (59 miles) S of Podgorica.
🏠 *11,000.* 🚌 🛈 *ulica 6 Novembra, (030) 412 595.* ⛴ *Fri.*

The southernmost city on the Montenegrin coast, Ulcinj is thought to be one of the oldest trading settlements in the Adriatic. Its Old Town (Stari grad) was mentioned as early as the 6th century BC, when it was home to a Greek colony. Its naturally defensive position atop a rocky peninsular made for an ideal vantage point over the sheltered harbour and was reinforced by mighty walls, rendering it virtually impenetrable to attack over the centuries. However, it succumbed to the Serbs, then the Venetians, and, finally, the Ottomans in 1571 before its integration into the new Montenegrin state in 1880. Today, the Old Town has been restored following widespread damage caused by the 1979 earthquake. The **Old Town Museum** (Zavičajni muzej) occupies many buildings on Slave's Square (trg Robova). Its archaeological collection, housed in a 16th-century Renaissance church, includes marble Turkish tombstones, medieval coins and a variety of pottery specimens. Traditional costumes are on display in the neighbouring 6th-century Bishop's Palace, while the 15th-century Balšić Tower is used for temporary exhibitions.

🏛 **Old Town Museum**
Stari grad. **Tel** *(030) 421 419.* ⬜ *May–Sep: 7am–noon & 3pm–8pm daily; Oct–Apr: 7am–2pm daily.* 📷 🔌

One of the remote beaches in Ulcinj

MONTENEGRO'S BEST BEACHES

Between Bar and Ulcinj, endless stretches of fine sandy beaches merge with the clear blue waters of the Adriatic. To the west of Bar, and only accessible by sea, is the Kraljičina (Queen's) Beach, favoured by Queen Milena, wife of King Nikola. To the east is the 1-km (0.5-mile) long Crvena (Red) Beach named after its unusual red sand. The Veliki Pijesak (Great Sand) Beach between Bar and Ulcinj or the 13-km (8-mile) long Velika Plaža (Great Beach) east of Ulcinj are the most isolated beaches. Naturists can also visit the beach at Ada Bojana, a small island at the end of Velika Plaža.

Budva's walled town with the striking tower of St Ivan's Catholic Church

Budva ❺

67 km (42 miles) SW of
Podgorica. 🏛 *17,000*. 🚌 🚏
ℹ️ *Mediteranska 4, (033) 402 814.*
www.budva.travel

With its fantastic beaches,
islands and bays, the enchanting town of Budva has become
extremely popular. One of
the oldest urban settlements
on the Montenegrin coast,
the town was successively
conquered by Greeks, Romans,
Serbs and various feudal rulers
before the Venetians gained
control in 1442. They strengthened its existing defences and
managed to resist the Ottoman
expansion that absorbed the

neighbouring towns of Bar,
Ulcinj and Podgorica in the
16th century. Budva stayed
under Venetian control until
1797, when it fell into Austrian
hands; it did not join
Montenegro until the
Allied defeat of the
Austro-Hungarian
Empire in 1918.

Perched on a
rocky bluff and
overlooked by
picturesque mount
ains, Budva's
atmospheric Old Town
(Stari grad) still has a distinct
Venetian flavour. Devastated
by an earthquake in 1979,
it has been painstakingly
restored. Today, its enchanting

alleys open on to charming
squares filled with shops,
bars and restaurants enlivened
by street performers. The
Budva Museum (Muzej Budve)
on the Old Town Square
(Starogradski trg) houses a
fascinating display of archaeological artifacts, many of
which were uncovered after
the upheaval of the 1979
earthquake. They include
Roman glassware and an
engraved 5th-century Illyrian
helmet. Smaller ethnographic
and historical exhibitions are
displayed on the upper floors
of the museum.

Standing next door is
St Ivan's Catholic Church
(Katolička Crkva Sv Ivana),
notable for its prominent
tower. Dating from the 7th
century, this is the town's
oldest church, although the
design was modified
following a severe
earthquake in
1667. Its simple
façade conceals
an interior with
a fine array of
17th-century
Venetian icons
as well as the 12th-century
Madonna of Budva icon,
believed to have miraculous
curative powers. The small
Franciscan **Church of St Mary**
(Crkva Svete Marije), tucked
away in the southwest corner
of the town, has a distinctive
triple-arched bell tower.
Founded in the 9th century, it
is now used to host occasional
cultural events.

A short distance out to
sea is the sloping St Nikola's
Island. Boats shuttle back
and forth during the summer
allowing visitors to climb to
the island's summit at 120 m
(395 ft), laze on its sandy
beaches or visit the small
St Nikola Church.

Painted arch, Church of
St Mary

SVETI STEFAN

Built on a rocky island to the south of Budva, Sveti Stefan
appears to float dreamily on the turquoise waters of the
Adriatic. The island's natural beauty, combined with ancient
stone houses converted into luxury apartments, earned it a
reputation in the 1970s and 80s as an exclusive summer
resort. Once a haven for medieval pirates and fishermen
resisting the Ottomans, it became the summer retreat of
royalty, such as Queen Elizabeth II and Hollywood stars
such as Sophia Loren and Sylvester Stallone. The Yugoslav
Wars abruptly curtailed its popularity, and although the
island reopened for business soon after, the resort remains
closed to the public and is scheduled to reopen shortly.

The fairy tale island resort of Sveti Stefan

🏛 **Budva Museum**
Petra I Petrovića 11, Stari grad.
Tel (033) 453 308. ⬜ *May–Sep:
8am–10pm Tue–Sun; Oct–Apr:
10am–8pm Tue–Fri, 10am–5pm
Sat & Sun.* 🖼️ 🚻

🔓 **St Ivan's Catholic Church**
Strarogradski trg. ⬜ *7am–7:30 pm
daily.* 🚻

🔓 **Church of St Mary**
Stari grad, southeast wall.
⬜ *8:30am–6pm daily.*

Tivat ❻

80 km (50 miles) W of Podgorica.
🏘 8,000. ⚓ 🚌 ℹ Palih Boraca 8,
(032) 671324. **www**.tivat.travel

Situated on the Bay of Kotor, Tivat has emerged as a major tourist attraction, where visitors promenade along the beachfront beneath palm trees as expensive yachts cruise in and out of the marina.

Wealthy aristocrats from Kotor were among the first to build their summer residences here in the Middle Ages. The **Buća-Luković Summer Palace** (Vila Buća-Luković) on the seafront was once the seasonal home of the Bućas, one of the wealthiest families of Kotor. The palace's stone tower and small Baroque church date back to the 15th century. The Renaissance building is now used for cultural performances and exhibitions throughout the summer.

North of the town centre, the Town Park is a pleasant retreat shaded by cypress, eucalyptus and oleander trees. The small Island of Flowers, connected to the mainland by a narrow isthmus, is home to the partially excavated ruins of the Monastery of Archangel Michael, founded in the 13th century by Benedictine monks.

🏛 **Buća-Luković Summer Palace**
Nikole Đurkovića br. 10. **Tel** (032) 674 591. ◻ summer: 8am–1pm & 7pm–noon daily; winter: 8am–1pm & 4pm–11pm Mon–Fri. ♿ 🅿 ▯

IGALO'S HEALING MUD

The town of Igalo, close to Herceg Novi, is famed for the healing *Igaljsko blato* (Igalo mud) found on its beach. First documented by an Austro-Hungarian physician in the 19th century, a spa treatment centre was built here, which now operates as a spa hotel (*see p542*). Visitors can also treat themselves for free by sunbathing on the beach with its therapeutic mud.

Visitor undergoing mud therapy

Evening stroll along the broad promenade in Tivat

Herceg Novi ❼

90 km (56 miles) W of Podgorica.
🏘 11,000. 🚌 ℹ Jova Dabovića 12, (031) 350 820.
www.hercegnovi.travel

Founded in the 14th century by the Bosnian King Tvrtko, Herceg Novi fell to the Ottoman Empire shortly after 1483. Following two centuries of intermittent battles, the Venetians took power in the late 17th century and stayed until 1797. The Austro-Hungarians then took over until 1918, when the town was finally absorbed into Montenegro. The 19th-century Austro-Hungarian Clock Tower (Sahat Kula) has been a symbol of the town ever since.

King Tvrtko left his mark by constructing the Forte Mare Castle on the seafront, while the Ottomans added to the defences with the **Bloody Tower** (Kanli Kula). The latter gained its gruesome moniker following its conversion to an infamous prison during Turkish rule. In the 1950s, part of the tower was turned into a summer amphitheatre with the Adriatic as its backdrop.

In the heart of the Old Town is the **Church of the Archangel Michael** (Crkva Sv Arhanđela Milaila), completed in 1911. It harmoniously combines Romanesque and Islamic architectural features, exemplified by the central cupola flanked by minaret-like turrets. Inside is a fine marble iconostasis made by Croatian masons.

🏛 **Bloody Tower**
Stari grad. ◻ 8am–8:30 daily.

⛪ **Church of the Archangel Michael**
trg Belavista. ◻ 8am–8:30pm daily. 🔼

The seaward bastion of Forte Mare Castle, Herceg Novi

Mist-covered hills forming a backdrop to Lovćen National Park

Kotor ❽

69 km (43 miles) W of Podgorica.
🏠 6,000. 🚌 ℹ️ Stari grad, (032)
325 947. **www**.tokotor.com

Located amidst breathtaking mountain scenery at the tip of Kotor Bay's furthest inlet, the medieval town of Kotor is encircled by ancient and imposing walls. Built between the 9th and 14th centuries, the walls stretch for 5 km (3 miles) and are up to 15 m (42 ft) thick and 20 m (66 ft) high. Thanks to these defences, Kotor withstood two Ottoman sieges, in 1537 and 1657.

The 17th-century clock tower in Kotor

During Roman times, the town (then known as Acruvium) was so well hidden that it escaped the devastating barbarian raids that brought down the Roman Empire. Its navy was also a formidable force; by the 18th century it

had a fleet of 300 ships and was trading as far afield as India and northern Europe. In 1979, after being hit by an earthquake, Kotor was designated a World Heritage Site. Today, the Old Town (Stari grad) is filled with visitors admiring the labyrinthine streets that connect its squares, ancient churches and splendid palaces.

Forming part of the western wall is the 17th-century Duke's Palace, facing the town's 1602 clock tower. Built in Renaissance style, it stands adjacent to the 15th-century armoury and was intended to house military offices.

The only building to escape damage by the earthquake was the single-nave **St Luke's Church** (Crkva Sv Luke), with both Orthodox and Catholic altars. Its brightest features are the Cretan icons within the small 18th-century Chapel of

St Spiridon. On the other side of town is the Romanesque **St Tryphon's Cathedral** (Katedrala Sv Tripuna), one of only two Catholic cathedrals in Montenegro. Its most precious treasure is St Tryphon's skull, which was brought to Kotor from Constantinople in 809 and kept in a silver casket. Other valuable items include a superb 15th-century engraved silver altar screen depicting Christ on a throne surrounded by saints.

🔒 **St Luke's Church**
trg Bokelijske Mornarice, Stari grad.
🕐 8am–8pm daily.

🔒 **St Tryphon's Cathedral**
trg Ustanka Mornara, Stari grad. **Tel**
(032) 322 315. 🕐 9am–6pm daily.

Lovćen National Park ❾
Nacionalni park Lovćen

37 km (23 miles) W of Podgorica.
🚌 from Podgorica. ℹ️ Bajova 2,
Cetinje, (041) 231 570.
www.nparkovi.co.me

Inaugurated in 1952, Lovćen National Park is the third largest of Montenegro's four national parks. Covering an area of 62 sq km (24 sq miles), it includes protected areas of ancient pine and beech forests that are home to over 200 species of birds and about 1,300 species of flora. The park is dominated by the twin peaks of Mount Lovćen. At the top of Jezerski Vrh (1,657 m/5,436 ft), Mount Lovćen's second highest peak, is the mausoleum of the Montenegrin poet and ruler Petar II Petrović Njegoš.

Aerial view of Kotor's sea-facing Old Town

For hotels and restaurants in this region see pp541–2 and p543

Cetinje ⑩

39 km (24 miles) W of Podgorica.
🏛 *16,000.* 🚌 ℹ️ *(041) 230 250.*
www.cetinje.travel

Once the capital of
Montenegro, Cetinje exudes
an inescapable air of faded
grandeur. Podgorica replaced
the town as capital in 1946
but despite the loss of its
official status, it is still considered to be the country's
historic centre; it was here
that King Ivan Crnojević
established the capital of the
old Zeta kingdom in the 15th
century. Pretty houses line
the streets and low rocky hills
frame the town on all sides.

The most significant
building here, the **Cetinje
Monastery** (Cetinjski Manastir),
was constructed in 1701 to
replace the 15th-century
Crnojević Monastery. As the
seat of Montenegro's religious
leader, Vladika, the monastery
attracted the country's influential figures and functioned as
the unofficial capital and
centre of organized resistance
against the Ottomans. Today,
the monastery is best known
for possessing what is believed
to be St John the Baptist's
right hand, a tiny fragment
of the original Holy Cross
and for its Treasury Museum.
Exhibits in the museum
include unique religious
manuscripts dating back to
the 13th century and decorative 16th-century crosses
painstakingly carved with
miniature biblical scenes.

Next to the monastery is
Bilyarda, a castle-like, single
storey palace, built in 1838
for Petar II Petrović Njegoš.
Surrounded by a wall with
towers, the palace now
functions as the **Njegoš
Museum** (Njegošev muzej),
where visitors can see
many of the king's personal
possessions, including period
furniture and a billiard table.

Nearby is the **Montenegrin
National History Museum**
(Istorijski muzej Crne Gore),
housed in the Government
House (Zetski Dom), which
was built in 1910 to accommodate government offices and
the national assembly. On
the ground floor is the

**Façade of the imposing
18th-century Cetinje Monastery**

History Museum, which
exhibits a vast array of Turkish
war trophies. Highlights
include the death mask of the
legendary Albanian ruler Karo
Mahmud Pasha Busatlija. On
the first floor is the museum's
absorbing collection of 19th-
and 20th-century Montenegrin
and Yugoslavian art.

Cetinje Monastery
Cetinje BB. *Tel (041) 231 021.*
⬜ *8am–6pm daily.* 📷 ℹ️

🏛 **Njegoš Museum**
trg Kralja Nikole, Biljarda.
Tel (041) 230 310. ⬜ *9am–5pm
daily.* 📷 ℹ️

🏛 **Montenegrin National
History Museum**
Novice Cerovića 7, Vladin
Dom. *Tel (041) 230 310.*
⬜ *9am–5pm daily.* 📷 ℹ️

Ostrog
Monastery ⑪
Manastir Ostrog

See pp536–7.

Durmitor National
Park ⑫
Nacionalni park Durmitor

140 km (87 miles) N of Podgorica.
🚌 *from Podgorica.* ℹ️ *ulica
Jovana Cvijića, (052) 360 228.*
www.nparkovi.co.me

Designated a national park
in 1952 and a UNESCO
World Heritage Site in
1980, Durmitor National
Park takes in a vast expanse
of spectacular scenery. One
of the oldest protected areas
in Montenegro, it is situated
on a 1,500-m (4,920-ft) high
plateau, from which numerous
peaks rise to heights of about
2,500 m (8,200 ft).

Known for its glacial lakes,
waterfalls and crystal-clear
rivers, the park has a broad
range of flora and fauna,
including mountain maple,
Bosnian iris, edelweiss,
Montenegrin bellflower, and
bears, wolves, golden eagles
and white-headed vultures. It
is also famous for its 400-year-
old black pine forest with
trees up to 50 m (165 ft) tall.

The superb mountain range around Durmitor National Park

Ostrog Monastery ⓫
Manastir Ostrog

Founded by St Basil in the 17th century, Ostrog Monastery was built into a sheer cliff face high above the Zeta river to guard it from the Ottomans. It comprises two complexes: Lower Monastery, which houses the administrative buildings, including the abbot's residence, and the Upper Monastery, which contains two cave-churches – the Chapel of the Honourable Cross and the Church of the Presentation of the Virgin Mary. Montenegro's most important place of pilgrimage, Ostrog has been associated with many healing miracles, attracting Catholic, Christian and Muslim pilgrims.

St Trinity Church
Part of the Lower Monastery complex, St Trinity Church is over 200 years old. Its barrel-vaulted interior is covered with intricate frescoes in gold and turquoise, which have been restored over time.

★ Upper Monastery
Completely rebuilt in the 1920s following a devastating fire, the Upper Monastery provides accommodation for Ostrog's 15 monks. The narrow corridors are decorated with lovely, colourful icons and mosaics.

STAR SIGHTS

★ Upper Monastery

★ St Basil's Relics

★ Chapel of the Honourable Cross

Lower Monastery
The 18th-century Lower Monastery stands beside St Trinity Church in the valley below the Upper Monastery.

Lower
Monastery
↓

★ St Basil's Relics
The Church of the Presentation of the Virgin Mary houses St Basil's bones. Pilgrims start gathering here from early in the morning, eager to catch a glimpse of the holy relics and in the hope of witnessing a miracle.

★ Chapel of the Honourable Cross
Nestled in the rock face above the Church of the Presentation is the Chapel of the Honourable Cross. The walls of the chapel feature splendid frescoes by the 17th-century painter Radul, depicting scenes from the life of Christ and venerated saints.

St Basil's Relics

ST BASIL

One of the Orthodox Church's most revered saints, St Basil founded the Ostrog Monastery in 1667 and remained here until his death in 1671. It was at Ostrog that he forged his reputation as a miracle-worker – a healer of the physically and mentally afflicted. The saint also assisted in the renovation of numerous monasteries, a practice forbidden by the Turkish rulers of the time.

Portrait of St Basil, patron saint of Ostrog

Vaulted Candle Room
Hundreds of flickering votive candles fill the atmospheric vaulted Candle Room; its frescoes are barely visible beneath the soot.

Practical & Travel Information

With the years of Communism and the recent Yugoslav Wars firmly behind it, tourism has picked up in Montenegro. There are plenty of tourist information centres across the country, although the staff may not be fluent in English. Public transport is good with frequent bus services connecting most towns, and additional minibus shuttles operating along the coast during summer. The country's only passenger railway line runs from Bar to Podgorica, from where it continues north to Belgrade. Those intent on exploring the more remote interior regions and the beautiful countryside are best advised to rent a vehicle.

WHEN TO VISIT

A good time to visit the country is during spring and autumn: late March to late June, and between September and October. July and August are the best months for those seeking sunshine and crowds, however this is high season, so room prices can be high.

DOCUMENTATION

Citizens of the European Union (EU), Switzerland, Norway, Iceland, Israel, the US, Cyprus, Croatia, Canada, Korea, Singapore, Australia and New Zealand can enter Montenegro with a valid passport for up to 90 days without a visa. Those needing visas should apply directly to the Montenegrin Embassy in their respective country.

Visitors are required to register with the police within 24 hours of their arrival; this is usually arranged by the hotel soon after arrival.

VISITOR INFORMATION

The **National Tourism Organization of Montenegro** is quite helpful, and there are several informative tourist websites, as well as Podgorica's free **In Your Pocket** guide, which also has its own website. There are tourist offices in all the main towns. These offer free maps and brochures and can provide information on hotels and local attractions, although not all staff members speak English. Smaller towns also have good sources of information, but again, not necessarily in English. There is, however, a 24-hour tourist information helpline in English.

HEALTH AND SECURITY

Visitors are advised to carry any medical prescription and essential medicines with them when travelling to Montenegro. They also need to be vaccinated against diphtheria, tetanus and polio prior to travel. Generally,

public clinics are not open to visitors and it is better to go to private hospitals where the standard of care is high and the doctors speak English. Private clinics and hospitals expect cash payment even for minor treatment; visitors are advised to have their own health insurance. Well-known hospitals in the capital include **As Mediph** and **Kbc**. Pharmacists sell over-the-counter medicines and can advise on minor ailments. People need to be wary of tick bites, especially when camping or hiking, and seek immediate medical assistance if bitten.

Montenegro has a low crime rate and travellers are unlikely to encounter anything more serious than pickpocketing and petty theft. It is safe for women travellers to walk alone at night, but they should exercise caution in lonely spots.

FACILITIES FOR THE DISABLED

There is little public awareness of the needs of the disabled in Montenegro although upmarket hotels and popular beach resorts may cater for travellers with disabilities. In Podgorica, most pedestrian crossings have sloped kerbs and the main crossings are equipped with sound signalling systems.

BANKING AND CURRENCY

The euro has been the country's official currency since 2002. ATMs can be found in all but the smallest towns. Credit cards are accepted in many large hotels, restaurants, shops and petrol stations. Banks are usually open from 8am to 5pm Monday to Saturday, and will exchange cash and traveller's cheques.

COMMUNICATIONS

Public payphones are very rare in Montenegro, so it is best to head to a post office to make a call. Phone cards, such as MonteCards, for use in phone booths, can be purchased in post offices as well as newspaper kiosks. However, these are usually

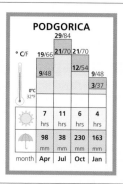

THE CLIMATE OF MONTENEGRO

The coast of Montenegro enjoys a Mediterranean climate with long, hot summers and short, wet winters. Summer temperatures average 28° C (82° F) and drop to around 8° C (46° F) in winter. Inland, the mountainous regions average 22° C (72° F) in summer and -3° C (27° F) in winter, with heavy snowfall.

PODGORICA

°C/F	Apr	Jul	Oct	Jan
	19/66	29/84	21/70	
	9/48	21/70	12/54	9/48
				3/37
hrs	7	11	6	4
mm	98	38	230	163

0°C 32°F

expensive. Using a local SIM card from cell phone providers such as T-Mobile, Promonte and M:tel is the cheapest way to stay connected. These can also be bought from kiosks, and work out cheaper than land-lines. International calls are best made in post offices. Most towns have Internet cafés and many hotels and restau-rants are free Wi-Fi spots.

ARRIVING BY AIR

Podgorica and Tivat both have international airports. Tivat is the best choice for those visiting the coast. Visitors can also use Dubrovnik's Čilipi airport, which is only 25 km (16 miles) northwest of Herceg Novi. As yet there are no budget airline routes to the country, but Montenegro is well served by national carriers. **Montenegro Airlines** offers thrice weekly direct flights from Podgorica to London. Serbia's **Jat Airways** has indirect flights from Rome, London, Paris, Frankfurt and Budapest to Podgorica and Tivat, while Slovenia's **Adria Airways** offers indirect European flights to Podgorica. **Croatia Airlines** connects Dubrovnik (Čilipi) to major European cities.

ARRIVING BY SEA

Those with private yachts can head for the marinas at Herceg Novi, Kotor, Budva and Bar, which all offer basic services. **Montenegro Lines** run daily car ferries from Bar to Bari and Ancona (Italy) in the summer. This service is reduced to three times a week out of season.

RAIL TRAVEL

Three trains a day make the 10-hour journey from Belgrade to Bar, along what is consi-dered to be one of the most spectacular railway lines in the world. Completed in 1979, the Montenegrin section carries passengers across the Mala Rijeka viaduct, the highest in the world at 200 m (656 ft), through the 6-km (4-mile) Sozina tunnel, and past a succession of dramatic rocky mountains. The railway journey from Belgrade to Podgorica takes 8 hours. Euro Rail also offers trips via Vienna, Budapest and Belgrade to Montenegro. Detailed time-tables are available on their website, **Montenegro Railways**.

TRAVELLING BY BUS

Public and private transport companies run an efficient network of buses, boosted by minibus shuttles in the summer. Tickets for local buses can be purchased on board. The country's more remote mountainous regions are connected by bus, but services are limited and timetables should be checked in advance. Tourist information offices can provide details of bus routes.

TRAVELLING BY CAR

Reckless local drivers present the greatest danger on Montenegro's roads. They frequently harass slower vehi-cles and overtake on blind corners. Lights should be kept on at all times, seat belts should be worn in the front and drunken driving should be avoided. Drivers need to carry an international or EU licence, the registration docu-ments of their vehicle and Green Card insurance. Car hire is available at both Podgorica and Tivat airports as well as through city rental agencies such as **Delta**, **Meridian** and **Evropa** – and should be booked in advance during high season.

Taxis, which are metered, are reasonably cheap, and can be ordered by phone. Most companies have English-speaking operators.

DIRECTORY

DOCUMENTATION

Council of Europe
Novaka Miloševa 6,
Podgorica.
Tel (020) 230 819.

EMBASSIES

Croatia
Vladimira Četkovića 2,
Podgorica.
Tel (020) 269 760.

United Kingdom
Ulcinjska 8, Podgorica.
Tel (020) 618 010.
www.ukinmontenegro.
fco.gov.uk

United States
Ljubljanska bb, Podgorica.
Tel (020) 225 417. www.
podgorica.usembassy.gov

VISITOR INFORMATION

National Tourism Organization of Montenegro
Rimski trg 47, Vektra
81000 Podgorica.
Tel (020) 235 155.
www.montenegro.travel

In Your Pocket
www.inyourpocket.com.

EMERGENCY NUMBERS

Ambulance
Tel 124.

Fire
Tel 123.

Police
Tel 122.

HEALTH AND SECURITY

As Mediph
Slobode 4, Podgorica.
Tel (020) 231 800.

Kbc
Podgorica bb, Podgorica.
Tel (020) 412 412.

ARRIVING BY AIR

Adria Airways
www.adria-airways.com

Croatia Airlines
www.croatiaairlines.com

Jat Airways
www.jat.com

Montenegro Airlines
www.montenegroairlines.
com

ARRIVING BY SEA

Montenegro Lines
www.montenegrolines.
net

RAIL TRAVEL

Montenegro Railways
www.zcg-prevoz.me

TRAVELLING BY CAR

Delta
www.rentacar-delta.com

Evropa
www.hotelevropa.co.me

Meridian
www.meridian-rentacar.
com

Shopping & Entertainment

There is no shortage of things to buy or places to shop in Montenegro. Painted icons, foodstuffs, such as olives and cheeses, and embroidered tablecloths make interesting gifts. The nightlife in Podgorica is vibrant, although it tends to fizzle out in the coastal towns during the off-season. Many festivals take place throughout the year, of which the Carnival of Kotor is perhaps the most colourful. The countryside is perfect for outdoor pursuits such as rafting through some of the world's deepest canyons, mountain biking and hiking.

MARKETS

Most towns have their own fruit and vegetable markets. At the daily market in Bar, women still dress in traditional outfits. In Kotor, the daily market on the seafront is a great spot to buy fresh vegetables and fish. It is also the place to find inexpensive tablecloths and curtains of handmade lace.

GIFTS AND SOUVENIRS

Wooden toys and utensils are sold in the markets of most towns, as is handmade lace. Colourful icons and other religious knick-knacks can be bought from church and monastery shops. Traditional folk music CDs make good souvenirs and are available in most gift shops.

FOOD AND DRINK

For olive products, it is worth paying a visit to the Olive Museum in Bar's Old Town. Honey from the Durmitor region, where bees graze on heather and wild flowers, is also particularly good.

Montenegro has a thriving wine industry and its red wine, vranac, is well known, as are krstač, crmničko, cabernet and chardonnay. Local brandies such as *šljivovica* (made from plums) and *loza* (made from grapes) are also popular.

JEWELLERY

Podgorica's Zlatarska (gold) street is lined with several jewellery shops, and the town of Ulcinj is famous for the work of its goldsmiths.

Budva's Old Town is crammed with trinket shops. Also worth buying is Montenegro's delicate silver filigree jewellery.

THEATRE

Theatre lovers should check what is on at the **Montenegrin National Theatre**, which hosts international performances. In summer, **Budva City Theatre** organizes drama, exhibitions and poetry readings.

NIGHTLIFE

Podgorica has numerous wine bars, clubs and cafés that stay open till late. **Porto Club**, with local DJs, **L'Ombelico**, with great live music, and **Nice Vice**, are some of the most popular. The coastal towns cater to visitors during summer with mainstream clubs and bars; Budva is also known for its all-night club scene.

FESTIVALS

Budva's open-air **Petrovac Jazz Festival** takes place in the last week of August, while Herceg Novi hosts the **Sunčane Skale** pop music festival in July. Kotor celebrates the **Carnival of Kotor**, a colourful procession of marked troupes through the Old Town, at the end of July.

OUTDOOR ACTIVITIES

Numerous agencies organize a wide range of outdoor activities. **Anitra Travel** and **Eco Tours** both arrange hiking, biking, climbing, rafting, jeep safaris, horse riding, skiing and paragliding. The **Pelikan Surf Club** organizes windsurfing on Lake Skadar,

while the **Dragon Surf Club** in Ulcinj offers courses in kitesurfing, windsurfing, sailing, skiing, paragliding and snowboarding. The **Diving Association of Montenegro** can provide information for scuba divers.

DIRECTORY

THEATRE

Budva City Theatre
13 Jul, Zgrada BSP, Budva.
Tel (033) 402 934.
www.gradteatar.cg.yu

Montenegrin National Theatre
ulica Stanka Dragojevića br. 18.
Podgorica. *Tel (020) 664 082.*
www.cnp.me

NIGHTLIFE

L'Ombelico
Hercegovačka 85, Podgorica.
Tel (067) 201 790.
www.lombelico.me

Nice Vice
ulica Slobode 82, Podgorica.
Tel (020) 230 394

Porto Club
ulica Stanka Dragojevića 34,
Podgorica. *Tel (067) 330 888.*

FESTIVALS

Carnival of Kotor
www.tokotor.com

Petrovac Jazz Festival
www.petrovacjazzfestival.
tripod.com

Sunčane Skale
www.suncaneskale.org

OUTDOOR ACTIVITIES

Anitra Travel
Atrium, Njegoševa 12, Nikšić.
Tel (040) 402 598.
www.tara-grab.com

Diving Association of Montenegro
Tel (067) 508 009.
www.mdiving.cg.yu

Dragon Surf Club
Ulcinj. *Tel (069) 624 429.*
www.dragonproject.net

Eco Tours
Kolasin. *Tel (020) 086 700.*
www.eco-tours.cg.yu

Pelikan Surf Club
Tel (069) 077 869.

Where to Stay in Montenegro

Montenegro has a mixture of hotels ranging from high-end establishments to state-run hotels. Away from the capital, hotels may be inexpensive, but they do not always match Western standards. Room rates gradually increase from April and peak during July and August, when they may nearly double.

PRICE CATEGORIES

Price categories are for a standard double room per night in high season, including tax and service charges. Breakfast is included, unless otherwise specified.

€ Under 30 euros
€€ 30–60 euros
€€€ 60–90 euros
€€€€ 90–150 euros
€€€€€ Over 150 euros

PODGORICA

Hotel Kerber   €€€

ulica Novaka Miloševa 6, 81000 **Tel** *(020) 405 405* **Fax** *(020) 405 406* **Rooms** *20*

Located above a shopping centre, Hotel Kerber is one of the city's few reasonably priced and centrally located options. It is a modern place, with brightly painted rooms that are comfortable and clean. Facilities include satellite TV, minibar and Internet access. **www.hotelkerber.co.me**

Bojatours   €€€€

Kralja Nikole 10, 81000 **Tel** *(020) 621 223* **Fax** *(020) 621 153* **Rooms** *18*

A few minutes from the city centre, Bojatours has elegant interiors with parquet floors and beautiful floral rugs. Rooms are clean and smartly furnished with central heating, minibar, TV and 24-hour Internet access. The fitness centre is free for all hotel guests, and there is a restaurant on site. **www.montenegrohotels.org**

Podgorica   €€€€€

Bul. Svetog Petra Cetinjskog 1, 81000 **Tel** *(020) 402 500* **Fax** *(020) 402 501* **Rooms** *44*

Built in 1967, this stunning hotel on the banks of the Morača river is a good example of early attempts to blend modern architecture with the natural environment. Rooms have stylish modern furniture and bathrooms. The best ones have terraces facing the river. **www.hotelpodgorica.co.me**

REST OF MONTENEGRO

BAR Inex-Zlatna Obala Complex   €€

Sutomore, 81355 **Tel** *(030) 312 259* **Fax** *(030) 312 249* **Rooms** *383*

Situated 4 km (2 miles) from Bar town, this idyllic complex stretches along the coast of the Ratac Peninsula. It offers standard hotel rooms as well as individual bungalows tucked away just metres from the beach. The bungalows are comfortably furnished and have kitchen facilities. **www.inexhoteli.com**

BAR Azalea Hotel Princess   €€€€

Jovana Tomaševića 59, 85000 **Tel** *(030) 300 300* **Fax** *(030) 312 510* **Rooms** *133*

This renovated four-star hotel lies right on a superb beach lined with palm trees. Rooms are spacious and well appointed, and staff provide an excellent standard of service. Two restaurants, two bars, a swimming pool, tennis courts and a fitness centre are among the many facilities on offer. **www.azalea-hotels.com**

BUDVA Slovenska Plaža Complex   €€€

trg Slobode 1, 85310 **Tel** *(033) 402 456* **Fax** *(033) 402 459* **Rooms** *719*

This seafront resort is a vast compex of small buildings interspersed with gardens with everything from souvenir shops, restaurants and fashion boutiques. The hotel has an impressive range of facilities including a circular outdoor pool. Each room has a balcony; suites have a kitchen and dining room.

BUDVA Šajo   €€€€

Jadranski Put bb, 85310 **Tel** *(033) 460 243* **Fax** *(033) 460 246* **Rooms** *26*

Like many of Budva's smart new hotels, the Šajo makes up for its distinct lack of character with a high standard of facilities and service. There is a sauna and fitness centre, and two restaurants, one in the hotel and the other in the garden. **www.sajohotel.com**

BUDVA Astoria Hotel   €€€€€

Njegoševa 4, Stari grad, 85310 **Tel** *(033) 451 110* **Fax** *(033) 451 215* **Rooms** *12*

This chic boutique-hotel has a fantastic location inside the walls of the Old Town. The elegantly furnished rooms have superb sea views. Its restaurant offers multinational cusine and it also provides magnificent sea views from its terrace. **www.hotelastoria.co.me**

Key to Symbols *see back cover flap*

CETINJE Hotel Grand

Njegoševa 1, 81250 **Tel** *(041) 231 652* **Fax** *(041) 231 762* **Rooms** *210*

Built in 1984, the Grand is one of the oldest hotels in Cetinje. The decor still exudes a Socialist-era charm, but all rooms have modern facilities. The indoor pool and sauna are still in working order and there are two restaurants, a snack bar and a large terrace. **www.hotel-grand.tripod.com**

HERCEG NOVI Vila Aleksandar

Save Kovačevića 64, Šetalište Pet Danica, 85347 **Tel** *(031) 345 806* **Fax** *(031) 345 804* **Rooms** *16*

This small hotel is right on the beach and all of its apartments have fabulous views of the sea. The rooms are simple yet comfortable with all modern amenities. Staff is polite and helpful and can arrange diving, sailing and hiking trips. **www.hotelvilaaleksandar.com**

HERCEG NOVI Mediterranean Health Centre (Igalo Spa Hotel)

Sava Ilića 5, Igalo, 85347 **Tel** *(031) 658 555* **Fax** *(031) 658 999* **Rooms** *380*

Established during the 1970s, this colossal seafront spa-centre utilizes the healing properties of Igalo's famous sea mud in many of the therapies offered to its guests. Rooms incorporate a computerized bell system to call the in-house physician. **www.igalospa.com**

HERCEG NOVI Perla Hotel

Šetalište 5 Danica, 85340 **Tel** *(031) 345 700* **Fax** *(031) 344 094* **Rooms** *18*

Overlooking the beautiful Kotor Bay, the front rooms of this well-furnished, medium-sized hotel come with fabulous views. All rooms have direct dial phones and TV. A variety of water sports is on offer. The staff speak good English. **www.perla.co.me**

KOTOR Cattaro Hotel

Stari grad 232, 85330 **Tel** *(032) 311 000* **Fax** *(032) 311 080* **Rooms** *20*

In the heart of the Old Town and housed in what was once an 18th-century mansion, the Cattaro is an atmospheric four-star hotel that occupies three buildings: the Rector's Palace, Old Town Hall and Town Guard. Pictures of naval heroes and sea battles adorn the walls. **www.cattarohotel.com**

KOTOR Vardar

Stari grad 476, 85330 **Tel** *(032) 325 084* **Fax** *(032) 325 074* **Rooms** *24*

Centrally located, this intimate establishment offers a wonderful opportunity to soak up the charm of Kotor's Venetian-influenced Old Town. Its modern makeover makes for a stylish contrast with original features such as exposed stone walls. The rooms are luxuriously furnished. **www.hotelvardar.com**

OSTROG MONASTERY Ostrog Monastery

Ostrog Monastery **Tel** *(040) 405 258* **Rooms** *20*

Constructed in the 17th century, Ostrog Monastery *(see pp536–7)* stands midway between the Lower and Upper Monasteries. There is dormitory accommodation for visitors. Dorms are single sex and guests are asked to be in bed by 10pm. A good option is to sleep under the stars at the Upper Monastery, which provides mattresses.

TIVAT Palma Hotel

Pakovo bb, 85320 **Tel** *(032) 672 288* **Fax** *(032) 672 261* **Rooms** *122*

With bright blue shutters and a red-tiled roof, this charming hotel is located right on the beach. The rooms have whitewashed walls with clean white bedding and comfortable chairs and sofas. The restaurant is a quiet place to sit and enjoy gorgeous views of the sea. **www.primorje.co.me**

TIVAT Pine Hotel

Obala bb, 85320 **Tel** *(032) 671 255* **Fax** *(032) 671 305* **Rooms** *26*

A home away from home, the Pine Hotel offers decent rooms at reasonable prices. Shaded by giant palm trees, its roadside restaurant, with tables and polka-dot cushioned chairs, provides expansive views of the beach. It also has friendly staff and excellent service. **www.htpmimoza.com**

TIVAT Vizantija

Kaluđerovina, 85320 **Tel** *(032) 680 015* **Fax** *(032) 680 020* **Rooms** *12*

Situated just outside Tivat, the Vizantija is a lovely small hotel with its own private beach as well as a heated indoor pool and fitness facilities. Standards are high, and the restaurant serves a range of local dishes which can be enjoyed on a spacious terrace overlooking the sea. **www.vizantija.com**

ULCINJ Velika Plaža

Velika Plaža, 85360 **Tel** *(030) 431 131* **Fax** *(030) 413 131* **Rooms** *139*

Shaded by trees and situated near Ulcinj Beach, the Velika Plaža is a pleasant holiday complex offering both hotel rooms and bungalows. The hotel rooms have minimalist furniture but are comfortable. Bungalows have their own kitchenettes. **www.velikaplaza.com**

ULCINJ Dvori Balšića

Stari grad, 85360 **Tel** *(030) 421 457* **Fax** *(030) 421 457* **Rooms** *21*

Once a royal palace, this magnificent stone building in Ulcinj's Old Town has since been converted into luxury accommodation. Rooms are classically furnished with wooden ceilings and have marvellous views of the sea. Wireless Internet is also available. **www.hotel-dvoribalsica-montenegro.com**

Key to Price Guide *see p541* **Key to Symbols** *see back cover flap*

Where to Eat in Montenegro

Restaurant menus along the coast tend to revolve around fresh fish dishes such as fish stew, baked mussels and roast squid. Pizza and pasta also feature. Traditional meat-based Montenegrin cuisine, such as lamb stewed in milk and thick meat soups, can be found further inland. Vegetarian dishes include salads, soups and potato dishes.

PRICE CATEGORIES
Based on the price per person of a three-course meal with half a bottle of wine, including cover charge, service and tax.

€ Under 20 euros
€€ 20–25 euros
€€€ 25–30 euros
€€€€ 30–35 euros
€€€€€ Over 35 euros

PODGORICA

Carine Centar €
ulica Slobode 43, 81000 **Tel** *(020) 402 400*

Located in the centre of the city, this popular restaurant has both indoor and outdoor seating. The menu offers a predictable range of pizzas, and pasta dishes cooked with fresh herbs are the speciality of this restaurant. Service is brisk and efficient.

Three Centuries €€€€
Hotel Podgorica, Bul. Svetog Petra Cetinjskog 1, 81000 **Tel** *(020) 402 500*

Housed in the luxurious Hotel Podgorica *(see p541)*, Three Centuries is the place to dine in style. With its striking modern decor and enviable location on the banks of the Morača river, this is the best place in Podgorica to sample the regional cuisine as well as Italian and Mediterranean dishes.

REST OF MONTENEGRO

BUDVA Garden Café €
Mediteranska bb, 85310 **Tel** *(033) 452 090*

Tall eucalyptus and oleander trees provide shade to this quiet restaurant just outside the Old Town. Its outdoor tables are spaced well apart and service is polite and efficient. The varied menu features plenty of salads and light Montenegrin dishes as well as grilled sandwiches and pies.

CETINJE Vinoteka €€
Njegoševa 103, 81250 **Tel** *(041) 679 936*

With well-designed interiors, Vinoteka is an inviting restaurant. Local specialities of smoked ham and cheese feature on the menu alongside beef steak, pizza and pasta dishes and there is a comprehensive selection of Montenegrin and international wines. Staff is friendly and extremely efficient.

HERCEG NOVI Konoba Krušo €€
Šetalište 5 Danica, 85340 **Tel** *(031) 323 238*

This seafront restaurant, cosily adorned with fishing nets and shipping paraphernalia, has great sea views from its covered terrace. Fresh fish dominates the menu and it is a good spot to try local specialities such as roast squid and fish stew. The wine selection is excellent.

KOTOR Le Bastion €€€€€
Stari grad, 85330 **Tel** *(032) 322 116*

Located in the centre of Kotor's Old Town, Le Bastion's atmospheric setting complements its excellent menu of Montenegrin favourites. Its peaceful terrace, with fragrant flowers and overlooking the Church of St Maria, is the perfect place to unwind after a hard day's sightseeing.

LAKE SKADAR Pelikan €
Lake Skadar, Virpazar, 81305 **Tel** *(020) 711 107*

Located on the shores of stunning Lake Skadar, this cosy family-run restaurant serves incredible home-cooked fish, fresh from the lake. Spicy fish soup, home-made bread, smoked carp and roasted eel are among the delicious offerings. The affable owner can also arrange fishing and bird-watching trips.

ULCINJ Miško €€€
Ada Bojana, 85360 **Tel** *(069) 022 868*

This scenic restaurant on Bojana Island, near Ulcinj, is immensely popular with both locals and visitors. The menu has a broad range of mouth watering fish dishes prepared with locally caught fish, which are grilled right before diners' eyes. The pleasant terrace is a lovely place to sit and laze over lunch.

SERBIA

L *ying at the crossroads of Europe, Serbia's history goes back to the Neolithic era. Settled by Slavs in the 6th century, the country was home to a thriving civilization in the Middle Ages, and many of the surviving churches and monasteries from the period are UNESCO protected today. Serbia's natural forests, pristine mountain lakes and karst rock formations add to its stunning natural beauty.*

Situated at the heart of the Balkan Peninsula, Serbia has played a central role in the history and culture of South Eastern Europe. A turbulent past has produced a nation that seems uncertain about the future, but is rarely lacking in cultural pride.

At the crossroads of history, Serbia's population of just under 7.5 million is composed of various ethnic groups. The majority are Orthodox Christian Serbs, although the northern province of Vojvodina is home to a large number of Catholic Hungarians, alongside small numbers of Slovaks, Romanians and Croats. In addition, there are significant numbers of Muslim Bosnjaks, who are mostly concentrated in the southeast.

HISTORY

The establishment of a Serb state dates back to the early 13th century, when the rulers of the Raška region (modern-day Novi Pazar) established a kingdom with an autonomous church. The state reached its zenith under Stefan Dušan (r. 1331–46), who conquered territories in modern-day Macedonia and Greece. However, Serbian power went into decline with the arrival of the Ottomans in the Balkans. Although the epic Battle of Kosovo (1389) held them at bay for a while, the constant conflict weakened the state and, after 70 years of resistance, Serbia fell to the Ottomans, ushering in four centuries of foreign occupation. In the

View of the 15th-century Nebojša Kula on the Sava river, Kalemegdan Park, Belgrade

◁ **The renovated Sopoćani Monastery, founded in the 13th century**

Massacre of Serbs, First Balkan War, 1912

late 17th century, Habsburg victories over the Ottomans persuaded thousands of Serbs to leave their homelands in Kosovo and seek a new life in the Habsburg-controlled region of Vojvodina, in the north of the country. This went on to become the centre of education and culture.

A series of uprisings against the Ottomans in 1830 led to the creation of a Serbian principality. This was upgraded to the status of a kingdom in 1878, and became the focus of the aspirations of people throughout the Balkans. The collapse of the Habsburg

Empire in 1918 led to the creation of the kingdom of Serbs, Croats and Slovenes (later renamed Yugoslavia). However, the lack of a common Yugoslav identity resulted in the collapse of the country when Germany attacked it in April 1941. In Serbia, resistance groups formed around the Serbian-nationalist Četnik Movement, and the pan-Yugoslav Partisans led by Communist Josip Broz Tito. In 1945, Tito established a federal Yugoslavia composed of six republics. The ethnically mixed Serbian regions of Vojvodina and Kosovo were made into autonomous provinces. After the death of Tito in 1980, Serbians launched a campaign to regain control of these regions. This upsurge of Serbian national sentiment was perceived as a threat by the other Yugoslav republics, and both Slovenia and Croatia chose to break away from Yugoslavia in 1991. In 1999, an Albanian insurgency was answered by a Serbian crackdown, leading to the NATO bombardment of Serbia.

Throughout the 1990s Serbian politics was controlled by the Nationalist-Communist Slobodan Milošević. He fell from power in 2000, leading to a process of democratization. Serbia is currently a parliamentary democracy, with hopes of joining the EU.

KEY DATES IN SERBIAN HISTORY

AD 600 Serb tribes settle in the Balkans

1219 Saint Sava establishes the Serbian Orthodox Church

1345 The Serbian Empire under Stefan Dušan reaches its height

1389 Serbs and Ottoman Turks fight at the Battle of Kosovo

1459 Serbia conquered by the Ottoman Empire

1690 Austrian-controlled Vojvodina is settled by Serbs from Kosovo

1804 First Serbian Uprising against the Ottoman Turks

1869 Principality of Serbia gains independence

1912–13 Serbia expands its territory during the Balkan Wars

1918 Serbia becomes part of the kingdom of Serbs, Croats and Slovenes

1945 Serbia becomes part of the Communist-ruled Yugoslav Federation

1991 Slovenia and Croatia leave Yugoslavia

1999 NATO bombards Serbia

2008 Kosovo declares its independence from Serbia

LANGUAGE AND CULTURE

Serbian is a Slavic language, related closely to Bosnian and Croatian and more distantly to Russian, Polish and Czech. It is traditionally written in the Cyrillic script.

Traditional song and dance play an important part in Serbia's rich folk culture. The Roma community has greatly influenced its musical heritage, and visitors may come across their energetic brass bands at weddings and village fêtes throughout the year.

Exploring Serbia

Serbia's lively capital, Belgrade, stands at the centre of the country's transport network. Beyond the capital are a number of impressive cultural monuments as well as picturesque towns. North of Belgrade are the flatlands of Vojvodina, home to the city of Novi Sad and its riverside fortress as well as the border town of Subotica, while to the south are the Sopoćani and Studenica monasteries. Travelling by bus is the preferred choice of transportation; trains are crowded and can get delayed.

Busy pavement cafés on Zmaj Jovina ulica, Novi Sad

SIGHTS AT A GLANCE

Belgrade pp548–55 **1**
Despotovac **4**
Niš **6**
Novi Pazar **7**
Novi Sad **2**
Sopoćani Monastery **8**
Subotica **3**
Studenica Monastery **5**

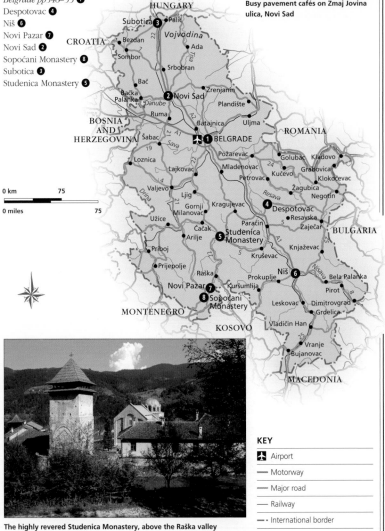

The highly revered Studenica Monastery, above the Raška valley

KEY

✈	Airport
─	Motorway
─	Major road
─	Railway
–·–	International border

Belgrade ❶

The capital of Serbia since 1840, Belgrade, today with a population of approximately seventeen million people, has been a site of strategic importance for a succession of imperial rulers. Over the second half of the 19th century it gradually took on the appearance of a modern European metropolis, although the magnificent Kalemegdan Fortress bears eloquent witness to its turbulent past. Situated between the main fortress and Kalemegdan Park is the Old Town (Stari grad), with remnants from Ottoman times. Today, Knez Mihailova is the centre of social and commercial life in the city. A long, pedestrianized street lined with handsome 19th-century buildings, it is busy with shoppers and strollers throughout the day and night.

SIGHTS AT A GLANCE

Ethnographic Museum ④
Fresco Gallery ②
Kalemegdan Fortress pp550–51 ①
Nikola Tesla Museum ⑨
Orthodox Cathedral ⑥
Palace of Princess Ljubica ⑤
Skadarlija ⑦
St Mark's Church ⑧
St Sava's Church ⑪
The Royal Compound ⑩
Tito's Mausoleum and the 25th May Museum ⑫
Vuk and Dositej Museum ③
Zemun ⑬

KEY

▨ Major sight / Place of interest
✈ Airport
🚉 Railway station
🚌 Bus station
ℹ Visitor information
🅿 Parking
✝ Church
▨ Pedestrian zone
━ Major road
━ Minor road
═ Motorway
─ Railway

Intricate stonework detail, Fresco Gallery

GETTING AROUND

Central Belgrade is easily explored on foot, with the lively Knez Mihailova serving as the main route from the city centre to the Kalemegdan Fortress. Attractions outside the city centre can be reached by tram, bus or trolleybus. Taxis are reasonably priced, although those booked in advance (hotel recep-tionists can make the call) are cheaper than those flagged down on the street. Driving in the city can be stressful due to heavy traffic, bad roads and limited parking.

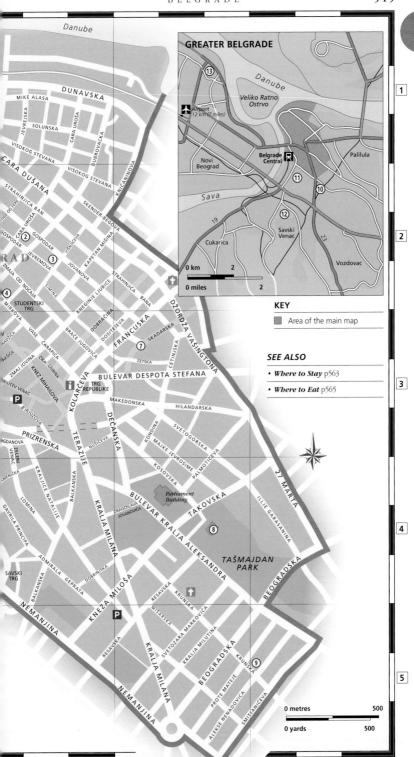

GREATER BELGRADE

Danube

Airport
12 km (7 miles)

Veliko Ratno
Ostrvo

Novi
Beograd

Belgrade
Central

Palilula

Sava

Cukarica

Savski
Venac

Vozdovac

0 km   2

0 miles   2

KEY

Area of the main map

SEE ALSO

- **Where to Stay** p563

- **Where to Eat** p565

Danube

DUNAVSKA

MIKE ALASA
JEVREJSKA
SOLUNSKA
VISOKOG STEVANA
CARA UROŠA
DUBROVAČKA
KNIĆANINOVA

CARA DUŠANA
VISOKOG STEVANA
SKENDER-BEGOVA

STRAHINJIĆA BAN
CARA UROŠA
GOSPODAR JEVREMOVA
VIŠNJIĆEVA
JOVANOVA
KAPETAN MIŠINA
SIMINA
STRAHINJIĆA BANA

ZMAJA OD NOĆAJA
KNEGINJE LJUBICE

STUDENTSKI
TRG

MIRKOVA
VASE ČARAPIĆA
DOBRAČINA
DOSITEJEVA
FRANCUSKA
SKADARSKA
ČETINJSKA
DŽORDŽA VAŠINGTONA

BRAĆE JUGOVIĆA
ZETSKA

ZMAJ JOVINA
ČIKA LJUBINA
KNEZ MIHAILOVA
KOLARČEVA
BULEVAR DESPOTA STEFANA
MAKEDONSKA
HILANDARSKA

OBILIĆEV VENAC
DEČANSKA
NUŠIĆEVA
KONDINA
SVETOGORSKA

B IRIUSOVA
TERAZIJE
MAJKE JEVROSIME
PALMOTIĆEVA

PRIZRENSKA
KOSOVSKA

ZELENI VENAC
KRALJICE NATALIJE
BALKANSKA
Parliament
Building
TAKOVSKA
ILIJE GARAŠANINA
27 MARTA

LOMINA
BULEVAR KRALJA ALEKSANDRA
DRAGOSLAVA JOVANOVIĆA

GAVRILA PRINCIPA
ADMIRALA GEPRATA
KRALJA MILANA
TAŠMAJDAN
PARK

SAVSKI
TRG
BALKANSKA
DOBRINJSKA
RESAVSKA
KRUNSKA
BEOGRADSKA

NEMANJINA
KNEZA MILOŠA
MILARSKA
SVETOZARA MARKOVIĆA
KRALJA MILUTINA
KRUNSKA

RESAVSKA
KRALJA MILANA
BEOGRADSKA
PROTE MATEJE

NEMANJINA
SVETOZARA MARKOVIĆA
ALEKSE NENADOVIĆA
SMILJANIĆEVA

0 metres   500

0 yards   500

D   F

Kalemegdan Fortress ①
Kalemegdanska tvrđava

Dominating the confluence of the Sava and Danube rivers, the Kalemegdan Fortress (*kale* meaning "fortress" and *meydan* meaning "field") was one of the most fought-over strategic points in South Eastern Europe. It was first settled by the Celts, then refortified by Serbia's medieval rulers and expanded during the Ottoman and Austrian occupations, evolving into an extensive complex of buildings blending various architectural styles. Today, it is Belgrade's most popular park, offering fine views of the Danube from its bastions.

Emperor Karl VI Gate, a triumphal arch, was built by the Austrians to celebrate the capture of Belgrade in 1718.

Nebojša Kula

Nebojša Kula
Also known as the "daredevil tower", this 15th-century hexagonal structure was used as a dungeon under the Ottomans.

★ **The Victor**
One of the best-known works by the Croat sculptor Ivan Meštrović (see p491), The Victor (Pobednik) was erected in 1928 to honour the tenth anniversary of the end of World War I.

STAR SIGHTS

- ★ The Victor
- ★ Chapel of Sveta Petka
- ★ Zindan Gate

Military Museum
Built in 1929, the Military Museum resembles a medieval fortress. Tanks, cannons and World War II machinery are on display.

★ Chapel of Sveta Petka
*Built in 1937, this chapel stands on
the site of a sacred spring associated
with St Petka, patron saint of families.
The spring is believed to have miraculous powers. It is thought that
St Petka's relics were kept in a
church here during the
Middle Ages.*

VISITORS' CHECKLIST

Kalemegdan. **Map** *C2.* 🚌
ℹ️ *(011) 262 0685.* **Military
Museum** *Tel (011) 334 3441.*
◻️ *10am–5pm Tue–Sun.*
Nebojša Kula ◻️ *10am–
9pm Sat & Sun.* **Sahat Kula**
◻️ *9am–9pm daily.* ♿ **www**.
beogradskatvrdjava.co.rs

Leopold Gate,
on the east side of
the fortress, was
built in honour of
Austrian Emperor
Leopold I, who
held Belgrade
briefly in the 1680s.

★ Zindan Gate
*This 15th-century fortified gate was
used as a zindan (dungeon) by the
Ottomans. There are good views
of the Danube from its two
barrel-like towers.*

The Cvijeta Zuzoric Art Pavilion,
used for high-profile art exhibitions, was named after a
celebrated poet and beauty
from 16th-century Dubrovnik.

Sahat Kula, a distinctive
clock tower, was built
by the Austrians in the
18th century.

Ivan Meštrović's
Memorial to France
*Meštrović's sculpture, which
depicts a bathing figure,
was built in honour of the
French troops who played a
major role in liberating
Serbia in 1918.*

Struggle by **Simeon Roksandić**,
(1874–1943) a Serbian sculptor,
depicts a naked fisherman
wrestling with a snake.

Fresco Gallery ②
Galerija fresaka

Cara Uroša 20. **Map** D2. **Tel** (011) 262 1491. ☐ noon–8pm Tue, Wed & Fri, noon–8pm Thu, 10am–noon Sat, 10am–4pm Sun. 🖾

Displaying copies of some of the remarkable medieval paintings that adorn the churches and monasteries in Serbia, the Fresco Gallery provides a stunning visual introduction to the Orthodox Christian culture that thrived in the region before the Ottoman occupation. In the 14th century, Serbia was at the forefront of religious art, blending traditional Byzantine styles with a new style of realistic, emotional portraiture. In particular, New Testament scenes from the monastery churches of Studenica (see p558) and Sopoćani (see p559) are reproduced here to great effect. There are also many paintings from the monastery of Kosovo-Metohija and frescoes from the 14th-century foundation at the Orthodox monastery of Dečani. Visitors can also view scale models of many of the churches in which the frescoes can be found, which helps to place the paintings in their architectural context.

Vuk and Dositej Museum ③
Vukov i Dositejev muzej

Gospodar Jevremova 21. **Map** D2. **Tel** (011) 262 5161. 🚌 26. ☐ 10am–5pm Mon, Tue, Wed & Sat, noon–8pm Thu, 10am–2pm Sun. 🖾

The Vuk and Dositej Museum honours two of Serbia's most important language reformers.

Traditional folk costumes on display in the Ethnographic Museum

The museum occupies one of the oldest houses in Belgrade. Featuring oriel windows and terracotta tiles, it is a fine example of the Levantine-style houses that characterized the city in the early 19th century.

The ground floor houses a display devoted to Dositej Obradović (1742–1811), a widely travelled educator who opened Serbia's first high school here in 1808. The first floor holds personal effects and manuscripts relating to Vuk Stefanović Karadžić (1787–1864), who is regarded as one of the most influential figures in modern Serbian history and culture.

Born into a simple, peasant family, Vuk Stefanović Karadžić spent much of his life compiling traditional songs and stories, amassing a huge body of Serbian folk literature that still exerts a profound influence over the nation's culture. He was also a linguist, responsible for standardizing Serbian grammar, and publishing dictionaries and books that set the standard for language teachers in his day.

Ethnographic Museum ④
Etnografski muzej

Studentski trg 13. **Map** D2. **Tel** (011) 328 1888. 🚌 31, 28, 29, 41. ☐ 10am–5pm Tue–Sat, 9am–2pm Sun. 🖾 🅿 **www**.etnografskimuzej.rs

The Ethnographic Museum offers a colourful and informative introduction to Serbia's rich folk traditions. It is housed in the former Belgrade Stock Exchange, a stark piece of Functionalist architecture built in 1934. The ground floor hosts interesting temporary exhibitions on various themes, often featuring items on loan from foreign museums.

The permanent collection begins on the first floor with a display of traditional Serbian textiles. The highlight here is a collection of vividly coloured woollen carpets from the east Serbian town of Pirot, decorated with a rich repertoire of geometric, floral and zoomorphic symbols. There are also examples of the vertical looms on which such carpets were handwoven, alongside the beautifully carved *preslice* (distaff) used to spin the wool, each adorned with sun and star motifs.

The top floor displays traditional folk costumes as well as examples of 19th-century urban dresses, top hats and umbrellas. There are also intricate scale models of village farmsteads and re-creations of typical urban and rural house interiors.

Reproduction of a fresco from the Orthodox Cathedral, Fresco Gallery

Palace of Princess Ljubica ⑤
Konak Kneginje Ljubice

Kneza Sime Markovića 8.
Map C3. **Tel** *(011) 263 8264.*
🕐 *10am–5pm Tue, Wed, Fri & Sat,
noon–8pm Thu, 10am–2pm Sun.* 📷

Situated a short distance from Belgrade's Orthodox Cathedral, this former royal residence is the finest surviving example of Ottoman-Serbian architecture from the early 19th century. It was built for Prince Miloš Obrenović in 1830, but he preferred his forest-fringed residence in Topčider Park southwest of the city centre, and left this building to his wife, Princess Ljubica, and their children Milan and Mihail.

The exterior is Oriental in appearance, with bay windows protruding from the upper floors and slender minaret-like chimneys emerging from the roof. Inside is a display of traditional Balkan decorations, with the ground floor *divanhane* (reception room) containing a raised platform carpeted with brightly coloured Oriental rugs. Cushioned benches, charcoal braziers, Turkish coffee jugs and tables inlaid with mother-of-pearl re-create the semi-European, semi-Levantine lifestyle enjoyed by the Serbian elite of the period. The top-floor rooms house a collection of 19th-century furniture and portraits of the Serbian Royal Family.

Mosaic, Orthodox Cathedral

Visitors enjoying a stroll through the cobbled streets of Skadarlija

Orthodox Cathedral ⑥
Saborna crkva

Kneza Sime Markovića 3. **Map** C3.
Tel *(011) 263 6684.* 🕐 *7am–8pm daily.* ✝

Built in 1837 on the orders of Prince Miloš Obrenović and dedicated to the Archangel Michael, the Orthodox Cathedral is a blend of Neo-Classical and Baroque styles. Inside, the gilded iconostasis carved by Dimitrije Petrović bears several tiers of icons. In front of it is a casket containing the bones of Prince Lazar, who was killed during the Battle of Kosovo in 1389. This battle ended in stalemate and the province of Kosovo has held special importance in Serbian national consciousness ever since. Outside the main entrance lie the tombs of cultural reformers Dositej Obradović and Vuk Karadžić. Opposite the cathedral, on Kralja Petra, is the **Café of the Question Mark** (Kafana "?") *(see p565)*, built in 1823 and the oldest functioning tavern in the city. It was originally called the Café at the Cathedral, but the church authorities objected to the name, leaving the owner to hang the "?" sign above the door as a symbol of protest.

Skadarlija ⑦
Skadarska

Skadarska ulica. **Map** E3. 🚍 *2, 5, 10, 79.*

Centred on a cobbled street, Skadarlija was early 20th-century Belgrade's bohemian quarter, where artists and poets would gather for a night of wine and song. Crowded with cafés and restaurants, it is one of the city's hot spots for dining and carousing.

Skadarlija's history as a hub for nightlife dates back to the 1880s, when Czech entrepreneur Ignat Bajloni established a brewery at the end of the street. A host of inns opened up in the vicinity and a regular clientele of artists and writers began to meet here. Today, Skadarska is still atmospheric, with most of the restaurants retaining their traditional furnishings.

Further down the street stands an Ottoman-style fountain, a replica of the Sebilj Fountain *(see p514)* in the Baščaršija district of Sarajevo.

Oriental façade of the Palace of Princess Ljubica

St Mark's Church ⑧

Crkva Svetog marka

Bulevar Kralja Aleksandra 17.
Map E4. 🚋 25, 26, 27, 32. ⛪

Completed in 1940, St Mark's Church is an architectural tribute to Serbia's medieval builders, being largely based on the 14th-century monastery church of Gračanica in Kosovo. With its cluster of green domes and striped red-and-ochre stonework, it is a more exuberant piece of work than the original, and features an angular modern belfry. Laid out beneath a 52-m (171-ft) high cupola, the interior of the church is comparatively bare, which draws attention to a glittering mosaic of the Last Supper set in the iconostasis. Set against the south wall of the nave is the sarcophagus of Serbia's greatest medieval ruler, Tsar Dušan.

Southeast of the church stretches **Tašmajdan Park** (Tašmajdanski park), named after the quarry that operated here during the Ottoman period; Tašmajdan means "stone quarry" in Turkish. Today, its leafy promenades attract a lot of visitors. A few steps west of the church is Serbia's **Parliament Building** (zgrada Parlamenta), famously stormed in October 2000 by protesters demanding the overthrow of the then president, Slobodan Milošević. The entrance to this Classical-style building features striking sculptures of muscular figures wrestling to control struggling horses, the work of the 19th-century Croatian sculptor Toma Rosandić.

Detail on the exterior of St Mark's Church

Section of the permanent exhibition space inside the Nikola Tesla Museum

Nikola Tesla Museum ⑨

Muzej Nikole tesle

Krunska 51. **Map** F5. **Tel** (011) 243 3886. 🚇 7, 12. 🚋 26, 27. 🕐 10am–6pm Tue–Fri, 10am–1pm Sat & Sun. 📷 🎥 ⛪ www.tesla-museum.org

Born to Serb parents in the Lika region of Croatia, Nikola Tesla (1856–1943) was one of the engineering geniuses of the Modern Age, carrying out pioneering work in the fields of X-rays, radio transmission and remote-control devices. One of his greatest achievements was demonstrating how electricity could be transmitted in the form of alternating currents, a system now used around the world.

Tesla is also credited with being one of the co-inventors of the radio, even though his Italian rival Guglielmo Marconi was the first to succeed in demonstrating the technology in action. Despite spending most of his adult life in North America, Tesla requested that his ashes be brought to Belgrade after his death; this memorial museum was established to house them. The display provides an informative overview of Tesla's life and work, with labels in Serbian and English. There are scale models of his laboratories, together with a replica of the remote-control boat

he first demonstrated to the public at Madison Square Gardens in New York in 1898.

The Royal Compound ⑩

Kraljevski dvorovi

Dedinje. **Map** D4. **Tel** (011) 334 3460. 🚌 Makedonska 5. 🕐 Nov–Mar: 11am & 2pm Sat & Sun. 📷 🎥 11am & 2pm Sat & Sun, call for bookings. www.royalfamily.org

Comprising two palatial villas and a landscaped park, the Royal Compound was built by King Aleksandar of Yugoslavia in the 1920s. It is located in Dedinje, a hilly suburb southwest of the centre. After the monarchy was abolished by a referendum in 1947, the compound was used by the then Yugoslav president Tito, and more recently, by the Serbian Nationalist-Communist leader Slobodan Milošević. After the fall of Milošević, the Royal Family returned to Dedinje, and the compound now serves as their home. The main royal residence has an entrance hall decorated with copies of medieval Serbian frescoes and a splendid dining room decked in Flemish tapestries. The basement is decorated in Muscovite style, with motifs from Russian folk art adorning its vaulted ceilings.

On the other side of the park stands the **White Palace** (Beli Dvor), originally built by Aleksandar for his sons; it now contains the royal art collection. Highlights include paintings by Poussin and Canaletto as well as Rembrandt's *Portrait of a Young Man*.

St Sava's Church ⑪
Hram svetog save

Krušedolska 2a. **Map** F2. 🚌 *9. 10. 14. 31, 33, 39, 47, 48.* ☐ *7am–7pm daily.* **www**.hramsvetogsave.com

Dedicated to St Sava, the Serbian prince and holy man who is regarded as the founder of the Serbian Orthodox Church, St Sava's Church is the largest working Orthodox church in the world. It is the result of a Herculean building project that has lasted several decades and is still in the process of completion. The location of the church is considered sacred, as it was here that the saint's remains were ritually burned by the Ottomans in 1595 after being seized from the Mileševa Monastery in southwest Serbia.

Begun in the 1930s, construction was halted midway with the onset of World War II and only resumed in 1984. The basic structure of the church is now in place. It is styled on the Byzantine cross-in-square model, with a central dome flanked by four half-domes. Faced with white-coloured marble plates, it has a luminous appearance. The interior, still unfinished, covers an area of 3,650 sq m (36,288 sq ft) and boasts a capacity of 10,000 worshippers.

Statue of Tito, 25th May Museum

Tito's Mausoleum and the 25th May Museum ⑫
Kuća Cveća, Muzej 25. maj

Botićeva 6. **Map** F2. **Tel** *(011) 367 1485.* 🚌 *40, 41.* 🚌 *94.* ☐ *10am–4pm Tue–Sun.* 📷 **www**.mij.rs

Communist leader Josip Broz Tito led partisan forces during World War II and was the architect of the federal Yugoslav state that emerged from the ashes of the war. He served as dictator of Yugoslavia from 1945 until his death on 4 May 1980, when his body was laid to rest in a mausoleum in western Belgrade called the House of Flowers (Kuća Cveća). Despite the fact that Tito's Yugoslavia no longer exists, his tomb continues to attract plenty of visitors curious about the statesman and his legacy. An adjacent building houses the 25th May Museum, where the former leader's Rolls Royce and a collection of relay batons are displayed. The batons serve as a reminder of the bombastic ritual surrounding Tito's official birthday (25 May), when relay runners crisscrossed Yugoslavia before converging on Belgrade on the momentous day.

The striking Millennium Monument in Gardoš, Zemun

Zemun ⑬

Map E1. 🚌 *15, 84, 704, 706.* 🛈 *Zemun Tourist Centre, Zmaj Jovina 14, (011) 219 2904.*

Sprawled along the west bank of the Danube, 4 km (3 miles) from central Belgrade, lies the suburb of Zemun. Unlike the rest of Belgrade, Zemun was part of the Austro-Hungarian Empire from the late 17th century until World War I, and retains the pleasant atmosphere of a small central European town.

The most interesting part of Zemun is Gardoš, an area of steep cobbled alleyways on a hillside overlooking the river. Towering over Gardoš from the top of the hill is the **Millennium Monument** (Milenijumski spomenik), a red-brick tower built by the Hungarians in 1896 to celebrate the 1,000-year anniversary of the creation of their state. From the foot of the tower, there is a wonderful view of central Belgrade, and key landmarks such as the Kalemegdan Fortress (see pp550–51) and St Sava's Church are clearly visible.

Zemun's other attraction is **Kej Oslobođenja** (Freedom Quay), a foot-and-cycle path that runs along the banks of the Danube and is popular with strollers on Sunday afternoons. This is also the heart of Belgrade's nightlife due to the long line of rafts moored here, most of which have been turned into restaurants, bars, pubs and clubs.

Monumental structure of St Sava's Church

Freedom Square, the spacious hub of Novi Sad

Novi Sad ❷

74 km (46 miles) N of Belgrade.
🏠 500,000. 🚉 🚌 ℹ️ *Bulevar
Mihajla Pupina 9, (021) 421 811.* 📷
EXIT Festival (Jul). **www**.turizamns.rs

A prosperous town on the
north shore of the Danube
river, Novi Sad is the administrative centre of the Vojvodina
region. The town owes its
existence to the strategically
located Petrovaradin Fortress
on the south bank of the
river. Fortified since Roman
times, Petrovaradin was
turned into an impregnable
garrison by the Austrians in
the 18th century, and the
civilian settlement of Novi
Sad grew up by its side.

Largely populated by Serbs
fleeing from the Ottoman
Empire, the town soon became
a major centre of Serbian
religion, culture and learning.
The first ever Serbian-language
theatre was founded here in
1861, and the key literary and
cultural society, Matica Srpska,
moved here from Budapest
in 1864. Modern Novi Sad
houses the cultural institutions
of Vojvodina's Hungarian,
Slovak, Romanian and Rusyn
(a different ethnic group to
the Russians) communities.

🏛 Pedestrian Zone
A cluster of pedestrianized
streets constitutes the centre
of Novi Sad. At their heart is
the Freedom Square (trg
Slobode), dominated by Ivan
Meštrović's statue of Svetozar
Miletić, a 19th-century politician and lawyer who fought
for the rights of Serbs within
the Habsburg monarchy.

Looming over the eastern end
of the square is the Neo-Gothic
St Mary's Cathedral (crkva sv
Marije), the city's main Catholic
church and the principal venue
for Hungarian and Croatian-
speaking masses. The
church's plain interior stands
in remarkable contrast to its
colourful stained-glass
windows, made by Czech
and Hungarian masters.

Stretching northeast from
the cathedral, Zmaj Jovina
ulica is distinguished by
several two-storey build-
ings painted in pastel
hues of yellow, ochre
and turquoise. At the
end of the street stands
the 19th-century
Bishop's Palace,
designed by Vladimir
Nikolić in a variety of
architectural styles. Just
around the corner is the
Orthodox Church of St George,
dating from 1742, which features a Rococo iconostasis and
vivacious Art Nouveau stained-
glass windows by local artist
Paja Jovanović.

St Mary's
Cathedral

Monument to Serbian statesman
Svetozar Miletić at Freedom Square

🏛 Museum of Vojvodina
Dunavska 35. *Tel* (021) 420 566.
🕐 10am–5pm Tue–Sun.
www.muzejvojvodine.org.rs
Located in the pedestrian
zone, this museum (Muzej
Vojvodine) displays Neolithic
pottery and tools unearthed
in the region. There is
also a wealth of finds from
the Roman city of Sirmium
(now Sremska Mitrovica),
just west of Novi Sad,
which served as Emperor
Galerius's capital city in
the late 3rd century. The
ethnographic diversity of
Vojvodina emerges through
a colourful display of Serb,
Hungarian and Slovak
costumes. There are also
painted wooden chests and
brightly decorated ceramics
in a range of traditional
folk designs.

🏛 Petrovaradin Fortress
Petrovaradinska tvrđava.
🕐 8am–5pm Tue–Sun.
City Museum *Tel* (021) 643
3145. 📷 9am–3pm (except
Mon). **www**.museumns.rs
A short walk east of
central Novi Sad,
Petrovaradin Fortress
(Petrovaradinska
tvrđava) stretches
along the high ground
on the south bank of
the Danube river.
Occupied first by the
Romans, then medieval
Hungarians and Ottoman
Turks, the fortress itself dates
from the arrival of the
Austrians in 1692. Eager to
consolidate their rule over
Central Europe, they saw
Petrovaradin as the focal point
of their southern defences and
set about building a fortress
so formidable that the
Ottomans would be dissuaded
from ever taking up arms
against Austria again. The
resulting stronghold comprised
a star-shaped pattern of bastions and trenches, with over
15 km (9 miles) of under-
ground galleries to house
30,000 defending troops.

Positioned high above
the river, the central citadel
offers magnificent views of
Novi Sad from its ramparts.
Inside, many of the barrack
blocks have now been
converted into artists'

View of Petrovaradin Fortress across the Danube river, Novi Sad

workshops and galleries, with atmospheric cafés and restaurants.

Petrovardin's former arsenal (topovnjača) is now occupied by the **City Museum** (Gradski muzej), home to a fine collection of period furnishings, porcelain and fine arts. Guided tours of the underground galleries (podzemne vojne galerije) offer the chance to explore a subterranean warren of gun positions and ammunition dumps.

Every July, Petrovaradin becomes the venue for the famous EXIT Festival (see p562), a four-day celebration of rock and pop that draws between 150,000 and 190,000 revellers from all over Europe.

Subotica ❸

178 km (111 miles) N of Belgrade.
🏠 100,000. 🚊 🚌 🚏 trg Slobode
1, (024) 670 350. 🎬 Palić Film Festival
(mid-Jul). **www**.visitsubotica.rs

Located close to the Hungarian frontier, Subotica is a typical multicultural border town with a mixed community of Hungarians, Serbs and Croats. First documented in the late 14th century as a free-trading post, the town is known for its Art Nouveau architecture, of which the monumental Town Hall (Gradska kuća) on the main square is an outstanding example. Designed in 1908 by architects Marcell Komor and Dezső Jakab, it is rich in Hungarian folk motifs, with colourfully patterned roof tiles, oriole windows and decorative floral designs adorning the façade.

North of the main square, at Synaogue square (trg Sinagoge) stands Subotica's Synagogue (Sinagoga), which showcases Komor and Jakab's flamboyant architectural style. Mixing red brick with green and yellow tiling and topped with a cluster of plump domes, it is an extraordinarily striking building. Set in one corner of the synagogue enclosure is a monument honouring Subotica's 4,000-strong Jewish population, transported to Nazi death camps in July 1944.

The nearby **Municipal Museum** (Gradski muzej) houses a colourful ethnographic collection rich in traditional Hungarian and Croatian costumes, and a display of African folk artifacts collected by famous local explorer Oskar Vojnić. East of the main square, the pedestrianized Korzo is full of fine buildings from the pre-World War I period. Most remarkable is the richly decorated apartment house at No. 4. The beehive symbol on its façade reveals its former function as a savings bank. Just round the corner from Korzo, the **Likovni Susret Gallery** (galerija Likovni Susret), covered in brightly coloured tulip motifs is an Art Nouveau gem. Built by architect Ferenc Rajhl to serve as a family home in 1904, it now hosts changing exhibitions of contemporary art.

Environs
Located 8 km (5 miles) east of Subotica, the lakeside settlement of **Palić** was developed as a health resort in the mid-19th century, and is now a popular spot for sunbathing and swimming in summer. Here, too, is an ensemble of buildings designed by Komor and Jakab, blending Art Nouveau style with Hungarian folk motifs. A cone-shaped vodotoranj (water tower), attached to a gateway of the lakeside park, is among them. The town's most distinctive building, however, is the Womens' Beach (Ženski strand), an all-timber waterside pavilion resembling a string of Transylvanian village huts.

🏛 **Municipal Museum**
trg Sinagoge 3. **Tel** (024) 555 128.
🕙 10am–4pm Tue–Fri, 10am–1pm,
Sat. 🈺

🏛 **Likovni Susret Gallery**
trg Ferenca Rajhl. **Tel** (024) 553 725.

Subotica's main square, graced by Art Nouveau buildings

Fortifications at the serene Manasija Monastery, Despotovac

Despotovac ❹

130 km (81 miles) SE of Belgrade.
🚶 33,000. 🚌 from Belgrade.
ℹ️ Cerska 3, (035) 613 672.
www.despotovac.com

Located in the Resava valley
30 km (19 miles) east of the
main Belgrade-Niš Highway,
the town of Despotovac is
renowned for the spectacular
medieval **Manasija Monastery**
(manastir Manasija), also
known as Resavska
after the local river.
Founded by Despot
Stefan Lazarević in
1418, the monastery
is surrounded by
fortifications, includ-
ing 11 castellated
towers. Inside are
some of Serbia's finest 15th-
century frescoes. The west wall
has a portrait of Stefan
Lazarević wearing gold-
embroidered robes, while the
north and south walls are covered with friezes of warrior-
saints wielding weapons.

Detail of fresco,
Manasija Monastery

Higher up, the walls are
decorated with scenes from
the gospel, while depictions of
Old Testament prophets adorn
the cupola.

Environs
The **Resava Cave** (Resavska
Pećina), one of Serbia's most
dramatic karst features, is situated 20 km (12 miles) southeast of Despotovac. Formed by
seeping water over an estimated period of 80 million years,
the cave features rock
formations. An 800
m (2,625 ft) stretch
of the cave is acces-
sible via a staircase.
Highlights include
the Beehive Hall,
characterized by
beehive-shaped sta-
lagmites, and the Crystal Hall,
which takes its name from its
chandelier-like stalactites.

🔺 **Resava Cave**
Tel (035) 611 610. ⬤ Apr–Nov:
9am–5pm daily. 📷
www.resavskapecina.rs

Studenica
Monastery ❺

135 km (84 miles) S of Belgrade.
Tel (036) 536 050. 🚌 from Belgrade.
⬤ 5am–8pm daily. ✝️

Nestled in a wooded valley,
Studenica Monastery is
regarded as the spiritual heartland of the Serbian Orthodox
church. It was founded in the
late 12th century by Prince
Stefan Nemanja, founder
of the medieval Serb state,
who became a monk in
1196. The monastery later
served as a base for his son
Sava, the first archbishop
of the Serbian Church and
the nation's patron saint.

Surrounded by a horseshoe-
shaped ring of buildings, the
main monastery is a Byzantine-
style basilica decorated with
a profusion of Romanesque
details, notably floral swirls
and animal motifs. Inside
are some of the most splendid
frescoes in the Balkans, in
which portraits of the holy
family, saints and apostles
combine Byzantine formality
with the realism of Western
European art.

On the northern side of
the monastery compound
stands the smaller **King's
Church** (Kraljeva Crkva),
built in 1314 by Stefan
Nemanja's great-grandson
King Uroš II Milutin. Among
several brilliantly executed
frescoes are a joyous *Birth of
the Virgin* on the north wall,
and portraits of Serbian rulers
in the south chapel.

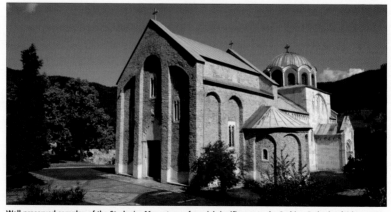

Well-preserved complex of the Studenica Monastery, of special significance to the Serbian Orthodox faith

Equestrian monument to the Liberation of 1878, Niš

Niš ⑥

235 km (146 miles) SE of Belgrade.
🏛 *250,000.* 🚉 🚌 ℹ *Voždova 7 (018) 523 118.*

Despite its fairly contemporary appearance, the town of Niš has an ancient pedigree. Believed to be the birthplace of Emperor Constantine the Great, who led the Roman world's conversion to Christianity, it was also an important Roman trading post. Conquered by the Ottomans in 1386, Niš became a part of the modern Serbian state after its liberation in 1878.

Today it is Serbia's third largest city and centres around the pedestrianized Kralja Milana Square, where there is an equestrian monument dedicated to the liberators of 1878.

North of the square, a bridge leads across the Nišava river towards the 18th-century **Tvrđava** (Fortress) built by the Ottoman Turks, which is now the town park. Entered via the Istanbul Gate (Stambul Kapija), the park contains some Ottoman buildings, including a domed bath house and the 15th-century Mosque of Bali Beg, which now serves as an art gallery.

South of the main square, the Copper-workers' Alley (Kazandžijsko Sokače) preserves some 19th-century craft workshops. About 3 km (2 miles) east of the centre stands the **Tower of Skulls** (Ćele Kula), a gruesome

Detail from the Tower of Skulls

monument dedicated to the origins of the Serbian Uprising of 1809, when insurgents blew themselves up to avoid capture by the Turks. The Ottoman authorities built a tower studded with the victims' heads to serve as a warning to others. It originally contained around 1,000 skulls, but many were stolen in the 19th century, leaving just 60 today.

Novi Pazar ⑦

270 km (168 miles) S of Belgrade.
🏛 *120,000.* 🚌 ℹ *28 Novembar 27, (020) 338 030.* **www**.tonp.rs

Situated in mountainous territory in southwest Serbia, Novi Pazar was founded in the mid-15th century as a way-station on the Dubrovnik-Constantinople caravan route. The town centre still has some Ottoman-era buildings and plenty of mosques – the majority of the locals are Muslim Bosnians. Highlights include the many-domed **Isa Beg Hammam** (Isa-begov hamam), a 15th-century bath house beside the Raška river. North of the river is the Lejlek Mosque, built a century later, with its arched portico overlooked by a minaret.

The area around Novi Pazar was once the heartland of the medieval Serbian state and is dotted with ancient churches and monasteries. North of the centre stands the 9th-century **St Peter's Church** (Petrova Crkva), the original seat of the bishops of Ras and the oldest

St Peter's Church in Novi Pazar, the oldest church in Serbia

surviving church in Serbia. West of the town centre is the monastery of Đurđevi Stupovi (George's Pillars), built by Stefan Nemanja in the 1170s.

Sopoćani Monastery ⑧

287 km (178 miles) S of Belgrade.
🚌 *from Novi Pazar.*

Located on a hill surrounded by mountains, the monastery of Sopoćani was founded in 1263 by King Uroš I, the grandson of Stefan Nemanja, who intended it to serve as his mausoleum. The monastery church is a three-aisled Romanesque basilica made from blocks of stone. The nave is covered with frescoes painted by masters from Constantinople, with a fine *Dormition of the Virgin* filling the west wall. Also in the nave are the tombs of Uroš I and his Venetian mother Anna Dandolo. The narthex contains more frescoes, with superb portraits of Uroš and his son Dragutin.

Evocative fresco of *Dormition of the Virgin*, Sopoćani Monastery

Practical & Travel Information

Serbia has largely missed out on the tourism boom enjoyed by other countries in Eastern and Central Europe, and facilities for visitors are a little less predictable than elsewhere in the region. However, tourist information is available in the most popular destinations, and banks, post offices and public transport ticket offices are efficient. There is a good network of rail and road services reaching all parts of the country, although standards of comfort in trains and buses vary widely.

WHEN TO VISIT

Serbia has a Continental climate that is prone to seasonal extremes. Spring, early summer and early autumn are the best times both for sightseeing and for catching regional festivals. Temperatures can be very high in August, while in mid-winter, they can drop to below freezing for long periods of time. Heavy snow can hamper transport in rural areas. Many museums have shorter opening hours from October until March and may stay closed on weekends. The skiing season is generally from December to March.

DOCUMENTATION

Citizens of the EU, US, Canada, Australia and New Zealand need only a valid passport to visit Serbia for up to 90 days. For more information about visas or extended stays, visitors should contact the Serbian Embassy or Consulate in their home country before travelling, or check the website of the **Serbian Ministry of Foreign Affairs**.

VISITOR INFORMATION

The country is still in the process of developing a tourist information infrastructure. Many smaller destinations may lack tourist information of any kind. However, cities such as Belgrade and Novi Sad have professional tourist information centres with English-speaking staff. Both cities are also well signposted, making it easy to tour the main sights on foot. Most towns in Serbia have official websites with information given in English, though these are not updated regularly. The **National Tourism Organization of Serbia** and the **Tourist Organization of Belgrade** have informative websites.

HEALTH AND SECURITY

No special vaccinations are required for visiting Serbia. Minor ailments can be dealt with by visiting a *apoteka* (pharmacy) where over-the-counter medication is available. Each city has one or more centrally located pharmacies that stay open 24 hours. Air quality in the capital, Belgrade, is poor especially in mid-winter and mid-summer. Serbia is generally a safe country in which to travel, and the only likely dangers are petty theft and pickpocketing. Visitors should keep their valuables out of sight or while using public transport services. They should also avoid leaving their bags unattended on trains.

FACILITIES FOR THE DISABLED

Few of Serbia's public transport facilities, museums or tourist attractions have been adapted for wheelchair users. Pavement ramps are being introduced in central Belgrade, but their provision elsewhere in Serbia is erratic. Hotels offering facilities for the disabled are mostly in the four- and five-star bracket and command high prices.

BANKING AND CURRENCY

Banks and *menjačnica* (exchange bureaus) offer better exchange rates than hotels and travel agencies. Banks are open from 8am to 5pm Monday to Friday and from 8am to 2pm on Saturday.

ATMs are widespread in towns and cities. However, not all accept the full range of plastic cards. If the logo of the card is not displayed on the ATM, the machine will reject the card. Major international credit cards are accepted in central shops as well as restaurants in Belgrade and other bigger cities. If travelling in small towns or rural areas, it is a good idea to carry sufficient cash to cover major items such as hotel bills as well as lesser expenses.

The currency of Serbia, the dinar (RSD or din), is rarely available in banks or exchange bureaus outside the country. However, there are exchange facilities at Belgrade's airport, train and bus stations and at road border crossings.

COMMUNICATIONS

Serbia's telephone network is straightforward and easy to use, and there is cell phone

THE CLIMATE OF SERBIA

Winters are cold and wet with heavy snow. Summers are rarely oppressively hot, although it can get quite humid in Belgrade during August. May, June and September are the perfect months to visit in terms of weather, although May and June are also the wettest. Early to mid-October is still warm, and excellent for cultural and outdoor activities.

BELGRADE

month	Apr	Jul	Oct	Jan
°C/F high	18/64	28/82 17/63	18/64	3/37
°C/F low	7/45		8/46	-3/27
sun (hrs)	6 hrs	10 hrs	3 hrs	2 hrs
rain (mm)	54 mm	61 mm	55 mm	47 mm

coverage almost everywhere in the country. Public telephones use Halo cards, which can be purchased from newspaper kiosks and post offices. Internet cafés are widespread in Serbian towns and cities, and an increasing number of hotels and restaurants in Belgrade offer free wireless Internet to guests carrying their own laptop.

Post offices stay open from 8am to 7pm Monday to Friday and from 8am to 3pm on Saturday.

ARRIVING BY AIR

Coming from the UK, there are several direct flights from London to Belgrade operated by both **British Airways** and **JAT Airways**, Serbia's national carrier.

Currently, the only low-cost airline flying to Belgrade is **Germanwings**, which operates direct services from several German airports. There are no direct flights from North America or Australasia to Belgrade, although most travel agents will offer a one- or two-stop flight to Belgrade, changing at a major European airport such as Amsterdam, Frankfurt, London or Vienna.

Belgrade's **Nikola Tesla Airport** is 20 km (12 miles) north of the city at Surčin. Local bus number 72 runs from the airport to the city centre every 30 minutes from about 5am until 11pm. There is also a comfortable JAT shuttle bus to the centre running approximately every hour.

RAIL TRAVEL

Rail travel in Serbia is slightly cheaper than bus travel, but journey times are slower and departures less frequent. There is a useful international service from Belgrade to Zagreb, with four departures per day. The 8-hour train trip from Belgrade to the Montenegrin capital Podgorica is one of South Eastern Europe's classic journeys, taking in breathtaking mountain scenery and spectacular viaducts. Train carriages on international services are clean and plush. The rolling stock used on domestic journeys is often old and less comfortable, and toilets may be filthy. As few domestic or international trains include a buffet car; passengers should purchase provisions before travelling. Both local and Intercity trains are crowded and can be late. Tickets and information on rail travel throughout the country is available on the **Serbian Railways** website.

TRAVELLING BY BUS

Bus travel is the most popular form of public transport in Serbia. The **Belgrade Bus Station** is the central bus station that serves most destinations in the country. Fast Intercity services link the main centres as well as rural destinations. Many buses may be old, especially in the rural south of the country, and are unlikely to be air conditioned.

Each town or city has a central bus station with clearly displayed timetables (*polasci* means departures, *dolasci* means arrivals). Tickets should be purchased in advance and usually include a seat reservation. When buying a ticket, passengers are also given a *žeton* (token) which provides access to the relevant departure platform. Both Belgrade and Novi Sad have daily international services to Zagreb, Sarajevo and in the summer months, to Dubrovnik. The Bulgarian capital Sofia can be reached twice a day from Niš.

TRAVELLING BY CAR

A valid international driving license is required to drive legally in Serbia. Insurance policies from countries that have signed the Vehicle Insurance Convention are valid. However, citizens of other countries must purchase an insurance policy when entering Serbia. The European Green Card vehicle insurance is now valid in Serbia. Well-maintained *autoput* (highways) run from Belgrade to Niš, Novi Sad and Subotica. Tolls are paid on these roads. Cars can be hired from service providers such as **Budget** and **Hertz**.

Shopping & Entertainment

Serbia's high streets have modern shops selling branded goods, however, traditional open-air markets where an array of fresh foodstuffs and craft items are available are a big draw. Serbia has a lively outdoor drinking culture, with cafés and alfresco bars particularly popular during the spring and summer months. The capital, Belgrade, has a thriving music and theatre scene with the season usually running from October to June. A busy schedule of music festivals takes over in the summer, with Novi Sad's EXIT festival drawing the biggest crowds.

CRAFTS AND SOUVENIRS

In Belgrade, the main upmarket shopping area is along Terazije and Knez Mihailova Streets. Open-air stalls along the main avenue in Kalemegdan Park (see pp550–51) in Belgrade display traditional Serbian handicrafts such as carpets, opanke (leather slippers), painted gourds and shoulder bags decorated with folk motifs. A good selection of items is also available at the **Ethnographic Museum**. For postcards, guidebooks, T-shirts and other souvenirs, head for the **Beoizlog** gift shop. The multimedia store **Mamut** has a number of English-language books and music, and also sells guidebooks and maps.

FOOD AND DRINK

The **Zeleni Venac** market in Belgrade is a good place to pick up dried red paprika, scented honey and herbs. The Serbian national drink, rakija (brandy), comes in several varieties although šljivovica (plum brandy) and lozovača (grape brandy) are the most common. Rakija and other spirits can be bought at supermarkets throughout Serbia, although **Rakia Bar and Gift Shop** outlets have a larger range of products.

MUSIC AND FESTIVALS

Serbia's national opera and ballet companies are based at the **National Theatre** in Belgrade. The **Belgrade Philharmonic Orchestra** performs most weeks in the Kolarac Hall. **Sava Centre** is the venue for musicals, variety shows and visiting symphony orchestras as well as major rock, pop and world music acts. Of the festivals, the **Belgrade Music Festival** in October brings top classical performers, while the **Belgrade Dance Festival**, held in April, features international dancers.

Serbia's biggest summer rock and pop event, the **EXIT Festival**, takes place in Novi Sad's Petrovaradin Fortress (see p556). In August, the **Guča Trumpet Festival**, sees Serbia's best brass bands perform in a village southwest of Belgrade.

THEATRE

For classical drama in the Serbian language, both the **National Theatre** and the **Yugoslav Drama Theatre** offer quality productions. Novi Sad is the home of the **Serbian National Theatre**, while Subotica has a dedicated Hungarian-language theatre, the **Dezső Kosztolányi Theatre**. The **Belgrade International Theatre Festival (BITEF)**, in September, is the leading festival of contemporary theatre in South Eastern Europe.

BARS AND CLUBS

Many of Belgrade's fanciest bars are located along Strahinjića Bana. Nearby is Skadarlija (see p553), whose restaurants and cafés preserve the atmosphere of the 1920s and 30s and feature live music. In spring and summer, nightlife shifts to the splavovi (rafts) which line the banks of the Sava and Danube rivers. A popular one is **Povetarac**, which plays rock music. Also famous are nightclubs such as **Plastic**, which play electronic music.

DIRECTORY

CRAFTS AND SOUVENIRS

Beoizlog
trg Republike 5, Belgrade.
Tel (011) 328 18 59.

Ethnographic Museum
Studentski trg 13, Belgrade.
Tel (011) 328 1888.

Mamut
Cnr Sremska and Knez Mihailova,
Belgrade. *Tel* (011) 263 9060.

FOOD AND DRINK

Rakia Bar and Gift Shop
Terazije 42, Belgrade.
Tel (011) 264 3158.

Zeleni Venac
Jug Bogdanova bb, Belgrade.

MUSIC AND FESTIVALS

Belgrade Dance Festival
www.belgradedancefestival.com

Belgrade Music Festival
www.bemus.co.yu

Belgrade Philharmonic Orchestra
Tel (011) 328 2977.
www.bgf.co.rs

EXIT Festival
www.exitfest.org

Guča Trumpet Festival
www.guca.rs

National Theatre
Francuska 3, Belgrade.
Tel (011) 328 1333.

Sava Centre
Milentija Popovića 9, Belgrade.
Tel (011) 220 6000.

THEATRE

BITEF Theatre Festival
www.bitef.rs

Dezső Kosztolányi Theatre
Subotica. *Tel* (024) 557 421.
www.kosztolanyi.org

Serbian National Theatre
Pozorišni trg 1, Novi Sad. *Tel* (021) 662 1411. www.snp.org.rs

Yugoslav Drama Theatre
Kralja Milana 50, Belgrade. *Tel* (011) 306 1900. www.jdp.co.yu

BARS AND CLUBS

Plastic
Cnr Takovska & Dalmatinski.
Tel (011) 324 5437.

Povetarac
Tel (063) 577 132.

Where to Stay in Serbia

With an increase in the number of visitors to Serbia, the accommodation facilities in the region are fast improving. To meet the growing demand, old hotels have been revamped and many new establishments have sprung up. Bigger cities such as Belgrade, Novi Sad and Niš offer a good choice of accommodation.

PRICE CATEGORIES
Price categories are for a standard double room per night in high season, including tax and service charges. Breakfast is included, unless otherwise specified.

🄳 Under 3,000 din
🄳🄳 3,000–6,000 din
🄳🄳🄳 6,000–9,000 din
🄳🄳🄳🄳 9,000–15,000 din
🄳🄳🄳🄳🄳 Over 15,000 din

BELGRADE

Green Studio Hostel
🅿 📋   🄳🄳   Map C4

Karađorđeva 69, 11000 **Tel** *(011) 263 3626* **Rooms** *10*

Just across the road from Belgrade's train and bus stations, the Green Studio offers a mixture of dormitory rooms and self-contained private units. Bright and airy common rooms, including a kitchen and TV lounge, make it a good place to socialize. Free tea and coffee are provided. **www.greenstudiohostel.com**

Travelling Actor
🍽 📋   🄳🄳🄳   Map D2

Gospodar Jevremova 65, 11000 **Tel** *(011) 323 4156* **Fax** *(011) 323 4821* **Rooms** *9*

An intimate bed and breakfast located in the restaurant-packed Skadarlija district, just round the corner of Strahinjića Bana. Squeezed into the lower floors of an apartment block, rooms are small but comfortable and equipped with flat-screen TV. Breakfast is served in the nearby Putujući Glumac restaurant. **www.travellingactor.rs**

Le Petit Piaf
🍽 📋   🄳🄳🄳🄳   Map E3

Skadarska 34, 11000 **Tel** *(011) 303 5252* **Fax** *(011) 303 5353* **Rooms** *13*

A charming boutique hotel located in a pleasant courtyard in the Skadarlija district, Le Petit Piaf is a short walk from the city's main sights. Rooms are decorated in warm colours and come with TV, safe and Internet. The hotel also offers a handful of well-furnished suites that have living rooms and kitchenettes. **www.petitpiaf.com**

Majestic
🅿 🍽 🛁 📋   🄳🄳🄳🄳   Map D3

Obilićev venac 28, 11000 **Tel** *(011) 328 5777* **Fax** *(011) 3284 995* **Rooms** *93*

A few steps away from bustling Knez Mihaila, the Majestic is a good mid-range choice. The hotel dates from the 1930s and retains a few Art Deco touches, although the rooms are relatively plain. All rooms have TV and Internet facilities. **www.majestic.rs**

Moskva
🅿 🍽 📋 ♿   🄳🄳🄳🄳   Map D4

Balkanska 1, 11000 **Tel** *(011) 268 6255* **Fax** *(011) 268 8389* **Rooms** *138*

Located on the central Terazije Square, Moskva is a Belgrade landmark. Dating from 1906, this imposing hotel in Art Nouveau style is one of the most striking buildings in the city. The rooms blend old-style furnishings and modern fittings and there is an atmospheric coffee shop on the ground floor. **www.hotelmoskva.co.yu**

Palace Hotel
🍽 🛁 📋   🄳🄳🄳🄳   Map C3

Toplićin venac 23, 11000 **Tel** *(011) 218 5585* **Fax** *(011) 218 4458* **Rooms** *86*

This elegant, slightly old-fashioned hotel is located on a relatively quiet street just off Knez Mihaila. Dating back to the 1920s, the rooms are decorated with period furnishings and provide Internet access. The Belgrade Panorama restaurant on the top floor offers excellent views of the Sava river. **www.palacehotel.co.yu**

Balkan
🍽 📋   🄳🄳🄳🄳🄳   Map D3

Prizrenska 2, 11000 **Tel** *(011) 363 3000* **Fax** *(011) 2687 466* **Rooms** *79*

The Balkan is one of the oldest hotels in Belgrade, although the present building dates from 1935. Located just off Knez Mihaila, the hotel offers elegantly furnished rooms with plasma screens and coffee-making machines. The popular restaurant, Orient Express, serves Serbian cuisine. **www.balkanhotel.net**

FURTHER AFIELD Chillton Hostel
🅿 📋   🄳

Katanićeva 7, 11000 **Tel** *(011) 344 1826* **Rooms** *3*

Situated in a residential street behind the historic St Sava's Church (*see p555*), Chillton offers comfortable dormitory accommodation. Facilities include a large common room with free Internet, satellite TV and a guest kitchen. The staff is well informed about local places of interest. **www.chilltonhostel.com**

FURTHER AFIELD Hyatt Regency
🅿 🍽 🏊 🍴 🛁 📋 ♿   🄳🄳🄳🄳🄳

Milentija Popovića 5, 11070 **Tel** *(011) 301 1234* **Fax** *(011) 301 2234* **Rooms** *302*

Located amidst the wide boulevards of Novi Beograd, the Hyatt has long had a reputation for high levels of comfort and service. Although not within strolling distance of the city centre, it offers a range of on-site shopping and leisure facilities. Some rooms have great views of the Old Town. **www.belgrade.regency.hyatt.com**

Map References see map of Belgrade pp548–9

REST OF SERBIA

NIŠ Hostel Niš

Dobrička 3A, 18000 **Tel** *(018) 513 703* **Rooms** *5*

Located midway between the bus station and Tvrđava Park, this small and simple hostel offers bunk-bed dormitories and two self-contained double rooms. It has a communal kitchen and a café-bar, and free coffee and tea are served throughout the day. It also offers free Internet facilities. **www.hostelnis.rs**

NIŠ Konak Duo D

Kopitareva 7, 24000 **Tel** *(018) 517 701* **Fax** *(018) 517 704* **Rooms** *12*

An old Ottoman word meaning "villa" or "palace", Konak lives up to its name, providing stylish guesthouse accommodation in the heart of the city. Built in the manner of old Serbian houses, the rooms feature a mix of modern and traditional furnishings; some have bright Balkan carpets. **www.konak-duod.com**

NIŠ My Place

Kej 29 Decembar bb, 18000 **Tel** *(018) 525 111* **Fax** *(018) 295 295* **Rooms** *30*

Situated beside the Nišava river, this striking four-star hotel is within easy walking distance of both Tvrđava Park and the city centre. Rooms have modern decor and come with flat-screen TV, Jacuzzi and wireless Internet. Guests have free use of the sauna and gym. **www.hotelmyplace.com**

NOVI PAZAR Tadž

Rifata Burđevića 79, 36300 **Tel** *(020) 311 904* **Fax** *(020) 316 838* **Rooms** *22*

This centrally located hotel combines modern architecture with Oriental touches. Minimalist modern decor and 1960s-style swivel chairs create a chic ambience in the reception area. The elegant rooms come with modern comforts such as TV, minibar and Internet access. **www.hoteltadz.rs**

NOVI SAD Hostel Sova

Ilije Ognjanovića 26, 21000 **Tel** *(021) 527 556* **Fax** *(020) 316 838* **Rooms** *9*

Occupying an apartment building just steps away from Novi Sad's city centre, Sova, meaning "the Owl", is a well-equipped hostel, which offers a couple of en suite double rooms as well as multibed dormitories with Internet access. A communal kitchen and spacious living room provide a homely feel. **www.hostelsova.com**

NOVI SAD Ile de France

Cara Dušana 41, 21000 **Tel** *(021) 636 2382* **Fax** *(021) 1939 784* **Rooms** *14*

An elegant Baroque building close to the city centre, Ile de France occupies a medium-sized apartment block in a residential area. Rooms are neat and bright and come with wooden floors, modern bathroom facilities, Internet access and TV. Buffet breakfast is served in a small dining room. **www.iledefrance.co.rs**

NOVI SAD Panorama

Futoška 1a, 21000 **Tel** *(021) 480 1800* **Fax** *(021) 480 1800* **Rooms** *12*

On the sixth floor of an office block overlooking the intersection of two of Novi Sad's busiest streets, Panorama is within walking distance of the town centre and entertainment venues. Several of the well-equipped rooms offer excellent views of the downtown area. **www.hotelpanorama.co.rs**

NOVI SAD Park

Novosadskog Sajma 35, 21000 **Tel** *(021) 488 8888* **Fax** *(021) 488 8888* **Rooms** *225*

Located near the Trade Fair, this ten-storey business hotel offers smart fully-equipped rooms. Note however that some rooms are equipped with shower cabins rather than bathtubs. Alongside an international restaurant there is "Tito's Salon", where the former president once celebrated New Year's Eve. **www.hotelparkns.com**

NOVI SAD Leopold I

Petrovaradinska Tvrđava bb, 21000 **Tel** *(021) 488 7878* **Fax** *(021) 488 7877* **Rooms** *59*

Situated in the heart of Petrovaradin Fortress *(see p556)*, Leopold I is named after the Habsburg emperor who captured the citadel in 1692. Period furniture and lush fabrics re-create the decor of the late Renaissance period. Staff frequently dress in period costumes. Rooms are plush and equipped with all amenities. **www.leopoldns.com**

SUBOTICA Patria

Đure Đakovića bb, 24000 **Tel** *(024) 554 500* **Fax** *(024) 552 320* **Rooms** *141*

This recently renovated six-storey hotel in the town centre looks rather plain on the outside, but has elegant and comfortable rooms. Tastefully furnished, they have a reasonable amount of desk space and en suite modern bathrooms. Wireless Internet access is available on the ground floor. **www.hotelpatria.rs**

SUBOTICA Gloria

Dimitrija Tucovića 2, 2400 **Tel** *(024) 672 010* **Fax** *(021) 488 7877* **Rooms** *32*

This recently opened, intimate four-star hotel is strategically located just off Subotica's main square. The chic coffee-and-crimson toned rooms come with minibar, desk and Internet access. The ground floor café is a good place to relax over coffee and sweet delicacies. **www.hotelgloriasubotica.com**

Key to Price Guide *see p563* **Key to Symbols** *see back cover flap*

Where to Eat in Serbia

Serbian cuisine is largely influenced by Mediterranean, Oriental and Hungarian culinary traditions. Many establishments specialize in regional dishes, which although somewhat heavy, are very appetizing. Most restaurants in Belgrade serve a great variey of grilled meats, although there is also a good choice of international dishes.

PRICE CATEGORIES
Based on the price per person of a three-course meal with half a bottle of wine, including cover charge, service and tax

din Under 1,000 din
din din 1,000–2,000 din
din din din 2,000–3,000 din
din din din din 3,000–5,000 din
din din din din din Over 5,000 din

BELGRADE

Kafana "?"
Kralja Petra I 6, 11000 **Tel** *(011) 236 5421* — Map C3

The oldest surviving café in Belgrade, the "question mark" dates back to 1823 and has changed little since then. The traditional decor features low tables and wooden chairs and simple local standards such as grilled meats with home-baked bread are served. An ideal place to take a break while sightseeing.

Ima Dana
Skadarska 38, 11000 **Tel** *(011) 323 4422* — Map E3

The cobbled Skadarlija ulica boasts a string of traditional-style restaurants serving Serbian food to locals as well as visitors. Ima Dana is one of the oldest and most authentic, offering a varied menu of traditional Balkan dishes and outdoor seating in a lovely inner courtyard. Live music every evening after about 8pm.

Ipanema
Strahinjića bana 68, 11000 **Tel** *(011) 328 3069* — Map E2

Despite the Brazilian-sounding name, Ipanema is an excellent Mediterranean restaurant offering superb salads, delicious pastas and expertly grilled fish dishes. Its location in the bar-lined stretch of Strahinjiča Bana makes it popular with the hip crowd; it is advisable to book in advance.

FURTHER AFIELD Salaš
Sinđelićeva 34, Zemun, 11080 **Tel** *(011) 219 0324*

A quaint and cosy restaurant in a stylishly decorated period house in the Gardoš district of Zemun, Salaš serves a combination of Serbian and Central European cuisine. The *ćuretina s mlincima* (turkey with baked shards of pasta) is the house speciality. It is a good idea to make a reservation.

FURTHER AFIELD Šaran
Kej oslobođenja 53, Zemun, 11080 **Tel** *(011) 618 235*

Occupying a historic single-storey house along the waterfront, Šaran (The Carp) specializes in local freshwater fish. The extensive menu also features appetizing Adriatic seafood and hearty Balkan meat dishes. The desserts are highly recommended. Book in advance.

REST OF SERBIA

NIŠ Nišlijska Mehana
Prvomajska 49, 18000 **Tel** *(018) 511 111*

One of the liveliest places for a night out in Niš, the Mehana, meaning "inn", features folksy tableware and ethnic wall hangings, as well as waiters in traditional costume. It is the perfect place to sample regional Serbian meat dishes, grilled to perfection and washed down with local spirits. Live music in the evenings.

NOVI SAD Plava Frajla
Sutjeska 2, 21000 **Tel** *(021) 61 3675*

A popular restaurant just southwest of the city centre, the "Blue Lady" features chequered tablecloths, chairs hanging from the ceiling, and black-and-white photographs of Novi Sad. The extensive menu features everything from grilled meats to Hungarian-influenced goulash. There are also excellent *palačinke* (pancakes) for dessert.

SUBOTICA Riblja Čarda
Obala Lajoša Vermeša, Palić, 24413 **Tel** *(024) 755 040*

This popular out-of-town destination near the shore of Lake Palić is the ideal place to sample local fish dishes. The in-house speciality is *riblji paprikaš* (fish stew rich in paprika), usually served with locally made pasta similar to tagliatelle. The dining room features exposed timber beams and there is an outdoor terrace facing the lake.

Map References *see map of Belgrade pp548–9*

ROMANIA

Although the country is unlikely ever to disassociate itself from the myth of Dracula, in recent years Romania has certainly managed to shake off its Communist-era image of grey uniformity. Beyond its prettily restored historic towns and cities lie breathtaking mountains and scenes of rural tranquillity that have changed little for generations.

Bordered by Ukraine to the north, Bulgaria to the south and Serbia and Hungary to the west, Romania has long been torn between its neighbours, particularly during the 18th and 19th centuries when the Russians and Austrians waged war against the Ottoman Empire on Romanian soil.

Despite its turbulent history, Romania has retained much of its traditional culture and a visit there is a rewarding experience. In Transylvania, the country's largest region, medieval castles neighbour modern ski resorts. To the northeast, Bukovina is home to beautiful monasteries, and to the south, Bucharest, the ancient capital of Wallachia, has superb museums and gardens.

HISTORY

The earliest evidence of human settlement in Romania is from the Neolithic period around 5,000 BC. Thracian tribes arrived in the first millennium BC, followed by Greeks, who settled along the Black Sea coast in the 7th century BC. The expanding Roman Empire conquered the region in the 1st century AD and named it Dacia. Subsequent centuries saw Dacia gradually split into three principalities – Transylvania, Moldavia and Wallachia – which were ruled by feudal leaders throughout the Middle Ages. Neighbouring Hungary conquered and controlled Transylvania in the 10th century and by the 13th

The spectacular snow-laden Făgăraş Mountains, Transylvania

◁ Well-preserved frescoes on the exterior of the Orthodox Moldoviţa Monastery, Bucovina century the principalities and their neighbours fought together to fend off the relentless Ottoman Empire. As the Ottoman grip weakened in the 19th century, Moldavia and Wallachia united to form the independent state of Romania in 1862. Carol I was made king of a constitutional monarchy in 1866 and full independence was declared in 1877. Fighting with the Allies in World War I brought the reward of unification with Transylvania in 1918, only to be lost again at the beginning of World War II, prompting Romania to take sides with Germany in the hope of regaining its territory. Romania changed sides towards the end of the war, ensuring the final return of Transylvania. In 1947, the Communist Party, with the support of Soviet troops, forced King Michael I (r. 1927–30) to abdicate and declared Romania a People's Republic. Gheorghe Gheorghiu-Dej (1901–65) was the first leader of the single-party dictatorship; upon his death in 1965, he was succeeded by Nicolae

Romanians protesting against Nicolae Ceauşescu, 1989

Ceauşescu (1918–89). However, Ceauşescu indulged in grand projects which consumed the nation's resources, leading to an economic crisis. In 1989, a series of violent demonstrations culminated in the resignation and subsequent execution of Ceauşescu. A brief period of instability followed as hard-line Communists attempted to regain power. Since 1990, however, the country has been ruled by a succession of democratic governments. In 2004, Romania joined NATO and on 1 January 2007, it became a member of the European Union.

LANGUAGE AND CULTURE

Romanian is the country's official language, although Hungarian is spoken by the large Hungarian minority in Transylvania.

The fascinating ethnographic museums scattered around the country provide an insight into Romania's rich cultural heritage. It has a diverse history of rural traditions involving music, dance and ritual. These are still preserved in towns and villages where most people have practised Orthodox Christianity for centuries, while the large, modern cities are very much on a par with many of their European counterparts.

KEY DATES IN ROMANIAN HISTORY

AD 101 Romans conquer and colonize Dacia

1003 Hungarian king Stephen conquers Transylvania

1456–1476 Vlad the Impaler brutally resists invading Ottoman forces

1526 Transylvania wins independence from Hungary

1600 Michael the Brave unifies Wallachia, Moldavia and Transylvania for a single year

1683 Transylvania is absorbed into the Habsburg Empire

1878 Treaty of Berlin recognizes the principalities of Moldavia and Wallachia as the independent state of Romania

1918 Transylvania is unified with Romania following World War I

1941 Romania joins Germany to fight the Allies under the dictatorship of Marshall Ion Antonescu

1947 Communists force King Michael to abdicate; Romania is proclaimed a People's Republic

1989 Following a bloody revolution, Romania becomes a democratic republic

2004 Romania joins NATO

2007 Romania becomes a member of the EU

Exploring Romania

With plenty of historic sites, Bucharest offers a rich taste of Romanian culture. Just north of the capital, in the foothills of the mighty Carpathian Mountains, are the medieval town of Braşov and Bran Castle, while further north, Suceava makes a good base for the Bucovina Monasteries Tour. The delightful towns of Sighişoara and Sibiu lie to the southwest the Carpathians. A network of railways connects many main towns and Bucharest has a bus service to most towns and villages across the country. The seaside resorts are best reached by bus or taxi from Constanţa.

The scenic tree-lined drive to Peleş Castle, southeastern Transylvania

SIGHTS AT A GLANCE

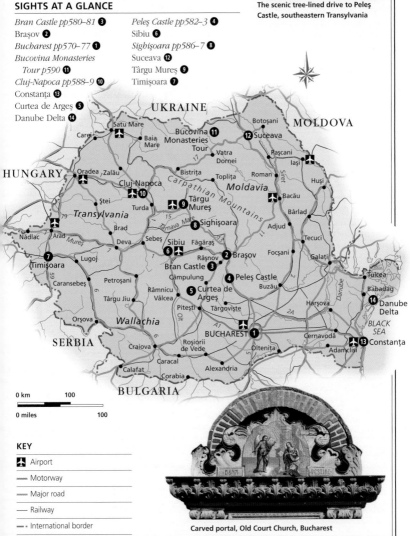

Carved portal, Old Court Church, Bucharest

KEY

✈ Airport
— Motorway
— Major road
— Railway
–·– International border

0 km 100
0 miles 100

Bucharest **❶**

In the Middle Ages, Bucharest served as the summer residence of the Wallachian court, but it gained notoriety as the seat of the brutal Vlad Țepeș (The Impaler) between 1456 and 1476. After periodic attacks by the Austrians and Russians, the city was eventually conquered by the Ottomans in the late 16th century, as a result of which it has a strong Turkish flavour. Heavy bombing in World War II, followed by a devastating earthquake in 1977, caused severe damage, and gave President Nicolae Ceaușescu an excuse to demolish huge swathes of the historic Old Town. However, this bustling, cosmopolitan capital still boasts an abundance of parks, churches, lavish mansions and French-style architecture that once earned it the title of "Little Paris". Its numerous high-class restaurants and boutiques, combined with a vibrant nightlife, add to its appeal.

SIGHTS AT A GLANCE

Communist Party Headquarters ⑥
George Enescu Memorial Museum ⑧
Herăstrău Park and Lake ⑬
Museum of Art Collection ⑩
Museum of Old West Art ⑭
Museum of the Romanian Peasant ⑫
National History Museum ②
Old Court Church ③
Palace of Parliament pp572–3 ①
Romanian Atheneum ⑦
Royal Palace and National Art Museum ⑨
Russian Church ⑤
Stavropoleos Church ④
Storck Museum ⑪

SEE ALSO

• **Where to Stay** p596

• **Where to Eat** p598

Fountains in Unity Square, with the Palace of Parliament visible in the distance

Herăstrău Park and Lake,
Museum of Old West Art
2 km (1 mile)

PARCUL KISELEFF

STR. ARH ION MINCU

BULEVARDUL ION MIHALACHE

STR. ȘOSEAUA KISELEFF

BULEVARDUL BANU MANTA

⑫

Piața Victoriei

ȘOSEAUA NICOLAE TITULESCU

BULEVARDUL ALEX IOAN CUZA

STRADA BERZEI

CALEA GRIVIȚEI

B-DUL GH. DUCA

STR OCCIDENT

Gara de Nord

BULEVARDUL DINICU GOLESCU

PIAȚA MATACHE

B-DUL SCHITU MAGU

STRADA MIRCEA VULCANESCU

STRADA BERZEI

CALEA PLEVNEI

STR STIRBEI VODĂ

STR GR. COBALC.

CALEA PLE

Izvor

STRADA IZVOR

B-DUL NAT

CALEA 13 SEPTEMBRIE

A   B   C

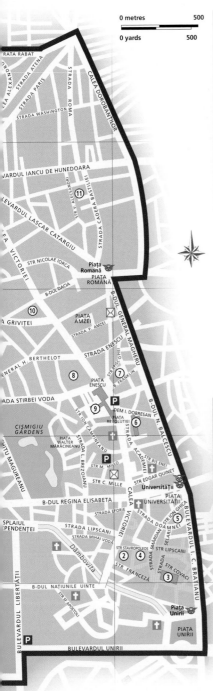

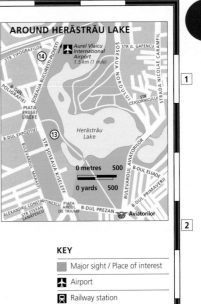

AROUND HERĂSTRĂU LAKE

STR TIPOGRAFILOR
B-DUL POLIGRAFIEI
Aurel Vlaicu International Airport
1.5 km (1 mile)
ȘOSEAUA BUCUREȘTI-PLOIEȘTI
ȘOSEAUA NORDULUI
STR G. GAFENCU
SOSAVA NICOLAE CARAMFIL
STR CEASORNICULUI
(14)
PIAȚA PRESEI LIBERE
B-DUL EXPOZITIEI
STR ȘOSEAUA KISELEFF
Herăstrău Lake
BULEVARDUL AVIATORILOR
B-DUL ELIADE
B-DUL PRIMAVERII
(13)

0 metres   500
0 yards   500

ALEXANDRU CONSTANTINESCU
STR ȘTEFAN SĂNĂTESCU
BULEVARDUL MARAȘTI
PIAȚA ARCUL DE TRIUMF
B-DUL PREZAN
Aviatorilor

KEY

	Major sight / Place of interest
✈	Airport
🚉	Railway station
🚇	Metro station
P	Parking
⊠	Post office
†	Church
	Pedestrian zone

Magnificent Neo-Classical colonnades of the Romanian Atheneum

GETTING AROUND

There is usually heavy traffic on the roads during the day, making travelling by car, taxi or bus tortuously slow. Sites of interest are spread widely across the city, so rather than walk it is a good idea to use the comprehensive metro system, which is clean, cheap and safe. However, metro maps and signs can be confusing. Taxis are cheap, but visitors should be wary of being overcharged.

D   E   F

Palace of Parliament ①
Palatul Parlamentului

Towering over the western end of Bulevardul Unirii, the Palace of Parliament is the second largest administrative building in the world, next to the Pentagon. Covering an area of 33 ha (82 acres), this colossal structure has 15 floors, 5 of which are underground. President Nicolae Ceauşescu ordered its construction in 1983, clearing a large area of historic Bucharest to make way for the project. The Romanian government continued the project after his death and in 1997 moved the Chamber of Deputies there, followed by the Senate in 2005. An estimated 10 per cent of the building remains unfinished.

The grand chandelier in the Palace Theatre

The 137-seat Senate, Romania's Upper House, was moved here in 2005 from Palatul Senatului in Revolution Square.

IIC Bratianu Hall, a venue for international conferences, features floor-to-ceiling marble panelling.

The 100-m (328-ft) corridor, the longest in the building, is separated by three sets of enormous sliding wooden doors.

★ **Alexandra Ioan Cuza Hall**
(Sala Alexandru Ioan Cuza)
One of the palace's many elegant rooms, the auditorium was intended for international meetings. The room opens on to a central balcony with sweeping views of Bulevardul Unirii.

Nicolae Bălcescu Hall, an imposing conference hall, has pink Transylvanian marble pillars adorned with gilt Corinthian capitals.

NICOLAE CEAUŞESCU (1918–1989)

Romania's former president, Nicolae Ceauşescu, joined the Romanian Communist Party at the age of 14. He rose to ministerial level follow-

Ceauşescu at his last session of the party congress

ing the Communist takeover in 1947 and succeeded Gheorghe Gheorghiu-Dej as First Secretary of the Party in 1965. During his leadership, he earned the respect of Western governments, but his megalomaniac vision of development caused immense suffering to the Romanian people. By the 1980s, poverty was rife and food and fuel shortages were crippling the country, giving rise to the Romanian Revolution of December 1989. On 25 December, Ceauşescu and his wife were tried by a military court and executed.

★ **Unification Hall (Unirii Hall)**
The largest room in the building, this hall has walls 15 m (49 ft) high, ornate marble columns and an immense glass ceiling. The two marble panels at either end of the room were intended to contain portraits of Nicolae and his wife Elena.

VISITORS' CHECKLIST

Bulevardul Libertăţii. **Map** C5.
🚌 *136, 385*. 🛈 *(021) 414 1426*. ⏰ *10am–4pm daily.* 📷
📷 📷 📷 **www**.cdep.ro
The National Museum of Contemporary Art *Tel (021) 318 9137.* ⏰ *10am–6pm Wed–Sun.* 📷 **www**.mnac.ro

The National Museum of Contemporary Art hosts temporary exhibitions of contemporary art from Romania and abroad in its opulent halls.

The palace was constructed exclusively from Romanian building materials, including locally quaried marble.

★ **Palace Theatre (Sala CA Rosetti)**
Marble pillars, ornate balconies and a gigantic central chandelier adorn this circular theatre. It has only been used for meetings because it lacks a backstage area.

Assembly Hall (Camera Deputaţilor)
Topped by a stunning glass dome, the Assembly Hall has, since 1997, been home to the 332-seat Chamber of Deputies, Romania's Lower House.

STAR FEATURES

★ Alexandra Ioan Cuza Hall

★ Unification Hall

★ Palace Theatre

National History Museum ②

Muzeul Naţional de Istorie

Calea Victoriei 12. **Map** E4. *Tel* *(021) 315 8207.* 🚍 *336, 601.* ⬜ *Apr–Oct: 10am–6pm Wed–Sun; Nov–Mar: 9am–5pm Wed–Sun.* 🖼️ 📷

Housed in a late 19th-century Neo-Classical building that served as the headquarters of the Romanian Postal Service until 1970, the eclectic National History Museum offers a great introduction to Romania's past. The museum's well-presented exhibitions are spread over 60 rooms. The central hall holds an enormous replica of the original Trajan's Column in Italy. A basement vault houses Romania's National Treasury, with jewellery and gold dating from the 14th century BC. The highlights of this collection are the beautiful gold earrings from the Hellenistic period (3rd–4th century BC) and the legendary Piretrosa Treasure, also known as The Hen and her Golden Brood, which was discovered by peasants in the Buzău region in 1837. The treasure is thought to have belonged to the Goths. Its 12 surviving pieces include brooches inlaid with semi-precious stones, a sacrificial dish engraved with images of gods, a 12-sided ceremonial goblet and several intricate necklaces.

Ornamental brickwork on the 16th-century Old Court Church

Old Court Church ③

Biserica Curtea Veche

Str Franceza 25–31. **Map** E4. 🚍 *116.* ⬜ *8am–8pm daily.*

The lovely Old Court Church, with its striped brick tower and ornamental niches, is one of Bucharest's oldest churches. Founded in the 16th century, it has undergone several renovations following fires and earthquakes, but has retained its original design. It was here that the Wallachian princes were crowned between the 16th and the 19th centuries. The interior is blackened from years of candle smoke, however parts of the superb murals and frescoes are still visible.

Stavropoleos Church ④

Biserica Stavropoleos

Str Stavropoleos 4. **Map** E4. *Tel* *(021) 313 4747.* 🚍 *336, 601.* ⬜ *7:30am–7pm daily.* **www.** stavropoleos.ro

Built in 1724 for the first Phanariot ruler, Nicolae Mavrocordat, this church has remained intact ever since, despite renovation work carried out in the 20th century. Four columns support the brilliant Byzantine-style arched porch and a series of framed icons adorn the church's façade. The interior, dominated by an 18th-century gilt iconostasis, features detailed biblical scenes from floor to ceiling. Next door is a small monastery complex, which was added to the church in the early 20th century and accommodates an active community of nuns today. The nuns maintain a valuable library of Byzantine manuscripts and a museum collection of icons and frescoes. Some of these priceless frescoes were rescued from the numerous churches that were torn down by Communist leader Nicolae Ceauşescu to make way for his grandiose scheme for the rebuilding of Bucharest's centre.

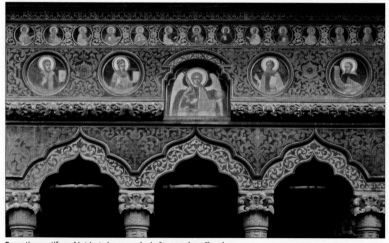

Byzantine motifs and intricate iconography in Stavropoleos Church

For hotels and restaurants in this region see pp596–7 and pp598–9

Colourful onion domes of the Russian Church

Russian Church ⑤
Biserica Rusă

Str Ion Ghica 9. **Map** E4. 🚌 *336, 601.* ⬜ *7:30am–7pm.*

The imposing Russian Church, with its seven onion domes, has stood opposite Bucharest University since 1909 when it was commissioned by Russian Tsar Nicholas II to serve the Russian Embassy's staff. Its splendid yellow brick façade is decorated with floral motifs and mosaics featuring images of saints. Intricate details such as fish head guttering add to its appeal. A portrait of St Nicholas stands over the entrance. Entered through a narrow passage, the church's interior is lit by candles, which have blackened the murals over the years. In 1992, the church became the official chapel of the academic community, but has remained open to visitors.

Communist Party Headquarters ⑥
Partidul Comunist Român

Piața Revolutiei. **Map** E3. 🚌 *300.*

Closely associated with the downfall of Nicolae Ceaușescu, the General Secretary of the Communist Party, Revolution Square (Piața Revolutiei) is overlooked by buildings which once housed Romania's Communist Party Headquarters. It was from the first floor balcony of this block that Ceaușescu gave his last speech to a gathering of 80,000 people on 21 December 1989, just a few days after thousands were killed by police in Timișoara *(see p585)*. Surprised by shouts of "murderer" and "Timișoara", the dictator famously faltered on live television. The crowd seized on his weakness and tried to storm the building. Ceaușescu's minister of defence, General Vasile Milea, was executed on the spot for refusing to order his troops to open fire on the protestors. Ceaușescu himself fled Bucharest in a helicopter from the roof of the building and was executed shortly thereafter.

Today, a huge marble needle stands opposite the building and forms the centrepiece of a memorial to the thousands killed during the revolution. The only other reminder of the event is the bullet-scarred façade of a building to the left of the square, which now houses government offices.

Romanian Athenaeum ⑦
Ateneul Român

Benjamin Franklin 1–3. **Map** E3.
Tel *(021) 315 0026.* 🚌 *131, 182, 301, 330.* ⬜ *9am–6pm Mon–Sat.* 📷

Designed by French architect Albert Galleron and completed in 1888 with the help of public donations, the impressive

Façade of the historic Communist Party Headquarters

Romanian Athenaeum is home to the George Enescu Philharmonic Orchestra. The concert hall is encircled by a 3-m (10-ft) high fresco depicting glorious moments in Romania's history. The auditorium, with plush red velvet chairs beneath a lavish dome featuring stucco sculptures of mythological creatures, can seat up to 600 people.

Detail, Neo-Classical colonnade of the Roman Athenaeum

George Enescu Memorial Museum ⑧
Muzeul Național George Enescu

141 Calea Victoriei. **Map** D3.
Tel *(021) 318 1450.* ⬜ *10am–5pm Tue–Sun.* 📷 www.georgeenescu.ro

The magnificent 20th-century Cantacuzino Palace was the one-time residence of Romania's most illustrious composer, conductor and musician, George Enescu. Enescu resided here briefly after his marriage to Princess Maria Cantacuzino in 1939, but the opulent Baroque palace was too much for him and he chose to live with his wife in the servants' quarters behind the building instead. After his death in 1955, the palace became the George Enescu Memorial Museum. Three of its stunning rooms feature an array of musical scores, manuscripts, photographs and memorabilia related to the musician's life and works.

Royal Palace and National Art Museum ⑨

Regal Palatul și Muzeul Național de Arta

Calea Victoriei 49–53. **Map** D3.
Tel (021) 314 8189. 178.
May–Sep: 11am–7pm Wed–Sun;
Oct–Apr: 10am–6pm Wed–Sun.
www.mnar.arts.ro

An imperial residence since the mid-19th century, the Royal Palace has undergone several renovations during its lifetime. King Carol I *(see p568)* was responsible for much of the current layout, redesigned in 1906. Further reconstruction took place after a catastrophic fire in 1926 and heavy bombing in World War II. Its location next to Revolution Square led to further damage from gunfire in December 1989.

Housed in the north wing of the palace, the National Art Museum was opened in 1950 to house the royal family's art collection. It closed in 1989 following the revolution when as many as 1,000 artworks were damaged, but reopened after complete renovation. The Gallery of Romanian Art includes sculptures by world-renowned sculptor Constantin Brâncuși and paintings by artist Nicolae Grigorescu. The European Art Gallery, spread over 15 rooms, boasts works by masters such as Rubens, Rembrandt, El Greco, Tintoretto and Monet.

Transylvanian biblical icons on stained glass, Museum of Art Collection

Visitors at the Royal Palace and National Art Museum

Museum of Art Collection ⑩

Muzeul Colecțiilor de Arta

Calea Victoriei 111. **Map** D3.
Tel (021) 212 9641. closed
for renovations, call in advance.

Housed in a Neo-Classical mansion with a surprisingly unassuming interior, the Museum of Art Collection has an intriguing variety of exhibits, of which the dazzling 17th-century gilt icon of Jesus Christ is the undisputed highlight.
An impressive range of Romanian artwork by masters such as Nicolae Grigorescu, Ștefan Luchian and Nicolae Tonitza occupies the ground floor.

Carpet, Museum of Art Collection

On the first floor, a display of traditional glass Transylvanian icons, remarkable for their bright colours and simplicity, can be seen alongside the Oriental collection, comprising 15th-century Chinese porcelain, 19th-century Japanese crockery, statues and a pretty wooden cupboard inlaid with mother-of-pearl, as well as Iranian ceramics and Turkish rugs. The same floor has a selection of antique European treasures which includes Austrian silverware, colourful Bohemian crystal and 19th-century French furniture and tapestries.

Storck Museum ⑪

Muzeul de Arta Frederic Storck și Cecilia Cutescu-Storck

Str V Alecsandri 16. **Map** D2.
9am–4pm Tue–Sun.

Built in 1913 by sculptor and architect Frederick Storck, this museum contains numerous works of art created or collected by Storck and his wife Cecilia. Delightful murals with floral and feminine motifs cover the walls of the central rooms, which took Cecilia four years to paint. Other pictures by Cecilia include seascapes painted at the family villa in Balchik (now in Bulgaria), portraits and still lifes. Particularly impressive among Storck's sculptures, which are exhibited next to his wife's work, are the bronze pieces inspired by Rodin. Several rooms are furnished with lovely ceramic stoves decorated with floral and bird motifs painted by Karl Storck, Frederick's father, who was the first Romanian teacher of sculpture in the Fine Arts Academy of Bucharest. There is also a small exhibition of medieval religious objects collected during the couple's travels.

Museum of the Romanian Peasant ⑫
Muzeul Ţăranului Roman

Str Şoseaua Kiseleff 3. **Map** C1.
Tel *(021) 317 9661.* 🚌 300.
🕐 *10am–6pm Tue–Sun.* 📷
www.muzeultaranuluiroman.ro

Housed in a red-brick edifice built in 1906, the Museum of the Romanian Peasant was intended as a celebration of the country's traditions at a time when industrialization was beginning to alter the rural face of Romania. With around 100,000 exhibits, the collection covers the regions of Romania. It includes mock-ups of craftsmen's workshops, a 19th-century classroom and numerous colourful traditional costumes. The highlight, how-ever, is an enormous wooden 18th-century windmill, which has been recon-structed on the ground floor alongside a mas-sive spiked *dărstă* (carding comb), which was used to prepare wool for spinning. A room at the back con-tains a replica of an Orthodox church, hung with icons dating back to the 17th century.

The Communism Exhibition, which has paintings and

Replica of a typical Romanian house at the Village Museum, Herăstrău Park

memorabilia relating to Romania's former Communist leaders, is worth a visit. Also of interest are the handmade wooden chairs collected from villages around the country, displayed on the first floor.

Herăstrău Park and Lake ⑬
Parcul Herăstrău

Costume display, Museum of the Romanian Peasant

Str Kiseleff 32. **Map** F1. 🚌
Village Museum ***Tel*** *(021) 317 9110.* 🕐 *9am–5pm Mon, 9am–7pm Tue–Sun.* 📷 **www**. muzeul-satului.ro

Bucharest's largest park was created in the 1930s under King Carol II after several marshes in the area were drained. Located to the north of the city, the park is popular today with cyclists, roller-bladers and joggers. Regular boat trips traverse the lake and smaller boats are available for individual hire.

Herăstrău is also home to one of Europe's oldest museum parks, the **Village Museum**. Inaugurated in 1936, it comprises a wonderful collection of reconstructed rural dwellings and work-shops. The buildings represent architectural styles from all over the country and range from 19th-century wood-tiled houses to wooden windmills and thatched Transylvanian cottages with beautifully painted window frames. There is even a half-buried house, designed to escape

the notice of invading tribes. However, the highlights of the museum are the oak houses from Maramureş county, which have beautifully carved hunting and animal scenes on their gateways. The museum shop stocks an excellent range of souvenirs.

Museum of Old West Art ⑭
Muzeul de Arta Veche Apuseana

Str Dr Minovici 3. **Map** F1.
Tel *(021) 665 7334.* 🚌
🕐 *9am–5pm Thu–Sun.* 📷

This charming red-brick Tudor-style house was built in the 1930s for Dumitru Minovici, who made his fortune in the oil industry and became an avid art collector. The house contains a collection of European art dating back to the 16th century and is fur-nished with antiques and Swiss stained-glass windows.

Passenger boat cruising on the calm waters of Herăstrău Lake

The grand building of the Museum of the Romanian Peasant

Hiking in the Făgăraș Mountains

European brown bear

Part of the Carpathian Mountains, the beautiful Făgăraș range offers some of Romania's most thrilling hiking routes, reaching heights of up to 2,544 m (8,346 ft). A combination of incredible views, glacial lakes, waterfalls, spruce forests, wildlife and hospitable shepherds ensures that a trip here is an unforgettable experience. However, the mountains are notorious for abrupt changes in weather, so inexperienced hikers are advised to join a group or hire a local guide. Severe winters restrict the hiking season to a few months between July and October.

Dianthus alpinus, *commonly known as Alpine pinks, bloom in late spring. They can be found growing above 2,000 m (6,561 ft) in the Făgăraș Alpine regions.*

Glacial lakes, *many at altitudes above 2,000 m (6,561 ft), are scattered throughout the mountains. Balea is the highest at 2,034 m (6,673 ft), and offers panoramic views as well as a lakeside mountain hut.*

Mountain huts, *or cabanas, are available on the northern side of the Făgăraș ridge, offering crackling log fires, dormitory beds and simple food. However, hikers intending to climb further south will need to carry camping equipment.*

Moldoveanu is Romania's highest peak at 2,544 m (8,346 ft). The country boasts a total of eight peaks over 2,500 m (8,202 ft).

Transfăgărășan, *Romania's highest road, crosses the Făgăraș Mountains and connects the regions of Transylvania and Wallachia as well as the towns of Sibiu and Pitești. The road has five tunnels; the longest is 884 m (2,900 ft).*

Hiking routes *in this region are well marked and easy to follow. However, all hikers should carry essential items such as maps, a compass, a first-aid kit, adequate food and water supplies, waterproofs and strong walking boots.*

Braşov ❷

168 km (104 miles) N of Bucharest.
🏛 *400,000.* 🚉 🚌 ℹ️ *Piaţa*
Sfatului 30, (0268) 419 078.
www.ghid-brasov.ro

Founded by German settlers
in the 13th century, Braşov
quickly grew into one of
the region's leading defensive
and commercial centres,
thanks to its position on
the southwestern border of
Transylvania. Today, this city
is one of the most visited
places in Romania.

Facing the Main Square
(Piaţa Sfatului) and built
into a line of Baroque
buildings is the façade of
the intriguing 19th-century
Orthodox Cathedral. Built in
Byzantine style, the church is
noteworthy for its beautiful
frescoes. In the centre of
the square stands the 15th-cen-
tury Town Hall, which now
houses the **History Museum**.
It has an excellent collection
of archaeological, medieval
and modern history exhibits.
Dominating the southwestern
corner of the square is
Transylvania's largest Gothic
building, the **Black Church**,
built in the 14th century.
Originally named St Mary's,
it came to be known as the
Black Church after a devastating fire in 1689 blackened
its walls. The church contains
Romania's heaviest bell,
weighing 6.3 tonnes (6.9 tons)
as well as its biggest organ.

Two streets south of the
Black Church is the imposing
Viennese and Art Nouveau

**View of the Gothic Black Church
and Tampa Hill, Braşov**

style **Temple
Synagogue**, built in
1899. In the north of
the city is the **Art and
Ethnographic Museum**,
displaying traditional
costumes from the
region and some
antique European and
Oriental ceramics and
glassware. This is also
the best place to see
Romania's largest
collection of exquisite
paintings by Nicolae
Grigorescu, one of the
forefathers of modern
Romanian art.

Of the city's ancient
fortifications, the most
striking is the south-
eastern Ekaterina Gate,
with a pointed central tower
surrounded by four corner
watch towers. For superb
views of Braşov, a cable
car ascends to the summit of
the forested 995-m (3,264-ft)
high Tampa Hill. Trekking up
the hill is not recommended
due to the threat of bears.

The Episcopal Church, Curtea de Argeş

🏛 Orthodox Cathedral
Piaţa Sfatului 3. ⬜ *9am–6pm daily.*

🏛 History Museum
Piaţa Sfatului. ⬜ *10am–6pm
Tue–Sun.* 📷

🏛 Black Church
Curtea Johannes Honterus 2.
⬜ *10am–5pm Mon–Sat.* 📷

✡ Temple Synagogue
Str Poarta Schei 27. ⬜ *9am–4pm
Mon–Fri, 9am–12pm Sat.*

**🏛 Art and Ethnographic
Museum**
B-dul Eroilor 21. ⬜ *10am–6pm
Tue–Sun.* 📷 **www**.muzeulartabv.ro

Bran Castle ❸

See pp580–81.

Peleş Castle ❹

See pp582–3.

Curtea de Argeş ❺

150 km (93 miles) NW of Bucharest.
🏛 *33,000.* 🚉 🚌

The small town of Curtea de
Argeş began as the 13th-
century capital of Argeş

county and later became
the capital of Wallachia. Its
most famous building is the
Episcopal Church, built in 1512
upon a 2-m (7-ft) high stone
platform within the grounds
of Curtea de Argeş Monastery.
Its elaborate design features
two domes and a pair of
cupolas with slanting narrow
windows set atop a box-like
building adorned with tiers of
niches and arabesque motifs.
According to legend, the chief
architect, Manole, was forced
to entomb his wife in the
walls of the church to keep
the building from collapsing;
popular belief at the time
held that ghosts were required
to keep buildings from falling
down. Upon completion of
the building, the church's
patron, Radu Negru, left
Manole and his fellow workers
stranded on the roof to ensure
they never built a greater
church. The whole group fell
to their death attempting to
fly using wooden wings made
from the roofing shingles.

Not far from the town centre
and to the north is one of
Wallachia's oldest churches.
Built in the 14th century, the
Princely Church is located
within the 13th-century complex of the Court de Argeş.
Its original frescoes have
been restored.

🏛 Episcopal Church
B-dul Basarabilor.
⬜ *summer: 8am–8pm daily;
winter: 8am–5pm.*

🏛 Princely Church
Court de Argeş. ⬜ *8am–6pm daily.*

Bran Castle 3

Castelul Bran

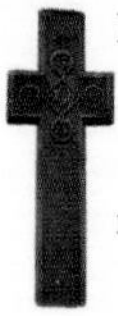

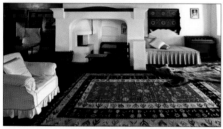

Tombstone at the castle

Perched on a rocky bluff, Bran Castle was built in the 13th century and first used as a defence against the Ottomans. Although the ruler of Wallachia, Vlad Ţepeş, better known as Dracula, never lived here, it is believed that he was briefly imprisoned here by the Hungarians. In more recent times, the castle was the favourite summer residence of Queen Marie (granddaughter of Queen Victoria of England), who refurbished the entire building and had electricity installed. Known today as Dracula's Castle, it is now a museum dedicated to the history of the Romanian Royal Family.

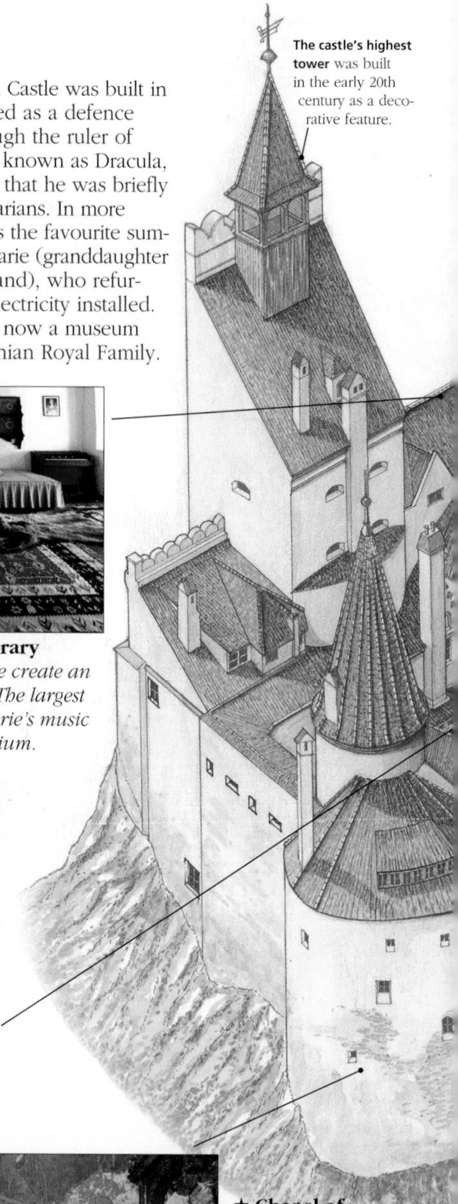

The castle's highest tower was built in the early 20th century as a decorative feature.

Queen Marie's Music Saloon and Library
Dark wooden floors and rustic furniture create an inviting atmosphere in this attic room. The largest room in the castle, it became Queen Marie's music room and housed her German harmonium.

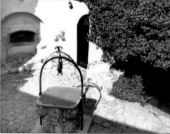

The Inner Yard Well
Converted into an elevator in 1921, this 60-m (197-ft) deep well led to a passage that opened out into a park in the valley.

★ Chapel of Prince Mircea
This chapel is dedicated to Queen Marie's first child, who died of typhus in 1916 at the age of three. The centrepiece is a dazzling gilt iconostasis brought from Mount Athos in Greece.

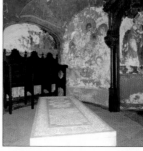

STAR FEATURES

- ★ Chapel of Prince Mircea
- ★ Gothic Room
- ★ Queen Marie's Bedroom

For hotels and restaurants in this region see pp596–7 and pp598–9

★ Gothic Room

Distinctly Gothic in style, this vaulted room is furnished with sculptures and furniture dating back to the 14th century. Among these is the 16th-century wooden sculpture of St Anne.

VISITORS' CHECKLIST

195 km (121 miles) NW of Bucharest. **Tel** *(0268) 238 332.* 🚌 from Braşov. ⬜ *May–Sep: noon–7pm Mon, 9am–7pm Tue–Sun; Oct–Apr: 9am–4pm Tue–Sun.* 🖻 🖪 🚹 **www**.brancastlemuseum.ro

The dining hall was used by Queen Marie to entertain royal guests. The massive wooden dining table is ornately carved with mythical images.

★ Queen Marie's Bedroom

Decorated in Art Nouveau style, the queen's bedroom contains several pieces of furniture she commissioned herself, including a rosewood Italian Baroque bed and an armchair adorned with carved vultures.

Secret Passages

Some of the castle's 60 rooms are connected by a network of underground passages, which were used either for hasty evacu-ations or to bring in food supplies in times of siege.

RÂŞNOV FORTRESS

Situated halfway between the towns of Braşov and Bran, Râşnov Fortress overlooks the small town of Râşnov from a hilltop. Founded in the 13th cen-tury by Teutonic knights, the fortress served as a refuge for the people of Râşnov during times of seige. The central courtyard contains a 143-m (469-ft) deep well, dug to supply drinking water to the inhabitants. A museum within the complex displays armour and various finds uncovered during excavations, among them a skeleton now encased beneath a glass floor.

Râşnov Fortress sitting on a hilltop

Peleş Castle ❹

Castelul Peleş

An extravagant palace built by King Carol I to serve as his summer residence, Peleş Castle is among the most impressive palaces in Europe. Built between 1873 and 1883 and redesigned in 1914, the castle stands in a vast forested park tucked away among the low hills of the Carpathian countryside. The German Neo-Renaissance façade recalls a fairy tale castle with its sharp Gothic profile and decorative woodwork. The interior design of its 170 rooms was overseen by King Carol I's wife Elisabeth and features lavish furnishings, ornate woodcarvings and numerous artworks. One of the last royal palaces to have been built in Europe, it was the first to be supplied with electricity, central heating and a lift.

The Renaissance-style dining room contains an exquisite set of silverware and Rosenthal crockery. Its stained-glass windows are framed by intricately carved columns of walnut and ash.

The walls of the French Passage are adorned with two valuable early 20th-century tapestries featuring Cleopatra and Marc Antony.

Statue of King Carol I

A towering statue of King Carol I, by Italian sculptor Raffaello Romanelli, overlooks the park.

★ Florentine Hall

The bright Murano glass chandeliers and Palanazzo marble fireplace provide a wonderful contrast to the dark ebony wall cabinets. Venetian mirrors reflect the ceiling paintings, which are reproductions of works by the Flemish artists van Eyck and Rubens.

STAR FEATURES

★ Florentine Hall

★ Theatre Room

★ Hall of Honour

For hotels and restaurants in this region see pp596–7 and pp598–9

★ Theatre Room
Originally designed as a theatre, this room was turned into a cinema in 1906. The highlight is the Art Nouveau wall frieze painted by Gustav Klimt in 1894 and elegantly framed with cream and gilt mouldings.

The Large Armory Hall has a fascinating collection of over 3,500 items dating back to the 15th century, including weapons from Japan, Persia, India and Turkey.

The abundance of carved woodwork on the building is typical of the German Neo-Renaissance style.

★ Hall of Honour
The castle's main entrance incorporates a striking three-storey display of Viennese walnut carvings that decorate the spiral staircase and arched balconies overlooking the Reception Hall. Light floods into the hall from the 16-m (52-ft) high sliding glass roof.

King Carol's office is lined with walnut panelling and portraits of the royal family.

Library
Among the king's collection of over 10,000 books are 40 novels written by Queen Elizabeth under the pseudonym Carmen Sylva. One of the beautifully carved bookcases conceals a secret passage leading to the royal bedroom.

The Music Room was occasionally used for literary evenings; its teak furniture was a gift from the Maharajah of Kapurthala.

Sibiu ❻

273 km (170 miles) NW of Bucharest. 🏘 170,000. ✈ 🚉 🚌
ℹ Str S. Brukental 2, (0269) 208 913. www.sibiu.ro

Founded in the 1190s, Sibiu is one of Romania's most charming cities. Its historic centre is filled with medieval, steep-roofed houses with attic windows and the narrow streets lead into wide open squares surrounded by the colourful façades of renovated mansions and churches.

The first recorded mention of the city dates back to the 12th century, when the region received two waves of Saxon settlers who had obtained privileges from the Hungarian rulers controlling Transylvania at the time. In 1241, invading Tatars prompted Sibiu's residents to raise fortifications. Successive centuries saw the city walls enlarged and strengthened, eventually transforming it into an impenetrable citadel. In the 15th century, Sibiu's craftsmen formed some of Europe's first guilds and the city developed into a prosperous trading centre.

In recent years, the Old Town has benefited enormously from European Union (EU) funding, and Sibiu served as European capital of Culture in 2007. Dominating the vast Large Square (Piaţa Mare) is an imposing Baroque palace built for Samuel von

Brukenthal, who governed Transylvania between 1774 and 1787. The grand façade bears Brukenthal's medieval coat of arms above the ornate entrance. The interior, with plush halls, stucco ceilings and embossed wallpaper, now houses Romania's oldest museum – the **National Brukenthal Museum**. This holds Transylvania's finest art collection as well as Romanian and Western works, including some by Romanian artists such as Nicolae Grigorescu *(see p576)*,

Tiles, Evangelical Cathedral

Theodor Pallady and the Abstractionist Hans Mattis Teutsch. The palace library holds over 280,000 volumes as well as a priceless collection of manuscripts.

The nearby **History Museum** is housed in an elegant 15th-century Gothic building that served as Sibiu's Town Hall for 500 years until 1948. The collection was moved here from the Brukenthal Palace in 1984 after the Town Hall's restoration. A secluded gateway leads into its cobbled courtyard overlooked by balconies festooned with colourful flowers. The ancient doors at the museum entrance open on to a surprisingly modern interior with original vaulted ceilings. Smartly lit glass

Houses and shops lining a street in Sibiu

cases display an absorbing collection of old coins, medieval weaponry and archaeological finds. Just a few streets away on Huet Square (Piaţa Huet) is the five-towered **Evangelical Cathedral**, whose exquisitely tiled spire can be seen from all over town. Constructed over an original 14th-century Roman church, the cathedral has a regal Gothic interior and contains the tombs of local nobles.

Situated in a dense forest just outside Sibiu is the **Museum of Traditional Folk Civilization**, Romania's largest outdoor museum. Over 300 replicas of traditional dwellings are scattered throughout the 101-ha (250-acre) complex, which can be explored either on foot or in the comfort of a horse-drawn carriage. Buildings include Dutch-style windmills, farmhouses, wooden churches and traditional inns.

🏛 **National Brukenthal Museum**
Piaţa Mare 4-5. *Tel (269) 217 691.*
⭕ 10am–6pm Tue–Sun. 🎟 📷 📹
www.brukenthalmuseum.ro

🏛 **History Museum**
Str Mitropoliei nr 2. *Tel (269) 218 143.* ⭕ 10am–6pm Tue–Sun. 📷
www.brukenthalmuseum.ro

⛪ **Evangelical Cathedral**
Piaţa Huet 1. ⭕ 9am–5pm Mon–Sat, 11am–5pm Sun.

🏛 **Museum of Traditional Folk Civilization**
Calea Rasinari. *Tel (0269) 242 599.*
⭕ May–Oct: 10am–6pm Tue–Sun.
www.muzeulastra.ro

The cobbled courtyard of the National Brukenthal Museum, Sibiu

For hotels and restaurants in this region see pp596–7 and pp598–9

Timişoara ⑦

347 km (216 miles) NW of Bucharest.
🏚 310,000. 🚉 ✈ 🚌 ℹ Str Alba
Iulia 2, (0256) 437 973.

Located close to the border of Serbia and Hungary, Timişoara claims to have been the first city in Europe to introduce electric street lighting, the first in Romania to have a public water supply and one of the first in the world to have had horse-drawn trams.

In the 14th century, Timişoara was a part of Hungary and the heavily fortified town became a focal point of resistance against invading Ottoman forces. The Ottomans conquered it in 1551 and it remained a military stronghold until the Habsburg Empire forced them out in 1716. The town was then completely rebuilt and the historic centre owes much of its present-day appearance to its Austrian conquerors. When Timişoara finally became part of Romania in 1920, it was still dominated by ethnic Hungarians and Germans, but most of them left following the end of World War II. Today, Timişoara has a majority population of ethnic Romanians and is venerated as the city that sparked events leading to the overthrow of Nicolae Ceauşescu in December 1989 (see p568).

Victory Square (Piaţa Victoriei), scene of the tragic events that saw police open fire on peaceful protesters in

The Baroque Roman Catholic Cathedral on Unity Square, Timişoara

1989, is now the city's thriving hub. Nearby is its best museum, the **Banat Museum**, which has excellent regional, historical, archaeological and natural history exhibitions. Founded in 1872, it has been located in Hunyadi Castle (Castelul Huniade) since 1948. This Venetian-style castle was constructed in the 15th century and is thought to be Timişoara's oldest building. To the south of Victory Square is the extravagant 20th-century **Orthodox Cathedral**, with 11 towers of differing sizes, each covered with patterned mosaic tiles. The striped brickwork is reminiscent of both Byzantine and Moldavian church architecture. A memorial to the victims of 1989 stands in front to mark the protests that took place in and around the church.

Detail, Banat Museum

To the north of the square is **Unity Square** (Piaţa Unirii), an expansive space lined with elaborate Austro-Hungarian mansions. In the 18th century,

it was used as a major commercial and ceremonial site. Two impressive Baroque cathedrals, both constructed in the late 18th century, stand here; to the west is the grand Serbian Orthodox Cathedral; to the east the Roman Catholic Cathedral. Located in another 18th-century building, just off Unity Square, is the **Memorial Museum of the 1989 Revolution** which documents events around the uprising with original video footage, photographs, military uniforms and newspapers. The adjoining chapel has been dedicated to the revolution.

🏛 **Banat Museum**
Piaţa Huniade 1, Castelul Huniazilor.
Tel (0256) 491 339. ⬜ 10am–4pm Mon–Sat. 🎫 🚻 www.muzeul
banatului.ro

⛪ **Orthodox Cathedral**
Piaţa Victoriei. ⬜ 8am–8:30pm daily.

🏛 **Memorial Museum of the 1989 Revolution**
Str Emanuil Ungureanu 8.
Tel (0256) 294 936. ⬜ 8am–4pm Mon–Fri, 10am–2pm Sat & Sun.

Ecstatic crowds after the overthrow of the regime

THE 1989 REVOLUTION

In December 1989, Romania's Communist regime was toppled by the most violent revolution in Eastern Europe at the time. The catalyst was a minor protest against the eviction of an ethnic Hungarian anti-Ceauşescu priest, László Tőkés, on 16 December. Around 1,000 lives were lost when police opened fire on demonstrators and the military was called to suppress the unrest. It culminated with the execution of Ceauşescu on 25 December.

The 11-spired Orthodox Cathedral near Victory Square, Timişoara

Sighişoara ❽

Perched high on a hill above the Târnava Mare river, Sighişoara was founded in the 12th century by German merchants and craftsmen who had been invited by the king of Hungary to settle in the region and defend its borders. The settlement grew into a major Transylvanian town but was almost abandoned following a devastating fire in 1676. Most of the buildings today date from the town's subsequent rebuild. The Old Town is one of Europe's few remaining inhabited medieval citadels, and is now a UNESCO World Heritage Site. Studded around it are a number of towers, many of which belonged to the town guilds; of the 14 towers originally built, only 9 have survived. Clustered behind the fortified walls is an ensemble of 17th-century buildings whose fading façades enhance the citadel's period charm.

The Gothic Venetian House, at the corner of Museum Square

Symbolic wooden figures on the 13th-century Clock Tower

🏛 Clock Tower

Piaţa Muzeului 1. *Tel (265) 771 108.* ⬜ *15 May–15 Sep: 10am–5:30pm Tue–Sun; 16 Sep–14 May: 9am–3:30pm Tue–Fri, 10am–3:30pm Sat & Sun.* 🏛

Built over the main gate in the 13th century, the Clock Tower (Turnul cu Ceas) is the dominant feature of the citadel. Designed as a defensive structure, its thick lower stone walls made it difficult for enemies to attack. It housed the town council offices until 1550. The fifth and sixth floors, as well as the clock, were added at the beginning of the 17th century. At midnight every day one of seven wooden figures, symbolizing day and night, emerges from the clock to face the town. The tower was destroyed by the Great Fire of 1676 and rebuilt in subsequent years. Today, it is occupied by the History Museum and a small Museum

of Torture, which includes among its exhibits a ladder that was used to roast people alive.

🏛 Monastery Church

Piaţa Muzeului. ⬜ *8am–7pm daily.*

Originally part of a 13th-century Dominican monastery, this Gothic church (Biserica Manastirii Dominicane) has been Lutheran since 1556. Its present appearance dates back to the late 17th century, when it was rebuilt following the Great Fire; the Baroque organ was installed in 1680. Its interior walls are decorated with 300-year-old Anatolian rugs.

🏛 Vlad Dracul's House

Str Cositorarilor 5. *Tel (265) 771 596.* ⬜ *10am–11pm daily.*

Despite its name, there is no historical evidence linking this building (Casa Vlad Dracul) to Vlad Dracul, father of Vlad Ţepeş, the Wallachian ruler

Sign outside Dracul's House

who was notorious for his methods of punishment. However, some of the murals inside the house, discovered during renovations, depict a figure bearing some resemblance to the infamous ruler. The ground floor is now a medieval-themed restaurant while the first floor is home to the Museum of Weapons.

🏛 Venetian House

Piaţa Muzeului.

Located on the corner of Museum Square (Piaţa Muzeului), the Venetian House (Casa Venetian) was once a mayoral residence. Built in the 16th century, it is named for its Venetian Gothic stone window frames, which were added during renovations in the 19th century. Today, the house is used by the German Evangelical parish and the German Democratic Forum, founded in 1989, which represent the town's remaining German residents.

Sighişoara Monastery Church seen across a cluster of rooftops

For hotels and restaurants in this region see pp596–7 and pp598–9

🏰 Shoemakers' Tower

Str Manastirii.

At the northernmost point of the citadel stands the 16-m (52-ft) high Shoemakers' Tower (Turnul Cizmarilor), built in 1594. The unusual hexagonal structure incorporates a watchtower over the Old Town. There was once an identical watchtower on the tower's opposite side, from where guards could survey the surrounding area. Although it retains much of its original appearance, the tower's main entrance and windows have been modified in recent years to accommodate a radio station and a newspaper office.

Shoemakers' Tower, offering a vantage point over the Old Town

🏰 Tailors' Tower

Str Manastirii.

This twin-arched 14th-century tower (Turnul Croitorilor) is one of three entrances to the citadel. The upper part of the tower was destroyed in the 1676 fire but was restored in 1935. Known as the Rear Gate, it was once defended by massive wooden doors secured with iron bars, and a small army of 30 tailors belonging to Sighişoara's oldest guild.

🏰 Furriers' Tower

Str Manastirii.

The 15th-century Furriers' Tower (Turnul Cojocarilor) is one of the smallest of the nine surviving towers. It is linked to the Butchers' Tower by an ancient gateway through which shepherds once took cattle out to pasture.

🏛 Church on the Hill

Str Scolii. ◯ 8am–7pm daily. 📷

Reached by a 400-year-old covered wooden staircase, the striking 14th-century Gothic Church on the Hill (Biserica din Deal) stands high above the citadel. Initially a Catholic church, it has since become part of the German Evangelical parish. During renovations between 1992 and 2003, its plain white façade was

Distinctive arches of the 14th-century Tailor's Tower

rebuilt and some of the original interior murals were discovered. The church's centrepiece is the 16th-century altarpiece of St Martin, which depicts scenes from the saint's life. It originally belonged to the Monastery Church and was transferred here after Russian Cossacks stole the original silver altar in 1601.

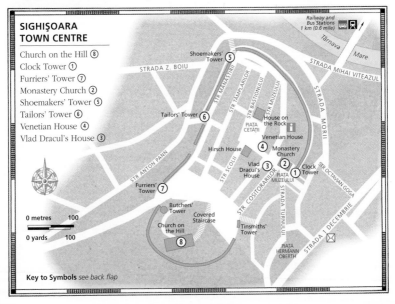

SIGHIŞOARA TOWN CENTRE

Church on the Hill ⑧
Clock Tower ①
Furriers' Tower ⑦
Monastery Church ②
Shoemakers' Tower ⑤
Tailors' Tower ⑥
Venetian House ④
Vlad Dracul's House ③

0 metres 100
0 yards 100

Key to Symbols *see back flap*

Târgu Mureş ❾

341 km (212 miles) N of Bucharest. 🏛 150,000. ✈ 🚉 🚌 ℹ *Str G Enescu 2, (0365) 404 934.* **www**.cjmures.ro

Although it currently lies within Romania's borders, the city of Târgu Mureş has always had a strong Hungarian influence and for many centuries was known by its Hungarian name Marosvásárhely. It was ceded to Hungary for four years during World War II and for 15 years, was an autonomous Hungarian province under Communist rule. Today, half of its population is ethnically Hungarian.

Târgu's most striking building, the **Palace of Culture**, stands right in the heart of the city. Built between 1911 and 1913, its main attraction is the Mirror Hall, with 12 stained-glass windows depicting Hungarian folklore. The art gallery within the palace exhibits works by famous Romanian painters. Classical concerts take place inside the palace every Thursday.

East of the city centre is the **Teleki-Bolyai Library**, where the Transylvanian chancellor, Count Samuel Teleki, opened the region's first library in 1802. Today, it holds over 200,000 ancient volumes, manuscripts and other documents.

🏛 **Palace of Culture**
Str G Enescu 2. ◯ *9am–4pm Tue–Fri, 9am–1pm Sat & Sun.* 🎫

🏛 **Teleki-Bolyai Library**
Str Bolyai 17. ◯ *10am–6pm Tue–Fri, 10am–1pm Sat–Sun.* 🎫

Broad and attractive pedestrianized streets in Târgu Mureş

Cluj-Napoca ❿

Now Romania's third largest city, Cluj-Napoca began life as a Roman colony, although it was abandoned in the 3rd century. Cluj was refounded in the Middle Ages by the Hungarians, who brought in Saxon immigrants to boost regional trade. Periods of Ottoman and Austrian rule followed, and not until 1918 did the town become part of Romania. In recent history, the 1989 revolution saw violent demonstrations here, resulting in many deaths. Today, Cluj-Napoca retains an air of small-town charm, and its wide pedestrianized streets are lined with 19th-century buildings connected by narrow alleys and courtyards.

Exterior of the Gothic St Michael's Church on Unity Square

🏛 **Ethnographic Museum of Transylvania**
Str Memorandumului 21. **Tel** *(0264) 592 344.* ◯ *9am–5pm Tue–Sun.* 🎫 **www**.muzeul-etnografic.ro
Founded in 1922, this museum (Muzeul de Etnografie din Transilvania) features a large collection of Transylvanian ethnographic objects. Housed in the 16th-century Reduta Palace, exhibits include traditional costumes, brightly patterned rugs and agricultural tools and pottery that date back 300 years. The museum also has an outdoor section with full-size replicas of rural dwellings and village churches.

🔒 **St Michael's Church**
Piaţa Unirii. 🔒
With a spire over 76 m (249 ft) high, this Gothic church (Biserica Sfântul Mihail) towers over the city. Its austere interior is adorned with stained-glass windows featuring a portrait of St Michael, a graceful cream and gilt altar and a superbly carved pulpit decorated with doves, angels and biblical characters.

🏛 **Art Museum**
Piaţa Unirii 30. **Tel** *(0264) 596 952.* ◯ *10am–5pm Wed–Sun.* 🎫 **www**.macluj.ro
Housed in the 18th-century Baroque Bánffy Palace, the museum's (Muzeul de Arta) collection is dominated by the works of French-influenced artists of the 19th and 20th centuries. Among them are Romanian masters Nicolae Grigorescu, Theodor Pallady and Ştefan Luchian.

🔒 **Orthodox Cathedral**
Piaţa Avram Iancu. ◯ *8am–7pm daily.* 🔒
Built between 1923 and 1933, this monumental cathedral (Catedrala Ortodoxa), with its massive central dome, dominates Avram Iancu Square. The highlight of its opulent interior is a huge gilt iconostasis comprising 18th- and 19th-century icons illustrating the life of Christ. In front of the church is a modernist statue of Avram Iancu, a 19th-century Romanian

Entrance to the Art Museum in the Bánffy Palace, Unity Square

The brightly painted National Theatre and Opera

VISITORS' CHECKLIST

440 km (273 miles) NW of
Bucharest. 🏠 340,000. ✈ 7km
(4 miles) NE of centre. 🚉 🚌 ℹ
B-dul Eroilor 6-8, (0264) 452
244. 🎬 Transylvanian Film Festival
(Jun). **www**.clujnapoca.ro

nationalist who led the 1848
revolt against the unification of
Transylvania and Hungary.

🎭 National Theatre and Opera

Piaţa Stefan cel Mare 24. **Tel** (0264)
592 876. **www**.operacluj.ro

Opened in 1906, the National
Theatre and Opera (Teatrul
National si Opera) started as a
Hungarian theatre. The majestic building was designed by
Austrian architects Ferdinand
Fellner and Hermann Helmer,
and it has been home to the
Romanian theatre and opera
since 1918. Its striking Art
Nouveau lobby leads into a
grand auditorium seating up
to 1,200 people. Regular
national and international
performances take place here.

🎓 Babeş-Bolyai University

Mihail Kogalniceanu nr1. **Tel** (0264)
405 300. **www**.ubbcluj.ro

Founded in 1581, this
(Universitatea Babeş-Bolyai) is
the largest university in
Romania. It started off as a
Jesuit Academy but was later
closed down when Romanians
were denied education in their
language and taught in
Hungarian instead. After the
country's liberation, two universities were established to
provide education in both
languages. In due course, the
institutions were merged and
adopted a name inspired by
the Romanian scientist Babeş
and Hungarian mathematician
Bolyai. Today, the university
has a student population of
45,000 and with 21 faculties.

🌺 Botanical Gardens

Str Bilaşcu. ◯ 9am–7pm daily.
🖼 ♿

Opened in 1920, the Botanical
Gardens (Botanice Grădini)
are located just outside the
city centre on a hillside park.
It has six greenhouses filled
with equatorial and tropical
plants, including specimens
from Japan, as well as flora
from all over Romania.

✡ Synagogue

Str Horea 21. **Tel** (0264) 596 600.
◯ varies, call in advance.

Built in the late 19th century,
this is the city's main synagogue (Sinagogă Neologă),
topped with four silver onion
domes. It has had a chequered
history, first attacked in 1927
by the Romanian fascist
organization, the Iron Guard,
and then during World War II.
It has now been restored
to its original design and
serves as a Holocaust
memorial for the city's
small Jewish community.

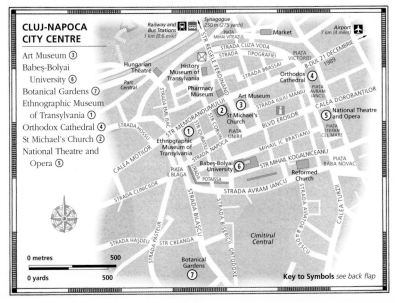

CLUJ-NAPOCA CITY CENTRE

Art Museum ③
Babeş-Bolyai University ⑥
Botanical Gardens ⑦
Ethnographic Museum of Transylvania ①
Orthodox Cathedral ④
St Michael's Church ②
National Theatre and Opera ⑤

0 metres   500
0 yards   500

Key to Symbols see back flap

Bucovina Monasteries Tour ⑪

The painted churches of Bucovina, a hilly region in northwestern Moldavia, were the illustrated Bibles of their time. Most were constructed during the reign of Stephen the Great (1457–1504), who welcomed Bulgarian and Serbian Orthodox Christian monks seeking refuge from the Ottoman Empire. After each victory against the Ottomans, Stephen commissioned a church to be built. Petru Rareş, his son, continued the tradition. Their beauty and rarity has earned the monasteries UNESCO World Heritage Site status.

Sucevita Monastery, the last church to be built before the Ottoman invasion

Sucevita ④
Founded in the late 16th century, this church is famous for its *Ladder of Virtue* mural, which depicts monks trying to climb to heaven with the help of Christ and his angels.

Putna ⑤
The most important monastery in the region, Putna was ransacked in the 17th century but has since been restored. Stephen, two of his wives, and his sons Petru and Bogdan are all buried here.

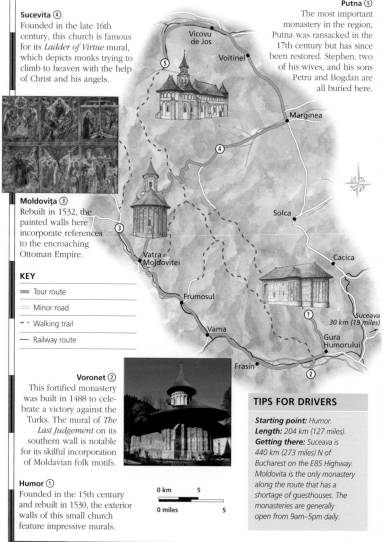

Moldovita ③
Rebuilt in 1532, the painted walls here incorporate references to the encroaching Ottoman Empire.

KEY

▬ Tour route

═ Minor road

- - Walking trail

— Railway route

Voronet ②
This fortified monastery was built in 1488 to celebrate a victory against the Turks. The mural of *The Last Judgement* on its southern wall is notable for its skilful incorporation of Moldavian folk motifs.

Humor ①
Founded in the 15th century and rebuilt in 1530, the exterior walls of this small church feature impressive murals.

0 km   5

0 miles   5

TIPS FOR DRIVERS

Starting point: *Humor.*
Length: *204 km (127 miles).*
Getting there: *Suceava is 440 km (273 miles) N of Bucharest on the E85 Highway. Moldovita is the only monastery along the route that has a shortage of guesthouses. The monasteries are generally open from 9am–5pm daily.*

Suceava ⓬

440 km (273 miles) N of Bucharest.
🏠 *107,000.* 🚉 🚌 ℹ️ *Str Stefan cel
Mare 23, (0230) 551 241.*

Once the powerful capital
of Moldavia, Suceava has
long since faded from glory.
Today, the town serves as
a base for visitors who
want to explore the marvellous monasteries in the
Bucovina region.

Suceava Fortress, on a
hill overlooking the town,
is the most impressive
sight here. Built during the
reign of Petru I Muşat and
occupied by a succession
of powerful rulers, it resisted
a number of seiges and
remained unconquered when
the Ottoman Empire ordered
its destruction. Only the ruins
of the citadel are
visible today.

Closer to the town
centre, the colour-
fully tiled roof of the
**Mirăuţi Church of
St George** can be
seen rising above
the surrounding pine
trees. Founded by
Petru I Muşat in about
1390, this is the town's oldest
church and was once used
for the coronations of
Moldavia's princes. It was
here that Stephen the Great
was crowned as prince of
Moldavia. Some of the original
murals can still be seen.

⚓ Suceava Fortress
Dealul Cetătii. 🕐 9am–6pm
daily. 🎫

🏛 Mirăuţi Church of St George
Str Mirăuţi. 🕐 8am–7pm daily.

The scattered ruins of ancient Tomis, Constanţa

Constanţa ⓭

223 km (139 miles) E of Bucharest.
🏠 *310,000.* 🛬 🚉 🚌 ℹ️ *B-dul
Tomis 221, (0241) 488 600.*

Romania's main port and fifth
largest city, Constanţa is also
one of the oldest cities in
Romania. Known as
Tomis in the 5th cen-
tury BC, Constanţa
started off as a Greek
colony. It was then
conquered by the
Romans around 20 BC
and was renamed
Constanţa by the
Roman Emperor
Constantine the Great. Today,
all that remains of the city's
glorious past is an uninspiring
array of unmarked Roman
walls, columns and fragments
of statues in the Archaeological
Park on Bulevardul Republicii.
More interesting is the **Tomis
Mosaic Museum**, housing a
colourful 800-sq-m (9,149-sq-ft)
mosaic floor from Tomis's
4th-century Roman forum. A
short walk from the museum
is **Mahmudiye Mosque**. Built
in 1910 during the reign of

*Detail in the
Mahmudiye mosque*

King Carol I, it is Romania's
largest mosque. The plain interior is brightened by a vast
Persian carpet, a gift from the
Ottoman ruler, Sultan Abdul
Hamid. One of the biggest
Turkish carpets in Europe,
it measures 144 sq m (1,550
sq ft). There are fine views of
the city from the 47-m (154-ft)
high minaret.

🏛 Tomis Mosaic Museum
Piaţa Ovidiu 12. 🕐 8am–8pm daily.
🎫 ℹ️

☪ Mahmudiye Mosque
Str Arhiepiscopiei 5. 🕐
9:30am–9:30pm daily. 🎫 ℹ️

Danube Delta ⓮

223 km (139 miles) E of Bucharest.
🚢 *from Tulcea.* ℹ️ *Str Garii 26,
Tulcea, (0240) 519 130.* 🚤 *Navrom
boat tours from Tulcea.*

Covering an area of 4,142 sq
km (1,599 sq miles), the
Danube Delta, a biosphere
reserve, is the largest and
best-preserved delta in
Europe. A UNESCO World
Heritage Site, it is home to a
variety of wildlife including
wolves, wild cats and around
300 bird species and 150
species of fish. The starting
point for exploring the
reserve is Tulcea, located at
the tip of the delta. From here,
three ferries a week make the
3-hour journey to Sulina,
once a bustling port. The
town's old lighthouse, built
in 1870, is now a history
museum detailing Sulina's
heyday as the headquarters
of the European Danube
Commission (1856–1938).
Sulina's vast 40-km (25-mile)
beach is also worth a stroll.

The old lighthouse in the coastal town of Sulina, Danube Delta

Practical & Travel Information

Romanians are generally polite and hospitable and will often go out of their way to help, especially in rural areas where foreign visitors are rare. The country's substantial size makes it a formidable area to explore. Public transport is adequate, but slower than using a car and although car hire is reasonably priced and cuts down journey time, it exposes travellers to the perils of Romania's reckless drivers. There are numerous airports around the country and those wishing to see as much as possible in a short space of time should consider taking domestic flights, which connect the most important places of interest.

WHEN TO VISIT

Spring and autumn are the best seasons to visit Romania, with warm, sunny days and cool nights. The capital, Bucharest, becomes unbearable in summer, when most residents escape to the coast or the hills, where temperatures are 10–15 degrees lower. The months of September and October are the best time to go hiking in Transylvania.

DOCUMENTATION

Since Romania's accession to the European Union (EU) in January 2007, EU citizens no longer require a visa and can enter the country with a valid passport or identity card. Citizens of the US, Canada, Australia and New Zealand can stay in Romania for up to 90 days without a visa, provided they show a valid passport. Citizens of other countries such as Russia, Albania, Bosnia and Herzegovina, Serbia, Montenegro and Macedonia require a visa.

VISITOR INFORMATION

Bucharest does not have a tourist information centre yet so visitors must rely on guide books, tourist websites or local English-language publications such as **In Your Pocket**, which provides up-to-date listings and is distributed at bars, restaurants and hotels. The guide also has a free website. City maps can be found at bookshops, kiosks and petrol stations. Most tourist destinations have tourist offices that provide brochures; they can also arrange car rental and hotel reservations.

HEALTH AND SECURITY

Although no vaccinations are officially required for travel to Romania, it is recommended that visitors are immunized against tetanus, hepatitis A, diphtheria and typhoid as well as polio. Medical services are are free of charge to EU citizens carrying their European Health Insurance Card (EHIC). However,

standards are not always high, so visitors are advised to take out medical insurance to cover private treatment. There have been no instances of malaria in Romania, but mosquitoes can be a problem around the Danube Delta in summer; repellent is recommended. However, there have been cases of rabies in recent years, and street dogs should be given a wide berth. For medical emergencies, it is best to go to the **Emergency Clinic Hospital** in Bucharest or in Braşov.

Violent crime against visitors is non-existent in Romania, but pickpockets can be a problem on crowded public transport in Bucharest and other cities. Travellers are advised to be vigilant and keep their valuables in a money belt or bag. When travelling on overnight trains, doors to sleeping compartments should always be locked and bags guarded.

FACILITIES FOR THE DISABLED

Public awareness of the needs of the disabled is low, but has improved in recent years. Hotels in bigger cities are more likely to have facilities than smaller hotels.

BANKING AND CURRENCY

The Romanian currency is the leu. Although most foreign currencies can be exchanged at banks, exchange bureaus and larger hotels, euros and dollars are preferred. Traveller's cheques are accepted only at major banks and hotels in the bigger cities and towns. Banks are open from 9am to 5pm Monday to Friday.

ATMs can be found in most places, but are less common in the more remote areas; visitors to these places are advised to carry sufficient cash. Similarly, credit cards can be relied upon only in larger hotels, restaurants, petrol stations and shops.

COMMUNICATIONS

Public telephones can be found across the country, and are operated with a

THE CLIMATE OF ROMANIA

The country has hot, dry summers with temperatures soaring up to 35° C (95° F) in June and July. Autumn is cool but dry, and beautiful when the fields and trees are colourful. Winters can be bitterly cold, with temperatures dipping as low as -8° C (18° F) in January. Snowfalls usually start in mid-December and continue until March.

BUCHAREST			
	29/84		
18/64	16/61	18/64	
5/41		6/43	
0°C 32°F			1/34
			-1/30
6 hrs	11 hrs	5 hrs	2 hrs
59 mm	53 mm	29 mm	46 mm
month Apr	Jul	Oct	Jan

Romtelecom card sold at post offices such as the **Bucharest Main Post Office** and at newspaper kiosks. Mobile phones with roaming will function everywhere, but those visitors staying longer in the country are advised to buy a local pre-paid SIM to reduce the cost of calls. Even the smallest towns usually have at least one Internet café. **Green Hours** in Bucharest and **Cyber Café** in Braşov are among these. Hotels, cafés and restaurants in larger cities often provide Wi-Fi access for those with laptops.

ARRIVING BY AIR

Bucharest's two international airports are both north of the centre. The smaller Aurel Vlaicu (Băneasa) airport is closer and is used by budget airlines such as **Wizzair**. Larger carriers, such as Romania's national airline **TAROM**, use the bigger Henri Coandă Otopeni airport, which lies 16 km (10 miles) from the centre. Sibiu, Timişoara, Cluj-Napoca and Constanţa all have international airports served by less frequent flights.

RAIL TRAVEL

Most international and domestic trains arrive and depart from Bucharest's Gara de Nord, which lies north of the centre. There are four classes of Romanian train – Intercity is the quickest and most comfortable; Rapid and Accelerat tend to stop more frequently; Personal trains are slow, uncomfortable and best avoided. The first three categories require seat reservations. Although it is not yet possible to book tickets online, the national railway website, **CFR**, has a railway timetable for the whole country. Visitors can book tickets through the agency **Wasteels**, which has an office in Bucharest.

TRAVELLING BY BUS

Instead of a central bus station, Bucharest has six smaller bus stations located around the edges of the city. Of these, **Filaret Bus Station** serves Thessaloniki, Athens and southeastern Romania; **Bucureşti Militari** serves northern destinations includ-ing Sibiu; **C&I Bus Terminal**

serves Braşov and Târges Mureş. Buses also leave for various destinations around the country from opposite Gara de Nord.

Tickets for local buses, trams and trolley buses can be bought at street kiosks and should be validated once on board.

TRAVELLING BY CAR

Driving in Romania is an unsettling experience, as Romanian drivers are very impatient, relying on tail-gating and frequent use of horns to intimidate other road users. In rural areas, horses and carts are a major hazard, particularly at night when they may not have lights. Drivers are required to carry an EU or international licence, Green Card insurance or its equivalent and vehicle registration documents. Car hire is available in most towns and cities. Major rental companies are: **Ecoline Car Rental**, **Prima** and **PanTravel**.

Taxis are also plentiful in bigger towns and cities. However, passengers should insist on the meter being used, or agree on a fare in advance.

DIRECTORY

DOCUMENTATION

www.ec.europa.eu

EMBASSIES AND CONSULATES

Australia
14–18, Buzeşti St,
Bucharest.
Tel (21) 316 7558.

United Kingdom
24 Jules Michelet,
Bucharest.
Tel (21) 201 7200.

United States
7–9, Tudor Arghezi St,
Bucharest.
Tel (21) 200 3300.

VISITOR INFORMATION

www.romaniatourism.com

In Your Pocket
www.inyourpocket.com

EMERGENCIES

Ambulance, Police
Tel 112.

HEALTH AND SECURITY

Emergency Clinic Hospital
Calea Floreasca 8,
Bucharest.
Tel (021) 599 2300.
Calea Bucureşti 25-27,
Braşov.
Tel (0268) 320 022.

COMMUNICATIONS

Bucharest Main Post Office
St Matei Millo 10,
Bucharest.

Cyber Café
St Republicii 58, Braşov.

Green Hours
Calea Victoriei 120,
Bucharest.

ARRIVING BY AIR

TAROM
www.tarom.ro

Wizzair
www.wizzair.com

RAIL TRAVEL

CFR
www.cfr.ro

Wasteels
Tel (021) 317 0369.
www.triptkts.ro

TRAVELLING BY BUS

Bucureşti Militari
141 Iuliu Maniu, Bucharest.
Tel (021) 220 8440.

C&I Bus Terminal
35 Ritmului, Bucharest.
Tel (021) 250 8669.

Filaret Bus Station
1 Gara Filaret Square,
Bucharest.
Tel (021) 336 0692.

TRAVELLING BY CAR

Ecoline Car Rental
Al Vlahuta St 10,
Braşov.
Tel (0268) 546 137.
www.ecoline.ro

PanTravel
St Grozavescu 13,
Cluj-Napoca.
Tel (0264) 420 516.
www.pantravel.ro

Prima
11 C Robescu, Ap. 10,
Sector 3, Bucharest.
Tel (021) 316 1080.
www.primarent.ro

Shopping & Entertainment

From small, busy markets to upmarket malls, Romania offers great shopping opportunities. Bucharest is by far the best place for most shopping needs. However, towns and villages often sell regional crafts and produce not found elsewhere. Bucharest is also the entertainment capital, hosting a wide range of classical music concerts, theatre, opera and ballet while the ever-expanding number of bars and clubs contribute to a lively nightlife. The country's wealth of natural beauty makes it very attractive to outdoor enthusiasts. Its mountains cater for all hiking levels, with well-marked routes for experienced walkers as well as organized trips.

OPENING HOURS

Local shops usually open from 9 or 10am to around 6 or 8pm on weekdays. Larger department stores stay open all day on Saturdays, while most shopping malls open from 10am to 10pm daily. Food stores open from 8am to 8pm Monday to Saturday but on Sundays they open only from 8:30am to 1pm.

MARKETS

Most towns have daily fruit and vegetable markets which offer an intriguing insight into local life. Bucharest's main markets are at Piața Obor and Piața Amzei. In rural areas, weekly markets are colourful affairs, with traders arriving in horsecarts from outlying areas, bringing home-grown produce and, sometimes, crafts such as wooden utensils and embroidered shawls.

MALLS

Bucharest has a host of shopping malls ranging from the country's largest, **Plaza Romania**, with 150 shops and an 11-screen cinema, to the central **Unirii Shopping Centre**, which was the exclusive preserve of the party elite during Communist times. These tend to sell well-known clothing brands at prices similar to other European cities. Bigger towns such as Timișoara, Brașov and Constanța also have large modern malls. **Iulius Mall Timișoara** has an ice rink during winter.

ANTIQUES

The Lipscani area of Bucharest, between Unity Square and University Square, is known for its numerous antique and second-hand shops, and is the best place to hunt for rarities and obscure Communist memorabilia.

GIFTS AND SOUVENIRS

Some of the best souvenirs can be found at the outdoor Village Museum and the Museum of the Romanian peasant *(see pp577)* in Bucharest; both stock a range of original crafts. **Romartizana**, in Bucharest, also has a good selection of crafts, and there are several small shops selling glassware, porcelain and hand-crafted crystal clustered around the courtyard of **Curtea Sticlarilor**. Textile weaving is popular across the country; embroidered rugs, folk costumes, tablecloths and wall hangings are found in most souvenir shops. Reproductions of religious icons are also worth looking out for.

Several high-end jewellery shops such as **Cellini** are located along Bucharest's B-dul Magheru and B-dul Balcescu. The bigger shopping malls also stock jewellery.

FOOD AND DRINK

Romanian cuisine is noted for its *ciorba* (soup), which is traditionally made with *ciorba de burta* (tripe), *ciorba de perisoare* (meatballs) or *ciorba de legume* (vegetables). Main dishes lack variety and tend to consist of grilled meat, but spicy stews such as *tocăniță* are worth trying. *Sarmale* is a delicious dish made of stuffed vine or cabbage leaves, which is found all over the Balkans.

Romania is one of the world's largest producers of plums and turns most of its harvest into the enormously popular, and potent *țuică* (plum brandy). Wine is also produced in large quantities; the sweet *moldavian grasă* and *tămâioasă* are two of the best wines in the country. Romania has a reputable beer brewing industry and Ciucaș, from Brașov, is popular.

BOOKS AND MUSIC

For English-language books in Bucharest, visitors should head for either **Nautilus**, which has a particularly good range of fiction, or the **Anthony Frost English Bookshop**. Those in search of traditional Romanian folk music should try Bucharest's Village Museum shop or **Muzica** in the city centre. The huge Sony Music Centre in the Unirii Shopping Centre has a good selection of mainstream music.

LISTINGS

Șapte Seri is Bucharest's best free weekly events guide. Written in a mixture of English and Romanian, its website has a full English-language version. **In Your Pocket Bucharest** provides comprehensive entertainment listings. Those who understand Romanian can consult *Time Out Bucharest*.

NIGHTLIFE

The country's nightlife is best experienced in Bucharest, where hundreds of clubs and bars cater to every taste and budget. Popular clubs with live music include **Club A** and **Arcade Café**. Larger towns and cities with a substantial population of students, such as Brașov, Timișoara and Cluj-Napoca, also offer good nightlife. In summer, numerous seasonal clubs and bars open in Constanța to entertain the influx of both Romanian and foreign visitors to the coast.

THEATRE

Bucharest is home to the country's modern **National Theatre** with regular plays in Romanian. Many smaller theatres are scattered around the city and occasionally feature foreign-language productions.

CLASSICAL MUSIC AND OPERA

The **Romanian Atheneum** in Bucharest is the best place to catch performances by the world class George Enescu Philharmonic Orchestra, which plays most days of the week. Opera fans should visit the **Bucharest National Opera**, **Opera Braşov** or **Cluj-Napoca National Opera**, which stage both opera and ballet. Timişoara and Constanţa also host regular performances.

FESTIVALS

In June every year, Bucharest's Village Museum holds a **Traditional Crafts Fair** with participants from all over the country. **Bucharest of Old**, in July, is a celebration of the city as it was in the 19th century, involving a street procession in traditional costume with horse-drawn carriages.

The atmospheric **Sighişoara Medieval Festival**, which takes place in the last week of July, is certainly worth visiting. Local culture is celebrated at folk festivals throughout August – the Romanian Folk Art Festival is one of the biggest. Sibiu hosts an **International Jazz Festival** in May. If visiting in late October, Halloween in Transylvania, revolving around Count Dracula, is not to be missed.

OUTDOOR ACTIVITIES

The country's most popular ski resort, **Poiana Braşov**, is located 12 km (7 miles) south of Braşov. Its runs range from easy to medium levels and ski equipment can be hired on site. The season lasts from December until March.

Romania's abundance of mountainous terrain offers endless possibilities for hikers, who usually head for the well-marked paths in the Făgăraş range. Bird-watchers should visit the Danube Delta, which attracts numerous species of rare birds; bird-watching boat trips can be arranged through various agencies in Tulcea. **Outdoor Holidays** organizes mountain-biking, bird-watching, hiking, horse riding, caving and rafting trips all over Romania.

DIRECTORY

MALLS

Iulius Mall Timişoara
Str Aristide Demetriade nr. 1, Timişoara.

Plaza Romania
Bulevardul Timişoara 26, Bucharest.

Unirii Shopping Centre
Piaţa Unirii 1, Bucharest.

GIFTS AND SOUVENIRS

Cellini
Bulevardul N Bălcescu 16, Bucharest.
Tel (021) 312 2202.

Curtea Sticlarilor
Str Selari 9–11, Bucharest.
Tel (021) 314 3228.

Romartizana
Calea Victoriei 16–20, Bucharest.
Tel (021) 313 1465.

BOOKS AND MUSIC

Anthony Frost English Bookshop
Calea Victoriei 45, Bucharest.
Tel (021) 311 5138.
www.librariaengleza.ro

Muzica
Calea Victoriei 41–43, Bucharest.
Tel (021) 313 9674.

Nautilus
Str Arh. Ion Mincu 17, Bucharest.
Tel (021) 222 5030.
www.nautilus.ro

LISTINGS

In Your Pocket Bucharest
www.inyourpocket.com

Şapte Seri
www.sapteseri.ro

NIGHTLIFE

Arcade Café
Str Smardan 30, Bucharest.
Tel (021) 314 5066.

Club A
Str Blănari 14, Bucharest.
Tel (021) 313 5592.

THEATRE

National Theatre
Bulevardul Bălcescu 2, Bucharest.
Tel (021) 314 7171.

CLASSICAL MUSIC AND OPERA

Bucharest National Opera
Bulevardul Kogalniceanu 70, Bucharest.
Tel (021) 314 6980.
www.operanb.ro

Cluj-Napoca National Opera
Piaţa Ştefan cel Mare 24, Cluj-Napoca.
Tel (0264) 597 175.
www.operacluj.ro

Opera Braşov
Str Bisericii Romane Nr. 51, Braşov.
Tel (0268) 415 990.
www.opera-brasov.ro

Romanian Atheneum
Str Franklin 1–3, Bucharest.
Tel (021) 315 2567.
www.fge.org.ro

FESTIVALS

Bucharest of Old
www.festivaluidimuzicaveche

International Jazz Festival
www.sibiujazz.ro

Sighişoara Medieval Festival
www.sighisoara-medieval.ro

Traditional Crafts Fair
www.muzeul-satului.ro

OUTDOOR ACTIVITIES

Outdoor Holidays
4th, Aleea Rotunda, BL H6; Apartment no 26, 032705, Bucharest.
Tel (021) 643 2402.
www.outdoorholidays.com

Poiana Braşov
Tel (0268) 417 866.
www.poiana-brasov.com

Where to Stay in Romania

Most Romanian towns and cities still have at least one Socialist-era relic recalling former Soviet splendour, but these are now outnumbered by new hotels providing high standards of comfort. From historic lodgings to budget-friendly hostels, the country has plenty of accommodation to cater for its influx of visitors in recent years.

PRICE CATEGORIES
Price categories are for a standard double room per night during the high season, including tax and service. Breakfast is not included unless specified.

ⓛ Under 110 lei
ⓛⓛ 110–220 lei
ⓛⓛⓛ 220–320 lei
ⓛⓛⓛⓛ 320–540 lei
ⓛⓛⓛⓛⓛ Over 540 lei

BUCHAREST

Funky Chicken Hostel
ⓛ

Str Gen. Berthelot 63 **Tel** *(021) 312 1425* **Fax** *(021) 610 2214* **Rooms** *4*   **Map** *D3*

Crammed into several rooms on the ground floor of a residential block, the Funky Chicken Hostel is both lively and chaotic. It has all the usual facilities, including Internet connection in all rooms and is run by cheerful staff. **www.funkychickenhostel.com**

Athenee Palace Hilton Bucharest
🄿 🍴 ⛱ 🛎 🛗 🗄 ♿   ⓛⓛⓛⓛⓛ

1–3 Episcopiei Str Sector 1, 10292 **Tel** *(021) 303 3777* **Fax** *(021) 315 3813* **Rooms** *271*   **Map** *E3*

Part of the international Hilton chain, the Athenee Palace effortlessly meets its five-star rating. Gleaming marble floors and columns give the lavish lobby a Classical feel, while the rooms are modern, spacious and comfortable. Facilities include a sauna, gym and basement pool. A good top-end choice. **www.hilton.com**

Golden Tulip
🄿 🍴 🛎 🛗 🗄 ♿   ⓛⓛⓛⓛ

166 Calea Victoriei, 10096 **Tel** *(021) 212 5558* **Fax** *(021) 212 5121* **Rooms** *83*   **Map** *D3*

Centrally located, the Golden Tulip offers spacious, comfortable rooms with modern interiors. High-speed Internet access is provided. Generous breakfasts are served in the top-floor restaurant from where guests can enjoy sweeping views of the city. **www.goldentulipbucharest.com**

FURTHER AFIELD Butterfly-Villa Hostel
⛱ 🄿 🗄   ⓛⓛ

Str Strbei Vodă 96, 10118 **Tel** *(021) 314 7595* **Rooms** *7*

Run by a pair of German ex-backpackers, the Butterfly-Villa is Bucharest's best budget option, with both dormitory beds and private rooms. Wireless Internet, tea and coffee and laundry are free and the breakfast is excellent. Pick-ups from the railway station and the airport can be arranged. **www.villabutterfly.com**

FURTHER AFIELD Tania
🄿 🗄   ⓛⓛⓛ

5 Selari Str 3rd District, 30067 **Tel** *(031) 104 2083* **Fax** *(021) 319 2756* **Rooms** *16*

Located in the heart of the Old Town, the Tania is a modern, mid-range hotel with clean, comfortable and tastefully decorated rooms. There is also the option of a smart top-floor maisonette with an office. The staff is polite, helpful and efficient. **www.taniahotel.ro**

FURTHER AFIELD Andy Hotel
🄿 🍴 🗄   ⓛⓛⓛⓛ

Str Witing 2 **Tel** *(021) 3003050* **Fax** *(021) 300 3052* **Rooms** *49*

Situated just a short distance from the railway station, this smart modern hotel offers immaculately clean and comfortable en suite rooms. Cheaper rooms with shared bathrooms are also available. Wireless Internet is also provided. **www.andyhotels.ro**

REST OF ROMANIA

BRAN The Guest House / Villa Jo
⛱ 🄿 🗄   ⓛⓛⓛ

Str Principala 365B, 507025 **Tel** *(0745) 179 475* **Fax** *(026) 831 6836* **Rooms** *6*

Set amidst lovely lawns and flowerbeds, the Guest House/ Villa Jo lies just a few minutes from Bran Castle *(see pp580–81)*. The rooms are spotless and the ground floor kitchen is open to guests. The complex has two new well-furnished guesthouses offering high standards of comfort. **www.guesthouse.ro**

BRAȘOV Casa Wagner
🄿 🗄   ⓛⓛⓛⓛⓛ

Piața Sfatului 5, 500031 **Tel** *(0268) 411 253* **Fax** *(0268) 410 871* **Rooms** *12*

Located on the main square, Casa Wagner is housed in a 15th-century building, formerly a German bank, with many of its original features intact. Its large rooms feature exposed beams and period furnishings; some face the Black Church. Incredibly helpful staff ensure a delightful stay. **www.casa-wagner.eu**

Map References *see map of Bucharest pp570–71*

BRAŞOV Villa Prato

Str St. O. Iosif 2, 500041 **Tel** *(0268) 473 371* **Fax** *(0268) 473 373* **Rooms** *6*

This wonderfully restored villa in the heart of Braşov has been turned into a delightful hotel offering spacious modern rooms with antique styling. Breakfast is served in a glass conservatory that overlooks the Old Town. Advance booking is advised. **www.villaprato.ro**

CLUJ-NAPOCA Capitolina

Str Victor Babeş 35, 400012 **Tel** *(0264) 450 490* **Fax** *(0264) 450 490* **Rooms** *24*

This smart new hotel lacks atmosphere, but the rooms are spacious and comfortable and it is just a few minutes from the city centre. Guests can also opt for a VIP suite with a hydro-massage facility. The standard rooms are good value. The staff is polite and efficient. **www.hotelcapitolina.ro**

CLUJ-NAPOCA City Central

Str Victor Babeş 13, 400012 **Tel** *(0264) 439 959* **Fax** *(0264) 439 951* **Rooms** *34*

The City Central's location, along with its cleanliness and good service, compensates to some extent for its lack of atmosphere. Modern, functional furniture fills the rooms, which are all provided with Internet and cable TV. The hotel also provides video surveyed car parking. **www.cityhotels.ro**

CONSTANŢA Voila

Str Callatis 22, 900744 **Tel** *(0241) 508 002* **Fax** *(0241) 508 007* **Rooms** *15*

Located close to the seafront, the Voila is a delightful small hotel run by a friendly team of staff. The modern interiors are furnished with some antique ironwork flourishes and several rooms have sea views. Its pleasant top-floor restaurant has a large terrace that overlooks the beach. Great service and good value. **www.voilahotel.ro**

CURTEA DE ARGES Confarg

Str Adresa Negru Voda 5, 115300 **Tel** *(0248) 728 020* **Fax** *(0248) 506 171* **Rooms** *22*

The three-star Confarg is a decent mid-range option with clean, spacious rooms as well as a sauna and fitness facilities. Overall it is a little dated, but is kept spotless by helpful, hard-working staff. Internet connection is provided. **www.confarg.ro**

PELEŞ CASTLE Bastion

2A Aleea Pelesului, Sinaia 106100 **Tel** *(0244) 315 595* **Fax** *(0244) 315 595* **Rooms** *12*

This recently renovated residence allows visitors to stay in the immediate vicinity of Peleş Castle *(see pp582–3)*. The mansion, with a grand lobby, successfully recreates a stately regal atmosphere. The rooms are bright, comfortable and spacious. **www.hotelbastion.ro**

SIGHIŞOARA Casa cu Cerb

Str Scolii 1, 545400 **Tel** *(0265) 774 625* **Fax** *(0256) 777 349* **Rooms** *10*

One of Sighişoara's oldest buildings, the Casa cu Cerb (House of the Stag) is located at the centre of the Old Town. This delightful hotel features barrel-vaulted ceilings, exposed brick walls, woodwork and plenty of period-style furniture. Staff is reasonably efficient. **www.casacucerb.ro**

SIGHIŞOARA Sighişoara

Str Scolii 4-6, 545400 **Tel** *(0265) 771 000* **Fax** *(0256) 777 788* **Rooms** *29*

Situated in the medieval heart of the Old Town, Sighişoara is housed in a wonderful 16th-century building. Its lovely rooms have vaulted ceilings, exposed original beams and antique-style furnishings. The attractive cellar restaurant is very atmospheric. **www.sighisoarahotels.ro**

SUCEAVA Bukovina

Str Ana Ipatescu 5, 720026 **Tel** *(0230) 217 048* **Fax** *(0230) 520 250* **Rooms** *116*

One of Romania's Socialist relics, the Bukovina has an exquisite 1970s wood-panelled lobby. All rooms have private bathrooms and superb views. Guests can choose between refurbished or non-refurbished accommodation. All rooms are provided with wireless Internet. **www.hotelbucovina.ro**

TÂRGES MUREŞ Concordia

Piata Trandafirilor 45, 540053 **Tel** *(0265) 260 602* **Fax** *(0265) 269 666* **Rooms** *34*

Concealed behind a classic 19th-century façade, Concordia is one of the city's smartest modern hotels, offering spacious and comfortable bedrooms and bathrooms. A small fitness centre and pool are available. The hotel restaurant *(see p599)* is highly recommended. **www.hotelconcordia.ro**

TIMIŞOARA Timişoara

Str Maraseşti 1-3, 300086 **Tel** *(0256) 498 862* **Fax** *(0256) 498 852* **Rooms** *150*

Located in the heart of Timişoara, this hotel has a relaxing and casual atmosphere. All rooms are spacious and well equipped, with a minibar and TV and offer excellent views of the city. Internet access is provided. **www.hoteltimisoara.ro**

TULCEA Delta

Str Isaccei 2, 820169 **Tel** *(0240) 514 720* **Fax** *(0240) 516 260* **Rooms** *117*

Situated on the waterfront with great views of the Danube, the Delta's Socialist-era interior will appeal to those seeking a flavour of Romania's Soviet past. It offers a decent range of facilities including a reasonably sized pool and sauna. A travel agency in the lobby organizes river tours. **www.hoteldelta.eu**

Key to Symbols *see back cover flap*

Where to Eat in Romania

Romanian restaurants rely heavily on the Italians for culinary inspiration – almost every restaurant menu features pizza and pasta. Bucharest has several international restaurants but the choice narrows outside the capital. Specialities include *ghiveci calugaresc* (vegetable stew) and *tochitură ardelenească* (Transylvanian stew).

PRICE CATEGORIES
Based on the price per person of a three-course meal with half a bottle of wine, including cover charge, service and tax.

ⓛ Under 60 lei
ⓛⓛ 60–70 lei
ⓛⓛⓛ 70–80 lei
ⓛⓛⓛⓛ 80–90 lei
ⓛⓛⓛⓛⓛ Over 90 lei

BUCHAREST

Caru Cu Bere ⓛⓛⓛ
Str Stavropoleos 5, 30081 **Tel** *(021) 313 7560*   **Map** E4

Built in 1899, the elegant Caru Cu Bere has retained much of its original style and features a high vaulted ceiling, stained-glass windows, ornate wooden balustrades and intricate floral murals. The menu is extensive and the wine list exhaustive.

Isoletta ⓛⓛⓛⓛ
Şoseaua Nordului 7, 14102 **Tel** *(021) 232 2177*   **Map** F1

The Italian-owned Isoletta has gained a reputation for its high-quality fish dishes prepared by an Italian chef, with fresh stock delivered from Italy twice a week. The restaurant is partly managed by a well-known Romanian actress and model, which adds to its appeal.

Trattoria Il Calcio ⓛⓛⓛⓛⓛ
Str B Franklin1–3, 10287 **Tel** *(0732) 528 140*   **Map** E3

Housed in a delightful 19th-century building opposite the Royal Palace *(see p576)*, the Trattoria Il Calcio offers an excellent choice of well-prepared pizza and pasta dishes. Comfortable chairs and shaded outdoor seating make for a relaxing environment.

FURTHER AFIELD Rossetya ⓛⓛⓛⓛ
Str Dimitrie Bolintineanu No. 9, 21061 **Tel** *(031) 805 9199*

The inviting interior of the Rossetya recreates a classic 19th-century Romanian restaurant. It specializes in the preparation of intricate traditional Romanian dishes and has a broad-ranging menu that covers vegetarian broths as well as duck, pork and mutton recipes.

REST OF ROMANIA

BRAŞOV Panoramic ⓛⓛ
Tampa Mountain **Tel** *(0268) 475 349*

The 955-m (3,133-ft) high Tampa Mountain looms over Braşov's sprawling streets. The best place to enjoy the view is from the Panoramic restaurant, which exploits its position with enormous glass windows, although it offers no more than a standard range of Romanian dishes. It can be reached by road or cable car.

BRAŞOV Casa Hirscher ⓛⓛⓛ
Piaţa Sfatului Nr. 12–14, 500025 **Tel** *(0268) 410 502*

Originally built in the mid-16th century as a residence for Apollonia Hirscher, the city judge's wife, the Casa Hirscher restaurant offers an imaginative choice of dishes served by polite staff in elegant surroundings. The interior is decorated with copies of ancient frescoes. The soups are particularly good and the wine list is excellent.

CLUJ-NAPOCA Ethno ⓛ
Str Memorandum 21, 400114 **Tel** *(0264) 590 501*

The restaurant's shaded outdoor seating fills the Ethnographic Museum's pleasant courtyard, while its superb medieval-style interior consists of a series of vaulted cellar rooms furnished with solid wooden tables. Grilled meat and pizza feature heavily on the menu.

CLUJ-NAPOCA Baracca ⓛⓛⓛⓛ
Str Napoca 8A, 400009 **Tel** *(0732) 155 177*

This funky restaurant features exposed brick walls, stripped wooden floors and enormous white shell-shaped lampshades. The atmosphere is pleasant and the clientele smart. The menu offers a good range of international cuisine as well as Italian staples.

Map References *see map of Bucharest pp570–71*

CONSTANŢA New Pizzico

Piaţa Ovidiu 7, 900745 **Tel** *(0241) 615 555*

The high ceilings and classic furnishings of the New Pizzico evoke a classy Italian restaurant. Although the standards are high, the reasonably priced menu is a straightforward mix of Romanian and Italian cuisine. The place is very popular with locals.

CONSTANŢA New Safari

Str Aristide Karatzali 1, 900746 **Tel** *(0241) 555 571*

One of the best located restaurants in town, New Safari has a wide open terrace directly overlooking the sea and a pleasant, simple interior with rough brick walls. Plenty of international dishes feature on the menu along with a good range of fish dishes.

PELEŞ CASTLE Cutitu d'Argint

Aleea Pelesului 2, Sinaia 106100 **Tel** *(0244) 312 243*

Surrounded by a forest and furnished to resemble a medieval inn, the Cutitu d'Argint fits in well with the neighbouring Peleş Castle *(see pp582–3)*. Its long wooden tables, low-hanging chandeliers and grand fireplace are the perfect setting in which to devour one of the restaurant's specialities: whole roasted piglet.

SIBIU La Trattoria

Str Brukental, 550178 **Tel** *(0730) 002 249*

This charming Italian restaurant has a great location, with outdoor tables on a cobbled street right next to the Brukenthal Museum. Its interior is intimate and welcoming and the menu offers a wide range of pizza and pasta as well as fish dishes.

SIGHIŞOARA Casa Vlad Dracul

Str Cositorarilor 5, 545400 **Tel** *(0256) 771 596*

This 15th-century house is popularly believed to have been the birthplace of Vlad the Impaler *(see p586)*, after murals depicting his likeness were uncovered here in the 20th century. It now houses a large and rather gloomy restaurant with exaggerated Gothic decor serving mid-range international cuisine.

SIGHIŞOARA Sighişoara Hotel

Str Scolii 4–6, 545400 **Tel** *(0256) 771 000*

Housed in an atmospheric 400-year-old building, the restaurant lies deep in the cellars of the Sighişoara Hotel and features exposed stonework and subtle Gothic decor. Meals are prepared to a high standard, with specialties such as roast duck with cabbage.

SUCEAVA Taco Loco

Vasile Bumbac 3, 72003 **Tel** *(0230) 220 032*

Situated just off the main street, the Taco Loco's Mexican menu of fajitas, burittos and chile con carne offers a refreshing alternative to the ubiquitous Romanian and Italian dishes elsewhere. Decorated in Mexican style inside, it also has outdoor seating in a secluded courtyard.

SUCEAVA Casa de Piatra

Str Humorului 961A, 717030 **Tel** *(0230) 526 854*

With a capacity of 450, the lovely Casa de Piatra is more suited to wedding parties than intimate dinners, but the cuisine is of a high standard. Typical sumptuous Bucovinian dishes can be sampled along with numerous other international options.

TÂRGU MUREŞ Leo

Piaţa Trandafirilor 43, 540053 **Tel** *(0265) 214 999*

Located on the central square, this simple restaurant split over two floors attracts a constant flow of diners. It offers a good selection of local dishes, pasta and pizza, all served in generous portions. The staff is extremely helpful and polite. Regular culinary art exhibitions are also held at the restaurant.

TÂRGU MUREŞ Concordia

Piaţa Trandafirilor 45, 540053 **Tel** *(0265) 260 602*

The Concordia is refreshingly modern in its design and has an excellent international menu; the beef steak is highly recommended. A separate Chinese menu prepared by a resident Chinese chef is also on offer. The restaurant can be accessed via the hotel lobby *(see p597)*.

TIMIŞOARA Cucina Moderna

Str Socrate 12, 300552 **Tel** *(0256) 202 405*

The Cucina Moderna is an inviting, family-run restaurant with an emphasis on both Romanian and Italian cuisine. The Italian-trained chef prepares exquisite daily specials to supplement the main menu, which features some delicious soups and an array of traditional drinks.

TULCEA Made in Italy

Tulcea Harbour

Decked out with pretty flower baskets and consisting of a few outdoor tables aboard an old ship in Tulcea's harbour, Made in Italy is a lovely spot for a meal. The cuisine is predictably Italian and features dishes that are reasonably good.

Key to Symbols *see back cover flap*

BULGARIA

Bulgaria's stunning scenery and Mediterranean climate have made it one of Europe's fastest-growing tourist destinations. Though famous for its Black Sea beaches and scintillating ski resorts, it offers the visitor many further rewards through the sheer diversity of its natural beauty spots, archaeological sites and picture-postcard villages.

With its warm climate and fertile soil, Bulgaria has attracted settlers from ancient times and remnants of former civilizations can be found everywhere, from prehistoric burial grounds to Ottoman mosques. Among its natural attributes, its sandy beaches are captivating and the mountains provide scope for hiking and skiing. The country's proud folk heritage contrasts with its recent transformation into a modern European nation, making Bulgaria a vibrant and invigorating destination.

HISTORY

Archaeological discoveries have shown that Neolithic people were living in the region as early as 5500 BC.

By 1000 BC, South Eastern Europe was falling under the Thracians, who established tribal states across Bulgaria, Romania and northern Greece. By AD 50, however, the Romans had taken control of the region. The Roman Empire was split in the 5th century and Bulgaria became part of the eastern Byzantine half. Migrating Slav tribes were allowed to settle and live peacefully throughout the region.

The Bulgars, a Turkic tribe from Central Asia, crossed the Danube in 681 and soon fused with the Slavs already living there, creating the Bulgarian nation. Bulgarian power reached its peak under Tsar Simeon (r. 893–927), who extended

The colourful Rose Festival being celebrated in central Bulgaria

◁ Beautiful 19th-century frescoes in Rila Monastery, south of Sofia the borders almost as far as Constantinople. However, a Byzantine resurgence halted further expansion.

The Ottoman Turks conquered Bulgaria in the 1390s and ruled it for almost 500 years, cutting the country off from Western Europe and weakening its language and culture. An upsurge of Bulgarian culture known as the National Revival took place in the 19th century, and young patriots planned a revolt. The so-called April Rising began in 1876 but was quashed by the Ottomans.

Bulgarian soldiers during the Second Balkan War, 1913

Outraged by the massacre that took place, public support in Russia and Western Europe took up the Bulgarian cause. Russia declared war on the Ottomans in April 1877, resulting in the creation of an independent Bulgarian state. The new Bulgaria was initially intended to include Macedonia as well but this was prevented by the European powers at the Congress of Berlin in 1878.

Eager to force the Ottomans out of Macedonia, Bulgaria was drawn into an alliance with Serbia and Greece.

In the First Balkan War of 1912, the three Balkan states defeated the Ottomans but disagreed on how to divide their conquests. Bulgaria declared war on Serbia and Greece but was defeated in the Second Balkan War of 1913.

In 1941, two years after the outbreak of World War II, Bulgaria joined Germany. However, it switched sides in 1944, hoping in vain to head off an invasion by the Soviet Red Army. Supported by the Soviets, the Bulgarian Communists staged a coup and ruled the country for the next 45 years. The Communist regime disintegrated in 1989 but economic collapse soon followed. Bulgaria's entry into the EU in 2007 marked a new phase in the country's voyage from post-Communist chaos to political and economic stability.

KEY DATES IN BULGARIAN HISTORY

1000–800 BC The Thracians begin to form powerful tribal states in Bulgaria

AD 50 Thracian lands are captured by the Romans

681 The Bulgars conquer the land south of the Danube

930 Rila Monastery is founded by St Ivan of Rila

1393 The Ottomans seize the capital of Bulgaria

1830 The National Revival gains momentum, bringing with it a flowering of the arts

1876 The April Rising

1877–8 The Russo-Turkish War ends in defeat for the Ottomans

1912–13 First Balkan War against the Ottomans

1913 Second Balkan War

1915–18 Bulgaria joins World War I on the German side

1944 Bulgarian Communists, supported by the Soviet Red Army, seize power

1946 Bulgaria becomes a republic

2004 Bulgaria joins NATO

2007 Bulgaria becomes a member of the EU

LANGUAGE AND CULTURE

The country's official language is Bulgarian, a Slavonic language related to Serbian, Russian and Croatian. It is written in the Cyrillic script, although Roman lettering is sometimes used on public signs.

With heritage playing a highly visible role in Bulgarian society, religious holidays, saints' days and folk festivals form the backbone of Bulgaria's festive calendar.

Exploring Bulgaria

Few capitals bear the imprint of history as clearly as Sofia, Bulgaria's largest city. Roman masonry juts from the walls of its churches, while fragments of Byzantine fortifications survive in pedestrian subways. To the south of bustling and sophisticated Sofia are fascinating highland villages such as Bansko and Borovets and the monasteries of Rila and Bachkovo; to the east, on the Black Sea, are the coastal towns of Varna and Nesebûr and the Golden Sands resort; while all over the country, medieval fortresses stand as reminders of Bulgaria's illustrious history. The country's rail network links all the major towns and cities, while rural Bulgaria is accessible by local bus. Taxis can also be used for long-distance journeys if arranged in advance.

Wooden houses along a street in the Old Town, Sozopol

SIGHTS AT A GLANCE

Bachkovo Monastery pp618–19 **7**
Bansko **5**
Borovets **4**
Burgas **17**
Golden Sands **13**
Kaliakra **14**
Koprivshtitsa pp622–3 **9**
Melnik **6**
Nesebûr **16**
Plovdiv pp620–21 **8**
Rila Monastery *pp612–15* **2**
Rila National Park **3**
Sofia pp604–611 **1**
Sozopol **18**
Stone Forest **12**
Sunny Beach **15**
Varna pp628–9 **11**
Veliko Tûrnovo pp624–7 **10**

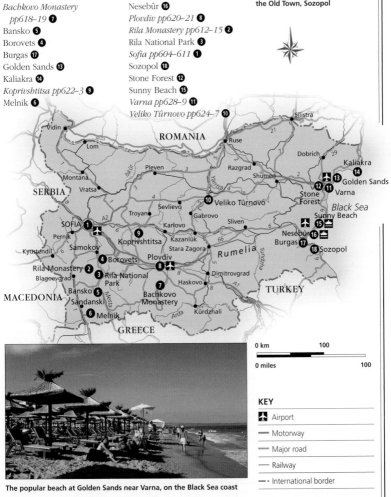

KEY

- ✈ Airport
- — Motorway
- — Major road
- — Railway
- – – International border

The popular beach at Golden Sands near Varna, on the Black Sea coast

For additional map symbols *see back flap*

Sofia ❶

With a population of over one million people, Sofia was founded more than 7,000 years ago and has been the capital of Bulgaria since 1879. Today, the city's historic centre bears witness to the diverse cultural influences that have shaped the country. Orthodox churches and an Art Nouveau synagogue are evidence of its rich religious heritage, while Roman, medieval and Ottoman-era buildings serve as reminders of the city's ancient origins. Adding to the city's grandeur are the monumental public buildings from the Communist period, dotting the downtown squares and intersections. Beyond the city centre, residential suburbs are broken up by attractive swathes of green parkland and the looming presence of Mount Vitosha.

The magnificent Aleksandûr Nevski Memorial Church

KEY

▨	Major sight / Place of interest
✈	Airport
🚆	Railway station
Ⓜ	Metro station
ℹ	Visitor information
🅿	Parking
✚	Church
C	Mosque
▬▬	Motorway
▬▬	Major road
═══	Minor road
▬▬	Pedestrian zone
───	Railway

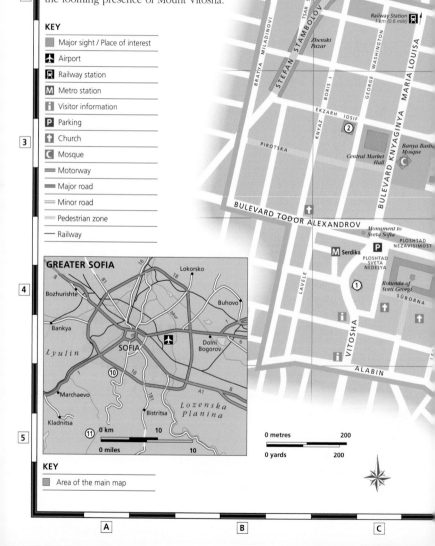

GREATER SOFIA

Lokorsko

Bozhurishte

Buhovo

Bankya

SOFIA ✈

Dolni Bogorov

Lyulin

⑩

Marchaevo

Bistritsa

Kladnitsa

Lozenska Planina

⑪

0 km   10
0 miles   10

KEY

▨ Area of the main map

0 metres   200
0 yards   200

Railway Station
1 km (0.6 mile) 🚆

Zhenski Pazar

Central Market Hall

Banya Bashi Mosque

Monument to Sveta Sofia

PLOSHTAD NEZAVISIMOST

Ⓜ Serdika 🅿

PLOSHTAD SVETA NEDELYA

Rotunda of Sveti Georgi

A   B   C

SIGHTS AT A GLANCE

*Aleksandûr Nevski Memorial
Church see pp608–609* ⑦
Archaeological Museum ③
Church of Sveta Nedelya ①
Church of Sveta Sofia ⑧
Mount Vitosha ⑪
National Art Gallery ④
National Gallery of
Foreign Art ⑨
National History Museum ⑩
Natural History Museum ⑤
Russian Church ⑥
Sofia Synagogue ②

GETTING AROUND

The city centre is easy to explore on foot, although
visitors may need public transport to reach some
outlying museums. An efficient tram network covers the
city centre and the inner suburbs, while buses and
trolleybuses are a convenient way of reaching Sofia's
outer fringes. Taxis are numerous and inexpensive, and
the single metro line runs across the city from northwest
to southeast, connecting a handful of sites of interest.

SEE ALSO

• *Where to Stay* pp636–7

• *Where to Eat* pp639–40

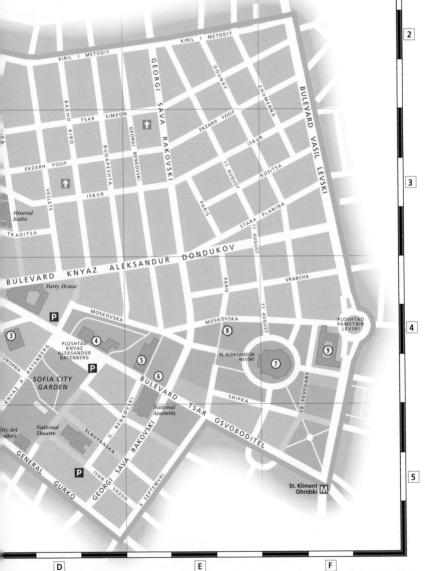

Church of Sveta Nedelya, one of Sofia's most important places of worship

Church of Sveta Nedelya ①
Църква "Света Неделя"

pl. Sveta Nedelya. **Map** C4. **Tel** (02) 987 5748. ☷ 1, 2, 7, 18. ☒

Set on an island in central Sofia, the Church of Sveta Nedelya (Tšurkvata Sveta Nedelya) was built on the site of a 10th-century church and has long been one of the city's principal places of worship. It serves as the seat of the bishops of Sofia and has now been given a cathedral status.

During the Ottoman period it was known as the Church of Sveti Kral – the Blessed King – because it held the relics of Stefan Urosh II Milutin, a 14th-century Serbian ruler who defeated the Bulgarian emperor, Mihail Shishman. The bones, believed to have

miraculous healing powers, are kept in a wooden casket beside the iconostasis. The church was rebuilt between 1856 and 1863, but was almost completely destroyed in 1925, when Communist extremists bombed it during a funeral service attended by Tsar Boris III. The arcades on the north side and the gilt iconostasis remain intact. Frescoes executed in the 1970s and a marble floor added in the 1990s give the interior a contemporary look.

Sofia Synagogue ②
Софийска Синагога

ul. Ekzarh Iosif 16. **Map** C3. **Tel** (02) 983 5085. ☷ 1, 2, 7, 18, 20, 22. Ⓜ Serdika. ◯ 9am–4pm Mon–Fri, 9am–1pm Sat, call in advance.

One of the largest in Europe, this synagogue (Sofiska sinagoga) can hold as many as 1,300 people. Designed by Austrian architect Friedrich Grünanger and completed in 1909, it is home to a brass chandelier weighing over 2,000 kg (4,400 lb). The interior also has some exquisite Moorish mosaics, painted pillars and scalloped arches. A Jewish Museum of History here tells the history of the Jews in Bulgaria. A visit to the museum might not always be possible since it might be closed.

Detail of the ornate Moorish exterior of the Sofia Synagogue

Archaeological Museum ③
Археологически Музей

ul. Sûborna 2. **Map** D4. **Tel** (02) 988 2406. ☷ 1, 2, 7, 18, 20, 22. Ⓜ Serdika. ◯ Nov–Feb: 10am–5pm Tue–Sun. ☒☐ museum annexe.

Many of Bulgaria's finest Thracian, Roman and medieval treasures are preserved in Sofia's Archaeological Museum (Arheologicheski Muzei). The building, once the Grand Mosque (Buyuk Dzhamiya), was built in 1494 and converted into the present museum in 1894. The former prayer hall, a cube-shaped space beneath nine graceful domes, perfectly complements an open-plan display of Greek, Roman and medieval sculpture. The side rooms are devoted to a superb sequence of treasures. Highlights include a finely crafted Golden Burial Mask belonging to a Thracian chieftain of the 5th century BC, a bronze helmet and a delicate golden laurel wreath found near Plovdiv (*see pp620–21).

Golden Burial Mask, Archaeological Museum

The ground floor features Roman finds, including finely carved tombs, while the first floor holds a host of valuable medieval icons and lavishly decorated pottery with animal, bird and floral designs.

National Art Gallery ④
Национална Художествена Галерия

pl. Knyaz Aleksandûr Batenberg 1. **Map** D4. **Tel** (02) 980 3325. ☷ 1, 2, 7, 20, 22. Ⓜ Serdika. ◯ 10am–6pm Tue–Sun. ☒ **Ethnographic Museum Tel** (02) 988 4191. ◯ Mar–Oct: 10am–6pm Tue–Sun; Nov–Feb: 5pm. ☒☐

The imposing National Art Gallery (Natsionalna Hudozhestvena Galeriya) occupies the west wing of the former royal palace. Built in 1873 for Sofia's

Ottoman rulers, it was adapted for the monarchs of independent Bulgaria after 1877. The building's palatial character persists. Many of the exhibition halls have pre-World War I parquet floors and intricate stucco ceilings.

Bulgarian fine art grew out of the icon-painting workshops of the 19th century, and the gallery's exhibition appropriately begins with works by the greatest of all Bulgarian religious artists, Zahari Zograf (*see p612*). His series of realistic portraits shows great psychological insight and effectively launched Bulgarian painting on a modern European course.

The gallery's collection traces the development of Bulgarian painting. Highlights include a room devoted to the work of local Impressionists, and that of Bulgarian painters of the interwar generation, in which modernist styles are fused with traditional native themes. Foremost among them are Vladimir Dimitrov-Maistora, Zlatyu Boyadzhiev and Tsanko Lavrenov. Exhibitions of contemporary art are often held in the gallery's ground floor rooms.

The **Ethnographic Museum** (Etnografski Muzei) in the east wing has a fascinating collection of traditional Bulgarian costumes. It also mounts temporary exhibitions devoted to aspects of Bulgarian folklore. The museum shop offers a range of traditional craft items.

Entrance to the interesting Natural History Museum

Natural History Museum ⑤
Национален Прироаонаучеh Музей

bul. Tsar Osvoboditel 1. **Map** E4.
Tel (02) 987 4195. 🚌 9, 94, 280, 306. Ⓜ Serdika. ⬜ 10am–6pm daily. ⬤ 1 Jan, 3 Mar, 25 Dec. 🎦 🖥 www.nmnhs.com

To the east of the National Art Gallery is the Natural History Museum (Natsionalen Prirodonauchen Muzei), which is devoted to European fauna and geology. The display begins with rows of rocks and crystals, then moves on to a large collection of stuffed birds and mammals, and an array of glass cabinets filled with insects. Live snakes and rodents are kept in glass enclosures alongside the staircases. The museum shop sells fine decorative stones and crystals.

Russian Church ⑥
Руска Църква

bul. Tsar Osvoboditel 3. **Map** E4.
Tel (02) 986 2715. 🚊 2. ⬜ 7:30am–6pm daily. 🎦

The Church of St Nicholas the Miracle-Worker (Tsurkva Na Sveti Nikolai Chudotvorets), popularly known as the Russian Church, is the most striking building in Sofia. Built to serve the city's Russian community, it was consecrated in 1914.

Modelled on 16th-century Muscovite churches, it boasts a cluster of gilt domes, one of which thrusts skywards at the tip of a pea-green spire. The porch, with a steeply pitched roof covered in bright green tiles, exudes a fairytale charm.

The church's interior, covered with frescoes derived from 17th-century paintings in Moscow and Yaroslavl, reveals the influence of exotic Eastern styles on Russian art. A door on the west side of the church leads down to the crypt, the resting place of Archbishop Serafim, leader of the Russian Church in Bulgaria from 1921 to 1950. Serafim's reputation for anti-Communism and his kindness made him popular with Sofians. Such is his enduring spiritual stature that his tomb is believed to be capable of working miracles. As a result, a regular stream of worshippers can be seen visiting the tomb to place prayers beside his sarcophagus.

Traditionally painted icons in elaborate gilt frames adorning the iconostasis in the Russian Church

Aleksandûr Nevski Memorial Church ⑦

Храм-паметник "Александър Невски"

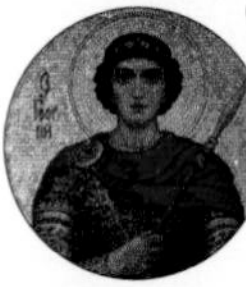

Mosaic portrait in the church

Crowned with a cluster of gilt domes, the Aleksandûr Nevski Memorial Church (Hram-pametnik Aleksandûr Nevski) was built in stages between 1882 and 1924 to commemorate Russia's military contribution to the War of Liberation of 1877–8. It is named after one of Russia's most revered medieval rulers, Prince Aleksandûr Nevski of Novgorod (1220–63), who defeated the Teutonic knights on the frozen waters of Lake Peipsi in Estonia in 1242. Modelled on Russian Neo-Byzantine churches, it is built in pale Bulgarian limestone. The solemn interior is bathed in amber light, enhanced by the glow of hundreds of flickering candles.

West window
Entrance to the crypt
Main entrance

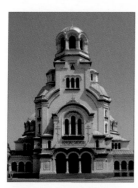

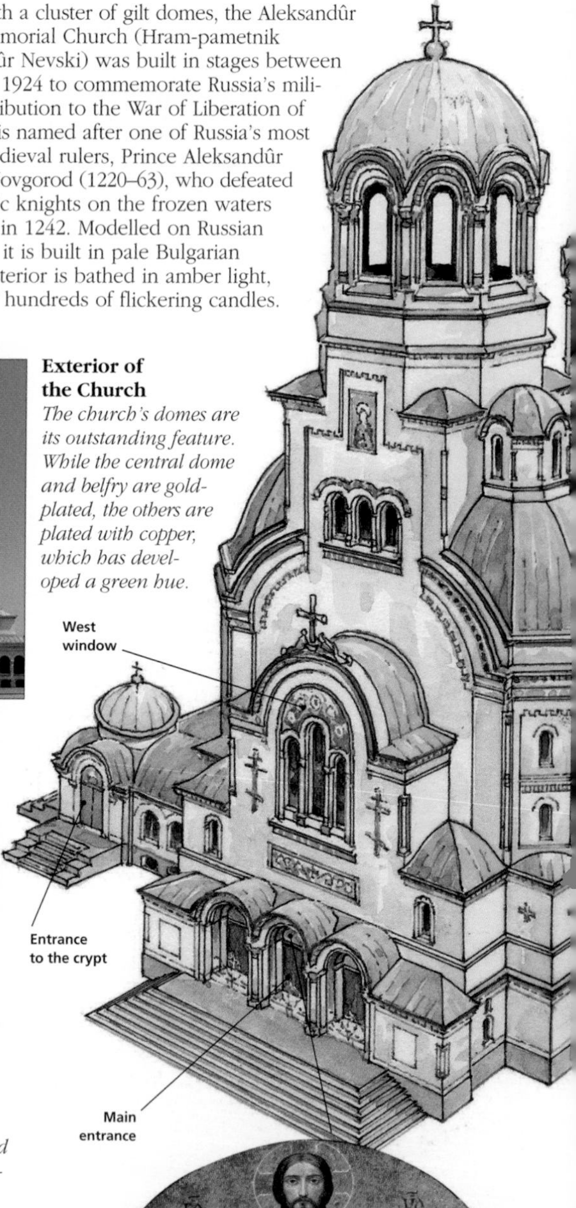

Exterior of the Church
The church's domes are its outstanding feature. While the central dome and belfry are gold-plated, the others are plated with copper, which has developed a green hue.

★ Icon Gallery in Crypt
With icons dating from the 12th to the 19th centuries and several delicately carved iconostases, this gallery contains the richest collection of religious art in Bulgaria.

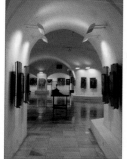

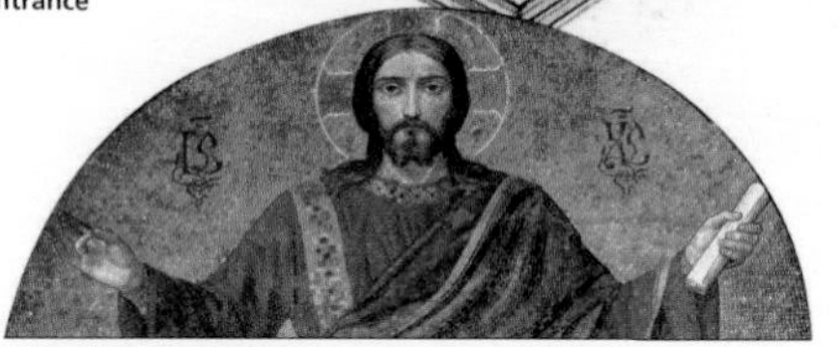

Mosaic of Christ
This mosaic of Christ, with arms outstretched, fills the tympanum over the portal's central arch.

STAR FEATURES

- ★ Icon Gallery in Crypt
- ★ Iconostasis

For hotels and restaurants in this area see pp636–8 and pp639–41

Dome Fresco

The dome fresco depicts God the Creator, with the Christ Child on his knee, looking down on the congregation. The frescoes were painted by Russian and Bulgarian artists.

VISITORS' CHECKLIST

pl. Aleksandūr Nevski. **Map** F4.
🚌 9, 280, 306. 🚊 1, 2, 4, 9, 11. **Main Church** ***Tel*** *(02) 988 1704.* ⬜ *Nov–Feb: 7am–6pm daily; Mar–Oct: 7am–7pm daily.* **Icon Gallery in Crypt** ***Tel*** *(02) 981 5775.* ⬜ *10am–5:30pm Tue–Sun.* 🚫 *1 Jan, 3 Mar, 25 Dec.* 📷✝ *9:30am Sun, 8am & 5pm daily (liturgy).*

Gold-plated dome

★ Iconostasis

The marble, onyx and alabaster iconostasis features carvings of grapes, palms and peacocks. The icons include portraits of Christ and the Virgin.

Tsar's Throne

Built for Tsar Ferdinand (r. 1886–1918), the throne is guarded by stone lions and crowned by a marble canopy. Behind it is a portrait of the tsar and his wife.

Clusters of Candles

Visitors to the church buy candles at the entrance and light them as a symbol of prayer.

Church of Sveta Sofia ⑧
Църква Света София

pl. Aleksandûr Nevski. **Map** E4.
Tel (02) 987 0971. 🚋 1, 2, 4, 9, 10, 11. 🚎 20, 22. ◯ 9am–6pm. 📷

The origins of Sofia's oldest surviving Christian church go back to the 6th century. It was built on the site of two 4th-century churches outside the city walls. The spot was also the town graveyard of Serdika, as Sofia was known in ancient times. The church remained Sofia's principal cemetery church well into the Middle Ages.

During the Second Bulgarian Kingdom (1185–1396), the church became the seat of the city's bishop. The city itself, known in Bulgarian as Sredets, gradually took the church's name, which means Holy Wisdom. After the Ottoman conquest, the church became a mosque, but was abandoned when an earthquake struck in 1858.

The church takes the form of a three-aisled Byzantine-style basilica. The interior is lofty, calm and peaceful, and the beautiful brickwork of the walls and arches is completely devoid of ornamentation. Some fragments of mosaic from a 4th-century church can be seen on the floor of the south aisle.

Outside the church, beside the south wall, is the Tomb of the Unknown Soldier, which commemorates the thousands of Bulgarian soldiers who died during World War I. The monument is guarded by a stately bronze lion.

National Gallery of Foreign Art ⑨
Национална галерия за чуждестранно изкуство

pl. Aleksandûr Nevski 1. **Map** F4.
Tel (02) 980 7262. 🚌 9, 280, 306. 🚋 1, 2, 4, 11. Ⓜ Sveti Kliment Ohridski. ◯ 11am–6:30pm Mon, Wed–Sun. 📷 📷
www.foreignartgallery.org

The pristine white building behind the Aleksandûr Nevski Memorial Church (see pp608–9) houses the National Gallery of Foreign Art (Natsionalna Galeriya za Chuzhdestranno Izkustvo). It opened in 1985 and comprises gifts made to the Bulgarian state, either by private individuals or by

Main entrance to the National Gallery of Foreign Art

countries allied to the ruling Communist regime at that time. On the ground floor are outstanding collections of African tribal sculpture and Japanese woodblock prints. Upstairs, a display of 19th- and 20th-century paintings includes a pastel drawing by Renoir, a lithograph by Picasso and some animated sketches by Eugène Delacroix. Thematic exhibitions are often held in the basement, where a barrel-roofed late-Roman tomb is on display.

The building itself is a modern reconstruction of the State Printing House of 1883, one of post-Liberation Bulgaria's finest Neo-Classical buildings, which was destroyed by Allied bombing raids in 1944.

National History Museum ⑩
Национален Исторически Музей

ul. Vitoshko Lale, Boyana. **Map** A4.
Tel (02) 955 4280. 🚌 63, 111, 107. 🚋 2. ◯ Nov–Mar: 9am–5:30pm (last ticket 4:45pm); Apr–Oct: 9:30am–6pm (last ticket 5:30pm). 📷 📷 📷 📷 **www**. historymuseum.org

Bulgaria's largest collection of historic artifacts is located 7 km (4 miles) from the centre of Sofia. It has a delightful setting in the foothills and showcases remarkable objects. The collections are displayed chronologically over three floors.

Lion guarding the Tomb of the Unknown Soldier, Church of Sveta Sofia

The building was once a Communist Party palace, so touring the vast rooms is interesting in itself, just to see how Communist leaders lived.

On the first floor, the prehistory section features a clay figure called the Earth Mother statue, found near Tûrgovishte in northeastern Bulgaria. Just 14 cm (5.5 in) high, it is believed to be about 6,500 years old. Other highlights include the 3rd-century BC Thracian gold treasures from Panagyurishte in western Bulgaria, which consist of eight richly decorated gold *rhytons* (drinking vessels).

The second floor of the museum includes displays from the 6th millenium BC to the late 19th century AD. Displays cover artefacts from the Neolithic, Chalcolithic and Bronze Ages, jewellery and treasure from the Thracian and Greek settlements as well as manuscripts from the 7th to the 14th centuries, including the richly decorated Tzar Ivan Alexzander's *Gospel*.

The third floor of the museum is devoted to modern history, with military uniforms, hardware and theatrical memorabilia. It also houses a collection of traditional costumes from all over Bulgaria, including metal *pafti* (belt buckles) embossed with animals, figures of saints and abstract designs. Cinema posters and other exhibits taken from the world of entertainment and popular culture are part of the display devoted to 20th-century life.

Fresco of the Last Judgment, National History Museum

Magnificent view of Cherni Vruh, Vitosha's highest point

Mount Vitosha ⑪
Витоша

12 km (7 miles) S of Sofia.
Map A5. 🚌 *66 to Aleko; 64, 93 to Dragalevtsi; 122 to Simeonovo; all from Hladilnika Bus Terminus (on tram route nos. 9 & 10).* 🛈 *(02) 989 5377.* **www**.park-vitosha.org

Rising above Sofia's southern suburbs, the granite massif of Mount Vitosha provides Bulgaria's capital with an easily accessible recreation area. The top of the mountain is relatively smooth, making it the ideal terrain for easy hikes. Acres of beech forest cover the lower slopes, while spruce and pine predominate further up. The mountain's highest point, the 2,290-m (7,500-ft) Cherni Vruh (Black Peak), is surrounded by a plateau covered in grassland, juniper bushes and bogs. Protected since 1934, Vitosha provides a safe, natural habitat for martens, deer, wild boar and, occasionally, brown bears.

Vitosha's main recreational centre, connected to the city by road and within easy reach of the summit, is Aleko. Built in 1924, the mountain hut here is a popular starting point for hikers in summer; in winter, it becomes the centre of a busy ski scene. The pleasant surburbs of Dragalevtsi and Simeonovo, nestling in the foothills, make a good base for exploring the region. The 14th-century **Dragalevtsi Monastery**, set in deep forest just above the su*burbs, contains stunning 15th-century frescoes.

Chairlifts and cable cars run from Dragalevtsi and Simeonovo, providing excellent views over Sofia. The summit of Cherni Vruh is about an hour's walk from Aleko, or a 30-minute walk above the last stop of the highest chairlift, when they are running.

On the western side of Mount Vitosha lies Zlatni Mostove, which features the spectacular Stone River, a popular natural attraction with huge, smooth boulders deposited by a glacier in the last Ice Age.

Conspicuous Stone River at Zlatni Mostove, Mount Vitosha

Rila Monastery ❷
Рилски манастир

Established in the 10th century by St Ivan of Rila, Rila Monastery (Rilski manastir) is Bulgaria's most impressive example of National Revival architecture. Generously supported by successive kings, the monastery flourished until Ottoman raids destroyed it in the late 15th century. While the Russian Church sponsored its renovation, Rila's monks played a crucial role in preserving Bulgaria's language and history during the most repressive periods of Ottoman rule. Devastated by fire in 1833, the monastery was rebuilt with funding from wealthy Bulgarians intent on cultivating national pride at a time of great hope for liberation from the Ottomans.

Rila Monastery, situated in the northwestern Rila Mountains

Arcades
The murals in the arcades vividly depict sinners thrown into an apocalyptic vision of Hell. This contrasts with the arcades' graceful structure of arches, slender columns and blind cupolas.

CHURCH OF THE NATIVITY
The exquisite Church of the Nativity, which stands proudly in the middle of Rila Monastery's courtyard, is the largest monastic church in Bulgaria. Its exterior is a busy but harmonious confection of stripes, curved domes and arches set at different levels. It is worth spending some time exploring the outside before entering the main body of the church.

Entrance to church

★ Murals
Magnificent murals adorn the church walls, illustrating characters and episodes from the Bible. Zahari Zograf, Bulgaria's greatest 19th-century painter, is the only one of the artists responsible to have signed his work.

The arcades are decorated with some of the monastery's finest murals

★ **Holy Relic of St Ivan**

A silver casket holds the nation's holiest relic: the preserved left hand of St Ivan of Rila. In the 16th century, the right hand was taken on a tour of Russia to raise funds for the monastery.

The three main cupolas contain murals of the Holy Trinity

★ **Iconostasis**

This masterpiece was created by a team of woodcarvers working under Atanas Telador between 1839 and 1842. The 10-m (33-ft) wide iconostasis, covered in gold leaf, is elaborately decorated with complex carvings of stylized floral elements, symbolic human and animal images, biblical scenes and wild animals.

Grave of Tsar Boris

The heart of Tsar Boris III, who was allegedly poisoned by the Nazis in 1943 for saving Bulgarian Jews, is buried here.

STAR FEATURES

★ Murals

★ Holy Relic of St Ivan

★ Iconostasis

St Ivan of Rila, patron saint of Bulgaria

ST IVAN OF RILA

The medieval hermit St Ivan of Rila (880–946) retreated into the Rila Mountains to escape what he believed to be the moral decline of society. He was venerated both for his wisdom and as a healer, and was persuaded by his followers to establish a monastery. After his death, pilgrims came to view his remains, which were believed to possess curative powers.

Exploring the Rila Monastery

Deep in the heart of a forest reserve, Rila Monastery has an imposing external presence. The entire complex is ringed by mighty walls, giving it the outward appearance of a fortress. Visitors usually enter through the Dupnitsa (Western) Gate, crossing over ancient stone slabs worn smooth by pilgrims' feet. Several floors of wooden balconies enclose the courtyard and the central Church of the Nativity, with Hrelyo's Tower to one side. To the right of the Dupnitsa Gate is the Treasury Museum, located in the south wing. The north wing, to the left of the gate, contains the old kitchen and leads to the Samokov (Eastern) Gate, which conceals the entrance to the Monastery Farm Museum and leads out to a cluster of restaurants and souvenir shops.

The beautiful intricate carvings on Raphael's cross

CHURCH OF THE NATIVITY

Construction of the Church of the Nativity began in 1835, two years after the monastery had been devastated by fire. It was done by 19th-century master builder Petûr Ivanovich, who had previously worked on Mount Athos in Greece.

The church's design was intended to be innovative and original, as befitted the National Revival period. For the interior, emphasis was placed on spatiality so as to draw worshippers into the centre of the building. The three large domes were positioned to allow maximum light to fall on the spectacular gilt iconostasis, while keeping the rest of the interior in sombre darkness. The murals on the inner walls are also typical of the period and were executed by the country's best painters. The biblical scenes that cover the walls are brightly painted and show an attention to detail that was the hallmark of the National Revival movement. Among the many artists responsible were Zahari Zograf and his brother Dimitûr, of the Samokov school of icon painters, which developed in a town near Sofia.

The walls are also filled with delightful displays of icons, some produced by 19th-century artists from Samokov and Bansko (*see p617*). Others date from much earlier. On the left-hand side of the church, usually hidden away in a wooden drawer, is the serene 12th-century Icon of the Virgin.

A chapel on the right of the church contains a smaller iconostasis and the simple grave of Tsar Boris III, marked with a plain wooden cross.

TREASURY MUSEUM

The museum collection includes about 20 miniature crosses, jewelled silver boxes containing ancient Bibles, a ruby-encrusted communion cup and other church silver. The highlight, however, is Raphael's Cross. Just 81 cm (32 in) high, the cross bears a series of biblical scenes carved with needles, each one enclosed in silver-plated frames no larger than a finger-nail. The work, completed in 1802, took 12 years and cost the monk Raphael his eyesight.

The lower floor has varied exhibits, including a 2-m (6-ft) long musket and several swords and pistols. Nearby is a collection of books from the monastery library. The oldest dates back to the 10th century and is written on parchment in the Glagolitic script of the old Slavonic languages. Also on display is the Suchava Tetra, a large Bible produced in 1529. Its embossed gold and enamel cover depicts Christ on the cross, with the four evangelists watching from each corner. Several other ancient Bibles are on show below some extravagantly jewelled icons.

A neighbouring glass case is filled with a selection of 19th-century gold church plate. At the far end of the room is a 14th-century ivory-inlaid bishop's throne that belonged to the original monastery church. Alongside

The Church of the Nativity, the courtyard's dominant feature

For hotels and restaurants in this region see pp636–8 and pp639–41

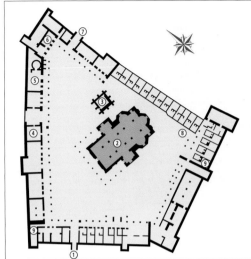

RILA MONASTERY PLAN

① Western Entrance
   (Dupnitsa Gate)

② Church of the Nativity

③ Hrelyo's Tower

④ Monastery Kitchen

⑤ Oven

⑥ Monastery Farm Museum

⑦ Eastern Entrance
   (Samokov Gate)

⑧ Treasury Museum

⑨ Public Toilets

KEY

▓ *See pp612–13*

☐ Rila Monastery Complex

are the skilfully carved original doors from **Hrelyo's Tower** and a pair of 14th-century icons of St Ivan of Rila.

MONASTERY COMPLEX

In contrast to the monastery's stern exterior, the courtyard is light and open. An elegant tracery of red, white and black striped arches deftly frame more than 300 monks' cells, mirroring the façade of the Church of the Nativity.

Hrelyo's Tower, the monastery's oldest surviving structure, was built by Hrelyo Dragoval, a feudal lord, in 1334. A small chapel on the top floor, with 14th-century frescoes, is occasionally open to the public. Today, access to this mini-fortress is via wooden steps but originally there was a removable stepladder.

An intriguing section of the north wing contains the **Monastery Farm Museum**, which is entered via the old guard house, off Samokov Gate. Here, muskets used by the guards are displayed alongside their red and white uniforms, which have metal breastplates featuring a portrait of St Ivan of Rila and the monastery. Next door is a bare-walled room that houses the monastery's water-powered mill, with a

display of hollow logs once used as sewage pipes. A 19th-century see-saw water pump used for fire fighting demonstrates the precautions taken after the fire that devastated the monastery in 1833. The enormous domed brick oven that takes up most of the next room is an impressive sight. Like the huge pots and cauldrons of the old kitchen, and the giant wooden ladles on display in the adjoining room, the oven's great size was essential to provide sufficient food for the hundreds of monks and pilgrims at the monastery. The kitchen ceiling curves into a huge blackened chimney that tapers elegantly through the four floors of the north wing.

AROUND RILA MONASTERY

The **Chapel of St Ivan of Rila** and the dark cave where he spent the last part of his life are an hour's walk north of the monastery and worth a visit just to get out into the surrounding countryside. Visitors can clamber through the narrow opening of the cave ceiling, a challenge once presented to visiting pilgrims: it is said that only the pure of heart can get through.

About 7 km (4 miles) northeast of the monastery is **Kiril Meadow**, an attractive leafy green picnic spot with cafés and a few places offering accommodation.

The 14th-century Hrelyo's Tower, in the monastery courtyard

View of Mount Malyovitsa, Rila National Park

Rila National Park ❸

Национален парк Рила

85 km (53 miles) S of Sofia. 🚌 from Sofia, Samokov. ⌂ campsites, and chalets can be booked via Bulgarian Tourism Union, (02) 980 1285. **www**.rilanationalpark.org/en/index.phtml

Bulgaria's largest national park, Rila National Park is located in the Rila Mountains, the highest range in the Balkan peninsula. The source of several Balkan rivers, the massif derives its name from the Thracian word *rula*, meaning "abundance of water". Its dense forests of spruce, fir and Macedonian pine are home to wolves, bears, boar, Balkan chamois and *suslik* (ground squirrels) as well as the rare wallcreeper and the Alpine chough. No fewer than 57 endemic plant species, including the divine primrose, Rila pansy and Bulgarian avens, also thrive here.

The national park is home to two forest reserves. Created in 2000, the Rila Monastery Forest Reserve covers more than 270 sq km (104 sq miles) around Rila Monastery *(see pp612–15)*. The Parangalitsa Reserve, on the southwestern slopes of the Rila Mountains, was established in 1933 to preserve some of Europe's oldest spruce forests. It is now a protected UNESCO Biosphere Reserve.

A network of hiking trails crisscrosses the park, reaching the spectacular peaks of Musala, at 2,925 m (9,596 ft), and Malyovitsa at 2,729 m (8,953 ft). One of the most popular hiking trails follows the Seven Lakes – a series of small glacial lakes set amidst beautiful scenery. Formed by melted glaciers, the lakes are set at ascending levels. A set of glacial pools, located below Mount Musala, are also popular with hikers.

Borovets ❹

Боровец

70 km (43 miles) S of Sofia. 🚌 🏔

Located just below the majestic peaks of the Rila Mountains, Borovets is one of Bulgaria's major ski resorts, clustered with large hotel blocks and lines of

wooden huts housing bars, restaurants, ski shops and souvenir stalls. During the winter season, visitors crowd the ski runs and lifts by day, and then move on to the bars and clubs for late-night partying.

The resort also offers a wide range of summer activities, including pony trekking, motorized safaris, hiking and abseiling, most of which can be arranged through the large hotels here. One option is to take the main gondola up to Yastrebets, a peak that rises to the height of 2,369 m (7,775 ft), from where hikers can follow a path to the Musala refuge before climbing to the lofty summit of Musala, the highest peak in the Balkans. Alternatively, the Sitnyakovo Express, a chairlift that operates only on weekends, whisks visitors up to the highest point among the Sitnyakovo ski runs, from where a path leads back down to Borovets.

The resort has one other highlight: the captivating **Bistritsa Palace**. This was built as a hunting lodge for Ferdinand, the prince of Bulgaria in the late 19th century, making Borovets the country's oldest mountain resort. The palace's impressive interior features luxurious Victorian fittings, elaborate Samokov woodcarving and hunting trophies.

🏛 **Bistritsa Palace**
3 km (2 miles) from central Borovets. **Tel** (0750) 32710. ⬜ 10:30am–3:30pm Tue–Sun. 🖼

Visitors enjoying skiing in Borovets, one of Bulgaria's major ski resorts

Painting with inscription in the Church of Sveta Troitsa, Bansko

Bansko ❺
Банско

160 km (100 miles) S of Sofia.
🚂 10,000. 🚉 🚌 🚲 ℹ️
pl. Nikola Vaptsarov, (0749) 885 800.
🎭 Pirin Sings (Aug, even years).
www.bansko.bg

The small mountain town of Bansko lies just below the jagged peaks of the Pirin Mountains. Founded in the 9th century, it remained obscure until the 19th century, when its prospering merchants began to fund the building of churches here. Famous as the birthplace of 19th-century scholar Neofit Rilski, the town is also closely associated with Bulgarian nationalism. Another of its famous sons is Father Paisii, whose seminal work *Slavo-Bulgarian History* provided the impetus for the beginnings of the National Revival.

Bansko's historic centre consists of a labyrinth of cobbled streets running between high stone walls, which conceal 19th-century timber and stone houses. In the Old Town stands the massive **Church of Sveta Troitsa**. Construction began in 1832 but the bell tower was added in 1850. Its carved wood interior contains an intricately designed iconotasis. Behind the church, along ulica Pirin, stands the **Neofit Rilski House-Museum**, former home of Rilski, revered as the founder of modern education

in Bulgaria. The remarkable **Nikola Vaptsarov House-Museum** stands on the corner of a square of the same name. This was the childhood home of Vaptsarov, a poet who was executed for anti-Fascist activities, and the museum contains his possessions.

Bansko's surburbs, mostly filled with hotels, reflect its recent development into a ski resort and weekend retreat.

Melnik ❻
Мелник

182 km (113 miles) S of Sofia.
🚂 250. 🚌 from Sofia.

Once a thriving centre of wine-making and a major focus of Balkan trade, the enchanting town of Melnik is tucked away in a valley formed by rocky hills crowned with pyramidal sandstone formations.

Wine has been Melnik's major export since the 13th century, when it had tax-free trade with Dubrovnik (*see pp454–60*). During this period, the despot Aleksei Slav made Melnik the capital of his principality, funding the construction of monasteries and churches in the vicinity. After the Ottoman conquest, Melnik fell into decline, but its fortunes revived in the 19th century, when the town's Greek population began to prosper from exporting wine and tobacco. Much of the

Bottle of wine from Kordopulov House

town of Melnik was destroyed during the Second Balkan War of 1913, however, and its remaining Greek residents left. Today, Melnik is officially Bulgaria's smallest town, but it continues to attract visitors, who come to admire the intriguing rock features and taste the famous wine that is still produced by a few local families.

Most of Melnik's attractions are at the top of a hill overlooking the town. The **History Museum** is housed in a building located right next to the Despot Slav hotel. The museum is a branch of the Regional History Museum of Sandanski. It has a fine collection of exhibits on display including terracotta wine vessels, regional costumes and photographs.

A little further on is **Kordopulov House**, a superb example of early National Revival architecture in which Western and Oriental motifs are combined on a grand scale. The interior features a central salon and an Ottoman-style raised seating area. Downstairs is a small *mehana* (tavern) connected to a labyrinthine wine cellar.

🏛 **History Museum**
Pashovata Kûshta. **Tel** (07437) 216.
◯ 9am–5pm daily.

🍷 **Kordopulov House**
Kordopulov House. **Tel** (07437) 265. ◯ Nov–Feb: 9am–5pm; Mar–Oct: 9am–6pm. 📷 🏛 📷

Melnik and its square konak, the Town Hall during Ottoman rule

Bachkovo Monastery ❼

Бачковски манастир

At the foot of Rhodope Mountains lies Bachkovo Monastery (Bachkovski manastir), the second largest monastery in Bulgaria after Rila Monastery *(see pp612–15)*. It was founded in 1083 by Grigori and Abbasi Bakouriani, Georgian brothers who were commanders in the Byzantine Army. In the 13th century, the monastery was sponsored by Tsar Ivan Asen II and his successor Ivan Aleksandûr. Destroyed by the Ottomans in the 16th century, it was restored by the 17th century. Today, its serene courtyards are filled with trees and drinking fountains, and, thanks to its architecture and frescoes, it has been added to UNESCO's World Heritage List.

The Ossuary
Located away from the main monastery complex, the ossuary is the only surviving part of the 11th-century monastery.

★ Last Judgment
In the porch of the Church of Sveti Nikola is a fresco of the Last Judgment by Zahari Zograf, with sinners falling into the fires of Hell.

Church of Sveti Nikola
A door to the left of the main courtyard leads to the Church of Sveti Nikola, which was built in 1834. It contains frescoes by Zahari Zograf and other renowned painters.

STAR SIGHTS

★ Last Judgment

★ Iconostasis

★ Refectory

Fresco in the Dome
The dome of the Church of Sveti Nikola is decorated with a fresco of Christ Pantocrator, encircled by exquisitely painted portraits of saints.

Church of Sveta Bogoroditsa

This 17th-century church is richly decorated with frescoes. Themes include the Devil addressing Christ from the mouth of a monster, and Death shadowing an angel.

Devotees gather here to kiss the silver-plated Icon of the Virgin, painted in 1310.

VISITORS' CHECKLIST

176 km (109 miles) SE of Sofia. *Tel* (359) 3327 277. from Plovdiv. 7am–9pm daily. compulsory for Refectory.

★ Iconostasis

The Church of Sveta Bogoroditsa also contains a highly ornate 17th-century gilt iconostasis, which gleams in the soft light of hundreds of flickering candles.

Main entrance

Ayazmoto

Ayazmoto

The nearby hills shelter three chapels near a locality known as Ayazmoto. The Icon of the Virgin was once hidden here from the Ottomans.

★ Refectory

A solid stone table and wooden benches stretch the length of the 17th-century refectory. The vaulted ceiling is covered with frescoes by pupils of Zahari Zograf.

PROCESSION OF THE MIRACULOUS ICON

The refectory wall on the left of the courtyard bears the largest panoramic wall painting in Bulgaria. Painted by Alexi Atanasov in 1846, it depicts the annual procession of the Icon of the Virgin on 15 August, the day of the Assumption of the Virgin. After Orthodox Easter, the icon is carried to Ayazmoto.

Procession of the miraculous Icon of the Virgin Mary

Plovdiv ⑧
Пловдив

Situated along the two banks of the Maritsa river, Plovdiv is Bulgaria's second largest city after Sofia. Settled as early as the 7th millennium BC, the city was held by the Romans between the 1st and 4th centuries. It rose to economic power in the 14th century under the Ottomans, becoming a centre of the Bulgarian National Revival in the 19th century when wealthy citizens built ornamented houses. In 1885, Plovdiv became part of Bulgaria. Today, it is a pleasant city, with a pedestrianized centre, mosques, churches, Roman ruins and National Revival mansions. An architectural reserve, the Old Town consists of steep cobbled streets lined with museum-houses and galleries all the way up to Nebet Hill, from where there are stunning views over the city.

Statue in the Roman Stadium

The well-preserved Roman Theatre, still used for performances

🏛 Roman Stadium
pl. Dzhumaya.
Crumbling marble terraces and columns, oddly incorporated into the concrete foundations of modern Plovdiv, are almost all that remains of the city's once huge Roman stadium. Built in the 2nd century AD, it could seat 30,000 spectators.

⛪ Church of Sveta Marina
ul. Dr Vulkovich 7.
The present church was built in 1783 on the site of a 16th-century church. It is renowned for its iconostasis, which is decorated with tiny figures painted by various artists including Zahari Zograf.

🏛 Roman Theatre
ul. Hemus. ◯ 9am–6pm daily. 🖾
This impressive amphitheatre, set in the hillside overlooking the city and the Rhodope

Mountains beyond, was discovered during construction work in 1972. It was built in the 2nd century AD, when Roman Plovdiv (Trimontium) was at its height, and formed part of the acropolis. Today, the theatre is used for plays and concerts.

⛪ Church of Sveta Bogoroditsa
ul. Metropolit Paisii. ◯ 7:30am–6:30pm daily. 🚹
The imposing Church of Sveta Bogoroditsa has a distinctive pink and blue bell tower which was added with Russian assistance in 1880, after the Liberation. Its murals echo the mood of the late 19th century. They depict Bulgarian Orthodox saints alongside leaders of the Liberation movement.

🏠 Hristo Danov House
ul. Mitropolit Paisii. ◯ 9am–noon, 2–5pm Mon–Fri. 🖾
Built on Taxim Hill (Taxim Tepe) and approached up steep steps, Hristo Danov House overlooks Plovdiv. Its arched gable is supported by four columns, and trompe-l'oeil pillars adorn the façade. The symmetrical interior layout is typical of National Revival architecture. Hristo Danov, founder of organized book publishing in Bulgaria, lived here from 1868 until his death in 1911.

🏛 State Gallery of Fine Arts
ul. Sŭborna 14a. ◯ 9am–5:30pm Mon–Fri, 10am–5:30pm Sat & Sun. 🖾 Thu (free entrance).
This gallery has a vast collection of 19th- and 20th-century Bulgarian paintings. Solemn 19th-century portraits hang alongside idyllic pastoral scenes and some vibrant works by Vladimir Dimitrov-Maistor. Large, bold canvases on the second floor represent more recent Bulgarian painting. Among the works here is *The Fire* (1977) by Svetlin Rusev, in which a figure walks away from a furnace carrying a glowing ember into the darkness.

🏠 Hipokrat Pharmacy
ul. Sŭborna. ◯ 10am–5pm Mon–Fri.
The fascinating Hipokrat Pharmacy has been preserved virtually as it was when it was a working pharmacy. It is lined with wooden drawers and contains bottles and jars neatly labelled in Latin.

The State Gallery of Fine Arts, in an imposing Neo-Classical building

For hotels and restaurants in this region see pp636–8 and pp639–41

� Icon Museum

ul. Sŭborna 22. ◯ 9am–12:30pm &
1–5:30pm Mon–Sat. ☑
This interesting museum is
home to a valuable array of
15th and 16th-century icons
collected from churches
under threat during the
Communist years.

Hindliyan House

ul. Artin Gidikov 4. ◯ 9am–5pm
Mon–Fri. ☑
This elegant house, its pale
blue outer walls decorated
with floral motifs, looks on to
a peaceful courtyard garden.
It was built between 1835 and
1840 for Stepan Hindliyan, a

Icon of Sts Cyril and Methodius in
the Icon Museum

Room in Nedkovich House, built for
a textile trader in 1863

wealthy Armenian merchant.
The interior has murals depicting the European cities that he
visited. The house also has a
hammam with a marble floor,
and a domed ceiling with tiny
windows. The first-floor salon
has a stunning panelled ceiling and a marble fountain.

Nedkovich House

ul. Tsanko Lavrenov 3. ◯ 9am–
noon, 1–5pm Mon–Fri. ☑
This grand house is a fine
example of National Revival
architecture. An interesting
feature is the courtyard structure with a window to the
street called the klyukarnik
(gossip room), where the
inhabitants could drink tea
and chat. The rooms contain
many original furnishings,

imported from the East and
West to blend European and
oriental styles.

History Museum

pl. Sŭedinenie. Tel (032) 229 409.
◯10am–5:30pm Mon–Sat. ☑ Thu
(free entrance). ♿
Housed in what was intended
to be eastern Rumelia's new
parliament building, the
museum documents the
reunification of Plovdiv
with Bulgaria in 1885.
Exhibits include declarations,
weaponry, uniforms and
photographs of soldiers.

Imaret Mosque

ul. Han Kubrat.
Dating from 1445, this is one
of more than 50 mosques
built in Plovdiv during the
Ottoman period. Imaret
means "shelter for the home-
less", and this was the
mosque's original function. Its
square walls support a central
dome and a minaret with
unusual zigzag brickwork.

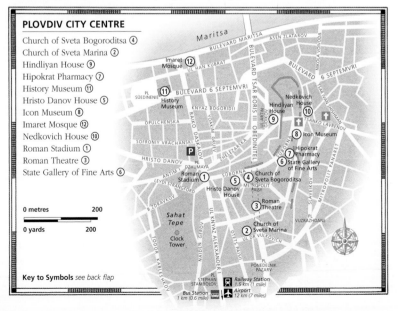

PLOVDIV CITY CENTRE

Church of Sveta Bogoroditsa ④
Church of Sveta Marina ②
Hindliyan House ⑨
Hipokrat Pharmacy ⑦
History Museum ⑪
Hristo Danov House ⑤
Icon Museum ⑧
Imaret Mosque ⑫
Nedkovich House ⑩
Roman Stadium ①
Roman Theatre ③
State Gallery of Fine Arts ⑥

0 metres   200
0 yards   200

Key to Symbols see back flap

Koprivshtitsa ⑨
Копривщица

Detail of murals in Lyutov House

Considered one of Bulgaria's most attractive towns due to its many fine National Revival houses, Koprivshtitsa was founded in the 14th century. It was originally a rich centre of cattle farming. Under Ottoman rule its citizens were granted autonomy in return for collecting taxes on behalf of the Ottoman Empire. In the early 19th century, Koprivshtitsa's prosperity attracted *kûrdzhali* (bandits), who plundered and torched the town on several occasions. It was during the ensuing period of reconstruction that its colourfully painted wood and stone houses were built. Koprivshtitsa was also the home of several of Bulgaria's leading revolutionaries, and it was here that the momentous April Rising of 1876 *(see p602)* was declared.

Kableshkov House, elegant home of the leader of the April Rising

🏛 Debelyanov House
ul. Dimcho Debelyanov. *Tel (0359) 7184 2077.* ⬚ *9:30am–5:30pm Tue–Sun.* 📷
This delightful house set above the town was the birthplace of the Symbolist poet Dimcho Debelyanov, who was killed in action in World War I. The house contains personal possessions, such as books, photographs and paintings, including a portrait of the poet by Georgi Mashev.

Statue in the garden of Debelyanov House

🔒 Church of Sveta Bogoroditsa
ul. Dimcho Debelyanov 26.
⬚ *irregular hours.* 🚩
The blue-walled Church of Sveta Bogoroditsa played a memorable role in Bulgarian history. On 20 April 1876, its

bell rang out to announce the beginning of the April Rising. The church was built in 1817 on the site of an earlier church that was destroyed by the *kûrdzhali*. Surrounded by thick stone walls, it was built slightly sunken into the ground so as to comply with Ottoman regulations governing the height of Christian churches. The three-storey bell tower was added in 1896. The church's interior is plain, but it has a superb iconostasis by woodcarvers of the Tryavna School. Some of its icons were painted by Zahari Zograf. Tragically, the church's original murals were replaced by newly painted icons in the course of misguided renovation.

🏛 Kableshkov House
ul. Todor Kableshkov 8. *Tel (0359) 7184 2054.* ⬚ *9am–5pm Tue–Sun.* 📷
This imposing building was the home of Todor Kableshkov, leader of the April Rising. He declared the start of the uprising with his Bloody Letter, written in the blood of the revolutionaries' first Turkish victim. The house was built in 1845 to a symmetrical design, the central salons on both floors flanked by identical rooms. The central bay on the upper floor has stepped windows and a decorated ceiling.

🏛 Bridge of the First Shot
ul. Todor Kableshkov.
A hallowed site in Bulgarian history, this humpbacked bridge in a quiet location southwest of the town centre is the spot where the first Turk was killed during the April Rising.

🏛 Lyutov House
ul. Nikola Belovezhdov 2. *Tel (0359) 7184 2138.* ⬚ *9:30am–5:30pm Mon, Wed–Sun.* 📷
Designed by master craftsmen from Plovdiv in 1854, Lyutov House features a huge curved gable, symmetrical layout and decorative features of Plovdiv architecture. In 1906, it was acquired by Petko Lyutov, a local merchant. The central salon has an elliptical vaulted ceiling edged with murals of the cities that Lyutov visited. The rooms on either side are furnished with Ottoman-style benches and European furniture. On the ground floor is

The Church of Sveta Bogoroditsa, whose bell proclaimed the April Rising an exhibition of 18th- and 19th-century grey felt rugs, made in Koprivshtitsa.

Oslekov House

ul. Garanilo 4. *(0885) 743 657.* 9:30am–5:30pm Tue–Sun.

This house was built in 1856 for the wealthy merchant, Nincho Oslekov. Due to space restrictions, it is asymmetrical, but is otherwise typical of the National Revival style, with separate winter and summer quarters. Murals throughout the building depict places Oslekov visited while on business. Views of European cities decorate the façade, while on the walls of the Red Room are paintings of mansions and the original symmetrical plan for the house.

The painted front façade of the Oslekov House

Karavelov House

bul. Hadzhi Nencho Palaveev 39. *Tel (0359) 7184 2191.* 9:30am–5:30pm Wed–Mon.

Home to one of the National Liberation movement's key ideologists, Karavelov House consists of two separate buildings. The winter quarters were constructed in 1810, while the summer house, built over the main entrance, was added in 1835. Lyuben Karavelov was a prolific writer, publisher and fervent revolutionary, responsible for publishing two newspapers out of Bucharest. The printing press is on display here in the winter quarters along with some of the publications he put together with fellow revolutionaries.

Benkovski House

ul. Georgi Benkovski 5. *Tel (0359) 7184 2030.* 9:30am–5:30pm Wed–Mon.

Georgi Benkovski, who was born as Gavril Hlutev, became a revolutionary in Romania. He returned to Koprivshtitsa in 1875 to form the legendary "winged" cavalry detachment that rallied support from local villages during the April Uprising. This was the Hlutev family home and the rooms contain his revolutionary flag, Winchester rifle and personal

VISITORS' CHECKLIST

110 km (68 miles) E of Sofia. 3,000. pl. 20 April, (0359) 7184 2191. Fri. Re-enactment of the April Rising (1–2 May), Intl Folk Festival (every five years, next in summer 2015). **www**.koprivshtitza.com

View of Koprivshtitsa from the Benkovski monument

photographs. The veranda has a replica of one of the cherry-tree cannons used in the uprising. The granite monument on the hillside above the house portrays a cloaked Benkovski astride a leaping horse looking over his shoulder to rouse his rebel army.

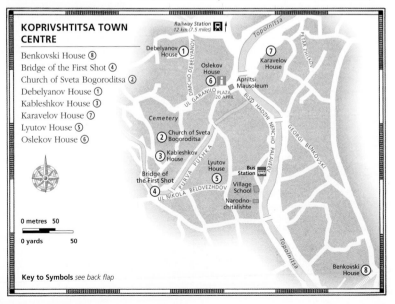

KOPRIVSHTITSA TOWN CENTRE

Benkovski House (8)
Bridge of the First Shot (4)
Church of Sveta Bogoroditsa (2)
Debelyanov House (1)
Kableshkov House (3)
Karavelov House (7)
Lyutov House (5)
Oslekov House (6)

Railway Station 12 km (7.5 miles)

Debelyanov House (1)
Oslekov House (6)
Apriltsi Mausoleum
Karavelov House (7)
PLAZA 20 APRIL
Cemetery
Church of Sveta Bogoroditsa (2)
Kableshkov House (3)
Bridge of the First Shot (4)
Lyutov House (5)
Bus Station
Village School
Narodno-chitalishte
Benkovski House (8)

0 metres   50
0 yards   50

Key to Symbols *see back flap*

Veliko Tûrnovo ⑩

Велико Търново

With a picturesque hillside setting, fine architecture and a wealth of historic sights, Veliko Tûrnovo is one of Bulgaria's most beautiful cities. Tall, narrow houses teeter on sheer cliffs that rise high above the meandering Yantra river, while to the east are the ruins of the majestic fortress of Tsarevets *(see pp626–7)*. The city has a proud history as the mighty capital of the Second Kingdom (1185–1393), and later as the seat of liberated Bulgaria's first National Assembly.

By day, Veliko Tûrnovo bustles with a mix of locals, students and visitors. After dark, the focus switches to the city's lively bars and clubs.

Detail of the Asenid Monument

🏠 House of the Little Monkey

ul. Vûstanicheska 14. 📷 *to the public.*

This house, one of many in Veliko Tûrnovo designed by the great local architect Kolyo Ficheto, dates from 1849. It is set on a hillside, with the ground floor accessible at street level, and entrances to the two upper floors at the rear. It features a pair of bay windows, attractive red-and-white brickwork, and a tiny statue of a monkey that gives the house its name.

🏠 Samovodska Charshiya

Varosh quarter.

In the 19th century, Samovodska Charshiya developed into a thriving bazaar, with stalls, workshops and a caravanserai for visiting merchants. It is located in the pleasant historic Varosh quarter of the city, which rises steeply above the Old Town. The attractive stone houses that line the bazaar's narrow cobbled streets are now occupied by souvenir shops selling local craft items.

An outdoor café in Samovodska Charshiya, Varosh quarter

🔒 Church of Sts Cyril and Methodius

ul. Slaveykov, Varosh quarter.
🕐 *8am–7pm daily.* 📷

Built by Kolyo Ficheto in 1860, this church lost its dome and belfry during an earthquake in 1913. A curved wooden balcony at the back of the church was designed for the segregation of female worshippers.

🔒 Church of Sveti Nikola

ul. Shipka, Varosh quarter.
🕐 *8am–7pm daily.* 📷

Kolyo Ficheto's design for this church features a simple stone exterior and a red-tiled roof. The iconostasis, with dragons, eagles and a central sun motif lighting the church's gloomy interior, is a stunning example of the work of the Tryavna School, Bulgaria's oldest school of icon painting. The bishop's throne has an allegorical carving of a dragon (Turkey) attacking a lion (Bulgaria) that is being suffocated by a snake (the Greek-speaking priesthood).

🏠 Asenid Monument

Asenovtsi Park.

Unveiled in 1985 to mark the 800th anniversary of the founding of the Second Bulgarian Kingdom, this monument features a mighty sword, with the figures of Asen, Petûr, Ivan Asen II and Kaloyan, the four tsars who ruled the kingdom from 1185 to 1241. The monument is an excellent point from which to admire the city's old houses, precariously perched on the cliffs opposite.

🏛 Art Gallery

Asenovtsi Park. **Tel** *(062) 638 941.*
🕐 *10am–6pm Tue–Sun.* 📷 📷
Nov–Feb: 10am–5pm.

Bulgarian paintings of the 19th and 20th centuries make up this fine collection. Charcoal landscapes by Boris Denev fill much of the ground floor, while the upper rooms hold works by Dimitûr Kazakov, with sharply outlined figures in abstract compositions. Some monumental works are *Veliko Tûrnovo in the Past* (1981) by Naiden Petkov and *People Say Goodbye to Patriarch Evtimii* (1969) by Svetlin Rusev.

🏠 Sarafkina House

ul. Gen. Gurko 88. **Tel** *(062) 626 6954.* 🕐 *9am–noon & 1–6pm Tue–Sat.* 📷

With stone walls below and whitewashed walls above, shuttered windows and a tiled

Church of Sveti Nikola, built by the 19th-century architect Kolyo Ficheto

For hotels and restaurants in this region see pp636–8 and pp639–41

Luxurious interior of Sarafkina House

roof, this house is typical of the city's 19th-century domestic architecture. It was built in 1861 for Dimitûr Sarafkina, a wealthy banker, and is set on sheer cliffs above the river. The wood-panelled interior displays Western-style furniture as well as family photographs and period outfits.

🏛 Archaeological Museum
ul. Pikolo 6. *Tel (062) 601 528.*
◯ *9am–5:15pm Tue–Sun.*
The courtyard of this building is littered with Classical columns and busts. Although several artifacts were stolen in 2006, most of this absorbing collection remains in place. The centrepiece is a replica of a burial site, Kaloyan's Grave. It was discovered in 1972 near the Church of the

Forty Martyrs in the Asenova quarter *(see pp626–7).* On the skeleton was a gold ring and seal bearing the name Kaloyan, which suggested that these may be the remains of Tsar Kaloyan. The gold seal of Tsar Ivan Asen II is displayed under a magnifying glass in an adjoining room. Downstairs are finds from the Roman city of Nikopolis ad Istrum, the ruins of which lie 20 km (12 miles) north of Veliko Tûrnovo.

Fine arcades of the grand old Archaeological Museum

VISITORS' CHECKLIST

220 km (137 miles) NE of Sofia.
🚉 66,900. 🚌 🚐 🚏 🛈 *ul. Hristo Botev 5, (062) 622 148.*
www.velikoturnovo.info

🏛 Museum of the National Revival and Constituent Assembly
pl. Sûedenenie 1. *Tel (062) 629 821.* ◯ *9am–6:30pm Mon & Wed–Sun.*
Built by Kolyo Ficheto for the city's Ottoman governor in 1872, this vast edifice became Bulgaria's first parliament building after the Liberation. It holds a copy of the new state's first constitution, signed in 1879, as well as a huge collection of material relating to the revolt against Ottoman rule.

🏛 Modern History Museum
pl. Sûedenenie. *Tel (062) 623 847.*
◯ *8am–noon, 1–5pm Mon–Fri.*
Housed in a former prison, the museum's exhibits cover the Balkan Wars and Bulgaria's role in World War I. A display recalls the life of one of the most popular Bulgarian prime ministers, Stefan Stambolov, who was born in Veliko Tûrnovo.

VELIKO TÛRNOVO CITY CENTRE

Archaeological Museum ⑧
Art Gallery ⑥
Asenid Monument ⑤
Church of Sts Cyril and Methodius ③
Church of Sveti Nikola ④
House of the Little Monkey ①
Modern History Museum ⑩
Museum of the National Revival and Constituent Assembly ⑨
Samovodska Charshiya ②
Sarafkina House ⑦

Key to Symbols *see back flap*

Veliko Turnovo: Tsarevets & Asenova Quarter
Царевец и Асенова Махала

The hilltop fortress of Tsarevets occupies a commanding position on a rocky hill that is almost completely encircled by the Yantra river. It was a sought-after vantage point from the 4th millennium BC and in 1186, Tsar Petûr made it the capital of the Second Bulgarian Kingdom. When the kingdom fell to the Ottomans in 1393, Tsarevets was reduced to rubble. Only a few buildings have been completely restored. Below the walls of Tsarevets and straddling the banks of the river, lies the Asenova Quarter. For centuries it was inhabited by a community of artisans and clerics, but they left after a devastating earthquake in 1913.

★ Light Show
A fantastic light show, with a soundtrack, takes place almost every night in summer. Waves of colour light up the fortress, and the spectacle culminates with fireworks and the ringing of bells.

Church of St George
Constructed in 1616, the church contains badly damaged and heavily restored frescoes of Orthodox saints.

The Church of the Dormition, dedicated to the Dormition of the Virgin, was built in 1923.

The Church of the Forty Martyrs, built in 1230, commemorates Ivan Asen II's victory over the Byzantines.

To Veliko Tûrnovo

Main Gate

Asenova Gate
Reconstructed in 1976, this three-storey gate tower was used by the inhabitants of the Asenova Quarter.

0 metres   50

0 yards   50

★ Baldwin's Tower
Named after Emperor Baldwin of Constantinople, who was held here in the 13th century, this tower guarded the southernmost point of the hilltop. Earlier, it was known as the Frenk Hisar Gate, and defended the merchants' quarter.

STAR SIGHTS

★ Light Show

★ Baldwin's Tower

★ Royal Palace

For hotels and restaurants in this region see pp636–8 and pp639–41

Church of St Demetrius

This church is dedicated to St Demetrius, patron saint of the Second Bulgarian Kingdom. Restored medieval frescoes decorate its interior.

VISITORS' CHECKLIST

Tsarevets. **Tel** (062) 636 954.
Apr–Oct: 8am–7pm daily;
Nov–Mar: 9am–4pm daily.
(062) 638 841.
Light Show (062) 636 952.

Church of Sts Peter and Paul
dates from the 13th century and is notable for its openwork capitals, frescoes of the two saints, to whom it is dedicated, and a depiction of the *pietà*.

Rock of Execution

At the northernmost point of the fortress, the Rock of Execution juts out above sheer cliffs, with the Yantra river far below. It was from here that traitors and criminals were pushed to their deaths.

Patriarchate

At the hill's highest point is the 13th-century Church of the Patriarchate. Defended by thick walls, it was once part of the patriarch's residential complex. Striking modern murals adorn the interior.

★ Royal Palace

Built in the 12th century, the Royal Palace was an enclosed complex with a central courtyard. Now partially reconstructed, it has modern concrete staircases enabling visitors to climb up for magnificent views of the surroundings.

Varna ⓫
Варна

With wide pedestrianized boulevards and a sandy beach, Varna has the tranquil air of a coastal resort, despite being a centre of commerce and Bulgaria's third largest city. As Varna's remarkable Archaeological Museum shows, the city's history goes back to the 5th millennium BC. In the 6th century BC, it was settled by Greeks. The thriving colony fell to the Romans in the 1st century BC, but retained its role as one of the Black Sea's key ports. Varna became part of Bulgaria in the 8th century. It was taken over by the Ottomans in 1393, but after the Liberation of 1878 it rapidly grew to become the bustling modern city, port and resort that it is today.

🏛 Archaeological Museum
bul. Maria Luiza 41. **Tel** (052) 681 011. ◯ 10am–5pm Tue–Sun. 📷 📹 🖥 🛈

Over 100,000 ancient artifacts discovered in and around Varna fill this museum. It was founded in 1888 by the Czech archaeologist Karel Škorpil, who pioneered the exploration of Bulgaria's ancient past. The collection is housed in 40 rooms on two floors. The most intriguing section is that devoted to Varna's necropolis, west of the modern city. It contains some stunning gold items. The upper floor has pottery, weaponry and religious art from the medieval period.

🛈 Cathedral of the Assumption
pl. Mitropolitska Simeon. **Tel** (052) 613 005. ◯ 7:30am–7pm daily. 🛈 🛈

The second-largest place of Christian worship in Bulgaria after the Alexandûr Nevski Memorial Church in Sofia (see

Archaeological Museum exhibit

pp608–609), this cathedral was built to commemorate the Russian soldiers who died in the fight for liberation from Ottoman rule. Funded by Varna's citizens and designed by Russian architect Maas, it was completed in 1886. The interior is covered with over-life-size murals painted under Russian supervision in 1949, and the vast iconostasis and splendid bishop's throne are the work of master craftsmen from Macedonia.

🏛 Ethnographic Museum
ul. Panagyurishte 22. **Tel** (052) 630 588. ◯ Nov–Feb: 10am–5pm Mon–Fri. 📷 🛈

Housed in a fine 19th-century National Revival-style house, this is one of Bulgaria's largest ethnographic museums. The ground floor is devoted to farming, with a wide array of tools for harvesting, beekeeping and viniculture. Upstairs, traditional costumes are on display, along with the

re-creation of a typical farmer's house used by the Gagauz, a Turkish-speaking Christian people who settled on the Black Sea coast in the 12th century.

🛈 Church of the Assumption
ul. Han Krum 19. **Tel** (052) 633 925. ◯ 7:30am–6pm daily. 🛈

This small church, built in 1602, is set below ground level, in accordance with the orders given by the Ottoman rulers that churches should be no higher than a man on horseback, lest they outshine mosques. The attractive wooden bell tower was added after the Liberation. The church contains Varna's oldest icon, a brilliant 13th-century depiction of the Virgin.

A surviving section of the Roman Thermae baths complex

🛈 Roman Thermae
ul. Han Krum. **Tel** (052) 600 059. ◯ Nov–Apr: 10am–5pm Mon–Sat. 📷

A monument to the ingenuity of Roman architects, this massive public baths complex covers over 7,000 sq m (75,000 sq ft). It was built in the 2nd century AD for what was then the Roman city of Odessos. Although in ruins, enough of the complex is still intact to give an idea of Roman bathing habits. The exorbitant amount spent on the baths is said to have caused their steady decline in the 3rd and 4th centuries.

🏛 City History Museum
ul. 8 Noemvri 3. **Tel** (052) 632 677. ◯ 10am–5pm Tue–Sun. 📷

Constructed in 1851, this building is one of Varna's oldest surviving houses.

Iconostasis made by Macedonian craftsmen, Cathedral of the Assumption

For hotels and restaurants in this region see pp636–8 and pp639–41

The torpedo boat, *Drŭzhki* at the entrance of the Navy Museum, Varna

The museum traces the history of Varna from the late 18th century, when it was a neglected coastal town, to the mid-20th century, when it became a major port and popular seaside resort.

🏛 Navy Museum

bul. Primorski 2. *Tel* (052) 731 523. ☐ 10am–5:30pm Mon–Fri. 🖼

The prize exhibit of the Navy Museum is the torpedo boat *Drŭzhki* (Intrepid) displayed outside the museum. In 1912, during the First Balkan War, the *Drŭzhki* secured the Bulgarian navy's only victory in the conflict when it sank a large Turkish cruise ship.

The museum itself holds exhibits relating to navigation on the Black Sea starting from the 6th century BC.

🌿 Sea Gardens

Aquarium *Tel* (052) 632 066. ☐ 9am–8pm daily. 🖼 🗲 www.aquariumvarna.com

Planetarium *Tel* (052) 684 441. ☐ Mar–Oct: 5pm, 6pm Tue–Sat, Nov–Feb: 5pm Tue–Fri. 🗲 shows for pre-booked groups only. 🖼

Dolphinarium *Tel* (052) 302 199. ☐ 1 May–1 Oct: 10:30am, 12pm, 3pm & 7pm Tue–Sun, Oct–Apr: 12pm. 🖼 🗲 📷 🅿 www.dolphinarium.festa. org

Begun in 1862, this urban park was designed by Czech landscape architect Anton Novak, with trees and plants from Bulgaria and around the Mediterranean. Among its flowerbeds and shaded paths are several family-friendly attractions, including an **Aquarium** with stingrays, a **Planetarium** and a **Dolphinarium** with regular shows. Stretching out below

the Sea Gardens is Varna's long, sandy beach. Lined with outdoor restaurants, cafés and bars, it is ideal for lazy days of swimming, sunbathing, eating and drinking. After dark, the beach is one of the Black Sea's liveliest spots, with clubs open until the small hours.

🏰 Evksinograd Palace

Tel (052) 393 100. ☐ 9am–3pm Mon–Fri, only for pre-booked groups of 10 or more. 🟢 July & Aug.

Located 8 km (5 miles) from central Varna, the spectacular Evksinograd Palace, built for Prince Aleksandŭr Batenberg I, was completed in 1886, and served as the summer residence for Bulgarian royalty until the Communists came to power in 1944. It was designed by famous Viennese architect Rumpelmeyer and its gardens were laid out by French landscape designers in the 19th century. Today, the palace is still a state property.

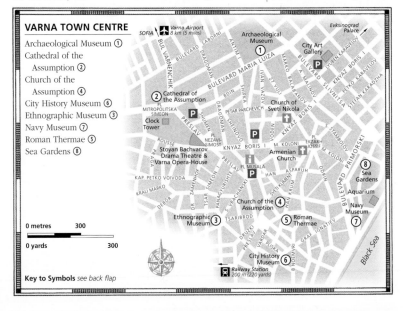

VARNA TOWN CENTRE

Archaeological Museum ①
Cathedral of the Assumption ②
Church of the Assumption ④
City History Museum ⑥
Ethnographic Museum ③
Navy Museum ⑦
Roman Thermae ⑤
Sea Gardens ⑧

0 metres 300
0 yards 300

Key to Symbols *see back flap*

Stone Forest ⓒ
Побитите камъни

420 km (260 miles) E of Sofia. 🚌

As the name suggests, the famous Stone Forest (Pobiti kamûni) is a cluster of tree-like stone columns. Spread over a barren landscape, they stand together in 7 groups of more than 300 each. Some of them are 6 m (20 ft) high and up to 9 m (30 ft) in circumference.

The stones are believed to be 50 million years old and their origins have long been the subject of scientific speculation. Among the numerous theories advanced by experts, it is generally agreed that they were formed when separate layers of chalk merged through a layer of sand. Some scientists, however, still support the theory that they are fossilized remnants of an ancient forest.

Massive tree-like pillars of the 50-million-year-old Stone Forest

Golden Sands ⓒ
Златни пясъци

455 km (283 miles) E of Sofia.
🚌 from Varna. 🚈
www.goldensands.bg

Bulgaria's second largest coastal resort after Sunny Beach, Golden Sands (Zlatni pyasâtsi) certainly lives up to its name. Wooded hills, which are part of the Golden Sands Nature Park, slope down towards the sea, rimmed by an almost continuous line of newly built hotels. The beach itself is an unbroken 3.5-km (2-miles) long stretch of fine white sand. The areas behind

Beach at Golden Sands, one of Bulgaria's most popular resorts

the beach feature well-tended gardens, outdoor pools and sports facilities for children. The resort has a wide range of restaurants and bars and offers a variety of water sports.

Environs
About 7 km (4 miles) inland from Golden Sands is the **Aladzha Monastery**. The hermits who settled here in the 6th century cut dozens of cells and chambers into the limestone cliff, and evidence of Stone Age dwellers has also been discovered. The caves are now linked by sturdy metal steps, but the monks accessed them by scrambling up and down perilous ledges, using footholds that are still visible in the cliff face. A museum at the entrance displays earlier models of the monastery, alongside ancient relics, including artifacts dating from around 5000 BC discovered in a Chalcolithic necropolis on the outskirts of Varna.

Kaliakra ⓒ
Калиакра

520 km (323 miles) E of Sofia.
🚌 from Varna. ⬜ 10am–7pm daily.
🚻 ⅱ 🖾 🏠

Meaning "fine nose" in Greek, Kaliakra is a rocky promontory that extends 2 km (1 mile) into the sea. Locals attribute the reddish colour of its limestone cliffs to the blood of the many people who died in battles for control of this strategic point. Kaliakra is now an extensive archaeological site, occupied by the ruins of a grand fortress dating back to the 4th century BC. It was successively held by Greeks, Romans, Bulgarians and Ottomans. According to legend, 40 maidens tied their hair together and jumped into the sea here to escape a worse fate at the hands of invading Ottoman soldiers. The spot affords stunning views of the imposing cliffs around the coast.

Ruins of the 4th-century BC fortress at Kaliakra

Sunny Beach ⑮
Слънчев бряг

430 km (267 miles) E of Sofia.
🚌 *from Burgas.* Ⓜ ⚓
www.sunnybeach.bg.com

Established in the 1960s, Sunny
Beach (Slûnchev Bryag) was
one of Bulgaria's first coastal
resorts. It is now the country's
largest, and it continues to
expand in all directions. Palatial hotels, apartment blocks
and Socialist-era leisure complexes stretch out behind a
beach 8 km (5 miles) long.
   Sunny Beach has earned
Blue Flag status in view of its
high environmental standards
and is particularly popular with
families and visitors on package holidays. The resort offers
a range of water sports, as well
as a multitude of shops.

Nesebûr ⑯
Несебър

435 km (270 miles) E of Sofia.
🏛 9,000. 🚌 *from Sunny Beach,
Burgas and Varna (in summer).*
⚓ *from Sunny Beach.* ⛴ *daily.*

Set on a rocky peninsula,
Nesebûr was first settled by
Thracians, but it was in the
13th and 14th centuries that
it reached its commercial and
cultural zenith. Today, it is a
UNESCO World Heritage Site,
and tends to become very
crowded in summer.
   The beautiful Old Town is
packed with historic houses
and attractive churches, many
in Byzantine style. Among the
churches, the **Old Metropolitan
Church**, founded in the 5th
century, is the largest and oldest. Although it is in ruins, it is
still the focal point of the Old
Town, and a popular meeting
point and concert venue.
In the 15th century, it was
supplanted by the **New
Metropolitan Church**, which
has a breathtaking interior
densely covered in 16th– to
18th-century frescoes, as well
as an ornate bishop's throne
and a wooden pulpit. The
Archaeological Museum provides a fascinating insight into
Nesebûr's long history, with
fine Thracian and medieval
collections, including an

Ruins of the Old Metropolitan Church, Nesebûr

outstanding array of icons,
gold jewellery and architectural elements. There is also
an Ethnographic Museum.

Burgas ⑰
Бургас

403 km (250 miles) E of Sofia.
🏛 193,000. 🚆 🚍 🚌 Ⓜ ⚓
daily. **www.**burgas.bg

Burgas had its heyday in the
19th century, when it enjoyed
an economic boom based on
craftsmanship and the export
of grain. It has benefited from
recent refurbishment and
has several fine churches
and museums.
   The **Church of Sts Cyril and
Methodius** was designed by
Ricardo Toskanini, an Italian
architect who strongly influenced Burgas's architecture in
the early 20th century. Nearby, the Ethnographic Museum
contains a good collection of
traditional costumes, while
the Archaeological Museum
has a small but captivating
display of items dating back
10,000 years. The town's Art
Gallery has some fine 18th-

Elegant façade of the Church of Sts
Cyril and Methodius, Burgas

and 19th-century icons as well
as works by modern Bulgarian
painters, including local artists.

Environs
Outside Burgas is **Lake Poda**, a
haven for rare birds and plants.
Managed by the Bulgarian
Society for the Preservation of
Birds, the lake and its environs
are internationally important.

Sozopol ⑱
Созопол

435 km (270 miles) E of Sofia.
🏛 4,400. 🚌 *from Burgas.* Ⓜ
⚓ *daily.* 🎭 *Apollonia Arts
Festival (first 10 days in Sep).*
www.sozopol.bg

With sandy bays to the north
and south, Sozopol stands on a
peninsula jutting out into the
Black Sea, its cobbled streets
lined with pretty old houses.
One of the First Bulgarian
Kingdom's major ports, it
remained an important centre
of shipbuilding, commerce and
fishing until it was overtaken
by Burgas in the 19th century.
   The collections in the
Archaeological Museum document Sozopol's long history,
including Greek pottery and
some fascinating figurines from
the ancient Greek necropolis.
Most of the town's medieval
churches were destroyed in
the Ottoman period, but later
examples remain, including
the 15th-century Church of
Sveta Bogoroditsa, with elaborate wooden iconostases,
and the Church of Sveti Zosim,
with icons by the famous artist
Dimitar of Sozopol. Sozopol
also hosts the Apollonia Arts
Festival, one of Bulgaria's
foremost cultural events.

Practical & Travel Information

With fine cities, beautiful beaches and ski resorts, Bulgaria is a mecca for sun-seekers and winter sports enthusiasts alike. Travelling to the country is relatively easy, with frequent flights and trains from most European countries. Although domestic travel may not be as quick and easy as in other European destinations, there are no serious obstacles, and Bulgarians are helpful and courteous towards foreign visitors.

WHEN TO VISIT

Bulgaria is an attractive destination all year round. On the Black Sea coast, the main holiday season runs from May to September, peaking in July and August when temperatures are at their highest and the beaches fill with holidaymakers. Bulgaria's historic cities, with their churches, museums and art galleries, are rewarding places to visit at any time of the year.

DOCUMENTATION

To enter Bulgaria, citizens of European Union (EU) countries do not need a visa but must show a valid passport. Citizens of Australia, Canada, New Zealand and the US do not need a visa for a stay of less than 90 days. Nationals of other countries should check current regulations with the Bulgarian Embassy or consulate in their country.

VISITOR INFORMATION

The availability of visitor information in Bulgaria differs greatly from one region to another. A useful resource is the National Information and Publicity Centre in Sofia, which is run by the **Bulgarian Tourism Authority** and provides information on the whole country. There are also some privately run regional information centres, mostly in those areas popular with hikers and skiers, and in towns such as Bansko *(see p617)* and Koprivshtitsa *(see pp622–3)*, which attract visitors on account of their historic and cultural interest. Visitor information centres in such places sell maps of the local area and can offer advice on accommodation in the vicinity.

Surprisingly, given its popularity with holidaymakers, there are very few tourist information centres on the Black Sea coast.

For details of local attractions and tourist excursions, and advice on local restaurants, visitors should enquire at the reception desks of their hotels, or go to a privately run travel agency in the nearest town or city.

HEALTH AND SECURITY

Basic medical advice is available at pharmacies but, as hospitals are underfunded, visitors should make sure that they have adequate medical insurance for private care in case of more serious problems. Every major town has a duty pharmacy with an emergency counter that is open 24 hours a day. However, it may be difficult to find one with English-speaking staff.

Although Bulgaria has a low crime rate, petty theft can be a problem in major towns and cities and in tourist spots. To minimise the risk of being targeted, take basic precautions and keep documents, money and credit cards hidden from view at all times; keep valuables in the safe in the hotel room and beware of pickpockets in crowded areas.

FACILITIES FOR THE DISABLED

Few public buildings, shops and visitor attractions in Bulgaria are adapted for wheelchair users. Pavements everywhere are uneven and unramped, many museums are in older buildings without lifts, and access to archaeological sites is also very difficult.

Although most of Sofia's five-star hotels are wheel chair-accessible, there is no guarantee that the rooms will have been adapted for disabled guests.

BANKING AND CURRENCY

Bulgarian towns and cities are well serviced by banks, and automatic cash machines can be found outside most major high-street branches. Credit cards are increasingly accepted in high-end hotels, restaurants and luxury shops, but are not widely used elsewhere. Most transactions, from paying for a stay in a hostel to buying souvenirs, are usually made in cash.

The currency of Bulgaria is the *lev*, which is divided into 100 *stotinki*. As *leva* are not widely available outside Bulgaria, visitors will need to withdraw currency on their arrival to the country.

THE CLIMATE OF BULGARIA

Bulgaria lies in two overlapping climate zones – Continental and Mediterranean – characterized by warm, dry summers and cold winters. Temperatures in summer, between June and September, average between 17° C (63° F) and 24° C (75° F). In winter, between December and February, they rarely rise above 6° C (43° F) but may drop to -1° C (30° F).

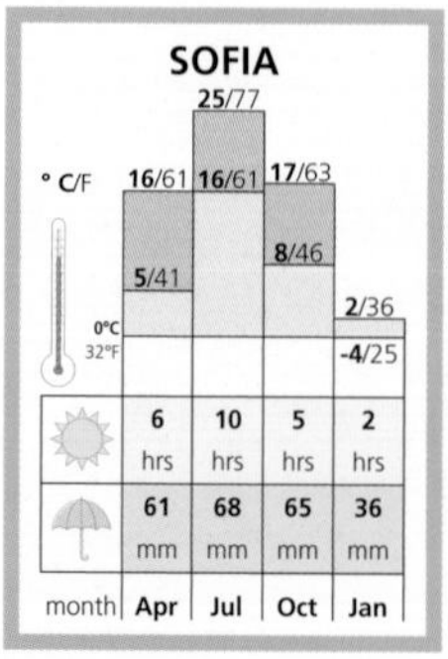

SOFIA
°C/F
16/61
5/41
25/77
16/61
17/63
8/46
2/36
-4/25
0°C
32°F
6 hrs
10 hrs
5 hrs
2 hrs
61 mm
68 mm
65 mm
36 mm
month
Apr
Jul
Oct
Jan

COMMUNICATIONS

Bulgaria's national telephone and postal systems, are reasonably efficient, although the postal service is a little slower than in some Western European countries. Visitors will have no trouble finding an Internet café, even in small towns.

Visitors can avoid high call charges by buying a pre-paid SIM card from a Bulgarian mobile phone operator, enabling them to make calls to local numbers at Bulgarian rates during their stay.

ARRIVING BY AIR

Sofia is well served by direct flights from other European countries. **Bulgaria Air**, the national carrier, has daily scheduled flights to Sofia from **Gatwick Airport** in London, Amsterdam, Paris and other European capitals. **British Airways** also provides scheduled flights to Sofia from **Heathrow Airport** in London. The low-cost airlines **easyJet** and **Wizzair** offer flights to Sofia, Varna and Burgas from the UK and parts of Central Europe. Direct flights to Bulgaria from North America and other non-European countries are rare. Most intercontinental routes involve flying to either London, Amsterdam or Frankfurt, then taking a connecting flight to Bulgaria.

Bulgaria's largest airport is **Sofia Airport**, which serves the capital. It has convenient transport connections with the city centre, which is about 10 km (6 miles) to the west. Much of western and central Bulgaria is easily accessible from Sofia. For visitors heading for the Black Sea coast, there are budget flights to Varna and Burgas.

RAIL TRAVEL

The total cost of travelling to Bulgaria by train is likely to be higher than by air. It may also be difficult to buy one ticket all the way from Western Europe to Bulgaria. From Continental Europe, the main routes to Bulgaria are from Budapest to Sofia via Belgrade or Bucharest. The country's rail network is operated by the **Bulgarian State Railways** (Bulgarska durzhavna zheleznitsa, or BDZ). Train tickets can be purchased at station ticket offices. Reservations are advisable for visitors travelling between Sofia and the Black Sea coast during summer. The best sources of information on train travel to Bulgaria are **Rail Europe** and **Trainseurope**.

TRAVELLING BY BUS

Bus services in Bulgaria are operated by several national and regional bus companies. Most towns and villages are accessible by bus. Intercity bus routes connecting Sofia with major towns and cites depart several times a day. Buses on these routes are modern, with comfortable seats and air conditioning.

Tickets can be bought from counters at bus stations, but not on the buses themselves. On intercity routes, advance reservations are advisable. Tickets and information on bus travel throughout Bulgaria is available from **Sofia Central Bus Station**.

TRAVELLING BY CAR

Exploring Bulgaria by car is an attractive option, as it gives greater freedom and allows visitors to explore more remote areas of the country that may not be well served by public transport. However, visitors should bear in mind that motorways are few, and that road conditions often leave much to be desired. Road signs on main intercity trunk roads are in Cyrillic and Roman scripts. Cars can be hired from reliable service providers such as **Avis**, **Budget** and **Europcar**.

DIRECTORY

DOCUMENTATION

www.mfa.bg/en

EMBASSIES AND CONSULATES

Canada
ul. Moskovska 9, Sofia.
Tel (02) 969 9710. www.
canadainternational.gc.ca

United States
ul. Kozyak 16, Sofia. *Tel*
(02) 937 5100. www.
bulgaria.usembassy.gov

United Kingdom
ul. Moskovska 9, Sofia. *Tel*
(02) 933 9222. www.
ukinbulgaria.fco.gov.uk

VISITOR INFORMATION

Bulgarian Tourism Authority
www.bulgariatravel.org

EMERGENCY NUMBERS

Ambulance
Tel 150.

Fire
Tel 160.

Police
Tel 166.

ARRIVING BY AIR

British Airways
www.britishairways.com

Bulgaria Air
www.air.bg

easyJet
www.easyjet.com

Gatwick Airport
www.gatwickairport.com

Heathrow Airport
www.heathrowairport.bg

Sofia Airport
www.sofia-airport.bg

Wizzair
www.wizzair.com

RAIL TRAVEL

Bulgarian State Railways
www.bdz.bg

Rail Europe
www.raileurope.com

Trainseurope
www.trainseurope.co.uk

TRAVELLING BY BUS

Sofia Central Bus Station
www.centralnaavtogara.bg

TRAVELLING BY CAR

Avis
Tel (02) 826 1100.
www.avis.bg

Budget
Tel (02) 870 0000.
www.budget.bg

Europcar
Tel (02) 981 4626.
www.europcar.bg

Shopping & Entertainment

Bulgaria has a wealth of shops, malls, open-air markets and stalls selling everything from Bulgarian-made soaps to *rakiya* (fruit brandy). In every town centre there is a market, its stalls stacked with fruit, vegetables and flowers, and street kiosks with meticulously arranged trays of dried fruit, nuts and sweets. The country's classical music, ballet and theatre season runs from the beginning of October to the end of June, when orchestras, opera and ballet companies perform at venues in Sofia and other major towns, and theatre companies stage productions of classical and contemporary plays. Bulgaria's summer folk festivals also provide an opportunity to see the country's vigorous folk culture.

OPENING HOURS

In major towns, cities and holiday resorts, shops open from 10am to 8pm from Monday to Saturday, and often later during the summer season. In Sofia and towns along the Black Sea coast, shops also open on Sundays, closing at various times between 2 and 6pm.

MARKETS

Every town in the country has an open-air market, where fresh fruit and vegetables and a great variety of Bulgarian cheeses and sausages are sold.

Several of Bulgaria's most picturesque outdoor markets sell not only fresh produce, clothing and household goods but also handicrafts. The liveliest of these are the daily **Zhenski Pazar** in Sofia, the daily market in Varna and the Sunday morning market in Bansko.

The daily **Bric-à-Brac Market** in front of the Aleksandŭr Nevski Memorial Church in Sofia is the best place for antiques, old postcards, and Communist-era medals and militaria.

HANDICRAFTS

High-quality craft items are abundant at Bulgaria's souvenir stalls, with ceramics, embroidery and traditional textiles among the most popular tourist buys. Pottery from the central Bulgarian town of Troyan, decorated with flowing patterns in bright colours, is a favourite Bulgarian

souvenir, and is available throughout the country. Traditional Bulgarian textiles include vividly patterned *kilims* (carpets) hand-woven on vertical looms by the womenfolk in highland villages. Other highland crafts include *guberi* (fleecy rugs), and *kozyatsi* (tufted goat-hair rugs). Brightly coloured blouses, delicately embroidered with folk motifs, are usually also of high quality.

Bulgaria is a major producer of attar of roses, an essential oil extracted from the damask rose, which is used all over the world in perfumes and beauty products. Locally made soaps, skin creams and eau de cologne made from Bulgarian attar are available from pharmacies and supermarkets throughout the country. Other items to look out for include traditional copper pots and coffee sets, and hand-painted copies of Orthodox icons.

Souvenirs can be found in market stalls and small shops in tourist resorts across the country. Specialist outlets selling fine handicrafts include the **Ethnographic Museum Shop** in Sofia. Shops in Veliko Tûrnovo are also good places to pick up good-quality items made by local crafts workshops.

FOOD, WINE AND RAKIYA

The most famous Bulgarian speciality is yogurt, considered very healthy due to a rare bacteria found only in Bulgaria. *Sirene* (salty white cheese) and *kashkaval* (cheese made from cow's milk) are also some good buys available

in most supermarkets. Most food shops also carry a wide selection of Bulgarian wines. While Bulgarian Merlot and Cabernet Sauvignon are on a par with red wines from elsewhere in Europe, domestic varieties, such as Melnik from the southwest, have a much more distinctive character. The highest quality wines are those produced by leading wineries such as **Todoroff** and **Damyanitza**. These are available in stores throughout the country. Bottles of *rakiya* (grape or plum brandy) make very good gifts. Bottles marked *otlezhala* (matured) are likely to be of superior quality.

NIGHTLIFE

Central Sofia is packed with clubs and bars, many of which have designer interiors and attract an equally style-conscious clientele. **Motto**, which serves cocktails and food in a trendy lounge-bar atmosphere, is typical of Sofia's contemporary bar scene. There is also a growing number of pubs, of which **JJ Murphy's** is one of the longest-established.

Dance clubs are informal and inexpensive, with long-standing venues such as **Yalta** and **Chervilo** ("Lipstick") attracting international DJs and a young crowd.

MUSIC, THEATRE AND DANCE

Bulgaria has a fine tradition of classical music and tickets for concerts are very reasonably priced. The Bulgarian Philharmonic Orchestra, which performs weekly at the **Bulgaria Concert Hall** in Sofia, is the country's most prestigious orchestra. Plovdiv, Varna and Burgas also have good symphony orchestras. Many of Bulgaria's best ensembles and soloists perform at **Varna Summer International Festival** in July.

Local bands playing rock and jazz standards are a frequent feature of bars and clubs in the cities and holiday resorts. Rock and pop stars perform at the **National Palace of Culture** in Sofia. International jazz musicians gather for the **Varna International Jazz Festival** in early August, and the **Bansko Jazz Festival** in mid-August.

Every sizeable town and city in Bulgaria has at least one theatre. Sofia's leading theatre, the **Ivan Vazov National Theatre**, is the base for Bulgaria's best actors and directors. Modern plays are also put on by the **Sofia Drama Theatre**, the **Aleko Konstantinov Satirical Theatre**, and **Tears and Laughter**, Sofia's oldest theatre.

The **Sfumato Theatre Workshop** is well known internationally for putting on contemporary and avant-garde plays. However, the main festival for challenging modern drama is **Scene at the Crossroads**, which takes place in Plovdiv in mid-September. Modern drama also forms part of **Sozopol's Arts Festival**, in early September. For visitors from other countries, the main disadvantage is that

almost all performances are in Bulgarian with simultaneous translations seldom provided. However, many are based on improvisation and movement rather than text, so they are accessible even to non-Bulgarian speakers.

The leading opera and ballet companies in the country operate under the aegis of the **National Opera and Ballet Sofia**. The **Plovdiv Opera and Philharmonic Society**, **Stara Zagora Opera** and **Varna Opera and Philharmonic Society** are the best regional companies.

Information and tickets for most cultural events in Sofia are available from the National Palace of Culture.

CINEMA

New Hollywood blockbusters and other international films reach Bulgaria a month or two after their release elsewhere. They are screened in

their original language, with subtitles in Bulgarian. Modern multiplex cinemas with comfortable seats and high-quality sound are common in Sofia. Outside the capital, cinemas tend to be old-fashioned and badly ventilated. Both in Sofia and elsewhere, cinema tickets are inexpensive.

FOLK FESTIVALS

Performances of traditional folk music and dancing are an important feature of the Bulgarian calendar. The leading folk festival, held in Koprivshtitsa, is the **International Folk Festival**, at which folk dancers and musicians from all over Bulgaria perform. This takes place every five years on a meadow outside the village.

The **Folklore Days Festival**, a smaller gathering featuring local folk singers and dancers, is held in central Koprivshtitsa in mid-August each year.

DIRECTORY

MARKETS

Bric-à-Brac Market
pl. Aleksandûr Nevski, Sofia.

Zhenski Pazar
bul. Stefan Stambolov, Sofia.

HANDICRAFTS

Ethnographic Museum Shop
pl. Aleksandûr Batenberg 1, Sofia. **Tel** (02) 805 2615.

FOOD, WINE AND RAKIYA

Damyanitza
www.melnikwine.bg

Todoroff
www.todoroff-wines.com

NIGHTLIFE

Chervilo
bul. Tsar Osvoboditel 9, Sofia. **Tel** (02) 981 6633.
www.chervilo.com

JJ Murphy's
ul. Kurnigradska 6, Sofia. **Tel** (02) 980 2870.
www.jjmurphys.com

Motto
ul. Aksakov 18, Sofia. **Tel** (02) 987 2723.
www.motto-bg.com

Yalta
bul. Tsar Osvoboditel 20, Sofia. **Tel** (02) 980 1297.
www.yaltaclub.com

MUSIC, THEATRE AND DANCE

Aleko Konstantinov Satirical Theatre
ul. Stefan Karadzha 26, Sofia. **Tel** (02) 988 1060.

Bansko Jazz Festival
Vaptsarov Square, Bansko.
www.bansko.bg

Bulgaria Concert Hall
ul. Aksakov 1, Sofia. **Tel** (02) 987 7656.

National Opera and Ballet Sofia
Dondukov Bul. 30, Sofia. **Tel** (02) 987 1366.
www.operasofia.bg

Ivan Vazov National Theatre
ul. Dyakon Ignatii 5, Sofia. **Tel** (02) 811 9227.
www.nationaltheatre.bg

National Palace of Culture
1 Vitosha, Sofia, **Tel** (02) 916 6300. www.ndk.bg

Plovdiv Opera and Philharmonic Society
Tel (032) 625 553.
www.ofd-plovdiv.org

Scene at the Crossroads
Tel (032) 630 476.
www.scenatepe.com

Sfumato Theatre Workshop
ul. Dimitar Grekov 2, Sofia. **Tel** (02) 944 0127.
www.sfumato.info

Sofia Drama Theatre
bul. Y Sakuzov 23a, Sofia. **Tel** (02) 944 2485.
www.sofiatheatre.en

Sozopol's Arts Festival
Tel (02) 980 7833.
www.apollonia.bg

Stara Zagora Opera
M M Kussev 30, Plovdiv. **Tel** (042) 622 431.
www.stateopera-starazagora.com

Tears and Laughter
ul Rakovski 127, Sofia. **Tel** (02) 987 5895.
www.salzaismiah.com

Varna International Jazz Festival
Chaika 50-D-47, Varna. **Tel** (052) 302 322.
www.vsjf.com

Varna Opera and Philharmonic Society
pl. Nezavisi-Most, Varna. **Tel** (052) 665 022.
www.operavarna.bg

Varna Summer International Festival
www.varnasummerfest.org

FOLK FESTIVALS

Folklore Days Festival
www.folklore-bg.com

International Folk Festival
www.folklore-bg.com

Where to Stay in Bulgaria

From luxurious hotels in major towns and cities to monasteries in isolated locations, Bulgaria offers an ever-increasing choice of places to stay. There is a profusion of hotels in Sofia, on the Black Sea coast and in skiing areas, though the choice in northern and central Bulgaria is more limited.

PRICE CATEGORIES
Price categories are for a standard double room per night in high season, including tax and service charges. Breakfast is included, unless otherwise specified.

€ Under 25 euros
€€ 25–50 euros
€€€ 50–75 euros
€€€€ 75–100 euros
€€€€€ Over 100 euros

SOFIA

Bulgari

€€€

ul. Pirotska 50 **Tel** *(02) 831 0060* **Fax** *(02) 931 1477* **Rooms** *12* **Map** *B3*

This is a small and friendly hotel in one of Sofia's oldest shopping areas. Rooms are low-ceilinged and simply furnished, but all have a small TV, desk space and Wi-Fi. While some bathrooms have a bath, others have a Bulgarian-style open shower. **www.bulgarihotel.net**

Scotty's Boutique Hotel

 €€€

ul. Ekzarh Yosif 11 **Tel** *(02) 983 6777* **Fax** *(02) 983 3229* **Rooms** *16* **Map** *C2*

In a historic district close to Sofia's main mosque, synagogue and market hall, Scotty's occupies the upper floors of a 19th-century apartment block. Rooms are decorated in contemporary, minimalist style and have TV, minibar and spacious bathrooms. Breakfast is not available but there are plenty of cafés nearby. **www.scottyshotel.info**

Light

 €€€€

ul. Veslets 37 **Tel** *(02) 917 9090* **Fax** *(02) 917 9010* **Rooms** *31* **Map** *D2*

Located in a stylish contemporary building in a tranquil 19th-century street, Light is just a short distance from the main sights of interest. Rooms are plush and cosy, although there is a touch of minimalism about the lobby and communal areas. There is a small gym and sauna on site. **www.hotels.light.bg**

Grand Hotel Sofia

 €€€€€

ul. Gurko 1 **Tel** *(02) 811 0800* **Fax** *(02) 811 0801* **Rooms** *122* **Map** *D5*

The centrally located Grand Hotel Sofia provides modern five-star comforts with spacious rooms, stylish furnishings and eager, attentive staff. The health centre offers a gym, solarium and beauty treatments. There is a restaurant, an elegant café and a piano bar in the basement. **www.grandhotelsofia.bg**

Radisson SAS

 €€€€€

pl. Narodno Sûbranie 4 **Tel** *(02) 933 4334* **Fax** *(02) 933 4335* **Rooms** *136* **Map** *E5*

This is one of Sofia's best hotels both in terms of comfort and location, with large en suite rooms offering views of the Aleksandûr Nevski Memorial Church *(see pp608–609)*. There is a restaurant on the top floor providing panoramic views over the city and a lively pub on the ground floor. **www.sofia.radissonsas.com**

Sheraton Sofia Hotel Balkan

 €€€€€

pl. Sveta Nedelya 5 **Tel** *(02) 981 6541* **Fax** *(02) 980 6464* **Rooms** *188* **Map** *C4*

Centrally located, the opulent Sheraton is a popular choice for those looking for five-star comforts. All the rooms have plush furnishings and bathtubs, while the executive-class rooms on the upper floors also feature flat-screen TVs, tea- and coffee-making facilities and antique furniture. **www.luxurycollection.com/sofia**

FURTHER AFIELD Niky

 €€

ul. Neofit Rilski 16 **Tel** *(02) 952 3058* **Fax** *(02) 951 6091* **Rooms** *23*

A bright, clean and friendly hotel in the heart of the city, Niky has a mix of cosy en suite double rooms and apartment-style rooms with a lounge space, TV, small kitchenette and spacious bathrooms. The ground floor grill-restaurant has an attractive garden and is a popular dining-out venue in the summer. **www.hotel-niky.com**

FURTHER AFIELD Red Bed and Breakfast

€€

ul. Lyuben Karavelov 15 **Tel** *(02) 988 8188* **Fax** *(02) 988 8188* **Rooms** *6*

Friendly and informal bed and breakfast in a central location, housed in the upper storeys of the Red House Cultural Centre. Rooms can be simply furnished or plushly decorated, with TV and antique wardrobe. Toilets and bathrooms are located in the hallway. Breakfast is delivered to your room at the time of your choice. **www.redbandb.com**

FURTHER AFIELD Rotasar

 €€

ul. Costa Lulchev 15a & Kosta Lulchev St. 1 **Tel** *(02) 971 4571* **Fax** *(02) 971 4574* **Rooms** *18*

A friendly, intimate hotel 2 km (1 mile) east of the city centre, Rotasar offers double rooms and studio apartments, each with homely furnishings, TV, en suite bathroom and Internet access. Unusual paintings and prints decorate the rooms. Optional breakfast costs a few euros extra. **www.rotasar.com**

Map References *see map of Sofia pp604–605*

FURTHER AFIELD The Rooms

ul. Pop Bogomil 10 **Tel** *(02) 983 6712* **Fax** *(02) 983 3508* **Rooms** *5*

Located in a converted 19th-century apartment building in a quiet residential street, this informal and youthful bed and breakfast offers a mix of single and double rooms, with high ceilings and antique furnishings. Some bathrooms are en suite, others are shared.

FURTHER AFIELD Apartment House Dunav

ul. Dunav 38 **Tel** *(02) 983 3002* **Fax** *(02) 983 3804* **Rooms** *14*

Located in an old-fashioned residential street, Dunav is suitable for both short and long stays. It has self-catering units ranging in size from two-person studios to two-room family apartments. All units feature wooden floors, pastel colours and modern bathrooms. Breakfast is served on request. **www.dunavapartmenthouse.com**

FURTHER AFIELD Diter

ul. Han Asparuh 65 **Tel** *(02) 989 8998* **Fax** *(02) 989 8998* **Rooms** *21*

A friendly establishment in a restored 19th-century mansion in a quiet cobbled street, Diter's rooms offer warm colour schemes, TV, minibar, Internet access and plenty of desk space. The bathroom showers are specially designed to give water massages and an atmospheric basement breakfast room adds to the charm. **www.diterhotel.com**

FURTHER AFIELD Sofia Plaza

bul. Hristo Botev 154 **Tel** *(02) 813 7979* **Fax** *(02) 813 7912* **Rooms** *50*

A medium-sized hotel within easy reach of Sofia's train and bus stations, the Sofia Plaza has pastel-coloured rooms with TV, minibar, Internet access. There are also some family rooms including a kitchenette. Other facilities include a sauna, solarium and gym. **www.hotelsofiaplaza.com**

FURTHER AFIELD Hilton

bul. Bulgaria 1 **Tel** *(02) 933 5000* **Fax** *(02) 933 5111* **Rooms** *245*

High standards of comfort and service in a large, modern hotel, just south of the centre but still within walking distance of the sights. Rooms, in pastel colours, have coffee-and tea-making facilities and spacious bathrooms. Other features include a fine restaurant, swimming pool and fitness facilities. **www.sofia.hilton.com**

FURTHER AFIELD Kempinski Zografski

bul. James Bouchier 100 **Tel** *(02) 969 2222* **Fax** *(02) 969 2223* **Rooms** *420*

The five-star Kempinski Zografski is 4 km (2 miles) south of the centre and has on-site shopping facilities, fitness rooms, a swimming pool and beauty salon. Rooms are well equipped and service is professional. The hotel has five restaurants, a casino, a Viennese-style café and two bars. **www.kempinski.bg**

FURTHER AFIELD Oborishte Residence

ul. Oborishte 63 **Tel** *(02) 814 4888* **Fax** *(02) 846 8244* **Rooms** *9*

A cosy and intimate hotel, the Oborishte Residence is located in a leafy, upmarket residential area on the eastern fringes of the city centre. Most of the accommodation is in the form of two-room apartments. Wooden floors and contemporary design flourishes help to create a stylish but homely atmosphere. **www.residence-oborishte.com**

REST OF BULGARIA

BACHKOVO Bachkovo Monastery

Bachkovo Monastery **Tel** *(03327) 277* **Rooms** *10*

A stay here is as close to monastic life as many visitors will experience. A number of the monks' cells have been refurbished and converted into guest rooms with simple wooden furniture and en suite bathrooms. Guests are guaranteed an early night as the monastery gates close at 9pm.

BANSKO Kempinski Hotel Grand Arena

ul. Pirin 96 **Tel** *(0749) 88888* **Fax** *(0749) 88565* **Rooms** *159*

Designed to look like the local houses, this five-star hotel complex stands next to the ski-lift base station. It is very luxurious and guests pay handsomely for their stay. The rooms are spacious and have fantastic mountain views. Facilities include indoor and outdoor pools, a spa centre and tennis courts. **www.kempinski-bansko.com**

BOROVETS Alpin

Tel *(07503) 2201* **Fax** *(07503) 2203* **Rooms** *8, plus 8 chalets*

Centrally located at the foot of the ski slopes and near the ski-lift stations, this small establishment offers a cosier alternative to the massive package-holiday-oriented hotels. Rooms are comfortably furnished and guests can also use the steam room and Jacuzzi. **www.alpin-hotel.bg**

BOROVETS Rila

Tel *(07503) 2441* **Fax** *(07503) 2531* **Rooms** *522*

Bulgaria's largest ski hotel, Rila is situated right at the heart of Borovets, next to the slopes and ski-lift stations. It provides excellent four-star facilities and caters mainly to tour groups. The rooms have wonderful views and there is a sauna, Jacuzzi, steam baths, fitness centre and a ski school. **www.borovets-bg.com**

Key to Symbols *see back cover flap*

BURGAS Bulgaria

ul. Alexandrovska 21 **Tel** *(056) 842 820* **Fax** *(056) 841 291* **Rooms** *203*

Burgas's most imposing landmark is the 16-storey Bulgaria hotel, built in 1976 to accommodate high-ranking bureaucrats and foreign diplomats. All rooms have TV, radio, en suite bathrooms and a fantastic view of Burgas and the coast. **www.bulgaria-hotel.com**

GOLDEN SANDS Berlin Golden Beach

Golden Sands **Tel** *(052) 384 151* **Fax** *(052) 355 113* **Rooms** *276*

A huge luxury complex right on the beach, the Berlin Golden Beach is a well-managed hotel offering high standards of service. All the rooms have fantastic sea views and it also has an attractive range of facilities including mineral-water pools, children's entertainment and tennis courts. **www.lti-berlin.net**

KOPRIVSHTITSA Tryanova Kûshta

ul. Geremilov 5 **Tel** *(00359) 8883 02313* **Rooms** *3* **Apartments** *1*

Built in 1895, the Tryanova Kûshta is an authentic wooden house in a tranquil spot on Koprivshtitsa's western hillside. Its three atmospheric rooms are decorated in red, blue and pink and have pine beds and colourful rugs. The downstairs apartment retains the original low wooden ceilings designed to conserve heat in winter.

MELNIK Litova Kûshta

Litov's House Complex **Tel** *(07437) 313* **Rooms** *12*

This upmarket hotel is built over one of Melnik's oldest wine cellars, cut deep into the rock. The large rooms are smartly furnished and have traditional wooden ceilings, panelling and floors. Hand-painted borders and coving provide a touch of style. Horse riding can be arranged. **www.litovakushta.com**

NESEBÛR Sveti Stephan

ul. Ribarska 11 **Tel** *(0554) 43604* **Fax** *(0554) 43604* **Rooms** *18*

Located opposite the New Metropolitan Church originally known as Sveti Stefan, this is a modern hotel whose façade mimics the style of Nesebûr's 19th-century National Revival buildings. Excellent service is combined with comfortably furnished rooms and sea views. There is also a fitness centre, sauna, Jacuzzi and solarium.

PLOVDIV Hebros

ul. Konstantin Stoilov 51a **Tel** *(032) 260 180* **Fax** *(032) 260 252* **Rooms** *10*

This atmospheric hotel consists of two adjacent 19th-century houses that have been lavishly renovated. Furnished with antiques, it features low wooden ceilings and subdued lighting and has an enchanting ambience. There is also an award-winning restaurant. Internet access is available. **www.hebros-hotel.com**

PLOVDIV Novotel

ul. Zlatyu Boyadzhiev 2 **Tel** *(032) 934 444* **Fax** *(032) 934 346* **Rooms** *330*

Overlooking the Maritsa river, this is Plovdiv's largest and most expensive hotel. Facilities include Wi-Fi, a fitness centre and an indoor pool, but the eye-catching interiors are the real attraction. Its restaurant, Evridika, is the most stylish in town. **www.icep.bg**

RILA MONASTERY Tsarev vrûh

Tel *(070) 542 280* **Fax** *(070) 542 285* **Rooms** *54*

Surrounded by trees, on the hillside a little beyond the monastery, the Tsarev vrûh is a large whitewashed hotel complex offering rooms with simple pine furniture. Some have balconies and most have lovely views of the valley. The hotel also has a restaurant.

SOZOPOL Orion

ul. Vihren 28 **Tel** *(0550) 23193* **Fax** *(0550) 22037* **Rooms** *16*

Set high on a hill in the new town, and facing the Sozopol and Burgas bays to the northwest, the Orion is one of the few hotels on the Bulgarian coast that offers romantic views of sunsets over the sea. The hotel is family-run, with clean rooms, and it has an excellent restaurant with an outdoor terrace. **www.hotel-orion.net**

SUNNY BEACH Neptun Beach

Sunny Beach **Tel** *(055) 426 605* **Fax** *(055) 422 011* **Rooms** *376*

Sunny Beach is full of hotels catering to visitors on package holidays. Standards vary, but the Neptun Beach has a reputation for consistently good service. It offers spacious rooms with superb sea views and many other amenities including children's entertainment, an outdoor Jacuzzi and a karaoke bar. **www.neptunbeach.com**

VARNA Grand Hotel Musala Palace

ul. Musala 3 **Tel** *(052) 664 100* **Fax** *(052) 664 196* **Rooms** *24*

The Grand Hotel Musala Palace is a central five-star hotel housed in a 19th-century building. Thick carpets, Art Nouveau decor, impeccably liveried staff and rooms with original works of art and flat-screen TVs are among the extravagant features on offer. The restaurant is equally fine. **www.musalapalace.bg**

VELIKO TÛRNOVO Comfort

ul. Panoyot Tipografov 5 **Tel** *(062) 628 728* **Fax** *(062) 623 525* **Rooms** *7*

This cosy hotel has wood panelling and parquet floors, and commands tremendous views of Tsarevets. All the rooms have large windows and some have balconies as well. It is also extremely clean and the staff provide friendly and helpful service. Internet access is available. **www.hotelkomfortbg.com**

Key to Price Guide *see p636* **Key to Symbols** *see back cover flap*

Where to Eat in Bulgaria

As new restaurants continue to open in Bulgaria, the range of eating options throughout the country is gradually increasing. The types of restaurant vary from eateries offering the best of traditional Bulgarian cooking to elegant establishments specializing in modern European cuisine.

PRICE CATEGORIES
Based on the price per person of a three-course meal with half a bottle of wine, including cover charge, service and tax.

€ Under 10 euros
€€ 10–20 euros
€€€ 20–30 euros
€€€€ Over 30 euros

SOFIA

L'Etranger
ul. Tsar Simeon 78 **Tel** *(02) 983 1417* €€€ **Map** D3

Located in an anonymous side street just off the bustling Knyaginya Mariya Luiza, this intimate, family-run French bistro is worth seeking out whether for a quick lunch or a multi-course meal. The food is excellent, authentic and not too expensive. Delicious desserts and a carefully chosen list of French wines add to the experience.

Gioia
ul. Lavele 11 **Tel** *(02) 986 0854* €€€ **Map** D3

For quality Italian food in an intimate setting, there is no better place in Sofia. The menu features innumerable varieties of fresh pasta. Main courses include veal cutlets and some highly recommended fish dishes. The wine list is as Italian as the food, and the espresso coffee is as dark and strong as you would expect.

Checkpoint Charly
ul. Ivan Vazov 12 **Tel** *(02) 988 0370* €€€€ **Map** D5

In this stylish eatery minimalist decor is melded with ironic Communist-era decorations, including place mats designed to resemble the propaganda-filled newspapers of the Socialist years. Quality international cuisine from steak to roast duck, and high-class live jazz at weekends – when you will need to reserve in order to get a table.

Ovtud aleya zad shkafa
ul. Budapeshta 31 **Tel** *(02) 983 5545* €€€€ **Map** D2

Housed in a beautifully restored Art Nouveau building in a quiet street northeast of the centre, "Beyond the Alley Behind the Cupboard" is one of Sofia's most atmospheric and charming restaurants. The menu features a mixture of Bulgarian and modern European dishes – all are excellently prepared.

FURTHER AFIELD Dani's
ul. Angel Kûnchev 18a **Tel** *(02) 987 4548* €

A deli-style café-restaurant on a quiet downtown corner, Dani's is furnished with a couple of narrow tables flanked by tall wooden stools. On the menu is an inventive range of sandwiches, salads, soups and pastas, many of which cater to vegetarians. Dani's is also famous for its refreshing home-made lemonade.

FURTHER AFIELD Jimmy's Sladoledena Kûshta
ul. Angel Kûnchev 11 **Tel** *(02) 980 3099* €

This renowned café-cum-sweet shop serves supremely palatable ice creams (to eat in or take away), as well as scrumptious pancakes and gateaux. It is also a good place to indulge in a decent cup of coffee, or a luxurious hot chocolate. There are several branches in the centre of the city.

FURTHER AFIELD Pod Lipite
ul. Elin Pelin 1 **Tel** *(02) 866 5053* €€

Pod Lipite (Under the Limes) recreates the atmosphere of a 19th-century country tavern, with a wood-beamed interior and delicious home-cooked food. The emphasis is on grilled and oven-baked meats, although there is a decent selection of vegetarian dishes on the starters menu. Reservations are required.

FURTHER AFIELD Pri Latsi
ul. Oborishte 18 **Tel** *(02) 846 8687* €€

A Hungarian-run restaurant located in a small and welcoming split-level space, Pri Latsi is decorated with folk-art textiles and ceramics. The specialities comprise several varieties of spicy paprika-rich goulash with home-made noodles or dumplings. For dessert, the shamloi galushki (syrup-covered balls of deep-fried dough) are irresistible.

FURTHER AFIELD Vagabond
ul. Svetoslav Terter 5 **Tel** *(02) 944 1465* €€

Vagabond has the homely and intimate feel of a domestic dining room. The menu has a genuinely international flavour, although it is the Russian-influenced dishes that stand out. Vodka with *selyodka* (marinated herring) makes a good starter, and the home-made *pelmeni* (meat-filled dumplings) are outstanding.

Map References *see map of Sofia pp604–605*

FURTHER AFIELD Mahaloto

bul. Vasil Levski 51 **Tel** *(0887) 617 972*

A welcoming city-centre restaurant in a red-brick cellar, offering a classy mixture of Bulgarian and international cuisine, backed up by a list of quality wines. Stand-out dishes include the trout with walnuts and the chicken breast with cream and mushroom sauce. In summer, head for the quiet, tree-shaded terrace behind the building.

FURTHER AFIELD Manastirska Magernitsa

ul. Han Asparuh 67 **Tel** *(02) 980 3883*

Located in a plushly decorated villa featuring flowery wallpaper and near-antique furnishings, Manastirska Magernitsa means "monastery refectory". Many of the dishes on offer were researched from the cookbooks of Bulgaria's monasteries; lentil, bean and pepper-based recipes feature strongly, alongside grilled meat dishes.

FURTHER AFIELD Pri Yafata

ul. Solunska 28 **Tel** *(02) 980 1727*

One of Sofia's most enjoyable folk-themed restaurants, Pri Yafata boasts a colourful collection of embroidered tablecloths, striped rugs and old muskets hanging from the walls. A range of Bulgarian specialities is enhanced by quality wines from every region of the country, as well as a long list of potent, fruit-flavoured rakiyas (brandies).

FURTHER AFIELD Sushi Bar

ul. Denkoglu 18 **Tel** *(02) 981 8442*

Smart without being overly formal, the Sushi Bar is around the corner from Sofia's main shopping street and is the perfect place for a quick lunch or a more leisurely Oriental meal. The extensive menu of expertly prepared sushi is available in small helpings, or in set menus featuring various types of sushi on one plate.

FURTHER AFIELD Chepishev

ul. Ivanitsa Danchev 27 **Tel** *(02) 959 1010*

This upmarket restaurant in the mountainside suburb of Boyana is perfect for a special night out. The Bulgarian and modern European dishes are prepared to gourmet standards. There is also an impressive list of international wines, although it is the huge selection of whiskies that really makes the place famous.

FURTHER AFIELD Uno Enoteca

bul. Vasil Levski 45 **Tel** *(02) 981 4372*

Combining exceptional standards of service with old-fashioned elegance, this is one of the best places in the city for formal dining. Expect modern European cuisine with a strong Mediterranean flavour, backed up by a wide-ranging list of vintage wines from Bulgaria and abroad.

FURTHER AFIELD Vishnite

ul. Hristo Smirnenski 45 **Tel** *(02) 963 4984 or (0890) 866 730*

Hidden away in the residential district of Lozenets, 3 km (2 miles) southeast of the centre, Vishnite is delightfully intimate and makes for a fine dining experience. The menu features several classic European dishes, accompanied by a small but well-chosen selection of wines. There are only four tables, so reservations are required.

REST OF BULGARIA

BACHKOVO Dzhamura

ul. Osvobozhdenya 74 **Tel** *(03327) 2320*

This large restaurant has a cosy interior warmed by a large open fire as well as a spacious open terrace overlooking the river and makes a good place to relax after visiting the monastery. Although vegetarians are catered to, grilled meat and fish dominate the menu.

BANSKO Mehana Hadzhi Rushovi

ul. Pirin 33 **Tel** *(0878) 805 532*

This intimate mehana (tavern) is concealed behind traditional stone walls and a hefty wooden door. The interior features bare walls hung with animal skins. Specialities include *kurvavitsa* (Bansko black pudding), patlazhan po Banski (Bansko-style aubergines) and yogurt with locally picked forest fruits.

BOROVETS Hunters

Tel *(0750) 32509*

The friendly restaurant owner, who is also a ski instructor and mountain guide, spent time as a chef in Turkey, which accounts for the menu's eclectic mix. Turkish bread and kebabs are offered alongside Bulgarian dishes, English and Swedish breakfasts and fried trout. The walls are decorated with tea towels donated by English guests.

BURGAS Vodenitsata

Morska Gradina (Sea Gardens), northern end **Tel** *(0897) 988 334*

One of several outdoor eateries in Burgas's peaceful Sea Gardens, the Vodenitsata (Watermill) is a bustling place particularly popular on balmy summer evenings when diners may have to queue for a seat. Some tables have sea views and service is usually efficient. Fresh fish, pizza, and Bulgarian cuisine are on the menu.

Key to Price Guide *see p636* **Key to Symbols** *see back cover flap*

GOLDEN SANDS Taj Mahal 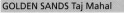 €€
Next to Admiral Hotel **Tel** *(0886) 600 030*

This atmospheric Indian restaurant, surrounded by lush green lawns, offers deliciously spiced food cooked by Indian chefs served in generous portions by waiting staff in saris and other traditional dress. Comfortable sofas scattered with colourful cushions surround the smart dining tables.

KOPRIVSHTITSA Dyado Liben €
Bul. Hadzhi Nencho Palaveev 47 **Tel** *(07184) 2109*

Housed in one of Koprivshtitsa's 19th-century mansions, the Dyado Liben is wonderfully atmospheric. Tables fill the wood-panelled salon and symmetrical rooms upstairs, while outdoor seating takes up the cobbled courtyard. The brief menu includes Bulgarian and Serbian cuisine, with an emphasis on grilled meat.

MELNIK Mencheva Kûshta €€
ul. Melnik 46 **Tel** *(07437) 339*

Dining tables and chairs are squeezed into various rooms in this atmospheric old house, which is decorated with antique knick-knacks and a small fish pond. The menu begins with a selection of over 30 *rakiyas* (fruit brandies) and moves on to traditional dishes such as nettle soup and *otshtipez* (minced meat with cheese).

NESEBÛR Kapitanska Sreshta €€
ul. Mena 22 **Tel** *(0554) 42124*

Nesebûr's medieval stone walls provide a fitting backdrop to this atmospheric restaurant, which occupies a lovely old house and has a wide, shaded terrace overlooking the harbour. Conger eel, shark and swordfish feature among the wide range of fish dishes. Diners pay a little extra for the restaurant's established reputation.

PLOVDIV Devetnaysti Vek €
ul. Tsar Koloyan 1a **Tel** *(032) 653 882*

The walls of this romanticized version of a 19th-century Bulgarian tavern are hung with antique rifles and other curiosities. Traditional tablecloths and brown-glazed crockery complete the effect. Specialities include *manastirski keremida*, a well-prepared mixture of tongue, intestines and mushrooms baked with cheese.

PLOVDIV Petr I €€€
ul. Knyaz Tseretelev 11 **Tel** *(032) 632 389*

An expensive Russian restaurant whose sumptuous decor borders on kitsch, Petr I nonetheless offers a delightful dining experience and has splendid city views from its terrace. Liveried staff provide good service and there is a nightly floor show featuring costumed dancers. The Russian-themed menu includes a whole page of vodkas.

RILA MONASTERY Drushliavitsa €€
Tel *(0888) 278 756*

A stream runs under the Drushliavitsa's outdoor terrace, beside the monastery walls. Hearty Bulgarian dishes served here include an excellent *shkembe* churba (tripe soup) and an equally good *bob churba* (bean soup). Freshly caught trout and beef steak are also on the menu. The restaurant is usually busy and provides good service.

SOZOPOL Rusalka €
ul. Milet 36 **Tel** *(0550) 23047*

The Rusalka is one of several restaurants situated on the south side of the Old Town peninsula. Waves crash against rocks directly below and diners have superb views of the main beach. The menu features a variety of seafood as well as pizza and pasta. The restaurant belongs to the Rusalka hotel.

SUNNY BEACH Hanska Shatra €€€
Tel *(0554) 22811*

A massive concrete replica of a "Khan's Tent", lit by neon lights on a hilltop north of Sunny Beach, this themed restaurant is flashy but fun. Diners can choose from a range of Bulgarian and international cuisine, and are entertained with endless floor shows performed by costumed dancers. The outdoor terrace has great views of the coast.

VARNA Tambuktu €€
On the seafront, close to the Aquarium **Tel** *(052) 610 864*

Located right next to the sea, this open-air fish restaurant evokes a vaguely desert island theme due to its use of rough wood furniture and proximity to the beach. Numerous small aquariums add to the decor. Baked salmon with whisky and broccoli sauce is among the specialities; there is also a sushi menu.

VARNA Musala Palace €€€
ul. Musala 3 **Tel** *(052) 664 100*

Varna's classiest restaurant, in the Grand Hotel Musala Palace *(see p638)*, is a wonderfully refined affair, with velvet upholstery, silver cutlery and impeccable staff. The award-winning chef prepares a small selection of European dishes, including roast duckling, venison and fresh Black Sea turbot. Daily specials supplement the menu.

VELIKO TÛRNOVO Klub na Arhitekta €
ul. Velchova Zavlka 14 **Tel** *(062) 621 451*

Reached by a flight of steps leading down off ul. Nikola Pikolo, this traditional-style tavern is built in the steep hillside above the Yantra river. Spring water trickles from the bare rock walls of its cave-like interior, while candlelight and hefty wooden tables create a snug environment popular with locals.

General Index

Zagreb (cont.)
Zagreb: the Upper Town **488–9**
Marconi, Guglielmo 554
Marconi, Henryk 180, 181
Marconi, Leonard 201
Margaret, Princess 355
Margaret Island 352, 355
Margit Kovács Ceramics Collection (Szentendre) **358**
Maria Alexandrovna, Tsarina 155
Maria Cantacuzino, Princess 575
Maria Stransky 407
Maria Theresa, Queen
  Bishop's Palace (Eger) 380
  Burgtheater 404
  The Royal Palace (Budapest) 339
  Városliget 354
Maribor 432, **440–41**
  hotels 447
  map 440
  restaurants 449
Maribor Castle and Regional Museum (Maribor) **440**
Marie, Queen 580
Mariinskiy Theatre, St Petersburg 155, 159
Maritime and Historical Museum of Croatia (Rijeka) 482
Maritime Museum (Dubrovnik) 459
Marjan Peninsula (Split) **467**
Market Colonnade (Karlovy Vary) **268**
The Market (Ljubljana) 420, 422–3
Markets 66
  Bulgaria **634**
  Croatia **500**
  Czech Republic **286**
  Estonia **114**
  Hungary **388**
  Latvia **90**
  Montenegro **540**
  Moscow and St Petersburg **158**
  Poland **216**
  Romania **594**
  Slovakia **326**
  Slovenia **442**
Markus, Géza 376
Martek, Vlado 493
Martinelli, Antonio 274
Martinelli, G. 308
Martin of Tours 362
Martin of Tours (painting) 352
Martinov, Petar 458
Marton, László 351
Martos, Ivan 130
The Martyrdom of St Thomas (Rubens) 239
Marulić, Marko 466
Marzio, Galeotto 341
Maso di Bartolomeo 460
Massys, Quentin 204
Master of Flemalle 149
Master of Litoměřice 251
Master of the Solčava Maria 423
Master of the Vyšší
  Brod Altar 251
Matejko, Jan
  Battle of Grünwald 44, 181
  Cloth Hall (Cracow) 185
  Raczyński Palace (Rogalin) 205
Matejko House (Cracow) 185
Matisse, Henri 134, 149
  La Danse 147
  Goldfish 134
Matkov Kot (Logarska Dolina) 433
Matk's Tub (Logarska Dolina) 433
Matsche, Franz 268
Matveev, Andrey 154

Mátyás Church (Budapest) 338, **342–3**
  map 342–3
  music and dance 388, 389
Mátyás Corvinus, King of Hungary 333, 334, 359
  Mátyás Church 342
  Mátyás Fountain 341
  The Royal Palace 339
Mátyás Fountain 338, 341
Mátyás Király Museum (Visegrád) 359
Mauelbertsch, F. A. 279
Mavrocordat, Nicolae 574
Mažvydas, Martynas 61
Maximilian Fountain (Bratislava) 302
Maximilian of Habsburg, Archduke 460
Maya 445
Mayerhoffer, András 352, 356, 376
Mayor's Salon (Prague) **256**
MEDEM 156, 157
Medgyaszay, István 366, 367, 384
Medical treatment **13** *see also* Health and Security
Medjugorje 521
Meer, Willem van der 210, 212
Meissner, Jakob 206
Meissner Palace (Toruń) 206
Melnik **617**
  hotels 638
  restaurants 640
Melnikov, Konstantin 133, 134
Melnikov, Viktor 134
Melnikov House (Moscow) 133, **134**
Memling, Hans 213
Memorial Museum of the 1989 Revolution (Timişoara) 585
Mendelsohn, Erich 200
Menshikov, Prince 142
Menshikov Palace (St Petersburg) 142, **152**
Mentzendorff House (Riga) **79**
Merchant's house (Cracow) 185
Meridian 539
Mesni Trg 420
Messerschmidt, Franz Xaver 308
Meštrović, Ivan 454, 491
  Ban Berislavic 477
  Distant Chords 467
  Memorial to France (Kalemegdan Fortress) 551
  Meštrović Gallery (Split) 467
  Meštrović Gallery (Zagreb) 489, 491
  Milesi Palace (Split) 466
  Monument of Bishop Gregory of Nin 495
  Pietà 488
  Račić Mausoleum (Cavtat) 461
  The Victor 550
  The Well of Life 492
Meštrović Foundation 491
Meštrović Gallery (Split) **467**
Meštrović Gallery (Zagreb) 489, **491**
Metelkova Mesto 444, 445
Methodius (monk) 33
Metric System 13
Metro 158, 159
Meyerhoffer, Andras 358
Michael, Archangel
  Archangel Michael and Gabriel Orthodox Church and Museum 514
  Cathedral of the Annunciation 127
  Cathedral of the Archangel 127
  Michael's Gate 305
  Orthodox Cathedral 553
Michael I, King 568
Michael's Gate (Bratislava) 302, **305**

Acknowledgments

Dorling Kindersley would like to thank the following people whose contributions and assistance have made the preparation of this book possible.

Main Contributors

Jonathan Bousfield was born in the UK and has been travelling in Central and Eastern Europe for as long as he can remember. A student of East European history and languages, Jonathan has lived at various times in Belgrade, Sofia, Zagreb, Rīga, Vilnius and Cracow. His first travel-writing job involved researching a guide to the former Yugoslavia in 1989. Since then he has authored the Dorling Kindersley *Eyewitness Travel Guide to Bulgaria*, Rough Guides to Croatia and the Baltic States, and co-authored the Rough Guides to Austria, Poland and Bulgaria. He has also been a magazine editor, feature writer and rock critic.

Matt Willis first encountered Central and Eastern Europe during an overland trip to Iran from his home town of Malvern, UK, in 1996. Since then, he has returned repeatedly to explore the region and has worked there both as a journalist and travel guide writer. He is the author of Dorling Kindersley *Top 10 Travel Guide to Moscow* and co-author of Dorling Kindersley *Eyewitness Travel Guide to Bulgaria*.

Additional Contributors

Stephen Brook, Tomasz Darmochwał, Božidarka Boza Gligorijević, Howard Jarvis, Jerzy S Majewski, John Oates, Tim Ochser, Małgorzata Omilanowska, Marek Pernal, Catherine Phillips, Chistopher Rice, Melanie Rice, Marek Rumiński, Jakub Sito, Neil Taylor, Craig Turp, Teresa Czerniewicz-Umer, Barbara Sudnik-Wójcikowska.

Fact Checkers

Višnja Arambašić, Talis Saule Archdeacon, Andrei Bogdanov, Joel Dullroy, Irena Jamnikar, Michal Jareš, Tomáš Kleisner, Brigita Pantelejeva, Petya Milkova, Marko Mirović, Karolina Montygierd, Natasa Novakovic, Jonathan Smith, Craig Turp.

Proofreader

Debra Wolter.

Indexer

Cyber Media Services Ltd.

Design and Editorial

Publisher Douglas Amrine
List Manager Vivien Antwi
Editorial Consultant Justine Montgomery, Hugh Thompson

Senior Cartographic Editor Casper Morris
Managing Art Editor (jackets) Karen Constanti
Jacket Design Kate Leonard
Senior DTP Designer Jason Little
Senior Picture Researcher Ellen Root
Production Controller Louise Daly

Editorial Assistance

Vicki Allen.

Cartographic Assistance

The map on page 512–13 is derived from © www.openstreetmap.org and contributors, licensed under CC-BY-SA, see www.creativecommons.org for further details.

DK Picture Library

Rose Horridge, Emma Shepherd, Romaine Werblow.

Additional Photography

Gabor Barka; Demetrio Carrasco; Jiri Dolezal; John Heseltine; Nigel Hudson; Dorota and Mariusz Jarymowicz; Dave King; Beata Kowalewska; Jiri Kopriva; Krzysztof Kur; Jamie Marshall; Stanislaw Michta; Frantisek Preucil; Rough Guides: Jon Cunningham, Eddie Gerald; Lucio Rossi; Tony Souter; Jonathan Smith; Peter Wilson; Gregory Wrona; Leandro Zoppe.

Special Assistance

Dorling Kindersley would like to thank the following for their assistance:
Alex Priscu at Bran Castle Museum, Roxana Lozneanu at Palace of Parliament, Protopresbyter Radomir Nikcevic and Nada at SPC Mitropolija Crnogorsko Primorska, Elena Obuhovich at The State Hermitage Museum, Anna Kotlyar at Tretyakov Gallery.

Photography Permissions

Dorling Kindersley would like to thank the following for their assistance and kind permission to photograph at their establishments:
Lea Ferjan at Bled Castle Museum; Ethnographic Museum, Belgrade; Fresco Gallery, Belgrade; Jože Šerbec at Kobarid Museum; Marta Kovac at The National Gallery, Slovenia; Veronica Leca at The National Museum of Art of Romania and The Museum of Art Collections; National Museum of Contemporary History; Irena Ribic at Postojna Caves; The Plečnik House. Works of art have been reproduced with the kind permission of the following copyright holders;
La Danse © Succession H Matisse/DACS 2009 147cr

Picture Credits

Placement Key- t=top; tc=top centre; tr=top right; cla=centre left above; ca=centre above; cra=centre right above; cl=centre left; c=centre; cr=centre right; clb=centre left below; cb=centre below; crb=centre right below; bl=bottom left; bc=bottom centre; br=bottom right; ftl=far top left; ftr=far top right; fcla=far centre left above; fcra=far centre right above; fcl=far centre left; fcr=far centre right; fclb=far centre left below; fcrb=far centre right below; fbl=far bottom left; fbr=far bottom right.

Every effort has been made to trace the copyright holders, and we apologize in advance for any unintentional omissions. We would be pleased to insert the appropriate acknowledgments in any subsequent edition of this publication.

The Publishers are grateful to the following individuals, companies and picture libraries for permission to reproduce their photographs:

4CORNERS IMAGES: Pavan Aldo 527b, 537tc; Simeone Giovanni 38-39; Kaos03 226; Panayiotou Paul 333b; SIME/Schmid Reinhard 332.

AKG-IMAGES: 32ca, 195cra; 125cr,/ Erich Lessing 44tl, 252cla, 253bc.

ALAMY IMAGES: Vladimir Alexeev 23br; Arco Images GmbH 23cb; Peter Barritt 1c; Pat Behnke 441tr; Gary Cook 87bl; Danita Delimont/Walter Bibikow 374tr,/Inger Hogstrom 126tl,/Janis Miglavs 71b; Don Davis 578cla; Diomedia 559br,/Snezana Negovanovic 33br; Sindre Ellingsen 57tl; I Capture Photography 581cra; James Davis Photography 400bc; johnrochaphoto 30clb; Ladi Kirn 427ca; Stan Kujawa 578bl; Kuttig - Travel 469tl; Yadid Levy 150bc; Nikreates 620br; PBstock 582cl; PhotoEdit 519cb; Nicholas Pitt 33clb; PjrFoto/Phil Robinson 588bl; Profimedia International s.r.o./Michaela Dusíková 253tr, 275c; Alex Segre 150cla; Snappdragon 517c; Ilian Stage 620cl; TTL Images 535br; Ivan Vdovin 559tr; Jan Wlodarczyk 22tr; Sven Zacek 106cla.

ARCHAEOLOGICAL MUSEUM, Zagreb: 32bl.

ARCHIVES MATISSE: 147cr.

AUSCHWITZ - BIRKENAU MEMORIAL & MUSEUM: 194tr, 194cl, 194bl, 194br, 195tc, 196cl, 197tl, 197tr, 197cb, 197br,/ Ryszard Domasik 195crb.

SZABOLCS BARANYAI: 364bl.

BRAN CASTLE MUSEUM: 580bc, 581tc.

THE BRIDGEMAN ART LIBRARY: Torun, Poland (engraving) (b/w photo), German School, (17th century)/Private Collection 21ca, Holy Roman Emperor Charles IV (colour litho), French School/Private Collection/The Stapleton

Collection 34ca, Matthias I, Hunyadi (oil on paper),/Kunsthistorisches Museum, Vienna, Austria 334tc, The Visitation, 1506, Master M.S., (16th century)/Hungarian National Gallery, Budapest, Hungary 340tl, ureus (obverse) of Diocletian (AD 284-AD 305) cuirassed, wearing a laurel wreath. (gold) Inscription: IMP C C VAL DIOCLETIANVS P F AVG, Roman (4th century AD)/Private Collection 469cra.

CORBIS: Atlantide Phototravel 30cla; The Art Archive/Alfredo Dagli Orti 34bl, 352cra; Bettmann 36cla, 96tr, 416tl; Tibor Bognar 30-31c; EPA 196bl; Owen Franken 585bl; The Gallery Collection 402tr, 403tl; E.O. Hoppé 491br; Hulton-Deutsch Collection 36tr, 72tl, 298tl, 452tl, 602tr; JAI/Ivan Vdovin 124cla; Barry Lewis 335tl, 347tl; The Picture Desk Limited/Gianni Dagli 155br; Carmen Redondo 196tr, 196cla; Roman Soumar 343cr; Sygma/Bernard Bisson & Thierry Orban 37tl,/ Pascal Le Segretain 568tr; Peter Turnley 37tr, 170tl.

THE CROATIAN MUSEUM OF NAÏVE ART: 492tl.

CROATIAN NATIONAL TOURIST BOARD ARCHIVES: 456cl, 460bc, 461tl, 461br, 462cr, 462bl, 463tl, 465br.

DANITA DELIMONT STOCK PHOTOGRAPHY: Russian Look 127tr.

DK IMAGES: Gabor Barka 342c, 343tl, 348cl, 349tl, 349cra, 349crb, 349bc.

EUROPEAN CENTRAL BANK: 15 (all images).

ETHNOGRAPHIC OPEN-AIR MUSEUM: 81cla, 81clb.

GETTY IMAGES: AFP 619br,/Dimitar Dilkoff 528tr,/ Gerard Fouet 572bl,/Stringer 30bc, 126tr; Bettmann 31br; Hulton Archive/Handout 33tr,/ Imagno 31bl; Stringer/Valentina Petrova 32cb; The Image Bank/Peter A°dams 8-9; Time & Life Pictures/Ben Martin 31bc.

THE GRANGER COLLECTION, NEW YORK: 9c, 30tr, 35ca, 35bl, 120tl, 165ca, 228tc, 411ca, 510tl; Rue des Archives 546tl.

IGALO SPA: 533tr.

IGOR JEREMIC: 536br.

JEWISH CULTURE FESTIVAL SOCIETY: *Mizrah* designed by Zbigniew Prokop, paper-cutting by Marta Gołąb 31cb.

KGB CELLS MUSEUM: 111c.

KLAIPEDA CLOCK MUSEUM: 60crb.

LONELY PLANET IMAGES: Richard I'Anson 125tc.

ERICA MARTINETTI: 537br.

Mary Evans Picture Library: 39ca.

Masterfile: Mike Dobel 487cr; Lloyd Sutton 227b.

National Geographic Stock: H. M. Herget 33bl; James L. Stanfield 32tr, 614tr.

Naturhistorisches Museum: 166bl.

Nikola Tesla Museum: 554tr.

Old Masters Gallery: 493c, 493bc.

Protopresbyter Radomir Nikcevic: 537cla, 537bl.

Palace of Parliament: 572tr, 572cl, 573tl, 573crb, 573bc.

Igor Palmin:133bc, 134clb.

Peleş Castle: 582clb, 583tl, 583cra, 583br.

Photo Tresor: 604tr, 619cra, 621cl.

Photolibrary: César Lucas Abreu 192bl; Alamer 29crb; Richard Ashworth 410-411; Henry Ausloos 530c; Gonzalo Azumendi 94, 401bc, 405br; Walter Bibikow 22clb, 164-165, 168, 317br, 414, 509b, 516tl, 526, 530tl; Barbara Boensch 297b; Sebastien Boisse 11cr; The Bridgeman Art Library 402cla; Wojtek Buss 40br, 43b, 62cl, 70, 600, 612cl, 619bl; The British Library 31tr; Wendy Connett 173tr; JD. Dallet 430tl; Peter Dawson 1-2; Cécile DéGremont 462tr; Günter Flegar 462cl; Raymond Forbes 465tl, 479tr; Kevin Galvin 451b; Gilsdorf Gilsdorf 398; Sylvain Grandadam 150clb; Gavin Hellier 20-21, 28clb; Hi Pix 579bl; Imagesource Imagesource 12tc, 22br, 249tc; John Warburton-Lee Photography/Christian Kober 557br; Jon Arnold Travel/Russell Young 95b; JTB Photo 25br, 42, 601b; Henryk T Kaiser 243cra, 296; Frank Krahmer 431br; Dinu Lazar 567b; Paolo Lazzarin 544; Günter Lenz 40cla; Holger Leue 454tr; Sheldon Levis 464cl; Lonely Planet Images/Grant Dixon 437cra; Oleksiy Maksymenko 118; Mary Evans Picture Library 33tl; Gotin Michel 31tl; Rainer Mirau 436bc, 450; Graham Monro 278bl; Don Mckinnell 35crb; S. Nicolas 614bl; Qinetiq

Qinetiq10cl; Jose Fuste Raga 169br, 483br; Rolf Richardson 618br; Robert Harding Travel/Ken Gillham 463br; Martin Siepmann 404cr, 437bc; Witold Skrypczak 494cla; Frédéric Soreau 478cl; Dimitar Sotirov 615br; Egmont Strigl 508; Yoshio Tomii 119b; Wolfgang Weinhäupl 511bl.

Photoshot: Hemis 463cra.

Pictures Colour Library: Simon Heaton 616br.

Prague Castle Picture Gallery: 234bc.

Private Collection: 31cra, 34tr, 34br, 35tc, 109cr, 151tr, 248br.

The State Hermitage Museum, St Petersburg: 144cla, 144clb, 144br, 145tl, 145cra, 145bl, 145br, 146cla, 146bc, 147tr, 147bc, 148c, 148cla, 149tr, 149bl.

Dusan Timotijevic: 545b.

Tretyakov Gallery: 136cla, 136clb, 136br, 137tl, 137cra, 137bc.

Velika Planina: 432br, 433br.

Wikipedia, The Free Encyclopedia: Public Domain 35tl.

Front Endpaper: 4Corners Images: Kaos03 ftl, SIME/Schmid Reinhard crb; Photolibrary: Gonzalo Azumendi fcr; Walter Bibikow tc, fcl, bl; Wojtek Buss fcr (Riga), fbr; Gilsdorf Gilsdorf tl; JTB Photo cr; Henryk T Kaiser ftl (Mountain); Paolo Lazzarin br; Oleksiy Maksymenko tr; Rainer Mirau cl; Egmont Strigl fbl.

Cover Picture Credits
Front Cover: Alamy Images: Stephen Bond (main); DK Images: Stanislaw Michta clb. Back Cover: DK Images: Jonathan Smith cla, clb, tl; Photolibrary: Superstock bl. Spine: Alamy Images: Stephen Bond t; DK Images: Dorota i Mariusz Jarymowiczowie b.

All other images © Dorling Kindersley
For further information see: www.dkimages.com

SPECIAL EDITIONS OF DK TRAVEL GUIDES

DK Travel Guides can be purchased in bulk quantities at discounted prices for use in promotions or as premiums. We are also able to offer special editions and personalized jackets, corporate imprints, and excerpts from all of our books, tailored specifically to meet your own needs.

To find out more, please contact:
(in the United States) **SpecialSales@dk.com**
(in the UK) **travelspecialsales@uk.dk.com**
(in Canada) DK Special Sales at **general@ tourmaline.ca**
(in Australia)
business.development@pearson.com.au

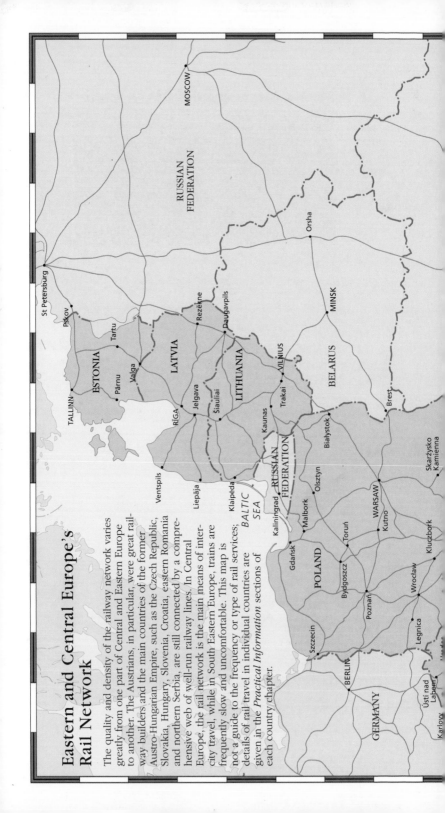

Eastern and Central Europe's Rail Network

The quality and density of the railway network varies greatly from one part of Central and Eastern Europe to another. The Austrians, in particular, were great railway builders and the main countries of the former Austro-Hungarian Empire, such as the Czech Republic, Slovakia, Hungary, Slovenia, Croatia, eastern Romania and northern Serbia, are still connected by a comprehensive web of well-run railway lines. In Central Europe, the rail network is the main means of inter-city travel, while in South Eastern Europe, trains are frequently slow and uncomfortable. This map is not a guide to the frequency or type of rail services; details of rail travel in individual countries are given in the *Practical Information* sections of each country chapter.